MANAGEMENT

A PACIFIC RIM FOCUS

ENHANCED EDITION

For Madeline Shira Tehillah,

another blessing to count

MANAGEMENT

A PACIFIC RIM FOCUS

ENHANCED EDITION

KATHRYN BARTOL   MARGARET TEIN   GRAHAM MATTHEWS   DAVID MARTIN

Boston   Burr Ridge, IL   Dubuque, IA   Madison, WI   New York
San Francisco   St. Louis   Bangkok   Bogotá   Caracas   Kuala Lumpur
Lisbon   London   Madrid   Mexico City   Milan   Montreal   New Delhi
Santiago   Seoul   Singapore   Sydney   Taipei   Toronto

McGraw·Hill Australia

A Division of The McGraw·Hill Companies

National Library of Australia Cataloguing-in-Publication Data

Management: a Pacific rim focus.
  Enhanced ed.

  Includes index.
  ISBN 0 07 471189 X.

  1. Management – Pacific Area. 2. Management. I. Bartol, Kathryn M.

658.4

Published in Australia by
McGraw-Hill Australia Pty Limited
Level 2, 82–84 Waterloo Road
Macquarie Park, NSW 2113, Australia
Sponsoring Editor: Ailsa Brackley du Bois
Developmental Editor: Jane Clayton
Supervising Editors: Amanda Phillips, Karen Enkelaar (Do Write, NSW)
Project Editor Enhanced Edition: Leanne Peters
Copy Editor: Christine Connor. Enhanced Edition: Diane Fowler, Megan Stansfield
Senior Marketing Manager: Sharon-Lee Lukas
E-Learning Director: Cameron Craig
Proofreader Enhanced Edition: Tim Learner
Cover and text design: Lucy Bal
Permissions Editor: Susan Gentle. Enhanced Edition: Colette Hoeben
Indexers: Puddingburn Publishing Services
Typesetter: Midland Typesetters. Enhanced Edition: Anne McLean (Jobs on Mac)
Printed by Best Tri Printing Limited

'It used to be that the big ate the small;
now the fast eat the slow'
Bartol, *Gaining the Edge*, p.189.

PUBLISHER'S FOREWORD

This text was first published in 1994 and since then has guided over 75 000 students through introductory management studies.

The acclaimed strength of our Australian adaptation has always been the wealth of locally relevant case studies. We have now taken this focus one step further, to ensure our cases remain current and responsive to learning needs and educational outcomes.

It is with the greatest pleasure that McGraw-Hill Australia now presents the Enhanced Edition of *Management: A Pacific Rim Focus*, containing:

○ sixty additional cases on real people, real organisations, and real strategies and decisions
○ new and original video cases on real issues affecting managerial decision making
○ new critical thinking questions that provide a genuinely critical approach to management.

In the competitive, electronic era in which we operate, it is essential that McGraw-Hill constantly raise our standards, every day and in every way to maintain our focus on delivering superior 'Content Today'. We recognise that the provision of quality content that responds to market needs is the key to both gaining and maintaining the edge. With that in mind, we surveyed the market extensively, asking 'What do you want, in addition to what you already have in this textbook?' The response, in consultation with instructors across Australia and New Zealand, is this enhanced package that delivers precisely what you wanted.

To our range of contributing authors and the academic community who have so staunchly supported this progressive product, we say thank you.

HOW TO USE THIS BOOK

Management: A Pacific Rim Focus is a pedagogically rich learning resource.
These pages show you how to fully utilise your text and study package.
Getting the most out of your text will help you to do better in management studies.

CHAPTER OUTLINE

Management: An Overview
What is management?
The management process

What managers actually do
Work methods
Managerial roles
Managerial work agendas

Managerial job types
Vertical dimension: Hierarchical levels
Differences among hierarchical levels
Promoting innovation: The entrepreneurial role
Horizontal dimension: Responsibility areas

Managerial knowledge, skills, and performance
Knowledge base
Key management skills
Performance

Managing in the 21st century
Managing change and innovation
Managing diversity: The workforce of 2000 and beyond
Developing a global perspective
The quest for total quality and continuous improvement

Chapter Outline
Each chapter opens with a quick summary of the sub-headings in the chapter you are about to study.

O L C Search for more on the management topics presented in the Chapter Outline using PowerWeb, an online bank of up-to-the-minute cases and articles on management from the local and international media, accessible from the Online Learning Centre that accompanies this text (www.mhhe.com/au/bartol).

Your PowerWeb card and pin-code may be packaged with your text, or purchased independently from your bookstore. Ask your bookseller for more information.

LEARNING OBJECTIVES

After studying this chapter, you should be able to:

○ Explain the four functions of management and other major elements in the management process.
○ Describe three common work methods managers use and 10 major roles managers play.
○ Identify the main factors influencing work agendas and the ways managers use such agendas to channel their efforts.
○ Delineate three major types of managerial skills.

Learning Objectives
Each new topic begins with a list of the chapter's learning objectives. These tell you what you should be able to do after you have finished reading that chapter, and are an excellent foundation for exam revision.

Striving for **excellence**

Organisations and their members have shown themselves to be capable of self-delusion as to their internal culture and morale. Slogans and words are easy to come up with, but the reality is identified in the actual processes. One such process is decision making. When all is said and done, and all the rhetoric has been verbalised, it is possible to actually see whether it is true or merely lip-service by examining the decision processes within an organisation.

Autoliv is no exception. In examining the processes it becomes obvious that it is teams and individuals who make decisions regarding activities which are within their areas of expertise. Other decisions are within the corporate plan's decisions framework—which are derived collaboratively at the senior management-team level.

Still there are a number of levels of analysis which need to be considered. As with all organisations which are part of a global entity, there is a corporate-level headquarters. However, this level sets parameters for a global structure and for the dividends which must flow from each national entity. Autoliv Australia is basically autonomous. The managing director, Bob Franklin, reports to the manager, Asia Pacific, who reports to the CEO in head office. Within guidelines, which for the most part focus on the financial reporting structures, delineate the specific territory it can operate in and dictate the products it takes to market, Autoliv Australia is left to carry on its activities as it sees best.

Within Autoliv Australia, the decision-making process starts at the bottom—issues focus on activities required to

Striving for Excellence
This progressive case, featuring car manufacturer Autoliv Australia, launches each chapter topic and shows you first-hand how an organisation puts the chapter theories into practice. Judge for yourself whether Autoliv's business strategies could have been managed differently to achieve better outcomes. It's much easier to learn new things when you understand why they are important.

they initiated was common because of magnification and interruption; a number of top managers saved their major brainwork for times outside the normal workday.

Verbal contacts and networks Managers in Mintzberg's (1980) study strongly preferred verbal communication through either phone conversations or meetings, instead of written communication such as memos and formal reports. For obtaining and transmitting information, they relied heavily on networks. A **network** is a set of co-operative relationships with individuals whose help is needed for a manager to function effectively. The network of contacts in Mintzberg's study included superiors, subordinates, peers and other organisation members, as well as numerous outside individuals. Some contacts were personal, such as friends and peers. Others were professionals, such as consultants, lawyers and insurance underwriters. Still others were trade association contacts, customers and suppliers.

Implications of Mintzberg's findings Although Mintzberg's study focused on top-level managers, his findings apply to a wide variety of managers (Kurke & Aldrich 1983; Gibbs 1994). For example, one study of factory supervisors found they engaged in between 237 and 1073 activities within a given workday—or more than one activity every two minutes (Guest 1956). Such research strongly supports the view that managers must develop a major network

network
A set of co-operative relationships with individuals whose help is needed in order for a manager to function effectively

Key Terms
The field of management has its own language. This book helps you learn this language through key terms that are bolded in the text and defined in the margin. The key terms are also presented in an alphabetical glossary at the end of the text. Learn the lingo as you go, and review it before exams.

⬤ Not in the plans

case in point

When one forms a relationship, one rarely plans for it to go wrong. Or should one do so?

Hans Stoehr learnt this the hard way when a deal that was finalised late last year dissolved into a bitter dispute five months later. Unexpected operational problems did put pressure on the partnership, but the problems stemmed from the original agreement.

In November 1997, Stoehr, the owner and manager of Vertigo Tree Services in Dubbo, New South Wales, won a contract that offered a tremendous growth opportunity. His tree-pruning service, established in 1996, had turnover of about $150 000 by June 1998. The new contract to manage green waste for 26 councils in central western NSW, which he won over much larger rivals, could increase turnover by $900 000.

The $395 000 mulching machine that Stoehr proposed to use for the job helped him to win the contract, but he did not have the cash or finance facility to buy one. Stoehr says: 'Other machines beat the product to a pulp, and

Case in Point

These short cases bring to life key concepts and issues being explained in the text, and invite you to diagnose particular management problems and identify the specific decisions, models and processes that are represented in each example.

How much impact does gender have on the management process, and what implications does it have for each chapter topic? Your e-CD contains all new *Gender Factor* cases that examine the changing roles of men and women in business and the new workplace realities that this creates. These cases challenge you to think about the impact of gender-related issues within the context of each chapter topic.

✖ Which theory is that?

crossroads

You are beginning to be exposed to the development of management theory. The closest example of this that you might have at the moment is how your lecturer manages your class. Consider which theory your lecturer is practising, then interview your lecturer and consider whether your perception of their practice is congruent with their statement.

Decision point

Consider these issues:

1 What is your lecturer's theory of learning (how people learn)?
2 What are your lecturer's views on the question of evaluation?
3 What is their role in the classroom?
4 Do you think that your lecturer's attitude to the students is affected by stereotypes of them? What are the stereotypes? Why did you come to that conclusion?

Crossroads

Crossroads cases describe the hard decisions managers have had to make in response to various threats and opportunities. Reflect on the possible outcomes of the management decisions presented and use the theory you have learned so far to devise new strategies and develop your own course of action!

⬆ Deming's 14 points on how to improve quality

management skills for the 21st century

In the course of his work, Deming developed 14 management points outlining what he believes managers, especially at upper levels, must do to produce high-quality products:

1 Make a long-term commitment to improve products and services, with the aim of becoming competitive, staying in business and providing jobs.
2 Adopt the new philosophy of concern for quality. We are in a new economic age. Western management must awaken to the challenge, learn its responsibilities and take on leadership for change.
3 Cease dependence on mass-inspection to achieve quality; build quality into the product in the first place.
4 End the practice of awarding business on the basis of price. Instead minimise total cost. Move to a single supplier for any one item, building a long-term relationship of loyalty and trust.

Management Skills for the 21st Century

These practical exercises help you to develop the basic skills critical to being a successful manager for example, creativity, self-analysis, entrepreneurship, quality assurance, and negotiation and delegation skills. Work through these skill-building activities and apply your newfound wisdom to your professional and student life.

@ Information is the key

managing the e-challenge

Regardless of the differences in their individual strategies, one thing Enterprise Resource Planning (ERP) companies have in common is the concept of the corporate 'portal'.

A portal is a site within a company's Intranet that aggregates all the information a particular user needs to do their job. The key to a successful portal is the ability to deliver concise information that lets a user make instant decisions—hence PeopleSoft's partnership with strategic planning specialist Cognos.

Andrew Barkla, PeopleSoft's regional vice-president, says, 'Portals are simply a door to go through to get what you want. The value is in the information, the community that you build around that'. Oracle has gone so far as to propose a set of

Managing the e-Challenge

How is technology impacting on businesses and organisations? *Managing the e-Challenge* cases examine the use of electronic tools by particular businesses to increase customer reach and productivity, and how technology interacts with and impacts on people and human endeavour.

Your e-CD includes additional cutting-edge, up-to-the-minute e-challenges to keep you up-to-date with the latest technology trends in business, and the new ways in which electronic tools have influenced management practices.

HOW TO USE THIS BOOK (CONT.)

 Turbosoft—Innovation and customer focus

gaining the edge

Turbosoft started as the research and development section of a systems integration company in 1984. In 1988 it became an independent whose product is called TTWIN—a terminal emulation package. Terminal emulation is a technology that allows a personal computer (PC) to act as a terminal. This technology is used primarily by large businesses and corporations.

Some of Turbosoft's clients in Australia include ATSIC, the ACT government, Big W, Carlton & United Breweries, Deloitte Touche Tohmatsu, the Department of Defence, Diners Club International, the RACV, and the Reserve Bank of Australia. International clients include MGM Grand (America), Oral B (America), Foxwoods Casino (America), Mitsubishi (Germany), B & S Card Services (Germany), the National Planning Authority (United Kingdom) and Bedfordshire Police (United Kingdom).

Turbosoft prides itself on the further development of existing products as well as the investment in new products which meet customers' changing needs—whether the client is one with few users or several thousands. Turbosoft endeavours to achieve customer satisfaction at all times. It encourages feedback from

Gaining the Edge

Take a critical look at an organisation whose management practices are exemplary in some way, and identify why they are successful. These short, inspiring examples enliven your learning and broaden your view of how management applies to your everyday life.

■ The subordinate's log

the reflective practitioner

In reviewing the theory of management styles, I realise that I had to assume a couple of styles which reflected the demands of the senior management. They demanded strong operational and financial controls. The CEO, recognising that I had little experience in that particular role, attempted to retain control until I settled into the job, however, he never gave over control. I have often felt that had he given me more latitude, I would have been able to assume the required control and handle the situation adequately. Hence the management style to satisfy those demands required keeping a lot of data, continuous reporting and therefore was very scientific in nature. This management style had to be applied to the people who reported to me as I needed to collect a lot of data, but at the same time I attempted to minimise that impact, as instinctively I felt that the consultants operated better with a looser management style.

This brought about a two-phase style on my part. Having worked with a number of the consultants, I had a fair idea of their strengths and weaknesses and how they related to clients. While I was in frequent contact with clients and made it my business to know what the consultants were doing in their projects, I took the approach that they were professionals and deference should be given to the skills which they demonstrated. Therefore provided I was happy with the approach they were taking and they could demonstrate a good result (both for our firm and the client), I was happy to let them work without requiring constant formal reporting or applying overly close supervision. I took on the role of a mentor who could provide advice and help problem solving rather than of a supervisor and boss.

I found that the tight management under which I was managed was very restrictive and I found that I was spending so much time reporting to my manager I had no choice but to adopt a non-management style with my subordinates. The result was I was resentful and ineffective to senior management and could not sufficiently direct my subordinates. I learned there was a balance between being a manager and a subordinate simultaneously.

The Reflective Practitioner

Theory is one thing—but what do people really think? In these fascinating interviews with a managing director and their first-line manager from the same organisation, we learn about the different perspectives and experiences each have had in relation to their performance and the chapter themes. *The Reflective Practitioner* provides a valuable insight into the working lives of the manager and the subordinate, and their different responses to similar situations.

Chapter summary

Organisations are affected by the external environment, the outside forces with potential to influence significantly the success of products or services. Broad conditions and trends in societies within which an organisation operates constitute an organisation's mega-environment. The mega-environment consists of five major elements: technological, economic, legal-political, sociocultural and international. Generally, mega-environment elements are beyond a single organisation's ability to alter directly, at least in the short run.

The task, or operational, environment is the specific outside elements with which an organisation interfaces in conducting its business. One such environment depends on the organisation's specific products and services, and the locations where it conducts business. A single organisation may be more successful in affecting its task environment than the mega-environment. Major organisational task environment elements typically include customers, competitors, suppliers, labour supply and government agencies.

Two important, but differing, perspectives on the relationship between organisations and their environments are the population ecology and the resource dependence models. Managers can analyse their organisation's environmental situation in terms of two key concepts: environmental uncertainty and environmental bounty, or capacity. Environmental uncertainty refers to the extent to which future conditions affecting an organisation can be accurately assessed and predicted. Environmental bounty refers to the extent to which the environment can support sustained growth and stability. The degree of environmental uncertainty is a function of two factors, complexity and dynamism.

Three major approaches to managing environmental elements are adaptation, favourability influence and domain shifts. Adaptation involves changing internal operations and activities to make an organisation more compatible with its environment. Methods of adaptation include buffering, smoothing, forecasting and rationing. Favourability influence focuses on altering environmental elements to make them more compatible with the organisation's needs.

Chapter Summary

The Chapter Summary recaps the key themes of the chapter topic. Use these summaries as a reliable pre-exam revision tool.

 Once you have read the chapter summary, get ahead of the class with MaxMark, a self-paced online assessment tool that contains thirty interactive questions per chapter, and is accessible via the Online Learning Centre that accompanies this book (www.mhhe.com/au/bartol).

Your MaxMark card may be packaged with your text, or purchased independently from your bookshop. Ask your bookseller for more information.

Questions for discussion and review

1 Describe each major function of management: planning, organising, leading and controlling. For a campus or other organisation to which you belong, give an example of a manager engaging in each of these functions. If one or more of the functions are lacking, what are the implications?

2 List three common managerial work methods identified by Mintzberg. How could a manager misuse these work methods to the extent they would lead to poor performance?

3 Explain the three general types of roles and 10 specific roles managers play. Suppose you opened a ski-and-surf shop near campus carrying clothing, skis and other accessories for recreation at ski resorts and beaches. Assume you have six employees. How might you use the 10 roles in managing your shop?

4 Outline three major sources of managerial work agendas. How do work agendas help managers channel their efforts toward appropriate levels of performance?

5 Contrast effectiveness and efficiency as they apply to organisational performance. What happens when you have one without the other?

Exercises for managing in the 21st century

Exercise 1
Self-assessment exercise: The kind of organisation I would manage

Select the response which best reflects the culture you would work to instil in an organisation you would manage.

1 = Strongly disagree
2 = Somewhat disagree
3 = Neither agree nor disagree

Decision making at ChocCo
on the rim—
in New Zealand

The setting is by a tranquil river bend, with a golf course nearby and splendid mountain views as a backdrop. ChocCo enjoys a tranquil life away from the hurly-burly of large cities, even though the factory is part of a multi-national group spanning the world. It employs some 200 factory workers (70 per cent are female) and supporting staff, and has been in its present location since the 1920s. The factory is geared to a continuous process operation in which production spans 24 hours daily, every day of the week. The plant is unionised.

The tranquillity of the surroundings has transferred to the management team, which was caught unprepared for a grass-roots movement among its employees wanting a change in their shift patterns. Traditionally they had worked a daily pattern of three 8-hour shifts but, in some parts of the plant, pressure was applied to management for a move to two 12-hour shifts. The proposal was for three weekly rotating shifts of 12-hours, framed around a six-day fortnight. As far as management could determine, workers were attracted by the idea of having more days off under this regime than the traditional shift pattern. Such a pattern of shifts suited women in particular with respect to their non-work-life activities. Management therefore did not initiate the change in shifts and had no agenda in mind except that of attempting to please its employees.

Although management did not initiate the proposal, it wished to be responsive to workers' desires and so agreed.

The sky's no limit
going global

From his 35th-floor office, Subhash Chandra has a stunning view of Bombay's skyline and, for as far as the eye can see, the Indian Ocean. It's a fitting perch for an entrepreneur poised atop India's booming satellite and cable television business—one whose sights are now set on expanding into cyberspace by providing Internet service and content, and into outer space by launching India's first private communication satellite.

To help finance his ambitions, Chandra plans to raise up to $1.5 billion by listing his flagship company, Zee Telefilms, on a US stock exchange this year. Which exchange is yet to be decided by Zee's board, but it would be the largest-ever international share offering by an Indian firm. Zee, India's biggest private media company, makes and buys TV programs, distributes them via satellite and cable, and produces entertainment and educational content for the Internet. Thanks to his 70 per cent holding in Zee, one of the best-performing stocks on the Bombay exchange, Chandra's net worth is estimated at $9 billion.

Chandra has stated that his goal is to make Zee television and Internet content available to anyone,

---

Questions for Discussion and Review
These short-answer discussion questions give you an opportunity to think about and discuss different situations directly related to the chapter you've just read. Learning to think critically about management will enable you to analyse problems and make decisions based on real business situations.

Your e-CD extends the book's critical approach with over 100 new high-level critical thinking questions that challenge you to think more strategically about organisational change, planning, organising, leading and controlling, as related to real examples.

Exercises for Managing in the 21st Century
Actively build the management skills you need to succeed as a manager in the 21st century by working through these rigorous applications. These exercises encourage you to think independently, as well as operate in a group.

On the Rim
These cases look closely at the management activities of different organisations doing business on the Pacific rim, within the context of the chapter theories. They are important because they highlight the management behaviours of Australia's main trading partners, and because doing business in different parts of the Asia-Pacific region varies markedly, particularly in terms of motivation and reward.

Additional *On the Rim* cases are accessible on your e-CD, further focusing your attention on regional management trends within neighbouring Pacific rim businesses.

Going Global
These extended cases focus on companies that are doing something notable on a worldwide basis, be they Pacific rim organisations with an international focus or overseas multinationals operating in the region. Read the case and build your critical thinking skills by undertaking the activities for discussion, analysis and further research.

Additional *Going Global* cases are available on your e-CD, and highlight the innovative international practices of well-known companies to help you understand how management theory can be applied globally.

End of Part

E-STUDENT

www.mhhe.com/au/bartol

MaxMARK

Unique to McGraw-Hill, MaxMark is a self-paced learning tool comprising thirty interactive, multiple-choice questions for every chapter of the text. MaxMark is designed to help you 'maximise your marks' by allowing you to randomise the questions, set time limits, and switch the extensive feedback option on or off.

MaxMark may be packaged with your text or purchased separately. Ask your bookseller for more information.

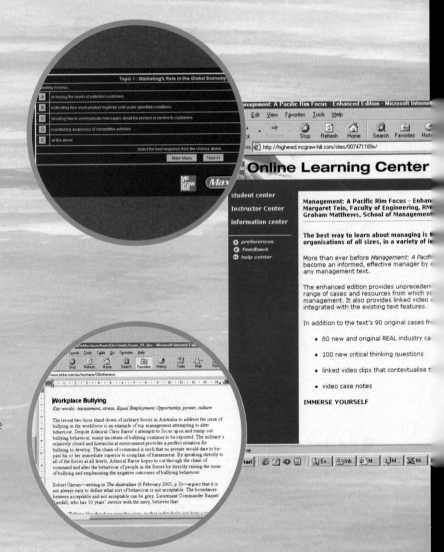

Management in the News

Current issues in management are explored in depth in a series of newsletters that help you extend your knowledge of management and keep you up-to-date with the latest trends and issues.

Weblinks

Over 80 links to management organisations, news services and interesting regional and global companies are provided here. Use these to investigate the management practices of leading organisations and to explore the variety of management resources available to you.

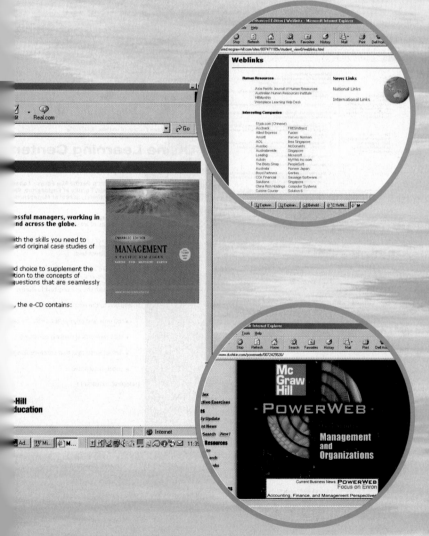

POWERWEB

Unique to McGraw-Hill, PowerWeb is your link to an endless, up-to-the-minute online bank of management case studies and articles to help you with study and assignments. Linking you to international breaking news specific to your discipline and updated every hour, as well as study tips on web research and over 6000 online journals, PowerWeb is great for researching essays and fostering an understanding of the subject that your peers and future employers will thoroughly respect.

Your access card to PowerWeb may be packaged with your text or purchased separately from your bookshop. Ask your bookseller for more information.

E–INSTRUCTOR

www.mhhe.com/au/bartol

Instructor's Manual

Written by Margaret Tein and Graham Matthews, and tied specifically to each chapter of the text, the Instructor's Manual features comprehensive lecture notes, teaching ideas, additional case studies and examples, and suggested solutions to discussion questions and case problems. An ideal resource for busy lecturers, the Instructor's Manual can be used in conjunction with the PowerPoint slides as part of a powerful teaching package.

Solutions to all Critical Thinking Questions and additional case studies on the e-CD are available on the Online Learning Centre.

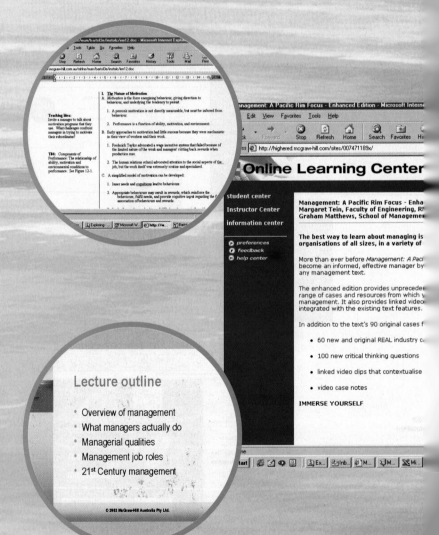

PowerPoint Slides

This text comes with a full suite of colour PowerPoint slides that distil key concepts from each chapter of the book. Present these slides in lecture theatres to reinforce management principles to your class, and distribute them as lecture notes.

Lecture outline

* Overview of management
* What managers actually do
* Managerial qualities
* Management job roles
* 21st Century management

© 2003 McGraw-Hill Australia Pty Ltd.

Test Bank
(for instructors only)

More than 900 multiple-choice questions are available in WebMCQ's powerful and flexible *online* quizzing format with tracking and reporting capabilities. With WebMCQ, you can deliver your own online revision quizzes or tests and adapt them to suit your individual or class needs. Exclusive to McGraw-Hill.

WebCT and
Blackboard Resources

WebCT and Blackboard are both Course Management Systems (CMS) that allow you to deliver and manage your course via the Internet. A Course Management System presents your own course content as web pages that typically include study tools such as lecture notes, quizzes, bulletin boards and calenders. McGraw-Hill can provide online material to supplement your existing material for your chosen Course Management System. Ask your McGraw-Hill sales representative for more information.

Welcome to McGraw-Hill's

It's all about flexibility. Today. You want to be able to teach your course, your way. McGraw-Hill offers you extensive choices in content selection and delivery backed by uncompromising service.

Your course: Connect your students with leading texts and study guides, websites, online readings, online cases, online course materials and revision programs. To assist you in teaching your course, McGraw-Hill provides you with cutting edge resources, including online testing and revision, instructor's manuals and guides, test banks, visual resources and PowerPoint slide shows. Your McGraw-Hill Academic Sales Consultant is trained to help match your course with our content, today.

Your way: Your McGraw-Hill Academic Sales Consultant, our instructional designer, and our E-learning team are trained to help you customise our content for your existing or new course. We carefully examine and match your course to our content and then discuss what, how, and when you would like it to be delivered—online or in print. It is that easy.

Your guarantee: Our programs are backed by our unique service guarantee. If you are a loyal McGraw-Hill customer, we will convert your course to our content each time your course changes—we use only qualified instructional designers or we consult with your own academic staff. Ask about our Course Conversion Program today!

your course

Text:
Management: A Pacific Rim Focus,
Enhanced Edition

Text supplements for academics:
PowerPoint Presentations, Instructor's Manual and Test Bank

Text supplements for students:
Student CD-ROM (containing additional cases, discussion questions and video footage) and PowerPoint Presentations

Text website:
Online Learning Centre

Cases & news online:
PowerWeb and Online Newsletters

Revision online:
MaxMark

your way

Online testing & revision:
WebMCQ

Online course delivery:
WebCT, Blackboard, PageOut

Custom publishing & cases

www.mcgraw-hill.com.au/contenttoday

TOTALLY INTEGRATED LEARNING PACKAGE

The enhanced edition of *Management: A Pacific Rim Focus*
is a totally new integrated learning package. Every new copy of the text comes with a free e-CD,
providing you with unprecedented currency, flexibility and choice.

How to use the integrated learning package:

EMPHASIS ON EXPERIENTIAL APPLICATION

- Video clips (and cases) linked to the text contextualise the chapter topics.
- 100 new critical thinking questions challenge students to diagnose specific management issues.

CURRENCY

- 60 new and original real industry cases keep students up to date with management debates.
- New issues (gender, SME's, globalisation) extend the text and allow you to develop your own focus.

BEST PACKAGE

- Active links between the text, the e-CD and the Online Learning Centre provide a totally integrated learning package.

CASES

Bring concepts to life with cases. The e-CD contains 60 new and original real industry cases focussing on gender issues, small businesses and globalisation. These cases expand on the issues already highlighted within the text so you can use them to extend the relevance of introductory concepts. Cases are placed within a chapter-by-chapter context or can be referenced by theme according to the case matrix.

VIDEOS

Local video clips on the e-CD contextualise the part themes within the text. You can reference or play the videos within your class knowing that your students can refer back to them, at home or in department labs, in their own time. Video case notes accompany each clip and explain how the footage relates to the chapter material.

CRITICAL THINKING QUESTIONS

Over 100 new critical thinking questions challenge students to diagnose specific management issues so that they learn to analyse problems and make decisions based on real business situations. The critical thinking questions are placed within a chapter-by-chapter context and can be used for in-class discussion or as home assignments.

PREFACE

The new enhanced edition of *Management: A Pacific Rim Focus* continues to equip students with the skills they need to become informed and effective managers by offering the most diverse and original case studies of any management text. We believe that current and diverse case studies and vignettes are essential for providing students with a foundation from which to develop the decision-making and analytical skills that they will need to deal effectively with managerial challenges.

The enhanced edition of Bartol is not a new edition, it is more a new approach to teaching. With a new accompanying CD-Rom the enhanced edition seamlessly provides 60 new and original case studies ensuring that you can provide your choice of the most current cases available on gender issues, SMEs, globalisation or engineering situations. Each case features real people, real organisations and real strategies and decisions, and is accompanied by critical discussion questions and includes weblinks to the Bartol online resources.

Our experience tells us that one of the most challenging things for lecturers in this field is to teach students to think critically and strategically about theories, and to develop decision-making and analytical skills. To that end, the e-CD extends each chapter of the text by providing 10 new critical thinking questions, as well as application exercises and true/false and multiple choice questions. Why are the questions so important? These questions invite students to evaluate more carefully contemporary management debates in a regional and global context, and inspire the development of analytical and decision-making skills.

The preface to previous editions has begun with the statement 'Management is about people'. To us, this is self-evident. However, ironically, of late our students have begun to question the relevance of a personal approach to management, perceiving that it is being replaced by technology. They see electronic messaging taking the place of verbal communication, e-commerce replacing the need for front-line interactions with customers or suppliers, and computer software performing many of the planning and control functions previously completed by managers.

The popularity of technology might lead students to believe that success will evade them unless they use and master such tools. However, while we maintain that the tools are relevant and that it would be foolish to disregard their value, they are, nonetheless, only tools. This is why we maintain the stance that management is about people. The use of current technology puts the competence of managers at risk, because it is too easy to rely on it, thereby ignoring the potency of the person-to-person interactions that result in true management excellence. We would like to stress that the e-CD too, is only a tool; it is the content and how you use it that will make you successful.

This book was conceived based on the philosophy that management is about human endeavour and people achieving results, and, in spite of many changes appearing in society, our convictions remain the same. As you work your way through this text, you will observe that our emphasis is still on the applications of theory to produce a culture and environment in which success is possible. If the use of tools determines the degree of success, this can be achieved by any individual or organisation with the skills to do so. How then, do organisations and individuals differentiate themselves when both have the resources to acquire, and the skills to use, the tools?

The key differences are found in examples of leadership; how individuals in organisations treat one another, their clients, their suppliers and their competitors—in other words, how people are managed. If business enterprise is about people and their aspirations to succeed, then it is the ability to direct the human energies generated in fulfilling these aspirations that constitutes the key to good management.

CONTRIBUTORS
TO THE ENHANCED EDITION

Just as teams are crucial to effective management in business, so too have they been essential to the creation of the enhanced edition of this text. We are extremely proud to acknowledge the contributions made by our diverse author team to this unique edition, and are especially grateful to those instructors who authored case studies and critical thinking questions for our interactive CD-Rom.

For our new and thought-provoking *E-Challenge* case studies, we are grateful to: **André M. Everett** (University of Otago), **John Paynter** (University of Auckland), **Ken Dooley** (Central Queensland University), and **Ravindra Bagia** and **Peter Lewis** (University of Technology, Sydney). Our topical *Gender Factor* case studies (entirely new to this edition) have been authored by an innovative team in management studies, comprising **Glenice Wood** (University of Ballarat), **Ella Henry** (UNITEC Institute of Technology) and **Elizabeth Hall**, **Virginia Phillips**, **Karen Henderson** and **Jodyanne Kirkwood** (University of Otago), and we are thankful for their contribution. **John Krasnostein** (Murdoch University) has further enhanced this edition with new and internationally relevant *Going Global* case studies, and we also express warm thanks to **Michael Schaper**, **Stephen Choo** (Curtin University of Technology) and **Ross Milne** (Auckland University of Technology) for our additional *On the Rim* case studies. **Timothy Bartram** (La Trobe University) has done a superb job of writing video cases that relate the local footage that accompanies this text back to key management concepts.

We gratefully acknowledge **Julian Teicher** and **Jo-anne Tui McKeown** (Monash University) for their exceptional work on the critical thinking questions that supplement every chapter of this text on the CD-Rom. The depth of their research has given this book an additional dimension, and one that further challenges students to think critically and intelligently about management in a real world context.

We also extend our gratitude to **George Sansbury** (La Trobe University), for his excellent work in updating the PowerPoint slides that accompany this enhanced edition.

Most of all we must thank those persistent characters at McGraw-Hill who have worked long and hard to bring this enhanced edition to fruition. The management of educational resource development and production is very much about managing people, and our Sponsoring Editor, Ailsa Brackley du Bois, will surely attest to this. She has the patience of a saint, with spurs. Our Developmental Editor Jane Clayton commissioned the fine suite of case study authors who contributed new material to this edition, and sourced the cutting-edge local video footage that supports and distinguishes this text. She also developed with Mark Waters Productions the interactive and expertly crafted CD-Rom that enlivens our enhanced edition. Project Editor Leanne Peters and designer Lucy Bal are also to be thanked for their tireless efforts in bringing the parts of this edition together, as are the marketing and sales team for their energy and commitment to the text. Without this dedicated team, this text would not be the success that it is today.

Margaret Tein & Graham Matthews

PAST CONTRIBUTORS

Throughout the life of this book many other people have provided ongoing and generous support, and we thank our colleagues, both at RMIT and other universities around the Pacific rim, for their suggestions and encouragement.

For their time and interest in this book we are grateful to Professor Israel Herszberg, Head of the Department of Aerospace Engineering at RMIT; Associate Professor Murray Ainsworth; and Bob Franklin and Cheryl Woollard of Autoliv Australia. We would also like to extend our thanks to Colin Innes (University of Technology, Sydney) for his work on writing our chapter on human resource management.

The numerous case study contributors deserve our gratitude for enriching the vitality of the text: Tony Cvorkov; Phillippe Cahill; L. Nash; Lindsay Nelson; Peter Holland; K. Walters; Tom Batley; J. Kirby; S. Dhume; C. Dawson; P. Switzer; S. Lloyd; P. Harmsen; Andrew Hutt; M.G. Harvey; Q. Hardy; A. Gome; Alexander Sibbald; K. Lee; J. Gordon; A.T. Cheng; Graham Elkin; Mark Weston Wall; C. Deutsch; N. Way; W.E. Deming; D. James; R. Garran; and S. Elegant and M. Hiebert.

Our appreciation also goes to the reviewers from institutions around Australia and New Zealand who took the time to offer constructive criticism on this text during its development. Special thanks go to John Dugas (University of Newcastle), Andrew Sense (University of Wollongong), Tony Jolley (management consultant), John Rodwell (Deakin University) and Clive Oliver (Edith Cowan University) for their comments.

In addition, we would like to acknowledge those who developed the supplementary material that accompanies this text: Rae Dorai, who has been invaluable in writing the answers to the case study questions that appear in the text for the Instructor's Manual; Loretta Inglis (Monash Graduate School), who has done an excellent job of writing the Computerised Test Bank; David Meacheam (University of Newcastle), who authored the original PowerPoint slides; and Ken Dooley (Central Queensland University), who wrote the rigorous self-assessment questions for MaxMark. We also thank Stephanie Miller (Victoria University) for authoring the online management newsletters that accompany this book.

Margaret Tein & Graham Matthews

CONTENTS IN BRIEF

Publisher's foreword		*v*
How to use this book		*vi*
e-student		*x*
e-instructor		*xii*
Preface		*xvii*
Contributors to the enhanced edition		*xvii*
Past contributors		*xviii*

Part One	**INTRODUCTION**		
	1	The challenge of management	3
	2	Pioneering ideas in management	31
	3	Understanding internal and external environments	63
	4	Social responsibility and ethics in management	93
Part Two	**PLANNING AND DECISION MAKING**		
	5	Managerial decision making	125
	6	Establishing organisational goals and plans	171
	7	Strategic management	203
	8	Fostering an innovative organisation	233
Part Three	**ORGANISING**		
	9	Basic elements of organisation structure	265
	10	Strategic organisation design	297
	11	Human resource management	329
Part Four	**LEADING**		
	12	Motivation	365
	13	Leadership	397
	14	Managerial communication	425
	15	Managing groups	455
Part Five	**CONTROLLING**		
	16	Controlling the organisation	491
	17	Managing organisations through change and conflict	575
Part Six	**ACROSS ALL FUNCTIONS**		
	18	International management	609
	19	The regional context	639
		Glossary	661
		References	681
		Credits	715
		Index	717

CONTENTS IN DETAIL

Publisher's foreword v
How to use this book vii
e-student x
e-instructor xii
Preface xvi
Contributors to the enhanced edition xvii
Past contributors xviii

Part 1   INTRODUCTION 1

Striving for excellence   4

**Management skills for
the 21st century**
How to build networks   8

Managing the e-challenge
Be part of the e-boom   18

Gaining the edge
Getting the balance right   20

Crossroads
When the unexpected hits   22

Case in point
Rag traders get some help
from an experienced hand   24

The reflective practitioner
The MD's diary   25
The subordinate's log   25

On the Rim
Getting the timing right   29

Chapter 1   The challenge of management 3
Chapter outline 3   Learning objectives 3
Management: An overview 5
What managers actually do 7
Managerial knowledge, skills and performance 12
Managerial job types 14
Managing in the 21st century 21
Focus on practice 26   Chapter summary 26   Questions for discussion
and review 27   Exercises for managing in the 21st century 28

Critical thinking questions and additional cases on e-management, gender issues,
small businesses and globalisation are available on your e-CD. See case matrix.

Striving for excellence   32

Case in point
The only person in the company
without a computer   39

Crossroads
Which theory is that?   42

**Management skills
for the 21st century**
Deming's 14 points on how
to improve quality   53

Managing the e-challenge
Information is the key   54

Gaining the edge
NGOs—A new power in world
politics   56

The reflective practitioner
The MD's diary   56
The subordinate's log   57

On the Rim
Ford Motor charges ahead
and into globalisation   60

Chapter 2   Pioneering ideas in management 31
Chapter outline 31   Learning objectives 31
The birth of management ideas 33
Preclassical contributors 33
Classical viewpoint 36
Behavioural viewpoint 42
Quantitative management viewpoint 48
Contemporary viewpoints 49
Focus on practice 57   Chapter summary 57   Questions for discussion
and review 58   Exercises for managing in the 21st century 59

Critical thinking questions and additional cases on e-management, gender issues,
small businesses and globalisation are available on your e-CD. See case matrix.

Chapter 3   Understanding internal and external environments 63
   Chapter outline 63   Learning objectives 63
  Types of external environments 65
  Analysing environmental conditions 73
  Managing environmental elements 78
  The internal environment: Organisational culture 81
  Focus on practice 88   Chapter summary 89   Questions for discussion
  and review 89   Exercises for managing in the 21st century 90

 Critical thinking questions and additional cases on e-management, gender issues, small businesses and globalisation are available on your e-CD. See case matrix.

Striving for excellence   64
Case in point
To rent or buy?   68
**Management skills
for the 21st century**
Keeping tabs on competitors   71
Crossroads
AYS Stevedoring—Changing
corporate culture   77
Managing the e-challenge
Peakhour—Serious business   83
Gaining the edge
Turbosoft—Innovation and
customer focus   85
The reflective practitioner
The MD's diary   87
The subordinate's log   88
On the Rim
In a changing environment ...   91

Chapter 4   Social responsibility and ethics in management 93
   Chapter outline 93   Learning objectives 93
  Organisational social responsibility 95
  Organisational social responsiveness 104
  Being an ethical manager 106
  Managing an ethical organisation 112
  Focus on practice 116   Chapter summary 116   Questions for discussion
  and review 117   Exercises for managing in the 21st century 118

 Critical thinking questions and additional cases on e-management, gender issues, small businesses and globalisation are available on your e-CD. See case matrix.

Striving for excellence   94
Managing the e-challenge
War of the Web   101
Gaining the edge
Honesty cashes in but not
on the exchange rates 102
Crossroads
Aye, captain—Managing
ethical quandaries   103
**Management skills
for the 21st century**
Questions to facilitate ethical
business decisions   110
Case in point
Recyclable Christmas trees   111
On the Rim
Hello Kitty—Hello madness   119
Going global
Video Ezy holds course for Asia 120

Part 2   PLANNING AND DECISION MAKING 123

Striving for excellence 126

Case in point
To fly or not to fly   135

Crossroads
On to the next thing   138

Managing the e-challenge
Bill paying online   144

Gaining the edge
Click for fresh fruit   147

**Management skills
for the 21st century**
How to be more creative   148

The reflective practitioner
The MD's diary   150
The subordinate's log   151

On the Rim
Decision making at ChocCo   155

Chapter 5   **Managerial decision making** 125
          Chapter outline 125   Learning objectives 125
The nature of managerial decision making 127
Managers as decision makers 130
Steps in an effective decision-making process 131
Overcoming barriers to effective decision making 135
Managing diversity: Group decision making 141
Promoting innovation: The creativity factor in decision making 144
Focus on practice 151   Chapter summary 152   Questions for discussion
and review 153   Exercises for managing in the 21st century 153

Critical thinking questions and additional cases on e-management, gender issues,
small businesses and globalisation are available on your e-CD. See case matrix.

Supplement to Chapter 5   **Planning and decision aids** 157
Forecasting 157
Project planning and control models 162
Other planning techniques 165
Quantitative aids for decision making 167

Striving for excellence 172

Case in point
Not in the plans   179

**Management skills
for the 21st century**
How to set goals   181

Managing the e-challenge
E-jobs in China   188

Gaining the edge
'Now the fast eat the slow'   189

Crossroads
Planning takes time   190

The reflective practitioner
The MD's diary   194
The subordinate's log   195

On the rim
Wood Veneer Products   198

Chapter 6   **Establishing organisational goals and plans** 171
          Chapter outline 171   Learning outcomes 171
The overall planning process 173
The nature of organisational goals 174
How goals facilitate performance 180
Linking goals and plans 185
Management by objectives 191
Focus on practice 196   Chapter summary 196   Questions for discussion
and review 197   Exercises for managing in the 21st century 197

Critical thinking questions and additional cases on e-management, gender issues,
small businesses and globalisation are available on your e-CD. See case matrix.

Chapter 7   **Strategic management 203**

Chapter outline 203   Learning objectives 203

The concept of strategic management 205

The role of competitive analysis in strategy formulation 208

Formulating corporate-level strategy 213

Formulating business-level strategy 221

Formulating functional-level strategy 223

Strategy implementation 224

Focus on practice 225   Chapter summary 227   Questions for discussion and review 227   Exercises for managing in the 21st century 228

 Critical thinking questions and additional cases on e-management, gender issues, small businesses and globalisation are available on your e-CD. See case matrix.

Striving for excellence 204

Managing the e-challenge
Risky business   210

Gaining the edge
Coming back to call back   213

Crossroads
Cuisine—Fast-food style   216

Case in point
The Pavlova Kitchen
(Dunedin, NZ) Ltd   220

The reflective practitioner
The MD's diary   226
The subordinate's log   226

On the Rim
The strategic development of
Melba's Chocolate Factory   229

Chapter 8   **Fostering an innovative organisation 233**

Chapter outline 233   Learning objectives 233

The nature and change of innovation 234

Organisational life cycles 236

The change management and innovation process 241

Organisational development 244

Innovation for competitive advantage 246

Key organisational change components 252

Focus on practice 255   Chapter summary 255   Questions for discussion and review 256   Exercises for managing in the 21st century 256

 How are the Japanese getting their staff to smile? The video footage is on your e-CD! Critical thinking questions and additional cases on e-management, gender issues, small businesses and globalisation are also available on your e-CD. See case matrix.

Striving for excellence 234

Crossroads
Business idea competition   238

Gaining the edge
The value of knowledge   243

Managing the e-challenge
Shaping up to the new guard   244

**Management skills
for the 21st century**
Checklist for choosing
intrapreneurial ideas   250

Case in point
Dough innovations   251

The reflective practitioner
The MD's diary   254
The subordinate's log   255

On the Rim
Uncharted territory   258

Going global
The sky's no limit   260

Part 3   ORGANISING 263

Chapter 9   Basic elements of organisation structure 265

Chapter outline 265   Learning objectives 265

The nature of organisation structure 267

Job design 271

Types of departmentalisation 276

Methods of vertical co-ordination 277

Promoting innovation: Methods of horizontal co-ordination 287

Focus on practice 292   Chapter summary 292   Questions for discussion and review 293   Exercises for managing in the 21st century 294

Critical thinking questions and additional cases on e-management, gender issues, small businesses and globalisation are available on your e-CD. See **case matrix**.

Striving for excellence 266

Case in point
Franchising: a structure
for success   269

Crossroads
Knock, knock   276

**Management skills
for the 21st century**
Guidelines for effective
delegating   282

Gaining the edge
The Williamstown Naval
Dockyard   283

Managing the e-challenge
An integrated distribution
package   288

The reflective practitioner
The MD's diary   291
The subordinate's log   292

On the Rim
Going solo   295

Chapter 10   Strategic organisation design 297

Chapter outline 297   Learning objectives 297

Designing organisation structures: An overview 298

Assessing structural alternatives 301

Weighing contingency factors 314

Matching strategy and structure 318

Promoting innovation: Using structural means to enhance prospects 320

Focus on practice 323   Chapter summary 323   Questions for discussion and review 324   Exercises for managing in the 21st century 325

Critical thinking questions and additional cases on e-management, gender issues, small businesses and globalisation are available on your e-CD. See **case matrix**.

Striving for excellence 298

Managing the e-challenge
Web site steers trucker's
business   300

Case in point
Bringing ends together   313

Crossroads
Tripac makes an unexpected
decision   313

Gaining the edge
Incubator nurtures small
businesses   319

The reflective practitioner
The MD's diary   322
The subordinate's log   322

On the Rim
Singapore Computer Systems
comes of age   326

Chapter 11   **Human resource management 329**
Chapter outline 329   Learning objectives 329
The human resource management framework 330
Establishing the employment relationship 335
Maintaining the employment relationship 343
HRIS, Internet, intranets and extranets 348
The future of work 350
Terminating the employment relationship 352
Focus on practice 355   Chapter summary 355   Questions for discussion
and review 356   Exercises for managing in the 21st century 357

Is psychological testing an ethical means of firing staff? The video footage is on your e-CD!
Critical thinking questions and additional cases on e-management, gender issues, small
businesses and globalisation are also available on your e-CD. See case matrix.

Striving for excellence 330
**Management skills
for the 21st century**
How to conduct an effective
interview   340
Case in point
Who rates the high rates?   341
Crossroads
Narrowing options   342
Gaining the edge
Hi-Tech Personnel   346
Managing the e-challenge
E-how turns knowledge into
power   350
The reflective practitioner
The MD's diary   354
The subordinate's log   355
On the Rim
From pills to bread making   358
Going global
Faulding   359

Part 4   **LEADING 363**

Chapter 12   **Motivation 365**
Chapter outline 365   Learning objectives 365
The nature of motivation 366
Needs theories 368
Cognitive theories 374
Reinforcement theory 380
Social learning theory 385
Focus on practice 388   Chapter summary 389   Questions for discussion
and review 389   Exercising for managing in the 21st century 390

Critical thinking questions and additional cases on e-management, gender issues,
small businesses and globalisation are available on your e-CD. See case matrix.

Striving for excellence 366
Case in point
Sue Riem-Tan   371
Crossroads
Stepping out safely   373
Gaining the edge
Time off   379
Managing the e-challenge
Reinforcing innovative culture 384
The reflective practitioner
The MD's diary   387
The subordinate's log   388
On the Rim
Performance and bonus systems:
How well do they relate?   391

Striving for excellence 398

Crossroads
How much can managers
manage?   404

Case in point
Female principals—Where
are they?   406

Gaining the edge
The grey hair brigade
leadership   411

Managing the e-challenge
Small businesses need to
log on   415

The reflective practitioner
The MD's diary   419
The subordinate's log   420

On the Rim
Surviving the crisis   424

Chapter 13   Leadership 397
Chapter outline 397   Learning objectives 397
How leaders influence others 398
Searching for leadership traits 400
Identifying leader behaviours 401
Developing situational theories 407
Promoting innovation: Transformational leadership 416
Are leaders necessary? 417

Focus on practice 421   Chapter summary 421   Questions for discussion
and review 422   Exercises for managing in the 21st century 422

Critical thinking questions and additional cases on e-management, gender issues,
small businesses and globalisation are available on your e-CD. See case matrix.

Striving for excellence 426

Case in point
Horizon Pacific Television   432

**Management skills
for the 21st century**
How to listen actively   438

Gaining the edge
The 12-step program   440

Crossroads
The cost of pour
communication   443

Managing the e-challenge
Big Cooke is watching!   446

The reflective practitioner
The MD's diary   447
The subordinate's log   448

On the Rim
Connecting to riches   452

Chapter 14   Managerial communication 425
Chapter outline 425   Learning objectives 425
The nature of managerial communication 427
Influences on individual communication and interpersonal processes 431
Group communications networks 438
Organisational communication channels 440

Focus on practice 448   Chapter summary 449   Questions for discussion
and review 449   Exercises for managing in the 21st century 450

Critical thinking questions and additional cases on e-management, gender issues,
small businesses and globalisation are available on your e-CD. See case matrix.

Chapter 15 **Managing groups 455**
Chapter outline 455 *Learning objectives 455*
Foundations of work groups 457
Work-group inputs 461
Work-group processes 467
Promoting innovation: Using task forces and teams 475
Focus on practice 479 Chapter summary 479 Questions for discussion and review 479 Exercises for managing in the 21st century 480

Discover the leadership tactics used to set up Virgin Blue. The video footage is on your e-CD! Critical thinking questions and additional cases on e-management, gender issues, small businesses and globalisation are also available on your e-CD. See case matrix.

Striving for excellence 456
Crossroads
New store, old store, no store 462
Case in point
Phone home? 465
Management skills for the 21st century
How to lead a meeting 472
Gaining the edge
Whistle while you work 473
Managing the e-challenge
I'll be watching you ... 474
The reflective practitioner
The MD's diary 477
The subordinate's log 478
On the Rim
Fisher and Paykel 483
Going global
No pride without lions 486

Part 5 **CONTROLLING 489**

Chapter 16 **Controlling the organisation 491**
Chapter outline 491 *Learning objectives 491*
Control as a management function 492
The control process 496
Types of controls 502
Managerial approaches to implementing controls 506
Assessing control systems 512
Focus on practice 515 Chapter summary 516 Questions for discussion and review 516 Exercises for managing in the 21st century 517

Critical thinking questions and additional cases on e-management, gender issues, small businesses and globalisation are available on your e-CD. See case matrix.

Striving for excellence 492
Case in point
Getting rid of less profitable customers 501
Gaining the edge
Benchmarking as a control mechanism 504
Crossroads
Balancing risks 508
Managing the e-challenge
e-control for e-savings 510
The reflective practitioner
The MD's diary 514
The subordinate's log 515
On the Rim
The kings of culture 518

Supplement 1 to Chapter 16 **Managerial control methods 521**
Major control systems 521
Total quality management 523
Financial control 526
Budgetary control 533
Inventory control 535

Supplement 2 to Chapter 16   Operations management 538
Defining operations management 539
Formulating operations strategy 541
Developing and implementing operating systems 543
Designing and utilising facilities 551
Promoting innovation: Process technology 552
Improving productivity 555

Supplement 3 to Chapter 16   Management information systems 557
Computer-based information systems: An overview 557
Types of information systems 562
Promoting innovation: Strategic implications of information systems 565
Developing computer-based information systems 567
Influence of information technology on organisations 570

Chapter 17   Managing organisations through change and conflict 575
Chapter outline 575   Learning outcomes 575
Managing change 576
Managing resistance to change 578
Managing conflict 583
The relationship between change and conflict 594
Focus on practice 600   Chapter summary 600   Questions for discussion
and review 601   Exercises for managing in the 21st century 602

Striving for excellence 576
Case in point
Changing to fit the time   581
Crossroads   586
Gaining the edge
Dealing with change—now!   591
Managing the e-challenge
Hackers breach Treasury site   597
The reflective practitioner
The MD's diary   599
The subordinate's log   600
On the Rim
Implementing a multimedia
super corridor   603

Learn more about the hotly debated merger between BHP and Billiton. The video footage is on your e-CD! Critical thinking questions and additional cases on e-management, gender issues, small businesses and globalisation are also available on your e-CD. See case matrix.

Part 6   ACROSS ALL FUNCTIONS 607

Chapter 18   International management 609
Chapter outline 609   Learning objectives 609
The nature of international management 610
Assessing the international environment 614
Gauging international strategic issues 620
Organising international business 623
Managing diversity: Adapting to cultural differences 626
Handling social responsibility and ethical issues 630
Focus on practice 633   Chapter summary 633   Questions for discussion and review 634   Exercises for managing in the 21st century 634

 Critical thinking questions and additional cases on e-management, gender issues, small businesses and globalisation are available on your e-CD. **See case matrix.**

Striving for excellence 610
Case in point
The cost of being an
expatriate   613
Gaining the edge
Crossing the boundaries for
partnerships   617
Crossroads
Going my way?   619
Managing the e-challenge
B2B   623
The reflective practitioner
The MD's diary   631
The subordinate's log   632
On the Rim
One country's food ...   635

Chapter 19   The regional context 639
Chapter outline 639   Learning objectives 639
The regional context 640
Focus on Singapore 642
Focus on New Zealand 645
Focus on Indonesia 648
Focus on Malaysia 651
Focus on Thailand 653
Japan's impact on the Region 655
Australia's position within South-East Asia 657

 Critical thinking questions and additional cases on e-management, gender issues, small businesses and globalisation are available on your e-CD. **See case matrix.**

Striving for excellence 640
The reflective practitioner
The MD's diary   658
The subordinate's log   659
Going global
The price of corruption   659

Glossary   661
References   681
Credits   715
Index   717

CASE MATRIX

Customise your case focus! Locate specific case studies in the text by first finding the 'case type' you require from the list below, and then running your finger along that row to see where in the book case studies of this type can be found, and if additional cases in this area are available on the e-CD that accompanies this edition.

	1	2	3	4	5	6
THE REFLECTIVE PRACTITIONER Reveals the contrasting viewpoints of MDs and their subordinates in relation to specific management issues	page 25	page 56	page 87	page 115	page 150	page 194
CROSSROADS Invites you to consider the threats and opportunities of a specific management decision	page 22	page 42	page 77	page 103	page 138	page 190
GAINING THE EDGE Profiles organisations whose practices are exemplary in some way	page 20	page 56	page 85	page 102	page 147	page 189
STRIVING FOR EXCELLENCE Provides a running snapshot of how Autoliv Australia puts management theory into practice	page 4	page 32	page 64	page 94	page 126	page 172
CASE IN POINT Highlights specific examples of the concepts and issues described in the chapter	page 24	page 39	page 68	page 111	page 135	page 179
ON THE RIM Focuses on regional trends within Asia-Pacific businesses within the context of chapter theories	page 29	page 60+ 💿	page 91+ 💿	page 119	page 155+ 💿	page 198
GOING GLOBAL Profiles organisations that have done something notable on a worldwide basis				page 120+ 💿		
MANAGING THE E-CHALLENGE Explores the use of electronic tools by particular businesses for planning and reaching customers	page 18+ 💿	page 54+ 💿	page 83+ 💿	page 101+ 💿	page 144+ 💿	page 188+ 💿
THE GENDER FACTOR Explores gender issues in the workplace and how the roles of men and women impact on perception and organisational structure	💿	💿	💿	💿	💿	💿
VIDEO CASES Summarises local video footage available on the e-CD and contextualises key management principles in action						

Chapters

7	8	9	10	11	12	13	14	15	16	17	18	19
page 226	page 254	page 291	page 322	page 354	page 387	page 419	page 447	page 477	page 514	page 599	page 631	page 658
page 216	page 238	page 276	page 313	page 342	page 373	page 404	page 443	page 462	page 508	page 586	page 619	
page 213	page 243	page 283	page 319	page 346	page 379	page 411	page 440	page 473	page 504	page 591	page 617	
page 204	page 234	page 266	page 298	page 330	page 366	page 398	page 426	page 456	page 492	page 576	page 610	page 640
page 220	page 251	page 269	page 313	page 341	page 371	page 406	page 432	page 465	page 501	page 581	page 613	
page 229+ [CD]	page 258	page 295+ [CD]	page 326+ [CD]	page 358+ [CD]	page 391+ [CD]	page 424	page 452+ [CD]	page 483+ [CD]	page 518+ [CD]	page 603+ [CD]	page 635+ [CD]	
	page 260+ [CD]			page 359+ [CD]				page 486+ [CD]		[CD]	[CD]	page 659+ [CD]
page 210+ [CD]	page 244+ [CD]	page 288+ [CD]	page 300+ [CD]	page 350+ [CD]	page 384+ [CD]	page 415+ [CD]	page 446+ [CD]	page 474+ [CD]	page 510+ [CD]	page 597+ [CD]	page 623+ [CD]	
[CD]	[CD]	[CD]	[CD]	[CD]	[CD]	[CD]	[CD]	[CD]	[CD]	[CD]	[CD]	[CD]
	[CD]			[CD]				[CD]		[CD]		

PART ①

INTRODUCTION

As we move into the 21st century, management is at a significant stage. Global competition is a way of life. Technology, international activities, business practices and changes in organisational social responsibility mean managers must reconsider their methods and goals, and increasingly emphasise innovation. In this section we consider some applications of basic management principles in this rapidly changing environment.

Chapter 1 overviews management process. It focuses on managers' actual activities and on skills and knowledge needed to be effective and innovative. However, any innovative practice does not emerge in a vacuum; it is built on the best ideas about management which have developed.

Chapter 2 analyses the roots of current approaches to management: the scientific, behavioural, quantitative and contemporary perspectives.

As **Chapter 3** shows, effective managers require knowledge of both the organisation's environment and internal culture. Successful managers can deal with external and internal factors in ways supporting organisational goal achievement.

Chapter 4 explores organisational social responsibility and managerial ethics. A broad perspective also considers the debate about how much social responsibility an organisation should assume relative to shareholders, employees, customers, community and the larger society.

The Challenge of Management

Chapter 1

CHAPTER OUTLINE

Management: An Overview
What is management?
The management process

What managers actually do
Work methods
Managerial roles
Managerial work agendas

Managerial job types
Vertical dimension: Hierarchical levels
Differences among hierarchical levels
Promoting innovation: The entrepreneurial role
Horizontal dimension: Responsibility areas

Managerial knowledge, skills, and performance
Knowledge base
Key management skills
Performance

Managing in the 21st century
Managing change and innovation
Managing diversity: The workforce of 2000 and beyond
Developing a global perspective
The quest for total quality and continuous improvement

LEARNING OBJECTIVES

After studying this chapter, you should be able to:

○ Explain the four functions of management and other major elements in the management process.
○ Describe three common work methods managers use and 10 major roles managers play.
○ Identify the main factors influencing work agendas and the ways managers use such agendas to channel their efforts.
○ Delineate three major types of managerial skills.
○ Distinguish between effectiveness and efficiency as related to organisational performance.
○ Explain how managerial jobs differ by hierarchical level and responsibility area.
○ Explain how managers at different hierarchical levels can foster innovation by use of the entrepreneurial role.
○ Describe how management education and experience prepare managers.
○ Identify four particularly influential management trends in the 21st century.

Striving for excellence

Autoliv presents itself as an organisation focused on high-quality technical leadership. As can be seen in the mission statement reproduced below, embedded within it is not only a technical focus, but an emphasis on people's welfare and development. While many organisations claim people are their key resource, Autoliv differentiates itself by reflecting this claim in its key objectives and values. This is further embedded in senior management's practices.

Robert Franklin, managing director, has a background in engineering with post-graduate qualifications in business and management. His many years of experience combine manufacturing, engineering and management with a focus on quality. Mr Franklin not only puts his name to documents expounding the organisation's values but practises them on a day-to-day basis. He makes it his responsibility to be the one to communicate the corporate plan and the company's performance indicators and outcomes to each and every employee. He does this by regular meetings in small groups of roughly 20, these being repeated until each staff member has participated. These interactions are held with natural work groups, giving these employees opportunity to raise issues of most concern to themselves.

Another aspect of this commitment to people is Robert Franklin's time on the shop floor. He attends AIMS meetings, which are weekly production floor team meetings looking at how each production cell has performed measured against quality and production targets.

Mr Franklin is a strong and positive role model to his senior management team, using these same objectives as part of every manager's competency-based performance review.

The Autoliv Australia business plan indicates that all of the key objectives are of equal value to the way the organisation assesses itself, and therefore how the managing director manages and leads his people.

Autoliv is the world leader in the development and manufacture of automotive-occupant safety systems. The Australian operation supplies the local and Asia-Pacific regions' vehicle manufacturers with seat belts, air bags, child restraints and steering wheels.

This book examines many organisations in considering critical management approaches to organisational success in the new millennium.

In the process, we highlight several themes particularly important to managers. For one, we will examine techniques especially effective for managing change and promoting innovation. These techniques help explain how a company can develop many new products. For another, we explore why forward-looking companies place so much emphasis on developing quality and initiating total quality management systems. Yet another theme is the importance of building and managing a diverse workforce. Statistics show that due to changes in population profile, women and minority groups make up a growing proportion of the workforce for the 21st century. Finally, we will highlight the need to adopt a global perspective, as managers must operate in an international context. We will be returning to these themes at various points through the book as we explore management.

We begin the current chapter by overviewing the nature of management and the basic processes involved. We then consider what managers actually do by describing the work methods used, different roles played and work agendas guiding their actions. We also examine the knowledge base and skills managers need to achieve high performance. We explore two major dimensions along which managerial jobs differ, and we consider how the entrepreneurial role at different levels of management fosters innovation. Finally, we investigate how becoming an effective manager includes understanding future trends and issues.

MANAGEMENT: AN OVERVIEW

For most of us, organisations are an important part of our daily lives. By **organisation**, we mean two or more persons engaged in a systematic effort to produce goods or services. We all deal with organisations when we attend classes, deposit money at the bank, buy clothing and attend a movie. Our lives are indirectly affected by organisations through the products we use (Jones 1995).

What is management?

Management is the achievement of organisational goals by engaging in the four major functions of planning, organising, leading and controlling. This definition recognises that management is an ongoing activity, entails goal attainment, and involves knowing how to perform management's major functions. Since these are crucial to effective management, we use them as this book's basic framework (Carroll & Gillen 1987; Jones 1995). Accordingly, text Parts Two to Five are devoted, in turn, to planning, organising, leading and controlling. In this section, we briefly overview these four functions (see Fig. 1.1). Then we consider their relation to other major aspects of managerial work.

Planning   **Planning** is the management function involving goal setting and deciding how best to achieve goals.

Organising   **Organising** is the management function focusing on allocating and arranging human and non-human resources so plans can be successfully carried out. Through the organising function managers determine the tasks to be done, how they can best be combined into specific jobs, and how jobs can be grouped into various units to comprise the organisation's structure. Staffing jobs with those who can successfully carry out plans is also part of the organising function.

organisation

Two or more persons engaged in a systematic effort to produce goods or services

management

The process of achieving organisational goals by engaging in the four major functions of planning, organising, leading and controlling

planning

The process of setting goals and deciding how best to achieve them

organising

The process of allocating and arranging human and non-human resources so that plans can be carried out successfully

Fig. 1.1 The functions of management

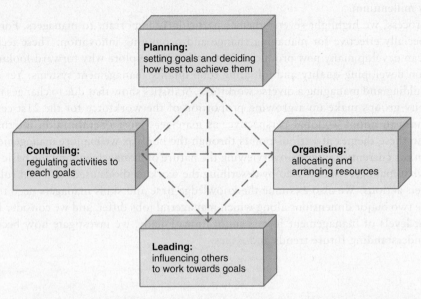

Leading **Leading** is the management function involving influencing others to engage in work behaviours needed to reach organisational goals. Leading includes communicating with others, helping to outline a vision of what can be accomplished, providing direction, and motivating organisation members to put forth the substantial effort required. This function also includes encouraging necessary levels of change and innovation.

Controlling **Controlling** is the management function regulating organisational activities so actual performance conforms to expected standards and goals (Newman 1975). To regulate, managers must monitor ongoing activities, compare results with expected standards or progress toward goals, and take any necessary corrective action.

The management process

While the four major functions of management form the basis of the managerial process, there are several further key elements in the process. Carroll and Gillen (1987) identified these elements on the basis of their review of major studies on managerial work. As Figure 1.2 shows, work methods and managerial roles, as well as work agendas, feed core management functions. A manager's knowledge base and key management skills are important in contributing to high performance (goal achievement). We consider each of these in more detail in the next two sections of this chapter. Throughout this discussion, remember that management process applies both to profit-making organisations and not-for-profit organisations (Lachman 1985). A **not-for-profit organisation** (sometimes called a non-profit organisation) is an organisation whose main purposes centre on issues other than making profits. Common examples are government organisations (the federal government), educational institutions (your university or college), cultural institutions (a symphony orchestra), charitable institutions (Salvation Army) and many health-care facilities (a large public hospital).

---

leading

The process of influencing others to engage in the work behaviours necessary to reach organisational goals

controlling

The process of regulating organisational activities so that actual performance conforms to expected organisational standards and goals

not-for-profit organisation

An organisation whose main purposes centre on issues other than making profits

Fig. 1.2   An extended model of the management process
(adapted from Carroll & Gillen 1987, pp. 38–51)

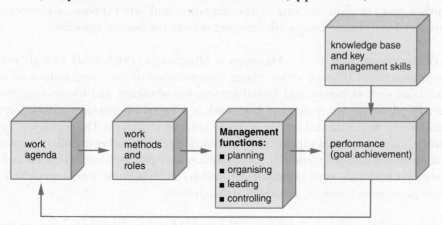

WHAT MANAGERS ACTUALLY DO

One of the most influential studies of managers was conducted by Mintzberg (1980) who followed several top managers around for a week each and recorded everything they did. In documenting their activities, Mintzberg reached some interesting conclusions about managerial work methods and several major roles managers play.

Work methods

Mintzberg (1980) found managers' actual work methods differed drastically from their popular image as reflective, systematic planners spending considerable quiet time in their offices poring over formal reports. Three of his findings provide glimpses into the world of high-level managers.

Unrelenting pace   Managers in Mintzberg's study started work the moment they arrived at the office in the morning and kept working until they left at night. Rather than take coffee breaks, the managers usually drank their coffee while they attended an average of eight meetings each day. Similarly, lunches were almost always eaten during formal or informal meetings. When not in meetings, managers handled an average of 36 pieces of mail per day, as well as other written and verbal communications. Any free time was usually quickly used by subordinates anxious to have a word with the boss.

Brevity, variety and fragmentation   Mintzberg found managers were handling a wide variety of issues through the day, ranging from a retirement presentation to discussing bidding on a multi-million-dollar contract. Many activities were surprisingly brief: about half the activities Mintzberg recorded were completed in less than nine minutes, and only 10 per cent took more than an hour. Telephone calls tended to be short, averaging six minutes. Work sessions at the manager's desk and informal meetings averaged 15 and 10 minutes respectively. Managers experienced continual interruptions from telephone calls and subordinates, and often stopped their own deskwork to place calls or request subordinates drop in. Leaving meetings before they finished was common. Because of fragmentation and interruptions, a number of top managers saved their major brainwork for times outside the normal workday.

Verbal contacts and networks   Managers in Mintzberg's (1980) study strongly preferred verbal communication through either phone conversations or meetings, instead of written communication such as memos and formal reports. For obtaining and transmitting information, they relied heavily on networks. A **network** is a set of co-operative relationships with individuals whose help is needed for a manager to function effectively. The network of contacts in Mintzberg's study included superiors, subordinates, peers and other organisation members, as well as numerous outside individuals. Some contacts were personal, such as friends and peers. Others were professionals, such as consultants, lawyers and insurance underwriters. Still others were trade association contacts, customers and suppliers.

network

A set of co-operative relationships with individuals whose help is needed in order for a manager to function effectively

Implications of Mintzberg's findings   Although Mintzberg's study focused on top-level managers, his findings apply to a wide variety of managers (Kurke & Aldrich 1983; Gibbs 1994). For example, one study of factory supervisors found they engaged in between 237 and 1073 activities within a given workday—or more than one activity every two minutes (Guest 1956). Such research strongly supports the view that managers must develop a major network of contacts to have influence and operate effectively (Luthans 1988). For some ideas on how you might be able to develop such contacts as a manager, see the Skills for the 21st century discussion, 'How to build networks'.

⬆ How to build networks

management skills
for the 21st century

Experts agree building networks of influence involves the principle of reciprocity. Reciprocity means people generally feel they should be paid back for various things they do and one good (or bad) turn deserves another. Mostly, individuals do not expect to be paid back right away or in specific amounts; approximations will usually do. Because individuals anticipate their actions will be reimbursed in one way or another, influence and networking are possible.

One way to think about the reciprocity principle in networking is to view oneself as a 'trader' and to use the metaphor of 'currencies' as a means of approaching the process of exchange. Just as there are many types of currencies used in the world, there are many different kinds of currencies to use in organisational life. Too often individuals think only in terms of money, promotions and status, but there are actually many possibilities.

Some possible currencies

Some possible currencies you might be able to trade include the following:
○ **Resources:** giving budget increases, personnel, space, etc.
○ **Assistance:** helping with projects or taking on unwanted tasks
○ **Information:** furnishing organisational and/or technical knowledge
○ **Recognition:** acknowledging effort, accomplishment or abilities
○ **Visibility:** providing the chance to be known by higher-ups

- **Advancement:** giving tasks that can aid in promotion
- **Personal support:** providing personal and emotional backing
- **Understanding:** listening to others' concerns

How to use currencies

In using currencies, it helps to consider four steps:

1   Think of each individual you have to deal with as a potential ally or network member. If you want to have influence within an organisation and get the job done, you will need to create internal network members or allies. Assume even a difficult person is a potential network member.

2   Get to know the world of the potential network member, including the pressures they are under, as well as their needs and goals. An important factor influencing behaviour is how performance is measured and rewarded. If you ask an individual to do things which may be perceived as poor performance within their work unit, you are likely to encounter resistance.

3   Be aware of your own strengths and potential weaknesses as a networker. Sometimes networkers underestimate the range of currencies they have available for exchange. List potential currencies and resources you have to offer. Then think about your own preferred style of interaction with others. Would-be networkers often fail to understand how their preferred style of interaction fits or doesn't fit with the potential ally's preferred style. For instance, does the potential ally like to socialise first and work later? If so, they may find it difficult to deal with someone who likes to solve the problem first and only then talk about weather, family or office politics. Skilled networkers learn to adapt their own style to others in dealing with potential allies.

4   Gear your exchange transactions so both parties can come out winners. For the most part, transactions in organisations are not one-time occurrences. Usually parties will need to deal with one another again, perhaps frequently. In fact, that is the idea of networks—to have contacts to call on as needed. The implication here is that in most exchange relationships there are two outcomes which ultimately make a difference. One is success in achieving the task goals at hand. The other is maintaining and improving the relationship so the contact remains a viable one. With networking, it is better to lose the battle than to lose the war (Cohen & Bradford 1989; Baker 1994).

Managerial roles

To make sense of the mass of data collected, Mintzberg (1980) categorised managers' various activities into roles. A **role** is an organised set of behaviours associated with a particular office or position (Mintzberg). Positions usually entail multiple roles. For example, roles for a salesperson position in a retail store might include information giver, stock handler and cashier.

The three general types of roles Mintzberg observed were interpersonal, informational and decisional. Interpersonal roles grow directly from a manager's position authority and involve developing and maintaining positive relationships with significant others. Informational roles relate to receiving and transmitting information so managers can serve as their organisational

role

An organised set of behaviours associated with a particular office or position

Table 1.1   Mintzberg's 10 managerial roles

Role	Description
Interpersonal	
Figurehead	Performs symbolic duties of a legal or social nature
Leader	Builds relationships with subordinates and communicates with, motivates and coaches them
Liaison	Maintains networks of contacts outside work unit who provide help and information
Informational	
Monitor	Seeks internal and external information about issues affecting organisation
Disseminator	Transmits information internally obtained from either internal or external sources
Spokesperson	Transmits information about the organisation to outsiders
Decisional	
Entrepreneur	Acts as initiator, designer and encourager of change and innovation
Disturbance handler	Takes corrective action when organisation faces important, unexpected difficulties
Resource allocator	Distributes resources of all types including time, funding, equipment and human resources
Negotiator	Represents the organisation in major negotiations affecting the manager's areas of responsibility

Source: Based on Mintzberg (1980).

units' nerve centres. Decisional roles involve making significant decisions affecting the organisation. Within these role types, Mintzberg outlined 10 more specific roles managers play (see Table 1.1).

Mintzberg's categorisation of managerial activities into roles gives insight into what managers actually do during their workday. The roles also give us clues about the kinds of skills managers will need to effectively carry out their work.

Mintzberg's role approach gives a different perspective on management to the four management functions. At first, it might seem Mintzberg's findings are incompatible with the view that planning, organising, leading and controlling are an important part of management. However, Mintzberg's study did not consider why managers were engaging in the different roles described. When the why is taken into consideration, it is clear the functions of management provide an important blueprint to help managers channel their role behaviours in ways that lead ultimately to goal achievement (Kotter 1982). For example, information transmission through the disseminator role or representing the organisation in the negotiator role has little meaning unless it is linked to a purpose such as a management function. But how do managers tie various activities and roles into the planning, organising, leading and controlling necessary to achieve goals? Part of the answer is suggested by another study, conducted by Kotter.

Managerial work agendas

Kotter's (1982) study focused on 15 general managers in nine companies from a wide range of industries. General managers typically are responsible for a major section of an organisation. From his findings, Kotter suggested managers focus their various efforts productively through work agendas.

Nature of work agendas   A **work agenda** is a loosely connected set of tentative goals and tasks a manager attempts to accomplish. Managers usually develop work agendas during their first six months on a new job, although they are continually subject to reassessment due to changing circumstances and new opportunities. Typically, such agendas address immediate and long-run job responsibilities and are used with more formal organisational plans. Kotter (1982) found that to put their work agendas into place, general managers established the extensive networks Mintzberg identified.

By making use of work agendas and networking strategies, the managers in Kotter's (1982) study were able to engage in short, seemingly disjointed conversations and still accomplish their missions. Consider the following interaction. Peter Barr is the New South Wales state sales manager and is preparing to chair the monthly review meeting of his sales team. His senior account executive, Harry, arrives at the meeting early.

'By the way, Peter, those figures on the 23 are rather good, aren't they?'

'They sure are. I hope we can match them again this month. And beat the Northern Region, as well. Did you pick up on that call Irene passed on to you?'

'Actually, Peter, I passed that on to Roxanne. You remember, we talked about giving her a first small account. Now about those guidelines ...'

'Harry, not now. I want to hear what your three musketeers come up with first.'

The above dialogue may seem somewhat disjointed to an outsider. That perception comes from unfamiliarity with what has gone before and specific business and organisational knowledge shared by the managers. For example, an outsider would be unable to identify Peter Barr, nor know that his business is food distributorship as the wholesale arm of a large food manufacturer and that item 23 is a range of soups. An outsider would also not be able to explain why beating the Northern Region, which is subtropical, on selling soups is rather important to the state sales office. In fact, the Northern Region is Queensland and for the past six years Queensland has sold more soups than New South Wales. Another item which would not be understood is who the three musketeers are and why Peter would want to know what they had to say before listening to Harry's comments.

However, the interchange had many worthwhile consequences. Peter learned that:

Harry is aware of the figure on item 23.

Harry has remembered to pass on an account to Roxanne, and which account it is.

Harry is concerned with the guidelines for restructuring the state's regions.

Peter has also passed on the following information:

He is concerned about the figures for the following month and he really wants them to show an increase over the Northern Region.

He wanted to ensure action was taken over the call Irene had passed on.

He wished to let the team given the task of working out guidelines for the restructure do it, and he did not wish to have this pre-empted by Peter.

---

work agenda

A loosely connected set of tentative goals and tasks that a manager is attempting to accomplish

This discussion demonstrates the fast pace, brevity, variety and fragmentation characteristic of a manager's workday. It also illustrates the use of verbal contacts and networks identified in Mintzberg's study. Read through the conversation again and see if you can identify where Peter used the monitor role in seeking information, the disseminator role in providing information, and the entrepreneur role in following up on issues which could affect the plans for the state. His words had purposes ultimately related to reaching his goals.

Without a work agenda (the manager's own working plan), similar discussions could actually be fairly random and far from efficient. Even with an agenda, managers need to ensure they work within its guidelines. Work agendas give rough guidelines for managers to determine how to orient their various activities and roles. But what factors influence work agenda content?

Factors influencing work agendas   According to Stewart (1982) there are three main factors likely to impact on a manager's work agenda: demands, constraints and choices.

Job demands are activities a manager must do in a job. For example, managers usually have responsibilities related to significant major organisation goals and plans (such as achieving a 10 per cent increase in sales).

Job constraints are factors, both inside and outside the organisation, which limit what a manager can do. Constraints include variables such as resource limitations, legal restrictions, union activities, technological limitations and the degree to which a manager's work unit is defined.

Job choices are work activities the manager can do but does not have to do. For example, without a directive to do so, a manager might initiate a proposal to develop a computerised customer service tracking system. Thus work agendas tend to reflect individual managers' personal preferences and career objectives.

MANAGERIAL KNOWLEDGE, SKILLS AND PERFORMANCE

For managers to develop work agendas, act out roles and engage in planning, organising, leading and controlling, they need a sound knowledge base and key management skills. In this section, we consider these essential management process elements and explain how they relate to the issue of performance.

Knowledge base

Although managers often switch companies working in different industries, they may have difficulties if they don't have a relevant, reasonably extensive knowledge base for their particular managerial job. This knowledge base can include information about an industry and its technology, company policies and practices, company goals and plans, company culture, the personalities of key organisation members, and important suppliers and customers. For example, Kotter (1982) found one reason why general managers could accomplish much within short periods of time was that they took action with only small bits of information at their disposal. Their extensive knowledge base enabled them to attach appropriate meaning to information fragments they obtained.

Key management skills

In addition to having a knowledge base, managers need certain skills to carry out the various functions of management. A skill is the ability to engage in a set of behaviours functionally related to one another and that lead to a desired performance level in a given area (Boyatzis 1982). For managers, three types of skills are necessary: technical, human and conceptual.

Technical skills   **Technical skills** reflect both an understanding of and a proficiency in a specialised field. For example, a manager may have technical skills in accounting, finance, engineering, manufacturing or computer science.

Human skills   **Human skills** are associated with a manager's ability to work well with others, both as a group member and as a leader who gets things done through others. Managers with effective human skills are typically adept at communicating with others and motivating them to develop themselves and perform well in pursuit of organisational goals.

Conceptual Skills   **Conceptual skills** relate to the ability to visualise the organisation as a whole, discern interrelationships among organisational parts, and understand how it fits into the wider industry, community and world contexts. Conceptual skills, coupled with technical skills, human skills and a knowledge base, are important elements in organisational performance.

Performance

What constitutes high performance in an organisation? Drucker (1967) points out that performance achieved through management is actually made up of two important dimensions: effectiveness and efficiency.

Effectiveness   **Effectiveness** is the ability to choose appropriate goals and achieve them. So organisations are effective when managers choose appropriate goals and then achieve them. Some years ago, for example, McDonald's decided on the goal of providing breakfast service to attract more customers. This choice proved very smart, for sales of breakfast food now account for over 30 per cent of McDonald's revenues (Jones 2000). Thus McDonald's illustrates what Drucker (1988) means when he points out that effectiveness is doing (accomplishing) the right things.

Efficiency   **Efficiency** is the ability to make best use of available resources in the process of achieving goals. Organisations are efficient when managers minimise input resources (labour, raw materials and component parts) or the amount of time needed to produce a given output or services. For example, McDonald's recently developed a more efficient fat fryer which reduces (by 30 per cent) the amount of oil used in cooking but also speeds up cooking of french

technical skills

Skills reflecting both an understanding of and a proficiency in a specialised field

human skills

Skills associated with a manager's ability to work well with others, both as a member of a group and as a leader who gets things done through others

conceptual skills

Skills related to the ability to visualise the organisation as a whole, discern interrelationships among organisational parts, and understand how the organisation fits into the wider context of the industry, community and world

effectiveness

The ability to choose appropriate goals and achieve them

efficiency

The ability to make the best use of available resources in the process of achieving goals

fries. Through such means, McDonald's illustrates what Drucker (1988) has in mind when he speaks of efficiency as doing things right.

In essence, organisations must exhibit both effectiveness (doing the right things) and efficiency (doing things right) to be good performers. Because these dimensions are so closely linked, we generally use the term 'effectiveness' in this book in reference to both effectiveness and efficiency. We do this for the simplicity and readability.

MANAGERIAL JOB TYPES

Although we have been discussing the nature of managerial work in general, managerial jobs vary somewhat on the basis of two important dimensions. One is a vertical dimension, focusing on different hierarchical levels in the organisation. The other is a horizontal dimension, addressing variations in managers' responsibility areas. We explore these dimensions and their implications in this section. Because of its importance in fostering innovation, we give special attention to the entrepreneurial role at various hierarchical levels (refer to Table 1.1).

Vertical dimension: Hierarchical levels

Along the vertical dimension, managerial jobs in fall into three categories: first-line, middle and top management. These categories represent vertical differentiation among managers because they involve different levels of the organisation, as shown in Figure 1.3.

first-line managers/ supervisors

Managers at the lowest level of the hierarchy who are directly responsible for the work of operating (non-managerial) employees

First-line managers: First-line managers (or supervisors) operate at the lowest hierarchical level and are directly responsible for the work of operating (non-managerial) employees. Their titles often include the word 'supervisor'. First-line managers are vital to the success of organisation goals as they are responsible for smooth day-to-day operations in pursuit of those goals.

Operating between management and the rest of the workforce, first-line supervisors often experience conflicting demands. At the same time, first-line supervisor power has eroded

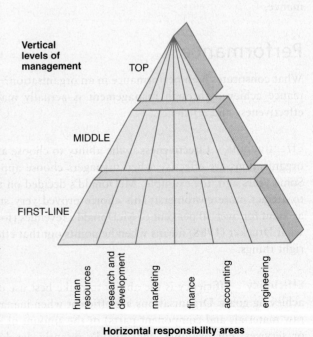

Fig. 1.3 Types of managers by hierarchical level and responsibility area

Vertical levels of management

TOP

MIDDLE

FIRST-LINE

human resources

research and development

marketing

finance

accounting

engineering

Horizontal responsibility areas

because of factors such as union influence, increasing worker education levels, establishment of work teams and use of computers to track activities formerly regulated by first-line managers. Consequently, first-line supervisors' jobs in future are likely to involve greater emphasis on dealing with internal human relations and representing the unit externally.

Middle managers: **Middle managers** are managers beneath the top hierarchical levels and directly responsible for the work of lower-level managers. They may have direct responsibility for other middle managers or first-line managers. Sometimes they may also supervise operating personnel, such as administrative assistants and specialists (e.g. engineers or financial analysts). Middle managers' titles include 'manager', 'director of', 'chief', 'department head' and 'division head'. They are mainly responsible for implementing overall organisational plans to achieve organisational goals.

Organisations, particularly large ones, traditionally tended to have several layers of middle managers. For example, at one point, General Motors had 14 or 15 management levels. This reflected a post-World War II trend to add layers of middle management to co-ordinate expanding activities. By the 1980s, however, the trend was reversed. Many companies cut managerial levels to lower costs, reduce layers involved in decision making and facilitate communication (Labich 1989).

Reducing middle management layers brings challenges and opportunities. A common result is that remaining middle-managers gain greater autonomy and responsibility. Unsurprisingly, pressure on middle managers also increases (Wysocki 1995). In one survey, more than half of respondents reported that middle managers in their organisations work longer hours than before, and a quarter said they spend more weekends in the office (Zemke 1988; Fisher 1992). For individuals who lose their jobs through downsizing, dislocation can be painful until another is found (Grossman 1996; Cascio 1993; Parker, Wall & Jackson 1997).

Though there may be fewer middle managers in future, Kanter (1989) argues the distinction between managers and the managed is also declining. She predicts less emphasis on hierarchical level and, instead, greater weight on horizontal influence, increased reliance on peer networks, greater access to information and more control over assignments at lower levels. As middle managers assume additional responsibilities, many of their current duties will be distributed to lower management levels, thereby raising the importance of these positions.

Top managers: **Top managers** are at the very top levels of the hierarchy and are ultimately responsible for the entire organisation. There are few of them and typical titles include 'chief executive officer' (CEO), 'president', 'general manager', and 'director'. Top-level managers are often referred to as executives, although the term 'executive' is also sometimes used to include upper-middle managers as well. Top managers are directly responsible for the upper layer of middle managers. They typically oversee overall organisation planning, work with middle managers in implementing the planning, and maintain control over the organisation's progress.

Differences among hierarchical levels

Although the same managerial process applies at all hierarchical levels of management, differences in emphasis occur. Major differences stem from the importance of the four functions of management, the skills needed to perform effectively, the emphasis on managerial roles at each level, and the use of the entrepreneurial role.

middle managers

Managers beneath the top levels of the hierarchy who are directly responsible for the work of managers at lower levels

top managers

Managers at the very top levels of the hierarchy who are ultimately responsible for the entire organisation

Functions of management: The relative importance of planning, organising, leading and controlling varies by managerial level (Mahoney, Jerdee & Carroll 1965; Gomez-Mejia, McCann & Page 1985). As indicated in Figure 1.4, planning is more important for top than for middle or first-line managers. This is primarily because top managers are responsible for determining the organisation's overall direction, which requires extensive planning.

Similarly, organising is more important for top and middle than for first-line managers. This stems from top- and middle-management levels being mainly responsible for allocating and arranging resources, though this is also performed by first-line supervisors.

In contrast, leading is much more important for first-line supervisors than for higher-level managers. Since first-line supervisors are in charge of goods or services production, they use greater amounts of communicating, motivating, directing and supporting—all associated with leading.

Finally, the management function common to all hierarchical levels is controlling. This reflects a common degree of emphasis on monitoring activities and taking corrective action.

Management skills: The three management levels also differ in the importance attached to key skills discussed before: technical, human and conceptual (see Fig. 1.5) (Katz 1974). Generally, conceptual skills are most needed by top management. These managers must see the organisation as a whole, understand how its various parts relate to each another, and associate the organisation with the outside world (Maruca 1994).

Fig. 1.4   Use of management functions at different hierarchical levels

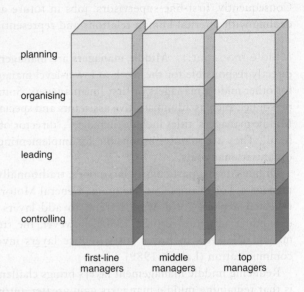

Fig. 1.5   Use of key management skills at different hierarchical levels

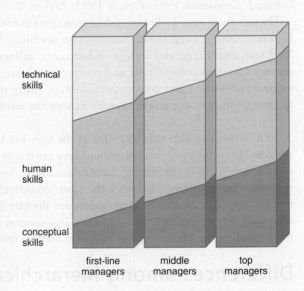

In contrast, first-line managers have the greatest need for technical skills, as they directly supervise most non-managerial technical and professional employees. Yet middle managers, too, often need technical skills so they can communicate with subordinates and recognise major problems (Torrington & Weightman 1987). Even top managers must have some technical skills, particularly when technology is important to their organisation's products or services. Otherwise, upper-level managers will be unable to foster innovation, allocate resources efficiently, or devise strategies to stay ahead of the competition.

Not surprisingly, all three levels of management require strong human skills because they all must get things done through people (Pavett & Lau 1983). Ironically, promotions to first-level management are often based on individuals' good technical skills, with little consideration given to assessing their human skills. Managers lacking sufficient human skills usually have serious difficulties attempting to deal with individuals both inside and outside their work units. In fact, studies focusing on the primary reasons executives derail suggests human skills are particularly important factors (see Table 1.2). Derailed executives are those who reach relatively high levels but then find little chance of further upward movement because their personal skills are insufficient (Van Velsor & Leslie 1995).

Table 1.2   Causes of executive career derailment

1.   Problems with interpersonal relationships
2.   Failure to meet business objectives
3.   Inability to build and lead a team
4.   Inability to develop or adapt

Source: Adapted from Van Velsor & Leslie (1995, p. 64).

Managerial roles   Although Mintzberg (1980) argued the 10 managerial roles he identified apply at all management levels (see Table 1.1), he did note some differences in emphasis at various levels. Subsequent research suggests the figurehead role and others such as liaison and spokesperson become more important as a manager moves up the hierarchy. On the other hand, the leader role appears to be more critical at lower levels, a finding which supports the idea that the leading function itself has greater importance for lower-level managers than for higher ones (Pavett & Lau 1983).

In a study of the importance of various roles, managers at all levels gave particularly high ratings to the entrepreneurial role (Pavett & Lau 1983). Several experts on innovation, however, argue the entrepreneurial role varies in some important ways depending on a manager's hierarchical level (Kanter 1982; Pearson 1988). Because of innovation's importance to organisation success, we explore the differences below.

@ Be part of the e-boom
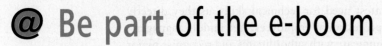
managing the e-challenge

Forrester Research has a stern warning for Australian businesses and governments: respond to the Internet or lose ground to those who do. The prediction is that e-commerce—the trade of goods and services in which the final order is placed over the Internet—will grow dramatically over the next three years to billions of dollars in the United States alone.

The contention is that for a country to succeed it must have a robust network infrastructure, and needs a foundation for e-commerce, laws adapted to digital trade, and domestic policy aligned to global treaties.

Forrester has developed the 'commerce threshold' model which outlines the 'window of opportunity' in which governments and businesses must act to fully participate in the growth of e-commerce.

Source: Adapted from Bryant, G. (1999).

Activities for discussion, analysis and further research

1 Investigate the degree to which countries like the United States, Canada, Britain, Germany and Australia are developing their e-commerce infrastructure.
2 What would be the preparedness factors which will impact on the ability of a government or business to take full advantage of e-commerce?

Promoting innovation: The entrepreneurial role

innovation

A new idea applied to initiating or improving a process, product or service

intrapreneurs

Individuals who engage in entrepreneurial roles inside organisations

intrapreneurship

The process of innovating within an existing organisation

idea champion

An individual who generates a new idea or believes in the value of a new idea and supports it in the face of numerous potential obstacles

An **innovation** is a new idea involving initiating or improving a process, product or service (Kanter 1983). The process of innovation is closely related to the entrepreneurial role in organisations, as this role relates to discovering and exploiting new opportunities. In fact, innovative activities, especially major ones, are often referred to as entrepreneurship within organisations. More recently, those engaging in entrepreneurial roles within organisations are called **intrapreneurs**. The term differentiates between innovators working inside existing organisations and those who innovate by creating new organisations (the latter are often called entrepreneurs). Similarly, the process of innovating in an existing organisation is referred to as **intrapreneurship**.

Encouraging innovation in organisations takes great effort. Furthermore, successful innovations are rarely produced by one person's work. Rather, the innovative process usually involves individuals at various levels fulfilling three types of entrepreneurial roles: idea generator or champion, sponsor and orchestrator (Galbraith 1982).

Idea champion: An **idea champion** is someone who generates a new idea or believes in its value and supports it in the face of numerous potential obstacles. Such individuals are known as entrepreneurs, inventors, creative individuals or risk takers. They are usually at lower levels in the organisation, recognise a problem and help develop a solution. First-line supervisors act as idea champions when they develop innovative ideas, nurture them in others, and fight tenaciously to help make the ideas a reality. However, because idea champions are relatively low in the hierarchy, they often do not have the power and status to get their innovations accepted. This situation creates the need for the next type of role.

Sponsor   A **sponsor** is an individual, usually a middle manager, who recognises an idea's organisational significance, helps obtain necessary funding for development of the innovation, and facilitates its implementation. Sponsors tend to be middle managers because their higher-level organisation position enables them to provide backing needed for an innovation's survival. While innovations in organisations are unlikely to occur without a sponsor, their occurrence also depends on an individual filling a third role.

Orchestrator   An **orchestrator** or high-level manager explains the need for innovation, provides funding for innovating activities, creates incentives for middle managers to sponsor new ideas, and protects idea people. Because innovations often constitute a challenge to established ways of doing things, those comfortable with or having a particular stake in the status quo often resist them. (For example, an expert in a process may resist a change making it outmoded.) An orchestrator maintains the balance of power so new ideas can be tested in the face of possible negative reactions. By filling the role of orchestrator, top managers encourage innovation.

Without all three roles, major innovations are much less likely.

Horizontal dimension: Responsibility areas

In addition to vertical differences, managerial jobs differ on a horizontal dimension which relates to the nature of the responsibility area involved (see Figure 1.3). In horizontal differentiation, there are three major types of managerial jobs: functional, general and project.

Functional managers   **Functional managers** are managers responsible for a specific, specialised organisation area (often called a functional area) and mostly supervise those with expertise and training in that area. Common functional specialisations include finance, manufacturing or operations, marketing, human resource management, accounting, quality assurance and engineering.

General managers   **General managers** are those with responsibility for a whole organisation or a substantial subunit including most of the common specialised areas. In other words, a general manager presides over several functional areas (hence the term 'general'). General managers have several titles such as 'division manager' and 'president', depending on circumstances. A small company will normally have just one general manager, who heads the entire organisation. Depending on how it is organised, a large company may have several general managers (in addition to the chief executive officer), and each usually presides over a major division.

Project managers   **Project managers** are responsible for co-ordinating efforts involving individuals in several different organisational units working on a particular project. Because individuals report to managers in their specific work units but also to their project manager, project managers usually must have extremely strong interpersonal skills to keep things moving smoothly (we discuss this issue further in Chapter 11). Project managers are frequently used in aerospace and other high-technology firms to co-ordinate projects, such as aeroplane or computer project development. They are also used in some consumer-oriented companies to launch or stay on top of market development for specific products, such as cookies or margarine (Stanley & Davis 1977).

Margin glossary

sponsor

A middle manager who recognises the organisational significance of an idea, helps obtain the necessary funding for development of the innovation, and facilitates its actual implementation

orchestrator

A high-level manager who explains the need for innovation, provides funding for innovating activities, creates incentives for middle managers to sponsor new ideas, and protects idea people

functional managers

Managers with responsibility for a specific, specialised area of the organisation who supervise mainly individuals with expertise and training in that area

general managers

Managers with responsibility for a whole organisation or a substantial subunit including most of the common specialised areas

project managers

Managers with responsibility for co-ordinating efforts involving individuals in several different organisational units all working on a particular project

Getting the balance right

Being a manager is considered to be a full-time job. In today's environment, it is often too easy to let that full-time job occupy more than its fair share of a normal 24-hour day. However, the truly successful senior manager finds a way to balance work and family or other commitments.

Daniel Petre, chairman of PBL Online, the Internet subsidiary of Kerry Packer's Publishing and Broadcasting Limited, is one of those who has discovered and satisfied the need for a proper balance between the demands of work and the needs of a family.

To fail in finding such a balance can be costly. Just how costly this can be was found by Peter Ritchie, chairman of McDonald's Australia, whose long hours spent building up the chain has been blamed for the breakdown of his relationship with his only son.

Balance is essential. Individuals must make sure that right through their year, there is time for regeneration of physical, mental and emotional energy. The demands made of the manager (and these increase with the level of the individual in the organisation) are to be productive and efficient. That takes an incredible amount of time, effort and energy. Yet there is also the expectation that managers will be sharing and caring members of families and will be able to enjoy satisfying personal lives. These expectations are frequently in conflict with each other, and cause role overload and role interference when there is not enough time or energy to meet all the conflicting and over-lapping demands of the multiple roles.

Mike Ferraro is a partner at Freehill Hollingdale & Page in Melbourne. He maintains balance by making sacrifices. He and his wife have attempted to stagger work hours so that their two children get parental attention. Ferraro has little time for other social outlets such as sports or catching up with old friends. He has invested his efforts in balance by ensuring that most of his non-working hours are devoted to family.

Gillian Franklin is the managing director of Creative Brands, a toiletries and cosmetics company, with a frenetic work life that sees her arriving at her Melbourne office at 7.15 every morning to start a 12-hour work day. Her self-imposed work style demands a 60 to 70-hour work week so she has to be organised, focused and committed. To achieve this and still have a balanced life, Franklin has a live-in housekeeper to help with the children and liberate her for activities she can share with her children and husband.

Over the past year, Barry Jackson, managing director of the manufacturing group Pacifica, has spent over 100 days away from home. He identifies the dangers of being insulated from the real world where diversity of thought and perspectives can balance the dilemma of how inward-thinking senior managers can be. His family weekends at Phillip Island in Victoria went a long way to keeping him in touch with what the people in the community were thinking.

Not all senior executives have been fortunate in achieving a healthy balance. Every McDonald's golden arch in Australia is a monument to Peter Ritchie's determination, ambition and capacity to focus on his goals. However, he looks back and sees a life out of kilter. His message to executives is: 'You can't just ignore your family while pursuing a career. As I discovered, you can't catch up for lost time either. In the end, it's just not worth it.' (Way, 1999 p. 73)

The CEO referred to here is not named. His action is extreme but revealing: 'One CEO said that, with over 300 days of leave accrued, he had instructed his secretary to log some of his work days as holidays, so that his total did not increase and embarrass him in the light of his edict that all executives take their due holidays.' (Way, 1999 p. 75)

Do boards of companies who pay their executives seven-figure packages own them 365 days a year, 24 hours a day? Some maintain that this is the case. Others don't agree. Petee maintains that there is no meeting that cannot be missed for the sake of a child or other family member. Brian Dyson, CEO of Coca-Cola Enterprises, says it a bit differently: 'Imagine life as a game in which you are juggling five balls in the air. You name them work, family, health, friends and spirit, and you are keeping them all in the air. You will soon understand that work is a rubber ball. If you drop it, it will bounce back. But the other four balls—family, health, friends and spirit—are made of glass.'

Source: Adapted from Way, N. (1999).

Activities for discussion, analysis and further research

1 Discuss why the maintenance of a balanced work and family life is considered to help 'gaining the edge' for senior executives.
2 Run a web search on the following senior executives from international organisations and try to determine what they do to maintain a balanced work and family life. Can you detect a pattern? What sacrifices do they make, if any?
  - Herman Z. Latif, chairman of Krama Yudha Tiga Berlian Motors (they assemble vehicles in Indonesia as part of a joint venture with Mitsubishi Motors Co.)
  - Carlos Ghosn, chief operating officer of Nissan Motor Co.
  - David Murray, CEO Commonwealth Bank (CBA)
  - Hilton Sack, CEO Visa International Australia
  - Steve Outtrim, CEO, Sausage Software
  - Brett Blundy, CEO Brazin
3 Make contact with a manager in a local organisation. Interview them with a view to discovering their views on the issue of life-activity balance, and identify the strategies they use to maintain a personal work and life balance.

MANAGING IN THE 21ST CENTURY

Successful managers must watch future trends likely to impact on the actions they must take to keep their organisations moving forward. As we mentioned at the beginning of this chapter, several important themes are emerging as researchers study trends relevant to managing in the 21st century. Here, we expand upon these four themes briefly and explain how they will be addressed throughout this book to help you become a successful 21st century manager.

Managing change and innovation

As we move into the 21st century, effectively managing change and innovation is becoming more critical. Change is any alteration of the status quo to which a company must respond. Innovation is a new idea applied to initiating or improving a process, product or service. Most companies confront serious competitive challenges due to the increasingly rapid rate and unpredictability of technological change. Changes in information technology will be most important in the 21st century. Firms face many other pressures, such as alterations in competitor strategies, shifts in economic conditions, or modifications in customer preferences (Seiders & Barry 1998). Companies will survive and prosper if their managers guide the process of change so the organisation makes needed adaptations faced with altered conditions (Anderson 1997). But they must do more. Increasingly, successful companies are those who emphasise opportunities available from innovation (Lengnick-Hall 1992; Bower & Christensen 1995).

We further discuss issues relating to managing change and innovation in an entire chapter (see Chapter 10). In addition, throughout the book we frequently refer to examples of organisations successful in managing change and innovation.

✖ When the unexpected hits

crossroads

Consider the following process in an organisation the author is familiar with but is not at liberty to name.

This organisation for a number of years has been running a very successful off-shore manufacturing facility. As a result of the financial crisis in South-East Asia, its export market all but disappeared. However, when the budget forecasts were done, the expected income from exports had been included. This meant that the organisation stood to make an enormous loss.

Source: M. Tein.

Decision point

1 If you were the general manager of this organisation what would you do? Why?

Reflection point

1 Senior management decided that what they would do is retrench all the team leaders, as they were the most expensive staff in the factory. What do you think happened? Why? What would you now do to overcome the resulting difficulties?

Managing diversity: The workforce of 2000 and beyond

To use all resources effectively, organisations are beginning to capitalise on their managers' and employees' country-specific or even continent-specific knowledge. For example, Coca-Cola takes advantage of its diverse foreign workforce's knowledge to develop effective marketing campaigns in its major global markets. At senior levels too, Coca-Cola takes up the challenge of global diversity by employing diverse managers to lead the company. Former Coca-Cola chairman Roberto Goizueta came from Cuba; other senior managers are from France, Brazil and Spain.

Many other companies rely on their diverse workforce's talents. For example, Jac Nasser, Ford's CEO since 1998, was born in Lebanon. He has extensive international experience, having headed Ford's Australian operations. Alex Trotman, former Ford US chairman, who pioneered Ford's global reorganisation, is English. Trotman acquired extensive knowledge of European customers' needs while in charge of Ford's European operations. This is important as managers who value their employees' diversity invest in developing these employees' skills and capabilities and link available rewards to their performance. They are managers who succeed in promoting performance in the long term (Cox & Blake 1991). Today, more and more organisations realise people are indeed their most important resource and developing and protecting human resources is crucial for management in a globally competitive environment.

A recent survey showed more than 70 per cent of *major* organisations in America have diversity management programs in place. Another 16 per cent are developing programs or have various initiatives at division levels (Society for Human Resource Management 1995). Most countries in the region, including Australia, are at present lagging on this issue. Why have so many organisations set up diversity programs? The motivations behind these efforts are varied. For one, companies are concerned about their ability to attract and retain the best talent available. Companies with positive reputations for managing diversity are likely to be at a competitive advantage in assembling talented individuals. For another, the customer base of most companies is also increasingly diverse.

Essentially in the coming millennium, managers themselves will reflect the emerging diversity and, at the same time, will need to be able to utilise effectively an increasingly diverse workforce. We discuss the diversity issue further in Managing diversity sections in several chapters and periodically spotlight important organisational efforts in this area through the use of Managing diversity boxes at intervals.

Developing a global perspective

Along with diversity initiatives, organisations must assume a global perspective in their business for three major reasons. First, businesses are facing more global competition. Second, more companies are likely to be operating in other countries.

Third, businesses are increasingly becoming globalised in the sense of operating as one company, despite far-flung operations. As these trends imply, managers must have a greater knowledge of international business in the 21st century. Accordingly, we devote an entire chapter to international management (see Chapter 19) and include international material in a number of other chapters. In addition, we frequently use international companies as examples so you can learn more about such organisations and how they do business.

The quest for total quality and continuous improvement

Due to increasing global competition, particularly from Japanese companies, many organisations have placed greater emphasis on quality and embracing concepts of continuous improvement. Such programs often are referred to as total quality management (TQM). Total quality management is a management system integrated into an organisation's strategy and is aimed at continually improving product and service quality so as to achieve high levels of customer satisfaction and build strong customer loyalty (Bounds, Yorks, Adams & Ramney 1994; Riecheld 1996).

Many companies have benefited from an emphasis on TQM; however, it requires considerable company-wide commitment to be successful. We, therefore, refer to quality issues in several chapters and provide extended coverage of this topic in Supplement 1 to Chapter 16 on quality and other managerial control methods.

In this chapter, we have provided an overview of the basic management challenge, including a forward glance at trends likely to influence the way managers work in the future. In the next chapter, we take a look back at the pioneering ideas which helped shape our knowledge of management today.

Rag traders get some help from an experienced hand

One of the biggest challenges facing young companies looking for equity finance is to find an investor with compatible business philosophies and goals. Two entrepreneurs, David Stewart, 36, and Chris Carr, 43, found a way around the problem. They already knew the person they invited to invest and work full-time in their new Geelong company. He was their old boss. With his experience, the founders avoided some costly mistakes, and the capital has put them two years ahead of their five-year plan.

For Stewart and Carr, starting their own clothing company was a long-held dream. They shared the same motivations: the satisfaction of seeing their clothes worn in the streets, the opportunity to push past the salary ceiling that came with working for someone else, and greater control over their own lives.

The impetus to act on their dream came from dissatisfaction with their employer, the Austin Group. After the company listed on the Australian Stock Exchange in 1993, Stewart and Carr felt that it became bowed down by bureaucracy. On 15 May 1997, they left to launch C&D Clothing, which trades as Henley Clothing Company.

The plan for their range of casual men's wear was simple: better quality, quicker turnaround, lower prices. The pair had a network of customers and suppliers, and were experienced in the clothing industry. They began with $200 000 working capital borrowed against their homes, but within three months they were in trouble. Demand for their products exceeded their expectations, drained working capital and left them struggling to fulfil orders.

Stewart and Carr lacked financial and administrative experience. They paid a premium to manufacturers in India and China to improve quality and turnaround, eroding their profit margin. The surge of orders, initially from independent retailers, kept them on the road, and the warehouse operations began to suffer.

Stewart and Carr needed help. They thought about their old boss, Ron Tenabel, 54, who was a founding director of Austin, and had hired Stewart in 1986 and Carr in 1992. Like Stewart and Carr, Tenabel disagreed with the new direction of Austin after the listing. He left in 1995, signing a restraint-of-trade agreement. Bored by early retirement, Tenabel started searching for private investment opportunities, but none fitted his requirement for a small, lean business. When Stewart and Carr approached him with a proposal to join their company, it was the opportunity Tenabel was looking for. He wanted a day-to-day role in operations and financial strategy, and a place for his wife, Sharon, 54, in accounts. His agreement not to compete against Austin had expired. Stewart and Carr agreed to keep the company lean and limit sales growth to $5 million a year. In October 1997, Tenabel and his wife joined the company, bringing more than $750 000 with them. Ron Tenabel was also made a director of Henley.

Stewart and Carr had designed, made and paid for their first range of stock before it was sold. It was a risk, but it gave them credibility in the market, and won orders. However, to improve cashflow and the swift movement of stock through the warehouse, Tenabel encouraged Stewart and Carr to pre-sell as much of the stock as possible.

Profit margins are tight, and Tenabel has introduced other operational efficiencies to help improve results. He put the delivery schedules on to a computer, and the team has aligned shipping dates as closely as possible with in-store dates by developing strong relationships with the overseas manufacturers. Stewart and Carr have learnt not to drop prices. The Tenabels track profitability, and the team works through the figures. Ron Tenabel says: 'We cannot bow to market pressure. If we can't get our margin, we don't sell'.

The company is ahead of its five-year plan. Since last year, it has been selling to Just Jeans, Myer-Grace Bros., Man-to-Man and other name retailers. The business plan was for a $5-million turnover in 2001–2: Henley turned over $4.4 million in 1998–9 and is on track to reach $5.5 million for 1999–2000. The Tenabels will work in the company for the foreseeable future. Over Christmas, the partners will discuss plans to reduce the Tenabels' majority share to 33 per cent by repaying some capital with retained earnings.

Source: Walters, K. (1999a).

Activities for discussion, analysis and further research

1 Identify the manner in which the managerial functions and responsibilities are being divided in the above organisation.

2 Identify the Mintzberg role as they are evidenced by the above organisation.

3 Find Austin on the Web and track down evidence of the bureaucratic processes that Stewart and Carr felt existed with their former employer.

■ The MD's diary

the reflective practitioner

If you talk about my role in the organisation and where I put my efforts the first area is in the strategic direction of the organisation. I have to provide that, so I spend some part of my time thinking about where the organisation is going and how we are going to move it there. The vision of the organisation and the strategic direction is of critical importance. I spend a lot of my time trying to communicate to the organisation, deploying the vision and the strategic direction to ensure that everyone in the organisation firstly understands what it is we're after. They then have a task to go away and come up with their own departmental business plans and their individual plans focused on the key objectives and strategies that will deliver that vision.

That's what I see as my role. I actually spend most of my time making sure that people are not losing sight of and are working towards that vision. And I have a saying that I use quite regularly. When people tell me 'I've got too many things to do. I don't know what I should do', I say, 'have a look at the vision, have a look at the strategic direction of the organisation. If it's contributing to that, you do it. If it's not, you don't'. So a lot of my time is making sure that I'm coaching, and directing and leading people in the direction that will deliver that vision and those key strategic objectives. That's where most of my effort goes.

Obviously, once we have that framework in place, I have a role to make sure that the resources are available. That we're able to, having set objectives, prioritise and make sure that we are resourcing those in dollars and in human resources. Not only for today but for the future. We do the work today but I try to maintain my focus out another year or two all the time and we're constantly making sure that whatever we are doing today is moving towards where we want to be in one or two or three years' time.

Apart from that are the normal operational requirements—making sure that programs are on time, that costs are under control, that quality and safety are addressed and that customers are being supported in the correct way. That's my time.

■ The subordinate's log

the reflective practitioner

I found that managing people was accurately described in the management subject I studied at university. It is fundamentally planning, organising, leading and controlling. It is also, like Mintzberg observed, lots of varied and unstructured tasks, or in other words—fighting fires.

Being a first-line manager means you are the meat in the sandwich. You have responsibilities for subordinates and are yourself a subordinate. For me, a number of challenges presented themselves, especially as I was promoted from the ranks. Individuals who were colleagues and friends yesterday were all of a sudden individuals I needed to direct. Further complications arose in the way one managed those individuals. This was impacted upon by instructions from above that I did not necessarily agree with. There arose an internal dissonance as I needed to deal with the personal internal conflict of what was best for the firm, what was best for my subordinates, what was comfortable for me, and satisfying senior management.

My previous management experience had been in organisations where jobs and tasks were more defined and less conceptually oriented, where the requirements on staff were less creative. The issue of close or loose supervision did not really arise. This took some getting used to, getting the right balance between the closer supervision that financial decisions dictated and the loose supervision that enables creative, talented and ambitious people to do what they do best.

The third issue was that I was promoted above, and had to manage, senior individuals with greater experience and knowledge of the business than I had.

The job involved a balance between selling the services of the organisation, overseeing the quality of the consulting services provided to clients, and the administrative and reporting functions that senior management required.

Focus on practice—Strategies for improving

1 Discuss with a manager of your acquaintance the proportion of time spent on each of the four categories of functions: planning, leading, organising and controlling. Based on the theory you have studied, is this an appropriate proportion?
2 Ask the manager of your acquaintance which of Mintzberg's 10 managerial roles he or she feels they are performing adequately. Why do they rank themselves in that manner?
3 What steps would you suggest to this manager to ensure that they possess the right skills appropriate to the level of management they are functioning at?

Source: Jones et al. (2000).

Chapter summary

Management is the process of achieving organisational goals by engaging in the four major functions of planning, organising, leading and controlling. While these functions form the basis of the managerial process, several other elements contribute to an understanding of how managers actually operate. For instance, work methods and managerial roles, as well as work agendas, feed into management functions aimed at performance. A manager's knowledge base and management skills are also important factors in reaching targeted performance.

Mintzberg's study of top managers found their work methods were characterised by an unrelenting pace, brevity, variety, fragmentation and heavy use of verbal contacts and networks. To make sense of the voluminous data he collected while observing the managers, Mintzberg isolated three major categories of roles: interpersonal, informational and decisional. Within these categories, he identified 10 specific roles: figurehead, leader, liaison, monitor, disseminator, spokesperson, entrepreneur, disturbance handler, resource allocator and negotiator. To a large extent, these work methods and roles are also characteristic of managers at other levels of organisations.

On the basis of his research on general managers, Kotter found managers channel their various efforts through use of work agendas, which are loosely connected sets of tentative goals and tasks a manager is attempting to accomplish. Work agendas usually develop from the demands, constraints and choices associated with a manager's job.

For managers to develop work agendas, act out roles and engage in planning, organising, leading and controlling, they also need a knowledge base and key management skills. The key skills fit into three categories: technical, human and conceptual. These skills, and other elements in the management process, impact performance. Performance comprises two important dimensions: effectiveness and efficiency. Effectiveness is the ability to choose appropriate goals and achieve them, while efficiency is the ability to make best use of available resources in the process of achieving goals.

Managerial jobs differ by hierarchical level (a vertical dimension) and responsibility areas (a horizontal dimension). They are generally divided into three hierarchical levels: first-line, middle and top. Managers at these levels vary in emphasis placed on planning, organising, leading and controlling. They also differ in the importance they place on key management skills and in the degree to which they use different types of managerial roles. Although managers at all levels rate the entrepreneurial role as highly important, the way they use this role to encourage innovation depends on their hierarchical level, as follows: idea champion (first-line), sponsor (middle) and orchestrator (top). In contrast, horizontal managerial job differences focus on responsibility area and involve three major types of managers: functional, general and project.

According to several recent informal surveys, managerial work in future is particularly likely to be affected by an increasing need to manage change and innovation, growing workforce diversity, the burgeoning globalisation of business, and expanding concern with issues of quality and continuous improvement.

Questions for discussion and review

1   Describe each major function of management: planning, organising, leading and controlling. For a campus or other organisation to which you belong, give an example of a manager engaging in each of these functions. If one or more of the functions are lacking, what are the implications?

2   List three common managerial work methods identified by Mintzberg. How could a manager misuse these work methods to the extent they would lead to poor performance?

3   Explain the three general types of roles and 10 specific roles managers play. Suppose you opened a ski-and-surf shop near campus carrying clothing, skis and other accessories for recreation at ski resorts and beaches. Assume you have six employees. How might you use the 10 roles in managing your shop?

4   Outline three major sources of managerial work agendas. How do work agendas help managers channel their efforts toward appropriate levels of performance?

5   Contrast effectiveness and efficiency as they apply to organisational performance. What happens when you have one without the other?

6   Describe how managerial jobs vary according to hierarchical level. What are the implications for managers?

7   Outline how managers at different hierarchical levels use the entrepreneurial role. What do you think is likely to happen if the entrepreneurial role is missing from middle or top organisation levels?

8   Indicate how managerial jobs vary according to responsibility area. What are the implications for managers?

9   Identify the four themes mentioned in the chapter as important trends likely to influence managing in the 21st century. How can learning more about these trends help you become a more effective manager?

Exercises for managing in the 21st century

Exercise 1
Skill building: Identifying management functions

You have just accepted a position as manager of a local pizza shop. You are reviewing management activities you will be expected to perform. You are aware they will be part of one of the four major management functions. Indicate which function would normally include each activity listed in the chart below.

Activity	Planning	Organising	Leading	Controlling
1. Decide whether to open a second pizza shop				
2. Assign job duties				
3. Check register slips to ensure proper prices are being charged				
4. Provide incentives for employees				
5. Check that pizzas are prepared on time				
6. Decide what new menu items to offer				
7. Hire experienced cooks				
8. Determine profit margins to be achieved for the year				
9. Institute an employee suggestion program				
10. Monitor the pizza shop opening and closing times as compared to the schedule				

Exercise 2
Management exercise: Producing the new binding machine

You are a first-line supervisor in the production department of a local concern manufacturing a variety of office products such as staplers, binders and cellotape holders. Recently, the research department developed an innovative small machine which binds reports in one easy operation. According to market research and early sales figures, demand for the new machine (on which the company holds the patent) is expected to be strong because the machine produces good-looking reports at a very reasonable price. Because sales of the machine are already brisk, the company has decided to add a new production unit. A new first-line supervisor will be hired to head the unit.

You, your boss (who heads the production department) and a few other first-line supervisors who report to your boss are having a working lunch in a small room off the company cafeteria. The purpose of the meeting is to discuss the basic requirements of the new job and the details to be explained to job candidates. It is likely that many candidates will not have management experience and, hence, may be somewhat unfamiliar with the nature of managerial jobs.

Using your knowledge of the management process and managerial job types, list the kinds of information the group might provide to candidates.

Getting the timing right

on the rim—in
Australia and Malaysia

CCK Financial Solutions is a wholly Australian-owned designer and developer of treasury solutions and services. Established since 1981, it now has offices in Australia, Malaysia and Singapore.

Its chairman and CEO, Joe Wong, has discovered that good business ideas never fade, they sometimes just take time to win a market. More than 20 years ago he designed treasury software that was obviously ahead of its time. This world-class treasury management system had been gathering dust until demand caught up with his work.

Today, Joe Wong, 50, sells his treasury systems to some of the biggest companies in Australia and is poised to go global and list on the Stock Exchange. His company had its origins as Campbell Cook and King (the original name of CCK), where Wong worked as an actuary. The treasury systems now so much in demand date back to 1978 when Joe Wong was asked, as part of his actuary work, to write a system for the merchant bank Westralian International. He did and it worked, but it was probably too advanced for its time, and Westralian disappeared from the merchant banking world.

CCK Financial Solutions has carved out a niche by offering a service that adds value to the work of banks, corporate treasurers and fund managers. Its software handles complex questions of dealing in money, shares, foreign exchange and the many derivatives that are being created almost daily.

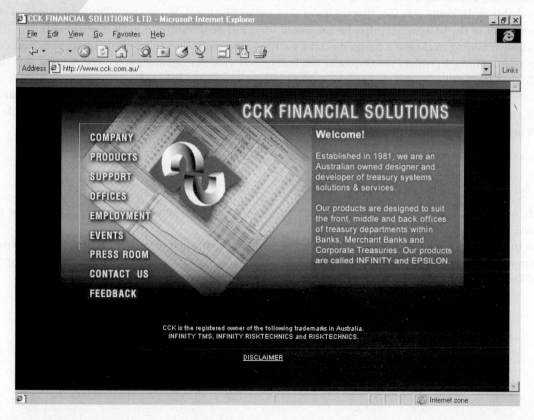

Internet home page of CCK Financial Solutions Ltd, a company whose existence demonstrates that innovation, technical skill and strategic planning are some of the strong managerial abilities of its CEO.

'Our software enables the dealer to analyse his portfolio and run what-if scenarios and simulate deals', Wong says. 'It helps them look at changed market conditions on their portfolios. That is just one facet of the system. It is a fully integrated system that handles the front office where the deals are done, the middle office where risk is managed, and the back office processing.'

Only Wong, his staff of 60 and the client users have the time, and inclination, to understand how the software works. The best way for the casual observer to grasp the value of the work lies in CCK's customer list which, in Australia, includes Westpac, Merrill Lynch, Deutsche Bank, AMP, Foster's Brewing Group, Unilever and Telstra. In Asia, the customer list includes Bank Negara Malaysia, Land Bank of the Philippines and Far East Bank and Trust. Each has signed with the Perth-based CCK because it is selling a unique niche product.

'I put it in the bottom drawer and it gathered dust', Wong says. That was until a friend working for the Philadelphia National Bank in Sydney called and asked what had happened to the old Westralian treasury management system. Wong's program, suitably upgraded, was back in business. After that first call, a request came from Australia's most infamous merchant bank, Rothwells.

Wong laughs when talking about Rothwells, a business that failed spectacularly in 1987, but it was that job that convinced him he could make a business out of CCK. He continued with his actuarial work, merging Campbell Cook and King into William M. Mercer and Co and becoming a principal of William M. Mercer. These days, Wong's time is largely devoted to building CCK, which has an annual turnover of $5 million. He is aiming much higher as international clients take a closer look at his business and its products. Earlier this year, Wong took CCK to the European trade fair and conference of SIBOS, an arm of the Swift international bank settlement organisation.

While exhibiting at SIBOS, Wong was visited by a senior Australian banking executive—a man who for years had been unreachable in Australia. ('Before that we never even got to first base', Wong says.) The banker was so impressed with what he saw in the CCK system that he has asked for a full demonstration back in Australia.

Wong is now planning to choose a partner to take CCK products into the global marketplace. The costs of global expansion and continued product development (including new risk management software) will be met through a planned float of the business 'later this year'.

In January of 2000, CCK obtained its first Singaporean client. RHB Bank Bhd will be implementing CCK's INFINITY treasury management system in its Singapore branch. With an established client base in Malaysia and the Philippines, CCK is forging ahead to becoming a regional player.

Sources: Adapted from Treadgold, T. (1999); www.cck.com.au

Activities for discussion, analysis and further research

1   Identify what roles Joe Wong takes on at CCK. How do you think those roles have changed over the past 20 years? Why have they done so?
2   Log on to CCK's web page at www.cck.com.au and find out what other activities the company has been active in during the past year. Have a look at the profile of its management team. Do you detect a pattern of specialisation? Examine their listed credentials and draw some conclusions about them.

Pioneering Ideas in Management

Chapter (2)

CHAPTER OUTLINE

The birth of management ideas
The evolution of management theories

Preclassical contributors

Classical viewpoint
Scientific management
Bureaucratic management
Administrative management

Behavioural viewpoint
Early behaviourists
Hawthorne studies
Human relations movement
Behavioural science approach

Quantitative management viewpoint
Management science
Operations management
Management information systems

Contemporary viewpoints
Systems theory
Contingency theory
Theory Z
The total quality philosophy

Promoting innovation: Contributions of the major viewpoints

LEARNING OBJECTIVES

After studying this chapter, you should be able to:

O Identify several early innovative management practices and explain the basic management theory evolution.

O Trace preclassical contributions to the field of management.

O Explain major approaches within the classical viewpoint of management.

O Describe major developments contributing to the establishment of the behavioural viewpoint.

O Explain major approaches within the quantitative management viewpoint.

O Discuss the relevance of systems theory and contingency theory to the field of management.

O Explain how management in Japan influenced the emerging Theory Z management viewpoint.

O Explain how current knowledge about management is the result of innovative processes involving many management pioneers.

Striving for excellence

As you will discover while studying how various management theories have developed over the decades, there is no such thing as an organisation which represents a pure model. Each organisation encompasses a number of styles which merge to give that organisation an identity and flavour of its own.

At Autoliv, the overriding management style is participative. There is a strong commitment to, and visible practice of, empowering individuals in the belief that every staff member at Autoliv has a stake in the success of the organisation.

One of the main aims of the organisation is job security. This philosophy means all staff can concentrate on what is really important, which is meeting organisational performance criteria in the most effective manner. Therefore, everybody accepts responsibility for quality. The shop floor is everybody's customer and consequently, this organisation truly practises the philosophies of TQM, zero defects, from the managing director's office to the shop floor.

Understanding various management theories and relating them to the workplace can enable managers to develop practices best-suited to their companies, as well as devise improvements for their futures.

Throughout this book, we discuss leading-edge approaches to management. New ideas, however, do not arise in a vacuum. They normally rise from a foundation of established ideas, as well as an awareness of the shortcomings of those ideas.

Thus, in this chapter, we explore the birth of management ideas. We briefly examine pioneering approaches of the preclassical contributors, individuals predating modern management thinking but who helped lay the groundwork. We consider the ideas of classical management, which covers the scientific, administrative and bureaucratic approaches. Next we analyse three major management viewpoints: the behavioural, quantitative and contemporary perspectives. Finally, we summarise the innovative contributions of the major viewpoints to modern management.

THE BIRTH OF MANAGEMENT IDEAS

The evolution of management theories

Although examples of management practice can be traced back several thousand years, the development of management as a field of knowledge is recent. Much of the impetus for developing management theories and principles came from the industrial revolution and factory growth in the early 1800s. With factories came a widespread need to co-ordinate large numbers of people in producing goods.

Some individuals began to think about ways to run factories more effectively. Later known as preclassical management contributors, they focused on particular techniques to solve specific problems (see Fig. 2.1). They were followed by individuals who developed broader principles and theories which formed the bases of the major viewpoints, or schools, of management: classical, behavioural, quantitative and contemporary. Several approaches contributed to the development of each of these viewpoints (see Fig. 2.1). We examine them after first focusing briefly on the preclassical contributors.

PRECLASSICAL CONTRIBUTORS

A number of individuals in the preclassical period of the middle and late 1800s offered ideas which became the basis for later, broader inquiries into the nature of management. Principal contributors were Robert Owen, Charles Babbage and Henry R. Towne (see Table 2.1).

Table 2.1   The preclassical contributors and their pioneering ideas

Contributor	Pioneering Ideas
Robert Owen	Advocated concern for the working and living conditions of workers
Charles Babbage	Built the first practical mechanical calculator and a prototype of modern computers; predicted the specialisation of mental work; suggested profit sharing
Henry R. Towne	Outlined the importance of management as a science and called for the development of management principles

Fig. 2.1   Major viewpoints in the development of modern management

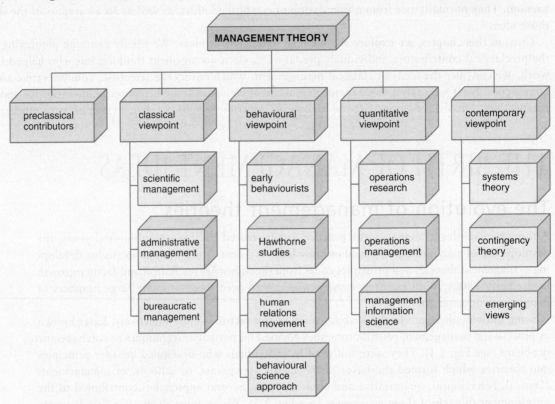

Robert Owen   A successful British entrepreneur, Robert Owen (1771–1858) was ahead of his time in seeing the importance of human resources. He was interested in his employees' working and living conditions while running a cotton mill in New Lanark, Scotland. As was common, the mill employed 400 to 500 young children, who worked 13-hour days including 90 minutes off for meals. Although his business partners resisted some of his ideas, Owen worked to improve employees' living conditions by upgrading streets, houses, sanitation and the educational system in New Lanark. At the time, Owen was seen as a radical, but today his views are widely accepted. His ideas laid the groundwork for the human relations movement, discussed later in this chapter (Wren 1994; Duncan 1989).

Charles Babbage   English mathematician Charles Babbage (1792–1871) is known as 'the father of modern computing'. His projects produced the world's first practical mechanical calculator and an 'analytical engine' with basic elements of modern-day computers (Duncan 1989). Difficulties in managing his various projects, however, led him to look at new ways of doing things. In the process, he contributed to management theory.

Babbage (1832) was excited by the idea of work specialisation, the degree to which work is divided into jobs. (Work specialisation is discussed further in Chapter 8.) He recognised that both physical work and mental work could be specialised. In this sense, he foresaw specialists, such as accountants who limit their practice to either personal or corporate taxes.

Babbage also developed a profit-sharing plan with two parts: a bonus awarded for useful suggestions and a portion of wages dependent on factory profits. His ideas foreshadowed some modern-day group incentive plans, such as the Scanlon Plan, in which workers suggest ways to improve productivity, then share in resulting profits.

Henry R. Towne   President of the Yale and Towne Manufacturing Company and a mechanical engineer, Henry R. Towne (1844–1924) explained the need to view management as a separate field on a par with engineering. He outlined his views in a paper titled 'The engineer as an economist', delivered in 1886 to the American Society of Mechanical Engineers in Chicago. He observed that although good engineering skills and good business skills were rarely combined in the same person, both were needed to effectively run an organisation. Accordingly, the paper called for the establishment of a science of management and the development of management principles. Although the engineering society itself was not a major force in developing management knowledge, a person attending Towne's presentation, Frederick Taylor, was later significant in developing the management field (Towne 1886; Noble 1977; Wren 1994).

Assessing the preclassical contributors   Although these early pioneers explored several avenues related to management, their efforts were unco-ordinated. They were largely focused on developing specific techniques to solve particular problems. For example, to prevent disorderly meetings, Henry Robert produced *Robert's Rules of Order*, a preclassical-era publication still used to run large, formal meetings.

Robert's Rules Bring Order

In the late 1800s, Henry Martyn Robert, a US brigadier general, during his military career as a civil engineer frequently attended meetings with people from many backgrounds. He often had to preside over these meetings.

He quickly learned the challenge of running meetings when the first meeting over which he presided, involving a group of Baptist ministers, ended in total chaos. Robert was puzzled because nothing was settled or resolved. He had prepared his subject well and gathered advice on how to conduct a meeting. He decided he would never again participate in such an encounter.

For the next seven years, he collected information on meeting conduct, and produced a 176-page book titled *Pocket Manual of Rules of Order for Deliberative Assemblies*. The book provided a set of parliamentary rules for conducting meetings.

He promoted the book, which he had published on his own, by sending 1000 copies to parliamentarians in the United States, including governors, legislators, the vice president and some attorneys, asking for comment. After receiving enthusiastic responses and some good suggestions, he modified the text, changing the title to *Robert's Rules of Order*. The book has become a classic source of guidance for running large, formal meetings and is used by many legislative bodies, government councils, associations and other organisations where decisions are made by member vote. First published in 1876, the book is still in print. Over four million copies have been sold across the English-speaking world. It has also been published in Braille (Sampson 1988).

Since they generally came from technical backgrounds, early pioneers did not see management as a separate field until Towne presented his paper. Still, they were important innovators laying foundations for later major management thinkers. Their forward-looking ideas have endured.

CLASSICAL VIEWPOINT

Henry Towne's call to establish management as a separate field generated a major approach called the **classical viewpoint**. This viewpoint emphasises managing work and organisations more efficiently. It comprises three different management approaches: scientific, administrative and bureaucratic. This viewpoint is called 'classical' because it includes early works and contributions making up the core of the field of management (Bluedorn 1986).

Scientific management

Scientific management is an approach within classical management theory emphasising the scientific study of work methods to improve worker efficiency. Representatives of this approach include Frederick Winslow Taylor, Frank and Lillian Gilbreth and Henry Gantt.

Frederick Winslow Taylor   Frederick Winslow Taylor (1856–1915) is called 'the father of scientific management'. Born into a relatively wealthy Philadelphia family, Taylor was an apprentice pattern maker and machinist for a local firm before moving to Midvale Steel. At Midvale, rising from labourer to chief engineer in six years allowed him to tackle a serious problem he saw—soldiering by workers (Duncan 1989). **Soldiering** is deliberately working at less than full capacity. Taylor believed workers did this for three main reasons. First, they feared increased productivity would cause them or other workers to lose their jobs. Second, management's wage systems encouraged workers to operate slowly. For example, some companies cut incentive pay when standards were exceeded, making workers reluctant to excel. Third, general methods of working and rules of thumb were often inefficient (Staudenmaier 1994; Benyon 1975).

Taylor believed soldiering could be avoided by developing a science of management based on four principles, shown in Table 2.2. Central to this was using scientific methods to find how tasks should be done rather than relying on past experience. Specifically, Taylor pioneered time-and-motion study (Taylor called it a time study). This involved breaking a task into various elements, or motions, eliminating those not needed, determining the best way to do the job, and then timing each motion to determine the level of production expected in a day (with allowances for delays and rest periods) (Taylor 1985).

Table 2.2   Taylor's four principles of scientific management

1. Scientifically study each part of a task and develop the best method for performing it.
2. Carefully select workers and train them to perform a task using the scientifically developed method.
3. Co-operate fully with workers to ensure they use the proper method.
4. Divide work and responsibility so management is responsible for planning work methods using scientific principles and workers are responsible for executing work accordingly.

To solve the problem of soldiering being encouraged by wage systems, Taylor supported using wage incentive plans. He argued workers should be paid from 30 to 100 per cent more for using scientifically developed work methods and reaching daily standards (Locke 1982).

---

classical viewpoint

Perspective on management emphasising finding ways to manage work and organisations more efficiently

scientific management

Approach emphasising the scientific study of work methods to improve worker efficiency

soldiering

Deliberately working at less than full capacity

A study by Taylor at Bethlehem Steel focused on shovelling. Until he introduced scientific management, workers used their own tools on the job. Taylor saw workers might use the same shovel for both iron ore and ashes, though the materials' relative weights were very different. From his studies, Taylor determined the optimum weight for shovelling was 9.5 kilograms. He argued it was sensible to have shovels of different sizes for different materials so the weight of what was being shovelled would be about 9.5 kilograms. Implementing his plan with company-owned shovels demonstrated that the average number of tonnes shovelled per worker per day increased from 16.3 to 60.2. Simultaneously average earnings per worker per day increased from $1.15 to $1.88, and the average cost of handling a tonne decreased from $0.072 to $0.033. Taylor's plan included additional worker incentive pay and benefits for the company (Locke 1982). Some managers, Bethlehem citizens and others opposed Taylor, arguing that he exploited workers by getting them to produce more and caused large reductions in Bethlehem Steel's workforce.

A strike at the Watertown (Massachusetts) Army Arsenal (1911–1912), where some of Taylor's ideas were being tested, led to a congressional investigation. The investigation found no evidence of workers being abused by 'Taylorism'. Still, the publicity slowed the spread of scientific management (Wren 1994). However, by World War I's end scientific management, aided by many French management experts, spread through Europe and was used in diverse places such as English chocolate factories, Icelandic fisheries, German paper mills and Swedish typewriter factories (Breeze 1986; Wregge & Perroni 1974; Wregge & Stotka 1978; Fry 1976; Locke 1982).

There is little doubt Taylor's ideas are still used today. As we will see in Chapter 8, the use of scientific management can lead to overspecialised jobs, resulting in worker resentment, monotony, poor quality, absenteeism and turnover.

The Gilbreths   Other major advocates of scientific management were the husband and wife team of Frank (1868–1924) and Lillian (1878–1972) Gilbreth. Though Frank qualified for admission to the Massachusetts Institute of Technology, he become a bricklayer because of the profession's importance at the time. As Frank became involved in training young bricklayers, he noticed inefficiencies handed down from experienced workers.

To remedy the situation, he proposed using motion studies to streamline the bricklaying process. Frank designed special scaffolding for different job types, devising precise directions for mortar consistency. On the basis of these and other ideas, Frank reduced bricklaying motions from 18½ to 4. Using his approach, workers increased bricks laid per day from 1000 to 2700 without increased physical effort (Wren 1994).

Meanwhile, Frank married Lillian Moller, who worked with him on projects while completing a doctorate in psychology. The two continued their studies to eliminate unnecessary motions, expanding their interests to explore ways of reducing task fatigue. Part of their work involved isolating 17 basic motions, each called a therblig ('Gilbreth' reversed, with the 't' and 'h' exchanged). Therbligs included motions such as select, position and hold—motions the Gilbreths used to study tasks in several industries. The Gilbreths also pioneered motion picture technology use to study jobs (Locke 1982).

Lillian's (Gilbreth 1914) doctoral thesis, published as *The Psychology of Management*, applied psychology's findings to the workplace. At the publisher's insistence, the author was listed as L. M. Gilbreth to disguise the book's author being a woman. She was interested in scientific management's human implications, arguing that its purpose was to help people reach their maximum potential by developing their skills and abilities (Wren 1994).

In 1924, Frank died of a heart attack, leaving Lillian with their 12 children, aged between 2 and 19. She continued their innovative studies and consulting work, finally becoming a professor of management at Purdue University (Wren 1994). Lillian Gilbreth ranks as the first prominent woman in the development of management as a science.

Henry L. Gantt   One of Taylor's closest associates was Henry Gantt (1861–1919), who worked with Taylor in several companies, including Midvale Steel and Bethlehem Steel (Wren 1994; Duncan 1989). Gantt later worked as an independent consultant, making his own contributions. The best known is the Gantt chart, a graphic aid to planning, scheduling and control that is still used. (A Gantt chart is in the supplement to Chapter 5.) He also devised a unique pay incentive system which paid workers more for reaching a standard in the allotted time and awarded supervisors bonuses when workers reached this standard. Thus the system encouraged supervisors to coach workers who had difficulties.

Bureaucratic management

bureaucratic management

Approach emphasising the need for organisations to operate in a rational manner rather than relying on owners' and managers' arbitrary whims

Another branch of the classical viewpoint is **bureaucratic management**, which considered the need of an organisation to operate rationally rather than relying on the arbitrary whims of owners and managers. The bureaucratic management approach is based mainly on prominent German sociologist Max Weber's work.

Weber (1864–1920) was born into an affluent family with strong political and social connections (Wren 1994; Eisen 1978; Duncan 1989). He worked as a consultant, professor and author. Among his most important management contributions were his ideas on the need of organisations to operate more rationally.

Weber reacted to prevailing norms of class consciousness and nepotism. For example, only individuals of aristocratic birth could become Prussian Army officers or attain high-level government and industry positions. Weber felt this was unfair and led to significant human-resource waste. He also believed running organisations on the basis of who one knows not what one knows, and engaging in nepotism (hiring of relatives regardless of competence), reduced organisational effectiveness.

To visualise how the large organisations evolving from the industrial revolution might operate ideally, Weber outlined the characteristics of 'ideal bureaucracy' (see Table 2.3). He coined the term 'bureaucracy' (based on the German *büro*, meaning 'office') to identify large organisations operating on a rational basis. Weber understood his ideal bureaucracy did not actually exist. In fact, he did not intend his ideas to be used as managers' guidelines. Rather, his purpose was to develop ideas to use as a starting point in understanding organisations (Weiss 1983; Stern & Barley 1996; Scott 1996). However, when his work was translated into English in the late 1940s, many management scholars used his ideas as a guide to how organisations could be more effectively managed.

Because of the possibility of carrying Weber's ideas to excess, the term 'bureaucracy' is sometimes used in a negative sense to mean red tape and excessive rules. Yet clearly the bureaucratic characteristics outlined by Weber have advantages.

Table 2.3   Major characteristics of Weber's ideal bureaucracy

Characteristic	Description
Specialisation of labour	Jobs are broken down into routine, well-defined tasks so members know what is expected of them and can become extremely competent at their particular subset of tasks.
Formal rules and procedures	Written rules and procedures specify behaviours desired from members, facilitating co-ordination and ensuring uniformity.
Impersonality	Rules, procedures and sanctions are applied uniformly regardless of individual personalities and personal considerations.
Well-defined hierarchy	Multiple levels of positions, with carefully determined reporting relationships among levels, provide supervision of lower offices by higher ones, a means of handling exceptions and the ability to establish accountability of actions.
Career advancement based on merit	Selection and promotion is based on members' qualifications and performance.

The only person in the company without a computer

case in point

The managing director of Sydney's Richard Hill & Associates is an eclectic practitioner. He specialises in finance advice for the smallest end of the listed sector. Amongst his business venues he lists China, New Zealand and even Port Moresby, where his clients are likely to bring in their accounts in a shoe box.

He believes in coming in at the inception of a venture so that he can be involved in deciding how to tackle it. This prevents having to compete in a tender process which saves time and money both for himself and the client. He sees his role as doing something imaginative for the project, not only running the numbers. His greatest difficulty is the recruitment of staff, for which he competes against larger firms.

In spite of the growing size of the company, Richard Hill refuses to have a computer on his desk, believing he gets better value from time spent in telephone discussions.

Source: Adapted from Thomas, T. (1999a).

Activities for discussion, analysis and further research

1   Imagine that you are one of Richard Hill's employees. Describe the type of management processes which might best be used to effectively manage this company. Why?

Administrative management

While scientific management's supporters looked to develop principles to help organise individual worker tasks more effectively and Weber struggled with the idea of bureaucracy, another branch within the classical viewpoint developed. The **administrative management** approach focused on principles to be used by managers to co-ordinate the internal activities of organisations. Major contributors include Henri Fayol and Chester Barnard, both executives of large enterprises.

administrative management

Approach focusing on principles used by managers to co-ordinate the organisations' internal activities

Henri Fayol   French industrialist Henri Fayol (1841–1925) was born into a middle-class family near Lyon, France (Wren 1994; Duncan 1989). Trained as a mining engineer, he joined a coal-and-iron combine as an apprentice and rose to managing director in 1888. He accomplished the arduous task of moving the company from severe financial difficulties to a strong position before retiring at 77. The company survives today as part of LeCreusot-Loire, a large mining and metallurgical group in central France.

Based on his experiences as a top-level manager, Fayol was convinced it was possible to develop management theories to be taught to individuals who had administrative responsibilities. His theories were published in a monograph titled *General and Industrial Management*.

Fayol attempted to isolate the main activity types in industry or business. Within the category of 'managerial activities', he identified five major functions: planning, organising, commanding, co-ordinating and controlling. This is known as the functional management approach. You may notice the similarity between Fayol's functions and the four functions of management (planning, organising, leading and controlling) used as the framework of this book. Many contemporary management books use a form of the functional approach with roots in Fayol's work.

Fayol outlined several principles (see Table 2.4) he found useful in running his large coal-and-iron concern. Although contemporary research found some exceptions to his principles (which will be discussed in later chapters), the principles are in general use (Eccles & Nohira 1992).

acceptance theory of authority

Theory arguing authority does not depend as much on 'persons of authority' who give orders as on the willingness to comply of those who receive the orders

Chester Barnard   Another major contributor to administrative management was Chester Barnard (1886–1961). Born in Massachusetts, he attended Harvard but did not complete his degree (Duncan 1989). After joining AT&T as a statistician, he rose rapidly, becoming president of the New Jersey Bell Telephone Company in 1927. Barnard recorded his observations about effective administration in a single classic book, *The Functions of the Executive*, in 1938.

One of Barnard's best-known contributions is his **acceptance theory of authority**. This theory argues that authority does not depend so much on 'persons of authority' who give orders, as on the willingness to comply of those who receive the orders. Thus, in Barnard's view, it is really employees who decide whether or not to accept orders and directions from above. From a practical point of view, Barnard felt managers can exert authority on a day-to-day basis because each individual possesses a 'zone of indifference' within which they are willing to accept orders and directions without much question.

On the basis of his view that authority flows from the bottom to the top, Barnard argued that employees are more willing to accept directions from a manager if they (1) understand the communication, (2) see the communication as consistent with the organisation's purposes, (3) feel actions indicated are in line with their needs and those of other employees and (4) view themselves as mentally and physically able to comply.

Table 2.4 Fayol's general principles of management

1. Division of work	Work specialisation can result in efficiencies and is applicable to both managerial and technical functions. Yet there are limitations to how much that work should be divided.
2. Authority	Authority is the right to give orders and the power to exact obedience. It derives from the formal authority of the office and from personal authority based on factors like intelligence and experience. With authority comes responsibility.
3. Discipline	Discipline is absolutely necessary for the smooth running of an organisation, but the state of discipline depends essentially on its leaders' worthiness.
4. Unity of command	An employee should receive orders from one superior only.
5. Unity of direction	Activities aimed at the same objective should be organised so there is one plan and one person in charge.
6. Subordination of individual interest to general interest	The interests of one employee or group should not prevail over the organisation's interests and goals.
7. Remuneration	Compensation should be fair to both employee and employer.
8. Centralisation	The proper amount of centralisation or decentralisation depends on the situation. The objective is optimum use of personnel capabilities.
9. Scalar chain	A scalar (hierarchical) chain of authority extends from top to bottom of an organisation and defines the communication path. However, horizontal communication is also encouraged as long as managers in the chain are kept informed.
10. Order	Materials should be kept in well-chosen places to facilitate activities. Similarly, due to good organisation and selection, the right person should be in the right place.
11. Equity	Employees should be treated with kindness and justice.
12. Stability of personnel tenure	Because time is required to become effective in new jobs, high turnover should be prevented.
13. Initiative	Managers should encourage and develop subordinate initiative to the fullest.
14. Esprit de corps	Since union is strength, harmony and teamwork are essential.

Source: Adapted from Fayol (1949, pp. 19–42).

Barnard helped integrate concern with authority, which grew out of the administrative and bureaucratic approaches, with emphasis on worker needs, which was developing at the same time within the behavioural viewpoint. He also knew about early behaviourists and the Hawthorne studies, a primary force in the development of the behavioural viewpoint, to which we turn next (Wolf, cited in Wren 1994; Barnard 1968).

✖ Which theory is that?   crossroads

You are beginning to be exposed to the development of management theory. The closest example of this that you might have at the moment is how your lecturer manages your class. Consider which theory your lecturer is practising, then interview your lecturer and consider whether your perception of their practice is congruent with their statement.

Decision point

Consider these issues:

1　What is your lecturer's theory of learning (how people learn)?
2　What are your lecturer's views on the question of evaluation?
3　What is their role in the classroom?
4　Do you think that your lecturer's attitude to the students is affected by stereotypes of them? What are the stereotypes? Why did you come to that conclusion?

Reflection point

1　Discuss and compare your answers to the last section with those of a couple of your peers. In what ways were they similar? Why do you think this was so? Are you prepared to give your lecturer some feedback? If so, how? If not, why?

BEHAVIOURAL VIEWPOINT

**behavioural
viewpoint**

Perspective on management
emphasising the importance
of attempting to understand
various factors affecting
human behaviour in
organisations

Classical theorists generally viewed individuals as production mechanisms. So they were primarily interested in finding ways for organisations to use individuals more efficiently. Despite Barnard's views, the idea that an employee's behaviour might be influenced by internal reactions to aspects of various job situations was generally not seen as relevant to the quest for greater efficiency. In contrast, the **behavioural viewpoint** emphasised the importance of attempting to understand various factors affecting human behaviour in organisations. In exploring this viewpoint, we examine four aspects of its development: early behaviourists' contributions, the Hawthorne studies, the human relations movement and the more contemporary behavioural science approach.

Early behaviourists

With growing interest in management, individuals from other backgrounds began to offer alternatives to the engineering focus of scientific management. Two early behaviourists, psychologist Hugo Münsterberg and political scientist Mary Parker Follett, contributed pioneering ideas which helped make the behavioural perspective a major viewpoint.

Hugo Münsterberg　Born and educated in Germany, Hugo Münsterberg (1863–1916) earned both a PhD in psychology and a medical degree. In 1892, he set up a psychological laboratory at Harvard and began seeking practical applications of psychology. Soon, his attention turned to industrial applications, leading him to publish an important book, *Psychology and Industrial Efficiency*, in 1913. The book argued that psychologists could help industry in three major ways. The first was closely linked to scientific management: psychologists could study jobs and find ways to identify individuals best suited to particular jobs. The second way psychologists could help industry was by identifying psychological conditions where individuals are likely to do their best work. The third was developing strategies to influence employees to behave in ways compatible with management interests. The ideas and examples Münsterberg provided led to the establishment of the field of industrial psychology, or the study of human behaviour in a work setting. Thus, Münsterberg is considered to be 'the father of industrial psychology' (George 1972; Landy 1977).

Mary Parker Follett   Another well-known early behaviourist was Mary Parker Follett (1868–1933). Born in Boston and educated in political science at what is now Radcliffe College, Follett was a social worker who became interested in employment and workplace issues.

Follett attributed much greater significance to group functioning in organisations than the supporters of the classical management view. She argued that organisation members are continually influenced by groups within which they operate (Parker 1984). In fact, she held that groups can control themselves and their own activities, a view re-emerging with recent interest in self-managed teams.

Another of Follett's ideas was her belief that organisations should operate on a principle of 'power with' rather than 'power over'. Power, to her, was a general ability to influence and produce change (Graham & Follett 1995). She argued that power should be a jointly developed, co-operative concept, having employees and managers work together, rather than a coercive concept based on hierarchical influence. Though her views probably influenced Barnard's acceptance theory of authority, Follett advocated sharing power where Barnard emphasised encouraging appropriate responses from below (Barnard 1968; Duncan 1989).

Follett suggested a way to foster the 'power with' concept was by conflict resolution through integration. By integration she meant finding a satisfactory solution for all parties. She cited an example of a dairy co-operative which almost broke down due to a controversy over the pecking order in unloading milk cans. The creamery was located part way down a hill, and members who came downhill and those who came uphill both thought they should be given precedence in unloading. The situation was locked until an outsider pointed out that changing the loading dock's position would allow both groups to unload their cans at the same time. Follett noted, 'Integration involves invention, and the clever thing is to recognise this, and not to let one's thinking stay within the boundaries of two alternatives that are mutually exclusive' (Metcalf & Urwick 1940, p. 32). Her integration ideas are echoed in modern conflict-resolution methods (see Chapter 15).

Follett emphasised what she called integrative unity, where the organisation operates as a functional whole with various interrelated parts working together to effectively achieve organisational goals. She saw the process of working together as a dynamic process because environmental factors demanded change. As we will see, her ideas anticipated the systems view of management (Wren 1994; Parker 1984; Linden 1995). A contemporary reviewer of her work argued its significance 'rivals the long-standing influence of such giants as Taylor and Fayol' (Parker 1984, p. 738). A new book of her writings was recently published by Harvard Business School Press (1995).

Hawthorne studies

Hawthorne studies

Group of studies conducted at the Hawthorne plant of the Western Electric Company during the late 1920s and early 1930s the results of which ultimately led to the human relations view of management

While Follett was working, other researchers were involved in the **Hawthorne studies**. These were conducted at Western Electric's Hawthorne plant during the late 1920s and early 1930s, and led to the human relations view of management, a behavioural approach emphasising concern for the worker. To understand their significance, we have to trace the studies from the start.

When they started, the Hawthorne studies reflected scientific management's tradition of seeking greater efficiency by improving the tools and methods of work—in this case, lighting. General Electric wanted to sell more light bulbs so, with other electric companies, it supported studies on the relationship between lighting and productivity conducted by the National Research Council. The tests were held at the Hawthorne Works (Chicago) of the Western Electric Company, an equipment-producing subsidiary of AT&T (Greenwood & Wrege 1986). Ultimately, three sets of studies were conducted.

First set of studies   The first set of studies, called the Illumination Studies, took place between 1924 and 1927 directed by several engineers. In one study, light was decreased progressively for the experimental group (the group for whom lighting was altered), while light levels were held constant for the control group (a comparison group working in a separate area). In both, performance increased, though lighting for the experimental group became so dim workers complained they could hardly see. At that point, the experimental group's performance finally declined (see Fig. 2.2). Researchers concluded factors besides lighting were operating (as performance rose in both groups), and discontinued the project (Greenwood & Wrege 1986). One possible explanation was that experimental and control groups were in contact and may have been competing.

Fig. 2.2   Actual versus expected results for experimental and control groups in one of the Hawthorne Illumination Studies

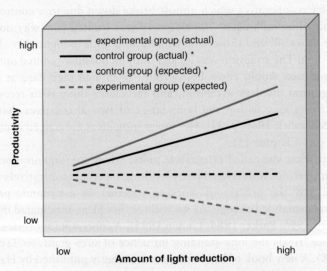

* lighting remained at the same level in the control group

Second set of studies   Intrigued with the positive changes in productivity, some engineers and company officials decided to attempt to determine the causes. So a second set of experiments was carried out between 1927 and 1933. The most famous study had five women assembling electrical relays in the Relay Assembly Test Room, where they were away from other workers and researchers could modify work conditions and evaluate results. Before the study, researchers were concerned about possible negative reactions from those included in the experiment. To lessen potential resistance, researchers changed supervisory arrangements so there would be no official supervisor. Instead, workers would operate under the general direction of the experimenters. Workers were given special privileges, such as being able to leave their workstation without permission, and received considerable attention from experimenters and management (Adair 1984). The study aimed to explore the best combination of work and rest periods, but other factors were also varied (sometimes simultaneously), such as pay, length of workday and free lunch provision. Generally, productivity increased over the study, regardless of how factors under consideration were manipulated (Greenwood & Wrege 1987).

A Harvard University research group (involved in assessing results) ultimately concluded that changes in supervisory arrangements were the major reason for productivity increases in the Relay Assembly Test Room study and two related studies with other work groups. Researchers felt that physical changes, such as rest periods, free lunches and shorter hours, as well as group incentive pay plans, were factors of lesser importance (largely because negative changes in some factors did not seem to decrease performance).

Since researchers set up supervisory arrangements before the study started, this change was not actually part of the study manipulations and was not intended to affect results. One study outcome was the identification of a famous concept which became known as the Hawthorne effect. The **Hawthorne effect** is the possibility that individuals being studied may improve their performance simply because of added attention from researchers, not because of any specific factors being tested (Rice 1982).

More contemporary investigations suggest the Hawthorne-effect concept is too simplistic to explain what happened in the Hawthorne studies and the concept itself is faulty. It appears likely that the Hawthorne plant results stemmed from workers interpreting what was happening differently from researchers (rather than from the idea workers simply reacted positively because of researchers' attention). Workers probably viewed the changes in supervision as a significant positive change in work environment, though this was not the researchers' intention (Adair 1984).

Third set of studies   The third set of Hawthorne studies built on the second set's findings. It included the famous Bank Wiring Observation Room study (1931–32), involving a group of male workers. Studying the group gave information about informal social relations in groups and the use of group norms in restricting output when this seems worthwhile to the group (Wren 1994; Bramel & Friend 1981).

Impact of the Hawthorne Studies   As a result of the Hawthorne studies, the focus of the study of management was altered drastically. In contrast to the classical approach's impersonal nature, the Hawthorne studies showed the impact a job's social aspects have on productivity, particularly the effects of the personal attention of supervisors and group-member relationships. As one writer put it, 'No other theory or set of experiments has stimulated more research

Hawthorne effect

Possibility that individuals singled out for a study may improve their performance simply because of the added attention received from researchers, rather than because of any specific factors being tested

and controversy nor contributed more to a change in management thinking than the Hawthorne studies and the human relations movement they spawned'. (Adair 1984, p. 334; Carey 1967; Shepard 1971; Bramel & Friend 1981; Greenwood, Bolton & Greenwood 1983; Sonnenfeld 1985).

Human relations movement

However flawed, the Hawthorne research set the stage for great interest in the organisation's social dimension. The key to productivity, from a managerial view, seemed to be showing greater concern for workers so they feel more satisfied with their jobs and are willing to produce more. Emphasis was put on building more collaborative and co-operative supervisor-and-worker relationships. Consequently, managers needed social skills in addition to technical skills. They also required a better understanding of how to make workers more satisfied with their jobs. While the Hawthorne studies provided some clues, managers needed more focused guidance. Two major theorists, Abraham Maslow and Douglas McGregor, were among those who developed ideas managers found helpful.

Abraham Maslow   Abraham Maslow (1908–70) received his doctorate in psychology from the University of Wisconsin, eventually becoming chairman of Brandeis University's psychology department. He developed a motivation theory based on three assumptions about human nature. First, human beings have needs, never completely satisfied. Second, humans aim to fulfil unsatisfied needs. Third, needs fit into a somewhat predictable hierarchy, going from basic, lower-level needs at the bottom to higher-level ones at the top (Duncan 1989). Maslow's hierarchy has five levels of needs: physiological (lowest), safety, belongingness, esteem and self-actualisation (highest). Self-actualisation needs refer to the need to develop our capabilities and reach our full potential (Maslow 1954).

Maslow's work showed managers that workers have needs beyond the basic drive to earn money to put a roof over their heads. This concept conflicted with scientific management's views, which emphasised the importance of pay. Of all management-related theories, Maslow's hierarchy of needs theory is probably the best known among managers today.

Douglas McGregor   The move to having managers see workers in a new light was also driven by Douglas McGregor (1906–1964). McGregor earned a doctorate at Harvard and spent most of his career as a professor of industrial management at the Massachusetts Institute of Technology. A six-year stint as president of Antioch College led him to realise that simply trying to have everyone like the boss (i.e. maintaining good relations with workers) offered inadequate managerial guidance.

He developed the concept of Theory X versus Theory Y to explain assumptions managers make about workers. McGregor believed these assumptions influence how managers operate. Theory X managers (see Table 2.5) assume workers are lazy, must be coerced, have little ambition and focus mainly on security needs. In contrast, Theory Y managers assume workers do not inherently dislike work, are capable of self-control, creativity and innovation, and generally have higher-level needs often unmet on the job.

Table 2.5   Theory X and Theory Y managerial assumptions

Theory X Assumptions

1. The average person dislikes work and will try to avoid it.
2. Most people must be coerced, controlled, directed and threatened with punishment to get them to work toward organisational goals.
3. The average person wants to be directed, shuns responsibility, has little ambition and seeks security above all.

Theory Y Assumptions

1. Most people do not inherently dislike work; the physical and mental effort involved is as natural as play or rest.
2. People will exercise self-direction and self-control to reach goals to which they are committed; external control and threat of punishment are not the only means for ensuring effort toward goals.
3. Commitment to goals is a function of rewards available, particularly rewards satisfying esteem and self-actualisation needs.
4. When conditions are favourable, the average person learns not only to accept but also to seek responsibility.
5. Many people have a capacity to exercise a high degree of creativity and innovation in solving organisational problems.
6. The intellectual potential of most individuals is only partially utilised in most organisations.

McGregor believed managers holding Theory X assumptions set up elaborate controls and attempt to motivate strictly through economic incentives. As a result, workers will respond in a way that reinforces the manager's assumptions.

In contrast, managers with Theory Y assumptions integrate individual and organisational goals. McGregor believed that this occurs when managers give workers latitude in performing their tasks, encouraged them to be creative and innovative, minimised use of control and attempted to make work more interesting and satisfying of higher-level needs. The result of Theory Y, according to McGregor, was that 'The limits of collaboration in the organizational setting are not limits of human nature but of management's ingenuity in discovering how to realise the potential represented by its human resources' (Jones, George & Hill 2000, p. 45). The managers' task was to encourage commitment to organisational goals and, by creating appropriate work settings, provide opportunities for workers to be imaginative and exercise initiative and self-direction. McGregor (1960) understood that some immature, dependent workers might require greater controls to develop the maturity needed for a Theory Y approach.

As with Maslow's hierarchy, McGregor's Theory X and Theory Y approach helped managers develop a broader view of the nature of workers and ways of interacting with them. The ideas appealed to managers looking for ways to operate more effectively. Their theories became very popular and are still widely applied.

Behavioural science approach

Maslow, McGregor and others developing the human relations viewpoint tried to show alternatives to the classical school's rational-economic view of workers. They depicted workers as social creatures, with varied needs to be met on the job. Still, they drew a fairly general and simplistic picture. Managers were often uncertain about actions to be taken and the implications of such actions. The need for a more complex view of work situations led to the behavioural science perspective.

behavioural science

Approach emphasising scientific research as the basis for developing theories about human behaviour in organisations, that is used to establish practical guidelines for managers

The **behavioural science** approach uses scientific research to develop theories about human behaviour in organisations. The theories are used to establish practical guidelines for managers. This approach draws on a variety of disciplines, including management, psychology, sociology, anthropology and economics. Concepts are tested in business organisations or laboratory settings before being recommended to managers. Behavioural science's ultimate aim is to develop theories to guide managers in assessing various situations and choose appropriate action. Since humans and their interactions with others are complex, the challenge is to understand organisations and their members.

An example of behavioural science is the idea that individuals perform better with challenging but attainable goals than without them. Of course, goals must be specific and measurable ('I want to get an A in my management subjects this semester') rather than vague ('I want to do well in my course this semester'). The idea that goal setting improves performance results from research by Edwin A. Locke and others (Locke, Shaw, Saari & Latham 1982; Pritchard, Jones, Roth, Stuebing & Ekeberg 1988). We consider the motivational aspects of goal setting more in Chapter 6.

QUANTITATIVE MANAGEMENT VIEWPOINT

The quantitative management viewpoint emerged during World War II. Because of the sheer magnitude of the war effort, the Allied military forces used quantitative methods to help decide the most effective uses of resources. For example, quantitative studies by the US Navy helped eliminate the 'catch-as-catch-can' method aeroplanes used to search for enemy vessels. Quantitative analysis showed a pattern for these searches which reduced numbers of search planes needed for a given area and gave greater coverage. This conserved scarce resources and led to the seizure of enemy ships and valuable cargo in the South Atlantic which aided the Allied effort (Gaither 1986). This and other important applications of quantitative methods caught the attention of business organisations, as quantitative specialists found jobs in civilian organisations after the war.

The quantitative management viewpoint focused on mathematics, statistics and information aids to support managerial decision making and organisational effectiveness (Miller & Feldman 1983). Three main branches have evolved: management science, operations management and management information systems.

Management science

Management science increases decision effectiveness by means of mathematical models and statistical methods. (Caution: This term is not synonymous with the term 'scientific management', discussed earlier.) Another name for management science is **operations research**. The increasing power of computers has expanded possibilities for using mathematical and statistical tools of management science in organisations. For example, management science was used at Avon, maker of beauty, health-care and fashion jewellery products. Group Vice President for Planning and Development, Robert W. Pratt, used statistical methods to analyse what would be the effect of changing the company's common practice of offering heavy discounts to generate larger orders. His results showed the company could significantly boost profits by reducing discounts, even if this meant smaller average orders per salesperson (Waldon 1985). In the Supplement to Chapter 5, we explain operations research tools, such as linear programming; queuing or waiting-line models; and routing or distribution models.

management science

Approach aimed at increasing decision effectiveness through use of sophisticated mathematical models and statistical methods

operations research

Another name used for management science

Operations management

Operations management is responsible for managing production and delivery of an organisation's products and services (Sawaya & Giauque 1986). It includes areas such as inventory management, work scheduling, production planning, facilities location and design, and quality assurance. Operations management often applies to manufacturing settings where aspects of production need management, such as production process design, raw materials purchase, employee work scheduling, and storing and shipping final products. Operations management applies to service delivery too. We consider some techniques in the Supplement to Chapter 5 and explore operations management in Chapter 16.

operations management

Function or field of expertise primarily responsible for managing production and delivery of an organisation's products and services

Management information systems

The term **management information systems** refers to the field of management that focuses on designing and implementing computer-based management information systems. These systems turn raw data into information for various management levels. They are important to many industries, as computer-based systems for handling large amounts of information are powerful competitive weapons for organisations. We discuss computer-based information systems for management more fully in Chapter 17.

management information systems

Field of management focused on designing and implementing computer-based information systems for use by management

CONTEMPORARY VIEWPOINTS

While classical, behavioural and quantitative approaches continue to contribute to management, others have emerged. These are contemporary, as they are recent innovations in management thinking. Two important contemporary viewpoints are systems and contingency theories. Also, at any time, emerging ideas influence the development of management thinking, without yet having the status of enduring viewpoints.

Systems theory

systems theory

Approach based on the idea that organisations can be visualised as systems

Systems theory is based on the view of organisations as systems (Kast & Rosenzweig 1972). A **system** is a set of interrelated parts operating as a whole in pursuit of common goals. The systems approach is based on biological and physical sciences (Bertalanffy 1951; Katz & Kahn 1978; Boulding 1956). In this section, we consider major systems components, open versus closed systems and open system characteristics.

system

Set of interrelated parts operating as a whole in pursuit of common goals

Major components: According to the systems approach, an organisation system has four major components (see Fig. 2.3). **Inputs** are the various human, material, financial, equipment and informational resources needed to produce goods and services. **Transformation processes** are an organisation's managerial and technological abilities used to change inputs into outputs. **Outputs** are the organisation's products, services and other outcomes. **Feedback** is information on results and organisational status relative to the environment (Ramaprasad 1983).

inputs

Various human, material, financial, equipment and informational resources required to produce goods and services

The systems approach has several advantages. First, it can analyse systems at different levels (Asmos & Huber 1987). For example, Miller developed a typology of hierarchical levels of living systems, ranging from an individual human cell including atoms and molecules, to a supranational system consisting of two or more societies (Miller 1978). Usually, managers consider the organism (individual), group, organisation and society levels, although increasing global emphasis means the supranational level moves increasingly into play. Second, the systems view gives a framework for assessing the interaction between the various parts of an organisation. Third, it shows that change in one part of the system affects other parts. In thinking about interrelationships among organisation parts, you might imagine parts being connected by rubber bands. A pull on one part may affect the position of others. Fourth, the systems approach considers an organisation's interaction with its environment—factors outside the

transformation processes

Organisation's managerial and technological abilities used to convert inputs into outputs

outputs

Products, services and other outcomes produced by the organisation

feedback

Information about results and organisational status relative to the environment

Fig. 2.3   A systems view of organisations

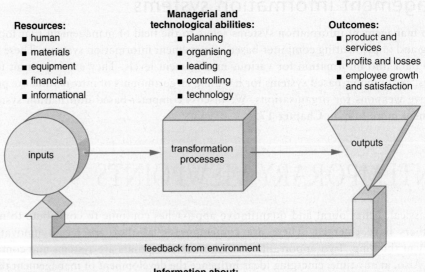

organisation which affect its operations. To consider the environment adequately, an organisation must operate as an open system.

Open versus closed systems: Systems can be open or closed. An **open system** continually interacts with its environment. Through such interaction the system gains new inputs and learns how its outputs are viewed by outside elements. In contrast, a **closed system** does not interact with its environment, receiving little feedback. Practically, all organisations are somewhat open, since an organisation cannot operate for long without interacting with the environment. Still, organisations differ tremendously in their position on the open–closed continuum. If an organisation operates too close to the closed end, it might not see important environmental factors until major problems emerge (Kast & Rosenzweig 1974).

Characteristics of open systems: Organisations operating closer to the open end of the continuum share characteristics that help them survive and prosper. Two major characteristics of open systems are negative entropy and synergy (Kast & Rosenzweig 1972; Katz & Kahn 1978).

Entropy refers to the tendency of systems to decay over time. In contrast, **negative entropy** is the ability of open systems to bring in new energy in the form of inputs and feedback from the environment, to delay or arrest entropy.

A second major characteristic of open systems is **synergy**, the ability of the whole to equal more than the sum of its parts. This means an organisation can achieve its goals more effectively and efficiently than if the parts operate separately.

According to the systems viewpoint, managers will be more successful if they operate their units and organisations as open systems tuned in to significant environmental factors. We discuss environmental factors in more detail in Chapter 3.

Contingency theory

The classical theorists, such as Taylor and Fayol, tried to identify 'the one best way' for managers to operate. If universal principles could be found, then becoming a good manager would mean learning these principles and their applications. Unfortunately, things were more complex. Researchers found that some classical principles, such as Fayol's unity of command (each person should report to only one boss), could be violated with positive results. Consequently, **contingency theory** developed. This theory argues that appropriate managerial action depends on the particular parameters of the situation. Hence, rather than universal principles for every situation, contingency theory identifies actions to take that depend on the characteristics of the situation (see Fig. 2.4) (Luthans 1973; Lee, Luthans & Olson 1982).

To be fair, Fayol and other classical theorists recognised that judgement was needed to apply their various principles. Still, they emphasised universal rules and were vague about when they might not apply (Lorsch 1979; Tosi & Slocum 1984).

Throughout this book you will meet theories and concepts related to the contingency viewpoint—that is, areas in which applications of management ideas depend on situational factors. The contingency approach applies very well in areas such as environmental factors, strategy, organisational design, technology and leadership.

---

open system

System operating in continual interaction with its environment

closed system

System doing little or no interacting with its environment and receiving little feedback

negative entropy

Ability of open systems to bring in new energy, in the form of inputs and feedback from the environment, to delay or arrest entropy

synergy

Ability of the whole to equal more than the sum of its parts

contingency theory

Viewpoint arguing that appropriate managerial action depends on the particular parameters of the situation

Fig. 2.4   The contingency managerial viewpoint

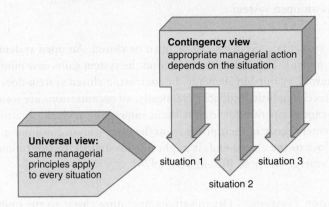

Theory Z

Japanese management

Approach focusing on aspects of management in Japan that may be appropriate for adoption in other countries

Theory Z

Concept combining positive aspects of American and Japanese management into a modified approach aimed at increasing managerial effectiveness while remaining compatible with the norms and values of American society and culture

Given that management is a complex endeavour, innovative approaches are always needed to advance the knowledge base. New approaches may develop into major viewpoints when research and managerial practice show they are effective, others wither after investigations show they are not worth pursuit.

One recent perspective gaining attention is best termed the **Japanese management** approach, since it focuses on aspects of management in Japan appropriate for adoption in other countries. Interest has arisen because of the success of Japanese companies, particularly in manufacturing items such as televisions, videocassette recorders and computer printers (Keys 1994).

On the basis of his research on both American and Japanese management approaches, Ouchi outlined Theory Z. **Theory Z** combines the positive aspects of American and Japanese management into a modified approach aimed at increasing US managerial effectiveness while fitting the norms and values of American society and culture (see Fig. 2.5). The Theory Z approach means giving workers job security; including them in decision making; emphasising group responsibility; increasing quality; establishing gradual-advancement policies, more informal controls and broader career paths; and showing greater concern for employees' work and non-work well-being. A number of companies, such as General Motors, the Ford Motor Company,

Fig. 2.5   **Characteristics of theory Z management (adapted from Ouchi & Jaeger 1978, pp. 308, 311)**

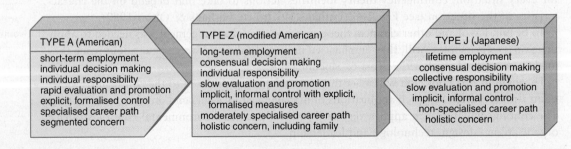

Hewlett-Packard and Intel, have adopted aspects of Theory Z, particularly concepts of involving workers in decision making, instituting more informal controls and encouraging group members to accept responsibility for their unit's work.

The total quality philosophy

In pursuing the competitive advantage of quality, some companies have adopted an interesting approach. This is **total quality management** (TQM), an approach highlighting collective responsibility for product and service quality, encouraging individuals in different but related departments (e.g. product design and manufacturing) to work together to improve quality. Originally called total quality control (TQC), the approach emphasises organisation-wide commitment, integrating quality improvement efforts with organisational goals and including quality in performance appraisals (Port 1987; Schroeder 1989).

TQM represents a change in how quality is perceived. The traditional approach to quality views it in terms of deviation from specified standards, products and services. In contrast, TQM aims to achieve zero defects, with the workforce striving to make a product or service conform exactly to specified quality standards (Schroeder 1989).

Although Japanese companies are often credited with pioneering TQM, the concept originated in America. The late W. Edwards Deming took his ideas on statistical methods for quality improvement to Japan in the late 1940s after being ignored in America. He promoted involvement of employees and various organisation units in quality efforts, developing 14 management points that defined his overall philosophy. Japanese companies welcomed his ideas; in fact, they appreciated his contributions so much they established the Deming prize, an annual award for excellence in quality control. In the 1950s Juran, another American, also helped Japanese companies in TQM efforts (Garvin 1987; Juran 1988). For ideas about how to improve quality in organisations, see the Skills for the 21st Century discussion on 'Deming's 14 points on how to improve quality'.

total quality management

Approach highlighting collective responsibility for product and service quality, and encouraging individuals to work together to improve quality

↑ Deming's 14 points on how to improve quality

management skills for the 21st century

In the course of his work, Deming developed 14 management points outlining what he believes managers, especially at upper levels, must do to produce high-quality products:

1 Make a long-term commitment to improve products and services, with the aim of becoming competitive, staying in business and providing jobs.

2 Adopt the new philosophy of concern for quality. We are in a new economic age. Western management must awaken to the challenge, learn its responsibilities and take on leadership for change.

3 Cease dependence on mass-inspection to achieve quality; build quality into the product in the first place.

4 End the practice of awarding business on the basis of price. Instead minimise total cost. Move to a single supplier for any one item, building a long-term relationship of loyalty and trust.

5 Constantly improve the system of production and service so quality and productivity also constantly improve and costs decrease.

6 Institute on-the-job training.

7 Institute leadership. The aim of supervision should be to help people, machines and gadgets do a better job.

8 Drive out fear so everyone may work effectively for the company.

9 Break down barriers between departments so people work as a team.

10 Eliminate slogans, exhortations and targets asking the workforce for zero defects and new levels of productivity. Such exhortations create adversarial relationships because most causes of low quality and low productivity can be traced to the production system and lie beyond the power of the workforce.

11 Eliminate work standards (quotas) and use of numerical goals on the factory floor. Substitute leadership instead.

12 Remove barriers robbing workers of the right to take pride in their work. Change the emphasis from sheer numbers to quality.

13 Institute a vigorous program of education and self-improvement.

14 Put everybody in the organisation to work on accomplishing the transformation. The transformation is everybody's job.

Source: Adapted from Deming (1986).

@ Information is the key managing the e-challenge

Regardless of the differences in their individual strategies, one thing Enterprise Resource Planning (ERP) companies have in common is the concept of the corporate 'portal'.

A portal is a site within a company's Intranet that aggregates all the information a particular user needs to do their job. The key to a successful portal is the ability to deliver concise information that lets a user make instant decisions—hence PeopleSoft's partnership with strategic planning specialist Cognos.

Andrew Barkla, PeopleSoft's regional vice-president, says, 'Portals are simply a door to go through to get what you want. The value is in the information, the community that you build around that'. Oracle has gone so far as to propose a set of industry standards, which would enable companies to easily construct portals from pre-configured interfaces. It is unlikely that ERP vendors will get their strategy right on the first try. E-business is emerging so rapidly that they go through a period of testing and ensuring that you have got your strategy right.

Source: Adapted from Howarth, B. (1999).

Andrew Barkla, regional vice-president of PeopleSoft.

Activities for discussion, analysis and further research

1 Find out what the issues are for ERP.

2 The following are ERP companies. Contact one of them to find out what they do.
Baan, JD Edwards, Oracle, PeopleSoft, SAP

3 Each of these companies has different strengths and operates with different partners, looking for various strategies to implement. Find out what those strengths are.

An important aspect of TQM is its emphasis on the cost of quality, the cost of not doing things right the first time (Monks 1987).

More recently, there has been a drift away from TQM or TQC as a tool for improvement or control, and a strong move towards adoption of quality as a managerial philosophy. This often translates into a search for continuous incremental improvements in all organisational processes instead of merely a bean-counting strategy for reducing manufacturing defects.

Promoting innovation: Contributions of the major viewpoints

Each major viewpoint has added important ideas to current knowledge of management and has changed how managers think about and behave in organisations (Hill & Jones 1995). The main contributions of major viewpoints are listed in Table 2.6.

Table 2.6   Main innovative contributions of major viewpoints

Viewpoint	Innovative contributions
Classical	Highlights the need for a scientific approach to management Points out work methods can often be improved through study Identifies a number of important principles useful in running organisations efficiently Emphasises pay's potential importance as a motivator
Behavioural	Spotlights the managerial importance of factors such as communication, group dynamics, motivation and leadership Articulates practical applications of behavioural studies Draws on findings of several disciplines such as management, psychology, sociology, anthropology and economics Highlights the importance of organisation members as active human resources rather than as passive tools
Quantitative	Provides quantitative aids to decision making Develops quantitative tools to assist in providing products and services Pioneers new computer-based information systems for management
Contemporary (systems and contingency)	Emphasises organisations can be visualised as systems of interrelated parts Points out the potential importance of the environment and feedback to organisational success Argues there is no one best way to manage, and identifies circumstances or contingencies influencing which particular approach will be effective in a given situation

NGOs—A new power in world politics

In January of 2000, the United Nations Conference of Trade and Development (UNCTAD) tenth session took place in Bangkok. Its general focus was: 'Developmental strategies in an increasingly interdependent world: applying the lessons of the past to make globalisation an effective instrument for the development of all countries and all people'.

Two months earlier a similar event took place. This one, in Seattle, was the meeting of the World Trade Organisation. Both of those organisations cross international borders and form super systems. Other such super systems are ones called NGOs (non-government organisations).

The NGOs of the new millennium are a powerful force. NGOs have gained influence by forming coalitions across borders, increasing their power by forming large groups and making alliances with other powerful groups such as unions. They are using resources such as the Internet to ease communication and build world-wide coalitions which can co-ordinate lobbying in many cities simultaneously.

Source: UNCTAD web site.

Activities for discussion, analysis and further research

1 Consider how mega-organisations such as UNCTAD and WTO are able to manage themselves across international boundaries. Which do you think would be the approach best suited to their survival?
2 Consider the systems approach and discuss how NGOs are effectively applying it to achieve their goals.
3 Do a literature search and identify some of the groups which were represented at the Bangkok UNCTAD Conference. Identify the breadth of those systems and discuss how the various management styles could be applied to them. Explain how the activities of groups such as UNCTAD might have an impact on what happens in Australia.

■ The MD's diary

My style is very much a consensus style. It's one that is based on making sure people are on board and understanding the direction we are going in and are agreeing with it. And then, supporting them, so it's also a supportive style. I do a lot of coaching, a lot of mentoring of people. I try to empower people, to make them feel that they own the process, that they are responsible and that they have the ability to deliver.

I tend to operate as a counter puncher. I am not the one who will throw all the ideas as to how we should do things on the table and expect people to run away and do them. My expectation is that I'll ask them to put the proposals forward, to do the ground work, how they are going to achieve what needs to be achieved, and then I tend to counterpunch by coming in behind that and saying: 'Well OK, I think what you're doing here is right but have you thought about this or I can support you with resources in this area.' So I continually try to leave the ownership for the process with them and coach or mentor them.

The subordinate's log   the reflective practitioner

In reviewing the theory of management styles, I realise that I had to assume a couple of styles which reflected the demands of the senior management. They demanded strong operational and financial controls. The CEO, recognising that I had little experience in that particular role, attempted to retain control until I settled into the job; however, he never gave over control. I have often felt that had he given me more latitude, I would have been able to assume the required control and handle the situation adequately. Hence the management style to satisfy those demands required keeping a lot of data, continuous reporting and therefore was very scientific in nature. This management style had to be applied to the people who reported to me as I needed to collect a lot of data, but at the same time I attempted to minimise that impact, as instinctively I felt that the consultants operated better with a looser management style.

This brought about a two-phase style on my part. Having worked with a number of the consultants, I had a fair idea of their strengths and weaknesses and how they related to clients. While I was in frequent contact with clients and made it my business to know what the consultants were doing in their projects, I took the approach that they were professionals and deference should be given to the skills which they demonstrated. Therefore provided I was happy with the approach they were taking and they could demonstrate a good result (both for our firm and the client), I was happy to let them work without requiring constant formal reporting or applying overly close supervision. I took on the role of a mentor who could provide advice and help problem solving rather than of a supervisor and boss.

I found that the tight management under which I was managed was very restrictive and I found that I was spending so much time reporting to my manager I had no choice but to adopt a non-management style with my subordinates. The result was I was resentful and ineffective to senior management and could not sufficiently direct my subordinates. I learned there was a balance between being a manager and a subordinate simultaneously.

Focus on practice—Strategies for improving

1 Select an organisation you are acquainted with and determine to what degree Fayol's 14 principles apply.
2 To what degree does this organisation fit Weber's ideal bureaucracy model?
3 If this organisation has a lengthy history, investigate whether the management style has evolved. How closely does it follow the evolution of management theory generally? What were the social and environmental factors which impacted on the changes of management style in this organisation?

Source: Jones et al. (2000).

Chapter summary

Although management practices can be traced to ancient times, much impetus for developing management theories and principles came from the industrial revolution and the need for better ways to run resulting factory systems. Preclassical contributors such as Robert Owen, Charles Babbage and Henry R. Towne provided initial ideas leading to identification of management as a significant field of inquiry. From this, four major viewpoints developed: classical, behavioural, quantitative and contemporary.

The classical viewpoint emphasises finding ways to more efficiently manage work and organisations. It includes three approaches. Scientific management, represented by the work of Frederick Winslow Taylor, Frank and Lillian Gilbreth, and Henry Gantt, emphasises the scientific study of work methods to improve worker efficiency. The bureaucratic approach, pioneered by Max Weber, focuses on the need for organisations to operate rationally instead of relying on the arbitrary whims of owners and managers. The administrative management approach, supported by Henri Fayol and Chester Barnard, explores principles used by managers to co-ordinate the organisation's internal activities.

The behavioural viewpoint tries to understand factors affecting human behaviour in organisations. Hugo Münsterberg and Mary Parker Follett were early behaviourists. The Hawthorne studies dramatically demonstrated that workers were more than mere tools of production. Though flawed, the studies produced insights leading to the establishment of the human relations movement, and emphasised concern for the worker. Abraham Maslow's hierarchy of needs theory and Douglas McGregor's Theory X and Theory Y provided managerial guidance but were still general. The behavioural science approach, emphasising scientific research, emerged to build more specific theories about behaviour in organisations to provide practical managerial guidelines.

The quantitative viewpoint focuses on mathematics, statistics and information aids supporting managerial decision making and effectiveness. It has three main branches. Operations research increases decision effectiveness through sophisticated mathematical and statistical methods. Operations management is responsible for managing production and delivery of an organisation's products and services. Management information systems focus on designing and implementing computer-based information systems for management use.

The contemporary viewpoints represent recent major innovations in ways of management thinking. They include systems and contingency theories as well as more recent views. The systems theory approach is based on viewing organisations as systems, including inputs, transformation processes, outputs and feedback. Contingency theory argues appropriate managerial action depends on a given situation's particular parameters. More recent viewpoints include promising approaches which may develop into major viewpoints if research supports them. Another view is Japanese management, represented by Theory Z. This theory combines positive aspects of American and Japanese management into a modified approach appropriate to business in America. Another important view is total quality management.

All major viewpoints contribute significantly to innovation in the field of management. Others will develop as the field progresses.

Questions for discussion and review

1 Explain how preclassical contributors helped set the stage for the development of management as a science. Identify a situation in which you have used the guidelines in Robert's Rules of Order or seen them used. Why have the rules been so popular over time?

2 Contrast the three major approaches within the classical viewpoint: scientific management, bureaucratic management and administrative management. Give examples of how these approaches are reflected in a familiar organisation.

3 Review Frederick Taylor's scientific management principles. How effective do you think these principles would be in eliminating soldiering? What might be some disadvantages of his approach? What did Frank and Lillian Gilbreth add to Taylor's approach?

4 Summarise Mary Parker Follett's contributions. For each, give an example illustrating the relevance of her ideas today.

5   Explain the development of the behavioural viewpoint. How could a flawed set of studies—the Hawthorne studies—help bring about the behavioural viewpoint of management?

6   Differentiate between the three major approaches within the quantitative management viewpoint. How have computers aided development of this viewpoint?

7   Explain major ideas underlying the systems viewpoint. Use this viewpoint to analyse your college or university. To what extent would you consider it to be an open system? Give reasons for your view.

8   Describe the reasoning behind the contingency viewpoint. Why did it emerge? What implications are there for managerial education?

9   Explain the Theory Z approach to management. Under which system would you prefer to work: American (Type A), Japanese (Type J) or modified American (Type Z)? Why? Which system would work best in the following work environments: research, production, mining, agriculture, service?

10 Show how current management knowledge results from innovative processes involving many management pioneers. What can we learn about innovation from studying these people's ideas?

Exercises for managing in the 21st century

Exercise 1
Self-assessment exercise: What kind of a manager am I?

Select the response best describing how you would manage a group of employees.

1 = Strongly disagree
2 = Somewhat disagree
3 = Neither agree nor disagree
4 = Somewhat agree
5 = Strongly agree

_____   1   I would normally give explicit instructions concerning both what is to be accomplished and how it is to be done.

_____   2   I would make sure subordinates know they could lose their jobs if they do not produce well.

_____   3   I would motivate mainly through an incentive awards program based on individual output.

_____   4   I would measure individual contribution based strictly on economic efficiencies.

_____   5   I would make an effort to recognise and develop individual skills.

_____   6   I would install a detailed monitoring system to ensure everyone follows proper procedures.

_____   7   I would attempt to arrange organisational and personal goals so both could be accomplished simultaneously.

_____   8   I would intervene immediately, at will, to modify an employee's behaviour to reach the organisation's goals.

_____   9   If I had to choose between using an employee for something today or having that employee gain experience for the future, I would emphasise output for today.

_____   10 I would rely on my subordinates' imagination and creativity to solve organisational challenges.

Exercise 2
Management exercise: Problems at the ice-cream plant

You are manager of a plant producing a special type of extra-creamy ice-cream. Sales had increased every quarter for the past four years, until last quarter. During that quarter: sales slipped 17 per cent; production was about 15 per cent below projections; absenteeism was about 20 per cent higher than in the previous quarter; and tardiness increased steadily. You believe the problems are management-related, but you are unsure about the causes or steps to take to correct them. You decide to call in a consultant to help determine what to do next. The consultant tells you they wholeheartedly support scientific management and usually look at problems from that point of view.

They mention other consultants in the area who tend to take other views. To get the fullest idea of what should be done at your plant, you call in five other consultants, each of whom supports one of the following approaches: administrative management, bureaucracy, human relations, quantitative management and systems theory.

Form a group with two classmates. Have each member select two of the six management approaches mentioned above. Ensure all approaches are included. Each member plays the role of a consultant for one approach they have selected and then repeats the process for their second role. The person should analyse likely problems at the ice-cream plant and offer solutions from the point of view of the management approach they represent. The other group members critique explanations presented by the consultant.

Ford Motor charges ahead and into globalisation

on the rim—
in Australia

Right around the world, through the mid-1980s, the automotive industry was experiencing a downturn. This state of affairs did not exclude Australia, nor did it exclude the Ford Motor Company. In fact, as a whole, the Ford Motor Company was haemorrhaging. Between 1979 and 1982, the company lost $3 billion. It had managed to acquire a reputation for producing cars designed for yesterday's consumers, and—worse—the quality was poor.

Cutting costs and raising quality were clear priorities. By the mid-1980s, the company had reduced its hourly workforce, cut back on white-collar workers and shut down eight plants in the US. The remaining 81 plants were revamped and upgraded technologically to make the work as efficient as possible. Computerised robots and upgraded inventory control were part of the massive changes. At the same time, Ford tied its efficiency and cost-cutting efforts in search of quality. It adopted the Japanese management view that higher quality ultimately means lower costs. Such changes reduced costs by $5 billion by the mid-1980s, with another $5 billion in savings by the early 1990s.

The company also redirected the design of its cars. Whereas in the past the tendency had been to follow the competition, top management now told designers to 'design the kind of cars you would like to drive'. With the new approach, Ford has produced a number of models that have sold well.

Some of the less visible changes at Ford related to its new approach to internal management. Once considered to have the most autocratic managers in the automotive industry, the company launched a program called Employee Involvement that has pushed decision making to lower levels, including the assembly line. For example, assembly-line workers are now authorised to stop the line if they see a problem. Ford emphasises teamwork and uses the team concept to involve individuals from various areas such as design, engineering and manufacturing in the development of new models. Ideas come from the bottom of the company as well as from the top.

The company is continuing to further dismantle the old corporate pyramid and place more emphasis on a matrix-type organisation structure, in which many parts of the organisation work together but retain their autonomy. As one part of the change, Ford eliminated separate North American and European engineering operations in favour of moving 15 000 employees into five worldwide product-development centres—four in Dearborn and one in Europe. Under this arrangement, instead of developing separate Escort-size cars for sale in Europe, the United States and Australia, the European centre would develop a basic design that could be modified for use in various markets. The other centres would be responsible for basic designs for other types of vehicles—for example, large cars and minivans or trucks. Through such an approach Ford had hoped to create excellent products within a shorter time period with increased efficiency so that vehicles can be sold at an affordable price. Within a year, though, the company was paring the number of centres back to three, an arrangement somewhat similar to the original one. Ford found that having so many centres was leading to confusion, duplicate work and turf battles. Purchasing was also to be globally integrated, but Ford is still struggling to make the approach work. Meanwhile, Ford has encountered price resistance to its cars, which are loaded with desirable new features but have hefty price tags. The company is quickly shifting gears to turn out low-priced, stripped-down models.

A major challenge facing Ford is to sell its products in more markets. Ford has targeted China and India as high-priority countries for expansion. Indonesia, Thailand and Vietnam also are important. In addition, the company is expending major efforts to build a greater presence in Latin America, particularly in Argentina, Brazil and Venezuela.

As the century turned, Ford hoped to be much more efficient. One of the issues facing the company is industrial safety. A philosophy of health and happiness was the driving force behind a radical new approach Ford Australia has taken to occupational health and safety when designing the new AU Falcon. For this, Ford Australia received the 1998 Victorian WorkCover awards which recognised Ford's 'Process safety review', an innovative approach to ergonomics and safety risk assessment which was introduced at the earliest design stages of the AU Falcon.

Safer, more ergonomically comfortable work practices on the assembly line have been designed into the product—a process which began the moment the first designer put pen to paper on the new car three years ago.

This award was a tribute to the teamwork and relentless commitment to safety improvement by many people throughout the company.

Source: Autoweb Pty Ltd and Web Publications.

Activities for discussion, analysis and further research

1 Identify influences from the classical, behavioural and quantitative viewpoints in the way the Ford Motor Company is managed today.

2 Use systems theory to contrast the way the Ford Motor Company operated at the time the Edsel was introduced with the way the company is currently operating, including its worldwide emphasis. You may need to visit the Ford web site to get some more information.

3 Explain the influence of Japanese management (Theory Z) on current management at the Ford Motor Company.

4 Identify some of Ford's competitors and log on to their web sites. Determine whether those organisations also went through similar evolutions. Why do you think that might have happened?

Understanding Internal and External Environments

Chapter **3**

CHAPTER OUTLINE

Types of external environments
Mega-environment
Task environment

Analysing environmental conditions
Views of the organisation–environment interface
Characteristics of the environment

Managing environmental elements
Adaptation
Favourability influence
Domain shifts

The internal environment: Organisational culture
Nature of organisational culture
Manifestations of organisational culture
Promoting innovation: An adaptive, entrepreneurial culture
Changing organisational culture
How leaders influence cultural change

LEARNING OBJECTIVES

After studying this chapter, you should be able to:

○ Explain the concept of mega-environment and outline its major elements.
○ Distinguish between the concepts of task environment and mega-environment and describe major task environment elements.
○ Contrast population ecology and resource dependence views of the organisation-environment interface.
○ Explain how environmental uncertainty and bounty impact on organisations.
○ Describe the major methods organisations use to manage their environments.
○ Explain the nature of organisational culture and its major manifestations.
○ Contrast entrepreneurial and administrative cultures as means of promoting innovation.
○ Explain how organisational cultures can be changed.

Striving for excellence

Autoliv holds a key position within the larger automotive industry. This industry membership has some interesting impacts. Any changes in the number of car sales in Australia impacts on the organisation's productivity requirements. Autoliv is a supplier to all four Australian car manufacturers and exports to KIA, Hyundai and Telco. Autoliv, through its business planning, attempts to buffer the ups and downs of individual manufacturers.

The larger political and economic activities of the nation impact on the organisation. Autoliv tries to keep things internal by winning and holding the hearts and minds of its people so that the external pressures have a minimal impact on internal activities.

While it is impossible to keep everything outside, the building up of a strong organisational culture will withstand what goes on in the external political environment and the ups and downs within the workplace of individual customer organisations.

**external
environment**

Major forces outside the
organisation with potential
to influence significantly a
product or service's likely
success

**internal
environment**

General conditions existing
within an organisation

**organisational
culture**

System of shared values,
assumptions, beliefs and
norms uniting members of
an organisation

An organisation's effectiveness is influenced by its **external environment**—by the major forces outside the organisation able to impact on the success of its products or services. In addition, organisations which might otherwise achieve spectacular success do not do so unless their **internal environment,** or general conditions existing within the organisation, is compatible with the external environment. The internal environment includes organisation members, the nature of their interactions and the physical setting they operate in. The term **organisational culture** is often used for an organisation's internal environment. Organisational culture is a system of shared values, assumptions, beliefs and norms uniting an organisation's members (Smircich 1983; Kilmann, Saxton & Serpa 1986).

In this chapter, we examine an organisation's external environment first. We consider both mega-, or general, environments within which an organisation functions, and more specific elements which comprise an organisation's task environment. We also explore views about the relationship between an organisation and its environment, and consider important environmental characteristics. Next we look at ways environmental elements can be managed. Finally, we examine the internal environment by looking at how an organisation's culture can influence prospects for success. Our discussion also considers the relationship between innovation and entrepreneurial culture.

TYPES OF EXTERNAL ENVIRONMENTS

The Warren Featherbone Company had a problem—recognising the ebbing of a lucrative market. This company built a thriving business about a century ago around a patented product, the featherbone. Used to stiffen corsets, collars, bustles and gowns, the featherbone was made of finely split turkey quills woven to form a cord. Though the company survived the Great Depression, technological advances such as plastic were emerging. It saw the trend and, in 1938, started making plastic baby pants to go over nappies, just as demand for the featherbone dropped. It then made a rocky move into baby clothing. Fortunately, its baby clothing had became a solid business by the mid-1960s, as the development of the disposable napkin destroyed demand for plastic pants (Morgenthaler 1989). As the Warren Featherbone Company's history shows, considering an organisation's environment is crucial. Organisations must always be prepared to change and innovate.

Systems theory highlights the importance of the environment to organisations. According to this view, an organisation will be more successful if it operates as an open system constantly interacting with, and receiving feedback from, its external environment (see Chapter 2). Consequently, organisations need managers to expend effort understanding their organisation's external environment. Their external environment can be divided into two segments: mega-environment, or general environment, and task environment. These segments and their elements are shown in Figure 3.1. (The internal environment, as related to the idea of organisational culture, is also shown. Organisational culture is discussed later in this chapter.)

Mega-environment

The **mega-environment**, or general environment, is the external environment segment reflecting broad conditions and trends in societies within which an organisation operates. The mega-environment consists of five major elements: technological, economic, legal-political, sociocultural and international (see Fig. 3.1) (David 1987; Hall 1987). Because these reflect major trends and conditions outside the organisation, they tend to be beyond a single organisation's ability to affect or alter directly, at least short term. The Xerox Corporation's mega-environment is shown in Figure 3.2.

mega-environment

The broad conditions and trends in societies in which an organisation operates

Technological element The **technological element** reflects current knowledge about production of products and services. Although specific organisations' technical knowledge and patents give them a competitive edge for a time, most organisations are affected, either positively or negatively, by technological progress.

Research in the minicomputer, cement and airline industries shows that technology evolves through periods of incremental change punctuated by technological breakthroughs which either enhance or destroy the competence of firms in an industry (Tushman & Anderson 1986; Barnett 1990). For example, Nobel prize-winning Bell Laboratory physicists invented the transistor in 1947 and pioneered the computer age. Subsequent microchip development affected businesses and their products in industries ranging from automobile and small-appliance manufacturing to home building.

To remain competitive, organisations must understand current technology developments affecting their ability to offer desirable products and services. Many sources provide information about environmental elements. Among these are major business periodicals (such as *Business Review Weekly*, *Forbes*, *Asia Week* and *Fortune*), various trade journals aimed at

technological element

Current state of knowledge regarding production of products and services

Fig. 3.1   The internal and external environments of the organisation

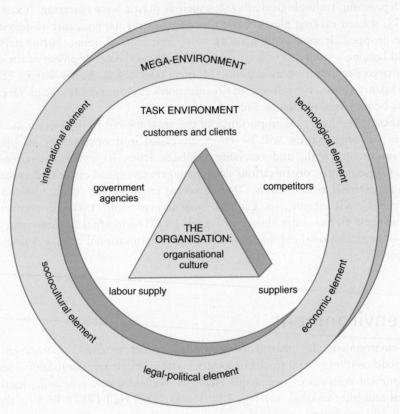

specific industries, government publications, business services (such as various Dun & Bradstreet indexes), and on-line services (such as LEXIS/NEXIS, a service providing access to many interesting publications and information sources).

Economic element   The **economic element** involves systems of wealth production, distribution and consumption. Companies operating in Western countries function largely in capitalist economies, though they may do business with and/or operate in countries with socialist economies. In a **capitalist economy**, market forces operate and individuals own the means of production, either directly or through corporations. In a **socialist economy**, the state owns the means of production, and economic activity is managed by plan.

In practice, countries are hybrid economies. Though Australia and New Zealand operate close to the capitalist end of the continuum, considerable government regulation occurs in areas such as mass communications. Today, the socialist end is represented by the People's Republic of China. The economies of most countries, such as Singapore, Thailand and Indonesia, fall somewhere between the extremes. Third-world countries (mainly poor countries with low per capita income, little industry and high birthrates) have different patterns as they struggle to decide to follow either capitalist or socialist models.

Fig 3.2   Elements of the mega-environment of the Xerox Corporation

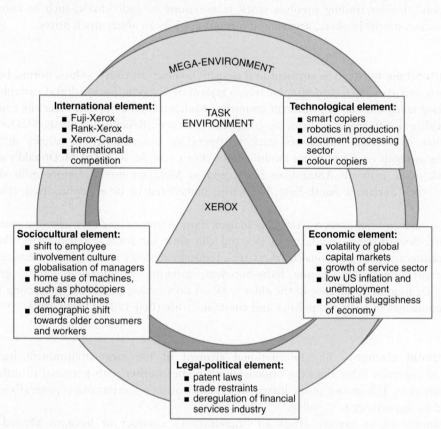

Because of these differences, organisations operating in a variety of countries face a range of economic ground rules (Standard & Poor 1993). Within any economic system, of course, organisations are influenced by economic factors they have little control over, such as inflation, interest rates and recessions.

Legal-political element   The **legal-political element** refers to legal and governmental systems within which an organisation functions. Trends in legislation, court decisions, politics and government regulation are important legal-political environment aspects.

For example, organisations operate within the general legal framework of every country in which they do business. They are governed by many laws specifically addressing their functioning (Salpukas 1994). Such laws may include Acts aimed at controlling pollution and occupational health and safety. Simultaneously, organisations are subject to growing numbers of lawsuits filed by interest groups, ranging from employees to clients. These have been motivated by juries awarding large sums of money, particularly in product liability cases (Finn 1987; Skrzycki 1989; Kesner & Johnson 1990).

Political processes also influence the legal system. Political issues may result in government regulation of various areas. For instance, share market scandals result in political pressure on

legal-political element

Legal and governmental systems within which an organisation must function

regulatory bodies for computerised tracking and criminal prosecutions of illegal stock trading by 'insiders'. Insider trading involves stock transactions by individuals, such as company officers or investment bankers, accessing information likely to affect stock prices.

sociocultural element

Attitudes, values, norms, beliefs, behaviours and associated demographic trends characteristic of a given geographic area

Sociocultural element   The **sociocultural element** involves attitudes, values, norms, beliefs, behaviours and associated demographic trends typical of a region. Sociocultural variables are often raised when considering different countries. Multinational companies face the problem of sociocultural differences influencing competitive success. Recognising these, McDonald's insists that its foreign franchisees stick to operating procedures, but allows different marketing methods or a few menu modifications. For example, in Brazil McDonald's sells a soft drink made from an Amazonian berry, and in Malaysia menus feature milk shakes flavoured with durian, a South-East Asian fruit considered to be an aphrodisiac (Deveny 1986).

Because sociocultural aspects change, managers must monitor trends for new opportunities or threats. Sociocultural trends mean demand can shift for some product types. Among current changes affecting regional markets are a tendency to delay marriage, the emergence of single-parent households, ageing baby-boomers, growing workforce diversity, greater longevity creating need for care of the elderly, recent downsizing trends and increasing influence of minorities in business, politics and community life (Bell 1987; Davies 1995).

international element

Developments in countries outside an organisation's home country with potential to influence the organisation

International element   The **international element** of the mega-environment includes changes in countries other than the organisation's home country with potential to influence the organisation. The impact of the international element on organisations is generally significant and its importance is growing.

International issues greatly affect an organisation's conduct of business abroad. For example, currency fluctuations influence an organisation's ability to compete globally. When the domestic currency's value is high against foreign currencies, companies find it difficult to compete internationally. Conversely, when the local currency falls against foreign currencies, new business opportunities arise.

Free-trade agreements, such as the North American Free Trade Agreement (NAFTA) (Canada, Mexico and the United States), offer opportunity for long-term growth. Typically these allow goods, services and funds to move more freely between participants, as tariffs and other trade barriers are gradually eliminated. Such agreements can cause major changes in the ability of individual businesses to compete (Bhagwati 1988). Thus international factors largely beyond the direct influence of an organisation can affect managers' efforts.

⬤ To rent or buy?

case in point

Imagine your washing machine breaking down. What would you do? Rush out to buy a new one? Not if you were Rolf Berglund. He simply asked Electrolux to deliver a free replacement.

In an innovative way to increase market share, Electrolux is now in the business of selling services as well as washing machines, refrigerators and vacuum cleaners. The company charges the client for using the machine. Rolf

Berglund's machine is monitored through an Internet connection and the local electricity company bills him on behalf of Electrolux.

Faced with narrowing margins in the manufacturing industry, Electrolux is only one of a growing number of manufacturers hoping to increase market share by selling services as well as products. Their aim is to build long-term relationships with consumers directly. Whirlpool Corp in the USA is also using the Internet to reinvent itself as a service provider.

This isn't a new process. In recent months, Australia has seen computer companies offer free computers in order to bind consumers through long-term service contracts. The mobile telephone industry subsidises the cost of hand sets in order to achieve the same results.

While this is a step towards the economy of the future being a service economy, people need convincing. In the case of the washing machine, the company makes more money through selling the service than they do through selling the machine, as most people only buy one machine every ten years or so. In time, consumers may think differently about domestic gadgets they have been buying in the same way for decades. But as their expectations change, so will the way in which manufacturing organisations do business. Electrolux, in collaboration with the Swedish power utility, have installed a 'smart energy meter' in Rolf Berglund's home. This enables his washing machine to be connected to a central data base via the Internet and on every monthly electricity bill, there is a listing of how many times the washing machine has been used.

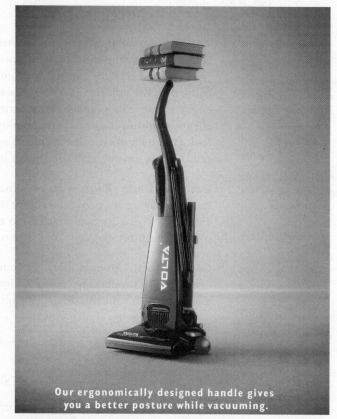

Our ergonomically designed handle gives you a better posture while vacuuming.

Advertisement for a Volta vacuum cleaner, a product of Electrolux. Electrolux is one company that has decided to sell related services as well as its physical products.

Source: Adapted from Dow Jones Newswires (2000).

Activities for discussion, analysis and further research

1 Find the Web site for Merloni Eletrodomestici SpA in Italy. See what you can find out about their attempt to introduce service delivery as well as sales of manufactured items to the public.
2 What factors are Electrolux taking into consideration when they are offering this type of service?
3 In what ways will this necessitate a change in their culture?
4 Do you think this will gain acceptance in Australia? Why? What factors of Australian culture will impact on this strategy being adopted?

Task environment

task environment

Specific outside elements
with which an organisation
interfaces in the course of
conducting its business

**customers and
clients**

Individuals and organisations
purchasing an organisation's
products and/or services

competitors

Other organisations either
offering or with a high
potential of offering rival
products or services

The **task environment** is the external environment segment made up of specific external elements an organisation faces in operating. This environment depends on an organisation's products and services and the locations where it operates. Any organisation will have difficulty directly influencing the mega-environment, but it may successfully affect its task environment. The organisation's major task environment typically includes customers and clients, competitors, suppliers, employees and government bodies. Each organisation must look at its own situation to decide its specific task environment. Elements of the Xerox Corporation's task environment are shown in Figure 3.3.

Customers and clients   An organisation's **customers and clients** are individuals and organisations buying its products and/or services. Many organisations try to stay close to the customer, paying particular attention to service and quality, listening to customers and trying to serve them better (*New York Times* 1995; Erlick 1995; Wyman 1996).

Competitors   An organisation's **competitors** are other organisations offering or potentially offering rival products or services. Organisations must be concerned with known competitors and monitor for potential new entrants (Kuntz 1995).

Fig. 3.3   Elements of the task environment of the Xerox Corporation

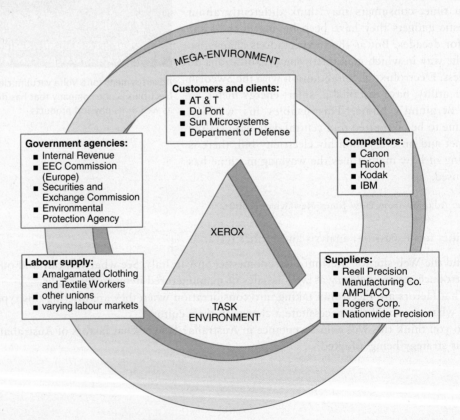

Organisations must be aware of the activities of their competitors. For example, Xerox benchmarks to estimate what competitors do and how much it costs. To understand Kodak's distribution and handling costs, for instance, Xerox managers ordered Kodak copiers, noting where they were shipped from, how they were shipped and even how they were packed (McComas 1986). For ideas about how organisations keep informed about competitors, see the Management skills for the 21st century discussion, 'Keeping tabs on competitors'.

 # Keeping tabs on competitors

management skills for the 21st century

Here are 10 legal ways to track what your competitors are doing:

1 Commercial databases are an easy way to obtain information. Databases contain published articles from newspapers, magazines and trade publications, as well as reports from stock analysts, patent applications, biographical information, etc. This information can be accessed by computer. Information about various databases is contained in the Directory of Online Data Bases, published by Cuandra/ Elsevier (New York). Also many companies have web sites containing useful information about new products, special promotions and other activities.

2 Specialty trade publications dealing with industries and product areas provide very up-to-date information about major personnel changes, product advertising, new product announcements, trade show notices and the like.

3 News clippings from local newspapers often provide specific information not available in national publications. You can hire a clipping service. Clipping services charge a basic fee, as well as a fee for each clipping. Check the telephone directory for clipping services.

4 Help-wanted advertisements can give clues about expansion plans and new technologies competitors are pursuing, and even financial status information may be embedded in them, especially in advertisements for senior personnel.

5 Published market-research reports can often be helpful.

6 Stock reports give information about public companies (stock is publicly traded) and their various subsidiaries through analysis by securities analysts at brokerage firms.

7 Trade shows and the product literature obtainable at them are good sources of information about product innovations, price changes and methods of marketing. Speeches and presentations given at trade shows are often helpful as well.

8 Public filings (federal and state) often provide information about financial data and future plans. The filings include reports public companies must submit to the Corporate Affairs Commission, records of bankruptcy cases and other court cases and government-required annual reports.

9 Advertisements give clues about competitors' marketing strategies. Advertising or clipping services can often obtain copies of advertisements for you. Information about competitors' advertising expenditures by product in various media (such as TV or magazines) can be obtained.

10 Personal contacts can provide many titbits of useful information about competitor activities. A contact base may include academics with knowledge about technological advances, suppliers, customers, purchasing agents, service technicians and financial analysts. Trade shows and professional conferences are also particularly good places to develop contacts (Fuld 1989; 1988).

suppliers

Organisations and
individuals supplying
resources an organisation
needs to conduct its
operations

Suppliers   An organisation's **suppliers** are organisations and individuals supplying resources (such as raw materials, products or services) to conduct operations. The conventional view was that it is best to have many suppliers to reduce dependence on any one. World competition is changing this. Companies find they can trim costs by reducing supplier numbers and contracting them. In 1980, Xerox got parts and components from 5000 vendors worldwide. More recently, with fewer vendors, Xerox set tougher quality standards, got better prices, and built more co-operative supplier relationships (Byrne 1987).

labour supply

Individuals potentially
employable by an
organisation

Labour supply and the importance of managing diversity   An organisation's **labour supply** consists of people employable by the organisation. The ability to attract, motivate and retain human resources to provide products and services is crucial for organisations (Pyatt 1986).

Employers can expect to recruit from an increasingly diverse labour supply (*Economist* 1990). For example, a breakdown of the Australian labour force by birthplace for 1998–99 is shown in Table 3.1.

In combination, diversity and the baby boomers are having a significant impact on workforce character. However, diversity's influence will increase and baby-boomer impact will lessen. Researchers have identified trends based on Australian Bureau of Statistics (ABS) data. Currently 75 per cent of workers are Australian born and approximately 60 per cent are from Australian-born parents. The others come from a range of countries, the majority still being

Table 3.1   Australian labour force by birthplace 1998–99

	Total
Birthplace	
Born in Australia	7 083 000
Born outside Australia	2 316 000
Total	9 399 000
Country of origin	
Oceania	284 100
Europe and former USSR	1 217 200
Middle East and North Africa	97 500
South-East Asia	284 500
North-East Asia	136 200
Northern America	53 300
Other	243 200
Total	2 316 000
Language	
Main English-speaking countries	987 300
Other countries	1 328 700
Total	2 316 000

Source: Adapted from ABS (2000).

from mainly English-speaking countries. The rate of increase in women in the labour force is slowing; six out of ten women of working age are in the labour force. This is becoming closer to men's labour participation rate, although more women are in part-time employment than men. Minorities are increasing in workforce participation. This is partially due to higher minority-group immigration rates and increases in labour participation by minority-group women. The labour force is still growing, but more slowly than during the 1970s and 1980s, when baby boomers entered the labour force in increasing numbers. Overall, by 2050, Australia's population is expected to be about 23 million, compared with 18.9 million in 1998 (http://www.immi.gov.au/facts/13pop.htm; http://www.immi.gov.au/facts/11fifty.htm; http://www.statistics.gov.au/websitedbs/c311).

Baby boomers, dominant in the workforce for two decades, will have less impact in the workplace. They will constitute less than half the labour force by 2005, from about 55 per cent in the mid-1980s. By 2005, baby boomers will move to the older-worker category of 55 years of age and above, as the first baby boomers are 55 years old in 2001. Older workers will constitute about 14.7 per cent of the workforce by 2005, compared with 12.3 per cent in 1998.

As a result of this diversity, many companies have instituted programs to help organisation members value and utilise a more diverse workforce.

Given increasing globalisation, workers (especially better-educated ones) in the future will migrate to countries needing their skills, despite immigration laws discouraging such movements (Johnston 1991; Eisenhardt & Brown 1998). Labour supply issues are discussed further in Chapter 10.

Government agencies   Various **government agencies** provide services and monitor compliance with laws and regulations at local, state or regional, and national levels. Usually an organisation's task environment involves interactions with representatives of specific government agencies (e.g. tax, consumer affairs, police, health, and workers' compensation).

ANALYSING ENVIRONMENTAL CONDITIONS

Although most researchers see the environment as influential, views differ on the relationship between organisations and their environments. In this section, we examine two major views of the organisation–environment interface, then explore major environmental characteristics.

Views of the organisation–environment interface

Among prominent approaches to explaining the nature of the interface are the population ecology and resource dependence models (Hall 1987; Ulrich & Barney 1984).

Population ecology model   The **population ecology model** focuses on populations or groups of organisations, arguing that environmental factors cause organisations with appropriate characteristics to survive and others to fail. Thus, organisations survive whether the specific

government agencies

Agencies providing services and monitoring compliance with laws and regulations at local, state or regional, and national levels

population ecology model

Model focusing on populations or groups of organisations and arguing that environmental factors cause organisations with appropriate characteristics to survive and others to fail

**natural selection
model**

Term sometimes used for the
population ecology model

environmental conditions suit them or not. Sometimes this is called the **natural selection model**. Since organisations do not change rapidly, the view is that managers have little opportunity to affect their organisation's fate (Hannan & Freeman 1977; Bennon & Dress 1985).

Environmental results are shown in a *Forbes* magazine study on its 70th anniversary in 1987. *Forbes* looked at which of the 100 largest companies (in terms of assets) in 1917 appeared among the largest 100 companies 70 years later. Only 22 companies on the original were on the 1987 list. Of these, 11 had the same name as in 1917 (American Telephone & Telegraph; Eastman Kodak; E. I. Du Pont de Nemours; Ford Motor; General Electric; General Motors; Pacific Gas & Electric; Procter & Gamble; Sears, Roebuck; Southern California Edison; and Westinghouse Electric). The other 11 had changed names. The 78 companies gone from the list had met a variety of fates. Some had grown too slowly to maintain position; some had been acquired; some faltered badly and faded. At now-defunct Baldwin Locomotive, for example, executives insisted new technology would not replace steam locomotives. In another case, Atlantic Gulf & West Indies Steam Ship Lines had lost ships (*Forbes* 1987). Could something have been done to make these companies prosper? Population ecology model supporters do not think so. However, the resource dependence model views the situation differently.

**resource
dependence model**

Model highlighting the
organisation's dependence
on the environment for
resources and arguing that
organisations attempt to
manipulate the environment
to reduce dependence

Resource dependence model   The **resource dependence model** sees organisations as being dependent on the environment for resources, arguing that organisations manipulate their environment to reduce dependence (Pfeiffer & Salancik 1978; Ulrich & Barney 1984). In this view, organisations cannot generate all resources (e.g. financing, materials and services) needed to operate. For example, General Motors buys many parts rather than making them. By forming relationships, organisations solve many resource problems. However, these create dependency and reduce organisation flexibility in making decisions and taking actions. So organisations try to be independent by controlling their critical resources or developing alternatives.

For example, IBM developed its PS/2 personal computer and contracted Microsoft to develop a new operating system called OS/2. By doing this, IBM sped up the introduction of the new computer. Unfortunately, Microsoft developed both the IBM system and a better one called Windows. Moreover, Windows could run on older IBMs, simplifying their use. One reason Microsoft developed Windows was that they did not want to be too dependent on the new PS/2. Ironically, the availability of Windows meant sales of IBM's new PS/2 computer slowed. IBM then developed its own competing software, but too late to gain market share over Windows (Zachary 1989; Burgess 1992). This situation illustrates how resource needs and dependence intertwine as organisations deal with their environments.

In contrast to population ecology, which sees managerial actions as limited in dealing with the environment, resource dependence argues that managers have strategic choices, or options, and these influence organisational success. Managers not only have choices in their reactions but also have options in attempting to influence the nature of the environment (Pfeiffer & Salancik 1978). Hence, in regard to the *Forbes* study, Baldwin Locomotive may have been better off had its managers paid more attention to environmental change. Even the Atlantic Gulf & West Indies Steam Ship Lines could have moved some part of the business to less risky ventures.

Reconciling the differing models   Both population ecology and resource dependence models are useful to managers. The population ecology model highlights the fact that organisations have little control over environmental factors influencing them and luck may be important in their success.

On the other hand, the resource dependence model shows managers often have options influencing environmental aspects, including inter-organisational relationships. Hence, they should monitor, understand and influence environmental elements, recognising that unforeseen elements can have major organisational impacts.

Characteristics of the environment

Assessing the environment accurately is difficult. From one view, an organisation's environment is objective reality—a set of perfectly measurable conditions giving managers complete information. In practice, however, managers are more likely to act on the environment as they perceive it. Thus, the environment may be more sensibly viewed as subjective reality, existing only in managers' minds (Weick 1995). Since managers act on their own perceptions they must verify these through alternative sources of information (perhaps others' opinions, as well as objective data) (Boyd, Dess & Rasheed 1993).

In analysing the environment of an organisation, it is useful to consider two key concepts: environmental uncertainty and environmental bounty, or capacity. Although the main focus here is task environment, relevant mega-environment trends have to be considered.

Environmental uncertainty **Environmental uncertainty** occurs when an organisation's future environmental circumstances cannot be assessed or predicted accurately (Pfeiffer & Salancik 1978). The more uncertain the environment, the more time and effort managers must spend monitoring it, assessing organisational implications and deciding actions to take. The degree of environmental uncertainty results from two major factors: complexity and dynamism (Dess & Beard 1984).

Complexity **Environmental complexity** is the number of elements in an organisation's environment and their degree of similarity. Environments with a relatively small number of similar items are homogeneous. In contrast, environments with a large number of dissimilar items are heterogeneous. As environmental elements become more heterogeneous, managers have more variables to deal with.

Dynamism **Environmental dynamism** is the rate and predictability of change in the elements of an organisation's environment. Environments where change is slow and relatively predictable are stable. Conversely, environments where change is fast and relatively unpredictable are unstable. As environmental elements become more unstable, the greater is the challenge for managers.

Assessing environmental uncertainty The concepts of complexity and dynamism can help assess the degree of environmental uncertainty. Such assessment can be done by looking at important task-environment elements and major potential influences in the mega-environment (see Fig. 3.4). As cell 1 in Figure 3.4 suggests, uncertainty is relatively low when both dynamism and complexity are low. This situation prevails in the funeral industry, with slow change and a steady stream of customers with similar needs. The situation in cell 2, low dynamism but high complexity, produces moderately low uncertainty. An example is the insurance industry, where companies serve a diverse set of customer needs but competitive elements change fairly slowly.

environmental uncertainty

Condition in which future environmental circumstances affecting an organisation cannot be accurately assessed and predicted

environmental complexity

Number of elements in an organisation's environment and their degree of similarity

environmental dynamism

Rate and predictability of change in the elements of an organisation's environment

Fig. 3.4   Assessing the degree of environmental uncertainty (adapted from Duncan 1979, p. 63)

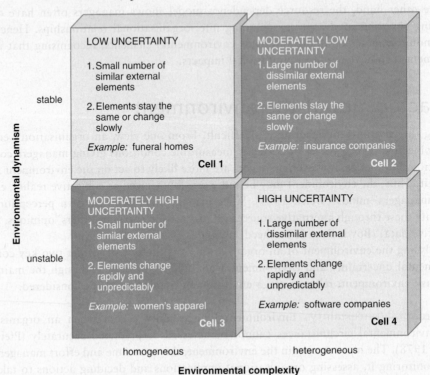

In cell 3, high dynamism but low complexity produces a situation of moderately high uncertainty. This characterises the women's clothing industry, in which customers and retailers constitute fairly homogeneous market segments but fashion trends move rapidly. Finally, cell 4 shows both high dynamism and complexity, resulting in high uncertainty. High environmental uncertainty occurs in the computer-software industry, where conditions change rapidly and a large number of environmental factors (technological change, vast numbers of diverse customers and strenuous competition) exert strong heterogeneous pressures.

Conditions of uncertainty may change over a period of time. For example, a relatively homogeneous and stable environment may change (perhaps gradually) to one with greater uncertainty. Then managers must reassess their situations.

environmental bounty
<hr>
Extent to which the environment can support sustained growth and stability

Environmental bounty   Another important environmental element is **environmental bounty**: the extent to which the environment can support sustained growth and stability (Aldrich 1979; Dess & Beard 1984). Environmental bounty ranges from relatively rich to relatively lean, depending on available organisational resource levels (Castrogiovanni 1991). Organisations operating in rich environments can build a cushion of internal resources, such as capital, equipment and experience. A high level of internal resources can fund innovations and expansions to help an organisation keep its position, as well as weather leaner times. Unfortunately, rich environments attract other organisations.

☒ AYS Stevedoring—Changing corporate culture

You may recognise the situation described under anonymous terms in the following exercise. If you do, look up information and newspaper reports of the incidents. Do you think the organisations concerned made appropriate decisions considering the circumstances of the environment they were operating in?

Assume there is a port where three companies carry out most of the stevedoring work. The companies are Stevedoring A, Stevedoring B and AYS Stevedoring (AYS is an acronym for At Your Service). AYS Stevedoring are a new entrant to the market. Stevedoring A and B had long-lasting, well-established contracts with little or no outside competition (or so they thought) and tended to give little thought to future customers or outside influences. In both Stevedoring A and Stevedoring B the culture was one of complacency.

The complacent cultures of Stevedoring A and B led them to believe that the new company would not be a threat, the market was considered 'closed' and the new competitor would not gain enough work to survive. They thought that the small contracts that the new competitor obtained would not be of great consequence. They were incorrect. In a short time AYS Stevedoring grew from strength to strength and gained many additional contracts on the way.

The factors that have contributed to the success of AYS Stevedoring are:

Customer service They had a positive attitude to work and were helpful towards both internal and external customers. Their outlook towards current and future business clients was highly professional. The ship owners, freight forwarders and numerous other port users were eager to trial the new company in an effort to increase their productivity, save money and improve their customer service.

Responsiveness Response times for the new company for most tasks requested were well in front of the competitors. This further highlighted a lack of enthusiasm from existing competitors.

Price As the company grew and acquired contracts it maintained a level of professionalism while offering competitive prices. This combination of professional service and competitive pricing has proved to be a powerful incentive to importers and exporters.

Personal contact The level of personal contact from senior management and supervisors helped to cement relationships and ensure customers were confident with the dealings of the company.

Source: Allison Powell, Australian Maritime College.

Activities for discussion, analysis and further research

1 The general manager of Stevedoring A seeks your advice as to how to improve the situation.
   What steps should be taken to change organisational culture?
   What can be done to embed and maintain the cultural change?
2 The manager of AYS Stevedoring asks you what can be done to ensure that they retain and increase market share in the changing environment.
   How can they ensure that the organisation will hang on to its market share?
   What steps can they take to increase their market share?

MANAGING ENVIRONMENTAL ELEMENTS

While recognising limitations in managing environmental factors, some organisational theorists (e.g. those advocating the resource dependence model) view environmental elements as responsive to action by managers and advocate proactive measures. For example, Carnival Cruise Lines, the world's largest cruise operator, has been successful attracting new passengers by aiming more at the mass market. Carnival's new cruises include using the amenities of a resort at a reasonable price (Booth 1992). Managers have three major options: adapt to existing environmental elements, attempt to influence environmental favourability and/or shift their operating domain away from threatening environmental elements and toward more beneficial ones (Thompson 1967; Kotter 1979). Major methods of implementing these are presented in Table 3.2. The feasibility of any or all of these depends on the situation, but prospects are enhanced if the environment has high bounty or if the organisation has built a resource cushion.

Adaptation

The adaptation approach involves changing internal operations and activities to make the organisation and its environment more compatible. This strategy accepts the existing environment as a given and seeks to develop a rational process for adjusting to it. Four common organisation methods to adapt to environmental fluctuations are buffering, smoothing, forecasting and rationing (Thompson 1967).

buffering

Stockpiling either inputs into or outputs from a production or service process to cope with environmental fluctuations

Buffering   The use of **buffering** involves stockpiling inputs into or outputs from a production or service process to cope with environmental variations. Buffering by stockpiling inputs is used when it is difficult to find reliable sources of inputs, such as supplies. Conversely, buffering by maintaining inventories of finished products is used when wide fluctuations in market demand make it hard to produce outputs efficiently as ordered. Buffering is not always feasible because of high expense, perishability of materials, or difficulty of stockpiling

Table 3.2   Approaches to managing environmental impacts

Approach	Methods
Adaptation	Buffering, smoothing, forecasting and rationing
Favourability influence	Advertising and engaging in public relations, boundary spanning, recruiting, negotiating contracts, co-opting, establishing strategic alliances, joining trade associations and engaging in political activity
Domain shifts	Changing domain completely or diversifying into some new areas

services, such as customer service in a restaurant. Furthermore, substantial buffering of inputs and finished products risks obsolescence before items are used or sold.

Smoothing   While buffering tries to accommodate market fluctuations, **smoothing** means taking actions to reduce the impact of market fluctuations. For example, electricity companies often discount rates at particular times to encourage energy use in slow-demand periods. Department stores run sales during slow months. Restaurants often make offers on certain weekday nights when business is normally slow. Such actions may avoid the inefficiency of expanding to meet peak demands which leaves resources underutilised during non-peak times.

Forecasting   Another way to deal with environmental fluctuations is forecasting, or predicting changing conditions and future events that significantly affect an organisation's business. To the extent future conditions can be predicted with reasonable accuracy, it may be possible to prepare to meet the fluctuations. For example, on the basis of customers' shopping habits, grocery stores frequently hire part-time staff to assist regular staff during expected busy periods. For situations such as this, forecasts based on experience with customer patterns may be accurate. When environmental fluctuations are related to more complex dynamic factors, such as economic trends, more sophisticated forecasting techniques may be needed. Many companies have staff economists and/or subscribe to services giving economic forecasts based on elaborate econometric models.

Rationing   Environmental fluctuations may be managed by **rationing**, or giving limited access to a high demand product or service. For example, universities may ration places in popular specialisations by having prerequisites, such as achievement of a certain first-year average. By rationing, the organisation avoids expanding capacity to meet a temporary demand increase. This is good, as many costs associated with capacity expansion (e.g. extra plants, equipment or classroom buildings) continue when demand drops. Rationing may be used when demand exceeds forecasts or when new production expands slowly (because of heavy costs and considerable risk if demand does not materialise). Rationing has a down side, however. In denying consumers a product or service, the organisation is turning away potential business (Fuhrman 1988).

Favourability influence

In contrast to adaptation strategies, a favourability influence approach means trying to alter environmental elements to make them more compatible with the organisation's needs. Instead of accepting environmental elements as givens, this approach holds that some environmental aspects can be changed by the organisation.

Organisations have many ways of attempting to influence significant environmental elements. These include advertising and engaging in public relations, boundary spanning, recruiting, negotiating contracts, co-opting, establishing strategic alliances, joining trade associations and engaging in political activities (Kotter 1979).

Advertising and public relations   One way to influence the environment is by advertising, using communications media to gain favourable publicity for products and services. Closely aligned to advertising is public relations, using communications media and related activities

smoothing
Taking actions aimed at reducing the impact of fluctuations, given the market

rationing
Providing limited access to a product or service in high demand

to create a favourable overall public impression of the organisation. In combination, advertising and public relations can promote positive feelings towards an organisation. For example, in addition to regular advertising, many major companies sponsor events such as Olympic participation, take part in charitable activities such as the Starlight Foundation, and donate time and money to groups including universities.

Boundary spanning   Another means of influence is **boundary spanning**, creating roles in the organisation that interface with important environment elements. People in these roles fulfil two different functions (Aldrich & Herker 1977; Tushman & Scanlan 1981). First, they have an information-processing function by collecting information about the environment, filtering out what is important and transmitting it to those inside the organisation to act on the information. Second, they perform an external representation function by presenting information about the organisation to outsiders. Boundary spanning roles include salespeople, purchasing specialists, personnel recruiters, admissions officers, shipping and receiving agents, receptionists, lawyers and scientists who maintain close ties with developments in their fields.

Recruiting   A further means of environmental influence is recruiting, or the finding and attempting to attract candidates capable of effectively filling job vacancies. This can help influence the environment when organisations seek job candidates with a knowledge of, and close ties to, a major environmental element. For example, organisations often hire executives from specific companies or in particular industries because of their environmental knowledge and connections. Many executives in rival computer firms began their careers at IBM.

Negotiating contracts   In some cases, attempts at influence are made by negotiating contracts, or seeking favourable agreements on important organisational matters. Specific agreements with customers and suppliers are a common way to create environmental favourability.

Co-opting   Another method of influence is **co-opting**, or absorbing key members of important environmental elements into an organisation's leadership or policy-making structure. A common example of co-opting is adding key members of the environment to the board of directors. For instance, most universities have prominent individuals on their councils. These individuals often help them deal more effectively with environmental elements, particularly for fund raising. Powerful and influential outside individuals, however, may raise questions about the organisation's practices and thereby constitute a threat to current management (Mizruchi 1983; Lesly 1995).

Strategic alliances   Increasingly organisations form a **strategic alliance**, an arrangement where two or more independent organisations form a co-operative partnership to gain mutual advantage (Miller & Dess 1996; Yoshino & Rangan 1995). Often strategic alliances involve joint ventures. A **joint venture** is an agreement between two or more organisations to produce a product or service through a jointly owned enterprise. Strategic alliances usually occur because of some mutual advantage for the organisations involved that would be difficult if each acted alone. Such alliances are increasingly common because cost, market and technological factors often encourage resource pooling for greater effectiveness (Anderson 1990).

boundary spanning

Creating roles within the organisation interfacing with important elements in the environment

co-opting

Absorbing key members of important environmental elements into an organisation's leadership or policy-making structure

strategic alliance

Arrangement where two or more independent organisations form a co-operative partnership to gain mutual strategic advantage

joint venture

Agreement involving two or more organisations arranging to produce jointly a product or service

For example, Toys 'R' Us and McDonald's (which owns a 20 per cent stake) formed a joint venture to establish a chain of toy stores in Japan, sometimes with McDonald's food outlets on the premises. So far, the venture has 6 per cent of the Japanese toy market, making it number one (Potts 1989; *Discount Store News* 1996). Unfortunately, 7 of 10 joint ventures do not meet expectations or are disbanded. Primarily this is because the technology or market doesn't materialise, a partner's objectives change, or managers in the two organisations find it difficult to work together (Levine & Byrne 1986).

Trade associations   **Trade associations** are organisations comprising individuals or firms with common business concerns. Members of trade associations include manufacturers, distributors, importers, brokers and retailers of a product or group of products. They may also be individuals or organisations supplying, transporting, or using the goods or services of a particular industry (Washington 1986). Because they represent pooled resources of many individuals or organisations, trade associations can conduct public relations campaigns, influence legislation through lobbying efforts and improve environmental favourability for their members.

> **trade associations**
> Organisations composed of individuals or firms with common business concerns

Political activity   The environment can also be affected by political activity, in which organisations try to enhance their competitive situations by influencing legislation and/or the behaviour of government regulatory agencies. Political activities may be carried out by a single organisation for itself or by several organisations or associations for collective group well-being.

Domain shifts

Another approach to managing environmental elements is to make **domain shifts**, or changes in the product and service mix offered, so an organisation will interface with more favourable environmental elements. One way of doing this is to move entirely out of a current product, service or geographic area and into a more favourable domain. Another way is to expand current domains through diversification, or expansion of products and services offered.

> **domain shifts**
> Changes in product and service mix offered so an organisation will interface with more favourable environmental elements

THE INTERNAL ENVIRONMENT: ORGANISATIONAL CULTURE

In this section, we examine the concept of culture more closely, considering its nature and manifestations, as well as how it can be used to promote innovation.

Nature of organisational culture

As mentioned before, organisational culture is a system of shared values, assumptions, beliefs and norms uniting organisation members (Smircich 1983; Kilmann et al. 1986). Culture reflects common views about 'the way things are done around here'. Organisational culture is sometimes called **corporate culture** because the concept is often used to describe the internal environment of major corporations. Yet organisational culture can also describe internal conditions in not-for-profit organisations, such as government agencies, charitable organisations and museums. Culture is important to organisations because as individuals act on shared values and other aspects of organisational culture, their behaviours can have a significant impact on organisational effectiveness.

Organisational cultures develop from many sources (Kilmann 1985). As new organisations form, cultures often develop reflecting the drive and imagination of individuals involved. Strong founders, too, may have a major impact on culture. For example, Ray Kroc, McDonald's founder, espoused 'quality, service, cleanliness and value', still the corporate creed. As reward systems, policies and procedures are set up, they influence culture by further specifying appropriate behaviour. Moreover, critical incidents, such as rewarding or firing an employee for pushing a major innovation, may add to individuals' perceptions of internal norms. Changes in environment, such as the emergence of new competitors, may force organisations to reassess acceptable norms in areas such as quality.

Three aspects of organisational culture are important in analysing the impact of culture on a given organisation: direction, pervasiveness and strength (Kilmann et al. 1986; Martin 1992; Schein 1992). Direction refers to the degree to which a culture supports, rather than interferes with, achieving organisational goals. Pervasiveness addresses the extent to which a culture is widespread among members or unevenly distributed. Strength refers to the degree to which members accept values and other culture aspects.

A culture can positively impact on organisational effectiveness when it supports organisational goals, is widely shared, and is deeply internalised by organisation members (Barney 1986). For example, a consistent and shared emphasis on innovation has helped 3M produce a stream of new products, as well as continually improve existing ones. In contrast, a culture can have negative impact when it is widely shared and well internalised but influences behaviours in directions that do not further (and possibly interfere with) organisational goals. Mixed situations have less impact. For example, a culture unevenly distributed and weakly held will have much less impact (either positive or negative), regardless of its direction.

Manifestations of organisational culture

An interesting feature of organisational culture is that values, assumptions, beliefs and norms constituting a particular culture are generally unobservable. Rather, we often infer the nature of a particular culture through manifestations such as symbols, stories, rites and ceremonials (Smircich 1983; Trice & Beyer 1993).

Symbols   A **symbol** is an object, act, event or quality serving as a vehicle for conveying meaning. For example, a very explicit symbol used to support an organisational value is Corning Inc.'s use of a 'quapple', a pin shaped like a combination of the letter 'Q' and an apple. Organisation members receive the pin after successfully completing their initial training course in quality improvement, and they wear it to show their commitment to quality (Dubashi 1987).

Stories   A **story** is a narrative based on true events, which (but not always) may be embellished to highlight the intended value. According to a story told at 3M, a worker was fired because he continued to work on a new product idea after his boss told him to stop. Despite being fired and taken off the payroll, the person continued to come to work, pursuing his idea in an unused office. Eventually, he was rehired, developed the idea into a huge success, and was made a vice-president. In this case, the story conveys an important value in the innovative 3M culture—persisting when you believe in an idea (Deal & Kennedy 1982).

Rites and ceremonials   A **rite** is an elaborate, dramatic, planned set of activities intended to convey cultural values to participants and, usually, an audience. A **ceremonial** is a system of rites performed at a single occasion or event.

> **rite**
>
> Relatively elaborate, dramatic, planned set of activities intended to convey cultural values to participants and, usually, an audience
>
> **ceremonial**
>
> System of rites performed in conjunction with a single occasion or event

@ Peakhour—Serious business

Peakhour is one of the first of its kind in Australia. It focuses on the business-to-business electronic commerce, rather than business-to-consumer Internet activities. The key attraction of this initiative is the target audience. It focuses on small and medium enterprises (SMEs) which are the fastest growing sector of the Australian economy. Its aim is to get SMEs online by offering domain-name registration, Internet access packages, free e-mail, Web site hosting packages, links, business guides and software. The next stage will be to help SMEs improve their online performance with a suite of integrated Web tools that drive the traffic to their Web site and enable companies to exchange banner advertising space, as well as provide advice on how to manage people and deal with the goods and services tax. All products are branded with the Peakhour name.

Peakhour aspires to be more than a SME service company. Once it has its customers in place, the company plans to migrate them to a sophisticated business application provider (ASP). In any ASP model, a company's software is hosted and managed offsite, and accessed through a private network or the Internet. For the client, this can eliminate any need for information technology staff—the only technology on the premises is the PCs or terminals used to access applications and the connection to the network.

In the next few years, online business-to-business markets will sprout like weeds. Once the battle for supremacy is over, those left standing will have five attributes: a business model, market size, industry expertise, branding and distribution, and management execution—the ability to carry out strategy.

Source: Adapted from Ferguson, A. (2000).

Activities for discussion, analysis and further research

1   What do these developments mean for the effective manager of a SME?
2   What are the factors which Peakhour must consider as it launches its developments?

Promoting innovation:
An adaptive, entrepreneurial culture

Mounting evidence shows successful organisations foster adaptive, entrepreneurial cultures. The organisation opportunity matrix (see Fig. 3.5) classifies organisations by the extent to which a firm's culture supports both a desire for change and a belief in its capacity to influence the competitive environment (Stevenson & Gumpert 1985; Kotter & Heskett 1992).

**Fig. 3.5   Organisation opportunity matrix (adapted from Stevenson &
Gumpert 1985, p. 93)**

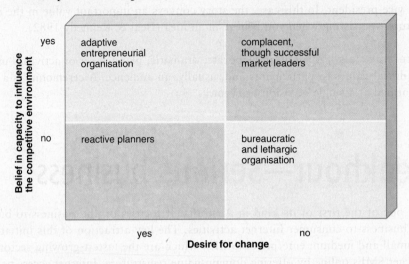

As the matrix shows, adaptive, entrepreneurial organisations tend to have cultures where members view growth and change as desirable and also believe they can affect the competitive environment to their advantage. Hewlett-Packard has a reputation for being an adaptive organisation. For example, the firm altered its competitive environment by halving the time taken to design and produce many products. The change allowed the company to produce a matchbox-sized disk drive, called the Kittyhawk, ahead of the competition (Hof 1992). In the opposite vein, bureaucratic and lethargic organisations are likely to have members preferring the status quo and with little faith in their ability to influence the competitive environment.

In more mixed situations, cultures may support a desire for change but foster little belief in the ability to influence competitive situations. These cultures are likely in reactive planner organisations, where managers try to plan for environmental change yet are not proactive in influencing the environment. Finally, cultures oriented to very slow change, coupled with a belief in their ability to affect the competitive environment, produce complacent organisations. Such organisations may be successful market leaders, but only while environmental changes occur slowly. For example, Baldwin Locomotive, mentioned before, was very successful until major technological change made its main product, the steam engine, obsolete.

The organisational culture continuum (see Table 3.3) differentiates cultures on several dimensions. At one end of the continuum are several characteristics associated with adaptive, entrepreneurial cultures. With such a culture, an organisation is better equipped to anticipate and respond to environmental changes. At the other end are characteristics of organisations with administrative cultures. These organisations are less likely than their adaptive counterparts to make necessary modifications as the environment changes.

Recently, researchers suggested culture may be common to an entire industry, such as the automobile industry. Such an interorganisational macroculture can occur when organisation-related beliefs are shared among managers across organisations in a whole or particular segment of an industry (Abrahamson & Fombrun 1994; Chatman & Jehn 1994). If an industry has a macroculture and is more toward the continuum's administrative culture end than the adaptive, entrepreneurial end, the entire industry may be slow to innovate and change.

Table 3.3 Characteristics of entrepreneurial versus administrative cultures

Dimensions	Entrepreneurial characteristics ⇔	Administrative characteristics
Strategic	Driven by perceptions of opportunity	Driven by controlled orientation resources
Commitment to seize opportunities	Revolutionary change within short period	Evolutionary change over long period
Commitment of resources	Many stages, with minimal exposure at each stage	A single stage, with complete commitment based on one decision
Control of resources	Use of freelance help and rental of required resources	Employment or ownership of required resources
Management structure	Few levels, with emphasis on informal communication patterns	Many levels, with emphasis on communication through formal hierarchy

Source: Adapted from Stevenson & Gumpert (1985, p. 89).

Turbosoft—Innovation and customer focus

Turbosoft started as the research and development section of a systems integration company in 1984. In 1988 it became an independent whose product is called TTWIN—a terminal emulation package. Terminal emulation is a technology that allows a personal computer (PC) to act as a terminal. This technology is used primarily by large businesses and corporations.

Some of Turbosoft's clients in Australia include ATSIC, the ACT government, Big W, Carlton & United Breweries, Deloitte Touche Tohmatsu, the Department of Defence, Diners Club International, the RACV, and the Reserve Bank of Australia. International clients include MGM Grand (America), Oral B (America), Foxwoods Casino (America), Mitsubishi (Germany), B & S Card Services (Germany), the National Planning Authority (United Kingdom) and Bedfordshire Police (United Kingdom).

Turbosoft prides itself on the further development of existing products as well as the investment in new products which meet customers' changing needs—whether the client is one with few users or several thousands. Turbosoft endeavours to achieve customer satisfaction at all times. It encourages feedback from customers and user groups to fuel the drive for product development, as well as setting the direction for new project innovation. An outstanding example of Turbosoft's determination to provide total customer satisfaction is the 24-hour, seven-day-a-week

TTWIN is the product of Turbosoft, a company whose three key focuses are to deliver quality products, quality services and quality management.

technical support service that the company provides to its clients or potential clients. Turbosoft insists that if a customer has a problem or query with its software the issue should be given attention and a prompt and appropriate solution be presented to the customer. Innovative use of the Internet has enabled Turbosoft to maximise client access on a global basis and decrease its response time.

One of its proud achievements is the use of its product TTWIN in a plan by UniDirect Ltd in the United Kingdom as part of a process to speed up the ordering process by hotels and restaurants to W. Pauley & Co. UniDirect distributed copies of TTWIN to these hotels and restaurants so they could connect to W. Pauley & Co by dialling into their system and ordering directly. The orders were received almost instantly so in most cases they could be assembled and delivered to the client the next day.

The company CEO and president, Bernie Snoek, has ensured that Turbosoft gains a strong reputation for providing both a high-quality product flexible to the needs of the market, and an unmatched level of customer service and support. Turbosoft's three key focus areas are quality product, quality support and quality management. The company is a firm believer in the total quality management philosophy and is constantly developing all areas of the organisation including development, design, production, marketing, sales and support of its own terminal emulation software and protocol software.

The thrust towards working in teams has been identified as the reason for Turbosoft's success both in Australia and abroad. The team includes distributors and resellers, both locally and around the world, to ensure that needs are recognised and met. Turbosoft's mission statement highlights this: 'To expand local and international markets for our connectivity solutions, through developing relationships with established quality, highly focused distribution channels in targeted markets'.

Source: Case study by Tony Cvorkov based on information from Turbosoft and www.ttwin.com.

Activities for discussion, analysis and further research

1 Consider Turbosoft's mission statement and determine what factors the organisation should be taking into consideration to meet its own goals.

2 Log on to the Turbosoft web site on www.turbosoft.com.au and check the company's complete mission statement. Look at other pages on the site and consider the external environment issues Turbosoft contends with.

3 Turbosoft takes a unique approach to marketing in that, from first contact, it works one-on-one with clients to respond to specific needs and requirements. In what way is this commitment in tune with current external environment demands? Consider the internal environment issues this might give rise to.

Changing organisational culture

Because they involve fairly stable values, assumptions, beliefs and norms, organisational cultures can be difficult to change (Lorsch 1986). One procedure for changing organisational culture involves five main steps (Kilmann 1985):

1 **Surfacing actual norms.** This step has organisation members list actual norms (expected behaviours in the organisation) they believe influence their attitudes and actions. The process typically occurs in a workshop and may involve a representative group of employees or many employee groups, depending on venue capacity. For organisations where the impact of culture on effectiveness is negative, these sessions often show norms such as 'Don't rock the boat', 'Don't enjoy your work', and 'Don't share information with other groups'.

2 **Articulating new directions.** In this step, group members discuss the organisation's current direction and behaviours necessary for organisational success.

3 **Establishing new norms.** In this step, members develop a list of new norms with a positive impact on organisational effectiveness.

4 **Identifying culture gaps.** This step involves identifying areas where there is a major difference (culture gap) between actual norms and those that would positively influence organisational effectiveness.

5 **Closing culture gaps.** This step entails agreeing on new norms and designing means of reinforcing them, such as developing reward systems encouraging members to follow new cultural norms.

While this process is useful as a general approach to changing organisational culture, leaders often have specific cultural changes they wish to implement.

How leaders influence cultural change

Despite inherent difficulties, some senior managers have achieved specific cultural changes they believe are critical to organisational success (Kotter & Heskett 1992). In doing so, they typically convince members a crisis has occurred or is likely to occur. Next, they communicate a vision outlining a new direction or strategy for the organisation. Finally, they motivate others to lead in implementing the vision and its corresponding strategy, including required cultural changes.

Additional approaches for achieving organisational change are discussed in Chapter 11. Meanwhile, the issue of values, beliefs and norms in organisations is also important to the topic of the next chapter, organisational social responsibility and managerial ethics.

 **The MD's diary**   the reflective practitioner

In terms of the culture we built in this organisation, the approach is very much one where I try to foster a learning environment and one where people are expected and encouraged to stretch their own abilities to take on things which they are perhaps a little uncomfortable with, knowing that the cost of failure is just that they have to regroup and do it differently. It isn't a situation where failure is frowned upon. What is frowned upon is that people don't stretch and don't have a go, and don't learn and deliver as a result of that whole process. I want it to be a non-threatening personal approach. My approach is always very very hard at the task but soft at the individual. Having said that, there must be a buy-off and there is a clear understanding what the end objectives are, and when I say buy-off, there will be a buy-off from both parties in terms of a clear understanding of what they've got to deliver and a clear commitment from me in terms of the resourcing that will be provided in support.

People are encouraged to take risks. We know that everything they do won't be right, but no risks means no try, means no progress, it's gone. So, I provide as much freedom to have a go as I possibly can. I try to foster an atmosphere where people always have access to me, where they can always bounce something off me so they don't have to go it alone. There is always someone there that they can talk to and say, 'This is where I'm at, this is what I'm doing.' So without trying to put too many controls in place, they don't have to put themselves out on too much of a limb.

We give people responsibilities, I think, beyond what most organisations do. For example, our production team leaders have responsibility for the customer and they have direct contact with the customer. They quite clearly accept that they have the responsibility to deliver what the customer needs, in the correct quantity, at the right quality, on time.

Similarly with our project teams and our engineering teams. Once again, they are given a clear mandate to deal with the customer as they see fit within the company guidelines, and my role in the way we manage that is to make sure that they are adopting the values and the codes of behaviour that are important to our organisation. If we've got them behaving the right way internally, and they understand how we want them to behave externally, then we give them the freedom and the ability to manage that external environment without a watchdog.

■ The subordinate's log the reflective practitioner

At the operational level of the organisation, the culture was open and supportive, consisting of a small group of talented individuals with a very direct communication style that engendered vigorous debate and effective problem solving. This effective communication style meant that personal rivalries and issues of organisational politics rarely if ever raised their ugly heads. At a broader organisation level, there was a climate of cynicism and reluctance to deal directly with senior management's confrontational style. This was largely based on poor communication from senior management. Decisions were sometimes perceived as unreasonable by the staff.

My approach to managing the internal environment was to justify and explain the communications from above; even those I did not necessarily agree with or believe were appropriate. It meant that I would have to justify my management style with operational staff to senior management whose natural inclination was to respond: 'if they don't like it they can leave'. This made me a stress and conflict sponge. It was a difficult role to play. I was trying to supply a mentoring, loose supervision environment, and ours being a small organisation, my staff knew exactly what the demands were from above. This meant that I had to demonstrate loyalty to the organisation, while not compromising the relationship with the people I had to manage.

The external environment for us was made up of large client organisations and large competitors. Only a handful of our competitors were of our size and, despite what senior management thought, were becoming very good at what they did and establishing a good client base in competition with our own. In a business environment which increasingly scrutinises the role of consultants it was becoming harder and harder to sell our services and maintain and extend our engagements. Our consultants did good work for clients generally but this was sometimes hampered by poor resourcing decisions from above and the need to place people on assignments to which they were not really suited. This was partly caused by high turnover and partly by costing decisions of senior management.

Clients being often located interstate or overseas added to my stress by needing to manage my staff from afar. This commercial reality as much as anything else dictated what I saw to be the need to strike the right balance between loose and close management.

Focus on practice – Strategies for improving

1 Consider the organisation you work for, or your university if you do not work. Examine the forces in the task environment which impact upon it the most. Are those forces going to necessitate changes in the way the organisation operates? How will those affect the organisation?

2 Repeat the above while considering the general environment.

Source: Jones et al. (2000).

Chapter summary

Organisations are affected by the external environment, the outside forces with potential to influence significantly the success of products or services. Broad conditions and trends in societies within which an organisation operates constitute an organisation's mega-environment. The mega-environment consists of five major elements: technological, economic, legal-political, sociocultural and international. Generally, mega-environment elements are beyond a single organisation's ability to alter directly, at least in the short run.

The task, or operational, environment is the specific outside elements which an organisation interfaces with in conducting its business. The task environment depends on the organisation's specific products and services, and the locations where it conducts business. A single organisation may be more successful in affecting its task environment than the mega-environment. Major organisational task-environment elements typically include customers and clients, competitors, suppliers, labour supply and government agencies.

Two important, but differing, perspectives on the relationship between organisations and their environments are the population ecology and the resource dependence models. Managers can analyse their organisation's environmental situation in terms of two key concepts: environmental uncertainty and environmental bounty, or capacity. Environmental uncertainty refers to the extent to which future conditions affecting an organisation can be accurately assessed and predicted. Environmental bounty refers to the extent to which the environment can support sustained growth and stability. The degree of environmental uncertainty is a function of two factors, complexity and dynamism.

Three major approaches to managing environmental elements are adaptation, favourability influence and domain shifts. Adaptation involves changing internal operations and activities to make an organisation more compatible with its environment. Methods of adaptation include buffering, smoothing, forecasting and rationing. Favourability influence focuses on altering environmental elements to make them more compatible with the organisation's needs. The resource dependence perspective argues that environmental areas organisations will attempt to influence are those on which they are most dependent. Major methods of favourability influence include advertising and engaging in public relations, boundary spanning, recruiting, negotiating contracts, co-opting, establishing strategic alliances, joining trade associations and engaging in political activities. Domain shifts are changes in the product and service mix offered so an organisation will face more favourable environmental elements. One domain-shift method is moving entirely out of a current product, service or geographic area and into a more favourable domain. Another method is diversification through product and service expansion.

Organisational culture is a system of shared values, assumptions, beliefs and norms uniting members of an organisation. A particular organisation's culture is typically inferred through their use of concrete elements, such as symbols, stories, rites and ceremonials. Entrepreneurial cultures encourage innovation, with members tending to view growth and change as desirable and believing they can affect the competitive environment. Changing organisational culture can be difficult and is likely to be a multistep process. Top managers often attempt to produce cultural change enhancing organisational prospects for success.

Questions for discussion and review

1 Outline major elements making up the mega-environment. Identify an important trend in each of these elements influencing the organisation in which you or some member of your family works.

2 Identify major elements making up the typical task environment of an organisation. Use these elements to develop an outline of the task environment of an organisation in which you or some member of your family works.

3 Contrast population ecology and resource dependence views of the organisation–environment interface. Identify a situation in which environmental change caused an organisation to go out of existence. What possible actions, if any, might management have taken to avoid the organisation's demise?

4 Explain how environmental uncertainty affects organisations. How would you assess environmental uncertainty for R.M. Williams, the Australian clothing maker?

5 Describe how environmental bounty influences organisations. How would you assess environmental bounty for R.M. Williams?

6 Outline major methods to help organisations adapt to their environmental elements. For each, give an example based on a familiar organisation.

7 Enumerate major methods used to help organisations influence their environments favourably. For five of these, give an example based on a familiar organisation.

8 Explain how domain shifts can help organisations cope with their environments. Give an example of an organisation making a major domain shift. Was the shift beneficial to the organisation? Why, or why not?

9 Explain the nature of organisational culture and list its principal manifestations. Give an example of each indicating the culture at your university or college. Briefly describe your perception of the culture at your university or college.

10 Explain the difference between an entrepreneurial and an administrative culture.

Exercises for managing in the 21st century

Exercise 1
Self-assessment exercise: The kind of organisation I would manage

Select the response which best reflects the culture you would work to instil in an organisation you would manage.

1 = Strongly disagree
2 = Somewhat disagree
3 = Neither agree nor disagree
4 = Somewhat agree
5 = Strongly agree

_____   1   For many projects, I would prefer to obtain needed additional professional human resources on a part-time or contract basis.

_____   2   I would prefer to indicate my support for a program/project by committing all resources required when I approve it.

_____   3   I believe change is often best accomplished by making major changes within a short time frame.

_____   4   Programs/projects usually are improved by many reviews through the chain of command.

_____   5   Current resource availability should dictate the size and type of long-term programs and projects attempted.

_____   6   I would be inclined to have very few levels of management.

_____   7   I would base resource commitments on successes at several points in a program/project.

_____   8   I would prefer owning all resources for a project/program so they would be immediately available when needed.

_____ 9 Normally it is relatively easy to recognise opportunities arising and to plan for them well in advance.

_____ 10 Most communication regarding programs/projects under development is best handled through the formal hierarchy.

Exercise 2
Management exercise: Assessing a ski-shop environment

Your best friend's sister and brother-in-law run a ski shop near your campus, but they have recently bought another type of business in another part of town. They want you and your friend to take over managing the ski shop. If you run it successfully, you and your friend will gradually be given substantial equity in the shop and eventually would own the whole business.

So far, the shop has been only marginally profitable. Although the shop carries ski equipment and clothing, it often runs out during the peak ski season. Extra merchandise ordered to meet demand often arrives so late it cannot be sold until the next season, if at all. In addition, the shop does very little business from October to April.

Due to a dispute over the size and prominence of an outside sign displaying the shop's name, the relationship with local government is poor. Tact and diplomacy are not major strengths of your friend's brother-in-law. As a result, the shop gets more than its share of inspections, and a recent effort to gain permission to expand the parking lot was turned down.

So far, other than minimal advertising, nothing has been done to make inroads on campus. Yet the campus should be lucrative. The student population includes many avid skiers, since good skiing is about an hour and a half away by car. Unfortunately, many of them purchase their ski equipment and clothing at the lodges. In part this is because lodges tend to have good arrangements for repair and maintenance of ski equipment.

Your initial assessment is that, so far, the ski shop has not adequately attempted to deal with its environment. There have been persistent rumours another ski shop may open nearby next year, creating a competitor. You and your friend (and possibly some other friends willing to give you advice) plan to get together soon to try to develop approaches to help manage the ski shop's environment better. This analysis is crucial to your decision about whether to manage the shop. Also, your friend's sister and brother-in-law want to hear your ideas.

First, outline the major elements in the ski shop's task environment. Then prepare a proposal showing how you would attempt to better manage the shop's environmental elements.

 # In a changing environment ...   on the rim— in Korea

Daewoo Motors is South Korea's second largest automobile manufacturer. In 1999, it produced 758 500 vehicles at its 17 facilities at home and abroad. However, due to many management difficulties, the Daewoo Group narrowly escaped bankruptcy when its domestic creditors agreed in June to delay repayment of $8.3 billion in debt for six months and extend $3.3 billion in new loans. In return for this stay of execution, the Group agreed to sell or spin off 13 units. Its 12 other units, including Daewoo Motor, were placed under a program that calls for creditors to turn debts into equity or delay debt payment. Although the government hasn't decided whether to sell Daewoo Motor to a foreign or local company, the stance of South Korea's Financial Supervisory Commission is that the prospective buyer must keep current production facilities, including the carmaker's subcontractors and workforce.

In spite of its difficulties, the carmaker has put other manufacturers under stress with its Matiz Micro. This has had incredible impact on the new car market in Australia. Until recently, the most dramatic change to the Australian market was during the mid-1990s when Hyundai priced its base model Excel at about $2000 below the price of most other small cars. This made even some second-hand cars more expensive than a new Excel. The outcome was that individuals who normally buy second-hand cars were attracted by the low drive-away prices.

Recently Daewoo has been making a similar impact by launching the Matiz Micro, a vehicle which, at $12 000, will include all dealer and delivery charges as well as many parts and servicing benefits.

Though Daewoo is facing financial crisis at home, it is struggling valiantly under the siege. It is divesting itself of everything it can in order to retain its core automotive business and convince its creditors to maintain its solvency. Daewoo, through all its diversification, became an unwieldy giant which grew far faster than it could handle. It now needs to restructure and this will take some time. Currently, it is seeking alliances to support it in this difficult stage.

Consequently, a number of international car manufacturers have been invited to submit bids for Daewoo. Among those are General Motors Corp. and Ford Motor Co., who have indicated they intend to bid for Korea's struggling automaker Daewoo Motor Co.

Source: Tuckey, Bill (1999).

Activities for discussion, analysis and further research

1 Consider Daewoo's pricing strategies to maintain a higher market share. What impact are these having on both the new and used car markets in Australia?
2 If you were selling used cars, what other elements would impact on your business?
3 What are the elements impacting on Daewoo in Korea? In Australia? On the international scene?

Social Responsibility and Ethics in Management

Chapter 4

CHAPTER OUTLINE

Organisational social responsibility
Major perspectives
Social responsibilities of management
Social stakeholders
Does social responsibility pay?
Promoting innovation: vanguard
    companies

Organisational social responsiveness
Monitoring social demands and expectations
Internal social response mechanisms

Being an ethical manager
Types of managerial ethics
Ethical guidelines for managers
Ethical career issues
Managing an ethical organisation
Situational factors influencing ethical
    behaviour
Mechanisms for ethical management

LEARNING OBJECTIVES

After studying this chapter, you should be able to:

O Explain three major perspectives on corporate social responsibility and identify major stakeholder groups frequently mentioned in conjunction with social responsibility.

O Assess the extent to which organisational social responsibility pays.

O Explain the characteristics of vanguard companies.

O Outline approaches used to monitor social demands and expectations.

O Describe internal social response mechanisms available to organisations.

O Contrast three major types of managerial ethics.

O Outline ethical guidelines for managers and explain actions they can take to handle ethical situations and avoid ethical conflicts.

O Describe situational factors influencing ethical behaviour and outline mechanisms for ethical management.

Striving for excellence

As you will see from the segment of Autoliv Australia's business plan reproduced here, Autoliv includes 'good corporate citizenship' as one of its key objectives. This includes community involvement, environmental health and safety practices and maintenance of a positive public profile.

Most large organisations have realised good corporate citizenship has a positive effect on the bottom line. The key discriminator is where an organisation is placed on the continuum which flows from a point of minimum exposure to one of active, though sometimes invisible, community contributions.

Autoliv tries to act locally and identifies activities in the neighbourhoods from which it draws its labour force. There is a great investment of time and effort with the local Hume Council as part of the Safe Cities Task Force, which concentrates on the strategic co-ordination and planning for all the human services agencies operating within the City of Hume. It examines the integration between the work of police, education and social welfare departments to make the environment a better place to live in. This model operates in a number of local government councils in Victoria. Autoliv commits time of one of its senior managers to help the local community achieve its aims. This type of involvement operates in tandem with other more visible ones. Sponsoring the Hume City Council Ball, for instance, makes the organisation's name visible, while involvement in the Safe Cities Task Force does not, yet it is far more important to the well being of the community that the organisation operates in.

On another front, aimed to directly involve all staff, Autoliv sponsors one charity a month with the workforce's participation. At the time of writing, all staff on site were proudly wearing bandannas to support Bandanna Day.

Staff at Autoliv may identify a cause they wish to support. For example, the staff decided to raise funds for the East Timor crisis. In every case the company matches funds collected.

Inside Autoliv's facilities. In any workplace, managers are obliged by law to ensure that occupational health and safety protocols are practised for the benefit of staff and the community.

Autoliv Australia Pty Ltd
CODE OF ETHICS AND CONDUCT

As an Employee of Autoliv Australia I am committed to:

+ Acting honestly and with the utmost integrity;
+ Respecting the rights of all people within the workplace regardless of race, sex, age, social status or religion;
+ The pursuit of excellence in all that I do;
+ The ongoing improvement of products and processes;
+ Conducting myself in accordance with all company policies and procedures with special consideration of safety requirements for myself and others;
+ Resolving difficulties through consultation;
+ Respecting the rights of co-workers, customers and suppliers to confidentiality;
+ Consistently providing excellent service to all customers;
+ Behaving at all times in a calm manner;
+ Working as part of the team.

Segment of Autoliv Australia's business plan.

Society is increasingly focusing attention on the social responsibility of organisations and the ethics of their managers. For example, one poll showed that 58 per cent of respondents saw the ethical standards of business executives as only fair or poor (Wildstrom 1987). Ethics refers to standards of behaviour and moral judgment differentiating right from wrong (Post, Frederick, Lawrence and Weber 1996). **Managerial ethics** are standards of conduct and moral judgment managers use conducting their business. In this chapter, we explore the nature and extent of the social responsibilities of organisations. We consider various methods organisations use to fulfil their social responsibilities, and we also look at managers' ethics. Finally, we examine the challenge of managing an ethical organisation.

managerial ethics

Standards of conduct and moral judgment used by managers of organisations in carrying out their business

ORGANISATIONAL SOCIAL RESPONSIBILITY

Organisational social responsibility refers to an organisation's obligation to act to protect and improve societies' welfare as well as its own interests. Organisational social responsibility is often called **corporate social responsibility** when the concept is applied to business firms. Views differ on how much organisations should consider social responsibilities in their operations (Bahree 1995).

Major perspectives

Concern with organisational social responsibility is relatively recent. The issue of social responsibilities emerged in the late 1800s when large organisations first developed. Anti-competitive practices (e.g. kickbacks and price-fixing) led to pressures from government and labour. Concern grew during the Great Depression, and after the stock market crash much

organisational social responsibility

The obligation of an organisation to seek actions protecting and improving society's welfare along with its own interests

corporate social responsibility

A term used in reference to the concept of organisational social responsibility as applied to business organisations

business regulation was enacted. By 1936 the CEO of Sears, General Robert E. Wood, argued for managerial, not just governmental, actions on social concerns. The 1960s social movements (e.g. civil rights, women's liberation and environmentalism) highlighted still further the idea of organisational social responsibilities (Carroll 1980).

These historical developments led to three contrasting views on corporate social responsibility: the invisible hand, the hand of government, and the hand of management (Goodpaster & Matthews 1982).

The invisible hand   The chief advocate for the invisible-hand, or classical, perspective of corporate social responsibility is Milton Friedman, but it can be traced to Adam Smith in the 18th century. The **invisible-hand** view holds that the corporation's entire social responsibility may be seen as 'make profits and obey the law'. Thus, each corporation works actively to increase legal profits. In this way, corporate responsibility is guided by the invisible hand of free-market forces, eventually ensuring the allocation of resources for the betterment of society. Otherwise, business executives will allocate resources, gaining excessive power with little accountability for their decisions. Friedman (1962) also argues that the charitable activities of corporations are not socially responsible because, in making such contributions, the corporation stops stockholders making their own decisions about disposal of funds.

The hand of government   Under the **hand-of-government** perspective, the role of corporations is to be profitable within the law. However, it argues that society's interests are best served by having the regulatory hands of the law and the political process, rather than the invisible hand, guide corporations' endeavours (Galbraith 1962; 1975). The hand of government controls the possible negative actions of firms with regard to employees (minimum wage, safety and equal employment opportunity legislation), customers (product safety and advertising control) and the wider community (hazardous chemical and pollution control). Neither the invisible-hand nor the hand-of-government approach gives corporate leaders latitude in social issues.

The hand of management   The **hand-of-management** perspective says corporations and their managers must act to protect and improve society's welfare as well as advance corporate economic interests (Post et al. 1996). Typically three arguments are raised supporting organisational social responsibility (Tuleja 1985). The **anti-freeloader argument** holds that businesses benefit from a better society, and should bear some of the cost of improving it by working to bring about solutions to social problems. The **capacity argument** states that the private sector, with considerable economic and human resources, must make up for government cuts in social programs. The **enlightened self-interest argument** holds that businesses exist at society's pleasure and, for their own legitimacy and survival, businesses should meet public expectations of social responsibility (Stevens 1995). Otherwise, eventually they suffer financially. This relates to the **iron law of responsibility**, which states 'in the long run, those who do not use power in a manner that society considers responsible will tend to lose it' (Post et al. 1996, p. 32). Generally, society's expectations regarding the social responsibilities of business are increasing. For example, one *Business Week*/Harris poll indicates most people believe businesses have social responsibilities beyond concentrating solely on shareholder profits (See Table 4.1) (Tuleja 1985). Thus, the hand-of-management approach is increasingly relevant to corporate action (Carton 1995).

invisible hand

A view holding that the entire social responsibility of a corporation can be summed up as 'make profits and obey the law'

hand of government

A view arguing that the interests of society are best served by having the regulatory hands of the law and the political process, rather than the invisible hand, guide the results of corporations' endeavours

hand of management

A view stating that corporations and their managers are expected to act in ways that protect and improve society's welfare as a whole as well as advance corporate economic interests

anti-freeloader argument

An argument holding that since businesses benefit from a better society, they should bear part of the costs by actively working to bring about solutions to social problems

capacity argument

An argument stating that the private sector, because of its considerable economic and human resources, must make up for government cutbacks in social programs

Table 4.1   Perceptions of business responsibility

Question: Which of the following statements do you agree with more strongly?	% responding
U.S. corporations should have only one purpose—to make the most profit for their shareholders—and their pursuit of that goal will be best for America in the long term.	5
or	
U.S. corporations should have more than one purpose. They also owe something to their workers and the communities in which they operate, and they should sometimes sacrifice some profit for the sake of making things better for their workers and communities.	95

Source: Business Week (11 March 1996, p. 65).

Social responsibilities of management

The idea that managers have social responsibilities stems, in part, from the growing interdependencies of present times. Such interdependencies have woven a web of common interests between corporations and their communities. This broad view of management's social responsibilities encompasses economic, legal, ethical and discretionary responsibilities, as shown in Figure 4.1 (Carroll 1979; Gatewood & Carroll 1991). Proportions shown in the figure suggest the magnitude of each responsibility for corporate leaders.

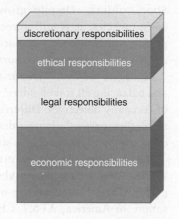

Fig. 4.1   Social responsibilities of management (adapted from Carroll 1979, p. 499)

enlightened self-interest argument

An argument holding that businesses exist at society's pleasure and that, for their own legitimacy and survival, businesses should meet the public's expectations regarding social responsibility

iron law of responsibility

A law stating that 'in the long run, those who do not use power in a manner that society considers responsible will tend to lose it'

Economic and legal responsibilities

The economic and legal responsibilities of management are recognised by all three perspectives on corporate responsibility—the invisible hand, the hand of government and the hand of management. These responsibilities involve making a profit and obeying the law (Zeigler 1995).

Ethical and discretionary responsibilities

The hand of management perspective recognises ethical and discretionary responsibilities, in addition to the economic and legal responsibilities that are dictated by the invisible hand and hand of government views. Ethical responsibilities include behaviours and activities expected of business by society. For example, in the 1980s, mounting public pressure, with managerial concerns about apartheid, resulted in many organisations discontinuing activities in South Africa though they were not legally obligated to do so (Post et al. 1996). Ethical responsibilities are ill-defined, frequently controversial and change over time. For this reason business leaders often have difficulty identifying such responsibilities.

On the other hand, discretionary responsibilities include voluntary activities not strongly expected of business by society. While organisations would not be viewed as unethical if they did not participate in them, some elements of society may view them as desirable. Examples of discretionary activities are philanthropic contributions, sponsoring AIDS clinics and training the economically disadvantaged. For instance, Merck provided the drug Ivermectin free to millions of people in Africa, South America and the Middle East to provide protection from the parasitic disease 'river blindness'. The program cost the company millions of dollars in forgone profits (*Business Week* 1988).

Social stakeholders

If corporations and managers are to be socially responsible, an important issue is to whom they are to be responsible. Six overlapping groups are identified: shareholders, employees, customers, the local community, general society (regional and national) and the international community (Tuleja 1985; Donaldson & Preston 1995). They are social stakeholders as they can be affected for better or worse by corporations' business activities.

Shareholders   Despite growing perceptions of the obligations of business to several constituencies, it is still agreed the main management role in public companies is to earn profits and dividends for shareholders (Post et al. 1996). Shareholders have provided capital allowing the companies to survive and grow.

Managers see themselves as responsible for the firm's survival, developing and expanding it, and balancing all stakeholders' demands so multiple demands do not jeopardise the achievement of company objectives. Different perspectives of shareholders and management sometimes lead to conflict, particularly over dividend levels (versus reinvestment allocations) or expenditures on executive perquisites such as stock options, club memberships and other fringe benefits.

Shareholders sometimes pressure for change in management's social stance. Currently, shareholders are concerned about CEOs being paid millions of dollars despite poor company performance. Moreover, top managers often do not disclose the full extent of their compensation. In America, AT&T CEO Robert E. Allen recently was widely criticised for taking a supplementary stock option of nearly $11 million as he announced layoffs of 40 000 workers—other important stakeholders (Byrne 1996). There are other less extreme examples reported in most countries.

Employees—Managing diversity   Businesses and other organisations must at least honour specific agreements made with employees and obey relevant employee–employer relationship laws. Laws and regulations specify employer responsibilities on equal employment opportunity, pensions and benefits, and health and safety. Increasing regulatory measures reflect growing recognition of workforce diversity and public displeasure at employer abuses (Robinson & Dechant 1977).

Although it is fashionable for top managers to refer to employees as 'family', employee treatment varies considerably. Extreme lack of concern for employees was shown in the case of Film Recovery Systems, Inc. Officials from their Chicago plant were found guilty of murder when an employee died from cyanide poisoning. The death occurred when workers, mostly non-English-speaking immigrants, were not warned about the use of cyanide to extract silver from film scraps and were only provided with minimal safety equipment (Trost 1985).

At the other end of the continuum of social concern for employees, Du Pont makes major efforts to help employees balance family and work pressures. For example, it spent

$1.5 million over three years to build and renovate child-care centres near company work sites. Du Pont also has a generous leave policy for birth, adoption or family illness. Employees have six weeks on full pay and up to six months of unpaid leave with full benefits (Weber 1991).

Du Pont's actions show efforts to manage diversity effectively. Managing diversity is planning and implementing organisational systems and practices to maximise employee potential to contribute to organisational goals and develop employee capabilities unhindered by group identities (such as gender, race or ethnic group) (Cox 1994). It is arguable that managers should manage diversity effectively because it is socially responsible. However, socially responsible actions are also good business. As Table 4.2 illustrates, social responsibility is one argument for building competitive advantage by managing diversity effectively.

Customers   Although *caveat emptor* ('let the buyer beware') was once many businesses' motto, consumers now expect more. Two current areas of social concern for consumers are health and safety matters and quality issues.

Product liability suits are becoming common, drastically affecting business prospects. For example, Bic Corporation's stock dropped when a number of suits were revealed claiming Bic lighters had exploded resulting in severe injuries and death (Potts 1987). Due to increases in product liability cases, many organisations find it hard to obtain liability insurance. As questions are raised about the social responsibilities of business, some people think the pendulum may have swung too far to the consumer. It is argued that a manufacturer should be liable for product safety only if they 'knew, or should have known, about its dangers'. However, this has perils, since it can be hard to determine the research a manufacturer needed to ensure all safety contingencies are considered. A 100 per cent requirement may mean most products would take years to reach the market—if at all—and would be most expensive. Consequently, businesses caring about consumers compromise by trying to be 99 per cent certain a product is safe, taking out large insurance policies and hoping for the best.

Quality has become increasingly prominent as a consumer issue. Keeping up with the competition is important and some companies have recognised quality is an issue linked to social responsibility. For example, when Harley-Davidson's quality dropped during the 1970s, customers became upset and the entire company's reputation suffered. A lot of effort was needed to fix the situation. Richard Teerlink, Harley-Davidson's CEO, notes: 'We are living

Table 4.2   Arguments in favour of managing diversity for competitive advantage

Socially responsible	Managing diversity can protect and improve society's welfare while advancing corporate economic interests.
Cost effective	Attracting workers is costly; firms effectively managing diversity will be able to attract and retain good workers.
Enhances prospects for customer satisfaction	A workforce mirroring customer-base diversity provides unique insight into the needs of customers, thereby enhancing prospects for customer satisfaction.
Encourages innovation	Innovations are more likely to emerge when diversity of thinking is applied to business problems.
Facilitates globalisation	Openness to other cultures and ways of doing things is helpful in successfully doing business around the globe.

proof that you can win your reputation back. But it's not easy' (Caminiti 1992, p. 76). Perrier learned the hazards of quality issues and social responsibility when it removed its mineral water from sale in 1990 due to benzene contamination. Though the amount of benzene was harmless, the company tried to protect its reputation with consumers. Unfortunately, during the four months taken to correct the problem, many consumers switched brands. The company was acquired by Nestlé, and the brand is struggling to regain its prominence (Brown 1991; Browning 1992; 1993).

Local community   In regard to social responsibility, the organisation's community is its local area of business influence (Post et al. 1996). Most communities have needs extending beyond available resources. As a result, businesses will get more requests for assistance than they can honour, meaning priorities must be set.

While communities often desire business aid, businesses need various forms of community support. Such support includes adequate transportation, equitable taxes, adequate school and recreational facilities, and complete public services, such as police, fire services, sewage, water, gas and electric services. Because of these complementary needs, businesses and their communities are interdependent and often function more effectively with mutual support (see Fig. 4.2) (Moskowitz 1989).

Society   Social responsibility at a societal level involves regional and national issues. For example, many business leaders are involved in educational reform so future labour-pool members will be adequately prepared. For instance, Aetna Insurance trains up to 700 employees a year in basic reading, writing and mathematics (Segal 1992; Bernstein 1992). When connections are weak between corporate social expenditures and business-related results, supporters of the invisible-hand view of social responsibility are likely to object. Conversely, the hand-of-government view favours government regulation of social expenditures, through higher corporate taxes allowing governmental allocation of funding.

Fig. 4.2   Possible levels of business and community mutual support
            (Frederick et al. 1988, p. 342)

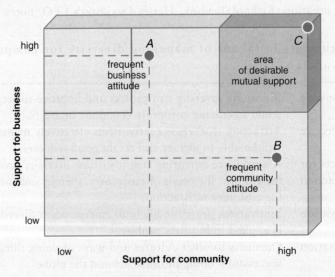

International community   Social responsibilities also involve international issues. The Union of International Associations in Brussels drew up a list of 10 000 global problems, and developed categories such as international tensions, scarce resources and increasing pollution (Cornish 1990). Many companies responded to these concerns by altering their practices (Ortega 1995).

Does social responsibility pay?

One interesting question is what impact being socially responsible has on financial success. Studies on this issue are problematic as it is difficult to accurately measure one firm's social responsibility against another's. This makes a definitive answer impossible; however, research shows no clear relationship exists between degree of social responsibility and financial success—at least short term (Arlow & Gannon 1982; Aupperle, Carroll & Hatfield 1985).

Research has suggested a firm's financial performance is a good predictor of its social responsibility, rather than a result of it. For example, organisations doing well financially may feel better placed to undertake socially responsible activities. There are also indications firms engage in social responsibility to develop stable relationships with major stakeholders and to help reduce the risk of lawsuits and government fines threatening organisational well-being (McGuire, Sundgren & Schneeweis 1988).

Research has found that announcing illegal corporate actions has an adverse effect on a firm's stock price, although the long-term impact is unclear (Davison & Worrell 1988). Ironically, research suggests generous charitable donations may contribute to perceptions of companies being socially responsible, even if they behave illegally (Wokutch & Spencer 1987). Corporate contributions for charitable and social responsibility purposes is called **corporate philanthropy**.

To balance conflicting expectations of stakeholders favouring socially responsible behaviour and those favouring concentration on profit, many corporations focus on socially responsible activities that affect their bottom line.

corporate philanthropy

Corporate contributions for charitable and social responsibility purposes

@ War of the Web

managing the e-challenge

Over the past, there have been a number of instances of attacks on Web sites which have brought forward the urgency of site security. One such attack has had political overtones. It has taken place between the People's Republic of China and Taiwan. In both countries Web sites have been attacked by hackers from the other side of the Straits. The official Web site of Taiwan's 'National Assembly' was assailed by a hacker who inserted statements supporting the ownership of Taiwan by the PRC. The main server went down soon after the attack and computer engineers found they could not reboot it because all the data and information stored therein were destroyed.

Meanwhile retribution took place as Taiwanese hackers struck back by logging on to the State Taxation Bureau in China inserting Taiwan independence messages on its home page.

Source: Adapted from Jiang Jingen (1999).

Activities for discussion, analysis and further research

1 Consider the ethics involved in organisations securing their Web sites against attacks by hackers.
2 It has often been said that programmers of software deliberately leave open back doors. Do a literature search to see what you can find out on the topic.
3 How does Web site security affect you on a day-to-day basis?

Promoting innovation: Vanguard companies

Although there may be no direct relationship between social responsibility and financial performance (at least short term), a number of firms score high on both social responsibility and success. O'Toole (1985) terms these 'vanguard' corporations. Some of his examples are John Deere, Honeywell, Levi Strauss and Motorola. Vanguard organisations have four common characteristics:

1 **They try to satisfy all their stakeholders.** The basic idea is that shareholder interests are best served in the long run when corporations attempt to satisfy all of stakeholders' legitimate concerns. Such organisations work hard to resolve conflicts and find ways to serve all constituencies at once.

2 **They are committed to a higher purpose.** These corporations see their role as providing society with needed goods and services, employment and wealth creation in profits to increase the general standard of living and quality of life. In this sense, profit is the means, not the end, of corporate efforts.

3 **They value continuous learning.** These companies recognise that flexibility, change and responsiveness are vital to organisational survival. As a result, they monitor environmental changes, assessing the applicability of their own strategies and practices.

4 **They aim high.** They are dedicated to be best in all they do. As a result, they emphasise innovation to help them reach high goals. Through commitment to these principles, vanguard companies have achieved high-level social responsibility and been financially successful too.

Honesty cashes in but not on the exchange rates

gaining the edge

Over the past months, with currency cross rates behaving like a see saw, many organisations have very carefully played the odds on the exchange rates. In Thailand, a number of exporters have taken advantage of the weakened Baht (the Thai currency unit).

One organisation, however, decided to deal very differently with their customers. Maenamkhong Karnkha Limited Partnership is a small exporter of construction materials, motorcycle tyres and parts, food and handicraft products, teak and steel furniture and many other manufactured items. It has clients in neighbouring countries to which it has passed on the exchange-rate gains in a bid to win loyalty and trust. The company felt that this would be a positive move to ensure long-term positive business relationships.

Over the past two years, the company has returned over Bt2 million in exchange-rate differential to customers in Vietnam, Laos, Cambodia and Burma. Though to individual clients it was small amounts, it made a strong and lasting impression—so much so that, in spite of a poor economic climate, Maenamkhong Karnkha has had sales revenue growth of 50 to 60 per cent in the two years of economic upheaval that the country has suffered.

The company was started in 1994 with a very small capital but massive support from overseas customers who transferred cash to it to source products. Managing director Surapan Sanitwong went solo after 25 years of experience working as a clerk in a variety of export companies trading with various parts of the world. With encouragement from several customers, he took the plunge. From these slim beginnings, the company struggled with help from the Export and Import Bank of Thailand from whom they received a loan of Bt2 million on the strength of their export proposal. Seven years down the track, the company revenue has topped the Bt100 million mark. Its major export products are highly diversified, as mentioned above.

When discussing the reasons for his success, Surapan identifies pricing strategy, good marketing and service, but above all the honesty with which the organisation is associated.

Source: Adapted from: Achara Pongvutitham (14 February 2000).

Activities for discussion, analysis and further research

1 Is it appropriate for an organisation to keep any gains it makes through the fluctuation of the currency it deals in? Why would returning those gains be seen as positive by the clients of this organisation?

2 Contact a number of local organisations who deal in foreign activities and pose the question to them. Find out if the fluctuation of currencies is an issue to them. How do they deal with it?

3 What would you do? Why?

✖ Aye, captain—Managing ethical quandaries

crossroads

Values define a person's beliefs. Ethics are concerned with what is right, what is wrong and with moral duty to your employees, your organisation and society. A situation may be further complicated by the fact that moral standards change with time, and by the complexity of conducting business in a multi-cultural environment. Ethics is very much concerned with the management of physical resources and operations, underpinned by human factors such as attitude and behaviour.

Consider the following situation:

A motor vessel was towing a barge from Singapore to Indonesia and had difficulty getting past Customs. The paperwork was in order but clearance was not given. It was hinted that a sum of money was the 'custom'. The Australian captain considered this to be morally incorrect and, being prepared to stand by his principles, went against the 'custom'. Consequently, the ship was held up for four days. The Company demanded an explanation for the delay. The payment of a sum of money was a known and accepted 'custom/norm' and several people ridiculed the captain's decision for going against the norm.

Source: Allison Powell, Australian Maritime College.

Decision point: the central question of right conduct

1 Although the outcome resulted in a financial and operational 'cost' in that the ship was held over and the sailing schedule was disrupted, the captain's intentions and underlying motives were good. Generally we tend to judge a person's character by the deeds they perform. A 'good' person, we normally think, is one who tries to do or habitually does what is 'right'. In the managerial context, ethical decisions frequently require us to make careful judgments of character. Therefore a manager has a moral duty to select employees whose moral integrity can be relied upon.

Reflection points

1 What are the ethical issues involved in the above situation?

2 If you were the Australian captain and it was hinted that a personal payment would ease the process, what would you do? Why? What do you think you should do and why?

ORGANISATIONAL SOCIAL RESPONSIVENESS

While managers hold a particular view of their organisation's social responsibilities, the concept becomes more concrete when managers actually respond to social responsibilities. **Organisational social responsiveness** refers to the development of organisational decision processes where managers anticipate, respond to, and manage areas of social responsibility. Organisational social responsiveness is also known as **corporate social responsiveness** because it is frequently applied to business organisations. Remember, though, social responsiveness is important for other organisations too. For example, not-for-profit schools and hospitals have to monitor various stakeholders' changing expectations and respond to them.

Two processes are essential to the development of organisational social responsiveness. First, methods must be established to monitor the social demands and expectations of the external environment. Second, internal social response mechanisms must be developed.

Monitoring social demands and expectations

Means to assess social demands and expectations relative to organisations include social forecasting, opinion surveys, social audits, issues management and social scanning. Each is discussed in turn.

Social forecasting　Social forecasting is a systematic identification of social trends, evaluation of organisational importance of those trends, and integration of these into an organisation's forecasting program. One approach is the use of **futurists**, individuals who track significant environmental trends and attempt to predict their organisational impact, usually 10 or more years ahead. Others use consultants and research institutes specialising in social forecasting.

Opinion surveys　Associations and business publications conduct surveys on various social issues. These frequently give feedback about various groups' perceptions of social responsibility. For example, one poll showed only 31 per cent of people rate business executives as having good moral and ethical standards (also see Table 4.1) (*USA Today* 1992).

Social audits　A **social audit** is the systematic study and evaluation of social, rather than economic, organisation performance. It includes assessment of the social impact of a firm's activities, evaluation of programs aimed at social goals, and a determination of areas needing organisational action. Conducting social audits is difficult as disagreements can arise on what should be included, results can be intangible and/or difficult to measure, and interpretations of adequate or good social performance vary. Nevertheless, companies increasingly assess their performance through social audits (Post et al. 1996).

Issues management　As applied to social responsiveness, **issues management** is the identification of a small number of emerging social issues particularly relevant to the organisation, analysing their potential impact, and preparing effective responses. Typically, 10 to 15 issues

Margin glossary

organisational social responsiveness

A term referring to the development of organisational decision processes where managers anticipate, respond to, and manage areas of social responsibility

corporate social responsiveness

A term used in reference to the concept of organisational social responsiveness as applied to business organisations

social forecasting

The systematic process of identifying social trends, evaluating the organisational importance of those trends, and integrating these assessments into the organisation's forecasting program

futurists

Individuals who track significant trends in the environment and attempt to predict their impact on the organisation

social audit

A systematic study and evaluation of the social, rather than economic, performance of an organisation

issues management

The process of identifying a relatively small number of emerging social issues of particular relevance to the organisation, analysing their potential impact and preparing an effective response

are identified, but this can vary depending on organisational circumstances. Issues management attempts to minimise 'surprises' from environmental forces and facilitate a proactive approach to environmental change (Fleming 1981; Wartick & Cochran 1985). At Monsanto, for example, the Executive Management Committee, chaired by the president, worked with various parts of the organisation to identify 170 social issues. Ultimately, the list narrowed to five critical issues in the Monsanto business environment: fair trade, biotechnology regulation, intellectual property rights, agricultural policy, and hazardous waste and public compensation. Through issues management, the company led the increasing co-operation between industry and environmental groups.

Social scanning   **Social scanning** is general surveillance of various task-environment elements to detect evidence of impending changes affecting organisational social responsibilities. Unlike issues management, social scanning is usually not formal and systematic. Executives draw on their own experiences of factors likely to have organisational implications. They may rely on data from systematic assessments, such as discussed above (Daft, Sormunen & Parkes 1988).

After assessing American social expectations, Sadahei Kusumoto, president and CEO of Minolta, urged the subsidiaries of Japanese companies to be more attentive to US corporate social responsibility standards. The subsidiaries had not engaged in corporate philanthropy in the United States, because the tax incentives for this kind of activity were lower in Japan and corporate giving was not common there. Kusumoto argued that the subsidiaries of Japanese companies in the United States must be more active in the US community or risk being branded as 'irresponsible outsiders' and 'dim their prospects for the future'. Thus Kusumoto had an important role in environment scanning and noting trends affecting Japanese companies operating in the United States. Recently, Japan doubled corporate tax deductions for foreign charitable gifts, causing Japanese corporate giving to double globally (Kusumoto 1989; Schroeder 1991). While monitoring social demands and expectations is important, organisations must develop appropriate response mechanisms.

social scanning

The general surveillance of various elements in the task environment to detect evidence of impending changes affecting the organisation's social responsibilities

Internal social response mechanisms

An organisation's internal social response mechanisms include departments, committees and human resources affecting its responsiveness to social environment changes (Strand 1987). Common effective social responses of organisations include individual executives, temporary task forces, permanent committees, permanent departments or combinations of these (Holmes 1978; Post et al. 1996).

Individual executives   The use of individual executives as a social response mechanism involves either appointing or allowing certain executives to handle critical social issues as they happen. This approach is more often used in small rather than large organisations.

Temporary task forces   This mechanism involves several people serving on a committee for a limited period to deal with a critical social issue. After action is taken, the committee or task force disbands. Temporary task forces are particularly effective when an important social issue arises suddenly requiring input from various parts of the organisation.

Permanent committees   There are many variations in the use of permanent committees. Almost 100 of the *Fortune* 500 companies have special committees on the board of directors to deal with social issues. These may be called public policy, public issues, social responsibility and corporate responsibility committees (Lovdall, Bauer & Treverton 1977). Alternatively, permanent committees made up of individuals at the executive level, committees of members from all management levels, and division-level committees channelling critical issues to higher-level committees may be used.

Permanent departments   Many companies have a permanent department co-ordinating ongoing social responsibilities, identifying and recommending policies for new social issues. This is often called the **public affairs department**. It may be responsible for co-ordinating government relations, community relations and other external activities. In a study of large and medium-sized business firms, 361 of 400 respondents had some type of public affairs unit, with one-third established since 1975. The trend to establishing such departments is continuing (Post, Murray, Dickie & Mahon 1983; Post et al. 1996).

Combination approaches   In practice, organisations use a combination of mechanisms to enhance social performance (Bhambri & Sonnenfeld 1988). For example, division-level committees may recommend to an executive-level committee; or a public affairs department to an executive-level committee; or a public affairs department to certain key executives. A novel use of permanent committees was pioneered by Levi Strauss, a company with a good reputation in social responsiveness. Involving employees across the organisation, the program is co-ordinated through regional and corporate community affairs departments.

> **public affairs department**
>
> A permanent department that co-ordinates various ongoing social responsibilities and identifies and recommends policies for new social issues

BEING AN ETHICAL MANAGER

Ultimately, organisational social responsibility and responsiveness depend on managers' ethical standards. Newspaper and magazine articles about ethical problems in business are common. In a recent study with simulated business situations, 47 per cent of top executives, 41 per cent of controllers and 76 per cent of graduate-level business students surveyed were prepared to commit fraud by understating write-offs, reducing the value of certain assets. Taking write-offs would lower company profit levels, which were about to be reported (Brief, Dukerich, Brown & Brett 1996). Faced with these difficulties, many companies are clarifying ethical standards. In one approach to help employees understand company standards, Citicorp and Lockheed Martin Corp. developed games including cards depicting situations and issues their employees are likely to confront. Game participants progress in the game by choosing correctly from among alternatives for handling the situation depicted. They gain or lose points depending on how their choices fit with company standards. Try answering some questions from the Lockheed Martin game in the 'Grey Matters' exercise at the end of this chapter (*Wall Street Journal* 1989; Myers 1992).

One issue is rising white-collar crime rates (crime, such as fraud or embezzlement, by a person in business, government or not-for-profit organisations, or by professionals in occupational activities) (*Webster's New World Dictionary* 1984). According to US estimates, street crime costs $4 billion a year, and white-collar crime costs $40 billion, ultimately from consumers and taxpayers. Reasons for the rise are the current emphasis on materialism and competitive pressures. Women, long non-participants, are increasingly involved in white-collar crime (Koepp 1987; Bowen 1987; Burrough 1987).

   The difficulties and concerns with business ethics raise three important issues about being an ethical manager: the types of managerial ethics in organisations, the kinds of ethical guidelines a manager might adopt, and the ethical career issues one may face.

Types of managerial ethics

Managerial ethics, as explained earlier, are standards of conduct or moral judgment managers use to carry out their business. These standards come from society's general norms and values; from an individual's experiences in family, religious, educational and other institutions; and from interpersonal interactions. Therefore, managerial ethics may differ between individuals (Post et al. 1996; Lee 1994; *Business Week* 1995) (see Fig. 4.3). Carroll (1987) notes that three major levels of moral, or ethical, judgment characterise managers: immoral management, amoral management and moral management.

Immoral management   'Immoral' and 'unethical' may be synonymous in business. Thus **immoral management** lacks ethical principles but actively opposes ethical behaviour. It is characterised by exclusive concern for company profit and success at any price, willingness to treat others unfairly, a view of laws as obstacles and a tendency to 'cut corners'. The key principle of immoral management is: 'Can we make money with this action, decision or behaviour?' Implicit in this is the view that other considerations matter little, if at all.

   An example of immoral management cited by Carroll (1987) involved plant managers at a GM truck plant. In a flagrant violation of the company work contract, they used a secret control box to override a control panel which set the assembly line's speed. Plant managers, under pressure from higher-level managers because of missed deadlines, began meeting

immoral management

An approach not only lacking ethical principles but actively opposed to ethical behaviour

Fig. 4.3   **Extract from *Business Week*/Harris Poll (*Business Week* 1995)**

BUSINESS WEEK/HARRIS POLL: IS AN ANTI-BUSINESS BACKLASH BUILDING?		
Q. How would you describe your own attitude toward business in this country … very favourable, somewhat favourable, somewhat unfavourable, or very unfavourable?	**A.** Very favourable	18%
	Somewhat favourable	54%
	Somewhat unfavourable	18%
	Very unfavourable	6%
	Not sure	4%
Q. How would you rate the ethical standards of business executives … excellent, pretty good, only fair, or poor?	**A.** Excellent	2%
	Pretty good	38%
	Only fair	46%
	Poor	12%
	Not sure	2%
Q. Do you think white-collar crime is very common, somewhat common, not very common, or not common at all?	**A.** Very common	49%
	Somewhat common	41%
	Not very common	7%
	Not common at all	2%
	Not sure	1%

production targets and being praised by their bosses. When the scheme was discovered, workers won a settlement to compensate them.

Amoral management   **Amoral management** is neither immoral nor moral but ignores or is oblivious to ethical issues. There are two types of amoral management: intentional and unintentional. Intentionally amoral managers do not include ethical concerns in their decisions and actions as they think general ethical standards are not appropriate to business. Unintentionally amoral managers do not think about ethical issues in their dealings as they are inattentive or insensitive to moral implications of their decisions and actions. Overall, amoral managers may be well-meaning, but pursue profitability as a goal, paying little attention to their behaviour's impact on others. They generally leave other managers to behave as they wish unless the behaviour leads to notoriety or pressure. The basic principle of amoral management is: 'Within the letter of the law, can we make money with this action, decision or behaviour?'

One example of amoral management is Nestlé's decision to market baby formula in third world countries. The Swiss company did not anticipate negative effects on mothers and babies of marketing formula in areas with impure water, poverty and illiteracy. Its indifference led eventually to a worldwide consumer boycott of Nestlé products.

Moral management   In contrast to both immoral and amoral management, **moral management** follows ethical principles and precepts. While moral managers want to succeed, they do so only within parameters of ethical standards and ideals of fairness, justice and due process. As a result, moral managers pursue twin business objectives of making profit and engaging in legal and ethical behaviours. They follow both the letter and the spirit of the law, recognising that moral management requires operating above what the law mandates. The central guiding principle is: 'Is this action, decision or behaviour fair to us and all parties involved?'

One example of moral management where an organisation assumed ethical leadership involved the chainsaw manufacturer, McCulloch Corporation. The dangers of chainsaws were highlighted in statistics showing they were involved in 123 000 injuries annually. Despite this data, the Chain Saw Manufacturers Association fought mandatory safety standards, arguing the statistics were inflated and provided insufficient justification for mandatory standards. Displaying moral leadership, McCulloch decided to put chain brakes on all its saws. Later, the company withdrew from the association after repeated attempts to persuade them to adopt higher safety standards failed.

Carroll (1987) believes the amoral management style predominates today. He argues, however, that a moral management stance is more likely to be in the best interests of organisations in the long term.

amoral management

An approach that is neither immoral nor moral, but ignores or is oblivious to ethical considerations

moral management

An approach that strives to follow ethical principles and precepts

Ethical guidelines for managers

Not everyone has the same ethical standards. For example, a survey by *INC.* (1992) had 43 per cent of respondents believing it was acceptable to pay suppliers within 60 days, while expecting accounts receivables to be paid in 30 days. Sixteen per cent of respondents agreed it was acceptable to make dealers buy more product than they are likely to need. Unfortunately, it is difficult to write hard-and-fast rules for all conditions, because situations differ. Furthermore, some are ambiguous, falling into grey areas. For example, when does a supplier's 'token gift' constitute a bribe? (Tuleja 1985). To help employees grapple with this issue, General Motors recently issued a policy on 'gifts, entertainment and other gratuities', outlined in a 12-page document with instructional scenarios involving fictional characters. One such scenario, with an explanation of proper application of General Motors policy, is shown in Table 4.3.

Despite the problems outlining specific ethical standards, some guidelines can help in thinking about the ethical implications of managerial decisions and behaviours. The guidelines given below are consistent with the principle of enlightened self-interest (O'Toole 1985).

Obey the law. A basic tenet of social responsibility and managerial ethics is obedience to the law, preferably in both letter and spirit.

Tell the truth. Telling the truth is important to build trust with relevant stakeholders. When a group of employees asked the Digital Equipment Corporation (DEC) to look at an apparently high miscarriage rate among women working on semiconductor assembly lines, DEC commissioned a study. The study, costing several hundred thousand dollars, revealed the miscarriage rate was 39 per cent in the semiconductor area compared to only 18 per cent in other company parts and the general population. DEC quickly informed employees of results and shared them with the Semiconductor Industry Association (Moskowitz 1987).

Show respect for people. The notion of treating people with respect has deep roots in the study of ethics. Respect for the individual is an important aspect of the recent emphasis on valuing diversity.

Stick to the Golden Rule. The Golden Rule, 'Do unto others as you would have others do unto you', provides a benchmark for evaluating the ethical dimensions of business decisions. In business terms, it means treating individuals fairly, just as managers would want the business treated if it were an individual (Tuleja 1985). When Cummins Engine announced closure of a components plant in Darlington, England, British trade union leaders went to

Table 4.3   General Motors revised gratuities policy

Guidelines for a specific scenario as set out in the GM Revised Policy on Gifts, Entertainment, and Other Gratuities

Scenario:
A distinguished investment banking firm has successfully concluded a major acquisition for GM and invites, at the firm's expense, all the GM employees who worked with it to a dinner in New York at which each will be given a nice mantle clock, appropriately inscribed, as a memento of the successful venture.

Policy:
The dinner and clock should be politely declined. While 'thank you' gestures are a nice custom socially, they can create wrong appearances if they are lavish or extravagant. Firms that provide high-value services should be rewarded by being considered for future work. There is no need or expectation that they 'thank' individual GM employees with gifts, entertainment or other gratuities. Consistent with business custom and management approval, items of no or nominal commercial value commemorating significant accomplishments or expressing appreciation for past GM support, such as a Lucite block, certificate or baseball cap, may be accepted from suppliers on an infrequent basis.

Source: Reprinted from the *Wall Street Journal* (1996).

company headquarters in Columbus, Indiana, to get the company to reverse its position. Although Cummins felt it had to stand by its decision, it offered funding for a program to help 500 displaced workers find new jobs. Union leaders praised the company for its sympathetic concern (Moskowitz 1987).

Above all, do no harm. (*Primum non nocere*). This principle—the first rule of medical ethics—is considered by some writers to be the bottom-line ethical consideration and one easily adaptable to business. H. J. Heinz told growers supplying fruit and vegetables for its baby foods that products could not be treated with chemicals being studied by federal agencies as possible health threats. This unprecedented step was taken even though the chemicals were legal to use at the time (Moskowitz 1987).

Practice participation, not paternalism. This principle is aimed at learning about stakeholders' needs, instead of deciding what is best for them. Weyerhaeuser, a forest-products company, built a good reputation among environmentalists by seeking their views before finalising plans for land or facility development.

Always act when you have responsibility. Managers have responsibility of taking action when they have the capacity or resources. Managerial action is particularly important if those nearby are in need and a manager is the only one who can help. For example, when Merck pledged to provide free supplies of Ivermectin to combat river blindness in third world countries, the company found no effective distribution system existed. So, Merck went further and organised a committee to oversee distribution of the drug.

For a guide to help you, as a manager, utilise these principles, see the Management skills for the 21st century discussion, 'Questions to facilitate ethical business decisions'.

⬆ Questions to facilitate ethical business decisions

management skills for the 21st century

When you face an ethical dilemma, you may find it useful to work through the following list of questions. These questions will help you clarify your thinking and decide what to do.

1 Have you defined the problem accurately?
2 How would you define the problem if you stood on the other side of the fence?
3 How did this situation occur in the first place?
4 To whom and to what do you give your loyalty as a person and as a member of the corporation?
5 What is your intention in making this decision?
6 How does this intention compare with the probable results?
7 Whom could your decision or action injure?
8 Can you discuss the problem with the affected parties before you make your decision?
9 Are you confident that your position will be as valid over a long period of time as it seems now?
10 Could you disclose, without qualm, your decision or action to your boss, your CEO, the board of directors, your family, or society in general?
11 What is the symbolic potential of your action if understood? If misunderstood?
12 Under what conditions would you allow exceptions to your stand?

Source: Nash (1981). Reprinted by permission of *Harvard Business Review*.

Ethical career issues

Like most managers, you will experience ethical dilemmas during your career. Typically, these come from grey areas, where different interpretations of a situation are possible. In addition to considering social responsibilities involved, managers must think about their personal values and self-protection in deciding how to handle such situations. They also must consider actions they can take to anticipate and avoid ethical conflicts (Bhambri & Sonnenfeld 1987).

Assessing values and protecting yourself   When you are faced with an ethical dilemma, three steps are important in career terms. First, seek expertise and support from a wide network of trusted people. At times others may accept a practice as ethical but you will be doubtful. In such cases, you should check with trusted friends, former schoolmates, peers and/or experts. This helps you clarify your own values on the issue and decide if further action is needed. Second, if necessary, take internal actions to achieve change. As a manager, ensure you have your facts straight before suggesting others' behaviour may be inappropriate or illegal. Then bring the matter to the attention of superiors and attempt to persuade them to take corrective action. If the dilemma persists, you may have to move to the third step, which is to take internal actions to protect yourself. As a manager in the chain of command, you may become a scapegoat for actions implicitly or explicitly condoned by those above. Arguing you were following orders will not get you off the hook if you have done something illegal. Instead, it is a good idea to write a memo for the file, outlining your objections and conversations with others. Talk with other employees about your concerns. Actively seeking another job is another step you should seriously consider. Above all, do not engage in illegal activities. Together, these actions build a strong case that you attempted to halt the ethical difficulty.

Anticipating ethical conflicts   Although it is often difficult to accurately predict the likelihood of ethical conflicts, some steps can be taken to help. First, when seeking employment, look for signals that indicate conflicts are likely. Ask your family, friends and teachers about the organisation. Check the library for recent articles and background information. Use job interviews to learn how the organisation operates. If possible, try to meet with some people you would be working with. Try to detect signs of serious dissatisfaction and dissension that might signal ethical conflicts. Second, check industry practices. Industries that have been stable for a period of time may develop informal networks encouraging collusion among competitors. Industries at the other end of the spectrum, with easy entry and a highly competitive environment, may be particularly susceptible to ethical difficulties due to severe market pressures. Third, avoid making even small ethical compromises: they can escalate out of control. Managers avoid such compromises, according to experts, by setting aside backup money in a bank account so they can walk out of an unbearable situation. Otherwise, managers could find themselves trapped.

 # Recyclable Christmas trees   case in point

Have you ever considered what happens to all those Christmas trees after the Christmas period is over? Well, if you were living in Singapore, you might be returning your tree to the Ikea store you purchased it from. In an effort to convince customers to return the 1743 trees purchased before Christmas, Ikea is offering a $5 Ikea voucher. The trees are collected by the recycling company, Meng Guan Landscape, and shredded into wood chips. Helping nature to take its course, chicken manure and other organic materials can be added to produce several grades of compost.

Ikea's general manager explained that this was simply a very small part of encouraging their customers to participate in making Singapore an eco-friendly place to live. More importantly, Ikea is having discussions with the Singapore Environmental Council on how to promote best green practices.

Source: Adapted from *Straits Times* (11 January 2000).

Activities for discussion, analysis and further research

1 What do you think of Ikea's activities as described above? Why do you think Ikea is doing this?
2 Are you aware of other organisations doing similar things? Do a web search and identify some of the socially responsible things that organisations do.

MANAGING AN ETHICAL ORGANISATION

Although it is easy to blame everyone else, individuals are ultimately responsible for their own actions. An important management challenge is to operate an organisation where business is conducted ethically. To do this, managers must be knowledgeable about environmental and organisational conditions that increase the likelihood of unethical behaviour. They can also use mechanisms facilitating ethical behaviour.

Situational factors influencing ethical behaviour

Much research on ethical versus unethical behaviour in organisations focuses on actual law breaking. These studies suggest several factors in an organisation's environment can be conducive to illegal, unethical behaviour (see Table 4.4) (Finney & Lesieur 1981; Baucus & Near 1991). Of course, managers' values also bear on whether individuals actually engage in unethical behaviour, though some situations make it more likely.

Table 4.4   Situational factors influencing ethical behaviour

External factors	Internal factors
Environmental competitiveness	Pressure for high performance
Environmental munificence	Labour dissatisfaction
Extreme dependency	Delegation
	Encouragement of innovation

For example, *environmental competitiveness* encourages unethical behaviour. Some industries with common price-fixing, such as the motor industry, paper cartons, plumbing fixtures and heavy electrical equipment, have strong competition, fairly similar products, and frequent price changes and negotiations. Competition can foster unethical behaviour in not-for-profit organisations too. Such behaviour shows in illegal payments to athletes, illegal political campaign contributions, and misrepresentations of the level of charitable contributions actually going to those in need.

Both low and high *environmental bounty* may also be conducive to unethical behaviour. When it is low, opportunities for success are limited. The struggle for financial performance in this environment may cause organisations to behave unethically. This happened to the Beech-Nut Nutrition Corporation, the second-largest US baby food manufacturer. Beech-Nut executives ignored chemists' warnings that the apple concentrate the company bought at below-market prices was probably extensively altered. Ultimately, two executives received prison terms and fines for their part in selling the completely synthetic juice, labelled '100 per cent fruit juice'. The scandal adversely affected sales of the company's baby food products. The executives had ignored warnings because the company was almost insolvent (Welles 1988; Queenan 1988).

On the other hand, high bounty may lead to unethical behaviour as organisations try to grow quickly and take advantage of a favourable situation. For example, an executive of Halsey Drug Co., a Brooklyn, New York, maker of generic drugs, was sentenced to 18 months in prison for conspiring to add ingredients unapproved by the Food and Drug Administration (FDA) to generic drugs for irregular heartbeats, meningitis and hyperthyroidism (Pereeira & Rebello 1995). The official was attempting to boost effectiveness of the drugs to take advantage of burgeoning markets for generics costing less but presumed to be therapeutically equivalent to brand-name drugs.

One ethical consideration of management is environmental protection, a responsibility of industry towards society.

A third important external factor influencing unethical behaviour is *extreme dependency* of one organisation on another. These dependencies create pressures for bribes and payoffs (Ingersoll 1989).

Internal organisational factors can also increase the likelihood of unethical behaviour. *Pressure for higher performance* and output induces individuals to take 'shortcuts' such as price fixing, secretly speeding up an assembly line or releasing unsafe products (Eichenwald 1992; *Economist* 1995).

Labour dissatisfaction may also produce unethical behaviour as anger replaces constrained, rational behaviour. Ironically, *delegation of authority* and *encouragement of innovation* may increase the likelihood of unethical behaviour because of increased latitude and creativity. For example, at Adam Opel AG, the German subsidiary of General Motors, three senior board members and several employees resigned amidst allegations they had accepted gratuities such as free work on their homes, or engaged in a kickback scheme involving awarding contracts. Opel chairman David Herman said that, in making cutbacks to become 'leaner', the company may have eliminated too many financial checks and balances. He warned, 'This is a word to the wise in other companies'. (Kurylko 1995, p. 36).

Since external factors and internal pressures increase the likelihood of unethical acts, managers must monitor such conditions. When the conditions exist, managers must spend greater effort in conveying the importance of ethical behaviour to organisation members.

One study suggests that middle- and lower-level managers may feel more ethical pressure than upper-level managers (Posner & Schmidt 1984). This implies that upper-level managers may be insufficiently aware of pressures on middle and lower levels and do not take enough action to counter the pressures.

Mechanisms for ethical management

An important issue is what managers can do to foster ethical behaviour in organisations. There are no easy ways to influence behaviour; however, some mechanisms can help managers create an ethical climate. These include the following (Post et al. 1996).

Increasing awareness of diversity   It is natural to view others from your own viewpoint, as you use your own attitudes, feelings, thoughts and experiences to guide your interactions. Appreciating diversity, however, requires awareness of others' attitudes and experiences. Diversity-awareness programs try to increase participants' awareness of (1) their own attitudes, biases and stereotypes and (2) the different viewpoints of managers, subordinates, co-workers and customers. These programs have a few common goals (Carnevale & Stone 1994) such as to:

○ provide participants with accurate information on diversity
○ uncover stereotypes and personal biases
○ assess personal beliefs, attitudes and values
○ overturn inaccurate stereotypes and beliefs
○ develop an atmosphere where people can share differing perspectives and viewpoints
○ improve understanding of those who are different

Top-management commitment   Managers can demonstrate their commitment by instituting a range of mechanisms set out below and setting positive examples by their own behaviours (Jones 1995). Vernon R. Loucks Jr, president and CEO of Baxter Travenol Laboratories Inc., argues that subordinates will pay more attention to what you do than to what you say.

Codes of ethics   It is estimated 90 per cent of major corporations have written codes of ethics. A **code of ethics** is a document prepared to guide organisation members when encountering

code of ethics

A document prepared for the purpose of guiding organisation members when they encounter an ethical dilemma

ethical dilemmas. While almost all companies with codes say it is helpful in maintaining ethical behaviour among employees, a study showed that only 36 per cent distribute the code to all employees and only 20 per cent display it across the organisation (Otten 1986). A comparative study of business firms in Britain, France and what was then West Germany showed only about 40 per cent had codes of ethics and the content varied considerably between countries due to political, legal and sociocultural differences (Langlois & Schlegelmilch 1990).

Ethics committees   According to a survey by the Ethics Resource Centre, about a third of *Fortune* 1000 companies have ethics committees. An **ethics committee** is a group charged with helping establish policies and resolve major questions of ethical issues facing organisation members in their work. The committee may oversee training programs on ethics. Often the committee consists of individuals from top management and/or the board of directors.

Ethics audits   Some organisations conduct **ethics audits**—systematic efforts to assess conformity to organisational ethical policies, aid understanding of these policies, and identify serious breaches requiring remedial action. Even with such efforts, ethical problems can be hard to identify. For example, Dow Corning had a model ethics program encompassing ethics audits, yet the company was embroiled in a serious ethical situation.

Ethics hot lines   An **ethics hot line** is a special telephone line set up to allow employees to bypass their normal chain of command, to report grievances and serious ethical problems. The line is normally handled by an executive designated to investigate and help resolve reported issues. A hot line facilitates internal handling of problems and thus reduces the likelihood of employees becoming external whistle-blowers. A **whistle-blower** is an employee who reports a real or perceived wrongdoing under the control of their employer to those able to take appropriate action. When a whistle-blower goes to an outside person or organisation, unfavourable publicity, legal investigations and lawsuits often result (Dozier & Miceli 1985; Near & Miceli 1995).

Ethics training   Many organisations use ethics training to encourage ethical behaviour. Such training may focus solely on ethical concerns or be integrated into training programs covering many organisational issues. By clarifying expectations and ethical standards, this training helps reduce unethical behaviour (Michael, Daniel, Hopper, George-Falvey and Ferris 1996; Garland 1998). Enhanced understanding of organisational standards helps managers and other employees engage in appropriate decision making, the subject of the next chapter.

ethics committee

A group charged with helping to establish policies and resolve major questions involving ethical issues confronting organisation members in the course of their work

ethics audits

Systematic efforts to assess conforming to organisational ethical policies, aid understanding of those policies, and identify serious breaches requiring remedial action

ethics hot line

A special telephone line established to enable employees to bypass the normal chain of command in reporting grievances and serious ethical problems

whistle-blower

An employee who reports a real or perceived wrongdoing under the control of their employer to those able to take appropriate action

■ The MD's diary   the reflective practitioner

To me, the sorts of behaviour that I like to see and that I like to encourage are those that see people deal with other people honestly and openly. It's one where I would expect or I would hope that people in the organisation both trust me and trust the organisation to be open and honest and completely without politics. It's one where mutual respect is absolutely given, where everyone's contribution to the organisation is valued, everyone has a contribution to make and that contribution is valued within the organisation. It's one of decency in terms of the way we operate. I expect that people will work in a way with each other that is not adversarial, that's not aggressive. But is assertive and very hard at the task. I believe that we can achieve and still treat people with respect, decency and honesty.

■ The subordinate's log
the reflective practitioner

Having been a consultant, I knew what demands the nature of the work and frequent travel placed on my family and myself. This awareness placed a personal responsibility on me to do my best to minimise impact on staff. I know from experience that you cannot get the best out of someone who has conflict at home due to unavoidable work pressures.

I therefore looked for ways of programming projects with realistic time frames. I am a firm believer in a 95 per cent solution on time, rather than a 100 per cent solution taking all night to complete. The personal repercussions could lose me a good staff member.

Conscientious staff sometimes built project plans with work scheduled for weekends. While I recognised the occasional need for weekend work, I insisted that such project plans were altered wherever possible. Client demands often needed to be negotiated so that balance could be maintained. Many clients, if not most, did display concern regarding the demand placed on their consultants, and their negotiations were based solely on the quality and cost of the output. Some clients effectively formed a partnership with the consultants and took an interest in their welfare as you would an employee.

Honest dealings were a non-negotiable demand of the organisation members and consequently of the clients. In one instance, one of our consultants responded to a potential client's offensive remarks with: 'no, we don't want your business'. I supported the position of the consultant, ahead of gaining new business. The CEO supported me.

Our organisation had a printed code of behaviour which stated the requirements for direct and honest communication. However, while on an industry basis there is no formal consulting code of ethics, we operated as most consultancies do: we maintained client confidentiality, we could not perform work which would conflict with our clients' interests, and consultants agreed not to compete for a certain period after leaving the firm.

Focus on practice—Strategies for improving

1 Does your organisation have a code of ethics? If not, how would you go about convincing your organisation of the need to develop one?
2 Develop a strategy to implement the development of a code of ethics in an organisation which has not believed they required one.
3 How would you ensure that managers in your organisation treat individuals equitably, rather than based on familiarity with their backgrounds?
4 Develop a plan for assisting managers in your organisation to understand and avoid stereotypes.

Source: Jones et al. (2000).

Chapter summary

Organisational, or corporate, social responsibility refers to a business firm's obligation to seek actions that protect and improve society's welfare as well as its own interests. Three major contrasting perspectives on the nature of corporate social responsibility are the invisible-hand, the hand-of-government and the hand-of-management. Due to expanding societal expectations regarding social responsibility of businesses and other organisations, the hand-of-management view is increasingly relevant to managers. The iron law of responsibility suggests socially responsible behaviour may have a positive long-run effect on organisational success.

The social responsibilities of management focus on six major stakeholder groups: shareholders, employees, customers, the local community, the wider society and the international community. Studies indicate no clear relationship between a corporation's degree of social responsibility and its short-run financial success. Nevertheless, it is possible to be both socially responsible and financially successful. Increasingly, organisations are attempting to orient their socially responsible activities to areas which can affect their bottom line and ultimately give a competitive edge.

Corporate social responsiveness refers to the development of organisational decision-processes where managers anticipate, respond to, and manage areas of social responsibility. Two processes usually are essential. First, it is necessary to establish methods of monitoring social demands and expectations. Major means are social forecasting, opinion surveys, social audits and issues management. Second, it is important to develop internal social response mechanisms. These include the use of individual executives, temporary task forces, permanent committees, permanent departments or combinations of these elements.

Ultimately, questions of corporate social responsibility and social responsiveness depend on managers' ethical standards. Three types of managerial ethics are immoral, amoral and moral. While amoral behaviour prevails, moral management is likely to be in the organisation's best long-run interests. Ethical guidelines for managers include: obey the law; tell the truth; show respect for people; stick to the golden rule; above all, do no harm; practise participation, not paternalism; and always act when you have responsibility. Ethical career issues for managers may involve assessing their own values and protecting themselves, as well as considering what actions they can take to anticipate and avoid ethical conflicts.

An important management challenge is operating an organisation so members conduct their business ethically. To do so, managers must be knowledgeable about what environmental and organisational conditions increase the likelihood of unethical behaviour. They should also use mechanisms facilitating ethical behaviour, such as top-management commitment, codes of ethics, ethics committees, ethics audits, ethics training and ethics hot lines.

Questions for discussion and review

1 Explain the three major perspectives on corporate social responsibility. What criteria might you use to determine whether an organisation's management subscribes most closely to the invisible-hand, hand-of-government, or hand-of-management view?

2 Identify at least one regulation in each hand-of-government control category for your local area. In what ways do these direct companies' actions or responsibilities?

3 Identify an organisation fulfilling some discretionary activities in your local area. In what ways will this impact on the community's perceptions of the organisation?

4 Identify, from your local business press, one example of shareholders' pressure producing change in management's social stance. Will this make further changes more likely? Why?

5 Identify six stakeholder groups often mentioned in conjunction with social responsibility. To what extent do these groups apply to your college or university? What other stakeholders might you add?

6 Evaluate the extent to which organisational social responsibility is likely to pay off financially. Universities are often recipients of corporate philanthropy. Identify two ways such philanthropy has helped your college or university. How might contributors benefit from such donations?

7 Identify the major approaches used to monitor social demands and expectations. Choose an organisation with which you are familiar and suggest how it might use these methods to monitor relevant social issues.

8 Explain several internal social response mechanisms available to organisations. Identify two mechanisms used by your college or university.

9 Distinguish between three major types of managerial ethics. Use *Business Review Weekly* or the *Wall Street Journal* to identify an example of one of these types.

10 Enumerate the ethical guidelines for managers discussed in the chapter.

11 Suggest some steps you could take when seeking employment to help you detect potential ethical problems. To what extent do your friends consider these issues when seeking jobs?

12 Describe the situational factors likely to influence ethical behaviour.

13 Outline the basic mechanisms for ethical management. Suppose you have just been appointed to a top-level position with a major contractor. How would you use these mechanisms to help prevent some ethical difficulties, such as misrepresenting costs on contracts, that are plaguing other contractors?

Exercises for managing in the 21st century

Exercise 1

Skill building: Business ethical dilemmas from Lockheed Martin's ethics game

Use the questions in the Management skills for the 21st century discussion ('Questions to facilitate ethical business decisions') in this chapter to help you choose what to do in each of the following situations taken from *Grey Matters: The Ethics Game* (Lockheed Martin 1992).

Situation 1

Since program funds are short, you have been directed by your supervisor to charge your time to an account you know to be improper. What do you do?

Potential answers to situation 1 (choose one):

A Explain to your supervisor that mischarging on a government contract is fraud.

B Refuse to mischarge.

C Mischarge as directed by your supervisor.

D Ask finance for an overhead number to charge your time to.

Situation 2

A company-sponsored training course in your field is being held in Orlando, Florida. You have no interest in the training but you are ready for a vacation and have never been to Disney World. What do you do?

Potential answers to situation 2 (choose one):

A Even though you have no interest in the training, ask your supervisor if he thinks it will benefit you.

B Obviously, or maybe not so obviously, it will be of some benefit to you, so you sign up.

C Reluctantly decline to go.

D Suggest that someone else go who has both a need and the interest.

Situation 3

On the bus going home at night, the woman sitting next to you mentions that she is being sexually harassed by one of her fellow employees. Although she does not work for you, you both work for the same company. You are a manager in the company. What do you do?

Potential answers to situation 3 (choose one)

A Listen politely, but since she doesn't work for you, stay out of it.

B Suggest she speak to her supervisor about it.

C Suggest she speak to either your company's equal-opportunity office or ethics officer.
D You contact your company's equal-opportunity officer or ethics officer.

Exercise 2
Management exercise: A question of ethics

After earning an undergraduate degree in history and an MBA in finance, Roberta was offered a position with a medium-sized real-estate development firm in her home town. Much to her liking, the job involved working in the firm's 'community projects' area, where she would oversee the books for the company's construction of low-cost housing projects.

The opportunity to work in finance while also aiding public good appealed to Roberta. She had been interviewed for other jobs in finance and real estate, but she didn't like the competitive atmosphere at larger firms, where size of salaries and bonuses seemed to be overriding concerns of most new employees.

After a few weeks, Roberta discovered a discrepancy in the books of one of her firm's projects. Six separate cheques for $10 000 each had been written by Roberta's boss over the past year, each made payable to cash with no further explanation. When Roberta approached her boss, she was told they were just another cost of doing business and she should inflate other items' costs to cover the payments.

On further investigation, Roberta learned the cheques were paid to inspectors so they would overlook the use of certain substandard materials. Roberta again protested to her boss, who responded with obvious irritation. He said such payments were common and the use of substandard materials wouldn't affect safety.

The boss implied that significant cost savings on materials were necessary if the firm was to build low-cost housing on a profitable basis. He noted that the cost of each unit would increase by only $2000 to cover the payments and the owners would probably expect to upgrade their units eventually anyway.

Roberta knows that, at the least, replacement or repairs would be needed after only two or three years because of substandard materials. Concerned a wrong was committed and fearful she might personally become entangled in the mess, Roberta protested to her boss's supervisor. The supervisor told Roberta he 'would look into it'. Roberta hasn't heard anything in three weeks and has just discovered that a seventh $10 000 cheque payable to cash has come through. What should Roberta do now?

Source: Adapted from *National Business Employment Weekly* (1987).

Hello Kitty—Hello madness

on the rim—
in Singapore

On New Year's Day 2000, the McDonald's chain in Singapore initiated a different kind of promotion. For every purchase of an Extra Value Meal, customers could also purchase a matched set of Hello Kitty and Dear Daniel dolls dressed in wedding garb. One week, the pair were dressed for a futuristic wedding; another week, they were dressed in traditional Malay wedding costumes. When McDonald's launched the promotion they apparently did not envisage the eagerness with which Singaporeans would pursue the acquisition of the doll pairs.

Every outlet in Singapore was besieged with extensive queues of people, some of whom lined up for hours in order not to miss out. Others blocked the drive-through lanes to order from the outside windows.

The attraction seemed to go beyond the ownership of the toys. It was anticipated that these would become collectors' items and would eventually be worth much more than the $4.50 each McDonald's was selling them for. A spokesman for McDonald's commented that the company's on-line auction of the entire line of Hello Kitty pairs had received bids as high as $950. Therefore in the expectations that their investment would appreciate, Singaporeans were purchasing as many sets as they could get away with. Given this, the McDonald's chain put a limit of four toys per person at any one time. Resourceful Singaporeans got around this by arranging for a number of family members and even the children's nanny to line up and buy the set meals in order to qualify for purchasing the Hello Kitty wedding pairs.

What happened to all the hamburgers purchased? Well, most of them ended up in the rubbish bin. More than one buyer was seen tossing the meals away as they left the stores. The attraction was the dolls, not the food.

Citizens themselves reacted strongly to this and a number of letters to the editor were printed in the *Straits Times* making suggestions to McDonald's. The company acted on those suggestions and provided charity option forms to customers, who were invited to ask for them at the restaurants when making unwanted purchases of food in order to obtain the dolls. At the end of the month-long Hello Kitty Promotion, the forms were collated and Extra Value Meals distributed across the 55 National Council of Social Service Charities.

Waste of food was not the only problem encountered as a result of this promotion. A number of the McDonald's Restaurants were the scene of fights. For example, in week three of the promotion, when the pair were available in traditional Korean wedding dress, customers were so keen to get their hands on them that one of the outlets had its glass door shattered, hurting seven people. In response to the number of fights that broke out, the fast-food chain announced that it would station security officers as part of crowd-control measures. A company spokesman expressed dismay at the euphoria surrounding the promotion and appealed to customers to remain calm and follow staff directions.

Sources: Adapted from Lai, F. (11 January 2000), Chong, C. K. (14 January 2000) and Santamaria, S. (7 January 2000).

Activities for discussion, analysis and further research

1 Consider the actions of the McDonald's chain. What do you think of this type of strategy to promote additional sales?
2 Should McDonald's have been able to predict the reactions of customers?
3 Discuss McDonald's responses to the throwing away of food.
4 Recently, a similar promotion at McDonald's in Australia ran into difficulty when the fast-food chain claimed that the participants in some of the games were cheating and using tokens from the previous year. Do a search to find information on how the class action which was started is progressing. Discuss the appropriateness of such activities on the part of a food retailer.

● Video Ezy holds course for Asia   going global

Australian home-video giant Video Ezy is pursuing its global ambitions despite doubts surrounding the future of its major international shareholder, the Malaysian conglomerate Berjaya Group, and rumours about its ownership structure. Video Ezy turns over about $250 million a year. It has 571 stores in four countries and, over the next few years, it wants to add at least another 300 stores and move into six more countries.

The Asian economic downturn has winded Berjaya. Its profit crashed by 98 per cent last year, from 723.6 million ringgit in 1997 to just 4.7 million ($A1.9 million). Industry sources say that Berjaya (Malaysian for 'success') had put its 60 per cent holding in Video Ezy on the market earlier this year with a price tag of $25 million, but received no offers and withdrew it.

Bob Maidment, Video Ezy's managing director and 40 per cent shareholder, says Berjaya is not a desperate seller, 'but if they suddenly found they could get the return they're seeking, they'd still probably sell'. Video Ezy's international managing director, Clinton Hayes, agrees: 'It's a timing issue. This is one of the few things they've got working well for them at the moment. So they're committed to it and have really just been doing the prudent thing, examining options for bringing their debt–equity ratios into line, including the possibility of liquidating assets.'

Maidment concedes Berjaya's uncertain future led to Video Ezy's market float. But Hayes insists there has been no change to plans to open stores in Malaysia and Thailand. 'We're pushing ahead, regardless. The proposed float was never a central funding plank of our international expansion', Hayes says. 'There have always been great growth opportunities for us in Asia. We'll simply be continuing the ongoing development of new territories as before, establishing corporate-store footholds and developing the franchise slowly. We don't want to over-stretch our resources. We're just happy taking it one territory at a time, making sure we have the infrastructure in place and that everything's running smoothly before we move on to somewhere else.'

Berjaya is a publicly listed company, turning over close to 7.5 billion ringgit in 1998. It has interests in gaming and lottery management, financial services, direct selling, hotels and resorts, recreation services and property investment and development. Apart from Video Ezy, its Australian interests include 55 per cent of the CarLovers carwash company and 37.5 per cent of the World Square development in Sydney.

Controlled by chairman and chief executive Tan Sri Dato Seri Vincent Tan Chee Yioun, Berjaya bought its stake in Video Ezy from Maidment in January 1996 for $9.6 million. Maidment is a former accountant who started operating a small chain of video stores in Canberra as a sideline. He joined Video Ezy as a franchisee in 1991 before taking over the company in 1993.

'I had a pretty straightforward business plan to develop the system and market it nationally', Maidment says. 'The idea was to be the McDonald's of the video industry and I think we're probably 95 per cent of the way there, now.'

Working with Berjaya, Video Ezy opened stores in Malaysia in 1996 and Thailand last year. It now has 556 stores in Australia and New Zealand, nine in Malaysia and six in Thailand. About 90 per cent of the stores, both in Australia and overseas, are franchised. The rest are company-owned.

Maidment and Hayes plan to have 150 more Video Ezy stores in Thailand within five years. Seventy now operate under the VO5 banner and will become Video Ezy outlets under the terms of a licensing and master franchise deal that was signed last year. Maidment and Hayes are also considering expansion into Singapore, Brunei, the Philippines, Mexico, Brazil and Britain.

Flat sales in the $750–800 million a year Australian video market and the growth of such rivals as Blockbuster Video are driving Video Ezy's overseas expansion. It has a strong share of the local market. 'Conservatively, one in three videos hired in Australia is hired from a Video Ezy', Maidment says. 'The market is flat, currently, but we are still experiencing growth in the marketplace at the expense of small independent traders. The business itself is also trading exceptionally well, recording growth in excess of 30 per cent over the past three years.'

Maidment says Video Ezy holds 29 per cent of the Australian market, followed by the United States-owned Blockbuster on 14–15 per cent and the local franchised group Civic Video on 13 per cent. 'It's a pretty commonly held belief now that the market place will settle down to two major players—Blockbuster and ourselves', he says. 'Blockbuster's stores are performing about par with us, but they don't have as many stores. Civic has as many locations but those stores are operating at about 60 per cent of our turnover per store.

'Blockbuster is opening new stores all the time. Its expansion is helping {build} the industry. When they entered the marketplace, they did us a favour. They brought a new standard, forcing us to provide better service to our customers and bringing some longevity and stability to the industry.'

Hayes says Video Ezy's move into Malaysia has been successful. 'We opened our first store about two or three months before the bottom fell out of the Asian economy, but we had a pretty good first year anyway', he says. 'Our second year was rougher because it was difficult for anyone to get finance to buy a franchise. But this year it's come back again and we're starting to get a lot more franchises on board.'

'On the consumer front, we've been largely immune, because videos are one of the few forms of entertainment and escape that is still affordable, even during a crisis. The sell-through market {video sales} certainly got kicked around, but the rental market has held its own.'

Hayes envisages that in the long term, the company will have 200–300 stores in Thailand, and more stores in Malaysia. The development of an unspecified regional market is also on the table. Hayes says it makes sense for Video Ezy to use its Malaysian and Thai operations as a springboard into Singapore, Brunei and the Philippines. The possibility of joint ventures in Mexico, Brazil and Britain is also being examined, although Hayes says nothing will happen in those countries until the year 2000.

Source: Cahill, P. (1999).

Activities for discussion, analysis and further research

1 What are the elements of the external environment which this organisation has had to deal with over the past three years? How has each of them impacted on the growth of the organisation?

2 In groups of three or four, conduct some research on the various countries which Video Ezy states it wants to enter. What has happened to the video rental market in the past two or three years? How has Video Ezy progressed with its intentions? What have been the factors that have impacted on the level of success in that venture?

3 Log onto **www.blockbuster.com**. This is Video Ezy's largest competitor world wide. Go into the sections 'About us' and 'Press releases'. Explore what Blockbuster is about to do and the directions it plans to take. Compare those to Video Ezy's plans and keep this information in mind as you study the chapters on Planning and Strategic management. Are the owners and managers of both companies going through the processes recommended by the theory you are studying? In what ways are they varying from the theory?

PART ② 2

PLANNING AND DECISION MAKING

The management function of planning involves setting goals and then deciding how best to achieve them. It includes consideration of what will encourage needed levels of change and innovation, as well as providing a basis for the other major functions of management (organising, leading and controlling) by mapping the course and providing the steering mechanism. This section, then, is geared to acquiring a basic knowledge of the planning function.

The kinds of problems that managers attempt to resolve through decision making, as well as the appropriate steps to take in the decision process, are the focus of **Chapter 5**. This chapter also addresses creativity, a vital ingredient in innovation.

Chapter 6 examines the overall planning process and explores how setting goals facilitates organisational performance. It will become clear that goals and the related plans necessary to achieve them vary in important ways according to organisational level.

One of the most important aspects of planning is strategic management. **Chapter 7** explores how managers formulate and implement large-scale action plans called strategies to attain a competitive edge for the organisation.

As innovation in organisations must be an integral part of the planning process, **Chapter 8** probes ways managers can effectively facilitate needed innovation and change.

Managerial Decision Making

Chapter 5

CHAPTER OUTLINE

The nature of managerial decision making
Types of problems decision makers face
Differences in decision-making situations

Managers as decision makers
The rational model
Non-rational models

Steps in an effective decision-making process
Identifying the problem
Generating alternative solutions
Evaluating and choosing an alternative
Implementing and monitoring the chosen solution

Overcoming barriers to effective decision making
Accepting the problem challenge
Searching for sufficient alternatives

Recognising common decision-making biases
Avoiding the decision-escalation phenomenon

Managing diversity: Group decision making
Advantages and disadvantages of group
    decision making
Enhancing group decision-making processes
Computer-assisted group decision making

**Promoting innovation: The creativity factor in
    decision making**
Basic ingredients
Stages of creativity
Techniques for enhancing group creativity

LEARNING OBJECTIVES

After studying this chapter, you should be able to:

○ Explain the major types of problems facing decision makers and describe the differences
  between programmed and non-programmed decisions.
○ Contrast rational and non-rational models of managers as decision makers.
○ Describe the steps in an effective decision-making process.
○ Explain how to overcome barriers associated with accepting the problem challenge and
  searching for sufficient alternatives.
○ Describe how to recognise common decision-making biases and avoid the decision-escalation
  phenomenon.
○ Assess the advantages and disadvantages of group decision making.
○ Explain three basic ingredients and four stages of creativity.
○ Describe the major techniques for enhancing group creativity.

Striving for excellence

Organisations and their members have shown themselves to be capable of self-delusion as to their internal culture and morale. Slogans and words are easy to come up with, but the reality is identified in the actual processes. One such process is decision making. When all is said and done, and all the rhetoric has been verbalised, it is possible to actually see whether it is true or merely lip-service by examining the decision processes within an organisation.

Autoliv is no exception. In examining the processes it becomes obvious that it is teams and individuals who make decisions regarding activities which are within their areas of expertise. Other decisions are within the corporate plan's decisions framework—which are derived collaboratively at the senior management-team level.

Still there are a number of levels of analysis which need to be considered. As with all organisations which are part of a global entity, there is a corporate-level headquarters. However, this level sets parameters for a global structure and for the dividends which must flow from each national entity. Autoliv Australia is basically autonomous. The managing director, Bob Franklin, reports to the manager, Asia Pacific, who reports to the CEO in head office. Within guidelines, which for the most part focus on the financial reporting structures, delineate the specific territory it can operate in and dictate the products it takes to market, Autoliv Australia is left to carry on its activities as it sees best.

Within Autoliv Australia, the decision-making process starts at the bottom—issues focus on activities required to meet customer needs. These are worked up as recommendations. Where a capital investment is required, the managing director has the final say, but he works on recommendations from the senior management team.

For the most part, employees are encouraged to make recommendations, and these are taken through established processes to the approval stage. An example is when employees wanted to pull down the smoking sheds for reasons of safety and aesthetics. The safety team suggested an extension to the canteen for smokers. A group of staff approached HR personnel, who put the recommended proposal to the senior management team on their behalf. This was further recommended to the managing director who signed off on it. Issues around safety and return on investment, and meeting the customers' requirements are never questioned and are always treated as first priority issues. It is interesting to note that many of those issues are raised by factory-floor staff, as they are the closest to them and their comments and suggestions are noted with care.

The decision process is facilitated by the fact that sign-off authorities are part of individuals' position responsibilities. These are not usually stated in terms of dollar values but areas of responsibility. Structures are set within the larger organisational context. Staff are expected to operate within their given guidelines and carry out responsibilities within them, and are given the authority and power to make and implement their decisions.

decision making

The process by which managers identify organisational problems and try to resolve them

In this chapter we explore the nature of managerial **decision making**, including the types of problems and decision-making situations managers can face. We evaluate managers as decision makers and consider the steps in an effective decision-making process. We examine how to overcome barriers to effective decision making, and weigh the advantages and disadvantages of group decision making. Finally, we show how managers can promote innovation through the use of creativity in decision-making processes.

THE NATURE OF MANAGERIAL DECISION MAKING

Managers make many different decisions in their work. While lower-level managers might not make decisions such as changing a revered product's formula, many smaller decisions at lower levels have a cumulative effect on organisational effectiveness. For example, Motorola built its reputation for high quality and innovation (in semiconductors, electronic pagers and mobile phones) in part by having people from design, manufacturing and marketing departments involved early in decision making for new projects (Therrien 1989). Good decision-making processes are important at all levels.

Effective decision making generally includes four steps as shown in Figure 5.1 (Elbing 1978). Some refer to the four steps as 'problem solving', and reserve 'decision making' for the first three steps up to, but not including, implementation and follow-up (Huber 1980). Here 'decision making' and 'problem solving' are used interchangeably for the process depicted in Figure 5.1. This is because 'decision making' is used more commonly in business, and it is clear when it is used in a narrower sense. We analyse the four steps in the process in more detail later in the chapter. First, though, it is useful to examine the major types of problems managers encounter and to consider differences in managerial decision-making situations.

One business component that involves decision making by managers is marketing, and an important market sector is the family, whose members are often group-decision makers themselves.

Fig. 5.1　Steps in the decision-making process (adapted from Huber 1980, p. 8)

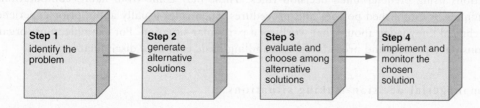

| **Step 1** identify the problem | → | **Step 2** generate alternative solutions | → | **Step 3** evaluate and choose among alternative solutions | → | **Step 4** implement and monitor the chosen solution |

Types of problems decision makers face

Managerial decision making centres on three types of problems: crisis, non-crisis and opportunity problems (Mintzberg, Raisignhani & Thoret 1976; Nutt 1985).

crisis problem

A serious difficulty requiring immediate action

Crisis   A **crisis problem** is a difficulty serious enough to require immediate action. An example of a crisis is a discovery of a severe cash-flow deficiency with the potential to become a serious loss. Coca-Cola faced a crisis when customers protested about the classic Coke formula's demise. New Coke appears as Coke II in some markets, but accounts for just one-tenth of one per cent of carbonated beverage volume (Collins 1995).

non-crisis problem

An issue requiring resolution but without the simultaneous importance and immediacy characteristics of a crisis

Non-crisis   A **non-crisis problem** is an issue needing resolution but without the importance and immediacy of a crisis. Many managerial decisions centre on non-crisis problems. Examples are a factory needing to be made to conform with new anti-pollution standards over the next three years and an employee often late for work. Once, poor earnings in Coke's food division, which produced Minute Maid juices, was a non-crisis problem. After a new president and CEO of the division was appointed, the situation improved significantly (Morris 1987).

opportunity problem

A situation offering strong potential for significant organisational gain if appropriate actions are taken

Opportunity   An **opportunity problem** is a situation offering potential for organisational gain if appropriate actions are taken. These problems typically involve new ideas and directions, and are major innovation vehicles. Coca-Cola's top management saw an opportunity in placing Coke's name on an extensive soft-drinks line. More recently, they have made adjustments for the Japanese market where consumers like a steady flow of new products. After setting up a new product-development centre in Japan, which is Coke's most profitable market, Coke released up to 50 new beverages a year there (Frank 1995). Opportunities involve ideas to be used, not difficulties for resolution. Non-innovative managers focus on crisis and non-crisis problems, and neglect opportunities. In a study of 78 managerial decision-making situations, 13 per cent were crisis problems, 62 per cent were non-crisis problems, and 25 per cent were opportunity taking (Nutt 1984). In addition to these three types of problems, managers also typically face different decision-making situations.

Differences in decision-making situations

Decision making overwhelms managers if they handle every problem as a completely new situation. Fortunately, it is not so. Generally, decision situations fall into two categories: programmed and non-programmed. Examples of each are shown in Table 5.1.

programmed decisions

Decisions made in routine, repetitive, well-structured situations by use of predetermined decision rules

Programmed decisions   **Programmed decisions** are for routine, repetitive, well-structured situations using predetermined decision rules. These may come from habit, computational techniques or established policies and procedures. Such rules usually apply prior experience or technical knowledge about what works in a particular situation. For example, most organisations have policies and procedures for handling basic employee disciplinary matters.

Table 5.1   Types of managerial decision-making situations

Type of organisation	Programmed decision	Non-programmed decision
Fast-food restaurant	Determine supplies to be reordered	Identify location for new franchise
University	Decide if students meet graduation requirements	Choose new academic programs
Car-maker	Determine work rates	Select new car design

Programmed decisions apply in routine, well-structured situations, but can be quite complex. Computers have simplified making sophisticated programmed decisions, because they can collect and analyse vast quantities of information to help programmed decision making. For example, when a person uses a credit card, a computer makes a programmed decision about authorising the purchase. However, if the charge is an unusually large amount or exceeds the limit for their account, a supervisor may have to make a further programmed decision based on policies and procedures for this situation.

Most first-line managers' decisions and many middle managers' decisions are programmed. Top-level managers make few programmed decisions (see Fig. 5.2).

Non-programmed decisions **Non-programmed decisions** occur when predetermined decision rules are impractical due to novel and/or relatively unstructured situations (Bazerman 1986). Most significant decisions that managers make are non-programmed. Non-programmed decisions, because of their nature, usually involve considerable **uncertainty**, where the decision maker must choose a course of action with incomplete knowledge of the consequences of implementation.

Decisions made under uncertainty involve **risk**, the possibility that a chosen action could lead to losses rather than the results intended (Taylor 1984). Uncertainty can come from many sources. For example, environmental elements that are difficult to predict or control can affect the success of a decision. Cost and time constraints limit information collection. Social and political organisational factors, such as poor inter-unit communication, make gathering relevant information hard. Situations change rapidly, so current information quickly becomes obsolete (Weisman 1989). Partially to cope with rapid change and exchange-rate variations, Annette Roux, head of France-based Chantiers Bénéteau, opened a manufacturing plant in South Carolina to produce the company's line of pleasure craft (Bass 1983; Keren 1996).

The number of non-programmed decisions managers must make increases at each hierarchical level (see Fig. 5.2). Because these decisions need effective decision-making skills—and, frequently, creativity—they are the biggest managerial decision-making challenges. This chapter focuses mainly on non-programmed decisions.

non-programmed decisions

Decisions for which predetermined decision rules are impractical due to novel and/or ill-structured situations

uncertainty

A condition in which the decision maker must choose a course of action with incomplete knowledge of consequences following implementation

risk

The possibility a chosen action could lead to losses rather than intended results

Fig. 5.2   Relationship of decision-making situation to management level in organisations (adapted from Daft & Steers 1986, p. 440)

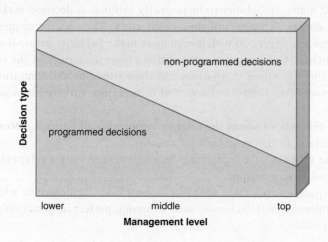

MANAGERS AS DECISION MAKERS

Because managers' decisions impact on organisation success, managerial approaches to decision making have been the subject of considerable research. In this section, we describe two major types of models of how managers make decisions: rational and non-rational.

The rational model

rational model

Model suggesting managers engage in completely rational decision processes, ultimately make optimal decisions, and possess and understand all information relevant to their decisions at the time they make them

The rational model of managerial decision making, popular in the first half of the 20th century, is based on economic theory of the firm. In developing theories about the economic behaviour of business firms, economists tended to make the basic assumption that managers would always make decisions in their firms' best economic interests. Many management theorists initially accepted this. According to the **rational model**, managers use totally rational decision processes, make optimal decisions, and have and understand all the information needed for decisions when making them (including all possible alternatives, potential outcomes and ramifications). If you recently purchased an item such as a personal computer or a car, you probably found it difficult obtaining perfect information and making an 'optimal' decision. As a result, the serious flaws in the rational managerial decision-making view (Simon 1955; 1956) will not surprise you. Nevertheless, it provides a reference point for comparison of actual managerial decision-making patterns.

Non-rational models

non-rational models

Models suggesting information-gathering and processing limitations make it difficult for managers to make optimal decisions

In contrast to the rational view, **non-rational models** of managerial decision making suggest that information-gathering and processing limitations make optimal decisions difficult for managers. Within the non-rational framework, researchers have identified three major models of decision making: satisficing, incremental and rubbish bin.

bounded rationality

Concept suggesting the ability of managers to be perfectly rational in making decisions is limited by factors such as cognitive capacity and time constraints

Satisficing model   During the 1950s Herbert Simon studied the behaviour of managerial decision makers. From his studies, Simon developed the concept of bounded rationality as a framework to understand actual managerial decision making (Bazerman 1986). **Bounded rationality** means that managers' ability to be perfectly rational in decision making is limited by factors such as cognitive capacity and time constraints. The concept suggests that some factors commonly limit the degree to which managers make perfectly rational decisions:

O Decision makers may have inadequate information about the nature of the issue to be decided and also about possible alternatives and their strengths and limitations.

O Time and cost factors often limit the amount of information gathered in regard to a particular decision.

O Decision makers' perceptions about the relative importance of various pieces of data may cause them to overlook or ignore critical information.

O The part of human memory used in making decisions retains only a relatively small amount of information at one time.

O The calculating capacities associated with intelligence limit the degree to which decision makers can determine optimal decisions, even assuming perfect information has been gathered (Huber 1980).

Rather than optimising their decisions, Simon argued, managers follow the **satisficing model,** which holds that managers seek alternatives only until they find one which looks satisfactory. Satisficing is best when the cost of delaying a decision or searching for a better alternative outweighs the likely payoff from such a course. For example, if one is driving on an unfamiliar road with little fuel left, it might be better to choose the petrol station in sight than wait for one's favourite brand. On the other hand, managers sometimes make a habit of using a simplistic satisficing approach even in situations where the cost of searching for further alternatives is justified given potential gain (Gupte 1988).

Incremental model   Another decision-making approach is the **incremental model,** which holds that managers make the smallest possible response to reduce the problem to a tolerable level (Huber 1980). This approach is geared more to achieving short-run alleviation of a problem than to making decisions facilitating long-term goal attainment. Like the satisficing model, the incremental model does not require managers to process a lot of information to take action. One researcher likened incrementalising to a homeowner's actions dealing with the problem of insufficient electric plugs by using various multi-outlet adapters. In the long run, the homeowner's incremental decisions may be unworkable, since additional electrical equipment (e.g. VCRs and personal computers) may cause fuses to blow (Cohen, March & Olsen 1972; Grandori 1984).

Rubbish-bin model   The **rubbish-bin model** of decision making holds that managers behave randomly in making non-programmed decisions. In other words, decision outcomes occur by chance, depending on those who happen to be involved, problems they happen to be concerned with at the moment, opportunities they happen to stumble upon, and favourite solutions available for a problem to solve. The rubbish-bin strategy is most likely when managers have no goal preferences, unclear means of achieving goals, and/or decision-making participants change rapidly (Weiner 1987; Kindel 1988; O'Neal 1988; *Economist* 1988). Desirable outcomes can sometimes be achieved with this strategy, but there can be serious difficulties.

Thus, while the rubbish-bin approach can lead managers to take advantage of unforeseen opportunities, it can also lead to severe problems. The rubbish-bin approach is often used in the absence of strategic management. (See Chapter 7 for a discussion of strategic management.)

STEPS IN AN EFFECTIVE DECISION-MAKING PROCESS

The models of managerial decision making just outlined are referred to as **descriptive decision-making models** because they try to document how managers actually make decisions. In contrast, models such as those outlined in Table 5.2 are referred to as **normative decision-making models,** as they try to prescribe how managers should make decisions. Decision-making experts note that managers are more likely to be effective decision makers if they follow the general approach in Table 5.2. Although following these steps does not guarantee all decisions will have the outcomes desired, it does increase the likelihood of success (Cowan 1986). While managers do not control many factors affecting the success of

satisficing model

Model stating managers seek alternatives only until they find one which looks satisfactory, rather than seeking an optimal decision

incremental model

Model stating managers make the smallest response possible to reduce the problem to at least a tolerable level

rubbish-bin model

Model stating managers behave in virtually a random way in making non-programmed decisions

descriptive decision-making models

Models of decision making attempting to document how managers actually make decisions

normative decision-making models

Models of decision making attempting to prescribe how managers should make decisions

Table 5.2   Steps in an effective decision making process

Step	Activities
Identify the problem	Scan the environment for changing circumstances
	Categorise the situation as a problem (or non-problem)
	Diagnose the problem's nature and causes
Generate alternative solutions	Restrict criticism of alternatives
	Freewheel to stimulate thinking
	Offer as many ideas as possible
	Combine and improve on ideas
Evaluate and choose an alternative	Evaluate feasibility
	Evaluate quality
	Evaluate acceptability
	Evaluate costs
	Evaluate reversibility
	Evaluate ethics
Implement and monitor the chosen solution	Plan the implementation of the solution
	Be sensitive to the decision's effects on others
	Develop follow-up mechanisms

their decisions, they do have substantial control over the process they use to make decisions. In this section, we discuss the four-step decision-making process in more detail.

Identifying the problem

The first step in decision making is identifying the problem. Part of identifying the problem, of course, is recognising one even exists. **Organisational problems** are discrepancies between a current state or condition and that desired. This step has three general stages: scanning, categorisation and diagnosis (Studer 1992; Fuhrman 1992).

Scanning stage   The scanning stage involves monitoring the work situation for changing circumstances signalling emergence of a problem. At this point, a manager may be only vaguely aware an environmental change could lead to a problem, or that an existing situation constitutes a problem. For example, during the 1970s, Swiss watchmakers noticed the appearance of inexpensive watches produced in Japan and Hong Kong (Taylor 1984).

Categorisation stage   The categorisation stage entails attempting to understand and verify signs that there is a discrepancy between the current state and that desired. At this point, the manager tries to categorise the situation as a problem or a non-problem, though it may be difficult to specify the exact nature of the situation. For example, sales of relatively expensive Swiss watches declined.

Diagnosis stage   The diagnosis stage involves gathering additional information and specifying both the nature and causes of the problem. Without appropriate diagnosis, it is hard to be successful in the rest of the decision process. At this stage the problem is to be stated in

organisational problems

Discrepancies between a current state or condition and what is desired

terms of the discrepancy between current conditions and those desired, and the causes of the discrepancy must be specified. At first, watchmakers thought cheaper watches would be a fad and soon disappear. By 1983, however, the situation had not improved, and Switzerland's two largest watchmakers, SSIH and Asuag, were deeply in debt. The two firms controlled several of the world's best-known watch brands—Omega, Longines, Tissot and Rado. It was clear that cheaper watches from Japan and Hong Kong were a serious threat to Swiss watchmakers. Banks holding debt for SSIH and Asuag called in Zurich-based management consultant Nicolas G. Hayek to help generate solutions.

Generating alternative solutions

The second step in decision-making is developing alternative solutions. This usually leads to higher-quality solutions (Osborn 1963), particularly when the situation needs creative and innovative ones. Development of alternatives can often be helped by **brainstorming**, a technique for enhancing creativity that encourages group members to generate as many novel ideas as possible on a given topic without evaluation. Four principles are involved:

1 Don't criticise ideas while generating possible solutions. Criticism during the idea-generation stage inhibits thinking. Also, as discussion tends to get bogged down when early ideas are criticised, only a few ideas are generated.

2 Freewheel. Offer even seemingly wild and outrageous ideas. Though they may never be used, they may trigger usable ideas from others.

3 Offer as many ideas as possible. Pushing for a high volume of ideas increases the probability some will be effective solutions.

4 Combine and improve on ideas already offered. Often the best ideas come from combinations of others (Maier 1963).

Although brainstorming is typically done in a group, individuals can use the principles too. For example, the manager jots down a number of possible solutions, including far-fetched ones, tries to generate a high volume of ideas, and combines or builds on the ideas. Brainstorming and other methods of generating ideas will be considered further when we discuss creativity later in this chapter.

It is important to emphasise that a number of alternatives should be generated during this phase of the decision-making process. For example, Hayek, the bankers, and the watch companies' heads developed several alternatives, such as liquidation, diversifying into other products, and merging the two companies and mounting an offensive against the overseas threat.

Evaluating and choosing an alternative

This step involves carefully considering the advantages and disadvantages of each alternative before choosing one. Each should be evaluated systematically according to six general criteria: feasibility, quality, acceptability, costs, reversibility and ethics.

Feasibility   The feasibility criterion refers to the extent to which an alternative can be accomplished within organisational constraints, such as time, budgets, technology and policies. Alternatives not meeting the feasibility criterion should be eliminated. In the case of the watch companies, at first they did not recognise the feasibility of fighting the overseas threat.

brainstorming

Technique encouraging group members to generate as many novel ideas as possible on a given topic without evaluating them

Quality   The quality criterion refers to how effectively an alternative solves the problem. Alternatives only partially solving the problem or representing a questionable solution are eliminated now.

Acceptability   This criterion refers to the degree to which decision makers and others who will be affected by the implementation of an alternative are willing to support it. Acceptability is recognised as an important criterion for assessing decisions (Gittler 1985).

Costs   The costs criterion refers both to resource levels required and the extent to which alternatives may have undesirable side effects. Thus 'costs' include not only direct monetary issues but also intangible issues such as possible competitor retaliation.

Reversibility   This criterion refers to the extent an alternative can be reversed, if at all. When the Coca-Cola Company had problems with its new formula for Coke, it reversed the decision by reintroducing the old formula as Coke Classic. Other decision types may be harder to reverse (*Forbes* 1995). In such cases, alternatives should be reconsidered carefully before selecting them. For example, liquidating the watchmakers would have been hard to reverse. Instead, the group decided to merge the two companies, creating the Swiss Corporation for Microelectronics and Watchmaking (known as SMH), with Hayek as chairman. SMH then launched an inexpensive, innovative plastic Swatch watch, assembled at low cost on a fully automated assembly line. By 1995, the company had sold more than 150 million Swatch timepieces and competed with Hattori Seiko of Japan to be the world's number-one watchmaker. Unlike its Japanese competitors, SMH also continues to produce both medium-priced and luxury watches (Stepp 1991a; 1991b).

Ethics   The ethics criterion refers to how compatible an alternative is with the organisation's social responsibilities and its managers' ethical standards. For instance, Hayek is a hero in Switzerland for saving the Swiss watchmaking industry and many jobs.

Implementing and monitoring the chosen solution

For successful decision making, managers must give a lot of thought to implementing and monitoring the chosen solution. A 'good' decision can be made in terms of the first three steps and the process can still fail because of difficulties at the final step.

Implementing the solution   Successful implementation depends on two main factors: careful planning and sensitivity to those involved in the process and/or affected by it.

In regard to planning, minor changes may need only a small amount of planning, but major changes may call for greater planning efforts such as written plans, co-ordination with units inside and outside the organisation, and special funding arrangements. In general, the more difficult a solution is to reverse, the more important it is to plan for effective implementation.

Implementation is also smoother when decision makers are sensitive to the reactions of those affected by the decision.

Monitoring the solution   Managers must monitor decision implementation to ensure progress is as planned and the problem triggering the decision-making process is resolved. The more important the problem, the greater the need for follow-up.

To fly or not to fly

The Y2K bug scare is now well in the past. However, not so long ago, major world airlines were making decisions whether to carry out normally scheduled flights during the dreaded 31 December 1999. As early as September, Ansett Australia announced that it would cancel domestic and international services for 13 hours from 11 pm on 31 December to noon on 1 January 2000. The reason for these actions was given as lack of demand during those periods.

Qantas and Air New Zealand indicated that they would be operating but with a reduced schedule. Again lack of demand was given as the reason.

Many experts questioned about the levels of preparedness of various key organisations were optimistic that all would go well. However, most of them admitted that they were making plans for contingencies, divulging a less optimistic personal view.

Source: Adapted from Head (1999).

Activities for discussion, analysis and further research

1 Put yourself in the place of one of the 455 'experts' interviewed for this article and analyse the two levels of decisions that were made—the professional and the personal. Which one might you have made at that time? Why?

2 Obviously hindsight is 20/20. Or is it? There is still uncertainty as to whether the Y2K bug was a big hype or whether we managed to avoid the problems by reacting promptly and properly to a threat. If you were requested to answer this by your manager, regarding your organisation, how would you go about finding an answer?

OVERCOMING BARRIERS TO EFFECTIVE DECISION MAKING

Unfortunately, as non-rational managerial decision-making models suggest, managers do not often follow the four-step process outlined. Despite this general approach being supported by experts in the field, managers may be unaware of it. As well, there are barriers to effective decision making. In this section, we discuss how to overcome four key decision-making barriers: accepting the problem challenge in the first place, searching for sufficient alternatives, recognising common decision-making biases, and avoiding the decision-escalation phenomenon.

Accepting the problem challenge

Researchers have identified four basic reaction patterns in the behaviour of individuals faced with a problem in the form of a difficulty or an opportunity. The first three—complacency, defensive avoidance and panic—are barriers to effective decision making. The fourth—deciding to decide—is a more effective approach for decision makers (Keinan 1987).

complacency

Condition in which individuals either do not see signs of danger or opportunity or ignore them

Complacency   **Complacency** occurs when individuals either do not see the danger or opportunity signs or ignore them. With complacency, failure to detect signs usually comes from poor environmental scanning. Ignoring signs is the 'ostrich' effect—putting one's head in the sand and hoping the danger or opportunity will fix itself. Complacency can occur even when someone seems to be responding. For example, an individual may immediately accept a job offer which seems a good opportunity, without devoting time or effort to properly assessing the situation.

defensive avoidance

Condition in which individuals either deny the importance of a danger or an opportunity or deny any responsibility for taking action

Defensive avoidance   With **defensive avoidance**, individuals deny the importance of a danger or an opportunity or deny responsibility for taking action. Defensive avoidance has three forms: rationalisation ('It can't happen to me'), procrastination ('It can be taken care of later'), or buck-passing ('It's someone else's problem'). All three forms came into play when Barings Bank officials in London ignored warning signs that their Singapore-based derivatives trader, 28-year-old Nicholas Leeson, was taking unwarranted risks leading to losses of more than $1 billion and the bank's collapse. Investigation showed bank officials had 'failed to follow up on a number of warning signals over a prolonged period'. Among the signals were unrealistically high profitability levels; unusually high funding to finance the Singapore office's trades; and earlier auditing reports which were never acted upon because of warring factions within the bank, showing controls were lax. Leeson was sentenced to 6½ years in prison on two fraud charges (Barbash 1995; *Washington Post* 1995).

panic

Reaction in which individuals become so upset they frantically seek a way to solve a problem

Panic   With **panic** or panic-like reactions, individuals become upset, frantically seeking a way to solve a problem. They hastily seize a quickly formulated alternative without seeing its severe disadvantages and not considering other, possibly better, alternatives. Panic is more likely with crisis problems (Nutt 1984).

deciding to decide

Response in which decision makers accept the challenge of deciding what to do about a problem and follow an effective decision-making process

Deciding to decide   With a **deciding-to-decide** response, decision makers accept the challenge of deciding what to do about a problem and follow effective decision-making processes. Deciding to decide is important in a legitimate problem situation. Of course, managers cannot attend to every potential problem, no matter how minor and remote, that appears on the horizon. Some guidelines are presented in Table 5.3.

Table 5.3   Guidelines for deciding to decide

Appraise credibility of information
Is the source in a position to know the truth?
If so, is the source likely to be honest?
Is there any evidence, and how good is it?
Ascertain importance of threat or opportunity
How likely is a real danger or opportunity?
If a threat, how severe might the losses be?
If an opportunity, how great might the gains be?
Determine the need for urgency
Is the threat or opportunity likely to occur soon?
Will it develop gradually, or is sudden change likely?
If some action is urgent, can part be done now and the rest later?

Source: Adapted from Wheeler & Janis (1980, pp. 34–5).

Searching for sufficient alternatives

For many decision situations, particularly non-programmed ones, it is impossible for decision makers to identify all potential alternatives and assess all possible pluses and minuses. Information acquisition is limited because of time and money. There are costs even when information gathering is simply checking with other organisation members are having a meeting. As a result, decision makers must decide how much time, effort and money to spend collecting information to help make a decision.

This information-gathering dilemma is shown in Figure 5.3. The horizontal axis indicates potential information about the decision, from 0 to 100 per cent. The vertical axis depicts the value and cost of additional information. As indicated by line a, as a decision maker collects more and more information, the value of additional information levels off. At the same time, as shown by line b, the cost of additional information during the initial search is not high but gets higher as one moves to obtaining perfect information. As a result the marginal, or incremental, value of additional pieces of information (line c) rises to an optimal point then declines as cost exceeds value for additional pieces of information. The area of optimal information gathering is shown.

Decision makers' efforts tend to be below the zone of cost effectiveness in identifying potential alternatives. For example, one study of 78 decision-making situations found little or no search for viable alternatives in 85 per cent of cases. Instead, decision makers copied another's solution, accepted a consultant's off-the-shelf solution, or seized on an idea of unknown or debatable value and tried to find support for it. Even in 15 per cent of cases where a deliberate effort to develop alternatives was made, the search process was cut off after a few possibilities were identified (McKean 1985). The tendency to skip or cut short the search for alternatives stifles innovation. Some approaches helpful in generating decision alternatives will be discussed later in the section on creativity. Of course, in many cases, managers may feel the time and effort involved identifying multiple alternatives is unwarranted.

Fig. 5.3   The cost of additional information (adapted from Harrison 1987, p. 47)

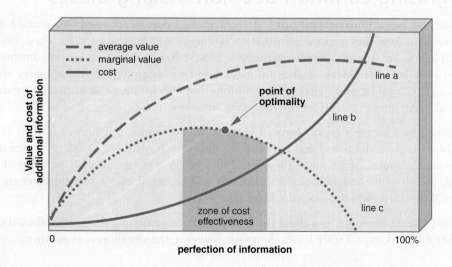

✖ On to the next thing

The name 'Red Earth' has been a familiar one on the Australian scene. For those in the cosmetics retail business, it conjures visions of exciting stock at high prices with a strong level of customer loyalty. At least it did, until February 1998.

The managing director of the Australian operations, Nick Chadwick, took over this position in June 1997, at the request of his equity partners. However, though being a great entrepreneur and innovative thinker, he was poor on detail, management, systems forecasting and stock control. Furthermore, he surrounded himself with people who did not challenge him. By the end of the Christmas period, the company showed a loss of A$1 million. So in January 1998, his partners sacked him and he lost his share of the company.

As a result of dramatic changes to the quality of the stock and its packaging, and to the pricing of stock, previously loyal customers are deserting in droves. In spite of feedback from the stores, service by the parent company is not improving. Products are being recalled, stock does not get delivered on time, and the range is decreasing. Many franchisees are in a situation where they have invested A$250 000 for the franchise and now have an asset which they cannot sell. Some are considering whether to start a class action or to attempt mediation.

Source: Gome, A. (1999).

Reflection point

1   Look up and read the complete report: Gome, A. (1999), 'The brand that fell to earth', *Business Review Weekly*, 11 June, pp. 98–103. Consider the issues for the franchisees. Think about contacting one in your local area and interviewing them. What factors are affecting their decision about whether to start a class action?

Decision point

1   Access the web site for Red Earth and seek information about purchasing a franchise. What factors would you take into consideration in order to make an appropriate decision?

Recognising common decision-making biases

Kahneman and Tversky, investigating how decision makers operate, pointed out several biases characteristic of how they process information (Dunegan 1993; Slovic 1995). These biases, explained below, are framing, representativeness, availability, and anchoring and adjustment. A related issue is the tendency of decision makers to be over confident. These biases affect decision makers' evaluation of alternative solutions, but also influence identification of difficulties and opportunities. Consider the following situation:

> Threatened by a superior enemy force, a general has a dilemma. Intelligence officers say his soldiers will be ambushed and 600 will die unless he leads them to safety by one of two available routes. If he takes the first, 200 soldiers will be saved. If he takes the second, there's a one-third chance 600 soldiers will be saved and a two-thirds chance none will be saved. Which route should he take?

If you are like most people, you chose the first alternative, reasoning the general should save 200 rather than risk even higher losses. Suppose, however, the situation is as follows:

The general again has to choose between two escape routes. But this time his aides tell him if he takes the first, 400 soldiers will die. If he takes the second, there's a one-third chance no soldiers will die and a two-thirds chance 600 soldiers will die. Which route should he take?

In this situation, most argue the general should take the second route. Their rationale is that with the first route, 400 will certainly be dead. With the second there is at least a one-third chance no one will die, and casualties will only be 50 per cent higher if the scheme fails.

Interestingly, most people draw one conclusion from the first problem and the opposite conclusion from the second problem. In the first problem, people favour the first alternative 3 to 1; in the second problem, they choose the second alternative 4 to 1. Yet a closer look reveals the problems in both cases are exactly the same: just stated differently. The first problem is stated in terms of lives saved, the second in terms of lives lost. The tendency to make different decisions depending on how a problem is presented is called **framing**.

To explain the paradoxical decision pattern exhibited in the general's dilemmas, Kahneman and Tversky (Bundescu & Weiss 1987; Fagley & Miller 1987; Neal, Huber & Northcraft 1987; Rachlin1989; Jegers 1991) developed **prospect theory**. Based on the belief that decision makers tend to be 'loss averse', prospect theory argues that they find the prospect of an actual loss more painful than giving up the possibility of a gain. Some industries seem to understand prospect theory. So customers may receive 'discounts for cash' rather than being charged 'credit surcharges' for using credit cards. Prospect theory suggests customers may be less willing to pay an extra charge for using credit cards (an actual loss) than they are to forgo a discount for paying cash (a potential gain). Even so, the system draws complaints from credit customers (Southerland 1994).

Linda is 31, single, outspoken and very bright. She majored in philosophy at university. As a student, she was deeply concerned with discrimination and other social issues and participated in anti-nuclear demonstrations. Which of the following statements is more likely?
1 Linda is a bank teller.
2 Linda is a bank teller and active in the feminist movement.

Most people decide that Linda is a bank teller and a feminist. Actually, however, the laws of probability suggest an occurrence (bank teller) is more likely on its own than in conjunction with another occurrence (bank teller and feminist). The Linda problem illustrates a common decision shortcut called **representativeness**, the tendency to be overly influenced by stereotypes in making judgments about the likelihood of occurrences. We increase the odds of decision-making difficulties when judgments run counter to the laws of probability.

In a typical English text, does the letter 'K' appear more often as the first letter in a word or as the third letter?

People generally judge the letter 'K' more likely to be the first letter in a word even though it is almost twice as likely to appear in the third position. We do this because of the bias of **availability**, the tendency to judge the likelihood of an occurrence on the basis of the extent to which other like instances or occurrences can be recalled easily. In this case, it is easier to recall words beginning with the letter 'K' than words in which 'K' is the third letter. Availability also shows in tendencies to overestimate likelihood of deaths due to vividly imaginable

framing

Tendency to make different decisions depending on how a problem is presented

prospect theory

Theory positing that decision makers find the prospect of an actual loss more painful than giving up the possibility of a gain

representativeness

Tendency to be overly influenced by stereotypes in making judgments about the likelihood of occurrences

availability

Tendency to judge the likelihood of an occurrence on the basis of the extent to which other like instances or occurrences can easily be recalled

causes such as aeroplane accidents, fires and murder and to underestimate more common, but less spectacular, causes such as emphysema and stroke (Lichtenstein, Slovic, Fischoff, Layman & Combs 1978). Managers fall victim to availability bias in many ways. For example, they may base annual performance appraisals on subordinates' most recent and easily recalled performance. Other examples are judging how well competitors' products are doing by the extent to which they have seen them in use, and gauging employee morale by relying on immediate subordinates' views.

A newly hired engineer for a computer firm in the Sydney metropolitan area has four years' experience and good all-around qualifications. When asked to estimate a starting salary for this employee, a chemist with very little knowledge of the profession or industry guessed an annual salary of $27 000. What is your estimate? (Bazerman 1986).

Most people do not think the chemist's guess influences their own estimate. Yet people tend to give higher salary estimates when the chemist's estimate is $60 000 than when it is $27 000. The tendency to be influenced by an initial figure, even when it is largely irrelevant, is known as **anchoring and adjustment**. For example, employers often ask a job candidate about their current salary and then use this as a basis for an offer, even though they may be under- or over-paid.

These information-processing biases suggest that decision makers should be cautious about the accuracy of their estimates regarding event likelihood. Evidence suggests that decision makers are often **overconfident**, tending to be more certain of judgments about a future event's likelihood than actual predictive accuracy warrants (Bazerman 1986). Ironically, overconfidence appears most likely when decision makers are working in unfamiliar areas (Schine 1995). This stems from a failure to fully understand potential pitfalls involved. Thus managers may be particularly susceptible to overconfidence when they are planning moves into new, unfamiliar areas of business (Koriat, Lichtenstein & Fischoff 1980).

Managers can avoid some ill effects of information-processing biases by being aware of how their judgments can be affected (Barney & Griffin 1992). Gathering enough information to be fairly well versed about issues associated with important decisions is helpful. In addition, decision makers should think about why their judgments might be wrong or far off target. Such thinking helps reveal contradictions and inaccuracies. Evidence suggests decision making also is influenced by other factors, such as emotions, habits and motivation about the subject (Keren 1996). Some quantitative methods to help decision makers are covered in this chapter's supplement.

anchoring and adjustment

Tendency to be influenced by an initial figure, even when the information is largely irrelevant

overconfident

Tending to be more certain of judgments regarding the likelihood of a future event than one's actual predictive accuracy warrants

Avoiding the decision-escalation phenomenon

When a manager makes a decision, it is often only one in a series about a particular issue. Further decisions may be necessary, depending on previous results. For example, suppose you hire a new employee because you expect they will be an excellent performer. However, after several months it is clear they are not performing acceptably. Should you fire them? Of course, you have invested considerable time and money training the new employee, and it is possible they are still learning the job. So you spend more time helping the worker, providing further training. Even with these additional inputs, two months later their performance is still not acceptable. What do you do now? Although there is more reason to 'cut your losses', you also have even more invested in making them productive. When do you discontinue your 'invest-ment'? (Bazerman 1986).

Decision situations like this present dilemmas for managers. Substantial costs have been incurred because of the earlier decision. On the other hand, future actions can either reverse the situation or compound initial losses. Such situations are referred to as **escalation situations**, as they signal a strong possibility of escalating commitment and greater losses (Ross & Staw 1993).

Research indicates that when managers incur costs for an initial decision, they often react by giving more resources to the situation even when prospects for improvement are dim. These situations become non-rational escalation. **Non-rational escalation,** or the escalation phenome-non, is the tendency to increase commitment to a previously selected course of action beyond that expected if an effective decision-making process was followed (Bowen 1987). As economists and accountants warn, previously incurred costs (e.g. time and money) are **sunk costs**. Such costs, once incurred, are not recoverable and should not be considered in future courses of action. Yet decision makers are often influenced by prior costs when they have made the initial decisions.

Part of the reason for the escalation phenomenon is that decision makers are loss-averse and reluctant to write off sunk costs. Thus the tendency may be related to prospect theory, discussed before. In addition, the decision maker may be concerned that changing the course of action may cause others to see the original decision as a mistake or failure. Methods of avoiding non-rational escalation include setting advance limits on how far to extend commit-ment, asking tough questions about why the commitment is being continued, reviewing costs involved, and watching for escalation situations constituting commitment traps (Rubin 1980; Brockner 1992).

escalation situations

Situations signalling a strong possibility of escalating commitment and accelerating losses

non-rational escalation

Tendency to increase commitment to a previously selected course of action beyond the level expected if the manager followed an effective decision-making process; also called escalation phenomenon

sunk costs

Costs which, once incurred, are not recoverable and should not enter into considerations of future courses of action

MANAGING DIVERSITY: GROUP DECISION MAKING

Major decisions in organisations are most often made by more than one person in order to take advantage of a diversity of outlooks (Gentile 1994). For instance, Gencorp Automotive geared its new reinforced plastics plant to run with just three levels: plant manager, team leaders, and 25 teams of 5 to 15 production workers. Each team makes most decisions involving its work area (Fowler 1988). In this section, we consider the advantages and disad-vantages of group decision making, as well as ways to enhance group decision-making processes (Huber 1980; Maier 1989).

Advantages and disadvantages of group decision making

Group decision making has several advantages over individual decision making. These advan-tages are summarised in Table 5.4. According to a study of more than 200 project teams involved in management-education courses, groups outperformed their most proficient group member 97 per cent of the time. In a group a diversity of ideas is brought to bear on a problem (Michaelsen, Watson & Black 1989).

Despite its advantages, group decision making also has several potential disadvantages in contrast with individual decision making. These are summarised in Table 5.4. One—group-think—requires further discussion.

Table 5.4   Advantages and disadvantages of group decision making

Advantages
1 More information and knowledge is focused on the issue.
2 An increased number and diversity of alternatives can be developed.
3 Greater understanding and acceptance of the final decision are likely.
4 Members develop knowledge and skills for future use.

Disadvantages
1 It is usually more time-consuming.
2 Disagreements may delay decisions and cause hard feelings.
3 One or a few group members may dominate the discussion.
4 Groupthink may cause members to overemphasise achieving agreement.

groupthink

Tendency of cohesive groups to seek agreement about an issue at the expense of realistically appraising the situation

Groupthink is the tendency of cohesive groups to seek agreement about an issue at the expense of realistically appraising the situation (Janis 1982). According to the theory of groupthink, group members are concerned about preserving group cohesion so they are reluctant to cause disagreements or provide information and unsettle discussion. National Aeronautics and Space Administration (NASA) officials and others attributed the Challenger tragedy to groupthink. Despite receiving contrary information, upper-level officials at NASA and at Morton Thiokol, the company making the solid rocket boosters, decided to go ahead with the mission. They ignored information from Morton Thiokol engineers and others about possible malfunctions due to unusually cold weather conditions. All seven crew were killed in the explosion at takeoff (Kruglanski 1986). Recent research suggests groupthink occurs even when groups are not highly cohesive, if the group leader early in the discussion has stated a particular preference (Aldag & Fuller 1994; Mullen, Anthony, Salas & Driskell 1994). Other researchers have criticised the groupthink concept, arguing that group decision making is more complex than groupthink suggests (Watson, Kumar & Michaelson 1993). Still, the groupthink idea may be useful in highlighting the need to follow an effective decision-making process, as outlined before, when operating in groups.

Enhancing group decision-making processes

Managers can take steps to help not only avoid the major pitfalls of group decision making but also reap its advantages. One step is involving the group in decisions when the group's information and knowledge are important to decision quality. That way, the time taken for group decision making can be justified.

Group design or composition is another factor in enhancing group decision making. For example, there is evidence that membership diversity improves group performance. In one study, culturally homogeneous groups (all members of the same national and ethnic background) initially performed more effectively than culturally heterogeneous ones (members from different national and ethnic backgrounds) (Ancona & Caldwell 1992; Jackson & Associates 1992). Over time, however, the heterogeneous groups caught up with, then surpassed, the performance of the homogeneous groups. Data showed heterogeneous groups had difficulty interacting effectively at first, but gradually learned to capitalise on diverse group perspectives (Zaheer 1995). With increasing workforce diversity and business globalisation, managers must be able to handle group dynamics to reap the available benefits of diversity (we discuss this issue further in Chapter 15) (Watson et al. 1993).

Another way of enhancing group decision-making involves other aspects of group composition. For example, including individuals who are likely to concentrate on major organisational goals can help overcome any tendency to self-interest (Browning 1994). Including someone skilled at encouraging the ideas of others can reduce problems caused by dominant individuals.

Yet another step facilitating group decision making is setting up specific mechanisms to avoid groupthink. For instance, managers may designate one or more **devil's advocates**— individuals who ensure negative aspects of attractive decision alternatives are considered. Managers can also encourage the group to use **dialectical inquiry**, a procedure where a decision situation is approached from two opposite points of view (Wheeler & Janis 1980; Schwenk 1990; Schwenk & Valacich 1994).

Computer-assisted group decision making

Advances in information technology can enhance group decision making with the assistance of computers. One method is teleconferencing—simultaneous communication among groups of individuals by telephone or via computer with specially designed software (Laudon & Price 1994). Such software is **groupware**, which is designed to support the collaborative efforts of group members, such as scheduling meetings, holding meetings, collaborating on projects and sharing documents. Group decision making can be aided by specialised computer-based information or group decision-support systems, which help decision makers work together on poorly structured problems. (See Chapters 14 and 19.) Groupware aims to help group member communication, where group decision-support systems focus more on a group actually making a decision.

Because using computers to assist decision making is fairly new, applicable research is just emerging (Hollinghead & McGrath 1995; Guzzo & Dickson 1996). Early results suggest computer-assisted groups interact and exchange to a lesser degree than face-to-face groups and take longer to complete their work. The performance impact appears to depend on the task. Computer assistance seems to help groups generate better ideas. On the other hand, face-to-face groups appear to perform better solving difficult problems and particularly resolving major conflicts. One analysis of 13 computer-assisted group decision-making studies suggested that consensus regarding the decision decreases, as does satisfaction with the process itself. It appears face-to-face meetings may be better when there are major opinion differences among group members and commitment of group members is critical to

devil's advocates

Individuals assigned the role of making sure negative aspects of any attractive decision alternatives are considered

dialectical inquiry

Procedure in which a decision situation is approached from two opposite points of view

groupware

Software designed to support collaborative efforts among group members, such as scheduling meetings, holding meetings, collaborating on projects and sharing documents successfully implementing the result. This could change as groupware and group decision-support systems improve and better studies assess circumstances under which computer assistance is helpful (McLeod 1996).

Computer assistance seems to aid generation of more creative ideas and may be useful during decision-making phases when creativity is important. Creativity is essential to decision-making because it generates novel alternatives leading to innovation and fosters unique perspectives on the nature of problems. In the next section, we discuss ways to encourage greater creativity in individuals and groups.

@ Bill paying online

managing the e-challenge

Microsoft and America Online have been waging war across a range of online services, from shopping to instant messaging, with the aim of building a dominant position in electronic commerce and communications. Internet bill-paying is expected to be a major battlefield because it is a way of locking in consumers and encouraging them to use other services.

Consumers can use the service to pay bills such as electricity and gas and fuel charges through an electronic fund transfer managed over the Internet. As consumers gain confidence in the technology, particularly the security precautions, the market is expected to take off.

Consumers will become more comfortable with the Internet as a transactional medium, not merely as an informational medium. For online hubs such as Microsoft's MSN network of Web sites, AOL and Yahoo Inc., online bill-paying is very attractive and potentially lucrative.

Source: Adapted from Blomberg, N. (1999).

Activities for discussion, analysis and further research

1 If you were going to consider paying your bills online, what factors would you take into consideration in order to make the decision? Having listed those factors, compare the list to the formal decision making process outlined in this chapter.

PROMOTING INNOVATION: THE CREATIVITY FACTOR IN DECISION MAKING

creativity

Cognitive process of developing an idea, concept, commodity or discovery viewed as novel by its creator or a target audience

Creativity is the cognitive process of developing an idea, concept, commodity or discovery viewed as novel by its creator or a target audience (Bazerman 1986). Hence creativity is identified by assessing outcomes (Amabile 1983). In fact, Amabile (Kohn 1987, p. 54) argues, 'Creativity is not a quality of a person; it is a quality of ideas, of behaviours, or products'. Creativity is crucial to solving problems in ways resulting in organisational innovations. As worldwide competition increases, greater emphasis is placed on creativity. Japan, particularly, works to overcome a reputation as a copycat of other countries' technology through increased creativity. For example, at Matsushita Electronics Corporation, semiconductor executives wear badges stating 'Create'. At Nippon Electric Company (NEC), posters and placards encourage workers to 'invent the new VCR' and offer $100 awards for creative ideas (Bylinski 1987, p. 43).

Try the classic creativity problem shown in Figure 5.4. Then look at Figure 5.5, which shows some solutions. Many people cannot solve the nine-dot problem because they assume lines cannot go outside the dots. As the problem shows, creativity needs both convergent and divergent thinking. **Convergent thinking** is solving problems by beginning with a problem then moving logically to a solution. One might compare convergent thinking to searching for oil by digging an ever bigger and deeper hole (de Bono 1968). **Divergent thinking**, on the other hand, is solving problems by generating new ways of viewing a problem and seeking novel alternatives. Rather than digging in the same hole, a divergent thinker digs in different places to generate new perspectives. In creativity, convergent thinking helps define a problem and evaluate possible solutions. Divergent thinking helps develop alternative views of problems, as well as seek novel ways of dealing with them. In this section, we examine the basic ingredients of creativity, describe stages in the creative process, and offer techniques for enhancing group creativity for managers.

convergent thinking

Effort to solve problems by beginning with a problem and attempting to move logically to a solution

divergent thinking

Effort to solve problems by generating new ways of viewing a problem and seeking novel alternatives

Fig. 5.4   The nine-dot problem. Without lifting your pencil from the paper, draw no more than four straight lines that will cross through all nine dots

Basic ingredients

According to Amabile (1983), the following three basic ingredients are necessary for creativity.

Domain-relevant skills   These skills come from expertise in a relevant field. They include related technical skills or artistic ability, talent in the area and factual knowledge.

Creativity-relevant skills   These skills include a cognitive style, or method, of thinking oriented to exploring new directions; knowledge of approaches used for generating novel ideas; and a work style conducive to developing creative ideas. A creative work style is characterised by an ability to concentrate effort and attention for long periods of time, the ability to abandon unproductive avenues, persistence and high energy level.

Fig. 5.5   Some possible solutions to the nine-dot problem (based on Adams, reprinted from Papalia & Olds 1985, p. 297)

This puzzle is difficult to solve if the imaginary boundary (limit) enclosing the nine dots is not exceeded. A surprising number of people will not exceed the imaginary boundary, for often this constraint is unconsciously in the mind of the problem-solver, even though it is not in the definition of the problem at all. The overly strict limits are a block in the mind of the solver. The widespread nature of this block is what makes this puzzle classic (Adams 1980, p. 24).

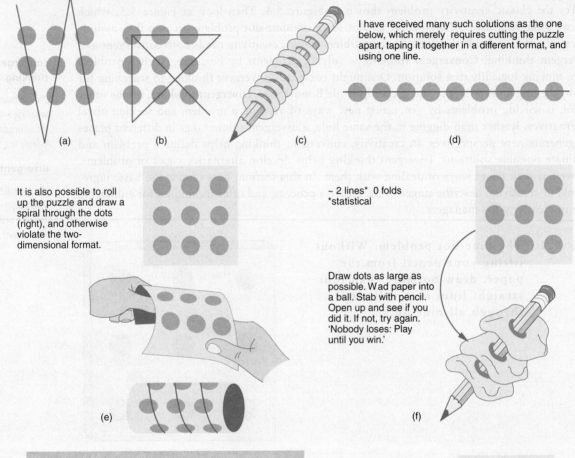

(a)   (b)   (c)

I have received many such solutions as the one below, which merely requires cutting the puzzle apart, taping it together in a different format, and using one line.

(d)

It is also possible to roll up the puzzle and draw a spiral through the dots (right), and otherwise violate the two-dimensional format.

~ 2 lines* 0 folds
*statistical

Draw dots as large as possible. Wad paper into a ball. Stab with pencil. Open up and see if you did it. If not, try again. 'Nobody loses: Play until you win.'

(e)   (f)

30 May, 1994
6 Rowan Road
Frankston, Vic

Dear Prof. James Adams,
    My dad and I were doing Puzzles from 'Conceptual Blockbusting'. We were mostly working on the dot ones, like ⋮⋮⋮ My dad said a man found a way to do it with one line. I tried and did it. Not with folding, but I used a fat line. It doesnt say you can't use a fat line.

    Like this

    ▬▬▬ ←

Sincerely,
Cathy Bush
age: 10

PS actually you need a very fat writing apparatus

(g)

1 line 0 folds

Lay the paper on the surface of the Earth. Circumnavigate the globe twice + a few centimetres, displacing a little each time so as to pass through the next row on each circuit as you 'Go West, young man'.

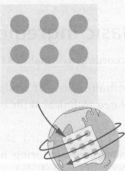

(h)

Click for fresh fruit

At 8.30 every morning, Desmond Lee (26), Adrian Lee (26) and Keith Tan (25) are at the Pasir Panjang wholesale centre in Singapore looking for the freshest produce they can find.

Having received orders over the Internet earlier in the day, they package and deliver the orders personally to your doorstep.

How did they get into this? Well, they were inspired by tales of successful online retail stores overseas. Investing their combined savings of S$40 000 they purchased a delivery van, bought a computer, and rented a small office to operate from. Placing advertisements on the web was one way of attracting attention, the other way was very 'low-tech': they distributed notices by hand into people's mailboxes. This paid off. In their first two months of operations they sold S$20 000 worth of produce.

How did they make the decisions as to the type of enterprise to start? Investigating their environment, they found that people liked the convenience as well as the certainty that they would get really fresh produce. Their target—people who want the best quality.

Source: Adapted from Koh, L. (2000).

Outdoor advertisements such as this one demonstrate that the managers of FRESHdirect have assessed their target markets and made decisions on the most effective ways of spending money to reach them.

Activities for discussion, analysis and further research

1 Log onto www.freshdirect.com.sg and explore the range offered to customers. Think about the factors the three might have needed to consider before embarking on this venture.

2 What were the risks they took? Compare the risk factor with the uncertainty factor. Would you have done it? Why?

3 In what way have these three young people gained an edge?

Task motivation The individual must be genuinely interested in the task for its own sake, rather than because of some external reward possibility, such as money. Recent evidence suggests primary concern with external rewards tends to inhibit creativity. For example, a scientist attempting to develop a new drug to obtain a bonus or prize is unlikely to be as creative as a scientist whose primary interest is learning more about a promising new direction (Amabile 1983). For some ideas on boosting your creativity, see the Management skills for the 21st century discussion, 'How to be more creative'.

 # How to be more creative

Some of the following suggestions, which are based on research and thinking on creativity, may help you be more creative in work and daily life.

What do you want to do?

○ Take time to understand a problem before beginning trying to solve it.
○ Get all facts clearly in mind.
○ Identify facts which seem to be most important before you try to work out a detailed solution.

How can you do it?

○ Set aside a sizeable block of time to focus on a particular problem, rather than attending to it in scattered sessions.
○ Work out a plan for attacking the problem.
○ Establish subgoals. Solve part of the problem and go from there. You don't have to do everything at once. Write out your thoughts. This allows you to capture important points and to come back to them later. It also allows you to look for patterns.
○ Imagine yourself acting out the problem. Actually act out the problem.
○ Think of a similar problem you've solved in the past and build on the strategy you used then.
○ Use analogies whenever possible. See whether you can generalise from a similar situation to your current problem.
○ Use several different problem-solving strategies—verbal, visual, mathematical, acting. Draw a diagram to help you visualise the problem, or talk to yourself out loud, or 'walk through' a situation.
○ Look for relationships among various facts.
○ Trust your intuition. Take a guess and see whether you can back it up.
○ Play with ideas and possible approaches. Try looking at the same situation in a number of different ways.

How can you do it better?

○ Try consciously to be original, to come up with new ideas.
○ Don't worry about looking foolish if you say or suggest something unusual or if you come up with the wrong answer.
○ Eliminate cultural taboos in your thinking (such as gender stereotyping) which might interfere with your ability to come up with a novel solution.
○ Try to be right the first time, but if you're not, explore as many alternatives as you need to.
○ Keep an open mind. If your initial approach doesn't work, ask whether you made assumptions that might be untrue.
○ If you get stuck on one approach, try to get to the solution by another route.
○ Be alert to odd or puzzling facts. If you can explain them, your solution may be at hand.
○ Think of unconventional ways to use objects and the environment. Look at familiar things as if you've never seen them before.

○ Consider taking a detour, which delays your goal but eventually leads to it.
○ Discard habitual ways of doing things, and force yourself to figure out new ways.
○ Do some brainstorming with one or more other people. This involves trying to produce as many new and original ideas as possible, without evaluating any of them until the end of the session.
○ Strive for objectivity. Evaluate your own ideas as you would those of a stranger.

Source: Reprinted from Papalia & Olds (1988).

Stages of creativity

The creativity process involves several stages. A commonly used model of creativity has four stages (Haefele 1962; Bazerman 1986), shown in Figure 5.6 and described below.

Fig. 5.6   Stages of creativity

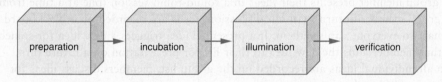

Preparation   This stage involves gathering initial information, defining the problem or task needing creativity, generating alternatives, and seeking and carefully analysing data related to the problem. At this stage, the person becomes immersed in every aspect of the problem. For complex technical problems, this may take months or years.

Incubation   This stage of creativity involves subconscious mental activity and divergent thinking to explore unusual alternatives. During this stage, the person generally does not consciously focus on the problem, allowing the subconscious to work on a solution.

Illumination   At this stage, a new insight is achieved, often by a sudden breakthrough in 'eureka' fashion.

Verification   This stage involves testing ideas to determine the insight's validity. At this point, convergent, logical thinking evaluates the solution. If the solution is not feasible, cycling back through all or some of the previous stages may be needed.

Techniques for enhancing group creativity

Whereas the preceding section looked at an individual's creative efforts, this section examines techniques to enhance group creativity. Two major techniques are brainstorming and the nominal group technique. (We discuss two other methods to enhance group creativity, the Delphi method and scenario analysis, in this chapter's Supplement.)

Brainstorming The brainstorming technique encourages group members to generate as many novel ideas as possible on a given topic without evaluation. The four basic rules—do not criticise during idea generation, freewheel, offer many ideas, and improve on ideas already offered—were discussed before. Recent research suggests computer-assisted brainstorming is better than face-to-face brainstorming in idea generation. This seems to be because there is more time for idea production because members offer ideas at the same time rather than having to listen to others or wait for them to stop speaking before offering an idea (Gallupe, Cooper, Grise & Bastianutti 1994).

nominal group technique (NGT)

Technique integrating both individual work and group interaction within certain ground rules

Nominal group technique The **nominal group technique** (NGT) enhances creativity and decision making by integrating individual work and group interaction within ground rules. The technique was developed to foster individual, as well as group, creativity and to overcome the tendency to criticise ideas when offered. The ground rules, or steps, of NGT are as follows:

1 Individual members independently prepare lists of their ideas on a problem.
2 Each group member presents their ideas in a round-robin session (one at a time from each group member in turn) without discussion. Ideas are recorded on a blackboard or flip chart so everyone can see them. If a presented idea triggers a new idea for someone else, that member adds the new idea to their list for presentation on a future turn.
3 When all individual ideas are recorded on the group list, members discuss ideas for clarification and evaluation purposes.
4 Members silently and independently vote on the ideas, using a rank-ordering or rating procedure. The final outcome is determined by pooling individual votes (Delbecq, Van de Ven & Gustafson 1975; Huber 1980).

Evidence generally supports NGT's effectiveness in developing large numbers of alternatives while maintaining group satisfaction. There is evidence NGT may be more effective than brainstorming at generating ideas when groups operate face-to-face, but less effective than computer-assisted brainstorming (Van de Ven & Delbecq 1974; Dennis & Valacich 1994).

Thus there are a number of means managers can use to encourage creativity and innovation at work. While this chapter has focused on understanding various aspects of organisational decision processes, the Supplement to this chapter highlights specific tools to assist organisation members in planning and decision making.

■ The MD's diary   the reflective practitioner

I would like to think that most decisions in the organisation are made in the team environment. I say this while realising that there always remains the need for a final point of arbitration, and in this organisation that rests with me.

However, generally decisions are not reached unilaterally, but through the broad involvement of all the stakeholders.

People, hopefully, are given a clear indication of their levels of authority. There are guidelines on how they operate and hopefully, clear agreement as to what the desired outcomes are. But generally our people are given the freedom they need to make whatever decisions are required to deliver the expected results.

Having said that—we are still a transitional organisation. We used to have two or three people in the organisation who tended to provide most of the direction and to some extent individuals here are still comfortable with that. Which, of course, means that they can be uncomfortable when the requirement is that they make decisions. Certainly it is my intention that as the organisation develops and matures that we may be able to devolve the decision making much deeper in the organisation. We are not there yet.

■ The subordinate's log   the reflective practitioner

My decision-making style varied according to the level I was working with. With the consultants, my style was consultative as they often had more experience in the area than I did. As they were the ones who had to implement the decisions, I encouraged their input to increase their sense of ownership of the decisions.

Most times a decision would be agreed upon. When I made a decision that was not popular, it would still be carried out and the staff felt comfortable enough to tell me why they did not agree, minimising potential conflict. Typically the consultative style worked as the consultants often came to me with the situation they were facing and their thoughts about what the solution should be.

At the senior levels of the firm, decision making was less consultative. Opinion was sought among senior management. Ultimately the CEO made the decision and this decision was conveyed to lower levels. The opinions and suggestions were taken into consideration but the consideration was largely about the congruence with his own opinions and the degree of likely resistance. For the most part, decisions were made autonomously and passed on to lower levels. His decision-making style was largely dictated by the fortunes of the firm. When business was good, he was more relaxed and his decision-making style was more open. When business was slow, he became much more directive.

Involving my staff in decision making felt right, but I was always wary of being perceived as too easily influenced and relinquishing control and power. In the early days I did make a number of poor decisions as a result of not taking sufficient control. If I relied too much on my staff and made a poor decision, the responsibility still lay with me. It becomes a very sobering lesson in the consequences of decision making.

Where appropriate I passed on to staff the consequences of those inadequate decisions. This resulted in a much greater trust level between myself and my staff and higher levels of co-operation. I took responsibility both because the responsibility was mine and also in the interest of buffering staff and I was fortunate that my staff did not take advantage of that. On the contrary, it created stronger linkages between them, and increased productivity and good will.

The CEO's decision-making style limited my ability and desire to make decisions of my own. Decisions were often made above me irrespective of my input or my abilities to implement them. This, I feel, in many ways deskilled me. I lost interest in making decisions as I had little control.

Focus on practice—Strategies for improving

1 Develop a strategy which will convince managers that it is not always possible to make optimal decisions, and that they must focus on making the best decision for the circumstances.
2 How would you encourage managers at the lower levels of an organisation to focus on generating as many options as possible as part of problem-solving processes?
3 Work with a group to get them to identify the impact of their preferences and interests on the options they have generated and the decisions which are ultimately made.
4 What strategies can you use to try to eliminate biases from the alternative generation and decision-making processes?

Source: Jones et al. (2000).

Chapter summary

Decision making is the process by which managers identify organisational problems and attempt to resolve them. Managers deal with three problem types: crisis, non-crisis and opportunity. Opportunity problems are major vehicles for organisational innovation. Because opportunities involve ideas to be used, rather than difficulties to be resolved, they sometimes receive insufficient attention.

Generally, managerial decision situations fall into two categories: programmed and non-programmed. Because of their nature, non-programmed decisions usually involve significant uncertainty and risk.

Two types of models have been developed to better understand the ways managers make decisions. The rational model suggests managers are almost perfect information handlers and, therefore, make optimal decisions. In contrast, non-rational models of managerial decision making, including satisficing, incremental, and rubbish-bin models, suggest information-gathering and processing limitations make it difficult for managers to make optimal decisions.

An effective decision-making process includes four major steps: (1) Identifying the problem involves scanning, categorisation and diagnosis stages. (2) Generating alternative solutions emphasises the importance of alternatives in achieving a high-quality solution. (3) Evaluating and choosing an alternative requires consideration of feasibility, quality, acceptability, costs, reversibility and ethics. (4) Implementing and monitoring the solution focuses on careful planning, sensitivity to those involved in implementation and/or affected by it, and design of follow-up mechanisms.

As non-rational models of managerial decision making suggest, managers sometimes do not follow effective decision-making processes. This is because they face four major decision barriers. Managers must be familiar with means of overcoming each one. The first entails accepting the problem challenge. This requires deciding to decide, rather than reacting with complacency, defensive avoidance or panic. The second involves searching for sufficient alternatives. The third focuses on recognising common decision-making biases, such as framing, representativeness, availability, anchoring and adjustment, and overconfidence. The fourth centres on avoiding the escalation phenomenon, or non-rational escalation. This phenomenon is the tendency to increase commitment to a previously selected course of action beyond the level expected if the manager followed an effective decision-making process.

Group decision making has several advantages and disadvantages. The advantages are that more information and knowledge is focused on the issue, an increased number and range of alternatives can be developed, greater understanding and acceptance of the final decision are likely, and members develop knowledge and skills for future use. The disadvantages are group decisions are usually more time-consuming, disagreements may delay decision making and cause hard feelings, discussion may be dominated by one or a few group members, and groupthink may cause members to overemphasise gaining agreement. Managers can take a number of steps to help minimise the disadvantages including taking advantage of diversity in group composition.

A major aspect of promoting innovation is the creativity factor. Creativity involves both convergent and divergent thinking. Basic ingredients of the creative process are domain-relevant skills, creativity-relevant skills and task motivation. The creativity process comprises four stages: preparation, incubation, illumination and verification. Techniques for enhancing creativity include brainstorming and nominal group technique.

Questions for discussion and review

1 Outline the major types of problems managers are likely to confront. Give an example of each type, which has occurred or could occur at your university.

2 Explain the difference between programmed and non-programmed decision situations. Choose an organisation with which you are familiar and identify two programmed and two non-programmed decision situations.

3 Contrast rational and non-rational models of managers as decision makers. Think of a recent non-programmed decision situation you have seen handled in an organisation (perhaps a student group or association to which you belong). Which of the following models best describes the decision process involved: rational, satisficing, incremental or rubbish bin? Explain why.

4 Describe each step in an effective decision-making process. We sometimes witness serious organisational problems, such as poor quality products or services, which go unresolved. What are some potential managerial reactions to problem situations, which might account for why such problems persist?

5 Explain the main decision barriers involved with accepting the problem challenge and searching for sufficient alternatives. How can these barriers be overcome?

6 Give an example of each common decision-making bias. Explain how these might influence evaluations of alternative solutions.

7 Explain the conditions under which the escalation phenomenon is likely to occur. What steps can a manager take to minimise the possibilities of falling prey to non-rational escalation?

8 Assess the advantages and disadvantages of group decision making. Give an example of (a) a situation in which you felt the advantages outweighed the disadvantages, and (b) one in which you felt the opposite was true. In the latter, what could have been done to prevent the decision-making difficulty? Could effectively managing diversity have helped?

9 Explain the main ingredients necessary for creativity.

10 Suppose you are chairing a bank task force charged with developing new ideas for enhancing customer service. What approaches might be used to facilitate the flow of creative ideas? Which one would you pick, and why?

Exercises for managing in the 21st century

Exercise 1
Skill-building exercise: Effective decision making

You own the Happy Hamburger chain of 10 restaurants in your local area. You were informed two weeks ago the competitor in your area has introduced 'funny' hamburgers in different shapes and sizes. These have been very popular with teenagers. You notice a drop in sales at several of your restaurants, and your managers tell you they are serving fewer teenagers. Yesterday you became aware of a device to cut ground meat into hamburgers of specific weights and a variety of shapes (e.g. round, cars, yachts and bicycles). You realise this could give you the capability to compete with the other restaurant. Further, your employees are currently making hamburgers by hand. These are round in shape and weigh about 150 grams. The hamburger cutter can be rented or purchased. Refer to Table 5.2 to determine which of the considerations would be included in each step of the decision-making process.

Table 5.2   Considerations in making the decision about hamburger shapes

Consideration	Identify the problem/opportunity	Generate alternative solutions	Evaluate/choose alternative	Implement/monitor solution
1 Could rent device				
2 Provides variety; competitor has device				
3 Device would save some money by precise weighing				
4 Could continue making present round shapes by hand				
5 If device is rented, could opt out				
6 Evaluate sales, costs and satisfaction monthly				
7 Could purchase device				
8 New shapes would appeal to younger buyers				
9 Costs $300 each per month to rent and $1750 each to buy				
10 Schedule an electrician to install the necessary wiring				

Exercise 2
Management exercise: Brainstorming

Objectives

O To learn how the brainstorming technique for stimulating creativity operates
O To gain experience in generating ideas in a brainstorming session

Instructions

1 Select a problem of common interest to group members. If the group has difficulty selecting a problem, try one of these:
   a How can students be more involved in developing your university's policies (e.g. new programs, admissions and transfers, and electives)?
   b What kind of game could be developed to help learn how to make better decisions?
   c What features would you like cars to have 10 years from now?
   d What new approaches could recent graduates use in developing job leads?
2 Spend 30 minutes brainstorming alternative solutions. Someone in the group should record all ideas. Even if the group runs out of steam after 15 minutes or so, keep brainstorming. Usually, the best ideas occur later in the session. Freewheel. Offer ideas even if they seem wild and impractical. Remember, no criticising is allowed during the brainstorming phase.
3 Go over the list and select the 10 best ideas. Evaluation is allowed in this phase of the process.
4 Narrow the list to the five best ideas, and then select the best idea.
5 Be prepared to discuss your top five ideas with the class as a whole.

Decision making at ChocCo

The setting is by a tranquil river bend, with a golf course nearby and splendid mountain views as a backdrop. ChocCo enjoys a tranquil life away from the hurly-burly of large cities, even though the factory is part of a multi-national group spanning the world. It employs some 200 factory workers (70 per cent are female) and supporting staff, and has been in its present location since the 1920s. The factory is geared to a continuous process operation in which production spans 24 hours daily, every day of the week. The plant is unionised.

The tranquillity of the surroundings has transferred to the management team, which was caught unprepared for a grass-roots movement among its employees wanting a change in their shift patterns. Traditionally they had worked a daily pattern of three 8-hour shifts but, in some parts of the plant, pressure was applied to management for a move to two 12-hour shifts. The proposal was for three weekly rotating shifts of 12-hours, framed around a six-day fortnight. As far as management could determine, workers were attracted by the idea of having more days off under this regime than the traditional shift pattern. Such a pattern of shifts suited women in particular with respect to their non-work-life activities. Management therefore did not initiate the change in shifts and had no agenda in mind except that of attempting to please its employees.

Although management did not initiate the proposal, it wished to be responsive to workers' desires and so agreed. The main difficulty was that not all sections in the factory were suited to 12-hour shifts. For example, seasonal production processes are not stable and therefore not conducive to 12-hour shifts. Initially, only those in the milk-processing area and the boiler house were granted a change to 12-hour shifts, but the idea soon spread to other areas of the plant, and management was besieged with demands to implement them on a universal basis. Management responded by granting 12-hour shifts to all workers. At no stage in its deliberations did ChocCo consult with outside parties, such as the unions.

After 12-months ChocCo management was unhappy with several aspects of the shiftwork changes. However, since their employees had been working the new shifts for such a lengthy time, in some cases for more than 12 months, the company felt unable to retreat from the new shifts. Management was aware by now that to rescind the arrangement would result in an adverse reaction by employees and for this reason was not prepared to revoke the 12-hour shifts. Moreover, since there was no change in productivity levels or staff turnover, ChocCo felt there were insufficient grounds to claim that the company was 'disadvantaged' to the extent that it was prepared to make an industrial issue of 12-hour shifts and run the risk of a major union dispute.

Management admits that the factory processes are noisy, repetitive and boring for employees. For this reason it is felt that the welfare and wishes of workers are important and should not be ignored or easily dismissed. ChocCo expressed the view that it was 'between a rock and a hard place' with respect to the present situation. On one hand it was deeply concerned about health and safety issues, but on the other hand realised that to withdraw 12-hour shifts at this point would be unacceptable to employees. Chief among the concerns was that the 12-hour regime extended by 50 per cent the 'normal' shift period, contributing significantly to fatigue, stress and accidents. In essence, workers were simply spending too much time on the factory floor, increasing their exposure to adverse work conditions. Accidents had increased, as had the incidence of stress claims and general absenteeism. The stress claims in particular were a matter of considerable concern and appeared to be solely due to the long-term effects of employees working for extended shifts in a noisy and stressful environment.

A further issue related to the rehabilitation of previously injured workers. Whereas returning to work, even on light duties, can be both desirable and possible in an 8-hour shift situation, this is difficult or even impossible where 12-hour shifts are involved, because of the dramatic increase in the length of shift. The fatigue factor over 12 hours compared with 8 hours was found to be excessive and workers were unable to continue at their stations for such a period of time. In another case, this time involving stress, the employee was only able to work for short bursts, a situation that is incompatible with 12-hour shifts.

The union was not involved with management discussions prior to the trials, but was aware of the mooted changes, and advised management to exercise caution before agreeing to 12-hour shifts. In fact neither the union nor management were supportive of the change but both felt that the ground-swell of opinion among workers was too strong to resist. According to union sources, management at ChocCo has a record of poor planning and decision making and it is regarded as a place 'where things just happen'.

The present situation is that ChocCo has a shift regime it does not want and neither does the union. However, the workers are strongly in favour and the company feels at a loss as to how to extricate itself from the present shift patterns, even though it notionally has union support. For its part, the union can see the folly in opting for 12-hour shifts, but is duty bound to support the wishes of its members. It is therefore most unlikely that the union would openly support any initiative by management to move back to 8-hour shifts. ChocCo is worried about the escalation in accidents and workers' compensation claims and the apparent adverse affect upon absenteeism, and is in a quandary as to what it should do next.

Source: Written by Lindsay Nelson and Peter Holland.

Activities for discussion, analysis and further research

1 Describe the decision-making process at ChocCo. Who were the parties involved? Who should have been involved? Why? How might you have ensured that they all were?

2 How could the decision-making process be made more effective?

3 What lessons can be learned from the experience at ChocCo? What would you do differently if you were to be a party to the process?

Planning and Decision Aids

Management science (also called operations research) is a management perspective aimed at increased decision-effectiveness by use of sophisticated mathematical models and statistical methods. (Management science is explained in Chapter 2.) Management science has a variety of quantitative techniques to help managers plan for and make decisions about complex situations. There are a number of aids available to help managers be competitive through innovations in planning and decision making areas (Halloran & Burn 1986; Labich 1987; *World Airlines News* 1995).

Generally, managers do not require in-depth knowledge of mathematics and computers to use management science tools. Rather, they need to have an understanding of the major tools so they can develop applications of these tools. In some conditions, managers must get assistance from experts. With the growing availability of packaged software, many techniques are increasingly accessible. As a result, the importance of these planning and decision-making aids will increase.

In this supplement, we describe several major planning and decision making aids. In doing so, we consider some forecasting methods, including one useful for promoting innovation. We also examine tools for planning and controlling projects and explore useful quantitative planning techniques. Finally, we investigate quantitative decision-making aids.

FORECASTING

Forecasting is making predictions about changing conditions and future events significantly affecting an organisation. Forecasting is important to planning and decision making because each relies on assessing future conditions. Forecasting is used in many areas, such as production planning, budgeting, strategic planning, sales analysis, inventory control, marketing planning, logistics planning, purchasing, material requirements planning and product planning (Mentzer & Cox 1984). Forecasting methods fall into three categories: quantitative; technological or qualitative; and judgmental (Wheelwright & Makridakis 1989).

Quantitative forecasting

Quantitative forecasting relies on numerical data and mathematical models to predict future conditions. Two main types of quantitative forecasting methods are time-series and explanatory methods.

Time-series methods **Time-series methods** use historical data to forecast the future. The assumption of time-series models is that patterns or combinations of patterns repeat. Time-series

---

forecasting

Process of making predictions about changing conditions and future events that may significantly affect the business of an organisation

quantitative forecasting

Type of forecasting that relies on numerical data and mathematical models to predict future conditions

time-series methods

Methods using historical data to develop future forecasts

models use extensive historical data, such as weekly sales figures, to identify patterns then base future projections on them.

Examples of patterns identified by time-series methods are shown in Figure 5s.1. A trend is a long-range general movement either up or down. For example, though coffee-house chains like Starbucks Coffee Co. are expanding rapidly, the market could become saturated as coffee consumption declines, particularly among individuals in their 20s, who average less than one cup per day (Mathews 1994). A seasonal pattern shows changes coinciding with particular points in a year, such as seasons. A cyclical pattern involves changes in a time-span of more than a year. For example, sunspot intensity varies over an 11-year cycle and affects agriculture (Gallagher & Watson 1980).

Fig. 5s.1   Examples of patterns identified by time-series methods (adapted from Gallagher & Watson 1980, p. 116)

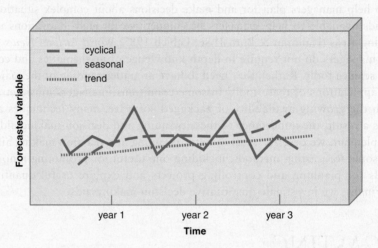

Because time-series methods are based on historical data, they are less useful predicting the impact of present or future actions managers might take to produce change. They are more suited to predicting broad environmental factors, such as general economic prospects, employment levels, general sales levels or cost trends, that may be influenced by past events. There are methods for analysing time series, many quite sophisticated and requiring computers. Time-series methods try to predict the future by identifying patterns, but are not concerned with patterns' causes.

Explanatory, or causal, models   Explanatory, or **causal, models** try to identify major variables related to or causing particular past conditions and then use current measures (predictors) to predict future conditions. Developing such models leads to better understanding of situations being forecast than time-series models. Explanatory models let managers assess the possible impact of changes in predictors. For example, a manager may estimate how future sales will be impacted by increasing sales personnel or expanding shelf space. Explanatory models are generally more use than time-series models in assessing the impact of managerial actions on the variables.

explanatory, or causal, models

Models attempting to identify major variables related to or causing particular past conditions and then using current measures of those variables (predictors) to predict future conditions

Three major types of explanatory models are regression models, econometric models and leading indicators. **Regression models** are equations that express fluctuations in the variable being forecast, in terms of fluctuations in one or more other variables. An example of simple regression, in which one variable (a predictor) helps predict a future level of another (forecast) variable, is shown in Figure 5s.2. Here, a firm selling burglar alarm systems for homes attempts to predict demand for alarm systems (forecast variable) by the number of information leaflets (predictor variable) the public requests. Leaflets are offered in a newspaper advertisement. Data points plotted in Figure 5s.2 show leaflets requested and sales within a month of the request. A simple regression states the relationship between predictor and forecast variables mathematically. The form is $y = a + bx$, where y is the forecast variable, x the predictor variable, a is a constant representing the point where the regression line crosses the vertical axis, and b shows how much y's value changes when the value of x changes by 1 unit. A statistical technique is used to develop the straight line best fitting the data points and providing values for a and b. Then future projections substitute different values for x in the equation and determine the impact on y. For example, if our equation came out to be $y = 1.5 + 0.07x$, then substituting 350 leaflets for x would predict sales of 26 alarm systems.

regression models

Equations expressing fluctuations in the variable being forecast in terms of fluctuations in one or more other variables (predictors)

Fig. 5s.2   Data points and regression line for number of leaflets requested and number of burglar alarm systems sold (adapted from Gallagher & Watson 1980, p. 134)

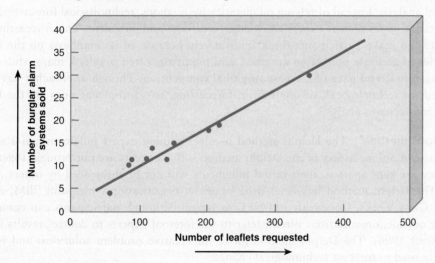

More complex regression models with multiple predictor variables are also used for forecasting.

The second major category of explanatory models is **econometric models**. This refers to multiple regression equations using several predictor variables to identify and measure economic relationships or interrelationships.

These models try to predict the economy's future directions and the impact that change such as changes to tax legislation may have on various economy segments. Econometric model development is complex and expensive. As a result, the models are beyond the scope of most

econometric models

Systems of simultaneous multiple regression equations using several predictor variables used to identify and measure relationships or interrelationships existing in the economy

managerial jobs, and all but the largest organisations. However, companies can subscribe to an econometric forecasting service. This gives a company the benefits of econometric forecasting at less cost than developing its own model.

The third major category of explanatory model is **leading indicators**, variables correlated with the phenomenon of interest but generally coming before the phenomenon. Generally using leading indicators is simple, though analytic methods can be complex. For example, the semiconductor industry uses book-to-bill ratio as a key leading indicator. This is based on comparing orders with shipments. Therefore, a ratio of .78 means that, of every $100 of products shipped, only $78 were ordered. Compared with a previous month's ratio of .79, the figure indicates a sales decline. However, a trend may take months to establish (Fisher 1996). The difficulty is to identify a leading indicator giving accurate predictions.

Promoting innovation: technological, or qualitative, forecasting

Technological, or **qualitative**, **forecasting** aims to predict long-term technology trends. Technology is emphasised, since organisations' innovativeness and competitiveness relates to opportunities from technological change (Ihrcke 2000). Technological, or qualitative, forecasting differs from quantitative approaches as it focuses on longer-term issues less suited to numerical analysis. Instead of relying on quantitative methods, technological forecasting relies on qualitative issues such as expert knowledge, creativity and judgment. This forecasting type is excellent to make participants think innovatively because of its emphasis on the future. Difficulties of accurate prediction are clear, and predictors often overlook major shifts, such as the magnitude and pace of increase of global competition. Though approaches have been developed for technological, or qualitative, forecasting, two prominent ones are the Delphi method and scenario analysis.

The Delphi method   The **Delphi method** involves gaining expert judgments on a specific future issue. A unique aspect of the Delphi method is that experts are not brought together to talk. They are kept apart so their initial judgments will not be influenced by others (Huger 1980). The Delphi method has been used by many organisations, including IBM, AT&T, Corning Glass Works, Goodyear, and NEC in Japan. Although participants can come from inside or outside, organisations often prefer to use internal experts to control results (Preble 1984; Wolff 1996). The Delphi method looks for creative problem solutions; and is most frequently used to forecast technological change.

There are three basic steps in the Delphi method:

1 An expert panel anonymously identifies scientific breakthroughs in an area over a specified long-term period (e.g. the next 50 years). They estimate when, within the period, breakthroughs can be expected. On the basis of this information, a list of possible breakthroughs is drawn up, including an estimated time-frame for each.

2 The list is returned to the experts, to estimate (often on a 50–50 basis) whether each will come before the average estimated time frame. They may specify they do not believe the breakthrough will occur during the time period (e.g. 50 years).

3 Experts are provided with a new list of information gathered in step 2. If there is agreement, those who disagree must explain. If participants differ they may be asked to

leading indicators

Variables tending to be correlated with the phenomenon of major interest but also to occur in advance of that phenomenon

technological, or qualitative, forecasting

Type of forecasting aimed primarily at predicting long-term trends in technology and other important, environmental aspects

Delphi method

Structured approach to gaining judgments of a number of experts on a specific issue relating to the future

justify their views. They can change estimates then. If wide divergence still exists, step 3 is repeated to reassess previous explanations.

These are the basic steps for the Delphi method; however, organisations make minor alterations to suit their circumstances.

Scenario analysis   Developed in France and widely used in Europe, **scenario analysis** (called scenario planning or La Prospective) argues that futures depend on issues such as actor interactions, whether current trends continue, regulatory and other constraints, and relative power of actors (Schoemaker 1995; Clemons 1995). As a result, organisations must consider alternative futures, try to make decisions and take actions without inhibiting further choices. Severe difficulties may result from rigid, irreversible actions if forecasts are wrong. Scenario analysis addresses many futures by assessing environmental variables and the likely strategies of significant actors (e.g. other organisations), devising counter-strategies, developing ranked hypotheses about variables, and devising alternative scenarios. Scenarios outline future events, including the paths leading to these conditions. Scenario analysis is increasingly common (Schoemaker 1995).

scenario analysis

Approach that addresses a variety of possible futures by evaluating major environmental variables, assessing likely strategies of other significant actors, devising possible counter-strategies, developing ranked hypotheses about the variables, and formulating alternative scenarios

Judgmental forecasting

Judgmental forecasting relies on individual judgments or committee agreements about future conditions. Although judgmental forecasting is the most widely used method, this approach relies on informal opinion gathering and is the least systematic forecasting method. As a result, judgmental forecasting is susceptible to common decision-making biases discussed in Chapter 5 (Wheelwright & Makridakis 1989). Two major approaches are the jury of executive opinion and sales-force composites.

judgmental forecasting

Type of forecasting relying mainly on individual judgments or committee agreements regarding future conditions

The jury of executive opinion   The **jury of executive opinion** is a forecasting method where executives meet and estimate, as a group, a forecast. However, since estimators are in contact, group power and personality factors may weight outcomes. The process can be improved by providing background material to executives before they meet.

jury of executive opinion

Means of forecasting in which organisation executives hold a meeting and estimate, as a group, a forecast for a particular item

Sales-force composites   The **sales-force composite** is a means of forecasting used to predict future sales and involves obtaining views of various salespeople, sales managers, and/or distributors regarding sales outlook. While salespeople and distributors are close to the customer, they often lack information about broad economic factors affecting future sales. On the other hand, when sales management make forecasts, the process may be subject to the same difficulties met by a jury of executive opinion. The process can be improved by giving salespeople and distributors economic trend information before they start.

sales-force composite

Means of forecasting used mainly to predict future sales and typically by obtaining views of various salespeople, sales managers, and/or distributors regarding the sales outlook

Choosing a forecasting method

Criteria for selecting a forecasting method and the general characteristics of each method are outlined in Table 5s.1. As this suggests, managers must consider factors including desired time horizon, type of accuracy needed, ease of understanding, and development costs. Each has advantages and disadvantages, depending on the forecasting situation's needs.

Table 5s.1   Criteria for choosing a forecasting method

Criteria	Quantitative	Technological	Judgmental
Time horizon*	short to medium	medium to long	short to long
Time required	short if method developed; long otherwise	medium to long	short
Development costs	often high	medium	low
Accuracy in identifying patterns	high	medium	medium to high
Accuracy in predicting turning points	low for time series; medium for other methods	medium	low
Ease of understanding	low to medium	high	high

*Short term = one to three months; medium term = three months to two years; long term = two years or more

Source: Adapted from Makridakis & Wheelwright (1981, p. 132).

PROJECT PLANNING AND CONTROL MODELS

Managers may manage projects—one-time sets of activities with a clear beginning and ending. For example, a manager may be responsible for designing and implementing a new computer system, building a new manufacturing plant, or developing a new product. Projects are unique, though the manager may have been responsible for similar projects before. For large and complex projects, managers may need a planning and control model to manage the project effectively. Two planning and control models are the Gantt chart and PERT.

Gantt charts

Gantt chart

Specialised bar chart developed by Henry L. Gantt showing current progress on each major project activity relative to necessary completion dates

One of the earliest and most flexible project planning tools is the **Gantt chart**, a specialised bar chart Henry L. Gantt developed (see Chapter 2), which shows current progress of every major project activity relative to necessary completion dates. A simple Gantt chart is shown in Figure 5s.3.

A project, in this case completing a management course, is divided into major activities listed on the chart's left side. The entire project's time frame is indicated at the top or bottom. A bar shows each activity's duration and scheduling, and each is shaded to show how complete the activity is. Thus each activity's status relative to project deadlines can be easily determined. You can construct a Gantt chart to help plan and control activities needed to complete a course or a whole semester. Checking the chart in Figure 5s.3 for 'Today' shows the individual has chosen a paper topic, has researched, and is ahead of schedule writing the paper. However, they are a bit behind studying for the mid-term examination and need to catch up.

Fig. 5s.3　Partial Gantt chart for completing a management course

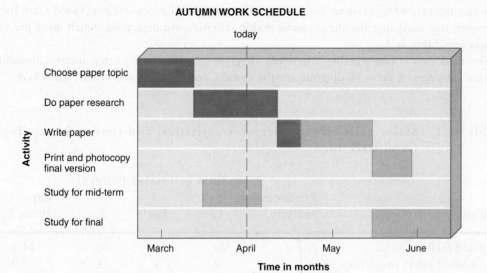

Gantt charts are popular, and software packages are widely available to help plan and control projects (Hack 1989). While Gantt charts are useful in many cases, they do have one weakness. They do not show the interrelationships of various activities. For small projects, these are obvious. For complex projects, more sophisticated methods are needed.

PERT

During the 1950s, the US Navy had to co-ordinate 11 000 contractors involved in developing Polaris, the first submarine to remain submerged while launching long-range ballistic missiles. The Defense Department, with Lockheed, invented the **program evaluation and review technique (PERT)**, a method of network planning for large projects. At the same time, Du Pont, with Remington-Rand, developed another network approach called Critical Path Method (CPM) (Dilworth 1993). Network planning involves breaking projects down into activities and determining the time needed for each, but it goes beyond Gantt charts by specifically considering the interrelationships of activities.

Setting up PERT to manage a major project involves six main steps:
1 All project activities must be clearly specified.
2 Sequencing requirements among activities must be identified (i.e. which activities must precede others).
3 A diagram reflecting sequence relationships must be developed.
4 Time estimates for each activity must be determined.
5 The network must be evaluated by calculating the critical path. Various activities can be scheduled.
6 As the project progresses, actual activity times must be recorded so any necessary schedule revisions and adjustments can be made (Adam Jr & Ebert 1992).

program evaluation and review technique (PERT)

Network planning method for managing large projects

In order to understand how PERT works, we will go through a simple example. Suppose an organisation providing nursing-home care, Good Care Inc., wants to expand and upgrade its services. Because of regulations the organisation must build a new facility. Good Care Inc.'s administrator must first list the project's major activities and determine which must precede others (see Table 5s.2).

network diagram
···
Graphic depiction of interrelationships among activities

The next step is constructing a **network diagram** graphically depicting interrelationships among activities. A network diagram for the Good Care project is shown in Figure 5s.4.

Table 5s.2   Major activities, predecessor activities, and time estimates for Good Care Inc.

Activity	Predecessor activity	Time estimates (weeks)			Expected time, T_e
		t_o	t_m	t_p	
A Build facility	None	20	24	30	24.3
B Conduct safety inspection	A	2	3	4	3.0
C Install equipment	A	8	10	20	11.0
D Decorate interior	B	3	5	9	5.3
E Recruit staff	None	2	2	3	2.1
F Train staff	E	4	5	6	5.0
G Perform pilot	C, D, F	4	5	9	5.5

Source: Adapted from Adam Jr & Ebert (1992, p. 342).

Fig. 5s.4   Network diagram, critical path and expected time for each activity in the Good Care Inc. project (adapted from Adam Jr & Ebert 1992, p. 343)

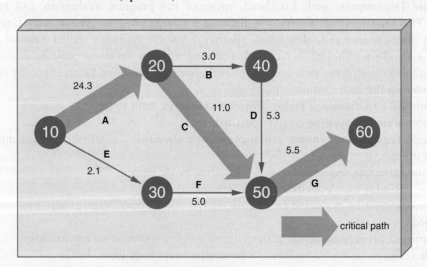

On the diagram an **activity**, or work component, is shown by an arrow. Activities take time. A **node**, or **event**, is an indication of network activities beginning and/or ending. It shows a single time point. Nodes are numbered for easy identification, usually in tens (e.g. 10, 20, 30) so additions can be made without renumbering. The diagram shows various activities' interrelationships. In Figure 5s.4, for example, building the facility (A) precedes safety inspection (B), and recruiting staff (E) precedes training staff (F). However, as the diagram shows, building and safety inspection processes (A, B) can be accomplished while recruiting and training staff (E, F).

Developing the diagram may include providing initial time estimates for each activity's duration. Unless times are well established, optimistic (t_o), pessimistic (t_p) and most likely (t_m) times necessary to complete each activity are estimated. Each activity's expected, or average, time is then calculated using the following formula, which gives heavy weight to the most likely time for activity completion:

$$t = (t_o + 4t_m + t_p)/6$$

Each activity's expected time (in weeks) is shown next to its respective arrow on the network diagram.

The next step is identifying the **critical path**, the network path taking longest to complete. This network has three different paths: 10-20-40-50-60, 10-20-50-60, and 10-30-50-60. By adding up each path's expected times, we can determine the path 10-20-50-60 will take longest (40.8 weeks) and is, therefore, the critical path. This means a delay in any activity on this path will delay project completion. Therefore, the manager must pay particular attention to this path. As well, allocating further resources to this path may shorten time taken to complete the project. For example, if time needed to install equipment could be shortened by two weeks, completion time could be reduced to 38.8. When activity times are significantly shortened, another path may become critical. This could happen if activity C (20-50) was cut to eight weeks. Then the path 10-20-40-50-60 becomes the critical path. On non-critical paths, there is latitude about when activities can be started without risking the entire project's completion date. This is referred to as **slack**.

Once the critical path is developed, actual time taken for various activities is recorded periodically and then the implications reviewed. For example, when critical path activities take longer than estimated, action must be taken to correct the situation. Otherwise, the entire project may be delayed. Similarly, if activity on a non-critical path takes substantially longer than expected, the critical path may change. Thus PERT helps managers plan and also control projects. (Issues of control are discussed further in Chapters 16 to 19.) Individual managers' ability to use PERT to plan and control both small and large projects has vastly increased with relatively easy-to-use software packages.

OTHER PLANNING TECHNIQUES

A number of other quantitative planning techniques exist that can assist managers. Some prominent ones include use of linear programming; queuing, or waiting-line, models; routing, or distribution, models; and simulation models. We discuss each of these briefly. Typically, effective application of these techniques requires a management science expert's help.

---

activity

Work component to be accomplished

node, or event

Indication of beginning and/or ending of activities in the network

critical path

Path in the network taking the longest to complete

slack

Latitude about when various activities on the non-critical paths can be started without endangering the entire project's completion date

Linear programming

linear programming (LP)

Quantitative tool for planning how to allocate limited or scarce resources so a single criterion or goal (often profits) is optimised

Linear programming (LP) is a quantitative tool for planning the allocation of limited or scarce resources to optimise a single criterion or goal (often profits). It is a widely used quantitative planning tool. Linear programming is applicable when a single objective (maximising profits) must be achieved, constraints exist, and variables are linearly related to the objective (Davis & McKeown 1984). A variable is linearly related to an objective when increasing (or decreasing) the variable leads to a proportional objective increase (or decrease) in the objective. For example, a linear relationship applies if one chair (variable) produced can be sold for $30 profit (objective), four chairs for $120 profit, and six chairs for $180 profit. The technique has been applied to situations that include minimising the cost of chicken feed while maintaining proper nutritional balance, finding the most profitable product mix in manufacturing, and oil refinery capacity maximisation (Pinney & McWilliams 1982).

Queuing, or waiting-line, models

queuing, or waiting-line, models

Mathematical models describing operating characteristics of queuing situations, in which service is provided to persons or units waiting in line

Managers are often responsible for providing services where persons or units needing service must wait in lines, or queues. **Queuing, or waiting-line, models** are mathematical models describing the characteristics of queuing situations. Many different models exist for different queuing situations (such as a single window at a small post office versus multiple service points in obtaining a driver's licence). Unlike linear programming, queuing, or waiting-line, models do not provide optimal solutions. Rather, they allow managers to vary situation parameters and assess probable effects.

Routing, or distribution, models

routing, or distribution, models

Quantitative models assisting managers in planning the most effective and economical approaches to distribution problems

Organisations may distribute a product or service to multiple customers. **Routing, or distribution, models** are tools to assist managers planning effective, economical approaches to distribution problems. The development and use of these models is network optimisation analysis.

Simulation models

simulation

Mathematical imitation of reality

Simulation is a mathematical imitation of reality. The technique is used when the situation of interest is too complex for narrower methods such as linear programming or queuing theory. Rather than a standardised set of formulas applicable to a broad set of problems, simulations are usually custom-made for a situation (Pinney & McWilliams 1982). As a result, they can be expensive to develop. Simulations let managers change parameters to evaluate different assumptions and/or approaches. Simulations have been used in production, inventory control, transportation systems, market strategy analysis, industrial and urban growth patterns, environmental control and many other areas (Huber 1980).

QUANTITATIVE AIDS FOR DECISION MAKING

Although the aids discussed so far are considered planning tools, they can assist managers make decisions during the planning process. In addition, a number of aids are aimed specifically at helping managers make particular decisions. Two well-known aids for decision making are payoff tables and decision trees.

Payoff tables

One helpful way to frame managerial decision situations is using a payoff table. The **payoff table**, a two-dimensional matrix, allows decision makers to compare different future conditions likely to affect the outcomes of two or more decision choices. The payoff table is referred to as a **decision matrix**. Typically decision alternatives are row headings in the matrix, and possible future conditions are column headings. The values where row and column intersect represent the **payoff**, the amount of decision-maker value from a particular decision alternative and future condition. An example will help clarify these concepts (Harrison 1981).

Assume you are a decision maker at a college where enrolments may increase but where existing classroom capacity is fully used. Three alternatives are found to increase space: Construct a new building, expand an old one, or rent or lease another. These alternatives are row headings in Table 5s.3. There are three possible conditions. Student enrolments may go up, down, or be unchanged. These are column headings in the table. Potential payoffs for each combination is shown at the intersections. If future events were clear then the simple solution would be to select the alternative with the highest payoff. Unfortunately, it is not possible to know which outcome will occur. However, on past experience, current enrolment trends, and personal judgment, the decision maker can assign probabilities to possible future outcomes. A probability is a decision maker's best estimate whether a future condition will occur. These estimates are usually put as a percentage. For example, as shown, the decision maker estimates a 50 per cent probability enrolments will increase, while probabilities they will drop or remain unchanged are each estimated at 25 per cent. Which alternative should the decision maker select?

payoff table or decision matrix

Two-dimensional matrix allowing a decision maker to compare how different future conditions are likely to affect respective outcomes of two or more decision alternatives

payoff

Amount of decision-maker value associated with a particular decision alternative and future condition

Table 5s.3 Payoff table for classroom space problem

| Alternatives | Possible future conditions | | | Expected value |
	Student enrolments up [.50]*	Student enrolments down [.25]	Student enrolments unchanged [.25]	
Construct new building	$500 000	($200 000)†	($100 000)	$175 000
Expand old building	$400 000	$100 000	$100 000	$250 000
Rent or lease another building	$400 000	($100 000)	$200 000	$225 000

*Numbers in brackets are probability estimates for possible future conditions.
†Numbers in parentheses represent losses.

Source: Adapted from Harrison (1987, p. 375).

Experts recommend choosing the highest expected value alternative. A given alternative's **expected value** is the sum of payoffs times respective probabilities for that alternative. For example, expected value (EV) for redeveloping an old building is as follows:

EV = .50(400 000) + .25(100 000) + .25(100 000) = $250 000

Likewise, expected value for constructing a new building is (notice when the payoff is a loss, a minus sign is used):

EV = .50(500 000) − .25(200 000) − .25(100 000) = $175 000

Similar calculations show for renting or leasing another building an expected value of $225 000.

Therefore, the alternative with the highest expected value in this case is to expand an old building.

The value of payoff tables is that they help decision makers evaluate situations where the outcomes of various alternatives depend on the likelihood of future conditions. As such, payoff tables are useful when a decision maker can determine major relevant alternatives, can quantify payoffs, and make reasonably accurate judgments about future probabilities (Huber 1980; Ferguson & Selling 1985). For example, payoff tables help decide which new products to introduce, which real-estate investments to select, crops to plant, and needed restaurant staffing levels (Barron 1985). Managers at Hallmark, the greeting-card company, use payoff matrixes to set production levels of unique products, such as a special Muppet promotion including albums, plaques, gift wrap, stickers, patterns and other items (Ulvila 1987).

Decision trees

A **decision tree** is a graphic model showing a series of alternative actions. These are usually payoffs associated with various paths, and probabilities associated with each potential event.

A decision tree is shown in Figure 5s.5. Here, the manager faces a decision about building a large or a small manufacturing plant, given uncertain future demand for a product. If a large plant is built and demand is high, the company will make $12 million profit. However, if demand is low, it will make a $2 million profit (low profit because of overhead on the large plant). This is less profit than made with a small plant when demand is either high or low ($8 million and $5 million, respectively). To help with the decision, each alternative's expected value is computed. The large-plant alternative's expected value is $8 million [(.60 × $12 million) + (.40 × $2 million)]. The small-plant alternative's expected value is $6.8 million [(.60 × $8 million) + (.40 × $5 million)]. This suggests the large plant should be seriously considered.

The decision tree can be used as a graphic alternative to a payoff table. However, the decision tree's major advantage is that it considers complex alternatives. For example, it may be worth considering building a small plant initially, then expanding it when demand increases. In our example in Figure 5s.5, building a small plant would raise the possibility of a second decision point later, when a manager could choose a number of possibilities ranging from a large plant expansion to no expansion. These can be considered and values expected could be calculated using decision trees with many decision points. Decision trees help identify options, and consider the potential impacts of alternative branches (Adam Jr & Ebert 1992).

Fig. 5s.5 Decision tree and expected values for building a large or a small manufacturing plant

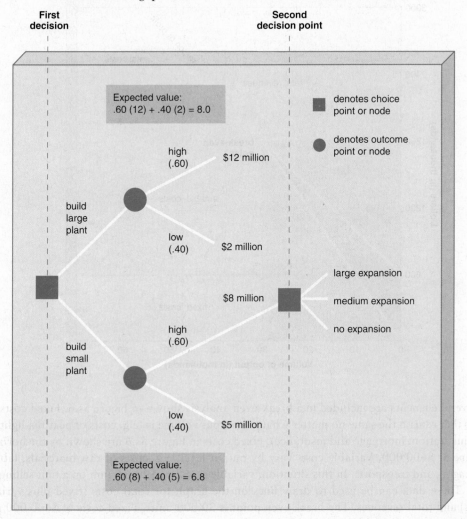

Break-even analysis

Break-even analysis is a technique helping decision makers understand the relationships between an organisation's sales volume, costs and revenues (Brealey & Myers 1991). Break-even analysis is often graphical, as in Figure 5s.6 and it also can be mathematical (Meecham 1995). The technique allows determination of the break-even point—the sales volume at which total revenues equal total costs. The break-even point is where the organisation neither loses nor makes money; it just breaks even. This point is important because only with greater sales volume can the organisation make a profit.

break-even analysis

Graphic model helping decision makers understand relationships between sales volume, costs and revenues in an organisation

Fig. 5s.6   Break-even analysis

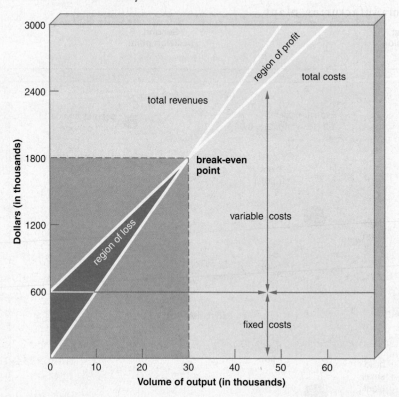

Several elements are included in a break-even analysis shown in Figure 5s.6. Fixed costs are costs that remain the same no matter what the output volume is (e.g. costs of heating, lighting, administration, mortgage and insurance). Fixed costs in Figure 5s.6 are shown by the horizontal line at $600 000. Variable costs vary by output level (e.g. costs of raw materials, labour, packaging and transport). In this situation, variable costs are $40 per unit on a unit selling for $60. These data can be used to draw lines on the graph for total costs (fixed plus variable costs) and total revenues. The break-even point is 30 000 units. Fixed costs of $600 000 plus variable costs of $1 200 000 [30 000 × $40 (variable costs per unit)] are $1 800 000. Revenues are also $1 800 000 [30 000 × $60 (sale price per unit)]. Hence the organisation breaks even at 30 000 units.

Break-even analysis is useful to determine how many units of a product or service the organisation must sell before it begins to make a profit. The analysis helps assess the impact of cutting costs when profits start. For example, if the organisation lowered fixed and/or variable costs, the total cost line in Figure 5s.6 would drop, lowering the break-even point.

Airlines often use break-even analysis in assessing fare discount levels (Meecham 1995).

Break-even analysis makes some simplifying assumptions. For instance, it assumes that the same price will be charged for all units (yet some customers may get discounts) and that fixed costs will remain the same across a range of outputs. Such assumptions show the technique is useful for doing rough analyses, rather than for fine-tuning volumes, costs and revenues. More complex types of break-even analyses are available when more precision is needed (Powers 1987).

Establishing Organisational Goals and Plans

Chapter 6

CHAPTER OUTLINE

The overall planning process
Major components of planning
Organisational mission

The nature of organisational goals
Benefits of goals
Levels of Goals

How goals facilitate performance
Goal content
Goal commitment
Work behaviour
Other process components
Potential problems with goals

Linking goals and plans
Levels of plans
Plans according to extent of recurring use
Time horizons of goals and plans
Promoting innovation: The role of the
  planning process
Potential obstacles to planning

Management by objectives
Steps in the MBO process
Strengths and weaknesses of MBO
Assessing MBO

LEARNING OBJECTIVES

After studying this chapter, you should be able to:

○ Describe major components in the overall planning process.
○ Explain the concept of organisational mission and purposes of a mission statement.
○ Outline the major benefits of goals and explain how they differ according to organisational level.
○ Describe various components helping explain how goals facilitate performance.
○ Explain how plans differ by organisational level and the extent of recurring use.
○ Assess the role of goals and plans in promoting innovation.
○ Outline the major steps in management by objectives and assess strengths and weaknesses of the approach.

Striving for excellence

At Autoliv, the planning process occurs on a five-year cycle. However, the organisation engages in a quarterly review and update. Management by business objective is the tool utilised.

The management team is involved in the quarterly review, with each department developing its own objectives. Every individual staff member with responsibility continuously monitors these objectives and measures achievement against objectives to report to the quarterly meeting

Excerpts of how the key criteria are allocated and how these are measured and rated within the larger picture are included below.

Examine the business-plan flowchart below. It shows how each idea and action is analysed as to how it affects the various sub-areas as detailed in the boxes. Similarly the boxes are assessed for their impact on ideas, actions and projects.

All that happens in the organisation must be related to the plan and its successful implementation. The flow chart graphically illustrates the whole process of the feedback loop. In management discussion, one often hears the phrase that 'What gets measured gets done'. The above is a reflection of the validity of such a comment.

An organisation without planning is like a yacht without a rudder. Without planning, organisations are at the mercy of the winds of environmental change, unable to take make use of the currents to choose their own direction. The management function of planning, setting goals and deciding how best to achieve them is crucial to the survival of organisations like Autoliv. The function includes considering how to achieve needed levels of change and innovation. Planning is the foundation of the other major management functions—organising, leading and controlling—by setting the course and steering.

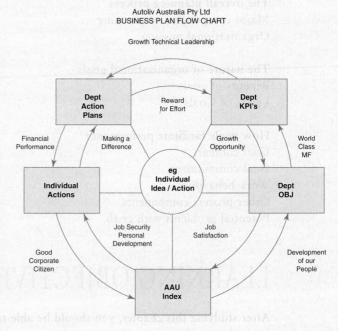

Autoliv Australia Pty Ltd
BUSINESS PLAN FLOW CHART

Growth Technical Leadership

In this chapter, we examine the overall planning process, including development of the organisation's mission. We also consider the nature of organisational goals and examine a model helping explain how goals facilitate performance. Next we probe the link between goals and plans, considering how plans differ according to level, the extent of recurring use, and time horizon, and we examine the role of goals and plans in promoting innovation. Finally, we explore steps in the management by objectives process and review MBO's major strengths and weaknesses.

THE OVERALL PLANNING PROCESS

Having a good idea of an organisation's overall mission, as well as more specific, written goals and carefully configured plans, is important to an organisation's success. In this section, we introduce these major components of the planning process.

Major components of planning

One could argue it is impossible for organisations to function without at least some goals and plans. A **goal** is a future target or end result an organisation wishes to achieve. Many managers and researchers use the term 'goal' interchangeably with 'objective'. Others consider 'goal' to be broader, encompassing a longer time horizon, and use 'objective' to refer to narrower targets and shorter time frames (Rue & Holland 1989). We use both interchangeably for simplicity. When a distinction between the two is important to the concepts being examined, it will be clear from the context whether a broad or narrow scope or a long or short time-frame is involved.

Where a goal is an end result an organisation wants to achieve, a **plan** is the means for trying to reach the goal. Planning, then, is the management function involving setting goals and deciding how best to achieve them. Managers make extensive use of decision-making skills, as well as various planning and decision aids (see Chapter 5 and the supplement to Chapter 5), in carrying out the planning function. An overall view of the process is shown in Figure 6.1. Hopefully, setting goals and developing plans leads to goal attainment and, ultimately, to organisational efficiency and effectiveness. As the diagram indicates, the planning process also involves the organisation's mission.

goal

Future target or end result an organisation wishes to achieve

plan

Means devised for attempting to reach a goal

Fig. 6.1   The overall planning process

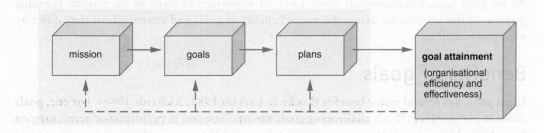

Organisational mission

Essentially, planning builds on the organisation's **mission**, the organisation's purpose or fundamental reason for existence. A mission statement is a broad statement of the basic, unique purpose and scope of operations distinguishing the organisation from others of its type (Pearce & Robinson 1988). A **mission statement** serves many purposes. For managers, it is a benchmark to evaluate success against. For employees, a mission statement defines a common purpose, nurtures organisational loyalty, and fosters a sense of community for workers. For external parties such as investors, government agencies and the public, it helps provide unique insight into the organisation's values and future direction (Nash 1988). In some organisations,

mission

The organisation's purpose or fundamental reason for existence

mission statement

Broad declaration of the basic, unique purpose and scope of operations distinguishing the organisation from others of its type

the mission is presented as a formal written document. In others, the statement is implicit. Of course, in the latter case, there is a danger various organisation members may have different perceptions of the mission, perhaps without realising it (Want 1986; Morrisey 1988).

One study estimates about 60 per cent of *Fortune* 500 companies have written mission statements (Pearce & David 1987). According to another study, which examined statements of 75 firms from the *Business Week* 1000, mission statements tend to comprise some or all of these nine components (David 1989):

1 **Customers**. Who are the organisation's customers?
2 **Products or services**. What are the organisation's major products or services?
3 **Location**. Where does the organisation compete?
4 **Technology**. What is the firm's basic technology?
5 **Concern for survival**. What is the organisation's commitment to economic objectives?
6 **Philosophy**. What are the organisation's basic beliefs, values, aspirations and philosophical priorities?
7 **Self-concept**. What are the organisation's major strengths and competitive advantages?
8 **Concern for public image**. What are the organisation's public responsibilities, and what image is desired?
9 **Concern for employees**. What is the organisation's attitude toward its employees?

Excerpts from mission statements matching each of these components are shown in Table 6.1. Nash (1988 p. 156) studies mission statements, and reports that her favourite statement hangs, yellowing, on the wall of a Boston shoe-repair shop. It reads: 'We are dedicated to the saving of soles, heeling and administering to the dyeing'.

THE NATURE OF ORGANISATIONAL GOALS

As we have seen, organisational goals form an important element in the overall planning process. In this section, we assess the major benefits of goals and examine how they differ by organisational level.

Benefits of goals

Using goals has several major benefits (Locke & Latham 1984; Richards 1986). For one, goals increase performance. When challenging goals are set, increases in performance occur, ranging from 10 to 25 per cent and sometimes even higher. Furthermore, such increases occur across employee groups, including clerical, maintenance, production, sales, managers, engineers and scientists (Pritchard, Roth, Jones, Galgay & Watson 1988).

Another benefit of goals is they help clarify expectations. With goals, organisation members have a clear idea of their expected major outcomes (Hammer & Champy 1993). Without goals, members lack direction. Thus, even when they all work very hard, they may collectively accomplish little—as if they were rowers independently rowing the same boat in different directions and making little progress.

Goals also facilitate controlling by providing benchmarks to assess progress so corrective action can be taken if needed. Thus goals help individuals gauge their progress and also assist managers maintain control over organisational activities (Siler 1989).

Table 6.1   Major components and sample excerpts

Major component	Sample excerpt
Customers	To deliver quality welfare service to New Zealanders in the most cost-effective way and in accordance with the policies of the government. (New Zealand Department of Social Welfare) The purpose of Motorola is to honourably serve the needs of the community by providing products and services of superior quality at a fair price to our customers. (Motorola)
Products or services	We will become a world leader in defining and delivering valued telecommunications services by setting new levels of excellence in service, quality and productivity, and through the application of leading-edge technology. (Optus) We deliver service of an international standard in a professional and personalised way. (ANA Hotel, Singapore)
Location	Sara Lee Corporation's mission is to be a leading consumer marketing company in the United States and internationally. (Sara Lee Corporation)
Technology	Du Pont is a diversified chemical, energy and speciality products company with a strong tradition of discovery. Our global businesses are constantly evolving and continually searching for new and better ways to use our human, technological and financial resources to improve the quality of life of people around the world. (Du Pont)
Concern for survival	To serve the worldwide need for knowledge at a fair profit by gathering, evaluating, producing and distributing valuable information in a way that benefits our customers, employees, authors, investors and our society. (McGraw-Hill)
Philosophy	It's all part of the Mary Kay philosophy—a philosophy based on the golden rule. A spirit of sharing and caring where people give cheerfully of their time, knowledge and experience. (Mary Kay Cosmetics)
Self-concept	Crown Zellerbach is committed to leapfrogging competition within 1000 days by unleashing the constructive and creative abilities and energies of each of its employees. (Crown Zellerbach)
Concern for public image	The company feels an obligation to be a good corporate citizen wherever it operates. (Eli Lilly & Company)
Concern for employees	The people of Airways Corporation are qualified, motivated professionals committed to providing—on a sound commercial basis—safe, efficient and cost-effective air-traffic management and related services which meet the needs of our customers. We aim to make the Corporation the best it can be—to work for and to do business with. (Airways Corporation of New Zealand)

Source: Adapted from David (1989, pp. 92–3).

Another benefit of goals is increased motivation. Meeting goals, feeling a sense of accomplishment, and receiving recognition and other rewards for reaching targeted outcomes all enhance motivation.

An interesting study by Latham and Locke (1979) shows goal setting's benefits. The situation involved truck drivers of a forest-products company in the western United States. Unionised drivers were concerned that, if their log-hauling trucks were overloaded, they could

Achieving organisational goals involves a cycle of assessment, planning, negotiation and commitment.

be fined by the highway department and lose their jobs. For this reason, they seldom loaded their trucks to more than 63 per cent of capacity. Interestingly, the company had not set any goals concerning expected load levels.

In an experiment, the company co-ordinated a plan with the union specifying the goal of loading to 94 per cent of legal truck capacity. Under the agreement's terms, no reprimands would be issued if the goal was not met. No monetary rewards or fringe benefits were offered as incentives. However, verbal praise was given when drivers loaded their trucks to greater levels than before. During the first month, trucks hauled 80 per cent of capacity, more than ever before. In the second month, however, performance decreased to 70 per cent of capacity. Interviews with drivers revealed they were testing management to see if action would be taken against drivers who did not reach the goal. When drivers realised no action was going to be taken, they increased their performance. Loading capacity reached over 90 per cent in the third month and remained there for more than seven years. Over the nine-month study period the company saved over $250 000 (Latham & Locke 1979). Thus the goal clarified expectations, helped increase motivation, provided a standard against which to assess progress, and led to improved performance. This is one of many studies supporting goal setting's organisational importance (Lee, Locke & Latham 1980).

Levels of goals

Organisations typically have three levels of goals: strategic, tactical and operational, as shown in Figure 6.2. (Also shown are three parallel levels of plans, discussed later in this chapter.)

strategic goals

Broadly defined targets or future results set by top management

tactical goals

Targets or future results usually set by middle management for specific departments or units

operational goals

Targets or future results set by lower management that address specific measurable outcomes required from the lower levels

Strategic goals   **Strategic goals** are broadly defined targets or future results set by top management. They typically address issues relating to the whole organisation and are stated in fairly general terms. Strategic goals are sometimes called official goals, as top management formally states them (Perrow 1961; Richards 1986).

Drucker (1974) suggests organisations set goals in at least eight major areas (shown in Table 6.2). These areas encompass aspects important to the health and survival of most profit-making organisations (Morrisey 1996).

Tactical goals   **Tactical goals** are targets or future results usually set by middle management for specific departments or units. Goals at this level spell out what must be done by various departments to achieve results outlined in strategic goals. Tactical goals are stated in more measurable terms than strategic goals.

Operational goals   **Operational goals** are targets or future results set by lower management addressing specific measurable outcomes required from lower levels.

Fig. 6.2   Levels of goals and plans

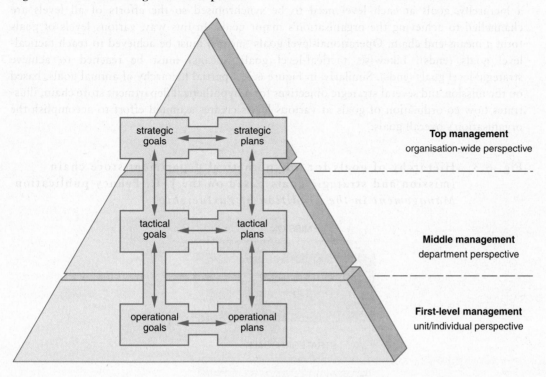

strategic goals ↔ strategic plans

Top management
organisation-wide perspective

tactical goals ↔ tactical plans

Middle management
department perspective

operational goals ↔ operational plans

First-level management
unit/individual perspective

Table 6.2   Eight major areas for strategic goals

Major area	Description
Market standing	Desired share of present and new markets, including areas in which new products are needed, and service goals aimed at building customer loyalty
Innovation	Innovations in products or services, as well as innovations in skills and activities required to supply them
Human resources	Supply, development and performance of managers and other organisation members; employee attitudes and development of skills; relations with unions, if any
Financial resources	Sources of capital and how it will be utilised
Physical resources	Physical facilities and how they will be used in the production of goods and services
Productivity	Efficient use of resources relative to outcomes
Social responsibility	Responsibilities in such areas as concern for community and maintenance of ethical behaviour
Profit requirements	Level of profitability and other indicators of financial well-being

Source: Based on Drucker (1974, pp. 103–17).

Hierarchy of goals   The three levels of goals can be thought of as forming a hierarchy. With a hierarchy, goals at each level need to be synchronised so the efforts of all levels are channelled to achieving the organisation's major goals. In this way, various levels of goals form a means-end chain. Operational-level goals (means) must be achieved to reach tactical-level goals (ends). Likewise, tactical-level goals (means) must be reached to achieve strategic-level goals (ends). Similarly, in Figure 6.3, a partial hierarchy of annual goals, based on the mission and several strategic objectives for a hypothetical department store chain, illustrates how co-ordination of goals at various levels creates a united effort to accomplish the organisation's overall goals.

Fig. 6.3   Hierarchy of goals for a hypothetical department store chain (mission and strategic goals based on the J. C. Penney publication *Management in the Tradition of Partnership*)

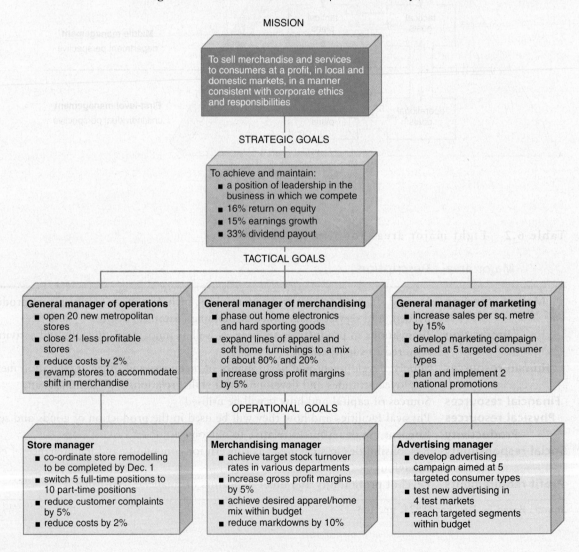

MISSION

To sell merchandise and services to consumers at a profit, in local and domestic markets, in a manner consistent with corporate ethics and responsibilities

STRATEGIC GOALS

To achieve and maintain:
- a position of leadership in the business in which we compete
- 16% return on equity
- 15% earnings growth
- 33% dividend payout

TACTICAL GOALS

General manager of operations
- open 20 new metropolitan stores
- close 21 less profitable stores
- reduce costs by 2%
- revamp stores to accommodate shift in merchandise

General manager of merchandising
- phase out home electronics and hard sporting goods
- expand lines of apparel and soft home furnishings to a mix of about 80% and 20%
- increase gross profit margins by 5%

General manager of marketing
- increase sales per sq. metre by 15%
- develop marketing campaign aimed at 5 targeted consumer types
- plan and implement 2 national promotions

OPERATIONAL GOALS

Store manager
- co-ordinate store remodelling to be completed by Dec. 1
- switch 5 full-time positions to 10 part-time positions
- reduce customer complaints by 5%
- reduce costs by 2%

Merchandising manager
- achieve target stock turnover rates in various departments
- increase gross profit margins by 5%
- achieve desired apparel/home mix within budget
- reduce markdowns by 10%

Advertising manager
- develop advertising campaign aimed at 5 targeted consumer types
- test new advertising in 4 test markets
- reach targeted segments within budget

Not in the plans

When one forms a relationship, one rarely plans for it to go wrong. Or should one do so?

Hans Stoehr learnt this the hard way when a deal that was finalised late last year dissolved into a bitter dispute five months later. Unexpected operational problems did put pressure on the partnership, but the problems stemmed from the original agreement.

In November 1997, Stoehr, the owner and manager of Vertigo Tree Services in Dubbo, New South Wales, won a contract that offered a tremendous growth opportunity. His tree-pruning service, established in 1996, had turnover of about $150 000 by June 1998. The new contract to manage green waste for 26 councils in central western NSW, which he won over much larger rivals, could increase turnover by $900 000.

The $395 000 mulching machine that Stoehr proposed to use for the job helped him to win the contract, but he did not have the cash or finance facility to buy one. Stoehr says: 'Other machines beat the product to a pulp, and you don't get a saleable product'.

After several months fruitlessly trying to raise funds from banks and finance companies, he turned to the Sydney-based equity matchmaker, Australian Business Angels, to find a partner. He wanted a loan of $100 000 to put a deposit on the machine and working capital of $50 000. He was prepared to offer a 5 to 10 per cent share of the profits for the period of the loan. 'I wanted to retain full control of the business', he says.

Australian Business Angels found Mark Sheridan of Moree, who had the skills and capital Stoehr could use, but the investor wanted more than was being offered. Sheridan met Stoehr in August. Sheridan insisted on forming a separate company, Vertigo Services, and wanted 50 per cent of the company and its profits. Stoehr thought the deal was unfair, but agreed to it. The deal was still under negotiation in November 1998, and Stoehr felt in danger of losing the contract altogether. He found such a prospect embarrassing as well as damaging to his business. Sheridan says Stoehr did not voice any concerns about the terms at the time. Stoehr denies this.

The project hit trouble almost immediately. The United States manufacturer of the mulcher claims it can handle 78 cubic metres of waste an hour. Stoehr cannot get this result. 'The lowest we have done is 30, and the average is 50', he says. Vertigo's income has been reduced.

Stoehr says the waste coming from the councils has had rocks and hard waste in it because ratepayers are not yet aware of the need to separate materials. The machine has been damaged repeatedly. Staff began sorting material before mulching it, but he has since told the councils that he will pass on the cost of repairs. The density of Australian hardwoods and tree stumps is also slowing the machine.

Sheridan says the reduction in income is caused by inadequate management of time and staff. He visited the work site in secret to watch the operation. 'The machine did not start working until 9.40 because they were waiting for fuel', he says. 'Then it stopped again at 10.30 because the cutters were blunt, but everyone had been sitting around for an hour and a half.'

Sheridan refused to put in more money. After observing the work, he asked Stoehr to make changes. He gave him a few weeks to do so, but was dissatisfied with the results and withheld the remaining $30 000 of the $150 000 he had pledged.

Stoehr was angered by Sheridan's visit, but says he did act on several of the recommendations. He says Sheridan is not entitled to withhold the extra funds, but there is insufficient time, money and inclination to dispute the point in court. Sheridan says Stoehr has breached the contract.

Stoehr's feeling of being ripped off has undermined the partnership. The problems have little to do with the size of Sheridan's share, yet Stoehr often refers to the unfairness of the deal, and to Sheridan's focus on finance. 'I just don't like bean counters', Stoehr says. 'The truck and the bobcat we funded through a loan [from a finance company] for $750 000 which is on my shoulders, not his. He has only put in $120 000.' Sheridan says the loan is $475 000. Stoehr is a guarantor. Sheridan is not.

Sheridan says the venture should have been profitable within three months and its difficulties stem from a lack of business skills. Stoehr admits he has fallen behind his financial projections, but says Sheridan has not been patient enough. He believes the problems are beyond his control. He is ploughing his wages back into the venture to keep it going, but is making enough to pay his two staff. He says the business will be profitable within six months.

Stoehr says Sheridan has made two offers: Stoehr could buy Sheridan out for $132 000 ($12 000 more than Sheridan contributed), or if Sheridan pays Stoehr say, $100, Sheridan will take over the company, debts and all. Sheridan confirms that the offers have been made. He says the $132 000 offer represents his contribution plus costs. He does not really want to take over the company: his offer to take over is simply one way of recouping his capital.

Source: Walters, K. (1999).

Activities for discussion, analysis and further research

1 It is obvious that there are problems in the company described above. Describe a plan which might have avoided some of those difficulties.

2 Develop a plan which might at this stage assist Stoehr resolve the problems and avoid his losing the company.

HOW GOALS FACILITATE PERFORMANCE

To make effective use of goals, managers must understand how goals can facilitate performance. The major components involved in enhancing performance are shown in Figure 6.4.

In this section, we consider these components, highlighting particularly goal content, goal commitment, work behaviour and feedback aspects.

Fig. 6.4   How goals facilitate performance (adapted from Lee, Locke & Latham 1989, pp. 291–326)

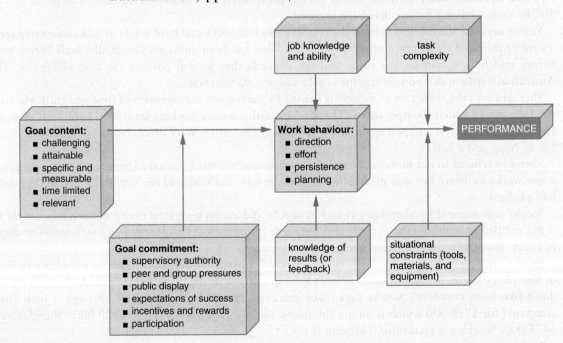

Goal content

Goals effective in channelling effort towards achievement at strategic, tactical and operational levels have a content reflecting five major characteristics. Goals should be challenging, attainable, specific and measurable, time-limited and relevant.

Challenging   Extensive research indicates that, within reasonable limits, challenging, difficult goals lead to higher performance. Assuming goals are accepted, people try harder when faced with a challenge. Interestingly, when individuals are asked to do their 'best', they do not perform as well as they do with specific, challenging goals.

Attainable   Although goals need to be challenging, they usually work best when attainable. If individuals make maximum use of their skills and abilities, they cannot achieve higher performance levels. Asking workers to meet difficult, but attainable, goals is more likely to promote sustained performance over time than continually asking them to do the impossible (Locke & Latham 1984). Still, research shows individuals perform better with difficult goals than with easy ones.

Specific and measurable   To be effective, goals must be specific and measurable so workers clearly understand what is expected and know when the goal has been achieved. When possible, goals should be stated in quantitative terms. Quantitative goals encompass relatively easy-to-verify objective numerical standards. At Rubbermaid Inc., a company with a reputation for innovative products, a quantitative goal is to derive 30 per cent of its sales from products less than five years old. In some cases, though, qualitative goals are more appropriate. Qualitative goals involve subjective judgment about whether or not a goal is reached. A qualitative goal at Rubbermaid is to develop an idea and prototype for a new useful, long-lasting, and inexpensive plastic desk accessory (Wright & Kacmar 1994; Mathews 1995).

Time-limited   Goals also need to be time-limited; that is, there should be a defined period of time within which a goal must be accomplished. Otherwise, goals have little meaning, since individuals can keep putting them off. In many organisations, goals are set annually but may be reviewed more often, such as quarterly (Latham & Wexley 1981).

Relevant   Goals are more likely to be supported when they are clearly relevant to the organisation's major work and the particular department or work unit.

For guidelines on how to set goals, see the Management skills for the 21st century discussion, 'How to set goals'.

 # How to set goals

management skills
for the 21st century

There are six main steps in setting goals to obtain optimal results:

1   Specify the goal to be reached or tasks to be done. What do you want to accomplish? Do you want to increase sales? Reduce costs? Improve quality? Boost customer service? Maybe, at the moment, you are thinking you would like to obtain an A in a particular course this semester (perhaps the one involving this textbook).

2 Specify how performance will be measured. Some outcomes can be measured more easily than others (e.g. number of units sold and dollar volume of sales). Work outcomes (the results achieved) are typically measured according to one of three parameters:

   Physical units: For example, quantity of production, market share, number of errors, number of rejects (quality control)

   Time: For example, meeting deadlines, servicing customers, completing a project, coming to work each day, being punctual

   Money: For example, profits, sales, costs, budgets, debts, income

   Similarly, many course-of-study outcomes can be measured in terms of physical units (such as the number of questions answered correctly on examinations and grades received on papers and assignments) and in terms of time (such as meeting deadlines for assignments and attending classes).

   Sometimes outcomes are difficult to measure, perhaps because measurement would be too costly or because outcomes are affected by factors beyond an individual's control. In such cases, it may be necessary to measure behaviours or actions instead of outcomes. For example, if a manager's goal of overcoming worker resistance to impending changes will be affected significantly by others' actions, it may be possible to measure crucial activities instead of outcomes. Such activities might include whether the manager clearly explains why change is needed, outlines how the change will affect others, and listens to employee's concerns. When possible, though, goal-setting should focus on outcomes.

3 Specify the standard or target to be reached. This builds on the type of measure chosen in step 2 by spelling out the degree of performance required. For example, the target might be producing 40 units per hour, reducing errors by two per cent, completing a project by 15 December, answering the telephone within three rings, or increasing sales by 10 per cent.

   In pursuing the objective of attaining an A in a particular course, you might set targets such as correctly answering at least 90 per cent of questions on mid-term and final exams, offering one knowledgeable point during discussion in each class, and fulfilling written assignments well enough to earn high grades. Setting subgoals, such as the number of textbook pages to be read and summarised each day, can also help goal achievement.

4 Specify the time span involved. To have a positive impact on performance, goals must have a time span within which they are to be completed. In a production situation, the goal may be stated in terms of production per hour or day. In a service situation, the goal may involve the time taken to deliver a service. For example, a photocopier repair service may have the goal of responding to customer calls within two hours. Other goals, such as major projects, may have time spans involving months or even years. For instance, your goals for the semester may involve a few months, while goals associated with obtaining your degree and developing your career may span several years.

5 Prioritise the goals. When multiple goals are present, as with most jobs, they need to be prioritised so effort and action can be directed in proportion to each goal's importance. Otherwise, individual effort can be focused poorly. For example, suppose in the course in which you want to obtain an A, examinations count 70 per cent, a paper counts 20 per cent, and discussion in class counts 10 per cent toward the grade. In this case, a goal related to examinations should be given first priority, while goals related to the paper and class discussion should receive second and third priority, respectively.

6 Determine co-ordination requirements. Before a set of goals is finalised, it is important to investigate whether achieving goals depends on other individuals' co-operation and contributions. If so, co-ordination with them may be needed. In organisations, vertical co-ordination is usually easy. It may be more difficult, but still important, to co-ordinate horizontally, particularly if some individuals report to other managers outside your work unit.

In the case of the course you are attempting to excel in, your efforts may require co-ordination with your boss (if employed) so your work schedule gives sufficient study time before exams. If you plan ahead, you may also be able to get parents, a spouse or friends to help with other duties at crucial times during the semester, such as right before exams, so you have plenty of time to review.

Source: Locke & Latham (1984).

Goal commitment

A critical element in effectively using goals is getting individuals and/or work groups to be committed to goals they must carry out. **Goal commitment** is one's attachment to, or determination to reach, a goal (Locke, Latham & Erez 1988). Without commitment, setting specific, challenging goals will not impact on performance. How, then, can managers foster commitment to important organisational goals? They can draw on five major factors positively influencing goal commitment: supervisory authority, peer and group pressure, public display of commitment, expectations of success, and incentives and rewards. A sixth factor, participation, is sometimes helpful.

goal commitment

One's attachment to, or determination to reach, a goal

Supervisory authority   Individuals and groups often commit themselves to a goal when the goal and reasons for it are explained by someone with supervisory authority. With this approach, goals are essentially assigned by a supervisor, who explains the reason for the goals to their employees while providing them with needed instructions. The explanation and instructions will be more effective when the supervisor is supportive, not authoritative. Instead of simply telling subordinates to meet goals, a supervisor must give encouragement and offer opportunities for questions to be asked.

Peer and group pressure   Pressure from peers and work-group members enhances goal commitment when everyone's efforts are focused. This is because enthusiasm becomes infectious. In addition, successful individuals serve as role models for others. However, peer and group pressure can reduce goal commitment, if goals are seen as unfair.

Public display   Recent evidence suggests commitment to difficult goals is higher when commitment is public (made in front of others) than when private.

Expectations of success   Goal commitment is more likely when individuals or groups have high expectations of success. That is, individuals become committed when they believe they have a good chance of performing well on tasks needed to reach the goal. If they believe they cannot accomplish the tasks, they are unlikely to be committed to the goal.

Incentives and rewards   Goal commitment is enhanced by incentives and rewards. Incentives are offered during goal-setting, while rewards occur upon goal achievement. Some are tangible, such as money, others intangible, such as job challenge, anticipation of or positive feelings about accomplishment, feedback, competition (as long as it is constructive) and recognition for goal attainment.

While positive outcomes foster commitment, negative outcomes inhibit it. For example, if workers fear increased production will lead to layoffs, commitment to high production goals will be low. It is important to ensure goal achievement is not associated with unfavourable consequences.

Participation   Although research shows participation is not needed to gain goal commitment, individual participation in goal-setting can foster commitment. Participation is particularly helpful in developing plans for implementing goals. For these reasons, managers often include subordinates in goal setting and in subsequent planning of how to achieve the goals (Locke et al. 1988).

Work behaviour

Given goals and commitment, how does goal-setting ultimately influence behaviour? Goal content and commitment affect an individual's work behaviour by influencing four factors: direction, effort, persistence and planning.

Direction   Goals direct attention and action toward activities related to the goals, rather than toward other activities. Thus, when individuals are committed to specific goals, those goals help them make better choices about activities they will undertake.

Effort   In addition to channelling activities, goals to which individuals are committed boost effort by mobilising energy. Individuals will try harder when goals are difficult than when easy.

Persistence   Persistence involves maintaining direction and effort to reach a goal. This means persistence may be required over time. Commitment to goals makes it more likely individuals will persist.

Planning   In addition to their effects on work behaviour in terms of direction, effort and persistence, goals have an indirect effect through their influence on planning. Individuals committed to achieving difficult goals are likely to develop plans or methods to attain those goals. With easy goals, however, little planning may be needed.

Other process components

Several other components influence goals' impact on job performance. For one, job knowledge and ability will affect an individual's work behaviour and prospects for goal attainment, even when there is strong commitment. For another, task complexity affects the influence of goal-directed work behaviour on job performance. According to related studies, the impact of goals on performance is greater with simple tasks (such as basic arithmetic, toy assembly tasks or basic typing) than more complex ones (such as supervision or engineering projects) (Wood, Meant & Locke 1987). Apparently, the effect of goals on direction, effort, work behaviour persistence and planning is diluted across a complex task.

Situational constraints are another element influencing the impact of goals on performance. Having proper tools, materials and equipment is important to achieve difficult goals. Finally, knowledge of results or feedback of progress toward goals is particularly influential in goal effectiveness. While goals set the target, knowledge of results influences goal achievement by allowing individuals to measure progress (Locke, Shaw, Saari & Latham 1981). Thus, goal setting is important in increasing productivity and quality. Still, it must be used properly.

Potential problems with goals

Although many positive aspects are associated with goal use in organisations, there are potential pitfalls (Locke & Latham 1984; 1990). These problems and solutions to each one are summarised in Table 6.3.

Table 6.3 Potential goal-setting problems and possible solutions

Potential problem	Possible remedies
Excessive risk taking	Analyse risk; avoid careless or foolish risks
Increased stress	Eliminate unnecessary stress by adjusting goal difficulty, adding staff and offering training in necessary skills
Undermined self-confidence	Treat failure as a problem to be solved rather than a signal to punish (due to failure)
Ignored non-goal areas	Make sure goals encompass key areas.
Excessive short-run thinking	Include some long-term goals.
Dishonesty and cheating	Set example of honesty, avoid using goals punitively, offer help in overcoming difficulties, give frequent feedback, and be open to information indicating goals are inappropriate.

Source: Based on Locke & Latham (1984, pp. 171–2)

LINKING GOALS AND PLANS

Goals and plans are closely related. Though an organisation may set strategic, tactical and operating goals, these will be meaningless unless thought is given to the actual process. While goals are desired ends, plans are the means to bring them about. The importance of plan development is clear when one considers there may be more than one way to reach a particular goal. Plans differ by organisational level and by extent of recurring use.

Levels of plans

As there are levels of goals, plans also differ by organisational level (see Fig. 6.2). Thus there are strategic, tactical and operational plans (Locke & Latham 1984).

Strategic plans   **Strategic plans** are detailed action steps mapped out to reach strategic goals. These address such issues as responses to changing conditions, allocation of resources, and the actions to be taken to create unified and powerful organisation-wide effort to achieve strategic goals (Thompson & Strickland 1987). Top management, in consultation with the board of directors and middle management, develop strategic plans. They typically cover a

strategic plans

Detailed action steps mapped out to reach strategic goals

time horizon of three to five years or more into the future. Organisations' strategic plans often include the mission and goals as these form the basis for action steps. We discuss issues related to strategic planning in the next chapter.

tactical plans

Means charted to support implementation of the strategic plan and achievement of tactical goals

Tactical plans   **Tactical plans** support strategic plan implementation and tactical goal achievement. These plans focus on intermediate time frames, usually one to three years. Generally, they are more specific and concrete than strategic plans. Tactical plans outline the major steps toward tactical goals. They are developed by middle managers in consultation with lower-level managers, before making commitments to top-level management. In developing tactical plans, managers may consider many possibilities before settling on a final plan (the plan is subject to change, should things not occur as expected). Tactical plans are important to the success of strategic plans.

operational plans

Means devised to support implementation of tactical plans and achievement of operational goals

Operational plans   **Operational plans** support the implementation of tactical plans and operational goal achievement. These plans generally consider time frames of below a year, such as a few months, weeks or even days. Operational-level plans are usually developed by lower-level managers in consultation with middle managers. They spell out what must be accomplished over short time periods to achieve operational goals. Unless operational goals are achieved, tactical and strategic plans will be unsuccessful and goals at those levels unachieved.

Plans according to extent of recurring use

Plans can be categorised by how frequently they will be used. There are two types of plans: single-use plans and standing plans (see Fig. 6.5).

single-use plans

Plans aimed at achieving a specific goal which, once reached, will most likely not recur in the future

Single-use plans   **Single-use plans** aim to achieve a specific goal which, once reached, will be unlikely to recur. There are two major types of single-use plans: programs and projects.

A **program** is a comprehensive plan co-ordinating a set of activities for a major non-recurring goal. Programs involve several different organisation units, comprise several different projects, and may take over a year to complete. Programs usually include six basic steps: (1) dividing what is to be done into major parts, or projects, (2) determining the relationships between parts and developing a sequence, (3) deciding who will take responsibility for each part, (4) determining how each part will be completed and the necessary

program

Comprehensive plan co-ordinating a complex set of activities related to a major non-recurring goal

Fig. 6.5   Plans according to extent of recurring use

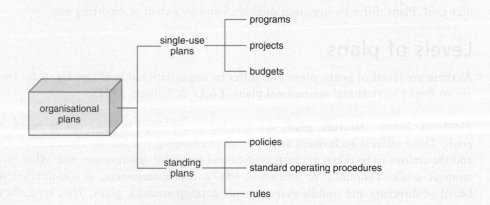

resources, (5) estimating time required for completion of each part, and (6) developing a schedule for implementing each step (Newman & Logan 1981). Programs frequently have their own budgets. A budget is a statement outlining financial resources needed to support various activities in the program.

A **project** is a plan co-ordinating a set of limited-scope activities not needing to be divided into major components to reach an important non-recurring goal. Like programs, projects often have their own budgets. A project may be one of several in a particular program.

Standing plans   **Standing plans** provide guidance for performing recurring activities. The three main types of standing plans are policies, procedures, and rules (Rue & Holland 1989).

A **policy** is a general guide specifying broad parameters within which organisation members operate in pursuit of organisational goals. Policies do not normally dictate specific actions. Rather, they provide general boundaries to action. For example, policies spell out important constraints. Many retail stores have a policy requiring returned merchandise be accompanied by a sales receipt. Similarly, policies may outline desirable actions (Sellers 1988).

A **procedure** is a set series of steps to be taken in certain recurring circumstances. Well-established and formalised procedures are called standard operating procedures (SOPs). Unlike policies, which are fairly general, procedures provide detailed, step-by-step instructions. Thus they do not allow flexibility or deviation. For example, banks have SOPs governing how tellers handle deposits. Because they specify desired recurring actions, SOPs are good for new employee training.

A **rule** is a statement spelling out specific actions to be taken or not taken in a situation. Unlike procedures, rules do not specify a series of steps. Instead, they dictate exactly what must be or must not be done, leaving no flexibility or room for deviation.

Time horizons of goals and plans

Different levels of goals and plans relate to different time horizons (see Fig. 6.6). Strategic goals and plans address long-range issues with time periods of five years or more. The period varies

Fig. 6.6   Time horizons for goals and plans

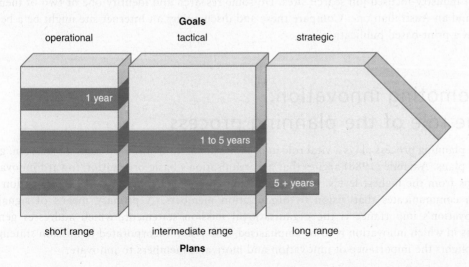

project

Plan co-ordinating a set of limited-scope activities which do not need to be divided into several major projects to reach a major non-recurring goal

standing plans

Plans providing ongoing guidance for performing recurring activities

policy

General guide specifying broad parameters within which organisation members are expected to operate in pursuit of organisational goals

procedure

Prescribed series of related steps to be taken under certain recurring circumstances

rule

Statement spelling out specific actions to be taken or not taken in a given situation

depending on the industry. In rapidly changing environments, long-range planning may focus on periods of less than five years. In stable environments (such as the power industry), long-range planning extends from 10 to 20 years. Tactical goals and plans address intermediate-range issues with periods between one and five years. Operational goals and plans are oriented toward short-range issues spanning periods of one year or less.

@ E-jobs in China

managing the e-challenge

Twelve months ago, *Career Post* was a 300 000 circulation classified advertisements broadsheet filled with job listings from hundreds of multinational firms and foreign joint-ventures. One of its owners, Norman Lui, recalls being trapped in a walk-in cupboard of a friend's apartment by mountains of freshly printed newspapers which were picked up by delivery boys in the evening.

From a twice-monthly newspaper, *Career Post Weekly* became 51job.com, charging 1000 yuan (A$185) per advertisement, which is about 10 per cent of the newspaper charge. The site is now packed with 15 000 listings. Online listings are apparently not cannibalising the newspaper. The benefits come from cross-marketing, says Lui, who believes that stripping down to the Internet only would not be profitable.

Fusing the traditional business and the Internet, a process known as 'clicks and mortar', has allowed 51job.com to expand from Beijing and Shanghai to Guangzhou without having to give up control to overseas investors. The enterprise is already profitable and expects to see four or five times revenue growth this year. When asked about foreign investors, Norman Lui says: 'We're not one of those companies which will die if the investment stops. We can choose the quality of our investors—what added value can they offer us in terms of technology and connections?' And to date, the answer appears to be 'none'.

Source: Adapted from Reuters (2000).

Activities for discussion, analysis and further research

1 What does the above case study indicate about the planning activities the owners of *Career Post* have been undertaking?

2 There are a number of industry-focused job search sites. Do some research and identify one or two of them. Log onto 51job.com and an Australian one. Compare these and discuss why an Internet site might be a better place to advertise than a print-based publication.

Promoting innovation: The role of the planning process

The planning process plays a vital role in organisational innovation through the mission, goals and plans. Amabile (1988) argues that an organisation's basic orientation toward innovation stems from the highest levels. Ideally, the CEO envisions a future based on innovation and then communicates that vision to organisation members. A primary means of signalling innovation's importance is the organisational mission statement, which addresses general areas in which innovation is to be emphasised. The vision incorporated in mission statements highlights the importance of innovation and motivates members to innovate.

The goals component of planning also supports innovation. For example, translating a mission into strategic goals might lead to the following: 'Within five years, the organisation will be the number-one provider of state-of-the-art semiconductor chips in a [specified broad] area'. The 'state-of-the-art' designation signals the need for product innovation. A corresponding tactical-level goal might be: 'Within two years, the programmable logic devices division will introduce 20 new products'. Finally, at an operational level, a particular work unit's goal might be: 'Within one year, the unit will have a working prototype meeting following general specifications...' Thus each level of goals encourages innovation.

The plans component of planning also has a role in innovation. While goals calling for innovative outcomes can be stated in general terms, actual plans for achieving such outcomes (e.g. new products) are often looser than plans for predictable situations. The greater flexibility reflects difficulty specifying exactly what should be done when seeking innovative breakthroughs and nurturing new ideas, particularly in product or service development. Of course, the likelihood of innovative goal achievement can be increased if managers ensure that organisational conditions foster innovation (Hill & Jones 1995). We discuss several of these conditions, such as organisational structure, resource levels, communication patterns and leadership, in later chapters.

Plans can help achieve goals which do not represent innovative outcomes but rely on innovative means. Even if a goal focuses on a traditional result, such as cost cutting or quality improvement, plan development can encourage innovative ways to reach the target (Ramanujam & Varadarajan 1989; Scheifer & Vishny 1994). In this way, emphasis is on developing innovative ways to reach goals not stated in terms of innovative outcomes.

'Now the fast eat the slow'   gaining the edge

'It used to be that the big ate the small; now the fast eat the slow.' So stated a partner in the venture-capital firm Redpoint Ventures. The impact of this on planning is revolutionary. Net-speed has forced all sorts of cultural changes. Customer expectations, not executive boards, guide big projects and their planning.

The five-year plan is dead, and so is the three-year version. In the information economy, organisations are writing and rewriting the plan every three months. An illustration of the required speed and changes required is Sun Microsystem's President Ed Zander, who holds weekly 'whack-o-meter' sessions to assess ways that rivals might 'whack' Sun in the market place.

Organisations are beginning to shy away from conventional thinkers who plan carefully and are determined to carry out the plan. What they need now is individuals who thrive on change and ambiguity and are prepared to throw plans out and start over often and regularly.

Source: Adapted from Stepanek, M. (1999).

Activities for discussion, analysis and further research

1 Log on to www.GoodHome.com, a company which went from idea to business plan to first round of venture capital to merger and launch in 10 weeks. Consider the issues which needed to be faced in order to achieve this process. Would it have been possible to plan it? Why and How?

2 When things have to move that quickly, it takes special activities to maintain morale and energy in your staff. What are some of the problems which such a situation might cause and how could they be overcome?

Potential obstacles to planning

Several potential obstacles threaten organisations' ability to develop effective plans. One is rapid environmental change, which makes planning more difficult. Another obstacle is that some managers view planning as unnecessary. This occurs when managers have at least a general idea about future directions and ways to reach organisational goals (*INC* 1989). Another potential barrier to planning is managers' day-to-day work pressures. Even when managers feel planning is beneficial, daily stress can focus their attention away from planning (Mintzberg 1980). Yet another obstacle is poor line-manager preparation in terms of planning knowledge and skills. Finally, effective planning may be thwarted if staff specialists come to dominate the planning process. This leads to low involvement by those managers ultimately implementing the plans (Grey 1986).

Organisations can reduce planning obstacles. One step is showing strong top-management support for the planning process. Top-level managers demonstrate commitment by personal involvement in the process and by maintaining interest in plan implementation. This commitment encourages lower-level managers to engage in and support planning. Another step is ensuring planning staffs, or corporate planners, have a helping role, rather than actually plan. **Planning staff** assist top-level managers develop various planning process components. Such staff typically help monitor both internal and external environments to generate data for top management's strategic decisions. They also suggest changes to organisational missions, goals and plans. From the 1960s to early 1980s corporate planners' influence grew, often dominating the planning process and leaving line managers in minor roles. Since then, the role of planning staff has been reduced (Rue & Holland 1989). For instance, when John F. Welch Jr became chairman at General Electric, he cut corporate planning staff from 58 to 33. Corporate planners were also eliminated across the company (*Business Week* 1984).

The GE moves are another step organisations can take to reduce planning obstacles. Top management can actively involve managers primarily responsible for carrying out the plans. In part, this means providing them with training in planning. Managers must be encouraged to review plans often, particularly in rapidly changing environments. To cope with these environments, managers can also use contingency planning. **Contingency planning** is developing alternative plans for use if environmental conditions evolve unexpectedly, making original plans unwise or infeasible.

planning staff

Small group of individuals who assist top-level managers in developing various components of the planning process

contingency planning

Development of alternative plans for use in the event that environmental conditions evolve differently than anticipated, rendering original plans unwise or infeasible

✖ Planning takes time   crossroads

Australiawide Loading, Melbourne-based transport company, took five years to find the right equity investors. During that time, they acquired market information that became critical to their company's success. They gained the support of important stakeholders in the industry. Furthermore, they had plenty of opportunity to rewrite and refine their business plan and financial strategy several times over.

Their determination was an asset in itself. By March of 1999 they had raised almost a million dollars, half from the Australian Government in the form of a concessional loan and the balance from an investor. In the time that it took them to organise this support, the cost of the hardware and software they needed had fallen and by leasing more of the equipment rather than buying it, they could lower start-up costs.

Source: Walters, K. (1999c).

The managers of Australiawide Loading use future investment planning, and openly display the company's goals in their offices.

Reflection point

1 To wait five years to implement a business is a long time. What do you think the partners John Bolton and John Williams might have done to shorten that time?

Decision points

1 Log into the Australiawide Loading web site www.alis.com.au and consider how the organisation does business.

2 What are some issues which this organisation should be taking into consideration as they develop their yearly plan of action?

MANAGEMENT BY OBJECTIVES

One method used by organisations to help linking goals and plans is management by objectives. **Management by objectives (MBO)** is a process by which specific goals are set collaboratively for the whole organisation and every unit and individual within it. These goals are then used for planning, managing organisational activities, and assessing and rewarding contributions. MBO incorporates considerable managerial and subordinate participation in setting the goals.

Although MBO's origins are unclear, General Electric appears to be the first organisation implementing the process, and Peter Drucker generally credited with being the first to write

management by objectives (MBO)

Process through which specific goals are set collaboratively for the organisation as a whole and every unit and individual within it; the goals are then used as a basis for planning, managing organisational activities, and assessing and rewarding contributions about it (Drucker 1954; Greenwood 1981). Over the years, MBO has been used by many organisations to help co-ordinate goal-setting and planning processes at various levels so organisation members' collective efforts ultimately support organisational goals. Organisations using MBO include Black & Decker, Texas Instruments, Boeing and Westinghouse (Raia 1974; Richards 1986).

Steps in the MBO process

There can be considerable variation in the way MBO is used in different organisations. Yet most viable MBO processes include the following six steps (see Fig. 6.7) (Raia 1974; Richards 1986):

1 **Develop overall organisational goals.** Goals at this stage are based on the organisation's mission, and address targets to be achieved by the whole organisation (e.g. a certain rate of return for a given period or a specific increase in market share). These goals are essentially strategic goals set by top management.

2 **Establish specific goals (or objectives) for various departments, subunits and individuals.** In this step, co-ordinating goals are set for various organisational levels so each goal helps reach the overall goals set in step 1. This stage begins when upper-level managers develop specific objectives they plan to accomplish, for their own departments or areas of responsibility (such as marketing or production). These goals are usually developed in collaboration with the next lower-level managers. For example, a head of a marketing department, together with regional sales managers, may set a goal of increasing a certain product's sales volume to 100 000 during the coming year. Then

Fig. 6.7   Steps in the MBO process

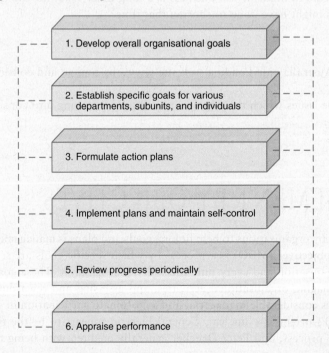

1. Develop overall organisational goals

2. Establish specific goals for various departments, subunits, and individuals

3. Formulate action plans

4. Implement plans and maintain self-control

5. Review progress periodically

6. Appraise performance

regional sales managers confer with their district managers in setting goals at regional levels. In the eastern region, for instance, a sales manager and district managers may decide on a goal of increasing sales volume to 25 000 for a particular product, thus contributing toward the 100 000 national-level goal. The process, referred to as cascading goals, continues until all units at various levels have specific goals for the coming year. At each level, goals are typically set in key areas, where results are critical to the organisation's success.

Although many organisations follow the top-down process just described, some use a bottom-up approach, in which goal setting begins at lower levels. These levels propose their goals on the basis of what they believe they can achieve. Tactical-level goals are then developed based on proposed goals provided by the operational level. The tactical goals are then proposed to the strategic level. Even with a bottom-up approach, however, goal setting usually follows some general guidelines developed at the strategic level. In any event, with MBO, there is some give-and-take among levels before goals at various levels are finalised.

3 **Formulate action plans.** Once goals are set, action plans must be developed focusing on methods or activities to reach particular goals. In essence, an action plan is a description of what is to be done, how, when, where and by whom to achieve a goal. Action plans contribute to feasibility of reaching goals, aid identifying problem areas, assist in spelling out areas needing resources and assistance, and facilitate search for more efficient and effective ways to achieve objectives. Such plans are usually developed by subordinates with their supervisors.

4 **Implement and maintain self-control.** A basic notion underlying MBO is once goals are set and action plans determined, individuals should be given latitude in carrying out their activities. The rationale with MBO is that individuals know what they are supposed to achieve, have mapped out plans, and can gauge their progress against set goals. Therefore, it is unnecessary for a supervisor to be involved in the individual's day-to-day activities as they might be without goals and action plans. The idea of self-control is especially true for managers. Of course, supervisors must be told about progress and unanticipated difficulties. They may need to provide coaching and support if subordinates have difficulties too.

5 **Review progress periodically.** Periodic reviews are important to ensure plans are implemented as expected and goals will be met. Such reviews provide a good opportunity for checking performance to date, identifying and removing obstacles, solving problems, and altering action plans not achieving expected results. Reviews also make it possible to assess continuing appropriateness of goals and to change them or add new ones as needed. How frequently these reviews are held depend on how quickly situations change, but quarterly reviews are common.

6 **Appraise performance.** At the end of a goal-setting cycle, which usually runs for a period of a year, managers meet with each subordinate to appraise performance over the cycle. This typically focuses on the extent goals were met, on shortfalls, reasons for them, and actions to be taken to prevent the same problems in future. The appraisal session includes praise and recognition for areas where the subordinate has performed effectively, as well as discussion of areas benefiting from future development of knowledge and skills. Goals and plans for the next cycle may also be discussed at this point.

As Figure 6.7 indicates, feedback from each step may lead to revising prior goals or setting future ones. While constant revision of goals defeats MBO's purpose, some revisions may be needed due to major changes in circumstances. The purpose of goal-setting and planning processes is to co-ordinate efforts toward important organisational goals. If those goals need changing, then efforts probably require adjustment too; hence, goals at various levels should also be changed.

Strengths and weaknesses of MBO

Management by objectives has a number of major strengths. On the other hand, MBO has several weaknesses. MBO's main strengths and weaknesses are summarised in Table 6.4 (Carroll & Tosi 1973; Raia 1974; Leonard 1986; Richards 1986).

Table 6.4   Strengths and weaknesses of MBO

Strengths	Weaknesses
1 Aids co-ordination of goals and plans from top management	1 Tends to falter without strong, continual commitment
2 Helps clarify priorities and expectations	2 Necessitates considerable training of managers
3 Facilitates vertical and horizontal communication	3 Can be misused as a punitive device
4 Fosters employee motivation	4 May cause overemphasis on quantitative goals

Assessing MBO

Because of these weaknesses, MBO has not always reached its potential. According to one estimate, MBO has been used in almost half the *Fortune* 500 companies, but has been successful only about 20 to 25 per cent of the time (Muczyk 1979). MBO system failures seem to stem from inadequate top-management support and poor goal-setting and communication skills among managers who must implement the system. According to a recent study, however, when top management commitment to the MBO program and processes was high, the average gain in productivity was 56 per cent (Rodgers & Hunter 1991). Hence, the way in which managers implement MBO may undermine its effectiveness. While overall organisational or strategic goals are important to the MBO process, they are also a critical element in strategic management, a subject that we explore in the next chapter.

 **The MD's diary**   the reflective practitioner

If I look at the organisation when I arrived and think about what I saw that I liked, the culture was very good. The people were happy to be here, everyone was very committed, everyone worked very hard, they were very customer-focused and, by and large, they delivered the results the customers required. And they did that in a very nice, co-operative, friendly environment.

What concerned me a little was that the organisation was moving into a growth phase. There were opportunities to grow the business that I saw quite clearly, but the organisation wasn't positioned for that growth in terms of the people, the skills and the organisation structure. It was an organisation that was very much structured for the there and then. That was appropriate, as we came out of an environment where the business wasn't profitable, we had very poor customer relationships, and we had a very savage industrial relations environment. I think the work that was done gave me a free start. But what it needed was to be developed so it would cope with the growth. I saw the important thing to do was to put in place a process which would enable the individuals in the organisation to grow and take on more responsibility. This enabled me to take the organisation, one where the previous Managing Director provided day-to-day direction, to one that encouraged and developed senior managers to take an increasing role in managing the operational requirements of the business.

What I try to do is encourage people in the organisation that have the ability to grow beyond their current position. These people are supported with a succession plan, a career path and a development strategy. Our aim is to ensure that we have the human capital within an organisation that will support the growth of our business for the next three to five years.

What I do worry about, though is having an organisation growing too quickly and losing focus on the fundamentals that have made us strong, like the customer focus, the quality and continuous improvement philosophy, all those things that should be driving the organisation. It's a case of understanding the needs of the organisation and keeping it moving forward without losing those things already in place.

Other things are important too. My role in the process is also to understand the customers and where they are going. The industry is changing rapidly, as is the industry direction, its global actions and the way business is done. If we are not careful, we will be left behind by not understanding how we need change to support our customers. My effort is in understanding the customer's thinking and integrating that into our planning processes.

■ The subordinate's log   the reflective practitioner

In a consultancy firm planning is utmost. I had learned the theory in my university course, but rapidly realised that applying the theory was quite another ball game. I could competently plan projects with defined outcomes and time frames. However, the level of business and strategic planning required my management role on an on-going basis without such clear boundaries, and this was much more difficult. The uncertainty of the business environment complicated this.

Planning is a critical skill you need to develop. You need to have clear objectives and be able to plan multiple tasks, including time and resources. The business environment is more complex and changes rapidly. In spite of the uncertainty and the changes, you have to draw a line. Business and life in general is about working with limited information. You need to be prepared to change directions as the information changes. You need to understand that good planning allows you to know where you are at any particular time. Business survival requires this both in terms of strategy and day-to-day operations and finance.

In my organisation, as I gained responsibility, my planning inexperience started to surface, leading to problems and conflicts with senior management. I learned some good planning skills from the CEO that reduced conflict, but more importantly helped produce better outcomes for both clients and staff. Without planning one cannot measure, cannot organise, cannot control. This impacts both on personal stress and the quality of outcomes. Planning therefore affected the quality of my decision making. Furthermore, planning adds a measure of security in spite of the environmental uncertainty and rapid changes. In my opinion, planning is probably the most important aspect of running a business, even more than having the right objectives, as good planning will help identify them and demonstrate whether you have the resources to reach them.

Focus on practice—Strategies for improving

1 Reflect on some plans which you made and which did not get implemented. Why did that happen? In what ways were those plans no longer appropriate and how did you go about changing them?

2 Monitor the planning processes in your organisation at all levels and develop means of rewarding managers who plan and implement processes to action those plans and review them.

Source: Jones et al. (2000).

Chapter summary

Major components of the overall planning process are the organisation's mission, goals and plans. The mission is the organisation's purpose or fundamental reason for existence. The mission statement, a broad declaration of the basic, unique purpose and scope of operation distinguishing the organisation from others of its type, has several purposes. The statement can be a benchmark to evaluate success against; a means of defining a common purpose, nurturing loyalty and fostering a sense of community among members; and a signal about values and future directions. A goal is a future target or end result an organisation wishes to achieve. A plan is a means devised for attempting to reach the goal.

Goals have several potential benefits. They can increase performance, clarify expectations, facilitate the controlling function and help increase motivation. Organisations typically have three levels of goals: strategic, tactical and operational. These levels of goals can be conceptualised as a hierarchy of goals.

A number of key components help explain how goals facilitate performance. Goal content is one component. Goals should be challenging, attainable, specific and measurable, time-limited, and relevant. Goal commitment is another key component. Commitment can usually be positively influenced through supervisory authority, peer and group pressure, public display of commitment, expectations of success, and incentives and rewards. Participation also may generate goal commitment. Work behaviour is also a major component. Goal content and goal commitment influence direction, effort, persistence and planning aspects of work behaviour. Other major components are job knowledge and ability, complexity of task, and situational constraints. Care must be taken to avoid a number of potential problems with goal setting.

In the same way that there are levels of goals, plans also differ by organisation level. Thus there are strategic, tactical and operational plans. Plans can also be categorised on the basis of their frequency of use. Single-use plans are usually not needed again and include programs and projects. Standing plans are used on a recurring basis and include policies, procedures and rules. Different levels of goals and plans relate to different time horizons. Strategic goals and plans are usually focused on long-range issues five years or more in the future, tactical goals and plans are aimed at intermediate-range issues one to five years in the future, and operational goals and plans are oriented to a year or less. Research suggests the planning process can help promote innovation in several ways. These include wording the mission statement so it signals the importance of innovation, setting goals aimed at innovative outcomes, and developing loose plans allowing latitude in the innovation process or focus on innovative means of reaching goals. Managers must take steps to reduce or avoid several obstacles to developing plans.

Management by objectives includes the following steps: develop overall organisational goals; establish specific goals for various departments, subunits and individuals; formulate action plans; implement and maintain self-control; review progress periodically; and appraise performance. MBO has several strengths and weaknesses. Failures of MBO systems seem to stem from a lack of adequate top-management support and poor goal-setting and communication skills among managers who implement the system.

Questions for discussion and review

1 Outline the major components in the overall planning process. Give examples of these components in an organisation with which you are familiar.

2 Define the concept of organisational mission, and explain the purposes of a mission statement. Think of an organisation you would like to establish. What type of mission would you develop?

3 Outline the major benefits of goals. Describe a situation in which you have observed these benefits.

4 Explain how goals and plans differ according to organisational level. Describe how goals and plans may be different at the various levels of management at your college or university.

5 Discuss the major components in the diagram (Fig. 5.4) indicating how goals facilitate performance. Describe a situation in which you have seen goals work well and one in which goals did not seem to work. Use the diagram to explain each situation.

6 Explain how to set goals. List four goals you might set for yourself during the coming semester.

7 Delineate several potential problems with goal setting. Discuss how two of these problems might apply in an organisation with which you are familiar (perhaps an organisation on campus). What steps might you take to avoid such problems?

8 Explain the various types of single-use and standing plans. Give an example of each type of plan at your college or university.

9 Assess the role of goals and plans in promoting innovation.

10 Explain the steps in the management by objectives process, and assess the strengths and weaknesses of MBO.

Exercises for managing in the 21st Century

Exercise 1
Skill building: What type of goal is it?

You are reviewing goals for the chain of ice-cream stores your family operates across a number of suburbs. You are aware of levels of goals used by organisations. Today you want to classify these goals according to the normal hierarchy:

1 strategic
2 tactical
3 operational

Classify the following:

_____ 1 Increase sales at least 18 per cent each year for the next two years.

_____ 2 Reduce staff turnover to 10 per cent in all stores during the next financial year.

_____ 3 During the next five years 40 per cent of revenues will come from our brand of products.

_____ 4 Improve customer service 15 per cent in all stores in the region.

_____ 5 Increase visibility of stores in the region.

_____ 6 Decrease shrinkage to 5 per cent in store X.

_____ 7 Achieve minimum stock turnover ratio of once each month at all stores within two years.

_____ 8 Remodel store Y by April.

_____ 9 In five years be the ice-cream/frozen yoghurt industry leader in these suburbs.

_____ 10 Achieve profits equal to $2000 monthly per employee in all stores this fiscal year.

Exercise 2
Management exercise: Working with MBO

You recently received your degree and accepted a position as a department head at a local hardware store that is part of a small, but growing, chain. The chain uses an MBO system. Some of the strategic goals are reaching $400 million in annual sales within five years, building a reputation for excellent customer service, and having a double-digit return on investment through the period. Some tactical goals include opening six new stores each year for the next three years, opening one new large experimental store in your district next year, reaching annual sales of $8 million, earning a return on investment of 14 per cent, increasing customer satisfaction by five percentage points on the annual survey, and having sales of $99 000 for each employee in the department.

On the basis of these strategic and tactical goals, draft some goals for the operational level of your own department.

Wood Veneer Products
on the rim— in New Zealand

Wood Veneer Products is a small firm in the South Island of New Zealand owned and managed by Peter Jones whose father started the business 40 years ago. The factory is run by a foreman who has 11 men on production, plus an engineer who maintains the plant and equipment and develops new machines for improving productivity. The main products are ice-cream sticks, toothpicks made from veneer, and medical tongue depressors (similar to ice-cream sticks). At present Wood Veneer Products is the only manufacturer of these products in New Zealand. Beech from the Southland forests is used exclusively for manufacturing the products, and negotiating the supply of timber is a critical management function. The selection of suitable trees requires considerable expertise since the core of the tree can be soft and unsuitable for making sticks. Peter buys the standing timber then arranges with a local contractor to cut and prepare the logs at the rate required by the factory.

The contractor cuts the trees and sends them by rail to the factory several hundred kilometres away. When the tree trunks arrive by road from the rail yard they are sawn and the bark is removed before they are steam cleaned. A modified lathe is used to turn each log of timber and slice off the thin veneer. After the veneers have been sorted to select the appropriate quality timber they are fed into one of three small presses which stamp out the sticks. These are then inspected, sorted and sterilised before being packed ready for dispatch to customers. Toothpicks are produced in a similar manner. The basic plant and machinery was designed and built 30 years ago by Peter's father, and has since been continuously improved. Productivity is probably as high as could be expected from the plant, and this provides a low-cost product. Several other small manufacturers have entered the market over the last 20 years but all have been forced out by the low prices which Wood Veneer Products can maintain.

Quality
The quality of ice-cream sticks produced must be high to satisfy the standards specified by the ice-cream manufacturers. The thickness of the sticks must be precisely accurate, and they must be perfectly flat and straight grained with no cracks. Any poor quality sticks can cause machine breakdowns at the ice-cream factory which are costly to rectify. Even one split stick in every 10 000 may cause daily machine breakdowns, with ice-cream workers standing idle for several hours while the problems are rectified. Consequently every stick is inspected visually before it leaves Wood Veneer Products.

The factory

The small factory is almost bursting at the seams. The buildings have been expanded seven times in the last 10 years to the point where further expansion is impossible. The factory is in a residential area with several houses close to the factory walls on all sides. Local residents have complained about the noise, particularly at night. Factory staff are usually working from 7.00 am to 10.00 pm to produce maximum output, but the local authority has refused to allow night-shift work because of disturbing the local residents.

Two years ago Peter bought one acre of industrial land outside the town in order to build a new factory. The position of this land is ideal because it has railway sidings alongside which would reduce transportation costs both for incoming timber and for distribution of the finished products. An outline plan for a new factory has already been approved. $1.25 million is required for the new buildings and Peter plans to raise this partly from his own assets and with the help of a commercial loan. Company profitability has been consistently good over the last five years and there should be no major problems raising the necessary capital. The local accountant has told Peter that the company return on assets has been remarkable. The present fixed assets are mostly old and therefore of low financial value.

Ice-cream stick market

The present output of sticks from the factory is approximately 100 million per annum. Sticks account for 65 per cent of sales turnover. This output was enough to satisfy the home market until four years ago, but approximately 210 million sticks per annum are now needed. The ice-cream manufacturers claim that the total market demand is expanding at approximately 20 per cent per annum, and this growth appears to be unaffected by general economic trends.

Only two ice-cream companies in New Zealand supply 85 per cent of market demand. Wood Veneer Products supplies one of these plus several smaller companies. One large company buys all imported sticks, mostly from Australia. Stick supply contracts are normally for 12 months' requirements; there are six months left to run on the present contracts. Imported stick prices are confidential to the companies concerned, but are said to be about the same as prices of Wood Veneer Products, marginally higher with the extra transport costs.

The two major buyers say they are happy with price and delivery of sticks from the company but quality is sometimes below standard, bent or split sticks causing stoppages of the ice-cream making machines. The buyers agree there is some loyalty towards Wood Veneer Products as a good supplier, but if there was an alternative cheaper stick available of the right quality they would have to carefully consider changing supplier.

Other products which last year made up the full output from Wood Veneer Products were:

O 4 million ice cream spoons—market demand dropping
O 12 million toothpicks often used as cocktail sticks—demand has been higher than supply in recent years
O 1.5 million medical tongue depressors—a good market but limited size

Peter has tried diversifying his product range and welcomes new ideas for items which could be manufactured with his present equipment. The most promising recent ideas with possibilities are

O cervical smear sticks for use in hospitals
O coffee stirrers used with vending machines
O packs of sticks with designs for children to build models
O sticks used in plant pots for naming flowers

New machinery

For two years Peter has been searching for modern machinery prior to building his new factory. He needs purpose-built semi-automatic machines to provide an increased capacity without increasing the size of the labour force. Recruitment of extra labour in the town is a problem. A number of new factories have been built locally during the last five years and they have taken on all the spare labour. New Zealand woodworking machine suppliers can find nothing to produce sticks efficiently in large quantities and efforts to find machines abroad have so far been in vain. Peter's search for better machinery has proved to be time-consuming and frustrating. He has written over 60 letters during the last two years in his search, mostly to overseas agencies. There are very few firms in the world making machinery to produce sticks, and the large ice-cream firms with big markets have developed their own. They are unwilling to sell their machinery or the designs.

A university mechanical engineering student spent three months on a practical project at the firm developing machinery to automatically sort bent sticks from straight ones. This help was useful and several minor improvements were made to other machines as a result of his assistance. The sorting machine worked but not as efficiently as was anticipated. The machine has persistent problems which make it unreliable, and a lot of time has been spent trying to improve it without success. Meanwhile two people are employed full-time on the manual inspection process which is a boring, repetitive job.

Extensive contact has been maintained with all the New Zealand machinery importers and suppliers who continue to search internationally for suitable machines, but so far without success.

During the last two years Peter Jones has corresponded with the New Zealand Trade Commissioners in London, Sydney, New York, Japan and Canada but without success. A machinery agent in London has searched Europe and located two possible sources:

O One is a German company who have experience in building to order all kinds of woodworking machines. They design, build and install. They would be expensive.

O The other is a Canadian company who manufacture ice-cream sticks and build their own machines. They are at present replacing their presses with new ones and would be willing to sell the old presses. These stamp out high-quality sticks at a rate of 300 per minute, whereas Wood Veneer·Products' presses run at 400 per minute. All correspondence with this company must be in French.

The machinery and equipment used at the factory could be moved to a new factory but there is a risk. Everything works well at present but a move might upset some of the more delicate parts, particularly the older pieces, and several weeks may be required to successfully move and eliminate teething troubles. In the meantime there would be little production output.

A new competitor

A large North Island New Zealand company has recently announced the intention of forming a new company for making stick products in association with the principal Australian stick manufacturer. The Australians have American machinery and technical expertise for stick production and hold the marketing rights for this equipment. The New Zealand company has sawmills in Taupo and supplies of radiata pine which is supposedly similar to the Australian timber used for stick production. The production capacity of the new factory will be 300 million sticks per annum initially, with enough factory space for expansion. (This information was gained from the Company's annual report which announced their intentions.)

The new factory and the machines are planned to operate in six months' time. The ice-cream companies have already been approached with sample sticks of high quality and at a competitive price. Stick-sorting machines, to select bent or split sticks, have been offered to the companies concerned. One of these machines (which are not expensive) can sort all the sticks used in a large factory. The new company manager claims that 75 per cent of the production will be for export, mainly to Australia. Peter Jones is very concerned about this new development and feels that the viability of his firm and his livelihood are threatened.

Source: Tom Batley, University of Otago, New Zealand.

Activities for discussion, analysis and further research

1 What is the most important problem that Peter Jones is faced with?
2 Should the firm go ahead and build a new factory with more production capacity?
3 Should Peter continue to spend time and resources trying to find or develop better machinery and equipment?
4 What can be done about quality problems?
5 What is the future for the business facing new competition from the large North Island company?
6 Produce a plan which would enable the company to overcome the difficulties you have identified.

Strategic Management Chapter (7)

CHAPTER OUTLINE

The concept of strategic management
The strategic management process
Importance of strategic management
Levels of strategy

The role of competitive analysis in strategy formulation
Environmental assessment
Organisational assessment

Formulating corporate-level strategy
Grand strategies
Portfolio strategy approaches

Formulating business-level strategy
Porter's competitive strategies

Formulating functional-level strategy

Strategy implementation
Carrying out strategic plans
Maintaining strategic control

LEARNING OBJECTIVES

After studying this chapter, you should be able to:

○ Explain the concept of strategic management and identify three main levels of strategy.
○ Outline the major components of the strategic process.
○ Describe the role of competitive analysis in strategy formulation and explain the major approaches to such analysis.
○ Enumerate the main generic strategies available at the corporate level.
○ Explain the three major portfolio-strategy approaches for use at the corporate level.
○ Describe Porter's competitive strategies for the business level.
○ Explain the role of strategies at the functional level.
○ Outline the process of strategy implementation.

Striving for excellence

The umbrella philosophy world-wide of the parent company is that Autoliv seeks to be the local supplier of choice to every car manufacturer. Therefore it has a presence in every country where there is an automotive manufacturing activity. Autoliv has made an impact on the industry. In some instance it has been the establishment of a green-field enterprise; in others it has been by take-overs or mergers. In Australia, Autoliv was established through take-over. Its key focus became one of technical and manufacturing leadership; its differentiation strategy identified as quality.

The strategies to achieve its goals did not all focus on the external environment. Autoliv set up internally to reflect its external strategies. The manufacturing plant was restructured to include customer-specific lines as well as product specific lines. Production teams were established which for the most part were self-managing, setting targets and developing and recommending strategies to achieve those targets, working with management to implement them.

It rapidly becomes obvious that strategies applied externally must be congruent with internal strategies in order to achieve the highest levels of effectiveness.

Autoliv Australia Pty Ltd
VISION, MISSION & KEY STRATEGIES

VISION:
TO BE THE PREFERRED TECHNICAL PARTNER AND OFFER SECURITY OF EMPLOYMENT BY BEING THE BEST AT WHAT WE DO.

MISSION:
THROUGH OUR PEOPLE WE ARE A FULL SERVICE PROVIDER OF WORLD CLASS RESTRAINT SYSTEMS FOR PERSONAL SAFETY IN VEHICLES.

KEY OBJECTIVES:

Growth	Ensuring the survival of the organisation
World Class Manufacturing	Being the best at what we do
Technical Leadership	Viewed by the Automotive Industry as the leader in restraint systems for personal safety in vehicles
Employee Development	Providing opportunity for staff development and growth
Good Corporate Citizen	Contributing to the community's well being

VALUES:

People: Our main and most important resource; people provide the basis for the quality of our products and our reputation in the market place is totally dependent on the abilities of our people. The involvement and the team work of our people is essential for our success.

Products: Our products are the end results of all employees' efforts and as our products are regarded, so are the people in the company. Good quality products competitively priced are a sign of a company with good people.

Profit: Profits are the ultimate measure of how efficiently we meet the needs of our customers. Profits are essential to our long term growth and survival and if we are profitable the company can share these profits with its employees.

In Chapter 6, we looked at different levels of goals and plans, including those at the strategic level. Strategic goals and plans are particularly important in the managerial planning function because they eventually determine the organisation's overall direction. Accordingly, in this chapter, we look more thoroughly at strategic-level planning issues, and how companies are managed strategically. We begin by examining the concept of strategic management. Then we consider how competitive analysis forms a basis for developing effective strategies to gain an edge over competitors. We next analyse policy formulation at corporate, business and functional levels. Finally, we probe the process of strategy implementation.

THE CONCEPT OF STRATEGIC MANAGEMENT

Most well-run organisations try to develop and follow **strategies**, which are large-scale action plans for interacting with the environment to achieve long-term goals (Jauch & Glueck 1988; Pearce & Robinson 1988). An organisation's strategic plan is a statement of its strategies, mission and goals (Thompson & Strickland 1992). To learn where these come from and how they are put into action, we must examine the aspect of planning called strategic management. **Strategic management** is the process where managers develop and implement strategies for achieving strategic goals, within existing conditions (Thompson & Strickland 1992; Rue & Holland 1989). This recognises that strategic management is oriented toward achieving long-term goals, weighs important environmental elements, considers major internal organisation characteristics, and involves specific strategy development. Thus the strategic management process is a major part of the planning process introduced in Chapter 5.

The strategic management process

The strategic management process comprises several major components, as shown in Figure 7.1. It begins with identifying an organisation's mission and strategic goals (see Chapter 6). Next, it involves competitive situation analysis, considering both external environment and organisational factors. After this analysis, managers develop, or formulate, strategies to reach strategic goals. The process of identifying the mission and strategic goals, conducting competitive analysis, and developing specific strategies is **strategy formulation**. In contrast, the process of carrying out strategic plans and controlling how they are carried out is **strategy implementation** (Thompson & Strickland 1992). Distinguishing strategy implementation is increasingly important in strategic management because even brilliantly formulated strategies will not succeed if they are implemented ineffectively.

Importance of strategic management

Strategic management is important for many reasons (Thompson & Strickland 1992). For one, the process helps organisations identify and develop a **competitive advantage**, or a significant edge over competition in dealing with competitive forces (Porter 1985).

Fig. 7.1   The strategic management process

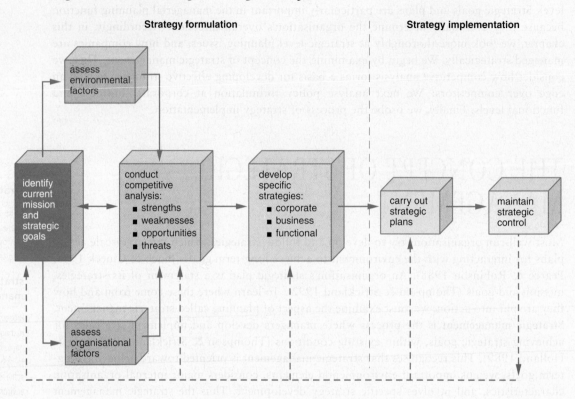

Strategy formulation | Strategy implementation

Strategic management is also important because it provides direction so organisation members know where to expend their efforts. Without a strategic plan, managers may concentrate on day-to-day activities, only to find that a competitor has achieved a more favourable position by taking a longer-term view of strategic directions.

Strategic management can also show a need for innovation, providing an organised approach for encouraging new ideas related to strategies (Schilit 1987). In addition, the process can involve managers at various levels in planning, making it more likely they will understand the resulting plans and be committed to them.

Research and development strategy is one component of the functional level of the strategic management planning process.

Fig. 7.2   Levels of strategy (adapted from Pearce II & Robinson Jr 1988, p. 9)

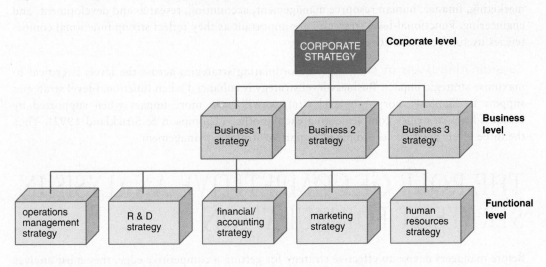

Levels of strategy

Many organisations develop strategies at three different levels: corporate, business and functional. The three levels are shown in Figure 7.2 (Thompson & Strickland 1992).

Corporate-level strategy   **Corporate-level strategy** addresses the businesses an organisation will operate, how those the strategies of those businesses will be co-ordinated to strengthen the organisation's competitive position, and how resources will be allocated among businesses. Strategy here is typically developed by top management, often with the assistance of strategic planning personnel, at least in large organisations.

The board of directors is involved in developing corporate-level strategy, although the degree of participation differs. Within the strategic management process, directors can typically be helpful advising on new growth directions, suggesting needed major strategy changes, and providing input on major investment timing (Mueller 1979).

Business-level strategy   Many organisations include strategic business units. A **strategic business unit (SBU)** is a distinct business, with its own competitors, managed independently of other businesses within the organisation (Rue & Holland 1989). **Business-level strategy** concentrates on how best to compete within a particular business while supporting corporate-level strategy. Strategies here aim at deciding the type of competitive advantage to build, determining responses to changing environmental and competitive conditions, allocating resources within the unit, and co-ordinating functional-level strategies. Most often, heads of business units develop business strategies, although typically subject to top management's approval. When an organisation is only a single business, corporate-level and business-level strategies are the same. Thus the corporate- and business-level distinction applies only to organisations with separate divisions competing in different industries.

Functional-level strategy   **Functional-level strategy** focuses on plans for managing a functional area in a business to support business-level strategy. Strategies here address the

---

corporate-level strategy

Type of strategy addressing what businesses the organisation will operate, how strategies of those businesses will be co-ordinated to strengthen the organisation's competitive position, and how resources will be allocated among businesses

strategic business unit (SBU)

Distinct business, with its own set of competitors, which can be managed relatively independently of other businesses within the organisation

business-level strategy

Type of strategy concentrating on the best means of competing within a particular business while also supporting corporate-level strategy

functional-level strategy

Type of strategy focusing on action plans for managing a particular functional area within a business in a way that supports business-level strategy

main directions for each major functional business area, such as manufacturing or operations, marketing, finance, human resource management, accounting, research and development, and engineering. Functional-level strategies are important as they reflect strong functional competencies useful for competitive advantage.

Co-ordinating levels of strategy   Co-ordinating strategies across the levels is critical to maximise strategic impact. Business-level strategy is enhanced when functional-level strategies support it. Similarly, corporate-level strategy will have more impact when supported by business-level strategies complementing each another (Thompson & Strickland 1992). Thus the three levels must be co-ordinated as part of strategic management.

THE ROLE OF COMPETITIVE ANALYSIS IN STRATEGY FORMULATION

Before managers devise an effective strategy for getting a competitive edge, they must analyse the organisation's competitive situation. This involves assessing both environmental and organisational factors influencing ability to compete effectively. Assessment can use SWOT analysis. **SWOT analysis**, a way to analyse an organisation's competitive situation, involves assessing organisational strengths (S) and weaknesses (W), environmental opportunities (O) and threats (T). Identifying strengths and weaknesses requires assessing internal characteristics, while detecting opportunities and threats requires evaluation of environmental factors.

For SWOT analysis purposes, a *strength* is an internal characteristic able to improve an organisation's competitive situation. In contrast, a *weakness* is an internal characteristic leaving the organisation vulnerable to competitors' strategic moves. An *opportunity* is an environmental condition offering significant hope for improving an organisation's situation. Conversely, a *threat* is an environmental condition with significant prospects to undermine the organisation's competitiveness.

Environmental assessment

In analysing opportunities and threats, managers must consider general, or mega-environment, elements which are able, for good or ill, to influence an organisation's ability to reach strategic goals. Such elements are broad factors such as technological, economic, legal-political, sociocultural and international influences. Managers must assess major organisation task-environment elements, including more specific external elements an organisation interfaces with conducting business. These include customers, competitors and suppliers. Elements of general and task environments are detailed in Chapter 3.

Porter's five competitive forces model   Porter developed the **five competitive forces model** to analyse the nature and intensity of competition in terms of five major forces. The forces are rivalry, bargaining power of customers, bargaining power of suppliers, threat of new entrants, and threat of substitute products and services. These forces collectively affect profit potential, or long-term return on investment, of businesses. Major reasons for lower profit potential are summarised in Table 7-1.

SWOT analysis

Method of analysing an organisation's competitive situation involving assessing organisational strengths (S), weaknesses (W), environmental opportunities (O) and threats (T)

five competitive forces model

Porter's approach to analysing the nature and intensity of competition in a given industry in terms of five major forces

Table 7.1   Porter's five competitive forces model

Competitive forces	Reasons for lower profit potential
Rivalry	Various competitive tactics among rivals lower prices that can be charged or raise costs of doing business.
Bargaining power of customers	Customers force price reductions or negotiate increases in product quality and service at the same price.
Bargaining power of suppliers	Suppliers threaten price increases and/or reductions in quality of goods or services.
Threat of new entrants	New entrants bid prices down or cause incumbents to increase costs to maintain market position.
Threat of substitute products or services	Availability of substitutes limits the prices that can be charged.

Source: Based on Porter (1980, pp. 3–28).

Rivalry is the extent to which competitors jockey for position by price competition, advertising battles, product introductions, and increased customer service or warranties. All these lower profits for competitors in an industry by lowering prices charged or by raising costs of doing business. This situation illustrates Porter's premise that the greater the rivalry, the lower the profit potential for businesses in an industry.

The *bargaining power of customers* is the extent customers can force prices down, bargain for higher quality or more service at the same price, and play competitors against each other. Customers are powerful when quantities purchased are large in proportion to a seller's total sales, when products or services are a significant portion of a customer's costs, or when standard items are needed (Alster 1989; Taylor 1994). The greater customers' bargaining power, the lower an industry's profit potential.

The *bargaining power of suppliers* is the extent to which suppliers exert power over an industry by threatening to raise prices or reduce quality of their goods and services. Suppliers are powerful when only a few sell to many businesses in an industry, when no substitutes exist for their products or services, or when they are critical to a buyer's business. The greater suppliers' bargaining power, the lower the industry's profit potential.

For example, French makers of champagne have a problem because of a shortage of grape-growing land in France's Champagne region. The region is famous for producing ideal grapes for the increasingly popular sparkling wine. Grape suppliers command premium prices. To remedy the shortage, Moët and other French champagne makers, such as Pommery et Greno and Laurent-Perrier, have purchased suitable wineries and land in Australia, Spain, the United States, Latin America and elsewhere. However, a debate rages over the virtues of grapes grown in France versus those from other locations. Some producers argue top-quality wine needs grapes from France's Champagne region, giving area growers considerable power as suppliers (Toy 1989).

The *threat of new entrants* is how easily new competitors can enter the same product or service market. New entrants add capacity and resources. This results in price wars and/or cost increases for existing businesses, which increase expenditures (additional advertising, larger sales force, better service, etc.) to maintain market position. The threat of entry depends on how hard it is to break into the market. High barriers exist when large capital investments are needed to start a business (as in the steel industry) or when economies of scale make it difficult for new entrants to start small and gradually build up volume (as with television manufacturing). High barriers also exist when established competitors have products or services perceived as unique (e.g. a brand-name perfume).

When barriers are high and new entrants expect a vigorous reaction from existing competitors, the threat of new entrants is low (Siler 1989). In contrast, with low barriers and new entrants expecting mild reactions from existing competitors, new entrant threat is high and, consequently, industry profit potential is low.

Threat of substitute products or services is the extent to which other products can substitute for others. For example, artificial sweeteners can substitute for sugar, electricity can substitute for gas in energy production, and paint can substitute for wallpaper. Substitute availability limits prices that firms in an industry (such as the coffee industry) can charge, since price increases encourage customers to switch to substitutes (such as cola drinks) (Mathews 1994). Thus, availability of substitute products or services reduces an industry's profit potential.

Hypercompetition   Conditions in some industries have shifted to hypercompetition (D'Aveni 1995). **Hypercompetition** is a state of rapidly escalating competition where competitors make frequent, daring and aggressive moves eventually creating continual disequilibrium and change. With hypercompetition, environments spiral to increasing uncertainty, dynamism and player similarity. Companies develop sources of competitive advantage that more quickly undermine competitors' advantages, aiming to disrupt the status quo and make more profits for a short period.

Hypercompetition makes it hard for organisations to sustain competitive advantage. Therefore, companies must disrupt their own competitive advantage by innovating continually. They must aggressively undermine their competitors' competitive advantages. Methods include finding new ways to satisfy customers, then using speed and/or surprise to implement them first. For example, Intel, the microchip maker, greatly increased the speed of incorporating new functions in its microprocessors, though holding over 80 per cent of the PC microprocessor market. Intel retooled its devices to include multimedia and communications functions. Previously these were performed by products from other specialised chip manufacturers. Intel's new microprocessors enable stereo sound and modems, making other auxiliary cards unneeded (Young 1996).

hypercompetition

State of rapidly escalating competition in which competitors make frequent, daring, and aggressive moves cumulatively creating conditions of continual disequilibrium and change in the industry

@ Risky business   managing the e-challenge

The biggest problem with e-commerce deals is that they are hammered together very quickly. Telstra Corporation played matchmaker to Solution 6 and Sausage Software. The merger is risky but could create Australia's first global Internet company. Two entrepreneurs, Chris Tyler of Solutions 6 and Wayne Bos at Sausage, combined with the partly privatised telecommunications carrier to dominate e-commerce services in the notoriously difficult small-business sector.

The Telstra Board does not consider the Solution 6–Sausage merger as a single play in a niche market, rather it sees it as a dress rehearsal for other e-commerce investments. Analysts say that the main motive behind the deal is a rush for scale and brand presence in the global e-market, particularly the international market for Internet-based professional services for small and medium-sized businesses. The deal is predicated upon the belief that the Internet has completely changed the dynamics of small and medium-sized companies and that services that would have been prohibitively expensive in the old economy are now viable on the online world.

Source: Kirby, J. (2000).

Activities for discussion, analysis and further research

1 Based on your studies around strategic management, what aspects do you think Telstra had to consider when it match-made this deal?
2 Why is the small-business sector described as 'notoriously difficult'?
3 Do a literature search to find out what has happened to the combination of Solution 6 and Sausage since March 2000.

Organisational assessment

While SWOT analysis includes in-depth assessment of environmental opportunities and threats, it also needs internal strength and weakness evaluation. An approach to internal assessment is referred to as the resource-based strategic view, because it focuses on evaluating an organisation's internal resources and the competitive implications of its capabilities (Miller & Shamsie 1996; Barney 1995).

An organisation's resources and capabilities include financial, physical, human and organisational assets for production of goods and services. Financial resources include debt, equity, retained earnings and related matters. Physical resources include buildings, machinery, vehicles and other material. Human resources include skills, abilities, experience and other work-related characteristics of people associated with the organisation. Organisational resources include the history of groups in the organisation, relationships, levels of trust, and associated culture dimensions, as well as the formal reporting structure, control systems and compensation systems.

In assessing the competitive implications of their resources and capabilities relative to their environments, organisations must ask questions about four major factors (see Table 7.2). These are critical to the organisation's ability to build competitive advantage using internal resources and capabilities.

The first critical factor is value. A resource or capability adds value to the extent it allows an organisation to capitalise on opportunities and/or nullify threats. For example, Sony Corp. possesses specialised expertise in designing, manufacturing and marketing miniaturised electronic technology. Sony uses this expertise to produce a range of successful products, including portable tape players, portable disc players and easy-to-handle video cameras, before competitors.

The second significant factor is rareness. A resource or capability is rare to the extent that it is uncommon among competitors. A valuable resource or capability other competing firms possess is typically a source of competitive parity—that is, it is necessary to equal competitors on a given dimension. Partially because Sony maintains and builds expertise by large research

Table 7.2   Four major factors of importance

Factors	Related questions
Value	Do the firm's resources and capabilities add value by enabling it to exploit opportunities and/or neutralise threats?
Rareness	How many competing firms already possess these valuable resources and capabilities?
Imitability	Do firms without a resource or capability face a cost disadvantage in obtaining it compared to firms already possessing it?
Organisation	Is the firm organised to exploit full competitive potential of its resources and capabilities?

Source: Based on Barney (1995, pp. 49–61).

and development expenditures, the depth of expertise has remained uncommon among competitors.

The third pivotal factor is degree of imitability. A resource or capability difficult for competitors to duplicate or substitute has low imitability. Duplication occurs when a competitor builds the same type of resources or capabilities as the organisation being imitated. Substitution comes when they can create an equivalent resource or capability no more costly to develop. Although competitors can quickly reverse-engineer new Sony products and develop competing offerings, Sony's ability to achieve high profits by being first with a stream of innovative new products affords the company sustained competitive advantage.

The fourth important factor is organisation. Organisational competitive advantage relies on the value of its resources and capabilities, rareness and imitability. Putting this competitive advantage in place, however, requires a firm to organise maximised usefulness of its resources and capabilities. Organisational components, such as formal reporting structures, control systems and reward systems, are complementary resources with limited ability to create competitive advantage. However, they can be combined with other resources and capabilities to maximise competitive advantage. For example, Sony's collaboration across various units which were expert in miniaturised electronic technology (such as tape recorders and earphones) helped lever Sony's expertise to produce innovative products. As Sony moved into the digital era, the company experienced difficulty with organisational issues. It has struggled to achieve competitive advantage by combining hardware expertise with a growing software-related entertainment empire including Sony Music Entertainment (formerly CBS Records) and Sony Pictures Entertainment (formerly Columbia Pictures) (Brull & Gross 1996).

Sustained competitive advantage cannot be achieved solely by analysing environmental factors and developing businesses where competitive forces are favourable. Gaining sustained competitive advantage also means developing valuable, rare and difficult-to-imitate resources and capabilities. A resource or capability that is valuable, rare and difficult to imitate is called a **distinctive competence**. Organisation factors using effective distinctive competencies are critical in building competitive advantage. (Note this resource-based strategic view has connections with the resource dependence model in Chapter 3. The resource dependence model, though, aims to reduce environmental dependence by attempting to control critical

distinctive competence

Unique strength competitors cannot easily match or imitate

resources. On the other hand, the resource-based strategic view emphasises a need to develop internal resources and capabilities to provide sustained competitive advantage. Thus the perspectives are complementary, helping managers focus on important issues involving organisation resources and effectiveness.) Carefully conducted organisational and environmental assessments support developing corporate-level strategies.

Coming back to call back
gaining the edge

Some time ago, call-back centres were said to be doomed in Singapore. Today, thanks to technology advances and a partial lifting of advertising legislation, the business is poised to make an unprecedented boom. With International Direct Dial phone rates declining, it was envisaged that call-back operations were a dying enterprise. However, these organisations, which use computer technology to provide a cheaper alternative to IDD, are enjoying a new lease of life.

Advances in technology have lowered the barriers to entry, and a partial lifting of advertising restrictions by the Infocomm Development Authority of Singapore (IDA) are a boon to operators. With such a huge revenue potential, the process is relatively simple. The tools of the trade include a computer which must have a Pentium 111, 500 MHz chip, a PPMS or pre-paid, post-paid management software which manages inbound and outbound calls and an ISDN card.

12U is one such operator in Singapore that started out with a base investment of S$100 000 which is expected to be returned within the year.

While such operations are legitimate, they are competing with SingTel but are unlikely to put a major dent in its annual IDD revenue.

Source: Written by Alexandra Hayes.

Activities for discussion, analysis and further research

1 Carry out some research on call-back centres and compare their rates with those of Telstra for IDD calls. In what ways are call centres a successful competitor to long-distance providers?
2 Would you consider them to be a threat? Why?

FORMULATING CORPORATE-LEVEL STRATEGY

Corporate-level strategy is the overall strategy an organisation follows. Its development involves selecting a grand strategy and using portfolio-strategy approaches to determine the various businesses making up the organisation.

Grand strategies

A **grand strategy**, or master strategy, provides basic strategic direction at corporate level (Pearce & Robinson 1988). There are several generic types, in three basic categories: growth,

grand strategy

Master strategy providing the basic strategic direction at corporate level

stability and defensive grand strategies (Rue & Holland 1989). These strategies and their major subcategories are shown in Figure 7.3.

Growth strategies   **Growth strategies** are grand strategies with organisational expansion as a major element. In business organisations, growth means more sales and earnings, though other criteria (such as number of geographic locations) are possible. Not-for-profit organisations grow in terms of revenue, clients served or other criteria. Three major growth strategies are concentration, vertical integration and diversification.

Concentration focuses on growing a single product or service, or a small number of closely related ones. Concentration occurs through *market development* (increasing current market share or expanding into new ones), *product development* (improving a basic product or service or expanding into closely related ones), or *horizontal integration* (adding one or more similar businesses, usually by purchase). For example, France-based Groupe Michelin increased horizontal integration by buying Uniroyal Goodrich Tyre Company, making Michelin the world's largest tyre maker. Indicative of the high concentration strategy, over 90 per cent of Michelin's annual sales are based on tyres (Browning 1990).

Vertical integration means growth through production of inputs previously provided by suppliers, or replacement of a customer role (such as a distributor) by disposing of one's own outputs

Fig. 7.3   Types of grand strategies

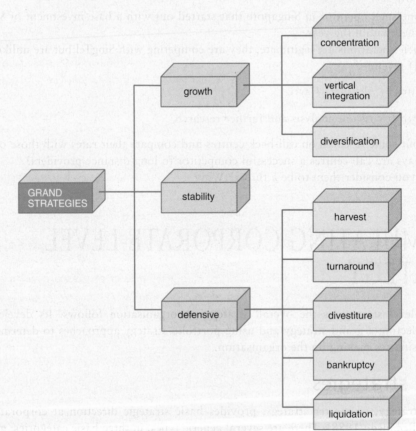

outputs. When a business grows by becoming its own supplier, this is *backward integration* (Kumpech & Bolwijn 1988).

When organisational growth includes occupying a role previously fulfilled by a customer, this is *forward integration*. According to one study, organisations use vertical integration when demand is reasonably certain, rather than highly uncertain (Harrigan 1985).

Diversification means growing through development of areas that are clearly distinct from current businesses. In addition to diversifying to grow, organisations often do so to reduce the risk of single-product or single-industry operations (Amit & Livnat 1988). Diversification comes in two types: conglomerate and concentric. *Conglomerate diversification* occurs when an organisation diversifies into unrelated main business areas. Organisations using a conglomerate diversification strategy are called conglomerates. For example, Rockwell International Corp., an $11 billion conglomerate, has about 48 per cent of revenue from electronics and industrial automation, 26 per cent from automotive components, 20 per cent from aerospace, and 6 per cent from printing presses. Some businesses are metal fabrication companies bending, welding, and fusing metals into components for cars, trucks and aircraft. Others are high-technology companies in telecommunications and industrial automation. The company gains synergy among different businesses by using high technology from some to keep the metal fabrication companies at the front of their industries (Lubove 1995). Because of the variety involved, conglomerates can be difficult for top management to administer. Concentric diversification occurs when an organisation diversifies into related, but distinct, businesses. With concentric diversification, businesses can be related by products, markets or technology.

All three growth strategies can be implemented by internal growth or acquisition, merger or joint venture. With internal growth, an organisation expands by building on its own internal resources. Core characteristics, coupled with technology and marketing changes, result in increased profit and growth (Pearce & Harvey 1990). **Acquisition** is purchase of all or part of one organisation by another, while a **merger** is the combination of two or more companies into one (see Chapter 11). Finally, a joint venture is when two or more organisations supply resources to support a given project or product (see Chapter 3). There are many alternatives for particular growth strategies.

Stability strategies   A **stability strategy** involves maintaining the status quo or growing slowly or methodically. Organisations might choose stability for many reasons. For instance, if a company is doing well, managers may not want the risks and hassles of aggressive growth. This often happens in small, privately owned businesses, which are the largest group to adopt a stability strategy (Jefferson 1990). Another reason for stability is it provides a chance to recover. An organisation stretched after a period of accelerated growth may seek stability before attempting more. On the other hand, if managers believe growth prospects are low, they may choose a stability strategy to maintain current market share. (Worsening situations call for defensive strategies.) Finally, a stability strategy may even occur by default if managers are unconcerned about their strategic direction.

Defensive strategies   **Defensive strategies** (or retrenchment strategies) focus on reducing organisational operations through cost reductions (such as cutting back on non-essential expenditures, and hiring no new staff) and/or asset reductions (selling land, equipment, and businesses) (Pearce & Robinson 1988). Defensive strategies include harvest, turnaround, divestiture and liquidation.

diversification

Approach entailing effecting growth through development of new areas clearly distinct from current businesses

acquisition

Purchase of all or part of one organisation by another

merger

Combining of two or more companies into one organisation

stability strategy

Strategy involving maintaining the status quo or growing in a methodical, but slow, manner

defensive strategies

Strategies focusing on the desire or need to reduce organisational operations, usually through cost and/or asset reductions

harvest

A strategy entailing minimising investments while attempting to maximise short-run profits and cash flow, with the long-run intention of exiting the market

Harvest entails minimising investments and maximising short-run profits and cash flow, with long-run intention to exit the market (Thompson & Strickland 1992). A harvest strategy is often used when future market growth is in doubt or requires investments that are not clearly cost-effective. For example, the vacuum-tube market collapsed with the transistor's invention and the subsequent development of advanced solid-state circuitry. Consequently, many vacuum tube producers (e.g. Western Electric, General Electric, and Westinghouse) phased out production (Willoughby 1987). With a harvest strategy, short-run profits are often used to build other businesses with better prospects.

turnaround

Strategy designed to reverse a negative trend and restore the organisation to appropriate levels of profitability

A **turnaround** is designed to reverse a negative trend and restore appropriate profitability levels. Such efforts often need temporary reductions to conserve funds. (The term 'turnaround' sometimes means a major shift from a negative direction to a positive one.) A **divestiture** involves selling or divesting a business or part of one. According to one study, if divestitures fit with corporate or business strategies, the firm's stock price is affected positively. Conversely, when divestitures are conducted without clear strategic goals, market effect is negative (Montgomery, Thomans & Kamath 1984).

Liquidation involves selling or dissolving an entire organisation and occurs when serious difficulties, usually financial, cannot be resolved.

✖ Cuisine—Fast-food style   crossroads

Cuisine Courier claims to be the world's largest multi-restaurant home-delivery company. The company, established in 1986, has more than 500 restaurants participating, which service Sydney and Melbourne. It offers more than 100 different styles of cuisine from these restaurants and delivers to customers' homes. Until recently the company depended on the use of a call centre to take orders efficiently and ensure the process was carried through and the orders despatched.

Exploring ways to expand their service, the logical extension was the establishment of an Internet site. This would improve the call-centre response time. This has had the added bonus of allowing the company to offer their call-centre and delivery infrastructure to other businesses that require goods delivery.

Source: Adapted from Banagham, M. (1999).

Decision points

1 If you were Matt Whitnall, the managing director of Cuisine Courier, what are the factors that you might have wanted to consider before you committed yourself to such an expansion?

2 Connect to their web site at www.cuisinecourier.com.au and consider what could be improved to make the site more user-friendly and facilitate service to customers.

Reflection point

1 In your opinion, is fast food home delivered via the Internet a good idea? Why?

A courier makes a delivery for Cuisine Courier, a company whose managers used strategic management processes to develop their new service—fast-food ordering via the Internet.

Portfolio-strategy approaches

While grand strategies address an organisation's overall direction, portfolio-strategy approaches help managers determine the types of businesses the organisation should be involved with. More specifically, a **portfolio-strategy approach** helps analyse the business mix in terms of individual and collective contributions to strategic goals. The concept is similar to when an individual attempts to assemble a group, or portfolio, of stocks providing balance of risk, long-term growth and other factors. Two frequently used portfolio approaches are the BCG growth-share matrix and the product/market evolution matrix. Each uses a two-dimensional matrix, measuring two dimensions to form four or more cells. Portfolio approaches help analyse existing or potential strategic business units.

BCG growth-share matrix   One early extensively used approach is the Boston Consulting Group's (BCG) four-cell matrix. The **BCG growth-share matrix**, shown in Figure 7.4, compares an organisation's portfolio of businesses on the basis of relative market share and market growth rate. Relative market share is the ratio of a business's market share (in unit volume) compared to its largest rival's market share. The growth rate is market growth during the previous year relative to growth in the whole economy (Rue & Holland 1989). In the BCG matrix shown in Figure 7.4, each business, shown by a circle, is plotted according to its position on both dimensions. The circle size indicates the business's per cent revenue relative to revenues generated by others in the portfolio. The resulting matrix divides businesses into four categories.

Fig. 7.4   BCG growth-share matrix (adapted from Pearce & Robinson 1988, p. 280)

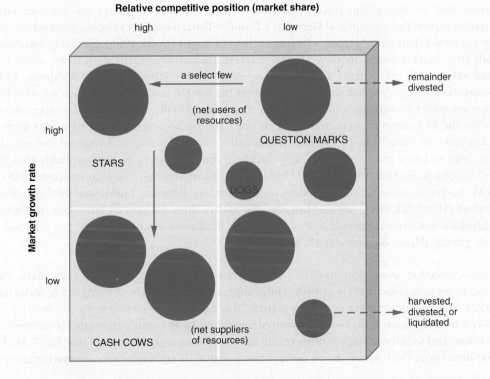

divestiture

Strategy involving an organisation's selling or divesting of a business or part of a business

liquidation

Strategy entailing selling or dissolving an entire organisation

portfolio strategy approach

Method of analysing an organisation's mix of businesses in terms of both individual and collective contributions to strategic goals

BCG growth-share matrix

Four-cell matrix (developed by the Boston Consulting Group) comparing various businesses in an organisation's portfolio on the basis of relative market share and market growth rate

The *star* has high market share in a rapidly growing market. Because of high growth potential, stars often initially require substantial investment capital beyond what they are able to earn themselves (Guyon 1988).

A *question mark* (or *problem child*) has low market share in a rapidly growing market. Question marks are a dilemma for organisations. Like stars, they require substantial investment to take advantage of a growing market, yet low market share means they have limited ability to generate large amounts of cash. They are thus 'cash hogs' (Phalon 1989). With question marks, managers must either provide enough cash to fuel growth or divest the business.

The *cash cow* has high market share in a slow growth market. As a result, it generates more cash than needed to maintain market position. Cash cows, often former stars, are valuable, being 'milked' to provide cash for stars and question marks (Phalon 1989).

A *dog* has low market share in a low-growth area. It generates only modest, or even a small negative, cash flow. Usually, dogs are harvested, divested or liquidated (Landro & Sease 1987; Guyon 1988).

Overall, the BCG matrix suggests using revenues from cash cows to fund the growth of stars and to build question marks which have the best market prospects. Dogs and remaining question marks are divested unless they provide sufficient positive cash flow to justify retaining them, at least short term. One study suggests dogs may generate more cash than is generally acknowledged, and managers, therefore, should evaluate them carefully before divesting (Hambrick, Macmillan & Day 1982).

The BCG matrix has flaws (Hambrick et al. 1982). One is that it does not directly consider the majority of businesses with average market shares in average growth markets (note that the matrix has only two categories, high and low, for each dimension). In addition, generalisations may be misleading, since organisations with low market shares are not necessarily question marks. For example, at Germany's Daimler-Benz, managers raise car production only after careful debate, lest Mercedes lose its exclusive image (Turner 1986). Similarly, businesses with large market shares in slow-growth markets are not necessarily cash cows. Some may need substantial investments to retain market position (Saporito 1988; Waldman 1989; Demetrakes 1995). Another shortcoming is that the matrix provides little guidance on which question marks to support and which dogs to salvage. Finally, one survey shows executives dislike the BCG terminology. According to one, 'We try to avoid the use of words such as "cash cow" or "dog" like the plague. If you call a business a dog, it'll respond like one. It's one thing to know that you are an ugly duckling; much worse to be told explicitly that you are' (Gupta & Govindarajan 1984). Despite these shortcomings, research indicates that the BCG matrix is valuable in its ability to differentiate between businesses thinking about strategy (Hambrick et al. 1998). However, the matrix does not specify strategies for various businesses, nor does it provide a way to identify businesses about to move into a period of high growth (Hofer & Schendel 1978).

Product/market evolution matrix   To facilitate identifying companies, particularly new ones, about to accelerate their growth, Hofer suggested a refinement (Thompson & Strickland 1992). The **product/market evolution matrix** (also called the *life-cycle portfolio matrix*) is a 15-cell matrix where businesses are plotted according to the unit's strength, or competitive position, and industry's stage in the evolutionary product/market life cycle (see Fig. 7.5). The first dimension, the business unit's competitive position, is similar to relative market share in

product/market evolution matrix

15-cell matrix (developed by Hofer) in which businesses are plotted according to the business unit's business strength, or competitive position, and the industry's stage in the evolutionary product/market life-cycle matrix

Fig. 7.5   Product/market evolution matrix (reprinted from Thompson & Strickland 1992, p. 204)

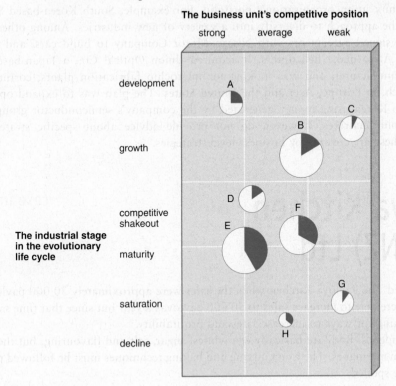

the BCG matrix, but includes an average category. On the second dimension the two approaches differ. Whereas the BCG matrix measures market growth rate, the product/market evolution matrix shows industry stage in the product/market life cycle. This starts with initial development and proceeds through growth, competitive shakeout, maturity and saturation, and decline stages. The maturity and saturation stage is important as it often lasts for some time. An industry has reached maturity when growth slows and a market moves to saturation, where demand is limited to product or service replacement (Hill & Jones 1989). The challenge in maturity and saturation is preserving or slowly expanding market share while avoiding decline (Schofield & Arnold 1988).

On the grid, each business is shown by a circle, with size proportional to size (measured by total industry sales) of the industry the business competes in. (Note the meaning of the circle differs from that in the BCG matrix, in which the circle represents the business's per cent revenue relative to revenues generated by others in the portfolio.) The pie slice within the circle shows the business's market share within the industry.

Data shown in Figure 7.5 suggest business A has good growth prospects and should be developed. Business B is in a weak competitive position and is a question mark in BCG matrix terminology. Business E is established and is a star, moving to maturity. Business F is gradually losing competitive position but is probably a cash cow. Business H is most likely a candidate for divesting or liquidating and a dog.

Assessing the portfolio matrixes   Each portfolio matrix offers a different perspective likely to be useful in strategy formulation. Therefore, one or both can enhance thinking about the business mix in an organisation's portfolio. For example, South Korea-based Samsung Group used the approach to diversify into a variety of new industries. Among other things, the company signed agreements with Nissan Motor Company to build cars, and France's Eurocopter S.A. to make helicopters. It acquired Union Optical Co., a Japan-based semiconductor manufacturer, and was looking for microchip fabrication plants, costing about $1 billion each, in Europe, Asia and the United States. The plan was to expand operations beyond South Korea using money generated by the company's semiconductor group (Glain 1995). Portfolio matrixes, however, do not provide advice about specific strategies for businesses. These are covered by business-level strategies.

● The Pavlova Kitchen (Dunedin, NZ) Ltd

case in point

Trevor and Evelyn Millar purchased The Pavlova Kitchen when the sales were approximately 30 000 pavlovas per year. After two years the Millars were able to increase sales to 50 000 pavlovas a year but since that time sales have levelled off, and they are now looking for ways to increase sales and profitability.

Pavlovas are very similar to meringues. Both are basically egg whites, sugar, salt and flavouring, but the baking process differentiates pavlovas from meringues. The exact mixing and baking techniques must be followed precisely for pavlovas or the product will be spoiled.

Manufacturing

Pavlovas are manufactured in a 900-square-foot building which also provides office and storage space. The production process consists of three sequential steps. First, the ingredients are placed in an electric mixer which must run for the precise amount of time to keep from ruining the product. The mix requires 3000 eggs to be cracked open in a week and the whites separated from the yolks. Next, the egg white mixture is moulded by hand, and later the pavlovas are baked and boxed.

The manufacture of pavlovas requires no special equipment. The 36 ovens used to manufacture pavlovas are ordinary 'cookers' similar to those found in the average home. The only other major equipment required for the process is a large mixer. The company also owns a delivery van and a computer used for bookkeeping, forecasting, and production and materials planning.

The consumption of pavlovas is very seasonal, with Christmas being the period of highest demand. The seasonality causes considerable production fluctuations. In November and December four times as many pavlovas are produced as in any other months during the year.

Because of the production fluctuations, the premises are rarely used to full capacity. During slow months, Trevor and Evelyn can produce the needed pavlovas by baking three mornings a week. Peak demand can normally be satisfied by working a full week plus overtime.

The business currently employs two part-time workers to help with the manufacturing and distributing of pavlovas. They are mothers who prefer part-time work because it allows them to spend some time with their children. The primary requisite for being hired is a willingness to work varying days and hours. During the winter (June till September) the women work very few hours a week, but as Christmas nears they work full-time.

Marketing

The Pavlova Kitchen sells its product through a number of different distribution channels. The major buyers are grocery stores, dairies, hotels, restaurants, coffee shops and caterers. They also sell directly to individuals who come to the factory. Freight charges are generally added to the cost of the pavlovas for customers afield.

Sales of pavlovas have plateaued recently and the Millars believe that exporting could be a good way to increase sales. Currently about 120 pavlovas per year are exported to Otaru in Japan which is Dunedin's sister city. Further efforts to export to Japan have taken a lot of time without realising future sales.

The Millars realise that they need to increase sales of pavlovas to improve profitability and have a comfortable lifestyle. They are considering a number of options that might increase their sales or decrease their operating costs. They are not sure what to do.

Source: Tom Batley, University of Otago, New Zealand.

Activities for discussion, analysis and further research

1 Develop a suitable mission statement for The Pavlova Kitchen, and a manufacturing policy, plus a SWOT analysis leading to appropriate strategies. In order to do this you will need to do a bit of research on the product. Develop a plan to enable you to carry out this task.
2 Develop a strategic plan for this organisation which will enable the Millars to meet their goals.
3 What are the main problems which face the owners of this business?
4 How can the owners satisfy market demand for their products without working excessive hours during the peak season?
5 What are the main aspects of quality management in this company and how could they be controlled?
6 What would you do with 3000 egg yolks per week?

FORMULATING BUSINESS-LEVEL STRATEGY

Business-level strategy is concerned with how a particular business competes. The best-known approach for strategy development at SBU level is based on Porter's research.

Porter's competitive strategies

Porter outlined three generic business-level strategies to gain competitive advantage over other firms operating in the same industry (Porter 1980). They are termed 'generic' as they apply to a variety of situations. Still, they are more specific than the generic corporate-level strategies discussed before. Porter's competitive strategies are cost leadership, differentiation and focus. Requirements for pursuing these strategies are summarised in Table 7.3.

Cost leadership   **Cost-leadership strategy** emphasises organisational efficiency so overall cost of providing products and services is lower than those of competitors. With this approach, attention must be paid to minimising costs in every business aspect. This means

cost leadership strategy

Strategy outlined by Porter involving emphasising organisational efficiency so overall costs of providing products and services are lower than those of competitors

Table 7.3   Common requirements for successfully pursuing Porter's competitive strategies

Generic strategy	Commonly required skills and resources	Common organisational requirements
Overall cost leadership	Sustained capital investment and access to capital	Tight cost control
	Process engineering skills	Frequent, detailed control reports
	Intense supervision of labour	Structured organisation and responsibilities
		Incentives based on meeting strict quantitative targets
	Products designed for ease in manufacture	
	Low-cost distribution system	
Differentiation	Strong marketing abilities	Strong co-ordination among functions in R&D, product development, and marketing
	Product engineering	Subjective measurement and incentives instead of quantitative measures
	Creative flair	
	Strong capability in basic research	
	Corporate reputation for quality or technological leadership	Amenities to attract highly skilled labour, scientists, or creative people
	Long tradition in the industry or unique combination of skills drawn from other businesses	
	Strong co-operation from channels	
Focus	Combination of the above policies directed at the particular strategic target	Combination of the above policies directed at the particular strategic target

Source: Reprinted from Porter (1980, pp. 40–1).

developing efficient production methods, keeping control tight on overhead and administrative costs, seeking savings by getting supplies at low prices, and watching other costs (such as promotion, distribution and service). Lower costs allow an organisation to offer lower prices and gain an edge over competitors. They can lead to above-average profits because of higher margins or large sales volumes (Cook 1989; Smart 1995).

For a cost-leadership strategy to be effective, lower costs cannot come at the expense of necessary quality.

A low-cost strategy is not without risks. To be effective, the strategy usually requires a business to be the cost leader, not just one of several. Two or more businesses vying for cost leadership can engage in a rivalry driving profits down to low levels. Therefore, the business must have a cost advantage not easily or inexpensively imitated, and must stay abreast of new technologies altering the cost curve. In addition, managers must make product or service innovations, at least those that are very important to customers. Otherwise, competitors with a differentiation strategy may lure customers with product or service improvements.

Differentiation   A **differentiation strategy** means attempting to develop products and services seen as unique by the industry. Successful differentiation allows charging premium prices, giving above-average profits. Differentiation can take many forms; for example, design or brand image (Oroton in handbags, Parker in Furniture), technology (Hewlett-Packard in laser printers, Coleman in camping equipment), customer service (IBM in computers, Optus in telecommunications), features (Bamix in kitchen appliances), quality (Xerox in copiers, SAAB in cars, Swarovski in rhinestones), and selection (Bunnings in hardware, Kambrook in electrical goods). With differentiation, perceptions of product or service uniqueness are more important than costs. However, a company still cannot afford to ignore costs.

There are a few vulnerabilities with a differentiation strategy. If prices are too high, customers may choose less costly alternatives, though they forgo desirable features. Also, customer tastes and needs change, so businesses following a differentiation strategy must assess customers' shifting requirements. Differentiation, of course, is best when the differentiating factor is important to customers and difficult for competitors to imitate. While differentiation is usually aimed at a broad market, a focus strategy concentrates on a narrow niche.

Focus   A **focus strategy** specialises by positioning for overall cost leadership, differentiation, or both, but within a particular portion, or segment, of an entire market. The segment may be a group of customers, a geographic area, or a part of a product or service line. The rationale is that a market segment can be more effectively served when an organisation specialises than when competitors attempt to cover the whole market. The focus strategy relies on a low-cost or differentiation approach, or perhaps both, to establish a strong position in a particular market segment, or niche. Differentiation within a focus strategy can occur by tailoring products to a market segment's specialised needs. This may produce a cost advantage too, since a firm that specialises may offer better prices on custom orders than a firm with the cost of leadership in serving the broader market's larger-volume needs.

Adopting a focus strategy has several risks a business must guard against. For one, costs for a focused firm may become very high compared to costs of less focused competitors. As time goes on, differentiation can become less of an advantage, since competitors serving broader markets may embellish their products. In addition, competitors may focus on a group within the customer population served by the focused firm.

There is growing evidence that it may be possible to combine two strategies, although combinations are difficult (Dess Gupta, Hennart & Hill 1995). Regardless of the generic strategy used, the ability to carry it out depends on distinctive competencies. Such competencies typically develop at the functional level.

FORMULATING FUNCTIONAL-LEVEL STRATEGY

Functional-level strategies spell out specific ways functional areas can bolster business-level strategy. For example, under a product differentiation strategy, the R&D department might accelerate the innovation process to provide new products in advance of competitors. Similarly, to support new product lines, marketing might develop a plan calling for premium

differentiation strategy

Strategy outlined by Porter involving attempting to develop products and services viewed as unique in the industry

focus strategy

Strategy outlined by Porter entailing specialising by establishing a position of overall cost leadership, differentiation or both, but only within a particular portion, or segment, of an entire market

prices, distribution through prestigious locations, and a special promotion scheme aimed at targeted market segments. Operations, the function responsible for actual production, might devise a functional strategy based on using excellent raw materials, incorporating the latest technology, and subcontracting some components to produce a premium product.

In essence, strategies at the functional level can be significant in supporting business-level strategy. Typically, functional areas develop distinctive competencies leading to potential competitive advantages. Such competencies rarely occur by chance. Instead, they need to be carefully conceived and may take several years to develop.

STRATEGY IMPLEMENTATION

While strategy formulation is important in strategic management, strategies are unlikely to have the impact intended unless implemented effectively. Strategy implementation involves management activities needed to put the strategy in motion, institute strategic controls for monitoring progress, and ultimately achieve organisational goals (see Fig. 7.6).

Fig. 7.6   The strategy-implementation phase of the strategic-management process

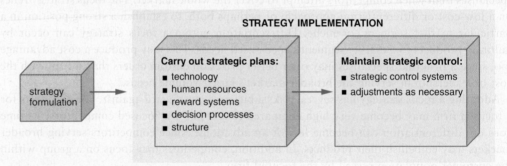

Carrying out strategic plans

Galbraith and Kazanjian (1986) suggest that several major internal aspects of an organisation may need synchronising to put a chosen strategy into place. Principal factors (shown in Fig. 7.6) are technology, human resources, reward systems, decision processes and structure. The factors are interconnected, so changing one will mean changes in others.

Technology   Technology comprises knowledge, tools, equipment and work techniques an organisation uses to deliver its product or service. Technology is important in implementing strategy because technological emphasis must fit strategic thrust. Organisational strategy, at all levels, must consider the technical functions of the business. For example, if an organisation pursues a low-cost strategy, changes in technology may help reduce costs. Following a differentiation strategy may entail technological change to develop and/or produce enhanced products or services.

Human resources   Human resources are individual organisation members. Having individuals with necessary skills in appropriate positions is a prerequisite for effective strategy implementation. This is managed by strategic human-resource planning, which links human-resource needs to strategies to be pursued. Furthermore, an organisation's human-resource skills and experience often provide competitive advantage.

A skilled workforce usually has greater ability to reduce costs or produce new products or services than less experienced staff. We discuss human resources more thoroughly in Chapter 10.

Reward systems   Reward systems include bonuses, awards or promotions, as well as intangible rewards such as feelings of personal achievement and challenge. Carefully considered reward systems constitute an important source of motivation to support given strategy. We discuss motivational issues further in Chapter 12.

Decision processes   Decision processes include means of resolving questions and problems occurring in organisations. Issues of resource allocation are important to strategy implementation because strategic plans will be more successful when resources needed are available. Decision-making processes can help resolve specific problems and issues arising while implementing the plan. We discussed managerial decision making at length in Chapter 5.

Structure   Organisation structure is the formal pattern of interactions and co-ordination that management designs to link individual and group tasks in achieving organisational goals. Such patterns help various organisation parts co-ordinate their efforts. The organisation's broad outline is often shown in an organisation chart. Research suggests strategies may be more successful when structure supports strategic direction. We discuss this further in Chapter 9.

Maintaining strategic control

While many factors must be considered in carrying out strategic plans, managers must monitor progress. They do so through strategic control. This means monitoring critical environmental factors affecting strategic-plan viability, assessing effects of organisational strategic actions, and ensuring strategic plans are implemented as intended. Instituting strategic control includes designing information systems that provide feedback on how strategic plans are carried out, as well as their effects. Such systems allow managers to adjust implementation of strategic plans, as needed. Issues related to strategic control are considered in Chapters 16 and 17. Chapter 19 investigates various management information systems used for strategic control purposes.

The strategy implementation process, of which strategic control is part, entails bringing about change and innovation. In the next chapter, we give special attention to the basic elements of organisation structure.

■ The MD's diary

This, to me, is the process of developing the strategy and implementing it in a way that will ensure that key objectives of the organisation and ultimately, the vision, are realised.

Everyone in the organisation must understand why they are here, where we are going and how we are going to get there. In this I cannot act in isolation. I may start the process, making sure that the vision and the key business objectives are deployed through the organisation, but it is at departmental level, at customer team level, and at the individual level that the drivers and the specific strategies are identified that will achieve the corporate goals in the most efficient way possible.

The process involves the deployment of the overall key objectives to specific strategies with key performance indicators, so that every individual in the organisation can see day-to-day how their activities and effort contribute to the organisation's development.

■ The subordinate's log

Strategic management largely rested in the hands of the CEO. This was his company; he knew where he wanted it to go. He communicated his long-term vision of the type of business the company would evolve to. However, there was a large gap between the strategic and the operational. The business had grown and evolved but there were some difficulties facing it, which hampered the fulfilment of those strategies. Desire to move the organisation in specific directions is well and good. However, the type of work we were doing was not always with the ideal clients, or in areas within our core expertise, or in the strategic directions the CEO wanted.

A number of senior managers globally were involved in attempting to develop the strategic directions of the firm. There was a lot of talk but little action. We had not got to the stage where we could actually achieve much because of the time constraints with the jobs we were doing. There were some discussions with the CEO, but typically he would decide and drive. Ultimately I felt that I had little impact on strategy. This is not a criticism, merely an observation, as the hardest thing is to take a step back from the business. For a business to grow and develop, it is crucial to step back and take a logical dispassionate look at it. Our CEO could do that fairly unemotionally but his demands on the operational aspects meant that no-one had the time or the desire to develop strategy, as everyone was too busy keeping their heads above the water. The climate to encourage strategy development was not created and maintained within the organisation culture.

Focus on practice—Strategies for improving

1 Develop a process which will ensure that a SWOT analysis is an automatic part of the planning process.
2 Develop a strategy to ensure that your staff understand the difference between planning and strategic management.
3 Find an old strategy which was analysed and implemented. Discuss any cost–benefits analysis which may have been performed and repeat it with the present outcomes in mind. To what degree was the analysis correct? What might have been done to increase the accuracy levels?

Source: Jones et al. (2000).

Chapter summary

Strategic management is a process by which managers formulate and implement strategies for optimising the achievement of strategic goals. Strategy formulation is the part of strategic management that includes identifying the mission and strategic goals, conducting competitive analysis and developing specific strategies. Strategy implementation is the part of the process that involves carrying out strategic plans and maintaining control over how they are carried out. The overall process helps organisations identify and develop a competitive advantage, a significant edge over the competition.

Organisations develop three different levels of strategy: corporate, business and functional. Corporate-level strategy addresses the businesses an organisation operates, how those businesses' strategies will be co-ordinated to strengthen the organisation's competitive position, and how resources will be shared among businesses. Business-level strategy concentrates on competition within a business while also supporting corporate-level strategy. Functional-level strategy focuses on action plans for managing a particular functional area in a business in a way that supports business-level strategy.

Before trying to devise effective strategy, managers must assess both environmental and organisational factors influencing an organisation's ability to compete effectively. One method is SWOT analysis, which involves assessing organisational strengths (S), weaknesses (W), environmental opportunities (O) and threats (T). Porter's five competitive forces model helps analyse the nature of the competition and its intensity in terms of five major forces: rivalry, bargaining power of customers, bargaining power of suppliers, threat of new entrants and threat of substitute products or services. The resource-based strategic view helps organisations assess internal resources and capabilities in terms of value, rareness, imitability and organisation.

Corporate strategy development involves selecting a grand strategy and using portfolio-strategy approaches to determine the various businesses making up the organisation. Three types of grand strategies are growth (including concentration, vertical integration and diversification), stability and defensive (including harvest, turnaround, divestiture, bankruptcy and liquidation). Two frequently used portfolio approaches are the BCG growth-share matrix and product/market evolution matrix.

At the business level, use of Porter's competitive strategies, including cost leadership, differentiation and focus strategies, constitutes the best-known approach. Functional-level strategies specify major ways functional areas can bolster business-level strategy.

In carrying out strategic plans, managers must consider major organisational internal aspects needing synchronisation. These include technology, human resources, reward systems, decision processes and structure. Strategy implementation also includes strategic-control maintenance. This involves monitoring critical environmental factors affecting strategic-plan viability, assessing the effects of organisational strategic actions, and ensuring strategic plans are implemented as intended.

Questions for discussion and review

1 Explain the concept of strategic management and the notion of competitive advantage. Identify an organisation you think has a competitive advantage in its industry, and describe the nature of its advantage.
2 Outline the major components of the strategic management process. Explain why engaging in strategic management is likely to be beneficial for an organisation.
3 Distinguish between three levels of strategy. Explain the role of each in an organisation with separate divisions competing in different industries.

4 Explain SWOT analysis. Conduct a brief SWOT analysis of your college or university by developing two items for each of the four SWOT categories.

5 Outline Porter's five competitive forces model. Use the model to assess the nature and intensity of competition in an industry with which you are familiar.

6 Explain how the resource-based strategic view can be used to aid organisational assessment. Use the view to assess an organisation's resources and capabilities in the industry you analysed in the previous question.

7 Describe three major generic strategies available at corporate level, and explain subcategories within each. For each generic strategy, identify an organisation appearing to be pursuing that particular strategy.

8 Contrast two major approaches to portfolio strategy at corporate level. If you were on the strategic planning staff of a major company with 35 different businesses, which approach would you recommend and why?

9 Describe Porter's competitive strategies for the business level. Assess the competitive strategy of an organisation with which you are familiar, and explain its usefulness in dealing with Porter's five competitive forces.

10 Outline the process of strategy implementation. Which corporate-level generic strategy do you believe is being pursued by your college or university? Evaluate the effectiveness of strategy implementation at your college or university.

Exercises for managing in the 21st century

Exercise 1
Skill building: What strategy is this?

Porter has proposed three generic strategies to gain a competitive advantage. Select the strategy the following characteristics could be expected to support.

Characteristic	Cost Leadership	Differentiation	Focus
1 Innovative products			
2 High quality and reasonable price			
3 Niche selling			
4 Buying resources in quantity			
5 Strong customer orientation; insurance sold primarily to active and retired military officers and families			
6 Culture supporting leading-edge software development			
7 Baked beans selling for an average of less than a dollar a can			
8 Homeowners' insurance sold primarily to wealthy people with expensive possessions			
9 Designer jeans			
10 Will not be undersold			

Exercise 2
Management exercise: Developing a strategy for a country school, NSW

You are an extremely successful restaurant manager. It is your ambition to eventually open up a restaurant of your own, but you do not have the necessary funds to do so. It has come to your attention the state government is in the process of closing some small country schools and selling the buildings. One of the schools for sale is one you attended as a young student. You are excited by the prospect that you might, by entering into a partnership with some of your old classmates, purchase the property and develop it in some way.

The school has six large classrooms, three offices and a medium-sized all-purpose room. The property also has a two-bedroom timber house on the grounds. You have had dinner with a group of your old classmates and some have indicated a willingness to participate in a joint venture if you could demonstrate some gain for them in doing so.

1 Jillian is a general practitioner working in a clinic in a harbourside suburb of Sydney who believes in holistic, preventative medicine. She would be able to invest approximately 20 per cent of the funds required to buy the property. Her comments indicate she might be persuaded to get involved beyond a simple investment.

2 Eric is a primary-school teacher at a large school in Wollongong. He thinks back fondly to the days of small schools and small classes and has indicated he is able to invest about 10 per cent of funds required to buy the property.

3 David is an accountant with a flair for giving his clients advice on creative business ventures. He does not wish to be directly involved in the enterprise but would be willing to assist in the development of it.

4 Joyce and Erica are sisters who own and operate two very successful beauty salons on Sydney's North Shore. They don't know how they could be of use but are willing to invest time and effort if it's appropriate as they do not have any funds available at the moment.

You can raise about 50 per cent of the purchase price yourself and really want to have a go at something. Develop a grand strategy for developing the school property and use a portfolio-strategy approach to analyse various business alternatives. Then use Porter's generic strategies to choose a strategy for each alternative you develop. Be prepared to explain the reasoning behind your choices.

The strategic development of Melba's Chocolate Factory

on the rim—
in Australia

Having been in the niche market of personalised logo chocolate-making and stylised chocolate dessert containers for several boutique hotels and restaurants in the Adelaide area for some time, Joy and Graeme Foristal recognised an opportunity to make old-fashioned confectionery from an historic site at Woodside, which is now a significant tourist attraction in the Adelaide Hills.

Graeme had developed a relatively inexpensive method of producing personalised logo chocolate moulds (his only competitor used an expensive laser method and lived in Queensland). He had decided to turn his part-time sideline into a full-time, single operator, chocolate workshop at Oakbank in the Adelaide Hills. He had adopted a focus strategy. He already had managed to achieve cost leadership as an owner-operator in a cottage industry. With a relatively inexpensive method for producing personalised logo moulds with few overheads, he could keep his costs down. His unique method of creating a mould for the personalised chocolates differentiated it from the only other known producer's method.

This intellectual property was invaluable. He wanted to keep the workshop small, but still entice visitors (e.g. tourists) to a workshop door-sales facility. Melba's Chocolates experienced strong growth. Personalised logo chocolates became highly fashionable in the early 1990s and soon, Melba's were servicing several boutique hotels, large restaurants and semi-government organisations.

At that time, the Adelaide Convention Centre wanted personalised up-market chocolate dessert containers and other products. The requirement was for something unique in the market, something quite distinctive. Graeme was able to create a personalised logo for the Adelaide Convention Centre, producing after-dinner chocolates using his special method of creating moulds. He won the contract. There was now pressure to expand their premises. Development regulations prevented the promotion of retailing so they concentrated on expanding the manufacturing side. Coincidentally, an Adelaide confectionery company announced a liquidation sale. The Foristals attended the auction intending to purchase cold-room panelling to extend their existing premises at Oakbank; however, the depressed economic climate enabled them to bring home five truckloads of confectionery-making equipment.

Immediately their plans changed. With so much equipment and the potential for growth that went with it, they now needed much larger premises than Oakbank. Recent government legislation prevented significant development in the Adelaide Hills without a great deal of report writing and deliberation, so they decided to look for large premises to lease or purchase. They found the Southern Farmers Cheese and Smallgoods factory at Woodside. It had been vandalised and abandoned for many years, and a sale contract had just fallen through. Seizing upon the opportunity, they bought it subject to the sale of their own house, set about scrubbing it clean, and painted it.

Within a short time, Graeme had set up the chocolate room to continue existing contracts, and expanded into floral cashell and sugar tableted lines using the equipment bought at the sale. Markets for their expanding confectionery lines needed to be developed; markets interested in the old-fashioned confectionery being produced. A direct reflection of the existing depressed economic climate was the prediction that tourism was to be the industry of the future. Obviously, historical confectionery equipment lent itself to the idea. Visitors could come and see the historical equipment in action producing the old fashioned confectionery as a tourist attraction. Graeme and Joy needed to find out more.

They discovered local tourist groups, who gave them several leads, including bus companies to contact. They contacted the South Australian Tourist Commission for advice, went to tourism meetings, and made sure they were on the tourist lists of destinations. They became familiar with the local council. They contacted bus companies to entice buses to visit on the way to other destinations. This enabled them to tap into the then lucrative senior citizens market.

Both Joy and Graeme realised that success in the tourism industry was based on numbers, on return visits, particularly in South Australia. One of the first groups to visit was a group of tourism and hospitality students. As part of their studies they were asked to design a tour brochure. The students were shown the newly established chocolate room and the Spartan residence within the factory, and given an insight into the future plans of the premises. What they saw enthused them and they expressed a desire to see it in six months' time. The catch phase 'See a factory in the making' was born. Progress became part of the attractions. A panning room, packing room, outfeed room or cold room, and toffee room were later established. Many groups regularly revisited to see the changes, particularly senior citizens who at that time were relatively affluent, keen travellers and very interested.

With these initiatives, the business emphasis was changing from a focus industry of personalised chocolates to an expanding, differentiating industry covering a wide range of old-fashioned products designed for the tourist market. Other general confectionery lines, such as truffles, and the hand-dipped lines of snowballs and biscuits were developed and a confectionery sales area was opened within the premises. Growth accelerated. A few months later the present day emporium-styled shop was built.

Buses destined east for Hahndorf or north to the Barossa Valley would detour via Melba's. Others from anywhere within two or three kilometres of Adelaide would visit because it was a new and exciting venture. Some months later, Melba's was featured in a documentary, together with Sovereign Hill, Ballarat, on 'Come on, kids' television program, which was invaluable.

Joy and Graeme noticed Sovereign Hill had a lolly shop, so contacted them for ideas and advice. They were invited to visit and returned home with some of Sovereign Hill's surplus equipment and a clearer vision for the future. Later, they were approached to make a traffic-light confectionery line for a particular company. The old-fashioned machinery, purchased especially for this, produced traffic lights relatively inefficiently and created many 'seconds'. A use was needed for this by-product. Within a short time, they started making old-fashioned inch liquorice blocks. Melba's was entered for the Tourism Award 'Best Retailer' in 1992 and won it for providing the best retailing experience in South Australia with their locally made confectionery. This proved a significant turning point as Melba's then went on to gain both State and National recognition.

The Foristals became heavily involved in the SA Tourism Commission, trade shows, and holiday and travel shows interstate. They recognised the need for 'destination marketing', which provides visitors with an experience and an opportunity to purchase goods at a number of destinations within the same area. Being part of a collection of other tourism products, and complementary destination operators, Melba's Chocolate Factory was promoted as one of the many attractions of the Adelaide Hills. This promoted the other attractions as well, and further fostered goodwill.

Melba's had a distinctive competence, a unique strength that any potential competitor could not easily match or imitate: its historical disposition, size and the historical nature of the Melba's building, the historical equipment and the historical confectionery lines made on this equipment were part of this. With the surrounding tourist attractions, they created an organisational synergy. Together they had greater impact on prospective visitors than by operating individually.

The disused heritage building next door and belonging to Melba's had been reclaimed and used by various single operators. Over time Joy and Graeme ensured that the premises were occupied by businesses operated seven days a week in line with the tourist trade, and provided products that were distinctively different and complementary to the other businesses on site. Some of these businesses are drawcards in their own right. Joy and Graeme constantly and carefully monitored critical environmental factors affecting the viability of their strategic plans.

When the senior-citizens tourists' dollar faded, Joy and Graeme developed the school excursion market, hoping children would coax their parents back. This, too, proved very successful. Since then, with their national recognition from tourism awards, television documentaries, magazines and newspaper features, their clientele come from all parts of the globe.

Today, Melba's Chocolate Factory is a thriving confectionery company serving local, interstate and international visitors and markets with enduring lines of highly successful confectionery, in particular, their own Melba's chocolates.

During Melba's development both Joy and Graeme held the belief that a good manager is able to work on the shop floor with everything and is able to take over anywhere if necessary. They have led by example. However, at present both Graeme and Joy are starting to delegate parts of their managerial roles. Joy is a very efficient and effective organiser, who was able to give production staff clear, well-defined instructions on organisational methods of operating. She was aware of when they needed more staff and was perceptive in selecting appropriate people for the various tasks. Joy administers the accounts and their payment, oversees office staff, meets with the present consultant and office staff, and manages the shop manager and overseas her activities. The shop manager has been carefully trained by Joy and Graeme and follows schedules produced by them. She is now responsible for providing pools of potential employees when needed, assessing these and reporting back as well as being responsible for workplace trials. Furthermore, the present shop manager now also handles the ordering. In both areas this delegation has been very successful. Joy has been responsible for the giftware and packaging. Having the negotiating skills and the familiarity with the market, she is able to get good prices on other purchases such as sugar prices, and dried fruit prices. She is decisive as she relentlessly chases markets, banks, insurance companies and other agents to keep costs down. This has had an extraordinary effect on the bottom line. Graeme is responsible for marketing and dealing with the public, and for maintaining and troubleshooting the machinery. He is responsible for wholesale manufacturing and in particular ordering raw materials for this. He is also responsible for the production manufacturing staff. Graeme also deals with service providers such as the bank manager, the accountant and the insurance agent.

This year, both Joy and Graeme have made a conscious decision to be 'hands off' on the production floor, except for Christmas and Easter. In February 1999 Joy worked seven days and nights. Now it is back to three days (sometimes five). She is trying to cut back. There has been an enormous reliance on her, so through 1999 and part of 2000 she has been writing operating schedules, and encouraging Graeme to do the same. She has been the final decision-maker in staff negotiations, occupational health and safety, workcover and general troubleshooter. Since February, Joy, Graeme and their family have moved offsite, for a change of life-style.

Recently they have engaged the services of a consultant for an evaluation of the present operating systems, to prepare them for the GST and to give them advice for future development in readiness for the new millennium. Both are committed to the idea of doing what they already do exceptionally well even better in the future.

Source: Written by Alexandra Hayes, based on interviews with Graeme and Joy Foristal.

Activities for discussion, analysis and further research

1 Describe the evolution of the strategic types which the Foristals have used.
2 Perform a SWOT analysis for the organisation as it exists today and discuss a number of strategies they might use to further expand their operations.
3 In order to become even more 'hands-off', what activities might the Foristals need to shed? How do you suggest they achieve this and not lose control of their organisation?

Fostering an Innovative Organisation

Chapter 8

CHAPTER OUTLINE

The nature of change and innovation
Distinguishing between change and innovation
Forces for change and innovation

Organisational life cycles
Four life-cycle stages
Organisational termination

Promoting innovation: The change and innovation process
An eight-step model
Organisational development

Innovation for competitive advantage
Product development principles
Intrapreneurship

Key organisational change components
Structural components
Technological components
Human resource components
Cultural components
Interrelationship among components

LEARNING OBJECTIVES

After studying this chapter, you should be able to:

○ Distinguish change from innovation and identify the major forces for change and innovation.
○ Enumerate four life-cycle stages of organisations and discuss organisational revitalisation and termination.
○ Explain the eight-step model of change and innovation.
○ Explain the meaning of organisational development and the techniques used in interventions.
○ Specify four factors necessary to link innovation and competitive advantage.
○ Describe common characteristics of intrapreneurs and factors inducing them to pursue new ideas in existing organisations.
○ Outline key organisational components usually needing to be altered in implementing major changes and innovations.

Striving for excellence

Given that one of the key objectives at Autoliv is technological excellence, the focus on innovation is a natural one, with the organisation constantly seeking ways to improve processes.

Innovation is managed on a global level; technology is shared around the world. Various parts of the company do not compete against each other. With global sourcing and pricing, technologies are dealt with on a world-wide level.

The cellular structure with the weekly meeting supports people talking about the way things are done and encourages people to have ideas. Ideas are respected and valued. Ideas which are implemented are rewarded. On a day-to-day basis, ideas are followed up. For example, someone says 'we should be doing this with five rather than six'—within minutes the whole team has changed to incorporate that idea. Listening is important, and asking in lots of different forums where ideas can be raised in a non-threatening environment.

R&D is expected but the quantum of innovation comes from individuals doing the day-to-day job. Ideas are assessed against viability. These require a business plan to be done, depending on whether they are classed as a major or minor project. Each then gets put to the management team for consideration. If the project is approved, it undergoes project-status review on a regular schedule. Every engineer presents existing and suggested projects to the status-review process. Existing projects are required to demonstrate progress and identify any barriers needing to be overcome. Suggested projects seek approval at this stage and are categorised as major or minor. The organisation operates with a feedback-loop system called APDS (Autoliv project/product development system). This serves as both as an instructional tool and a record.

In this chapter, we consider the nature of change and innovation, including the major forces pressuring organisations to change. We examine the effect of organisational life cycles on the need for management of change and innovation. We also consider the process involved in change and innovation management, and consider how innovation can build competitive advantage. We then outline the key organisational components useful in implementing change.

THE NATURE OF CHANGE AND INNOVATION

Increasingly fierce domestic and foreign competition emphasises organisational innovation and change (*Business Week* 1984; Jones et al. 2000). To illustrate, the video cassette recorder, originally designed by Ampex and RCA in the 1960s, was not developed into a successful product by US manufacturers. Eventually, Japanese manufacturers succeeded, and now monopolise the whole VCR market (Resberger 1987). Events such as this have increased interest in change and innovation. In this section, we look more closely at these concepts, and consider the major forces exerting pressure on organisations to change and innovate.

Distinguishing between change and innovation

In looking at change and innovation, differentiating the two terms is useful. **Change** is an alteration to the status quo, while **innovation** is more specialised. Innovation is a new idea used in initiating or enhancing a process, product or service (Kanter 1983; Ihrcke 2000). So long as the idea for improvement is seen as new by those involved, it is considered to be an innovation, even though outside observers may believe it exists elsewhere (Zaltman, Duncan & Holbek 1973; Van de Ven 1986). All innovations imply change; but not all change is innovation, since some changes may not use new ideas or be major improvements—and may cause difficulties (for example, a storm damaging a factory).

Organisational innovations range from radical breakthroughs (laser technology) to small improvements (an improved computer-printer paper tray). Both have value (Gersick 1991). Japanese companies, in particular, are known for product and service enhancements through a series of small, incremental changes. For example, at Matsushita Electric Industrial Company, 100 technicians, PhD scientists and factory engineers worked for eight years on improving a lens for projection televisions and laser-based products, including video disc systems and compact disc players. The new lenses cost 90 per cent less than existing ones. So a modest goal—enhancing a product component—led to greater market share for Matsushita's lenses, particularly in compact disc players (Gross 1989).

As Rosabeth Moss Kanter points out, innovation has a combination of particular features. For one, innovation has some uncertainty, as it may be hard to predict progress and results. For another, it is knowledge-intensive, as those involved in the innovation may have most situational knowledge, at least during development. Still another feature is that innovation may be controversial, as resources used for innovation could be used elsewhere. Finally, innovation may cross organisational boundaries, as development and implementation often involve more than one business unit, making things more complex. Therefore, managers must understand the major aspects of change and plan for the special needs of the innovation process.

Increasing pressure from competitors, both global and domestic, means organisations must become nimble and innovative. This means organisations must use change management— where managers make organisations more proactive in changing and innovating for competitive advantage. Through this chapter, we use 'change' to mean an organisational status quo alteration, including an innovation. We use 'innovation' more narrowly as a new idea for improvement. At times, we use both, or 'change management', to show the importance of both change and innovation.

Forces for change and innovation

Many forces influence organisational change and innovation. Some stem from external factors, while others from factors mainly inside organisations.

External forces   Organisations' external forces create a need for change and innovation (see Chapter 3's discussion of the environment). For example, insurance companies have to consolidate and innovate faster due to various forces—from earthquakes and hurricanes, to greater government regulation and increased competition One approach has been to have some field representatives, such as those selling insurance to financial services groups, work from their

change

Any alteration of the status quo

innovation

New idea applied to initiating or improving a process, product or service

homes with company-supplied laptop computers, fax machines and mobile phones (Funk 1996). Thus, while external forces make organisations change undesirably, the forces may lead to innovative ideas being applied (Haveman 1992).

Internal forces   Internal change and innovation forces come from many sources. Forces include strategy and plan changes, ethical difficulties from employee behaviours, decisions on change and innovation, culture shifts, restructures, technological and leadership changes (Machan 1991; Ihrcke 2000). Successful organisations have employees receptive to new and different ideas, a clear vision of the future, permission to take risks and be unconventional (see Fig. 8.1).

Of course, many internal changes can be traced to environmental factors. Some needs for internal change facing organisations are predictable, as organisations follow certain life cycles.

Fig. 8.1   Cultural barriers (Ihrcke 2000, p. 14; Droege & Co. AG).

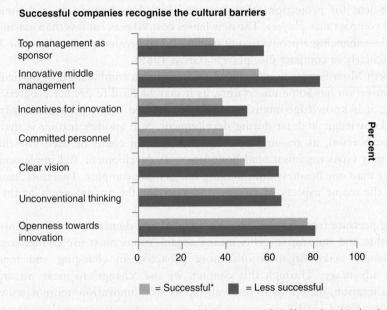

Successful companies recognise the cultural barriers

☐ = Successful*   ■ = Less successful

* Top 20% of the companies measured as a % of the turnover contributed by products introduced in the last three years

ORGANISATIONAL LIFE CYCLES

life cycles
Predictable stages of development organisations typically follow

organisational termination
Process of ceasing to exist as an identifiable organisation

Life cycles are development stages organisations typically follow. Evolving through each stage requires changes for organisations to survive and grow. Otherwise, **organisational termination,** or ceasing to exist in an identifiable way, may occur.

Organisational terminations are common. Many new businesses fail in the first five years. If you consider your local shopping centre or business district, you probably can name several businesses which started but did not survive.

Four life-cycle stages

Organisations move through four stages (Siler & Atchison 1991). These stages and their characteristics are shown in Table 8.1. Each requires changes in operating methods for organisation survival and prosperity. Oddly, unless managers plan for and encourage innovation, these same changes may eventually stop further innovation. The potential effects of the four life-cycle stages on innovation are shown in Figure 8.2.

Table 8.1   Characteristics associated with the four life-cycle stages

Characteristic	Entrepreneurial stage	Collectivity stage	Formalisation and control stage	Elaboration of structure stage
Structure	Little or none	Informal	Functional; centralisation	Self-contained; decentralisation
Focus	Survival; seeking resources	Growth	Efficiency; co-ordination	Restructuring
Innovation	Invention	Enhancement	Implementation	Renewal
Planning	Little or none	Short range	Long range	Long range; opportunistic
Commitment	Individual sense	Group sense	Complacency	Recommitment
Managers	Entrepreneurs	Entrepreneurs and early joiners	Professional managers	Professional managers and orchestrators

Source: Based on Greiner (1972) and Quinn & Cameron (1983).

Entrepreneurial stage   At the entrepreneurial stage, a new organisation is created, supporting an invention or innovation. It is formed from a single individual's initiative and is a one-person show, though others may be involved. Since the organisation is in its infancy, there is little planning and co-ordination. The prime inventor, or entrepreneur, makes the decisions.

The need for resources results in a crisis. Then, the entrepreneurial enterprise fails or moves to the next stage. For example, Howard Head, metals expert, ski enthusiast and inventor of Head skis, worked over three years developing a metal ski. His attempts met with acute scepticism from ski professionals, who often came back from the ski slopes with broken and twisted skis. When his company ran out of money, he had a resource crisis. The company was saved by investor funds in return for 40 per cent firm ownership. The design was perfected some years later, and the product was so good the skis were called 'cheaters' (Quinn 1979). Involving others as investors and helpers, however, took the Head company to the next development stage.

✖ Business idea competition   crossroads

A best business idea competition is being held again to encourage creative thinking and shrewd enterprise. The contest, now in its seventh year, is again organised by the National University of Singapore Entrepreneurial Society and the NUS Centre for Business Research and Development. Over the years the search for individuals with new services or products, or creative improvements to existing products, backed by sound business plans has attracted a large number of responses. The search is open to NUS graduates and undergraduates and aims to tap the pool of innovative business ideas as well as to provide an avenue for them to market ideas.

Reflection points

1 Why do you think such a competition was initiated?

2 What kind of organisations do you think might sponsor such a contest? What would their motivation be?

Decision points

1 Discuss how you might go about setting up a similar competition in your city or state. Who should host it? Why? Which organisation would you see as approachable for sponsorship? Why?

2 Find out whether there is already such a competition in your city or state.

Fig. 8.2   Potential effects of the four life-cycle stages on innovation

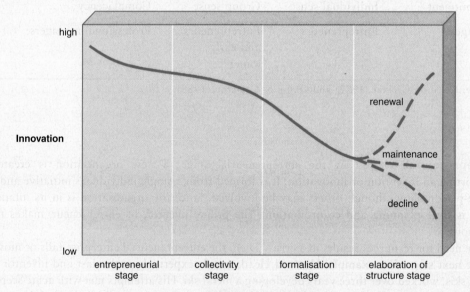

Collectivity stage   At the collectivity stage, others believing in the idea join the entrepreneur. The organisation is in its youth. There is strong group identification and a sense of mission. Organisation members put in long hours, show high commitment levels, and receive much pay in stock that is relatively worthless as yet. The vision is of better days to come.

Structure and communication patterns are informal; major decisions involve the group. Innovation is still high.

A crisis occurs as growth increases and this stage's informal management systems give poor leadership direction and control. Often entrepreneurs starting the organisation are unsuited in temperament or ability to manage a larger organisation, so they introduce professional managers. At Apple, John Sculley came from Pepsi-Cola to serve as the computer maker's president. Apple had problems cofounder Stephen Jobs felt could be handled better by an experienced manager. In two years, Jobs left after Sculley removed him as executive vice-president of Macintosh due to delays and development problems (Uttal 1985).

Formalisation and control stage   At the formalisation and control stage, the organisation's structure is more formal. Departments usually are organised into major specialisation areas such as finance, manufacturing or marketing. Emphasis is on efficiency and market-share maintenance. For co-ordination, rules and procedures are common and control is centralised. With the organisation moving to adulthood, this stage helps it consolidate, achieve better direction, and grow further. Innovation is replaced by a conservative stance, discouraging risk taking and further innovation. As growth continues, the organisation becomes harder to co-ordinate.

In this stage, competitive challenges, technological change and other factors increase the hierarchy's information-processing needs, making response slow. A crisis comes when organisation members are limited by red tape and centralised control. Levi Strauss, for example, had so good a market they could not match demand. However, procedures from the growth period meant the jeans giant could not react quickly to the slowing in the jeans market and the move to more fashionable options. One former employee said the company had 'enough staff and organisation to run General Motors' (*Business Week* 1983, p. 56). At this point, an organisation is ready for the next stage.

Elaboration-of-structure stage   At the elaboration-of-structure stage, managers look to streamline bureaucratisation from the formalisation and control stage. Decision making is decentralised, often reorganising around specific products or services. Emphasis is on co-ordinating individuals at similar levels in different work units. This means setting up temporary or continuing groups addressing interdepartmental issues. (We discuss these in Chapter 15.) In the organisation structure changes, managers work to cut costs, re-emphasising promising strategic directions.

The chief point of efforts in the elaboration-of-structure stage is **revitalisation**, renewal of the organisation's innovative vigour (Galbraith 1982). Not all try or succeed at revitalisation. Some stabilise and maintain themselves for a time. Others decline, despite efforts, failing eventually (Gray & Ariss 1985). Unfortunately, these organisations suffer dysfunctions, making them less manageable (Cameron et al. 1987). These dysfunctions, explained in Table 8.2, make renewal and revitalisation harder.

revitalisation

Renewal of innovative vigour of organisations

Table 8.2   Dysfunctional consequences of organisational stabilisation and decline

Consequence	Explanation
Curtailed innovation	No experimentation is conducted; risk aversion is prevalent and scepticism exists about activities not related specifically to current major directions.
Scapegoating	Leaders are blamed for pain and uncertainty.
Resistance to change	Conservatism and turf protection lead to rejection of new alternatives.
Turnover	The most competent leaders tend to leave first, causing leadership anaemia.
Conflict	Competition and infighting for control predominates when resources are scarce.

Source: Adapted from Cameron, Whetten & Kim (1987).

Organisational termination

Recently we have seen many organisational terminations. These occur when organisations have difficulties and cease to operate as separate entities. Termination occurs for several reasons (see Table 8.3).

Frequently, organisations terminate because they cannot innovate and change rapidly enough. Termination can occur at any life-cycle stage. Managers must think about where their organisation is in the life cycle. This helps determine types of changes needed to move the organisation to the next development stage.

Table 8.3   Methods of organisational termination

Bankruptcy	An organisation unable to pay its debts can seek protection from creditors while it tries to regain financial stability; if the problems continue, its assets will be sold in order to settle debts with creditors.
Liquidation	The sale or dissolution of an entire organisation for reasons usually associated with serious business difficulties and seemingly insurmountable obstacles.
Merger	The combining of two or more organisations into one.
Acquisition	The purchase of all or part of one organisation by another.
Take-over	The purchase of a controlling share of voting stock in a publicly traded company.

THE CHANGE MANAGEMENT AND INNOVATION PROCESS

Change management and innovation are difficult as they involve significant new ideas. Managers typically face two change types. **Reactive change** is when action is taken in response to perceived problems, threats or opportunities. As one is reacting to events, it is hard to analyse the situation properly and prepare a considered response. In one example, Johnson & Johnson had a crisis in the early 1980s when seven people died after taking cyanide-laced Extra-Strength Tylenol capsules (see Chapter 4). The company recalled 31 million bottles of pain reliever at a cost of $100 million. Then, after market-share dropped, J&J increased advertising by over 30 per cent. The company regained all but a fraction of its market share in what was termed 'one of the greatest marketing feats in our industry' (*Business Week* 1984, p. 137). The Tylenol story shows managers cannot anticipate every problem and sometimes events force them to react.

However, many situations allow **planned change**, which involves actions based on a carefully developed process anticipating possible difficulties, threats and opportunities. For example, although everyone hoped the Tylenol crisis was an isolated incident, J&J put the product into a tamper-resistant container. Four years later, following another death from a cyanide-laced Tylenol capsule, J&J showed the company was ready for a possible crisis. Chairman James E. Burke was on television almost at once, announcing they were stopping using the capsule, using instead a capsule-shaped tablet he called a 'caplet', and he showed a large model of a caplet. This decision cost millions of dollars and the company's offer to replace all capsules with caplets cost another $150 million. The speed and forthrightness of these steps showed J&J's managers had planned in case another crisis occurred and had conceived a course of action, including an implementation plan (Siwolop & Ekhund 1986).

When managers operate reactively, they increase the chances of serious mistakes, as they make changes without proper planning. As a result, effective managers engage in planned, or managed, change and innovation whenever possible.

reactive change

Change occurring when one takes action in response to perceived problems, threats or opportunities

planned change

Change involving actions based on a carefully thought-out process anticipating future difficulties, threats and opportunities

An eight-step model

Managers will be more effective in achieving change and innovation if they follow the process in Figure 8.3 (Kotter 1995; Zaltman et al. 1973; Maidique 1980). There are eight basic steps in the process.

1 **Gain recognition of an opportunity or a problem**. Major changes and innovations begin when a person or group identifies a problem situation or an opportunity. It is easy to recognise problems when things go badly. For example, when IBM spun off its printer operations, everyone realised the business had not been doing well and things would change (Flanagan 1994). When Roberto Goizueta became CEO at Coca-Cola, the company seemed to be doing well. Goizueta, however, found that its fountains business (retail outlet sales, like McDonald's, use systems called fountains to dispense Coca-Cola for immediate use) was earning less than the cost of capital. He got managers to consider returns from other company parts. They, too, were losing money. Goizueta says a belief

Fig. 8.3   The change management and innovation process

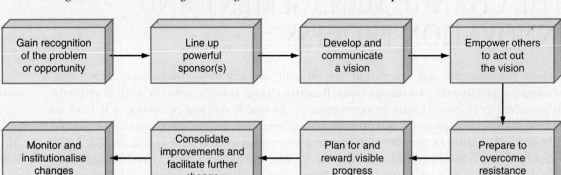

in the company that the soft-drink industry was mature led managers to overlook many options for growth (*Fortune* 1995). Opportunities were easy to miss.

Peter Drucker argues that a reason managers are not innovative is the tendency to consider immediate problems and ignore opportunities. Drucker has suggestions for increasing opportunity focus. He notes that the managers of most companies want an operations report each month. Typically, the first page lists areas where performance is below expectations. Drucker (1985) suggests adding a second 'first page' listing things going better than expected, drawing attention to possible opportunities. Another of Drucker's ideas is meeting every six months or so, having three or four managers report on entrepreneurial activities going well and that others might adopt.

2   **Line up powerful sponsor(s).** Change and innovation need the support of powerful individuals to gather needed resources and influence others for support. Major renewals need a coalition of several sponsors.

3   **Develop and communicate a vision.** To achieve change and innovation, it is important to develop a picture of the future which is easy to communicate and appeals to those who must change or support the process (Ettorre 1995).

4   **Empower others to act out the vision.** Managers need to embolden employees to act on behalf of the vision. Managers must remove obstacles stopping employees from doing so. At Lexmark, teams were set up to improve production line efficiency and raise quality. One assembly-worker team totally redesigned the laser printer production process.

5   **Prepare to overcome resistance.** That one group, even if it is top management, decides to change does not mean others will agree. At Lexmark, when the assembly worker team showed their new laser-printer production process to their boss for approval, he said each member would have to sign the plans before he would sign. The team hesitated to take the responsibility that comes with empowerment. The team took a month before they showed a redesign they were willing to sign. Later, we describe reasons employees resist change, and ways to overcome resistance.

6   **Plan for and reward visible progress.** Major change and innovation takes time, and it is possible people will lose focus or give up. One way to keep momentum is to have some projects or phases that are likely to be successful in 12 to 24 months. Celebrations,

recognitions and other rewards send a message that changes are important and it is important to focus on the vision (Fisher 1995).

7 Consolidate improvements and facilitate further change. With change processes and quests for innovation, it is easy to achieve clear improvements and then stop. At Lexmark, the first goal was to be profitable. Given the competition, though, it had to keep lowering costs and making product improvements. To do that, Lexmark management emphasised empowering the workforce, and this emphasis is still there. Worker teams still seek further advances in production, inventory and shipping.

8 Monitor and institutionalise changes. Unfortunately, renewal progress and strides to innovation can revert quickly unless they become part of corporate culture. Therefore, it is important to emphasise the need for new behaviours and their connection to company success until they are integrated into how things are done (Ettorre 1995). Companies known for innovation, such as 3M and Hewlett-Packard, have cultivated cultures supporting innovation and consider them part of their competitive advantage.

The value of knowledge

gaining the edge

Globalisation is changing the rules of commerce, and what managers bring to an organisation will no longer be enough to furnish an enterprise with competitive advantage. Management skills have become a necessary but not sufficient condition for survival. Managers who do not look outside their discipline are at risk in the global economy.

Such are the thoughts of the authors of 'Funky Business', Jonas Ridderstrale and Kjell Nordstrom. They state that management is on the way out and many external certainties are evaporating. They make the claim that workers own the means of production—knowledge. It is, however, questionable whether knowledge can be owned. It cannot be divested, lost or sold. Perhaps this means that knowledge assets is not the possession of knowledge but the conversion of that knowledge into information, or business processes, or customer relations.

Many of the boundaries which characterised the industrial era are dissolving, To make sense of such a high-degree change requires an ability to cross-reference different areas of activity without necessarily having a detailed knowledge of them. Enterprises are starting to employ staff for their attitudes rather than their skills. This is under-pinned by the belief that individuals will be able to acquire the required skills as they need them. While efficient production is important, it is no longer enough. Motivation and connection with the customer is more vital and this requires a motivated workforce.

Source: Adapted from James, D. (2000).

Activities for discussion, analysis and further research

1 In what ways do innovation and change assist an organisation to adapt to global business requirements?
2 What kind of institutions suit the global economy?
3 Herb Keller of South West Airlines says that he recruits for attitude and then trains for skills. This is especially true for industries where knowledge is perishable. Find examples of industries where this is appropriate.

Shaping up to the new guard

managing the
e-challenge

One of the key problems facing big 'legacy' (e-speak for traditional) companies in devising and implementing e-commerce strategies is to acquire the appropriate management skills. An equally pressing problem is to work out a way to sell products and services online without destroying existing relationships with customers, suppliers and staff. Executives who believe that e-commerce is little more than computer-industry hype can be found at every level of corporate Australia.

Here is a list of some of our blue-chip organisations who have entered the e-commerce field in a big way.

Company	Main e-trade rivals	Fightback plan
Coles Myer	Dstore, shopfast, CDNow, AOL-Wal-Mart, Amazon.com many others	Web development by Harris Technology, Coles online, order fulfilment service for other companies' Web sites
Holden	Autobytel, cars.com, CarPoint, drive.com.au	Online auctions among suppliers within 12 months, online sales to corporate fleets
Qantas	Travel.com, Microsoft	Boost e-tickets for international flights, online selling to frequent flyers and corporate accounts, links with banks
Southcorp	Winepalnet, Winepros, Liquorlink	Artesian portal, online sales direct to consumers
Westpac	Wizard, E*Trade, E-Loan, Commonwealth Securities	Aiming for tenfold increase in online customers, marketing alliance with John Fairfax Holdings, WAP phone trials with Telstra

While we may not clearly identify these as innovations currently, these are so for those organisations as they get into them for the first time.

Source: Adapted from Kirby, J. (2000).

Activities for discussion, analysis and further research

1 Why is it so necessary for those organisations to enter this area?
2 Why is this an innovation for those organisations, and why have they waited so long to do so?

organisational development (OD)

Change effort planned, focused on an entire organisation or a large subsystem, managed from the top, aimed at enhancing organisational health and effectiveness, and based on planned interventions

ORGANISATIONAL DEVELOPMENT

Organisational development (OD) is a change effort to improve interpersonal working relationships and organisational effectiveness through strategies using a change agent or third party who is well versed in behavioural sciences (Beckhard 1969; Beer 1980). The change agent, or consultant, comes with a fresh perspective and knowledge of behavioural sciences and acts as a catalyst to help people and groups approach old problems in new or innovative ways. This can be an outside consultant, an OD specialist in the organisation, a new manager, or an enlightened one able to look beyond the traditional.

OD was originally seen as a way to handle large-scale organisational change; however, much actual focus has been on improving working relationships. As such, OD efforts fit the change management and innovation process discussed before. OD efforts involve three major steps: diagnosis, intervention and evaluation (see Fig. 8.4) (French & Bell 1978; Huse & Cummings 1985; Mohrman, Mohrman, Ledford, Cummings, Lawler & Associates 1989).

Fig. 8.4 The organisational development process

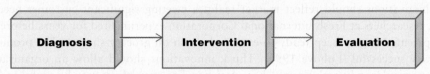

Diagnosis The first step, diagnosis, often draws attention to members' shared beliefs, values and norms which may interfere with effectiveness. The change agent and others helping the process use many ways to gather data, such as interviews, questionnaires, employee-behaviour observation, and internal documents and reports (Reibstein 1986).

Intervention Once the situation has been diagnosed, intervention is next. OD interventions, or change strategies, are designed and implemented with the change agent's help. There are many OD change strategies. Four techniques used by OD specialists are described below (French & Bell 1978; Huse & Cummings 1985).

Process consultation is concerned with the interpersonal relations and dynamics of work groups. The OD change agent, or consultant, watches the group and gives feedback on problems with communication patterns, conflict handling and decision making. The goal is helping group members gain skills to identify and resolve group dynamics issues.

Team building helps work groups develop effective task accomplishment. Like process consultation, it has OD consultant feedback on communication and conflict resolution. It also includes consultant help assessing group tasks, member roles, and strategies for work-task achievement.

Third-party intervention helps people, groups or departments resolve serious conflicts related to specific work issues or caused by ineffective interpersonal relations. The OD consultant helps the parties resolve differences by problem solving, bargaining and conciliation.

Technostructural activities help improve work technology and/or organisational structure. In this approach, the OD consultant helps members enhance work effectiveness by showing them how to evaluate and make changes in work methods, task design and organisation structure.

Evaluation Step three is evaluation. As with any change, the effectiveness of OD efforts must be monitored. The ability to evaluate the effects of OD interventions depends on how well the diagnosis stage identified areas needing change, and specified desired results.

INNOVATION FOR COMPETITIVE ADVANTAGE

Innovation does not guarantee business success. To gain competitive advantage from innovative activities, four factors are important (Lengnick-Hall 1992; Ihrcke 2000). First, innovations should be hard to imitate so competitors cannot easily duplicate an activity. Second, innovations should reflect market realities meeting significant customer needs. For example, researchers at Fresh International Corporation experimented for years before developing a patented bag to keep ready-to-eat salads fresh on grocery shelves. The product was immediately successful (Lubove 1995). Third, innovations should allow an organisation to exploit a particular industry's timing characteristics. For example, it may be useful to be first to offer an innovation. This is true in brand-name situations where customers can commit to a product or service before competitors react. In others situations, early followers may gain cost advantages. For example, relatively inexpensive copies of designer clothing are produced soon after their introduction on fashion runways or in chic boutiques in Milan, Paris and New York. Sometimes, copies appear even before originals reach stores. Fourth, innovations should rely on capabilities and technologies readily accessible to the organisation, but not to competitors.

Product development principles

Managers can enhance organisational ability to innovate new goods and services and increase competitive advantage. They can organise and control product development to reduce time, maximise fit to customer needs, maximise quality, manufacturability and efficiency. This can be done by use of four principles (Jones et al. 2000):

Principle 1: Establish a stage-gate development funnel: A mistake managers make in product development is starting too many new projects at once (Clark & Wheelwright 1989). The result is resources are spread thinly over too many projects, so no project has the resources to succeed.

Given this, managers need a process to evaluate product-development proposals and decide which to support and which to reject. A common solution is to establish a stage-gate development funnel, a planning model forcing managers to choose among competing projects so organisational resources are not spread thinly (Clark & Wheelwright 1989). The funnel gives managers control over product development and lets them intervene as needed (see Fig. 8.5).

At Stage 1, the funnel has a wide mouth, so managers can encourage employees to develop many new product ideas. Managers can reward employees coming up with ideas. Organisations can run 'bright idea programs' rewarding employees whose ideas are adopted.

New product ideas are presented as brief proposals. Proposals come to a cross-functional team, who evaluate the proposal at Gate 1. The team considers a proposal's fit with organisation strategy and feasibility. Proposals fitting with organisation strategy and assessed as technically feasible pass through Gate 1 into Stage 2.

The goal in Stage 2 is to draft a detailed product-development plan. This specifies all information needed to make a decision about mounting a full-blown effort. The plan includes

Fig. 8.5 A stage-gate development funnel

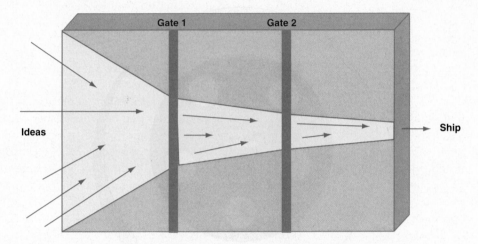

strategic and financial objectives, analysis of potential product market, desired features list, lists of technological needs, as well as financial and human resource needs, a detailed development budget, and a time line with specific milestones.

This takes about three months. Once completed, it is considered by a committee at Gate 2 (see Fig. 8.5). The focus is on plan details to see if the proposal is attractive (market potential) and viable (whether there are enough technological, financial and human resources to develop product). Senior managers in this review need to remember all other product-development efforts of the organisation. One goal at this point is to ensure limited organisational resources are used effectively.

At Gate 2 projects are rejected, sent for revision, or allowed to pass into Stage 3, the development phase. Product development starts with formation of a cross-functional team with primary responsibility for product development.

The Stage 3 development effort can last from six months to 10 years, depending on the industry and product type.

Principle 2: Establish cross-functional teams: A smooth-running cross-functional team is critical to successful development. Others besides core members work on the project as the need arises, but core members (generally from three to six) stay with the project from inception to completion of development (see Fig. 8.6).

Using a cross-functional team assures high-level co-ordination and communication among managers in different functions, increasing group cohesiveness and performance.

Principle 3: Use concurrent engineering: Traditional product development involves five steps: opportunity identification, concept development, product design, process design and commercial production (see Fig. 8.7a). Opportunity development occurs at Stage 1 of the funnel (see Fig. 8.5), commercial production at Stage 3, and others at Stage 2. The problems with sequential product development are long product-development times, poor quality and high manufacturing costs if there is no direct communication between marketing managers

Fig. 8.6 Members of a cross-functional product-development team

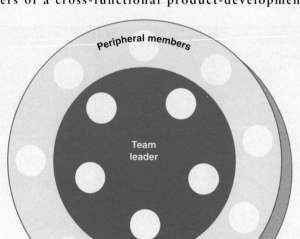

developing the concept, engineering or R&D managers designing the product, and manufacturing managers. In many cases engineers in R&D design a product then 'throw it over the wall' to manufacturing. The result can be costly to manufacture. If solving this requires redesign, manufacturing sends the product back to design, lengthening development time.

Cross-functional teams help solve this problem, and are helpful in altering the process so it is partly parallel, not sequential. In partly parallel product development, each step begins before the prior one is finished, and managers from one function are familiar with what goes on in others (see Fig. 8.7b). The goal is facilitating concurrent engineering, the simultaneous design of product and manufacturing process (Heartly 1992). The usual outcome is an easy-to-manufacture product. Concurrent engineering reduces manufacturing costs and increases product quality. The other benefit of a partly parallel process is reduced development time, for two reasons. The whole process is compressed, and concurrent engineering reduces costly and time-consuming product redesigns.

Principle 4: Involve both customers and suppliers: Many new products fail in the marketplace as they were designed with no attention to customer needs. Product development needs inputs from more than organisation members;

Organising brainstorming and cross-functional teams are effective ways of generating ideas and seeing them through.

Fig. 8.7   Sequential and partly parallel development processes

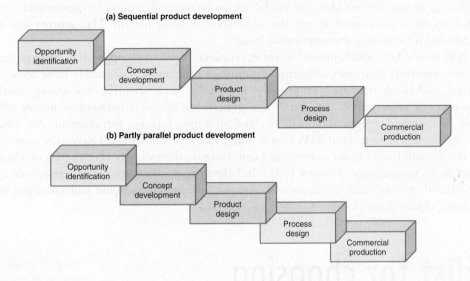

inputs from customers and suppliers are needed too (Avishai & Taylor 1989; Sounder 1988; Zinger & Maidique 1990).

In sum, managers must recognise that successful product development cuts across roles and functions and needs high-level integration. They need to recognise the importance of common values and norms promoting high levels of co-operation and cohesiveness to build an innovation culture. They must be careful to reward successful innovators and make heroes of employees and teams developing new products. Finally, managers should utilise four principles of product development for the process.

Intrapreneurship

To foster innovation, some organisations have encouraged individuals to assume entrepreneurial roles, such as idea generator or champion, sponsor and orchestrator (see Chapter 1). These are referred to as intrapreneurial roles when carried out by those inside existing organisations.

Although individuals in any of the three roles fit the intrapreneurial category, the idea champion is most often called an intrapreneur. This is because the idea champion has hands-on responsibility for turning an idea into reality (Pinchot 1985). The idea champion is the person who generates a new idea or recognises its value and supports it despite obstacles.

Intrapreneurs tend to have characteristics which can be learned, at least to a degree, if one wants to become intrapreneurial. For one thing, they tend to visualise what they wish to create. Their vision comes from taking time thinking about an idea. Intrapreneurs are also action-oriented, very dedicated, and willing to do mundane tasks to avoid delaying projects. They set goals for themselves beyond those asked of them, have high internal work standards, and recover from mistakes and failures. For example, Phil Palmquist worked on reflective coatings at 3M even though told to stop as it was not his job. Working four nights a week from 7 to 10 pm, eventually he produced the reflective coating used on most roads. It is over

100 times brighter than white paint (Pinchot 1985). Of course, part of a good intrapreneur's task is to choose a good idea. For guidelines on recognising a good intrapreneurial idea and what to do if it is rejected, see the Management skills for the 21st century discussion, 'Checklist for choosing intrapreneurial ideas'.

Why would individuals pursue an entrepreneurial idea in a company (i.e. be intrapreneurs) rather than start their own company? Established companies, particularly large ones, offer a strong technological base (proprietary knowledge and scientific resources), marketing resources (a known name, sales staff and advertising funds), a network of people who can help, established production facilities, and in-house finance. Intrapreneur Art Fry, who championed development of 3M's Post-it note pads, sees it this way: 'I have only so much time in my life and I want to do as much as I can. I can do things faster here as part of 3M and so I get to do more things' (Pinchot 1985). In helping turn ideas into reality, intrapreneurs take on official or unofficial management tasks and, like managers, must understanding how to manage organisation change.

 # Checklist for choosing intrapreneurial ideas

management skills
for the 21st century

Good intrapreneurial ideas must meet three kinds of needs: yours, the customer's and the company's. Otherwise, the intrapreneurial endeavour will not be successful. To test an idea, you can use the following checklist.

Fit with your skills and experience:
- Do you believe in the product or service?
- Does the need it fills mean something to you personally?
- Do you like and understand the potential customers?
- Do you have experience in this type of business?
- Do the basic success factors of this business fit your skills?
- Are the tasks of the intrapreneurial project ones you could enjoy doing yourself?
- Are people who would work on the project ones you will enjoy working with and supervising?
- Has the idea begun to take over your imagination and spare time?

Fit with customers and the market:
- Is there a real customer need?
- Can you get a price giving you good margins?
- Would customers believe in the product coming from your company?
- Does the product or service you propose produce a clearly perceivable customer benefit significantly better than that provided by competing means of satisfying the same basic need?
- Is there a cost-effective way to get the message and product to the customer?

Fit with the company:
- Is there a reason to believe your company could be very good at the business?
- Does it fit the company culture?
- Can you imagine who might sponsor it?
- Does it look profitable (high margin, low investment)?
- Will it lead to larger markets and growth?

What to do if your idea is rejected

Frequently, as an intrapreneur, you will find your idea has been rejected. There are a few things you can do:

1 Give up and select a new idea.
2 Listen carefully, understand what is wrong, improve your idea and presentation, and try again.
3 Find someone else to whom you can present your idea by considering:
   a Who will benefit most if it works, and can that person be a sponsor?
   b Who are the potential customers, and will they demand the product?
   c How can you get to people who really care about intrapreneurial ideas?

Source: Tanzer (1987), pp. 124–5.

◉ Dough innovations

case in point

When you take a business from an apartment in Sydney's eastern suburbs to a mountain location employing 26, you would suspect that the owners are really rolling in dough. Warwick Quinton literally is rolling dough, with a bread-making business that consumes three-and-a-half tonnes of flour a week and has an annual turnover of almost $1.5 million.

Not bad for someone who got into baking bread simply because he kept telling friends that he made better bread in his Waverley flat than you could find in the shops.

'Dallas bread was one of the first well-accepted organic breads people were buying', Mr Quinton said. 'But I kept telling friends that I made better. So, they said put your money where your mouth is.'

In his early days in the late 1980s he and his wife Vanessa used to run the gauntlet at the famous Paddington Markets selling bread off trays strapped around their necks.

In those days you were not allowed to sell food there so they were always evading market management and council rangers. 'In fact, the markets sit between three council boundaries and we used to be chased from one council area into the other', Mr Quinton remembers.

Was this difficult start rather discouraging? 'No, after selling 120 loaves in an hour, we knew we were in the right business.' Soon they escaped their apartment, going into partnership with another party to run Heaven's Leaven in the Sydney beachside suburb of Clovelly. After the partners went their separate ways, the Quintons waved goodbye to Sydney to head up to the Blue Mountains to start Quintons' Bakery Café at Leura, a town on the way to a tourist revival.

'Six years ago when we opened up as a bakery and café there were five food places in Leura and now there are 35', Quinton explained. When asked about the reason for their success, this self-taught baker thought it was his desire to combine his love of organic bread and gourmet food to produce a more consumer-friendly product. 'When I started there were a lot of farmers with organic grain who were dying to supply bakeries but there wasn't the volume', he said.

Quinton's Bakery in Leura, the Blue Mountains, uses innovation on all fronts: in its location, products and distribution.

'I suggested to some of them that they should mill a lighter flour and that has made the difference to the bread I make.' Two of his bakers are from Switzerland and Germany and together with the Quintons, they have produced a bread with a 'Euro–San Francisco' taste.

His latest innovation is to join up with people he hails as some of the best producers in NSW to supply produce for the Growers Market at Fox Studios. 'It's a very competitive market with specialty small retailers and restaurants key customers—but you can be knocked off by new producers, so the markets give us a chance to go straight to the consumer', he said.

This retail development is the plan of the future for Quinton. A number of small Sydney outlets are on the way. Coincidentally, communal markets were important in the past for the Quintons and will figure prominently in the future. Standing in the old showground arena where the Fox Studio markets are held, Mr Quinton made an observation: 'It's ironic that we're doing this on the doorstep of the old Royal Agricultural Showground'.

Source: Switzer, P. (2000).

Activities for discussion, analysis and further research

1 Identify the innovations the Quintons have come up with.
2 How have the Quintons managed their innovative processes?
3 Make suggestions for their next set of innovations

KEY ORGANISATIONAL CHANGE COMPONENTS

Significant change or innovation usually means altering one or more of the key components of structure, technology, human resources and culture (see Fig. 8.8) (Leavitt 1964; Huse & Cummings 1985). Since these are interrelated, change in one may demand adjustment in others.

Structural components

Organisation structure is the pattern of interactions and co-ordination designed to link individual and group tasks to achieve organisational goals. Structure includes factors such as how jobs are defined and clustered into work units, and various mechanisms to facilitate vertical and horizontal communication (e.g. delegation and use of interdepartmental teams) (Child 1977). As structures must adapt as circumstances change, reorganisations are common. Reorganisations influence change by altering interaction and co-ordination patterns (Russell 1987). (Specific structures are discussed in Chapters 9 and 10.) Minor structural changes also occur in most organisations, although many 'fine-tune' a previous reorganisation. Research suggests reorganisations representing quantum change—concerted and dramatic change—are more often associated with later high performance than piecemeal, incremental reorganisations (Miller & Friesen 1982; Romanelli & Tushman 1994).

Technological components

Technology is the knowledge, tools, equipment and work techniques an organisation uses to deliver products or services. Technological changes appear in new products and services (e.g.

Fig. 8.8   Key components for implementing change (adapted from Leavitt, in Cooper, Leavitt, & Shelly 1964, p. 56.)

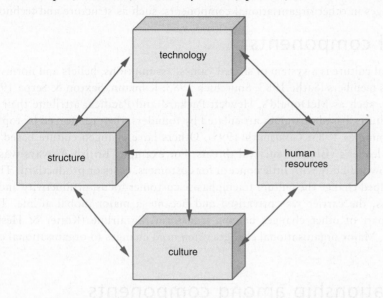

computer scanners and Internet connections) and improvements to current products and services. Technological change is important for international competition. When two Japanese companies, Yamaha Motor and Honda Motor, competed for the local motorcycle market, Yamaha said it would beat Honda. Unfortunately for Yamaha, Honda reacted by flooding the market with new models, often one per week. Forced continually to discount obsolete models, Yamaha Motor lost $300 million in two years (Tanzer 1987).

Technological innovations change work methods. For example, word-processors and personal computers eliminated the need to retype whole documents after corrections. Access to data banks gives more, better information to specialists such as doctors, engineers, educators and research scientists. In biotechnology, robot apprentices help scientists study deoxyribonucleic acid (DNA), the raw material of genes, by performing in hours tests previously taking a trained chemist weeks or months (Chase 1986). Technological changes often affect staff levels and types of skills needed.

Human resource components

Changing individuals in the workplace involves altering knowledge, skills, perceptions and behaviours needed for a job. The change relies on training and development activities, with performance appraisal and reward systems reinforcing needed behaviours. Frequently, recruitment and selection systems must change to reflect the need for people with different skills. Having people with knowledge and skills to handle changing circumstances needs careful planning. For example, Motorola is well known for extensive employee training programs. One of these, the Vice-President Institute (VPI), helps vice-presidents learn and practise innovation and leadership skills. Vice-presidents need these skills to sustain Motorola's growth. The program helps Motorola manage diversity, since vice-presidents from different countries and cultures can build networks (Eller 1995). Effective human resource systems are discussed at length in Chapter 11. Changes in these are needed to enhance the value of changes in other organisational components, such as structure and technology.

Cultural components

Organisational culture is a system of shared values, assumptions, beliefs and norms linking an organisation's members (Sathe 1983; Smirchich 1983; Kilmann, Sexton & Serpa 1986). Many organisations, such as McDonald's, Hewlett-Packard and Pacifica, attribute their success to distinctive cultures based on values articulated by founders, then reinforced by top executives (Huse & Cummings 1985; Goldsmith 1995). Others have changed culture based on factors such as their leader's vision or survival threats. For example, British Airways was a money-losing, state-owned body with little concern for customers, costs or productivity. Then, strong leadership helped change the culture to emphasise customer focus, productivity and initiative. In the process, the carrier was privatised and became a major global airline. The culture change was part of other changes helping transform the airline (Kotter & Heskett 1992; Dwyer 1992). Major organisational changes often need changes to organisational culture (see Chapter 3).

Interrelationship among components

Though minor changes may relate to only one change component, major changes may encompass all four. This is because a major change in one component has impacts on others. You might think of components as being connected by rubber bands. If you change one component, tensions are created on others until they are adjusted accordingly.

Of course, major innovation and change efforts also need an in-depth understanding of people's motivation. In the next chapter, we explore motivational processes and see how managers can effectively motivate others.

■ The MD's diary   the reflective practitioner

To me, Innovation is the process which delivers improved value to our customers or improved returns to our stake-holders. In this I do not differentiate between process or product. Ultimately innovation is what ever we do that provides a competitive advantage to our organisation.

Ours is an industry that has seen reduction of real prices in the market place. Effectively the only opportunity to maintain a stable business is to reduce costs through innovation; if we want to remain competitive and profitable, then we have to be able to innovate at a greater rate than the competition. This will grow the business by growing our market share and growing our penetration of products in the market place.

Innovation is of itself fundamentally essential to the survival of Autoliv, but at the end of the day it will not happen unless it can provide security to all the Autoliv Team. For me to be able to make a personal commitment to our people we have to ensure that our rate of growth will absorb the people realised through innovation.

For Autoliv then, our strategies of growth and innovation are absolutely linked. Innovation generally delivers reduced costs. With growth I am able to provide opportunities for our people to take on other roles which provide increased job satisfaction knowing that their basic security needs are looked after.

■ The subordinate's log   the reflective practitioner

The very nature of the organisation's work demanded that our people be creative and innovative. There was an expectation of innovation and it was acknowledged. However, that acknowledgment never really translated into real rewards for those involved.

Development and innovation within our service delivery tended to be ad hoc, and largely resulting from client need, depending on the project at the time and the skills of the consultant involved. Staff turnover meant that we lacked a stable environment in which innovation could be fostered, and this affected our competitive edge. We repeated ourselves, as new consultants had to learn. Activities, which were leading-edge years earlier, were no longer attractive to clients who could do those things for themselves.

Focus on practice—Strategies for improving

1 Discuss strategies for encouraging employees to take risks and become more innovative, and consider how to implement these strategies.
2 Consider strategies for avoiding a culture of risk aversion in your organisation.
3 Develop up-to-date usage skills for information management systems to ensure high quality data for innovative decision making.

Source: Jones et al. (2000).

Chapter summary

Largely due to increased competition, management of change and innovation is increasingly important to organisational survival and prosperity. Change is an alteration in the status quo, while innovation is a new idea applied to initiating or improving a process, product or service. Change forces can be external or internal. As they grow, organisations go through four life cycles, or predictable development stages: entrepreneurial, collectivity, formalisation and control, and elaboration of structure. Moving through these stages requires changes to operating methods, but these may inhibit innovation unless managers plan and encourage it. Failure to adapt to changed conditions may lead to organisational termination through bankruptcy, voluntary liquidation, and merger, acquisition or take-over.

Although managers may be forced to react to unpredictable situations, effective managers attempt to plan for major changes and innovations when possible. They typically follow an eight-step process: (1) gain recognition of problem or opportunity, (2) line up powerful sponsor(s), (3) develop and communicate a vision, (4) empower others to act out the vision, (5) prepare to overcome resistance, (6) plan for and reward visible progress, (7) consolidate improvements and facilitate further change, and (8) monitor and institutionalise changes.

Organisational development (OD) is a change effort aimed to enhance interpersonal working relationships and organisational effectiveness by planned interventions made with a change agent well versed in behavioural sciences. Organisational development has three major stages: diagnosis, intervention and evaluation. Intervention techniques used by OD specialists include process consultation, team building, third-party intervention and technostructural activities.

To gain competitive advantage by innovation, four factors are important. Innovations should be difficult to copy, reflect market realities, exploit industry timing characteristics, and rely on capabilities and technologies readily accessible to the organisation. Intrapreneurship is increasingly important in organisations, and intrapreneurs have characteristics which are learnable, such as being visionary, action-oriented, and willing to set goals associated with new ideas.

Major changes involve adjustments to one or more of the key organisational change components: structure, technology, human resources and culture. Since components are interrelated, a change in one needs adjustments in others to carry out successful change and innovation efforts.

Questions for discussion and review

1 Explain the differences between change and innovation. Think of some changes you have noticed on campus in the past year. In each case, explain the extent to which forces for change were external or internal. Which changes would you classify as innovations? Why?

2 Describe the four life-cycle stages of organisations. Choose an organisation you are familiar with and determine its stage in the organisational life cycle. On the basis of your analysis, what changes are likely to be needed in the future?

3 Explain the eight-step model of change and innovation process. Use this model to develop a plan for getting a student group to take advantage of an unexploited opportunity.

4 Explain the concept of organisational development. Suppose that you are helping with an OD project at your college or university. What major steps will be involved? What data-collection methods would you suggest for the diagnosis step?

5 Delineate the major intervention techniques used by OD specialists.

6 Specify how an organisation can use innovation to bring about competitive advantage. What possibilities for using innovation as a competitive-advantage tool appear to exist at your college or university?

7 Describe some common characteristics of intrapreneurs. Assuming these characteristics are learnable, how might you go about acquiring them?

8 Enumerate key organisational components needing to be adjusted in implementing major changes and innovations. Identify a recent change at your college or university aimed mainly at one of these components. To what extent did the change in that component alter the rest?

Exercises for managing in the 21st century

Exercise 1
Skill building: Strategies for innovation

Peter Clyde has recently been appointed as CEO to Edgemount Industries. He is 41 years of age and interested in finding new ways to do things. Edgemount Industries is a family company which has been in business for 83 years. In this generation, there is no family member able or willing to take on the management of the organisation. Consequently, Peter Clyde has been appointed.

Over the past three months, Peter has discovered some alarming facts. The average employee age is 54 and average length of service is 22 years. While things have been ticking over comfortably, the company has had no real growth in nine years and its products have shown no change in almost two decades. Peter Clyde has decided to introduce a culture of innovation. Make suggestions as to strategies he could use.

Exercise 2
Skill building: Attitudes to innovation scale

Indicate the extent to which each statement below describes the way you are, or intend to be, on the job. Use the following scale for your responses:

5 = Almost always true
4 = Often true
3 = Not applicable
2 = Seldom true
1 = Almost never true

1 I discuss with my boss how to get ahead.
2 I try new ideas and approaches to problems.
3 I take things or situations apart to see how they work.
4 I welcome uncertainty and unusual circumstances related to my work.
5 I negotiate my salary openly with my supervisor.
6 I can be counted on to find new uses for existing methods or equipment.
7 Among my colleagues and co-workers I will be first, or nearly so, to try out new ideas or methods.
8 I translate communications from other departments for my work group.
9 I demonstrate originality.
10 I will work on a problem that causes others great difficulty.
11 I provide critical input toward a new solution.
12 I provide written evaluations of proposed ideas.
13 I develop contacts with experts outside my firm.
14 I use personal contacts to manoeuvre myself into valued work assignments.
15 I make time to pursue my own pet ideas or projects.
16 I set aside resources for pursuit of risky projects.
17 I tolerate people departing from organisational routine.
18 I speak out in staff meetings.
19 I work in teams to solve complex problems.
20 If my co-workers are asked, they will say I am funny.

Scoring To determine your score, total the numbers associated with your responses to the items. Then compare the score to the following norm group (comprised of graduate and undergraduate business school students, all in full-time employment).

Score	Percentile*
39	5
53	16
62	33
71	50
80	68
89	86
97	95

*Percentile indicates the percentage of people expected to score below you.

Source: Adapted from Erlie & O'Keefe (1982).

Uncharted territory

After years of weak earnings, Japanese electronics-maker Pioneer finally looks like having bet on a winner. The company has emerged as a leading designer and maker of DVD players—a format for showing movies in the home that's proving a hit in markets as diverse as China and the United States, and is tipped to supersede video-cassette players.

Already, Pioneer has managed to carve out a 20 per cent share of the global DVD, or digital video disc, market—currently worth about ¥88 billion ($800 million) a year—and is expected to grow almost five-fold by 2003. And it has even bigger plans. 'Our goal is to be industry leader by 2005', says Kaneo Ito, the company's president.

This is not the first time Pioneer has put a video-disc technology at the heart of its ambitions, and it has paid a high price for its previous involvement. The company clung to the unwieldy laser-disc format, which got off to a promising start in 1981 before sales stalled and eventually collapsed in the mid-1990s in the face of the persistent popularity of video cassettes. This time the threat comes not from other formats but from other industry rivals: South Korean firms that are building cheaper players, and Sony whose new PlayStation 2 console comes with a built-in DVD player.

Pioneer has 'very, very good technology, but the problem is their profitability', says Masahiro Ono, an analyst at Warburg Dillon Read. On its own, he believes DVD 'won't make them much money' because competition is already bringing down the price of players.

That's where Pioneer has an ace up its sleeve. It recently launched the world's first recordable DVD system—a player that enables the user to record movies just as they do on video cassettes, or even to edit TV programs or home videos.

Still, it's pursuing a risky strategy by putting so much of its focus on DVD technology. As Ono explains, Pioneer, unlike industry giants like Sony and Matsushita, simply hasn't got the deep pockets or diverse product line-up to soften the blow if its DVD plans don't work out.

For now, investors seem willing to buy Pioneer's strategy and have pushed up its stock price by about 30 per cent in the past year, matching the percentage gains in shares of Matsushita and Sony and the benchmark Nikkei 225 stock index.

Pioneer has spent 25 years refining its optical-disc research, which Ito says gives the company an edge over its rivals. That could be the key to protecting its share of the DVD market, one of the fastest growing segments of the consumer electronic business.

Pioneer is counting on its DVD business to help it recover from a ¥1.9 billion group loss in the half year to September 1999. Thanks in part to the strong demand for DVD players overseas, the company expects to hit its full year net profit forecast of ¥5 billion—a five-fold gain from the previous year. Worryingly though, DVD prices have been falling nearly as fast as the market has been expanding. South Korean players sell in the United States for as little as $299, about $100 less than Pioneer's cheapest model and around half of what they were selling for not too long ago.

Of course, lower prices should boost sales, but Japanese manufacturers must reduce their costs in order to remain competitive. Pioneer and Matsushita are racing to move production off-shore to plants in China and South-east Asia. 'It's really unfortunate that manufacturing of such high-value-added product is being shifted overseas so soon after its introduction, but we really don't have a choice', says Yoichiro Maikawa, manager of the corporate planning office at Matsushita Electric Industrial, which already makes 10 per cent of its players in China.

Another challenge comes from Sony which appears willing to write off its own DVD-player business to spur sales of the PlayStation 2 home video game. The PS2 console, which sells for ¥39 800 in Japan, includes a DVD player that Sony says matches the quality of much more expensive stand alone DVD units sold by Matsushita and Pioneer. Officials at these companies insist that the DVD market is too big to be swallowed whole by the PS2, and say the game player might even help by making more DVD-compatible software available. But some analysts aren't so sure. 'DVD players will be forced to compete with the PlayStation 2', says Dresdner Kleinworth Benson analyst Kimihide Ttakano. 'This will kill the DVD market.'

Pioneer's answer to the PS2 is the DVR-1000, the world's first DVD capable of recording like a standard video-cassette recorder. The player was introduced in Japan in December, and the company hopes it will encourage holdouts to abandon the VCR for the cheaper image and crisper sound of DVD.

'We've finally created an optical disc which can be used over and over again to record', boasts Pioneer's Ito. 'It's like a dream come true.' The ¥250 000 price tag means it won't be on too many shopping lists in the near future, but Pioneer hopes to increase the current output of 10 000 players a month to cut production costs through economies of scale. One way to do that is by starting sales in foreign markets such as the US, where the technology has been held up by wrangling about the methods used to protect copyrighted works from illegal duplication. Pioneer officials say they hope to have the issue resolved later this year.

By getting a jump on the competition, Pioneer hopes to set the de facto industry standard for recordable DVDs. But as analyst Ono points out, 'Pioneer has had no success in the past setting de facto standards'. And with two other groups also trying to be the industry's standard setters—one led by Sony and Philips, the other by Matsushita and Toshiba—Pioneer is unlikely to find the going any easier in the future. None of these formats are compatible with each other, raising the spectre of the sort of battle seen in the VCR market in the 1980s between the Betamax and VHS.

But Pioneer is already looking beyond that battle and working on the next generation of DVDs, which will use blue lasers in quadruple storage capacity on individual discs.

Having decided last year to drop the second half of its old name, Pioneer Electronic, and revamp its logo to reflect its 'devotion to the spirit of the next millennium', Pioneer seems determined to show it has learned from its mistake of sticking with the laser disc in the face of falling sales. It has come up with a new business plan called 'Vision 2005' that outlines its strategy to become the leading company in DVDs, and further expand its production of plasma display panels for wall-hung TVs, advanced cable-TV set top boxes and car navigation systems. Ito says his company is also working with Sony to develop Memory Stick technology for new devices that can download data such as music and films directly onto computer chips instead of intermediate media such as disks.

Longer-term, Pioneer is developing a system code-named 'Agent' that aims to link all major consumer electronics through a voice-activated computer network. This would allow a user, for instance, to instruct his DVD player over a mobile phone to record a favourite movie.

'We want to allow anyone to watch anything, anytime', says Ito. With so much riding on its recordable DVD plans, that may in the end be Pioneer's only sure-fire strategy.

Source: Dawson, C. (2000).

Activities for discussion, analysis and further research

1 Outline the factors required in an organisation which will encourage innovation. Do you think Pioneer possesses those characteristics? Why? Do you identify any weaknesses? What are they? How may they be overcome?

2 Log on to the Pioneer home page and explore their company objectives. How do those reflect an innovative culture?

3 Blue laser technology was developed by a Japanese engineer called Shuji Nakamura while working for Nichia Chemical Industries. Do some literature research to discover why Nakamura has left Japan to take on a research position at the University of California at Santa Barbara. Can you identify which of the factors promoting an innovative culture that his original employers were disregarding?

○ The sky's no limit

From his 35th-floor office, Subhash Chandra has a stunning view of Bombay's skyline and, for as far as the eye can see, the Indian Ocean. It's a fitting perch for an entrepreneur poised atop India's booming satellite and cable television business—one whose sights are now set on expanding into cyberspace by providing Internet service and content, and into outer space by launching India's first private communication satellite.

To help finance his ambitions, Chandra plans to raise up to $1.5 billion by listing his flagship company, Zee Telefilms, on a US stock exchange this year. Which exchange is yet to be decided by Zee's board, but it would be the largest-ever international share offering by an Indian firm. Zee, India's biggest private media company, makes and buys TV programs, distributes them via satellite and cable, and produces entertainment and educational content for the Internet. Thanks to his 70 per cent holding in Zee, one of the best-performing stocks on the Bombay exchange, Chandra's net worth is estimated at $9 billion.

Chandra has stated that his goal is to make Zee television and Internet content available to anyone, anywhere, at any time. The company's plans include delivering Internet content using high-speed cable TV lines, adapting TV content for Web sites and creating educational Web sites about South Asia. Given the prediction that India's population of Internet users is expected to soar to 70 million by 2003 from just three million today, Zee hopes to use its brand recognition from TV to vault into a dominant role in the new media too.

Bombay analysts are confident that Zee can achieve this. Zee is at the top of the country's media universe. It is the country's only media company with software production and world-wide broadcasting and distribution through cable and satellite. Last year, Zee acquired full control of India's No 1 cable TV distribution network SitiCable, giving it a head start because it is able to offer faster Internet access through fibre-optic cables than is available through India's slow, unreliable phone lines. Zee has also acquired a licence to set up Internet service providers all over India.

Simultaneously, analysts also warn that Chandra faces serious challenges. They say Zee will need to hire top-flight talent to oversee the expansion and to run the company more professionally. It also needs to stay ahead of aggressive competition such as Sony and Rupert Murdoch's Star TV, while tightening control over its cable distribution business. Furthermore, Chandra must ensure that concerns over his plans to acquire a foundering satellite-phone company don't cool investor ardour about Zee.

Chandra's background, which tells of a journey from small-town north Indian rice trader to media tzar, shows his willingness to take dramatic risks. He set up India's first plant to make plastic tubes and founded one of the country's first amusement parks, both of which he still owns. In 1992, he ventured into the TV industry with Zee.

An early grasp of the potential of cable and satellite, an instinct for gauging the Indian tastes and a no-frills operation have been key to the 49-year-old's success in building Zee from a single channel in 1992 to a network of seven. During prime time, one-third of the 25 million Indian homes that have cable TV tune in to a Zee channel to watch its dramas, music shows, movies and news. Outside the sub-continent, Zee has about a million subscribers, mainly among the Indian diaspora in Britain and America. The company's profits have grown—they're estimated at $14 million for the nine months ending 31 December 1999, which is about the same as the whole of the previous fiscal year—and its share price multiplied 17 times in 1999.

Unlike rivals such as Star TV, Zee has virtually ignored India's English-speaking elite. Instead it provides Hindi entertainment to 'the masses, not the classes', while keeping staff to a minimum and salaries and perks low. 'We have the nose to smell this earth', says Chandra of the popular appeal of Zee's programs. The company has recently launched channels in the Bengali, Marathi and Punjabi languages. It also plans to start two English-language channels in March and a sports channel is likely this year. SG Securities forecasts that India's cable TV audience will rise to about 300 million by 2005 from 125 million today.

The $1.5 billion expected to be raised by Zee's US share offering will be used to fund the expansion of its television empire and its Internet plans. Chandra says the listing not only aims to raise capital but also to 'benchmark Zee's stock against other global players'. The US listing will enable Zee to build partnerships with other media companies through share swaps and strategic investments.

Analysts caution that Chandra's ambitions will require much more than money. First, they say Zee's top managers, while competent, lack the marketing skills and grasp of fast-changing technology needed to build a multinational company. Chandra says he's aware of the need for high-calibre, professional management. He has hired a headhunter to recruit up to 20 senior managers who will be groomed as future chief executives of his TV and Internet businesses.

Analysts also say Zee must stay ahead of arch-rival Sony Entertainment Television. In two years, Sony's flagship channel has claimed a quarter of India's prime-time cable TV viewers, largely by copying Zee's success with Hindi shows. Kunal Dasgupta, Sony's chief executive, says his company has what Zee lacks— international backing which gives it access to cutting-edge technology, expertise and global partnerships.

Moreover, Chandra acknowledges that Zee must tighten control over its cable-TV distribution: local cable operators, who collect monthly subscriptions, often report only one in five customers. Zee plans to deal directly with customers in areas where cable operators are short changing it.

One venture that may not go down well with investors is Chandra's purchase in November 1999 of a 26 per cent stake in ICO Global Communications, a yet-to-be-launched global satellite telephone service under bankruptcy protection. He is teaming up with US investor Craig McCaw to pump $1.2 billion into rescuing ICO. Chandra sees ICO's troubles as an opportunity to buy it cheap. Besides it's part of his strategic vision: for countries like India with poor telephone infrastructure, he says, satellites will play a much more important role in delivering data, voice and multimedia than in developed countries.

In 2002, ASC Enterprises, another company Chandra owns, is due to launch a $869 million satellite called Agrani that is being built by Lockheed Martin. Chandra says Agrani will provide low-cost satellite-phone services in India. With a pan-Asian 'footprint' Agrani will also lease its transponders to Zee and other TV companies. That will reduce Zee's dependence on Asiasat. It seems the sky's no limit for Chandra: 'Nothing is impossible if there is enough desire and conviction to achieve it.'

Source: *Far Eastern Economic Review* (2000).

Activities for discussion, analysis and further research

1 Discuss the planning and strategic planning issues in the case material presented.
2 Consider the mega environment factors that Zee must confront if it is to achieve the goals set by Chandra.
3 Discuss the issues requiring Chandra's attention as he launches Zee on the US stock exchange.
4 Do some literature search and locate a Web site for the company. Track its establishment as a listed company on the US stock exchange and its progress towards Chandra's goals and objectives.

PART ③

ORGANISING

Planning, as we saw before, is a crucial management function for setting organisational direction. Nevertheless, even carefully devised strategic, tactical and operational plans mean little if there is no effective way to carry them out. That is where organising becomes important. To perform the organising function, managers allocate and arrange human and other resources to enable plans to be successfully achieved. In the process, the organising function fosters innovation and facilitates needed change.

Chapter 9 presents the basic elements of organisation structure. Organisation charts, job design, types of departmentalisation, and methods of vertical and horizontal co-ordination are important to a well-structured organisation.

Yet the way one successful organisation is structured may not suit the needs of another equally successful one. As **Chapter 10** explains, managers must take a strategic approach to organisation design, assessing alternatives and considering contingency factors that influence structural choice effectiveness.

Organising, though, is not simply development of charts and means of co-ordination: people are the core of any organisation structure. **Chapter 11** looks at the strategic use of human resources to enhance the effectiveness of an organisation's workforce by means of human resource planning, staffing, development, evaluation and compensation.

Basic Elements of Organisation Structure

CHAPTER OUTLINE

The nature of organisation structure
Organisation structure defined
The organisation chart

Job design
Approaches to job design
Managing diversity: Alternative work schedules

Types of departmentalisation

Methods of vertical co-ordination
The role of formalisation

Span of management: The trend toward
  downsizing
Centralisation versus decentralisation
Delegation
Line and staff positions

**Promoting innovation: Methods of
  horizontal co-ordination**
Slack resources
Information systems
Lateral relations

LEARNING OBJECTIVES

After studying this chapter, you should be able to:

○ Describe the four elements making up organisation structure.

○ Explain the importance of organisation charts and the chain-of-command concept.

○ Outline the main approaches to job design, including the principal alternatives to traditional work schedules.

○ Explain the five major methods of vertical co-ordination, including formalisation, span of management, centralisation versus decentralisation, delegation, and line and staff positions.

○ Explain how slack resources and information systems can be used to co-ordinate horizontally.

○ Describe the major types of lateral relations and explain their usefulness in facilitating horizontal co-ordination.

Striving for excellence

At Autoliv the structure is fluid. The most recent organisation chart (2000) is in its fourth or fifth iteration. Given the nature of the organisation the structure is project driven, with the current projects driving the fluidity and adjustments to the structure to ensure best completion of the projects at hand.

In keeping with this philosophy, functions have changed as to their needs and appropriateness of those changes. Marketing and Materials and purchasing departments were separate, but they are interdependent areas. Engineers in fact do a lot of marketing so their skills were updated. The stores area was moved to the manufacturing zone. Another example of projects driving structure is that the Technical and Marketing departments are based around servicing the customer. Therefore, there is a program manager for Toyota whose responsibilities span both the technical and marketing aspects.

It is a common error of organisations that they produce structure charts which bear no resemblance to what happens on site. Autoliv's structure chart mirrors the practicalities of the work place. For example, the stores area, which in reality is interdependent with the manufacturing function, was physically moved to the manufacturing zone. This is reflected by the organisation chart.

Autoliv Australia—Departmental Organisation Chart

Managing Director's Office
Managing Director
Managing Director's Secretary

CRASH TEST OPERATIONS
MANAGER TEST OPERATIONS
—Crash Test Centre
—Production Testing
—Commercial Test Operations

FINANCE
FINANCE MANAGER
Org. Financial Management
Accounts Payable
Accounts Receivable
Insurance Administration
Information Technology

HUMAN RESOURCES
HUMAN RESOURCES MANAGER
Employee Relations
Training & Development
Occupational Health & Safety
Payroll   Buildings & Grounds
Security   Corporate Citizenship
Greenhouse Challenge Champion

KLIPPAN
KLIPPAN GENERAL MANAGER
Marketing & Sales
Product Development
Manufacturing

MANUFACTURING
MANUFACTURING MANAGER
Manufacturing
Material Control
Stores Operations
Maintenance
Industrial Engineering

MATERIALS
MATERIALS MANAGER
Purchasing Function
Contract Negotiation
Supplier Management

QUALITY
QUALITY MANAGER
Quality Function
Environmental Management
Korean Business Unit

TECHNICAL/MARKETING
TECHNICAL & MARKETING MANAGER
Product Development
Customer Development

Organising is important to managers because it is the way they match work with resources so organisational plans and decisions (discussed in Part 2) can be made and effectively carried out.

Often, a way of organising which works in one situation is less effective when the situation changes. As a result, organising is a constant management function. Managers must often consider organising issues to keep the company on target. In the first chapter of Part 3, we look at the nature of organisation structure. We explore major considerations in dividing work in meaningful ways to energise individuals to perform at their best. Then we review major ways to group jobs and units to develop an organisation's structure. We next investigate several methods of co-ordinating efforts across the hierarchy. Finally, we examine ways of co-ordinating horizontally which help various departments and units synchronise their efforts but also encourage innovation.

THE NATURE OF ORGANISATION STRUCTURE

Like most people, you may have had a problem and wanted to speak to a supervisor or someone from the next organisational level. If you were told that no-one knew who was supervising, or who was to handle complaints, you would respond with disbelief. We expect these issues to be worked out by organisations wishing to survive. In essence, we expect organisations to develop reasonably effective organisation structures.

Organisation structure defined

Organisation structure is the formal pattern of interactions and co-ordination that management designs to link the tasks of individuals and groups to achieve organisational goals. The word 'formal' refers to structures created by management for a specific purpose and which therefore are official, or formal, outcomes of the organising function. Organisations do have informal structures, or interaction patterns, not designed by management but emerging from common interests or friendship. We discuss informal patterns of interaction when considering groups in Chapter 15.

Organisation structure consists of four elements (Child 1977):

1 assignment of tasks and responsibilities defining jobs of individuals and units

2 clustering individual positions into units and units into departments and larger units to form an organisation's hierarchy

3 various mechanisms facilitating vertical (top-to-bottom) co-ordination, such as the number of people reporting to any given manager and the degree to which authority is delegated

4 various mechanisms fostering horizontal (across departments) co-ordination, such as task forces and interdepartmental teams

The process of developing an organisation structure is **organisation design**. An aid to visualising structure is the organisation chart. Therefore, we describe this chart before analysing the four main organisation structure elements in more detail.

The organisation chart

The **organisation chart** is a line diagram showing the broad outlines of an organisation's structure. Charts differ in detail, but typically show major organisation positions or departments. They also indicate how positions are grouped into specific units, reporting relationships from lower to higher levels, and official communication channels. Some charts show titles of positions, as well as their occupants. An organisation chart showing major managerial positions and

organisation structure

Formal pattern of interactions and co-ordination designed by management to link the tasks of individuals and groups in achieving organisational goals

organisation design

Process of developing an organisation structure

organisation chart

Line diagram depicting broad outlines of an organisation's structure

Developing and supervising an organisation chart is an overall responsibility of management.

Fig. 9.1   Organisation chart for the Acacia Mutual Life Insurance Company

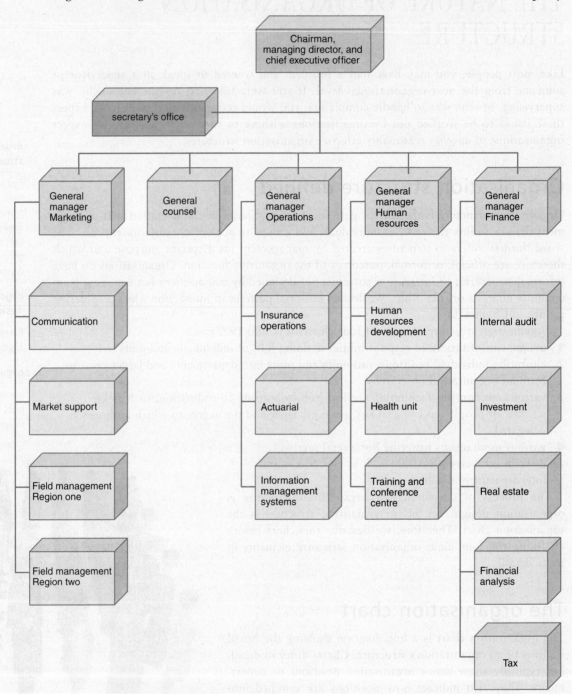

departments in the Acacia Mutual Life Insurance Company, based in Washington DC, is shown in Figure 9.1.

These charts provide a visual map of the chain of command. The **chain of command** is the unbroken authority line ultimately linking each person to the top of the organisation by a managerial position at each layer (Duncan 1989). The basic idea is that each individual in an organisation should be able to identify their boss and trace the line of authority through the organisation to the top position. In designing organisations managers need to follow one basic principle—that the chain of command must be kept to a minimum—that is, the hierarchy should always have an absolute minimum number of levels in order to effectively and efficiently use its human resources (Jones et al. 1999)

Most organisations of more than a few people have organisation charts showing the chain of command and basic organisation structure. These give a broad view but they do not give all aspects of the picture. For example, organisation charts do not normally give information about dividing work into specific jobs. Yet, as noted before, job design is an important structural aspect. It is the subject we turn to now.

chain of command

Unbroken line of authority ultimately linking each individual with the top organisational position through a managerial position at each successive layer in between

● Franchising: a structure for success   case in point

Gerry Harvey is Australia's most recent billionaire and the chairman of Harvey Norman Holdings Limited. Harvey started a partnership in Arncliffe in 1961 with co-founder Ian Norman, when they opened their first electrical store, Norman Ross Electrics. The decision by businessman Mr Alan Bond to sack them both, on his acquisition of the Norman Ross company in the 1980s, proved a disaster for the company. Under the control of Bond it went broke and Ian and Gerry formed Harvey Norman, which became one of the most successful retail chains in the country.

Apart from the sale of homewares and electrical goods, other principal activities of Harvey Norman Ltd include Franchisor, a subsidiary that handles provision of advertising and advisory services to Harvey Norman franchisees, provision of consumer finance, property investments and lessor of premises to Harvey Norman franchisees. The company is listed on the Australian Stock Exchange and has averaged an annual rate of return to shareholders of 46.5 per cent over the last ten years. If you had invested $1000 in the company in 1994 it would now be worth over $6000.

Luck plays no part in the layout of a Harvey Norman store. From the selection of the site demographically, to the final design of the store, it is all carefully planned by senior management. The Marion store, in South Australia, is a good example of this. With a total floor area of 10,000 square metres, the store contains four departments, bedding, furniture, computers and electrical, and it also has a large on-site carpark and warehouse.

Demographically, this store is situated on a main traffic route and close to a very large Westfield shopping complex. Being situated on the main road is one obvious advantage. Another is its ability to attract curious or unsatisfied Westfield shoppers through its doors. Design of the store is carefully planned. Shoppers are required to walk through the furniture and bedding sections, which are pleasantly merchandised, before entering the computer and electrical departments. With this floor plan, the company is able to get a lot of mileage for their advertising dollar. Why? The store design encourages browsing. A customer responding to a computer advertisement seen on television the night before might be seen walking out with a few other purchases made in other departments. The company promises a big range and it delivers that promise with large, impressive showrooms. This set-up responds to the customer who 'needs it now' with interest-free finance and, in the case of computers and electrical goods, stock on hand.

To the untrained eye, a Harvey Norman store looks like a big shop selling many things, and it is. However, there are actually four businesses under one roof. Not only are store location and design strong success strategies, but these are built upon by the synergy and sense of community that is created within individual departments.

A crucial part of the Harvey Norman jigsaw is the structural path of franchising the company. But don't come knocking with a bag of money, as stores cannot be bought. Only suitably qualified people, generally from within the organisation, get the chance to become proprietor of a Harvey Norman store. As Harvey says 'the people-management side of the business is more important than anything else . . . there is nothing more important for me than picking the right people and spending a lot of time with them'. This enables senior management to focus on grand plans while still maintaining control.

The responsibility for the operation of individual departments is put in the hands of that particular department's owner. In other words operational duties such as managing staff, merchandising and, of course, motivating the sales force are challenges the proprietor of each section needs to meet. For proprietors, the hours are long, the days are demanding, and dealing with the public sometimes can be difficult. However, it may just be worth your while considering the average proprietor is capable of earning between $300 000 and $400 000 per annum. By delegating the operational tasks to department proprietors, senior management are then 'freed up' to continue with the group's corporate-level strategy. A part of that strategy is the search for and selection of suitable sites to continue the store roll outs.

The economic conditions of the past few years have been good for retailers in general, with low interest rates and minimal inflation. This often means people are more comfortable spending money. With an advertising budget 'in excess of $30 million a year' and a simple advertising slogan on television which contains a 15 second voice over 'You want it we got it, at Harvey Norman', people are invited to spend at the store. Sales revenues that jumped from around $33 million in 1997 to over $69 million in 1998 indicate that the advertising is extremely effective. Not only is it effective in bringing shoppers in, it has shown itself as extremely cost effective on a store-by-store basis. The company takes advantage of 'economies of scale'. Retailing is an extremely competitive business and what sets these businesses apart is competitive advantage, and preferably a distinct competence.

To identify one for this company would be like trying to choose a colour from a kaleidoscope—there are many. One hundred and one visible stores across the country is one major benefit. As people relocate from other states they already know of a company that can help them 'set-up' home again. This size compared to others in the market place offers other advantages too. Besides competitors' awareness of the chain, manufacturers and suppliers see the company as a way to grow their own businesses as a result of the high-volume sales the company generates. Manufacturers enthusiastic to do business with Harvey Norman need to meet some tough measures, generally relating to price and advertising subsidies. There is no doubt who holds the strong bargaining lever.

Harvey Norman is set to take advantage of the changes that are occurring in technology and in consumer spending due to the changes in taxation law. Sales of computers for the company have been boosted due to the increased usage of the Internet. Sales of electrical products are expected to increase with the federal government reducing wholesale sales tax to 10 per cent in July 2000 and the introduction of digital TV the following year. Perhaps foolish to think otherwise, senior management at Harvey Norman have adopted a growth strategy. The acquisition of the Joyce Mayne stores in 1998 will provide a vehicle for the company to concentrate its efforts in a different market. These will be renamed Doymane and will involve a new lifestyle concept in retailing, offering homewares and furniture with a focus on high-spending shoppers.

With the growth of the Internet and the stories of millions made on it by retail-type investors, Harvey Norman is cautious. In a recent interview with Channel 9, Gerry Harvey was pessimistic about the use of the Internet as another market for the company to pursue. 'Everyone's on this Internet thing, you know and how wonderful it is and how much money they're going to make out of it . . . but I don't see proof of that.' Harvey, still not a believer in the possibilities of profits on the Internet, feels he had better 'keep his toe in the water' to avoid claims from other commentators that he is 'a dinosaur and out of touch'. Despite this, plans are already under way for the opening of the Harvey Norman 'Supersite' store, possibly before Christmas. The directors of the company are aware that the growth the company has achieved in recent times will not continue for ever. Besides continued store roll-outs in Australia, management is looking into countries in South-East Asia as possible locations for future expansion.

Source: Case prepared by Andrew Hutt. References: http://Hwww.brw.com.au/; Schmidt, L. (1999); Featherstone, T. (ed) (1999); Annual Report 1998, Harvey Norman Holdings Limited; http://businesssunday.ninemsn.com.au/; www.comsec.com.au.

Activities for discussion, analysis and further research

1 Using the theory studied in this chapter, identify the structure of this organisation.
2 Identify another organisation which franchises its stores. Determine the conditions for the franchisees and compare them to the ones Harvey Norman uses. Which of the two would you prefer to join? Why?
3 Consider the structure of the store and the management issues which result from it.
4 Locate the closest Harvey Norman store and make an appointment with the manager to interview them.
5 Discover the issues they feel are primary concerns to the success of their venture.

JOB DESIGN

Different job types can involve very different activities. A buyer's job for Grace Brothers, the Sydney-based department store chain, may involve contact with suppliers in an area (such as shoes), previewing new ranges, developing sources of in-house brands, and studying consumer taste trends. In contrast, a salesperson's job includes learning a department's new items, keeping displays neat, helping customers and registering sales. The buyer's and salesperson's different activities reflect **work specialisation**, the degree to which work to achieve organisational goals is divided into various jobs. Without specialisation, most organisations could not function. This is because every member could have all skills needed to run an effective organisation.

Conversely, jobs may have similar titles but involve very different activities. For example, an administrative assistant's job may include typing, filing and photocopying, or such activities as co-ordinating meetings and travel, investigating problems, and making decisions about a range of issues. What a given job includes depends on **job design**, or specified task activities associated with a particular job.

Job design is important to organising for two reasons. One is that task activities must be grouped logically. Otherwise, it may be hard for organisation members to function efficiently. The other is that how jobs are configured, or designed, influences employee motivation. (We discuss motivation further in Chapter 12.) Managers need to consider efficiency and motivational issues when designing jobs to produce effective performance.

Approaches to job design

There are four major job-design approaches: job simplification, job rotation, job enlargement, and job enrichment (Milkovich & Glueck 1985).

Job simplification   **Job simplification** is the designing of jobs to have only a small number of narrow activities (see Fig. 9.2a). Adam Smith, nearly a century ago, pointed out the advantages of work specialisation and simplification. Using an example involving pins, Smith (1910) noted that a person working alone could make 20 pins a day, while 10 who specialised

work specialisation

Degree to which work necessary to achieve organisational goals is broken down into various jobs

job design

Specification of task activities associated with a particular job

job simplification

Process of configuring jobs so job-holders have only a small number of narrow activities to perform

Fig. 9.2   Major approaches to job design

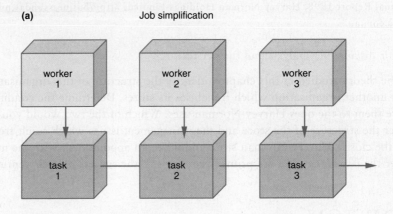

(a)   Job simplification

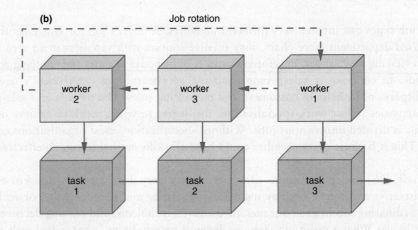

(b)   Job rotation

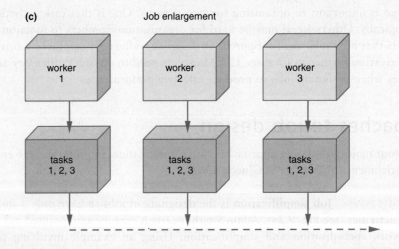

(c)   Job enlargement

could make 48 000 pins a day. Simplification was further popularised by Frederick Taylor through scientific management, which emphasises reducing jobs to narrow tasks and training workers in how to do them best (see Chapter 2).

Because jobs involved in simplification are simple and repetitive, workers are undifferentiated, making training new ones easy. The obvious job simplification example is an assembly line. Unfortunately, job simplification can go too far, creating narrow, repetitive jobs. Such jobs have negative effects, such as boredom, low job satisfaction, absenteeism, turnover, sabotage and inflexible customer service (Hackman & Oldham 1980).

Job rotation   **Job rotation** is periodic moving of workers through a set of jobs in sequence (see Fig. 9.2b). The approach aims to reduce the boredom of job simplification with some task variety. Rotation cross-trains workers (training them for tasks in several jobs) for more flexible job assignments. Although job rotation can help with monotony and boredom, its advantage may be short lived. With simple jobs, employees learn new jobs quickly and become bored again.

Job rotation is generally more successful for employee development. In this approach, employees rotated through more challenging jobs to increase their capabilities, expand job assignment flexibility and enhance understanding of various organisation aspects (Waterman 1988). Job rotation across different units or geographic locations may help innovation, as it helps exchange ideas. A recent study suggests seeking job rotation opportunities as they may lead to promotions, increased pay and other career benefits (Campion, Cheraskin & Stevens 1994). Potential problems with job rotation are departments may view rotating individuals as temporary help (giving them trivial things to do) and doubt their loyalty to the department.

Job enlargement   **Job enlargement** is allocation of a wider range of similar tasks to a job to increase the challenge (see Fig. 9.2c) (Kilbridge 1960). Enlargement increases **job scope**, the number of different tasks an employee performs in a job. Although an improvement over narrow job specialisation, job enlargement has limited success in employee motivation. This is because a few extra similar tasks do not give enough challenge and stimulation. So while the larger job of a Subway food server has a wider range of tasks than one from McDonald's, this will not necessarily reduce the boredom or increase motivation (Jones et al. 1999). In fact, if overdone, job enlargement reduces job satisfaction, efficiency and mental overload, increases errors, and reduces customer satisfaction (Campion & McClelland 1993).

Job enrichment   **Job enrichment** is the process of upgrading the job–task mix to increase potential for growth, achievement, responsibility and recognition. Enrichment was pioneered by Herzberg (1966), whose work showed the value of job content as a significant motivator. Job enrichment increases **job depth**, the degree to which individuals plan and control their work.

To guide job enrichment, Richard Hackman and Greg Oldham (1980) developed the **job characteristics model**. The model, shown in Figure 9.3, has three main elements: core job characteristics, critical psychological states, and outcomes. There are five core job characteristics:

1 Skill variety is the extent to which a job entails a number of activities requiring different skills.

2 Task identity is the degree to which a job allows completion of a major identifiable piece of work, rather than just a fragment.

---

job rotation

Practice of periodically shifting workers through a set of jobs in a planned sequence

job enlargement

Allocation of a wider variety of similar tasks to a job to make it more challenging

job scope

Number of different tasks an employee performs in a particular job

job enrichment

Process of upgrading the job-task mix in order to increase significantly potential for growth, achievement, responsibility and recognition

job depth

Degree to which individuals can plan and control work involved in their jobs

job characteristics model

Model developed to guide job-enrichment efforts including consideration of core job characteristics, critical psychological states, and outcomes

skill variety

Extent to which the job entails a number of activities requiring different skills

task identity

Degree to which the job allows completion of a major identifiable piece of work, rather than just a fragment

task significance

Extent to which a worker sees job output as having an important impact on others

autonomy

Amount of discretion allowed in determining schedules and work methods for achieving required output

feedback

Degree to which the job provides for clear, timely information about performance results

growth-need strength

Degree to which an individual needs personal growth and development on the job

alternative work schedules

Schedules based on adjustments in the normal work schedule rather than in the job content or activities

flexitime

Work schedule specifying certain core hours when individuals are expected to be on the job and then allowing flexibility in starting and finishing times as long as individuals work the total number of required hours per day

3 Task significance is the extent to which the worker sees job output as having an important impact on others.

4 Autonomy is the amount of discretion allowed in determining schedules and work methods for achieving required output.

5 Feedback is the degree to which the job provides for clear, timely information about performance results.

The more these core characteristics are reflected in jobs, the more motivating they are likely to be.

The motivational value of these characteristics comes from workers experiencing three critical psychological states: feeling work is meaningful, knowing they are responsible for outcomes, and finding out about results. According to the model, these lead to outcomes (listed in Figure 9.3) that include higher work motivation, greater growth-need satisfaction, higher job satisfaction, and increased work effectiveness. Increased work effectiveness usually comes from higher work quality, although quantity may be greater, due to improved work flow.

Research shows workers react differently to changes in core job characteristic (see moderators in Fig. 9.3). Not surprisingly, individuals are likely to be motivated more by job changes if they have the knowledge and skills to perform well in the redesigned jobs, if they have high **growth-need strength** (the degree to which they need personal growth and development on the job), and if satisfied with other job context aspects (such as supervision, pay, co-workers, job security) (Lohner, Noe, Moeller & Fitzgerald 1985; Griffin 1991).

Considering job content is one way to organise work to meet organisational and worker needs; another is devising alternative work schedules.

Managing diversity: Alternative work schedules

One aspect related to designing jobs is setting up **alternative work schedules**, based on adjustments to normal work schedules rather than content or activities. This approach's objective is to increase workers' job satisfaction and motivation by setting schedules that allow workforce flexibility by balancing work and personal life. Alternative work schedules help workers juggle work and family responsibilities, and are useful in other situations too. Three major alternative work schedules are flexitime, compressed workweek, and job sharing.

Flexitime   **Flexitime** specifies core hours when individuals must be on the job, but flexible starting and finishing times as long as required total are hours worked. For example, core hours may be 10 am to 3 pm (with an hour for lunch). Workers may then choose various schedules, such as 7 am to 4 pm or 10 am to 7 pm, making eight hours of work a day, including core hours. One recent study showed the most popular core is 9 am to 3 pm.

Flexitime's advantages include better employee morale, accommodation of working parents' needs, reduced lateness, and reductions in traffic problem as workers avoid peak times. There is often lower absenteeism and turnover. Major disadvantages include periodic lack of supervision, unavailable key people, understaffing, and co-ordination difficulties if some employees' outputs are inputs for others. Also, tracking various schedules may mean more administration. Overall, however, flexitime has been successful, and seems to be more common (Golembiewski & Proehl 1978; Ronen & Primps 1981; Dalton & Mesch 1990; Trost 1992).

Fig. 9.3   Job characteristics model (reprinted from Hackman & Oldham 1980, p. 90)

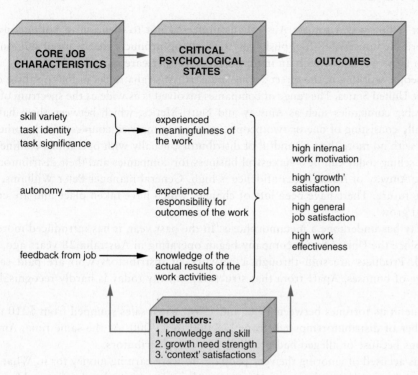

Compressed work-week   The **compressed work-week** is a schedule where four 10-hour days or a similar combination is worked, instead of a normal five 8-hour days. Some companies close three days each week. This gives operating economies, such as energy reductions resulting from no heating and cooling for days off (*Business Week* 1989).

Other organisations schedule employees to open five days a week. The basic idea of a compressed workweek, or 4/40 workweek, is to increase job attractiveness by having three (usually consecutive) days a week off. Disadvantages include fatigue, productivity losses, and accidents, as well as difficulties interacting with organisations operating on traditional schedules. More research on the compressed workweek's effects is needed. According to one study, a compressed schedule did lead to increased job satisfaction and performance, but positive effects disappeared within two years (Ivancevich & Lyon 1977). A 9/80 schedule is popular at a number of companies. With a 9/80 arrangement, employees work a nine-hour day Monday to Thursday and an eight-hour day on alternate Fridays, so they can have the other Friday off. Employees then get one free Friday in each two-week period (Genasci 1995).

Job sharing   **Job sharing** is where two or more people share one full-time job. With job sharing, one person works in the morning, the other in the afternoon, or they can work on alternate days or develop another schedule. Individuals sharing jobs may be parents sharing work and family responsibilities, or mothers combining home and work activities (Thomas 1987; Cohn 1995).

compressed work-week

Work schedule whereby employees work four 10-hour days or some similar combination, rather than the usual five 8-hour days.

job sharing

Work practice in which two or more people share a single full-time job

✖ Knock, knock

There was a time when direct selling was a subject Australians preferred not to mention in polite conversation. Door-to-door sales people were the housewife's foe, pushy shysters selling products that were of dubious quality. The exceptions were the Avon lady or a friend with an invitation to a Tupperware party.

In terms of the number of people working in the direct-selling industry, Australia ranks in the top three countries, alongside New Zealand and the United States. The range of companies involved is as wide as the spectrum of products now available. At the top are big companies such as Amway and Nutri-Metics, which between them have almost 200 000 distributorships (usually consisting of one or two people, most often married couples). At the other end are small, independent companies with no more than a handful of distributors, usually with operations confined to their local area. Big or small, direct selling today can be a successful business for companies and their distributors alike.

At the giant of the business, Amway of Australia, confidence is high. General manager Peter Williams, 45, says: 'We are very bullish about the future. There have been lots of changes which have taken place and are continuing to take place as we evolve and grow'.

In the past five years, Amway has undergone a metamorphosis. In the past year, it has introduced more changes than in the previous decade. Since the United States company began operating in Australia 28 years ago, the basic structure has barely changed. Products are sold through a network of distributors who are paid sales-based commissions and a wide range of bonuses. Apart from that structure, Amway today is hardly recognisable as the same organisation.

Amway suffered a big decline in its fortunes between 1992 and 1996, when sales slumped from $210 million to $148.1 million, and the number of distributorships fell from 128 000 to 71 000. At the same time, Amway was suffering severe image problems because of alleged bad practices by some distributors.

The Australian company was accused of ignoring the very people who were earning money for it. What had been the star performer of the global Amway network was on the nose with its masters at head office in Michigan.

Williams says those issues have been resolved. The number of Amway distributorships in Australia jumped from 71 000 in 1995–96 to 100 000 in 1998–99.

Source: Adapted from Lloyd, S. (1999).

Activities for discussion, analysis and further research

1 What are the issues that you would need to consider before you agreed to be a distributor for an organisation such as Amway?

2 Do some research on the structure of Amway and comment on the strategies used to co-ordinate the activities of the distributors.

3 Attempt to draw an organisation chart for Amway.

TYPES OF DEPARTMENTALISATION

departmentalisation

Clustering of individuals into units and of units into departments and larger units to facilitate achieving organisational goals

How individual jobs are arranged is an important dimension of organisation structure, and another is departmentalisation.

Departmentalisation is grouping individuals into units, and units into departments and larger units to achieve organisational goals. Different departmentalisation patterns are referred to as organisation designs.

Four common departmentalisation patterns are functional, divisional, hybrid and matrix (Duncan 1979; Robey & Sales 1994). Functional structures put positions into units based on expertise, skill, and similarity of work activity (e.g, marketing, accounting, production or operations, and human resources) (Bounds 1995). In contrast, divisional structures group them based on product or market similarity (e.g. separate divisions for each of several products). Hybrid structures combine aspects of functional and divisional forms, with some activities grouped by function and others by products or markets (Jones 1998). Finally, matrix structures superimpose, or overlay, horizontal divisional reporting relationships over an hierarchical functional structure. We discuss these methods of departmentalisation, or organisation design, in detail in Chapter 10.

Regardless of design, managers must focus on vertical and horizontal co-ordination to make the structure effective. In the next section, we discuss vertical co-ordination methods.

METHODS OF VERTICAL CO-ORDINATION

Although functional, divisional and hybrid types of departmentalisation types provide basic structures within which people carry out organisational activities, there are other mechanisms important to effective vertical co-ordination. **Vertical co-ordination** is linking activities at the top of the organisation with those at middle and lower levels to achieve organisational goals. Without co-ordination, organisation parts cannot work together. Five particularly important ways to achieve effective vertical co-ordination are formalisation, span of management, centralisation versus decentralisation, delegation, and line and staff positions (Daft 1998; Child 1984).

The role of formalisation

A common way to achieve vertical co-ordination is formalisation. **Formalisation** is how much written policies, rules, procedures, job descriptions, and other documents specify actions to take, or not to take, in a set of circumstances (Hall 1996; Child 1984). Formalisation helps vertical co-ordination by specifying expected behaviours in advance (Moutkheiber 1995). For example, policies provide general guidelines for organisation members' operations; procedures spell out actions to be taken under recurring circumstances; and rules specify what should or should not be done in a situation (see Chapter 6). Job descriptions detail a particular job's tasks and activities (see Chapter 10).

Most organisations are formalised. For example, major student organisations will have written policies about basic qualifications for office, as well as procedures on the conduct of elections. Without such formalisation, these issues would need to be decided every year, a time-consuming activity which might lead to inequities. On the other hand, extensive rules and procedures can stifle and discourage necessary change and innovation (Marcus 1988; Brown 1998).

When organisations are small, they can be informal, with few written policies and procedures. As they grow, organisations increase formalisation to co-ordinate the increased numbers. The challenge is to avoid becoming too formalised.

vertical co-ordination

Linking of activities at the top of the organisation with those at the middle and lower levels to achieve organisational goals

formalisation

Degree to which written policies, rules, procedures, job descriptions and other documents specify what actions are (or are not) to be taken under a given set of circumstances

Span of management:
The trend toward downsizing

Span of management, or **span of control**, is the number of subordinates reporting to a specific manager. Span of management impacts on vertical co-ordination because it defines how much managers interact with, and supervise, subordinates. With too many subordinates, managers become overloaded, find co-ordination difficult, and lose control of their work units' activities. On the other hand, with too few subordinates, managers are underutilised and tend to supervise excessively, giving little discretion (Child 1984).

Factors influencing span of management   Generally, spans of management can be wider under the following circumstances (Dewar & Simet 1981; Van Fleet 1983; Barkdull 1963; Child 1984):

O **Low interaction requirements** When work is such that subordinates can operate without frequent interaction with each other and/or with their superiors, managers can supervise more individuals.
O **High competence levels** High job-related skills and abilities of managers and/or subordinates make it possible for managers to handle more subordinates.
O **Work similarity** When employees in a given unit do similar work, it is easier for a manager to give adequate supervision than when they vary widely.
O **Low problem frequency and seriousness** When problems, particularly serious ones, are infrequent, there is less need for managerial attention.
O **Physical proximity** When subordinates are located closely to each other, managers can co-ordinate activities more easily.
O **Few non-supervisory duties of manager** Managers can handle more subordinates when they have few non-supervisory duties to perform, such as doing part of the work themselves.
O **Considerable available assistance** Managers can supervise more subordinates when they have considerable additional help, such as assistant and secretarial support.
O **High motivational possibilities of work** When the work offers a high challenge, subordinates are more likely to increase performance levels due to opportunities to exercise discretion, making it less necessary for continual managerial involvement.

Levels in the hierarchy   Spans of management for various managerial positions directly influence the number of organisational hierarchy levels. A **tall structure** has many levels and narrow spans of control. In contrast, a **flat structure** has few levels and wide spans of control.

To understand span of control's links to the number of levels, compare two hypothetical organisations shown in Figure 9.4. Organisation A, on the left, has seven levels; while organisation B, on the right, has five. If we assume a span of control of four in organisation A, then manager numbers (beginning at the top) would be 1, 4, 16, 64, 256 and 1024, for a total of 1365 (levels 1 to 6). At the seventh (bottom) level, there would be 4096 non-managerial employees. Then, if we assume organisation B has a span of control of eight, then manager numbers (beginning at the top) would be 1, 8, 64, and 512, for a total of 585 (levels 1 to 4). Organisation B also has 4096 employees in its bottom level, which is level 5. Thus, organisation A needs 811 more managers than organisation B (Robbins 1990).

Fig. 9.4   Contrasting spans of control (reprinted from Robbins 1990, p.88)

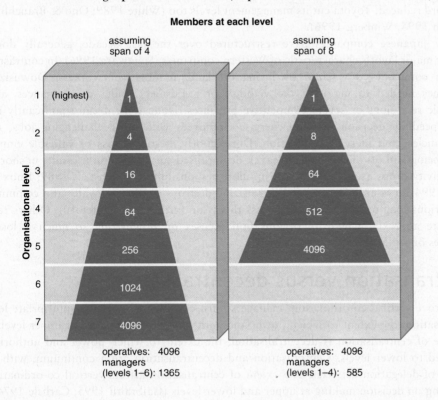

If one wanted to cut organisation A's number of hierarchical levels without reducing employees at the bottom, you would increase spans of control. Of course, in a real organisation, spans of control vary across the whole organisation, as in Figure 9.4. Still, the principle is the same. When average spans of control are narrow, the organisation will have a tall structure. Very tall organisations raise administrative overheads (more managers to be paid, given office space, etc.); result in slow communication and decision making (because of many levels); make it harder to see who is responsible for various tasks; and encourage dull, routine jobs.

Because of these problems with tall structures, many companies have downsized. **Down-sizing** is the process of significantly reducing middle management layers, increasing spans of control, and shrinking workforce size for better organisational efficiency and effectiveness (Smallwood & Jacobsen 1987; Bailey & Szerdy 1988; Freeman & Cameron 1993). A term synonymous with 'downsizing' is 'restructuring'. **Restructuring** is a major change in organisation structure by reducing management levels and possibly changing some major components of the organisation through divestiture and/or acquisition (Horton 1988; Bailey & Sherman 1988). Again, the purpose is to boost efficiency and effectiveness. Restructuring often means reducing the workforce size.

In an example of downsizing, Ford Motor Company reduced its management levels after finding it had 12 layers of management, compared with seven at Toyota (Nienstedt & Winter-mantel 1987). Ford's additional levels were expensive overhead not carried by a major competitor, which was a competitive disadvantage for Ford. The greater number of levels

downsizing

Process of significantly reducing middle-management layers, increasing spans of control, and shrinking workforce size

restructuring

Process of making a major change in organisation structure often involving reducing management levels and possibly changing components of the organisation through divestiture and/or acquisition, as well as shrinking workforce size made it harder for the company to be nimble in an increasingly competitive situation. Soon after Ford reduced, Toyota cut its management levels too (White 1989; Ono & Brauchli 1989; Reitman 1995; Winberg 1996).

Many Japanese companies have restructured over the last decade, generally doing so without major layoffs characteristic of Western companies (Sugawara 1996). In contrast many Western companies downsized by laying off large numbers of workers. Downsizing is sometimes needed to maintain the viability of a business under circumstances such as economic recessions or severe competitive pressures. Done well, it can significantly reduce costs, speed up decision making, energise employees with more challenging jobs, reduce redundancies, and increase innovation. Done poorly, it causes loss of valuable employees (either being laid off or deciding to leave), demoralised survivors, and it results in short-term productivity drops as employees pick up more responsibilities (Nienstedt 1989; Knox 1992; Burne 1994). It is argued continual downsizing destroys employee loyalty and commitment, with serious long-term effects (we discuss this issue further in Chapter 10). Others refer to corporate anorexia, where an organisation focuses on downsizing so much it loses the resources or will to grow (Wysocki 1995).

Centralisation versus decentralisation

centralisation

Extent to which power and authority are retained at the top organisational levels

decentralisation

Extent to which power and authority are delegated to lower levels

To improve vertical co-ordination, managers must consider what is the appropriate level of **centralisation**, the extent to which power and authority will be retained at upper levels. The opposite of centralisation is **decentralisation**, the extent to which power and authority are delegated to lower levels. Centralisation and decentralisation are a continuum, with many degrees of delegation between. The extent of centralisation affects vertical co-ordination by impacting on decision making at upper and lower levels (Galbraith 1995; Carlisle 1974).

Centralisation has some positive outcomes. If all major decisions are made at top levels, it is easier to co-ordinate the activities of units and individuals. Co-ordination from the top reduces effort and resource duplication by ensuring different units do not carry on similar activities (Rubel 1996). In additional, top managers may have more experience and make better decisions than those at lower levels. Similarly, the broader perspective of top-level managers can better balance the needs of various organisation parts. Finally, centralisation helps strong leadership as power stays at the top.

Decentralisation has some major advantages too (Carlisle 1974). Encouraging lower-level decision making eases executive workloads, leaving time to focus on major issues. Decentralisation enriches lower-level employees' jobs by offering them the challenge of making significant decisions affecting their work. This leads to faster decision making at lower levels, because most decisions do not have to be referred up the hierarchy. Those at lower levels may be closer to the problem and better placed to make decisions. Finally, decentralisation often helps set up independent units, such as divisions, whose output is easier to measure than functional units. It is worth noting that a divisional structure is not synonymous with decentralisation. In some divisional structures, power and authority is still held at the top, and most significant decisions referred to executive levels.

Given both approaches have advantages, how does top management decide on how to balance centralisation with decentralisation? There are four main factors tilting the scale away from centralisation's end of the continuum and toward decentralisation (Child 1984; Jones 1998):

- **Large size** It is difficult for top-level managers in large organisations to have time or knowledge to make all major decisions.
- **Geographic dispersion** Top executives often find it impossible to keep up with operational details at various locations.
- **Technological complexity** It is typically difficult for upper management to keep up technologically.
- **Environmental uncertainty** Rapid change interferes with top management's ability to assess situations quickly enough.

Delegation

Another method of vertical co-ordination closely related to centralisation-decentralisation is delegation. You are the new manager of a restaurant which is part of a chain. You are one of 10 managers reporting to a district manager. When you took over as manager, you expected to have **responsibility**, the obligation to carry out duties and achieve relevant goals. For example, you might be responsible for keeping the restaurant open during certain hours, seeing food is served, ensuring customers are satisfied, and producing a certain profit. You also expect to be given **authority**, the right to make decisions, act and direct others in matters related to their duties and goals. For example, as manager, you might expect to be able to hire employees, assign work, and order needed food and supplies. You would also expect to have **accountability**, to be required to give good reasons for major changes to duties or expected results.

Carrying the story further, suppose you soon found when making decisions, such as hiring a new worker, that the district manager interfered, frequently reversing your decisions. Yet, at the end of the month if you had not achieved the expected profit margin (largely due to the district manager's interference), you were still held accountable for the shortfall. Under these circumstances, you might conclude you had been given the responsibility but not the authority to do your job.

In this situation, the district manager has inadequately used **delegation**, the assignment of part of a manager's tasks to others, along with the responsibility and authority to achieve the results expected. Delegation means moving decision-making authority and responsibility from one organisational level to the next lower level. Delegators are still responsible for results and will be accountable to their own bosses. Delegation is important to vertical co-ordination as it allows the hierarchy to be more efficient and more effective by having work done at the lowest possible level (Duncan 1989). In addition, delegation develops subordinates to fill future managerial positions, increasing future prospects of adequate vertical co-ordination. Generally, more delegation occurs in a decentralised structure than in a centralised one. Even within a centralised structure, though, top managers do some delegating. They cannot do everything themselves.

Though even classical theorists emphasised the need to delegate, many managers still find it difficult. Some are reluctant because they fear blame if subordinates fail, believe they lack time to train subordinates, or want to hold on to their authority and power. Others avoid delegating as they enjoy tasks subordinates could perform, feel threatened by competent subordinates and worry they may make the manager look poor in comparison, or simply are concerned about ensuring work is done properly (Leana 1986; *Management Review* 1995).

Failure to delegate hurts managerial careers. A study by the Centre for Creative Leadership showed over-managing, or the inability to delegate and build a team, was one 'fatal flaw'

responsibility

Obligation to carry out duties and achieve goals related to a position

authority

Right to make decisions, carry out actions, and direct others in matters related to the duties and goals of a position

accountability

Requirement to provide satisfactory reasons for significant deviations from duties or expected results

delegation

Assignment of part of a manager's work to others, along with both responsibility and authority necessary to achieve expected results

causing fast-track executives to derail (McCall & Lombardo 1983). For guidelines on delegating, see the Management skills for the 21st century discussion, 'Guidelines for effective delegating'.

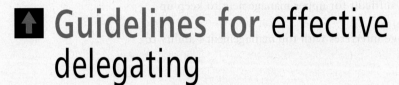

⬆ Guidelines for effective delegating

These will help you be an effective delegator:

○ The secret of delegating is determining what each member of a work unit can do. Carefully choose the subordinate to take on the project. Usually it is someone immediately below you in the corporate hierarchy. If you want to skip down two ranks, work through that person's supervisor.

○ Next, decide whether you want the subordinate to pinpoint the problem or propose a solution. If the latter, should they take action or just present you with alternatives? And do you choose the solution jointly or by yourself?

○ Once you define your goals, consider whether the person you have chosen can handle the responsibility. Will the task be a challenge, but not so difficult the subordinate gets frustrated? According to one expert, the art of managing is to figure out what each person is capable of, and create assignments within their reach, or slightly above, so they can learn.

○ Do not make the mistake of spelling out in detail how the subordinate should approach the task. Be clear in your objectives, though, because some people fear they will appear ignorant if they ask questions. Encourage questions. To give a sense of purpose, explain why the task is important. If it is something that seems menial or insignificant, note that it is a prelude to more meaningful assignments later on.

○ Make sure the subordinate has the time, budget, and data or equipment needed to get the job done on a deadline. If someone needs training to accomplish the task, be prepared to make the investment. Yes, you could do the job yourself in the time it takes to train someone else, but the hours spent training the individual will be recouped many times over in future. Unless the project is relatively simple, set up specific checkpoints to review progress so both you and your subordinate can be sure work is progressing as planned. That way you can provide additional help, if needed, before the project is in serious trouble. If things are going well, you can let the subordinate know you appreciate good work.

○ Be prepared, too, to live with a less-than-perfect result. Let subordinates know you will support the outcome of their efforts, good or bad. Take responsibility for an occasional blooper, says an expert, and you will have loyal followers for life.

Source: Adapted from Baum (1987).

Line and staff positions

Another issue related to vertical co-ordination is configuration of line and staff positions. A line position has authority and responsibility for achieving the organisation's major goals. A staff position has the primary purpose of giving line positions specialised expertise and assistance. Sometimes the term 'staff' refers to personal staff, those assisting a particular position as needed (e.g. administrative assistant to a division head).

Positions and related departments considered line or staff vary with organisation type. For example, in a grocery chain, line departments might be store operations, pharmacy, and food (directly linked to major organisational goals), staff departments might be human resources and consumer affairs (indirectly related to major goals). In a manufacturing organisation, production and sales are typically line departments, while purchasing and accounting are normally staff. Among departments seen as staff in many organisations are human resources, legal, research and development, and purchasing. However, organisations must be evaluated in terms of their own major goals to differentiate line and staff (Nossiter 1979). For instance, in a law firm, legal function would be line, despite being a staff department in other organisations.

The value of distinguishing between line and staff becomes clearer when one considers differences between line authority and staff authority. Line departments have **line authority**, or authority following the chain of command set by the formal hierarchy. On the other hand, staff departments have **functional authority**, or authority over others in the organisation in issues related directly to their respective functions. For example, in the bank's structure shown in Figure 9.5, line departments get authority through the chain of command leading to the managing director. The bank's staff departments have functional authority related to other departments; that is, authority in their area of staff expertise. Staff departments help vertical co-ordination by providing their expertise where needed, not following a strict chain of command.

Still, conflicts arise. For example, staff departments can grow, beginning to oversee departments they should assist. Before being trimmed, growing staff at Xerox second-guessed managers until new-product development steps took two years instead of two to four weeks due to continual staff unit reviews (*Business Week* 1983). Such conflicts are not inevitable, if responsibility areas are clarified and line and staff personnel operate as a jointly accountable team for final results.

Recently, there has been a trend toward reducing the number of corporate-level staff personnel, as companies attempt to cut costs and speed up decision making. Small central offices monitor budgets, cash flow, and overall operations (Moore 1987). Improving vertical co-ordination in organisations is a structural issue; promoting horizontal co-ordination is another.

line authority

Authority following the chain of command established by the formal hierarchy

functional authority

Authority of staff departments over others in the organisation in matters related directly to their respective functions

Achieving competitive advantage through new patterns of work: The Williamstown Naval Dockyard

gaining the edge

Flexible patterns of work have emerged as a key factor in enhancing organisational efficiency and competitiveness. In Australia this has been of particular interest as the globalisation of the marketplace has further increased competitive pressure. The ability of an organisation to respond in a flexible manner to increasing competition and

Fig. 9.5   Line and staff departments of a bank

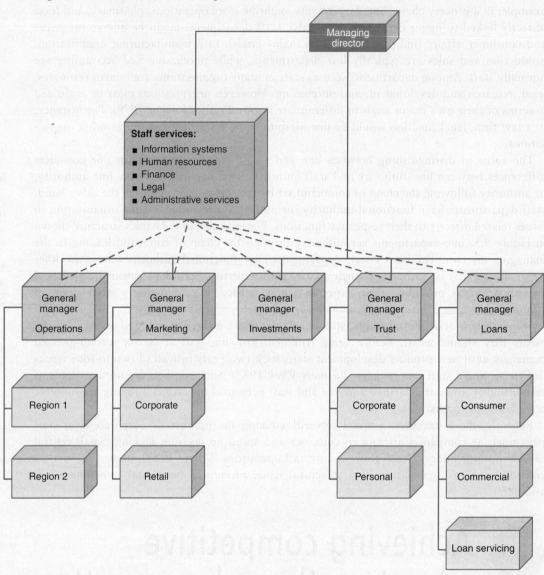

uncertainty through more effective and efficient use of resources, particularly human resources, is becoming increasingly important. This has made the management of human resources a key element in developing competitive organisations. The development of flexible patterns of work can be wide and varied, depending upon the needs of the organisation. It can mean the development of a wider range of skills for the workforce, to allow employees to be deployed according to demand. It can also mean a greater variation in the employment relationships with the outsourcing or sub-contracting of non-core production or services.

The Williamstown Naval Dockyard (WND) is Australia's premier naval shipbuilding facility. For many years the efficiency and performance of the dockyards had been a constant problem. Through the 1980s, productivity loss attributed to industrial unrest, and cost over-runs led to a Royal Commission of Inquiry. The Committee reported that the dockyard had fallen into a state of shambles. This led to the dockyard being given the nickname of the 'iron-lung' and described as Australia's worst worksite.

The continued losses and lack of international competitiveness, underpinned by archaic work practices and antagonistic industrial relations, forced the federal government to announce the sale of the Williamstown Naval Dockyard in 1987. This was to be the first major privatisation of a public utility in Australia.

Significantly, trade unions at the dockyard and the peak union body, the Australian Council of Trade Unions (ACTU), agreed to co-operate with the sale process. The ACTU position was that it was not opposed to the privatisation of the dockyard because of its poor industrial record and despair in almost all quarters at resolving the problems.

In December 1987 the federal government announced the sale of the dockyard to the Australian Marine Engineering Corporation (AMEC). The purchase of the dockyard by AMEC, a private consortium, took place on 1 January 1988. At the same time a restructuring of AMEC itself was in train. By May 1988 the Transfield Group, trading under the name AMECON, had acquired total ownership of the dockyard.

The development of a competitive shipbuilding industry meant the removal of highly regulated and restrictive work patterns, the multiplicity of trade unions and the conflictual approach to industrial relations at the dockyard. Prior to the sale of the dockyard, the workforce of 2400 employees was represented by 23 trade unions and 30 industrial awards. Demarcation was endemic and there were 390 work classifications. In addition to these classifications, there were a further 180 allowances. Work practices at the dockyard were further entrenched by policies which took no account of workload demands. This manifested itself in idle time for many employees stretching to more than 12 months.

The major focus for the new dockyard owners was the development of human resource management policies to increase efficiency. The key area that management sought to restructure was work patterns and practices. The first process in AMECON management's raft of reform was the modification of rules and regulations of work practices. Provision for an enterprise agreement (the first in Australia) was agreed upon with the ACTU. This agreement was the platform for further reforms that management wished to implement in order to create a marine engineering centre able to compete with the best in the world. The key aspect of this new agreement was the development of dispute-avoidance mechanisms, skill-enhancement provisions, the use of sub-contracting and elimination of restrictive work practices—in other words, a demarcation-free workplace with full flexibility in work allocation.

The focus on the removal of lines of demarcation and on skills-enhancement policies within the industrial agreement, and the need to involve unions relevant to the marine engineering industry, logically meant a reduced number of trade unions representing dockyard employees. This policy was supported by the ACTU and the federal government as it was part of a wider agenda to develop a modern trade union movement of 20 industry-based unions. Despite initial industrial unrest, AMECON argued that for the dockyard to increase productivity it was essential that the number of trade unions be reduced to those that were relevant to the dockyard's core work. The ACTU demarcation panel agreed upon three manufacturing-specific trade unions.

The ACTU and the dockyard management also negotiated new work practices into the enterprise agreements. A central theme in the development of an efficient and competitive dockyard for management was a labour force that would be responsive and adaptable to the needs and demands of a market-driven environment. With the enterprise agreement and three unions representing the workforce, the climate in which to undertake these reforms was in place.

The first step in the development of new patterns of work was the restructuring of job structures and classification. The process began with the reduction of work classifications from 390 to 2 (tradesperson and non-tradesperson), which immediately eliminated many lines of demarcation. AMECON also invested heavily in training and development, through its training board, which comprised management and employee representatives. The major development of this group was the establishment of the Skill Enhancement Program, which provided employees with the opportunity to develop a broad-based spectrum of skills linked to career progression. The board oversaw the design, development and evaluation of these programs.

The development of total quality management and team-based programs were also part of the board's brief from management to develop an adaptable, multi-skilled workforce. In addition, a Management Development Program for dockyard managers was developed in conjunction with local education institutions.

A key aspect in the more efficient utilisation of human resources is the ability to adjust the size of the workforce to the level of economic activity at short notice and with relative ease. The traditional model of recruitment at the dockyard had constrained work being undertaken outside the dockyard or by sub-contractors. Consequently, recruitment was geared to peak workloads. This combined with the extensive and complex lines of demarcation led to extensive 'idle time'.

The enterprise agreement provides for the use of contractors to facilitate work in the dockyard as and when required. The integration of sub-contractors focuses on the need to supplement normal procedures or to provide specialised work. The need to have the option of using external labour allows for whole sections of work to be sub-contracted. This maintains a compatible level of activity on-site and enables sub-contractors to carry out activities that cannot be economically performed by the company's employees on site. The integration of these work practices allows recruitment to be geared to program troughs rather than peaks.

To further develop and maximise the use of the 'core' workforce, variations in worktime are also provided for in the enterprise agreement. While work hours are specified within the agreement, incremental variations within the period specified (between one and four weeks) allow a maximum of 10 hours per day, with special provision to work up to 12 hours a day subject to the ACTU Code of Conduct on 12 hour shifts and in accordance with Occupational Health & Safety regulations. In addition, variations in the spread of work may be undertaken by mutual consent.

The use of shift work is also provided for in the enterprise agreement, specifically where unimpeded production is required, or for short periods in relation to the production schedules within the context of appropriate regulations and agreements. Provision for the use of overtime is also encompassed in the agreement.

The adoption of these new patterns of work have seen the dockyard reduce its core workforce from 2400 to 900 employees supported by up to 900 contractors. The elimination of restrictive work practices, idle time and lines of demarcation and the gearing of the size of the workforce to supply and demand has seen the dockyard increase its productivity by 700 per cent. Lost time has decreased from 10 per cent to 0.1 per cent per annum.

What has emerged from these changes is an increasing realisation of the importance of developing a strategic and integrative approach to the organisation's human resources as a way of improving performance. Underlying the development of these work patterns at the Williamstown Dockyard has been the integration of human resources drawn from both internal and external labour markets.

From being described as the 'iron lung', and notorious as the worst worksite in the country, the Williamstown Naval Dockyard has achieved world competitiveness by attracting both national and international contracts. Its achievements have also been acknowledged by its inclusion in the Australian Best Practice Development Program as an Australian Organisation that has achieved World's Best Practice.

Source: Peter Holland.

Activities for discussion, analysis and further research

1   What was the catalyst for these dramatic changes at the dockyard?
2   What were the advantages in developing these new work patterns and practices?
3   What factors helped the Williamstown Naval Dockyard develop these work patterns and practices?

PROMOTING INNOVATION: METHODS OF HORIZONTAL CO-ORDINATION

Suppose you purchase a television set at a department store on the understanding it would be delivered in three days, but it did not arrive. Imagine you call to inquire about the delay, and your call is passed up the hierarchy until you are talking with the regional manager of the store chain. You will begin to wonder about an organisation where a regional manager is drawn into what is a routine transaction between sales and shipping. If all problems were handled vertically, organisations would become paralysed.

Instead, organisations facilitate **horizontal co-ordination**, linking activities across departments at similar levels. Horizontal co-ordination helps processing of organisational information (Capowski 1993). Galbraith (1977) argues that the more organisations need to process information to produce their product or service, the more horizontal co-ordination is needed. Organisations typically have to process more information when facing complex and/or changing technology, environmental uncertainty, and increased size. (We discuss these issues further in Chapter 10.) For example, when William H. Wilson founded Pioneer/Eclipse Corporation, a small company specialising in a floor-cleaning system, he provided most of the co-ordination himself within a traditional functional structure. As the company grew, it lost money due to insufficient horizontal co-ordination. In one case, the sales department started a promotion only to find manufacturing and purchasing knew nothing about it and did not have enough materials and stock to fill orders. In another instance, the credit department denied credit to a major account before the sales department could solve the problem amicably. 'The left hand', said one observer, 'did not know what the right hand was doing' (Rodes 1988).

As horizontal co-ordination helps process information across the organisation, it also promotes innovation (Tushman & Tushman 1986; Kanter 1988). There are three reasons for this. First, new ideas are more likely when a range of views exist. Second, awareness of problems and opportunities spark creative ideas. Third, involving others in developing ideas often makes them more willing to help implement them (see Chapter 11).

By helping exchange information across units at similar levels, horizontal co-ordination mechanisms supplement the basic hierarchy and other vertical co-ordination methods. Three major means that are useful for promoting horizontal co-ordination are slack resources, information systems, and lateral relations (see Fig. 9.6) (Galbraith 1977).

horizontal co-ordination

Linking of activities across departments at similar levels

Slack resources

An interesting way to support horizontal co-ordination is the use of **slack resources**, a cushion of resources helping adaptation to internal and external pressures, as well as change initiation (Bourgeois 1981). You will have benefited from available slack resources in your own life. For example, in your family, a slack resource might be an extra car or television set, or your own telephone. Through co-ordination and tight programming of schedules, your family might manage with less, but this would take more effort and make quick changes in plans difficult. Because organisations face similar choices, they, too, often use slack resources, such as extra people, time, equipment and inventory, to reduce the need for constant co-ordination among units and to provide some flexibility in resource use.

slack resources

Cushion of resources that facilitates adaptation to internal and external pressures, as well as initiation of changes

Fig. 9.6   Horizontal co-ordination methods for increasing information-
            processing capacity as needed

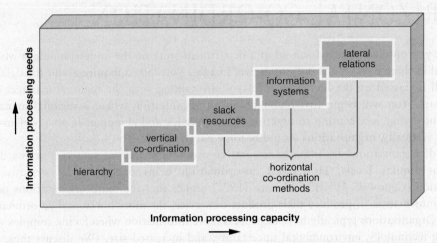

Slack resources can help foster creativity and innovation (Bourgeois 1981). For example, 3M has researchers spend 15 per cent of their time on projects of their own choice with potential for long-term payoff (a practice the company calls 'bootlegging'). In essence, this promotes slack resource use (time, equipment and materials) to enhance chances for innovation.

Information systems

An important, growing means of horizontal co-ordination is the use of information systems, mainly computerised ones, to co-ordinate parts of the organisation (Marcia 1995). For example, due to its international operations and use of divisional structures, Citicorp had horizontal co-ordination difficulties. Frequently the company was embarrassed when a client of one Citicorp unit would use other units' services, perhaps elsewhere in the world, and receive different advice. Even when advice did not conflict, fragmented guidance offered to clients did not maximise Citicorp's service capacity. The solution? Citicorp enhanced departments' ability to exchange information by setting up a new computerised conferencing system. Called PARTICIPATE, the system lets offices around the world communicate and co-ordinate efforts quickly (Mishkoff 1986). (We consider computerised information systems again in Chapter 19.)

@ An integrated distribution package

managing the e-challenge

The biggest change at Amway has been its vigorous move into e-commerce, which Peter Williams, Australian general manager, believes will be responsible for an important share of the company's future growth. If the Internet has triggered a communications revolution, it is likely to do the same for Amway and other direct-sales companies. To a large degree, his plans for Amway indicate the direction for the entire direct-sales industry.

In December 1997, Amway launched ELVIS (electronic link via Internet services), a product-ordering system that cost $500 000 to develop. Distributors have welcomed the new system, and today more than half of Amway's distributorships use it. According to Williams, about 7500 distributors place at least one order a week through the system.

On average, Amway processes and ships 50 000 orders a month from its head office in the north-west Sydney suburb of Castle Hill. Williams says one-third of those orders are being placed through the ELVIS system.

'As a totally integrated package for our distributors, it was leading-edge at the time', he says. 'It is not merely a batch-processing system where we take orders on the Internet, but a 24-hour-a-day facility. When a distributor places an order on ELVIS it interacts in real time with our back office, which can provide a huge range of information.

'We have come from a position where most of our people knew very little about the Internet to where now, I think, we have a very Internet-savvy group of distributors.'

However, ELVIS is only the start of Amway's presence on the Internet. In March next year, a new product will be launched that Williams predicts will trigger a surge in the number of orders placed over the Internet and will become an important means of generating new business and attracting new distributors. It will also help to streamline the company's distributor network.

Developed in conjunction with IBM, the new Internet system has been code-named A0A2K. Williams will not disclose how much Amway has invested in the project, citing a confidentiality agreement between the two parties. However, he says the savings to Amway will be about $3 an order once the system is in place.

'A0A2K is a whole new approach. A lot of the functionality of ELVIS will be retained, but the new system will give distributors much better direct access to Amway and will help them manage their business by providing so much more information than at present. It will give them what is basically a virtual Amway office.'

A0A2K has also been designed to simplify the way in which Amway deals with distributors and vice-versa. For the first time, Amway will put its distributors into categories under a model known as IMC, an acronym for independent business operator/member/client.

Williams says: 'At the moment we have what we would call business builders, people who are just members and people who are just clients, but we treat them all as distributors and do not differentiate too much between them. A0A2K will allow us to segment and target those people, provide services to better meet their needs, depending on whether they are active business builders, or whether they are members who just want to buy our products at preferential prices, or just a client.

'There are people who might have wanted to be associated with us in the past but really did not want to be a distributor. Now there is a home for them. We have always recognised that they are important but we haven't had the mechanisms to deal with them.'

Source: An excerpt from Loyd, S. (1999).

Activities for discussion, analysis and further research

1 Access Amway's ELVIS and consider how it responds to the needs of distributors.
2 Discuss the impact this new way of doing business has had on the distributors of Amway.

Lateral relations

Another increasingly common horizontal co-ordination approach is **lateral relations**. This is co-ordination of efforts by communicating and problem solving with peers in other departments or units, instead of referring issues up the hierarchy for resolution. This collaboration promotes innovative answers to difficulties and helps find creative answers to opportunities.

lateral relations

Co-ordination of efforts through communicating and problem solving with peers in other departments or units, rather than referring most issues up the hierarchy for resolution

Major lateral relations methods are direct contact, liaison roles, task forces, teams and managerial integrators (Galbraith 1977).

Direct contact   One means of lateral relations is **direct contact**, or communication between two or more persons at similar levels in different work units for purposes of co-ordinating work and solving problems. Direct contact allows issues to be resolved at middle and lower levels without having to involve upper-level managers. In fact, problems can frequently be handled better by lower-level managers because they may be more familiar with the issues involved.

direct contact

Communication between two or more persons at similar levels in different work units to co-ordinate work and solve problems.

Liaison roles   A **liaison role** is a role to which a specific individual is appointed to facilitate communication and resolution of issues between two or more areas. Liaison roles are reserved for situations where there is a need for continuous co-ordination between departments to function effectively. For example, an engineer may be appointed to set up contact between engineering and manufacturing departments (Reynolds & Johnson 1982).

Liaison roles are becoming more common between businesses and major customers. Here the liaison person improves horizontal co-ordination by working with internal departments and the customer, to facilitate customer needs. The benefit of liaison roles in dealing with customers is shown by a steel company executive's comments (who wished to remain anonymous). This company keeps a full-time liaison person on site at Honda's Marysville, Ohio, plant. He explained that if a problem occurs with stamping steel for body panels and there was no liaison person, the scenario would be as follows. Honda people affected by the problem would go to the purchasing department. Purchasing would contact the steel company's salesperson. The salesperson would complain to their product office. The product office would pass the issue to the department making the steel for Honda. At that point, said the executive, the offending department denies responsibility, arguing that 'it's a Honda stamping problem' (i.e. the problem is not caused by the way the steel is made but by Honda's stamping) (Flint & Heuslein 1989). A liaison person cuts through the red tape, dealing directly with departments where the problems are.

liaison role

Role to which a specific individual is appointed to facilitate communication and resolution of issues between two or more departments.

Task forces and teams   A task force is a temporary interdepartmental group formed to recommend on an issue. These recommendations are advice. Whoever appointed the task force can decide whether or not to follow the recommendations. Task forces promote horizontal co-ordination by getting people from a range of organisational areas to share ideas on issues and plan actions (Farnham 1994).

Teams, meanwhile, are temporary or permanent groups set up to solve problems and apply solutions on a particular issue or area. Teams may be from different departments, but may comprise members from the same unit (Jones 1998). At its nylon fibre plant in Pensacola, Florida, Monsanto combines liaison roles and teams in its Adopt A Customer program, which aims to offer excellent customer service. In the program, Monsanto matches top customers with key employees to act as liaisons. When problems appear, the liaison person becomes a 'resource team leader', helping resolve problems quickly. For example, if a customer tells the liaison that yarn is breaking during processing, the liaison person then becomes an internal resource team leader. They notify technical salespeople and quickly assemble a team with expertise and resources to solve the problem and offer innovative solutions. 'The whole idea of Adopt A Customer is to give top priority to that problem not in three days, but on day one, with the first phone call from our customer', says Monsanto's manager of technical sales (Flint & Heuslein 1989). We discuss teams and task forces further in Chapter 15.

Managerial integrators   A managerial integrator, another means of lateral relations, is a separate manager who co-ordinates related work across several functional departments. They have titles like 'project manager', 'product manager' or 'brand manager' and do not belong to departments whose activities they help co-ordinate. Project managers usually co-ordinate a particular project until completed. They are used in the aerospace, defence and construction industries, where large, technically complex projects must finish on schedule and at a contracted price (*Supervisory management* 1995). Product managers launch new products and services and may continue co-ordinating interdepartmental work on them. Brand managers co-ordinate organisational efforts on name-brand products, often in the soap, food and toiletries industries. Brand managers devise and implement brand strategies and plans, monitor results and correct problems. In essence, managerial integrators are horizontal co-ordinating agents (Child 1995). They permit rapid reaction to environmental change and the efficient use of resources as they can be moved between projects. In addition, managerial integrators can sponsor innovative ideas.

Managerial integrators typically lack line authority over people and departments they co-ordinate, so they must obtain the co-operation of functional managers, who control resources (Denton 1995). They compete with those (e.g. managerial integrators for other projects) who also want the help of various functional departments to make their projects, products or brands successful. As a result, managerial integrators must use knowledge, competence, personality, group management skills and persuasion abilities to work with functional managers and those working in functional departments assigned to their project (Adams & Kirchof 1984; Vlasic & Kerwin 1996).

In this chapter, we considered several major elements of organisation structure, including vertical and horizontal co-ordination methods. In the next, we explore links between strategy and organisation structure in improving organisational effectiveness.

■ The MD's diary   the reflective practitioner

The organisation structure has been developed so as to provide our customers and partners with the support they need that would make them totally comfortable with us taking the full responsibility for the whole process from design to development to production to delivery.

Our strategy is to add value to our customers through the way we support them. A detailed understanding of their business together with the appropriate organisational structure aligned to their needs will reduce the customers' requirement to resource at their end, reducing their cost and consequently increasing our competitive advantage.

If we are successful, ultimately it makes it less desirable for our customer ever to go elsewhere. So I guess the best structure is one which adds value to the customer and provides security and long-term commitment from the customer to our organisation.

Our structure here developed primarily from a need to support the strategy, so if I look at it in terms of how we developed our structure, we first developed our five-year business plan and our business strategy. From that we looked at what we do in terms of making sure that we had an organisation in place that gave us the best chance of achieving the corporate objectives—our key objectives in terms of customer service, in technical leadership, and in development of our people. What we needed to do with our structure was make sure that we were able to be very responsive to our customers needs; that we were able to be very nimble in terms of addressing issues, and we were able to innovate in as rapid a way as possible. So the structure that we have in place for an organisation our size supports that. It remains a very hands-on organisation and there is my predisposition away from having a lot of staff positions. I prefer having a structure whereby the line operators have responsibility for all aspects of their business and this has driven the organisation to take the shape it has.

■ The subordinate's log   the reflective practitioner

The organisation's Melbourne office with two consultants and senior managers for every administrative staff, officially had three levels and effectively four depending on the stream. This structure was replicated at other offices. Globally, the organisation had about 20 consultants and senior managers supported by about 10 administrative staff members.

Officially, the CEO had three global office heads reporting to him, and all other staff reported to the office heads. Variations were that within consulting teams, there was a senior or lead consultant by virtue of experience and organisational practicality, rather than any official designation. Some of those more involved directly with marketing the organisation would have a direct reporting role to the CEO as well as to the office heads. This made for a dual reporting line, which led to difficulties within the offices. It meant that the CEO made marketing decisions but responsibility was never really clear. Because the structure was so flat, the office heads had too much to manage and could spend too much time doing tasks which should be delegated. Even if tasks were delegated, the responsibility fell on the office heads. This caused great stress and conflicts throughout the organisation.

Focus on practice—Strategies for improving

1   Consider an organisation which has changed the range of products or services it provides. How does this impact on its structure? Should the organisation change the way in which it manages its processes?
2   Consider what strategies an organisation can use to keep its operational levels to a minimum.
3   What could an organisation do to retain an organic nature when it increases or significantly changes the number or kind of customers it attracts?

Source: Jones et al. (2000).

Chapter summary

Organising is the process of arranging work and resources so planned goals can be achieved. An important part of the organising function is developing organisation structure. This comprises four main elements: job design, departmentalisation of positions and units, vertical co-ordination methods and horizontal co-ordination methods. Organisation charts give a graphic depiction of an organisation's structure and help employees trace the chain of command.

There are four main job design approaches: simplification, rotation, enlargement and enrichment. The job characteristics model guides job enrichment efforts by showing the importance of core job characteristics, critical psychological states, and high growth-need strength to job outcomes. A related aspect of designing jobs is alternative work schedules, which often help with a diverse work force's needs. Major alternative schedules include flexitime, compressed workweek and job sharing.

Among common departmentalisation forms are functional, divisional, hybrid and matrix. There are five major ways to achieve vertical co-ordination, or linking activities at the top of the organisation with those at middle and lower levels: formalisation, span of management, centralisation versus decentralisation, delegation, and line and staff positions.

Three means particularly useful in facilitating horizontal co-ordination are slack resources, information systems and lateral relations. Slack resources give a cushion of resources allowing adaptation to change, while information systems enhance information exchange. Lateral relations, involving co-ordinating efforts with peers in other departments and units, has several main forms: direct contact, liaison roles, task forces, teams and managerial integrators. Horizontal co-ordination helps promote innovation as it facilitates idea exchange across organisational units.

Questions for discussion and review

1 Explain the four elements making up organisation structure. What evidence can you see of them at your college or university?

2 Describe the relationship between an organisation chart and its chain of command. If you were new to an organisation, how could the chart help orient you?

3 Contrast various major job design approaches. Use the job characteristics model to explain how you might enrich a particular job.

4 Distinguish between the three main alternative types of work schedule. What changes might be needed to accommodate non-traditional work schedules?

5 Explain the role of normalisation in vertical co-ordination. Give an example of a policy or rule likely to have a dysfunctional impact on organisational effectiveness. How should things be changed to have a positive influence?

6 Explain the relationship between span of management and the extent to which an organisation is flat or tall. Why are many major organisations flattening their structures? What are the potential pitfalls of downsizing?

7 Contrast the advantages of centralisation and decentralisation, and explain when each is appropriate. Why is delegation important to both?

8 Explain the differences between line and staff positions. Which type would you prefer? Why?

9 Explain slack resources and computer-based information systems as applied to horizontal co-ordination. Explain how each helps horizontal co-ordination in organisations.

10 Distinguish between the various types of lateral relations. How could they be used in your college or university?

Exercises for managing in the 21st century

Exercise 1
Skill building: Understanding organisation structure

Managers carrying out the organising function must understand organisation structure concepts. Significant issues about an organisation's structure are in the left column. Match these with examples from the right column.

Organisational issues

1. ____ Chain of command
2. ____ Organisation chart
3. ____ Job simplification
4. ____ Job rotation
5. ____ Job enlargement
6. ____ Job enrichment
7. ____ Flexitime
8. ____ Compressed workweek
9. ____ Job sharing
10. ____ Departmentalisation
11. ____ Vertical co-ordination
12. ____ Formalisation
13. ____ Span of control
14. ____ Centralisation
15. ____ Authority
16. ____ Accountability
17. ____ Line authority
18. ____ Functional authority
19. ____ Slack resources
20. ____ Lateral relations

Definition/example

a. Written policies, procedures (rules for purchasing equipment)
b. Provide reasons for significant deviations (explain change in production from 40 to 90 units)
c. First, second, third and fourth levels working together (four levels of managers in manufacturing meet to discuss possible new technology)
d. A cushion of resources used to meet unprogrammed requirements (additional trucks to deliver unusual number of orders)
e. Work four 10-hour days (6 am to 4 pm Monday to Thursday)
f. Authority related to specific function (pay policy enforced by director of human resources)
g. Authority follows chain of command (CEO decides which three plants will be closed following reorganisation)
h. Line of authority (John reports to Sue)
i. Number of reporting units (seven divisions reporting to director of operations)
j. Adding variety of similar tasks (assume the functions of peer in addition to current job)
k. Assigned only a few specific activities (make new files; file papers)
l. Line diagram reflecting structure (organisation has nine SBUs)
m. Elastic work hours; core hours (9 am to 5 pm; 6 am to 2 pm; 10 am to 2 pm)
n. Power and authority retained (need permission from headquarters)
o. Upgrading job task-mix (taking on budgeting, planning and other functions)
p. Co-ordination with other units/departments (engineering, sales and manufacturing working out a problem)
q. Two employees/one job (John works mornings, Joe works afternoons)
r. Right to make decisions (can spend up to $75 000 per purchase)
s. Clustering into work groups, units, divisions (assembly team, motors division)
t. Shifting workers through functions (sales, then human resources, then finance)

Exercise 2
Management exercise: Designing an innovative organisation

You have landed a job as the administrative assistant to the CEO of Chameleon Technology, a fast-growing high-technology firm. You took the job to learn more about how to manage high-technology firms. Also, you figure that, with the company growing rapidly, good career opportunities will open up soon.

Chameleon had great success with its initial product, a small hard-disk drive for personal computers which holds more data and costs less than competitors' products. Recently, the company introduced a high-resolution video screen for personal computers, also selling better than anticipated. Because the company is growing rapidly, the CEO is having difficulties handling long-range planning as well as day-to-day developments in a dynamic environment. For example, recently some sales were made but products were not shipped in a timely fashion. In another case, though production was expanded to meet rising demand, the human resources department was not notified of the need for additional workers. In both situations, the problems happened because the CEO's office did not co-ordinate these activities as well as previously.

In addition, the CEO wants to foster the kind of innovative thinking which leads to improvements in existing products and to new offerings. The CEO feels Chameleon is too dependent on its two products and the company is not moving fast enough to improve the disk drive and develop new products.

Because of your recent management studies, the CEO asks you to develop some ideas about how to better co-ordinate company activities and foster innovation. Chameleon is currently organised functionally, with major departments in manufacturing, sales, human resources, finance and accounting, and engineering. The company has about 600 employees.

Prepare a proposal for the CEO outlining steps to achieve better vertical and horizontal co-ordination and encourage more innovation.

 # Going solo

on the rim—
in China

T. S. Wong, the Malaysian chief executive of MyWeb Inc.com, always knew his push into China would be a solo ride, not a team effort with a Chinese partner.

'As an Internet company, you need to move very fast', said Mr Wong, a 28-year-old ethnic Chinese whose company provides Internet access via television sets. 'It's easier to move fast when you are alone.'

Increasing numbers of foreign investors ploughing into the Chinese market want to run their own show. In the first ten months of last year, 48 per cent of the funds pledged from overseas went to wholly owned foreign-owned enterprises. The rest was ear-marked to joint ventures.

On 15 November 1999, China and the US signed an agreement that paves the way for China's entry into the World Trade Organisation (WTO) after 13 years of negotiations. Assuming that the world trade body will make China a more transparent place to do business and help improve regulations, the number of wholly-owned foreign enterprises would multiply. This will bring pressure on the state-owned enterprises which are now struggling to become more competitive.

It is becoming easier for foreign companies to go it alone in China. Firstly, more talented state employees have been allowed to leave for well-paid positions at foreign enterprises. In the past, officials strictly enforced the rules requiring permission from the employee's previous employer.

'Increasingly, companies have their own China expertise, and it's possible for them to hire very competent local staff at senior level', says Michael Furst, executive director of the American Chamber of Commerce in China. 'Also, companies who have had bad experiences with joint ventures are unlikely to repeat them.'

China opened its doors to foreign investors in 1979 as part of a push for free-market reforms. Lured by the potential market of more than a billion consumers, companies swooped in to make China the biggest site for foreign investment in the world after the US. Precise figures on the number of joint ventures in China are unavailable. Foreign companies grabbed a foothold in industries ranging from car manufacturers to chemicals and accounting, though many needed a local partner to receive permission form local authorities. About 20 per cent of China's industrial production comes from companies that are at least partly foreign-owned.

There's another reason foreign companies prefering to go it alone. Many were burned by joint ventures that got snarled in red tape. Others found that business in the world's most populous country wasn't profitable, as economic growth there has slowed.

WTO membership will almost certainly move the goal posts. Foreign companies will be able to pick their own partners in areas such as insurance. They'll also gain access to key markets such as communications and the Internet, though they will still only be allowed to own up to 50 per cent of such projects.

Joint ventures will persist in a country where political connections can still make or break a business plan. But the risks of going solo no longer dampen its appeal.

Source: Harmsen, P. (2000).

Activities for discussion, analysis and further research

1 Discuss the strategic choices made by organisations who invest in foreign countries.
2 What are the structural contingencies which will impact on the structures of organisations who choose to go solo as distinct from the ones who opt for a joint venture?
3 Undertake a literature search to determine the conditions which have led to China being accepted into the WTO and how this will affect the way foreign organisations will be able to conduct business in China.

Strategic Organisation Design

Chapter 10

CHAPTER OUTLINE

Designing organisation structures: An overview
Which comes first—strategy or structure?
Factors influencing organisation design

Assessing structural alternatives
Functional structure
Divisional structure
Hybrid structure
Matrix structure
Emerging structures

Weighing contingency factors
Technology
Size
Environment

Matching strategy and structure
Promoting innovation: Using structural means to enhance prospects
Vital roles
Reservations
Differentiation paradox
Transfer process

LEARNING OBJECTIVES

After studying this chapter, you should be able to:

○ Summarise current views about the link between strategy and organisation structure.
○ Explain functional, divisional, hybrid and matrix types of departmentalisation.
○ List the major advantages and disadvantages of each type of departmentalisation, and discuss the basic circumstances in which each is likely to be effective.
○ Explain the stages of matrix departmentalisation.
○ Identify emerging types of structures.
○ Assess how contingency factors, such as technology, size and environment, impact organisation structure.
○ Delineate how to match strategy and structure.
○ Indicate how structure can enhance prospects for innovation.

Striving for excellence

Autoliv is very much a demonstration of structure following strategy. The strategy of linking teams to customers is evident in the restructuring which amalgamated the technical and marketing departments. The key objectives which are the foundations of the strategies of this company are the determinants of the structure.

There is continuous evidence that the environment is one of the key influences on the structure of Autoliv. This is true of both the internal and external environments. Internally, the focus on empowerment and demand that people take responsibility shows in the cascading down and consistency of decision-making processes. This is combined with the customer-focus structure, which is also an environment-driven strategy, and the result shows in the following example.

Teams at Autoliv use a decision tool called the Global 8Ds. This is a problem-solving and professional management technique used by Ford. It is standardised and linked strongly into the customer. Through this process all the individuals working on the products for a particular customer make decisions using the same parameters. It is easy to maintain and not overly costly. What it does mean is that engineers, testing people, materials people and so on, all are making decision the same way from the same base of understanding.

Over the past four years, there have been many changes in the way Autoliv has carried out its production. This strategy is congruent with the customer focus that the total organisation is implementing. As will be discussed further in the chapter on group processes, this strategy necessitated many adjustments on the part of staff members.

DESIGNING ORGANISATION STRUCTURES: AN OVERVIEW

As mentioned in Chapter 9, developing organisation structure is called organisation design. In organisation design, what factors must managers consider? According to one study, an important issue is an organisation's strategy.

Which comes first—strategy or structure?

Alfred D. Chandler (1962) studied the origins of large US firms. He was interested in whether strategy development came before or followed organisation structure design. Chandler concluded companies generally follow a pattern of strategy development, then structural change, rather than the reverse.

In Chandler's view, organisations often change strategy to use resources to more effectively fuel growth. Changes in strategy lead to management difficulties as current structures do not fit the new strategies. Unless organisations then adjust their structures, the new strategies cannot be successful and inefficiencies will occur.

The structure-follows-strategy thesis was seen as simplistic. It seems that particular structures can influence the strategies organisations choose (Frederickson 1986). For example, former Eastman Kodak CEO Colby Chandler estimated the company lost $3.5 billion in sales between 1981 and 1985. This was because Kodak's functional structure did not permit specific strategies needed for its multiple businesses, so they were not developed. Colby Chandler reorganised the $17-billion-a-year company into 34 divisions, ranging from colour film to copiers, to operate as strategic business units. In two years, all units developed specific strategies, almost all gained market share, and Kodak's exports grew 23 per cent (Taylor 1989). There may therefore be causal linkages both ways between structure and strategy. Structure may follow strategy first; then the new structures may influence new strategy development. In any event, Alfred Chandler's work suggests strategy and structure mismatches can lead to organisational difficulties.

Factors influencing organisation design

While strategy and organisation structure are linked, the effectiveness of a particular type of structure is influenced by contingency factors, such as dominant technology used or organisation size (Nadler & Tushman 1988). Further, structural means for promoting innovation may facilitate implementation of strategy and organisational goal attainment. These components and their relationships to organisation structure are shown in Figure 10.1. We will explore these further in this chapter, but first we begin by examining the major types of organisation structure, or departmentalisation, raised in Chapter 9, as they represent the principal available structural alternatives.

Fig. 10.1   Major components influencing the design of effective organisation structures

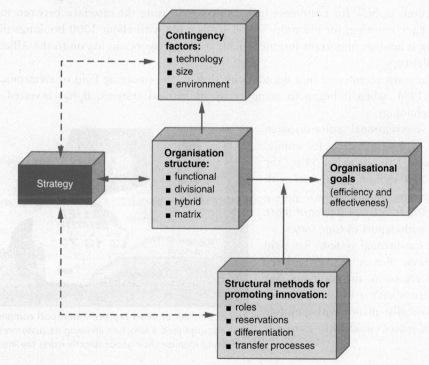

@ Web site steers trucker's business

When the Sydney transport company Allied Express went on to the Internet nearly three years ago, it wanted its site to be much more than just another pretty face on the Web. It intended to exploit Internet technology to achieve growth.

In its first phase, the Allied site was essentially a brochure put online, but the company had a much broader aim. General manager Michelle McDowell says: 'The benefit for us was to actually book and track our jobs over the Internet'. Allied spent eight months on electronic-commerce development, and opened the next stage for business a year ago. Customers can now book jobs, track parcels and access scanned proof-of-delivery signatures on the site, all in real time.

McDowell says: 'We wanted it set up so that the minute you book a job with us through the Internet it would be straight into our main dispatching system and printed out in one of our vehicles. We saw little point in having an Internet booking printed out on paper back at the base'. Internet security issues were an important concern. McDowell says: 'Getting the security right was critical. We did not want people booking things on other people's accounts or looking up information that wasn't theirs'.

Allied regards its e-commerce strategy as a medium-term investment. It is not looking at the number of Internet bookings as the measure of success. It says the real value lies in its potential for competitive advantage and value-added customer services. Hernani Inacio, senior executive in charge of management information systems at Allied, says: 'Over the past year, we have won lucrative contracts with several big customers because of the Internet. Our Internet services provide reasons for them to trade with us because they can track parcels in real time and do electronic commerce'.

Allied now processes transactions in bulk for customers including Foxtel, using the interface between its Web server and its dispatch system. Each morning, for example, Foxtel sends a file with about 1000 bookings directly to Allied's Internet server. Dulux is another important Internet client; store managers can log on to the Allied Web site, book jobs, then track the delivery.

Allied's Internet strategy is the most recent step in a decade-long shift to the emerging field of electronic technology. Allied says that since 1991, when it began to computerise its manual systems, it has invested about $18.5 million in information technology.

Before 1990, Allied had a conventional voice-dispatch system for managing a fleet of 130 vehicles. Its annual revenue was about $9 million. This financial year, the company expects turnover of $78 million, compared with $59 million last year. Its computers process 20 000 jobs a day, helping a national staff of 300 to manage a fleet of more than 1000 vehicles and drivers with depots in four states.

'Our strategy to computerise our manual systems has paid off resoundingly', McDowell says. 'But at the start of the decade, with Australia deep in recession, the company was viewed as a huge gamble. There wasn't a lot of computer savvy around in our industry. Basically, anyone with a mobile phone, a vehicle and a group of mates could form a courier company.'

Part of the fleet of Allied Express, a transport company that has organised a structure allowing its customers to order and monitor their goods directly using the Internet.

Technology alone does not account for the rapid growth of Allied—acquisitions have played a big part. In 1996, for example, Allied acquired its airfreight division, Skytrax. It has also bought smaller courier companies and taxi-truck companies.

'We look for businesses that we can simply add to our existing structure, which is built for high-volume sales', McDowell says. 'Without much effort, we can add $100 000 to our turnover. It has generally been quite easy.'

Source: Hanvey, M. (1999).

Activities for discussion, analysis and further research

1 How has Allied used e-technology to improve service to its customers?
2 Recently a staff member was relocated from the US to Australia. She was given a tracking number to track her shipment and see its progress. Try logging on to the Allied system and examine how you could track a removal around the world.

ASSESSING STRUCTURAL ALTERNATIVES

As discussed briefly previously, the four commonest departmentalisation types are functional, divisional, hybrid and matrix. They are often called organisation structures or designs. Each has major advantages and disadvantages (Duncan 1979; Robey & Sales 1992).

Functional structure

Functional structure is a type of departmentalisation where positions are grouped into functional (or specialisation) area. In other words, positions are combined on the basis of similarity of expertise, skill and work activity.

functional structure

Structure in which positions are grouped according to their main functional (or specialised) area

Common functions   Several specialties are common to functional structures (Robey & Sales 1992). For example, production, or operations, combine activities for product manufacture or service delivery. Marketing promotes and sells products and services. Human resources attracts, retains and enhances effectiveness of organisation members. Finance obtains and manages financial resources. Research and development produces unique ideas and methods leading to new and/or improved products and services. Accounting and financial reporting meet the needs of internal and external sources. Finally, the legal function handles the organisation's legal matters. Notice that in organisation structure, the term 'function' (specialised area of expertise) does not have the same meaning as in management's major functions (that is, planning, organising, leading, and controlling). The functional organisation structure of the Denver-based herbal tea company Celestial Seasonings is shown in Figure 10.2. It includes many functional areas discussed above.

An organisation developing a functional structure must consider specialised areas relevant to its own needs. For example, a functional design for a power company might have an energy department equivalent to the production, or operations, department in other organisations, as the company produces energy. It might also have a distribution department as a major

Fig. 10.2   The functional structure of Celestial Seasonings

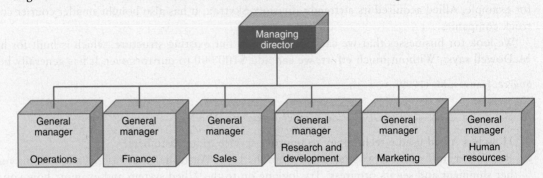

function. However, a bank's functional structure might include one department for investments and another for loans.

Advantages of functional structure   The functional organisation form has several major advantages, summarised in Table 10.1. One is that it encourages expertise development as employees specialise in a single function. For example, as director of human resources in a functional structure, you might develop specialists in recruiting, compensation and training. Another advantage is that employees have clear career paths in their particular function, encouraging them to develop expertise. In addition, a functional structure helps efficient resource use, as it is simple to shift individuals between projects when they work in the same department. Economies of scale may be possible too, as large amounts of work can be handled when individuals specialise or work volume justifies major equipment. A further advantage is that functional structures may ease co-ordination within departments, since activities are all related to the same area (Galbraith & Kazanjian 1986). Consider a situation in which people knowledgable in logistics, finance and sales were in the same functional group, managed by an electrical engineer. The diverse nature of these people's expertise would make it extremely difficult for the manager to co-ordinate or assess their activities individually. Finally, functional grouping increases potential for development of specialised technical competencies for a strategic advantage.

Table 10.1   Major advantages and disadvantages of a functional structure

Advantages	Disadvantages
In-depth development of expertise	Slow response time on multifunctional problems
Clear career path within function	Backlog of decisions at top of hierarchy
Efficient use of resources	Bottlenecks due to sequential tasks
Possible economies of scale	Restricted view of organisation among employees
Ease of co-ordination within function	Inexact measurement of performance
Potential technical advantage over competitors	Narrow training for potential managers

Disadvantages of functional structure   Functional designs also have disadvantages, summarised in Table 10.1. One is that co-ordination across functions is needed to handle complex problems and this may delay responses, as issues and conflicts are passed up the chain to resolve. Also, bottlenecks develop as a function waits for another to complete its work. In addition, specialists' orientation may narrow, and they may become unable to understand needs of other functions or overall organisation goals. At the same time, it may be hard to measure a particular unit's performance as various functions contribute to overall results. Finally, a functional structure limits managers' training as they move within a function and have only limited knowledge of others.

Uses of functional structure   The functional form is often used in small and medium-sized organisations too large to co-ordinate activities without some formal structure, but not large enough for co-ordination across functions to be difficult. Such organisations frequently have a few related products or services or deal with a relatively homogeneous customer or client set. For example, Pizza Hut, which deals mainly in pizza and related food items, has a functional structure, with operations, distribution, and finance and administration as functional departments. The design is useful in large more diverse organisations, such as insurance companies, normally operating in relatively stable environments where change occurs slowly enough for the functions to co-ordinate their efforts. In addition, a functional structure may be used by large organisations when considerable co-ordination is required among products (Child 1984).

Divisional structure

Divisional structure is a departmentalisation type with positions grouped by product, service or market similarity. Figure 10.3 shows the differences between functional and divisional structures. In a divisional structure, each division has major functional resources to pursue its own goals without relying on other divisions. For example, Figure 10.4 shows the structure for the seven telephone divisions of Bell Atlantic Corporation, a regional operating company giving local telephone service to customers in several US states. If the divisions were organised functionally, all telephone operators would be grouped in a central operations department and all field repair personnel grouped in a central repair services department. Instead, with a divisional structure, telephone operators and repair personnel are allocated to divisions so each can operate fairly independently. In this case, divisions operate as separate companies. Divisional structures are called self-contained structures as each division generally contains all major functions.

Forms of divisional structure   There are three major forms of divisional structure: product, geographic and customer. A simplified example of each is shown in Figure 10.5. Which form is used depends on the rationale for forming divisions.

    Product divisions concentrate on a single product or service or a relatively homogeneous set of products or services. When this structure is chosen, there are large differences in product or service lines making co-ordination within a functional design slow and inefficient. With a divisional structure, each department has its own functional specialists, such as marketing, manufacturing and personnel, performing work associated with their specific division's product only.

    Geographic divisions serve different geographic areas. This type of departmentalisation is often adopted to provide products and services tailored to different regions' needs. So the

---

divisional structure

Structure in which positions are grouped according to similarity of products, services, or markets

product divisions

Divisions created to concentrate on a single product or service or at least a relatively homogeneous set of products or services

geographic divisions

Divisions designed to serve different geographic areas

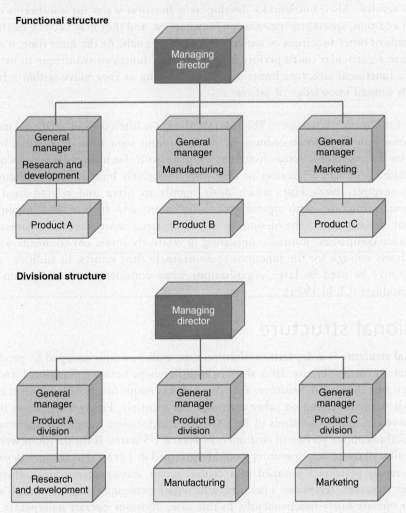

Fig. 10.3 Functional versus divisional structure

Functional structure

Managing director

- General manager — Research and development → Product A
- General manager — Manufacturing → Product B
- General manager — Marketing → Product C

Divisional structure

Managing director

- General manager — Product A division → Research and development
- General manager — Product B division → Manufacturing
- General manager — Product C division → Marketing

Fig. 10.4 Seven divisions of the Bell Atlantic Corporation

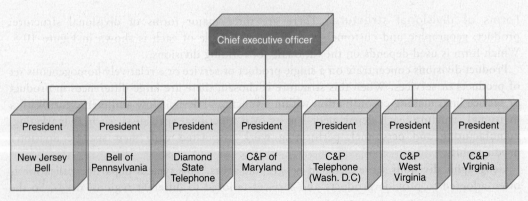

Chief executive officer

- President — New Jersey Bell
- President — Bell of Pennsylvania
- President — Diamond State Telephone
- President — C&P of Maryland
- President — C&P Telephone (Wash. D.C)
- President — C&P West Virginia
- President — C&P Virginia

Fig. 10.5 Major forms of divisional structure

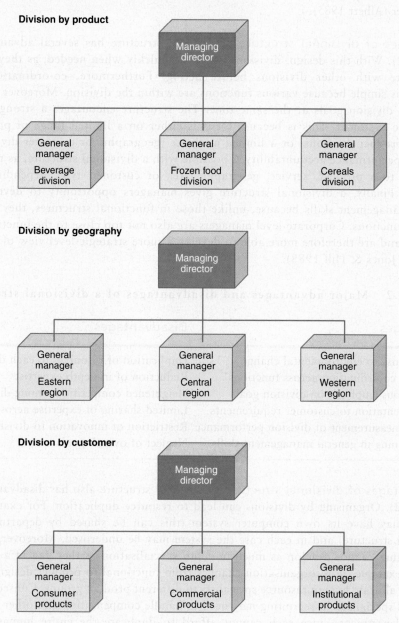

Division by product

Managing director

General manager — Beverage division

General manager — Frozen food division

General manager — Cereals division

Division by geography

Managing director

General manager — Eastern region

General manager — Central region

General manager — Western region

Division by customer

Managing director

General manager — Consumer products

General manager — Commercial products

General manager — Institutional products

Bell Atlantic telephone divisions shown in Figure 10.4 represent divisions organised by geography. If the geographical sector is very great, sufficient differences across divisions...

Customer divisions service particular types of clients or customers. This design is best when major differences among types of customers exist, making adequate co-ordination of customers' various needs within a standard functional structure difficult. With customer

customer divisions

Divisions set up to service particular types of clients or customers

divisions, each department has individuals performing functions necessary for a specific type of customer (Albert 1985).

Advantages of divisional structure   Divisional structure has several advantages (see Table 10.2). With this design, divisions can react quickly when needed, as they need not co-ordinate with other divisions before acting. Furthermore, co-ordination across functions is simple because various functions are within the division. Moreover, functions emphasise division goals at the same time. The structure encourages a strong focus on serving the customer. This is because focus is either on a limited range of products or services (product divisions) or a limited audience (geographic or customer divisions). In addition, performance accountability is possible with a divisional structure, as results can be linked to a product, service, geographic area or customer type, depending on the structure. Finally, a divisional structure gives managers opportunity to develop more general management skills because, unlike those in functional structures, they deal with multiple functions. Corporate-level managers are also not too close to the functional-level activities and are therefore more able to develop a more strategic-level view of divisional activities (Jones & Hill 1988).

Table 10.2   Major advantages and disadvantages of a divisional structure

Advantages	Disadvantages
Fast response to environmental change	Duplication of resources in each division
Simplified co-ordination across functions	Reduction of in-depth expertise
Simultaneous emphasis on division goals	Heightened competition among divisions
Strong orientation to customer requirements	Limited sharing of expertise across divisions
Accurate measurement of division performance	Restriction of innovation to divisions
Broad training in general management skills	Neglect of overall goals

Disadvantages of divisional structure   Divisional structure also has disadvantages (see Table 10.2). Organising by divisions can lead to resource duplication. For example, each division may have its own computer system (this can be shared by departments in a functional structure) and in each case the system may be underused. Moreover, people in this structure cannot develop as much in-depth specialisation as they can in a functional one. For example, if an organisation changes from functional to product design, management may allocate human resource specialists to different product groups. Consequently, an individual specialised in recruiting may need to handle compensation and other issues in a product department, since each cannot afford to duplicate the entire human resource department from the previous arrangement. Another disadvantage is divisions become absorbed with their own concerns and engage in destructive resource rivalries (Duncan 1979; Robey & Sales 1992). Often sharing of expertise and innovations is limited across divisions. If the geographical spread is very great, sufficient differences across customers may exist to cause dissatisfaction to emerge (Bounds 1995). Finally, with a divisional structure, employees may focus on immediate divisional goals to the detriment of longer-term organisational goals.

Uses of divisional structure   A divisional structure is likely in fairly large organisations with substantial differences across either products, services, geographic areas or customers served. It sometimes is infeasible to organise into self-contained units if the organisation's nature requires sharing common resources, such as expensive manufacturing equipment.

Hybrid structure

Hybrid structure is a form of departmentalisation with both functional and divisional structure elements at the same management level (Daft 1998; Robey & Sales 1992). It incorporates both structures' advantages. Many organisations, especially large ones, combine functional and divisional departments. Functional ones are created to benefit from resource usage efficiencies, economies of scale, or in-depth expertise. At the same time, divisional departments are used when potential benefits come from a stronger focus on products, services, or markets. IBM's hybrid structure is shown in Figure 10.6. At IBM, functional departments handle areas such as communications, finance, human resources, and research—areas where in-depth expertise is important and resources are more effectively used in a functional arrangement. Then there are four major product divisions concentrating on product development in areas needing different expertise and dealing with rapidly changing technology. IBM chose not to give each division a sales and service group. Instead, IBM centralised the sales and service function in a separate division organised by geography. Functional departments in a hybrid design are called corporate departments as they typically have staff authority relative to divisional departments, and authority from the organisation's top, or corporate, level.

> **hybrid structure**
> Structure adopting both functional and divisional structures at the same management levels

Advantages of a hybrid structure   Generally a hybrid structure has several advantages (see Table 10.3). With a hybrid design, an organisation can achieve specialised expertise and economies of scale in major functional areas. As well, adaptability and flexibility handling diverse product or service lines, geographic areas, or customers are possible by a partial divisional structure. Finally, a mix of functional and divisional departmentalisation helps align divisional and corporate goals.

Table 10.3   Major advantages and disadvantages of a hybrid structure

Advantages	Disadvantages
Alignment of corporate and divisional goals	Conflicts between corporate departments and divisions
Functional expertise and/or efficiency	Excessive administrative overhead
Adaptability and flexibility in divisions	Slow response to exceptional situations

Disadvantages of hybrid structure   Managers must be alert to the hybrid structure's disadvantages to minimise potential weaknesses (see Table 10.3). Hybrid organisations tend to develop excessively large staffs in corporate-level functional departments. As corporate departments grow, they may try to increase control over divisions, causing conflict. Finally, hybrid structures can be slow to respond to exceptional situations requiring co-ordination

Fig. 10.6   IBM's hybrid structure

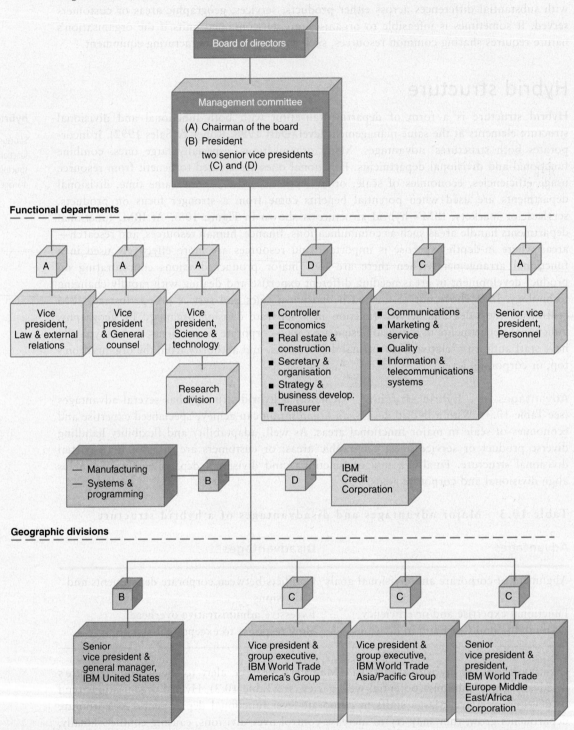

Board of directors

Management committee

(A) Chairman of the board
(B) President
    two senior vice presidents
    (C) and (D)

Functional departments

A — Vice president, Law & external relations

A — Vice president & General counsel

A — Vice president, Science & technology
    Research division

D — ■ Controller
    ■ Economics
    ■ Real estate & construction
    ■ Secretary & organisation
    ■ Strategy & business develop.
    ■ Treasurer

C — ■ Communications
    ■ Marketing & service
    ■ Quality
    ■ Information & telecommunications systems

A — Senior vice president, Personnel

— Manufacturing
— Systems & programming   B

D   IBM Credit Corporation

Geographic divisions

B — Senior vice president & general manager, IBM United States

C — Vice president & group executive, IBM World Trade America's Group

C — Vice president & group executive, IBM World Trade Asia/Pacific Group

C — Senior vice president & president, IBM World Trade Europe Middle East/Africa Corporation

between a division and a corporate functional department. For example, a personnel matter needing an exception to policy may be slower to resolve with a hybrid structure than either functional or divisional departmentalisation.

Uses of hybrid structure A hybrid structure is used in organisations facing considerable environmental uncertainty best met by a divisional structure but requiring functional expertise and/or efficiency. Typically, the approach is reserved for medium-sized or large organisations with sufficient resources to justify divisions and some functional departmentalisation.

Matrix structure

A **matrix structure** as a type of departmentalisation superimposes a set of divisional horizontal reporting relationships onto a hierarchical functional structure. Thus the structure is both functional and divisional at the same time. There are two chains of command, one vertical and one horizontal. A basic matrix structure is shown in Figure 10.7. In this case, the vice presidents of operations, marketing, finance, engineering, and research and development represent

matrix structure

Structure superimposing a horizontal set of divisional reporting relationships onto a hierarchical functional structure

Fig. 10.7 Matrix organisation structure

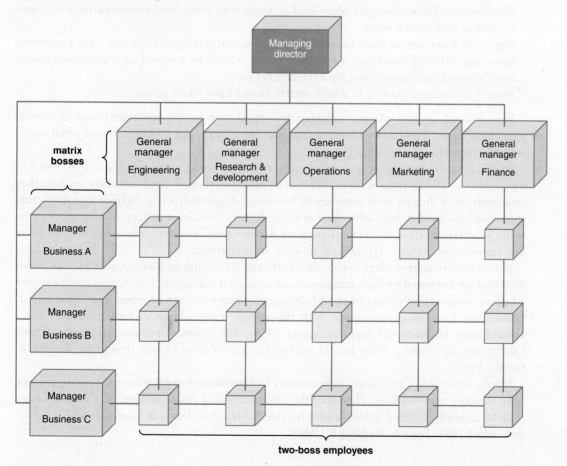

functional departments, making up the vertical hierarchy. Simultaneously, managers of businesses A, B and C represent divisional units operating horizontally. Heads of functional and divisional departments making up the matrix (e.g. vice presidents and business managers in Figure 10.7) are referred to as matrix bosses.

One major characteristic of a matrix structure is that workers within the matrix report to two matrix bosses. For example, as Figure 10.7 shows, a marketing researcher might report up the vertical chain to the vice-president of marketing, and across the horizontal chain to business A's manager. This dual authority system violates the classical principle of unity of command (an individual should have only one boss at any given point in time), making a matrix structure complex to operate.

Matrix stages Organisations adopting a matrix structure go through several identifiable structural stages (Davis & Lawrence 1977):

Stage 1 is a traditional structure, usually functional, following the unity-of-command principle.

Stage 2 is a temporary overlay, where managerial integrator positions are created to manage particular projects (e.g. project managers), oversee product launches (e.g. product managers), or handle issues of finite duration needing co-ordination across functional departments. These managers often lead or work with temporary interdepartmental teams created to address the issue.

Stage 3 is a permanent overlay, where the managerial integrators operate on a permanent basis (e.g. a brand manager co-ordinates issues related to a brand on an ongoing basis), often through permanent interdepartmental teams.

Stage 4 is a mature matrix, in which matrix bosses have equal power.

Even though a true matrix incorporates equal power for functional and divisional managers, stages 2 and 3, involving managerial integrators (see Chapter 9), are often called matrix structures.

Each stage gives increasing horizontal integration, but with greater administrative complexity (Jerkovsky 1983). Even with managerial integrators, there is dual authority because they frequently work directly with members of functional departments (e.g. engineers or marketing specialists) assigned to help with their project. In their capacity managerial integrators informally supervise work of individuals assigned to their projects, though they rarely have direct line authority over them. Typically, teamwork is emphasised.

With a mature matrix, there is true dual authority (Galbraith & Kazanjian 1986). All major decisions are approved by both functional and divisional managers. The mature matrix is used when an organisation's functional and divisional dimensions are of prime and equal importance. Dow Corning experimented with this design, even adding a third dimension for a simultaneous international focus (Goggins 1974). For international operations the 'Think locally, but act globally' view should explain the activities of matrix structures (Bartlett & Goshal 1992).

Matrix structures, particularly in temporary and permanent overlay forms, operate successfully in many organisations. However, the advantages and disadvantages of a matrix design must be carefully weighed before is adopted (see Table 10.4) (Davis & Lawrence 1977; Adams & Kirchof 1984; Ford & Randolph 1992).

Table 10.4   Major advantages and disadvantages of a matrix structure

Advantages	Disadvantages
Decentralised decision making	High administrative costs
Strong project or product co-ordination	Potential confusion over authority and responsibility
Improved environmental monitoring	Fast response to change
Heightened prospects for interpersonal conflicts	Excessive focus on internal relations
Flexible use of human resources	Overemphasis on group decision making
Efficient use of support systems	Possible slow response to change

Advantages of matrix structure   With a matrix design, decisions can be made by divisional project and functional managers. This allows upper-level management to concentrate on long-term strategic issues. Moreover, using the matrix adds strong horizontal co-ordination to projects (or products or brands) beyond that possible in a functional design alone, increasing the probability of success. The arrangement facilitates monitoring environmental conditions both for projects and functional areas, and is therefore a structure often used when organisations are moving more in international operations (Hill 1997). Often, a matrix structure can react quickly to change, as many decisions are made at lower levels. Still another advantage is functional specialists can be added to, or reassigned from, projects as needed, allowing effective human resource use. Finally, support systems, computers, special equipment and software can be allocated among many projects as needed, reducing the costs of such systems.

Disadvantages of matrix structure   Because a matrix arrangement adds a layer of project managers and their support staff to a functional hierarchy, administrative costs are increased. Moreover, with two bosses, workers in a matrix may be unable to determine who has authority and responsibility for decisions. The increased communication needed and the dual-authority arrangements increase the possibility of conflicts, particularly between project and functional managers. Individuals can become preoccupied with internal relations, at the expense of clients and project goals. In addition, matrix designs can encourage group decision making until relatively minor decisions are made in groups, causing a serious productivity erosion. Finally, while a matrix can adapt to change, it can also respond slowly if participants' interpersonal skills are poor, or upper management tries to retain control.

When to consider a matrix structure   Many organisations are unsuited to matrix designs. For example, Texas Instruments abandoned its matrix structure after blaming it for failure to keep up with the competition (Katz 1982). On the other hand many companies have found the structure works particularly well for them (*Supervisory Management* 1995; Farnham 1994; Denton 1995). The need for horizontal co-ordination must be high to justify additional administrative complexity at lower levels. Matrix designs are usually appropriate when three conditions exist (Davis & Lawrence 1977):

1 There is considerable environmental pressure necessitating a simultaneous strong focus on both functional and divisional dimensions. For example, diverse products may need a product orientation, but increasingly sophisticated engineering technology may argue for a functional orientation.

2 Demands on the organisation are changing and unpredictable, requiring large capacity for information processing and co-ordination of activities quickly. For example, in the microchip industry, foreign competitors often make technological improvements, and lower prices at the same time.

3 There is pressure for shared resources. For example, in competitive markets, organisations may need flexibility in use of functional resources across projects or products.

Evidence is growing that matrix designs need a corresponding change in organisation culture to support greater need for collaborative decision making (Joyce 1986; *Marketing* 1995). As well, managers and other employees may require special training, particularly in interpersonal skills, to function effectively in the structure (Kolodny 1979; 1981). Many organisations do not need a mature matrix structure; however, temporary and permanent overlay stages are increasingly common, particularly in the form of temporary and permanent cross-functional teams.

Emerging structures

Although many different types of organisational structures are possible as organisations experiment with new ways of doing things, two emerging types of structures are interesting: the process structure and networked structure, or virtual corporation (Galbraith 1995).

process structure

Type of departmentalisation where positions are grouped by a complete flow of work

Process structure   A **process structure** is a type of departmentalisation where positions are grouped by a complete flow of work. The basic idea is that individuals from each function working on a process are grouped into process teams and given beginning-to-end responsibility for the process or identifiable work flow. Under this type of structure, divisions have names like new product development, order fulfilment or customer acquisition and maintenance— signifying processes they are responsible for. The structure is referred to as the horizontal organisation, because they tend to be relatively flat. Functional specialties working in a team environment permit most operating decisions to be made at low organisation levels by teams (Child 1995).

networked structure

Form of organising where many functions are contracted out to other independent firms and co-ordinated by use of information technology networks to operate as if they were within a single corporation

Networked structure   The **networked structure** is a form where functions are contracted out to other firms and co-ordinated by information technology networks to operate as if they were within a single organisation. This structure is called the virtual corporation, performing as if it were virtually one corporation (Marcia 1995; *Economist* 1995). For example, Benetton, the Italian clothing maker, contracts manufacturing to about 350 small firms, but achieves economies of scale by buying materials for all of them. By having small firms do the labour-intensive sewing and packing, Benetton gains flexibility in response to rapid fashion shifts. One disadvantage of the virtual corporation is proprietary information may need to be exchanged, creating potential competitors (Chesborough & Teece 1996).

While managers weigh the advantages and disadvantages of various structural alternatives in developing appropriate organisation design—including emerging structures—they must consider major contingency factors affecting structural requirements. We review these next.

● Bringing ends together

The message has been around for some time that outsourcing is the way of the future. One Sydney manufacturer, in taking this message to heart, has outsourced his entire labour force. Tripac International (Australia) has adopted a strategy which has turned losses into profits, retained some of the staff which were about to be laid off and boosted productivity.

The story starts with the diversified whitegoods manufacturer, Email, who owned the subsidiary named Muller, a large, long-established car-parts manufacturer in Sydney's south-west. Email had an arrangement with Ford Australia to make air-conditioning parts for Falcons, Fairlanes and LTDs. While apparently a good deal, this made chronic losses for the organisation and Muller was on the verge of shutting down. Tripac International purchased Muller, introduced a number of efficiencies at the plant and adopted a blanket outsourcing policy. Only top management is actually employed by the company. Everyone else is hired by an 'employee leasing' firm which has the right to hire and fire. Tripac can concentrate on making the plant as efficient as possible as it no longer has to focus on personnel requirements.

EL Australia's search and recruitment division, EL Blue, employs and supplies staff as needed by the Tripac factory. Half of them are hired directly on a permanent contract basis while half are casual. This staff structure has given Tripac a flexible workforce that has been financially successful.

Source: Adapted from Tabakoff, N. (1999).

Activities for discussion, analysis and further research

1 What were the imperatives which prompted the changes in structure for Tripac?
2 What might be some of the consequences of this complete outsourcing?
3 Consider the impact on Ford when Email finally decided to off-load the unprofitable business. Ford could not build cars without the component Muller was supplying and they needed continuity. When Email could not be convinced to retain Muller, Ford started to attempt to persuade whoever took over to maintain production. Where are the organisation boundaries for Ford?

✖ Tripac makes an unexpected decision

Consider the organisation Tripac that was discussed in Case in point in this chapter. Ford needed the continuity of parts production for the air-conditioning system of its top-of-the-range cars. Muller, the organisation that made them, was losing money to the tune of six figures every month. So when Tripac was considering buying Muller the key issue was whether the business could be made a going concern. Tripac's initial intention when assessing Muller was merely to buy the manufacturing assets of the business. With pressure from Ford, Tripac decided to investigate the possibilities for turning the company around.

Source: Adapted from Tabakoff, N. (1999).

Reflection points

1 What were the issues that needed to be considered in making this decision?

2 Consider the impacts on the organisation's structure of this complete outsourcing process?

Decision points

1 Investigate how the process of entire workforce outsourcing is being undertaken in the United States. Look up the US National Association of Professional Employer Organisations (NAPEO) on the Internet.

2 The push to complete outsourcing lies in the trend for companies to concentrate on core activities, and the complexities of industrial relations laws. Consider how the spread of such a trend in Australia will impact on organisational structure.

WEIGHING CONTINGENCY FACTORS

Early in the study of management, classical theorists (see Chapter 2) tried to develop an ideal organisation structure. Instead, they found that a structural configuration, which worked for one organisation, was not effective for another. Gradually, contingency theory emerged. This viewpoint argues that appropriate managerial action depends on a particular situation's parameters (see Chapter 2). It was realised the best structure for an organisation depends on contingency factors such as technology, size and environment.

Technology

Different organisations need different structures partly because of **technology**—the knowledge, tools, equipment and work techniques used by an organisation to deliver its product or service. Two critical aspects of technology are technological complexity and technological interdependence (Fry 1982).

Technological complexity Research highlighting the importance of technology was conducted during the 1950s by a team led by Joan Woodward (1958; 1965). The team set out to determine the extent to which the classical theorists' management principles were actually practised by a group of 100 British manufacturing firms.

The researchers were surprised to find there did not seem to be any connection between use of classical principles in structuring organisations and a firm's success. Actual practices varied widely. After careful study, Woodward determined that three different technology types were reasonably predictive of structural practices of firms studied:

1 In **unit and small-batch production**, products are custom-produced to meet customer specifications or are made in small quantities primarily by craft specialists. Examples are diamond cutting in New York's diamond centre and production of stretch limousines.

2 In **large-batch and mass production**, products are manufactured in large quantities, frequently on an assembly line. Examples are production of most automobiles and manufacture of microchips for computers and related products.

3 In **continuous-process production**, products are liquids, solids, or gases made through a continuous process. Examples are petroleum and chemical products.

technology

Knowledge, tools, equipment and work techniques used by an organisation in delivering its product or service

unit and small-batch production

Type of technology where products are custom-produced to meet customer specifications or are made in small quantities primarily by craft specialists

large-batch and mass production

Type of technology where products are manufactured in large quantities, frequently on an assembly line

continuous-process production

Type of technology where products are liquids, solids or gases made through a continuous process

The team noted technologies are increasingly complex to manage, with small-batch and unit production being least complex and continuous-process production most complex. Increasing complexity stems from use of more elaborate machinery and its greater work process role. This technological complexity, in turn, seemed to explain differences in structural practices used by firms being studied (see Table 10.5).

For example, researchers found increasing complexity associated with more levels of management (a taller structure), more staff personnel per line worker, and larger spans of control at upper-management levels. Woodward's results also indicated formalisation and centralisation both tended to be high in organisations using large-batch and mass-production technology, where large numbers of workers' efforts need to be standardised. In contrast, formalisation and centralisation were low in organisations with unit and small-batch, as well as continuous-process, technologies, where appropriate work decisions must be made at lower levels.

At first-line supervisor level, the span was greatest with large-batch and mass-production technology, as one supervisor could handle a large number of workers doing fairly routine work. It was smallest for continuous-process where very serious problems can result from process difficulties (Woodward 1965; Collins & Hull 1986).

Overall, Woodward's research indicated more successful firms had structural characteristics close to the median for their particular technology. Research since Woodward's study supports technological complexity's importance in influencing organisation structure (Fry 1982; Hull & Collins 1987).

Technological interdependence   Another technology aspect impacting organising considerations is **technological interdependence**, the degree to which different organisation parts must exchange information and materials to perform needed activities (Fry 1982). There are three major types of technological interdependence: pooled, sequential and reciprocal (Thompson 1967).

The type involving least interdependence is **pooled interdependence**, where units operate independently but individual efforts are important to the whole organisation's success (hence 'pooled'). For example, you go to your bank's local branch and that branch will rarely need

technological interdependence

Degree to which different organisation parts must exchange information and materials to perform required activities

pooled interdependence

Relationship in which units operate independently but individual efforts are important to the whole organisation's success

Table 10.5   Woodward's findings on structural characteristics and technology*

Structural characteristics	Small batch	Mass production	Continuous process
Levels of management	3	4	6
Executive span of control	4	7	10
Supervisory span of control	23	48	15
Industrial workers vs. staff (ratio)	8:1	5.5:1	2:1
Formalisation	Low	High	Low
Centralisation	Low	High	Low

*Data are medians for organisations within each technological category.
Source: Woodward (1965, pp. 52–82).

to contact another branch to complete your transaction. If, however, the branch's performance is poor, losing you and other customers, this will ultimately affect the whole bank's health.

In contrast, in **sequential interdependence**, one unit must finish its task before the next unit in the sequence can start. For example, a strike at one General Motors Holden plant may cause workers at other plants to be stood down temporarily. This occurs when parts manufactured by the striking plant are needed for the sequentially interdependent assembly at non-striking plants.

Finally, the most complex situation is **reciprocal interdependence**, where one unit's outputs are inputs to another unit and vice versa. When an aeroplane lands, the flight crew hands the plane to the maintenance crew. After refuelling, replenishing supplies, and other needed activities, the maintenance crew releases the plane to flight crews so the plane can go on its journey. Thus the flight crew's output is the maintenance crew's input, then the process reverses. Clearly, reciprocal interdependence needs more horizontal co-ordination than the other two. Managers need to think about technological interdependence, and complexity, in designing organisation structure. Organisation size is also sometimes relevant.

sequential interdependence

Relationship in which one unit must complete its work before the next in the sequence can begin work

reciprocal interdependence

Relationship in which one unit's outputs become inputs to another unit and vice versa

Size

Woodward's research also investigated the relationship between size and structural characteristics, finding nothing definitive. Since then other studies have tried to untangle the relationship between size and structure, with modest success. Part of the problem is that size is one part of the equation. Other factors, such as environment and technology, also affect organisation structure. In addition, size can be measured in many ways, such as gross sales or profits or number of employees (most typical), making comparisons difficult.

Four trends have been identified by studies of size effects on structure:

1   As organisations grow, they tend to add departments and levels, producing increasingly complex structures. With functional structures, this pressures for a change to divisional structure (Astley 1985; Cullen, Anderson & Baker 1986).
2   Growing organisations increase the number of staff positions to help top management cope with increased size. This levels off when a critical mass has been achieved (Cullen et al. 1986), but it leads to the third trend.
3   Additional rules and regulations go with organisational growth. While guidelines are useful for achieving vertical co-ordination, the growth in rules and regulations leads to excessive formalisation and lower efficiency (Gooding & Wagner 1985).
4   As organisations grow, they become more decentralised. This is probably due to additional rules and regulations acting as guidelines for lower-level decision making (Robbins 1990).

Because of potential size effects, many divisionalised companies ensure subunits are kept small by creating new divisions when existing ones become unwieldy. To reap the advantages of smaller size and encourage innovation, Johnson & Johnson has over 150 autonomous divisions (Dumaine 1992). These companies' approach fits research showing larger organisational subunits are often less efficient than their smaller counterparts. While size bears on structural requirements, environment is also a factor.

Environment

Burns and Stalker (1961) conducted one study on environment's effects on organisation structure. In studying 20 British industrial firms, they discovered different structural characteristics, depending on whether it was a stable environment with little change or an unstable environment with rapid change and uncertainty.

Mechanistic and organic characteristics   Firms operating in a stable environment had relatively **mechanistic characteristics**, highly centralised decision making, many rules and regulations, and hierarchical communication channels. Much emphasis was on vertical co-ordination, with limited delegation between management levels. Firms were able to operate and be reasonably successful as environmental changes occurred gradually, allowing upper management to stay on top of changes.

In contrast, firms operating in highly unstable and uncertain environments had more **organic characteristics**, such as decentralised decision making, few rules and regulations, as well as hierarchical and lateral communication channels. Horizontal co-ordination was emphasised, with considerable delegation between levels. Firms developed these characteristics as their environments of rapid change meant individuals at many levels had to monitor the environment and decide on a response. Mechanistic and organic organisation characteristics are summarised in Table 10.6.

> **mechanistic characteristics**
>
> Characteristics such as highly centralised decision making, many rules and regulations, and mainly hierarchical communication channels
>
> **organic characteristics**
>
> Characteristics such as decentralised decision making, few rules and regulations, and both hierarchical and lateral communication channels

Table 10.6   Characteristics of mechanistic and organic organisations

Mechanistic	Organic
Work is divided into narrow, specialised tasks.	Work is defined in terms of general tasks.
Tasks are performed as specified unless changed by managers in the hierarchy.	Tasks are continually adjusted as needed through interaction with others involved in the task.
Structure of control, authority and communication is hierarchical.	Structure of control, authority and communication is a network.
Decisions are made by the specified hierarchical level.	Decisions are made by individuals with relevant knowledge and technical expertise.
Communication is mainly vertical, between superior and subordinate.	Communication is vertical and horizontal, among superiors, subordinates, and peers.
Communication content is largely instructions and decisions issued by superiors.	Communication content is largely information and advice.
Emphasis is on loyalty to the organisation and obedience to superiors.	Emphasis is on commitment to organisational goals and possession of needed expertise.

Source: Adapted from Burns & Stalker (1961, pp. 119–22).

Differentiation and integration   Lawrence and Lorsch went further with the idea that environment influences organisation structure. They thought organisational environments might have different effects on various organisation units. To test this, they studied three departments—manufacturing, sales, and research and development—in three industries with different environments—plastics, food processing and containers. They focused on **differentiation**, how organisational units differ from each another in their members' behaviours and orientations and formal structures (Lorsch 1976). As expected, Lawrence and Lorsch found differentiation among the units studied. R&D departments concentrated on new developments, operated fairly informally, and were concerned with long-term success. In contrast, sales departments looked to immediate customer satisfaction, operated more formally, and were interested largely in short-term sales results. In between were manufacturing departments, concerned primarily with efficiency, which operated less formally than sales departments but more formally than R&D departments, and in an intermediate-term time frame. Interestingly, differentiation among departments was greatest in the plastics industry, with the most unstable environment, and least in the container industry, operating in the most stable environment.

But differentiation was only one element. When considering effectiveness, the most effective firms attempted to balance differentiation with **integration**, the extent to which departments need to co-ordinate their efforts by collaboration. Greater differentiation among departments due to environmental instability was matched by greater efforts at integration in successful companies. For example, successful container companies used a functional hierarchy, rules and regulations, to achieve needed integration. Successful plastics companies, however, used several vertical and horizontal co-ordinating methods to integrate in the face of high differentiation (Lawrence & Lorsch 1969). Horizontal co-ordination methods, discussed in Chapter 9 (e.g. teams and managerial integrators) were very important.

differentiation

Extent to which organisational units differ from one another in terms of behaviours and orientations of members and their formal structures

integration

Extent to which there is collaboration among departments needing to co-ordinate their efforts

MATCHING STRATEGY AND STRUCTURE

In addition to considering contingency issues, managers must try matching strategy and structure to achieve effectiveness. Miller (1986; 1988) matched strategies similar to Porter's competitive strategies (see Chapter 6) with appropriate structures. Miller considered four main choices:

Niche differentiation. This strategy aims to distinguish one's products and services from those of competitors for a narrow target market (equivalent to Porter's focus strategy with differentiation).

Cost leadership. This strategy emphasises organisational efficiency so products and services can be offered at lower prices than those of competitors (equivalent to Porter's cost-leadership strategy).

Innovative differentiation. This strategy aims to distinguish one's products and services from those of competitors by leading in complex product or service innovations (similar to Porter's differentiation strategy but more narrowly oriented, specifically to sophisticated innovations).

Market differentiation. This strategy aims to distinguish one's products and services from those of competitors through advertising, prestige pricing and market segmentation (similar to Porter's differentiation strategy but more narrowly oriented, specifically to market approaches). Product and service designs may not be better than those of competitors, but may offer attractive packaging, good service, convenient locations and product or service reliability.

Miller's matches of structure and strategy are shown in Table 10.7. In making these matches, Miller also considered environment appropriateness for strategy–structure combinations, following the logic involved in contingency approaches.

Table 10.7   Major matches of structure and strategy

Type of departmentalisation	Strategy
Functional	Niche differentiation, or focus
Functional	Cost leadership; possibly market differentiation
Divisional or hybrid	Market differentiation or cost leadership at division level
Matrix, integrators	Innovative differentiation

Source: Based on Miller (1986; 1988).

With niche differentiation or focus strategy, the organisation is typically small or medium sized, dealing with a relatively homogeneous set of customers and clients, making a functional structure appropriate. A functional structure supports a cost leadership strategy, even in a large organisation, when limited numbers of related products or services are involved. Similarly, market differentiation strategy may be feasible with a functional structure when products and services offered have a narrow range and can be effectively co-ordinated across functional units.

The divisional or the hybrid structures generally match with market differentiation. A cost leadership strategy can work with these structures while strategy occurs at a division level.

The matrix structure is generally compatible with an innovative differentiation strategy. Matrix structures emphasise flexibility and collaboration across specialists, conditions useful to new product development.

Incubator nurtures small businesses

gaining the edge

What do you do when you make a decision to concentrate on clients with turnovers between $15 million and over $100 million and you also have a growing number of clients who are too small for that bracket? This is the issue faced by Boyd Partners on St Kilda Road in Melbourne. Within a few years, those small companies would have grown to a size which would make them worthwhile clients under the new policies.

The strategy Boyd Partners developed was to establish a new firm for those clients. The motivation was clear: once those small companies had established a relationship with another firm, it would be almost impossible to win them back. The new firm subleases premises from Boyd Partners, uses their facilities and equipment at concessional rates and outsources some book-keeping work to keep its own overheads low. Herc Koutas, new chief of this new venture, looks after the clients until they grow large enough to need the higher level services of Boyd Partners. These clients don't like paying high per-hour rates for compliance work. For more complex issues like business restructure, they can be referred to Boyd Partners as required.

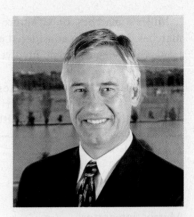

Members of the Boyd Partners' management team, which added a new firm to the company's structure in order to service an additional component of its market.

Herc Koutas is carefully growing the business with clients who, though they lack the business sophistication of the larger clients, show their appreciation for the care and attention displayed to them by paying their bills promptly.

Source: Adapted from Thomas, T. (1999).

Activities for discussion, analysis and further research

1 Discuss the imperatives of structure which have determined the validity for starting this new venture.
2 Describe how this additional portion of the organisation will gain a competitive advantage for Boyd Partners.

PROMOTING INNOVATION: USING STRUCTURAL MEANS TO ENHANCE PROSPECTS

Structure's ability to support strategy can be enhanced by using structural means to encourage innovation. Innovation is critical to various differentiation strategies (especially an innovative differentiation strategy). In this section, we consider four major means of using organisation structure to facilitate innovation: the roles vital for innovation, the need for innovative units called reservations, the differentiation paradox and the transfer process (Galbraith 1982).

Vital roles

Successful innovations are rarely only one person's work. The innovative process is more likely to occur when three vital entrepreneurial roles are filled: idea champion, sponsor and orchestrator. We discussed these in Chapter 1 and briefly review them here.

An idea champion generates a new idea or believes in a new idea's value, supporting it in the face of potential obstacles. These are often entrepreneurs, inventors, creative individuals or risk takers. Since they are generally low in the hierarchy, they often have difficulty getting their innovations accepted without a sponsor's help. A sponsor, usually a middle manager, recognises the organisational significance of an idea and helps obtain funding needed to continue the development of an innovation, facilitating the actual implementation of the new idea. However, innovations also need an orchestrator's help. An orchestrator is a high-level manager, who articulates a need for innovation, provides funding for activities, creates incentives for middle managers to sponsor innovative ideas, and protects ideas people. Orchestrators are vital as innovations disturb the status quo and are resisted by those who have to adjust to accommodate new ideas. These roles are important and their effectiveness can be enhanced by creation of special units called reservations.

Reservations

Breakthrough ideas are more likely if early efforts are differentiated, or separated, from the organisation's operating units (Maidique 1980). The reason is that most operating units aim to perform similar recurring tasks efficiently (e.g. produce the millionth automobile, process the millionth cheque or serve the millionth hamburger). Focusing on completing assigned tasks, operating units are not adept at developing new ways to do things. So many organisations that are seeking to encourage innovation set up **reservations**, which are organisational units devoted full-time to the generation of innovative ideas. The aim is to create 'garage-like' atmospheres where people can try new approaches. Steven Jobs and Steven Wozniak created the first Apple computer in a garage, which was a reservation for their work.

Reservations can be ongoing, relatively permanent units, such as research and development departments. **New venture units** can be set up either as separate divisions or specially incorporated companies for developing new products or business ideas and initiatives (Burgelman 1985; Bart 1988).

Reservations can be temporary task forces or teams of individuals relieved of their normal duties to develop a new process, product or program. These are **new venture teams**. Though differentiation, particularly setting reservations up, is effective in encouraging innovation, there is an associated paradox.

Differentiation paradox

The **differentiation paradox** occurs when separating innovative efforts from the rest of the organisation increases the probability of radical idea development, but when such differentiation also decreases the possibility the ideas will be implemented. The reason is that new ideas often are seen as being so different that they are threatening or even rejected. The paradox is strongest with a radical innovation that must be put in place by an organisation's operating units. Under these circumstances, units may reject the ideas. For example, during the 1970s at Xerox's Palo Alto Research Centre, scientists invented the first personal computer, the mouse, picture-oriented layout based on icons, and word processing software displaying fonts as they appear on the page. Unfortunately, the whole organisation did not appreciate the value of these inventions and Xerox never capitalised on them (Chakravarty 1994). Instead, Apple,

reservations

Organisational units devoted to the generation of innovative ideas for future business

new venture units

Either separate divisions or specially incorporated companies created to develop new products or business ideas and initiatives

new venture teams

Temporary task forces or teams made up of individuals relieved of normal duties to develop a new process, product or program

differentiation paradox

Idea that although separating innovation efforts from the rest of the organisation increases the likelihood of developing radical ideas, such differentiation also decreases the likelihood radical ideas will be implemented

Microsoft and others benefited from them. The PARC situation at Xerox illustrates the differentiation paradox and the need for concern about technological transfer.

Transfer process

As the differentiation paradox suggests, the more innovators are separate from the organisation, the more difficulty encountered in making innovations into marketable products or services. For example, Bell Labs has averaged around a patent a day since being founded in 1925 to provide cutting-edge research support to AT&T. Yet AT&T has generally been unable to translate Bell's research into products and services to fuel company growth (Schrage 1987).

It is best to see the effective transfer, or transition, process as a set of stages. In the first stage, an idea generator, or champion, works on an idea in a reservation. If initial tests are positive but the idea needs more work, others with expertise from the rest of the organisation hone it. Then, if results are still positive, the next stage involves testing the idea in an operating division. In the final stage, the new innovation is implemented. Of course, it may not be smooth and may be easier when the innovation represents incremental change. However, to develop and implement significant innovations consistently, innovative efforts must be fostered and new ideas transferred from innovating units to the whole organisation.

Sometimes, organisations establish separate new venture units and, when large enough, bring them into the main organisation as separate divisions, lessening transfer difficulties.

This chapter focused on designing structure in support of organisation strategy. In the next, we consider another aspect of the organising function, human resource management.

The MD's diary
the reflective practitioner

This very much concerns the people side of our business because as I said the key business objectives are growth, customer focus, technical leadership and the development of our people. The other thing that needs to be in place if we are to deliver these objectives is to have a structure which provides responsibility and authority at as low a level in the organisation as possible, so there isn't the need for constant monitoring and review up and down. We have, and I encourage continuous communication. I do not encourage the need to constantly monitor what and how people do things. The structure is meant to provide as much flexibility and latitude as possible. It encourages people to accept responsibility, and in a way which recognises an individual's capabilities. We very much have a philosophy here that there is no clearly defined role for an individual; that within the structure there is sufficient flexibility for those people who are capable of taking on greater responsibility and capable of working at a higher level, that they are able to do so.

The subordinate's log
the reflective practitioner

The organisation's structure was, to a degree, determined by the geographic location of the offices, which allowed progressive access to larger markets, initially to English-speaking and subsequently to non-English-speaking countries. This was rather effective.

The other issue about the structure is the nature of the ownership. The structure allowed the CEO to keep strong control over the organisation keeping it flat with constant and detailed reporting and regular face-to-face meetings. This is very much a sales-driven organisation. Therefore individuals more directly involved with sales reported more to the CEO as well as the office head. This dual reporting responsibility placed stress on the marketing people, while sometimes disempowering the office heads.

Two insights resulted from this. Responsibilities and reporting lines cannot be blurred. They must be well defined if effectiveness is to be the outcome. Otherwise you end up with frustrated, ineffective staff. You must have distinct lines of responsibility. Because the focus and structure emphasised sales and marketing, there was a division between the sales and marketing people and the client-consulting people, resulting in communication gaps between the two groups. I also learnt that to be effective in my role I had to actively bring the two groups together. There needed to be consulting input into the sales and marketing and, once the contract was obtained, there needed to be a marketing input to the consulting people as the marketing staff owned the relationship with the client.

Focus on practice—Strategies for improving

1 In today's environment, it is proposed that an organisation should remain organic in nature. Discuss this concept with reference to an organisation which alters the range of products or services it offers.
2 Consider what outsourcing and therefore the establishment of a network organisation does to an organisation's ability to maintain strict control processes and therefore a mechanistic structure.
3 If an organisation has quality or innovation as part of its key strategies, what can it put into place to ensure that it will stay decentralised?

Source: Jones et al. (2000).

Chapter summary

Chandler's study of the origins of large US firms helped establish the idea managers should design organisation structures to support organisation strategy. At the same time, structures needed to reach organisational goals effectively and efficiently are likely to be influenced by major contingency factors and structural methods for promoting innovation.

Four common forms of departmentalisation are functional, divisional, hybrid and matrix. Functional structure combines positions on the basis of similar expertise, skills and work activities. Divisional structure groups positions by similar products, services or markets. The three major forms of divisional structure are product, geographic and customer. Hybrid structure adopts both functional and divisional structures at the same management level. A mature matrix is a structure that is simultaneously both a functional and a divisional organisation, with two chains of command (one vertical and one horizontal). Matrix structures progress through several stages, beginning with a traditional structure then moving to a temporary overlay, permanent overlay, and, perhaps, mature matrix stage.

Matrix structures are appropriate when environmental pressure needs a strong focus on both functional and divisional dimensions; changing, unpredictable demands need rapid processing of large amounts of information; and there is pressure for shared resources. Functional, divisional, hybrid and matrix structures all have advantages and disadvantages. Differences exist in the circumstances under which each will be effective. Emerging structures include process and networked structures.

The best organisation structure depends on contingency factors such as technology, size and environment. Higher levels of technological complexity and interdependence require greater horizontal co-ordination. Increasing size leads to more departments and levels, a greater number of specialists, more staff positions, and an eventual tendency toward decentralisation. Organisations in more stable environments have relatively mechanistic characteristics, while those in more unstable environments have relatively organic characteristics. Unstable environments are associated with greater differentiation among units, increasing the need for integration. Integration is achieved by means of horizontal co-ordination.

Some matches of structure and strategy are more likely to be successful: functional structure and niche differentiation, cost leadership, or, perhaps, market differentiation; divisional or hybrid structure and market differentiation or cost leadership at a division level; and matrix structure and innovative differentiation.

Enhancement of organisational prospects for innovation is possible by several structural mechanisms. The vital roles of idea champion, sponsor and orchestrator are important for innovation. Organisations must designate reservations, or units devoted full time to innovation. However, the differentiation paradox must be considered. On one hand, innovation is more likely if innovating units are separated from the organisation physically, financially and/or organisationally. On the other hand, separation makes it hard to transfer innovations to other organisation elements.

Questions for discussion and review

1 Summarise current views about the link between strategy and organisation structure. To what extent can these differing views be reconciled?

2 Contrast functional and divisional departmentalisation types, including their respective advantages and disadvantages. Given your particular career interests, develop a list of advantages and disadvantages for (a) working in a company organised by function and (b) working in a company organised by product.

3 Describe hybrid, or mixed, departmentalisation. How does this structure help incorporate some advantages of both functional and divisional types?

4 Outline the advantages and disadvantages of matrix departmentalisation. How do they relate to conditions where it is appropriate to use matrix structures?

5 Contrast the two critical aspects of technology: technological complexity and technological interdependence. Give examples of small-batch, mass-production and continuous-process technologies. Alternatively, provide examples of three types of technological interdependence.

6 Explain the four trends identified by studies of size effects on structure. Can you present evidence of these trends in familiar organisations?

7 Contrast mechanistic and organic characteristics of organisations. To what extent do you view your college or university as having mechanistic or organic characteristics? Cite examples to support your view. Why might organisations with organic characteristics need more managerial efforts at integration?

8 Outline how strategy and structure could be matched to help enhance organisational success. What implications would this have for subsequent changes in strategy or structure?

9 Explain the notion of a reservation applied to encouraging organisational innovation. How does the differentiation paradox help explain AT&T's difficulties using Bell Labs' innovative ideas in marketable products?

10 Describe the typical stages in an effective innovation transfer process.

Exercises for managing in the 21st century

Exercise 1
Skill building: Recognising structural strengths and weaknesses

The four basic alternative types of organisation structure are functional, divisional, hybrid and matrix. Each has certain characteristics, advantages and disadvantages. Indicate the structure type the following statements best fit by placing the first letter of that structure type in the blank.

Functional Divisional Hybrid Matrix

1 _____   Corporate and divisional goals can be aligned.
2 _____   These organisations can react quickly to changes in the environment.
3 _____   Employees generally have clear career paths.
4 _____   Functional specialists can be added or removed from projects as needed, allowing effective use of human resources.
5 _____   These organisations tend to develop excessively large staffs in the corporate functional departments.
6 _____   Goals may conflict with overall organisational goals.
7 _____   These organisations focus on the development of in-depth expertise.
8 _____   Response time on multifunctional problems may be slow because of co-ordination problems.
9 _____   Line of authority and responsibility may not be clear to individual employees.
10 _____   Specialised expertise and economies of scale can be achieved in major functional areas.
11 _____   Employees work for two bosses.
12 _____   Department performance is easily measured.

Exercise 2
Management exercise: Developing an organisation structure

The Sun Petroleum Products Company, a subsidiary of Sun Company Inc., is a successful refining company. Its six refineries manufacture three main business products: fuels, petrochemicals and lubricants. The products are sold to Sunmark Industries (another Sun subsidiary), chemical manufacturers, industrial plants, the auto industry and a variety of other customers. The $7 billion company has a workforce of about 5400.

Sun Petroleum currently has a functional organisation structure, with the following positions reporting directly to the CEO: chief counsel; the directors of financial services, technology, planning and administration (including human resources), and operations (to whom the managers of marketing and manufacturing and supply distribution report).

Because of changing markets for the company's main products, Sun Petroleum is thinking about changing its organisation structure to a hybrid design. In the process, the president is considering adding a senior vice-president of resources and strategy to oversee the company's strategic planning.

First, draw an organisation chart depicting Sun Petroleum's current organisation structure.

Second, draw a chart showing the proposed change from Sun Petroleum's current structure to a hybrid organisation structure.

Third, be prepared to discuss the advantages and disadvantages of the proposed new structure and some possible ways of promoting innovation (Ackerman 1982).

Singapore Computer Systems comes of age

With 21 years of operations behind it, Singapore Computer Systems has strict targets for the future. SCS started as a software development house for the Chartered group of companies. Over the years, Mr Tay Siew Choon, current chairman, and general manager from 1985 to 1991 and managing director from 1991 to 1995, has steered the company until it is now one of the largest providers of IT services in the region with capabilities in IT consulting, systems integration, outsourcing, networking, e-commerce services and R&D in product development.

Among his achievements are the results from SCS's research efforts, crossing the $100 million revenue point, listing of the company on the Stock Exchange of Singapore, the introduction of news services and the start of regional operations.

SCS's research capabilities began with an in-house technical team in 1998 focusing on two areas—object-oriented technology and database intelligence.

Mr Tay is proud that both turned out to be major IT trends today, and the efforts benefited SCS in areas such as e-commerce and health care systems. Research, he said, allows the team to see many new technologies at work as well as provide added value to SCS's system integration projects. One of the earliest fruits of SCS's R&D efforts has been spun off into a company in the US called D2K. D2K has developed a product called Tapestry which is a software infrastructure that routes information rather than just data to anyone who needs it irrespective of where the database is located in any operation.

Tapestry is already in the market, with three out of five Singapore banks already using it. Other customers include Xerox, Synopsis and Corning.

When Mr Tay, an electrical engineer, was hired in December 1985 by Mr Phillip Yeo, then chairman of the Singapore Technologies group, to run SCS, he was challenged to break the $100 million revenue mark by 1990. He achieved it in four years, one year earlier than the set target, by injecting the company with a sense of entrepreneurship. He also widened the scope of the company by setting up regional operation in Malaysia and expanding the product offerings with services like business recovery. The first customer signed up was Singapore Airlines in 1987. From an in-house IT focus, SCS moved away from serving its sister companies. The bulk of its business comes from the commercial and public sector.

Fulfilling a charter to turn SCS into a commercial entity, he ensured that his staff could respond to rapid changes in technology. This response had not only to cover the technical evolution but also to put them in a position to help customers evolve and change with the technological demands of their own business environment. SCS places a high degree of emphasis on quality as it pertains to people, training, and both processes and systems.

'The company has a five-pronged strategy—internationalisation; growth through mergers, acquisitions and alliances; focus on key domains; product development; and increasing services and outsourcing businesses.

'Through internationalisation, it is hoped to increase our presence in existing territories as well as move into

The strategic organisational design of Singapore Computer Systems means that its own R & D team is used to contribute to the revenue of the company.

new ones. SCS already has operations in Malaysia, Brunei, Thailand, the Philippines, New Zealand, China, Hong Kong, the US, Australia and the UK. Each of those operations has its own unique capabilities that the other operations can tap in on. Mergers, acquisitions and alliances will help us to grow. It's also a way for us to stand on the shoulders of our partners and get into foreign markets.'

Besides just growing in breadth, the SCS is also aiming for depth of coverage, digging into various vertical industries such as health care, education, oil and gas, government, and banking and finance. The organisation has very strong teams that specialise not only in integrating solutions but also developing new products for these industries. For example, one team based in Singapore and Malaysia has successfully developed health care and financial services products. It is intended to spin off some of those teams into companies as the developed products become commercially viable. An example of this is the health care system which SCS has developed. This has been successfully implemented in hospitals and medical practices in Singapore and elsewhere in the region. It is planned to spin off this team in the very near future. Such spin-offs allow the companies to be more fleet footed while being supported by a large and financially strong SCS.

SCS is putting a lot of emphasis on service excellence. The organisation is e-ing every part of the business. Technical capabilities can no longer differentiate SCS from its competitors because everyone is doing the same thing. The company is committed to the thought that service excellence is the way to distinguish themselves. Through e-commerce, SCS can provide new value to a wider range of customers. In 1999, SCS achieved the Singapore Quality Class and is aiming for the Singapore Quality Award. A number of programs have been introduced to ensure that staff are conscious of delivering service excellence—training staff to understand what good service is as well as a reward system that is based on service excellence.

The organisation conducts frequent customer polling to gather feedback. This allows them to put their fingers on the pulse of the business with the aim of having customers associate excellence in service with SCS.

For the future, SCS is moving into a number of IT businesses, not only providing IT systems but also IT-based services. The strategy is to go into partnership with people who have the domain knowledge and market reach in the business. For example SCS has teamed up with a number of key players from the Singapore Secondhand Motor Vehicle Dealers' Association to set up an online used-car auction business. Their partners have the used-car expertise and SCS have the technical knowledge. Another example of such partnerships is the one formed with General Electric Internet Services (GEIS) to provide global electronic procurement services.

The changing face of the competition is another force for change. SCS is no longer competing against traditional competitors. These days competition can come from anywhere. Telecommunication companies and banks are getting involved in e-commerce. Systematic planning is the only way to eliminate guesswork. A strategic group gathers information, examines mergers and integration and keeps watch over the industry to identify trends. This group undertakes scenario planning and helps avoid the surprises which can throw the organisation off balance.

The greatest challenge for the organisation is maintaining a team of talented individuals who will grow the business and look for new e-ventures. SCS's greatest strength and competitive advantage is its international network of subsidiaries and alliances. These give the company a lot of leverage as each operation can rapidly replicate its key capabilities to other territories.

With SCS reaching the age of majority, Tay's new challenge is reaching the $1 billion mark by 2003. His outlook—confidence!

Source: *Straits Times* (2000).

Activities for discussion, analysis and further research

1 Discuss the imperatives of structure which have affected this organisation over the past 20 years.
2 How have Mr Tay's roles and responsibilities changed in that time? Have these been influenced by the structural imperatives? How?

Human Resource Management

Chapter 11

CHAPTER OUTLINE

The human resource management framework
The regulatory framework

Establishing the employment relationship
Acquiring human resources
Job analysis
Methods of job analysis
Recruitment
Methods of recruitment
Selection

Maintaining the employment relationship
Remuneration and benefits
Training and development
Performance appraisal
360 degree feedback

HRIS, Internet, intranets and extranets
The future of work
Flexible employing organisations
Flexible employees
Terminating the employment relations

LEARNING OBJECTIVES

After studying this chapter, you should be able to:

○ Describe the legislative and business framework within which human resource management is conducted.
○ Explain the three phases of the employment relationship.
○ Describe the importance of job analysis and its relationship to other functions of human resource management.
○ Identify the strengths and weaknesses of internal and external recruitment.
○ Describe the main selection techniques and explain how the selection interview can be improved.
○ Explain the relationship between remuneration and other functions of human resource management.
○ Describe three strategic rationales for training and development.
○ Assess the impact of the Karpin Report on the need for training and development.
○ Identify five reasons for undertaking performance appraisal.
○ Assess the impact of information technology on human resource management.
○ Explain the ways in which flexible work practices impact upon workers and the way that jobs are defined.
○ Identify the main issues associated with terminating the employment relationship.

Striving for excellence

In Autoliv's recruitment practices, there is an effort to target individuals who will challenge the status quo. The culture is forward looking, not historical—challenging the status quo is encouraged and rewarded.

Autoliv attempt to retain staff by encouraging career development and ensuring that staff do not remain in positions which do not utilise their competencies to the fullest. This is a management philosophy which, when properly implemented, keeps a better balance and helps individuals gain promotion within the company. When looking for people to be promoted to the management team, there is a preference for people who have been in more than one role in the company. The philosophy has always been for internal promotion rather than external recruitment. While this is not always appropriate or possible, the skill set is what determines the recruitment process. This must be carefully done as one of the Human Resources Department's performance measures is the percentage of internal promotions over external recruitment.

As do all the departments at Autoliv, the Human Resources Department has its own Key Objectives and Performance Criteria. As mentioned above, one of those performance criteria is the percentage of internal promotions against external recruitment. This percentage reflects the degree of success of the Training and Development Plan which must be developed for every individual on staff. This involves a Performance Plan and a Performance Development Review. Every person holding a staff position is reviewed against performance standards, which accurately reflect the efficiency and effectiveness of employee output. The Autoliv performance management system is based on two separate elements. The first element is clearly identified management competencies. The five management competencies identified for senior managers are: 1. Manage operations, 2. Manage people, 3. Manage finance, 4. Manage information and 5. Strategic management. The second element of the performance management system is Key Performance Indicators (KPIs) which are agreed and reviewed every six months.

The development of staff performance is key to the survival of an organisation if it is to grow and meet customers' needs. Research has shown that both motivation and performance improve when staff understand the expectations and standards of the employer. Therefore, Autoliv has a system which is transparent and to which staff are invited to contribute.

THE HUMAN RESOURCE MANAGEMENT FRAMEWORK

human resource management

Those management functions concerned with attracting, maintaining and developing people in the employment relationship

If the five basic functions of management are planning, organising, staffing, leading and controlling, then **human resource management** is concerned with the staffing function. That is, it deals with those functions concerned with attracting, maintaining and developing people in the employment relationship. The following diagram introduces a basic human resource management (HRM) framework (Fig. 11.1).

This HRM framework places the core functions of HRM within two inter-related contexts.

Within the 'business context', an organisation's plans and objectives influence the nature of its activities. Small entrepreneurial organisations are more likely to recruit on a needs basis and have informal HRM policies and procedures. Large divisionalised organisations with greater job specialisation have formal systems to provide structure and accountability. The

Fig. 11.1 Human resource management framework

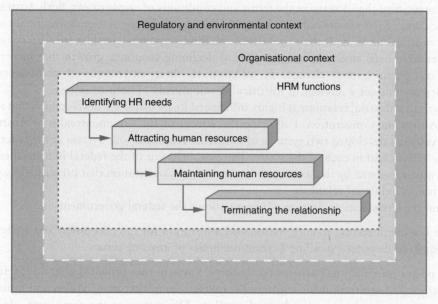

human resource management functions of acquiring, maintaining and developing human resources will be different for these two organisation types.

Within the 'regulatory and environment context', organisations are influenced by compliance with different forms of legislation, while responding to different environmental factors.

With HRM's emergence as a specialist field in the early 1980s, theorists looked at the interplay between these different organisational contexts. Beer and Spector (1985) proposed a set of assumptions underlying HRM policies. These included:

○ a shift from reactive interventions to proactive, system-wide interventions emphasising the fit between HRM and strategic planning and cultural change;

○ the concept of people as human capital, capable of development instead of being viewed as a straight organisation cost;

○ the ability to develop common interest between stakeholders instead of assuming inevitable conflict between stakeholders.

Fombrun, Tichy and Devanna (1988) suggested management's critical task was to align formal structure and HR systems of selection, appraisal, reward and development to drive the organisation's strategic objectives. In this way, single product, functional organisations would have functionally oriented selection processes using subjective criteria, highly subjective appraisal systems and unsystematic reward systems. Meanwhile multi-product, multinational organisations would use both functional and generalistic selection criteria, using systematic criteria, impersonal and objective appraisal measures and reward systems based on multiple planned goals.

The regulatory framework

The regulatory framework is responsible for influencing the contract of employment between employers and employees and the role of unions in representing employees. **Unions** are

unions

Membership groups formed to represent employees and to negotiate collective agreements with management that determine the terms and conditions of employment

membership groups formed to represent employees and to negotiate collective agreements with management that determine the terms and conditions of employment. Both Australia and New Zealand have experienced significant change in regulatory and organisational contexts. Both countries have had their industrial relations systems deregulated. Likewise both countries have been emerging from periods of declining economic growth that incorporated significant organisational change. In addition to these environmental constraints, it is necessary to consider a number of historical developments in both countries.

Australian industrial relations is highly influenced by its historical development and its links to the Australian Constitution. Following the advent of the Commonwealth of Australia in 1901, Australia developed two systems of industrial relations—one system at the federal level and one system within each of the states. The establishment of the federal industrial relations system was influenced by the section of the Australian Constitution that prescribed its powers in relation to industrial relations.

Within the Constitution, Section 51(xxxv) allows the federal government to:

make laws with respect to conciliation and arbitration for the prevention and settlement of industrial disputes extending beyond the limits of any one state

This power provided the basis for establishing a system that provided guaranteed access to conciliation and arbitration for registered employers, employer associations and unions that would ensure a resolution of industrial conflict. The states, at the same time, developed similar systems offering conciliation and arbitration to settle industrial disputes while maintaining the power to legislate directly on matters of industrial relations, a power the federal government was denied due to the interpretation of the Constitution and in particular Section 51(xxxv).

The benefits of such a system included the certainty of achieving an outcome, access to specialised industrial relations experts and the establishment of a system of minimum wages and conditions embodied in legally binding determinations called 'industrial awards'. The problems of such a system included the inability to respond quickly to changing environments, entrenched conflict as a means of determining wage increases, and highly regulated and inflexible awards. Additionally the highly centralised nature of the system at both federal and state levels meant that organisations tended to minimise the development of appropriate conflict-resolution procedures and skills within the organisation.

Major changes to this system of industrial relations occurred during the ACTU–ALP Accords from 1983 with the election of the Australian Labor Party, up to its defeat in 1996. These changes were iterative attempts to respond to significant economic and social pressures that highlighted the need for reform without specifying what shape that reform should take. Through a series of national wage case hearings conducted by the Australian Industrial Relations Commission (AIRC), the very nature of the system was transformed over a relatively short number of years. The involvement of the ACTU with the Labor government resulted in significant restraint being exercised by the unions in return for benefits derived from the 'social contract' elaborated within each of the Accords. The more significant of these changes occurred from 1987 onward. In 1987, the AIRC implemented the Accord proposal requiring employers and unions to identify cost-cutting measures that would help pay for increases to Award minimum rates of pay. While not wholly successful, this decision represented a significant mind-shift away from adversarial industrial relations toward a system of consensus. In 1988, building on the previous experience, the AIRC again implemented the

Accord proposal of undertaking significant reform of the Award system using the principles of structural efficiency. Again this required employers and unions to form a consensus on the way in which work would be structured, developed and rewarded, with benefits flowing to both employers and employees.

While maintaining the principles associated with structural efficiency, in 1991 the AIRC agreed (however reluctantly) to allow employers and unions to negotiate enterprise agreements following guidelines set down by the AIRC. From an entrenched adversarial system that imposed decisions upon the parties, the system had been transformed in a matter of only seven years to one that encouraged agreement-making at the enterprise level with reduced input from the AIRC. These reforms were further enhanced when the Labor Party introduced new industrial relations that, for the first time, utilised external affairs powers and corporations powers of the Constitution to allow the federal government to regulate more aspects of employment conditions than at any other time. As a result, the legislation imposed duties upon employers in areas such as unfair dismissals and allowed for the establishment of non-union enterprise agreements.

These changes had direct impact on organisations and their management of human resources. The Accords from 1987 onward required organisations to review their work systems, the structure of jobs, encouraged a shift to skills-based training and the linking of job structures to careers and the linking of wages and salaries to the reformed work systems.

The election of a conservative government in 1996 after 13 years of Labor government saw the introduction of the *Workplace Relations Act 1996*. Continuing on with the reforms of the Labor Party, this Act moved quickly to devolve responsibility for workplace relations (previously termed 'industrial relations') down to the workplace. It also reduces the influence of unions in negotiating collective enterprise bargaining agreements, and reduces the power of the AIRC to intervene or to use conciliation and arbitration to settle disputes, unless both parties in dispute are in agreement. At the same time there has been a strengthening of employers' prerogatives in the setting of conditions of employment through the use of individual contracts, known as 'Australian workplace agreements' or AWAs, which can override both federal collective agreements and state-based collective agreements. Problems with AWAs become evident when the negotiating power between parties is uneven, such as when low-skilled workers are required to deal with employers individually or when there is an oversupply of labour and hence pressure to accept what is offered.

The New Zealand system had developed a system of conciliation and arbitration in a similar fashion to Australia. In recent years the principle influence in industrial relations was the *Employment Contracts Act 1991*, legislation which when introduced radically overhauled industrial award agreements, reduced the rights and powers of unions in negotiating collective agreements, and allowed for individual contracts to be negotiated. The extent of reform was possible due to the lack of any parliamentary 'house of review' such as exists with the Australian Senate. The legislation significantly shifted the power in industrial relations matters toward employers, away from unions, and reduced the ability of third parties to intervene, as has happened more recently in Australia.

The election of a coalition government in 1999 that includes New Zealand Labour as a senior partner will see the introduction of new employment relations legislation which is likely to result in a partial restoration of powers to unions, though how much has yet to be determined.

Legislation does not operate in isolation. At the best of times it is open to interpretation and at the worst times it is used to advantage one party over another. The outcomes from the 1998

Patricks waterfront dispute demonstrated that the Workplace Relations Act in its current form has required parties in conflict to resort to legal challenges and legal remedies instead of having access to traditional conciliation and arbitration processes through the Industrial Relations Commission. Implicit in the Workplace Relations Act is the assumption that parties in negotiations are always able to reach agreement. The waterfront dispute demonstrated the consequences of parties who are unable to reach agreement. Recourse to legal intervention to resolve protracted industrial conflict is more likely under these circumstances.

Other Acts and regulations in both Australia and New Zealand deal with discrimination, equal employment opportunity, human rights, occupational health and safety, and environmental management, and all influence the employment contract. Some examples of relevant legislation include:

Australian legislation
Workplace Relations Act 1996
Equal Opportunity for Women in the Workplace Act 1999
Human Rights and Equal Opportunity Commission Act 1986
Sex Discrimination Act 1984
Race Discrimination Act 1975
Disability Discrimination Act 1992
Commonwealth Employees' Rehabilitation and Compensation Act 1988
Federal and state occupational health and safety Acts, regulations and codes of practice
Federal and State Environment Management Acts and Regulations, including
Clear Air Act
Clean Water Act
Noise Pollution Act
Ozone Protection Act

New Zealand legislation
The *Employment Contracts Act 1991* (to be replaced by Labor's draft employment relations legislation)
Accident Rehabilitation and Compensation Insurance Act 1992
Disabled Persons Employment Promotion Act 1960
Employment Contracts Act 1991
Equal Pay Act 1972
Minimum Wage Act 1983
Wages Protection Act 1983
Parental Leave and Employment Protection Act 1987
Health and Safety in Employment Act 1992
Dangerous Goods Act 1974
Explosives Act 1957
Higher Salaries Commission Act 1977
Holidays Act 1981
Immigration Act 1987
Machinery Act 1950
Industry Training Act 1992
Human Rights Act 1993

ESTABLISHING THE EMPLOYMENT RELATIONSHIP

Acquiring human resources

All organisations undertake planning for different purposes. **Human resource planning** involves determining future human resource needs in relation to an organisation's business objectives or strategic plan, then devising ways to meet these objectives (Walker 1980; Lengnick-Hall & Lengnick-Hall 1988). This section deals with the first staffing phase—the processes of attracting the 'right' number of people with the 'right' skills at the 'right' time and place. It shows the importance of defining jobs correctly through job analysis, then outlines recruitment and selection methods.

Job analysis

Two friends make surfboards on weekends and demand for their boards is high. They might make a business of their weekend pastime. To turn it into a business they will continue to make surfboards, but more of them. They will face many issues such as marketing, cost control, sales and bookkeeping. As small business operators, they may need to do everything themselves, with little thought as to whether they have skills or knowledge for these tasks. However, if the business grows and profits allow them to hire someone, they will have to decide who to hire and what the new person is going to do. It is one thing to wait until a surfboard sells to make money. It is different to have to pay someone whether or not any surfboards are sold. Even worse is employing a person who cannot work quickly or accurately enough to meet customer demand.

The staffing issues facing these two friends are similar to those faced by larger organisations. Before an organisation can recruit and select 'the right people' to achieve organisational goals, it has to determine tasks to be grouped together into jobs to achieve business objectives. It will also need to determine the employee specifications required if the job is to be done properly. **Job analysis** is the systematic process of collecting information on a job's task functions and identifying employee specifications for job success (Fig. 11.2). Two outcomes of job analysis are the development of job descriptions (what a job entails) and job specifications (skills, abilities, education and previous work experience required to perform the job).

human resource planning

Determining future human resource needs in relation to an organisation's business objectives or strategic plan, then devising ways to meet the objectives

job analysis

The systematic collecting and recording of information about the purpose of a job, its major duties, the conditions under which it is performed, the required contacts with others and the knowledge, skills and abilities needed to effectively perform it

Fig. 11.2   Job analysis process

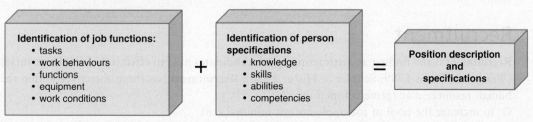

Job analysis is an important foundation for other human resource management processes. It can improve all of the following:

Recruitment and selection—Job descriptions allow an organisation to accurately describe the job to potential applicants, and job specifications give important decision criteria in candidate selection for the job.

Performance appraisal—Clearly defined tasks and specifications establish performance baselines against which an individual's performance may be measured.

Remuneration—Accurate job descriptions and specifications allow organisations to value the job relative to the market and to other employees in the organisation.

Training and development—Job analysis outcomes allow planning of initial and consequent training requirements and for later development opportunities.

Job design and redesign—The systematic processes in job analysis can ensure jobs meet regulatory requirements (occupational health and safety standards) and can be used to redesign jobs as organisations change.

Methods of job analysis

Gathering information about job content and specifications is a major communication exercise, requiring much planning. Information can be collected on existing jobs by interviews either with individuals or groups of employees. Sometimes supervisors familiar with the jobs are interviewed. Another way to gather information is observation, where people are directly observed doing a job and physical activities are recorded. Observation is not suited to jobs needing much thinking, or where the nature of tasks constantly changes. Observation may be combined with interviewing to get a representative sample of behaviours and tasks. Structured questionnaires can also be used, where employees choose tasks from lists of choices or rate the frequency of given activities. Another way employees can record their activities is by using employee journals or log books, where each activity and its duration is recorded. However, this method can result in inflated recordings of activities employees perceive to be important.

Whether using interviews, questionnaires or observation methods, it is important to ensure that employees understand their purpose. One organisation sent out a detailed questionnaire asking people to respond by the following Monday, without further explanation or briefing. It is not surprising this organisation received no completed questionnaires as most people believed information would be used to cut jobs.

Thorough job analysis processes can be time-consuming and costly, therefore organisations must ensure methods of gathering information are appropriate for their needs. There is no point in a 12-month job-analysis process if jobs change significantly every three to six months. On the other hand, a superficial process may have serious implications for an organisation if recent recruits leave because the job described was significantly different from the real job.

Recruitment

recruitment

The process of finding and attracting job candidates capable of effectively filling job vacancies

Recruitment is the finding and attracting of job candidates able to effectively fill job vacancies (Werther & Davis 1989; Schuler & Huber 1990). Recruitment has three objectives within the human resource management function:

O to increase the pool of job applicants at minimal cost

○ to ensure the organisation complies with legislative requirements such as equal opportunity or non-discriminatory processes
○ to improve the overall selection process by only attracting appropriately qualified and skilled applicants.

In situations where an existing job becomes vacant, there are some key questions to be asked before committing to the recruitment process:

Does the business need still exist? Work requirements may have changed so that the position is no longer relevant or required. (This should not be confused with downsizing, where an organisation reduces their workforce while expecting the same or more performance outcomes.)

If there is still a business need, is the job description of the vacant position appropriate? A job vacancy gives an opportunity to undertake a quick job analysis, especially where the nature of work has recently changed.

Can the business need be met by redesigning existing jobs? An opportunity exists to consider reallocating tasks between existing jobs or redesigning them to achieve better efficiencies. Managers must be conscious of any industrial relations implications of undertaking major workplace reforms.

If, after asking these questions, the position still needs to be filled, then the recruitment process can proceed. Recruitment can be either internal or external. Each has advantages and disadvantages.

For example, banks traditionally recruited new employees at entry level, then promoted internally in conjunction with internal training. While this ensured these employees developed loyalty and strong knowledge of organisational culture, they were less likely to be innovative. In a traditional, stable business environment, this was not a problem, but as the financial market was deregulated and the nature of banking changed, it became important for banks to reassess their recruitment strategies. New forms of retail banking, such as adopted by Colonial State, require different skills to traditional banking forms, and thus a change in recruitment strategy.

Table 11.1   Advantages and disadvantages of internal vs external recruitment

Internal recruitment

Advantages	Disadvantages
Improves morale	Closed group; inbreeding
Better assessment opportunity	'Nepotism'
Motivates staff	Infighting for promotion
Maintains organisational knowledge	Induction and training costs

External recruitment

Advantages	Disadvantages
Fresh blood	Harder to assess
New knowledge and experience	Lowers morale of internal applicants
Gain competitor insights	Adjusting to different work cultures

Methods of recruitment

A number of recruitment methods are available to organisations. These include the following:

Internal promotions—low cost, improves morale but no guarantee of finding right person

Advertisements—able to target local, state or national markets, also able to promote positive image of company; cost increase with increased content and style

Employee referrals—can be low cost, generates loyalty but may be limited talent pool

Employment agencies—useful for low-skilled or temporary fills, but at a cost

Executive recruitment ('head-hunters')—high fee-based search service which 'hunts out' senior management replacements; this method assumes the best person may not be looking to leave their existing job

Campus interviews—large pool of talent in one location, but it is important that academic qualifications are not the only criteria

Contractors—less permanent, reduces on-costs, useful for project work but not good for loyalty

The most recent method of recruitment has been through the Internet. Job and career sites give excellent opportunities for people not only to access job opportunities at any time and from any Internet site, but also provide the benefit of applicants being able to apply and download their CV directly onto the organisation's database. Sites in Australia include:

Monster Board Australia and New Zealand
    http://www.monsterboard.com.au; http://www.monster.co.nz/
Australian Job Search
    http://www.jobsearch.deetya.gov.au
nzjobs.co
    http://www.nzjobs.co.nz/
Fairfax Jobs Market
    http://www.market.fairfax.com.au/jobs
Employment.com.au
    http://www.employment.com.au/
mycareer.com.au
    http://www.mycareer.com.au/
Careers Online
    http://www.careersonline.com.au/
888 Casuals
    http://www.ozemail.com.au/~cm888
Fairfax IT Jobs
    http://www.itjobs.fairfax.com.au/

Advertising rates on the Internet are significantly less than for traditional display advertisements. When coupled with improvements in CV scanning software, organisations can achieve significant efficiencies. However, concerns about this medium of recruitment relate to issues of privacy and of appropriateness. While accessible, they do not guarantee sufficient numbers of appropriately skilled applicants will be searching the Internet for a job.

Selection

The recruitment process provides an organisation with a number of applicants to be considered for a vacant position. The **selection process** is the decision-making system applied to these applicants. As the importance of the vacant position increases, so do the consequences of an incorrect decision as to who should fill the position. The selection process tries to refine the decision-making process to optimise the fit between person and position. It is an attempt to predict who will be most successful in the position and, as with all predictions, it is always possible to get it wrong.

Reliability and validity **Reliability** in selection refers to how much the decision process will consistently measure the same thing. Drawing short straws to make a decision is unlikely to give the same result consistently, but a standardised set of questions related to job requirements is likely to give consistent results if repeated.

Validity in selection refers to whether the decision process actually measures what it sets out to measure. If the decision process for a vacant position is based on the school the applicant attended, then the organisation should be able to demonstrate the relationship between a particular school and job ability. The same applies to using psychological tests—there must be validated studies demonstrating a particular test is an accurate predictor of what it says it is predicting.

Selection devices There are several selection devices organisations use, individually or in combination, but there are some standard components which seem to be used universally.

Application forms request job candidate details from applicants and may be as simple as personal contact details (name, address, contact numbers) through to extensive biographical details of qualifications, experience and achievements.

Weighted application forms aim to provide a systematic, objective analysis of different factors, and when weighted appropriately to reflect job-relatedness, can be a valid predictor for those jobs. The difficulty with weighted application forms is they should be validated for each position, which is costly and time consuming.

Written tests include tests of intelligence, ability, aptitude and interest. Their use has seen a recent resurgence as they become more refined and demonstrate their ability to successfully predict suitable applicants for specific jobs. Some organisations justify their use due to the costs of making incorrect selection choices, but the issue remains one of validity and reliability.

The *selection interview*, in combination with application forms, is a well established device used for almost any job. Its attractiveness as a selection device is balanced against debate as to its value as a predictor (see, for instance, Arveny & Campion 1982). Its attractiveness in selection may have more to do with people's desire to actually meet the person they choose than whether the interview was a valid or reliable predictor of job performance. However, the interview's validity and reliability can be improved. Clark (1992) reports several measures to improve interviews, including these:

○ training of interviewers
○ combining interviews with other selection devices
○ clearly identifying what is being sought in a candidate
○ improving validity by looking for specific items whose relevance have been established
○ using interviews to identify disqualifying data rather than qualifying data

selection process

The decision-making system used to identify which job applicants are best suited to the vacant position

reliability

The degree to which the decision process will measure the same thing consistently

validity

Whether the decision process actually measures what it sets out to measure

○ using panel interviews to improve validity over sequential interviews
○ using interviews to assess interpersonal motivations and career aspirations, which may be difficult to identify by other means

Assessment centres provide an opportunity to evaluate applicant performance in simulated tests of the tasks related to the position. Trained assessors evaluate candidates as they operate in simulated situations they are likely to face in the position. Activities may be a combination of problem-solving exercises, leadership and team exercises, interviews and business-decision simulations. The ability to predict job performance in management positions well can be attributed to the identification of relevant job tasks, the combination of selection devices used and the training assessors receive. Assessment centres can therefore usually justify the high cost of establishing and conducting them.

In addition to risking the cost of an incorrect choice, organisations must operate within a regulatory context which imposes penalties for not conducting the selection process equitably. Large organisations have to make many selection decisions on a regular basis, and it is in their interest to ensure managers making selection decisions are at least trained and aware of the relative strengths and weaknesses of available selection devices.

 # How to conduct an effective interview

management skills
for the 21st century

You have a job vacancy in your unit and must interview several job candidates. What should you do? There are several steps to take before, during and after the interview to increase the likelihood of getting useful information to make your decision.

Before the interview

Much of the secret of conducting an effective interview is in the preparation. The following guidelines will help.

Determine job requirements. Using the job description and specification, draw up a list of characteristics the person must possess to perform the job. For example, suppose you are a bank manager and have an opening for a teller. Important characteristics would include oral communication skills, willingness to check for errors, ability to get along with others, and a service orientation to customer handling. Once these are identified, you can develop an interview guide.

Prepare a written interview guide. A written guide of what you wish to cover during the interview ensures all major points are addressed with each interviewee. You must plan questions assessing the degree to which candidates possess characteristics you identified as needed for the job.

Since past performance is a good predictor of future performance, a useful method is to frame questions in terms of examples of what a person has done, instead of focusing on generalities or speculations about what they will do in the future. For example, a *poor* question aimed at assessing how well an individual interacts with customers might be: 'How well do you handle problem customers?' Clearly candidates are unlikely to answer they have difficulty handling problem customers, even if it is true.

An *improved* approach asks questions as to how the individual has dealt with customers previously. For example, you might ask, 'Please describe a time when a customer paid you an especially nice compliment because of something you did. What were the circumstances?' You might follow up by asking, 'Tell me about a time when you had to handle a particularly irritating customer. How did you handle the situation?' Answers to these types of questions give insights into how a candidate is likely to treat customers and handle difficult situations. (If the individual has no job experience, questions can be adjusted; for example, '. . . a time when you had to handle a particularly irritating person'.)

Next, prepare a step-by-step plan of how to present the position to the candidate. Develop a similar plan for points to be made about the work unit and organisation. These plans help you present information in an organised way and ensure you cover all important points.

Review the candidate's application and/or résumé. This familiarises you with the candidate's specific experiences and accomplishments relevant to job requirements. Read these background materials before the interview; otherwise you will be unprepared for the interview. It is easy to miss gaps, discrepancies and relevant experience when background materials are reviewed quickly in front of the candidate.

During the interview

Your carefully prepared questions help maintain control during the interview. Here are additional guidelines.

Establish rapport. Small talk at the start of an interview can help put the candidate at ease. Comment on a résumé item, such as a hobby you have in common or a place you have both lived. Be careful, though, not to let the interview get too far off track with extended discussion of, say, your football team.

Avoid conveying the response sought. Suppose you try to determine a candidate's ability to work with other tellers, all working in a relatively small area. You ask, 'Will you be able to work well with other tellers, especially given our space constraints?' A bright interviewee realises quickly, from your question, the answer you are seeking and replies, 'Of course, no problem'. A better approach would be: 'We all sometimes have unpleasant experiences with co-workers. Tell me about the most difficult time you ever had working with someone else'.

Listen and take notes. Be sure to do a great deal of listening. Experts recommend the interviewer talk for 20 to 30 per cent of the time and allow the interviewee to talk for 70 to 80 per cent. You need to learn as much as you can about the candidate in the available time. So take notes to help remember important points.

Ask only job-relevant questions. Interviewers can stray into asking potentially discriminatory questions. One example is asking a female applicant the type of work her spouse does. Such a question is discriminatory since it is rarely asked of a male candidate and is irrelevant to job requirements or the person's qualifications. The best policy is to ask only questions clearly and directly related to job requirements.

After the interview

Write a short report right after the interview, scoring the candidate on the characteristics you identified as important to effective job functioning. Briefly indicate your rationale, using examples or summaries of responses. By documenting your ratings right after the interview, you will have good data to help your selection decision.

Source: Based on Janz, Hellervik & Gilmore (1986); Jenks & Zevnik (1989); Gatewood & Feild (1990).

 # Who rates the high rates?   case in point

Chris Anderson, chief executive of Cable and Wireless Optus, states that when he joined Optus in August 1997, he made sure executives are measured on performance. At Optus, all staff own shares and get part of their bonus in the form of shares. That way everyone is conscious of the share price of the company. That is important to the company because it makes staff feel more responsible for what the share price is doing.

This process forms part of the issues around the salary packages for chief executives. Much of the attention on chief executives' salaries comes after publicity in the business media. In the past four years, more than half of the top 50 listed companies in Australia have changed leaders. This trend is expected to continue as most chief executives here are said to be overpaid. Hart Consulting contends that targets are set too soft, and that incentives are being paid regardless of whether or not performances are measuring up.

What makes a good value chief executive? Hilmer of Fairfax says that the key is to keep moving the company forward aggressively and keep costs under control. Morris of Computershare says that a chief executive should be able to balance work and family life, focus on long-term issues rather than short-term shareholder return, and understand the importance of globalisation.

Source: Adapted from Ferguson, A., & De Clercq, K. (1999).

Activities for discussion, analysis and further research

1 Research the salary packages of senior chief executives and draw some conclusions regarding the links between the reward package and the performance measures.

2 Research the manner used by small and large organisations to develop remuneration packages for staff at various levels.

✖ Narrowing options

crossroads

Consider the Tripac story in Chapter 10. From the employer's perspective, this is a rosy tale. However, from the perspective of the Australian Manufacturing Workers' Union (AMWU) this is perceived as another nail in the coffin of workers' rights. The state organiser for the union describes the development as a nightmare for those who worked there. During the Email sale staff had good jobs with good conditions and pay but the sale suddenly placed them in jeopardy. Staff could not refuse contracts with EL Blue because the current industrial relations legislation meant they would not get the dole if they had knocked back a job offer.

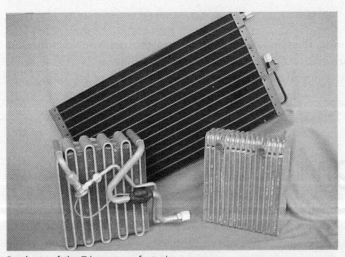

Products of the Tripac manufacturing company.

The Tripac strategy meant that there was effectively a union membership shut out. The company had stopped taking payroll deductions for union membership. Consequently, membership of the union decreased from 99 per cent to 10 per cent.

Because these strategies are acceptable within the Howard Government's industrial relations laws, the union is focusing on the issue of workers' privacy. It claims that worker information about staff already held by the previous employer, which should have remained private, was unfairly passed on to EL Australia by unknown parties.

Many of the staff are employed as casuals and do not receive the usual benefits that permanent staff receive. The factory's permanent workforce has decreased form 120 to 60 members.

The union contends that workers need to be very guarded and to make sure that there are clauses in their enterprise agreements to stop their jobs being contracted out.

Source: Adapted from Tabakoff, N. (1999).

Reflection points

1 Investigate the changes to industrial relations legislation and discuss what would have happened to workers who did not wish to undertake contracts with EL Blue prior to the new legislation.
2 What do you think of the denial of choice embedded in the new legislation?

Decision point

1 What can the AMWU do to ensure continued membership under the new work conditions?

MAINTAINING THE EMPLOYMENT RELATIONSHIP

Remuneration and benefits

This section deals with employee pay and benefits. In Australia the pay component of an organisation is referred to as 'remuneration', whereas in the US it is known as 'compensation'. Since compensation in Australia is associated with payment of wages or salaries to workers injured in workplace accidents, we refer to pay as 'remuneration' rather than 'compensation'. **Remuneration**, in this context, is financial payments to employees in return for work.

Remuneration has direct links with job analysis, in correctly identifying task functions and groupings which can then be valued. It is also linked to recruitment and selection. The value of positions has to be linked with remuneration offered to successful applicants. Having attracted and selected appropriately skilled people, it is necessary to reward them so they will accept the job, but not pay them so much the organisation loses money through weight of salaries and wages paid to employees.

Remuneration links to the regulatory framework, in that pay rates are often determined after negotiations between employer and employee representatives collectively or with the employee directly. Negotiated awards and enterprise agreements specify minimum rates to be paid to workers, as well as conditions within which they work. Individual contracts are legally binding and specify rates of pay and services to be performed for that pay.

Remuneration links to training and development. Organisations can offer lower-than-average wages or salaries if they can offer unique benefits and training or development opportunities otherwise unavailable. Alternatively they may be willing to accept high turnover rates if there are plenty of potential candidates and positions involve low skill-levels. Some call centres and commission pay jobs fall into this category.

As salaries can be more than 60 per cent of an organisation's costs, they should try to have some form of regularly reviewed salary system. A major purpose of salary systems is to achieve internal and external pay relativity.

remuneration

The financial payment to employees in return for their work

Internal relativity comes when salaries or wages are remunerated at levels where employees believe they are being paid a reasonable rate relative to other workers in other jobs within the organisation. External relativity is achieved when wage and salary rates for employees are comparable with rates paid by external organisations.

This does not mean all organisations try to pay the same as everyone else. If an organisation wishes to set up a reputation as a market leader, both in terms of product and service, then the organisation may choose to pay above average wages or salaries to attract and retain suitably skilled employees. Conversely if an organisation pays below market rates, an organisation would have to accept a high turnover or have a strategy to retain employees (due to non-salary benefits or unique work opportunities).

Training and development

Organisations must attract and retain an adequate supply of people with skills and competencies to meet organisational objectives. They have three choices in employee selection:

1 They can select employees who already have the skills and competencies necessary to achieve organisational objectives.
2 They can select employees with the ability to acquire necessary skills and competencies.
3 They can have a mixture of the two.

training

The process of equipping people with skills and competencies in a systematic manner

development

To broadly prepare the employee for future opportunities through the acquisition of new knowledge, skills and attitudes

Each option will impact on the amount and type of training offered in the organisation or acquired from external sources. **Training** is the equipping of people with skills and competencies systematically, while **development** aims to broadly prepare employees for future opportunities through acquisition of new knowledge, skills and attitudes. The aim of training is to increase skills, knowledge and competencies to be able to better achieve performance objectives. It is usually structured, may be formal, informal, on or off the job, during or after work hours. Training is directly related to recruitment and selection, and is linked to performance management and review.

Clark (1992) states that there are three broad strategic rationales for training. They are as follows:

1 The *proactive approach*—This is designed to meet a company's long-term objectives and to anticipate rather than react to organisation needs.
2 *Reactive approaches*—These are usually driven and prompted by immediate problems which could, if not addressed, adversely impact on the achievement of performance objectives.
3 *Enhancement of employee motivation, commitment and retention*—In this way, training is motivational. It is a means whereby employee expectations can be met, of providing career pathways, improving job security and increasing job satisfaction.

One of the most significant influences on how training is viewed within Australia has been the Karpin Report. In 1995, David Karpin chaired a task force with a brief to:

○ analyse Australia's current situation and performance from a management perspective;
○ consider how Australia's performance compared with what was happening in the rest of the world;
○ examine current trends and future changes in Australia's business environment;
○ consider the inevitable challenges Australia will be facing in the next decade; and

O propose strategies for change to help position Australia for strong international competitiveness by 2010.

Karpin released the task force report which found that:

> Australian enterprises, training providers and educational institutions are not moving quickly enough to address the new paradigm of management. Many of their counterparts overseas, and especially the leaders in various fields of industry and education, are changing more rapidly and more extensively, and will be better prepared for the next century.

The report identified that, by 2010, organisations will be learning organisations, with leaders encouraging learning within the organisation. Likewise, managers will be result-driven MBA graduates who, having completed several overseas job tasks, will need to cope with significant pressure while delegating to an internationally based workforce.

The Karpin Report issued five key challenges that the task force believed would influence development of management skills. They were:

O a positive enterprise based culture, through education;
O upgrading vocational education and training and business services;
O capitalising on talents of diversity;
O achieving best-practice management development; and
O reforming management education institutions

The heavy emphasis on management development, education and utilising workforce diversity in these five key challenges for Australian business emphasised the extent to which training and development contributes to organisation success.

Caudron (2000a) reports one of the biggest challenges organisations face is that, while CEOs are sold on learning, they do not see a link between training and business performance. Training has failed to demonstrate its impact upon the bottom line, been limited by compartmentalised content-based solutions and often operates in isolation, failing to understand core business or to establish links with the core mission. Caudron believes the challenge for organisations is to embed learning into core business processes. This can be achieved by:

O linking training objectives to business strategy, ensuring everyone is pointed in the same direction;
O addressing corporate culture—to create long-lasting organisational change trainers can't ignore the influence of corporate culture;
O focusing on outcomes, not activities;
O de-emphasising 'classroom' training and emphasising learning on the job;
O allowing employees time to process what they've learned; and
O demanding the same strategic change in practices from training suppliers as expected from within the organisation.

When linked to corporate strategy and organisational objectives, training and development can help organisations improve their ability to respond to rapidly changing environments. They can become critical to achievement of an organisation's core business objectives, but must move from an activity-focused event to outcomes-based integrated learning opportunities.

HiTech Personnel

Ray Hazouri started the company in 1993. His brother Sam became general manager in 1996. Both have backgrounds in information technology. When Ray Hazouri first tried to get a job as a programmer in the 1980s, the recruitment companies asked 'all the wrong questions'. He moved into information technology management roles and when he went back to recruitment agencies to find staff, nothing had changed. Hazouri decided to become an information technology personnel specialist.

Hazouri was disadvantaged by launching the business during a recession. His first strategy was to target blue-chip companies but he found they were shedding staff. It was flexible, small and medium enterprises that were growing and hiring, so he shifted the company's marketing focus.

HiTech solves a communication problem between information technology people and the rest of the world. The company consults technical staff as well as human-resources staff and management before recruiting. Technical staff may specify a position title and assume knowledge that human resources staff and managers do not have. What HiTech does is hone in on those assumptions. HiTech helps some clients write job specifications. The company makes its own assessment of the appropriate job titles before recruiting.

Sam Hazouri says the company's turnover doubled in the past twelve months. The company will open offices in Sydney, Brisbane and Melbourne this year. From day one, HiTech used the Internet as well as print media to recruit, but two years ago Hazouri changed the balance. All placements are now advertised over the Net. HiTech takes initial details from clients and candidates on line.

Hazouri predicts a flurry of mergers and acquisitions as the industry consolidates, driven in part by the need to recruit globally to find qualified candidates. The Internet will be the dominant medium for information technology recruitment.

Some members of the information technology personnel specialists, HiTech.

Source: Adapted from *BRW* (15 March 1999).

Activities for discussion, analysis and further research

1 Discuss the recruitment strategies used by HiTech to satisfy the needs of both the clients and the candidates.
2 How did changing the marketing focus of the organisation assist HiTech in achieving its goals?
3 Find the Web address of HiTech and log on to investigate how they carry out the initial recruitment contact. Is this a good way of recruiting staff? Why?

Performance appraisal

Performance appraisal is the process of appraising the job performance of employees. Clark (1992) identifies five reasons for appraising performance:

- O to mould employee behaviour according to company-determined norms;
- O to enhance consistency between employee actions and corporate goals;
- O to improve quality of human resource planning, in particular training and succession;
- O to improve quality of salary reviews; and
- O to provide a record in cases of dismissal, demotion, grievance or appeal.

Traditional appraisals are usually performed by line managers. The human resource department has a role in designing the system, training end-users and collecting and collating data from appraisals (Clark 1992).

Supporters of appraisal argue it serves as a key link in the human resource management system. Performance appraisal is linked to other human resource functions in the following way:

- O Job analysis provides job descriptions and criteria to which jobs are to be performed. These are the criteria by which an employee's performance can be judged.
- O Job requirements and employee duties are communicated during recruitment and selection process. Performance appraisal processes should align with criteria communicated at the time (unless later reviewed and agreed by employee and manager).
- O Performance appraisals may help identify effectiveness of both job analysis and recruitment and selection processes. Consistent failures in a position may identify weaknesses in either determination of job components or adequacy of applicants chosen to do the job.
- O Performance appraisal gives a rationale for an organisation's remuneration system. In some organisations there is a direct link between performance and pay, performance and promotion or performance and bonuses.
- O Performance appraisal links into training and development by identifying skills and knowledge deficits.
- O Appraisal outcomes may be the basis of instituting disciplinary action against an employee. If dismissal procedures are instituted, managers must ensure regulatory requirements for appropriate dismissal are followed.

Performance appraisal methods   The forms of performance assessment fall into the following categories:

> observations
> demonstration and questioning
> pen and paper tests and essays
> oral tests
> projects
> simulations
> portfolios
> computer-based assessments

As with methods used in recruitment and selection, performance appraisal methods must be:

- O valid—measure what they say they measure
- O reliable—consistent and repeatable
- O fair and equitable—not disadvantage any group

performance appraisal

A judgmental process of the job performance of employees

Critics of performance appraisal point to levels of dissatisfaction with the process by employees and lack of adequate skills of managers to effectively perform fair and equitable appraisals.

Employees are often dissatisfied with performance management system methods and managers are frequently reluctant to engage in a process which communicates levels of dissatisfaction with performance. The process may enforce an unhappy employee's compliance. Problems may also occur if individual appraisals are performed on team members who operate interdependently.

Organisations usually undertake appraisals for two purposes: to identify pay/bonus/promotion opportunities and to provide feedback linked to developmental opportunities. However, these purposes can be counterproductive, which is why it is recommended the two processes be completed separately, with the first to assess any developmental or training needs and the second to assess whether or not performance warrants increased or decreased salary and bonuses. As a result of these criticisms and difficulties, interest is growing in the process of 360-degree feedback.

360-degree feedback Traditional appraisal systems reinforce a hierarchical approach to organisations—managers appraise supervisors who appraise employees. This approach assumes the more senior person is the only one able to provide feedback. 360-degree feedback begins with the belief that it is useful to receive feedback not only from one's immediate supervisor but from peers and subordinates. The collection of ratings or views from subordinates, peers and supervisors are collated to provide a multi-source means of assessment.

The feedback from different appraiser groups or categories provides different perspectives and insights into how an employee is seen to be performing at different levels in an organisation. Benefits come from having a larger sample of appraisals and opportunity to represent outcomes graphically. Where the employees rate themselves, graphical outcomes give useful starting points in discussing perceived strengths, weaknesses, similarities and differences. There are, however, problems with maintaining anonymity in small groups or teams and ensuring adequate training in the system's use.

HRIS, INTERNET, INTRANETS AND EXTRANETS

An early function of the human resource department was collection and storage of employee details. This data was needed to meet legislative requirements or for use in transaction processing. Originally stored in hard copies on paper files, this data eventually found its way onto computer databases which processed transactions more easily and quickly. Again, reactively, reports could be generated identifying cost breakdowns, cumulative totals and exception reports on issues such as pay, leave entitlements and sick leave taken. It was not until database systems began to manipulate data into quality information linking data to organisational objectives that these computerised systems began to allow human resource management departments to operate strategically.

Information technology's impact on business continues to outpace other forms of organisational change. Access to stored databases and knowledge bases has increased with convergence of the Internet, intranets and extranets. The **Internet** is a global connection of computer servers interconnected by telecommunication systems through which individuals can access stored information from their own computer and modem. **Intranets** are closed networks of information databases and systems within an individual organisation, whereas **extranets** are closed networks of information systems between a group of organisations.

Coupled with the explosion in the use of e-mail, these changes are significantly impacting on HRM. Organisations are adopting Web-based strategies because of benefits of platform independence, access to wide-ranging information and potential to access information-rich multimedia files. The Internet is a powerful business tool because it represents a convergence of closed network intranets within an organisation and extranet closed networks between organisations. The issue for HR departments is to find how these networks can help them provide improved service provision, cost savings and value-added services.

Networks can deliver the following HR services:

O improved internal communication (speed and consistency of message, collaborative groups, etc.);

O distribution of HR policy, news and information and employee surveys;

O training and development activities on-line;

O recruitment over the Internet;

O HR self-service—employees accessing and changing personal details, travel bookings and claims, etc.;

O 360-degree feedback and traditional performance monitoring data input; and

O collaborative work groups independent of location or time zone

There are also other possibilities. The list only represents forms of transaction processing. To become more flexible and competitive, companies are moving from legacy information systems to integrated business management systems. Companies use enterprise-wide systems (such as PeopleSoft and SAP) to streamline business processes and improve information sharing to compete in the rapidly evolving business world. Human resource management systems are an important component of integrated software. Today, they drive recruiting, payroll systems, employee databases, succession planning benefits calculations and workflow solutions. But these systems' success hinges on many complex factors and involves more than the technical expertise of HR and information technology departments. The organisation's historical focus has typically been one of relatively narrow HR and IS issues, rather than on the larger business context. Without a core platform and a central strategy to drive decisions about hardware, software and work processes, the entire organisation can find itself shackled with automated inefficiency. Organisations must focus on the new systems' strategic contribution to achieving business objectives, and recognise HR's vital role as an active business partner with senior management and a critical service provider to business units.

Despite its benefits, introducing information technology into HR brings its own challenges. With widespread take-up of e-mail, there is a need to develop clear and comprehensive policies on access, use and misuse of e-mail (see Supplement 3 for Chapter 16). Legal issues arise when employees use e-mail to distribute pornography to unsuspecting recipients or to harass or threaten. Other legal issues emerge if organisations move to dismiss these employees without having established clear policies, communicated them and followed regulatory guidelines for dismissals. Privacy issues arise in terms of access to confidential data. Copyright and intellectual property rights are an issue when material is developed on the Internet or when material is used from the Internet.

Internet

A global connection of computer servers interconnected by telecommunication systems through which individuals can access stored information from their own computer and modem

intranets

Closed networks of information databases and systems within an individual organisation

extranets

Closed networks of information systems between a group of organisations

@ E-how turns knowledge into power

Courtney Rosen spent frustrating hours searching fruitlessly for advice on how to fix in-line skates. Rosen's insight was that though the Internet has a lot of information, it had little advice. Consequently, she quit her job at Anderson Consulting to create Ehow, a new Web site offering step-by-step instructions in everything imaginable. Unveiled in August 1999, Ehow lists more than 4000 'e-how' tutorials and hundreds more are being produced every week. Each 'e-how' ends with a list of items needed for the task and links to sites where the items can be purchased.

Many of the efforts are aimed at building communities of value, the Web phrase that is supposed to give you a better valuation than the earlier 'site stickiness'. For all of Ehow's high tech helpfulness, the real power lies in the old-fashioned sell. Ehow's how-to blurbs build interest, give people confidence in the outcomes, and make it easier for them to buy.

Source: Hardy, Q. (1999).

Activities for discussion, analysis and further research

1 Log onto the Ehow and determine to what degree it is effective in giving instructions for a problem of your choice.
2 Describe how this site might be of use to managers.

THE FUTURE OF WORK

Widespread use of flexible working arrangements has given functional and numerical flexibility. This flexibility has given major benefits to business and to those employees able to maintain a job, but has led to reduced labour demand in industries applying such practices. There has also been a trend to reduce numbers of core, permanent employees and increase numbers of part-time, casual or temporary employees.

Organisations have also attempted to have a more flexible workforce through teleworking. Teleworking enables workers to work remotely using telecommunications, but rather than being the final form of flexible work, teleworking is only one option among others. Even within teleworkers, there is a difference between skilled managers and professionals with freedom to choose when and where work activities are to be completed, and unskilled data-entry or call-centre employees whose work is highly structured, regulated and supervised.

Hotdesking is another way organisations are trying to respond to changing work demands more flexibly and efficiently. The term refers to removal of dedicated individual workspaces and offices, which are replaced by desks booked on demand. Supporting files, facilities and documents are also scheduled and delivered. Some organisations are redesigning workspaces to enable individuals to work collaboratively, combining software solutions with furniture facilitating group or collaborative work.

Temporary agency work, short-term hires, regular part-time work, on-call workers and contract workers have been used to deal with workload fluctuations or absences, and these are likely to increase in future. In addition, firms are increasingly using agency-placed contingent and contract workers. What we are seeing is use of contract workers for highly skilled occupational groups such as engineers, computer analysts and architectural services. Other areas also growing include management and public relations, research and development and scientific testing services. Use of personnel supply firms are increasing for lower-skilled workers such as administrative support workers and helpers, with firms relying on temporary help to supply workers in occupations such as office and clerical work, for which firm-specific skills are not usually needed.

Caudron (2000b) reports a consequence of these changes is that traditional jobs are often too rigid for today's workplaces. Job classifications and descriptions, pay structures and promotion charts are disappearing from new-style organisations. Koch Industries and Amazon.com have both abandoned traditional human resource structures. The customary way a person is hired, paid and trained to do a specific job is too rigid for an ever-changing marketplace.

As a result, new work relationships will be established between employer and employee. Traditional employment relationships previously based on exclusivity ('you are *my* employee', 'this is *my* job') and on permanence of employment, have previously led to situations where those employees remaining from downsizing exercises face an increased workload to cover for missing employees. In the current environment of rapid change, this attitude to job ownership is flawed. Organisations are increasingly required to adapt their employment relationships from one of fixed designated jobs to relationships based on flexible project demands. Employees must embrace a work future closer to an independent contractor than an employee, and employers will have to view their workforce as a dynamic mix of currently required skills and knowledge, not a fixed establishment of dedicated employees.

While this is no different from how some professional service groups operate now, such as IT, engineering and legal services, the challenge for future organisations is to translate this model to the wider workplace. It does not stop employees being engaged in a full-time capacity, but changes the criteria for engaging them.

The biggest hurdle for organisations is in moving from being a traditional employer to a flexible employer of knowledge and services. It requires expertise to successfully transform the organisation and establish new human resource policies and procedures. It also assumes the organisation can accurately forecast its needs and manage the workforce.

Many organisations would like to engage and disengage workers as needed, but are constrained by factors such as limited resources to manage such variable demands, legislative constraints or unionised workforces. Likewise employees may still seek full-time employment for fear of being unable to locate enough 'work on demand' and be unemployed for long periods.

Flexible employing organisations

Companies reducing their workforces as a straight downsizing exercise are unlikely to get medium-to-long term benefits. Downsizing not linked to a strategic plan is likely to result in greater staff hire costs to make up for lost skills. In these circumstances companies need to manage flexible staffing requirements from a strategic, rather than from a cost-minimisation perspective. Rather than seeking last minute short-term low-skilled employees, successful organisations will form strategic alliances with staffing agencies to guarantee supply of skilled and reliable contract and temporary staff. These agencies will offer one-stop shopping for business solutions and staffing services, and a broader service range including contract and temporary hires, payroll administration, human resource and training services.

Flexible employees

In a climate of scarce full-time jobs, high unemployment and changing job markets, searching for a full-time position with one employer becomes daunting. For many, the only option has been to go into business themselves, either in a small business or as consultants. The difficulty is that traditional employment markets see these people working very long hours for little return. An alternative is for the person to contract themselves to a staffing agency, offering their knowledge, skills and time to major projects on a full-time basis or to multiple small jobs in different companies. This is the same principle as working as a consultant, except they may work as part of a project team supervised by the staffing agency or provide services to multiple employers sourced and supervised by the staffing agency.

To maintain their value to the agency, it is in the workers' interests to maintain and upgrade their skills by training. Worker loyalty to the agency can be based on receipt of pro-rata benefits such as leave and health insurance. Handy (Ettorre 1996) refers to this as the development of 'portfolio workers', of selling a package of skills to their employer or clients. But where Handy fears these workers will work longer and harder, reducing their productive capacity as they age, this is less likely if organisations adopt these flexible work arrangements as a norm, and where workers feel confident to set their own level of time or work commitment to the agency, by limiting the hours they will contract themselves for.

Although these portrayals of flexible workplaces and employees are major challenges to current beliefs about work and employment, they only focus on the most obvious aspects of work changes in the future. A complete analysis of future work should consider the more complex issues of the inevitable dislocations of workers whose skills and knowledge become redundant as we move through a transition from traditional to new work systems and practices.

TERMINATING THE EMPLOYMENT RELATIONSHIP

Because the employment relationship is a legal contract between employer and employee, it is necessary to consider how the relationship is terminated. This section of the chapter deals with both voluntary and involuntary forms of termination and their implications for human resource management.

Voluntary termination involves employees giving an agreed minimum notice of intention to leave the employment relationship. Reasons for voluntary termination include resignation and retirement. Resignation may be due to the employee being offered another job, changed personal circumstances allowing them to leave employment, dissatisfaction with the existing job or as part of a voluntary redundancy offer. Voluntary redundancy involves an employer reducing the workforce size by asking employees to voluntarily leave the employment relationship, usually in return for an improved termination pay package. Retirement involves the employee reaching a specified age where they are eligible to retire and access super-annuation savings and/or any relevant pension scheme. Compulsory retirement, once widely practised, is now considered discriminatory and hence illegal.

Involuntary termination includes retrenchment, redundancy and dismissal. **Retrenchment** refers to the forced termination of the employment relationship due to financial, technological or organisational circumstances, and often reflects an attempt by an employer to reduce labour costs in order to remain in business. **Redundancy** is also a forced termination of the employment relationship but results from the permanent deletion of specific positions within an organisation due to the positions no longer being required. **Dismissal** is where the employer gives the required notice to terminate the employment relationship. Legal dismissal may be as a result of disciplinary action over time, or may be immediate if due to a serious breach of the employment contract, such as wilful damage to property, significant theft or violent behaviour toward other workers.

Various forms of legislation provide the basis for determining whether involuntary terminations are either legal or illegal. In Australia, the provisions for unfair dismissal instituted by the Australian Labor Party in 1993 were often criticised as being biased in favour of employees, making it extremely difficult to dismiss someone. The provisions of the current federal and NSW state legislation have established the principle of a 'fair go all round', meaning that all factors need to be considered in determining if the dismissal was fair (hence legal) or unfair (hence illegal).

The termination phase of the employment relationship raises a number of issues for human resource management. Organisations require sufficient knowledge and skill to be able to determine when dismissal is warranted and how it should be enacted. They also need to be aware of any provisions under existing industrial award or enterprise bargaining agreements dealing with retrenchments and redundancies, as well as the financial cost involved in settling retrenchment and redundancy cases.

From a more general perspective, organisations need to monitor and review the nature and extent of terminations. In addition to maintaining computerised HR systems, organisations often institute exit interviews for voluntary terminations, being the final interview immediately prior to or just after separation from the organisation. The interview is an opportunity to review the reasons for leaving and may also be used to offer counselling or assistance in finding a new job.

Some organisations engage out-placement consultants to provide a range of services to employees who are leaving or are being retrenched. Services may include career counselling, résumé preparation and advice, serviced office facilities and, in some cases, finding alternate employment. The cost involved for organisations undertaking such services can be returned many times over by the good will established with those employees leaving and in their consequent description of the organisation in public.

Finally the rate of employees leaving an organisation will influence the level of activity in other phases of human resource management. When employees leave, an organisation has the choice of either recruiting new replacements or reallocating work within the remaining employees. Either way, if staff turnover is excessive, those remaining are likely to suffer, as is the organisation's ability to achieve its objectives.

retrenchment

The forced termination of the employment relationship due to financial, technological or organisational circumstances, often reflecting an attempt by an employer to reduce labour costs in order to remain in business

redundancy

A forced termination of the employment relationship resulting from the permanent deletion of specific positions within an organisation due to the positions no longer being required

dismissal

The employer giving the required notice to terminate the employment relationship

■ The MD's diary

Our HR policy is driven by two things—firstly the strategy and the needs of the organisation. And we try to focus on policy and not on the organisation as it stands today but we are really quite focused on making sure that we have in place an HR policy that will provide the organisation that we need in three years' time, typically. Our view is that we must be setting up an organisation that will deliver what we need into the future, and the quality of people and their ability to grow must be consistent with that. Our view is that if we do that it means that we will be forced to recruit and develop people that probably have a greater capability than the organisation needs today. And our thinking is that it will do two important things for us. Firstly, it will give us the type of organisational skills that we need in three years' time. Secondly it will give us a capable work force today that will drive the strategy and drive the business growth that we need. So, my view is if we employ the people we will need in the future, then those people are going to be much more capable of driving and achieving those outcomes in the meantime.

The other thing that concerns me is the career opportunities that you can offer people. My feeling is that within most jobs for the more capable, more career minded individuals, you struggle to maintain enthusiasm in a position beyond three years—it seems to be the number—after three years, they're looking to move on; and if you are recruiting people you have to be able to have an organisation that will make sure that in three years' time they're still going to be challenged. If you can do that and do that well, then people who would normally think about continuing their career elsewhere will stay. In terms of our policies on the way we want to treat people, it is aimed at the same thing. It is aimed at making sure that people are motivated, that they're committed and that their contribution is recognised and rewarded because it is important to us that we can retain skills we have. We are working in an industry where innovation in technology is moving very very quickly, and it's not possible to continue to bring people up from scratch to keep pace with that so we do need to retain good people. So we look at ways to make sure that they are motivated, that they are challenged and that they can grow. Hence our policy of providing flexible position descriptions and flexible roles for them so that people can grow at the rate they are capable of. Our job is then to make sure that we take out all the blockages to that development, that we continue to stretch people, that we continue to find opportunities for them, that we continue to develop them.

Succession planning is a key strategy of our HR policy. It's not something that I think we are doing particularly well, but its something we're very focused on. In essence our HR philosophy is to position our organisation where we want to be in the future, and not where we want to be today. We need to continue to develop our people internally so that they can take up some of the more senior roles in the future. Our succession planning is not restricted to senior levels. We try to push that strategy right through the organisation. We are not interested in creating two sets of policies depending on whether you work on the shop floor progressing a less ambitious career or whether you are in senior management. We try to break down the inner barriers between the organisational levels. Everyone works to the same set of rules; there are no lines of demarcation between functions or between levels of the organisation. Wherever possible we are providing the same sorts of development opportunities to the shop floor level that we are to more senior levels of management. All our people recognise that there is a career opportunity with Autoliv if they want it. They all have the chance to access training programs and they are all encouraged to take as much responsibility as they feel comfortable with, and hopefully that reflects in some committed, high performance individuals who see a long-term career opportunity at Autoliv.

■ The subordinate's log

The organisation had a very open hiring policy in that there was no limit to background. The CEO expressed the opinion that a diversity of backgrounds was highly valuable to the firm.

The organisation size meant that we did not have an HR specialist and staff recruitment and selection was for the most part in the hands of senior people. Sales and marketing staff were finally vetted by the CEO as he saw those specifically as crucial to the organisation. Recruitment was done historically in house, but more recently, a personnel firm was employed to handle it. Salary and benefits were flexible. Once an overall package was agreed, its structure was developed to suit the employee. The working hours policy was flexible also, acknowledging that people worked hard and were able to schedule their own hours. A flexi-time approach was practised.

The organisation did not have a consistent reward policy. The marketing staff had to have a very good year to get any bonuses, and incentives were not effective as they were very difficult to achieve. The consultants themselves had a bonus structure if they could acquire more business, but effectively that was rarely paid because it was difficult to determine exactly who was responsible, as things were generally a team effort. Team incentives were considered at one stage but never implemented.

When a new employee was recruited, they were interviewed by as many of the staff as were available to participate, as it was felt that 'fit' within the organisation was exceptionally important, given the long pressured hours which staff worked together. If any member of staff felt strongly against the candidate, that person was not employed.

Focus on practice—Strategies for improving

1 Human resource planning processes are the key to maintaining the right skills mix. Consider a position in an organisation of your choice and attempt to plan and analyse the skills which will be required by the person doing this job in 15 years.
2 List the selection criteria and tools you might use to select the appropriate candidate for the job mentioned above in 15 years' time.
3 Design steps to carry out an informal performance review for the job mentioned above.
4 Treat employees with respect and consideration when giving any manner of feedback after performance appraisal. Consider how you might give negative feedback for unsatisfactory performance in a respectful and considerate manner.

Source: Jones et al. (2000).

Chapter summary

Human resource management is an integral part of the management of any organisation. In broad terms it involves the management of three phases of the employment relationship: establishing the relationship; by acquiring human resources; maintaining the relationship; and managing the termination of the relationship. These functions occur within an organisational context at the same time as interacting with a regulatory and environmental context.

Industrial relations systems are part of the regulatory context, inputting directly into the way in which the terms and conditions of employment are established. These systems were shown to influence human resource management functions through legislative and regulatory intervention. Other forms of legislation govern aspects of safety, environmental management, discrimination and equal opportunity within an organisation.

Human resource planning involves determining future human resource needs in relation to an organisation's business objectives or strategic plan, then devising ways to meet these objectives. Job analysis is an important component that helps establish human resource needs and produces position descriptions and specifications. Job descriptions allow an organisation to accurately describe the job to potential applicants, and job specifications provide important decision criteria when making a selection from candidates for the job. Job analysis can be used to improve job design and redesign, performance appraisal, remuneration and training and development. When used appropriately it forms the basis upon which an organisation ensures that organisational objectives are met.

Recruitment and selection processes ensure that an organisation is able to attract suitable applicants and to then decide which applicants best contribute to organisational objectives. Advantages and disadvantages have been identified in both internal and external recruitment, with the final choice contingent upon the organisational circumstances.

Maintaining employment relationships involves active processes aimed at aligning employee effort with organisational goals. Human resource management functions in this phase include establishing appropriate remuneration levels that take into account internal and external relativities. Managers need to ensure that the work effort of employees is effectively managed and evaluated and that feedback is provided in an accurate and unbiased manner. Training and development provides an opportunity for an organisation to increase the ability of its employees to perform efficiently and effectively.

Attempts by organisations to increase the flexibility of their workforce, and hence to increase its effectiveness and efficiency, has greatly influenced the way in which the workforce is defined. Increasing use of part-time and casual employees is changing the nature of the workforce, while trends such as teleworking and hot-desking are additional examples of flexible organisations.

Information technology impacts on the ability of organisations to harness the knowledge and expertise of its employees. The Internet, intranets and extranets are all being utilised to improve organisational knowledge and capacity, while computerised human resource systems are contributing to the strategic capacity of the organisation.

Organisations need to manage carefully the final phase of the employment relationship. Organisations must have systems in place by which terminations occur effectively and legally. Managers and supervisors require skills to ensure that their own performance as managers does not contribute to staff turnover or place the organisation at risk of prosecution for unfair dismissal.

Finally, changes in the flow of human resources through an organisation will have an impact on other human resource management functions. Increased turnover rates will have an impact upon those employees remaining, and on the need for increased numbers of new employees. Increased employee recruits will influence productivity, impact upon resources and may generate additional training demands.

Questions for discussion and review

1 Describe what impact the changes to Australia's industrial relations system since 1987 have had on the relationship between management, unions and employees. How has the election of the Liberal/National Party Coalition in 1996 changed these relationships?
2 Define job analysis and describe how it relates to other human resource functions, especially recruitment and selection, performance appraisal, remuneration and training.

3 The chapter noted the emergence of internet-based recruitment sites. Outline and discuss the benefits and pitfalls for managers and for applicants of this new form of recruitment.

4 Define and explain reliability and validity in the selection of new staff.

5 Identify the factors that allow assessment centres to provide good predictions of job performance. Discuss why the process is not used more often.

6 What would be the human resource implications for an organisation that did not maintain internal relativity for its remuneration system? Likewise, what human resource implications would there be for not maintaining external relativity?

7 What can organisations do to better integrate training and learning into core business functions? Discuss what organisational barriers exist to stop this from occurring.

8 Explain the benefits of 360 degree performance feedback over traditional performance appraisal processes.

9 Outline and discuss the impact of intranets and extranets on the three phases of attracting, maintaining and terminating human resources.

10 Debate the extent to which governments should impose conditions upon the termination of the employment relationship.

Exercises for managing in the 21st century

Exercise 1
Skill building: Linking HRM components with specific activities

Several important components of the human resource management process are listed below. Please match these components with the 15 specific activities/issues shown. Indicate the appropriate human resource management component by putting the first letter of that component in the appropriate blank.

Human resource management process components:

Selection	Human resource planning
Training and development	Performance appraisal
Compensation	Labour relations
Recruitment	

1 _____ Employees plan to organise
2 _____ Management by objectives
3 _____ Orientation, technical skill, management development
4 _____ Assessment centre
5 _____ Halo, contrast, leniency, severity, self-serving bias
6 _____ Job descriptions
7 _____ Job posting
8 _____ Skills inventory
9 _____ Replacement planning
10 _____ Interview
11 _____ Needs analysis
12 _____ Internal equity
13 _____ Realistic job preview
14 _____ Promotion
15 _____ Graphic rating scales

Exercise 2
Management exercise: Managing human resources in retail hardware

You have accepted a position as a department head in a large hardware store. The owner, and store manager, likes to involve others in decisions. During your job interviews, he mentioned that if you became a department head, he would seek your views on improving the store's human resource management. He is very interested in your input because he wants to open up other stores. (In fact, you took the job partly because you believe the expansion will help your career.)

The manager said he, with the assistant manager and nine other department heads, is planning to hold strategic planning meetings soon to consider the impact of human resources on expansion plans. He anticipates holding other meetings focusing on different human resource management aspects. He further states he wants to maintain a stimulating, challenging and exciting working environment.

From what you have learned, the store's 18 per cent annual growth and 15 per cent return on investment could be improved. In addition human resource management seems currently to be non-existent.

Questions

1 What issues will you suggest to consider as part of human resource planning?
2 What will you discuss about recruiting and selecting human resources?
3 What suggestions for training, performance appraisal and remuneration will you make?

 # From pill making to bread making   on the rim— in Singapore

One does not tend to associate Singapore with retrenchment. Rather the opposite is believed to be the case. Singapore has for years suffered an acute labour shortage which has necessitated the import of large numbers of foreign workers. These workers are needed particularly in the hospitality sector, as staff in hotels and restaurants. Others work as household help as maids and nannies. In order to use foreign workers, Singaporean employers must pay a monthly tariff to the government which is almost equal to the monthly pay of those individuals.

It is therefore not usual to discover cases of retrenchment and of workers needing to be retrained in order to remain employable. This was the case recently when SmithKline Beecham retrenched eleven of its pill-making workers. The issue of retrenchment and retraining is one that the National Trades Union Congress (NTUC) is taking very seriously. Consequently it has initiated an on-going program under the umbrella of the Skills Redevelopment Program (SRP) which is aimed at retraining older workers who often have little formal education.

This is a shift for the NTUC. In the past it would have assisted with negotiations on behalf of the workers to gain retrenchment benefits and then attempt to place them in new jobs. This was felt to be a short-term response. Now, the aim is to provide these individuals with new skills to ensure continued employability.

The scheme was launched in December 1996 with the goal of retraining 1500 people for jobs in the manufacturing sector. The retrenched SmithKline Beecham workers were the first batch of workers to take part in this initiative, their training preparing them for positions in the baking industry. Their course, a one-year basic bakery course at the Baking Industry Centre, carries a fee of S$28 000 per person which was paid by the four parties involved. Eighty percent came from the Skills Development Fund and the balance from SmithKline Beecham, NTUC and the trainees themselves.

This initiative marks the beginning of a new human resource era in Singapore, with the NTUC taking steps to negotiate with a number of companies so that workers may be retrained rather than retrenched into unemployability. Workers may be retrained and placed in different jobs within the same company, or equipped with the skills to access jobs in other industries, such as has been the case with the SmithKline Beecham group.

The NTUC expects to expand the program so that some workers might be retrained for the service industries, which are the ones for which foreign workers are mainly recruited.

Source: Adapted from Yap, E. (1997).

Activities for discussion, analysis and further research

1 Whose responsibility is it to ensure retraining for retrenched staff? Why is the Singapore government taking it on as their responsibility?
2 What are the implications for Singapore of organisations beginning to retrench staff when in certain industries there is such an acute shortage of labour that foreign workers are being imported?

 Faulding   going global

The Faulding company is one of South Australia's success stories. Faulding was established on Rundle Street in Adelaide by Francis Hardy Faulding in 1845. It developed a variety of products such as soluble eucalyptus oil (Solyptol) in 1887 and, on the government's request, it created a barrier cream in 1941 for industrial dermatitis. Faulding made Penicillin commercially available to the Australian public in 1943. Since its humble beginnings, Faulding has expanded its business into three related complementary areas. It has become increasingly global with its activities and today operates in over 70 countries, employing over 4000 people (http.//www.faulding.com).

Faulding is a dynamic company and an excellent example to any business. It has maintained strong levels of growth over the years, through innovation and intelligent management. The company's image is one of 'gold'. The company's values include performance, creativity, teamwork, communication, empowerment and integrity. Creativity is especially valued, as innovation is considered essential in the company's future success. These values are aimed at achieving the company's mission, which can apply to all employees, defining their objective of 'Delivering innovative and valued solutions in health care'. Faulding acknowledges a social responsibility to the wider community and supports and sponsors a variety of events and awards. These awards are not only in the scientific field, but also in programs that benefit the wider community, such as the Adelaide Festival of Arts and student international exchange scholarships through AFS (American Field Service).

Over the past few years Faulding has reviewed its businesses in order to restructure the company into three main divisions. Control is improved with the clear distinction among these business areas. Business-level strategies must support the corporate-level strategy of differentiation through innovative products. Businesses were evaluated in respect to present and future profitability in the businesses' environment and their ability to contribute to the company's corporate strategy. Through this process new businesses were acquired, while some were closed down. For instance, the US-based medical-device business which developed the 'Safe Connect' valve and related products was considerably successful, yet was terminated as it did not fit in with Faulding's corporate strategy.

Twelve months following the completion of the restructure, 'business is booming'. Following the restructure, Faulding now consists of three main divisions, Faulding Healthcare, Faulding Oral Pharmaceuticals and Faulding Hospital.

One of the most important and time-consuming tasks in the restructure was the identification of potential in the US pharmaceuticals market. The company realised its opportunity to integrate the US Oral Pharmaceuticals business with Faulding. After buying out foreign owners, Faulding has been able to solely manage the business and incorporate it into the company. The acquisition has played a major role in the restructure of the company, making Faulding more efficient and effective in sharing resources and skills amongst their businesses.

Faulding boasts a competitive advantage of having the fastest product approval in the generic injectable-product industry. Faulding Hospital believes that the significant factor for streamlining this process has been its relationship with the approval agencies. Faulding Hospital had 15 products receive approval last financial year. This fast approval process attracts many other businesses to in-license products for Faulding to manage and market. Faulding Oral Pharmaceuticals and Faulding Healthcare also have fast approval rates.

Faulding Healthcare is the largest distributor of products to hospitals and community pharmacies in Australia. Faulding Retail, as part of Healthcare, has around 600 aligned pharmacies throughout Australia. The Faulding Healthcare sector contributed 78 per cent of the Group's sales and 49 per cent of the Company's total earnings before income tax. Healthcare CEO David Murphy attributes this success to having the courage to stick by long-term strategies 'aimed at developing an integrated business with strong brands'. Upgrading technology in several of the company's distribution complexes is believed to have also played a major role in the increased productivity. Some popular products in the consumer division include the 'Banana boat' suncream range and 'Betadine' dermaceutical products.

Faulding Oral Pharmaceuticals is one of the top ten producers of generic and value-added oral pharmaceutical products in the US. The business product approval rate is currently ranked seventh, however Intellectual Property Associate Terri Young states their aim is 'to be the first in future new drug approvals'. Faulding Oral Pharmaceuticals have benefited through Faulding's development and marketing skills. Since Faulding has owned the business, sales have increased by 16% while earnings before income tax rose from $43.7 million to $45.2 million.

Faulding Hospital Pharmaceuticals is one of the largest manufacturers of generic injectable cancer medicines in the world. The business has the widest geographical span for an injectable generic company. Faulding Hospital continues to focus on niche markets, while concentrating on adding value through established products. Faulding Hospital targets for growth include Latin America, where local distributors introduce Faulding's products. This way, products receive exposure at a low cost to Faulding, enabling it to assess its potential in the new market place. Faulding learns about each particular business environment by adopting a 'market by market approach'. The US is the world's largest market and a targeted new growth area for Faulding. It believes this can be achieved through regular new products and good customer relations.

Faulding has been strengthening its human resources through training and support. The responsibilities of managers have expanded while rewards to senior management and employees are based on specific targets being reached. Employee incentives for performance include performance payments or opportunities to invest in the company at a lower cost than the market price. This is important as it aligns personal and shareholder interests. Higher productivity has been recorded in most areas, especially in Mulgrave in Victoria, where 50 million units were recorded, which was double the output of five years ago. Sales of over $2 billion for the last financial year were recorded, with earnings before income tax figure in excess of $100 million.

A leadership initiative program has been developed for employees. The aim of this program is to strengthen existing management teams and develop skills for future management positions. Therefore, opportunities for leadership in management are developed within the company as well as through an external recruitment program. A 'Wellness strategy' has been adopted by the company which addresses the need for maintaining a healthy balance between work, family and personal needs. Faulding believes 'The quality of Faulding's people is demonstrated by the way in which significant structural chance has been smoothly implemented during the year'.

The Faulding Development sector includes operations in China, Soltec Research and Faulding's Innovation Group. Innovation is essential to a company like this. 'Faulding is rated as being among the Top 50 innovative Australian companies' (*Business Review Weekly* survey, 8 June 1998). It invests almost $50 million per year on research and development. This investment is considered necessary for the long-term sustainable growth of the company.

Faulding conducts a large portion of its research with the Commonwealth Scientific and Industrial Research Organisation (CSIRO). Combining resources they are able to develop breakthrough therapies and hence earn access to new product opportunities. New product development is also critical. Faulding is at the leading edge in technology with current projects including a gene therapy to treat prostate cancer. The Commonwealth Government has granted $90 000 to this project while Faulding has already spent over $2 million dollars of its own in research.

For the first time operations in the People's Republic of China have resulted in a small profit. The result was attributed to focus on improving 'Good manufacturing practice and cost control at the Foshan facility'. Operations in China are strategically important for Faulding, as within 15 years China is expected to be the third largest pharmaceutical market in the world.

Growth strategies over this vast company emphasise concentration, market development and horizontal integration. Faulding has organisational synergy, where the units of the company have a greater ability to succeed with the greater resources and skills available. When a new business is established overseas Faulding's products are made available through a distributor, and a local manager will be appointed to report constantly on the progress. This process is currently occurring in targeted countries all over the world, such as in Latin America and parts of Europe.

The primary objective for the company is to deliver shareholder value, through being successful in providing innovative and valued healthcare solutions. Business continuity plans are in place after it has assessed the potential risks associated with the year 2000, and necessary action has been taken. It appears through sound management Faulding is ready to catapult into the next millennium, and one should not be hesitant in investing in this 'star'.

Source: Written by Rebecca Crilley.

Activities for discussion, analysis and further research

1 What are the structure issues discussed in the case above?
2 What processes has Faulding put into place for dealing with structures of the external environment?
3 Access the Faulding Web site and find an organisational chart. Discuss the reporting lines between the Australian site and the other sites around the world.

PART 4

LEADING

While planning provides direction and organising arranges resources, the leading function adds the action ingredient. Leading involves influencing others' work behaviour toward achieving organisational goals. In the process of leading, effective managers become catalysts in encouraging innovation. Thus leaders kindle the dynamic spirit for success.

The energy of an organisation comes from its workers' motivation. As **Chapter 12** notes, managers can use several motivational approaches focusing on individual needs, the thought processes involved in deciding whether or not to expend effort, and available reinforcements and rewards.

Does leadership depend on inherent traits or can anyone learn and apply effective leader behaviours to various situations? **Chapter 13** considers these possibilities in exploring leadership. In order to have influence, leaders must be able to communicate their ideas and visions, and have workable methods of learning about others' thoughts. **Chapter 14** discusses the nature of managerial communication, including an exploration of different types of communication and channels involved.

At the same time, many managers have realised that groups of teams can be powerful means of accomplishing organisational goals. As **Chapter 15** explains, understanding group dynamics and being able to encourage the power inherent in group activities are important to the leading function.

Motivation

Chapter 12

CHAPTER OUTLINE

The nature of motivation

Need theories
Hierarchy-of-needs theory
Two-factor theory
ERG theory
Acquired-needs theory
Assessing need theories

Cognitive theories
Expectancy theory
Equity theory

Goal-setting theory
Assessing cognitive theories

Reinforcement theory
Types of reinforcement
Schedules of reinforcement
Using reinforcement theory

Social learning theory
Major components
Using social learning theory

LEARNING OBJECTIVES

After studying this chapter, you should be able to:

○ Define motivation and outline the motivation process.
○ Compare and contrast the major need theories of motivation.
○ Describe each of three major cognitive theories of motivation and explain how they facilitate the motivation process.
○ Explain reinforcement theory of motivation and discuss how it can help managers.
○ Discuss the social learning theory of motivation.

Striving for excellence

In discussing motivation, our contact at Autoliv found it difficult to separate this concept from the other concepts and activities in the company. In her opinion, motivation at Autoliv is strongly linked to communication. The organisation continuously runs customer-satisfaction surveys and the results of these are communicated to all the areas which work for that particular customer. Autoliv's approach fosters a culture of openness and approachability in which the staff of the organisation have no hesitation in 'shirt fronting' any senior manager and discussing the issues which concern them.

The outcome of this culture is an environment in which people want to do their best. This is further enhanced by the work done by the HR staff to build the self-esteem specifically of the manufacturing staff. They are a vital part of the organisation's success and all efforts are made to ensure that they understand and recognise this. Team leaders are put through a course to help develop their skills. This is important in an environment where many of the workers are women. Many of them need to be encouraged to believe in their own skills and abilities.

It is difficult to assess accurately whether the culture of the organisation is the motivation for the performance or whether the culture is the reward for the performance. In either case, Autoliv is an example of how a strong and positive culture is a motivator to exceptional performance.

motivation

Force energising behaviour, giving direction to behaviour, and underlying the tendency to persist

Motivation is the force energising or giving direction to behaviour. In this chapter, we explore the basic nature of motivation and consider a general model of it. Next, we examine theories of motivation based on individual needs, such as the need for achievement. We also look into motivational approaches that emphasise cognitive aspects, focusing on how individuals think about where to direct effort and how to evaluate outcomes. Then we analyse reinforcement theory, which emphasises the power of reward. Finally, we review the contemporary extension of social learning theory.

THE NATURE OF MOTIVATION

Because motivation is an internal force, we cannot directly measure the motivation of others. Instead, we infer their motivation by watching their behaviour. For example, we might conclude an engineer friend who works late every evening, goes to the office on weekends, and continually reads the latest engineering journals is highly motivated. Conversely, we might suspect an engineer friend who is usually first through the door at the end of the day, who rarely puts in extra hours, and generally spends little time reading on new developments in the field is not motivated to excel.

In the end, how successful these two are on their projects will depend not only on their motivation, as shown by their efforts, but on their ability to handle engineering subject matter. Working conditions may affect their performance. Many interruptions, extra assignments or cramped office space may affect performance negatively. On the other hand, a quiet workplace, assistants' help, and support resources such as equipment, may affect project performance positively. Actual performance is thus a function of ability, motivation and working conditions, as shown in Figure 12.1 (Campbell & Pritchard 1976).

As a result, it is important managers hire those with ability to do what is needed. They must try to be sure people are motivated to contribute the required inputs, that these inputs are

Fig. 12.1   The relationship between performance and ability, motivation and working conditions

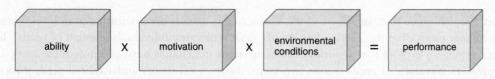

ability   X   motivation   X   environmental conditions   =   performance

used well or are directed to high performance, and that this performance results in workers reaching desired outcomes.

Then the challenge is to provide working conditions which nurture and support individual motivation to work to organisational goals (Ronen 1994).

The main elements of the motivation process are shown in Figure 12.2. As the diagram shows, our inner needs (food, companionship and growth) and cognitions (knowledge and thoughts about efforts we might put forth, and expected rewards) lead to various behaviours. Assuming these are appropriate to the situation, they may result in rewards. These rewards then help reinforce our behaviours, fulfil needs and influence cognitions about links between our behaviours and possible rewards. Alternatively, lack of reward leads to unfulfilled needs, leaves behaviours unreinforced, and influences our thinking about where to put future effort. Since motivation is complex, the major motivational theories address various elements in the process (see Fig. 12.2). To understand the implications of these elements for managers, we explore the respective theories in later sections of this chapter, beginning with need theories.

Fig. 12.2   The motivation process

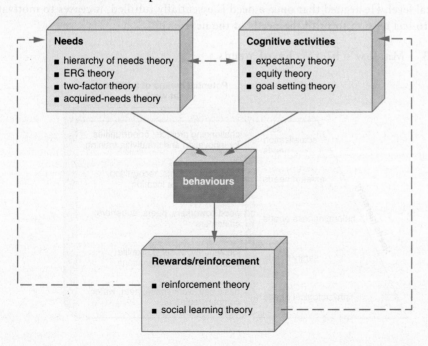

Needs
- hierarchy of needs theory
- ERG theory
- two-factor theory
- acquired-needs theory

Cognitive activities
- expectancy theory
- equity theory
- goal setting theory

behaviours

Rewards/reinforcement
- reinforcement theory
- social learning theory

NEED THEORIES

Need theories argue that we behave as we do due to the internal needs we attempt to fulfil. These are content motivation theories as they specify what motivates individuals (content of needs). In this section, we explore four theories examining needs individuals have and how these work as motivators: hierarchy-of-needs theory, two-factor theory, ERG theory and acquired-needs theory.

Hierarchy-of-needs theory

One motivation theory is **hierarchy-of-needs theory**, developed by Abraham Maslow and popular during the early 1960s. It argues that individual needs form a five-level hierarchy (shown in Fig. 12.3).

According to the hierarchy, our first need is survival, so we focus on basic **physiological needs**, such as food, water and shelter, until we feel sure these are covered. Next, we are concerned with **safety needs**, or the desire to feel safe, secure and free from threat. Once we feel safe and secure, we turn to relationships with others to fulfil our **belongingness needs**, which involve a desire to join with and be accepted by others. With this support, we focus on **esteem needs**, which are a two-pronged desire to have a positive self-image and have our contributions valued and appreciated. Finally, we reach the highest level, **self-actualisation needs**, or the development of our capabilities and attaining our full potential. We are concerned with testing our creativity, seeing our ideas put into practice, pursuing new knowledge and developing our talents. Needs at this level are never fulfilled, because as we develop capabilities, our potential and needs for self-actualisation grow. Some work-related ways to fulfil needs in the hierarchy are shown in Figure 12.3.

Maslow recognised that a need might be incompletely fulfilled before we move to the next hierarchical level. He argued that once a need is essentially fulfilled, it ceases to motivate and we begin to feel tension to fulfil the needs of the next level.

Fig. 12.3   Maslow's hierarchy of needs

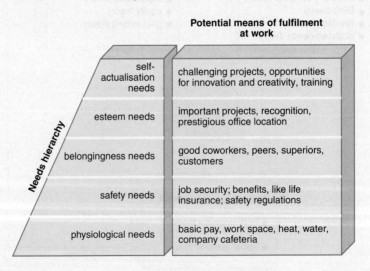

hierarchy-of-needs theory

Theory (developed by Maslow) arguing that individual needs form a five-level hierarchy

physiological needs

Survival needs such as food, water and shelter

safety needs

Needs pertaining to the desire to feel safe, secure and free from threats to our existence

belongingness needs

Needs involving the desire to affiliate with and be accepted by others

esteem needs

Needs related to the two-pronged desire to have a positive self-image and to have our contributions valued and appreciated by others

self-actualisation needs

Needs pertaining to the requirement of developing our capabilities and reaching our full potential

While Maslow's hierarchy stimulated thinking about individuals' various needs, it has some flaws. Research suggests needs may cluster in two or three categories, not five. Also, the hierarchy may not be the same for everyone. Entrepreneurs may pursue dreams for years despite relative deprivation of lower-level needs. Finally, individuals seem to work satisfying several needs at once, though some may be more important at a given point (Wahba & Bridwell 1976; Mitchell & Moudgill 1976).

The increasingly global economy means managers must realise that people from different countries may differ in needs they attempt to satisfy through work (Ronen 1994). Research has indicated some differences, with people from Greece and Japan being more motivated by safety needs and those from Sweden, Norway and Denmark by belongingness needs (Adler 1991; Hofstede 1980).

Furthermore, in poor countries with low standards of living, physiological and safety needs are likely to be the prime motivators of behaviour. As countries become wealthier and have higher standards of living, it is likely that needs related to personal growth and accomplishment (such as esteem and self-actualisation) become important as motivators of behaviour.

Two-factor theory

Building on Maslow's work, Frederick Herzberg interviewed accountants and engineers (Steers, Porter & Bigley 1996). He asked them to describe situations where they felt very good about their jobs and some where they felt very bad about them. Analysis showed a pattern. Factors making individuals satisfied with their jobs were associated with job content. These were labelled **motivators**. On the other hand, factors making individuals dissatisfied were associated with job context. These were labelled **hygiene factors** (see Fig. 12.4).

Herzberg's **two-factor theory** argues that hygiene factors keep workers from feeling dissatisfied, but motivators help workers feel satisfied and motivated. The implications are clear:

motivators

Factors seeming to make individuals feel satisfied with their jobs

hygiene factors

Factors seeming to make individuals feel dissatisfied with their jobs

two-factor theory

Herzberg's theory that hygiene factors are necessary to keep workers from feeling dissatisfied, but only motivators can lead workers to feel satisfied and motivated

Fig. 12.4   Herzberg's two-factor theory (Jones et al. 2000)

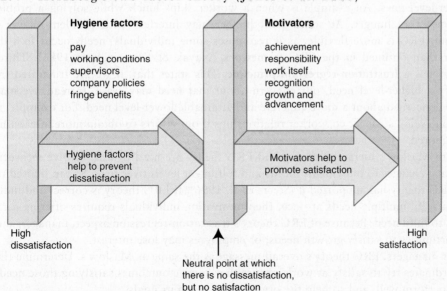

Hygiene factors

pay
working conditions
supervisors
company policies
fringe benefits

Motivators

achievement
responsibility
work itself
recognition
growth and
advancement

Hygiene factors help to prevent dissatisfaction

Motivators help to promote satisfaction

High dissatisfaction

High satisfaction

Neutral point at which there is no dissatisfaction, but no satisfaction

(1) provide hygiene factors that reduce worker dissatisfaction, and (2) include motivators, as they are the only factors to motivate workers and lead to job satisfaction. The two-factor theory has been criticised on the grounds that researchers have been unable to obtain the same pattern of results when using other study methods (King 1970; Locke 1976). Nevertheless, the theory is significant as it helped focus attention on the need to provide motivators and enhanced our understanding of motivation.

ERG theory

Because of criticisms of Maslow's hierarchy-of-needs theory, Clayton Alderfer (1972) proposed an alternative, **ERG theory**. The name comes from combining Maslow's five needs levels into three: existence, relatedness and growth. **Existence needs** include physiological desires, such as food and water, and work-related material wants, such as pay, fringe benefits and working conditions. **Relatedness needs** address relationships with significant others, such as families, friendship groups, work and professional groups. They deal with our need to be accepted by others, achieve mutual understanding on matters important to us, and influence those we interact with on an ongoing basis (Baumeister & Leary 1995). **Growth needs** produce creativity and innovation, and the desire to have a productive impact on our surroundings.

According to ERG theory, we concentrate first on existence requirements. As these are resolved, we have more energy available to concentrate on relatedness needs. Then, as relatedness needs are fulfilled, we have energy and support to pursue growth needs. Thus ERG theory incorporates a **satisfaction-progression principle** similar to Maslow's hierarchy, since satisfaction of one need allows concern with the next.

Aside from focusing on three levels not five, ERG theory differs from Maslow's hierarchy in three ways. First, though the general idea of a hierarchy is kept, Alderfer argues that we can be concerned with more than one category at once. Lower-levels needs may not be well satisfied before we focus on others. However, lower-level-need satisfaction lets us attend to higher-level ones. An example is when a worker skips lunch while solving a problem and becomes very hungry. At some point hunger may interfere with problem-solving efforts. Second, ERG is more flexible, as it recognises some individuals' needs occur in a different order than outlined in the ERG framework (Nayak & Ketteringham 1986). Third, ERG theory has a **frustration-regression principle**. This states that, if we are frustrated trying to satisfy a higher-level need, our concern about that need may cease. Instead, we may grow more concerned about a more concrete and attainable lower-level need. For example, we may try to develop stronger co-worker relationships if our efforts to obtain more interesting work are ignored.

Both Maslow's hierarchy theory and ERG theory are hard to test, involve measuring and tracking changes to individuals' needs and fulfilment levels over time. So far, limited research on ERG theory has supported it (Steers et al. 1996). If ERG theory is correct and individuals try to fulfil multiple needs at once, then motivating individuals requires offering a range of ways to fulfil need. Because of ERG theory's frustration-regression aspect, managers must give opportunities to satisfy growth needs, or employees may lose interest.

For managers, ERG theory's overall message is the same as Maslow's. Determine the needs subordinates try to satisfy at work, ensure they receive outcomes satisfying those needs when they perform well, and so help the organisation reach its goals.

● Sue Riem-Tan

case in point

Sue Riem-Tan claims she only goes to her office twice a year. The balance of her work days she spends in the lounge of Melbourne's Sheraton Hotel where a table is permanently reserved for her. She maintains that she does not like offices and would not know how to work in one.

Her company, Mirason Asia, with 30 staff, was built on her willingness to be different. Mirason sometimes spends months getting to know a client; it even undertakes work for which it charges no fees. However, when an invoice is sent, it must be paid within 24 hours.

Her decision to study computer-science part-time while working in the computer field has paid off. She found her job a more effective learning environment than university, reading everything she could get her hands on. Her job with the Bureau of Statistics in Canberra proved an excellent information-technology training ground, with the biggest databases in the southern hemisphere and expertise in systems design and development.

Riem-Tan's learning was always of an unconventional nature. Instead of attending formal training sessions, she borrowed the manuals, took them home and read them in her spare time. She absorbed knowledge on how to design IT systems, implementation and user involvement. While with the Bureau of Statistics, she established the first e-mail system in the Australian government sector and introduced the first PCs to the Bureau of Statistics.

She worked for a decade in situations that she describes as 'boring' but were useful as stepping stones to running her own business. Riem-Tan admits that when she is bored, she is dangerous. She goes off and learns things.

Source: Adapted from Schmidt, L. (1999).

Activities for discussion, analysis and further research

1   From the above material, describe what you think motivates Sue Riem-Tan.
2   Which of the motivation models would you apply to her?

Acquired-needs theory

While hierarchy-of-needs and ERG theories see some needs as a basic part of our makeup, David C. McClelland has another perspective, **acquired-needs theory**. McClelland argues that our needs are acquired or learned though experience. Although such needs are produced by a range of conditions, sometimes a specific event can deeply influence our desires (Fierman 1987).

McClelland mainly studied three needs: achievement, affiliation and power. He measures these using the Thematic Apperception Test (TAT), in which stories are written about purposely ambiguous pictures. These stories are scored by the achievement, affiliation and power themes they contain. The assumption is that individuals write on themes important to them (Spangler 1992). For most, test results show a blend of achievement, affiliation and power needs, not a high level of one and an absence of the rest.

McClelland's (1985) initial work looked at the **need for achievement (nAch)**, the desire to accomplish challenging tasks and achieve excellence in one's work. Individuals with high nAch seek competitive situations, achieving results by their own efforts and receiving relatively immediate progress feedback. They pursue moderately difficult goals and take calculated risks. Yet, contrary to common belief, high nAchs avoid very difficult goals due to high risk of failure. As they like problems needing innovative, novel solutions, high-nAch individuals can be an organisational source of creativity and innovative ideas (Steers 1987).

acquired-needs theory

Theory (developed by McClelland) stating that our needs are acquired or learned on the basis of our life experiences

need for achievement (nAch)

Desire to accomplish challenging tasks and achieve a standard of excellence in one's work

need for affiliation (nAff)

Desire to maintain warm, friendly relationships with others

need for power (nPow)

Desire to influence others and control one's environment

personal power

Need for power in which individuals want to dominate others for the sake of demonstrating their ability to wield power

institutional power

Need for power in which individuals focus on working with others to solve problems and further organisational goals

It is estimated that about 10 per cent of the general population has a high nAch. Managers trying to motivate high achievers must ensure they have challenging, but reachable, goals giving immediate progress feedback. McClelland argues high-nAch individuals may be not be motivated by money per se (as they get satisfaction mainly from achievement). Nevertheless, they may still see money as a source of feedback on their progress (McClelland 1976; 1985).

McClelland also addressed the **need for affiliation (nAff)**, the desire to have warm, friendly relationships with others. High-nAff individuals tend to work in professions demanding inter-action with others, such as health care, teaching, sales and counselling. To motivate, managers must provide a co-operative, supportive work environment where they can meet performance expectations and high affiliation needs by working with others. High-nAff individuals can be assets in situations needing high-level co-operation with and support of others, including clients and customers (Steers 1987).

McClelland gradually saw the **need for power (nPow)**, the desire to influence others and control one's environment, as a significant organisational motivator. Need for power takes two forms, personal and institutional. Individuals needing **personal power** try to dominate others to show they have power. They expect followers to be loyal to them, not the organisation, which may mean larger goals go unachieved. In contrast, individuals needing **institutional power** work with others to solve problems and achieve organisational goals. These people want things done in an organised way. They can sacrifice some of their own goals for the organisa-tion's good (McClelland 1976; 1985). Motivating individuals with high need for institutional power means giving them opportunities to hold positions to organise other's efforts.

McClelland analysed the relationship of various needs to managerial effectiveness. He first thought those with high achievement need would be best managers. His later work suggests high-nAch individuals focus on their own results instead of the development and perfor-mance of others. So, high-nAch people make good entrepreneurs. Individuals with high need for affiliation may be managerially weak, trying to keep good interpersonal links instead of achieving goals. Those with personal-power orientation have problems as managers, often trying to use others' efforts for their own benefit (McClelland 1985).

McClelland's work suggests those with a high institutional-power need make best managers due to their co-ordination of others' efforts to reach long-term organisation goals (Andrews 1967; McClelland & Boyatzis 1982). Thus the need profile of successful managers, in compet-itive environments, includes (1) moderate-to-high institutional power need, (2) moderate achievement need to help in early career activities, and a desire for the organisation to be competitive as they move to higher levels, and (3) a minimum need for affiliation to give enough sensitivity to influence others. McClelland's newest research shows need for achieve-ment is more important than power for small companies, and for large, decentralised ones when operating like small companies which must improve and grow cost-efficiently (McClelland 1995).

What if you want to be a manager but don't have an appropriate need profile? McClelland argues we can develop needs in ourselves and others. He increased individuals' need for achievement by training. Those trained were promoted faster and made more money than those not trained. The training involved tasks requiring goal achievement, and the situations became more challenging as individuals became more able. Trainees also saw the behaviour of appealing entrepreneurial models. The same methods can foster need for institutional power (McClelland 1965; 1985; McClelland & Burnham 1976). Other needs, such as affilia-tion, may be harder to develop by these means.

Assessing need theories

Needs identified in the four theories are compared in Figure 12.5. It is agreed that higher-level needs are important for motivation. Given the demand for new ideas, improved quality and greater capacity for change implementation, fostering growth needs is crucial. For example, Hewlett-Packard has an open-stock policy where engineers can take parts home from laboratory stock. The policy assumes this fosters original thinking and innovation. In one story, when Bill Hewlett, a company founder, found the stock area locked one Saturday, he used a bolt cutter to remove the padlock. He left a note saying, 'Don't ever lock this door again. Thanks, Bill.' (Peters & Waterman 1982). The open-stock policy fosters employee growth, helping Hewlett-Packard's reputation for innovation in electronics.

Fig. 12.5   Comparison of needs in four theories (adapted from Gordon 1987, p. 92)

Maslow: hierarchy of needs theory	Alderfer: ERG theory	Herzberg: two-factor theory	McLelland: acquired needs theory
physiological	existence	hygiene	
safety and security	existence	hygiene	
belongingness and love	relatedness	hygiene	need for affiliation
self-esteem	growth	motivators	need for achievement; need for power
self-actualisation	growth	motivators	need for achievement; need for power

✕ Stepping out safely

crossroads

Indonesia has very high unemployment rates. To overcome some of those stresses, it has attempted to expand its overseas labour force. Indonesia will have to work hard to catch up with the Philippines which supplies eight million overseas workers. Over the last five years, Indonesia has exported 1.6 million documented overseas workers who have sent home a cumulative $5 billion.

At the same time as lobbying foreign governments to open their doors to Indonesian workers, the Indonesian government is trying to better prepare workers for life overseas. A three-day course has been designed to equip workers with skills to assert their rights and avoid exploitation.

Source: Adapted from Cohen, M. (2000).

Reflection points

1 If you were an Indonesian unskilled or semi-skilled worker, what might motivate you to go overseas to work?
2 Try to find out why those workers send so much money home.

Decision points

1 What are the abuses that such a worker might face and how can those be avoided?
2 Consider what the Indonesian government might do to better protect its labour exports.

COGNITIVE THEORIES

cognitive theories
Theories attempting to isolate thinking patterns we use in deciding whether or not to behave in a certain way

Need theories try to identify internal desires directing behaviour, but they do not explain involved thought processes. In contrast, **cognitive theories** attempt to isolate thinking patterns used in deciding whether or not to act in a certain way. Cognitive theories do not conflict with need theories; rather, they look at motivation differently. Because they focus on the thought processes of motivation, cognitive theories are called process theories. The three major cognitive theories of work motivation are expectancy, equity and goal-setting theories.

Expectancy theory

expectancy theory
Theory (proposed by Vroom) arguing that we consider three main issues before we expend effort necessary to perform at a given level

The **expectancy theory** of motivation, proposed by Victor H. Vroom, argues that we consider three main issues before expending the effort needed to perform at a given level. These can be seen in the circles of Figure 12.6, which shows the basic components of expectancy theory.

effort-performance (E→P) expectancy
Our assessment of the probability our efforts will lead to the required performance level

Effort-performance expectancy When considering **effort-performance (E→P) expectancy**, we assess the probability our efforts will lead to required performance levels. Our assessment means evaluating our abilities, and considering the adequacy of contextual factors such as resource availability. To see how effort-performance expectancy works, imagine your boss asks you to start a major special project. The project involves designing and implementing a new computerised tracking system for customer complaints to improve customer service and identify complaint trends more quickly. Firstly you might consider the probability of being able to achieve needed performance levels, given your abilities and related environmental factors. If you feel you know little about such system development and/or resource availability is inadequate, you might assess the probability success as low. That is, your E→P expectancy for this assignment might be low. On the other hand, if you feel well qualified for

Fig. 12.6   Basic components of expectancy theory

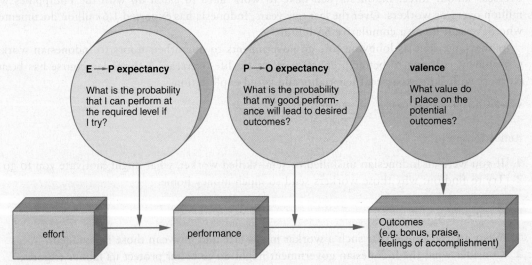

the project and available resources are adequate, you might assess the probability success—the E→P expectancy—as high. However, assessment of effort-performance expectancy is only part of the evaluation.

Performance-outcome expectancy With **performance-outcome (P→O) expectancy**, we assess the probability successful performance will lead to particular outcomes. Major outcomes considered are potential rewards (such as a bonus, promotion, or feeling of accomplishment), although we also consider possible negative results (such as loss of leisure time or family disruption due to extra job hours). In your special-project situation, your boss may have a history of giving rewards, such as recognition and bonuses, to individuals taking on special projects. If so, you might assess P→O expectancy for taking on the project as high. On the other hand, past experience with special projects may show the boss sometimes arranges for rewards but other times forgets. In this case, you might view the P→O expectancy as medium (perhaps a 50–50 probability rewarded). In the worst case, if your boss never rewards extra effort, you might assess P→O expectancy as virtually zero—at least for rewards available from the boss.

In any situation, many potential rewards can be linked to performance. Rewards provided by others, bonuses, awards or promotions, are **extrinsic rewards**. In addition to monetary rewards managers can use many non-monetary rewards to improve motivation. On the other hand, rewards related to our internal experiences with successful performance, such as feelings of achievement, challenge and growth, are **intrinsic rewards**. Considering various possible outcomes (both positive and negative), we assess the probability our performance will lead to desired outcomes. If our assessment of P→O expectancy is high, it contributes to our motivation. If assessment is low, expectancy reduces our willingness to perform at a high level. Still, there is another motivational component—the importance of various outcomes to us.

Valence With the **valence** component, we assess the anticipated value of various outcomes. If available rewards interest us, valence is high. However, possible negative-value outcomes, such as loss of leisure time or family disruption, may offset the reward value in a situation. Available rewards will motivate only when we attach a high overall valence to the situation. In the special-project example, you might view a special bonus from the boss very positively. Alternatively, if a rich aunt just left you $3 million, the bonus may be less important. However, you may attach high value to resulting intrinsic rewards if you develop the innovative project.

The importance of valence to expectancy is pointed out by Jones, George and Hill (2000) who note that overseas assignments, despite their stress, can have especially high valence for managers due to high levels of autonomy and the opportunities for learning they provide. International assignments are attractive as they allow people to learn about different cultures and different ways of operating, skills which will assist them in managerial roles (Loeb 1995).

Combining the elements Expectancy theory argues that in deciding whether to expend any effort, we consider all three elements: E→P expectancy, P→O expectancy, and valence. Research shows individuals make global judgments about each element in a situation, then combine elements into expectancy theory's general formula: (E→P) × (P→O) × valence = motivation (Staw 1984). For example, in the special-project situation, assume you assess all three elements as high. Chances are you will be highly motivated to pursue the project: high

performance-outcome (P→O) expectancy

Our assessment of the probability our successful performance will lead to certain outcomes

extrinsic rewards

Rewards provided by others, such as bonuses, awards or promotions

intrinsic rewards

Rewards related to our own internal experiences with successful performance, such as feelings of achievement, challenge and growth

valence

Our assessment of anticipated value of various outcomes or rewards

E→P expectancy × high P→O expectancy × high valence = high motivation. On the other hand, assessing any element as zero means the whole equation equals zero, regardless of the levels of the other two elements. This is because you will not pursue the project if you (1) believe there is a zero (or extremely low) probability of performing adequately, (2) assess a zero (or extremely low) possibility to the chance successful performance will lead to certain outcomes, or (3) attach a zero (or extremely low) valence value to potential outcomes. In more mixed situations, with no element with extremely low ratings, you will compare the situation with alternatives and choose one giving best chances of valued outcomes. In the special-project situation, you might negotiate with your boss for better prospects of good outcomes or to change assignments so you receive a task with greater motivational potential.

Expectancy theory has helped predict whether individual naval officers would retire voluntarily; foretelling the job a given undergraduate student would take on graduation; and determining the MBA program a particular graduate would select (Parker & Dyer 1976; Arnold 1981; Wanous, Keon & Lattack 1983; Steers & Porter 1991).

Implications for managers   Expectancy theory has several managerial implications. For one, managers must encourage high P→O expectancy formation by linking rewards carefully to high performance. To clarify, consider three scenarios with Alissa, Bob and Christen. In the first scenario, Alissa performs well, receives a bonus, and concludes that high performance has a good chance of leading to a valued outcome (enhanced P→O expectancy). In the second, Bob performs well but the boss does not even say 'good job', much less give a bonus. So Bob decides high performance does not pay, at least in organisational outcomes (reduced P→O expectancy). In our third scenario, Christen does little work but receives a substantial year-end bonus. Christen is likely to see high performance as unnecessary to receive valued organisation outcomes (reduced P→O expectancy). As a result, Bob and Christen will be less motivated in future, while Alissa will have increased motivation. In Bob's case, reduced P→O expectancy is due to the manager's failure to reward high performance; but in Christen's case, low performance was rewarded.

Aside from issues related to P→O expectancy, expectancy theory has other managerial implications. For one, managers must foster high subordinate E→P expectancy. Their high expectancy contributes to high motivation to succeed (Kaufman 1995). They foster this by having clear performance expectations; setting challenging, but achievable, performance goals; ensuring employees are trained and have resources to reach performance levels required; and providing encouragement. Managers can encourage motivation by giving reward opportunities (extrinsic and intrinsic) with a high employee valence (Nadler & Lawler 1983).

Managers can also boost subordinates' expectancy levels and motivation by providing training so they will have the expertise needed for high performance. Then the combination of training and high expectancy and motivation enhances the chances of success (Milbank 1995; *Wall Street Journal* 1995a; 1995b).

Although expectancy theory gives useful guidelines, managers may not obtain results expected from motivational efforts unless employees see outcomes as equitable, an issue addressed by equity theory.

Equity theory

To explain how we identify and react to situations we see as inequitable, J. Stacy Adams (1965) developed equity theory.

According to **equity theory**, we prefer situations of balance, or equity, which exist when we see our inputs: outcomes ratio to be equal to that for a comparison other (or others). The selection of with whom to compare ourselves depends on our view of appropriate comparisons. For example, looking at the equity of a pay rise, a person might compare their pay with some co-workers, peers in other units, and/or a friend at another company with similar credentials. In making these judgments, we view equity in relative terms (comparison with another) not absolute terms (comparison with a set standard). Inputs we consider to assess our inputs: outcomes ratio relative to that of others cover many variables, such as educational background, skills, experience, hours worked and performance results. Outcomes include issues of pay, bonuses, praise, parking places, office space, furniture and work assignments. The inputs and outcomes we use to assess a situation's equity are based solely on our perceptions of relevance.

The theory notes that two inequity types produce tension. Firstly, under-reward, when our inputs: outcomes ratio is seen to be less than that of a comparison other. In the second, over-reward, our inputs: outcomes ratio is seen to be greater than of a comparison other. Not surprisingly, equity theory research shows we adjust to over-reward conditions quickly—concluding that our inputs are worth much more than originally thought (Locke 1976; Mowday 1991). Under-reward situations are harder to resolve.

Reducing or eliminating inequity Although an individual's actions depend on what seems feasible in a given situation, Adams suggests maintenance of self-esteem is particularly important. As a result, an individual tries to maximise outcomes and resist costly input changes. Changing perceptions of others' inputs and outcomes or attempting to alter their side of the equation is more acceptable than changing perceptions of our own inputs or altering one's own side of the equation. Leaving the situation will be done only in cases of high inequity when other alternatives are not feasible. Finally, an individual will resist changing the comparison others, especially if they are stable.

Adams's equity formulation considered a situation at a point in time, but recent work shows perceptions of inequities endure. The addition of time explains why people blow up over small inequities. Previous inequity residues have built up until a small incident becomes the 'straw that breaks the camel's back', and we react strongly (Cosier & Dalton 1983).

Implications for managers Equity theory suggests ways to implement the recommendations of expectancy theory. For one, managers must communicate two-way with subordinates so they know their equity perceptions. For another, subordinates must know the 'rules' of outcome allocation relative to inputs. Also, since a pattern of inequity can result in major difficulties, managers must maintain good communication with subordinates and with superiors, peers, customers and other individuals associated with the job. Differing views inherent in the workforce's growing diversity may increase inequity feelings in organisations. As a result, many companies have set up diversity management programs to increase mutual understanding and ensure equitable treatment.

equity theory

Theory arguing that we prefer situations of balance, or equity, which exists when we perceive the ratio of our inputs and outcomes to be equal to the ratio of inputs and outcomes for a comparison other

The basis of motivation, however, is highest when most people in an organisation see themselves as being treated equitably, with inputs and outcomes balanced. The best performers are motivated to continue at a high level as they receive outcomes they deserve. Meanwhile, mediocre contributors and performers understand that to increase their outcomes, they must increase inputs.

Goal-setting theory

The value of setting goals across the organisation, as well as how to do so, are discussed in Chapter 6. Here, we summarise goal-setting theory in relation to motivation. Goal setting was seen as a technique; it has now developed into a motivational theory as researchers seek to better understand cognitive factors influencing its success. It is argued that it works by focusing attention and action, mobilising effort, increasing persistence, and encouraging the development of strategy to achieve goals. Feedback on results is essential (Locke & Latham 1984; 1990).

The success of goal setting in motivating performance depends on setting goals with the right aspects. They must be specific and measurable, challenging, attainable, relevant to the organisation's major work, and time-limited (i.e. achieved in a defined time). At Intel, which makes microprocessor chips or personal computers' 'brains', goals have helped reduced time taken to develop and produce new chips. The company used to develop new chips every four years. Now Intel's cycles overlap, with the development of the next generation two years before the Pentium chip hit markets (Hof 1995).

Goal commitment, or attachment to or determination to reach a goal, is important to goal setting. Goal commitment is influenced by the major elements of expectancy theory: effort-performance expectancy (can I reach the goal?), performance-outcome expectancy (will I be rewarded if I reach it?) and valence (do I value potential rewards?). Individuals are more committed to attaining goals when they hold high expectations of reaching them, see strong connections between goal accomplishment and rewards and value the rewards (Locke, Latham & Erez 1988). Thus expectancy and goal-setting theory fit with each other.

Goal setting's usefulness in improving performance has research support and managers will find it a helpful motivational tool.

Assisting with goal creation, motivating and evaluating performances are three requirements of the sales team leader.

Assessing cognitive theories

Each cognitive motivation theory gives a different view, although the three are complementary. Expectancy theory advises managers to help employees develop positive views of effort-performance expectancy by means of training and encouragement. It also highlights the value of clear links between performance and outcomes, as well as the need to offer employees rewards with positive valence (valence clues come from need theories). Goal-setting theory fits with expectancy theory as it helps pinpoint performance levels associated with effort-performance and performance-outcome expectancies. Finally, equity issues influence individual assessment of the value of maintaining equity in motivation.

 # Time off

gaining the edge

Only the best-behaved pupils jump the queue at this school's canteen. That is one of the rewards bestowed on well-behaved pupils at Tahuna Normal Intermediate School as part of its YIP ('Yes, it's positive') behaviour-modification plan. Its architect, deputy principal Keith Hutton, said the plan was based on the assumption that most pupils were well behaved. The majority of children are good but all too often the minority, just one or two in every class, upset the apple-cart.

That was happening in the school near the end of 1995, when staff started thinking that most children were getting a bad deal because of the behaviour of a troublesome handful. Worried that his staff might be right, Mr Hutton created a card-based behaviour modification plan. All pupils start the year with a green card which gives them rights taken for granted at most schools, such as invitations to school socials and the chance of leading a sports team. During the year staff reward people for positive behaviour, such as being considerate and showing consistently high effort, by giving them blue cards of recognition.

Pupils collect these cards to gain bronze, silver and gold awards and their associated privileges. These privileges include being able to jump the queue at the school canteen and being able to stay indoors unsupervised during intervals. Plans include photographs in the school foyer of the best-behaved students, an afternoon tea in town and a common room.

Although positive reinforcement is the main thrust of the program, staff now have a new form of punishment at hand: pupils who misbehave have their bronze, silver or gold awards—and their associated privileges—taken away.

While behaviour was hard to measure, the number of offences noted by staff had almost halved after the program had been working only a term. Although the number of offences had started to rise again, it was still below the level considered usual before the program started.

A recent anonymous survey of pupils suggested the plan was on the right track. A large majority supported the program, and suggestions for improvements included more cards being given out or more privileges being allowed. 'The kids are competitive and materialistic,' said Mr Hutton. 'They want to be rewarded.'

Source: G.Elkin and the *Otago Daily Times*.

Activities for discussion, analysis and further research

1   What do you see as the main strengths and weaknesses of the school's behaviour modification plan?
2   How would you feel if you were a pupil without a bronze, silver and gold card and found that card-holders walked in front of you in the canteen queue and that you were denied access to the common room? Would you feel motivated to improve your behaviour?
3   Have you any ethical objections to the techniques being used to modify the behaviour of the pupils?

REINFORCEMENT THEORY

reinforcement theory

Theory arguing that our behaviour can be explained by consequences in the environment

law of effect

Concept stating that behaviours having pleasant or positive consequences are more likely to be repeated and behaviours having unpleasant or negative consequences are less likely to be repeated

behaviour modification

Use of techniques associated with reinforcement theory

The reinforcement motivation approach is the reverse of cognitive theories, and is not concerned with an individual's thought processes to explain behaviour. One **reinforcement-theory** approach, pioneered by B. F. Skinner, is operant conditioning or behaviourism. According to this theory, behaviour can be explained by environmental consequences, and there is no need to look for cognitive explanations (Luthans & Kreitner 1975). Instead, the theory relies on the concept of the **law of effect**, which states behaviours with pleasant or positive consequences are more likely to be repeated than those with unpleasant or negative ones.

The way reinforcement works is that a stimulus cues a response or behaviour, followed by a consequence. If we find this rewarding, we are more likely to repeat the behaviour when the stimulus occurs again. If we do not find it rewarding, we are unlikely to repeat the behaviour. For example, assume you manage a marketing-research unit in a consumer-products company. A product manager from another unit asks you for urgent help with market research data (stimulus). You move some of your people from other priorities, even working late to produce data needed (behaviour). If the product manager ensures your unit is recognised for its efforts (pleasant consequence) you will be likely to make extra effort to help in future. On the other hand, if the product manager complains about a minor error (unpleasant consequence) saying nothing about the rest of the data or the extra effort you have made (less than pleasant consequence), you will be unlikely to help in future. Using reinforcement theory techniques is **behaviour modification**.

Types of reinforcement

In behaviour modification, four types of reinforcement influence behaviour: positive and negative reinforcements, extinction and punishment. Positive and negative reinforcements aim to increase a behaviour, while extinction and punishment focus on decreasing it (see Fig. 12.7). Skinner argued positive reinforcement and extinction encourage individual growth, while negative reinforcement and punishment foster immaturity in individuals, ultimately contaminating the whole organisation.

positive reinforcement

Technique aimed at increasing a desired behaviour, which involves providing a pleasant, rewarding consequence to encourage that behaviour

shaping

Successive rewarding of behaviours closely approximating the desired response until the actual desired response is made

Positive reinforcement Aimed at increasing desired organisationally-useful behaviour, **positive reinforcement** uses pleasant, rewarding consequences to encourage it. Rewarding outcomes, including praise, a pay rise, or time off, are positive reinforcers if a desired behaviour is repeated. Since people differ in what they find pleasant and rewarding, managers must watch the effects of a reinforcer to see if it encourages desired behaviour.

As individuals generally do not carry out a new behaviour exactly as required, managers encourage new behaviours by shaping. **Shaping** is rewarding of behaviours similar to that desired until the desired response is made. For example, a manager training a new salesperson may compliment their way of greeting customers (if this approximates the desired response). The manager may suggest questions the salesperson might ask customers to get a better idea of their needs. The manager then rewards the person's efforts to ask better questions and make further suggestions. By this process individual behaviour is gradually shaped to competency.

Fig. 12.7   Types of reinforcement situations according to Skinner

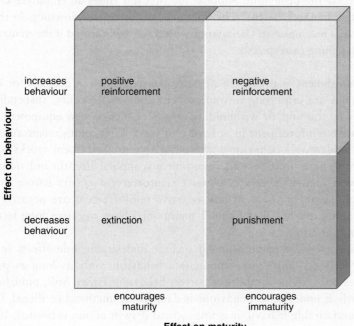

Negative reinforcement   Like positive reinforcement, **negative reinforcement** focuses on increasing desired behaviour, but in a different way. Negative reinforcement means presenting noxious (unpleasant) stimuli so an individual will engage in the desired behaviour to stop the stimuli. In other words, the desired behaviour is reinforced, but negatively because the individual must engage in the desired behaviour to stop an unpleasant state. For example, an engineer may try to finish a project on time (desired behaviour) to stop (consequence) the chief engineer's nagging or yelling (noxious stimuli). With negative reinforcement, either noxious, or unpleasant, stimuli are present or very likely to occur unless the desired behaviour is produced. For instance, the chief engineer may already be nagging about the deadline; or the chief engineer may not be yelling or nagging yet, but the engineer knows from past experience late projects trigger such behaviour. In either case, negative reinforcement increases the likelihood the project will be finished on time.

   Though negative reinforcement encourages desired behaviour, it also makes the individual feel negative toward the provider of the negative reinforcement. If this happens, the individual may react by doing only what is required and not putting in extra time when it might help, or even by leaving the organisation. Managers should use positive reinforcement whenever possible. Negative reinforcement produces an unpleasant work environment and possibly a negative organisation culture. Nagging, threats and other negative outcomes may cause subordinates to resent managers and even try to get back at them. Negative reinforcement fosters immature behaviour. For example, it may encourage the engineer to complete projects on time only if the boss is in the office.

negative reinforcement

Technique aimed at increasing a desired behaviour, that involves providing noxious stimuli so an individual will engage in the desired behaviour to stop the noxious stimuli

extinction

Technique involving withholding previously available positive consequences associated with a behaviour to decrease that behaviour

Extinction   **Extinction** involves stopping previously available positive outcomes from a behaviour to decrease the behaviour. Suppose the first few times an employee clowns during a staff meeting, the manager laughs. The laughter reinforces the clowning so the behaviour becomes disruptive. The employee's behaviour would be extinguished if the manager refrained from (withheld) laughing in response.

punishment

Technique involving providing negative consequences to decrease or discourage a behaviour

Punishment   **Punishment** is providing negative consequences to decrease or discourage a behaviour. Examples are criticising unwanted behaviour as it occurs, suspending a person without pay, denying training, or withholding resources such as new equipment. Punishment differs from negative reinforcement in at least two ways. First, punishment aims to decrease or discourage an undesirable behaviour, where negative reinforcement works to increase or encourage a desirable behaviour. Second, punishment is applied after the individual has shown an undesirable behaviour. Conversely, negative reinforcement occurs before they display a desirable behaviour. Both punishment and negative reinforcement are negative methods of behaviour change, approaches that Skinner maintained have negative long-term effects on individuals and organisations.

Arguments against the use of punishment include undesirable side effects (e.g. punisher-focused negative feelings) and it may eliminate a behaviour only as long as punishment is threatened. It does not provide a model of correct behaviour either. Still, punishment may be needed, particularly if undesirable behaviour is dangerous, unethical or illegal. Using extinction to decrease undesirable behaviour is impractical if swift action is needed. If punishment must be used, it will be most effective if there are recognised company policies applying to the situation; if the punishment is given as soon as possible after the undesirable behaviour; if the punishment is moderate, not severe; and is consistently applied (Arvey & Ivancevich 1980; Beyer & Trice 1984). In all cases its public application must be avoided. While the use of punishment can serve a useful instructional purpose in some cases, it will almost always serve to produce strong negative consequences later (Jones 2000)

Schedules of reinforcement

schedules of reinforcement

Patterns of rewarding that specify the basis for and timing of positive reinforcement

Reinforcement theory argues that positive reinforcement produces desired behaviours. Different reward patterns affect time taken to learn a new behaviour and level of behavioural persistence. These patterns, or **schedules of reinforcement**, specify positive reinforcement's basis and timing. There are two major schedules: continuous and partial. In continuous reinforcement, behaviour desired is rewarded when it occurs. For example, a manager praises a worker performing a task correctly. This is effective during initial learning, but becomes impractical. Further, desired behaviour stops quickly (rapid extinction) unless reinforcement continues. With a partial schedule, desired behaviour is rewarded sometimes. During initial learning, behaviour is often rewarded to encourage repetition, and less so later. There are four main partial reinforcement schedules: fixed interval, fixed ratio, variable interval, and variable ratio (see Fig. 12.8).

fixed-interval schedule of reinforcement

Pattern in which a reinforcer is administered on a fixed time schedule, assuming the desired behaviour has continued at an appropriate level

Fixed interval   In a **fixed-interval reinforcement schedule**, reinforcers are given on a fixed time schedule, assuming the desired behaviour has occurred. An example is a plant manager visiting a plant section every day at the same time, praising efforts to increase product quality.

Fig. 12.8   Types of partial reinforcement schedules (adapted from Arnold & Feldman 1986, p. 70)

		FIXED INTERVAL	FIXED RATIO
Spacing or timing of reinforcers	fixed	Reinforcement administered every *x* minutes	Reinforcement administered every *x*th occurrence of the behaviour
		VARIABLE INTERVAL	VARIABLE RATIO
	variable	Timing of reinforcers varies randomly around some average time period	Number of occurrences of the behaviour required to receive reinforcer varies randomly around some average number
		passage of time	number of times behaviour occurs

Basis for determining frequency of reinforcement

Fixed-interval schedules produce uneven responses, with desired behaviour peaking just before reinforcement is due, then dropping until the next reinforcement is due. With this schedule, extinction is quick if reinforcement is late or stops.

Fixed ratio   In a **fixed-ratio reinforcement schedule**, reinforcers are given after a fixed number of cases of desired behaviour, not on a fixed time schedule. For example, awards for innovations might occur after five usable ideas are given. Piecework pay systems for making a set number of units are another fixed-ratio reinforcement. Fixed-ratio schedules give high response rates, but extinguish rapidly if reinforcement stops even temporarily.

Variable interval   In a **variable-interval reinforcement schedule**, a reinforcer is given on a variable, or random, time schedule which averages out to a specified frequency. For example, a plant manager visits a plant section praising efforts to increase product quality on average five times a week, but at varying times. This schedule promotes a high, steady response rate which slowly extinguishes.

Variable ratio   In a **variable-ratio reinforcement schedule**, a reinforcer comes after varying, or random, frequency of desired behaviour (not on a varying time schedule) so the reinforcement pattern averages out to a specified ratio of events per reinforcement. For example, special awards for new ideas might be given on a ratio average of one award per five innovative ideas (i.e. an award after three ideas once, then after seven, etc.). Poker-machine payoffs, giving rewards after a variable number of lever pulls, are a variable-ratio schedule. This gives

fixed-ratio schedule of reinforcement

Pattern in which a reinforcer is provided after a fixed number of occurrences of the desired behaviour

variable-interval schedule of reinforcement

Pattern in which a reinforcer is administered on a varying, or random, time schedule which averages out to a predetermined time frequency

variable-ratio schedule of reinforcement

Pattern in which a reinforcer is provided after a varying, or random, number of occurrences of the desired behaviour in such a way the reinforcement pattern averages out to a predetermined ratio of occurrences per reinforcement

a high response rate and is the partial reinforcement method extinguishing slowest. Variable-ratio reinforcement was used in the McDonald's Monopoly promotion, where customers were given game pieces with stamps representing a Monopoly game board's properties. Although the odds of winning the top prize in this promotion were very long, immediate reinforcement was provided by giving customers chances to win instant food prizes at much better odds. The promotion was so successful it has been repeated twice.

Using reinforcement theory

Suggestions have been made to help managers use the reinforcement approach. They advise managers to encourage desired behaviours by positive reinforcement and tell subordinates what behaviours will be rewarded. Once desired behaviours have been learned, variable-interval and variable-ratio reinforcement patterns are effective approaches to behaviour maintenance. Finally, if punishment is needed, it should be moderately severe administered quickly and consistently to give best results (Beyer & Trice 1984; Hamner 1991).

@ Reinforcing an innovative culture

managing the e-challenge

In 1995, John Chaplin and Damien Mair wanted to develop a multimedia company based on good design. They had the vision but no money. They approached Apple Computer's Adelaide offices with a proposal. If Apple provided them with free computers and office space, they would interrupt their work to demonstrate the capabilities of Apple Computers to potential clients. Apple agreed and gave Fusion its boardroom to use as an office. Apple then provided Chaplin and Mair with their first two clients. One was Magpie Theatre Company which needed a CD-Rom to showcase its programs. A year later Apple Computers moved and Fusion went with them, taking its five staff members. By the end of 1996, Fusion had six staff and an annual revenue of $500 000, and its own office.

Initially, Fusion specialised in designing CD-Roms; however, as soon as they saw the first Internet browser, it was obvious that the Internet was going to be a part of what they did.

By 1998, Chaplin and Mair faced a number of new challenges. They needed to create a culture that would keep employees from being poached by competitors.

The rapidity of their expansion and growth meant that they had to learn how to manage effectively very quickly. They took to reading management books and journals. They decided that to be able to give their staff interesting projects they needed to expand. They also realised that they needed to step back from day-to-day operations and take a more strategic focus. When the average age of staff is 25, it is very difficult to spend ten minutes briefing an employee rather than quickly do it yourself.

Headquarters for Fusion, a multimedia company that leads the way in creating Internet solutions for other organisations.

Chaplin and Mair built their own project management software to improve time and expense management. At the touch of a button the program records the activities of all staff on an electronic time sheet.

When a new client is signed up, Fusion studies the business carefully to devise e-commerce strategies. Change is rapid. In the old economy, it was common for organisations to develop two- or three-year business plans. In the new economy, two or three years is a lifetime. Fusion plans on being Australia's highest quality Internet solutions provider and is quickly finding the ways to get there.

Source: Gome, A. (2000).

Activities for discussion, analysis and further research

1 In your opinion, what drives Chaplin and Mair in what they do?
2 What kinds of things would the partners have had to learn to manage their expanding company?

SOCIAL LEARNING THEORY

On the basis of his work on reinforcement theory, Albert Bandura was convinced the approach's apparent success could not be explained without allowing for individuals' cognitive or thinking capacity. Accordingly, he and others developed **social learning theory**, arguing that learning occurs by continuous interaction between our behaviours, personal factors and environmental forces. Individuals influence their environment, which affects how they think and behave. In other words, we learn much behaviour by observing, imitating and interacting with the social environment. Although social learning theory combines cognitive and reinforcement approaches, it is discussed here because it builds on reinforcement theory.

Major components

Social learning theory argues that three cognitively related processes are important in explaining behaviour: symbolic processes, vicarious learning and self-control (Bandura 1977; Krietner & Luthans 1991).

Symbolic processes   Social learning theory argues that we depend on **symbolic processes**, or the ways we use verbal and imagined symbols to process and store experiences (words and images) guiding future behaviour. By use of symbols, we solve problems without trying all courses of action. We can visualise a South Pacific holiday spot even if we have never been there. Images of desirable futures let us set goals and act to achieve those goals. Our symbolic processes have a cognitive element, **self-efficacy**, the belief in one's abilities to perform a specific task. Although similar to the effort-performance expectancy element of expectancy theory, self-efficacy is more oriented to our beliefs about our own capacities. It may help explain levels of goals we set, as well as task effort and persistence. One study found that faculty members feeling competent at research and writing produce more articles and books, which, in turn, increases self-confidence and likelihood of future productivity. Similar findings have come from studies of sales performance among life insurance agents (Barling & Beattie 1983; Taylor, Locke, Lee & Gist 1984).

Vicarious learning   **Vicarious learning** or observational learning is our ability to learn new behaviours and/or assess outcomes by observation. It is an important concept because,

social learning theory

Theory arguing learning occurs through continuous reciprocal interaction of our behaviours, various personal factors and environmental forces

symbolic processes

Various ways we use verbal and imagined symbols to process and store experiences in representational forms to serve as guides to future behaviour

self-efficacy

Belief in one's capabilities to perform a specific task

vicarious learning

Our ability to learn new behaviours and/or assess their probable consequences by observing others

modelling

Actually observing and attempting to imitate behaviours of others

contrary to reinforcement theory, we do not have to perform a behaviour to learn its consequences. The process of observing and copying others' behaviours is **modelling** (see Fig. 12.9). If you learn to swim or play tennis by imitating another's behaviour (perhaps a skilled friend or an instructor), you were modelling. Modelling has four stages. In the attention stage, we choose a model for observation, usually because they are skilled and successful, and we pay attention to relevant behavioural aspects. In the retention stage, we retain information about behaviour in mental images and words. In the reproduction stage, we try to reproduce a behaviour, but may be only partially successful, needing to further adjust our behaviour based on feedback. In the motivation stage, we are motivated to adopt a model's behaviour. For this stage to lead to actual adoption of behaviour, reinforcement must occur, usually from one of three sources. First, behaviour can be reinforced by consequences in a similar way to reinforcement theory. Second, reinforcement occurs vicariously by observing results of others behaving that way. Third, we can self-reinforce through self-control.

Fig. 12.9   The modelling process

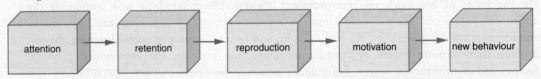

self-control

Our ability to exercise control over our own behaviour by setting standards and providing consequences for our own actions

Self-control   Self-control, or self-regulation, is the ability to exercise control over our own behaviour by setting standards and providing consequences (rewards and punishments) for our own actions (Boslet 1994). Self-control increases performance when we make self-rewards dependent on reaching high performance levels (Bandura 1977). Examples are promising ourselves a 15-minute break if we finish an assignment by a certain time, treating ourselves to something new when we get an A on an exam, or internally congratulating ourselves on a job well done. Since social learning theory recognises self-reinforcement, it gives more credit for control over our own behaviour than reinforcement theory (Engardio 1994).

Using social learning theory

Social learning theory has considerable research support, although investigators have only recently begun to explore its organisation implications (Davis & Luthans 1980; Evans 1986). The theory has two major managerial implications beyond those of other motivational theories. First, providing positive models seems to accelerate learning appropriate behaviours, especially with opportunities to try new behaviours in a supportive setting and receive feedback (Labate 1993). Modelling therefore can be very useful for training new workers. Second, vicarious learning indicates employees will draw conclusions about prospects for rewards and punishments, not just from their own experiences but also that of others (Betts 1992).

As these theories suggest, to promote high motivation, managers should reward organisational members based on performance levels, so high performers receive more than low performers (other things being equal) (Lawler 1981; *Newsweek* 1995). Thus social learning theory and other motivational theories discussed in this chapter are assets in influencing organisational behaviours (Jacob 1995; Norman 1994; Tully 1994). They are critical in effective leadership, to which we turn in the next chapter.

■ The MD's diary

I am driven by the need to understand my own limitations and what I can achieve. I need to be challenged. I know that, if I'm not challenged, then my whole demeanour changes very quickly. I'm not a person who sits comfortably with the status quo. I need to see change, I need to see things moving and happening. I am constantly looking at ways that I can challenge the organisation and challenge myself to reach new targets. I am typically a very high target-setter. I set very high expectations and targets for myself and it is only in recent years that I have started to accept that I don't always get where I want to when I want to. Maybe that is part of the art of target-setting. To me, the whole reason for working and for being is to improve. To improve what I'm doing, to improve the organisation I'm with, to just improve the outlook and the opportunities for everyone I come in contact with. That's where I get my buzz and excitement. And I guess the whole thing feeds on itself and when I have some success it drives me to the next level. My whole approach is all about being better tomorrow than I am today. My expectation of the organisation and the people around me is that they will have that same thinking, and that is what will drive them as well.

It does get me into trouble but at the end of day what it does, I think, is that it generates enthusiasm in people. I think that people recognise now that I do set high hurdles and I expect people to achieve them, and I get the feeling that people get caught up in that to some extent. That there is a level of excitement that gets generated by going after something that's a little bit outside your thinking in terms of what can be done, what is possible. I think it's infectious and if people see that I am prepared to take risks and that I am prepared to go after those extra bits, then they also will.

So what motivates me is change, by things happening, by improvement, by being better today than I was yesterday and, hopefully, doing better yet tomorrow. I suppose what I tend to do as a result is attract people around me who are also driven by the need to want to get better at what we do. I often talk to people around here about what's different about this organisation from some of the others I've been in—and it's the fundamental belief that what most people in this organisation come here for is to improve what we've got. They don't come to make seat belts or air bags. They come to do what they do today better. And I myself am constantly reassessing the way we do things and looking at ways to change it, to improve it. And I suppose where some people look at a strategy and think if it's not broken don't fix it, I tend to go the opposite way. I look at everything. 'If it's not broken then break it'—maybe there is a better way to do it. I like change. I like to look at ways to do things differently and to improve upon what we've got, and the people who work for me, by and large, feel the same and that in itself makes for a lot of motivation.

How do we reward people? The largest way we reward people is simply by valuing what they do, by recognising it and by making sure that everyone else understands that we recognise it. We certainly reward performance, achieving the outcomes is important to us—but we also reward the effort and the process on the way through, so we constantly provide feedback to people that they are behaving and working in a way which is consistent with our strategic directions and our values and our work ethics. So the vast majority is simply recognition and opportunity. People that perform are given the opportunity to grow within their own role, within the organisation. Every individual in this organisation to some extent, even if they are in a similar role, may well be operating in quite a different way, depending on how well they're performing and how much confidence we've got that they will deliver results. So some people might be subject to greater review and control than others in a similar role. We try to reward people by giving them greater flexibility; by empowering them and allowing them to make their own decisions, and in doing that in a way that means that we'll never let them get into too much trouble, but they feel as though they own the process and they have the ability to influence not only the outcome but also the way they deliver the outcome.

It's interesting in terms of money. It depends on the level, of course. At the shop-floor level, where the need may be more basic and you're looking to pay the bills and put the kids through school and clothe and feed them, then money's important. But in terms of motivation, in terms of job satisfaction, in terms of performance, I have never found that throwing dollars at people increase their motivation or performance. We want to attract the best people to our organisation so we have to pay better in terms of a salary. On the shop floor, we need to be competitive but in terms of the cost considerations for our products and attracting the right labour, we need to find that balance, and in those areas you need to make sure that people have sufficient financial capabilities to live at a reasonable level. So that when they come to work they are not focused on the problems outside work. That doesn't serve any useful purpose.

■ The subordinate's log   the reflective practitioner

One of the things I have learned is that money is a hygiene factor. Most people demand to be paid fairly. There are people who respond purely to money. But mostly, individuals appear to be motivated by the challenges inherent in their responsibility rather than the money. Money is also a comparative instrument. Staff will get upset if they learn that someone earns more than they do for exactly the same job—but at the end of the day, people do not leave or take jobs purely because of money issues.

The consultant typically is motivated by a degree of freedom which allows them to maintain a balance between personal and work life, allows them to learn and achieve personal objectives, the opportunity to make useful contacts, and ultimately become more marketable commodities. Interestingly I found that most of the consultants were not interested in more responsibility within the firm, because that meant dealing directly with the CEO, having more administrative duties for little gain. They were interested in taking leadership in consulting projects as that increased their freedom and control.

I learned that I liked having a degree of freedom in what I do and how I do it. I tend to seek out mentors, individuals from whom I can learn and be inspired by. I realised that I accepted the role of office head because I felt that a closer relationship with the CEO would enable me to learn from him.

Focus on practice—Strategies for improving

1 Performance will improve when you treat employees with confidence and let them know that you expect successful performance from them.
2 Develop ways to ensure that you have the authority to reward employees in the manner most likely to gain their commitment to the task.
3 Make sure that individuals are aware of the exact value of the outcomes required and their priority to the organisation.
4 Give examples of and contrast a positive and negative reinforcer for a particular behaviour.

Source: Jones et al. (2000).

Chapter summary

Motivation energises behaviour, directs behaviour, and underlies the tendency to persist. Actual performance results from ability and working conditions, as well as motivation. Efforts to understand the motivational process have centred on several major elements: needs, cognitive activities, and reward and reinforcement issues.

Need theories argue we behave as we do due to internal needs we work to fulfil. These are content theories as they focus on what motivates others. For example, Maslow argues our needs form a five-level hierarchy, from physiological to self-actualisation needs. Herzberg's two-factor theory contends hygiene factors keep workers from dissatisfaction, but only motivators lead to feelings of satisfaction and motivation. ERG theory updates Maslow's approach by suggesting three need levels and including a frustration-regression principle and satisfaction-progression explanation of movement among need levels. While hierarchy of needs and ERG theories see some needs as inherent, McClelland's acquired-needs theory argues needs are acquired or learned from our life experiences. His work focused on needs for achievement, affiliation and power, as well as on how they affect managerial success.

Cognitive theories, or process theories, isolate thinking patterns used in deciding to behave in a certain way. Expectancy theory argues that in deciding how much effort to use, we consider three issues: effort-performance expectancy (probability our efforts will lead to performance levels required), performance-outcome expectancy (probability successful performance leads to certain outcomes) and valence (anticipated value of various outcomes or rewards). Equity theory indicates we prefer situations of balance, or equity, which occurs when we perceive that the ratio of our inputs and outcomes is equal to the ratio of the inputs and outcomes of a comparison other (or others). Goal-setting theory highlights importance of goal commitment, specific and challenging goals, and feedback. Goal setting directs attention and action, mobilises effort, increases persistence, and encourages development of strategies to achieve goals.

Reinforcement theory argues our behaviour can be explained by environmental consequences. The four major reinforcement types are positive reinforcement, negative reinforcement, extinction and punishment. Schedules of reinforcement specify the basis for, and timing of, positive rewards. Rewards include fixed-interval, fixed-ratio, variable-interval, and variable-ratio schedules. Social learning theory argues learning occurs through continuous interaction of behaviours, personal factors and environmental forces. Three cognitively related processes are particularly important: symbolic processes, vicarious learning and self-control.

Questions for discussion and review

1 Briefly describe the concept of motivation and explain motivation process. Describe a situation illustrating the idea that performance is a function of ability and working conditions, as well as motivation.

2 Explain the hierarchy-of-needs theory. Assume you are manager of a large fast-food outlet. How could this theory help you motivate various individuals who work for you?

3 Outline the hygiene factors and motivators identified by Herzberg. Why might managers find this theory appealing and useful?

4 Identify the major differences between ERG and hierarchy-of-needs theories. Suppose you are the new manager of a work unit. How could ERG theory assist you assess how to motivate members of your new unit?

5 Describe the acquired-needs theory of motivation. According to McClelland's work on need for achievement, what are some difficulties in trying to motivate high-nAch individuals in organisations? How could you encourage need for achievement in others? How might you encourage need for institutional power?

6 Outline the expectancy theory of motivation. Suppose you are in charge of a group of engineers responsible for completion of various projects. How would you use expectancy theory to motivate them to perform at a high level?

7 Explain equity theory. In part, equity theory argues that our judgments of equity (or inequity) are based on our own perceptions of situations. What difficulties does the perceptual aspect of equity judgments present for managers?

8 Explain the four main types of reinforcement. For each, identify a situation where you have seen it used and assess the outcome.

9 Contrast the four major types of partial reinforcement schedules. Provide an example of each type from your own experience.

10 Explain the social learning theory of motivation. Describe an instance where you obtained important information through vicarious learning. Also describe a situation in which you learned through modelling. To what extent can you identify the modelling process steps in your own situation?

Exercises for managing in the 21st century

Exercise 1
Skill building: Learning about reinforcement schedules

Positive reinforcement is particularly significant to both manager and employee. Understanding reinforcement schedules will help selecting correct types to use at particular times. Match the type of partial reinforcement schedule with the examples indicated by placing the first letters of titles in the blanks.

Fixed Interval   Fixed Ratio

Variable Interval   Variable Ratio

1 _____ Monthly pay cheque
2 _____ Jackpot on a poker machine
3 _____ A free trip for two after making sales of $300 000 in a year
4 _____ The general manager visits the plant on average every two months to let everyone know their efforts are appreciated
5 _____ Lottery
6 _____ Certificate and pin for 25 years of service
7 _____ Monthly attendance award
8 _____ Sports tickets given to employees—usually once or twice a year depending on availability
9 _____ Restaurant waiter/waitress receives an award for serving the chain's half millionth customer
10 _____ Refreshment break every morning and afternoon
11 _____ Boss brings in snacks about every two or three weeks to treat everyone in the work unit
12 _____ $10 each for the first 100, $12 each for the next 30, $15 each for the next 30, and $19 each for all others produced during a work shift

Exercise 2
Management exercise: Marketeer or entrepreneur

Lee Brown has been a market planning specialist for the Sweet Tooth Company for the last two years. This is her first job following graduation from university, and she is pleased with her progress in the organisation. She has received three merit pay rises and expects to be promoted soon to the position of senior market planning specialist. She enjoys her work, and her immediate boss is one of the finest market planners she could ever hope to work with. Her boss gives her autonomy, support and resources when she needs them. Similarly, he seems to know when she needs help and gives it to her in a way which brings out the best in her. Lee frequently wonders how anyone could be happier than she is with her job and company.

Last week she met Jamie Wilson, a former schoolmate, at the local shopping centre. Lee recalled that Jamie, an excellent student who majored in human resource management, had accepted a position as a compensation analyst with a local health-care company. While catching up on the events of their lives over the last two years, Jamie said she had a business proposition she had been considering for some time but did not believe she could pursue alone. She needed a partner and suggested Lee could be that person.

Her proposition was that child-care centres were desperately needed in their area. The city of about 35 000 people had only one small child-care facility, which had a very long waiting list and very high rates. Jamie's research had revealed three different churches in the area would gladly support additional child-care centres by furnishing their facilities, at little or no cost, provided the centres were managed as separate businesses. Jamie had located a building which could be developed into an excellent child-care centre. Jamie reasoned she and Lee could start the business in one or more of the churches and expand into the building she had found. Financially, the return from operating one child-care centre would not quite equal Lee's current total compensation. However, two or more centres would yield a very nice income for both partners. Jamie had found appropriate licences could be obtained in a few weeks and the financing required to start the business was available at favourable rates. Other materials and supplies were readily available as well.

Lee was intrigued with this proposition and told Jamie she wanted a week to think it over. She intends to discuss her interest in this proposition with Jamie tomorrow.

Requirement

Using expectancy theory, indicate the factors impacting on Lee's decision and strength of her motivation to participate in the proposed business.

Performance and bonus systems: How well do they relate?

on the rim—
in New Zealand

Otago Steel Foundry Ltd, a company located in Dunedin in the South Island of New Zealand, has taken a strategic decision to introduce a bonus incentive scheme for the manufacture of a high-quality, high-value product. However, negotiations between management and the New Zealand Engineering, Printing and Manufacturing Union (Engineers' Union) have been prolonged and acrimonious, and are now at an impasse.

Company background
The company in its present form arose out of a merger some six years ago between two smaller companies operating in different markets, essentially dictated by product size. Corstorphine Steel Foundry Ltd produced

castings at the bottom end of the weight range, from a few pounds weight to about two tonnes, while Waverly Steel Foundry Ltd focused on the larger size of casting, from one tonne to about twenty tonnes. Typical products are, respectively, rollers for conveyor belts and generators used in the electricity supply industry. Both Corstorphine and Waverly continued manufacturing their own products after the merger. The Otago board of directors located the head office at the Corstorphine works, and promoted its general manager to chief executive of the new company. It also filled other key managerial positions in Waverly from the ranks of its sister operation. Waverly staff saw the tie-up as a take-over of their company, and not a joining of two equal partners.

No redundancies resulted from the merger, even although both markets have experienced some recession. On the other hand a lucrative opportunity has emerged for Waverly in the shape of high-quality fabricated castings.

However, differences in culture, as well as product type, also separated the two companies, in that Waverly's management ran a family-style of operation, whereas Corstorphine executives were in constant conflict with the unions. Their production employees had operated under bonus incentive conditions for many years, both prior to and since the merger. The Engineers' Union represented the majority of production employees in both works. White-collar staff in both plants are not paid bonuses.

Over the past six years senior management have introduced incentive schemes into all production areas in Waverly, despite much strife. Management frequently pointed out that productivity had increased by 110 per cent, wages had risen by 30 per cent, and no one lost their job, as a result of the changed working practices. While the production employees reluctantly accepted the changes, it was against the advice and wishes of the union delegates, most of whom are skilled craftsmen.

The welding shops

Because of production-process defects, all castings require rectification, achieved through repair welding. The weld is polished by a grinder operator to flush with the rest of the casting.

All repair welders, in common with the other production operators, are paid a basic rate per hour. This excludes bonus payments, and cannot be lowered under the existing collective contract. The top-paid production operators in Otago, in terms of basic rates but not total pay, are the moulders, followed by the furnacemen, and then the repair welders.

A bonus supplements the basic rate, based on the application of an incentive system, known as the 75/100 Straight Proportional Incentive Scheme, in which earnings are directly proportional to results achieved, subject to meeting a bonus starting performance of above 75. (Up to 75 performance, only basic rate is paid). That is, a proportionate increase in performance gives an equal proportionate increase in pay. Table 12.1 below gives more details of the relationship between pay and performance. For the purpose of budgeting and costing of its products, Otago aims that its workforce achieves at least Standard Performance, designated as 100. This rewards the worker with a third bonus (33.33 per cent). There is no ceiling limit on the bonus earning potential of employees.

Standard Performance is that level of performance that a qualified worker, suitably trained, following the method and quality specification for the job, taking the appropriate rest, and motivated by an incentive, would achieve over a working shift of eight hours without over-exertion. Personnel department staff, usually ex-craftsmen specially trained in work measurement techniques, determine the time required to work on particular jobs for the achievement of Standard Performance. This 'standard time' includes an allowance for rest and relaxation. From an analysis of the welders' recorded times spent on jobs compared to the work measured times, the personnel department calculates actual performance, which determines pay as shown in Table 12.1.

All existing incentive schemes operate on a small-group basis. Earnings are pooled, with each group member (e.g. welders) receiving an equal money share, irrespective of their own individual performance.

Table 12.1   75/100 Straight Proportional Incentive Scheme—Repair welders

Performance	Total pay as a percentage of basic rate	Repair welders— total pay per hour $
0	100.00 %	15
20	100.00 %	15
50	100.00 %	15
60	100.00 %	15
75	100.00 %	15
80	106.66 %	16
90	120.00 %	18
100	133.33 %	20
110	146.66 %	22
120	160.00 %	24
130	173.33 %	26
150	200.00 %	30

Notes:

(1) In the middle column, basic rate equals 100%, and total pay (including bonus), is expressed as a percentage of it. Bonus payment commences above 75 performance, where the relationship between total pay and performance is calculated by the formula:

Total pay = 1.33 × Performance

For example, a performance of 90 gives total pay of 120%, which comprises 20% bonus and basic rate (100%).

(2) The right-hand column shows the actual total pay per hour in dollars, and includes bonus. Welders' basic rate is $15 per hour. Only the best repair welders achieve performances of 120 and above. Over the past five years the actual average performance achieved by Waverly repair welders was just over 100, which is about 5 per cent lower than the average for Corstorphine.

Fabrication welding

In response to a new demand for fabricated products, which are complex shapes and cannot satisfactorily be directly cast but can only be produced by welding castings together, Otago management recently introduced fabrication welding at its Waverly plant. It is a much more intricate skill than repair welding, and requires a very high standard of work.

The company initially selected Waverly repair welders for fabrication duties on the basis of welding tests, resulting in a 60 per cent rejection rate. Those passing the test underwent a ten-week intensive training program, being tested a further three times. This resulted in another 15 per cent failing to satisfy the skill requirements, meaning that only 25 per cent of the original repair crew qualified as fabrication welders.

Late last year Otago provisionally agreed with the Engineers' Union that fabrication welding would carry a temporary fixed-rate pay rate of $20 per hour, irrespective of output, pending work measurement times becoming available for use in the introduction of a 50/100 Geared Incentive Scheme. In this arrangement, earnings are not directly related to results achieved. That is, a proportionate increase in performance gives less than a proportionate increase in pay, subject to a bonus starting performance of above 50 (up to 50 performance only basic rate is paid). Standard Performance (100) gives a third (33.33 per cent) increase in pay. There is no ceiling limit on the bonus earnings potential of employees. Table 12.2 below shows more details about the relationship between performance and pay.

Personnel department carried out fabrication welding time-studies over a period of two months, at the end of which they produced time standards for fabrication welding. Management then announced it wanted to introduce the 50/100 Geared Incentive Scheme immediately, and that each fabrication welder would earn his own bonus based on performance, that is, dispensing with the small-group arrangement. (All production employees are male in both works.)

Table 12.2   50/100 Geared Incentive Scheme—Fabrication welders

Performance	Total pay as a percentage of basic rate	Repair welders— total pay per hour $
0	100.00 %	15
20	100.00 %	15
50	100.00 %	15
60	106.66 %	16
75	116.66 %	17.50
80	120.00 %	18
90	126.66 %	19
100	133.33 %	20
110	140.00 %	21
120	146.66 %	22
130	153.33 %	23
150	166.66 %	25

Notes:
(1) In the middle column, basic rate equals 100%, and total pay (including bonus) is expressed as a percentage of it. Bonus payment commences above 50 performance, where the relationship between total pay and performance is calculated by the formula:
Total pay = 0.66 × Performance + 66.66
For example, a performance of 90 gives a total pay of 126.66%, which comprises 26.66% bonus and basic rate (100%).
(2) The right-hand column shows the actual total pay per hour in dollars, and includes bonus. Welders' basic rate is $15 per hour.
(3) Only the best fabrication welders will achieve a performance of 120 and above.

There is a good export market for fabrication castings, and an excellent profit possible, provided the rejection rate holds below 2 per cent and the welders achieve at least Standard Performance. Castings will be quality tested in the foundry at various production stages, and also by the customers at their own plants, mainly overseas. Otago Steel itself will meet the cost of fixing returned products: management intend that the fabrication welders would be paid only the basic rate for working on rejected castings.

Management also believed that the performance of 80 recorded during the derivation of time standards by the personnel department, and retrospectively calculated by them, arose because the welders received a temporary fixed rate of $20 per hour, irrespective of actual production achieved. Personnel department stood by the fairness of its work-measured times. Not surprisingly the welders dismissed both of these assertions, and on the contrary claimed that the bonus times were impossible to achieve, and thus they couldn't attain a decent bonus.

There is strong support among the workforce for the Union, perhaps surprising given the success of the *Employment Contracts Act 1991* in reducing union power in New Zealand. The Engineers' Union proved an able negotiator in the past, particularly in the Waverly plant.

Fabrication welders told their union officials they were rejecting the fabrication welding incentive scheme, and instead wanted a fixed rate of $25 per hour. They further commented that all incentive schemes in both works should operate on an individual basis. There is a great demand for their high-quality welding skills in the North Island and Australia. District basic rates for repair welders varied between $12 and $19 per hour.

Unexpectedly, the personnel director informed the Engineers' Union yesterday that he was giving the fabrication welders four weeks' notice of termination of their temporary fixed rate of $20 per hour: they would revert to their basic rate of $15 and not get bonuses until the incentive scheme was up and running. In an immediate reaction, the Engineers' Union called a mass meeting of workers in both plants, which intimated to management that industrial action would commence in all production areas, unless the welders' demands were met.

Source: Alexander Sibbald, University of Otago, New Zealand.

Activities for discussion, analysis and further research

1 How would you resolve the dispute?
2 What are the main personnel issues in the case?
3 Compare the 50/100 and 75/100 incentive schemes, and make any appropriate comments.

Leadership

Chapter 13

CHAPTER OUTLINE

How leaders influence others
Sources of leader power
Effective use of leader power

Searching for leadership traits

Identifying leader behaviours
Iowa and Michigan studies
Ohio State studies
The leadership grid
Managing diversity: Female versus male
   leader behaviours

Developing situational theories
Fiedler's contingency theory
Normative leadership model
Situational leadership theory
Path–goal theory

Promoting innovation: Transformational leadership
Are leaders necessary?
Substitutes for leadership
Leadership and the organisational life cycle

LEARNING OBJECTIVES

After studying this chapter, you should be able to:

○ Outline the major sources of leader power and explain how leaders can use power to encourage subordinate commitment.

○ Describe the current state of efforts to identify leadership traits.

○ Explain the different findings of Iowa, Michigan and Ohio State studies of leader behaviours and discuss their implications.

○ Describe the leadership grid approach to leadership and assess the extent to which females and males behave differently as leaders.

○ Delineate Fiedler's contingency theory of leadership.

○ Contrast the following situational approaches to leadership: normative leadership model, situational leadership theory and path–goal theory.

○ Describe transformational leadership and explain its link to innovation.

○ Evaluate the extent to which leaders are needed in organisations.

Striving for excellence

The leadership of an organisation sets the tone for absolutely everything which happens within it. This is demonstrated by Bob Franklin's leadership style. Bob operates in a consultative manner, takes advice and is perceived by his people to respect opinions of others. He is open about the status of things and trusts people with information. These practices are a strong success factor in setting a cultural standard for organisational culture.

Bob Franklin meets with other staff members face to face.

Once a quarter at the management conference, actual performance is measured against the business plan. All staff are involved from the evolution to the implementation of the business plan.

This leadership style cascades down the organisation to the shop floor. Bob Franklin spends time on the shop floor—not as an ad hoc activity but as a planned and scheduled one. He attempts to know all staff by name and build a personal relationship. It is his philosophy that he models a leadership role which he expects to be mirrored in all of his activities.

In the words of one of his staff who described him: 'He not only talks the talk, he walks the walk.'

In this chapter, we explore methods leaders have to influence others. We consider the possibility leaders have common traits, and review attempts to identify universal leader behaviours that leaders can use in any situation. We then probe recent efforts to develop situational approaches helping leaders decide when certain types of behaviour are applicable. Next, we examine transformational leadership and its link to innovation. Finally, we consider the question of whether and under what circumstances leaders are needed.

HOW LEADERS INFLUENCE OTHERS

leadership

Process of influencing others to achieve organisational goals

Why do people accept a leader's influence? Often they do so because the leaders have power. Yet as Katharine Graham notes, 'Nobody ever has as much power as you think they do' (*Forbes* 1987). In this section, we examine major power sources and ways leaders can use available power effectively.

power

Capacity to affect the behaviour of others

Sources of leader power

legitimate power

Power stemming from a position's placement in the managerial hierarchy and the authority vested in the position

Power is the capacity to affect others' behaviour (Mintzberg 1983; Pfeiffer 1981). Organisation leaders can rely on some or all six major types of power (French & Raven 1959; Raven 1993).

Legitimate power comes from a position's place in the managerial hierarchy and the authority vested in the position. When accepting a job, we know we will be directed in our work by an immediate boss and others in the hierarchy. Normally, we accept these directions as legitimate as these persons hold positions of authority.

reward power

Power based on the capacity to control and provide valued rewards to others

Reward power is based on the ability to control and provide valued rewards to others (Fierman 1995). Most organisations offer rewards under a manager's control, including pay rises, bonuses, interesting projects, promotion recommendations, a better office, support for training programs, high visibility assignments in the organisation, recognition, positive feedback and time off.

Coercive power depends on the ability to punish others if they do not display desired behaviours. Forms of coercion or punishment a manager may have available include criticisms, reprimands, suspensions, warning letters to go into an individual's personnel file, negative performance appraisals, demotions, withheld pay raises, and terminations.

Expert power is based on possession of expertise valued by others (Lopez 1994; *HR Magazine* 1994; Pottinger 1994). Managers often have considerable knowledge, technical skills and experience that are critical to subordinates' success.

Information power comes from access to and control over distribution of information about organisational operations and future plans (Raven & Kruglanski 1970; Grove 1993). Managers can usually access more information than subordinates and have discretion over how much is given to work-unit members.

Referent power comes from being admired, personally identified with, or liked by others (Fierman 1995; Bird 1994). When we admire people, want to be like them, or feel friendship toward them, we follow their directions more willingly and exhibit loyalty toward them.

Effective use of leader power

Although all power types are influential, they may produce different levels of subordinate motivation (Yukl 1994; Phillips-Carson, Carson & Roe 1993). Subordinates may react to a direction with commitment, compliance or resistance. With commitment, employees respond with enthusiasm, working hard toward organisational goals. With compliance, employees give minimal effort to give average, not outstanding, performance. With resistance, employees seem to comply but do an absolute minimum, even trying to sabotage organisational goal attainment.

The relationship between a leader's use of different power sources and likely subordinate reactions is shown in Table 13.1. As the table shows, expert and referent power generally lead to subordinate commitment, while legitimate, information, and reward power lead to compliance. Using coercive power often produces subordinate resistance (Norman 1988; Jackson 1990). Unsurprisingly, effective leaders minimise coercive power use (Rose 1993).

Table 13.1   Major sources of leader power and likely subordinate reactions

Likely subordinate reaction to power source

	Resistance	Compliance	Commitment
Power source	Coercion	Legitimate Information Reward	Referent Expert

Empowerment   Many managers integrate into their leadership styles an important aspect of power use: empowering their subordinates. In the process subordinates assume some leadership responsibility and authority, such as the right to enforce quality standards, check your own work, and schedule activities. Empowered subordinates are given the power to make decisions which leaders or supervisors did before.

Empowerment aids leadership in several ways:

○ Increased managerial ability to get things done with support and help from subordinates who have special work knowledge.

○ Increased worker involvement, motivation and commitment, as they work toward organisational goals.

○ Increased opportunity for managers to concentrate on significant issues and less time spent on daily supervision (Jones & Hill 1999).

Effective managers realise empowerment's significant benefits; ineffective managers try to keep control over decision making and force agreement from subordinates. The leadership style of managers who empower subordinates develops subordinates' ability to make good decisions, as well as guiding, coaching and inspiring subordinates (Burton 1995; Nakarmi 1995).

Managers usually rely on different types of power to be effective (Rapaport 1993). While power helps explain issues behind leader influence, we must look at other concepts, such as leadership traits and behaviours, to understand how leaders influence organisationally.

SEARCHING FOR LEADERSHIP TRAITS

After much discussion on effective leadership, army psychologists looking for methods to select officers during World War I set the stage for postwar research (Stogdill 1948). Early researchers saw it as logical to identify those traits distinguishing effective leaders from non-leaders (Jago 1982). **Traits** are an individual's internal qualities or characteristics, such as physical (e.g. height, weight, appearance, energy), personality (e.g. dominance, extroversion, originality), skills and abilities (e.g. intelligence, knowledge, technical competence) and social factors (e.g. interpersonal skills, sociability and socioeconomic position).

traits

Distinctive internal qualities or characteristics of an individual, such as physical characteristics, personality characteristics, skills and abilities, and social factors

Early researchers generally measured various individuals' traits, then put them in leaderless groups (without formal leaders) to see if certain traits would predict which individuals the group would identify as leaders. Researchers abandoned the trait approach during the 1950s when studies showed no traits separated leaders from non-leaders consistently (Stogdill 1948; Mann 1959).

Recent efforts, however, suggest the trait approach may have been abandoned too soon. Sophisticated statistical methods now allow better assessment of results across studies. Results show some traits originally studied are associated with individuals identified as leaders by others—specifically, intelligence, dominance, aggressiveness and decisiveness (Lord, De Vader & Alliger 1986).

Future research may find traits that predict leaders, at least in some cases. For example, a study at AT&T found that traits such as oral communication and human relations skills, need or motive for advancement, resistance to stress, tolerance of uncertainty, energy and creativity predicted managerial advancement (Bray, Campbell & Grant 1974). However, it is still uncertain whether a set of traits, if identified, would predict leadership performance. Many believe performance is more a case of things leaders do than their traits. Thus, recent leadership research looks at leader behaviours.

IDENTIFYING LEADER BEHAVIOURS

A number of researchers focused on the idea that specific behaviours make some leaders more effective than others (Richman 1988). Traits may be hard to change but, if universally effective behaviours were identified that led to successful leadership, most people could learn these behaviours. In this section, we review efforts at identifying significant leader behaviours. The research grew from work at the University of Iowa, the University of Michigan and Ohio State University. We also explore whether females and males display different behaviours in leadership positions.

Iowa and Michigan studies

At the University of Iowa, Kurt Lewin and colleagues made early attempts to identify effective leader behaviours (Lewin & Lippitt 1938). They considered three leader behaviours or styles: autocratic, democratic and laissez-faire. **Autocratic** leaders make unilateral decisions, dictate work methods, limit worker knowledge of goals to the next step, and give punitive feedback. In contrast, **democratic** leaders involve the group in decision making, let them decide on work methods, make overall goals known, and use feedback for coaching. **Laissez-faire** leaders generally give the group complete freedom, provide needed materials, participate only to answer questions, and avoid giving feedback—in other words, do very little.

To determine the most effective leadership style, Lewin's researchers trained adults in the styles then put them in charge of groups in preadolescent boys' clubs. They found on every criterion, groups with laissez-faire leaders underperformed when compared with both autocratic and democratic groups. On the other hand, quantity of work was equal in groups with autocratic and democratic leaders, while work quality and group satisfaction was higher in democratic groups. Thus it seemed democratic leadership could lead to both good work quantity and quality, with satisfied workers. Perhaps effective leadership's key had been found.

Unfortunately, more research produced mixed results. Sometimes democratic leadership gave higher performance than autocratic but other times performance was poorer than or just equal to the autocratic style. Results on follower satisfaction were consistent. Satisfaction levels were higher with a democratic leadership style than an autocratic one (Bass 1981).

These findings created a managerial dilemma. While a democratic leadership style produced more satisfied subordinates, it was not always accompanied by better, or even equal, performance. Furthermore, many managers were unused to operating democratically. To help resolve this dilemma, particularly in decision making, Robert Tannenbaum and Warren H. Schmidt (1973) developed the leader behaviours continuum shown in Figure 13.1. The continuum shows leadership behaviour gradations, ranging from an autocratic (boss-centred) approach on the left to a democratic (subordinate-centred) approach on the right. A move from the autocratic end is a move toward the democratic end and vice versa. In developing the continuum, the researchers softened the meaning of 'autocratic'. In their terms, it does not necessarily include punitive tendencies or keeping the task's ultimate goal hidden from subordinates. At the continuum's autocratic end, it means the boss makes the decision and lets others know what they are to do, instead of involving them in the decision.

autocratic

Behavioural style of leaders who tend to make unilateral decisions, dictate work methods, limit worker knowledge about goals to just the next step to be performed, and sometimes give feedback that is punitive

democratic

Behavioural style of leaders who tend to involve the group in decision making, let the group determine work methods, make overall goals known, and use feedback as an opportunity for helpful coaching

laissez-faire

Behavioural style of leaders who generally give the group complete freedom, provide necessary materials, participate only to answer questions, and avoid giving feedback

Fig. 13.1   Continuum of leader behaviours (Tannenbaum & Schmidt 1973, p. 164)

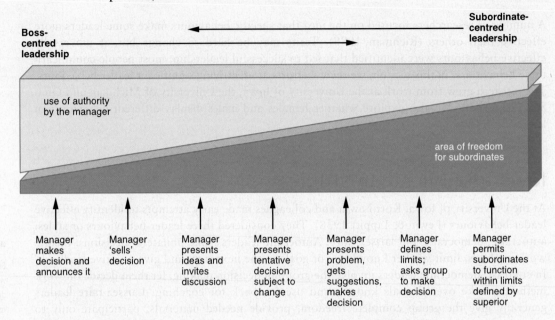

According to Tannenbaum and Schmidt, managers, when deciding on a leader behaviour pattern to adopt, must consider forces within themselves (e.g. comfort level with various options), within subordinates (e.g. readiness to assume responsibility), and the situation (e.g. time pressures). In the short term, managers must be flexible in their leader behaviour depending on the situation. In the long term, researchers advised managers to try to move to the subordinate-centred end of the continuum, on the basis that such leader behaviour will increase employee motivation, decision quality, teamwork, morale and employee development.

Further work at the University of Michigan confirmed the usefulness of the employee-centred approach compared to a more job-centred, or production-centred, approach. In an employee-centred approach, leaders build effective work groups dedicated to high performance goals. With a job-centred approach, leaders divide work into routine tasks and closely supervise workers, ensuring specified methods are followed and productivity standards met. However, output varied: an employee-centred approach might result in low output and a job-centred approach high output (Bass 1981; Likert 1961; 1979). Further study was needed.

Ohio State studies

A group at Ohio State University had another strategy for studying leadership. First they identified important leader behaviours. Then they developed a questionnaire to measure different leaders' behaviours and track factors such as group performance and satisfaction to see which behaviours were the most effective. Although several different leader behaviours, or styles, were identified, two seemed important: initiating structure and consideration.

Initiating structure is the degree to which a leader defines their own role and those of subordinates in achieving unit goals. It includes basic managerial functions of planning, organising

initiating structure

Degree to which a leader defines their own role and the roles of subordinates in terms of achieving unit goals

and directing, and focuses mainly on task issues. Initiating structure is similar to the Michigan studies' job-centred leader behaviour, but with a wider range of managerial functions. It emphasises task-related issues (Taylor 1993).

Consideration is the degree to which a leader builds mutual trust with subordinates, respects their ideas, and shows concern for their feelings. A consideration-oriented leader will be friendly to subordinates, maintain good two-way communication, and encourage participation in decision making (Gupta 1995; Jacob 1995; *Wall Street Journal* 1994). Consideration is similar to the Michigan studies' employee-centred leader behaviour. It emphasises people-related issues (King 1995).

In a major departure from both the Iowa and Michigan studies, which considered leadership dimensions to fall at opposite ends of the same continuum, Ohio State researchers saw initiating structure and consideration as independent behaviours (Chester 1979). This meant the behaviours were on separate continuums. A leader could be high on both, low on both, high on one and low on the other, or display gradations of both. The Ohio State two-dimensional approach is shown in Figure 13.2. The configuration was appealing, as many leaders seemed to display both initiating structure and consideration.

The two-dimensional approach led to the idea a leader could emphasise task issues and also produce high subordinate satisfaction levels by exhibiting consideration behaviour at the same time. While initial studies supported the view that a leader showing both high initiating structure and high consideration would produce best results, the idea of the great high-high leader was later viewed as a myth (Larson, Hunt & Osborn 1976). The reason the high-high approach lost favour was that, like the Iowa and Michigan studies, the studies were simplistic. Research accumulated, showing that situational elements, such as subordinate

consideration

Degree to which a leader builds mutual trust with subordinates, respects their ideas and shows concern for their feelings

Fig. 13.2   Ohio State two-dimensional model of leader behaviours

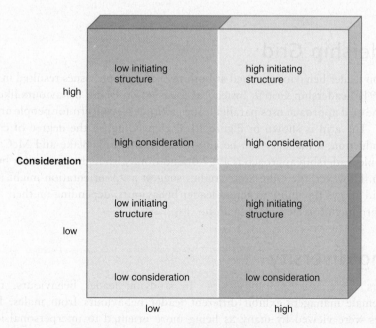

expectations and task nature, affected leadership behaviours' success (Kerr, Schriesheim, Murphy & Stogdill 1975; Greene 1979).

✖ How much can managers manage?　crossroads

Contemporary trends in management have brought in a new order of co-operation, partnership and consensus which is challenging the very basis upon which management exists—its right to manage, to control corporate destiny.

The conventional wisdom is that good management is all about consultation with workers. However, consultation takes time, and speed and timing are often crucial in today's rapidly changing business environment.

Consider the reflections of Robert Franklin, managing director of Autoliv, whose diary you will find in this chapter's The reflective practitioner. He has definite ideas about his leadership style and what works for him.

Decision point

1 The shift to more consultative and participative leadership is making organisations more competitive, especially as they will retain staff who are more involved in their organisation. Discuss the leadership characteristics of a manager who can shift between the consultative and the autocratic approach of leadership. Under what other circumstances besides issues of health, safety and product integrity might a manager forgo the consultative approach?

Reflection point

1 Review the leadership theories discussed in this chapter and discuss which might apply to a participative, consultative approach.

The Leadership Grid

The emphasis on leader behaviours aimed at both task and people issues resulted in Blake and McCanse's (1991) Leadership Grid®. Instead of focusing on leader behaviours like the Ohio State studies, the grid approach uses parallel leader attitudes—concern for people and concern for production. The grid is shown in Figure 13.3. Depending on the degree of concern for people and production, a manager can be anywhere on the grid. Blake and McCanse argue the most desirable leadership approach is a 9,9 orientation, with high concern for both people and production. However, the Ohio State studies suggest a 9,9 orientation might not always be best. The grid allows flexibility in actual leader behaviours, depending on their assessment of people and production issues in a situation.

Managing diversity

Female versus male leader behaviours In studying leader behaviours, researchers wondered if female managers exhibit different leader behaviours from males. Early data showed females were viewed by many as being more oriented to interpersonal issues and, therefore, ill-suited for leadership positions. Males were seen as more oriented to task issues

Fig. 13.3 The Leadership Grid (reprinted from Blake & McCanse 1991, p. 29)

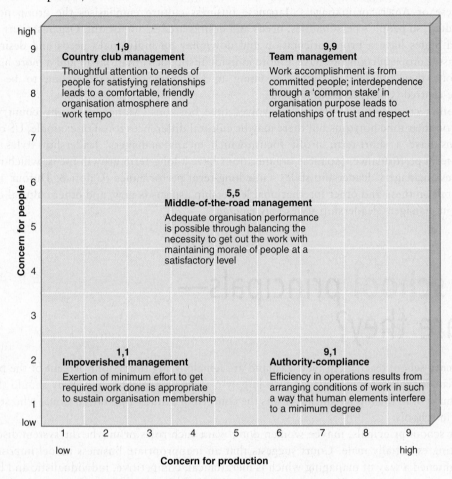

and better candidates for leadership responsibilities (Bass, Krusell & Alexander 1971; Rosen & Jerdee 1978). As it turns out, both stereotypes are incorrect. Most studies show female and male leaders are similar in the interpersonal and task behaviours exhibited, or that the differences are small. They are equally effective in gaining subordinate job satisfaction and performance (Bartol & Martin 1986; Dobbins & Platz 1986; Powell 1993).

Despite this there are few women in top-level positions in major companies (Dunkel 1996). There have been investigations into the 'glass ceiling', a term referring to barriers to women's upward mobility in organisations. These have proposed workforce diversity programs, expansion of traditional executive recruitment networks, and establishment of formal mentoring and career development programs to stop channelling women and people from minority groups into positions with low prospects for promotion to executive positions (Redwood 1996; Eagly, Karau & Mukhijani 1995).

Leadership styles across cultures   Evidence suggests leadership styles vary across countries or cultures. One suggestion is that European managers are more people-focused than either Japanese or American managers. Japanese business culture emphasises the group not the individual, so people's personalities, needs and desires are less important. Organisations in the United States have a profit orientation and downplay an individual's needs and desires. In contrast, European countries have a more individualistic focus than Japan and a more human-istic one than the United States, resulting in European managers tending to be more people-centred (Calori & Dufour 1995).

Another cross-cultural difference involves time horizons. Managers in any country will differ on their time horizons but there may be cultural differences too. For example, US organ-isations have a short-term profit focus, which means managers' leadership styles value short-term performance. Japanese organisations have a long-term growth focus, which means Japanese managers' leadership styles value long-term performance (Calori & Dufour 1995). Research on these and other international leadership aspects is new, and other cultural differ-ences in managers' leadership styles may emerge.

◖ Female school principals— Where are they?

case in point

Seventy-six per cent of primary school teachers in New Zealand are female. Only thirty-four percent of the princi-pals are female. A largely female workforce is managed by a largely male management group. Why should this be so and why so few women make it to the top in education was the concern of a study by Marian Court who studied Taranaki middle managers in schools.

Perhaps men make better school principals, maybe women don't want such roles or maybe the system discrimi-nates against women by being essentially male. Court suggests that an inappropriate business model imposed on schools since 1990 has heightened a way of managing which is hierarchical, competitive, individualistic and highly task orientated, in which people are only valued as means to an end. This is often characterised as a male model of management and leadership. Obviously there is huge variation between men and other men and between women and other women. Legislation has sought to level the playing field so that women can rise through the glass ceiling. The newly level playing field may be imbedded with this male way of doing things.

Court suggests that three strategies are available to women to succeed. One is to manage like a male, the second is to withdraw to the traditional nurturing roles at work, and the third is to seek to change the way leadership and management are perceived and carried out. That some women behave more like typical males than males and succeed is clear. That some women decide not to compete is true as well. Court maintains that a new generation of women is taking this challenge head on, drawing on skills and attitudes developed from their shared experience as women that emphasise collaboration and participation through the building of relationships, sharing information and valuing the views and contributions of all organisational members.

Research shows that schools with female principals have fewer discipline problems, higher staff and student morale and higher student achievements. Collegial decision making and collaborative ways of working have been shown to be effective in developing schools where staff, students and parents are well motivated towards learning.

Source: Written by G. Elkin, based on Court, M. (1994) and Sadker, M., Sadker, D. and Klein, S. (1986).

Activities for discussion, analysis and further research

1 In what ways is female leadership style different from a male's style?
2 Consider managers you have worked for and compare that of a female manager and that of a male manager. Which would you prefer to work for? Why?
3 Consider another industry where the workforce is largely female, such as nursing and social work. What can you find out about the proportion of females in leadership roles in that industry?

DEVELOPING SITUATIONAL THEORIES

Although trying to identify effective leader behaviours that work in every situation, researchers on the behavioural approach to leadership eventually found leader behaviours that worked well in one situation were often ineffective in another. As a result, leadership theories emerged involving situational factors. These are called **situational theories** due to their focus. They are also called contingency leadership theories as they hold that appropriate leader traits or behaviours are contingent, or dependent, on situational characteristics. Since many factors could influence leader effectiveness, different approaches have evolved. Among these are Fiedler's contingency model, the normative leadership model, Hersey and Blanchard's situational theory, and path–goal theory. Each gives managers useful guidance.

Fiedler's contingency model

Fred Fiedler and associates (Fiedler 1967; Fiedler & Garcia 1987) developed a **contingency model** which is a situational approach. The model argues that leaders differ in degree of orientation toward the task versus toward people. This makes leaders more effective in some situations but not others. Fiedler's contingency model identifies types of situations where each is likely to do best.

LPC orientation   The contingency model is based on a leader's **LPC orientation**, a personality trait measured by the least preferred coworker (LPC) scale. The LPC scale consists of 18 sets of bipolar adjectives. The leader is asked to describe the 'person with whom [he or she] can work least well' by rating them on a range of 1 to 8 points for each set. An example of a set is:

Pleasant :   :   :   :   :   :   : Unpleasant
          8   7   6   5   4   3   2   1

If a leader describes a least preferred coworker in negative terms on the LPC scale, they are likely to be task-motivated and put 'business before pleasure'. If the leader describes the least preferred coworker in relatively positive terms, they are likely to be people-motivated, believing a close relationship with coworkers is important to team success. The basic idea behind the model is that the leader's LPC orientation must be matched carefully to situational factors favouring that type of leader's prospects for success.

Assessing the situation   The contingency model identifies three situational factors affecting the degree of favourability or of situational control for a leader:

situational theories

Theories of leadership taking into consideration important situational factors

Fiedler's contingency model

Situational approach (developed by Fiedler and his associates) which suggests leaders differ in the degrees of their orientation toward the task versus toward the people

LPC (least preferred value of coworker) orientation

Personality trait indicating the extent to which an individual places a higher priority on task accomplishment than on personal relationships

Leader–member relations is the extent a leader has group members' support. It is an important situational variable. To assess this, a leader asks 'Will the group members do what I tell them, are they reliable, and do they support me?'

Task structure is the extent a task's goals, methods and performance standards are clearly specified. When assignments are vague, it is hard to know what should be done and to assess one's progress. Therefore, low task structure reduces a leader's favourableness, or situational control, while high task structure raises it. To analyse this, a leader asks 'Do I know what I am supposed to do and how the job is to be done?'

Position power is the amount of power the organisation gives the leader to accomplish necessary tasks. It is related to their ability to reward and punish. To evaluate this, a leader asks 'Do I have the support and backing of the "big boss" and the organisation in dealing with subordinates?'

Matching leadership style and situation   The contingency model combines different levels of these three situational factors into eight situations, or octants, representing different degrees of favourability, or situational control (see Fig. 13.4). For example, a combination of good leader–member relations, high task structure, and strong position power—octant 1—is most favourable. The boxes below the octants show which type of leader (low LPC or high LPC) matches the situation and will be most effective. According to the contingency model, in situations of either high (octants 1, 2, and 3, on the left) or extremely low favourability (octant 8, on the far right), a low-LPC leader does best; in moderate favourability situations (octants 4 through 7), a high-LPC leader excels.

The logic behind the model is that when a situation is very unfavourable, the leader must emphasise the need for task accomplishment strongly to move the group toward its goal. Alternatively, when it is very favourable, a task-oriented leader easily obtains the group's co-operation in doing what is needed to complete the task, because they willingly involve themselves. When the situation is moderately favourable, either because of poor leader–member relations or an unstructured task, a supportive, relationship-oriented leader

Fig. 13.4   Fiedler's contingency model of leadership (adapted from Jago 1982, p. 324)

Elements of situation	leader–member relations	good				poor			
	task structure	high		low		high		low	
	position power	strong	weak	strong	weak	strong	weak	strong	weak
Octant		1	2	3	4	5	6	7	8
Characteristics of leader	relationship-oriented (high LPC)	mismatch	mismatch	mismatch	match	match	match	match	mismatch
	task-oriented (low LPC)	match	match	match	mismatch	mismatch	mismatch	mismatch	match

Decreasing situational favourability/control →

Note: Leaders perform best when there exists a match between characteristics of leader and elements of situation

emphasises good working relationships across group members or provides support as they try to cope with an unstructured task (Fiedler & Chemers 1976; Rubello 1995).

Fiedler believes managers cannot change LPC orientation or management style easily. As a result, he argues that they must understand their leadership style and analyse the degree of favourability, or situational control. If the match is not good, a leader must make changes (e.g. increase task structure) or find a more suitable situation. Fiedler calls this 'engineering the job to fit the manager'.

Recent analyses of studies of Fiedler's contingency model support its value for managers. However, the analyses suggest other factors are at work that are not accounted for in the contingency model (Strube & Garcia 1981; Peters, Hartke & Pohlmann 1985). Managers may need to rely on other situational leadership theories, such as the normative leadership model.

Normative leadership model

The **normative leadership model** was designed for a fairly narrow, but important, purpose. It helps leaders assess critical situational factors affecting the degree to which they should involve subordinates in decisions (Vroom & Jago 1988).

The model has five management decision method types for use on group problems (problems where the decision affects more than one subordinate in the work unit). The methods are shown in Table 13.2. Each is designated by a letter and a number. 'A', 'C' and

normative leadership model

Model helping leaders assess critical situational factors affecting the extent to which they should involve subordinates in particular decisions

Table 13.2   Normative leadership model decision styles

Symbol	Definition
AI	You solve the problem or make the decision yourself using the information available to you at the present time.
AII	You obtain any necessary information from subordinates, then decide on a solution to the problem yourself. You may or may not tell subordinates the purpose of your questions or give information about the problem or decision on which you are working. The input provided by them is clearly in response to your request for specific information. They do not play a role in the definition of the problem or in generating or evaluating alternative solutions.
CI	You share the problem with relevant subordinates individually, getting their ideas and suggestions without bringing them together as a group. Then you make the decision. This decision may or may not reflect your subordinates' influence.
CII	You share the problem with your subordinates in a group meeting. In this meeting you obtain their ideas and suggestions. Then you make the decision, which may or may not reflect your subordinates' influence.
GII	You share the problem with your subordinates as a group. Together you generate and evaluate alternatives and attempt to reach agreement (consensus) on a solution. Your role is that of chairperson, co-ordinating the discussion, keeping it focused on the problem, and ensuring critical issues are discussed. You can provide the group with information or ideas that you have, but you do not try to 'press' them to adopt 'your' solution, and you are willing to accept and implement any solution supported by the entire group.

Source: Reprinted from Vroom & Yetton (1973).

'G' stand for 'autocratic', 'consultative' and 'group', respectively. Autocratic and consultative methods each have two variations, designated I and II. The methods become more participative when moving from AI (decide yourself) to GII (let the group decide).

To help managers choose the best method to use, the normative leadership model has eight basic questions about decision problem aspects (see the top of Fig. 13.5). Mainly the questions are clear. However, two points of clarification may help. First, in question QR 'technical quality' means the extent to which the solution facilitates reaching external objectives (e.g.

Fig. 13.5   Decision trees for normative leadership model (reprinted from Vroom & Jago 1988, pp. 184–5)

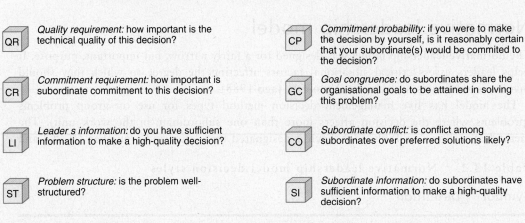

QR *Quality requirement:* how important is the technical quality of this decision?

CP *Commitment probability:* if you were to make the decision by yourself, is it reasonably certain that your subordinate(s) would be commited to the decision?

CR *Commitment requirement:* how important is subordinate commitment to this decision?

GC *Goal congruence:* do subordinates share the organisational goals to be attained in solving this problem?

LI *Leader s information:* do you have sufficient information to make a high-quality decision?

CO *Subordinate conflict:* is conflict among subordinates over preferred solutions likely?

ST *Problem structure:* is the problem well-structured?

SI *Subordinate information:* do subordinates have sufficient information to make a high-quality decision?

Development-driven decision tree

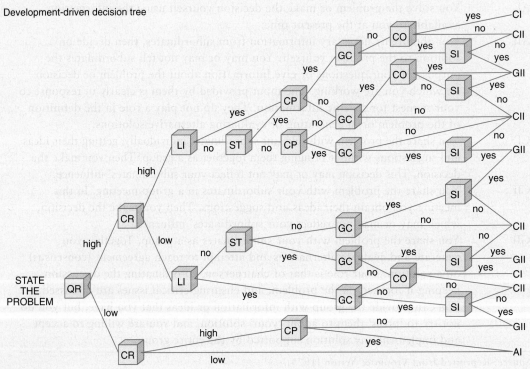

better quality, lower cost, longer lasting). Second, the structure aspect of question ST (problem structure) is similar to the structure issue in Fiedler's contingency theory. With structured problems, it is generally clear where you are, where you want to go, and what to do to get there (e.g. deciding when to schedule manufacture of extra batches of existing product). Unstructured problems are 'fuzzier' in regard to understanding the present situation, formulating goals, and deciding how to achieve them (e.g. deciding what new products to develop).

The eight questions are used with the two decision trees in Figure 13.5. The development-driven decision tree is used when subordinate development is more important than speed in the decision process. The time-driven decision tree is used when speed is more important than subordinate development.

The grey hair brigade leadership

gaining the edge

John Greaves has left behind a job as finance director of John Fairfax Holdings and become chairman of One.Tel and non-executive director of Spike Networks and Reckon. Greaves belongs to a growing list of prominent company executives and directors who have left old-economy companies to try their hands at the new. Among them can be found former New South Wales Premier Nick Greiner, who left the board of Coles Myer to become chairman of the online department store 'dstore'. Peter Shore, former managing director of Telstra's commercial and consumer division group, quit to join an Internet start-up called MyPrice. Two weeks later, Lindsay Yelland, former head of Telstra's business solutions division, moved to Solution6 as chief operating officer. The smart new-economy entrepreneurs understand the value of the grey brigade. They know that after the inevitable shake-out, money will gravitate to the companies with the best business plans, corporate governance and business principles. Well-known business people can help the small companies build the brands, customer loyalty and supply chains, as well as assist in strategic planning, development and financing. The e-commerce side speaks for itself. Now they need the grey hair and the business sense. Part of the attraction for older executives is to be involved in a completely new way of doing business.

There are good reasons for these individuals leaving the large, more traditional companies for the smaller, fleeter start-ups. As the old-economy becomes less relevant and, more importantly, their boards become less relevant, the directors are not nearly as able to influence the directions of the company as they did in days gone by. It is going to be a problem for quite a while for big icon companies like AMP to attract the best people. Old-economy companies will also have difficulty holding on to Internet-savvy senior and middle executives who are being offered half to two-thirds of their current salaries and 2 to 5 per cent equity in the new economy and they are having fun.

Source: Adapted form Gome, A. (2000).

Activities for discussion, analysis and further research

1 What sort of leadership is being expected from those 'grey brigade' individuals?
2 Why would start-up organisations value their leadership?
3 Do a literature search of recent newspapers or the business press and see if you can track down any others who have left old-economy companies and have joined start-ups.

Situational leadership theory

Another useful contingency theory is **situational leadership theory**, developed by Hersey and Blanchard (1988). It is based on the premise that leaders must alter their behaviours depending on one situational factor—follower readiness.

The situational theory focuses on two behaviours similar to the initiating-structure and consideration behaviours identified by Ohio State researchers:

Task behaviour refers to how much the leader spells out duties and responsibilities of an individual or group. It includes telling people what to do, how to do it, when to do it, where to do it, and who is to do it.

Relationship behaviour refers to how much the leader uses two-way or multiway communication. It includes listening, facilitating and supportive behaviours.

Since these behaviours, like the Ohio State leader behaviours, are seen to be two independent dimensions, a leader could be high on both, low on both, or high on one and low on the other (see the four quadrants in Fig. 13.6).

Fig. 13.6   Situational leadership theory® (adapted from Hersey & Blanchard 1993, p. 197)

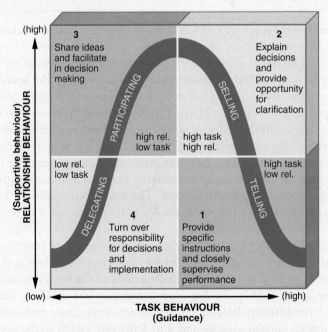

To determine the combination of leader behaviours for a given situation, under situational leadership theory, a leader must assess an interesting factor: the follower readiness. This is follower ability and willingness to accomplish a task. *Ability* (job readiness) includes ability, skill, knowledge and experience needed for a specific task. *Willingness* (psychological readiness) consists of confidence, commitment and motivation to complete a task. As can be seen at the bottom of Figure 13.6, the readiness continuum has four levels: low (R1), low to moderate (R2), moderate to high (R3) and high (R4).

The bell-shaped curve running through the four leadership quadrants specifies appropriate leadership style for a given level of readiness:

Telling is used in low-readiness situations, when followers are unable and unwilling or too insecure to be responsible for a given task. The telling style means giving individuals directions on what to do and how to do it.

Selling is used for low-to-moderate readiness, when followers are unable to take responsibility but are willing or feel confident to do so. The selling style gives specific directions, but it is supportive of individual willingness and enthusiasm.

Participating is used for moderate-to-high readiness, when followers can take responsibility but are unwilling or too insecure to do so. Since they can perform, a supportive, participating style that emphasises two-way communication and collaboration is most effective.

Delegating is used for high readiness, when followers are able and willing or confident enough to take responsibility. At this point, they need little support or direction; so the delegating style has the best chance.

To apply situational leadership theory, leaders decide the task areas they want to influence, assess the individual's readiness level, and select the leadership style corresponding to that level. The theory's underlying idea is that leaders should increase task-related readiness of followers quickly by changing their leadership style to move through the cycle from telling to delegating. Results of a comprehensive test of situational theory indicate its best application may be with newly hired employees or employees in new jobs. These are most likely to benefit from the telling style's highly structured leadership behaviour (Vecchio 1987; Graeff 1983; Blank, Weitzel & Green 1990).

Path–goal theory

The last situational leadership theory we consider, **path–goal theory**, explains how leader behaviour can influence motivation and job satisfaction of subordinates (House & Mitchell 1974). It is called path–goal theory as it focuses on the way leaders influence subordinates' perception of work goals and paths to achieve both work (performance) and personal goals (intrinsic and extrinsic rewards) (Evans 1970; House 1971; Wofford & Liska 1993).

Path–goal theory is based on expectancy motivation theory. As discussed in Chapter 12, expectancy theory has three main elements: effort-performance expectancy (probability our efforts will lead to required performance level), performance-outcome expectancy (probability our successful performance will lead to certain outcomes or rewards) and valence (anticipated value of outcomes or rewards). Path–goal theory uses expectancy theory to determine ways a leader might make achievement of work goals easier or more attractive.

path–goal theory

Theory attempting to explain how leader behaviour can positively influence the motivation and job satisfaction of subordinates

Leader behaviours   To affect subordinate perception of paths and goals, path–goal theory identifies four major leader behaviours:

Directive leader behaviour means letting subordinates know what is expected of them, giving guidance on work methods, developing work schedules, identifying work evaluation standards, and indicating a basis for outcomes or rewards. It is similar to task orientation.

Supportive leader behaviour means showing concern for subordinates' status, well-being and needs; doing things to make work more pleasant; and being friendly and approachable. The behaviour is similar to relationship-oriented or consideration behaviour.

Participative leader behaviour is characterised by consultation with subordinates, encouraging their suggestions, and considering their ideas carefully in decision making.

Achievement-oriented leader behaviour means setting challenging goals, expecting subordinates to perform at their highest level, and conveying a high level of confidence in subordinates.

Situational factors   In assessing how the four behaviours can enhance subordinates' path–goal motivation and job satisfaction, leaders must consider two situational factor types: subordinate characteristics and context characteristics. *Subordinate characteristics* are subordinates' personality traits, skills, abilities and needs. For example, a subordinate with low task-skills will be motivated by directive leadership, while someone highly skilled will appreciate a participative leader.

Context characteristics fall into three categories: task, work group, and the organisation's formal authority system (hierarchical levels, degree of decision centralisation, and nature of formal reward system). For example, supportive leadership may help motivation on a boring task, while achievement orientation may increase motivation on an interesting one.

Choosing leader behaviours   In using path–goal theory to select appropriate leader behaviours, leaders must diagnose the effects of various situational factors on the three expectancy theory elements (the path) and ultimately on desired end results (the goals). A practical approach to this involves three steps. First, think in terms of expectancy-theory elements. Second, diagnose situational factors to be changed to improve expectancy-theory elements (operate to increase motivation). Third, initiate appropriate leader behaviours to change situational factors (Norton 1994). Several examples of path–goal theory application are shown in Figure 13.7.

Since it is a situational leadership approach, path–goal theory argues that leadership behaviour effective in one situation is not necessarily so in another. For example, using directive leadership to clarify already clear task demands will have little effect as it is redundant. At worst, employees will be frustrated and this reduces the work's intrinsic valence. Notice that unlike Fiedler's contingency approach, path–goal theory assumes leaders can behave flexibly and learn to use any of its four leader behaviours as required (Gabor 1994).

Path–goal theory covers many leader behaviours and a large number of situational variables operating at the same time. Its flexibility gives managers a framework for considering the impact of their behaviours on subordinate motivation, goal attainment and job satisfaction (Yukl 1994).

---

directive

Leader behaviour involving letting subordinates know what is expected of them, providing guidance about work methods, developing work schedules, identifying work evaluation standards, and indicating the basis for outcomes or rewards

supportive

Leader behaviour entailing showing concern for the status, well-being and needs of subordinates; doing small things to make work more pleasant; and being friendly and approachable

participative

Leader behaviour characterised by consulting with subordinates, encouraging their suggestions, and carefully considering their ideas when making decisions

achievement-oriented

Leader behaviour involving setting challenging goals, expecting subordinates to perform at their highest level, and conveying a high degree of confidence in subordinates

Fig. 13.7   **Examples of path-goal theory (adapted from Yukl 1981, pp. 148, 150)**

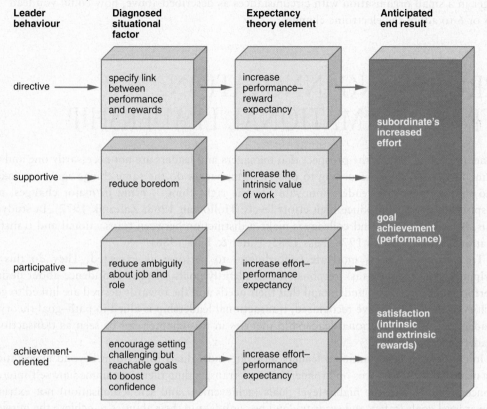

@ Small businesses need to log on

The tax office estimated in early 2000 that as many as 1.1 million small businesses is Australia are purely paper-based. The benefits of being computerised and on line are obvious for medium and large organisations. Yet the benefits for small businesses are even more profound. It provides instant access to national and global markets, instant communications to clients and suppliers, and it is the conduit to a wealth of information resources.

In 1999, only one in eight small businesses reported selling products or services via e-commerce. In order to counteract small business fears about the cost of getting Internet ready, the tax office has sent small registered organisations a software package called E-Records. This has been developed to help small organisations complete the required business activity statements, and will generate records about a business's cash profits and loss position and the pattern of revenue and expenditure.

The tax department claims that E-Records will save time, minimise administration costs, provide better information for the business owner and help them monitor cash-flow. The changes to the tax system, it is claimed, provide an unprecedented opportunity for small businesses to reap the benefits of electronic tools such as Internet and electronic record keeping to make them even more competitive.

Source: Adapted from Head, B. (2000).

Activities for discussion, analysis and further research

1 If you were a manager in a small organisation with circumstances as described above, how could you lead your small staff of 5 or 6 to adopt the electronic changes?

PROMOTING INNOVATION: TRANSFORMATIONAL LEADERSHIP

transactional leaders

Leaders who motivate subordinates to perform at expected levels by helping them recognise task responsibilities, identify goals, acquire confidence about meeting desired performance levels, and understand how their needs and the rewards they desire are linked to goal achievement

transformational leaders

Leaders who motivate individuals to perform beyond normal expectations by inspiring subordinates to focus on broader missions transcending their own immediate self-interests, to concentrate on intrinsic higher-level goals rather than extrinsic lower-level goals, and to have confidence in their abilities to achieve the extraordinary missions articulated by the leader

charisma

Leadership factor comprising the leader's ability to inspire pride, faith and respect; to recognise what is really important; and to articulate effectively a sense of mission, or vision, to inspire followers

One interesting issue is the prospect that managers and leaders are not necessarily one and the same (Zalezni 1990). According to one view, managers do the same things again and again (do things right), but leaders innovate (do the right things), bring in major changes, and inspire followers to produce high effort levels (Holloman 1968; Zaleznik 1977). In studying this, Bernard M. Bass and colleagues make a distinction between transactional and transformational leaders (Burns 1978; Bass 1985; Hater & Bass 1988).

Transactional leaders motivate subordinates to perform as expected. They do this by helping them recognise task responsibilities, identify goals, acquire confidence about desired performance levels, and understand that their needs and the rewards desired are linked to goal achievement. As you have recognised, transactional leadership is allied to path–goal theory of leadership. Other situational leadership theories in this chapter can be seen as transactional leadership approaches.

In contrast, **transformational leaders** motivate individuals to perform beyond expectations by inspiring them to: focus on broader missions transcending their own immediate self-interest; concentrate on intrinsic higher-level goals (achievement and self-actualisation) not extrinsic lower-level goals (safety and security); and be confident in their abilities to achieve the missions given by the leader (*Dealerscope* 1995; *Wall Street Journal* 1995; Nakarmi 1994).

Transformational leadership does not substitute for transactional leadership. It supplements for it with an add-on effect: performance above expectations (see Fig. 13.8). The logic is that even the most successful transformational leaders need transactional skills to manage effectively day-to-day events forming the broader mission's basis.

According to Bass, three factors are significant to transformational leadership: charisma, individualised consideration and intellectual stimulation. Of these, charisma is crucial. **Charisma** is the leader's ability to inspire pride, faith and respect; recognise what is really important; and to explain a sense of mission, or vision, inspiring followers (Sprout 1995). Individuals such as Martin Luther King, Mahatma Gandhi, John F. Kennedy and Franklin D. Roosevelt have been described as charismatic (House & Singh 1987).

Researchers have attempted to identify behavioural elements of charismatic leaders. Their efforts suggest these leaders try to change the status quo, project future goals or idealised visions that are very different from the present, and behave unconventionally and counter to existing norms. The studies indicate charismatic leaders rely heavily on referent and expert power and attempt to get others to share their radical vision of change (Conger & Kanungo 1987).

The second factor of transformational leadership, **individualised consideration**, means delegating projects to enhance each follower's capabilities, paying attention to the needs of

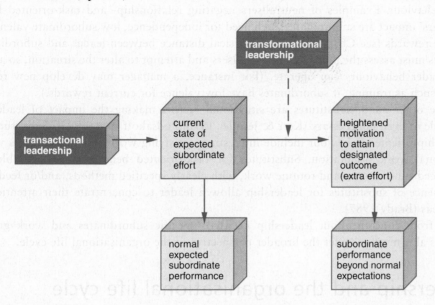

Fig. 13.8   Add-on effect of transformational leadership (adapted from Bass 1985, p. 23)

each, and treating them as worthy of respect. The third factor, **intellectual stimulation**, means offering new ideas to stimulate rethinking old ways of doing things, encouraging followers to look at problems from several vantage points, and fostering creative breakthroughs.

Not everyone agrees transformational leaders must have charisma. There seems to be agreement that such leaders must provide a vision of a desired future state, mobilise commitment, and generate changes to help followers to reach the vision (Howell & Frost 1989; Tichy & Ulrich 1984).

ARE LEADERS NECESSARY?

Some argue that leadership's importance is overrated and in many contexts will make little difference (Yukl 1989). In this section, we explore the prospect of leadership substitutes, and consider the organisational life-cycle approach to understanding the applicability of different leadership styles.

Substitutes for leadership

An interesting aspect of path–goal theory is that situational factors may make some leader behaviours unneeded and/or ineffective. However, path–goal theory does not specify conditions under which leader behaviour may not be needed due to situational factors. The **substitutes for leadership** approach tries to specify some situational factors likely to make leader behaviours not needed or negate their effectiveness (Kerr & Jermier 1978; Podsakoff, Niehoff, MacKenzie & Williams 1993).

---

individualised consideration

Leadership factor involving delegating projects to help develop each follower's capabilities, paying personal attention to each follower's needs, and treating each follower as an individual worthy of respect

intellectual stimulation

Leadership factor involving offering new ideas to stimulate followers to rethink old ways of doing things, encouraging followers to look at problems from multiple vantage points, and fostering creative breakthroughs in obstacles which seemed insurmountable

substitutes for leadership

Approach attempting to specify some main situational factors likely to make leader behaviours unnecessary or to negate their effectiveness

neutralisers

Situational factors making it impossible for a given leader behaviour to have an impact on subordinate performance and/or satisfaction

According to this approach, **neutralisers** are situational factors stopping a leader behaviour influencing subordinate performance and/or satisfaction. In other words, negating effects of leader behaviour. Examples of neutralisers negating relationship- and task-oriented leader behaviours' impact are subordinates' high need for independence, low subordinate valence for available rewards (see Chapter 12), and physical distance between leader and subordinates. Managers must assess the presence of neutralisers and attempt to alter the situation, so appropriate leader behaviours can operate. (For instance, a manager may develop new reward choices, such as training, if subordinates have low valence for current rewards.)

substitutes

Situational factors making leadership impact not only impossible but also unnecessary

On the other hand, **substitutes** are situational factors making the impact of leadership impossible or even unnecessary (Kerr & Jermier 1978; Podsakoff et al. 1993). Substitutes for relationship-oriented behaviour include interesting, satisfying work and subordinates with a professional work orientation. Substitutes for task-oriented behaviour include able and experienced subordinates and routine work, with clearly specified methods, and/or feedback. The presence of substitutes for leadership allow a leader to concentrate their attention on other areas (Brady 1987).

Aside from concern about leadership needs of specific subordinates and work groups, managers also must consider the broader perspective of the organisational life cycle.

Leadership and the organisational life cycle

The idea of organisations having life cycles, or predictable development stages (see Chapter 11), provides guidance about whether transactional or transformational leadership is most appropriate (see Table 13.3) (Baliga & Hunt 1987). When an organisation is at an entrepreneurial, or beginning, stage, transformational leadership is instrumental in creating a vision allowing the organisation to be born and take a few steps. At collectivity stage, additional workers join the initial core group, and transactional leadership becomes important to handle accelerating growth. By the formalisation and control stage, organisational growth needs greater emphasis on transactional leadership to maintain direction and control. By the elaboration of structure stage, high formalisation and control may reduce innovation to a low level, so heavy emphasis on transformational leadership is needed again. Though both transactional and transformational leadership styles can be used at every stage of effective organisations, the emphasis is different in each. Managers need to understand both leadership approaches to function effectively. Inherent in practising these approaches is the need to be well versed in organisational communication processes, a subject we turn to in the next chapter.

Table 13.3 Leadership and the organisational life cycle

Organisational life-cycle stage	Most important leadership emphasis
Entrepreneurial	Transformational
Collectivity	Transactional
Formalisation and control	Transactional
Elaboration of structure	Transformational

■ The MD's diary

In terms of leadership, the way I lead has two facets to it, two sides to it. Firstly I am very hands on, I am very much involved in every aspect of the business and very much wanting to be able to relate, at every level, with every individual in the organisation, so that I am able to at least understand what drives them, what motivates them, but also to make sure that I am communicating to them the sort of vision and direction that I'd like to see the organisation take. My style of leadership tends to be supportive, facilitative; I rarely ever will direct people in terms of how to work or how to behave. I see where I can add the greatest value is in providing and continuing to provide the overview in terms of what they're doing and whether in fact its leading towards the ultimate objectives of the organisation.

It's such a difficult question. I've never been able to tell people who ask me: 'why do you do what you do?' 'I just don't know, it just makes sense.' I am certainly not a directive sort of leader. I certainly do not tell people how to do things. I make sure we both sign up in terms of what the outcomes are—we both agree on that. And from there part of my role tends to be more of a coach, making sure that they are staying focused on the direction and putting their effort in the best way. I see myself as a counter-puncher to some extent, in that I like to ask people first to explore what is the right way to go about it, how they want to achieve something and then sell it to me. My role is to add some experience that I've had, add some knowledge, some skills. Providing for them some thinking that will allow them to review what they've proposed, that will input some other experiences that I've had that may change the direction a little bit. I tend to continually act as sources of review. Someone for them to bounce ideas off. That works very well for me. It's important that they retain ownership of the process, of the project or whatever.

I have one or two managers that are very proscriptive and what I tend to do is explore with them why they are making those decisions, why they are directing their people the way they are. I look for a way to force them to back away from it a little bit. It can be difficult. Managers have been trained in an era when we went through a lot of restructuring, a lot of change, and it was an era where it needed a lot of direction. Those people tend to accept direction, and in some cases prefer direction, but are also very directive themselves in the way they operate. They're the most difficult. What I try to do is take the ownership away from the manager and force them to hand it over to the person they're supporting and I'll do that by formally handing the ownership of the project to the individual. For example, if I have a manager who is not letting people get on with things in the way we've talked about, I will ask them to set up a project review, and get that person to report back to the management team in terms of what they are proposing. That helps to squeeze that manager a little bit to one side. Sometimes I can be quite brutal with it. This generally is successful. It's a little manipulative, but at the end of the day, it enables people to take ownership of what they should have ownership of. To me that's essential.

My kids ask me what I do when I get home of a night time, and I tell them I don't know because I do very little myself but I do a lot of reviewing of what others are doing. I structure it that way both in a formal and informal way. I have an open-door policy and people are encouraged to come and ask me questions. More often than not, they go out with a lot more questions than when they came in because I take every opportunity I can to challenge people's thinking about what they are doing and why they're doing it. I talk to them of my thinking, how I would approach it, some alternatives they might consider or some experiences that I've had. I don't see myself as a teacher. It seems to be a bit arrogant that I could sit back and say that my role in life is teaching and mentoring, but I guess that's a lot of what I do. I refuse to talk about problems. I am only interested in talking to them or supporting them with solutions or ideas.

I will generally not give anyone an answer as to how they should do something—unless it gets to a critical point—and there are those instances where things are absolutely critical and some decisions and actions have to be taken in a very proactive way. I will step in and say this has to be done now—this is how you will do—now go and do it. This is very rare and I am very hesitant about doing that.

I learned very early that the best way to get someone to do what you want them to do is if it is their idea. I do that constantly. I walk the shop floor and I talk to them about the things that are important to the organisation. My time of greatest satisfaction, where I think I'm really succeeding, is the time when people repeat messages I've given them in the past that they have taken on board as their own.

■ The subordinate's log

Leadership, to me, means the ability to make people want to do something for you, and the confidence to use that to achieve results. I think there are two aspects—you need to be able to influence them and have the power to direct them. One without the other does not work. I have the personal belief that leadership skills can be learnt and honed but that there is a core element which needs to be there. You cannot make something out of nothing. This may be against current accepted theory.

In my organisation, the CEO used to say that he doesn't believe in leadership. His view was that you should not have to lead or motivate people to do the job. You employ someone to do the job and they should do it. A team leader should not have to lead. People should just do their job. Resources, skills, techniques are one thing but in my opinion there needs to be something which binds the individuals together. I think that that binding is achieved by the attributes of the person who is the leader, and these attributes are in the person who assumes that role. I found that the critical part of a manager's skills is to identify leadership skills in their subordinates, because those are the people who are likely to make the best managers. I found that it is easier to teach management skills to someone with leadership qualities than it is to teach leadership attributes to someone with management skills.

Given that my CEO and I had different views of leadership and its practices, this affected the way I could do my job. He was less concerned about the opinions of his subordinates than I was, and this was both for sales and the allocation of consulting resources. He often disregarded interpersonal dynamics and he simply expected people to get the job done without consideration of the leadership issues.

My observations in a number of client organisations have revealed that the style of the head of a division, department or section crucially affects that area. The differences across the divisions of the same organisation can be very noticeable.

If I could choose my own leader, I would want one who is confident of their own abilities and sure of the directions they want to take. They need to be attuned to different personalities and be able to deal with them both as individuals and as a group. It is important that I can like the person but more important that I can respect them both professionally and personally.

Effective managers will engender other people's confidence in them, to follow their lead.

Focus on practice—Strategies for improving

1 In a situation where one of your staff was relationship-oriented, how would you make certain that the situation would lead to the satisfaction of their need?
2 How might you remove obstacles to success in order to enable your staff to succeed?
3 How would you enable a subordinate to know how their activities contribute to the success of the organisation?
4 Sharing organisational problems and issues with staff often leads to innovative and creative ideas. Design a process where you might make this a regular part of the weekly activities.

Source: Jones et al. (2000).

Chapter summary

Leadership is the process of influencing others to achieve organisational goals. Leaders use six major types of power to affect others' behaviour: legitimate, reward, coercive, expert, information and referent. Leaders must use their power carefully to encourage commitment and increase power, not diminish it.

Researchers have had limited success identifying common traits distinguishing leaders from non-leaders. Their efforts suggest some general traits, such as intelligence and dominance, and some that may apply only in specific situations.

Studying leader behaviours provided a more promising research direction. The Iowa, Michigan and Ohio State studies represent initial efforts identifying effective leadership behaviours, or styles. The Ohio State researchers found two leadership styles, initiating structure and consideration, viewed as independent dimensions not opposite ends of a continuum. Unfortunately, leaders showing both high initiating structure and high consideration did not always get the best results. The Leadership Grid emphasised concern for people and for production. Studies indicate female and male managers are similar in the levels of interpersonal and task behaviours exhibited.

Situational leadership theories grew from recognising that leader behaviours that work well in one situation are often not as effective in another. Fiedler's contingency model holds that a leader's effectiveness depends on whether the leader's LPC orientation fits the situation as set by leader–member relations, task structure and position power.

The normative leadership model aids leaders determine how much they should involve subordinates in decisions. Situational leadership theory argues that leaders must alter their combination of task and relationship behaviours according to follower task readiness. The path–goal theory of leadership relies on expectancy motivation theory and attempts to explain how leader behaviour influences subordinate motivation and job satisfaction.

Transformational leadership can be important in innovation as it motivates individuals to perform above normal expectations pursuing new visions. It adds-on to transactional leadership, as both are required.

There is some evidence leadership may make little or no difference in some contexts. One reason why it may not be so important is that there are substitutes for leadership. Also, the organisational life cycle may affect the emphasis placed on transactional and transformational leadership.

Questions for discussion and review

1 Outline the major power types available to managers. Think of a situation you were a leader in. What power types were available to you? Which ones did you use most? What follower commitment, compliance and resistance did you experience?

2 Explain the status of current research efforts identifying leader traits. What traits can you identify in an individual you consider to be a good leader? Do other familiar leaders possess any of the same traits?

3 Describe the continuum of boss- (authoritarian) and subordinate-centred (democratic) behaviours. Identify situations in which you have seen a democratic leader in action and situations in which you have seen an authoritarian one. How did followers react? Did situational factors make a difference in followers' reactions?

4 Explain the different findings of Iowa, Michigan and Ohio State researchers investigating leadership. Use the findings to give advice to managers on how to lead more effectively.

5 Outline the basic ideas in Fiedler's contingency leadership model. Analyse a student association or other leadership situation in terms of leader–member relations, task structure and position power. On the basis of Fiedler's model, what type of leader behaviour would the situation need?

6 Describe the normative leadership theory. Consider a leadership situation you have experienced in which a decision had to be made. Use the appropriate decision tree to determine the extent to which the group should have been involved. How closely does the decision tree's recommendation match what was done? What were the results?

7 Explain the basic ideas making up the path–goal leadership theory. Use it to determine how a leader might improve motivation in a familiar group.

8 Contrast transactional and transformational leadership. Identify a transactional leader and a transformational leader. To what extent is each one's leadership emphasis appropriate, given the life-cycle stage of the organisation each manages?

9 Differentiate between neutralisers and substitutes for leadership. Give two examples of each in a familiar organisation.

10 Explain how leadership relates to organisational life cycle. Analyse a familiar organisation in terms of appropriate use of transactional and transformational leadership.

Exercises for managing in the 21st century

Exercise 1
Self-assessment: Do you have charisma?

Charisma has helped many leaders in accomplishing goals. It may assist you in the future. The following questions will help in identifying your current charisma level.

1 I worry most about:
 a my current competitors
 b my future competitors

2 I'm most at ease thinking in:
 a generalities
 b specifics

3 I tend to focus on:
  a our missed opportunities
  b opportunities we've seized

4 I prefer to:
  a promote traditions that made us great
  b create new traditions

5 I like to communicate an idea via:
  a a written report
  b a one-page chart

6 I tend to ask:
  a 'How can we do this better?'
  b 'Why are we doing this?'

7 I believe:
  a there's always a way to minimise risk
  b some risks are too high

8 When I disagree with my boss, I typically:
  a coax him/her nicely to alter his/her view
  b bluntly tell him/her, 'You're wrong'

9 I tend to sway people by using:
  a emotions
  b logic

10 I think this quiz is:
  a ridiculous
  b fascinating

Source: Fortune (1996).

Exercise 2
Management exercise: The question of subordinate involvement

Case: Purchasing decision problem

You have just been appointed director (purchasing) for a manufacturing company. The company has seven plants, all located in the eastern states. Historically, the company has operated in a highly decentralised way with each plant manager encouraged to operate with only minimal control and direction from head office. In the area of purchasing, each purchasing executive who reports to the plant manager does the purchasing for their plant. There is little or no co-ordination among them, and relationships are largely competitive.

Your position was created when it appeared to the chief executive the company was likely to face increasing difficulty in securing certain essential raw materials. To protect the company against this possibility, the present haphazard decentralised arrangement must be abandoned or at least modified to meet current problems.

You were chosen for the position because of your extensive background in corporate purchasing with another firm which operated in a much more centralised fashion. Your appointment was announced in the last issue of the company house magazine. You are anxious to get started, particularly since the peak buying season is only three weeks away. A procedure must be established to minimise likelihood of serious shortages, and secondarily achieve economies associated with the added power of centralised purchasing (Vroom & Jago 1988).

Instructions

Get together with a group designated by your instructor, and use the normative leadership model to determine the degree to which you should involve subordinates in the purchasing decision.

 # Surviving the crisis

on the rim—
in Malaysia

Lim Kim Hong, now 48, is a native of Muar in the Malaysian state of Johor. He began life in a poor family, forced to leave school at 13 to become an apprentice carpenter. By age 14 and dissatisfied with earnings of $2.10 a month, he quit to set up a backyard furniture business. Within six months, Lim had a staff of eight—and the rest is history. His company, Sumurwand, began as a sole proprietorship set up by Lim in 1969. In 1980, Lim incorporated it as Lim Kim Hong Holdings Sdn Bhd, which was then renamed Sumurwand Sdn Bhd in 1984. From furniture, Lim expanded to spring mattresses in the late 1970s and stainless steel pipes in the early 1990s. He started the first Malaysian manufacturing operations in China by opening a mattress factory in Tianjin in 1984. By 1996, the China operations had expanded to 10 plants.

With funds realised from the sale of mattress flagship Kanzen Bhd (formerly knows as Dreamland Holdings Bhd), Lim is looking around for something to buy. He has set his sights on Neico as a vehicle to penetrate the electrical appliances industry. Lim is totally focused on strengthening Neico by providing new impetus and expanding its business. He feels a sense of pride that domestic companies have the resources to take over companies badly hit by the recession.

Lim is proud of Sumurwand's track record. He built up Dreamland spring mattress business against the then market leader Dunlop, penetrated the spring mattress market in China, and successfully entered the US market for stainless steel pipe fittings in the early 1990s. However, his pride is balanced with realism. He knows that he cannot fight the big boys head-on. His strategy is to focus on Islamic countries where the government has been promoting Malaysia's image and manufacturing capabilities. It is believed that if Sumurwand can build up a good brand image and knows how to market its electrical products effectively, especially in niche markets like the Middle East, it is likely to be successful. However, the mattress and electrical appliance businesses are different. This will be a major test of Lim's entrepreneurial skills.

Over the past twenty years. Lim has developed from a small businessman into a tycoon who has overcome his early handicap of low educational background to overcome many obstacles.

Though Lim has had very little formal education, he has always placed a high importance on learning, attending a number of courses in Taiwan. He also surrounds himself with highly qualified managers and professionals. As a manager, he is said to be direct, straightforward and results oriented. His philosophy is that he will not ask his employees to do something he would not do himself. He leads by example.

Certainly, Lim is one of a select group of Asian business tycoons who have survived the regional crisis with their fortunes intact. With the benefit of hindsight, reasons for his resilience appear obvious: conservative and focused management, healthy cash surpluses, low gearing and an impeccable sense of timing in sniffing out bargains.

Source: Lee Min Keong (1999).

Activities for discussion, analysis and further research

1 What kind of leader do you think Lim Kim Hong is? Why?
2 What issues must he take into consideration to keep on expanding his business?
3 Find out if Sumurwand Sdn Bhd has a web site. If it does, log onto it and look up the company's objectives and mission. See if you can find out anything about Lim Kim Hong's leadership style.

Chapter 14

Managerial Communication

CHAPTER OUTLINE

The nature of managerial communication
Types of communication
Managerial communication preferences
Basic components of the communication process

**Influences on individual communication and
   interpersonal processes**
Perceptual processes
Attribution processes
Semantics

Managing diversity: Cultural context
Communication skills

Group communication networks

Organisational communication channels
Vertical communication
Horizontal communication
Informal communication: The grapevine
Using electronics to facilitate communication

LEARNING OBJECTIVES

After studying this chapter, you should be able to:

○ Explain the major types of managerial communication and discuss managerial communication
   preferences.
○ Outline the basic components of the communication process.
○ Describe how perceptual processes influence individual communication.
○ Explain the role of attribution processes, semantics, the cultural context and communication
   skills in communication by individuals.
○ Assess the usefulness of centralised and decentralised group communication networks.
○ Distinguish between major organisational communication channels and explain their role in
   managing effectively.
○ Discuss the growing potential of electronics in regard to organisational communication
   channels.

Striving for excellence

In the past organisation charts were not released to the staff. This was done to prevent staff from seeing labels and pitching themselves into boxes. To disseminate the organisational chart therefore was a risk, but a strategy had to be developed where communication of the chart was possible while eliminating the risks.

At that stage, the concept of blue jackets for everyone was brought in. However, that proved not to be sufficient. The jackets did not sufficiently establish a sense of identity. This was graphically demonstrated a year after their introduction in the following incident. There was a problem on the line which should have easily been averted if the person on the line had told the engineer of the potential difficulties. The person on the line must have known that a particular process would not work but, when the person was questioned as to why the engineer had not been warned, the answer was 'He wears a tie'. At the next management-team meeting, the decision was taken that ties were not necessary on site. Male staff were requested not to wear ties or business shirts on site unless expecting external guests or customers. This decision brought out issues for some of the longer-serving staff. One in particular had been with the company for over 20 years, and every Friday he wore a bow tie. He objected and was allowed to continue wearing a tie. This staff member gradually gave up wearing a week-day tie but always wore his bow tie on Friday. Upon retirement, he presented this bow tie to his successor. However, on the first tieless day, every female staff member put on a tie—again an indicator of a strong, healthy, positive culture.

While symbols can be powerful communicators, other mechanisms can be very powerful as well. Toolbox is a memo system, the symbol representing a memo which is required reading by everyone. It focuses on what is going on around the place and should be known by all. It used to be circulated with a circulation list which had to be signed by all. In manufacturing, where language might be a problem, the team leader was required to read it and lead a discussion. Furthermore, Toolbox was posted on the bulletin boards and could be accessed by individuals who wanted to chat over it or reflect on it.

Toolbox was challenged by Management Systems, who wanted to reduce paper consumption. It is now e-mailed and this is causing a problem as it is possible to delete it unread. Furthermore, e-mail systems are not perfect and if an error occurs, it can easily be missed. Thought is being given to finding ways to overcome this with the assistance of the IT people. Toolbox is still posted on the notice boards but this removes the immediacy and perhaps lowers the level of commitment. Toolbox has been a valuable communication tool with high reliability, fostering an esprit de corps and discipline across the company.

Each team leader holds a morning meeting with their team using a set agenda which includes any Toolboxes, suggestions from the shopfloor, OH&S and HR issues. The team leaders then meet with the production managers and suggestions and issues are added to an action list to be dealt with by the end of the week and often by the end of the day.

Good organisational communication and interpersonal processes are crucial elements of organisational effectiveness (Goldhaber 1993). Effective communication is vital to all major management functions; it is especially important to the leading function as it provides the channel for interaction with and impact on others. In this chapter, we examine managerial communication and associated interpersonal processes, including different types of communication managers use, their communication preferences, and the basic components of the communication process. We consider factors which either block or enhance individuals' communication and interactions. We briefly look at group communication networks. Finally, we consider communication channels in organisations, investigate how the use of multiple communication channels promotes innovation, and explore electronics use in organisational communication.

THE NATURE OF MANAGERIAL COMMUNICATION

Communication is the exchange of messages between people to achieve common meanings (Baskin & Aronoff 1980). Unless meanings are shared, managers cannot influence others.

Communication is critical to every manager's job. In fact it has been estimated that managers spend about 85 per cent of their day in some communication activity (Adams, Todd & Nelson 1993). Without effective communication, even brilliant strategies and best-laid plans will fail (Thomas & Sireno 1980; Hildebrandt, Bon, Miller & Swinyard 1982). There will also be a great many more accidents and potentially risky activities when communication is ineffective (Winslow 1995; *Wall Street Journal* 1995)

communication

Exchange of messages between people to achieve common meanings

Types of communication

Managers use two major communication types: verbal and non-verbal. Each is important in effective transmission of organisational messages.

Verbal communication   **Verbal communication** is the written or oral use of words to communicate. Both written and oral communications pervade organisations.

There is a variety of written communication forms, such as letters, memoranda, reports, résumés, written telephone messages, newsletters and manuals. The cost of producing a single letter or memo has risen, and has been estimated at between $7 and $25 for an average memo (Max 1985; Chesanow 1987). Yet over 80 per cent of managers judged the quality of written communications they received as being either fair or poor. Further, 55 per cent of them saw their own writing skills as fair or poor (Kiechel 1982).

verbal communication

Written or oral use of words to communicate

Despite poor skills, written communication has advantages over oral. It gives a record of the message, can be circulated widely with little effort, and allows the sender to carefully consider the intended message. Written communication also has disadvantages, including preparation expenses, its impersonal nature, potential receiver misunderstanding, and delayed feedback on the message's effectiveness (Lewis 1980).

Oral communication, or the spoken word, occurs in face-to-face conversation, in meetings and telephone conversations. Oral communication is fast, generally more personal than written communication, and provides rapid feedback from those in the conversation. Among oral communication's disadvantages are that it is time-consuming, it can be difficult to finish, and more work is needed to document the communication if a record is wanted (Lewis 1980).

Given the advantages and disadvantages of written and oral communication, it is not surprising managers use both types of verbal communication. Later in this chapter we consider managerial preferences for written and oral communication. First, we consider another type of communication important to managers.

Oral communication by senior managers, either one to one, in meetings or on the phone, occupies a large amount of their time.

non-verbal communication

Communication by means of elements and behaviours that are not coded into words

kinesic behaviour

Body movements, such as gestures, facial expressions, eye movements and posture

proxemics

Influence of proximity and space on communication

paralanguage

Vocal aspects of communication that relate to how something is said rather than to what is said

object language

Communicative use of material things, including clothing, cosmetics, furniture and architecture

Non-verbal communication   **Non-verbal communication** is the use of elements and behaviours not coded into words. Studies estimate non-verbal aspects are 65 to 93 per cent of what is communicated (Birdwhistell 1972). Of course, verbal communication is impossible without some accompanying non-verbal communication. Important categories are kinesic behaviour, proxemics, paralanguage and object language.

Kinesic behaviour (or 'body language') is body movements, such as gestures, facial expressions, eye movements and posture. In assessing people's feelings on an issue, we draw conclusions not only from their words but also from non-verbal behaviour, such as facial expressions.

Proxemics is the impact of proximity and space on communication. For example, managers may arrange their offices with an informal area where people can sit without feeling the spatial distance and formality of a big desk. Another familiar example of proxemics is that it is more likely you will get to know students you sit near in class than those elsewhere in the room.

Paralanguage is the vocal aspects of communication, or how something is said rather than what. Voice quality and tone, laughing and yawning are in this category.

Object language is use of material things, such as clothing, cosmetics, furniture and architecture, to communicate (Baskin & Aronoff 1980; Nabers 1995). If you prepared a job résumé lately, you probably gave some thought to layout and the type of paper to print it on. These are object language aspects, you communicating information about yourself beyond the words on the page. These non-verbal elements are important to managers' messages.

Evidence shows that when verbal and non-verbal elements contradict, receivers will see non-verbal communication as accurate (Hayes 1973; Baskin & Aronoff 1980). This means managers must attend to both non-verbal and verbal parts of their messages (Schmitt 1997). In addition, to better understand others' thoughts and feelings, managers should consider both non-verbal and verbal parts of messages they receive.

Managerial communication preferences

As noted before, managers spend much time communicating in one form or another. Studies show they prefer oral to written communication, largely as oral communication is more informal and timely (Mintzberg 1973; Kurke & Alrich 1983). One study showed four top managers in four different types of organisations spent 74 per cent of their working hours communicating orally with others, through informal and formal meetings, telephone calls and organisation tours (see Fig. 14.1) (Smeltzer & Fann 1989; Mintzberg 1975). They spent about 50 per cent of that time interacting with subordinates. Most of the remaining time was spent with the board of directors, peers, trade organisations, clients and suppliers. Although the study focused on top-level managers, other levels also prefer spoken over the written word (Lewis 1980; Smeltzer & Fann 1989).

Managers serve as communication centres through the managerial roles discussed in Chapter 1 (such as monitor, disseminator and spokesperson). Managers in these roles are the basis of the organisation's communication network. If managers and those they interact with do not communicate effectively, there can be serious repercussions, not only for their work unit but the rest of the organisation (Petzinger 1997).

On the other hand, efforts to promote effective communication can be a key to an organisation's success.

Fig. 14.1   **Proportion of time top managers spent on various activities (based on Kurke & Aldrich 1983, p. 979)**

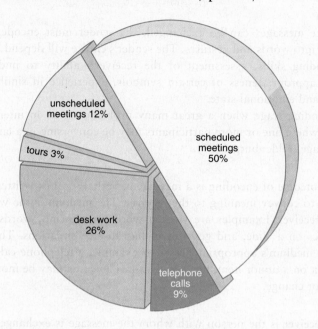

Basic components of the communication process

A look at the communication process's basic components helps one appreciate the challenge of effective organisational communication (Krone, Jablin & Putnam 1987). It also highlights the fact that the only way we interact with others is by communication. The components of the process are shown in Figure 14.2.

Fig. 14.2   **Basic components of the communication process (adapted from Lewis 1980, p. 55)**

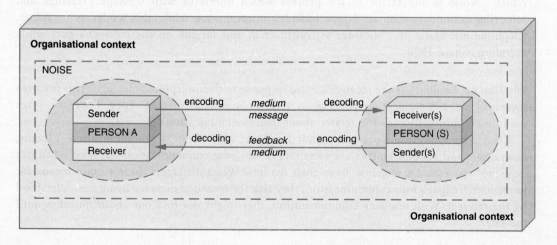

sender

Initiator of the message

Sender   The **sender** initiates the message. This is usually in response to an outside stimulus, a question, a meeting, an interview, a problem or report.

encode

Process of translating an intended message into words and gestures

Encoding   Before messages can be exchanged, the sender must **encode**, or translate the intended meaning into words and gestures. The sender's choice will depend on factors such as the sender's encoding skills, assessment of the receiver's ability to understand symbols, judgments about appropriateness of certain symbols, experience in similar situations, job status, education and emotional state.

It is in the encoding stage when a great many problems occur in international business communications, where one or more participants may be conversing in a language other than their native language (Oldenburg 1989).

message

Encoding-process outcome, which consists of verbal and non-verbal symbols developed to convey meaning to the receiver

Message   The outcome of encoding is a **message** of verbal (oral or written) and non-verbal symbols designed to convey meaning to the receiver. The **medium** is the way the message is conveyed to the receiver. Examples are written words in a memo, words spoken over the telephone, graphics on a slide, and gestures in face-to-face situations. The message sender must consider the medium's appropriateness. For example, a telephone call may be effective resolving a conflict on a minor item, but a face-to-face meeting may be more appropriate for negotiating a major change.

medium

Method used to convey the message to the intended receiver

receiver

Person with whom the message is exchanged

Receiver   The **receiver** is the person with whom the message is exchanged. If no exchange takes place (i.e. the receiver does not receive the message), there is no communication. There may be only one receiver, in a conversation between two individuals, or many, with a report sent to organisation members.

decode

Process of translating symbols into the interpreted message

Decoding   When the message is received, the receiver **decodes**, or translates symbols into the interpreted message. With effective communication, sender and receiver achieve common meaning. However, the decoding process may result in problems if the receiver does not decode the message as intended.

noise

Any factor in the communication process interfering with exchanging messages and achieving common meaning

Noise   **Noise** is any factor in the process which interferes with message exchange and achieving common meaning. Noise includes interruptions while the sender is encoding, telephone line static as a message is transmitted, and fatigue on the receiver's part while decoding (Chase 1998).

feedback

Receiver's basic response to the interpreted message

Feedback   **Feedback** is the receiver's basic response to the interpreted message. This involves reversing the communication process so receiver and sender swap roles. Feedback gives preliminary information to the sender about their communication's success.

one-way communication

Communication resulting when the communication process does not allow for feedback

When communication does not permit feedback, it is **one-way communication**. Memos, newsletters and announcements are examples of one-way communication—at least when not explicitly requesting a response from their readers. When managers do not build means for immediate feedback into communication, they risk the intended message being misunderstood by the receiver. With one-way communication, they might not find out about mistakes until too late.

Conversely, when communication specifically includes feedback, as in Figure 14.2, it is **two-way communication**. This communication type is more likely to give accurate exchange of common meaning (Chase 1998). Still, effective two-way communication needs careful attention to the process, particularly if many organisation layers are involved in transmission. This is needed for two reasons. First, each additional link increases the possibility that encoding and decoding processes and/or noise will distort information. Second, subordinates are reluctant to give negative information to upper hierarchical layers as they expect criticism (O'Reilly & Roberts 1974; Kaplan, Drath & Kofodimos 1984). So managers must work hard for accurate information even with two-way communication.

In addition to the normal communication difficulties involved in encoding, decoding, noise and subordinate reluctance to give negative information, there may be stresses in a situation that are likely to cause communication breakdown.

INFLUENCES ON INDIVIDUAL COMMUNICATION AND INTERPERSONAL PROCESSES

You may have experienced the frustration of arriving at a meeting only to find that some anticipated participants did not seem to know about it. How is it some people receive a particular communication and others do not? While miscommunications may be due to misdirected mail and lost messages, they may result from individual factors influencing organisational communication. These include perceptual issues, attribution processes, semantics, cultural context and communication skills.

Perceptual processes

Perception is the process of acquiring and making sense of information in the environment. It is a complex process involving three main stages. The first is *selecting*, filtering stimuli so only some information receives our attention. For example, suppose a manager taking over a new unit hears a rumour an individual in the unit has a short temper. If the manager is not careful, this information may cause them to focus on situations where the person is impatient or angry.

The second stage of the process is *organising*, patterning of information from the selection stage. Slowly say each of the following four words (Luthans 1995):

M-A-C-T-A-V-I-S-H
M-A-C-D-O-N-A-L-D
M-A-C-B-E-T-H
M-A-C-H-I-N-E-R-Y

Like many, you may have said the last as 'MacHinery.' This happens because the pattern has us expect another word with the same type of pronunciation. This exercise illustrates a perception characteristic: the tendency to organise information into expected patterns. In the example of the person rumoured to have a short temper, the manager may organise selectively perceived behaviour into a pattern of incidents where the person was angry.

two-way communication

Communication resulting when the communication process explicitly includes feedback

perception

Process individuals use to acquire and make sense out of information from the environment

The third stage is *interpreting*, giving meaning to selected and organised information. In our example, the manager may begin to (perhaps unfairly) interpret information showing the person has a short temper.

Individuals' perceptions are affected by many factors such as experiences, needs, personality, culture and education. As a result, individuals differ in their perceptions of the same situations and messages. Several distortions apply to managerial communication and interactions. These are stereotyping, the halo effect, projection and perceptual defence (Gordon 1996; Luthans 1995). Awareness of these can help managers avoid problems such distortions create.

Stereotyping   **Stereotyping** is the tendency to attribute characteristics to someone on the basis of a group to which they belong. When a manager engages in stereotyping, two steps occur. First, the manager classifies the person as belonging to a group whose members are seen as having some common characteristics. Second, the manager uses those perceived characteristics to draw conclusions about the individual's characteristics, rather than getting information directly.

Stereotyping is a problem when generalisations are inapplicable or do not apply evenly to all group members or when people generalise about less specifically related matters. Then, managers may convey inappropriate expectations (Mathewson 1988).

Halo effect   The **halo effect** is the use of a general impression, based on one or a few characteristics of a person, to judge other characteristics of theirs. For example, a manager may have a general impression based on one thing a worker does, such as compiling reports well or poorly, to judge their ability in other areas, such as customer handling. To avoid the halo effect, interviewers and managers must gather enough data to make reasonable judgments in areas they are trying to evaluate.

Projection   **Projection** is the tendency to assume others share your thoughts, feelings and characteristics. Unfortunately, projection encourages managers to use one-way communication, assuming they know how their employees feel on all issues. Using two-way communication to learn how others feel about various issues can help avoid projection's effects.

Perceptual defence   **Perceptual defence** is the tendency to block out or distort information one finds threatening or challenging to one's beliefs (Luthans 1995). So managers or workers may be unreceptive to some information. This can lead to the 'shoot the bearer of bad news' syndrome, where a person 'beheads' the bad-news bearer though they were not the problem's cause. Thus some managers get angry at employees providing information about serious problems which cannot be ignored, even though the manager needs to be aware of them.

Sidebar definitions

stereotyping

Tendency to attribute characteristics to an individual on the basis of an assessment of the group to which they belong

halo effect

Tendency to use a general impression based on one or a few characteristics of an individual to judge other characteristics of that same individual

projection

Tendency of an individual to assume others share their thoughts, feelings and characteristics

perceptual defence

Tendency to block out or distort information one finds threatening or which challenges one's beliefs

● Horizon Pacific Television   case in point

On 6 June 1997, Television New Zealand (TVNZ) announced that the Horizon Pacific Network was to be restructured. This involved all five regions in New Zealand: Auckland, Hamilton, Wellington, Christchurch and Dunedin. The entire network was to be axed. One hundred and twenty jobs were to be lost as a result. A major reason for the restructuring of TVNZ and the loss of the regional network was cost cutting. The Horizon network was unprofitable.

However, it is important to note that before the stations went to air on 19 March 1995, TVNZ had stated that the network had three years to prove they could break even.

The other major reason for the sudden death of the Horizon network was to signal a change of direction in the marketplace. Increased competition occurred with the launching of TV4 in early July 1997. TVNZ felt threatened by a new station snapping up a segment of the market. They felt they needed to act quickly to cope with the increased competition. The axing of Horizon Pacific Television meant that the UHF frequencies could be used to broadcast a youth channel straight from a satellite, a cost-effective way to provide a service to the new market.

The closure of the stations was announced to staff on Monday at midday by TVNZ executives throughout the country. The previous Friday TV3 announced on the news bulletin that Horizon Pacific Television was to close down. Soon after this news bulletin and throughout the whole weekend, staff heard rumours and wondered whether or not they were correct. The decision by the board had been made the week before the official announcement. A leaked memorandum quickly spread around the Auckland advertising agencies and to TV3's news bulletin.

Diary from a staff member

Friday 6 June 1997
After saying goodbye to my work mates, I left work ready for a good weekend. That night my friend rang to say TV3 had announced that all the stations were to close down and the News would finish next Friday. I didn't know what to think, obviously it couldn't be true or else we would have heard about it. Finally I said to my stressed-out friend, 'Don't worry about it, we still have jobs.' After the phone call I didn't think much more about it and carried on with my weekend.

Saturday 7 June
I got up as usual to drink my coffee and read the paper. To my disbelief the *Otago Daily Times* was also saying that my work would cease. I didn't know what to think and rang a work mate who also didn't know what was going on. The fact that a memo got leaked meant something serious was happening. However, why did everyone leave work on Friday thinking we still had permanent jobs to go back to? All day and night I was getting angrier and angrier because I had no idea what was going on and hearing from the media that I had no job made me even more upset.

Sunday 8 June
Woke up feeling dreadful because I couldn't sleep properly. This afternoon my boss phoned to say there would be a meeting on Monday with TVNZ executives. I kept asking him what was happening, but he said, 'I can not comment, you will find out tomorrow.' I couldn't believe it, my own boss wouldn't give me any answers. I hung up feeling even more frustrated and annoyed about the whole thing.

Monday 9 June
I got up early absolutely dreading having to go to work. Everyone was very solemn. We all knew whatever happened would be for the worst. After waiting around until midday everyone went to the meeting with the people from TVNZ. Basically everything the media said was true, the News was to finish this Friday therefore nearly half of us would be unemployed in four days. Because I worked in sales and programming it meant I would be employed until the end of the month. TVNZ organised for a human resources organisation to counsel us and help out with CVs. This didn't make me feel any better. As soon as the meeting ended everyone went back to their desks stunned. For the rest of the day I refused to do anything and decided to make some heavy toll calls to Australia in spite of TVNZ.

Source: Elkin, Graham, based on course work by Kesh Gilmore, University of Otago (1999).

Activities for discussion, analysis and further research

1 Comment on the communication process in this case.

2 Suggest ways TVNZ could have improved the process and the outcome for the staff.

Attribution processes

attribution theory

Theory attempting to explain
how individuals make
judgments or attributions
about the causes of
another's or their own
behaviour

One way to understand how perceptions influence managerial communication and interpersonal processes is attribution theory. **Attribution theory** explains how people make judgments or attributions about causes of another's or their own behaviour (Luthans 1995). These judgments form a basis for later actions. According to the theory, we make causal judgments that are either dispositional (attributed to internal causes, such as personality traits or a person's own efforts) or situational (attributed to external causes, such as equipment or luck). For example, if Jane fails to complete an assignment on time, should we attribute it to internal factors like lack of effort or ability, or do we decide some work context or issue is to blame? In making these judgments we consider consensus (the degree the behaviour is similar to how most act in a given situation), consistency (the degree to which the person behaves in the same way in this or similar situations at other times), and distinctiveness (the degree to which the person behaves differently in other situations). Thus, if other staff completed the same task on time, Jane has had trouble completing similar assignments on time before, and she has missed deadlines on other types of assignments, we would probably make a dispositional judgment about why the assignment was late. On the other hand, if others were late completing the assignment, Jane normally completes on time, and usually finishes other types of assignments by the deadline, we are likely to attribute the difficulty to situational factors. The attributions influence how we handle the late assignment.

**fundamental
attribution error**

Tendency to underestimate
importance of situational
influences and overestimate
the importance of
dispositional influences in
explaining behaviour

In making causal judgments, managers must consider the **fundamental attribution error**—the tendency to underestimate situational influences and to overestimate dispositional influences in explaining behaviour. We are likely to make this error when explaining others' behaviour. Moreover, if success and failure is involved, we are likely to succumb to **self-serving bias**. This bias is the tendency to see oneself as responsible for successes and others for failures (Tosi, Rizzo & Carroll 1986; Johns 1996). This sets the stage for communication problems between managers and subordinates. For instance, a manager attributes subordinates' successes to their own effective leadership but concludes failures are due to subordinates' shortcomings. Subordinates, meanwhile, see successes as coming from their own hard work and ability and view failures as stemming from bad luck or work environment factors, including areas managed by their supervisor (DeGregoria & Gillis 1980; Meyers 1983).

self-serving bias

Tendency to perceive oneself
as responsible for successes
and others as responsible for
failures

Semantics

semantic net

Network of words and word
meanings a given individual
has available for recall

Words are symbols, so their meanings are different for everyone. The study of meanings and word choice is semantics. A **semantic net** is the network of words and word meanings a person has available for recall (Lewis 1980). Everyone has their own net, which overlaps, but does not correspond exactly, with those of others. **Semantic blocks** are blockages or communication difficulties coming from word choices (Munter 1987). Such blocks are common because various meanings and shades of meanings individuals give to words depend on their semantic

semantic blocks

Blockages or communication
difficulties arising from word
choices

net. Receivers decode words and phrases to conform to their own semantic networks, which may differ from the sender's (Axley 1984). The examples presented in Table 14.1 show the high potential for semantic blocks between manager and subordinate.

Within organisations, different units can have terminology that has evolved through tradition or that is related specifically to the work being done. A common cause of semantic blocks is use of *professional jargon*, language related to a specific profession but unfamiliar to those outside. Such language must be used with care because it can bewilder newcomers, customers or visitors. Nevertheless, organisation-specific language helps build cohesion among employees, reinforces corporate culture, and, as it does at the Walt Disney Company, supports a competitive edge (Bormann 1983).

At many firms, employees speak a language of their own:

A hipo, a Wallenda, and an imagineer order drinks at a bar. They do a little work—edit a violin, non-concur with a wild duck, take care of some bad Mickey—and then ask for the bill. 'This is on the mouse,' says one of them. Who picks up the tab?

Organisations often create their own language, which becomes part of daily communication among employees. In fact, outsiders may need translations.

For example, a veteran employee at IBM says a 'hipo' (short for 'high potential') is a designation for an employee who appears to be on the fast track to success. Another IBMer claims that an employee seen as having low potential is known as an 'alpo.' IBM employees do not disagree with their bosses; instead, they 'non-concur'. An individual who non-concurs fairly frequently, but constructively, is known as a 'wild duck'. The 'wild duck' label was a favourite of a former chairman, Thomas Watson Jr, who borrowed it from Kierkegaard.

Corporate slang can be prevalent in publishers, whose employees have a way with words. At *Newsweek*, top editors are often called 'Wallendas', after the famous family of aerialists. The designation recognises the editors' job vulnerability. Writers at *Newsweek* refer to the weekly's top national story as the 'violin'.

Table 14.1 **Examples of semantic blocks in communications between manager and subordinate**

What the manager said	What the manager meant	What the subordinate heard
I'll look into hiring another person for your department as soon as I complete my budget review.	We'll start interviewing for that job in about three weeks.	I'm tied up with more important things. Let's forget about hiring for the indefinite future.
Your performance was below par last quarter. I really expected more out of you.	You're going to have to try harder, but I know you can do it.	If you screw up one more time, you're out.
I'd like that report as soon as you can get to it.	I need that report within the week.	Drop that rush order you're working on and fill out that report today.

Source: Reprinted from Hodgetts & Altman (1979, p. 305).

In one move, the Walt Disney ·Company consciously set up its own corporate jargon to support its efforts to have employees think of Disney theme parks as stages. At orientation and training sessions, they are taught to say they are 'onstage' when working in the theme park itself and 'backstage' when in lower environs, where they cannot be seen by the public. They learn to refer to co-workers as 'cast members'. An imagineer is a member of Disney's Imagineering division, an innovative group responsible for dreaming up new ideas and figuring out how to make them work.

Jack Herrman, a former Walt Disney World publicist, remembers co-workers would label anything positive a 'good Mickey' and anything negative (like a cigarette butt on the ground) a 'bad Mickey'. When employees take someone to lunch on the Walt Disney World expense account, they say it is 'on the mouse'. 'You're immersed in the jargon they impose upon you as a way of life,' Herrman says. Through such language, the company constantly reminds members of their roles in the theme parks. In this way, Disney uses language to support their competitive edge (Miller 1987).

Managing diversity: Cultural context

Culture also influences communication and interpersonal processes. One means of cultural influence is the importance placed on the context of the communication (Hall 1959; 1976; Kennedy & Everest 1991). Context includes situational factors such as participants' roles, nature of existing relationships, and non-verbal communication. **High-context cultures** emphasise establishing and strengthening relationships in communication while exchanging information. Countries with high-context cultures include Mexico, Saudi Arabia, India and China (see Fig. 14.3). For individuals from these countries, the circumstances, or context, and non-verbal communication will be as important as what is said. In **low-context cultures** emphasis is on information exchange and less focused on building relationships by communication. Countries with low-context cultures include Australia, Canada and the United States. Individuals from low-context countries will place more emphasis on the words spoken and pay less attention to circumstances or non-verbal communication. For example, many Asian cultures show deference to those higher in the social structure by not looking them in the eye; but an individual from a low-context country ignores such subtleties. There are also differences between country and city dwellers from the same country, and between genders (Tannen 1995a; 1995b). So those from low-context areas and high-context areas may have difficulties communicating with each other unless they allow for their differences.

An implication is that, if a low-context supervisor tries to give performance feedback to a high-context subordinate, they will experience difficulty if they concentrate on objective facts

high-context cultures

Cultures where the emphasis in the communication process is on establishing and strengthening relationships in the course of exchanging information

low-context cultures

Cultures where the emphasis in the communication process is on exchanging information and is less focused on building relationships

Fig. 14.3   Continuum of low-context and high-context cultures

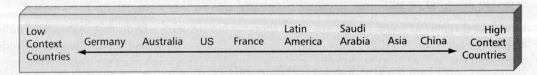

without focusing attention on building trust and building the relationship. Strong communication skills can help them adjust more readily to cultural context matters.

Communication skills

To be effective communicators in various settings, managers need strong listening and feedback skills. These are critical because managers spend so much of their time communicating orally.

Listening skills   As earlier discussion suggests, receivers must ensure they have decoded and interpreted the message the sender intended. Since managers rely heavily on information inputs from oral communication, their listening skills are crucial (Lewis & Reinsch 1988). Listening experts often differentiate between listening as relatively passive, in which the listener follows the word's general gist, and active listening. **Active listening** is where a listener actively participates in attempting to grasp facts and the speaker's feelings. Actively listening for both content and feelings is important to understand the message's total meaning (Gordon 1987). Managers are disadvantaged when they are not good listeners (Lenzner 1995). For guidelines to enhance listening skills, see the Management skills for the 21st century discussion, 'How to listen actively'.

> **active listening**
>
> Process in which a listener actively participates in attempting to grasp facts and feelings being expressed by the speaker

Feedback   Other interpersonal communication skills important for managers centre around feedback, both giving and receiving. Effective feedback has several characteristics. It focuses on relevant behaviours or outcomes, not the person. It deals with specific, observable behaviour, not generalities. Perceptions, reactions and opinions are labelled as such, rather than given as facts. Finally, feedback spells out how individuals can improve (Kaplan et al. 1984). Being skilled in feedback makes guiding subordinates easier and increases prospects for mutual success.

In addition to giving feedback, receiving it is important. Typically, most individuals have no difficulty receiving positive feedback. Receiving negative feedback is generally more of a problem. Yet the way managers and others react to feedback often influences how much they receive (Kaplan 1984). When receiving negative feedback, it is helpful to paraphrase what is being said (so you can check your perceptions), ask for clarification and examples regarding any unclear points or points with which you disagree, and avoid reacting defensively (Centre for Creative Leadership 1976).

Organisations are learning that it pays to get feedback from customers, particularly dissatisfied ones. For example, Roger Nunley, manager of industry and consumer affairs at Coca-Cola, says studies show only one dissatisfied consumer in 50 complains; the rest switch brands. Yet when a complaint is addressed, the individual is likely to remain a customer. As a result, companies such as

Good communication skills in a manager include actively listening to others in order to provide constructive feedback.

Coca-Cola, American Express, and Mattel have contact numbers to allow customers to voice complaints (Sellers 1988; Quintanilla & Gibson 1994).

⬆ How to listen actively

The following guidelines will help you be an active listener:

1 Listen patiently to what the other person has to say, although you may believe it is wrong or irrelevant. Indicate simple acceptance (not necessarily agreement) by nodding or injecting an occasional 'um-hm' or 'I see'.

2 Try to understand the feelings the person is expressing, as well as intellectual content. Most of us have difficulty talking clearly about our feelings, so careful attention is required.

3 Restate the person's feeling, briefly but accurately. At this stage, simply serve as a mirror and encourage them to continue talking. Occasionally make summary responses, such as 'You think you're in a dead-end job' or 'You feel the manager is playing favourites'. In doing so, keep your tone neutral and try not to lead the person to your pet conclusions.

4 Allow time for discussion to continue without interruption, and try to separate conversation from more official communication of company plans. That is, do not make the conversation any more 'authoritative' than it already is by virtue of your organisational position.

5 Avoid direct questions and arguments about facts; refrain from saying 'That's just not so', 'Hold on a minute, let's look at the facts', or 'Prove it'. You may want to review evidence later, but a review is irrelevant to how a person feels now.

6 When the other person does touch on a point you want to know more about, simply repeat their statement as a question. For instance, if the person remarks, 'Nobody can break even on their expense account', you can probe by replying, 'You say no one breaks even on expenses?' With this encouragement, they will probably expand on the previous statement.

7 Listen for what isn't said—evasions of pertinent points or perhaps too-ready agreement with common clichés. Such omissions may be clues to a bothersome fact the person wishes were not true.

8 If the other person appears to genuinely want your viewpoint, be honest in your reply. But in the listening stage, try to limit the expression of your views, since these may condition or suppress what the other person says.

9 Focus on message content; try not to think about your next statement until the person is finished talking.

10 Avoid making judgments until all information has been conveyed (Gordon 1987).

Source: Gordon (1987, p. 230).

GROUP COMMUNICATION NETWORKS

communication network

Pattern of information flow among task-group members

When tasks need several people's input, managers must look at the **communication network**, the patterns of information flow among task-group members. Research has assessed the impact of different networks on communication and task performance. Five major options are shown in Figure 14.4.

Fig. 14.4   Group communication networks (adapted from Baskin & Aronoff 1980, p. 77)

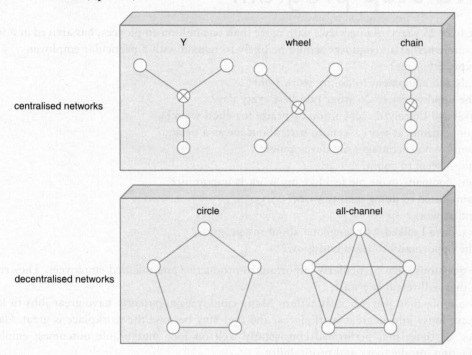

Three networks are fairly centralised, since most messages pass through one person. In the wheel network, the most centralised, all messages flow through the person at the centre. In the chain network, some members can communicate with more than one member of the network, but the individual in the centre of the chain emerges as message controller. In the Y network, the person at the fork of the 'Y' usually becomes the central person. The last two networks shown in Figure 14.4 are decentralised, since communication flows readily among members. In the circle network, each can communicate with the individual on either side. Finally, in the star network, the most decentralised; each member can communicate with any other.

For relatively simple, routine tasks, centralised networks are faster and more accurate. This is because in centralised networks, the person in the central position (marked with an '×' in Fig. 14.4) tends to be co-ordinator, and facilitates routine task completion. In contrast, on more complex tasks, decentralised networks are often faster and more accurate, with the star network being best. With complex tasks, free exchange of information in the circle and star facilitates the process and helps creativity.

An interesting finding is that group morale in the networks was higher in decentralised ones, regardless of task type. This is a managerial dilemma. Centralised networks are best for accurate performance on simple tasks, especially when time is short. However, morale suffers. For more complex tasks, decentralised networks give both high performance and morale. From a practical standpoint, many organisational tasks are complex (Shaw 1981). If tasks are simple and call for more centralised communication networks, managers can lift morale by giving subordinates a chance to work on more complex tasks, allowing involvement in a more decentralised network.

The 12-step program

The Gallup Organisation, over 25 years' of interviews with more than one million employees, has arrived at a series of 12 questions that measure whether an employee would be likely to remain with a particular employer.

1 Do I know what is expected of me?

2 Do I have the materials and equipment to do my work right?

3 At work, do I have the opportunity to do what I do best every day?

4 In the past seven days, have I received recognition or praise for good work?

5 Does my supervisor, or someone at work, seem to care about me as a person?

6 Is there someone at work who encourages my development?

7 At work, do my opinions seem to count?

8 Does the mission of my company make me feel like my work is important?

9 Are my co-workers committed to doing quality work?

10 Do I have a best friend at work?

11 In the past six months, have I talked with someone about my progress?

12 At work, do I have the opportunity to learn and grow?

The responses to those questions seem particularly important to productive and talented employees. They reveal aspects of the workplace that will retain key staff.

The research focused on more than just job satisfaction. Many employees apparently have great jobs in lousy workplaces, and others have lousy jobs in great workplaces, and they stay because the workplace is great. Gallup defined 'great workplaces' as those that performed consistently well on four measurable outcomes: employee retention, customer satisfaction, productivity and profitability.

Source: Onsman, Harry (1999).

Activities for discussion, analysis and further research

1 Which of the above questions does not refer in some way to the communication process?

2 Explain how the communication process underpins each of the factors at the core of the twelve questions.

3 Consider your job, or if you do not work, ask someone you know who does, and answer those twelve questions. Is the workplace involved a 'great workplace'?

ORGANISATIONAL COMMUNICATION CHANNELS

communication channels

Patterns of organisational communication flow representing potential established conduits through which managers and other organisation members can send and receive information

One point in assessing organisational communication is the flow of information through the company. When information does not reach individuals and groups who need it, effectiveness and efficiency problems emerge. Organisational **communication** patterns are called **channels** as they represent ways managers and other members can send and receive information. In this section, we consider two organisational flow directions: vertical and horizontal. We also examine an informal form of communication flow, the 'grapevine'. Finally, we consider consequences of communication channel usage for innovation, as well as increased use of electronics facilitating organisational communication.

Vertical communication

Vertical communication is message exchange between two or more organisational levels (see Fig. 14.5). Thus vertical communication may involve a manager and a subordinate or several hierarchical layers. It can flow down or up. Studies find managers spend about two-thirds of communication time in vertical communication (Porter & Roberts 1976).

Downward communication   When vertical communication flows from higher to lower organisation levels, it is **downward communication**. This takes many forms, such as staff meetings, company policy statements, newsletters, informational memos and face-to-face contact. Most of this communication involves information in one of five categories: (1) job instructions on specific tasks, (2) job rationales explaining relationships between tasks, (3) organisation procedures and practices, (4) feedback on individual performance and (5) attempts to encourage a sense of mission and organisational goal dedication (Katz & Kahn 1978).

Downward communication across several levels can be very distorted. A middle manager survey shows received information quality is poor (Harcourt, Richerson & Wattier 1991). As shown by Figure 14.6, 80 per cent of top management's message is lost within five levels. There are three main reasons for distortion. First, faulty message transmission due to sender carelessness, poor communication skills, and difficulties clearly encoding a message for individuals at many levels. Second, managers overuse one-way communication, using memos, newsletters and manuals, with little immediate receiver feedback possible. Third, some deliberately or accidentally filter communications by withholding, screening or manipulating information. Deliberate filtering occurs when a manager enhances personal power by controlling organisational information tightly (Baskin & Aronoff 1980; Lewis 1980).

Fig. 14.5   Vertical and horizontal organisational communication (adapted from Pace 1983, p. 40)

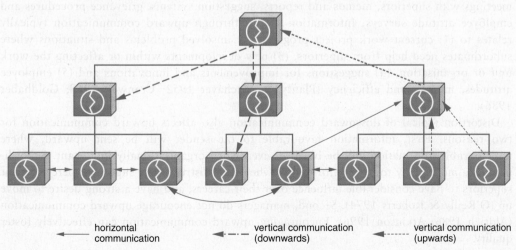

horizontal communication

vertical communication (downwards)

vertical communication (upwards)

vertical communication

Communication involving a message exchange between two or more levels of the organisational hierarchy

downward communication

Vertical communication flowing from a higher level to one or more lower levels in the organisation

Fig. 14.6   Levels of understanding as information is transmitted down the
organisation (adapted from Lewis 1980; and Scannell 1970)

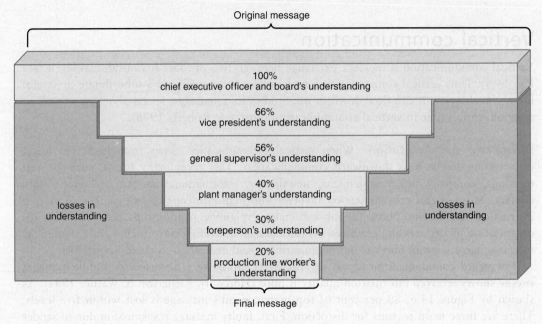

A way to increase downward communication's effectiveness is use of multiple channels and repetition (Ansberry 1991). Another way to improve downward communication is to encourage feedback through upward communication.

Upward communication   When vertical flow of communication is from lower levels to one or more higher levels in the organisation, it is known as **upward communication**. Upward communication includes one-to-one meetings with your immediate superior, staff meetings with superiors, memos and reports, suggestion systems, grievance procedures and employee attitude surveys. Information spread through upward communication typically relates to (1) current work project progress, (2) unsolved problems and situations where subordinates need help from superiors, (3) new developments within or affecting the work unit or organisation, (4) suggestions for improvements and innovations and (5) employee attitudes, morale, and efficiency (Planty & Machaver 1952; Cranwell 1969; Goldhaber 1986).

Distortion typical of downward communication also affects upward communication for two reasons. First, information favourable to the sender will be sent upward, where unfavourable information will be blocked, even when organisationally important. Subordinates are more likely to filter information when they distrust their superiors, perceive their superiors to have considerable influence over their careers, and have a strong desire to move up (O'Reilly & Roberts 1974). Second, managers do not encourage upward communication (Aldrich 1986; Atkinson 1996). Encouraging upward communication can effectively foster quality.

upward communication
....
Vertical flow of communication from a lower level to one or more higher levels in the organisation

Horizontal communication

Horizontal communication is lateral or diagonal message exchange within work-units, involving peers reporting to the same supervisor, or across work-unit boundaries, involving those reporting to different supervisors (see Fig. 14.5). Horizontal communication can take many forms, including meetings, reports, memos, telephone conversations and face-to-face discussions. Managers spend about one-third of their communication time in horizontal communication (Porter & Roberts 1990) related to one or more of the following: (1) task co-ordination, (2) problem solving, (3) information sharing, (4) conflict resolution and (5) peer support (Pace 1983).

Three major factors impede necessary, work-related horizontal communication. First, rivalry can lead employees to hide information damaging to themselves or aiding others. Second, specialisation may mean people are more concerned about their own unit's work and have little concern for the work and communication needs of others. For example, scientists in an R&D unit focusing on long-term projects may not want to interrupt their work to help with customer problems identified by sales. Third, motivation may be low when horizontal communication among subordinates is not encouraged or rewarded. Committees, task forces and matrix structures are ways managers encourage horizontal communication, mainly at work-unit boundaries (see Chapters 8 and 9) (Goldhaber 1986).

horizontal communication

Lateral or diagonal message exchange either within work-unit boundaries, involving peers reporting to the same supervisor, or across work-unit boundaries, involving individuals who report to different supervisors

 # The cost of pour communication   crossroads

Many years ago I was second mate on a ship loading bauxite in Weipa. The ship was nearly loaded to its marks but was trimmed a little too far by the stern. The mate made some rapid calculations and called to the leader operator, 'Pour 50 tons in number one'. He was understood by the operator to call for '450 tons in number one'.

Since this was a nine-hatch ship, the impact of an extra 400 tons in the forward hatch (No.1) was that we left Weipa trimmed heavily by the head and over our marks, as Weipa had no facilities for off-loading cargo. The outcome was that from then on, all communication relating to ship loading was written on a simple order sheet and passed to the operator.

The ship was loaded with sulphuric acid to discharge to a terminal on the Manchester Ship Canal. It came into the place of another ship that was to bring oil but was delayed at sea by weather. The wharfies were in a Christmas mood. Without the cargo papers being checked, the ship of sulphuric acid was connected to the oil tanks. Some railway tank wagons were also filled. After a few hundred tonnes of cargo had been discharged, a manager from the terminal realised that a mistake had been made—a very expensive mistake. All the oil in the shore tanks as well as the railway wagons was contaminated.

Source: Powell & Grewal, Australian Maritime College.

Reflection points

1 Given what you have studied about managerial communication in this chapter, analyse both the situations using the components of the communication process to structure your answer.
2 What factors or barriers impeded the communication?
3 How could the communication have been improved?

Informal communication: The grapevine

Vertical and horizontal communication patterns are formal patterns, or channels, because communication follows the official hierarchical structure and task requirements. You might see **formal communication** as associated with an organisational position. In contrast, **informal communication**, or the **grapevine**, occurs without reference to hierarchy or task requirements. Informal communication relates to personal, not positional, issues (Pace 1983). For example, personal relationships unrelated to organisational positions exist among employees who ride to work in the same car, attend the same church, or have children in the same school. Grapevine communications stem largely from relationships which may overlap, but may not coincide with hierarchy and task communication requirements.

The term 'grapevine' can be traced back to the American Civil War, when telegraph lines strung from tree to tree in grapevine-like patterns gave garbled intelligence messages (Davis 1972). Grapevines exist in all organisations, and grapevine patterns include both vertical and horizontal elements. A classic study looked at four configurations for grapevine chains (see Fig. 14.7). In a single-strand chain, communication moves from person A to B to C and so on. In the gossip chain, person A seeks out and communicates with others. When following a probability chain, person A spreads a message randomly, as do individuals F and D. In a cluster chain, person A gives the message to three others, and one gives it to three others. According to the study, the cluster chain predominates. This finding suggests individuals who are part of grapevines will be selective about those to whom they relay information and only some of those people will, in turn, pass the information further (Davis 1980).

Overall, grapevines are fast, carry large amounts of information, and produce data between 50 and 90 per cent accurate (Friedman 1981; Goldhaber 1986; Zaremba 1988). Although the grapevine is seen as inaccurate, the problem stems largely from misinterpretation of incomplete details (Pace 1983; *Wall Street Journal* 1989).

Although not officially set up or sanctioned, grapevines are a part of every organisation and cannot be abolished. They create problems when they carry gossip and false rumours, but have many good aspects if managed properly. By dwelling on errors, grapevines may be valuable in communicating organisational rules, values, morals, traditions and history.

Fig. 14.7   Types of grapevine chains (reprinted from Davis, in Ferguson & Ferguson 1980, p. 59)

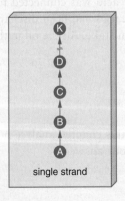
single strand

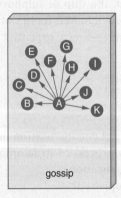
gossip

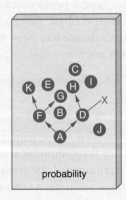
probability

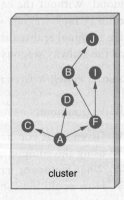
cluster

Grapevines give employees time to consider possible changes and can help employees' organisational goal contributions (March & Sevon 1984; Weick & Browning 1986; Mishra 1990). As well, they foster innovation by enhancing communication across the organisation.

Using electronics to facilitate communication

Electronic advances have given managers new methods, channels and concerns of communication. Four prominent advances are electronic mail systems and the Internet, voice mail, teleconferencing and videoconferencing, and interest is growing in groupware.

An **electronic mail system** allows the exchange of high-speed written messages through computerised text-processing and communication networks. Anyone with a computer terminal can write and send a written message to anyone else with a computer mailbox. It is reported managers say they save about seven hours per week as their electronic mail system increases decision-making speed (Crawford 1982). Other managers estimate their system saves them about three hours per week, by eliminating unreturned phone calls and reducing internal correspondence (Nyce & Groppa 1983).

There is also evidence electronic mail leads to information exchanges among managers previously not communicating either by mail or by telephone, and that managers receive new types of information (Rice & Case 1983; Kiesler 1986). Electronic mail systems improve vertical and facilitate horizontal communication (Huseman & Miles 1988; *Inc* 1995).

One disadvantage of electronic mail is that it has no non-verbal cues (facial expressions, body movements, and voice tone) which aid face-to-face communication (*Wall Street Journal* 1995). (Of course, regular mail has fewer non-verbal cues than face-to-face messages too.) Another is the speed and seemingly temporary nature of e-mail may lead people to vent anger (or 'flaming') in an e-mail message they never would have sent had they committed it to paper. Accordingly, handling significant misunderstandings on a face-to-face basis when possible is best; use extreme caution in resolving difficulties via e-mail. Still another disadvantage is that the ease of sending mail electronically can cause some to receive excessive amounts of irrelevant mail (Zachary 1994). A growing concern is that the seemingly anonymous nature of the process makes employees feel secure and use the system inappropriately (McMorris 1995; Bryan 2000).

Electronic mail is the first step to the Internet, which is a global computer network used by people around the world to communicate. About 77 million people in the United States alone use the Internet on a regular basis (*CyberAtlas* 2000). It is also estimated that managers in over 21 000 companies communicate this way (Eng 1995).

Managers and companies use the Internet for many reasons, communicating with: suppliers and contractors; distant offices; customers and potential customers; recruitment; the general public; as well as locating information on competitors (GCC Group 2000).

Internet use for communication is increasing. Nevertheless, some are concerned about security. Ironically, the very purpose of the Internet, allowing senders and receivers of messages to share enormous quantities of information, raises the issue of security. Experts believe the Internet can be made quite secure. However, only time will tell whether it can be secure enough for it to be used for many business transactions.

In addition to securing communication over the Internet, managers face other Internet problems. When employees surf the Net on company time for fun, costs increase and they may use it for inappropriate purposes (Bryan 2000; Kirby 2000).

electronic mail system

Mail system which allows high-speed exchange of written messages by use of computerised text-processing and communication networks

voice mail

Recording system providing senders with opportunity to leave messages for receivers by telephone

An allied form of electronic communication is **voice mail**, a recording system enabling senders to leave messages by telephone. With voice mail, non-verbal cues (voice quality and tone of voice) are present. Voice mail is useful with short messages not requiring further discussion. In another development, the use of voice recognition, computers and telephone technologies have made possible electronic secretaries. This strategy permits people to interact with their voice mail programs in a far more active way (Bulkeley 1995; Wildstrom 1995; Hartnett 1999; Carter 1999).

teleconferencing

Simultaneous communication among a group of individuals by telephone or via computer using specially designed software

Another electronic communication form, **teleconferencing**, is simultaneous communication among a group of individuals by telephone or via computer using specially designed software (Laudon & Laudon 1994). The software is referred to as groupware because it helps message sharing among group members communicating together. Groupware allows meetings among group members at different locations. However, it can also facilitate meetings among group members in one location. In this case, group members each sit in front of a computer. Groupware co-ordinates simultaneous messages and displays them on a special screen all can see. Messages are anonymous, and most communication is done through computers. Sometimes no one speaks a word (Kirkpatrick 1992; Bartino 1992).

Groupware is likely to be successful (Rifkin 1995; *Business Week* 1995) when work is group- or team-based, and members are rewarded for group performance, and with top management's full support. Furthermore, the culture of the organisation must not be too rigid, allowing for a high degree of flexibility, with the program being viewed as one tool in the group's best interest. Finally all participants must be sufficiently trained and comfortable in the use of the whole system.

videoconferencing

Holding meetings with individuals in two or more locations by means of closed-circuit television

A related form of electronic communication is **videoconferencing**, holding meetings with individuals in two or more locations by closed-circuit television. One quite creative application of the technology has diners facing a video screen interacting with others seemingly engaged in the same process, but a considerable distance away (Ziegler 1995). Teleconferencing use is growing (Hellweg, Frieberg & Smith 1984; Aldrich 1986). Companies with their own private television networks include Optus, Ford, Merrill Lynch and Xerox (Meeks 1988).

Since communication occurs with groups, managers find it helpful to have a knowledge of group dynamics. We explore this topic in the next chapter.

@ Big Cookie is watching!
managing the e-challenge

Next time you use the Internet, imagine there's a hidden camera following your mouse as it roams around the screen. It records where you linger, what links you click on, how often you go to your favourite cyber hang-outs. While it's doing that, an electronic scribe is noting what kind of computer you are using, who your Internet service provider is and whether you favour Internet Explorer or Netscape Navigator.

It's all anonymous, of course. But when you sign up for that free newsletter on fly fishing, pet care or travel, you give your name and e-mail address and maybe your post code. Suddenly the watchers on the other side of the screen can match your online roamings to your real world address, your mother's maiden name, your shopping habits and the make of the car you drive.

This is exactly what online advertising company DoubleClick is doing. DoubleClick uses 'cookies', tiny identifying files to follow people around as they browse the Web. The cookies help them to decide which advertisements to show users, and thousands of Web sites use them. But when DoubleClick bought a direct marketing firm called Abacus, it began to match the records to create detailed dossiers on individuals. Welcome to the world of Little Brother.

Source: Gibbons, P. (2000).

Activities for discussion, analysis and further research

1 In what ways are communications theories by-passed when the Internet is being used?
2 Consider all the sites you enter during a typical week. How many times do you submit forms with personal information? See if you can track what happens to that information.
3 Track a cookie to see how it compiles a dossier on you.

 The MD's diary   the reflective practitioner

We do have formal communication processes. We have a very regular process whereby any decision and policies that we want to communicate to people are formally communicated through Toolbox. This takes the form generally of a written communication, which is disseminated through the organisation. As well as that I take the opportunity, at least once a year, sometimes twice, depending on the circumstances of the organisation, to run formal communication sessions with everyone in the organisation. There would normally be a small group of 20-odd individuals and myself and I will take an hour to talk to them about the business, about the vision, about the strategy, and do that in a more formal way. So, they are all getting a consistent message in terms of what we are trying to achieve. The management meetings we have, once again, are very formal processes. Management meetings in this organisation are generally report-back meetings, rather than discussing issues or solving problems. The reason for them is for the managers to feedback to me—and when they run their departmental meetings, it's for their people to feed back to them the information about what is happening in their part of the organisation. That tends to formally feed its way back up the organisation and into the strategic thinking of the senior management team.

But I think that the most effective form of communication is one on one. I encourage my people to spend as much time as possible on the shop floor. I try to spend an hour on the shop floor myself every day. And I try over the course of a few weeks to talk to every individual that is on the shop floor. They found it quite amusing when I first came here that I would actually walk into every line and say hello to every individual and talk to them. I find that enormously successful because you can talk to them about the things that interest them one on one, the things that are getting in their way. That gives you an enormous opportunity to fix the little problems that they have. Through this you develop respect and trust. I continually try to challenge my people, my managers, to find the ways to fix the little problems, because if we can fix the little problems that are getting in the way of our people doing their job, the job that we want, then they're going to return that tenfold. That to me is the most effective form of communication that we can use. It's achievable in an organisation our size—it becomes more difficult as the organisation gets bigger. I think it's much more valuable than formal communication.

The grapevine at Autoliv is very powerful, and it's used to reasonable effect. If you want to send a message—particularly a negative message when something has gone wrong—then the grapevine works extremely well—as long as you don't leave it at that, but come in with the supportive communication. It's always a constant balance in the organisation not to be the 'good news guy' the whole time. It's nice to go down and tell people on the shop floor that everything is wonderful, but at times there needs to be some balance in that, so it is often that informal grapevine that sends the message out that there is something that needs to be addressed. So people have a chance to think about things and when the formal communication takes place they're prepared for it, they've thought about it, they understand, and they hopefully have some ideas about how to fix it. So they're not feeling threatened or vulnerable when issues or problems need addressing.

I allow people to get very close to me in terms of understanding how I feel and how I think. I'm not a particularly volatile person. I don't shout, I don't rant, I don't rave. I'm very calm, most of the time. If I do become a little shorter, a little more terse, or a little more direct, people seem to understand that there is something amiss and they need to be a little careful in terms of what they're doing and how they're behaving. A lot of what the people on the shop floor see of me is when I walk around the shop floor and I talk to them. I like to learn a little bit about as many of them as I possibly can; get to understand what their interests are, what their thinking is. At the same time I'm always getting some feedback about what's happening in the organisation; whether they're being treated correctly; whether the relationship between them and their supervisor is as it should be; whether they're getting the attention they need.

 # The subordinate's log   the reflective practitioner

Communication processes are the mortar that holds the bricks of the organisation together. I found that part of my role was as a filter of communication both up and down the organisation. That filtering role was both as a way of increasing the effectiveness of the communication and also in the interest of making my job easier or manipulating the outcome as I preferred it. A legitimate part of my role, as I saw it, was sometimes to convey to the CEO what I felt he needed to know. Given his very directive style of management, it was sometimes better to manage a situation myself and report it carefully rather than give too much information and have the whole issue escalate unnecessarily. Another filtering situation was that if I had to implement something I knew would not be popular, I would sometimes present a decision with a different spin to soften the blow or outline the benefits to the staff rather than just say that is the way it is. Generally speaking, though, the organisation had a fairly direct communication style, and most things especially at the operational level were discussed openly and dealt with directly. This I found to be very effective in managing people and maintaining a stable environment.

Focus on practice—Strategies for improving

1   Draw up a list of criteria to determine whether a communication should be face to face or whether e-mail is adequate.
2   Check with a number of organisations to discover if they have any policy regarding the use of company e-mail for personal use.
3   How would you go about establishing a sense of trust in the organisation in order to discourage distortion of information along the grapevine.
4   Think about a number of people you interact with. How do their cultural and linguistic differences impact on the meaning of their communications? How do you go about avoiding those problems?

Source: Jones et al. (2000).

Chapter summary

Effective communication and interpersonal processes are important in gaining and maintaining the competitive edge in organisations. Communication is the exchange of messages between people for the purpose of achieving common meanings. In their work, managers use two types of communication: verbal (including written and oral) and non-verbal. When the elements contradict each other, the receiver is most likely to interpret the non-verbal communication as the true message. Managers tend to prefer oral to written communication, spending approximately 75 per cent of their working hours communicating orally with others.

The communication process has several basic components: sender, encoding, message, receiver, decoding, noise and feedback. When communication provides for relatively immediate feedback, it is called two-way communication. Without a feedback provision, it is known as one-way communication.

A number of factors affect individual communication. Perception is susceptible to four major types of distortion: stereotyping, the halo effect, projection and perceptual defence. Attribution theory helps explain how individuals use communicated information to make judgments about the causes of another's or their own behaviours. Semantic blocks sometimes occur because the various meanings and shades of meanings that individuals attach to words depend on each person's semantic net. An individual's cultural orientation to high or low context also can have a major impact on communication and interpersonal processes. Individual communication is facilitated by the development of skills in such areas as listening, giving feedback and receiving feedback.

When tasks require input from several individuals, managers need to give some thought to the communication network among task-group members. Centralised networks are the wheel, chain and Y; decentralised networks are the circle and the star. For relatively simple, routine tasks, centralised networks tend to be faster and more accurate. When tasks are more complex, decentralised networks are likely to be faster and more accurate.

Managers need to be concerned with the flow of information among the various parts of the organisation. Formal communication in organisations follows channels specified by the official hierarchical organisation structure and related task requirements. It flows in two main directions, vertical and horizontal. When vertical communication flows from a higher level to one or more lower levels, it is known as downward communication. When it moves from a lower level to one or more higher levels, it is known as upward communication. Horizontal communication is lateral message exchange. Informal communication, better known as the grapevine, takes place without regard to hierarchical or task requirements or organisational position. Electronic mail systems, voice mail, teleconferencing, and videoconferencing are examples of the communication aids available to managers through advances in electronics.

Questions for discussion and review

1 Explain the major types of communication managers use, and discuss their communication preferences. For a familiar organisation, identify examples of each type. Classify non-verbal communication examples in terms of kinesic behaviour, proxemics, paralanguage and object language.
2 Outline the basic components of the communication process. Identify these in a conversation you witness.
3 Delineate several common tendencies to distort perceptions. Give an example of how each could adversely affect communication.
4 Describe attribution theory, including fundamental attribution error and the concept of self-serving bias. Identify an example of the fundamental attribution error based on a situation you have witnessed.
5 Explain the notion of semantic blocks. List some words used at your university or college which might cause semantic blocks to outsiders unfamiliar with the terminology.

6 Differentiate between high-context cultures and low-context cultures in terms of the emphasis in the communication process. How could you use the high/low context concept to help you supervise more effectively?

7 Outline the major types of centralised and decentralised group communication networks. Explain conditions under which centralised and decentralised networks will result in the best performance. Evaluate how well suited they appear to be for the situations involved.

8 Differentiate between vertical and horizontal communication. Identify the major methods used in your college or university for downward communication from senior administrators to students and for upward communication from students to senior administrators. What mechanisms exist for horizontal communication among students?

9 Assess the organisational implications of the grapevine. What evidence points to the existence of a student grapevine in your department at your college or university?

10 How can managers use electronic mail systems, teleconferencing and videoconferencing to their advantage in communicating? What potential problems exist with each?

Exercises for managing in the 21st century

Exercise 1
Self-assessment: Listening self-inventory

The purpose of this exercise is to gain insight into how well you listen. Please complete the following 15-item questionnaire twice. The first time check the appropriate response (yes or no) for each question. In checking your response, please think in terms of your behaviour in the last few meetings or conversations in which you participated. The second time through the questionnaire, place a plus (+) or a minus (–) in the third column. Mark a plus (+) next to your answer if you are satisfied with that answer, a minus (–) next to the answer if you wish you could have answered that question differently.

	Yes	No	+ or –
1 I frequently attempt to listen to several conversations at the same time.	—	—	—
2 I like people to give me only the facts and then let me make my own interpretations.	—	—	—
3 I sometimes pretend to pay attention to people.	—	—	—
4 I consider myself a good judge of non-verbal communications.	—	—	—
5 I usually know what another person is going to say before he or she says it.	—	—	—
6 I usually end conversations that don't interest me by diverting my attention from the speaker.	—	—	—
7 I frequently nod, frown or whatever to let the speaker know how I feel about what they are saying.	—	—	—
8 I usually respond immediately when someone has finished talking.	—	—	—
9 I evaluate what is being said while it is being said.	—	—	—
10 I usually formulate a response while the other person is still talking.	—	—	—
11 The speaker's delivery style frequently keeps me from listening to content.	—	—	—
12 I usually ask people to clarify what they said rather than guess at the meaning.	—	—	—
13 I make a concerted effort to understand other people's point of view.	—	—	—

14 I frequently hear what I expect to hear rather than what is said. — — —
15 Most people feel that I have understood their point of view when we disagree. — — —

Your instructor will provide instructions for tabulating your answers.

Source: Glenn & Pood (1989).

Exercise 2
Management exercise: A question of inferences

Read the story presented below, and indicate whether you believe the statements that follow the story are true (T), false (F) or unknown (?). Then get together with a group designated by your instructor, and determine as a group whether each statement is true, false or unknown.

Haney test of uncritical inferences

The story
A businessman had just turned off the lights in the store when a man appeared and demanded money. The owner opened a cash register. The contents of the cash register were scooped up, and the man sped away. A member of the police force was notified promptly.

Statements about the story
1 A man appeared after the owner had turned off his store lights.   T / F / ?
2 The robber was a man.   T / F / ?
3 The man who appeared did not demand money.   T / F / ?
4 The man who opened the cash register was the owner.   T / F / ?
5 The store owner scooped up the contents of the cash register and ran away.   T / F / ?
6 Someone opened a cash register.   T / F / ?
7 After the man who demanded the money scooped up the contents of the cash register, he ran away.   T / F / ?
8 While the cash register contained money, the story does not state how much.   T / F / ?
9 The robber demanded money of the owner.   T / F / ?
10 A businessman had just turned off the lights when a man appeared in the store.   T / F / ?
11 It was broad daylight when the man appeared.   T / F / ?
12 The man who appeared opened the cash register.   T / F / ?
13 No one demanded money.   T / F / ?
14 The story concerns a series of events in which only three persons are referred to: the owner of the store, a man who demanded money, and a member of the police force.   T / F / ?
15 The following events occurred: someone demanded money, a cash register was opened, its contents were scooped up, and a man dashed out of the store.   T / F / ?

Source: Haney (1986).

Connecting to riches

If you had wanted to invest in a boring but steady Hong Kong stock, you might have opted for property and construction company China Rich Holdings Ltd, with its real-estate portfolio and developments in south-eastern China.

But suddenly China Rich has become much more than a simple property and construction play. Now it is venturing into two hot but very diverse growth areas: the Internet and retirement services. In 1991 China Rich co-founder Robert Yip Kwong smelled money in Guangdong real-estate development. A native of Guangdong and a former cadre in the province, Yip had an edge over many other Hong Kong property developers: political connections or guanxi. Before immigrating to Hong Kong in 1978, he had worked as an officer in the Guangzhou Petrochemical Industries Bureau and had friends in the city government.

Those connections helped him earn a bundle trading goods between Hong Kong and China in the 1980s. And they helped him and his partner Kelly Cheng Kit Yin, both now 47, profit in the 1990s from real-estate developments. One deal in the city of Shunde, an hour's drive from Guangzhou, netted them more that $18 million.

By the time Guangdong property prices crashed in 1995, Yip and Cheng were seeking new ventures. An opportunity presented itself in 1997 when Hong Kong-listed construction company WingFai International Ltd was teetering on the edge of bankruptcy. The pair executed a reverse stock-market listing in September 1997. Renaming the company China Rich Holdings in May 1998, Yip and Cheng phased out unprofitable divisions and injected China Rich's core profitable asset: Regal Gardens, a condominium complex with six 23-storey towers in Shunde.

'We always wanted to be a publicly listed company,' says Yip, China Rich's chairman and chief executive officer. 'A publicly listed company allows us to raise the capital to achieve our goals.' Yip's goals were shaped by years of study of high-tech trends and the demographics of overseas Chinese, says China Rich chief financial officer Cheng, a woman who earned a bachelor's degree in mathematics and a master in computer science before starting a 21-year career in banking and finance.

Members of the China Rich property development company.

Yip made his plans public in two announcements in May and June 1999. The first was the $4.5 million acquisition of a 50 per cent stake in Hong Kong-based Outblaze, a leading designer of Internet portal sites. That announcement boosted China Rich's share price, which had languished since the October 1997 crash, by 50 per cent over the next few days.

The second announcement was the Evergreen Club, several multi-million-dollar retirement residential parks in Guangdong province to cater for elderly, middle-class overseas Chinese. 'For HK$400 000 (US$52 000), we'll take care of you from the age of 60 until the day you die,' says Yip. 'The price includes your meals, your residence and even the urn for your ashes and a temple to store your urn.' Yip says he has lined up a number of banks willing to finance the full cost for qualified retirees.

China Rich has built the condominiums and villas at the Regal Park complex in Shunde where there is a residents' club, a gym, restaurants and a dance floor; free medical check-ups at a state-of-the-art hospital in Guangzhou that China Rich acquired last year; and, finally, interment in a China Rich-owned temple park complex in Fado on the outskirts of Guangzhou. Club members also get free transportation between all three destinations and Hong Kong.

'Many overseas Chinese will want to come back to China,' says Yip. The Evergreen Club is capable of housing 2000 members. At HK$400 000 each, the sums are easy to calculate and this leaves a high profit while providing a high level of service.

The club is also available on a time-share basis for HK$3600 which allows retirees to live there for three months every year for three years.

While the Evergreen Club is Yip's pet project, high-tech investment Outblaze is clearly Kelly Cheng's. Most people can talk about the Internet business, says Cheng, but most of these people can't do it. Outblaze is unique and Cheng feels that there is a growing market which should be pursued.

Outblaze specialises in converting Web sites into portals or search engines and has grown at light speed. Barely a year old, Outblaze has converted 3500 Web sites into portals with free e-mail accounts, chat rooms and other electronic services. Those portals have a combined membership of 800 000 people and receive 20 million page views a month. Outblaze, though it creates the portals for free, gets a percentage of all advertising revenue from them. Founder Siu says he hopes to break even sometime next year.

Outblaze is a clear indication that the US Internet boom—which has allowed loss-making 'dot.com' companies to make millions on the stock market—is arriving in Asia. Outblaze is a good example of this. Upon hearing of the possibility of buying into Outblaze, Yip gave the go-ahead. The deal was sealed after only three weeks of negotiations. While some are saying that the China Rich investment is only temporary, it has the potential of making a 100 per cent profit within a year or two. While China Rich's bread and butter is construction which does not make large profits, Yip and Cheng do have their long-term hopes pinned on Outblaze and the Evergreen Club.

Source: Cheng, A.T. (1999).

Activities for discussion, analysis and further research

1 See if you can locate the Outblaze site on the Web. Explore it to identify its strengths as a communication tool.
2 Consider how an international or regional organisation might utilise a Web site as a means for communication, internally, with its customers.

Managing Groups

Chapter 15

CHAPTER OUTLINE

Foundations of work groups
What is a group?
Types of work groups
How informal groups develop
How work groups operate

Work-group inputs
Managing diversity: Work-group composition
Member roles
Group size

Work-group processes
Group norms
Group cohesiveness
Group development

Promoting innovation:
Using task forces and teams
Task forces
Teams

LEARNING OBJECTIVES

After studying this chapter, you should be able to:

O Differentiate among different types of groups in the workplace and explain how informal groups develop.
O Use a systems approach to describe factors influencing the way groups operate.
O Describe major work-group inputs, including group composition, member roles and group size, and explain how they affect teamwork.
O Explain the significance of group process factors, such as group norms, group cohesiveness and group development.
O Discuss how task forces and teams can be used to promote innovation.

Striving for excellence

Over the recent past, the management of groups at Autoliv has undergone a tremendous change. To adequately understand this, one must understand how the factory has been operating. The factory historically had been set up as two distinct types of operations. The sub-assembly, which is all the buckles for the Australian lines and the export market, was set up as a flow-through process.

The retractor lines and the airbag lines were team-based operations. The sub-assembly is gradually being moved into a teams operation, but this is difficult because of the nature of the tasks.

The goal for the factory floor is to have everyone operating within customer-specific work cells. This requires a shift from static work stations, where individuals had specialised sets of skills, to standing teams of people whose skill sets merged and supported one another.

The real task was to achieve a sense of cohesiveness and it took time to foster the relationships and the acceptance of interreliance amongst the workers of a particular team. The early ones were very time consuming but as the lessons were learned, experience identified the processes which worked better than others, and successes came faster. While the transition was at its most fragile, two human-resources staff members literally lived on the line in order to keep situations calm and communications active. It was crucial that HR staff were not only visible but seen to be committed to the process and a part of it.

Teams at work at Autoliv.

When using a team strategy, managers realise those working in effective groups can be a powerful force. To take advantage of a team's power, managers must understand group behaviour or group dynamics, because of the characteristic processes of groups and teamwork. They must also be conscious of their potential to influence groups and teamwork as part of the leading function.

In this chapter, we examine group characteristics, including work-group types, informal group development and group operations. Next, we look at inputs and processes affecting group outcomes. We also explore how task forces and teams can foster innovation.

FOUNDATIONS OF WORK GROUPS

What is a group?

A **group** is two or more interdependent individuals interacting and influencing each other in collective pursuit of a common goal (Shaw 1981; Alderfer 1987). This definition differentiates a group from a simple gathering of individuals. Strangers leaving by the same door at a theatre or studying in a library's reference section are not a group. In neither case are people interdependent, nor are they interacting and influencing each other collectively trying to reach a shared goal. Similarly, groups are different to organisations as the latter involve systematic efforts (such as using the four major management functions and a formal structure), and goods or services production. Groups do not use as much systematic effort as organisations and may or may not produce goods or services. Teamwork happens when groups work together efficiently and effectively to achieve organisational goals. We discuss teamwork later, focusing on how work groups operate.

Though groups have always been central to organisations, they are increasingly seen as important assets. Organisations using groups and teamwork power come in all sizes (Magnet 1988; Yerak 1994).

> **group**
>
> Two or more interdependent individuals interacting and influencing each other in collective pursuit of a common goal

Types of work group

There are different types of workplace groups. They fall into two categories: formal and informal. These and some subcategories are shown in Figure 15.1.

Formal groups A **formal group** is officially created by an organisation for a particular purpose. There are two types of formal groups: command and task.

A **command**, or **functional**, **group** is a formal group consisting of a manager and all subordinates reporting to that manager. Each work unit (manager and subordinates) in an organisation is a command group. For example, if you stay in a large hotel, your room will be cleaned by a housekeeper who reports to a housekeeping supervisor. With other housekeepers reporting to the same supervisor, they make up a command group. If you attend a lunch, the individuals who wait on your table and report to a catering supervisor form part of another command group. Each supervisor reports to a higher-level manager and belongs to the higher-level command group. In this way, supervisors link lower-level and higher-level groups. A linking pin is an individual who co-ordinates different levels of command groups by fulfilling a supervisory role in

> **formal group**
>
> Group officially created by an organisation for a specific purpose
>
> **command or functional group**
>
> Formal group consisting of a manager and all the subordinates who report to them

Fig. 15.1 Types of work group

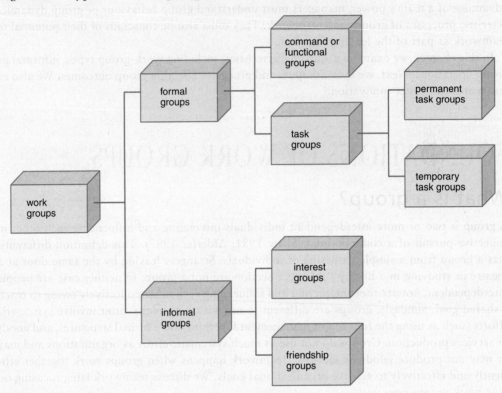

task group

Formal group created for a specific purpose, supplementing or replacing work normally done by command groups

standing committee

Permanent task group of individuals charged with handling recurring matters in a narrowly defined subject area over an indefinite, but generally long, time period

informal group

Group established by employees, not the organisation, to serve group members' interests or social needs

a lower-level group and a subordinate role in a higher one. Organisations are thus made up of command, or functional, groups in a pyramid, with linking pins holding them together.

A **task group** is a formal group created to supplement or replace work that a command group normally undertakes. Task groups can be permanent or temporary. A permanent task group, or **standing committee** or team, handles recurring issues in a narrow subject-area over an indefinite, generally lengthy, period of time. A temporary task group deals with a specific issue in a specific time frame. For example, as part of its Profitability Improvement program, Heinz has temporary teams of managers from different departments look for and prioritise projects for major cost savings (Saporito 1985). Temporary task groups, or ad hoc committees, may be called task forces, project groups or teams (Stech & Ratliff 1985). Names vary, so it is important to ask about time frames in establishing whether a task group is permanent or temporary. We discuss task forces and teams in greater detail later.

Informal groups   An **informal group** is set up by employees, not the organisation, to serve members' interests or social needs. These groups may or may not also further organisational goals. An informal group may have the same members as a formal group, for example when members of a work group eat together. Other times, an informal group comprises only some of one or more formal groups (see Fig. 15.2).

There are two major types of informal groups: interest and friendship.

Fig. 15.2   Formal and informal groups in an organisation

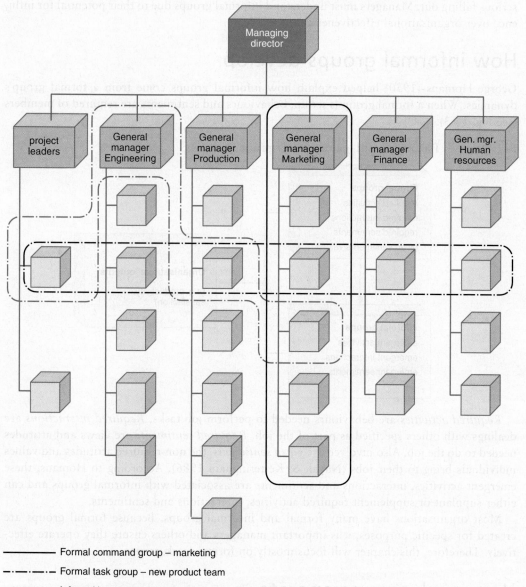

———— Formal command group – marketing

–·–·–·– Formal task group – new product team

–·–·–·– Informal interest group – members of local private golf club

An interest group is an informal group set up to help employees in common concerns. The interests producing informal groups can be wide, such as a new technology that is impractical for now (but which a group of engineers study informally), a sport (e.g. volleyball), or a desire to have the company alter one of its policies. A friendship group is an informal group existing mainly to meet employee social needs. These groups stem from mutual attraction, based on common characteristics such as similar work, backgrounds, and/or values. Informal groups can help an organisation by aiding information flow and reinforcing employees' readiness to work together. They can be harmful, when group concerns are put above work goals or there is a serious falling out. Managers must understand informal groups due to their potential for influence over organisational effectiveness.

How informal groups develop

George Homans (1950) helped explain how informal groups come from a formal group's dynamics. When a formal group is set up, behaviours and sentiments are required of members (see Fig. 15.3).

Fig. 15.3   The informal-group emergence process

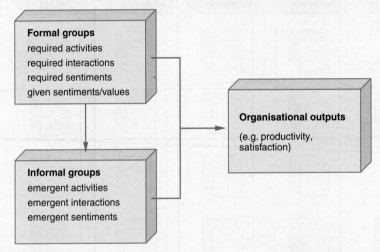

Required activities are behaviours needed to perform job tasks. *Required interactions* are dealings with others specified as part of the job. *Required sentiments* are views and attitudes needed to do the job. Also involved are *given sentiments*, the non-required attitudes and values individuals bring to their jobs (Nayak & Ketteringham 1986). According to Homans, these emergent activities, interactions and sentiments are associated with informal groups and can either supplant or supplement required activities, interactions and sentiments.

Most organisations have many formal and informal groups. Because formal groups are created for specific purposes, it is important managers and others ensure they operate effectively. Therefore, this chapter will focus mostly on formal work groups.

How work groups operate

Several factors affect teamwork and formal work-groups' effectiveness. In analysing these, it helps to view groups as systems using inputs, engaging in various processes or transformations, and producing outcomes (see Chapter 2 for a discussion of the systems approach to organisational analysis). Figure 15.4 lists several factors helpful in understanding group interactions and outcomes. These are grouped into categories of input, process and outcome. Note important outcomes are not simply group measures of performance such as quantity, quality and costs, but also member satisfaction. Moreover, in effective groups, teamwork increases effective operations and members' preparedness to work together again.

Fig. 15.4   A general model of work-group behaviour

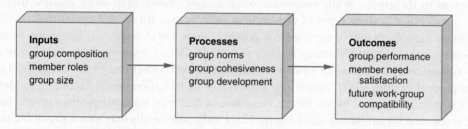

WORK-GROUP INPUTS

For groups to operate, they must have certain basic inputs. Some inputs affecting groups and teamwork are group composition, members' roles and group size.

Managing diversity: Work-group composition

Work-group composition bears on a group's ultimate success. So managers must carefully consider who will be a member of a work group. Two crucial factors to consider in selection are potential member characteristics and why they are attracted to the group.

Member characteristics   Managers must consider three types of member characteristics in setting up work groups (Hackman 1987). One is that group members must have task-relevant skills. Another is members must have correct interpersonal skills. Finally, for challenging tasks, a degree of diversity (e.g. personalities, gender, ethnic group, attitudes, background or experience) in group makeup is useful (Blackmon 1998). If they are too homogeneous, members may get along but not have sufficient different perspectives to generate new ideas (Jackson, Many & Whitney 1995). Alternatively, if the group is too heterogeneous, the advantages of breadth of talent may be lost due to problems of co-ordinating diverse efforts. Studies show diverse groups are more creative, more flexible when requirements change, and make better decisions (see Chapter 5) (Goodman, Ravlin & Argote 1986; Cox & Blacke 1991).

Managers must realise they need patience to benefit from group diversity. A study of culturally homogeneous versus culturally diverse groups (different nationalities and ethnic backgrounds) showed culturally diverse groups performed poorly at first, but over time performed better than homogeneous ones in assessing and solving business situations (Watson, Kumar & Michaelson 1993). Managers can facilitate the benefits of diversity by including members trained to function well in groups (Woodruff & Miller 1995). Some organisations offer diversity training to ensure members understand, appreciate and use individual differences effectively. For example, General Electric developed a vision statement for its diversity program: 'To be recognised as one of the world's most competitive companies due to our ability to value and fully utilise the contributions of all employees from all cultural and social backgrounds' (Capowski 1996, p. 14). Managers can promote benefits from diversity by monitoring groups to ensure they develop properly (Blackmon 1998).

Attraction to the group   Another consideration in group make-up is potential members' attraction to the group. While employees often cannot choose their work groups, they may have some choice in some types of task groups, such as task forces and committees.

Why do individuals join or participate in groups? (Shaw 1981). Some may like group members or be attracted to them (Armstrong & Holyoke 1995). Others may enjoy the group's activities, such as considering new ideas in an area of technical interest. Others may value the group's goals or purposes (Engardio 1988). People also join because of affiliation needs. According to McClelland's acquired-needs motivation theory, these will be higher in some people than others, but all have some need for affiliation (see Chapter 12). Lastly, individuals may join a group because it helps achieve a goal beyond the group (e.g. joining a committee to meet people from a work unit one would like to obtain a job in). Individuals join groups for any or all of these reasons.

New store—Old store—No store   crossroads

Metarlong imports and sells Indian handcrafts in its Rasa shops across Victoria and Queensland. In the midst of a growth push, two stores were opened at great speed over a period of two weeks.

In order to staff them, a very experienced manager, Glenda, was transferred from the Bourke Street store where she had been for two years, to undertake the launch of the new shop at Knox Shopping Centre in Melbourne's eastern suburbs. Other experienced staff were 'borrowed' from established stores to help start the two new stores and newly appointed staff were placed in the established stores to learn the ropes.

Within days there were complaints from staff in the established stores that these stores did not feel the same any more, in particular the one from which Glenda had been transferred.

Source: M. Tein.

Reflection point

1 Explain why the established stores did not feel the same any more.

Decision point

1 What were the factors considered which led to Glenda's transfer to the Knox Centre store? What other strategies might have worked successfully to staff the new stores?

Epilogue

The Bourke Street store no longer exists. There are many reasons for this. However, the decline started with Glenda's transfer. Keeping in mind what you have learned about group processes, explain why one person's transfer might have caused the decline of a store.

role

Set of behaviours expected of an individual occupying a particular position in a group

Member roles

Why do we expect a committee's nominated chair will call a meeting to order, someone from finance will give relevant financial expertise, and the nominated secretary will take notes? This is because each fulfils a **role**, a set of behaviours expected of someone occupying a group position. When in a work group, individuals have many roles. For example, a person may be an expert in a given area, may represent a command group and also be a workforce member interested in the consequence of some change.

In addition, the fact that an individual is a member of a group brings with it other roles. Common roles in groups fall into three categories: task, maintenance and self-oriented roles (Benne & Sheats 1948; Allcorn 1985).

Group-task roles help the group develop and accomplish goals. Among these are the following:

- **Initiator-contributor:** Proposes goals, suggests ways of approaching tasks, recommends procedures for approaching a problem or task
- **Information seeker:** Asks for information, viewpoints and suggestions about a problem or task
- **Information giver:** Offers information, viewpoints and suggestions about a problem or task
- **Co-ordinator:** Clarifies and synthesises various ideas in an effort to tie together members' work
- **Orienter:** Summarises, points to departures from goals, and raises questions about discussion direction
- **Energiser:** Stimulates the group to higher levels of work and better quality

group-task roles

Roles helping a group develop and accomplish its goals

Group maintenance roles do not address the task directly but help foster group unity, positive interpersonal relations among group members, and the development of members' ability to work together effectively. Group maintenance roles include:

- **Encourager:** Expresses warmth and friendliness toward group members, encourages them and acknowledges their contributions
- **Harmoniser:** Mediates disagreements between other members and attempts to help reconcile differences
- **Gatekeeper:** Tries to keep lines of communication open and promotes participation of all group members
- **Standard setter:** Suggests standards for how the group will operate and checks whether members are satisfied with the group's functioning
- **Group observer:** Watches the group's internal operations and provides feedback on how participants are doing and how they might be able to function better
- **Follower:** Goes along with the group and is friendly but relatively passive

group-maintenance roles

Roles not directly addressing a task itself but, instead, helping foster group unity, positive interpersonal relations among group members and development of their ability to work effectively together

Self-oriented roles relate to group members' personal needs and may negatively influence the group's effectiveness. These include the following:

- **Aggressor:** Deflates contributions of others by attacking their ideas, ridiculing their feelings and displaying excessive competitiveness
- **Blocker:** Tends to be negative, stubborn and resistive of new ideas, sometimes to force the group to readdress a viewpoint already dealt with
- **Recognition seeker:** Seeks attention, boasts about accomplishments and capabilities, and works to prevent being put in an inferior position in the group
- **Dominator:** Tries to assert control and manipulates the group or certain group members by flattery, giving orders or interrupting others

self-oriented roles

Roles related to the personal needs of group members and often negatively influencing group effectiveness

Group leaders may assume many task roles. In addition, they may use some maintenance roles to help group progress. However, a leader cannot assume all needed task and maintenance behaviours without assistance from others in the group. In leaderless groups (with no appointed leader), individuals likely to emerge as leaders (be perceived as leaders) are active participants who adopt task roles (Bass 1990).

informal leader

Individual, other than the formal leader, emerging from a group as a major influence and perceived by members as a leader

Even with a formal leader, other informal leaders may emerge. An **informal leader** is someone, other than the formal leader, who emerges from the group with major influence and is seen as a leader by members. Although some members may try to use informal leadership despite the formal leader's behaviour, emerging informal leaders are most likely when a formal leader has trouble facilitating group progress (Eddy 1985). In addition to roles, another important input factor is group size.

Group size

Research on small groups gives some understanding of the effects of group size. One area of research has looked at how different numbers affect interactions, and another at how group size affects performance (Shull, Debecq & Cummings 1970; Shaw 1981).

Size and group interactions   The number of people in a group affects members' interactions. With two-person groups, or dyads, the two are either likely to be very polite, attempting to avoid disagreements, or likely to disagree frequently, causing relations to be strained. Adding another person rarely solves interaction problems as the group tends to split into 'two-against-one'. Groups with four or six members often deadlock as groups split into equal factions.

In contrast, groups of five or seven have some benefits. For one, deadlocks cannot occur, due to the odd numbers. For another, they are large enough to produce different ideas but small enough to let members participate.

As groups grow above seven members, particularly above 11 or 12, it is harder for active participation. As a result, group interaction is increasingly centralised, with some having more active roles than others. Disagreements occur more often and group satisfaction declines unless participants work at group maintenance roles. Moreover, interactions may be drawn out on complex issues (Altier 1986; Schiller 1988).

Size and performance   What impact does size have on group performance? This is not easy to answer because the effects of size depend partly on the nature of the task. For example, in a group in which members work independently (such as waiters in a restaurant) the effects are different from a group in which members co-ordinate efforts closely (such as a rescue team). Generally, though, the effect of size on group performance forms an inverted 'U' (see Fig. 15.5) (Cummings, Huber & Arendt 1974; Goodman et al. 1986). Thus, as more workers are added to a group, performance improves; but after a point, the added impact of more workers levels off and may even deteriorate.

social loafing or free riding

Tendency of individuals to expend less effort when working in groups than when working alone and to benefit from the group's work without bearing a proportional share of costs involved

Why does performance stabilise and even drop with increased group size? One reason is **social loafing**, or people's tendency to use less effort working in groups than alone (Gooding & Wagner 1985; Karau & Williams 1995). Effects snowball if other members detect social loafing and reduce their own efforts (Kidwell & Bennett 1993). Individuals who engage in social loafing are called free riders as they benefit from the group's efforts without giving a proportional share of costs (Albanese & Van Fleet 1985). Thus, social loafing is called **free riding**. There is evidence that those who tend to individualism are more likely to free ride as

Fig.15.5   Effects of group size on performance

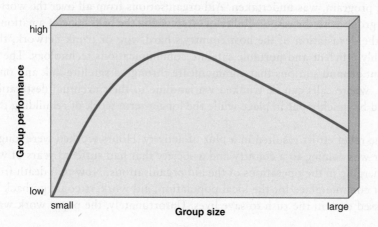

group-size increases than those leaning toward collectivism. **Individualism** is where personal interests are given more weight than group needs. Individualists are self-oriented and will ignore group interests if conflicting with their own. **Collectivism** occurs where group demands and interests are given precedence over individual desires and needs. Collectivists make personal sacrifices for the group's good (Wagner 1995).

Managers can reduce the likelihood of social loafing (Karau & Williams 1995). Assigning just enough people to do the work is one way. Other ways are having each person do different tasks, making individual work visible, providing individual feedback, having likely loafers work with respected people, giving a standard for measurement of group progress, and making rewards depend on individual, as well as group, performance. Finally, since social loafing is less likely with a group committed to the task, managers must design interesting, challenging tasks or choose group members who are committed to the task (Karau & Williams 1995; Jackson & Harkins 1985; Zaccaro 1984).

individualism

Condition where personal interests are given more weight than the group's interests

collectivism

Condition where the demands and interests of group interests are given precedence over desires and needs of individuals

 # Phone home?   case in point

Most employees with access to a company phone have made personal calls in business hours and without the explicit permission of their employer. Indeed, these calls in all but the very few organisations that expressly forbid them are considered if not exactly as a right, then as a basic privilege of employment. This largely tacit deal between the employer and the employee hinges on notions of what is reasonable in the circumstances. The employer seems to concede that a blanket prohibition on the use of company phones for personal calls would be a mean spirited and ultimately counterproductive thing to impose. On the other hand, the employee's concession is that calls made will not be too frequent or too long, and they will not be trivial or time wasting.

So it seems that the employment relationship can tolerate the implied terms that are encompassed in the employee making the occasional, short and important personal call from work. But what happens when a large contingent of employees is temporarily located overseas, in a developing country, and with telephone access only to an extremely expensive satellite communications network? Let's see.

In response to one of the world's more recent humanitarian disasters, an international relief effort, including an in-country infrastructure rebuilding program, was undertaken. Aid organisations from all over the world deployed to assist and amongst these was one group with the responsibility of establishing the backbone of a national telecommunications capability. In light of the devastation of the host country's hard wire or trunk network, the decision was made to use expensive but highly efficient and portable satellite communications technology. The equipment utilised effectively act as independent ground stations that communicate through a satellite link and on to permanent facilities, in this case offshore, where calls can be trunked via landline to their eventual destination. Thus a telecommunications capability could be quickly put in place while the longer-term work of rebuilding the network took place.

The first five or six months of the relief effort resulted in a blur of activity. Hours worked were long and hard, but slowly some semblance of order was coming to a country and a society that had suffered years of warfare and terror. Similarly, some order was emerging in the operations of the aid organisations. Now that death from disease, injury or starvation was at least not commonplace for the local population, aid workers could go back to some of the tasks that were put aside or passed over in the rush to save lives. Unfortunately, the paper work was about to catch up with a vengeance.

One of the more pressing post-emergency tasks was to get a clear picture on aid expenditure so far and to begin settling with some very patient creditors. Almost immediately this work began, alarm bells started to ring. Invoices for international telephone calls were way up on estimates. In fact they were hundreds of thousands of US dollars over what was considered appropriate. After itemised accounts were procured, it was revealed that a massive number of calls had been placed to one Pacific Rim country in particular. Of these, so many different numbers had been used that it was obvious that these could not be work related calls to, say, suppliers or parent organisations.

As the investigation began to uncover more of the story, it soon became clear that the numbers called were largely private and centred on one particular urban area. This area was easily identified as the one from which the staff operating the satellite communications equipment had been drawn. Further enquiry revealed that these staff had been making personal calls with sometimes alarming frequency.

Eventually it came to be known that most staff with access to the satellite phone system had made personal calls to their home country. Of these, a small number could be classified as high-order users with one notable for making two or more half-hour calls per day for a total cost equivalent to a reasonable annual salary. Mid-order users, with two or three calls per week, comprised a much larger group; however, it was the low-order users, with an average of one short call each fortnight, that formed the majority.

At this stage, it needs to be pointed out that while management had never given permission for staff to make personal calls, on the other hand it had not been expressly denied either. Additionally, the facts that some managers were themselves making personal calls, and that most managers and supervisors were aware of the practice, need to be considered. Similarly it should be remembered that this was an organisation that quietly acquiesced to personal calls in its home country.

In the fullness of time it was decided to separately bill individuals for all personal calls attributable to them and to issue a written instruction prohibiting all future calls. While pressure had been brought to bear to initiate criminal charges against all users, it was the restraint of the entirely reasonable low-order users and the fact that calls were common knowledge that argued against this. Unfortunately, in the clamour to lay blame, the magnificent effort of those that resisted temptation day to day while operating in often dangerous and lonely outposts went unacknowledged.

Source: Case study prepared by Mark Weston Wall.

Activities for discussion, analysis and further research

1 Most of us would probably agree that those who refrained from using the communications system to make personal calls were in the right in this case study. However, what can be said about those who did use the system and in particular the low-order users?

2 From the case study it is clear that managers and supervisors were not only aware of the fact that staff were making personal calls, they were also making their own calls. Does this somehow excuse or at least mitigate the behaviour of the staff?

3 From the perspective of the management of groups, what might be done to ensure that this problem is resolved without causing undue divisiveness in the work teams involved, and retaining the group cohesiveness required in this type of organisation?

4 If itemised international accounts had not been available, what techniques might management have employed to identify the cause of the exorbitant call costs?

5 Reactive management is one thing; however is there something management might have done to prevent this situation from arising? What might have been reasonable in the circumstances?

WORK-GROUP PROCESSES

Why do some groups accomplish little, while others with similar inputs accomplish a great deal? In part, the answer lies in *group processes*, the dynamic, inner workings of groups. As group members go about their work, some energy must go to developing and operating the group. This energy is diverted from the task, and is called process loss, since it is lost energy which could have been devoted to the task (Shepperd 1993). Some process loss is inevitable, given the characteristic interdependence among group members.

On the other hand, tremendous gains can flow from the combined force, or synergy, of group members (Hackman, 1987). **Positive synergy** is when combined gains from group interaction (as opposed to individuals alone) are greater than group process losses. When there is positive synergy, the whole (the group's total effect) is greater than the sum of its parts (tasks members could achieve individually). **Negative synergy** occurs when group process losses are greater than gains from combining group members' forces. If you have used a group that is so ineffective you could have done the job faster alone, then you have witnessed negative synergy. We next discuss three major group-process factors affecting group synergy and effectiveness: norms, cohesiveness and group development.

Group norms

Norms are expected behaviours sanctioned by a group which regulates and fosters uniform member behaviours (Goodman, Ravlin & Schminke 1987). For a behaviour to be a norm, group members must recognise it as expected for group membership.

Work groups do not regulate all behaviour by norms. Rather, they develop and enforce norms related to central issues (Goodman, Ravlin & Schminke 1987). For example, groups develop norms about production processes. These norms relate to quality and quantity standards, as well as how to do the job. Informal social arrangements are another area for norms. That is,

positive synergy

Force resulting when combined gains from group interaction are greater than group-process losses

negative synergy

Force resulting when group-process losses are greater than gains achieved from combining the forces of group members

norms

Expected behaviours sanctioned by a group that regulate and foster uniform member behaviour

groups often set norms about when and where to have lunch; the type of social function, if any, to have when someone leaves; and appropriate socialising at and outside work. Finally, work groups often have norms about resource allocation, such as materials, equipment, assigned work area (e.g. near a window) and pay (Lubin 1995).

Typically norms develop through one of four mechanisms: explicit statements, critical events, primacy and carryover behaviours (Feldman 1984).

Explicit statements   Explicit statements by supervisors and co-workers can give information about group members' expectations. These provide a good opportunity for a supervisor to influence the group's norms. Supervisory statements may be especially important when a new group is formed or a new person joins a group (Magnet 1988; *Fortune* 1994).

Critical events   In any group, there are critical events in a group's history which set precedents for the future.

Primacy   Primacy as a source of norms is the tendency for the first behaviour pattern a group displays to establish group expectations.

Carryover behaviours   Many norms are carryover behaviours from other groups and organisations. When group members share similar past experiences (such as working on similar company committees), norms are established quickly. Otherwise, they may evolve more slowly (Bettenhausen & Murnighan 1985; Prinzinsky 1996).

Group cohesiveness

group cohesiveness

Degree to which members are attracted to a group, are motivated to remain in it, and are mutually influenced by one another

Another factor related to group process is **group cohesiveness**, the degree to which members are attracted to a group, are motivated to stay in it, and are influenced by one another. We look at the consequences of group cohesiveness before exploring its determinants (Luthans 1995; Arnold & Feldman 1986).

Consequences of group cohesiveness   Group cohesiveness can have very positive outcomes for communication and job satisfaction. Members of cohesive groups communicate more often and are more sensitive to each another, and are generally better able to gauge other group members' feelings. Members of highly cohesive groups are more satisfied with their jobs and team members than those of less cohesive groups (Dobbins & Zaccaro 1986). Group cohesiveness leads to **organisational citizenship behaviours**, discretionary actions that are not part of job requirements but contribute to attaining organisational goals (such as assisting a co-worker who is struggling with a task) (Organ & Ryan 1995). Although some negative possibilities exist (such as too much communication among group members), the improved communication and job satisfaction resulting from group cohesiveness are organisationally valuable.

organisational citizenship behaviours

Discretionary actions that are not part of job requirements but contribute to attaining organisational goals

Group cohesiveness influences the hostility and aggression levels one group shows to another. Whether this is an organisational asset or liability depends on where the energy is channelled. For example, cohesiveness may help when friendly competition emerges among groups doing the same type of work but not dependent upon each other to get work done. Aggressiveness from group cohesiveness can energise a group against outside competition (Dallas 1995). On the other hand, when groups depend on one another to reach organisational goals, hostility or aggression results in little co-operation and other negative consequences, such as missing deadlines, raising costs and frustrating customers.

Another area influenced by group cohesiveness is performance—in highly cohesive groups members' performance levels are more similar. This is because members avoid letting the group down by underperforming or showing up other group members by a significantly higher-level performance.

The impact of cohesiveness on actual group performance levels, however, depends both on the group's degree of cohesiveness and on existing performance norms. This is shown in Figure 15.6. Groups perform at their highest when group cohesion and performance norms are high, encouraging all group members to perform at the same high level. In contrast, when group cohesion is high but performance norms are low, group performance tends to be lower (Seashore 1954; Stogdill 1972). Here, high group cohesion bolsters adherence to low performance norms. The effects can be seen in an example from a former MBA student, whose summer job was in a highly cohesive lawn-care crew with low performance norms. As he vigorously raked grass clippings on his first work day, crew members, even the crew leader, told him to slow or they would all get tired if they worked at that rate. Then the crew leader showed him how to use a handkerchief to mop his brow while leaning on his rake so it would look like he had been working hard and just stopped to wipe off the resulting perspiration. The handkerchief routine was used if one was caught not working when the supervisor drove up on periodic work-crew checks.

Group cohesiveness can also affect a group's readiness to innovate and change. Change is more difficult when opposed by a highly cohesive group, but can be much easier with such a group's strong backing (Serwer 1995).

**Fig. 15.6   Effects of cohesiveness and performance norms on group
                performance**

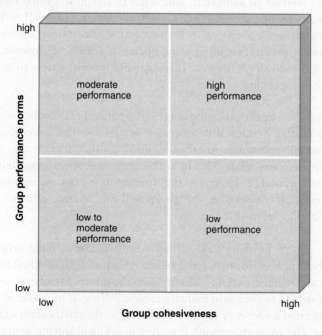

Determinants of group cohesiveness   Many factors influence group cohesiveness positively. For example, similar attitudes and values mean individuals can communicate, find common ground and develop mutual understandings. External threats, such as fierce outside competition or survival challenges, give compelling reasons for a group to pull together as a cohesive unit. Major successes produce strong positive feelings about group membership, forming links between group members (Mullen & Copper 1994). Difficulty in joining a group, based on factors such as high standards (university), sacrifice (Australian Volunteers Abroad) or difficult training (the Special Air Service) can build a common bond. Finally, group size can be a factor. Cohesiveness is easier when groups are small, and it is more difficult to achieve and maintain as groups grow larger (Brown 1988; *Forbes* 1989; Labarre 1995).

Group development

New groups, such as new work units, committees and task forces, are constantly forming in organisations. Even established groups change as members leave and new ones are added. These changes affect groups' processes.

Researchers argue groups go through relatively predictable developmental stages. Understanding these helps managers participate effectively in groups and assist those they are responsible for. One approach to analysis of group development identifies five major stages: forming, storming, norming, performing and adjourning (see Fig. 15.7) (Tuckman 1965; Tuckman & Jensen 1977).

New groups may progress through these phases, but if membership changes, development may briefly regress to an earlier stage.

forming

Stage in which group members try to assess ground rules applying to a task and to group interaction

Stage 1: Forming   In the group's **forming** stage, members try to assess the ground rules of task and group interaction. At this point, members seek information about the task, evaluate how the group might interact to achieve it, and begin to test how valued their input will be. Members may test acceptability of behaviours, such as engaging in small talk, making jokes, sarcasm or leaving to make telephone calls. Because of the uncertainty, members may depend on a powerful person, if present, or on existing norms, if commonly known. Because of the need to understand ground rules, groups at this stage often require time to get know the task and each other before proceeding.

storming

Stage in which group members frequently are in conflict with each other as they locate and resolve differences of opinion about key issues

Stage 2: Storming   During the **storming** stage, group members conflict with each other as they find and try to resolve opinion differences on key issues. The issues might involve task requirements and possible resistance. Another common conflict area centres on interpersonal relations, how group members relate. Often, at this stage, members struggle for leadership if a leader has not been appointed. Listening and attempting to find acceptable resolutions of major issues are important. Otherwise, the group will not operate effectively, not progress beyond this stage, and may even disband.

norming

Stage in which group members begin to build group cohesion, as well as develop a consensus about norms for performing a task and relating to each other

Stage 3: Norming   In the **norming** stage, group members start to build group cohesion, and reach a consensus about task performance and relationship norms. Individual members' idiosyncrasies are accepted, and members start to identify with the group. Member roles are clearer, and the group shows it is willing to engage in mutual problem solving. If no leader is appointed or the leader is weak, an informal leader may emerge. At this stage, the clarification of norms and roles, cohesiveness building, and using the group's resources in problem solving are important.

Fig. 15.7 Stages of group development

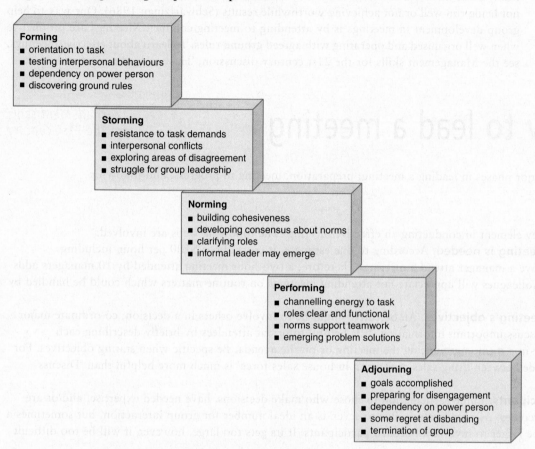

Forming
- orientation to task
- testing interpersonal behaviours
- dependency on power person
- discovering ground rules

Storming
- resistance to task demands
- interpersonal conflicts
- exploring areas of disagreement
- struggle for group leadership

Norming
- building cohesiveness
- developing consensus about norms
- clarifying roles
- informal leader may emerge

Performing
- channelling energy to task
- roles clear and functional
- norms support teamwork
- emerging problem solutions

Adjourning
- goals accomplished
- preparing for disengagement
- dependency on power person
- some regret at disbanding
- termination of group

Stage 4: Performing   The **performing** stage is when energy is channelled toward a task and when norms support teamwork. Solutions emerge from the previous stage's problem solving. Group members' roles become clear and more effective as the group works to achieve positive synergy and group goals. Not all groups reach this stage. Those which do will be effective so long as they work at the task and maintain good group relationships.

Stage 5: Adjourning   During the **adjourning** stage, group members prepare for disengagement as the group nears successful goal completion. While members may be pleased with finishing their tasks, they may regret the imminent group dispersal. The adjourning stage is more often applicable to temporary task groups such as committees, task forces or limited duration teams. With permanent formal groups, adjournment applies less often. However, reorganisations, take-overs and mergers can cause the stage to occur.

Do all groups have these stages? The five group development stages apply mainly to newly formed, unstructured groups. They are less likely in groups with members working together often or those with well-established operating methods or ground rules (Seeger 1983).

An important place for group development is meetings. Senior executives spend on average 23 hours a week in meetings, and middle managers about 11 hours per week (Hymowitz 1988).

performing

Stage in which energy is channelled toward a task and in which norms support teamwork

adjourning

Stage in which group members prepare for disengagement as the group nears successful completion of its goals

Many other members are in meetings several hours per week. Meetings are often criticised for not being run well or not achieving worthwhile results (Schwartzman 1986). One way to help group development in meetings is by attending to meeting conduct. Meetings are productive when well organised and operating with agreed ground rules. To learn about effective meetings, see the Management skills for the 21st century discussion, 'How to lead a meeting.'

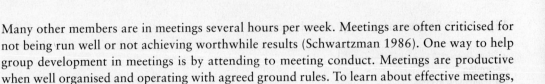

⬆ How to lead a meeting

management skills
for the 21st century

There are three major phases in leading a meeting: preparation, meeting in progress, and follow-up.

Preparation

Preparation is a key element in conducting an effective meeting. The following steps are involved:

1 **Ensure the meeting is needed**. According to one estimate, it costs about $100 per hour, including overhead, to have a manager attend a meeting. Therefore, a two-hour meeting attended by 10 managers adds up to $2000. Colleagues will appreciate not attending meetings on routine matters which could be handled by a memo.

2 **Define the meeting's objectives.** An objective might be to involve others in a decision, co-ordinate major activities, or discuss important information. It is helpful to orient attendees by briefly describing each objective either in a memo announcing the meeting or on the agenda. Be specific when stating objectives. For example, 'Decide between using sales reps or an in-house sales force' is much more helpful than 'Discuss sales'.

3 **Identify participants.** Limit participation to those who make decisions, have needed expertise, and/or are affected by outcomes. As noted before, five to seven is an ideal number for group interaction, but sometimes a meeting must be larger to involve all needed participants. If its gets too large, however, it will be too difficult to handle.

4 **Prepare an agenda.** When there is time, circulate the agenda before the meeting and get feedback. The agenda should be a short list of main topics to be discussed. It helps key participants focus on the preparations they need to make for the meeting and assists in ensuring important topics are covered. Send the final agenda out two or three days in advance.

5 **Distribute needed background information.** Consider the information participants will need in advance, and send it out with the final agenda. Avoid sending huge reports participants are unlikely to read. A better strategy is to send a summary and note the full report is available if needed.

Meeting in progress

Good preparation helps the meeting progress more smoothly. Actually running the meeting involves these five steps:

1 **Review the agenda.** Start on time, and review the agenda and major objectives. This helps focus participants on why they are there and what outcomes are needed. It helps to print the agenda on a blackboard or flip chart for easy reference.

2 **Get reports from individuals with preassigned tasks.** This should be done as soon as feasible, although it may be necessary to wait for a particular agenda item to ask for a report or presentation. Getting reports as early as possible ensures presenters have enough time and provides recognition for their pre-meeting work. It also gives some background information for other parts of the agenda.

3 Encourage participant input. Group effectiveness and member satisfaction will be greater when all members are able to provide input in their areas of expertise. A meeting leader should ensure the meeting is not dominated by one faction or a few members. If someone speaks too much, the leader might say, 'Well, Joan, let me see if I understand what you are saying.' Then, after summarising, the leader might follow with, 'Perhaps others have views on this issue.' If an individual has said little, the leader might say, 'Jim, we haven't heard from you yet. What are your views?'

4 Keep the meeting on track. If discussion wanders, refer to a point made just before the digression to get discussion back on track. If an issue is raised which cannot be resolved due to insufficient information, ask someone to look into it and report back.

5 Summarise and review assignments. Summarise what has been agreed upon or accomplished in the meeting. Also, review what each person has agreed to do and make sure deadlines are set. Review plans for the next meeting if that is appropriate. End the meeting on time.

Follow-up

The meeting leader should follow up on the meeting:

1 Send out a memo summarising the meeting. The memo should summarise the main things accomplished, and it should specify actions each person agreed to take and deadlines set.

2 Follow up on assignments where appropriate. This involves checking with various individuals about their progress, usually in preparation for a subsequent meeting.

Meeting leadership takes practice. It is usually a good idea for individuals to chair small, lower-level meetings early in their careers to gain experience (Jay 1976; Huber 1980; Whetten & Cameron 1998; Bailey 1987; Dressler 1995).

Whistle while you work　　　　gaining the edge

Not so long ago, while walking down the corridor of my work place, I heard a colleague say to a couple of others: 'Who's laughing in here? Don't you know it is against policy to have fun? The boss might think you're not doing your job!'

In spite of this, humour has been demonstrated to be of high benefit in managing work groups. It has been known to lower absenteeism, improve job-satisfaction ratings, lead to higher productivity, promote better retention rates and lower staff turnover, and even reduce customer-service complaints and problems.

Other benefits in the use of humour as a management tool include a rise in creativity and faster problem solving, as people see solving problems as a way to have fun. When people are having fun, they enjoy doing so together and more effective team-work is often the result.

There is no way to ban humour from the workplace. It will appear in guerrilla warfare form unless it is part of the culture of the organisation. Think of the number of e-mails and faxes you may have received which are bitter-sweet forms of humour taking a dig at something happening in the organisation.

Source: Stauffer, D. (1999).

Activities for discussion, analysis and further research

1 Develop a number of strategies which might encourage a culture which accepts fun and humour as part of 'the way we behave around here'.
2 Southwest Airlines is famous for its over-the-top having fun culture. Go into their web site and find some examples of the type of activity they engage in which livens up the work day and the workplace.
3 Look up the newsletter *Humour and Health*, whose editor is Joseph Dunn, and find some articles on how to introduce humour in the workplace. Describe the benefits expected from such actions.

@ I'll be watching you ...

managing the e-challenge

In early March 2000, six staff of Centrelink became some of dozens of Australians who have been fired for misusing e-mail and the Internet at work. At least one in five large organisations in Australia have installed surveillance software capable of recording the type of activity undertaken by staff on line. Over the past 12 months, the number of companies using such software rose by 10 per cent.

Companies claim that diminished productivity, potential legal liability and information theft are the three key dangers they have a right to protect themselves against. As expected, workers and unions object to this practice on the grounds of ethics and privacy. However, there have been a number of cases where judgments have been brought against employers for defamation in an internal e-mail, or a lawsuit over racially inflammatory comments sent over a work-based network.

Monitoring is recognised to be important because of the possibility of harassment and discrimination, as employers are obliged to take reasonable steps to prevent these. Employers face the issue of balancing employee privacy with legal accountability.

Wespac, Telstra and National Australia Bank each admits to having installed monitoring software which they say is only used when a specific complaint is lodged by a fellow staff member. Colonial and ANZ have each sacked staff for distributing pornography, and maintain a search for pre-set keywords deemed 'inappropriate'.

With three million Australian workers using the Internet, it has been estimated that the Net is responsible for $1 billion a year in lost productivity. NetComm, an Australian modem company, arrived at this estimate after investigating inexplicable traffic on its own network, and consequently added WebSpy to its own product range. Another such program is Investigator, with comprehensive capabilities for monitoring every action taken by staff on a network. To date there are over 100 licences in Australia, 62 of them in two government departments.

Though monitoring tools grow increasingly invasive, there is no legislation addressing the issue of computer privacy in the Australian workplace. Such legislation was attempted and failed in California recently on the grounds that it would leave companies legally accountable and damage their ability to monitor performance and guard intellectual property.

However, there is encouragement for organisations to produce policy and ground rules which are explicit and appropriate. Peter Leonard, partner of Gilbert and Tobin, went to the extent of developing an electronic communications policy that indicates what is acceptable monitoring and what is not.

Companies like Telstra, Colonial, NAB, ANZ and Westpac, for instance, allow staff a reasonable level of personal Internet use. Their view is that online banking or shopping takes less time than a lunch-time errand, and lunch-time surfing helps staff increase their skills.

Source: Adapted from Bryan, M. (2000).

Activities for discussion, analysis and further research

1 Does your organisation monitor staff usage of e-mail and the Internet? Does it have a policy about this?

2 Identify the organisation culture issues which are revealed when an organisation monitors staff activities secretly.

3 What should a manager do if they suspect that an employee is abusing the Internet and e-mail access? Why?

PROMOTING INNOVATION: USING TASK FORCES AND TEAMS

Groups are used when organisations can benefit from the experience and ideas of two or more people. Increasingly, group efforts are tapped when creativity and innovation are needed for organisational success. In this section, we investigate some special uses of teams.

Task forces

A **task force** is a temporary group formed to recommend on a specific matter (Altier 1986; Guzzo & Dickson 1996). It may be called an **ad hoc** or temporary **committee** (Stech & Ratliffe 1985; Kiechel 1991). Because they deal with issues involving several organisation parts, task forces often comprise individuals from command groups affected by an issue (Markels 1995). These people are needed to give expertise, furnish information about their command groups' needs, and help develop creative ideas for problem solving or opportunity taking (Birchard 1995). As task forces promote interaction among individuals from diverse departments, they are suited to fostering creativity and innovation.

task force

Temporary task group formed to recommend on a specific issue

ad hoc committee

Another term for a task force

Teams

A **team** is a temporary or an ongoing task group whose members work to identify problems, form a consensus about action, and implement needed actions on a particular task or organisational area. Two characteristics separate a team from a task force. First, team members typically identify problems in an area (rather than deal with them after identification by others). Second, they reach a consensus about what should be done and actually implement decisions as a team (rather than make recommendations implemented by others; Armstrong & Holyoke 1995). Of course, members (unless they are top-level managers) usually keep their superiors informed, as necessary. Also, they need the agreement of their superiors on decisions with major implications for others and the organisation,

Teams are often, but not always, task groups of individuals across command groups. Temporary teams handle a specific project to completion, where permanent teams have continuing responsibilities in a given area (Updike, Woodruff & Armstrong 1995). Teams may have a fluid membership of individuals who join when their expertise is needed and leave when their work is done.

team

Temporary or ongoing task group with members charged to work together to identify problems, form a consensus about what should be done, and implement necessary actions in relation to a particular task or organisational area

Teams have been very successful in a wide range of organisations, including such firms as Heinz, General Motors, Boeing, Hewlett-Packard, Xerox and Tenix. The use of teams has gained attention, especially as a way to foster innovation, increase quality and facilitate successful change (Reich 1987). According to an estimate, 80 per cent of organisations with 100 or more members use teams in some way, and 50 per cent of their employees are part of at least one team (Gordon 1992; Coradetti 1994; Fenn 1995; *Wall Street Journal* 1994). Three types of teams of particular importance are entrepreneurial, self-managing and virtual teams.

entrepreneurial team

Group of individuals with diverse expertise and backgrounds brought together to develop and implement innovative ideas aimed to create new products or services or significantly improve existing ones

Entrepreneurial teams   An **entrepreneurial team** is a group with varied expertise and backgrounds assembled to develop and implement innovative ideas to create new products or services or significantly improve existing ones (Rosow in Davidson 1986; Brahm 1995; Loeb 1994). Entrepreneurial teams focus on new business by pioneering different types of endeavours or by devising novel products and services fitting with existing business lines (Stevens 1995).

self-managing team

Work group with responsibility for a task area without supervision, and given authority to influence and control group membership and behaviour

Self-managing teams   A **self-managing team** is responsible for a task area without supervision and with authority to influence and control group membership and behaviour. It can be responsible for setting pay and bonus levels (Byrne 1995). Self-managing teams are also known as autonomous work groups. The Swedish automobile manufacturer A. B. Volvo pioneered these groups at its Kamar plant in the early 1970s. There, autonomous work teams of about 20 workers put together entire units of cars, such as the electrical system or engine (Lohr 1987).

A growing number of companies have experimented with self-managing teams (Dumaine 1990; Tjosvold 1993). One study indicates those in self-managing teams report more favourable work attitudes, higher job satisfaction and greater organisational commitment than those in traditionally designed jobs. Other studies obtained mixed results (Cordery, Mueller & Smith 1991; Guzzo & Dickson 1996).

Even in high-performing teams there will be some who do not measure up, and in self-managing teams disposing of these people is difficult for the team (Markels 1995). Similarly, the issue of evaluating team-member performances and setting members' pay can cause some groups to defer to management (Lublin 1995).

One major block to the success of self-managing teams is the tendency to label a work group as a 'self-managing team' without providing the necessary training and support. Four important steps are needed to increase prospects of success (Hackman 1987). First, before forming the team, the value of self-managing teams must be assessed, as well as determining the tasks and degree of authority to be delegated. Second, in forming a team, thought must be given to group composition and necessary resources allocated. Third, as the group moves through group development stages, training in effective team work and guidance in setting appropriate norms are needed. Finally, managers must help by removing performance obstacles and assisting the group to learn. Experts warn productivity may decline at first as new self-managing teams develop. In fact, assuming the steps are followed, it may be 18 months or more before productivity increases (Sims 1995).

virtual team

Physically dispersed work group using information technology as a means to interact but rarely, if ever, meeting physically

Virtual teams   **Virtual teams** comprise members who rarely if ever meet, interacting through different information technology means including phones, faxes, e-mail, computer nets and video conferencing. Virtual teams are increasingly important for global organisations with widely dispersed activities, and as knowledge becomes further specialised (Pape 1997;

Townsend, DeMarie & Hendrickson 1998; Kodama 2000a). Virtual teams permit creation of problem solving or exploration teams, overcoming the problem of having members unable to work in the same physical location (Kodama 1999).

Duarte and Snyder (1999) identify organisational factors critical to effective use of virtual teams. These include the following. Firstly, established appropriate reward systems together with non-traditional work arrangements are acceptable to the organisation. Secondly, continual training opportunities are provided for the team members and their organisational community. Thirdly, team processes are commonly understood and sufficiently flexible in nature. Fourthly, technological support resources must be widely available, as must adequate training in their use. Fifthly, cultural diversity must be valued and the overall culture must be one of trust. Sixthly, leaders must model the use of technology and high levels of performance. Finally, all team members and leaders must be experienced in the application of the technological tools, and comfortable in their virtual environments.

To use this strategy effectively there must be an understanding of the task's technological demands and how these must be matched to take full advantage of the relative strengths of rapidly evolving technology (Duarte & Snyder 1999; Vokola, Rezgul & Wood-Harper 2000). As well as this understanding, there must also be a clear realisation of the impact of both organisational and other cultural levels (Rockett, Valor, Miller & Naude 1998).

Setting up a virtual team requires a process of six steps (Duarte & Snyder 1999). These are: identification of significant sources of organisational influence or power; development of a clear statement of purpose or mission; team participant identification; orchestrated initial contacts across the team; in possibly the only face-to-face contact the team will have, orient members to the virtual team processes, and at that session establish team control and management processes (Miesing 1998; Thite 1999).

Virtual teams allow managers to forget spatial dispersion, setting up teams of members who are knowledgeable, expert and experienced for specific problems or a particular opportunity (Townsend et al. 1998; Cook 1999). Virtual teams can even have members from other organisations; for example, an outsourced supplier (Pape 1997). This form of team allows managers to move beyond the traditional boundaries of the organisation (Holmqvist 1999; Kodama 2000b).

■ The MD's diary

the reflective practitioner

One of the things that concerned me about this organisation when I started here was that we still very much had this chimney mentality, or people working in boxes. It concerns me that people try to put boundaries around their roles or their functions in such a way that makes it quite clear as to where their responsibilities start and finish. This is a very safe way to work but it reduces the value and the contribution that people can make. Right from the day that I arrived here, I have tried to break down this thinking, especially among the management team. I tried to encourage a culture whereby every one of us should be prepared to be challenged about what we think and what we say—if we are making a decision as an organisation, that affects others within the organisation, it is always subject to scrutiny and challenge, and I believe that by doing that, it does two things. It allows people to stretch their wings in terms of getting involved in things that are perhaps outside their direct functional responsibility and learn some new skills, and it means that the decision-making process would be much better. The other thing that it does is cut down the communication times. It breaks down all the barriers which lead to getting sign-off by all the functional heads for every decision that is taken. So, if one of the things that we are trying to do is to grow and grow quickly, and one of the ways we're trying to grow is to make sure that we are innovative, and not only that we are innovative but that the pace of innovation is fast, then we must break down all those barriers.

The other reason that we need to work in a group environment is because I have this fundamental belief that innovation is of itself not important but that the pace of innovation is crucial. It's not much good being innovative if you're second to the market. You have to be there first and if you are going to have this sequential way of doing things in terms of making decisions or in terms of getting a program in or a product in place, then that takes far too long. We have to have concurrent engineering of our programs, or our policies, or our products.

The area that we still struggle with is that it provides an opportunity for people in those groups to turn around and say, 'Well, it's no longer my individual responsibility any more, it's the group responsibility'. You tend to find people hiding a little bit behind the group. And that is something that we are really struggling to overcome. And there is certainly more work required from the organisation's point of view in quite clearly defining the dynamics of groups and the way we want them to work, but also in understanding and recognising what the drivers are for forming those groups. And how we recognise the individual's performance as well as the group's performance. How we can maximise people's commitment and ownership of their role within those groups. It's an interesting process that we are going through. It's a whole different way of operating that we are slowly working through. Some groups work much better than others—you need the right dynamics. You need the right mix of skills within the groups.

We have a training program that we put people through. We take individuals out of a very specialised area and ask them to make contributions in a broader group, and I think that takes some time. We still have some work to do to find the best way to motivate individual performance within the group. There is a thought that the best way for groups to work is to have this total consensus approach. The reality is that it doesn't work. It's inefficient, and it's time consuming. There is a subtle balance in the way those groups should work. Individuals within the group have specialist skills and can best deliver certain outcomes which are subject to review by the groups and sign-off by the group. So we try to find a way of best fostering that correct mix of individual responsibility and effective dynamics within the group.

■ The subordinate's log

the reflective practitioner

I have found that managing groups is both easier and harder than managing individuals. With individuals you can alter your style according to the person you have to manage, whereas you need to be more consistent with a group. However, managing a group also has the advantage of being able to use the group to manage itself. The difficulty is to be able to make the individuals in the group still feel like individuals and act like team members.

In the case of consultants, the hard part is to bring a bunch of strong individuals together to act as a cohesive group. Generally speaking I did not find managing groups terribly difficult because the members of the group in the consultancy situation tend to all want the same outcomes (they all want the project to be successful), and once you get over the initial storming phase of group development, outcomes are typically superior to individual work. The downside is that you have to be careful of time and resource costs, as groups can require more of these.

The CEO tended to treat the organisation as a number of groups. These included the senior people, the sales and marketing people, the consultants and office staff. Each group was treated slightly differently. There were instances when the total organisation needed to be treated as one large team as all members were important to the success of large projects and interdependent on each other. Typically, though, the various groups were managed significantly differently.

Focus on practice—Strategies for improving

1 Assist all members of the group to understand how they gain from particular goal-oriented activities. How will this benefit the organisation?

2 How do you need to individually reward individuals whose tasks are interdependent?

3 Develop strategies which will enable members of a work team to understand the linkages between their various roles.

Source: Jones et al. (2000).

Chapter summary

Work groups are increasingly important to the competitiveness of organisations. There are two major work-group types: formal and informal. Formal groups include command, or functional, groups and task groups. Informal groups include interest and friendship groups. Required aspects of formal groups lead to emergent behaviours, interactions and sentiments of informal groups.

One way to analyse groups is to view them as systems which use inputs to engage in processes or transformations and produce outcomes. Important group inputs are group composition, particularly member characteristics and reasons for group attraction; member roles, including task, maintenance and self-oriented; and group size.

Work-group processes have positive synergy. Important factors influencing group processes are norms, cohesiveness and development. Group norms come from the explicit statements of supervisors and co-workers, critical events in a group's history, primacy and carryover behaviours. Many factors lead to group cohesiveness. Cohesion, in turn, has major consequences for group communication, satisfaction, performance, hostility and aggression toward other groups, and willingness to innovate and change. New groups pass through five stages of development: forming, storming, norming, performing and adjourning. Size influences group interactions and encourages social loafing or free riders. Those leaning to individualism rather than collectivism are more likely to display social loafing. Important outcomes to consider in evaluating effectiveness are group performance, member need satisfaction and future work-group compatibility.

Some major mechanisms organisations use to tap the creativity and innovative capacity of groups include task forces, or ad hoc committees, and teams, particularly entrepreneurial and self-managing teams.

Questions for discussion and review

1 Outline the major work-group types. Identify several groups at your college or university. Classify them by work-group type.

2 Explain how informal groups develop. Choose an organisation with which you are familiar and identify two informal groups. Trace how the groups came about.

3 Explain the basic inputs groups require to operate. Analyse inputs of a work group you think runs effectively. What are member characteristics that help it operate successfully? What attracts various members to the group? What roles do members play? How does the number of members affect group interaction?

4 Explain the significance of norms and cohesiveness in group functioning. Think of a group to which you belong. What are four important norms in the group? How did they develop? Assess the level of group cohesiveness and its consequences.

5 Explain how groups develop. Trace the development of a group in which you have participated.

6 Describe how size influences group performance and interactions. Include an assessment of social loafing and possible effects associated with individualism and collectivism. To what extent have you seen these factors at work in groups?

7 Differentiate between task forces and teams. Explain how each can promote innovation. Identify examples of task forces and teams in the business section of your local paper, in the *Financial Review*, and/or magazines such as *Business Review Weekly* and *Asia Week*.

8 Explain why self-managing teams have been so successful. If you were a manager, why would you like or not like to have them in your organisation?

9 Explain the process of setting up a virtual team. What difficulties might emerge if any one step were overlooked?

Exercises for managing in the 21st century

Exercise 1
Skill building: Assessing group cohesiveness

Cohesiveness can be a favourable work-group characteristic. This exercise is designed to assist in assessing cohesiveness of a work group you are currently a member of. This could be a group preparing a paper for a class, a group developing a solution to a case or exercise, a group where you work, or any other group effort. If you are not involved in a particular work group, please refer to the most recent work group in which you participated.

		Disagree	Agree
1	Individual members of the group are respected by the others.	1 2 3 4 5 6 7 8 9 10	
2	The group goal is enthusiastically supported by group members.	1 2 3 4 5 6 7 8 9 10	
3	The group has quickly established norms to facilitate accomplishing our goal.	1 2 3 4 5 6 7 8 9 10	
4	Group members share similar work values.	1 2 3 4 5 6 7 8 9 10	
5	The group is able to bring out the best performance from each member.	1 2 3 4 5 6 7 8 9 10	
6	Group members' attitudes toward the ultimate goal are positive.	1 2 3 4 5 6 7 8 9 10	
7	Group members' commitment to the goal increases the longer we work together.	1 2 3 4 5 6 7 8 9 10	
8	Communications within our group improve steadily as we progress.	1 2 3 4 5 6 7 8 9 10	
9	A feeling of 'we' versus 'I' is evident in our group.	1 2 3 4 5 6 7 8 9 10	
10	The group pulls together, making the task easier.	1 2 3 4 5 6 7 8 9 10	
11	Everyone believes their contribution is important.	1 2 3 4 5 6 7 8 9 10	
12	The group seeks input from everyone prior to making decisions.	1 2 3 4 5 6 7 8 9 10	
13	The group interaction seems to bring out the best in each member.	1 2 3 4 5 6 7 8 9 10	
14	The size of the group helps promote a feeling of mutual support.	1 2 3 4 5 6 7 8 9 10	
15	If one member of the group needs help, other members are quick to respond.	1 2 3 4 5 6 7 8 9 10	

Your lecturer will tell you how to interpret your score.

Exercise 2
Management exercise: Shipwrecked

Wreck survivors' situation sheet

A private yacht, sailing through an archipelago located between the 10th and 20th parallels in the Pacific Ocean, is caught in a sudden storm and runs aground on a coral reef. The passengers and crew reach the sandy shores of one of the islands. Shortly before the impact, they tried a MAYDAY message on the radio with approximate co-ordinates; it was impossible to repeat the distress message or to receive a reply because of the rush of events. Unfortunately, the chances of the message getting through—in view of atmospheric conditions, quality of transmission, and distance—were poor.

The situation can be summarised as follows:

1 The island is small and uninhabited. There is plenty of tropical vegetation, and among the plants abound coconuts, mangoes and bananas. It rains in the afternoon most days, but the climate is mild and does not require heavy clothing. At low tide, fish and shellfish can be seen just offshore.
2 Nobody had time to pick up any supplies from the yacht. Passengers' and crew members' pockets contain some cigarettes, matches, two lighters and a pocket knife. Among them, they have three watches.
3 The lagoon between the beach and reef where the yacht ran aground is about 900 metres in diameter and has an area of deep water.
4 Only a few of the passengers and crew are good swimmers.
5 Most certainly, all equipment aboard the yacht (i.e. radio transmitter, radar, generators) was destroyed on impact.
6 The crew predicts the yacht will be dragged along the reef and will sink at high tide about eight hours later.

The total group has decided the wrecked yacht must be reached before it sinks in order to recover those items necessary for future survival. The best swimmers will go to analyse the situation on board the yacht and attempt to bring supplies back to the shore. The group needs to prepare a list of those items it considers most valuable for the group, selecting them in order of priority. Anticipating this, some crew members have compiled lists of items they think will be needed. Because time is valuable, it is decided the total group's list will include 15 of these items (the most retrievable in the time available), listed in order of priority. Each person may suggest one alternative item not on the original list, which they may place on the list of 15 if so desired.

Wreck survivors' individual task sheet

During this task, do not communicate with anyone. Your task is to rank, in order of priority, 15 items from the following lists. In addition, you can add one item of your choice which in all probability was left on board the yacht. Next to the number 1 write the name of the item you believe is most important. Continue until you reach number 15, the least important. You will have 15 minutes to complete this task.

These items are the choices of five members of the crew.

Chris	Pat	Dale	Kelly	Robin
axe	bed sheets	suntan lotion	rope	marine charts
hammer and nails	blankets	toilet articles	binoculars	pistol and ammunition
knives	cooking pots	mirror	water tanks	wooden planks
fishing tackle	canned food	condensed milk	large plastic sheet	tool box
transistor radio	beverages	chocolate bars	bottles of rum	flippers and harpoon
plastic buckets	first-aid kit	mosquito netting	life jackets	shark repellent

Item of your choice, if any:

Individual ranking

1. _____
2. _____
3. _____
4. _____
5. _____
6. _____
7. _____
8. _____
9. _____
10. _____
11. _____
12. _____
13. _____
14. _____
15. _____

Wreck survivors' group task sheet

The subgroup members now have to agree on a single list, which they write on newsprint—15 items in order of priority, including those items most likely to ensure survival. It is important to remember:

○ You must reach a consensus regarding the ranking given to each item.
○ 'Consensus' means each member of the subgroup agrees to the plan, at least to some degree. Coercion and methods of conflict avoidance such as averaging, voting and 'horse-trading' are not recommended.
○ The subgroup may organise as it wishes to obtain the best results.

The subgroup has 45 minutes in which to complete this task.

Group ranking

1. _____
2. _____
3. _____
4. _____
5. _____
6. _____
7. _____
8. _____
9. _____
10. _____
11. _____
12. _____
13. _____
14. _____
15. _____

Source: Adapted from Pfeiffer, J. W. (1994).

Team-development at Fisher and Paykel: The introduction of 'Everyday workplace teams'

on the rim— in New Zealand

The Fisher and Paykel Range and Dishwasher Division, based in Dunedin, New Zealand, is part of the Fisher and Paykel Whiteware and Health-Care manufacturing company. The Range and Dishwasher Division is responsible for the manufacture of all cookware products. The Division employs approximately 570 staff, with 400 employees in manufacturing roles and 170 support staff.

Following loss of market share in the wake of removal of export tariffs, the company was determined to succeed through a culture of change and innovation. This culture would be built on skilled and autonomous teams, focused on low cost/no cost improvement activity. The Division's responses to the company-wide focus on team working was to establish planning meetings between several key individuals in the Division, which were held over several months in 1994/1995, and to pilot teamwork sessions.

People working at Fisher and Paykel, a company that piloted various teamwork sessions to evolve successful group-work strategies.

Vision of 'Everyday workplace teams'

The outcome was a vision of a self-managing team culture with the concept of 'Everyday workplace teams' (EDWT) at its heart. While team working already existed to some extent with small work groups managed by supervisors, it needed to be strengthened and formalised. EDWT captured the belief that being a team member should be an integral part of employees' everyday work. The planning team identified that an Everyday workplace team would:

- encourage contributions from members
- have a unified vision
- understand and use quality tools
- have a positive focus
- be responsible for plans linked to goals
- have a plan to develop the team, the members and the process

Implementation process

A project team, initially called the *Understanding team* (later called the *Implementation team*) was set up, comprising the company accountant, a trainer, a production planner, the maintenance manager and an area leader who had already begun team-training sessions. Their project brief was to ensure that an understanding of EDWT was communicated throughout the division. This team would also identify the boundaries of particular teams, as some measure of restructuring was required, and would also be involved in the start-up of the teams.

Over the years several initiatives had been launched in the company with initial enthusiasm, but had fizzled out. It was feared that many would see EDWT as another management fad that would quickly fade. The challenge was to introduce radical and ongoing change which staff would accept but which would certainly threaten some long established 'comfort zones'. The aim was to end the mentality of 'leaving your brain at the door' which existed in some quarters in the division, and to develop new expectations of staff which went beyond their manufacturing and assembly roles. Such a change could be expected to meet with some opposition but also promised great opportunities for personal as well as organisational benefit.

The EDWT workbook

Realising the enormity of their task, the team adapted their brief to move further and faster into the implementation process itself. The outcome was the development of an EDWT workbook, which would operate as a standardised team training tool for start-up and for on-going reference. Production would stop for an hour while the team leader (with support initially from the training department) facilitated a team session using the EDWT workbook. This was a significant measure of the company's commitment to the EDWT concept. The highly inter-active workbook contained such modules as communication skills, team building, working together, and running meetings. The latter part of the workbook was more geared to teams becoming involved in activities to improve the running of their work area. The key aims of the workbook were:

- the development of functional teams
- the development of supporting team skills in individual team members
- linking the team to divisional goals
- prompting the team to direct energy to improvement activities in their work area.

All teams would use the workbook in order to develop a Division-wide common understanding of team working. It was expected that it would take approximately twelve months to work through the book. At the completion of the workbook, teams would give a presentation to senior management on their team development and improvement activities.

Cost savings

Team members with limited support from engineering are now able to drive projects, to monitor cycle times and to rebalance workflows as necessary. Downtime and wastage have fallen. Increased control over the work area has led to greater acceptance and implementation of change. Previously, an introduction of a new product line or radically different model would incur high implementation costs and long lead-times to markets. Recently, however, a product design change was accomplished on the Rangeline with no impact to the production schedule, and this is quickly becoming the norm across all assembly areas.

Skill development

Team members have developed skills in addition to the assembly work. Recognition of up-skilling in generic skills such as communication, data collection and analysis, and team skills has been captured (to some extent) by a competency-based pay scale for team members. Linking in the pay scale has been significant in achieving 'buy-in' from team members to this cultural change. However, it has not worked as well for those already at or near the top of the pay scale. How to reward both team performance and individual performance still needs to be further debated.

EDWT is part of the daily practice and language of the company. However, the division's experience suggests cautious use of language, as buzzwords invite reinterpretation, which although humorous can constitute barriers to change. EDWT is popularly known in the division as 'Everyday waste of time' which, in fact, belies the changes that have occurred and the enthusiasm for change in many team members who value the enhanced scope for personal development. There is also a large measure of passive acceptance. Outright resistance is still evident but not dominant.

Approximately 20 per cent of the teams have stalled in their efforts to complete the workbook, due in some cases to time commitment, in others to lack of management support. Some teams, particularly in salaried areas, feel that the workbook is neither necessary nor appropriate for them. Solutions might lie in customising the workbook for certain teams (e.g. engineering) and in providing additional facilitation support.

Team leaders

Perhaps the role that has been most affected by the change is that of the team leader. Previously the team leader (then called charge hand) was the technical expert or senior operator. The role now requires a high level of people-management skills in facilitating team sessions, coaching and developing team members, as well as in developing business plans, monitoring production and daily problem solving. There has been a difficult transition. Several former team leaders have stepped down from the role since the change and returned to the line. Recruitment of predominantly external candidates has filled these vacancies and newly created positions.

Some lessons from implementation

The question begs to be asked whether Fisher and Paykel would drive team development using the same process again. Hindsight has indicated that several factors could have been improved in the implementation process. Many team leaders expressed some concern that the initial development was not done in sufficient consultation with them, which is generally agreed within the Division to have been an important oversight. The excitement and challenge of implementing the vision perhaps obscured some of the more detailed planning required. In particular, resistance may have been minimised and 'buy-in' increased had team leaders had training in facilitation skills prior to running the sessions with their teams.

However, it is also interesting to consider what the outcome would have been with increased consultation. The up-skilling of both team leaders and team members has required strong shifts out of comfort zones and into new ways of thinking and working. It could be argued that had the team leaders been part of the development process, the change could have been more watered down, perhaps with team sessions being facilitated by trainers, or even derailed.

This leads to the final point to consider when moving to a cultural shift. However much the change process is driven, the momentum can quickly die when initiating any sort of change in the workplace. There was enormous effort involved in this initiative and there were many low points for its champions when resistance threatened to overwhelm it. Ensuring that the change has full management support and is visibly encouraged would have prevented some of the teams from stalling. Better contingency planning for barriers that could inhibit or stifle change could have been considered more thoroughly before moving into the implementation period.

In summary, the move towards a formal team structure at the Range and Dishwasher Division has provided a platform for growth and spawned up-skilling and improvement activities in teams. As the change becomes further embedded into the environment, it becomes more difficult to remember what the environment was before. Team sessions have become a weekly event in many parts of the division with teams working continually on low-cost/no-cost improvements. Measuring the success has become almost intangible. The focus now turns to where the organisation moves to next, and to constructing a measurement for how team activities are contributing to the bottom line. The division is in the process of reviewing the initiative to date and reflecting on what has been learned about implementation of significant cultural change.

Change begets change and the key challenge for the division now is to keep the momentum going and meet ever-increasing expectations from staff for involvement and for seeing that their input is indeed valued and enacted.

Source: Dr Mary Mallon, Tania Kearney, Fisher and Paykel.

Activities for discussion, analysis and further research

1 Fisher and Paykel encountered some difficulties in reconciling the exciting development of a new vision and culture with the detailed planning required for implementation. How would you ensure these two factors were given appropriate consideration?
2 Why did some people resist the introduction of team working, even though it enabled them to develop more generic skills and encouraged their contribution to change? How could this resistance be overcome?
3 Design a training program for those charge hands now expected to operate as team leaders.
4 When introducing team-working, what other aspects of organisational systems need to be reviewed and potentially changed?

● No pride without lions   going global

In July 1991, the creative excellence of Australian advertising was the hottest topic of conversation at the International Advertising Festival in Cannes. Australia's tally of 17 gold, silver and bronze Lions, the global advertising industry's equivalent of the Academy awards, placed it third behind the traditional big winners, the United States and Britain. It was a different story at Cannes this year. Australian advertising agencies won only five Lions for television and cinema advertising and Australia shared seventh place with Spain. The Netherlands and Argentina were amongst the countries ahead of them.

Although the result was not as bad as many in the industry had predicted, the failure to win more than one gold Lion this year did little to dispel the view that advertising in Australia is suffering a dearth of creativity. This perception is not new. Only a year after Australia's big success at Cannes, it fell back to sixth and has not been higher in any year since.

Some senior advertising executives say there are two main reasons for the perceived decline in creative standards: the correlation between advertising and general economic conditions; and the increasing globalisation of the industry.

Many in the industry say the most arresting and original work is usually done in the healthiest economic periods. In recessions, clients are reluctant to allow advertising that might risk their bottom lines and agencies are more than usually careful to avoid conflict with clients that could endanger accounts.

What is disturbing many agency executives is that, for two years, despite a booming economy and high consumer confidence, standards of creative advertising have remained mediocre. Neil Lawrence, the Australian jury member at the 1999 Cannes advertising festival, says: 'I've observed that a lot of the best work comes out in buoyant economies, with United States work, for example, very edgy and interesting at the moment'. Lawrence, who is chief executive and creative director of Sydney agency Whybin Lawrence TBWA, adds: 'In the best of times, clients relax and are prepared to take risks, but the trouble in Australia is that we seem to have developed a very risk-averse culture in general, which is evident in the marketing community'.

Lawrence also points to deregulation of the domestic advertising industry five years ago, which lifted restrictions that had prevented foreign advertising appearing on local TV. 'Now that we have a situation where advertising has become internationalised', he says, 'it is tough for this country to compete with the rest of the world'. He says deregulation has meant far fewer commercials being made in Australia, less money in the business as a whole and less experimentation. 'Many of the best (commercial) directors now work exclusively overseas', he says, 'where, of course, they are being paid a lot more'.

One of the few advertising agencies in Australia to have been a consistent winner at Cannes in the past decade is Clemenger Melbourne, which won the only gold Lion this year with a TV commercial for milk. Clemenger Melbourne has won 11 Lions in the past 10 years.

The agency's chairman, David Blackley, agrees with Lawrence that the economy and globalisation have conspired to depress local creative standards. He says: 'Creativity went flat because of the recession at the beginning of the 1990s. This caused clients to be less brave, while agencies were scared of losing business. The globalisation of the marketing industry has hit like an express train, and a lot of major advertising accounts with the creative work done in Australia have bled out. Australian agencies are fighting against their overseas counterparts and trying to satisfy clients who are able to pick from the best in the world. You have to produce the best work in the world's best practice ... if we produce a TV commercial that is not as good as a client can get from overseas, then we shouldn't be doing it'.

One of the more vexed questions over creativity relates to effectiveness. While the creative community places much store in 'great' creative advertising, the client's need is to sell its product. Is one possible without the other?

Lawrence says: 'the problem in this debate is that there is selling on one hand and creativity on the other, but you can't separate the two. Some creative ads sell well, some don't, and there are some highly original ads that fail'.

At the Australian Magazine Advertisement of the Year Awards in July, Ted Horton, a prominent freelance creative director in the local industry, commented on the National Australia Bank's 'Tailoring banking to your needs' campaign: 'I know of few people, if any, who liked watching those ads featuring a couple and their bank manager in front of a computer figuring a way to cut 14 years and $100 000 from their mortgage, but I also know of few campaigns that have been more successful'.

Other creative directors say that to be noticed, it is essential to produce an outstanding idea to 'cut through' the clutter of advertisements. In 1992–93, the American agency Leo Burnett, studying the effectiveness of advertising creativity, examined the world's 200 most-awarded commercials. It concluded that acclaimed commercials were 2.5 times more effective in raising consumer awareness and selling product than advertisements that had received no recognition.

Concern that creative standards have fallen sharply is reflected in the formation of an industry lobby group with the objective of reversing the decline. The group, Creative Voice, was started a year ago by J Walter Thompson (Melbourne) creative director Darren Woolley; Euro RSCG chairman Tom Moult; Saatchi senior writer Jane Caro; and Les Gock, the chairman and creative director of commercial music production house Song Zu. With a notional membership of 2000 copywriters and art directors, Creative Voice is seeking to address the issue of creativity mainly through education.

The group believes much of the slide has been due to a lack of understanding among the many Australian companies of the value of creative advertising and the failure of agencies to impress this upon clients.

Gock says: 'Throughout this very tough decade, there's been a lot of very short-term thinking in business, and many clients have viewed advertising as a cost, not as an investment. This has led to what are perceived to be lower standards in creative output. You can certainly apportion some of the blame to a lot of clients not understanding what the creative job is. Some clients will be happy to have the brief regurgitated and call that the creative answer. A lot of clients' exposure to the creative process is very limited. It is not necessarily their fault but we should bring it to their attention that it is worthwhile'.

Gock says agencies must also accept responsibility: 'Many agencies have lacked foresight and, hence, have not been at all effective or even particularly interested until recently in doing anything other than winning a piece of business at all costs. You can't blame people in a tough business environment for wanting to do that. But creatives can no longer be packed in cotton wool away form the harsh realities of their clients' business. They must show they have a deep understanding of it, not just glossing over it. Then a client will have the confidence to listen and say, 'Now how would you solve this problem since you understand my business?' There are a lot of lazy creative people out there who are not really interested, won't put in the extra effort, and come up with a half-baked idea. That is what makes clients lose confidence and be mistrustful'.

Through education forums, Creative Voice hopes to convince business of the value of excellence in creative advertising because it is always in the client's best interests. Gock says: 'Clients need to want to seek and demand the best creative, and reject ordinary creative for their own business's sake, not for any artistic reasons but because they'll be a lot less competitive unless they refuse ordinary creative and constantly demand the best'.

Source: Lloyd, S. (1999b).

Questions

1 Consider the concepts you have studied in this section of the text. Identify applications of these concepts in the case materials you have just read.
2 What forms of motivation are there for creativity practitioners, for their clients?
3 How should these motivations be communicated, according to Gock?
4 Where should the leadership for those activities be coming from?
5 Do some research and find out who won the Lions in the year 2000. What was Australia's share of the awards? Do you think that the organisation Creative Voice has had any impact?

PART 5

CONTROLLING

As we learned previously, the planning function provides direction, the organising function arranges resources, and the leading function adds the action ingredient. Still, how does a manager ensure an organisation performs to standard and achieves its intended goals? The controlling function adds the vital regulatory element, allowing managers to use a variety of methods to monitor performance and take corrective action when needed. Controls must be used flexibly, though, because too much control can stifle innovation.

In exploring the controlling function, **Chapter 16** takes a close look at the overall control process, including steps in the process, the major types of controls, the various managerial approaches to implementing available controls, and problems associated with attempting to control innovation.

In **Chapter 17**, we examine the ways managers attempt to control organisations by managing conflict caused by change. Conflict needs to be both controlled and managed. This is a subtle difference which many managers do not understand adequately. This chapter explores the ways organisation members respond to particular situations and how these responses impact on the organisation's success.

Controlling the Organisation

Chapter (16)

CHAPTER OUTLINE

Control as a management function
Significance of the control process
Role of controls
Levels of control

The control process
Steps in the control process
Deciding what to control: A closer look

Types of controls
Major control types by timing
Multiple controls
Cybernetic and non-cybernetic control

Managerial approaches to implementing controls
Bureaucratic control
Clan control
Market control
Promoting innovation: Controlling while nurturing innovation

Assessing control systems
Potential dysfunctional aspects of control systems
Overcontrol versus undercontrol
Characteristics of an effective control system

LEARNING OBJECTIVES

After studying this chapter, you should be able to:

- Explain major roles of controls in organisations.
- Describe how control responsibilities change with management levels.
- Outline the general process applicable to most control situations.
- Delineate principal conditions managers need to consider in deciding what to control.
- Explain major control types based on timing and use of multiple controls.
- Differentiate between cybernetic and non-cybernetic control.
- Describe the basic managerial approaches to implementing controls.
- Outline the potential dysfunctional aspects of control systems and explain the implications of overcontrol and undercontrol.
- Delineate the major characteristics of effective control systems.

Striving for excellence

The organisation has very strict control measures. These apply to all staff, as everyone has performance criteria which demand that they be measured against their subset of the business plan.

As part of their personal plan, each staff member has key criteria which are a part of the three-year plan. Each of these key criteria is assessed, the measures are rated, weighted and monitored.

For example, the shop floor has extremely intense measures. These follow the AIMS, which stands for Autoliv Integrated Manufacturing System. So the parts per million defects are measured and the constant aim is for zero defective parts per million. Another aspect which is measured is cycle time. All of these measures are reported to an AIMS meeting which is attended by the managing director of HR, the manufacturing and production managers and the team leader of each cell. These weekly meetings not only discuss the results and the strategies which were utilised to achieve those, but involve diagnostics as well where corrective strategies are discussed and developed as appropriate.

As we saw before, the planning function provides direction, the organising function arranges resources, and the leading function adds the action ingredient. But how does a manager ensure an organisation meets standards and actually reaches goals set? The controlling function is the regulatory element, allowing managers to use a variety of ways to monitor performance and take corrective action when needed. Controls must be flexible, because too much control smothers innovation.

We devote the next chapter and supplements to various aspects of controlling, the fourth major management function. In this chapter, we consider control's significance as a management process. We examine the control process itself and discuss how managers decide what to control. We also review major control types and when they are appropriate. We then describe different approaches managers can take to implement controls, including how to control without hampering innovation. Finally, we analyse how managers can assess the control systems they use.

During the control process, managers use systems to increase the probability of meeting organisational goals. Supplement 1 to Chapter 16 focuses on four of these: quality, financial, budgetary and inventory.

Another major control system is operations management, which is overseeing processes in producing a product or service. As Supplement 2 to Chapter 16 points out, a key element of operations management is productivity. Managers must develop operations strategies, develop operating systems, utilise facilities, and promote innovative technology with productivity in mind.

Finally, as Supplement 3 to Chapter 16 shows, information systems are important control methods. Computer-based systems give managers information to help make decisions needed in adjusting performance to meet goals. Information systems do not simply help improve organisational operating efficiency. They can be used innovatively to give an organisation a competitive edge.

CONTROL AS A MANAGEMENT FUNCTION

controlling

Process of regulating organisational activities so actual performance conforms to expected organisational standards and goals

All managers face issues related to the controlling function. **Controlling** is regulation of activities so performance conforms to organisational goals and standards (Newman 1975; Brand & Scanlan 1995; Rose 1995). As this suggests, controlling means that managers develop standards, compare performance against them, and ensure corrective actions are taken as needed. Since organisational activity depends on human behaviour, controlling ensures employees behave in ways to reach organisational goals. So controls highlight needed behaviours and discourage unwanted ones (Merchant 1985; Flamholtz 1996). For instance, during their two-year training, management trainees working to become McDonald's franchisees work their way through a thick guide laying out various aspects of what to do and what not to do in running a McDonald's outlet (March 1989; *McDonald's Corporation* 1995). To be effective, though, they need to do three things: have sufficient flexibility to cope with the unexpected; permit accurate assessments of organisational events; and provide the information as soon as possible (Jones et al. 2000).

Significance of the control process

As is expected, the controlling function is related to the other three major management functions: planning, organising and leading. It builds on the planning function by allowing monitoring and adjusting performance so plans can be reached. Controlling also supports the organising and leading functions by ensuring resources are used for organisational objectives (see Fig. 16.1). For example, control feedback might show a need to reorganise, increase training, clarify communication, increase leadership influence, or other activities associated with organising and leading functions.

During the control process, managers set up control systems. A **control system** is a set of mechanisms to increase the likelihood of achieving organisational standards and goals (Flamholtz 1979). Control systems regulate any area seen as important. They may relate to quantity produced, resources expended, profit margins, product or service quality, client satisfaction, delivery timeliness, or specific activities producing a product or service. For example, McDonald's has a seven-step procedure workers follow when cooking and bagging french fries to ensure quality. This procedure is one operation that corporate evaluation teams check during unannounced outlet inspections (Deveny 1986).

control system

Set of mechanisms designed to increase probability of meeting organisational standards and goals

Fig. 16.1 Relationship of controls to the other functions of management

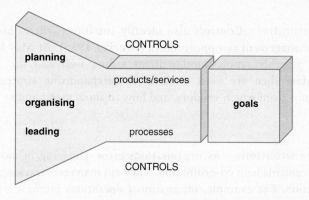

Role of controls

In evaluating the role of controls, consider what can happen with inadequate controls. Daiwa Bank, Japan's tenth-largest bank, was forced to close in the United States when it was revealed that a bond trader in Daiwa's New York office amassed a staggering $1.1 billion in losses and hid them over an 11-year period. In one of several letters to Daiwa's management, Toshihide Iguchi, the trader, told how the New York office did not detect a $100 million discrepancy. Iguchi noted the incident was 'indicative of how dysfunctional [controls] were at Daiwa' (Shirouzu 1995, p. A16).

Controls can help managers avoid these problems. Specifically, controls are important to assist managers with five challenges: coping with uncertainty, detecting irregularities, identifying opportunities, handling complex situations and decentralising authority.

Coping with uncertainty   Uncertainty arises because organisational goals are set for future events on the basis of the best knowledge available at the time, but things may not go to plan. Many environmental factors produce changes in customer demand, technology, and raw material availability. In control system development, managers watch specific activities, reacting quickly to significant environmental changes. For example, by controlling all phases of manufacturing, Italy-based Luxottica Group S.p.A. produced high-quality spectacle frames cheaply. CEO Leonardo Del Vecchio bought out many frame distributors. Thus Luxottica slowly controlled both manufacturing and distribution of its products. Recently, Luxottica started to gain control over retailing its frames by purchasing the owner of LensCrafters spectacle chain (Kindel 1995).

Detecting irregularities   Controls help detect irregularities such as poor quality, cost overruns or staff turnover. Early detection saves time and money by stopping minor problems becoming major ones. Finding problems early helps avoid problems that are difficult to fix, such as missing deadlines or selling faulty products. For example, Daiwa Bank might have avoided international embarrassment and loss of business if it had better operational control. Among other things, Daiwa did not follow the normal financial practice of cross-checking daily trades against monthly summaries and balance statements (Shirouzu 1995).

Identifying opportunities   Controls also identify situations where things go better than expected, alerting management to opportunities (Drucker 1985). At May Department Stores, managers prepare monthly reports noting items selling well and the amount of money generated. These data then are used to develop merchandising strategies for all stores, including what to buy, from which vendors, and how to show merchandise (Dunkin & O'Neil 1987).

Handling complex situations   As organisations grow, engaging in more complex operations and projects, controls help co-ordination. They aid managers tracking major elements to ensure synchronisation. For example, international operations increase complexity and also increase need for controls as shown by Daiwa's situation.

Decentralising authority Another major control role is giving managers more latitude. With controls, managers can move decision making lower in the organisation but still monitor progress. As you might expect, though, control issues vary by managerial level.

Levels of control

Just as planning responsibilities differ by managerial level (see Chapter 6), there are parallel control responsibilities at each level (see Fig. 16.2). Strategic, tactical and operational levels of control increase chances of realising plans at different levels (Lorange, Morton & Ghoshal 1986; Schreyoff & Steimann 1987; Simons 1995).

Strategic control means monitoring critical environmental factors to ensure strategic plans are implemented as set, assessing organisational strategic action effects, and adjusting plans when needed. Strategic-level control is mainly for top-level managers, who take an organisation-wide perspective. Inherent in strategic control is the need for these managers to be sure core competencies are developed and maintained to ensure the organisation's ability to pursue its strategic goals (Lorange et al. 1986; Schreyoff & Steimann 1987; Simons 1995). For strategic control, managers concentrate on long time frames, such as quarterly, semi-annual and annual reporting cycles, and longer. Although if environments are unstable and/or competition keen, shorter cycles may be used.

strategic control

Control type involving monitoring critical environmental factors which could affect viability of strategic plans, assessing effects of organisational strategic actions, and ensuring strategic plans are implemented as intended

Fig. 16.2 Levels of control (adapted in part from Lorange, Morton & Ghoshal 1986, p. 12)

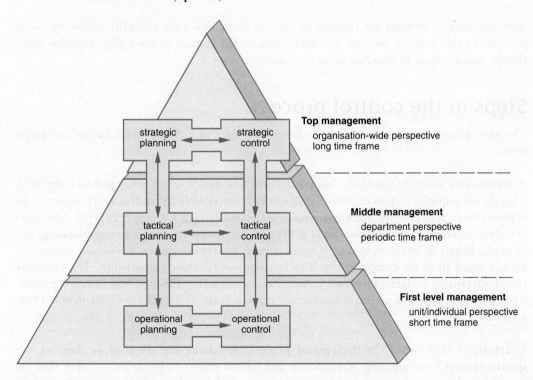

Top management
organisation-wide perspective
long time frame

strategic planning ↔ strategic control

Middle management
department perspective
periodic time frame

tactical planning ↔ tactical control

First level management
unit/individual perspective
short time frame

operational planning ↔ operational control

Though mainly concerned with strategic issues, top-level managers may use tactical and operational control to ensure tactical and operational plans are implemented as intended at middle- and lower-management levels.

tactical control

Control type focusing on assessing implementation of tactical plans at department levels, monitoring associated periodic results, and taking corrective action as needed

operational control

Control type involving overseeing implementation of operating plans, monitoring day-to-day results, and taking corrective action as required

Tactical control focuses on assessing department-level tactical plans, monitoring results and making corrections as needed. Tactical-level control involves middle managers who focus on department-level objectives, programs and budgets. They concentrate on periodic or middle-term time-frames and use weekly and monthly reporting cycles. They test environmental reaction to their departments' tactical initiatives (Marcom 1991). Though mainly concerned with tactical control, middle managers engage in strategic control by providing information to upper-level managers on strategic issues. They are involved in operational control by checking critical aspects of operating plan implementation.

Operational control means overseeing operating plan implementation, monitoring day-to-day results, and making corrections when needed. Operating-level control is largely lower-level managers' responsibility, and they are concerned with schedules, budgets, rules and specific outputs associated with individuals. Operating control gives feedback on what is being done very soon to achieve both short- and long-term organisation goals.

To be effective, control levels—strategic, tactical, and operational—must be clearly inter-related, as different level planning systems are integrated.

THE CONTROL PROCESS

Although control systems are tailored to specific situations, they generally follow the same process. In this section, we first consider steps in the control process then examine more closely issues related to deciding what to control.

Steps in the control process

The basic process used in controlling is shown in Figure 16.3. The process has several major steps.

1 Determine areas to control   Managers must first decide which areas will be controlled. Choices are required as it is expensive and virtually impossible to control every aspect of an organisation's activities. In addition, employees resent having too much control. Managers usually base controls on organisational goals and objectives developed during planning. For example, Briggs & Stratton, maker of small engines for lawn mowers, has closely monitored market share since the company began to face serious Japanese competition. The company raised advertising budgets, increased research and engineering funding, and lowered production costs to regain and maintain the former market share of over 50 per cent (Cook 1986; Croghan 1996).

2 Establish standards   In the control process, standards are essential as they set out specific criteria for evaluating performance and related employee behaviours. Often they are incorporated into goals set in the planning process, so they only need reiteration. Sometimes

Fig. 16.3 Steps in the control process

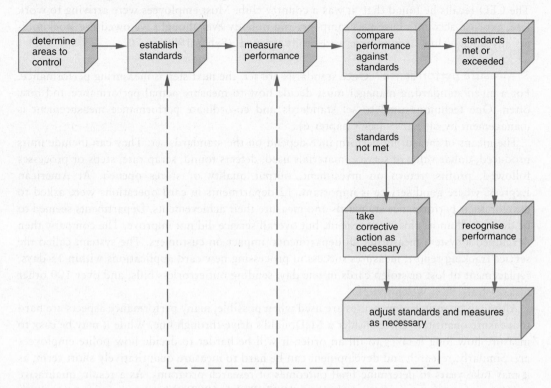

they must be developed during the control process. When one company began its service-improvement program, it found that salespeople took an average of 10 minutes approaching a customer. To improve things, the company set up training programs, incentives for sales-people, and a computerised scheduling program assigning salespeople to areas where they were most needed. As a result, they established a standard of two minutes to approach customers. Each salesperson also has daily sales goals set for them (Hamilton 1987; Calloway 1990; Richman 1993).

Generally, standards serve three major purposes for employee behaviour (Merchant 1985). For one, standards mean employees can understand what is expected and how their work will be evaluated. This helps them be effective. For another, standards are a basis for finding job problems related to members' personal limits. These can stem from lack of ability, training or experience, or any other job-related deficiency preventing proper performance. Timely identification means action can be taken before difficulties become serious or unresolvable. Finally, standards help reduce negative effects of goal incongruence. **Goal incongruence** occurs with major differences between organisation member goals and the goals of the organisation. This occurs for many reasons, such as lack of support for organisational objectives (e.g. an employee views a job as temporary and just does the minimum work), resulting in behaviours incompatible with organisational goal attainment.

A common example of goal incongruence is employee theft, including wasting organisa-tional resources as well as taking equipment, materials and money (Hollinger & Clark 1983). Wasted resources almost led to the death of one small company. A new CEO, who saved them

goal incongruence

Condition where there are major incompatibilities between goals of an organisation member and those of the organisation

from bankruptcy, set standards in areas such as working hours and expense account usage. The CEO recalls he found that 'it was a country club. Most employees were arriving to work late, expense account abuse was rampant, and nobody ever thought we owed the stockholders anything. Values around here were really warped' (Behar 1988, p. 70).

3 Measure performance　Once standards are set, the next step is measuring performance. For a given standard, a manager must decide how to measure actual performance and how often. One technique used to set standards and co-ordinate performance measurement is management by objectives (see Chapter 6).

The means of measuring performance depend on the standards set. They can include units produced, dollar value of service, materials used, defects found, scrap rate, steps or processes followed, profits, return on investment, output quality or stores opened. At American Express, where good service is important, 12 departments in card operations were asked to develop their performance standards and measure their achievements. Departments seemed to be doing well under this arrangement, but overall service did not improve. The company then developed a system measuring all departments' impact on customers. The system, called the service tracking report, measures success in processing new card applications within 15 days, replacement of lost or stolen cards in one day, sending out errorless bills, and over 100 other tasks (Uttal 1987; Welch 1992).

Although quantitative measures are used when possible, many performance aspects are hard to measure quantitatively. Consider a McDonald's drive-through line. While it may be easy to measure how long it takes to fill an order, it will be harder to decide how polite employees are. Similarly, research and development can be hard to measure quantitatively short-term, as it may take years to determine final outcomes of research programs. As a result, qualitative judgments by peers are often used (Uttal 1987; Welch 1992). Most organisations combine both quantitative and qualitative performance measures for control.

Once measurement means are selected, managers must decide how often to measure performance. In some cases, they must have control data on a daily, hourly or more frequent base (as for supervisors of air traffic controllers). In other cases, weekly, monthly, quarterly, semi-annual or even annual data may suffice. The period of measurement depends on how important a goal is, how quickly the situation can change, and how difficult and expensive it is to fix a problem if one occurred. Nuclear power plants, for example, have elaborate control systems constantly providing data on operational aspects. Extensive controls are needed given the consequences of a power plant accident.

4 Compare performance against standards　This step is comparing performance measured in step 3 against standards set in step 2. Managers often base comparisons on information in reports summarising planned versus actual results. Such reports may be oral, written or computer generated. Through computer networks, managers can get up-to-the-minute status reports on many quantitative performance measures.

Computer systems are suited to **management by exception**, a control principle suggesting managers should be told of events only if control data show a major deviation from standards (Newman 1975). Use of this principle, with or without computers, helps managers save time by bringing to their attention only cases needing action. While this can be used effectively, managers must be careful not to become so focused on problems they ignore subordinates' positive accomplishments.

management by exception

Control principle suggesting managers should be informed of a situation only if control data show a significant deviation from standards

Managers often compare performance and standards by walking around work areas, observing conditions, a practice called management by wandering around. For example, executives of a discount store chain are well known for habitual visits to stores, to check displays, talk with employees and meet customers (Saporito 1992). Other organisations have set up 360-degree feedback systems, which give an individual performance ratings from many sources, such as superiors, peers and customers (see Chapter 10).

5a Recognise positive performance   When performance meets or exceeds set standards, managers must recognise this. Recognition given can vary from a spoken 'well done' for a routine achievement to more substantial rewards, such as bonuses, training opportunities or pay raises, for major achievements or consistently good work. This is congruent with motivation theories, including expectancy theory and reinforcement theory, which emphasise rewarding good performance to sustain it and encourage more improvement (see Chapter 12) (Hamilton 1987; Galloway 1990).

5b Take corrective action as necessary   When standards are not met, managers must assess why and take corrective action. While doing this, they check standards and other performance measures to see if they are realistic. Managers may conclude standards are inappropriate—due to changed conditions—and corrective action to meet standards is undesirable. More often, though, corrective actions are needed.

6 Adjust standards and measures as necessary   Control is dynamic. So managers must check standards to ensure their relevance and for associated performance measures. For one, these may be a problem being set inappropriately to begin with or due to changed circumstances. For another, bettering a standard may mean unforeseen opportunities, potential to raise standards, and/or a need for major adjustments to organisational plans. Finally, even if standards are met, changing conditions, such as improvements in employee skill levels, may mean it is possible to raise standards in future. Conversely, a manager may see that achieving a standard takes too many resources and decide to lower the standard. Managers use the control process to track activities, but must review the process to ensure it meets current needs.

Deciding what to control: A closer look

Well-developed objectives, strategic plans and supporting goals give focus to what is organisationally important. They then suggest control areas. While managers collect data on how much desired ends are achieved, they may have to control elements leading to those ends.

One approach to help managers decide what to control is the **resource dependence** viewpoint (Green & Welsh 1988). This approach says managers must consider controls where they depend on others for resources needed to reach organisational goals. In this context resources can be parts, information, service, funding or any other resource a manager might need to reach objectives. However, a dependency does not mean the area must be controlled. Four conditions must be met before a final determination. Areas meeting all four conditions are **strategic control points**, performance areas chosen for control as they are important in meeting organisational goals. Conditions and a related decision tree are shown in Figure 16.4.

resource dependence

Approach to controls which argues managers need to consider controls mainly in areas in which they depend on others for resources necessary to reach organisational goals

strategic control points

Performance areas chosen for control because they are particularly important in meeting organisational goals

Fig. 16.4 Resource-dependence decision tree (adapted from Green & Welsh 1988, pp. 287–301)

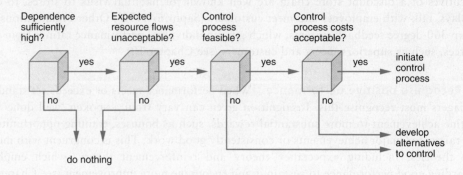

Four conditions for control   The first two conditions refer to whether controls are needed or not. The second two assess whether controls are feasible and practical.

The first condition is relatively *high dependence* on the resource. The more important dependence is and less it can be sourced elsewhere, the higher dependence is. If running a McDonald's outlet, you would find yourself highly dependent on resources such as food, food containers, water, napkins and working equipment. These are crucial resources. On the other hand, if a resource is unimportant or easily substituted (e.g. replacement for a trampled shrub), then there is no need for elaborate controls.

The second control condition is a strong chance *expected resource flow will be unacceptable*. In other words, a manager anticipates problems with the resource or is unsure. Anticipated problems can relate to any aspect, but are usually tied to resource quantity, some characteristics (e.g. specifications and quality) and timeliness. The more a manager feels a resource will cause problems, the greater control needed. For example, as a McDonald's outlet manager, it might be hard to stockpile food (lettuce, hamburger buns and milk) which can spoil. Yet changing customer patterns affect usage, making food inventory control important. On the other hand, though water is an important resource, water supplies are reliable, so a formal control system is not needed.

The third condition influencing whether to institute controls is *control-process feasibility*. Sometimes a basic control process—setting performance standards, measuring performance, comparing performance to standards, feeding back information on discrepancies and taking corrective action—is not feasible. Typically, this is an issue when it is difficult to specify performance standards or when it is difficult to measure performance or to do so in a timely way. For example, McDonald's cannot establish fixed standards on overseas price competition. In Japan, McDonald's ran a six-week sale, and cut regular hamburger prices from $1.75 (about 224 yen) to $0.83. The promotion was so successful the chain ran out of buns. McDonald's in Japan suspended the sale in half of its outlets until more buns could be produced. Meanwhile, they offered medium french fries for $0.83 not the usual $2.00. In this case, price and promotion issues were controlled locally because it is not feasible for McDonald's to assess these issues from headquarters (*New York Times* 1992).

Finally, an important consideration influencing whether to institute a control process is *cost acceptability*. Managers must weigh the costs of control against the benefits. Sometimes, a control system can cost more than the organisation gains. Again, McDonald's is a good illustration. The company's headquarters could have more control over outlets by setting up a videoconferencing network, including a two-way video-audio connection to every store (see Chapter 14). At this point the cost would be too high given possible gains.

Alternatives to control   What happens if the first two conditions (questions on the left in Fig. 16.4) show controls are needed, but the process is not feasible or too costly? Then managers must develop alternatives.

One way is to change dependence relationships so control is not needed. For example, a manager might have several suppliers so controls are less important. Because of few local suppliers in Saudi Arabia, for example, the Saudi Big Mac has Mexico sesame seeds and onions, buns from Saudi wheat, Spanish beef patties and lettuce, American pickles and special sauce, and New Zealand cheese (*McDonald's Corporation* 1994). Alternatively, managers can work with a source of dependence to make it more reliable, reducing the need for controls. This happened when McDonald's experts helped Thai farmers learn to grow Idaho russet potatoes, the key in McDonald's french fries (Deveny 1986).

Another approach is to change the nature of the dependence to one that is more feasible and/or cost-effective to control. For instance, redesigning complex jobs to involve narrower, simpler tasks reduces dependence on experienced workers. Although job simplification has disadvantages (see Chapter 8), it may make a situation easier to control when labour is tight.

Still another approach is to eliminate dependence. This can happen by vertical integration, where the organisation produces inputs previously coming from suppliers or replaces a customer role by disposing of its own outputs (see Chapter 7). McDonald's used this approach after problems with supplies of hamburger buns in Britain, finally, with two partners, by building its own plant (Deveny 1986). Alternatively, goals and objectives can be changed to no longer be dependent on a source. Changing goals is drastic and unlikely until other alternatives are exhausted. Still, it may be best in some cases.

● Getting rid of less profitable customers

case in point

Qantas and Ansett Australia both run successful but costly customer-loyalty programs. One of the biggest issues for the airlines is maintaining service to their loyalty-scheme members, most of whom do not actually fly frequently. Both programs grade customers according to how often they fly, and the higher the grade, the greater the benefits. However, customers are no longer entitled to remain on a particular grade forever.

In August 1999, Ansett introduced a system of tier credits, so that customers who fail to earn enough credit to remain in one of the 'sapphire', 'platinum' or 'diamond' tiers are downgraded. Qantas has a similar tier system for its frequent flyer program, which has 2.3 million members. The airline spends $12 million every year administering the program. Last year, it took a big step in its customer management regime: the airline introduced a $20 account service fee, charged every two years, in addition to the $75 fee to join the program. For blue, silver and gold level members the fee is waived. Qantas will not release precise figures but a spokeswoman for the frequent flyer program says that more than half the members have to pay the fee to stay in the program. The fee was introduced to cover the cost of maintaining the records of members and updating them. The cost for the top tiers of the frequent flyers has been absorbed because the economies of scale allowed that to happen. Qantas is not revealing how many customers have fallen out of the scheme.

Loyalty programs appear to have created a rod for the airlines' backs, in that the task of shedding unprofitable customers is highly sensitive. If the program is made financially unacceptable to stay in, then you will get customers who drop out. The difficulty for the airlines was how to achieve this without jeopardising the brand's image.

Source: Adapted from Lloyd, S. (2000).

Activities for discussion, analysis and further research

1 Organisations have to control such things as costs. Discuss how the above processes are examples of Qantas attempting to control its costs.
2 Other organisations who cull the less lucrative customers are banks, insurance companies and accounting firms. Do a literature search to identify how this happens.

TYPES OF CONTROLS

In addition to deciding which areas to control, managers must consider which control types to use. In this section, we discuss major control types based on timing, consider multiple control use, and contrast cybernetic and non-cybernetic control types.

Major control types by timing

Using a systems view, one can see an organisation's productive cycle as including inputs, transformation processes, and outputs occurring at different times (see Chapter 2). Thus, controls can be classified on the basis of timing, or stage in the productive cycle, depending on whether the focus is on inputs, transformation processes or outputs (see Fig. 16.5). Managers have options about the transformation cycle stage at which they will institute controls. Three types of controls based on timing are feedforward, concurrent and feedback.

feedforward control

Regulation of inputs to ensure they meet standards necessary for the transformation process

Feedforward control Feedforward control focuses on input regulation to ensure inputs meet standards necessary for the transformation process (see Fig. 16.5). Inputs subject to feedforward control include materials, people, finances, time and other organisational resources. The emphasis of feedforward control is on prevention of later difficulties in the productive process. Feedforward control is also called precontrol, preliminary, preventative or steering control.

Though feedforward controls often contribute significantly to organisational effectiveness, they may not cover every possible alternative (Lippert & Lupo 1988; *Detroit News* 1995). Other control types may be needed.

concurrent control

Regulation of ongoing activities which are part of the transformation process to ensure they conform to organisational standards

Concurrent control Concurrent control involves regulation of ongoing activities as part of the transformation process to ensure they conform to organisational standards. The emphasis is on identification of difficulties in the productive process that could mean faulty output (see

Fig. 16.5 Major control types by timing

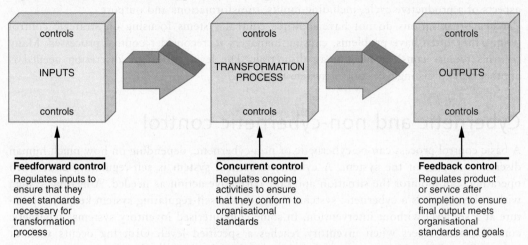

Feedforward control	**Concurrent control**	**Feedback control**
Regulates inputs to ensure that they meet standards necessary for transformation process	Regulates ongoing activities to ensure that they conform to organisational standards	Regulates product or service after completion to ensure final output meets organisational standards and goals

Fig. 16.5). Concurrent control or screening or yes-no control often has checkpoints where decisions are made about continuing progress, taking corrective action, or stopping work altogether. Since concurrent control means regulating current tasks, it requires clearly specified standards on how various activities are to be conducted (Ouchi & Maguire 1975).

Feedback control   Feedback control is regulation exercised after a product or service has been finished to ensure the final output reaches organisational standards and goals (see Fig. 16.5). Feedback control, or post-action control or output control, has important functions.

For one, it is often used when feedforward and concurrent controls are not feasible or too costly. For example, a sales manager will find it difficult to use concurrent control to regulate daily activities of salespeople visiting customers. Instead, the sales manager will use feedforward control by carefully selecting new people and then use feedback control comparing sales quotas (standards) with actual sales.

Feedback control is often used when the exact processes involved in producing a product or service (e.g. performing complex surgery) are hard to specify in advance. This control type can serve as a final check for deviations undetected before. Recently, many companies have worked to improve quality so feedback control is not needed or there are few deviations to find and therefore little scrap or rework to be done (see Chapter 17).

Feedback control also provides information to help planning. This includes numbers of units made or sold, cost of various production parts, quality measures, return on investment, or clients served. The data helps revise existing plans and formulate new ones. Finally, feedback control gives output information useful in rewarding employee performance.

Multiple controls

Organisations typically use **multiple control systems**, combining feedforward, concurrent and feedback control processes and using several strategic control points. As mentioned, strategic control points are performance areas chosen for control as they are important in meeting

feedback control

Regulation exercised after a product or service has been completed to ensure the final output meets organisational standards and goals

multiple control systems

Systems using two or more of the feedforward, concurrent and feedback control processes and involving several strategic control points

organisational goals. Multiple control systems develop due to needing to control various aspects of a productive cycle, including inputs, transformations and outputs.

When organisations do not have multiple control systems focusing on strategic control points, they often have problems, causing managers to reconsider control processes. Many controls require considerable human discretion. The level of human discretion needed is another way to distinguish control system types.

Cybernetic and non-cybernetic control

A basic control process can be cybernetic or non-cybernetic, depending on how much human discretion is part of the system. A **cybernetic control system** is self-regulating and, when operating, can monitor the situation and take corrective action as needed. A heating system with a thermostat is a cybernetic system. Once set, the self-regulating system keeps temperature at a set level without intervention. In some computerised inventory systems, cybernetic control places orders when inventory reaches a specified level. Ordering occurs without human discretion, such as managerial approval before the order is placed.

Although growing computer use increases options for cybernetic control, most organisational systems are non-cybernetic. A **non-cybernetic control system** relies on human discretion as a part of its process. By their nature, areas needing to be controlled typically go wrong in ways that are hard to predict. They are also complex enough to need human discretion in deciding the correction needed. Strictly speaking, even systems needing little human discretion, such as a computerised inventory system with automatic ordering capacity, produce reports for humans. They typically have built-in monitoring systems to alert an organisation member if things do not go as intended. Still, computers allow more controls closer to the cybernetic continuum end.

cybernetic control system

Self-regulating control system which, once operating, can automatically monitor the situation and take corrective action when necessary

non-cybernetic control system

Control system relying on human discretion as a basic part of its process

Benchmarking as a control mechanism

gaining the edge

A few years ago, a pharmaceutical company benchmarked its delivery methods against a competitor's.

The rival was combining product shipments from different divisions, enabling it to negotiate bigger, thus cheaper, shipping contracts. The company decided it would do the same.

It never happened: its logistics staff insisted they already had the lowest prices; then the data-processing people insisted they were too busy to check the historical transport costs, which might have proved otherwise; and the sales people insisted that only carriers dedicated to their products could guarantee on-time deliveries. 'It's three years later and the company still hasn't changed', says Thomas Slaight, a vice-president of A. T. Kearney, the consulting firm that helped with the initial benchmarking.

Ever wonder why companies are so amenable to letting others study and emulate those things they do best? Why give away the trade secrets? Probably because benchmarking, even with competitors, is a lot less risky than it sounds. Darrell Rigby, a director at the consulting firm Bain & Company, says: 'Chains like Wal-Mart and Target don't make any secret about what they do to succeed, because they know most companies just aren't capable of adopting their approach'.

Rigby should know, because he recently helped a floundering discount-store chain to benchmark its marketing and customer service procedures against industry leaders, only to see his client's employees botch attempts to implement what they learned.

Not so long ago, just ferreting out who had the best practices and setting up teams to study them was a big deal in itself. That problem can now be solved through trade association records, Internet and intranet databases, consultants and, increasingly, managers whose full-time job is co-ordinating benchmarking efforts.

Kevin Dehoff, a vice-president of the New York consulting firm Booz Allen & Hamilton, says: 'Doing the benchmarking attacks only 10 per cent of the problem. The other 90 per cent involves changing your culture, your processes, your whole philosophy, so that you encourage your employees to learn and share ideas'. Even the best-designed benchmark program can founder on many shoals.

Old habits die hard When employees complained a few years ago about slow reimbursement of expenses, Xerox Corporation studied 26 companies to find a way of speeding things up. The problem was that the new system entailed new forms, did away with cash advances and required people to carry more than one corporate credit card. It took months longer than management expected for employees to adapt to the new system. Warren Jeffries, manager of customer services benchmarking for Xerox, says: 'Everyone resisted the changes, even those that were unhappy with the old way'.

Egos have a dark side It is never easy to convince employees that a competitor does something better, when that rival otherwise has a reputation as a mediocre company.

Compensation systems may be out of sync Ford Motor Company recently benchmarked General Electric's success in getting managers to share ideas. But there was a hurdle: sharing ideas is a basis for bonuses at GE but not at Ford. Mark Slagle, Ford's process benchmarking champion, says that instead the emphasis was put on benefits to the organisation as a whole, and it used its intranet to guide people in implementing an idea-sharing process.

Higher-ups may be left out of the loop... Kathleen Mallette, benchmarking manager at AT&T, says: 'The people who implement the changes have to be the ones visiting other companies and getting a first-hand look at what can or cannot be applied to our environment'. Jack Hugus, vice-president for best practice at Lockheed Martin, says management must also be charged with prodding the implementation along. 'Maybe they didn't budget for training, or maybe it just wasn't high priority, but too often the divisional chiefs let the process of implementing get stuck.'

Of course, there is always the problem that corporate cultures differ. How do you get employees to make quicker decisions if they have always been rewarded for following orders, or to take risks when they have seen colleagues fired for failing?

Perhaps the companies that can best navigate these obstacles are those in such deep trouble that employees know their jobs depend on turning things around. When Continental Airlines was swimming in red ink in the mid-1990s, it went to the healthy Southwest Airlines to see if it could adopt Southwest's practice of cross-utilising personnel; for example, using the people who load baggage to also process customers.

Mark Erwin, Continental's senior vice-president of airport services, says employees grumbled about doing more work for the same pay, but they did not rebel. 'It's a lot easier to get a buy-in when people know that without more efficiencies you may have to lay them off.' Continental threw in a sweetener, asking employees to list all the particularly 'dumb, non-value-added things' they did each day. Then it dispensed with many useless chores, such as filing a daily report of how many tickets they collected at the gate when all tickets were sent to accounting for tallying anyway.

Source: Deutsch, C. (1999).

Activities for discussion, analysis and further research

1 Identify and explain the factors which need to be controlled when one benchmarks against another organisation.
2 Why do organisations benchmark? Does it have to be an organisation in the same industry? Why?
3 Identify an organisation you are familiar with that has benchmarked and try to find out how it went about it. What steps did the organisation take to implement what they had learned?

MANAGERIAL APPROACHES TO IMPLEMENTING CONTROLS

In addition to the control types they use, managers also have choices about mechanisms used to put controls in place. There are three managerial control approaches: bureaucratic, clan and market. It is useful to think of them in terms of how control is exercised—whether by bureaucratic rules, the clan or the market. All three will be used to some extent.

bureaucratic control

Managerial approach relying on regulation through rules, policies, supervision, budgets, schedules, reward systems and other administrative mechanisms aimed at ensuring employees exhibit appropriate behaviours and meet performance standards

Bureaucratic control

Bureaucratic control uses regulation by rules, policies, supervision, budgets, schedules, reward systems and other mechanisms to ensure employees show expected behaviours and meet performance standards. Several results of heavy bureaucratic control use are shown in Table 16.1. As shown, control sources are mostly external to the individual, emphasis is on a fixed set of tasks often defined narrowly, and on top-down hierarchical control.

With bureaucratic control, rules and policies develop to handle a range of recurring conditions. When unexpected events or infrequent exceptions occur, supervisors decide the corrective action, if any, that is needed. Supervisors also check to see people follow rules and other mechanisms.

Table 16.1 Characteristics associated with bureaucratic and clan control

Characteristics	Bureaucratic control	Clan control
Means of control	Rules, policies and hierarchy	Shared goals, values and tradition
Source of control	Mainly external mechanisms	Mainly internal motivation
Job design	Narrow subtasks; doing, rather than thinking	Whole task; doing and thinking
Definition of duties	Fixed	Flexible; contingent on changing conditions
Accountability	Usually individual	Often team
Structure	Tall; top-down controls	Flat; mutual influence
Power usage	Emphasis on legitimate authority	Emphasis on relevant information and expertise
Responsibility	Performing individual job	Upgrading performance of work unit and organisation
Reward emphasis	Extrinsic	Intrinsic
Innovation	Less likely	More likely
Likely employee reactions	Compliance	Commitment

Source: Adapted from Walton (1985, p. 81).

While bureaucratic control helps predictable activities run smoothly, heavy use has disadvantages. Bureaucratic control does not help innovation, inhibits needed change when environments change quickly, and produces compliance, not commitment, in employees by focusing on following regulations developed by others (see Chapter 13). For these reasons, organisations attempt to emphasise clan control more.

Clan control

Clan control relies on values, beliefs, traditions, corporate culture, shared norms and informal relationships to regulate employee behaviour and help reach organisational goals. Several results related to heavy clan control use are listed in Table 16.1. In contrast to bureaucratic control, clan control emphasises internal motivation, flexible duties and broad tasks, and influence based on relevant information and expertise instead of hierarchical position.

With clan control more emphasis is on groups, and teams are the focus of responsibility. This control type is common in situations with professionals, where training and norms, as well as group identification, substitute for the strong emphasis on rules and regulations characteristic of bureaucratic control.

Clan control improves commitment to organisational objectives and generally raises employees' willingness to bring about workplace change. For these reasons, some organisations with routine jobs are putting greater emphasis on clan control. For example, at Corning, teams vary in size between 10 and 25 persons, and make many operational decisions on a broad task range. Teams monitor their performance against established goals and appraise team members for feedback and development. The plant has a skill-based pay plan, where most employees get pay rises for learning new jobs. Since the greater emphasis on clan control, the plant has significantly improved productivity, defect rates, inventory costs, injury rates, and time required to complete a customer order (Liebowitz & Holden 1995). Increasingly, teams are used in a range of businesses, including insurance, automobile, aerospace, electronics, food-processing, paper, steel and financial services industries (see Chapter 15) (Hoerr 1988; 1989; Tang & Crofford 1995–96).

Market control

Market control uses market mechanisms to set prices for specified goods and services an organisation requires, relieving managers of the need to set up more elaborate controls over costs. To use market control, there must be competition in the relevant goods or services and needs must be clearly set out. For example, purchasing departments often develop specifications for goods the organisation needs, then set up a competitive bidding process. Without detailed specifications and bidding process (or at least comparable sources for goods or services), purchasing agents would have to decide if particular prices were reasonable on the basis of processes involved. Trying to control costs in this way involves much time and effort.

The use of market control is increasing because of outsourcing. **Outsourcing** is the process of using an outside vendor to perform a normal organisation function. For example, General Motors pressured its divisions to become more efficient making parts or lose work to outside sources. Until recently, it had produced about 70 per cent of parts used in its cars. Decisions about who makes some parts are being made through market control by comparing price and

clan control

Managerial approach relying on values, beliefs, traditions, corporate culture, shared norms and informal relationships to regulate employee behaviours and facilitate reaching of organisational goals

market control

Managerial approach relying on market mechanisms to regulate prices for certain clearly specified goods and services needed by an organisation

outsourcing

Process of employing an outside vendor to perform a function normally carried on within the organisation

quality available from outside suppliers to GM's internal costs and quality (Sedwick 1996; Vlasic 1996).

Market control often regulates internal operations by setting up profit centres for service units, such as photocopying or computer services, then charging other organisation parts for services. Generally, market control works poorly when it is difficult to specify requirements precisely due to uncertain or changing circumstances (e.g. customer requirements) or when little or no competition exists to base pricing on (e.g. R&D projects).

✖ Balancing risks

crossroads

Manufacturers have been exploring the potential of the Internet for direct sales to consumers. If they cut the intermediaries out of the supply chain, they can reduce the cost of their products. Another trend is the 'virtualisation' of manufacturing, which involves outsourcing the physical manufacturing to the lowest cost supplier while retaining control over product design, brand marketing and business relationships. A couple of issues have been identified. If manufacturers sell direct they risk damaging existing distribution networks. Another risk is that overseas manufacturers will use e-commerce to sell direct to consumers in this market.

Decision point

1 What factors should an organisation consider before it makes the decision to 'virtualise'? By doing a search on the Web, track down an organisation that has done this. Contact the organisation and seek information on what factors they retain control of.

Reflection point

1 E-commerce can reduce costs by reducing inventory levels and speeding the ordering and delivery process. These result in capital savings as well as a reduction in the need for real estate and warehousing services. What else can an organisation outsource while still maintaining control over its own business?

Promoting innovation:
Controlling while nurturing innovation

A managerial challenge is to engage in the controlling function without halting the creativity and innovation needed for long-term survival. In this section we consider how managers balance four strategic control levers to foster innovation, while regulating organisational activities. We also review the incrementalist approach to controlling innovation projects.

Four levers for strategic control: A balancing act   Managers have four major levers they can use in effective strategic control (Simons 1995). Together the levers encourage accountability, enable empowerment and allow shifts in strategic direction. The four levers, shown in Figure 16.6, are associated with planning (see Chapters 6 and 7) but are part of the controlling function to monitor strategic directions and take needed corrective action.

Fig. 16.6 Four levers of strategic control

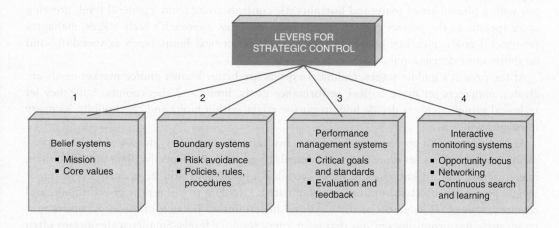

1 **Belief systems** are the ways by which managers communicate and reinforce an organisation's basic mission and values. Mission statements, credos and slogans provide inspiration and general direction, guiding organisational efforts and long-term effectiveness. Belief systems use is strongly associated with clan control.

2 **Boundary systems** define the acceptable domain of activities for organisational members. Through such means as policies, rules and procedures, organisations work to reduce risks that organisational members will waste or misuse the firm's resources and energies by setting boundaries to operate within. Boundary systems are closely linked to bureaucratic control.

3 **Performance management systems** focus on ensuring specific goals set are achieved. Such systems let managers check progress on specific targets and facilitate evaluation and feedback relative to achievement of those targets. Performance management systems are associated with bureaucratic control. They can be used with clan control by specifying end results needed, but letting members determine the best means.

4 **Interactive monitoring systems** encourage search and learning so the organisation can identify and adapt to new opportunities. Without a concerted effort focusing on new opportunities and developing new strategic competencies, organisations may blindly pursue previously established plans now obsolete or less than optimal due to changing environmental and competitive circumstances. Such efforts involve scanning the environment, gathering internal data on areas that are going better than expected, and encouraging individuals through the organisation to seize unexpected opportunities and deal with problems. Such systems involve those at all organisational levels in continuous challenge and debate about data, assumptions and action plans.

Incrementalist Approach When controlling innovative efforts such as R&D projects, James Brian Quinn (1979; 1985) says the ideal process should be seen as 'controlled chaos'. On one hand, it is unpredictable and chaotic. On the other, it can be controlled by mixing

incrementalist approach

Approach to controlling an innovative project that relies on clan control but also involves a phased set of plans and accompanying bureaucratic controls beginning at a general level and growing more specific as the project progresses

reliance on clan control with carefully set up bureaucratic controls. Using the **incrementalist approach** gives control over the process without stifling it. The approach relies on clan control but with a phased set of plans and bureaucratic controls going from a general level, growing more specific as the project goes on. In the incrementalist approach's early stages, managers set general goals, pick key people for the project, set critical limits (such as spending) and establish some decision points to check progress.

At the project's middle stages, technical aspects are better known and/or market needs are clearer, managers set more critical performance goals, limits and checkpoints. Still, they let technical group members decide how to pursue goals, within limits and checkpoints, as many questions will remain.

At later innovation process stages, when many variables are clearly demonstrated in experiments, managers may set more concrete controls to go with more specific planning. Even then, many factors are not known, and many technical options may still be opened. However, at review points, unsuccessful options are eliminated. Deciding to kill a project is difficult, and requires managerial judgment as there are still uncertainties. Because of these, managers may retain some less promising options that need lower resource levels. Smaller-scale options often give significant innovations, while the planned option fails. Sony's Walkman, a miniature stereo cassette player with lightweight earphones, grew from an attempt to produce a miniature stereo tape recorder. The idea of combining the miniature player, created by one engineering group, with earphones from another came from honorary chairman Masaru Ibuka, Sony's founder. Still, originally little money and personnel went into the product, as the Walkman was seen mainly as a young people's toy (Nyak & Ketteringham 1986).

The incrementalist approach means managers must strike a balance between control approaches to encourage innovation. Otherwise, control systems can stifle innovation, inhibiting long-term organisational effectiveness.

@ e-control for e-savings
managing the e-challenge

When e-commerce first appeared, it promised to revolutionise the way companies sold goods. Now it seems that the biggest benefit for most companies will be in the way they buy goods.

Electronic procurement is becoming one of the first entry points for companies keen to enter the world of business-to-business e-commerce. Companies can expect savings of 15 to 20 per cent without having to change the operational model or losing control of their own business.

That opportunity has been sufficient for outsourcing service provider Ausdoc to make a 4.5 million investment in local e-procurement software developer Streamlink. Best known for its document exchange and print-on-demand services, Ausdoc has bought a 15 per cent stake in Streamlink, a developer of Internet-based software for purchasing goods and services from multiple suppliers, over the Internet. Ausdoc will install Streamlink's e-procure software internally over the next six months, and from mid-2000 will offer an electronic purchasing capability to its customers.

Inside the Ausdoc warehouse. Ausdoc is planning software designed for the Internet that will facilitate its customers' control processes.

Ausdoc's e-procurement will consist of a Web portal designed for each customer's business, where they will purchase goods and services from a catalogue of suppliers. The ability to deliver a single bill from several suppliers is an attraction for customers, as it reduces their invoice processing costs.

Source: Adapted from Howarth, B. (2000).

Activities for discussion, analysis and further research

1 Consider what factors are controlled in this instance. In what ways will this new way of purchasing help organisations embed more effective control processes?
2 Find out what strategies were used to make lower cost purchases by small-volume buyers before the e-procurement initiative.

ASSESSING CONTROL SYSTEMS

Whether controls are intended to facilitate innovation or for other purposes, managers must continually assess control systems to ensure they achieve the results expected. In this section, we consider the potential dysfunctional aspects of control systems. The presence of any of these shows the control system needs adjusting. We also examine overcontrol and undercontrol, and conclude by looking at characteristics of effective control systems.

Potential dysfunctional aspects of control systems

As you might imagine, not all control system effects are positive. Poorly designed and/or excessive controls may give one or more of four major dysfunctional side effects: behavioural displacement, game playing, operating delays or negative attitudes (Merchant 1985).

behavioural displacement

Condition in which individuals engage in behaviours encouraged by controls and reward systems though they are inconsistent with organisational goals

Behavioural displacement   Behavioural displacement occurs when behaviours encouraged by control and reward systems are inconsistent with organisational goals. In one case, a research laboratory used the number of patents filed as an indicator of effectiveness. Unfortunately, the number of patents filed increased but the number of successful research projects decreased (Kotter, Schlesinger & Sathe 1979). Displacement comes from three basic causes: poor analysis of the relationship between controls and desired outcomes, overemphasis on quantification of control measures when qualitative aspects are important, and overemphasising activities rather than necessary end results.

Game playing   Game playing with controls occurs when managers improve their standing on performance measures by manipulating resource usage and/or data by not achieving actual performance improvements. Resource usage manipulation means getting more resources than needed so objectives can be easily met or exceeded. Some resource-level slack may be helpful, buffering against unforeseen events; carried too far though, it can weaken an organisation's competitive position through higher costs. Manipulating data means faking performance data or influencing performance results during data reporting.

Operating delays   Operating delays may come from actions needed by feedforward and concurrent controls. If excessive, such controls can cripple organisational goal attainment. This provokes actions undermining the effects of controls. For example, in a study of a diversified corporation, 74 per cent of general managers reported receiving expenditure approvals after money had been spent (Merchant 1984).

Negative attitudes   Controls may lead to negative attitudes, especially if the controls are excessive or poorly designed (Greenberger & Strasser 1986). Professionals particularly will resist controls. Most often, they oppose bureaucratic controls which do not seem to help organisational goal attainment.

Overcontrol versus undercontrol

As excessive control increases the chance of negative outcomes, managers must avoid overcontrol. **Overcontrol** is limiting individual job autonomy to the point where it seriously inhibits job performance. Managers must also avoid going too far the other way, producing a situation of undercontrol. **Undercontrol** is giving autonomy to an employee to where the organisation loses the ability to direct efforts to organisational goal achievement. In fact, undercontrol is often cited as the reason organisations do not achieve their goals (Jaworski, Stathakopoulos & Krishnan 1993; Merchant 1982).

Characteristics of an effective control system

Effective control systems have common characteristics (Merchant 1985; Stoner & Wankel 1986). To assess existing or proposed control systems, managers should use these as a checklist of essential features.

Future-oriented   To be effective, control systems must regulate future events, not fix blame for past ones. A well-designed control system lets managers know work's progress toward unit objectives, showing areas where future corrective action is needed, and uncovering unforeseen opportunities for development—all aids to future action.

Multidimensional   In most cases, control systems must be multidimensional to catch relevant major performance issues. For example, a GM plant would have difficulty quickly if it focused on quantity without considering issues such as quality, scrap rate and overhead.

Cost-effective   The cost of controls is important. One factor controlled at McDonald's is rest-room cleanliness. The company manual specifies frequency of rest-room cleaning, and both outlet manager and company inspection teams check this factor (Moser 1988). Still, McDonald's could control cleanliness more by dedicating one person at all outlets to do nothing but ensure this. The costs of this may be greater than the benefits of the additional control, as McDonald's already has a very good reputation for cleanliness. Essentially, controls benefits should outweigh its costs.

Accurate   Since controls are a basis of future actions, accuracy is crucial. Inaccurate control data is worse than none, as managers may make poor decisions based on such data.

Realistic   Control systems should have realistic views about what can be achieved. Otherwise, employees will view the control system as unreasonable and ignore or sabotage it.

Timely   Control systems give data on a production cycle or process at a specific time. For example, data may come in a monthly sales report, a weekly project update, a daily production report, or from a production line's quality inspections. For managers and employees to respond promptly to problems, control systems must give information soon enough for corrective action.

overcontrol

Limiting individual job autonomy to the point where it seriously inhibits effective job performance

undercontrol

Granting autonomy to an employee to the point where the organisation loses its ability to direct individual effort toward achieving

Monitorable   Control systems should be designed for ease of monitoring to ensure they perform as expected. One way of checking a control system is to introduce an imperfection, such as a defective part, and observe how long before the system detects and reports it to the correct person. Obviously, the test must be monitored to ensure the imperfection does not cause problems if the control system fails (as in a maintenance-quality test for aeroplanes). Other monitoring control system methods include various kinds of audits.

Acceptable to organisation members   Control systems operate best when accepted by organisation members affected by them. Otherwise, members may override and undermine them. Employees will accept control systems when they focus on important issues compatible with organisational goals, when they give useful data, when data collected give a fair and accurate picture of employee performance, and when the data are used for improvement (as opposed to blaming).

Flexible   Just as organisations must be flexible to changing environments, control systems must be able to meet new or revised needs. Accordingly, they should be designed to be able to be changed quickly to measure and report new information and track new endeavours.

During the 1990s, Japanese companies were in trouble due to exchange rates and competitors lowering costs by copying Japanese manufacturing innovations (e.g. total quality management). Losing their advantage, Japanese companies looked to improve efficiency. Many focused on output controls—goals and budgets—but without stopping innovation. One approach was moving responsibility for budgets and profit targets to first-line supervisors and workers (Jones 1999). This was to show employees the direct impact of their activities on profit. Another approach came from the realisation that a large proportion of costs went to buying components. In response companies worked with suppliers to reduce costs and raise product quality. Members from a range of organisational functions were put into cross-functional teams to reduce costs, one strategy being to teach suppliers to use budgets and goals effectively. The focus on output control has been very useful.

■ The MD's diary   the reflective practitioner

The controls we put in place are the traditional financial imperatives that are imposed upon us to some extent by our shareholders and head office. So, I would describe what we do as 'monitor and shepherd' more than control. If we have the right strategies in place, the right process, the right organisation, and people are focusing all their attention on making sure that they deliver the desired outcomes then our role is really to make sure that we have enough information feeding back in to us to make sure that it's not drifting off track. So we use a lot of indicators. They're specific indicators. So, for example, I will look at things like the air freight costs. That will tell me if our schedules are right because if we are planning and processing our inventory in the correct manner then we should not have to pay air freight because everything is coming in by the lowest cost option. Air travel is another indicator of how effectively our programs are in place. Because if they're not, we're running all over the world to fix major problems.

I tend to try and find indicators which are not hard indicators but that allow me to have a good feel for where the business is hurting. So I identify the symptoms and if I can see where the symptoms are then I can diagnose the cause. But it's not control. It's very much monitoring and marshalling, and shepherding, and making sure that we get early indicators back in.

The whole concept of control for me is not about reacting once things are out of control, but about identifying trends which show that things are slowly moving towards an out-of-control position and making sure that things shift a little bit. So if you have those early indicators, those early symptoms, you can very quickly get in and make sure that there are countermeasures in place very early. This helps to make sure that you don't go out of control but that you also don't deviate. It's all about trying to keep things as close to the mean, in terms of the way you want people to perform, as possible. That's, to me, effective control.

We do have a formal process whereby we take the overall strategic objectives of the organisation, we break those down into key strategies, and we look at what the desired outcomes are and we find a whole range of key performance indicators that will measure our success at doing that. That is aimed less at control as it is at continuous improvement. While it is a form of control, it's not my preferred method of control because it is measuring after the event. It measures your rate of improvement and provides some feedback indicating whether your effort is making a difference. But in terms of control, it's too late. It's an effective tool for monitoring continuous improvement. It's not the most effective tool, in my opinion, to determine if your efforts going forward are being directed in the most effective manner.

■ The subordinate's log

the reflective practitioner

The best theories and ideas in the world are all useless if you are not able to control your people and your resources. Control can have a negative connotation in that it implies trying to limit performance or people. I see control as a means of identifying whether your performance is meeting your plan. I found that control requires two aspects. Effective control requires information, and the ability to interpret the information and decide what to do with it. I think the former is the hardest. I have found that people, as a rule, are reluctant to complete any sort of formal reporting. I found the balance between an appropriate level of reporting to be able to make the right control decisions, and creating an administrative imposition on subordinates is a difficult one. Sometimes staff are reluctant to give complete and accurate information in order to protect themselves against perceived threats or embarrassment. Some people also withhold information as a means of maintaining power.

The information requirements for adequate decisions demand that staff be comfortable enough to report completely. I have found that there is no substitute for numbers. Anecdotal evidence is not adequate when making corrective decisions.

Focus on practice—Strategies for improving

1 Design strategies to evaluate behavioural control systems which enable the organisation to maintain the culture it desires.
2 How do you achieve the right balance of direct supervision and bureaucratic control to monitor progress towards goals?
3 Devise strategies to involve subordinates in any consideration and implementation of corrective action.

Source: Jones et al. (2000).

Chapter summary

Controlling is the regulation of organisational activities so actual performance conforms to set goals and standards. Controls are important to help managers handle five challenges: coping with uncertainty, detecting irregularities, identifying opportunities, handling complex situations and decentralising authority. Just as planning responsibilities differ by level, control responsibilities exist at strategic, tactical and operational levels.

The basic control process has several major steps: (1) determine areas to control; (2) set standards; (3) measure performance; (4) compare performance to standards; (5a) if standards are met or exceeded, recognise performance; (5b) if standards are not met, take corrective action as needed; (6) adjust standards and measures as needed. The resource-dependence approach to controls argues managers must consider controls in areas where they depend on others for resources to reach organisational goals. Four conditions that help show when controls should be used are: a high dependence on the resource; an expectation resource flows may be unacceptable without controls; feasibility of instituting a control process; and acceptable process costs.

There are different control types. Major types based on timing are feedforward, concurrent and feedback. Managers may need multiple control systems that use two or more of feedforward, concurrent, and feedback control processes and involve some strategic control points. Finally, systems can be cybernetic or non-cybernetic, depending on how much human discretion is part of the system.

Managers have options about approaches they will use to implement controls. The three basic ones are bureaucratic, clan and market. Managers have four strategic control levers to help them regulate activities and encourage motivation: belief systems, boundary systems, performance management systems and interactive monitoring systems. The incrementalist approach helps control specific innovation projects. It relies on clan control but involves a phased set of plans and accompanying bureaucratic controls beginning at a general level and growing more specific as the project progresses.

Potential dysfunctional control system aspects are behavioural displacement, game playing, operating delays and negative attitudes. To decrease chances of these effects, managers must avoid either overcontrol or undercontrol. Effective control systems must be future-oriented, multidimensional, cost-effective, accurate, realistic, timely, monitorable, acceptable to organisation members and flexible.

This chapter focuses on basic concepts for organisational control systems, and the following supplements examine specific managerial control methods, such as financial and quality control.

Questions for discussion and review

1 Explain the five major roles of controls. Give three examples from your college or university of controls fulfilling at least one of these roles.

2 Describe three levels of controls in organisations. For an organisation with which you are familiar, identify a control at each level.

3 Outline a general process applicable to most control situations. Using this, explain how you would develop a system to control home delivery staff at a local pizza shop.

4 Explain the principal factors, or conditions, managers need to consider in deciding what to control. Use these to assess a control existing at your college or university.

5 Describe the major types of controls by timing. Suppose you are managing a small factory making specialised microchips for a well-known computer manufacturer. Explain how you would use each control type to help maintain adequate control over manufacturing. What strategic control points would you establish?

6 Differentiate between cybernetic and non-cybernetic control. Explain how you might use these two types of control in a managerial position.

7 Explain the three basic approaches to implementing controls. For each approach, give an example based on a familiar organisation.

8 Explain the four strategic control levers. How does development of Sony's Walkman illustrate this approach?

9 Identify the major potential dysfunctional aspects of control systems in organisations. How could overcontrol or undercontrol contribute to these?

10 Delineate the major characteristics of effective control systems.

Exercises for managing in the 21st century

Exercise 1
Skill building: Timing the use of controls

The timing of control use is very important to organisational goal achievement. Controls at the proper point in development can give valuable information about quality, quantity, whether expectations are met or not, and possible solutions or opportunities. Following are examples of controls concerning timing. Indicate whether the type shown is a feedforward (FF), a concurrent (C) or a feedback (FB) control by placing the appropriate letters in the spaces provided.

1 _____ Road testing a new car

2 _____ Daily cash flow report

3 _____ Testing components from vendors prior to assembling a final product

4 _____ Ensuring employees are properly trained prior to starting a particular function

5 _____ Constantly checking woollen material for irregularities as it is being produced

6 _____ Certification of doctors prior to allowing them to practise

7 _____ A governor (a mechanical device for automatically controlling engine speed by regulating fuel flow) which controls the speed of a car or truck

8 _____ A final check of a report before it is sent to a client

9 _____ Individual employees check their work to ensure it is correct before passing it to someone else

10 _____ Sampling a batch of pills to ensure the correct amount of proper chemicals is included therein

Exercise 2
Management exercise: Opportunity knocks

You and a friend have what you believe to be the opportunity of a lifetime. You are both graduating this year, and your friend's father has asked whether the two of you would like to buy the air-conditioning and heating business he founded and has operated for the last 30 years. It has been very lucrative for him; today he is a millionaire many times over. His firm is the leader in its field in the area, and you and your friend see the possibility of expanding because many new homes are being built locally.

Your friend's father will finance the buyout through a loan, to be paid off over the next 10 years. Both you and your friend have some degree of expertise in the heating and air-conditioning field, as you have both worked for his father during the past four summers. His father has agreed to be a consultant to the two of you for a year or so in case his advice is needed.

The firm has almost 60 well-qualified employees, a large inventory, 40 service trucks in excellent condition, and a well-established list of clients. At the same time, return on investment has been lower than average for the past three years, labour costs are very high, and the company has attracted only a few new clients during the past two years. In addition, there is an indication the firm is not carrying the most up-to-date heating or air-conditioning equipment, and the four large buildings housing showrooms and service centres badly need refurbishing.

You and your friend are discussing the possibility of buying the firm. In considering the situation, the two of you are reviewing forms of control and control process which should be implemented.

Exercise requirement

Discuss the types of control you and your friend would use and the control process the two of you would implement as new owners of the firm.

 # The kings of culture

Peter O'Connor remembers well his first day at The Body Shop. Walking through head office in the south-eastern Melbourne suburb of Mulgrave, he was spotted by Graeme Wise, a director and one of the founders of The Body Shop in Australia. Wise not only said hello, he knew O'Connor by his first name. If he ever had any doubts about joining The Body Shop as production manager, that casual hello ended them.

O'Connor has now been at The Body Shop, a niche retailer selling personal-care products, for two years. Before that, he worked at a small manufacturing plant that sold machinery parts to about 15 countries around the world. Although O'Connor loved the overseas travel involved in that job, he found it too stressful. Relations with other staff, union and non-union, were poor.

That was not the only reason O'Connor joined The Body Shop. He and his wife, Ali, who works full-time at The Body Shop in customer service, wanted to have a family, and constant overseas travel did not fit into the plan. In addition, the Mulgrave head office has a creche. Job satisfaction, a healthy pay packet, a friendly work environment and convenience. What more could O'Connor want?

O'Connor's story is not atypical. Eight employees were interviewed, their length of service ranging from 11 years to 4 weeks. All spoke in glowing terms about their employer, and their sense of loyalty to an organisation that trains them, rewards initiative, has ethical standards they respect and does not expect their last drop of sweat during a day's work. A staff member in the Frankston shop comments on the support from every level—colleagues, management and the retail support centre (the in-house term for head office).

Are such comments typical of most of the 232 permanents, 76 part-timers and 295 casuals who serve behind the counters of the 66 stores in prime retail sites around the country as well as the Mulgrave headquarters? The Body Shop selected the eight employees who were interviewed but management did not sit in on the lengthy interviews. It must be remembered that this is the retail industry which is characterised by cut-throat competition and tight margins.

There are also other factors to challenge the squeaky clean image of The Body Shop. On the ethical front, the company was accused in Britain in the mid-1990s of failing to meet its widely proclaimed standards not to sell products tested on animals.[1] Although the case was disproved, the company was badly hurt by the subsequent media exposure. The firm is often accused of exploiting ethical and environmental issues as a selling point. And the absence of union involvement at The Body Shop prompts some in organised labour circles to suggest its human resources policies are better characterised as benign dictatorship than genuine employee empowerment.

No doubt there would be an element of truth in the critics' claims. But they must be kept in perspective—and not just because eight employees seem to genuinely believe that they are in employment nirvana. Legal sources say they

[1]The accusations made were disproved and the accusers successfully sued by The Body Shop.

Products from The Body Shop. For effective control of its human resources, The Body Shop uses a sensitive, 'people-first' approach with its staff.

cannot remember an unfair dismissal case being run against The Body Shop. Since it first opened the doors of its first outlet in 1983 in Melbourne's CBD, there have been only 12 retrenchments, of which 8 were voluntary.

Checks with industrial tribunals reveal no breaches of award conditions under which The Body Shop staff are employed. Staff turnover in 1999 was 22 per cent group wide and 15 per cent at head office. Consider that these numbers include Christmas casuals, who swell staff numbers by about 200, and that the business has 91 per cent female employees, many under 30 years of age, and an average length of service of 5.4 years, and it is clear that the company boasts a stable staff. Also, most of the part-timers and full-timers begin with the company by working as casuals. While there were seven compensation claims in 1999, none resulted in lost time.

Staff appreciate the balance between lifestyle and the work attitude of the company. Many industry observers despair about such issues as service and training in the retail sector. Interestingly, they largely absolve The Body Shop of these sins. In doing so, they are not making a direct comment on the retailer's human resources policies. However, it would seem fair to equate a committed workforce with good service. Not only industry observers strike a positive note about The Body Shop. Morris Wagenheim is the managing director of Esprit and in direct competition through Esprit's 100% ownership of Red Earth. Therefore, he has no vested interest in promoting The Body Shop. However, his comments are telling. 'The Body Shop is an excellent retailer. Their products are outstanding and they sell them with a clear message in the market place that takes account of growing community concerns about ethical, social and environmental issues. I have nothing but respect for this organisation.'

Wagenheim's comments about the ethical message in all aspects of The Body Shop's operations also intrigues industry analysts. What this company seems to have achieved is the coalescing of its aims, its philosophies, with that of the staff. It is a rare achievement in business, particularly in retail. A big positive for The Body Shop is that the staff seem to fit the culture. It seems to me their people believe in the concept, they believe in the brands. Certainly they appear to know their products. Many retailers would like to have staff identify with their corporate message but just cannot achieve it. The Body Shop has.

However, there appears to be a factor more important than the staff identifying with the corporate culture—it is the customer identifying with it. The Body Shop probably works very hard to ensure that it is in tune with its customers.

It would seem that critics who claim that The Body Shop jumps on the ethical issues for purely bottom-line motives may not be wrong. But perhaps this is irrelevant. If the staff and customers of The Body Shop believe The Body Shop message, that is all that counts. Even the public relations disaster that engulfed the company in the mid-1990s over animal testing did not find the true believers questioning the values underpinning the organisation.

As a private company in Australia, The Body Shop jealously guards its profit-and-loss statements. General manager Paul Bird is tight lipped, even on turnovers and margins. So critics, employees and customers alike are in the dark on just what effect the ethical and environmental campaigns and an enlightened human resources policy actually have on the bottom line. For the eight employees interviewed for this article, it obviously does not matter.

Source: Way, N. (2000).

Activities for discussion, analysis and further research

1 Identify the factors which The Body Shop have to control in order to achieve their outcomes.
2 Discuss the control strategies which the company appears to employ. Are they effective? How do you know?
3 Identify competitor companies to The Body Shop. If practical for you to do so, visit one of their outlets and attempt to establish how these compare to the culture of The Body Shop. Do you think the control mechanisms are applied in a similar manner as they are at The Body Shop? Explain your conclusions.

Managerial Control Methods

MAJOR CONTROL SYSTEMS

Looking at major control systems in organisations such as Telstra, Coca-Cola or American Express, you would probably find the systems shown in Figure 16s1.1 (Flamholtz 1996; Anthony, Dearden & Bedford 1984). Control systems increase the chances of achieving organisation goals and standards. For example, total quality management helps improve the quality of products and services. Financial control systems help track overall financial issues, such as whether the organisation is profitable or too much in debt. Budgetary control systems provide quantitative tools to monitor the revenues of various activities and match costs to plans. Inventory control systems ensure inputs are ready as needed and costs are minimised. Operations management means controlling the processes of producing a product or service. Finally, computer-based information systems help maintain better control over information and other functions. We discuss operations management and computer-based information systems in supplements 2 and 3, respectively. (Management by objectives, another control system, is described in Chapter 6.)

For the remainder of this supplement, we look at quality, financial, budgetary and inventory control systems. Before considering each, we explore how they differ by the management level they are oriented to and their timing emphasis.

Fig. 16s1.1   Major organisational control systems

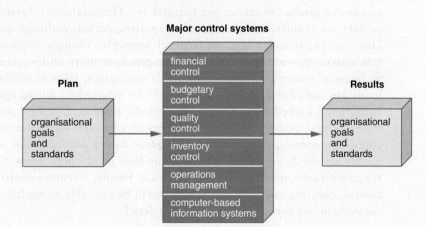

Managerial level

Control systems differ in how much they are used by different managerial levels (see Fig. 16s1.2). For example, total quality management (TQM) is used across the organisation, but it must be built into the strategic levels to be effective. However, for TQM to operate, all organisation levels must be involved. Financial control systems are mechanisms used by top management because they show overall organisation financial health. Middle managers watch financial matters affecting their own area. Middle- and lower-level managers mainly use budgetary controls. Top management monitors overall budget performance and deviations. Finally, inventory control rests with lower- and middle-level managers, although upper managers may evaluate costs.

Fig. 16s1.2   Major control systems by managerial level and timing

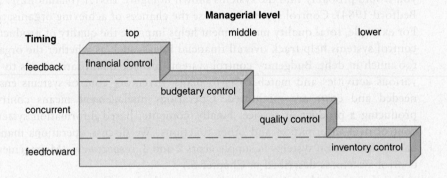

Timing emphasis

Major control systems have different timing emphases. Timing refers to when controls occur, before (feedforward), during (concurrent) or after (feedback) the transformation process results in a product or service (see Chapter 16). Financial control systems are feedback control as data are evaluated at the end of a reporting period. Although too late to make changes affecting the particular data, the feedback helps plan changes. Since computer-based information systems provide financial data, managers have more up-to-date information. In contrast to financial control, budgetary control is concurrent, since it regulates activities so budget levels are met. For example, budgets may be referred to during spending decisions. When budgets are looked at only after set periods, budgetary control moves closer to feedback control. Total quality management applies to all of the transformation process; it is more a concurrent control, since checks are frequent during production or service process to ensure quality standards are met. If checks occur after production, when materials are scrapped or rejected if faulty, quality control is feedback. Finally, inventory control is mainly feedforward control, ensuring materials and products will be available as needed. In the remainder of this supplement, we consider these in greater detail.

TOTAL QUALITY MANAGEMENT

Total quality management (TQM) in some form is quite common (Conference Board 1994a). One major impetus toward concern for quality has been fierce global competition from Japan-based companies offering products and services of superior quality, often at quite low prices. There are many views of total quality management (and in some cases, names other than TQM are used). For our discussion, we define **total quality management (TQM)** as an organisation-wide management system integral to an organisation's strategy and aims to improve product and service quality continually to achieve high levels of customer satisfaction and build customer loyalty (Bounds, Yorks, Adams & Ranney 1994; Reicheld 1996).

Although quality has been defined in many ways, the American Society for Quality Control offers this definition: **Quality** is the totality of features and characteristics of a product or service that bear on its ability to satisfy stated or implied needs (*Quality Progress* 1992; Reeves & Bednar 1994). This definition recognises that quality involves every aspect of a product or service, that quality affects ability of a product or service to satisfy needs, and that customer needs for quality may not always be explicitly stated or calculated in the same way.

In examining issues of quality and need for quality control, we explore quality's strategic implications, probe major assumptions underlying the philosophy of TQM, examine TQM change principles with intervention techniques, and consider issues related to TQM's actual practice.

Strategic implications of quality

David A. Garvin (1987) argues that quality can be used strategically to compete effectively. Choosing an appropriate strategy, though, depends on understanding quality's important dimensions. Therefore, we explore these before considering how to compete on quality.

Eight dimensions   From a strategic point of view, there are eight important dimensions of quality.

Performance involves the product's primary operating characteristics. For a car, performance includes acceleration, braking, handling and fuel use. For service industries, such as fast-food restaurants, airlines, or hotels, performance means prompt service (Hostage 1975; Sherden 1988; White 1988).

Features are supplements to the product or service's basic functioning characteristics. Examples are free newspapers for hotel guests, extra options on autofocus cameras, or stereo CD players in automobiles.

Reliability is the likelihood a product will not work properly or will break down in a specific period. Since significant use is involved in assessing reliability, this dimension does not apply as easily to products and services used immediately.

Conformance refers to how well a product's design or operating characteristics meet established standards. Products and services are developed for standards or specifications (White 1988).

Durability is how much use a product will get before it deteriorates or breaks down to where replacement is more sensible than repair. For instance, home appliance durability

total quality management (TQM)
Management system integral to an organisation's strategy and aimed at continually improving product and service quality so as to achieve high levels of customer satisfaction and build strong customer loyalty

quality
Totality of features and characteristics of a product or service bearing on its ability to satisfy needs stated or implied

varies, ranging from 5.8 to 18 years for washing machines and 6 to 17 years for vacuum cleaners (Yepsen 1987).

Serviceability refers to promptness, courtesy, proficiency and ease of repair. For example, Hoover has a free-call number customers can call when an appliance breaks down. For easy-to-fix items, they can buy parts which are mailed with directions.

Aesthetics refers to how the product looks, feels, sounds, tastes or smells—all issues dependent on personal judgment and preference.

Perceived quality is individuals' subjective assessments of product or service quality. These may use incomplete information, but perceptions count with customers.

Competing on quality   While some quality dimensions reinforce each other, others do not. For example, adding features often reduces reliability, and aesthetics may affect durability. Thus, organisations rarely try to compete on very high quality on all eight dimensions at once.

Most companies select a quality niche that customers see as important (Yepsen 1987). Of course, another crucial issue is providing the intended quality level.

⬆ Deming's 14 points on how to improve quality

W. Edwards Deming developed 14 management points summarising what he believed managers, especially at upper levels, must do to produce high-quality products:

1 Create constancy of purpose toward improvement of product and service, with the aim to become competitive and to stay in business, and to provide jobs.

2 Adopt the new philosophy. We are in a new economic age. Western management must awaken to the challenge, must learn their responsibilities, and take on leadership for change.

3 Cease dependence on inspection to achieve quality. Eliminate need for mass inspection by building quality into the product in the first place.

4 Stop awarding business on the basis of price. Instead, minimise total cost. Move to a single supplier for any item on a long-term relationship of loyalty and trust.

5 Improve constantly and forever systems of production and service, to improve quality and productivity, and thus constantly decrease costs.

6 Institute training on the job.

7 Institute leadership. The aim of supervision should be to help people, machines and gadgets to do a better job. Supervision of management needs overhauling as well as supervision of production workers.

8 Drive out fear so everyone may work effectively for the company.

9 Break down barriers between departments. People in research, design, sales and production must work as a team to foresee problems of production and use which may be encountered with the product or service.

10 Eliminate slogans, exhortations and targets for the workforce asking for zero defects and new levels of productivity. Such exhortations only create adversarial relationships, as most causes of low quality and productivity belong to the system and lie beyond the workforce's power.

11 **a** Eliminate work standards (quotas) on the factory floor. Substitute leadership.

   b Eliminate management by objectives. Eliminate management by numbers, numerical goals. Substitute leadership.

12 a Remove barriers robbing the hourly worker of their right to take pride in their work. The responsibility of supervisors must be changed from sheer numbers to quality.
    b Remove barriers robbing people in management and engineering of their right to take pride in their work. This means, inter alia, abolishing the annual merit rating and management by objectives.

13 Institute a vigorous program of education and self-improvement.

14 Put everybody in the company to work to accomplish the transformation. The transformation is everybody's job

Source: Deming (1986).

TQM philosophy

Japanese companies are generally credited with pioneering total quality management; however, the concept actually started in the United States. W. Edwards Deming developed statistical methods to improve quality, but took his concepts to Japan after being ignored. He promoted the idea of involving employees and organisation units in the quality effort, and set out 14 management points for his philosophy. For Deming's 14 points, see the Management skills for the 21st century discussion, 'Deming's 14 points on how to improve quality'.

Japanese companies, eager to rebuild after World War II, embraced Deming's ideas. In fact, his contributions were so valued they established the Deming prize, an annual award for quality management. During the 1950s, J. M. Juran also helped with total quality management efforts. Kaoru Ishikawa is also seen as important (Evans & Lindsay 1996; Juran 1988).

Deming, Juran and Ishikawa saw the organisation's main aims as to stay in business, to aid community stability, have useful products and services meeting customer needs, and foster organisational members' work satisfaction and growth. Although there are some differences, these three authorities show the basis for TQM's philosophy (Hackman & Wagemen 1995).

Good quality costs less than poor work quality. One basic assumption of TQM is that costs of poor quality (inspection, rework, scrap rates, lost customers and other factors) greatly exceed costs of high-quality products and services (training, proper equipment and tools, process improvement and other factors). According to one estimate, a factory without TQM spends about 20 and 25 percent of their budget on finding and fixing mistakes (Port 1987).

Employees try to improve quality while they are supported. A second TQM assumption is that employees will make quality changes when given the tools and training. Related to this, management must listen to employees' ideas.

Quality improvement needs cross-functional efforts. A third TQM assumption is that most quality problems do not fit into one functional area. For example, to produce high-quality products, design specialists must work closely with manufacturing during the design phase.

Quality improvement needs top management's strong commitment. The reasoning behind this fourth TQM assumption is that senior managers control the organisational systems that design and produce products and services. Employees' ability to do high-quality work is a direct result of the quality of the systems that managers create.

TQM change principles

According to three TQM authorities, four TQM change principles should guide organisational quality-improvement interventions. These are as follows (Hackman & Wagemen 1995):

1 *Focus on work processes.* The quality of products and services ultimately goes back to the processes producing them. It is, therefore, not only necessary to specify a need for higher quality, but to train and coach employees to analyse work processes to improve them.

2 *Analyse and understand variability.* The main cause of quality problems, in TQM's view, is process or outcome variation. For example, due to printing technology limitations, a small variation in photo reproduction in a book, such as this, is expected (the quality of photos being reproduced is important). However, if the variation is unacceptable, causes must be sought (poorly calibrated printing presses, untrained operators or paper problems). Only when the causes of product or service variability are found can employees seek better quality.

3 *Manage by fact.* Data must be collected everywhere in the problem-solving cycle and from all organisation levels. Data help identify priority problems, trace causes, and choose and analyse a solution's impact. Although writers vary in emphasis, all rely on data collection, statistics, and solution testing before implementation.

4 *Emphasise continuous learning and improvement.* The idea that improvement is vital to long-term organisation health is important. Focusing on continuous improvement means employees always learn and try to do better.

TQM intervention techniques

To implement change principles, TQM argues for several techniques. Some common ones are:

The cost of quality analysis helps assess the potential cost savings of doing the work right in the first place. This means determining the costs of setting quality at a desired level (such as cost of avoiding quality problems) compared with the costs of producing at poor quality. The latter include appraisal costs (constant inspections), internal failure costs (scrap and rework), and external failure costs (customer complaints and returns). Cost of quality analysis helps find where quality changes give savings (Evans & Lindsay 1996).

Quality improvement teams, another TQM technique, are small employee groups solving specific quality and productivity problems, often with stated targets. Typically, the teams are responsible for work areas targeted by quality improvement efforts, and are cross-functional. Management or workers may identify problems, and groups compete then set improvement goals. A survey of manufacturing firms showed most used TQM, and about 90 percent of service firms using TQM had these teams (Gerber 1986; Conference Board 1991). Quality improvement teams (other names are used) are good for finding causes of poor quality and productivity, and correcting them. For example, Monsanto set up a team when Ford Motor had trouble with Saflex, a product for laminated windscreens. The material's dimensions changed before delivery. In two months, the team traced the problem to packaging, designed a prototype, tested it, and set up a new process (Goldbaum 1988).

Training is important to TQM. TQM's philosophy emphasises proper training and tools for workers to produce high quality and improve continuously. One survey (Conference Board 1991) shows that 92 percent of manufacturing and 75 percent of service companies using TQM provide training. Almost all senior and middle managers are trained, 80 percent of first-line supervisors and 50 percent of non-managerial employees. One survey found the most common areas of training (in descending order) were personal interaction skills, team

quality improvement teams

Small groups of employees who work on solving specific problems related to quality and improvement of productivity, often with stated targets for improvement

building, meeting conduct, statistical process control (explained later), supplier qualification training and benchmarking (Olian & Rynes 1991).

Benchmarking is identifying best practices and approaches by comparing productivity in one company with that of others inside and outside the industry (Weatherly 1992). Benchmarking was common as companies using quality management adopted the approach (Main 1992).

Collecting customer data systematically is another TQM technique. Since TQM aims to satisfy customers and gain loyalty, understanding customer needs and satisfaction is vital. Methods range from focus groups to surveys and complaint monitoring (Hinton & Schaeffer 1994; Rabbitt 1994). One survey found 93 percent of TQM companies thought customers would have higher expectations in the next three years (Conference Board 1994b).

Working with suppliers is also important to TQM. The benefits of partnering with suppliers were shown by Japanese car manufacturers. One benefit is product development. By involving suppliers, superior products and services can result. Other benefits include better financial results and productivity-based supply reliability (Conference Board 1994c).

Statistical process control is a method of taking periodic random samples during production to see if quality levels are met or correction is needed. A common TQM technique, it assesses quality during production so problems can be fixed rapidly. Since the focus is stopping poor output during the process, this is concurrent control. Most production processes have variations, so statistical process control tests to see when the variations fall outside acceptable quality limits. Variations beyond the range signal a production process malfunction.

benchmarking

Process of identifying best practices and approaches by comparing productivity in specific areas within one's own company with that of other organisations both within and outside the industry

statistical process control

Statistical technique using periodic random samples taken during actual production to determine whether acceptable quality levels are being met or production should be stopped for remedial action

TQM: Does it work?

It is hard to answer the question, 'Does TQM work?'. Many case studies and reports suggest TQM can provide major benefits (Goldbaum 1988; Houghton 1987; Griffiths 1994).

Sometimes, other changes occurring while TQM is being introduced make it difficult to separate out the effects attributable strictly to TQM (McCartney 1994). For example, companies starting TQM often increase employee involvement, emphasising greater employee participation in decisions and moving decisions as low as possible in the organisation (Lawler 1994; Hackman & Wagemen 1995). TQM companies also use teams (see Chapter 15) more than before, making it hard to assess effects of TQM over the use of teams.

Some companies have put much time and effort into TQM with no worthwhile benefits. In fact, in one case, a winner of the Malcolm Baldrige National Quality Award filed for bankruptcy two years later (Fuchsberg 1992; Liebman 1992).

A reason for TQM programs' poor results may be that too much is tried too quickly. It may be better to concentrate on a few significant changes then build on these successes rather than initiate many changes at once. Another reason for difficulties with TQM programs occurs when total quality is introduced with fanfare in an organisation, but the philosophy, principles and interventions are not taken seriously and/or properly implemented (Brown, Hitchcock & Willard 1994; Houlder 1994). Senior management may not realise the significant shift in organisational culture needed (Houlder 1994). Finally, companies may err by working to improve quality in unimportant areas and compromise quality in important ones (Greising 1994; Meigs & Meigs 1994).

As discussed before, quality is a strategic issue, and it is important that quality efforts be focused on improving customer satisfaction and loyalty (Houlder 1994; Naj 1993; Greising 1994). Overall, TQM efforts can be successful when set up properly, and it is a valuable tool. Quality is not the only issue: financial controls are used too.

FINANCIAL CONTROL

Suppose you are a top-level manager in an organisation. What financial controls could you use? Here, we review some basic financial control methods, including financial statements, ratio analysis and comparative financial analysis. We also consider how managers can avoid financial controls' pitfalls.

Financial statements

financial statement

Summary of a major aspect of an organisation's financial status

A **financial statement** summarises a major part of an organisation's financial status. Information in these statements is essential to maintaining organisational financial control. Two types of financial statements used by business are the balance sheet and income statement (Meigs & Meigs 1993). Financial statements are prepared at the end of reporting periods (quarterly and annually) though computers aid more frequent preparation.

balance sheet

Financial statement showing an organisation's assets and claims against those assets at a point in time

Balance sheet   A **balance sheet** shows an organisation's assets and claims on those assets at a point in time. A balance sheet for The Coca-Cola Company is shown in Table 16s1.1. You may think of a balance sheet as a financial 'snapshot' with two sections. The top half shows current assets, and the bottom half shows claims against assets (Baker 1987).

Assets, or organisation resources, fall into two categories: current and fixed. Current assets are cash and other assets usually converted to cash or used in a year. (Examples are marketable securities, accounts receivable or credit sales which have not been paid for yet; and inventory.) Fixed assets have a useful life of over a year (such as property, buildings and equipment). In Coca-Cola's case, the balance sheet shows the company has $5.4 billion in current assets, $4.3 billion in investments and other assets, $4.3 billion in fixed assets (after depreciation), and $944 million in goodwill and other intangible assets, for total assets of $15 billion.

The balance sheet's bottom half shows claims, both liabilities and shareholder' equity. Liabilities are claims by non-owners on company assets (in other words, non-owner debts, such as banks). Liabilities fall into two categories: current and long-term. Current liabilities are normally paid in a year (accounts payable, current company bills and short-term loans). Long-term liabilities are usually paid over a period of more than a year (such as bonds). Coca-Cola has current liabilities of $7.3 billion, $1.1 billion long-term debt, $966 million other liabilities, and $194 million of deferred income taxes, a total of $9.6 billion.

Shareholders' equity is claims by owners against assets. As expected, shareholders' equity equals company assets minus liabilities. Shareholders' equity is the organisation's net worth. It is shown on the balance sheet by stock and retained earnings (funds accumulated from organisation profits). In Coca-Cola's case, shareholders' equity is $5.4 billion. As shareholder equity is assets less liabilities, putting assets ($15 billion) on top and liabilities and shareholder equity ($9.6 billion plus $5.4 billion, a total of $15 billion) on the bottom, the sheet

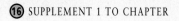

Table 16s.1 The Coca-Cola company and subsidiaries

Comparative balance sheet 31 December 1994 and 1995 (in millions of dollars)	1995	1994
Assets		
Current assets:		
Cash and cash equivalents	$1 167	$1 386
Marketable securities	148	145
Trade accounts receivable	1 695	1 470
Finance subsidiary receivable	55	55
Inventories	1 117	1 047
Paid expenses and other assets	1 268	1 102
Total current assets	5 450	5 205
Investments and other assets	4 311	3 928
Fixed assets:		
Land, buildings and improvements	2 177	2 035
Machinery, equipment and containers	4 480	4 122
Total fixed assets	6 657	6 157
Less: Accumulated depreciation	2 321	2 077
Net fixed assets	4 336	4 080
Goodwill and other intangible assets	944	660
Total assets	$15 041	$13 873
Liabilities and shareholders' equity		
Current liabilities:		
Accounts payable and accrued expenses	$ 2 894	$ 2 564
Loans and notes payable	2 371	2 048
Current maturity of long-term debt	552	35
Accrued taxes	1 531	1 530
Total current liabilities	7 348	6 177
Long-term debt	1 141	1 426
Other liabilities	966	855
Deferred income taxes	194	180
Total liabilities	$9 649	$8 638
Shareholders' equity:		
Common stock, $.25 par value	428	427
Capital surplus	1 291	1 173
Reinvested earnings	12 882	11 006
Unearned compensation related to outstanding restricted stock	(68)	(74)
Foreign currency translation adjustment	(424)	(272)
Unrealised gain on securities available for sale	82	48
	14 191	12 308
Less: treasury stock, at cost	8 799	7 073
Total shareholders' equity	5 392	5 235
Total liabilities and shareholders' equity	$15 041	$13 873

Source: The Coca-Cola Company 1995 Annual Report.

'balances'. Using a comparative sheet showing figures from one year to the next (as in Table 16s1.1), trends can be tracked in asset growth, liabilities and current net worth.

income statement

Financial statement summarising financial results of company operations over a specified time period, such as a quarter or a year

Income statement   A balance sheet looks at the organisation's overall financial worth at one point in time, while an **income statement** summarises the company's financial results over a specified period, a quarter or year. Income statements show revenues and expenses. Revenues are assets from selling goods and services. Expenses are costs of producing revenue (such as cost of goods sold, operating expenses, interest expense and taxes). The difference between the two represents profits or losses over a period of time and is referred to as the bottom line.

As with balance sheets, income statements for different time periods are often compared. A comparative statement for The Coca-Cola Company is shown in Table 16s1.2. The statement shows net income (revenues less expenses) is about $3 billion, up from about $2.5 billion.

Table 16s1.2   The Coca-Cola company and subsidiaries

Consolidated statement of income 31 December 1994 and 1995 (in millions of dollars)	1995	1994
Net operating revenue	$18 018	$16 181
Cost of goods sold	6 940	6 168
Gross profit	11 078	10 013
Selling, administrative, and general expenses	6 986	6 297
Operating income	4 092	3 716
Interest income	245	181
Interest expense	272	199
Equity income	169	134
Other income (deductions)—net	20	(104)
Gain on issuance of stock by Coca-Cola Amatil	74	—
Income before taxes	4 328	3 728
Income taxes	1 342	1 174
Net income	$ 2 986	$ 2 554

Source: The Coca-Cola Company 1995 Annual Report.

Ratio analysis

ratio analysis

Process of determining and evaluating financial ratios

In assessing financial data's significance, managers may use **ratio analysis**, the process of determining and evaluating financial ratios (Meigs & Meigs 1993). A ratio is a measure of one variable relative to another, shown as a percentage or a rate. Ratios are meaningful only in comparison with other information. As they are often compared to industry data, ratios help understand company performance relative to that of competitors and help track performance over time. Four financial ratios are important to managerial control: liquidity, asset management, debt management and profitability. Formulas and data for The Coca-Cola Company for the four ratios are shown in Table 16s1.3.

Table 16s1.3 Ratio analysis for the Coca-Cola company and its subsidiaries

Ratio	Formula		Calculation		Current year	Industry averages
Liquidity ratios						
Current ratio	Current assets		5 450			
	Current liabilities	=	7 348	=	.74x	.90x
Asset management ratios						
Inventory turnover	Cost of goods sold		6 940			
	Inventory	=	1 117	=	6.2	6.5
Debt management ratios						
Debt ratio	Total liabilities		9 649			
	Total assets	=	15 041	=	64.2%	82.2%
Profitability ratios						
Net profit margin	Net income		2 986			
	Net sales*	=	18 018	=	16.6%	7.7%
Return on investment	Net income		2 986			
	Total assets	=	15 041	=	19.8%	6.4%

Source: The Coca-Cola Company 1995 Annual Report & Troy (1995).

*Coca-Cola refers to net sales as net operating revenue in its financial statements.

Liquidity ratios   Liquidity ratios are ratios measuring the degree to which an organisation's current assets can pay current liabilities (current debt obligations). A major liquidity ratio is current ratio, or the company's ability to meet short-term creditors' claims by current assets. The current ratio in Table 16s1.3 shows Coca-Cola has $0.74 in current assets for every dollar in current liabilities. Coca-Cola's ratio is below the industry average of $0.90 for large beverage companies, but given their long-term success, this may mean good use of funds creating shareholder value.

Asset management ratios   Asset management ratios (or activity ratios) measure the effectiveness of an organisation's asset management. One asset management ratio is inventory turnover.

Inventory turnover measures how well inventory is managed. Low turnover may mean excess or obsolete inventory. High turnover means effective inventory handling relative to sales patterns, because less money is tied up in inventory waiting to be sold. An inventory turnover ratio can be too high. This would occur if sales are lost when items ordered were not in stock. Coca-Cola's inventory turnover of 6.2 (shown in Table 16s1.3) is similar to the industry average of 6.5.

Debt management ratios   Debt management ratios (or leverage ratios) assess how much an organisation uses debt to finance investments, as well as how well it can meet long-term obligations. The more debt finances needs, the more must be committed for interest and

---

liquidity ratios

Financial ratios measuring the degree to which an organisation's current assets are adequate to pay current liabilities (current debt obligations)

asset management ratios

Financial ratios measuring how effectively an organisation manages its assets management

debt management ratios

Financial ratios assessing the extent to which an organisation uses debt to finance investments, as well management as the degree to which it is able to meet its long-term obligations repaying principal. As debts increase, so does the risk the organisation may not meet its debts and become bankrupt. Thus an important ratio is the debt ratio, the measure of total asset percentage financed by debt (including current liabilities). The higher the percentage, the more organisation assets come from creditors not owners. Coca-Cola's debt ratio of 64.2 percent (shown in Table 16s1.3) shows creditors have supplied about 64 cents in every dollar of assets, and the industry average is 82.2 percent. The lower-than-average debt ratio may be good if they need to take on more debt. Future creditors may provide favourable loans due to the lower risk of the lower debt ratio.

profitability ratios

Financial ratios helping measure management's ability to control expenses and earn profits by use of organisational resources

Profitability ratios   **Profitability ratios** measure expense control and earnings through organisational resources (Meigs & Meigs 1993). Two profitability ratios are net profit margin and return on investment.

The net profit margin shows how much of each sales dollar is left after deducting all expenses. In Coca-Cola Company's case, net profit margin (shown in Table 16s1.3) is 16.6 percent. According to this, Coke earns about 16½ cents on every sales dollar, much better than the industry average of 7.7 percent. Comparatively, Coca-Cola seems to be expanding sales or managing expenses, or both.

The return on investment, or ROI (also called return on assets), measures management's overall effectiveness in gaining profits from its assets. The ROI for Coca-Cola (shown in Table 16s1.3) is 19.8 percent. Given an industry average of 6.4 percent, Coke's ROI is very good. The ratio suggests the company makes good investment decisions and ensures that benefits from those investments are gained.

Top managers in most companies make strong use of financial controls.

Comparative financial analysis

Financial statements and ratios are useful in comparing data against a standard. Managers must explain variances (positive and negative) so top-level executives can see why variances occur and their implications. The three standards managers use most often to compare data are management goals, historical standards and industry standards.

Management financial goals are set during planning. Then they form standards to compare actual achievements against during the control process. In The Coca-Cola Company, top management sets goals higher than industry averages on most ratios shown in Table 16s1.3, and for the period shown, they have exceeded industry averages on most measures (*Fortune* 1995).

In contrast to management goals, which project future standards, historical financial standards are data from past statements or ratios used to compare the current financial performance. The balance sheet and income statement for The Coca-Cola Company illustrate historical standard use as they include the previous year's data for comparison.

Another means of comparison is using industry financial standards, data based on industry averages. Financial ratios for many industries are available. The discussion of The Coca-Cola Company's financial ratios and data in Table 16s1.3 shows use of industry standards.

Financial controls can help top management, but six pitfalls can reduce their value. These are summarised in Table 16s1.4 (Cowen & Middaugh 1988). Managers need to carefully consider how they set up and use financial controls to benefit.

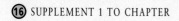

Table 16s1.4   Six potential financial control pitfalls

1. Failing to tailor financial controls to specific organisation requirements
2. Neglecting to link financial controls to the strategic planning process
3. Instituting controls which send mixed messages about desired behaviours
4. Allowing financial controls to stifle innovation and creativity
5. Forcing the same financial controls on subunits with different control requirements
6. Implementing financial controls that are too sophisticated for organisational needs

Source: Cowen & Middaugh (1988).

BUDGETARY CONTROL

While financial controls are vital to top management, budgetary controls are important to middle managers. Lower-level managers in turn use budgets to track their own unit's progress. **Budgeting** is the process of stating in quantitative terms, normally dollars, planned organisational activities for a given time period. Budgets, the quantitative statements coming from the budgeting process, may include projected income, expenditures and profits. Budgets are helpful as they translate diverse activities and outcomes into a common measure, such as dollars.

Budgets are prepared for the whole organisation, and for subunits (divisions and departments). For budgetary purposes, organisations call subunits responsibility centres.

Responsibility centres

A **responsibility centre** is a subunit with a manager responsible for achieving one or more goals (Maciariello 1984). Organisations can be seen as a hierarchy of responsibility centres, with small subunits at the bottom and large ones at the top. For example, a Telstra phone store and Telstra's marketing division are different levels of responsibility centre. There are five main responsibility centre types: standard cost, discretionary expense, revenue, profit and investment. A unit's particular designation for budgetary purposes depends on how much it controls major elements, such as revenues and expenses, that support profits and return on investment.

Standard cost centres   A **standard cost centre** is a responsibility centre where budgetary outcomes depend on achieving goals by operating within standard cost constraints. Because standard costs are set by engineering methods, this type of centre is also an engineered expense centre. With a standard cost centre, managers must control input costs (e.g. labour, raw materials) so predetermined standards are not exceeded (Waldman 1989; Bohn 1994). A standard cost centre is appropriate only if (1) cost standards of producing a product or service can be estimated fairly accurately and (2) the unit cannot be held responsible for profit levels as it has no significant control over other expenses and/or revenues.

Discretionary expense centres   A **discretionary expense centre** is a responsibility centre where budgetary outcomes are based on achieving goals by operating within expense limits

budgeting

Process of stating in quantitative terms, usually dollars, planned organisational activities for a given period of time

responsibility centre

Subunit headed by a manager responsible for achieving one or more goals

standard cost centre

Responsibility centre whose budgetary outcomes depend on achieving its goals by operating within standard cost constraints

discretionary expense centre

Responsibility centre whose budgetary outcomes are based on achieving its goals by operating within predetermined expense constraints set through managerial judgment or discretion set by managerial judgment or discretion. Discretionary expense centres are departments such as research and development, public relations, human resources and legal units, where it is hard to set standard costs or measure the direct profit impact of a unit's efforts.

revenue centre

Responsibility centre whose budgetary outcomes are measured primarily by its ability to generate a specified revenue level

Revenue centres   A **revenue centre** is a responsibility centre where budgetary outcomes are measured by its ability to generate set revenue levels. Revenue centres include sales and marketing, judged on sales (and revenues) generated in relation to resources allocated (Saporito 1988). Revenue centres are used when the unit is responsible for revenues but has no control over costs of a product or service, which makes it hard for them to be responsible for profit levels.

profit centre

Responsibility centre whose budgetary outcomes are measured by difference between revenues and costs—in other words, profits

Profit centres   A **profit centre** is a responsibility centre where budgetary outcomes are measured by the difference between revenues and costs—in other words, profits. Profit centres are appropriate only when the unit controls both costs and revenues, since these set profit levels (Olins & Waples 1996). The whole organisation is also a profit centre.

investment centre

Responsibility centre whose budgetary outcomes are based on return on investment

Investment centres   An **investment centre** is a responsibility centre where budgetary outcomes are based on return on investment. The ROI ratio is not just revenues, but also costs and assets used making the profit. Thus investment centres ensure managers focus on making good investment decisions in facilities and other assets. Of course, this type of centre works best if the unit has some control over investment decisions, as well as over both revenues and expenses (Serman 1989).

Uses of responsibility centres   The uses of responsibility centres depends on the organisation's structure (see Chapter 9). Standard cost, discretionary expense, and revenue centres are more common in functional organisations and in functional units in matrix designs. Manufacturing or production units are usually standard cost centres, while accounting, finance and human resources are usually discretionary expense centres. Sales or marketing units are normally revenue centres.

In contrast, with a divisional organisation design, profit centres can be used because large structural divisions usually have control over both expenses and revenues associated with profits. Of course, within divisions, departments may operate as other types of responsibility centres. Companies operating divisions as separate, autonomous businesses use investment centres for budgetary purposes.

Types of budgets

For budgetary control, organisations have a master budget including other budgets which together summarise the organisation's planned activities. Two major budget types typically included in the master budget are operating and capital expenditures budgets (Meigs & Meigs 1993).

operating budget

Statement that presents the financial plan for each responsibility centre during the budget period and reflects operating activities involving revenues and expenses

Operating budgets   An **operating budget** presents the financial plan for each responsibility centre during the budget period and reflects operating activities involving revenues and expenses (Maciariello 1984; Baker 1987). The operating budget lets management assess profit levels after looking at anticipated revenues and expenses across responsibility centres. If profits are low, managers can plan to raise revenues (having a marketing promotion to increase sales) and/or reduce expenses (cutting proposed travel expenditures or delaying non-essential equipment purchase).

Capital expenditures budgets A **capital expenditures budget** is a plan for acquisition or divestiture of major fixed assets, such as land, buildings or equipment. These are capital investments. As these take a long time to be paid for and companies may borrow to cover investments, they are significant organisational decisions. As a result, top-level managers are usually heavily involved, and the decision process often includes the board of directors.

Impacts of the budgeting process

Depending on their use, budgets can positively or negatively impact on managerial behaviour. On the positive side, budgets can keep managers up to date on organisational activities, enhance inter-unit co-ordination, and ensure future investments. They also provide standards for evaluating managers, and a way to adjust when corrective action is needed. Budgets can also have negative effects, if used rigidly and managers are concerned about fair treatment. Poorly run budgetary processes may result in negative managerial behaviours. These include politicking to raise budget allocations, overstating needs to increase allocations, and abandoning possible innovations because the fight for resources is too hard (Irvine 1970; Tosi 1974).

INVENTORY CONTROL

Another major control system type is inventory control. **Inventory** is the stock of materials used for production or to satisfy customer demand. There are three major inventory types: raw materials, work in process and finished goods (Schroeder 1989; Dilworth 1993).

Raw materials inventory is the parts, ingredients and other inputs to production or service. For example, McDonald's raw materials inventory has hamburgers, cheese slices, buns, potatoes and soft-drink syrup. Raw materials inventory at a bicycle factory includes chains, sprockets, handlebars and seats.

Work-in-process inventory is the items being made into a final product or service. For McDonald's, work-in-process inventory includes hamburgers being assembled, and syrup and soda water being mixed to make a soft drink. A bicycle frame with handlebars and seat attached would be work in process at a bicycle factory.

Finished-goods inventory is items produced and awaiting sale or transit to a customer. At McDonald's, finished-goods inventory includes hamburgers on the warmer. Bicycles are finished-goods inventory at a bicycle factory. Organisations largely providing services, not products, such as hospitals, beauty salons or accounting firms, do not have finished-goods inventory, as they cannot stockpile finished goods (e.g. operations, haircuts and audits).

Significance of inventory

Inventory serves several major organisational purposes (Schroeder 1989; Dilworth 1993). For one, it helps deal with uncertainties in supply and demand. For example, having extra raw

capital expenditures budget

Plan for acquisition or divestiture of major fixed assets, such as land, buildings or equipment

inventory
Stock of materials used to facilitate production or to satisfy customer demand

raw materials inventory
Stock of parts, ingredients and other basic inputs to a production or service process

work-in-process inventory
Stock of items currently being transformed into a final product or service

finished-goods inventory
Stock of items produced and awaiting sale or transit to a customer inventory

materials may avoid shortages holding up a production process. Having extra finished-goods inventory means customers can be better served. Inventory also enables more economic purchases, since materials may be cheaper in large amounts. Finally, inventory can help deal with anticipated changes to demand or supply, such as seasonal variations or expected shortage. However, predicting changes requires caution (Rebello & Burrows 1996).

Costs of inventory

item cost

Price of an inventory item

ordering cost

Expenses of placing an order (paperwork, postage and time)

carrying, or holding, cost

Expenses associated with keeping an item on hand (storage, insurance, theft, breakage)

stockout cost

Economic consequences of running out of stock (loss of customer goodwill and sales)

economic order quantity (EOQ)

Inventory control method developed to minimise ordering plus holding costs, while avoiding stockout costs

reorder point (ROP)

Inventory level at which a new order should be placed

Inventory is important to organisations as it is costly. For one thing, there is **item cost**, the item's price (cost of handlebars or seats). Then there is **ordering cost**, the expense of placing an order (paperwork, postage and time). There is also **carrying, or holding, cost**, the expense of keeping an item available (storage, insurance, theft, breakage). Finally, there is **stockout cost**, the economic impact of running out of stock. Stockout costs include lost customer goodwill and sales because the item is unavailable (Rebello & Burrows 1996). Inventory control minimises inventory costs (including stockout costs). An approach to minimising these costs is the use of the inventory method called economic order quantity.

Economic order quantity

Economic order quantity (EOQ) is an inventory control method used to minimise ordering and holding costs, and avoid stockout costs. The method uses an equation including annual demand (D), ordering costs (O), and holding costs (H). Assume a bicycle manufacturer estimates annual demand of 1470 bicycle frames for manufacturing, ordering costs at $10 per order, and holding costs of $6 per unit per year. Putting these into the equation shows economic order quantity as 70 frames:

$$\text{EOQ} = \sqrt{\frac{2DO}{H}} = \sqrt{\frac{2(1470)(10)}{6}} = 70$$

The EOQ equation helps managers decide what to order, but they also need to know the **reorder point (ROP)**, the inventory level a new order should be placed at. To determine reorder point, managers estimate *lead time (L)*, time from ordering to receiving. In the case of the bicycle manufacturer, lead time for getting frames from a producer is seven days. In the ROP equation, lead time is multiplied by average daily demand (annual demand ÷ 365 days). Conceptually, frames should be ordered when just enough frames are on hand to making bicycles until the new frames arrive. Substituting data for the bicycle manufacturer into the ROP equation shows an order should be placed when stock reaches 29:

$$\text{ROP} = (L)\frac{D}{365} = (7)\frac{1470}{365} = 28.19, \text{ or } 29 \text{ (rounded)}$$

The EOQ inventory control system needs continuous inventory monitoring, is shown in Figure 16s1.3. Although the assumption is that demand and unit costs are constant, demand may vary and suppliers may give discounts and special offers. Still, EOQ provides some help. (We consider more sophisticated inventory issues in Supplement 2.) In using EOQ, an organisation often adds fluctuation, or safety, stock. This is kept on hand for unforeseen events like quality problems or reorder delays (McLeavey & Narasimhan 1985). Alternatively, companies may approach inventory control by using 'just-in-time' methods.

Fig. 16s1.3   EOQ inventory control system

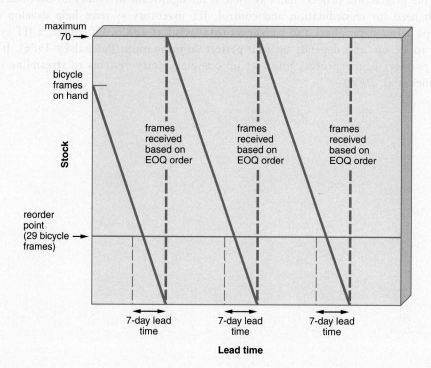

Just-in-time inventory control

Just-in-time (JIT) inventory control means materials arrive as needed (Schroeder 1989). The JIT inventory approach is part of a broader JIT philosophy of manufacturing. Accordingly, organisations must work to eliminate all sources of waste, including non-value-adding activities, by having the right part at the right place at the right time. Applying JIT to inventory means having materials arrive as needed, not keeping backup in inventory. This means an organisation can reduce holding costs and save space used by inventory waiting in the production area (Burck 1982). In its focus on waste avoidance, JIT's philosophy calls for using workers' full capabilities, giving them more responsibility for production processes, and making them part of ongoing efforts to improve the production process.

For inventory handling, JIT uses **Kanban** (Japanese for 'card' or 'signal'), a simple parts-movement system using cards and containers to pull parts from one work centre to another. With Kanban, workstations along the production process are given containers and produce enough to fill them. They produce again when they receive a card and an empty container from the next workstation, showing more will be needed. If the process stops due to machine breakdowns or quality problems, all workstations in the process produce only until their

just-in-time (JIT) inventory control

Approach to inventory control emphasising having materials arrive just as needed in the production process

Kanban

Simple parts-movement system depending on cards and containers to pull parts from one work centre to another

containers fill and then stop. The system means it is much simpler to identify sources of variation in production (Jones et al. 2000)

With a JIT system, high quality is vital. As suppliers deliver materials or various internal work centres make them just before they're needed, items must be perfect. Otherwise, there is waste and the production process halts as there is no significant inventory to cover. Because of the high need for co-ordination and control, JIT inventory systems help develop close relationships between suppliers and customers (Mangelsdorf 1989). Of course, a JIT system takes time to set up, and depends on near-perfect co-ordination (Pulchalsky 1996). It also means all partners in the process must set up complementary systems to streamline interactions (Jones et al. 2000)

Operations Management

Operations management is part of the controlling function because emphasis is on regulating the productive processes critical to reach organisational goals. In looking at operations management, we first explore its basic nature, and examine the productivity link. We next see how operations management can link to overall organisation strategy. We then consider other operations management aspects, such as operating systems, facilities, re-engineering and use of other process technology in promoting innovation. Finally, we look at major steps in improving operations management productivity.

DEFINING OPERATIONS MANAGEMENT

Operations management is management of productive processes converting inputs into goods and services (Chase & Aquilano 1992). Because of its manufacturing association, operations management is also called production-operations management. Recently, the term 'production' is being dropped in favour of 'operations management', which has less manufacturing connotation. The operations management function is carried out by the part of the organisation that produces the primary goods and services.

In a manufacturing organisation the operations management function includes plant managers and all other managers working in the factories (e.g. production managers, inventory control managers, quality assurance managers and line supervisors). In an organisation with a corporate level, operations include manufacturing or operations senior managers, with related corporate operations staff (those primarily concerned with production, inventory, quality, facilities and equipment).

In a service industry such as a hotel, the operations management function includes hotel managers (e.g. housekeeping, food and beverage and general management). Again, if a corporate level exists, operations comprise managers and staff at that level directly involved in actually running hotels (as opposed to managers from other functions, such as marketing and finance). Whether the organisation produces a service, a product, or both, operations managers must focus on productivity.

The productivity–operations management linkage

Productivity is an efficiency concept relating the ratio of outputs to inputs in a productive process (Mahoney 1988). In Chapter 1, we discussed organisational effectiveness and efficiency in performance. Effectiveness is the extent to which performance achieves organisational goals. In contrast, efficiency is resources (inputs) used achieving outcomes (outputs). Productivity is

operations management

Management of productive processes converting inputs into goods and services

productivity

Efficiency concept gauging the ratio of outputs relative to inputs into a production process assessing organisational performance efficiency—the ratio of outputs to inputs. As such, productivity helps managers track progress to more efficient resource use in production of goods and services.

Organisational productivity is often measured by this equation:

$$\text{Productivity} = \frac{\text{goods and services produced (outputs)}}{\text{labour + capital + energy + technology + materials (inputs)}}$$

total-factor productivity

Productivity approach considering all inputs involved in producing outputs

This approach considers all inputs in producing outputs and is called **total-factor productivity**. Managers also use **partial-factor productivity**, an approach considering total output relative to a specific input, such as labour. For example:

$$\text{Productivity} = \frac{\text{goods and services produced (outputs)}}{\text{labour hours (labour input)}}$$

partial-factor productivity

Productivity approach considering the total output relative to a specific input, such as labour

Managers develop particular ratios to assess productivity from specific outputs and inputs. Examples include sales per square metre of floor space, profit per sales dollar, return on investment, claims processed per employee, and tests completed per dollar of labour cost.

While expenses per sales are one measure, they show why managers must consider productivity. If competitors get more output (dollars of sales) from fewer inputs (expenses), they are more profitable and have more to improve their competitive position. Manufacturing and service organisations differ in their influences over productivity.

Manufacturing versus service organisations

Manufacturing and service organisations differ (Schroeder 1993). Manufacturing organisations transform inputs into tangible goods (soft drinks, cars or VCRs). Products can be stored (at least somewhat), and the ultimate customer is not present during the process. So, manufacturing can be central, and products shipped to customers. In addition, wasted capacity can be avoided in slack periods by using capacity to produce inventory before future sales. Manufacturing organisations can control when and how they will run, and organise to maximise productivity.

Service organisations transform inputs into intangible outcomes (education, health care or transportation). These are produced and consumed almost simultaneously, cannot be stored, and involve the customer. For example, in a service organisation you attend a class, see a doctor, visit a bank, catch a flight or have a haircut. You participate in all of these to receive the service, and none can be stored. Unlike manufacturing, service organisations cannot use idle capacity to produce stored inventory, and may have dispersed operations close to customers, since services cannot be stored and shipped. Compared to manufacturing, service organisations have less control over operations, as they depend on customer volume and needs, which are hard to determine in advance.

As shown in Figure 16s2.1, some organisations (factories, farms and mines) produce largely goods. Others (consulting firms, hospitals or government agencies) produce largely services. Of course, many organisations provide a combination of goods and services. For example, as well as cars, Ford and General Motors Holden provide services such as financing, insurance and repairs. Similarly, at a Hungry Jack's/Burger King outlet, you get services in order taking, filling and table availability, and a product in the shape of a cheeseburger.

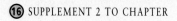

Fig. 16s2.1   Continuum of goods and services

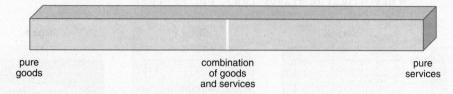

pure
goods

combination
of goods
and services

pure
services

Organisations can be classified by degree of service provided by measuring percentage of production process time spent in contact with customers (Chase 1978; Chase & Aquilano 1992). A pure goods producer has zero contact with end customers, and a pure service producer 100 percent. High customer contact lowers organisational efficiency and productivity, since arrival patterns vary and may need customised service. For example, lines are slower at Hungry Jack's/Burger King when non-standard items are ordered, such as a Whopper without pickles.

The operations management process

In transforming inputs into goods and services, operations management involves several elements (see Fig. 16s2.2). One is *operations strategy*, operations management's role in formulating and implementing strategies to reach organisational goals (see Chapter 7). Another is *operating systems*, methods to achieve efficiency and effectiveness in manufacturing and service operations. A third is *facilities*, land, buildings, equipment and other physical assets affecting the organisation's ability to deliver goods and services. Finally, *process technology*, used to transform inputs into goods and services, is significant to operations management. We consider each in the next sections.

Fig. 16s2.2 Operations management process

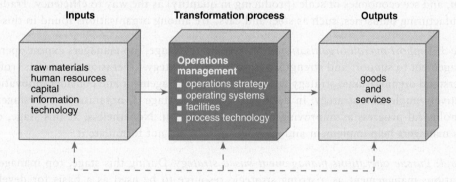

Inputs

Transformation process

Outputs

raw materials
human resources
capital
information
technology

**Operations
management**
■ operations strategy
■ operating systems
■ facilities
■ process technology

goods
and
services

FORMULATING OPERATIONS STRATEGY

Operations management has different roles in determining strategy, depending on the stage of an organisation's strategic role (Wheelwright & Hayes 1985). The four stages are shown in Figure 16s2.3.

Fig. 16s2.3 Stages in operations management strategic role (based on
Wheelwright & Hayes 1985, pp. 99–109)

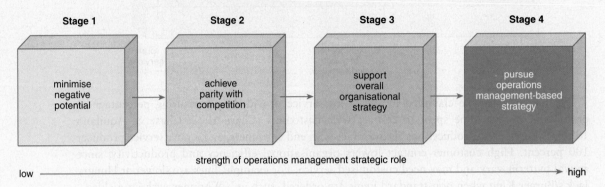

Stage 1: Minimise negative potential. In this stage, top managers try to neutralise negative impacts of internal organisation operations. This is because they see operations management as neutral, or as not affecting organisational competitive success positively. So they use detailed measures and controls to ensure the function does not go too far off track before correcting. Generally, top managers minimise involvement in operations. However, they are concerned with major investment decisions (such as new facilities or important equipment purchases) through capital budgeting. Stage 1 is typical of many consumer-products and service companies.

Stage 2: Achieve parity with competition. In this stage, top managers work to have operations management stay even with competitors. Organisations work to maintain equality by adopting industry practices on workforce issues, equipment purchases and capacity upgrades. Typically, they see new equipment and facility investments as good to get ahead of the competition, and see economies of scale (producing in quantity) as the way to efficiency. Traditional manufacturing industries, such as steel and cars, are among organisations found in this stage.

Stage 3: Support overall organisational strategy. In this stage, top managers expect operations management to support and strengthen organisation strategy. Operations managers' role is to understand organisational strategy developed by top management and consider innovations to effectively implement strategy. In contrast to those at stage 2, organisations at stage 3 see technological progress as improving competitive position. Nonetheless, at this stage, operations managers help implement and support strategy but not formulate it.

Stage 4: Pursue operations management-based strategy. During this stage, top managers see operations management as a strong strategic resource to be used as a basis for developing strategy. Therefore, they include operations managers in strategy development and formulate one largely on operations capabilities. Operations managers try to anticipate potential technological advances affecting operations, and to gain internal expertise well before implications are obvious. At this stage, organisations try to use innovation to make small strategic jumps before competitors. Stage 4 is characteristic of all world-class manufacturers or service providers. These companies typically emphasise their own innovations, particularly improving processes in producing goods and services.

DEVELOPING AND IMPLEMENTING OPERATING SYSTEMS

Applying operations strategy effectively requires the design and implementation of well-set-up operating systems, major methods to achieve efficiency and effectiveness. Primary operating systems in operations management are forecasting, capacity planning, aggregate-production planning, scheduling, materials-requirements planning, and purchasing (see Fig. 16s2.4). In this section, we consider aspects of service delivery systems. Quality control, important in operations management, is discussed more in Chapter 17.

Forecasting

Forecasting is predicting future conditions and events affecting an organisation's business. Forecasting methods are set out in Supplement 1 to Chapter 5.

For operations management purposes, forecasting tries to predict demand for goods or services. Demand forecasts can be short- to long-term and depend on quantitative and judgmental methods. Short-term forecasts (up to a year, but often between one and three months) are important as they affect short-run conditions, such as production schedules and material availability (Barrett & Kistka 1987). Forecasting intermediate-term (one to five years) or long-term (five years or more) demand impacts on expansion decisions, such as getting important equipment and new facilities.

After making demand forecasts, managers use information in two ways. As shown in Figure 16s2.4, demand forecasts influence capacity and aggregate-production planning. We consider capacity planning first.

Capacity planning

Capacity planning is deciding the people, machines and physical resources, such as buildings, needed to meet production goals (Schroeder 1993). Capacity is a unit's maximum output in a time period. For example, a car wash can handle so many cars an hour due to its physical limits. Common capacity measures by organisation type are shown in Table 16s2.1.

capacity planning

Process of determining people, machines and major physical resources, such as buildings, necessary to meet production objectives of the organisation

Table 16s2.1 Measures of capacity according to type of organisation

Type of organisation	Capacity measure
Airline	Available seat-kilometres
Brewery	Kegs of beer
University	Classes
Restaurant	Seats and tables
Power company	Megawatts of electricity
Cannery	Tonnes of food
Retail store	Square metres of selling space
Car repair shop	Service bays

Fig. 16s2.4   Major systems used in operations management

Time horizons   Capacity planning has three time horizons: long-, medium-, and short-range. Each involves different capacity issues (Monks 1987; Schroeder 1993).

Long-range capacity planning focuses on human, physical and financial resources to reach long-term organisational goals. As increasing long-term capacity needs capital expenditures for facilities and employment, decisions are top management's.

Medium-range capacity planning gives information on facility capacities, as well as ways to make some intermediate and short-term adjustments. These include employee hiring and laying off, overtime use and inventory increases.

Short-range capacity planning works to ensure current major facility capacity is used effectively in the master production schedule context. Planning in this horizon uses **capacity-requirements planning** to determine needed personnel and equipment to meet short-term production objectives (see Fig. 16s2.4).

Aggregate-production planning

Short-term demand forecasts, and intermediate- and short-range capacity planning, influence aggregate-production planning (Monks 1987; Dilworth 1993). **Aggregate-production planning** is planning how to match supply and product or service demand over about a year (see Fig. 16s2.4). Although generally spanning a year, the plan is revised, perhaps monthly. Aggregate planning is attainment of a balance between market demand and organisation capacity. It is called 'aggregate' because production plans are given in output unit, such as number of cars, tonnes of steel, or seat-kilometres, not car models, specific steel products or specific airline flight.

Aggregate planning assumes two things. First, facility capacity, such as plants, retail outlets, major equipment, cannot be changed quickly. Second, short- and intermediate-term demands change due to uncertainty, seasonal variation or other market factors. As a result, operations managers must plan to meet changing demand given fixed facility capacity.

Operations managers can use many approaches to satisfy short- and intermediate-term varying demand. These are summarised in Table 16s2.2.

Table 16s2.2   Major approaches to coping with fluctuating demand

Major approach	Related issues
Pay overtime	Expensive, but cheaper than hiring extra workers who are idle some of the time
Hire temporary workers	Helpful for predictable demand increases of some duration; may be hard to obtain necessary skills
Hire part-time workers	May be more helpful to address demand peaks in service than in manufacturing
Develop multiskilled staff	May involve considerable time and expense, but allows workers to help out where needed
Build inventory	May be good utilisation for slow periods; risks inventory becoming obsolete; increases holding costs; not usually appropriate for service
Take back orders; have customer returns policy	Customers may be dissatisfied and/or go to a competitor; may be effective if time frame is reasonable
Subcontract work to vendors	Expensive; less control over quality
Offer premiums/discounts for customer flexibility	Provide discounts for orders/service during slow periods or charge less for service flexibility (e.g. surface mail)

capacity-requirements planning

Technique for determining what personnel and equipment are needed to meet short-term production objectives

aggregate-production planning

Process of planning how to match supply with product or service demand over a time horizon of about one year

Scheduling

Aggregate planning is the basis for the next step, creating a master production schedule (see Fig. 16s2.4). The **master production schedule (MPS)** translates an aggregate plan into a formal production plan for specific products or services and capacity needs over a set period. Master scheduling means trial-and-error work and begins with a tentative schedule which is then revised.

Time horizon   A master schedule's time horizon ranges from a few weeks to a year or more, depending on product or service characteristics and lead times for sourcing materials. Within a master schedule, various activities are often broken down on a weekly basis. Some organisations use weekly intervals for 13 weeks (a quarter) and then monthly intervals.

MPS advantages   Using a master production schedule is useful. For one, it helps managers assess different schedules. Many computerised production and inventory control systems let managers simulate proposed production schedules. The simulation allows planners to determine materials lead times and delivery dates coming from various schedules. Another advantage of the process is that it helps determine materials required. It does so by giving specific information on products or services to be produced. This ensures materials are purchased and delivered to meet scheduled production. Still another advantage is that MPS gives specific information on immediate needs (such as labour and equipment resources) used in capacity-requirements planning (see Fig. 16s2.4). If needs exceed available capacity, schedule adjustments, such as delaying item or service production, may be needed. On the other hand, capacity underutilisation may mean producing some items ahead of schedule or generating greater demand (through a special promotion). Finally, a master schedule helps share relevant marketing information (such as customer deliveries), inventory and human resource matters (such as staffing needs).

Materials-requirements planning

While master schedule development is important, production cannot occur unless materials needed are in place at the right time for the job. One way to manage these issues is use of materials-requirements planning, which need to be closely co-ordinated with the master production schedule (see Fig. 16s2.4). **Materials-requirements planning (MRP)** is a computer-based inventory system projecting needed materials for goods and services listed in the master schedule and starting actions for acquiring materials.

MRP systems can handle different inventory types, but are best for **dependent-demand inventory**, or raw materials, components and subassemblies for production of an end product or service. For example, if a business makes wheelbarrows, components such as tyres, wheels and axles are dependent-demand inventory items used in products (wheelbarrows), not end products themselves. In other words, inventory demand for these is dependent on need for end products. In contrast, **independent-demand inventory** is end products, parts for repairs, and other items where demand is tied to market issues. MRP systems are common in manufacturing and they are just beginning to be applied in service organisations. They can yield productivity enhancements in areas such as restaurants, hotels, legal offices and health care.

Inputs to MRP systems   MRP systems use three inputs: a master production schedule, bill-of-materials information, and inventory status information. The MRP system gets information on products to be made from the master production schedule.

The system then consults a bill of materials for each product and model to determine needed materials. A **bill of materials (BOM)** lists all components, including partially assembled pieces and basic parts, that make an end product. The BOM usually has part numbers and quantities needed per unit of product. It is often hierarchically arranged to determine basic elements as well as subassemblies. For example, Figure 16s2.5 shows a product structure tree with BOM levels for a wheelbarrow. As the figure indicates, bars and grips at level 2 are assembled to make the handle assembly in level 1. Similarly, the tyre at level 3 (the most basic) and axle, bearings, and wheel at level 2 make up the level 1 wheel assembly. The top level (0) shows the end product. Bill-of-materials information is kept in computer files for access by the MRP system so needed materials for a proposed master schedule can be quickly found. The more levels in a BOM, the more an MRP system is needed to help manage production materials (Finch & Cox 1988). The MRP system uses computerised inventory information to set levels of materials on hand, schedule receipts of materials ordered, and orders released.

In service applications, a bill of activities replaces the bill of materials. Combined with a master production schedule and inventory data, the bill of activities determines activities and

bill of materials (BOM)

Listing of all components, including partially assembled pieces and basic parts, making up an end product.

Fig. 16s2.5   **Bill-of-materials levels for a wheelbarrow (reprinted from Monks 1987, p. 444)**

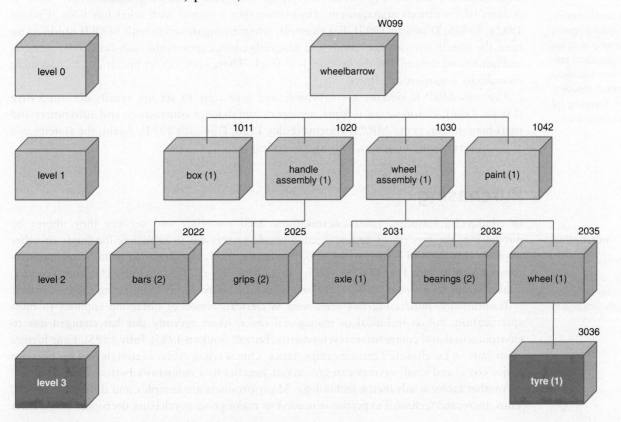

personnel needed to produce services. If materials are important, a bill of materials may be used. In an application of MRP at an electricity company, connection requests are put into a computer setting out a detailed list of labour, materials and tasks. These are then combined to check capacity. Ultimately, crews are given work orders from the system. They report back to it as work is completed (Schroeder 1993).

Benefits from MRP systems   MRP systems provide four outputs. First, the system triggers material orders. Orders go to purchasing or internal departments for needed components. Second, the system provides data to master production schedulers, identifying difficulties getting materials interfering with the master schedule. Third, it provides data to those managing capacity planning. Then they make short-run changes, move equipment and add people (through capacity-requirements planning) or longer-run changes from trends. Fourth, the system provides data on costs, quality and supplier activity.

MRP systems operate differently from the just-in-time (JIT) approach (Chapter 17). Like JIT, MRP reduces inventory costs and keeps the production line supplied with materials. However, MRP does so by planning and using lead times to order as needed on the basis of master production schedules (with a small amount of stock to allow for changes).

Manufacturing-resource planning   Given the success of materials-requirements planning systems, some organisations have expanded MRP. **Manufacturing-resource planning (MRP II)**, a computer-based system, combines MRP's production planning and control activities with financial, accounting, personnel, engineering and marketing information. MRP II systems tie operations management information into a system with other functions (Chopra 1982a, 1982b; Dilworth 1993). For example, when an organisation with MRP II produces an item, the system analyses the labour and materials costs, captures the cash-flow consequences, and notifies marketing that the product is in stock. These activities let operations management co-ordinate organisation efforts.

Although MRP II systems are expensive and take time to set up, results are impressive (Cockel 1986). Pharmaceutical firms, aerospace and defence contractors, and automotive and parts manufacturers use MRP II systems (Foley 1988; Dilworth 1993). Again, the systems can apply to service organisations, but are not widespread.

Purchasing

In conducting business, most organisations need materials and services they obtain by **purchasing**, the process of getting needed goods or services in exchange for funds or other payment (Monks 1987; Dilworth 1993). Purchasing needs are identified by materials-requirements planning (see Fig. 16s2.4). Then purchasing occurs. This includes checking vendors' qualifications to provide supplies, seeking substitute sources, and negotiating the best prices.

Traditionally, purchasing has been seen as clerical, aimed at obtaining supplies to meet specification, not as technical or managerial tasks. More recently this has changed due to environmental and competitive developments (Burt & Soukup 1985; Tully 1995). Four factors contribute to purchasing's growing importance. One is rising costs. Materials and supplies are major costs, and small savings can give major benefits to a company's bottom line.

Another factor is advancing technology. Many products are complex and difficult to assess. Thus, increased technical expertise is needed to make good purchasing decisions. Companies

---

manufacturing-resource planning (MRP II)

Computer-based information system integrating production planning and control activities of basic MRP systems with related financial, accounting, personnel, engineering and marketing information

---

purchasing

Process of acquiring necessary goods or services in exchange for funds or other remuneration

are hiring MBAs with technical focus to manage purchasing in specialist areas. Another factor is needing to get quality materials and services. Without quality input, organisations find it harder to produce the quality outputs to compete effectively.

Finally, rapid technological change increases innovation and shortens lead times. Organisations shorten development time and reduce expenses by getting more from other vendors and involving them in designing the product or service. For example, General Electric's jet engine division used 16 design teams on aspects of its new commercial engine. Each had members from purchasing so vendors could be part of the design process. GE expects this involvement to lower product development costs by 20 percent.

The service delivery system

As noted already, service delivery differs from manufacturing in many ways. Services differ as well. A service delivery system aims to maximise customer benefits relative to service provision costs. We first consider service differences by the matrix of service characteristics. We then see how organisations manage customer contact so service is effective and efficient (Dilworth 1993; Fitzsimmons & Fitzsimmons 1994; Schneider & Bowen 1995).

Matrix of service characteristics   The matrix of service characteristics puts services in four groups based on service complexity and degree of customisation needed (see Fig. 16s2.6). Complexity is based on the needed level of knowledge and skill or capital investment. The customer can perform services shown on the matrix's right side, but needs practice and time. Consumers purchase these to save time and money. Services on the left need more knowledge or equipment than readily available to the average consumer. Customisation refers to the degree to which a service is tailored to specific customer needs. Services shown in the matrix's top half need much customisation, while those in the bottom are quite standardised.

Services in all quadrants have customer contact, so businesses in all quadrants need workers with good skills to interact with customers. For services in quadrants II and IV, businesses can train workers to required service levels, but those in quadrant II must be flexible in tailoring services to customers. Services in quadrant I need professionally trained workers. High-level investments in facilities and equipment are wanted for services in quadrant III. Costs of special training for workers in this quadrant are often high, but economies of scale help lower prices to individual consumers. For success, quadrant III organisations must offer an attractive range of services for large numbers of customers.

Managing customer contact   Experts say the degree of service efficiency is linked to customer contact level. The more contact, the more likely are unusual requests, customer instruction changes, customer desire to chat, and other behaviours reducing efficiency of service delivery. By their scope, some services, such as mail service or mail-order catalogue shopping, need lower customer contact levels. Others, such as restaurants and hotels, need moderate levels. Still others, such as doctor's care or counselling, normally require high-level customer contact.

A common way to aid service delivery efficiency is to avoid customer contact with operation parts that do not need customer interaction. In hotels, for example, some functions,

Fig. 16s2.6   Matrix of service characteristics (adapted from Dilworth 1993, p. 371)

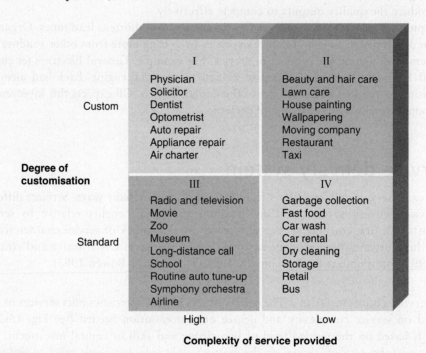

Table 16s2.3 Examples of service operations with front and back offices

Operation	Front office	Back office
Bank	Tellers, customer service officers	Posting clerks, encoders
Stock broker office	Brokers	Transaction clerks, data entry operators
Restaurant	Waiting staff	Chefs, cooks, dishwashers
Library	Reference desk	Purchasing, reshelving
Garage	Reception	Mechanics
Laundry	Pickup counter	Pressers, folders

Source: Reprinted from Dilworth (1993).

such as check-in, bell captain and cashier, demand heavy customer contact and efforts to set a friendly, responsive atmosphere. These are front office functions. Others, such as cleaning rooms, are conducted without guests as far as possible. These are back office operations. Some operations with front and back offices are shown in Table 16s2.3. Besides restricting customer contact, another benefit of back office operations is that they can be set up in inexpensive areas and centralised to achieve economies of scale.

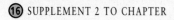

DESIGNING AND UTILISING FACILITIES

Facilities are closely tied to capacity planning. **Facilities** are land, buildings, equipment and other physical inputs which determine capacity, require time to change, and involve major capital input. Facilities issues for managers include expansion and contraction decisions, facilities location and layout.

Expansion and contraction decisions

Decisions on expanding or contracting facilities available relate to long-range capacity planning. Facility decision processes involve four steps (Buffa 1983). First, managers use forecasts of future demand for product or services. As it may takes at least two years to build and commission facilities, forecasts must extend beyond this, increasing uncertainty.

Second, managers compare capacity and future demand. Current capacity is the current maximum possible output. By comparing this with future demand, managers can see if it is sufficient, inadequate or excessive.

Third, when capacity is insufficient or in excess, managers generate and evaluate alternatives. In many cases, options for facility changes are wide. In others, it may be hard to develop any alternatives. These typically involve location issues, which we discuss below.

Fourth, managers consider risks and decide on a plan with capacity expansion or contraction timings, if any. Facilities decisions usually are high risk because more facilities raise fixed costs even if expected demand does not emerge. Conversely, insufficient capacity may allow competitors to attract your customers (Ingrassia & Stertz 1988; Taylor 1992).

Facilities location

Plant, warehouse and service facility location is important to facility decisions. In fact, most decisions on extra facilities are linked to location issues. Most location problems fall into one of four categories: single facility, multiple factories and warehouses, competitive retail outlets and emergency services. Each has different decision criteria for facility location.

A single-facility location involves a facility with no need to interact with any others the organisation has. A single factory or warehouse or a single retail store fits this category. Location decisions for a single facility involve many criteria, such as labour costs, labour supply, raw materials, transportation availability, services and other relevant issues.

Multiple factory and warehouse locations usually mean costs of product distribution are critical. For complex problems with multiple facilities, operations research methods help find locations minimising distribution costs (Ridnitsky 1982, 1987). The use of just-in-time inventory methods also means manufacturing organisations consider sites close to major customers.

Locating competitive retail outlets means the possible revenue obtainable from various locations must be considered. For example, locating a bank, shopping centre, or cinema in relation to both customers and competitors bears on a facility's revenue. Some computer programs use census and other data to aid retailers, such as Woolworths, choose retail outlet locations (Dawson 1988; Dilworth 1993).

facilities

Land, buildings, equipment and other major physical inputs that substantially determine productivity capacity, require time to alter, and involve significant capital investments

Emergency services are often located based on response times. For example, police and fire stations must be located to provide an acceptable level of service, including short response times for emergencies.

Facilities layout

Another facility aspect is layout, or the processing components (departments, workstations and equipment) placed in the production configuration. There are three main facility layouts: process, product and fixed position (Adam & Ebert 1992; Buffa 1983).

Process layout   A **process layout** is a configuration where processing components are grouped by function. The product or client being served moves between functions depending on specific needs. As a result, demand for a function is intermittent, since some products or clients may not need a given function. With intermittent demand, functions can be idle sometimes and overloaded other times. A process layout is best when several products and services are produced or when product or service variations need several functions. See Figure 16s2.7 for process layout examples for a product (machine shop) and a service (medical clinic).

process layout

Production configuration in which processing components are grouped according to type of function performed

Product layout   A **product layout** is a configuration where processing components are put in a specialised line along which the product or client passes during production. With this arrangement, the product or service is produced through a standardised production sequence set specifically to the product or service's characteristics. Product layout examples for a product (a separate assembly line for each of three products) and a service (a driver's licence centre set up for one service) are shown in Figure 16s2.8. Other examples of product layouts are automatic car washes and cafeteria lines.

Product layouts are used producing a standard large volume product or service. Each needs the same or a similar process, with limited variations.

product layout

Production configuration in which processing components are arranged in a specialised line along which the product or client passes during the production process

Fixed-position layout   A **fixed-position layout** is a configuration where the product or client stays in one spot and tools, equipment and expertise are brought to it. This is used when it is not feasible to move the product—due to size, shape or other characteristics—or when it is sensible to take the service to a client. For example, a fixed-position layout is often used building ships, locomotives and aircraft. It can be used for services, such as heating repair (where equipment, supplies and repair expertise are brought to the building) or a mobile CAT scanner (where the unit is taken to different hospitals due to economics). Having facilities is critical to the operations management aspect of process technology.

fixed-position layout

Production configuration in which the product or client remains in one location and tools, equipment and expertise are brought to it, as necessary, to complete the productive process

PROMOTING INNOVATION: PROCESS TECHNOLOGY

Process technology is used to transform inputs into goods and services. It includes tools, methods, procedures, equipment and production steps (Schroeder 1993). Process technology is increasingly important to competitive success. One reason is the interest in re-engineering,

Fig. 16s2.7 **Process layouts for (top) a machine shop and (bottom) a medical clinic (reprinted from Buffa 1983, p. 32)**

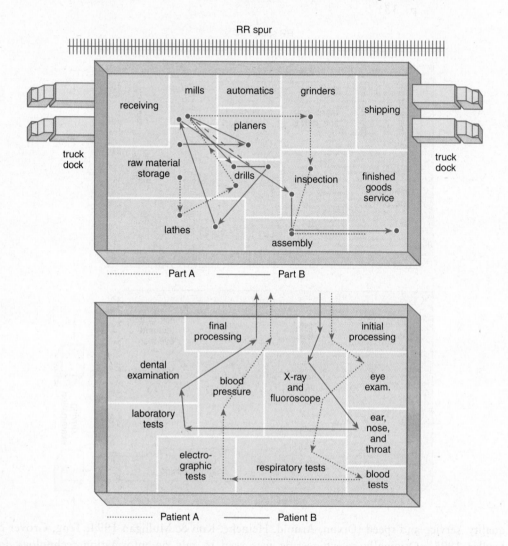

which aims to develop innovative ways for the transformation. Another is greater use of sophisticated technology producing goods and services due to accelerating advances in computer software, computer-controlled machines, and robots. In this section, we explore re-engineering, innovations in computer-integrated manufacturing, and advanced technology's use in service organisations.

Re-engineering

Organisations have used re-engineering for advantage in operations and other areas. **Re-engineering** (also called business process redesign or BPR) is analysis and radical business process redesign to achieve breakthroughs from critical performance criteria, such as cost,

re-engineering

Thorough analysis and radical redesign of existing business processes to achieve breakthrough improvements by focusing on critical performance criteria, such as cost, quality, service and speed

Fig. 16s2.8   Product layouts for (top) a three-product plant and (bottom) a driver's licence processing centre (reprinted from Buffa 1983, p. 33)

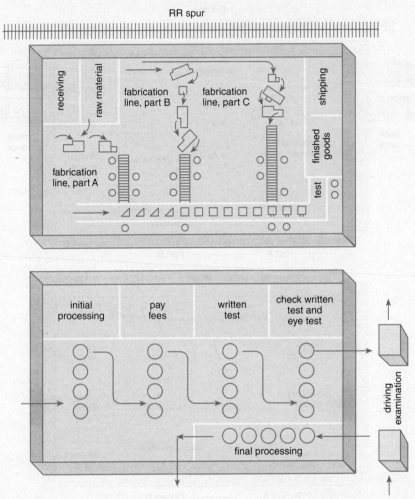

quality, service and speed (Dixon, Arnold, Heineke, Kim & Mulligan 1994; Teng, Grover & Fiedler 1994). Originally re-engineering was seen to rely on information technology for radical change. While information technology is influential, a study of 23 re-engineering projects saw that a key driving force for re-engineering efforts was a major goal change, such as new emphasis on cost, quality or cycle-time reduction. Senior management sets goals, and supports re-engineering efforts. This support is critical. Re-engineering efforts also involved cross-functional teams working together to recommend and put in place newly designed processes (Dixon et al. 1994; Connors 1996).

computer-integrated manufacturing (CIM)

Computerised integration of all major functions associated with production of a product

Computer-integrated manufacturing

Computer-integrated manufacturing (CIM) is the integration by computer of all major functions in production. These include product design and engineering, machine instruction, materials handling, inventory control and process direction. Operations using CIM are called 'factories of the future' as they use new technology creating world-class facilities. CIM systems also use sophisticated materials-requirements planning (MRP) systems. They rely on other computerised systems too, such as computer-aided design and manufacturing, as well as flexible manufacturing systems.

Computer-aided design   **Computer-aided design (CAD)** uses computers to prepare, review and evaluate product designs. With CAD, engineers and designers can easily alter and evaluate initial designs. The system needs less time and expense than conventional methods such as physical mock-ups. Because design is in an electronic data base, it can be accessed later for more work and tests. CAD systems also let designers test stress tolerance and reliability factors by computer.

Computer-aided manufacturing   **Computer-aided manufacturing (CAM)** uses computers to design and control production processes. To put products in production, CAM systems access computer-stored information on designs developed by CAD. With CAM, machine set-ups can be changed by computer, as well as materials and work in progress from one machine to another. For simple parts, the process from transmission of CAD materials to manufacture can take half an hour (Bylinsky 1996).

Flexible manufacturing systems   Computer-integrated manufacturing involves another concept, flexible manufacturing systems. **Flexible manufacturing systems (FMS)** use computers for control so many types of parts or product configurations can come from the same production line. Flexible manufacturing uses **group technology**, or classification of parts into families (groups of parts or products similar in manufacture) so members of the same family can be produced on the same line. Grouping products allows an FMS to be rapidly programmed to set up machines for both very small and large quantities of parts in the same production process (Williams 1994). This flexibility makes it cost-effective to manufacture lots as small as one, and increases manufacturers' responsiveness (Nemetz & Fry 1988; Avishai 1989; *PR Newswire* 1995).

Service applications

Advanced technology also gives opportunities for innovation in service industries, though the potential is only just being tapped (Heskett 1986).

Super Valu, a grocery wholesaler serving independent supermarkets, has a program called SLASH (Site Location Analysis Strategy Heuristic) to help its customers select good store locations. The program has a CAD system enabling architects to assess over 100 store plans on a screen (Fierman 1990; Hwang 1992; Hirsch 1996). Using advanced technology in service organisations needs careful identification of areas where the technology can influence services offered and productivity.

IMPROVING PRODUCTIVITY

At 12 noon in Appleton, Wisconsin, all 500-members of staff of the Aid Association for Lutherans (AAL), a fraternal society operating as a large insurance business, piled their

computer-aided design (CAD)

System using computers to geometrically prepare, review and evaluate product designs

computer-aided manufacturing (CAM)

System using computers to design and control production processes

flexible manufacturing system (FMS)

Manufacturing system using computers to control machines and the production process automatically so different types of parts or product configurations can be handled on the same production line

group technology

Classification of parts into families (groups of parts or products with similarities in how they are manufactured) so members of the same family can be manufactured on the same production line

belongings on chairs and rolled them to other areas of headquarters. Corridors were jammed as 'organised chaos' reorganised insurance operations. Within two hours, the move changed a functionally organised bureaucracy into self-managing teams (see Chapter 15) with fewer supervisor layers. Under the new set up, all policies related to one customer were handled by a single team, instead of being routed to separate departments. Within a year, productivity rose 20 percent—a significant change, especially for a service organisation (Hoerr 1988).

These results are only an example of what can be done when productivity improvements are given high priority. Within organisations, productivity improvement—that is, generating more outputs from the same or fewer inputs—relies on the following five-step process:

1 *Establish a base point to assess future improvements against.* Managers use a base point such as the number of claims processed daily, dollar income per square metre of selling space, amount produced per day, percentage of output passing inspection, percentage of repaired items returned for more repairs, or customers served per hour. It is important to choose measures which focus on important productivity aspects for the organisation or work unit (Naj 1993; Dumaine 1994). The continuous improvement principle of total quality management (see Chapter 17) also can help encourage productivity improvement.

2 *Set goals to establish desired productivity level.* Many studies in a range of jobs and industries support goal setting's usefulness as a way to raise productivity levels.

3 *Review methods for increasing productivity.* Managers have options to increase productivity. Useful methods include improved employee selection techniques, putting people in jobs matched to their qualifications, training workers in job-related skills, redesigning jobs to give workers more control over their own productivity, giving financial incentives carefully tied to productivity, and using feedback and performance appraisals to let workers know their progress (Guzzo 1988; Ilgen & Klein 1988). Other approaches to improve productivity involve many operations management techniques discussed before.

Managers may overemphasise cutting costs in current processes, seeing it as best to increase productivity, and not adopt new process technologies leading to significant productivity and competitiveness advances (Skinner 1986). Often, rethinking the work process, as suggested by re-engineering discussed already, can produce breakthroughs.

4 *Select a method and implement.* Managers should choose the method appearing to have the best chance of success in a situation (Gourlay 1994). Implementation will involve considering how to bring about change (see Chapter 11).

5 *Measure results and modify as necessary.* Further modifications are needed only if productivity does not improve as planned. Met goals, of course, lead to new ones, since productivity increases are a continuing challenge for successful organisations (Hammer & Champy 1993).

The productivity challenge can be met by judicious information technology use, the subject of the next supplement.

Management Information Systems

COMPUTER-BASED INFORMATION SYSTEMS: AN OVERVIEW

Information technology is causing major changes in how organisations handle and use information. For one, the number of personal computers has increased exponentially. This allows managers to have more, better information available. To use these opportunities, managers must understand computer-based information systems and their characteristics.

The nature of information systems

Despite their sophistication, information systems' basic concepts are straightforward. To understand them, it helps to differentiate between data and information, as well as to use a systems view to examine the nature of information processing.

Data versus information Although 'data' and 'information' are often used interchangeably, computer professionals distinguish between the terms. **Data** are unanalysed facts and figures. For example, when you buy a litre of milk at a supermarket, the cash register linked to a central computer records a litre of milk as sold. However, the data has little direct value.

To be useful, the data must be changed to **information**, data that have been analysed or processed into a form that is useful. For instance, data on the milk purchase may be processed with other data to produce current store milk inventory figures. This information is useful to those in charge of purchasing, delivery and stocking. The data may be processed to develop figures on store sales—broken down by shift for the store manager, day for the district manager, and week for upper management. Thus the milk-purchase data is an analysed element in these and other reports.

The difference between data and information is important to managers (Carlyle 1988). To be useful, information must be relevant to managers' decisions, accurate, timely or available as needed, complete or dealing with areas needed for a decision, and concise or giving information summarised for the decision maker (Cremillion & Pyburn 1988). With computers, it is easy to generate reports which do not meet managers needs and damage productivity.

Information processing: A systems view To obtain information for their purposes, organisations develop information systems. An information system is similar to the systems approach in understanding organisations (see Chapter 2). Information systems involve inputs, transformations and outputs. An information-processing system's elements are shown in Figure 16s3.1.

data

Unanalysed facts and figures

information

Data which have been analysed or processed into a meaningful form for decision makers

Fig. 16s3.1   Basic components of an information system

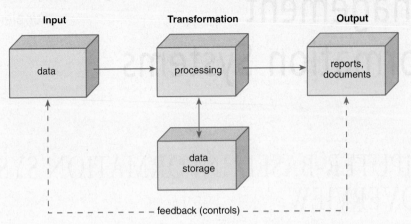

In an information system, data collected from the organisation or environment are inputs. The data is transformed, or processed. Processing uses forms of data manipulation and analysis (classifying, sorting, calculating and summarising) to transform data into information. Information-processing systems then use data storage for later retrieval. Outputs are reports, documents and other sources of information needed by decision makers. Feedback ensures outputs are appropriate and serve their intended purposes. Such safeguards can check the system to verify accuracy (as much as possible) of data and processing, and the usefulness of outputs to users.

Given this, an **information system** is a set of procedures set up to collect (or retrieve), process, store and disseminate information to support planning, decision making, co-ordination and control (Laudon & Laudon 1994). Information systems need not be computerised. For example, one could use a hand-made spreadsheet instead of a computerised one such as Microsoft's Excel (although it is more difficult without the computer). However, we are focusing on **computer-based information systems (CBISs)**. Thus when we discuss information systems, we mean those using computer technology.

information system

Set of procedures designed to collect (or retrieve), process, store and disseminate information to support planning, decision making, co-ordination and control

computer-based information systems (CBISs)

Information systems involving computer technology use

computer hardware

Physical computer equipment, including the computer itself and related devices

Computer-based information system technology

Computer-based information system technology fall into three categories: hardware, software and telecommunications technology (see Fig. 16s3.2).

Hardware   Computer hardware is the equipment used to input, process and output data in a computer-based information system. This includes input devices (keyboards and optical scanners), the computer's central processing unit (main memory and computer-processing section), storage devices (magnetic tape and optical disks), output devices (printers and on-line display terminals), and media connecting these devices.

Once, electronic information processing used mainframe computers in a central data-processing department. Microcomputers, and the lower cost and greater capacity of workstations and minicomputers, widened organisation information-processing options. On

Fig. 16s3.2 Basic components of a computer-based information system

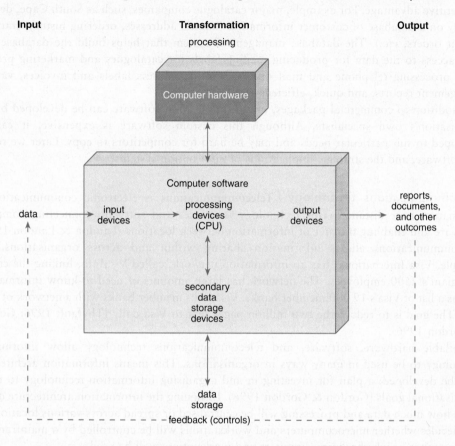

average, for the past two decades computer processing capacity has doubled, and the cost of production halved approximately every 18 months or so (Jones et al. 2000). Microcomputers are now so powerful that they can be used in organisational networks, linked to others, to telecommunication devices or larger computers. Supercomputers, with their vast speed, have allowed solving of problems needing complex and time-consuming calculations, such as predicting the weather. Overall, the trend to more computer hardware power at less expense is reducing differences between computers.

Software   **Computer software** is programs and documentation that control and co-ordinate a system's hardware elements. Most computers can perform many tasks, such as calculating an individual's appropriate pay, tracking a customer's fees or assessing inventory levels. The software gives instructions enabling the computer to perform tasks.

There are many software packages. Among them are word processing packages (e.g. WordPerfect and Word) and spreadsheets (e.g. Excel and Quattro Pro). There are also database packages (e.g. Access and Paradox). A **database** is an efficiently organised set of data in a central location serving several information system applications. A **database management system** is software letting an organisation build, manage and provide access to stored data

computer software

Set of programs, documents, procedures and routines associated with the operation of a computer system which makes hardware capable of various activities

database

Set of data organised efficiently in a central location to serve a number of information-system applications

database management system

Software which allows an organisation to build, manage and provide access to its stored data

(Laudon & Laudon 1994; Sanders 1987). Increasingly, organisations use databases for competitive advantage. For example, major catalogue companies, such as South Cape, depend heavily on a database of customer information (names, addresses, ordering history, status of current orders, etc.). The database management system that helps build the database also gives access to the data for producing mailing labels for catalogues and marketing promotions, processing telephone and mail orders, printing address labels and invoices, various management reports, and quick, efficient customer service.

In addition to commercial packages, unique application software can be developed by the organisation's own specialists. Although this custom software is expensive, it can be developed to suit particular needs and may be hard for competitors to copy. Later we revisit this software, and the strategic implications of information systems.

tele-communications

Electronic communication of information over a distance

Telecommunications technology Telecommunications is electronic communication of information over distance. This technology is devices and software connecting computer hardware and enabling transfer of information between locations (Laudon & Laudon 1994). Telecommunications allows information sharing within and across organisations. For example, Visa International has an information network, called VisaInfo, linking the credit-card giant's 2500 employees. The network has large amounts of need-to-know information, such as a list of Visa's 19 000 member banks. Visa links member banks with a network of their own. The goal is to reduce the two million pages sent to Visa daily (Thyfault 1996; Gordon & Gordon 1996).

information architecture

Long-range plan for investing in and organising information technology to facilitate reaching organisational goals

Available hardware, software, and telecommunications technology allow information technology to be used in many ways in organisations. This means **information architecture** must be developed: a plan for investing in and organising information technology to reach organisational goals (Gordon & Gordon 1996). Designing the information architecture determines how much data and processing will be centralised or spread across various locations. It also decides whether microcomputers and workstations will be controlled by a mainframe or minicomputer or whether minicomputers and workstations will be used.

Information needs by organisational level

knowledge workers

Specialists, such as engineers, architects or scientists, who design products, services or processes and create new knowledge for organisations

In designing information systems to enhance information use, it must be realised information needs differ by level. This is expected, since managerial responsibilities in planning and organising differ by level (Gordon & Gordon 1996). For now think in terms of the four general organisational levels in Figure 16s3.3. Strategic-level systems serve senior managers' need for long-range planning and control. Tactical-level systems help middle managers with planning, decision making and monitoring. Knowledge-level systems assist technical specialists or knowledge workers create and integrate new organisation knowledge. **Knowledge workers** are specialists, engineers, architects or scientists, who design products, services or processes and create new organisation knowledge. They are highly educated professionals. They are supported by **data workers**, who process and disseminate documents, messages and other information. They include secretaries, filing clerks or managers processing and distributing information others create. Operational-level systems support operating personnel and monitor their activities.

data workers

Individuals who mainly process and disseminate documents, messages and related information

Fig. 16s3.3   Examples of information systems for various functional areas by management level (reprinted from Laudon & Laudon 1994, p. 36)

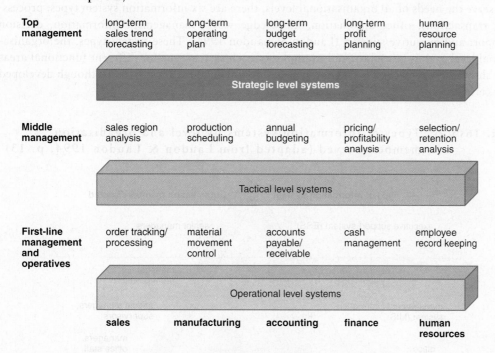

Information needs by specialised area

In most cases, information needs also vary by area, such as manufacturing, finance and human resources. When organisations began to use computers extensively, computer specialists saw a future where information needs of all areas would be joined in one large information system. The realisation has grown that a single system cannot meet all the organisation's information needs, especially large ones such as Telstra or General Motors Holden. In addition, the information requirements of various organisational parts are dynamic and change rapidly, making one system more unlikely.

A more realistic view is that information system efforts will be more effective if they work to develop systems for specific area needs, such as manufacturing and accounting (see Fig. 16s3.3). Data used and information produced are shared increasingly by other systems.

To help share such information, organisations are setting up **local-area networks (LANs)**, interconnections (usually by cable) allowing communications between computers in a single building or in close proximity. Many companies are establishing **wide-area networks (WANs)**, to allow long-distance communications between computers (Barnes & Greller 1994). Recently, many companies have been developing intranets. An intranet is an internal organisational network using Internet technologies so employees can browse and share information. An intranet is a private form of the Internet's World Wide Web and can be accessed only by people in the organisation or others with permission to use the information, such as customers and suppliers.

local-area networks (LANs)

Interconnections (usually cable) allowing communications between computers within a single building or in close proximity

wide-area networks (WANs)

Networks providing communications between computers over long distances, usually through telecommunications companies

TYPES OF INFORMATION SYSTEMS

To serve the needs of all organisational levels, there are six information system types: processing transactions, office automation, knowledge work, management information, decision support and executive support (Laudon & Laudon 1994). These system types, the organisational level each is geared to, and examples of each system type for different functional areas are shown in Figure 16s3.4. Of course, these are often used at several levels, though developed for certain need types.

Fig. 16s3.4   Types of information systems by level and organisation members served (adapted from Laudon & Laudon 1994, p. 13)

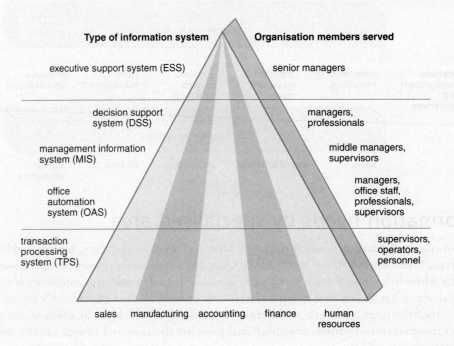

Transaction-processing systems

A **transaction-processing system (TPS)** is a computer-based information system which executes and records day-to-day transactions in an organisation's business. For example, each time you use a credit card at a service station, enrol at college or university, renew a driver's licence, or draw money from a bank account, a computerised transaction-processing system operates. Transaction systems are used in highly structured and repetitive situations when tasks and criteria are clear. The structured nature of the situation makes it possible to write detailed and unequivocal instructions enabling the computer to handle and record transactions properly. A TPS gives help to an organisation's operational level. TPSs produce data used by other computer-based information system types in an organisation.

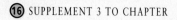

Office automation systems

An **office-automation system (OAS)** is a computer-based information system that helps communication and increases data workers' productivity by document and message processing. The best-known OASs are word-processing systems, where text can be created, edited and printed quickly and easily. Increasingly popular OASs are electronic mail (e-mail) systems, which allow high-speed exchange of written messages by means of computer text processing and communications networks (see Chapter 14). Other important OASs include the following (McLeod 1986; Laudon & Laudon 1994):

Voice mail: a method of recording a telephone message then storing it in secondary computer storage for later retrieval by the receiver

Electronic calendaring: a method of electronically maintaining an appointments schedule

Teleconferencing: simultaneous communication between a group of individuals by telephone or via computer using specially designed software

Document retrieval: use of one or more electronic devices to store documents as digitised images or other medium and facilitate the later location and copying of the stored images

Facsimile (FAX) transmission: means of sending documents over telephone linkages arriving in printed form at the receiving location

Groupware: software designed to support collaborative efforts among group members, such as scheduling meetings, holding meetings, collaborating on projects and sharing documents

Graphics: means of creating charts and diagrams

office-automation system (OAS)

Computer-based information system aimed at facilitating communication and increasing the productivity of managers and office workers through document and message processing

Knowledge work systems

A **knowledge-work system (KWS)** is a computer-based information system assisting knowledge workers create new organisational knowledge. Knowledge workers use office automation systems, but knowledge-work systems give them more tools for designing new products, services and processes and developing useful organisational knowledge. Knowledge workers may use workstations capable of advanced graphics, complex calculations and large database access. Workstations are used in areas such as medical diagnosis, legal document searches, scientific analysis and computer-aided design (Magnet 1992).

knowledge-work system (KWS)

Computer-based information system which assists knowledge workers in creation of new knowledge for the organisation

Management information systems

A **management-information system (MIS)** is a computer-based system that produces routine reports and often has on-line access to past and present information for middle and first-line managers. MISs focus on tactical and operational issues and are useful for planning, decision making and controlling. They often summarise transaction-processing information for managers and supervisors in routine and exception reports. For example, operations management's materials-requirements planning system (see Chapter 18) provides information to master schedulers about possible procurement problems affecting the schedule. MISs also provide capacity planners with information on necessary short- or long-run capacity changes.

management-information system (MIS)

Computer-based information system that produces routine reports and often allows on-line access to current and historical information needed by managers mainly at the middle and first-line levels

As well, they produce first- and middle-level managers' reports on costs, quality and supplier activities.

The term 'management-information systems' can be used broadly to describe computer-related systems for management, including the six types of systems discussed here. The term designates the management field focusing on designing and applying computer-based information systems for management. Here we use 'computer-based information systems' or 'information systems' to denote all such systems for various management levels. We keep the term 'management-information systems' for the narrower meaning above.

Decision-support systems

A **decision-support system (DSS)** is a computer-based information system supporting managerial decision making in poorly structured situations. These systems do not give 'answers' or show optimal decisions for managers. Rather, they work to improve the decision-making process by providing tools to analyse situations clearly. In essence they work to assist managers to make better non-programmed decisions (Turban 1988).

There are differences between a DSS and an MIS. For one, compared to an MIS, a typical DSS gives more advanced analysis and greater access to models managers can use to see a situation more fully. For another, a DSS often uses information from external, as well as from internal, sources that are largely the domain of the TPS and MIS. Finally, a DSS is more interactive than an MIS. It lets managers communicate directly (often back and forth) with computer programs controlling the system, and obtain results of various analyses quickly.

One specialised DSS type is a **group decision-support system (GDSS)**, a computer-based information system helping decision makers operate together on poorly structured problems. A GDSS focuses on solving a problem or making a decision, while groupware is more focused on helping communication.

Another specialised DSS type is the **expert system** (Turban & Watkins 1986; Finlay 1994). These are computer-based systems applying an expert's knowledge to solve specialised problems. In fact, in such systems, designers work with experts to find information and heuristics, or decision rules, experts use on particular problem types (Simon 1987).

Expert systems are a product of **artificial intelligence,** a field of information technology aimed at developing computers with human-like capabilities, such as seeing, hearing and thinking (Leonard-Barton & Sviokla 1988). Artificial intelligence is an inquiry area, not an end product such as an expert system. One development is fuzzy logic, a rule-based approach involving pattern recognition and inferences from incomplete or somewhat inaccurate data. For example, Ford Motor Co. is developing a fuzzy logic system for parking a simulated truck, based on a few rules such as 'IF the truck is near jack-knifing, THEN reduce the steering angle'. Computers still cannot conceptualise or reason (Laudon & Laudon 1994). Nevertheless, efforts on artificial intelligence have laid foundations for other developments, such as expert systems.

Executive-support systems

The **executive-support system (ESS)** is a computer-based information system supporting top-level decision making and effective functioning. These are sometimes called executive-information systems (EISs) (Watson, Rainer & Koh 1991).

decision-support system (DSS)
Computer-based information system supporting the process of managerial decision making in poorly structured situations

group decision-support system (GDSS)
Computer-based information system supporting decision makers working together to solve structured problems

expert systems
Computer-based systems that apply an expert's substantial knowledge to help solve specialised problems

artificial intelligence
Field of information technology aimed at developing computers with human-like capabilities, such as seeing, hearing and thinking

executive-support system (ESS)
Computer-based information system supporting decision making and effective functioning at the top levels of an organisation

Unlike the more narrowly focused DSS, an ESS has more general computing capabilities, telecommunications, and display options (such as graphs and charts) applicable to different problems. An ESS uses less analytical models than a DSS, gives information from several sources as needed, and allows interactive general queries (Gelfond 1988; Boone 1991).

ESSs are systems tailor-made for the needs of executives in some situations, and are often geared to managers' individual work habits. The characteristics of executive support systems, as well as of other major system types, are summarised in Table 16s3.1.

Table 16s3.1   Characteristics of information-processing systems

Type of System	Information inputs	Processing	Information outputs	Users
ESS	Aggregate data; external, internal	Graphics; simulations; interactive	Projections; responses to queries	Senior managers
DSS	Low-volume data; analytic models	Interactive; simulations; analysis	Special reports; decision analyses; responses to queries	Professionals; staff managers
MIS	Summary transaction data; high-volume data; simple models	Routine reports; simple models; low-level analysis	Summary and exception reports	Middle managers
KWS	Design specifications; knowledge base	Modelling; simulations	Models; graphics	Professionals; technical staff
OAS	Documents; schedules	Document management; scheduling; communication	Documents; schedules; mail	Clerical workers
TPS	Transactions; events	Sorting; listing; merging; updating	Detailed reports; lists; summaries	Operations personnel; supervisors

Source: Reprinted from Laudon & Laudon (1994).

PROMOTING INNOVATION: STRATEGIC IMPLICATIONS OF INFORMATION SYSTEMS

During the 1980s, strategic planning experts saw the innovative possibilities and strategy implications of information technology (Benjamin, Rockart, Morton & Wyman 1984; Porter & Millar 1985). Previously, top managers viewed computers as a way to improve internal processes to enhance efficiency. Today information technology is seen as valuable in gaining competitive advantage. Many large companies have appointed a chief information officer (CIO), a high-level executive responsible to recommend and oversee implementation of information systems to enhance an organisation's competitive position.

In thinking about how information technology can help develop strategies for competitive advantage, managers may use the strategic options matrix in Figure 16s3.5. The matrix is related to Porter's competitive strategy work (see Chapter 7). The matrix uses two dimensions: competitive strategies and strategic linkages (see Fig. 16s3.5) (Neumann 1994; Miller & Dess 1996; Wiseman & MacMillan 1984; Porter 1980).

Fig. 16s3.5   Matrix of strategic options related to information technology

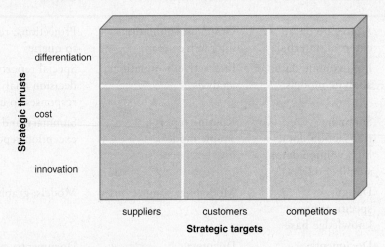

Competitive strategies

According to the matrix, organisations can combine information technology with three major competitive strategies for competitive advantage. The strategies are differentiation, cost leadership and quick response (see Chapter 7).

Differentiation   The goal of differentiation is either to increase an organisation's differentiation advantages in relation to others (suppliers, customers or competitors) or to decrease the differentiation advantages of others relative to the organisation.

Cost leadership   A cost approach works to reduce an organisation's costs in relation to others' costs (suppliers, customers or competitors), helping suppliers or customers reduce their costs so they want to do business with the organisation, or increasing competitors' costs (Wessel 1987; *The Wall Street Journal* 1987; Brown 1988).

Quick response   The quick response approach focuses on recognising, adapting to, and meeting changing customer needs more rapidly than competitors (Miller & Dess 1996). This is associated with organisation speed in improving products or services or customer responsiveness (Bartholomew 1996).

Strategic linkages

The matrix (see Fig. 16s3.5) suggests three areas where strategic information systems linkages can be made for competitive advantage. The linkage targets are suppliers, customers and alliances.

Supplier linkages   Suppliers include providers of raw materials, capital, labour or services (Wiseman & MacMillan 1984).

Customer linkages   Customers include organisations which retail, wholesale, warehouse, distribute or use a company's products or services (Datamation 1988).

Alliance linkages   Strategic alliances occur where independent organisations form a co-operative partnership to gain a mutual strategic advantage (see Chapter 3) (Miller & Dess 1996; Yoshino & Ranga 1995). They can be set up in the same industry or by firms in different industries. In the context of information technology, organisations with strategic alliances exchange information electronically, trade expertise in information technology or share resources (Santosus 1996; Pastore 1996).

Sustaining competitive advantage

An issue in pursuit of competitive advantage by information technology is sustainability (Neumann 1994). A competitive advantage is sustainable if it can be maintained long term despite competitor action or industry factors. In practice, few competitive advantages can be sustained for long without more improvements. One survey suggests strategic information systems give competitive advantage for about 12 to 18 months (Sullivan-Trainor & Maglitta 1990). Potential advantage for information technology comes from three factors. The first is a pre-emptive strike—that is, being first with a strategic information system. The second is improving the strategic information system in important ways. The third is using strategic information systems to complement and support other competitive advantages (Neumann 1994).

DEVELOPING COMPUTER-BASED INFORMATION SYSTEMS

Development of computer-based information systems can be difficult and expensive, particularly if applications are large and complex. In fact, time and cost overruns are common. In one study, only 9 percent of software projects were on time and budget (Fabris 1996).

Furthermore, resulting systems may give errors causing serious business problems (Port 1988). Because of the scope of such problems, and information technology's strategic value, managers must have a general idea of what the development of information systems requires.

The systems-development life cycle

**systems-
development life
cycle**

Series of stages used in the
development of most
medium- and large-sized
information systems

Traditionally, new information-system development follows the process of the **systems-
development life cycle** (see Fig. 16s3.6). This is a series of stages used in developing most
medium- and large-sized information systems. It is often used more informally in small-scale
system development. Typically, development is the responsibility of a project team of managers,
users, systems analysts, programmers and other technical personnel needed for the project.

There are three stages in the life cycle: definition, physical design, and implementation and
operation.

Fig. 16s3.6   The systems-development life cycle

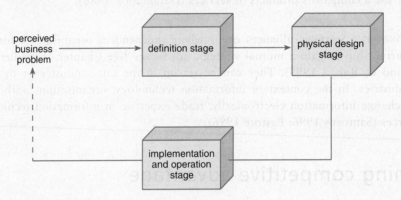

Stages in the systems-development life cycle   The *definition stage* aims to evaluate the
proposed idea and define system parameters. This stage is significant as, by one estimate,
mistakes and omissions not detected until later can cost between 10 and 100 times more to
fix than if detected during this stage (Sanders 1987).

The *physical design stage* takes a project from concept to reality. The stage includes a
detailed systems design, performing necessary programming and debugging, and planning
implementation.

The *implementation and operation stage* includes system implementation, effectiveness
evaluation and effective operation maintenance. A typical medium-sized project takes about
two years to be implemented and has an expected life span of five to eight years. Ongoing
maintenance will be needed and operating costs incurred (Laudon & Laudon 1994).

Assessing the life-cycle approach   The life-cycle approach has benefits. For one, it gives
a set of stages and phases to guide major systems-development efforts. For another, it focuses
effort on early definition of necessary functions and system outputs. Finally, it allows for
potential user involvement, particularly at the definition stage.

Unfortunately, the life-cycle approach has disadvantages. One drawback is that the cycle is
costly. Another is that intended users may have difficulty specifying all system functions and
outputs early in the life cycle, as needed. Yet another disadvantage is that the life-cycle
approach may discourage changes in system definition once that stage is done. Finally, there
may be a backlog of projects to enter the cycle.

Overall, the approach seems to be best with very large and/or complex projects or when applications are well structured so parameters can be well defined early in the project. Evidence suggests systems-development efforts that run into difficulty have not followed the life-cycle steps (Licker 1985; Tait & Vessey 1988).

Alternative means of systems development

Given the potential problems of information systems developed through the life cycle and that a long time-frame is needed for design and implementation, other alternatives have emerged. Among those are applications software packages, prototyping, end-user development and outsourcing (Laudon & Laudon 1995; Gremillion & Pyburn 1988).

Applications software packages **Applications software packages** are programs for sale or lease from commercial sources. They are geared to handle specialised areas needed by many organisations. For payroll, inventory control, work scheduling, accounts receivable and graphics, many software packages are available. Commercial vendors risk the expense of developing packages as they can profit by selling the same programs again. This means that organisations can get commercial packages more cheaply than in-house, custom-developed software.

There are disadvantages to commercial packages. The main one is the fact that the packages are generic. Though usually with many options, they may not manage unusual circumstances or procedures. On the other hand, if savings are great, it may be feasible to change organisational practices to comply with the software package's parameters. Another disadvantage is that using commercial packages to exploit information technology before competitors may make it easy for them to copy quickly. Finally, the packages may have major errors or cause serious problems.

Prototyping **Prototyping** is the building of a rough, working model of all or parts of an information system for preliminary evaluation and further refinement. Unlike a traditional approach, which involves trying to specify all user needs in early stages, the approach is based on providing a quick response to poorly defined user specifications. The prototype system then goes through several modifications and enhancements before meeting evolving user needs. Companies using prototyping report that it can cost 25 percent less than the traditional approach, usable results come more quickly, and systems generally are more accepted by users because they meet their needs (Gremillion & Pyburn 1988; Arthur 1992).

User-developed systems For information systems, a **user** is someone who is not an information system professional but is engaged in development and/or management of computer-based information systems. (A user is an **end user**.) End-user computing, development and/or management by users, is an interesting trend (Benjamin 1982).

User-developed systems are created with little aid from information-system professionals. The trend to **end-user computing** comes from several sources. First, microcomputer or personal computer popularity has let users gain basic computer experience. Second, the availability of applications software packages and other user-friendly tools means individuals who are not computer professionals can tackle information-system development. Third, as many

---

applications software packages

Software programs available for sale or lease from commercial sources

prototyping

Process of building a rough, working model of all or parts of a proposed information system for purposes of preliminary evaluation and further refinement

user

Individual, other than an information system professional, engaged in the development and/or management of computer-based information systems

end user

Same as a user

end-user computing

Development and/or management of information systems by users

projects are held up waiting to be developed by information-system departments, users have been forced to take issues into their own hands. Finally, end-users may be best placed to identify innovative information system ideas for competitive advantage (Gerrity & Rockart 1986).

However, end-user development may not always be best. Some systems may be too complex for non-professionals. Also, poorly designed systems may have errors undetected until much damage has occurred. As well, the systems may not link well with other organisational systems. Finally, if systems are developed by people who do not document the program's workings, others may have difficulty with it if the key person leaves.

Outsourcing   Outsourcing is employing an outside vendor for a function normally done by the organisation (see Chapter 16). For information systems, outsourcing is most frequent in computer-centre operations, telecommunications networks, or applications development. As an applications development option, outsourcing is good in providing specialised expertise, lower costs, and flexibility (additional help can be found as needed instead of hiring in-house staff). A disadvantage is that it is harder to gain competitive advantage when an outside vendor develops the system. They can then use the new expertise to develop similar systems for others or offer similar services to others. Thus, outsourcing systems development is best kept for systems with low potential for competitive advantage, which do not involve proprietary information handling, and do not lose control over systems crucial to organisational operations (Gordon & Gordon 1996).

Selecting a development approach

Three criteria help determine the best development approach (Gremillion & Pyburn 1988). The first is *commonality*, how likely there is a common need for the type of system in other organisations. When it is high, commercial software packages should be looked at instead of custom development. Also outsourcing may be possible. For example, organisations are outsourcing payroll processing. The second criterion is *impact*, how much the system affects the organisation, or the number of individuals affected, the importance to day-to-day operations, or the potential for competitive advantage. With greater impact it is important to have in-house information system professionals involved in development. The third criterion is *structure*, how much the problem and probable solution are understood. When structure is low, prototyping is better, particularly if the system has high impact.

INFLUENCE OF INFORMATION TECHNOLOGY ON ORGANISATIONS

As computers become more common, information technology has much influence on many organisational aspects. Areas include organisation structure, individual jobs, communication patterns and organisational risk (Davis & Olson 1985).

Organisation structure

Aside from organising the information system function itself, CBISs are impacting the overall structures of organisations. It was thought computers would reduce the need for middle managers, cause top management to assume more responsibility for innovating and planning, and allow organisations to recentralise decision making (Leavitt & Whisler 1958). Indeed, there is a trend to flatten organisations by eliminating some middle-management levels (Davidow & Malone 1992). This is possible because top-managers have increased ability to get information they need through computers. However, widespread use of microcomputers was not predicted, and this allows information sharing and decentralised decision making through horizontal information flows. In terms of organisation structure impact, computers seem to widen managers' structural options. They do so through decentralised decision making while allowing higher-level managers increased control by being up-to-date through computer networks (Applegate, Cash & Mills 1988; Malone & Davidow 1992).

Individual jobs

Computers influence individual jobs in several ways. Three significant effects are changes in job design, job-related stress and health consequences of computers, and options about work location.

Nature of jobs   The impact of personal computers in the workplace has been difficult to gauge. For clerical jobs, trends suggest computers can lead either to very simple jobs which require little skill or to jobs needing considerable creativity and skill (Attewell & Rule 1984). For professionals, computers seem to reduce routine tasks, and increase their ability to communicate with others and use decision-making tools developed for managers. For managers, computers offer new aids for decision making, communication and control.

Stress and health consequences   Stress and health issues centre on computers' impact on lower-level white-collar jobs. One topic is the effects of **electronic monitoring**, the practice of continually using computers to assess employee performance. For example, computers can monitor telephone and computer use. Critics argue that this reduces customer service and increases stress (Gelbspan 1987). One study concluded that monitoring lowers the quality of customer service and of the work environment. However, it also found that some workers internalised system standards, used data for feedback on progress, and were not bothered by monitoring. It may be more effective using computers to give direct, regular feedback to employees, but providing feedback to supervisors less frequently (Grant, Higgins & Irving 1988).

Long periods of computer use have caused health-related complaints. Most common is repetitive stress injury (RSI), occurring when muscle groups repeatedly go through the same motions. A common RSI type is carpal stress injury (CSI), affecting wrist muscles. There are over 332 000 reported RSI-related cases each year. Annual workers' compensation payments for RSI are over $2 billion. Proper posture, stretching often, and ergonomic office furniture help avoid these injuries (Adhikari 1996).

electronic monitoring

Practice of using computers to continually assess employee performance

Form of working at home made possible by using computer technology to remain in touch with the office

logical office

Concept that portable microcomputers allow an individual's office to be where the individual is, not restricted to a specific location

Location of work   Information technology advances give work location options. One is **telecommuting**, working at home using computer technology to stay in touch with the office. Yet telecommuting may be unsatisfactory because some people need social interaction with co-workers and because of the difficulties separating work and home roles. One study found that, if given a choice between telecommuting or working in the office, 56 percent of people prefer the office, 36 percent would split time between home and office, and 7 percent would work only at home (Kotlowitz 1987).

Another possibility is the **logical office**, with portable computers allowing an office to be where the individual is, not restricted to one location. Portable computers that run on batteries and can be plugged into phone jacks for transmission, are laptop computers. Managers using laptops while travelling have to manage inconveniences such as security scrutiny at airports, flat batteries, and poor phone-jack options in hotels (this is improving) (Bulkeley 1990).

Communication patterns

Computer-related communications tools, such as e-mail, teleconferencing, groupware and group decision support systems, have increased communication channels and methods (see also Chapter 14) (Barnes & Greller 1994). They have altered information exchange flows within and between organisations. Telecommunications technology makes information exchange easier locally and across the globe. The technology also allows electronic data interchange (EDI), direct exchange of transaction documents between the computers of two organisations (Laudon & Laudon 1994). EDI has permitted electronic partnerships between suppliers, producers, distributors and retailers.

Ultimately it is argued that information technology will alter the hierarchical nature of organisations by enhancing options for employee co-operation and collaboration at different levels within organisations (Harris & Foust 1987).

Organisational risk

Despite possible benefits, information technology poses some organisation risks. The most significant risks are possible errors, physical calamities, theft, sabotage and security breaches, invasion of privacy and resistance to major systems.

Errors   With major software, it is impossible to test for every possible error. Thus, errors and problems occur (Keller 1990).

Physical calamities   Physical damage by fire, flood, power failure, earthquake and other factors can disrupt organisation information flows (Keller 1990; Burgess 1988).

Theft   Theft committed through computers is over $5 billion per year in the United States alone. Computer theft is often internal. In one incident, employees wired $54 million from the Union Bank of Switzerland's London office to another bank with all needed codes. They were caught when the other bank's computer malfunctioned, and auditors identified the transaction. While a typical bank robber steals about $5000, electronic theft averages $500 000 per incident (Hafner 1988).

Sabotage and security breaches Sabotage and security breaches are increasing. Computer sabotage is deliberate disruption of computer-related activities and/or equipment, software, or data destruction. Computer security breaches include unauthorised entry to computers or computer networks, as well as accessing stored data.

Sabotage may be employee or hacker pranks. **Hackers** have a good knowledge of computers and may gain unauthorised entry to, and possibly tamper with, computer networks and organisation files they have no affiliation with. In December 1987, a West German law student used an academic research network to access IBM's 145-country e-mail network, planting a seemingly innocuous picture of a Christmas tree and a holiday message. To clear the greeting, individuals were told to type 'Christmas'. However, by doing so, they triggered a program and the greeting was reproduced and sent on in chain-letter fashion. Before long, the whole system shut down (Burgess 1987; Hafner 1988). The tool used in the prank was a **computer virus**, a small program, often hidden in another program, which replicates itself and surfaces at a set time to disrupt and possibly destroy. After press reports on a virus called 'Michelangelo', programmed to destroy data on 6 March each year (the Italian Renaissance artist's birthday), many companies have installed programs to detect many virus types. According to one estimate, over 7500 viruses are known, four times the number in 1990, and new ones emerge frequently. Virus damage cost companies worldwide $12 billion in 1999 (www.infowar.com), up from $996 million in 1995 (Stahl & Violino 1996). Inventive hackers are always working to beat antivirus programs.

Data security can also be threatened. Crucial databases and software can be compromised. According to a survey of 1290 companies, one in five had actual or attempted computer break-ins. The total number may be much higher as only half of the companies were confident such attempts would be detected (Violino 1996).

As a result of these problems, many companies are increasing computer security. They are using more elaborate password systems, dial-back systems which check whether an incoming call comes from an authorised number, and encryption hardware which disguises data by coding it to make it hard for others to decipher.

Privacy issues Widespread information technology use has created some privacy issues. For one, the data security issues already described threaten the privacy of personal data, including personnel, medical and credit records. For another, organisations can build databases with ease, collecting large quantities of individuals' data (Novack 1995).

Related to this is the privacy of companies' e-mail and voice mail communications. Courts support employers' right to monitor and retrieve employees' voice and e-mail communications, under published policy. These policies should make it clear that voice, e-mail and other systems (Internet access) are company assets, are all company property, and that they should not be seen as private. Policies like this are wise as in some cases company communication facilities have been used for hacking and sexual harassment. (Indeed, employees should note that even though an e-mail message may be erased, facilities running e-mail can hold message copies for a long time.) However, such a policy's major function is to provide guides for the use of communication facilities in order to avoid these problems (*1996 Executive File: Hot Employment Issues* 1996). Employers have complained that another area of misuse is employees wasting time on computer games or the Internet in non-business activities (Weiss 1996).

hackers

Individuals who are knowledgeable about computers and who gain unauthorised entry to, and sometimes tamper with, computer networks and files of organisations with which they have no affiliation

computer virus

Small program, usually hidden inside another program, which replicates itself and surfaces at a set time to cause disruption and possibly destruction

Resistance   It is possible resources might be put into systems development which managers and subordinates will resist. People may fear senior managers will check and interfere with their work more with the new system. New applications of information technology are vital to the future efficiency and effectiveness of most organisations.

Managing Organisations through Change and Conflict

Chapter (17)

CHAPTER OUTLINE

Managing change
Diagnosing the need for change
Introducing change to organisations
The change cycle
Resistance to change
Why individuals resist change
Overcoming resistance to change
Managing conflict
Conflict between individuals and organisations

Causes of conflict
Benefits and losses from conflict
Reducing and resolving conflict
Managing intergroup conflict through resolution

The relationship between change and conflict
Types of intergroup conflict
Changing views on conflict
Stimulating conflict

LEARNING OBJECTIVES

After studying this chapter, you should be able to:

O Identify internal and external factors leading to a need for change.
O Indicate why employees resist change.
O Explain how to overcome resistance to change, including the use of force-field analysis.
O Identify the differences distinguishing conflict between an individual and an organisation to that between groups.
O Explain the causes of conflict and how to reduce, resolve and stimulate conflict.
O Explain benefits and losses which can be incurred as a result of organisational conflict.
O Discriminate between different styles of conflict management and describe circumstances where each may be appropriate.
O Explain the relationship between change and conflict.
O Explain how both functional and dysfunctional conflict impact on group behaviour.

Striving for excellence

The key process at Autoliv is consultation. For example, as in every organisation in Australia, a key focus is the Enterprise Bargaining Agreement (EBA). Through a process of consultation with the Consultative Committee, shop stewards and the unions involved at the workplace, Autoliv Australia was able to achieve agreement which was not only good news for its employees but met the company's business plan strategies.

One of the issues facing the organisation is the number of new employees. Almost one hundred new employees joined the company between late 1999 and 2000. This presents challenges to the management to maintain the strong existing culture which has been built up through employees with a long history with the company. Winning the hearts and minds of employees without that history and maintaining the strong quality and team work existing will require specific HR strategies. The growth rate is due to new Asian business from Korea, India and Japan. Autoliv is an exemplar in many areas. Its turnover is 0.8 percent with an absenteeism rate of 1 percent of all working days. In an industry that is reputed for having had a savage industrial relations history, this is certainly a benchmark.

As you examine the change process closely, you will identify similarities with the control process discussed in Chapter 16. The management of change and conflict must be closely aligned and integrated with all managerial functions.

Successful organisations are not static. In earlier chapters we learned that the environment in which organisations function is ever-changing due to many factors. Consequently, organisations must change even if all they want to do is maintain their relative position in that context. If they want to alter or improve their position, the change must be greater.

In this chapter we consider the impact of change on organisational members and their reactions to it. We examine reasons for people's resistance to change, and conflicts ensuing from this resistance. Furthermore, we explore strategies to overcome resistance to change, and to manage and use conflict in a manner supporting organisational growth and development. Finally, we analyse ways conflict within and between groups can be managed, presenting possibilities for reducing or stimulating conflict.

Throughout this chapter, we refer to Chapters 3 and 7. This is because environmental awareness is a basis for effective change management. Further, innovation and any process leading to change may cause organisational conflict. Material presented here will include a brief review of material covered earlier as it fits with the topic's development.

MANAGING CHANGE

In today's ever-changing environment, success demands keeping a competitive advantage. To achieve this, effective managers recognise change as a matter of fact for organisation survival.

Diagnosing the need for change

The competent manager applies the skills discussed before, and scans the internal and external environments. Data is collected on both internal and external organisational trends. A careful watch is maintained on values, goals and activities to ensure they fit with customers' demands and needs. If there is a deficiency or gap, an effective manager works to remedy the situation (Lessem 1991).

Therefore, to manage change effectively, one must be aware of the need for change. There are many factors influencing organisational need for change (Jick 1993). These factors can be classified as external and internal (as seen in Fig. 17.1). They result from trends in external and internal environments.

Internal factors   As you saw in Chapter 3, there are many internal environment factors managers must be constantly aware of. This is a basis for accurate planning, as it is for accurate control mechanisms. The factors include all aspects of human and industrial relations regulation, balance of cultures and values among organisation staff, and changes of work processes imposed by new technology, just to name a few. Consider a familiar work place and identify changes from internal factors.

External factors   Simultaneously the external environment must be monitored and changes there must be examined for potential impact on the organisation. In many cases, these will demand organisation change, if it is to maintain a sustainable competitive advantage. Organisations constantly benchmark to keep up with industry developments. They carefully watch the activities of their competitors, suppliers and customers. Failure to do so can cause performance problems and threaten an organisation's survival (Isabella 1993).

In Chapter 7, we discussed planned and reactive change processes. We also discussed organisational change components. Figure 17.2 shows a simple version of the concept, emphasising how much organisational components are integrated in an organisation where change can be

Fig. 17.1   Internal and external factors causing the need for change in organisations

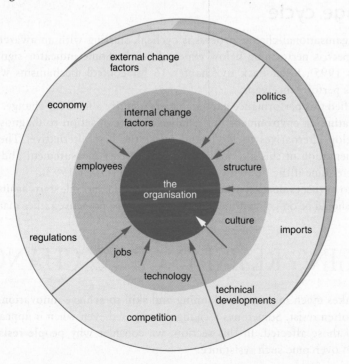

Fig. 17.2   Factors impacting on organisational activities

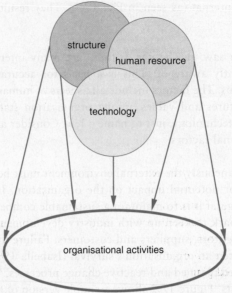

implemented. It is impossible to change any one area without impacting all other organisation areas.

The change cycle

The effective organisational-change process is cyclical, starting with an awareness that some organisation aspect is performing below expected levels. Some indicator signals a need for action (Luthans 1995). Refer back to Chapter 16 for control mechanisms which can alert managers of this performance gap.

Having identified this performance gap, managers identify a need for change. Then they can take action, creating an environment that enables the organisation to diagnose the problem accurately, develop alternatives to fix it and select the best alternative. The change cycle requires implementation of this alternative and that further measurement and evaluation be conducted to determine if the desired outcome is reached (Fisher 1993).

This will lead to further evaluation of actual performance and the cycle starts again (see Fig. 17.3). In fact the cycle should be on-going if the organisation is to be proactive rather than reactive.

MANAGING RESISTANCE TO CHANGE

One reason it takes much managerial planning and skill to achieve innovation and change is because people often resist. Sometimes a change is opposed even when it appears to be in the best interests of those affected. In this section, we consider why people resist change, and examine ways to overcome such resistance.

Fig. 17.3   The change cycle

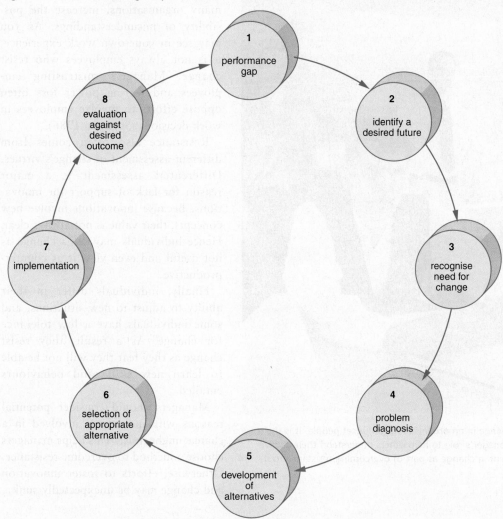

Why individuals resist change

Why are people—including ourselves—sometimes against change? Although there are many reasons for resistance, several stand out (Kotter & Schlesinger 1979).

One reason is self-interest. When people hear about a change, they ask, 'How will this affect me?' If someone sees the answer as 'adversely', resistance effort may be made. How much will depend on how strongly they feel their self-interests are affected. Citicorp lost many top investment bankers when integrating its international commercial and investment banking businesses. The departing investment experts saw the change as intruding on their turf (*Dun's Business Month* 1986).

Another reason for change resistance is misunderstanding and a lack of trust. People are often against change when they don't understand it. As well, low trust levels between

Change in an organisation can upset people. It is the manager's role to help others understand their involvement in change as part of overcoming resistance to it.

managers and employees, common in many organisations, increase the possibility of misunderstandings. As you may see in your own work experience, it is not always employees who resist change. Managers mistrusting employees and fearing power loss often oppose efforts to involve employees in work decisions (Saporito 1986).

Resistance also often comes from different assessment of change's virtues. Differential assessment is a major reason for lack of support for innovations. Because innovations involve new concepts, their value is not always clear. Hence individuals may see a change as not useful and even view it as counterproductive.

Finally, individuals differ in their ability to adjust to new situations, and some individuals have a low tolerance for change. As a result, they resist change as they fear they will not be able to learn new skills and behaviours entailed.

Managers should consider potential reasons why individuals involved in a change might resist. This helps managers choose a method to overcome resistance. Otherwise, efforts to foster innovation and change may be unexpectedly sunk.

Overcoming resistance to change

One approach to beating resistance has been offered by Kurt Lewin, who divides the change process into three steps (Lewin 1947; Huse & Cummings 1985). The first step, *unfreezing*, means developing initial awareness of a change need. The second, *changing*, focuses on learning needed new behaviours. The third step, *refreezing*, centres on reinforcing new behaviours, usually by positive results, feelings of accomplishment, and/or rewards from others. Lewin's approach helps managers recognise an unfreezing period is needed before individuals will change willingly. Furthermore, refreezing is important to reinforce and maintain changes.

Managers can adopt several methods to overcome initial change resistance and to facilitate unfreezing (Kotter & Schlesinger 1979). These options, situations where they are commonly used, and advantages and disadvantages of each are summarised in Table 17.1.

Table 17.1   Methods of overcoming resistance to change

Approach	Commonly used in situations	Advantages	Drawbacks
Education + communication	Where there is a lack of information or inaccurate information and analysis	Once persuaded, people will often help with the implementation of the change	Can be very time-consuming if lots of people are involved
Participation + involvement	Where the initiators do not have all the information they need to design the change, and where others have considerable power to resist	People who participate will be committed to implementing change, and any relevant information they have will be integrated into the change plan	Can be very time-consuming if participators design an inappropriate change
Facilitation + support	Where people are resisting because of adjustment problems	No other approach works as well with adjustment problems	Can be time-consuming and expensive and still fail
Negotiation + agreement	Where someone or some group will clearly lose out in a change, and where that group has considerable power to resist	Sometimes it is a relatively easy way to avoid major resistance	Can be too expensive in many cases if it alerts others to negotiate for compliance
Manipulation + co-optation	Where other tactics will not work or are too expensive	It can be a relatively quick and inexpensive solution to resistance problems	Can lead to future problems if people feel manipulated
Explicit + implicit coercion	Where speed is essential and the change initiators possess considerable power	It is speedy and can overcome any kind of resistance	Can be risky if it leaves people angry with the initiators

Source: Reprinted from Kotter & Schlesinger)1979, p. 111).

 # Changing to fit the time   case in point

He's the CEO of Telstra, but he works for an entirely different company. Ziggy Switkowski doesn't devote all his energies to Australia's biggest company. He's not all that interested in the continuation of the steadily successful telephone giant. Mainly because he's too busy working for the company Telstra is going to be: a very different, almost unrecognisable entity. And because he's going at it like there's no tomorrow, Telstra will probably have one. Not the local-and-long-distance-business-and-residential-narrowband-fixed-wire model. But the mobile-information-data-Internet-transaction-entertainment-broadband one.

Even being the biggest company in the country doesn't let you rest on your laurels any more. And fixing what ain't broke is no longer a TQM issue. Telephony giants becoming Internet providers? Computer suppliers getting into cars? The world's biggest stockbrokers chasing online upstarts? These aren't ripples, they're sea changes. How do you get in front of the wave?

Source: *Business Review Weekly*, Telstra advertisement.

Activities for discussion, analysis and further research

1 Explore the change issues for someone like Ziggy Switkowski. What processes will he need to follow to achieve changes in Telstra?
2 Do a literature search on the changes that the American telephone scene went through a number of years ago. Draw some conclusions as to what could perhaps happen in the Australian market. What changes are currently happening on the Australian telecommunications scene which could allow Australia to go the way of the US in that industry? What factors predicate against it?

One strategy to overcome resistance to change is *education and communication*. This means giving enough information and ensuring the change is clearly communicated to those it affects (Kotter & Schlesinger 1979).

Another way to overcome resistance to change is *participation and involvement*. Resistance is less pronounced when those affected by change participate in planning and implementing it. At Corning, worker involvement is a key in cost-saving efforts. For instance, a maintenance employee suggested using a flexible tin mould for several fixed moulds to shape wet ceramic material to be baked into automobile catalytic converters. This saved $99 000 per year (McComas 1986). There is evidence managers under-utilise participation to overcome resistance to change (Nutt 1986).

Facilitation and support can overcome resistance. When individuals react to impending change with fear and anxiety, managerial encouragement and help often reduce resistance. Other methods of facilitation and support include training and providing proper equipment and materials.

Another approach to reducing resistance to change is *negotiation and agreement*. Negotiation can be an important strategy when one group sees it will be hurt by change and is in a position to cause a change effort to fail. If other strategies, such as education and participation, falter, negotiation may be needed to gain co-operation (Schlesinger 1987).

Another way to overcome resistance is *manipulation and co-optation*. Manipulation involves giving selected information on a change so it seems to potential resisters to be more attractive or needed. Ethical questions arise when selective information use distorts the change's potential negative aspects. In co-optation, a leader or an influential person among potential resisters is given an apparently desirable role to gain their co-operation. Usually, the role is symbolic, as they have little say in the change process. However, it may be good enough for the person to obtain their support. The danger with manipulation and co-optation is that this strategy can backfire if they recognise what is being done and feel manipulated.

Finally, *explicit and implicit coercion* can overcome change resistance. This involves use of direct or indirect power to make change resisters conform. Tactics focus on direct or veiled threats about job loss, or loss of promotion, pay and other benefits. Individuals may be transferred or fired. With coercion, it is probable pressure targets will resent it even if they yield. Furthermore, coercion may escalate resistance (Kirkpatrick 1986). If a change is not popular but needs to be implemented quickly, managers may have to use the strategy. Evidence shows that managers use coercion more often than needed, and fostering subordinates' negative feelings may block future changes (Nutt 1986).

Of course, it is not just employees resisting change. Employers can resist it too. This happened to B. Thomas Golisano, sales manager for Electronic Account Systems Inc., a small computerised payroll-processing organisation. Electronic catered to large companies, but Golisano saw there might be a market with smaller companies. He presented his idea to his bosses, but no one listened. So he started his own company, Paychex, now the second largest payroll-processing company in the United States. His former employer says, 'He was right and we were wrong' (Cowan 1986; Meeks 1989; Taylor 1995).

Force-field analysis   To overcome resistance to change, managers can use **force-field analysis**. Developed by Kurt Lewin, this involves analysing two types of forces, driving and restraining forces, influencing proposed change and assessing how to overcome resistance. **Driving forces** are factors pressuring for a particular change, where **restraining forces** are factors pressuring against a change. At a point in time, the two force types push in opposite directions, giving an equilibrium defining current conditions, or the status quo. To change the status quo to a desired condition, it is necessary to increase driving forces, to decrease restraining forces, or do both. Although managers think of increasing driving forces, this, according to Lewin, is likely to produce a balancing increase in resistant forces. Managers can best achieve a successful change if they work to reduce restraining forces (Lewin 1951; Strebel 1994).

Faced with serious overseas competition, Xerox set a goal of halving manufacturing costs at its copier operation near Rochester, New York. This included plans to have wiring harnesses subcontracted, a move to lower costs but also eliminate about 150 jobs. As union leaders wanted to save jobs and as company-union relations had been historically good, union leaders met managers to consider ways to keep the harness work in plant.

Figure 17.4 shows a force-field analysis of major driving and restraining forces maintaining the status quo—costs too high for Xerox to effectively compete. The wider the arrow, the stronger the force. In considering possible solutions, union leaders suggested relaxing some rules so workers could make minor repairs on machines rather than wait for maintenance workers to fix equipment. Union leaders and management studied ways to save money which finally led to eliminating six paid days off, medical insurance cuts, and developing ways of controlling absenteeism. In return, the company promised no layoffs for three years. By working on restraining forces, the company and union were able to agree on changes giving lower plant cost levels without contracting the wiring harness work out (Kirkpatrick 1986).

MANAGING CONFLICT

In organisations, conflicts within and between groups are common. By **conflict** we mean a perceived difference between two or more parties resulting in mutual opposition (Robbins 1974) and which may occur at three levels: within the individual (intrapersonal); between individual and organisation; and between organisational groups.

For our purposes here we will consider conflicts between individual and organisation and conflicts between organisational groups. While intrapersonal conflict can be destructive to individuals and in turn the organisation, it generally results in conflict between individual and organisation.

force-field analysis

Method involving analysing the two types of forces, driving forces and restraining forces, that influence any proposed change, then assessing how best to overcome resistance

driving forces

Factors pressuring for a particular change

restraining forces

Factors pressuring against a change

conflict

Perceived difference between two or more parties resulting in mutual opposition

Fig. 17.4   Force-field analysis of the forces maintaining high cost level at Xerox plant

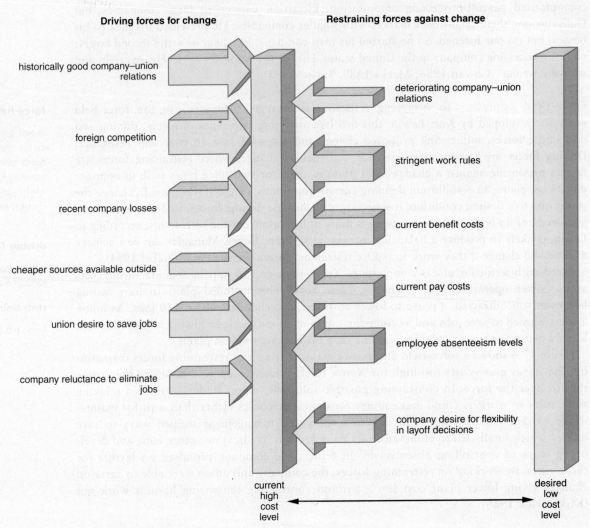

Driving forces for change

Restraining forces against change

historically good company–union relations

deteriorating company–union relations

foreign competition

stringent work rules

recent company losses

current benefit costs

cheaper sources available outside

current pay costs

union desire to save jobs

employee absenteeism levels

company reluctance to eliminate jobs

company desire for flexibility in layoff decisions

current high cost level

desired low cost level

Conflicts between individuals and organisations

As people mature, they move from:

○ a state of infant passivity to increasing adult activity;

○ a state of dependence on others to relative independence;

○ having a few ways of behaving to having many diverse ways;

○ having many shallow, casual, erratic interests to a few deep ones;

○ having a short time perspective (behaviour dictated by present events) to a longer one (behaviour determined by past, present and future events in combination);

○ being a subordinate person to being a teacher or supervisor (from child to parent or trainee to manager);

○ having a poor understanding of themselves to a greater understanding of and control over themselves as adults.

Unfortunately for efficiency and effectiveness, organisations increase task specialisation, unity of command, and formalisation to produce a standardised product with people whose work is regulated. Table 17.2 shows outcomes of this. As you consider it, think back to our earlier discussion of Taylor and scientific management in Chapter 2.

Table 17.2   Consequences of organisational standardisation

Individuals have little control over their work; control is often taken over by machines.
Individuals will be passive, dependent and subordinate.
Individuals will have only short-term work horizons.
Individuals are given repetitive jobs requiring minimum skill and ability.

Therefore, many job structures conflict with a healthy personality's basic growth needs. The degree of conflict is a function of several factors.

Conflict will be strongest with:
○ very mature employees;
○ highly structured organisations;
○ formalised rules and procedures; and
○ fragmented and mechanised jobs.

Hence, strongest conflict should come at lower organisation levels, among blue-collar and clerical workers. Managers have less mechanised jobs that are less subject to formalisation. For example, when cost cutting measures were introduced at Heinz's Dandenong plant in Victoria, the cafeteria manager started to charge 10 cents for a piece of toast, until then free of charge. This affected only the organisation's rank and file, as management had an executive dining room which charged an all-inclusive fee. Production workers' reaction to this change, which was neither discussed nor announced, was an almost complete walkout.

When conflict occurs, employees must choose to:
○ leave the organisation or work to climb into upper management;
○ use defence mechanisms to defend their self-concepts;
○ psychologically dissociate from the organisation (e.g. lose interest in their work or lower their standards);
○ concentrate on the organisation's material rewards;
○ find allies among other workers and all adapt by use of quota restrictions, strikes and sabotage.

While conflict is generally seen as negative, it can have either constructive or destructive consequences. Some of the destructive ones are well known. For example, conflict means individuals or groups can become hostile, withhold information and resources, and interfere with each other's efforts. It can cause delays in projects, increase costs, and cause valued employees to leave. Alternatively, conflict can have constructive outcomes. For one, conflict highlights problems and a need for solutions. For another, it promotes change as parties work to resolve the problem. Conflict can raise morale and cohesion, as members deal with the concern and frustration. Finally, conflict can stimulate interest, creativity and innovation, encouraging new ideas (Tjosvold 1984).

As a result, some conflict is useful, but too much can harm organisational performance (see Fig. 17.5). Very low conflict levels may mean problems are being hidden and new ideas stifled. In contrast, too much conflict means high amounts of energy are being wasted in dissension and opposition. Accordingly, managers must understand conflict's causes, how to reduce or resolve it and, when needed, to stimulate it positively.

Fig. 17.5   Effects of conflict on group performance

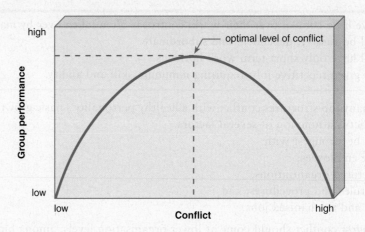

✖ 'We'll just sit here until you have got a problem.'

crossroads

The principal of a private school in Victoria had the following story to tell me:

'My school has two kindergarten units. Each has its own directress, both of whom are excellent teachers and really terrific with the children. But, for some reason, they just didn't get on. The tension between them had got to the point where the parents of the children were actually commenting on it to me. I really didn't know what to do, but I knew I had to do something. I did not intend to lose either one of them. So I invited them to my office and left instructions that we were not to be disturbed. There they both were seated side by side across the desk from me. I looked at them and said: 'I believe the two of you are having some problems?'

Both of them denied that they had any difficulty and looked ready to leave my office. I could not let that happen so I told them that in that case we would just have to sit there until they did have a problem. I picked up a file and started reading, ignoring my two staff members. Forty-five minutes later, one of them burst into tears and the other followed seconds later. As I passed around the box of tissues, I knew I was going to be successful in my wish and I would be retaining two good staff members.'

Source: Margaret Tein.

Reflection points

1 What strategies did the principal use to resolve conflict between her two staff members? Why did they work?
2 What conflict response did the kindergarten directress display?
3 What conflict management style did the principal use?

Decision points

1 What alternative strategies might have been used to resolve the conflict between those two staff members? What might have been the outcomes?
2 What were the risks involved in the strategy which was used?

Causes of conflict

Many factors contribute to conflict (Walton & Dutton 1969; Robbins 1983). Several are discussed below.

Communication factors   Managers ascribe many organisational conflicts to poor communication. If we define communication as the construction of a picture in the receiver's mind corresponding exactly to that intended by the sender, then perfect communication is rare. Given this, many chances occur for misunderstanding. Conflict stemming from unsuccessful communication is different from that based on substantive differences, yet it can still be harmful. For example, a manager who does not communicate clearly to subordinates who is responsible for performing an unpleasant task in the manager's absence may later find subordinates in conflict and the task still not done.

Structural factors   Organisational members may be conscious of a feeling of discomfort with how things are done. The processes followed may seem cumbersome. This may be due to organisational structure aspects. These may occur as a result of growth without planning.

Size   Reviewing studies on the relationship of conflict to organisational size, Robbins (1994) found consistent evidence of greater conflict in larger organisations. Size increases were associated with less goal clarity, greater formalisation, increased specialisation, more supervisory levels and increased opportunity for information distortion.

Participation   It is reasonable to expect more subordinate participation (for example, in decision making) to reduce conflict. From the human relations perspective it is argued that inviting subordinate participation satisfies a drive for involvement. Research, however, shows that with greater subordinate participation, conflict levels rise. This may occur because increased participation raises awareness of individual differences. However, increased conflict from greater participation is not necessarily undesirable (Barrett 1995; Cotts 1998). If participation's results, and consequent conflict, enhance overall work-unit performance then conflict's existence can be productive.

Line–staff distinctions   A frequently mentioned source of conflict is the distinction between line and staff units. Line units have jobs directly related to core organisational activities. In a manufacturing organisation, production would be a line unit, while in a customer-oriented organisation, a marketing or sales department would be considered line. Staff units support line functions. Examples of staff departments include research and development, public relations, human resources and industrial relations.

Conflict occurs between line and staff groups because of differences in functions, diverse goals, and members' values and backgrounds. Line groups are normally more operations oriented, while staff groups are further away from core activities. Line personnel more often accept their firm, while staff personnel are more critical of company practice. In fact, staff people identify more with their professional group than their organisation. Lastly, the two groups' time horizons differ, with staff people concerned with long-range, and line people more with short-term or day-to-day matters. Given these differences, it is not surprising line and staff personnel experience a high degree of conflict.

Reward systems   If one person or group gets rewards at another's expense, conflict arises (Kohn 1986, 1987). How mutually exclusive reward systems operate may not be clear. For example, staff people are rewarded for being innovative identifying a need for change. By suggesting and attempting to induce change, they demonstrate usefulness to the larger organisation. On the other hand, line people prefer to avoid change: for them it is disruptive and inconvenient. In fact, line people are rewarded for productive uninterrupted activity.

Resource interdependence   Groups typically compete for organisational resources (Friedkin & Simpson 1985). With increasing resources, conflicts may not occur. However, increasing resources are uncommon in organisations. Thus, conflict and lack of co-ordination and co-operation between groups are likely (Zachary 1995). This lets task interdependence become a conflict source.

Task interdependence   Two types of task interdependence are very prone to conflict. One is sequential interdependence, where one individual or work unit is reliant on another. For example, waiters are more reliant on cooks than the reverse because waiters depend on cooks to produce good meals in a timely manner. The second form of task interdependence is reciprocal interdependence, where individuals or work units are mutually interdependent. For example, purchasing agents want to be given generic specifications to be able to purchase at lowest cost. Users need materials of a particular quality with specific characteristics and find it simpler to specify a particular brand name (Strauss 1964).

Power   Organisational power distribution can also produce conflict. If a group feels less powerful than it should be, or it believes another group holds too much power, it will challenge the situation (Davies 1998a, 1998b; O'Reilly 1997). If departments that are ostensibly equal hold different amounts of power, discontent arises. For example, staff people must justify their need to exist, understand line departments' problems, and constantly get along with line personnel. The reverse is not true for line personnel, as they normally have greater authority. The imbalance increases tension in a difficult situation.

Personal behaviour factors   Another conflict source is individual differences. People's values or perceptions may generate conflict (Petzinger 1995). An example is a manager valuing the idea of employees 'paying their dues'. The manager might argue that they spent many years in a mundane low-level organisation position and others will benefit from the same experience. Imposing this on ambitious subordinates creates serious conflict. Similarly, managers who see people in a particular way (for example, inferred laziness or incompetence from limited evidence) will generate conflict by their response to certain situations. In addition, some people enjoy being argumentative and combative. For individuals whose personal style is especially conflict-prone, life is a series of hostilities and battles (Siler 1989; Bailey 1990).

Communication styles   Conflict may come from communication problems and inter-personal misunderstandings. For example, different linguistic styles means some men in work teams will talk more, taking more credit for ideas, than women in those teams. This produces conflict when men incorrectly assume the women are not interested or less capable because they participate less, and women incorrectly assume the men are being bossy and are not interested in their ideas as they seem to talk more (Jones et al. 2000).

Workforce diversity   Diversity can also generate conflict. An older worker may feel uncomfortable or resent reporting to a younger supervisor, an Asian may feel singled out in a group of white workers, or a female top manager may feel her mostly-male top-management team are ganging together when one of them disagrees with a proposal of hers. Whether the feelings are justified or not, they will cause recurring conflicts.

Differences in goals   As organisational subunits specialise, dissimilar goals develop. A production unit's goal may be low production costs and few defects. The research and development unit's goal may be innovative ideas convertible into successful new commercial products. These goals lead to different member expectations and conflict occurs because of varied goals. An example of this incompatibility surfaced at Heinz's Dandenong plant during the company's early drive to introduce TQM. For purchasing, TQM meant obtaining lowest-priced potatoes. However, for production, this meant minimum wastage due to bruising and marks on the potatoes. Low-cost potatoes had many bruises and marks needing to be removed by hand, raising the process's labour cost and reducing yield. This led to intense interaction until the conflict's cause was identified and resolved.

Reward structures   Intergroup conflict is likely when rewards are linked to individual group, not the organisation's overall, performance. When rewards link to individual-group performance, performance is seen as an independent variable, though group performance is very interdependent (Kohn 1986, 1987).

Differences in perceptions   Goal differences come with differing world perceptions, and disagreements lead to conflict (Behar 1995). Organisation groups develop different views of reality due to different goals and time horizons, status incongruence and inaccurate perceptions.

Time perspectives influence a group's perception of reality. Deadlines influence priorities and importance given to different activities. A company's research workers' time perspective may be several years, while manufacturing engineers operate with time frames up to a year. Furthermore, upper management focuses on five- to ten-year time periods, while middle managers use shorter spans. With such time-horizon differences, problems and issues one group sees as critical may seem unimportant to another, and conflicts erupt.

Conflicts about different groups' relative status occur and influence perceptions: an organisation may have many different status standards, resulting in a range of hierarchies (Naughton & Kerwin 1995). For example, conflicts may be produced by work patterns, such as which group initiates work and which responds. A production department, for instance, may view a change as damaging to its status because it involves work being initiated by a salesperson. This status conflict may be aggravated purposely by the salesperson.

Inaccurate perceptions often cause groups to stereotype others. Differences may be small; however, each group exaggerates them. When differences are emphasised, stereotypes are reinforced, relationships deteriorate and conflict develops.

The increased demand for specialists   Conflict between staff specialists and line generalists is a common source of intergroup conflict. With increased organisational demand for technical expertise, staff roles expand and conflicts increase. The point is that line and staff persons view each other and their organisational roles differently.

Benefits and losses from conflict

As noted before, conflict can have positive and negative outcomes. If an organisation eliminates conflict, then the organisation is in trouble. Conflict is a sign of a vital organisation and it is a problem only when excessive. Excessive conflict leads to wastage of valuable resources. Harmful, or dysfunctional, conflict is discussed later in this chapter.

Benefits   Benefits occurring when conflict is moderate are as follows:

Productive task focus. When groups have moderate conflict levels, intragroup differences are minimised, and task focus increases. Natural differences occur between groups (such as age, education, attitudes and clothing) to suit the task. These enable departments to excel at specific tasks.

Cohesion and satisfaction. Group identification increases cohesion. Members are attracted to a group, receiving satisfaction from belonging. Members co-operate and defer personal goals in achievement of departmental goals. Membership under conditions of mild intergroup conflict also increases member satisfaction.

Power and feedback. The occasional flare-up of intergroup conflict balances interdepartmental power relationships, giving feedback on departmental status. Employees' perceptions of their roles and relative importance are often inaccurate, so they expect and demand organisational resources inappropriate to their actual importance. Conflict blunts these excesses as it focuses on organisational problems and reduces intergroup disparities. Feedback lets groups correct these perceptions, and regulates intergroup power or resource balances.

Goal attainment. An organisation's goal-achievement ability is related to energy directed at department level goals. Moderate competition and conflict stimulate participants to work. Cohesion leads to an enjoyable work atmosphere. But complacency can be as bad as too much conflict. So an organisation can prosper and achieve its goals only when subgroups are effective.

Losses   When conflict is too strong, there may be negative consequences. Conflict losses are as follows:

Energy diversion. One consequence is diversion of departmental time and effort to winning a conflict rather than achieving organisational goals. When the most important outcome becomes defeating other departments, resources are wasted. In extreme cases, people withhold information or even vital innovative action, or sabotage may occur.

Distorted judgment. A finding from intergroup research is that judgment and perceptions become less accurate as conflict increases. Then after a group makes a mistake, it may blame perceived opponents instead of seeing its own flaws. People involved in conflict are also unreceptive to competitors' ideas.

Loser effects. Another aspect of interdepartmental conflict is someone loses. The loser undergoes significant change, tends to deny or distort reality and seeks scapegoats for the loss. Cohesion is reduced as losers display low co-operation and concern for other departments' members' needs and interests.

Poor co-ordination. The final problem is emphasis on departmental goal achievement. These goals energise employees, but should not become all-consuming. They must be integrated with organisational goals. Under intense conflict, integration does not happen. Collaboration between groups decreases as contact reduces and each group becomes unsympathetic to other viewpoints. Under intense conflict, departmental goal achievement and enemy defeat are a priority. Compromise is not possible.

 # Dealing with change—now!   gaining the edge

We have decided to make some significant changes to the organisation. You may even have reasoned that the ability to change should become a 'core competency' of the organisation—something absorbed into the structure and expected of all employees.

So what is the best way to do it? A short, sharp shock, or in stages? The benefit of doing it quickly is that employees do not have time to be apprehensive. The risk is that they will be unable or unwilling to adapt to the changes.

As with most management questions, the answer is 'it depends'. Businesses in trouble often have little choice but to make changes quickly. Others may choose to change slowly in order to be more adaptable in the future. An Anderson Consulting study demonstrates that the aim is ultimately not to rely on one person for change. It says that leaders have to communicate the message frequently and passionately to all members of the organisation by many different means. Managers often want to know how quickly they should implement change but time is not a factor. For example, in the merger of Westpac with the Bank of Melbourne, timing was not important, but thoroughness was. What the change agents worked on was the spirit of the merger, not the quick fix.

Three things are necessary to implement change effectively:
○ the engagement of staff;
○ the necessary training or plant and equipment; and
○ the requisite number of people who can manage the processes of change.

There are different opinions about the speed of change. Some believe that if managers concentrate on managing speed they will achieve 90 percent of their aims. Some believe that other questions are more important. First senior management must determine how much it wants to manage change, then it should determine the extent of delegation. Only then does speed become a consideration. The speed of change must be managed as an independent variable. Many organisations treat managing the consequences of change as incidental to the mechanics of it. The renewed emphasis on change management may spell the end of the 'empowerment' trend. A common theme in the change management literature is that employees do not like change and the implication is that they have to get used to it. This unfortunately infers a return to a more autocratic style of management.

The concentration on 'capabilities' rather than 'action' also represents a more aggressive form of autocracy. Employees are not only being asked to perform tasks efficiently, they are expected to develop an adaptive character.

Source: James, D. (1999).

Activities for discussion, analysis and further research

1 Compare the change strategies suggested in this article to the models studied in this chapter. In what ways do they differ?
2 Why should the speed of a change be treated as an independent factor?

Reducing and resolving conflict

avoidance

Conflict-handling mode involving ignoring or suppressing a conflict in the hope it will go away or become less disruptive

accommodation

Conflict-handling mode focusing on solving conflicts by allowing the other party's desires to prevail

competition

Conflict-handling mode involving attempting to win a conflict at the other party's expense

compromise

Conflict-handling mode aiming to solve issues by having each party give up some desired outcomes to get other desired outcomes

Since managers cannot escape intergroup conflict, they must manage it. Thus we need to examine techniques used to resolve dysfunctional intergroup conflicts. Most involve exchange between conflicting parties, suggesting resolution may be facilitated by constructive negotiation.

Changing situational factors. An obvious way to reduce conflict is to change the situational factors causing a problem. So a manager might seek to provide more resources, reorganise to reduce interdependencies, redesign the reward system, or improve communication processes.

Appeal to superordinate goals. If situations of excessive conflict are difficult to change managers may be able to refocus individuals or groups on superordinate goals. These are major common goals requiring all parties' support and effort. Examples are ensuring organisational survival and beating highly visible competition. The success of superordinate goals is dependent on identifying goals sufficiently important to all parties.

Use an interpersonal conflict-handling mode. Aside from a situation change or appealing to superordinate goals, interpersonal modes are another way to resolve conflict. Managers have five major interpersonal modes to reduce or resolve conflict (Thomas 1977; Reitz 1987).
○ **Avoidance** ignores or suppresses a conflict in the hope it will go away or not become too disruptive.
○ **Accommodation** solves conflicts by allowing the other's desires to prevail. In essence the manager voluntarily allows the other party to have their way instead of continuing the conflict.
○ **Competition** attempts to win a conflict at the other party's expense. In other words, one party wins and one loses.
○ **Compromise** solves conflict by having all parties give up some desired outcomes to obtain others. Compromise often involves bargaining by parties and needs a situation

offering all parties a chance to be in a better position or at least in no worse position after resolving the conflict. With compromise each person wins some major issues and loses others.

○ **Collaboration** resolves conflicts by devising solutions allowing all parties to achieve desired outcomes. In other words the solution allows both parties to win at least their major issues. Collaboration frequently requires considerable creativity developing solutions suited to the conflicting parties' needs.

collaboration

Conflict-handling mode striving to resolve conflicts by devising solutions allowing both parties to achieve desired outcomes

Although collaboration is good in handling conflict as both sides may be satisfied, there may be reasons to use other approaches. Table 17.3 summarises situations where each conflict-handling mode applies, as reported by 28 chief executives.

Although people may be tempted to see some styles of conflict management to be more effective than others (for example, collaborating versus avoiding), there is reason to believe each works best in some situations.

Table 17.3   Situations in which to use the five conflict-handling modes, as reported by chief executives

Conflict mode	Situation
Competing/forcing	1. When quick, decisive action is vital; e.g. emergencies 2. On important issues where unpopular actions need implementing; e.g. cost cutting, enforcing unpopular rules, discipline 3. On issues vital to company welfare when you know you're right 4. Against people who take advantage of non-competitive behaviour
Collaborating	1. To find an integrative solution when both sets of concerns are too important to be compromised 2. When your objective is to learn 3. To merge insights from people with different perspectives 4. To gain commitment by incorporating concerns into a consensus 5. To work through feelings which have interfered with a relationship
Compromising	1. When goals are important, but not worth the effort or potential disruption of more assertive modes 2. When opponents with equal power are committed to mutually exclusive goals 3. To achieve temporary settlements to complex issues 4. To arrive at expedient solutions under time pressure 5. As a backup when collaboration or competition is unsuccessful
Avoiding	1. When an issue is trivial, or more important issues are pressing 2. When you perceive no chance of satisfying your concerns 3. When potential disruption outweighs benefits of resolution 4. To let people cool down and regain perspective 5. When gathering information supersedes immediate decision 6. When others can resolve the conflict more effectively 7. When issues seem tangential or symptomatic of other issues

Accommodating	1. When you find you are wrong, to allow a better position to be heard, to learn, and to show your reasonableness
	2. When issues are more important to others than to yourself, to satisfy others and maintain co-operation
	3. To build social credits for later issues
	4. To minimise loss when you are outmatched and losing
	5. When harmony and stability are especially important
	6. To allow subordinates to develop by learning from mistakes

Source: Reprinted from Thomas (1977, p. 487).

Managing intergroup conflict through resolution

Since managers must live with intergroup conflict, they must confront managing it. Thus we need to examine techniques used in resolving dysfunctional intergroup conflicts. Most involve some exchange between conflicting parties, suggesting resolution may be facilitated by constructive negotiation.

Problem solving   The confrontation method of problem solving reduces tension by face-to-face meetings between conflicting groups, their purpose being to identify conflicts and resolve them. The groups openly debate various issues and bring together all relevant information until a decision is reached. Effective problem solving requires conflicting parties to display willingness to work collaboratively towards an integrative solution satisfying the needs of all concerned. Problem solving is effective in increasing solution commitment by incorporating everyone's concerns into a consensus.

While problem solving is a desirable approach to conflict resolution, it can be difficult to implement effectively. The greatest obstacle to be overcome is the win–lose mentality often characteristic of conflicting groups. Unless parties involved rise above this, problem solving is unlikely to be successful.

Expansion of resources   As noted before, a major cause of intergroup conflict is limited resources. What one group obtains comes at another group's expense. The scarce resource may be a particular position, money, space and so on. Expanding resources is a successful technique for solving conflicts since it enables almost everyone to be satisfied. Unfortunately, however, resources are not always easily expanded.

Smoothing   Smoothing emphasises common interests of conflicting groups and de-emphasises differences. The belief behind this is that stressing shared viewpoints helps achieve a common goal. If differences between groups are serious, smoothing—like avoidance—is a short-term solution. Smoothing may contribute to low-quality decisions whose full implications are unrealised.

Bureaucratic authority   Bureaucratic authority means rules, regulations and formal authority are used to resolve or suppress conflict. This technique's disadvantage is that it does not change attitudes and treats only the immediate problem. The method is effective short-term when agreement cannot be reached on a solution to a particular conflict.

Limited communication Encouraging small amounts of communication between departments stops misperceptions developing. When departments are in severe conflict, controlled interaction helps resolution. Often interaction is limited to issues over which departments have a common goal. Having a common goal requires departments to talk and co-operate to achieve the goal. The technique is most effective when decision making and interaction rules are clear. It may not help much with attitude change.

Confrontation and negotiation Confrontation occurs when those in conflict deal with each other directly to work out differences. Negotiation is the bargaining process occurring during confrontation, enabling parties to reach a solution. Both techniques bring parties' representatives together.

Confrontation and negotiation are risky, because discussion may not focus on the conflict and emotions may get out of hand. However, if members can resolve conflict through face-to-face discussions, they will find new respect for each other and future collaboration is facilitated. Relatively permanent attitude change is also possible through negotiation.

Confrontation can be used positively if it is seen as a means of starting the negotiation process.

Confrontation succeeds when managers develop a 'win–win' strategy. This means both groups adopt a positive attitude, striving to resolve conflict to the benefit of both. If negotiations deteriorate into a win–lose strategy (each group trying to defeat the other), confrontation will be ineffective.

Intergroup training Another conflict reduction strategy is intergroup training. When other techniques are inappropriate for the organisation, group members may need special training. For this, department members attend a workshop away from regular work problems. The technique is expensive, but can achieve attitude change.

The steps involved in intergroup training are as follows:

1 Conflicting groups come to a training setting with the stated goal of exploring perceptions and relationships.

2 Conflicting groups are then separated and each discusses and lists its perceptions of both groups.

3 Groups come together again and group representatives describe perceptions while group members listen. The objective is to report accurately to the other group each group's private images.

4 Before exchange occurs, groups return to private sessions to consider the information; reports generally show a gap between self-image and that reported by the other group. The next session seeks to analyse causes of discrepancies, which makes each group review its behaviour to the other and possible consequences of that behaviour, regardless of intention.

5 Representatives of each group publicly share discrepancies identified and possible reasons for them, focusing on actual, observable behaviour.

6 After this, the two groups explore the now-shared goal of identifying reasons for perceptual distortion.

7 Exploration of how to manage future relations to minimise conflict recurrence then takes place. After this process, understanding is improved and leads to improved working relationships.

THE RELATIONSHIP BETWEEN CHANGE AND CONFLICT

Change is a process and as such it has several stages which occur in sequence if the process is to be successful; however, we are frequently unaware of the stages. Sometimes they do not occur overtly and we are uncomfortable with change.

As you can see by the two flow diagrams in Figure 17.6, how we feel about change depends largely on the part we play in it. Regardless of whether change is welcome or not, it is almost always a case of going from the known to the unknown and as such will create a state of apprehension. This state inevitably leads to conflict.

Fig. 17.6   Personal responses to change

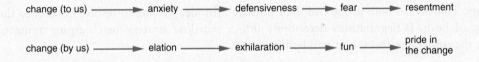

change (to us) ⟶ anxiety ⟶ defensiveness ⟶ fear ⟶ resentment

change (by us) ⟶ elation ⟶ exhilaration ⟶ fun ⟶ pride in the change

Types of intergroup conflict

Conflict is inevitable in organisations. As intergroup conflict can be both a positive and a negative force, management should not strive to eliminate all conflict, only conflict with disruptive effects on the organisation's efforts to achieve goals. Some type or degree of conflict may be beneficial if used as an instrument for change or innovation. The critical issue is not conflict itself but how it is managed. Using this approach, we can define conflict in terms of the organisation effect it has. In this respect, we shall discuss both functional and dysfunctional conflict.

Functional conflict   A functional conflict is a confrontation between groups which enhances and benefits organisational performance. Without this type of conflict, there would be little commitment to change, and groups would stagnate.

Dysfunctional conflict   A dysfunctional conflict is confrontation or interaction between groups that is harmful to the organisation or hindering goal achievement. Management must try to eliminate this conflict. Beneficial conflict can turn into bad conflict, but generally, the point when functional conflict becomes dysfunctional cannot be precisely identified. Certain levels of stress and conflict may help healthy and positive movement to goals in one group. The same levels, however, may prove disruptive and dysfunctional in another (or at a different time for the first group).

Behavioural scientists have spent 30 years researching and analysing how dysfunctional intergroup conflict affects those experiencing it. They have found groups in conflict situations react in predictable ways. We now examine a number of changes occurring within groups and between groups as a result of dysfunctional intergroup conflict.

Types of changes in groups in dysfunctional conflict   Changes occurring during inter-group conflict are as follows:

1 Group identification is strong when members share a common mission or purpose. Members see their group as separate and distinct from others. Pride develops and there are signs of the 'we feelings' characterising an in-group.
2 The presence of another group invites comparison and members prefer the in-group to the out-group.
3 A group perceiving conflict with another group becomes more tightly knit and cohesive. Members present a solid front to defeat the other group. The group tends to become more formal and accepting of a leader's autocratic behaviour.
4 Members tend to see other groups as an enemy not a neutral object.
5 Members experience feelings of superiority, overestimating their own strengths and achievements.
6 Intergroup communication decreases. If it does occur, it is characterised by hostile negative statements, with group members not listening or giving credibility to the other group.
7 Members lose cohesion when a group loses a conflict. Member tension and conflict increases in the group and a scapegoat is sought to blame for the failure.

Conflict, changes in perception, and hostility are not abnormal. They are natural, occurring when members are healthy and well adjusted.

@ Hackers breach Treasury site   managing the e-challenge

Hackers infiltrated the Federal Treasury's Internet Web site inserting a home page headed InSaNiTy ZiNe cOrp. While it was not clear whether the group had altered other pages on the site, this would be examined by its managers.

However, the Treasury site which contains economic statistics and information on economic policy was closed down for repairs after several hours of running the bogus home page. The new home page said: 'Hi department of the treasury of Australia, this one is our most important hack! Our defacement #14'.

It offered greetings to 'The Brazilian groups that are interested in changing our country to a better country, that's all we want'. The page had a link to the Treasury's true home page, and the rest of the site appeared not to be altered.

InSaNiTy ZiNe cOrp listed 12 other sites defaced in recent weeks, many of them in Brazil, but gave few clues about the group's identity.

Source: Garran, R. (2000).

Activities for discussion, analysis and further research

1 This sort of behaviour is the result of conflict. Identify the parties involved in the conflict.

2 Indicate why this is an aspect of the e-environment which needs to be managed.

3 Do a search to identify other incidences of e-attack. Why do they happen and what are the outcomes of such activity? How may managers prevent them from happening?

Changing views on conflict

The image of conflict has changed. Until the mid-1940s, it was seen as harmful and unnecessary. Its existence was seen as a sign something needed correction. According to this view, conflict serves no useful purpose, distracting managers and sapping energy and resources. Conflict thus should be avoided. In addition, conflict was thought to result from poor management and trouble-makers. Through effective management techniques and removal of trouble-makers, conflict could then be eliminated and optimal performance achieved.

More recently, the view of conflict has shifted. Today, it is seen as inevitable and necessary to produce high organisational performance. That conflict can be harmful is undeniable, but some forms of conflict encourage development of new tactics and strategies, helping overcome stagnation and complacency. Conflict as a motivator for effort can be desirable. The focus of this contemporary view is successful conflict management, not its elimination.

Successful conflict management involves sustaining a specific conflict level and selecting a conflict-reduction strategy. In addition, managers may consciously create conflict. In situations needing creativity or when development of alternatives is needed (as when resisting groupthink), conflict stimulation is advisable.

In itself, conflict is neither desirable nor undesirable. It is only by its performance effects that its value can be assessed.

Identifying an optimal conflict level for a situation is not simple. It requires good understanding of those involved and their tasks. A manager also must be creative when determining strategies and tactics to change the conflict level. Simply increasing conflict when seen as necessary will not foster creativity; it must be channelled and directed. Maintaining conflict at an optimal, or 'Goldilocks', point is a significant managerial challenge.

Stimulating conflict

Since apathy, lethargy and poor performance result from too little conflict, managers may need to stimulate conflict. This must be introduced positively and carefully, to avoid destructive levels. There are several ways to increase constructive conflict in a group (Robbins 1983). Adding members with diverse backgrounds is one. Another is communicating information to cause members to discuss the need for change. Still another means is encouraging internal competition (Peters 1988). Of course, in conflict stimulation, managers must monitor and control the situation carefully.

The management of change and conflict can be classified as part of organisational co-ordination processes. Managers have to stimulate co-operation among individuals and work groups of various sizes. They involve themselves in negotiations required to resolve conflicts and differences. To do this, managers need to use competencies in the Focus on Others cluster

(Boyatzis 1982). Some have been mentioned before. One is self-control. To be effective in a conflict resolution role, the manager must beware of personal involvement in the issue. Self-control must be shown to retain some objectivity. This leads to another competency in that cluster—perceptual objectivity. This means the manager's view is not limited by excessive subjectivity or personal biases or perspectives. Managers unable to achieve this when needed lose subordinates' respect rapidly. It is necessary for managers to be able to view an event from a multitude of perspectives simultaneously, and to distance themselves from emotional involvement.

■ The MD's diary   the reflective practitioner

I have a fundamental belief that a certain amount of conflict and a certain amount of stress in people is a very positive thing. I need a certain amount of stress in my life. I need to be challenged, as I have said before. I am never happy with just maintaining the status quo. So the way that I try to do that is to try and instil in my management team and in all the people in the organisation, that change is normal; that change is welcome. I try to encourage people to take risks. I reward risk taking at a much higher level than that at which I punish failure. So failure is not encouraged but to do nothing is much worse than to take a risk. I will be quite critical of people if I see that there is nothing happening, and I guess by nature I encourage people into the organisation and around me that are by nature risk takers. No one will be criticised for taking a reasonable risk. There is no fear about doing something and getting it wrong. If we change ten things today, chances are we will get five of them right. What about the other five—it's simple. Tomorrow I'll just change them back. So you can't lose. If you don't change anything, you can't improve. So what I have to reward and what I have to encourage is not maintenance and not consistency with what they did yesterday.

I'm always looking for and always encouraging change. And I tell people quite openly when they ask what we do in this organisation. 'As an aside we make seat belts and air bags but what we really do all day is get better. We change things every day.' It's amazing that after a period of time people get to accept that change is normal. Once you've accepted that it is normal and are not threatened by it in terms of your own personal security, in terms of how failure is viewed within the organisation, then it no longer becomes a problem to people. I do not see anyone in this organisation who is profoundly afraid of change. People get nervous, people get stressed, people lose a little bit of sleep but I hope they don't feel threatened. I have not seen that they do. It's a case of making sure that people are encouraged to make the changes and that people have ownership of them as well. It has to be their idea. Change is much easier when it's our idea so if you encourage that and you reward risk taking and reward success at a much higher level than you punish failure, on balance most people will be prepared to take the risks. We also make sure that our recognition process works. That those people who are successful, people that perform well and are able to make changes and to make it in a positive way—that their achievements are recognised. We play down the failures, we play up the successes.

Our change process here is incremental. I do not encourage huge change, big step change. I encourage small step change, very very small step. Every change that we make should take place today. If we go down to the shop floor, ask them to demonstrate their continuous improvement program, it's a board of ideas which at any one time will have roughly 30 to 40 ideas on it of which they will strive to achieve at least half every week. They are small ideas for improvement. If we talk about the big picture and talk about quantum leaps in change, you will frighten the living daylights out of people. If you talk about where I want to be in five years and we have our business plan structured in the correct way, and we break that business plan down into small manageable lumps, and we break it down into daily lumps, then the consequences of getting something wrong become insignificant. You look at what you did today. If the change moves you towards achieving your strategic objectives, then, it's great. If it's not, then you change it back. There's no opportunity for people to make monumental mistakes.

It's an interesting process when you're in an organisation and are absolutely flat out ten hours a day just doing the things that you need to do and every now and again I have to take my management team aside so they can reflect where they were 12 months ago. It is only then that they see the magnitude of the change. They are then amazed at what they have achieved. If I were to ask them up front to take on those changes, their answer would be no. So what we do is set the vision and the strategic objectives, without necessarily putting time lines on them but we work every day at moving towards it. It's a very successful way of managing continuous change in a non-threatening way.

 # The subordinate's log

the reflective practitioner

I had to manage various levels of conflict. At the operational level, consultants were constantly in conflict with sales staff who would make promises to prospective clients to win business and attempt to encourage consultants to greater efforts. Consultants would then attempt to modify the brief and overcome the ambitious claims and promises made by sales staff. My role often involved negotiating a position between the two groups.

Conflicts with the CEO arose periodically over various general business decisions. Unfortunately staff witnessed confrontations which had a negative impact on their motivation and my ability to lead.

Positive conflict arose during vigorous debate between members of project teams. This often led to superior project decisions and outcomes.

Focus on practice—Strategies for improving

1　Determine the differences between compromise and collaboration as conflict-handling styles. Which one fits you best? Why? Under what circumstances?
2　How would you go about ensuring workers understood the constraints and pressures of other jobs in the organisation, thus reducing conflict?
3　How would you determine whether conflict is due to structure or culture in a given organisation?

Source: Jones et al. (2000).

Chapter summary

Although they may be forced to react to unpredictable situations, effective managers try to plan for major change and innovation through use of a six-step model which includes perceiving an opportunity or a problem, diagnosing the situation and generating ideas, presenting a proposal and adopting change, planning to overcome resistance, implementing change and monitoring results. Planning to overcome resistance to implementing change needs a knowledge of reasons why people resist change. Major reasons are self-interest, misunderstanding and lack of trust, different assessments, and low change tolerance. Managers must be aware of ways to overcome resistance to change, including education and communication, participation and involvement, facilitation and support, negotiation and agreement, manipulation and co-optation, and explicit and implicit coercion. Force-field analysis helps understand driving forces and restraining forces producing the status quo. It is then more effective to reduce restraining forces than to increase driving forces for change.

Managing conflict is an important group skill. Causes of conflict include task interdependence, scarce resources, goal incompatibility, communication failures, individual differences, and poorly-designed reward systems. Methods of reducing or resolving conflict include changing situational factors, appealing to superordinate goals, and using interpersonal conflict-handling modes. In addition, managers may have to simulate conflict to encourage creativity and innovation.

Conflict between organisation groups is inevitable, and it may be positive or negative, depending on the impact of organisational goal attainment. Functional conflict helps and benefits organisational performance, while dysfunctional conflict hinders organisational goal achievement. While most managers try to eliminate conflict, evidence is that an optimal level of conflict benefits organisational performance. Dysfunctional conflict produces changes to and between groups. A group will increase cohesiveness, develop autocratic leadership and a task focus, as well as emphasise member loyalty. Changes between groups result in distorted perceptions, negative stereotypes and decreased communication.

One difficult managerial task is conflict diagnosis and management. Techniques for intergroup conflict resolution include problem solving, resource expansion, avoidance, forcing, smoothing, compromise, and changing people or organisation structure. Each is useful at different times. Conflict management techniques also exist for situations where the level of conflict is too low. Conflict stimulation techniques include using communication channels, bringing in new members and changing organisational structure. The point is that to be effective, conflict management must involve both resolution and stimulation.

Questions for discussion and review

1 Consider the university or college you are currently studying at and list internal and external factors which might help its administration identify need for change.

2 Explain why the change process is cyclical and not a straight line.

3 Outline the main reasons why employees resist change.

4 Explain the major approaches for overcoming resistance to change. Suppose you are a manager in a small manufacturing plant facing increased competition from foreign-made products and needing to increase productivity. Design a plan to overcome employees' resistance to changes and innovations needed to increase productivity. What is your preferred strategy? What is your least preferred strategy?

5 Explain force-field analysis. Suggest three situations where it might be useful to help analyse a change situation.

6 Explain Lewin's model for overcoming resistance to change and link those steps to a situation you have experienced.

7 Managers often believe putting rules and regulations into place will help overcome if not eliminate conflict. What are the consequences of such an approach? Why?

8 What are major causes of conflict in organisations? Can you make links between causes of conflict and the conflict management styles managers adopt?

9 Discuss strategies managers can use to overcome conflict situations in organisations. Give an example from your own experience.

10 If there is a proven relationship between conflict and change, how can managers best manage change to minimise the possibility of dysfunctional conflict?

Exercises for managing in the 21st century

Exercise 1
Skill building: Diagnosing resistance to change

Understanding why people resist change is the key to implementing new structures, procedures, methods and technologies. Five major reasons people resist change are shown below. Typical comments associated with the reasons are listed. Indicate the reason normally associated with each comment.

Self-interest   Different assessments
Misunderstanding   Lack of trust
Tolerance (low) for change

1 I don't want to take the job because my family will have to move again.
2 We've done it that way for years.
3 I still have trouble following the explanation about why we need this new complicated machine.
4 Management thinks it's an improvement; I have a different view.
5 Upper management won't admit it, but this merger will cost us jobs.
6 Their explanation wasn't very clear regarding how working with them is going to help our unit.
7 The last time they asked to make a change like this, our benefits ended up being reduced.
8 It appears producing buggy whips is not what our organisation should be doing in two years.
9 I just perfected using this method, and now there's another change to cope with.
10 I can't see where that job will help my career.
11 I'm not sure my manager has been candid about the likely impact of the new procedure.
12 Marketing believes we need field representatives, engineering doesn't believe they are required, and production wants to control costs. Are they really necessary?

Exercise 2
Management exercise: Force-field analysis

Specification
Think about a situation in which you would like to make a change or institute an innovation, but you face resistance. (The situation might involve getting a better grade in a course, instituting an innovative project in a student organisation, overcoming a challenge at work, or improving a relationship with a peer or friend.) Write a sentence or two describing the status quo. Then write a brief description of the situation as you would like it to be if you could change it.

Analysis
List the major driving forces, the factors pressuring for change, and then list major restraining forces, the factors pressuring against change. Draw a force-field analysis diagram like the one in Figure 17.4. Remember, the wider the arrow, the stronger the force.

Solution
Select two or three restraining forces in your diagram and develop a means for reducing the degree of resistance. Be prepared to explain your diagram and solutions to another class member, who will act as your consultant (Lewin 1951).

Implementing a multimedia super corridor

on the rim—
in Malaysia

Asian governments are scrambling to attract high-tech know-how and financing to boost their economies. How they try to lure the best brains and biggest investments varies widely. This story examines the roller-coaster ride of Malaysia's Multimedia Super Corridor. Premier Mahathir's pet project was once in danger of turning into a white elephant. Now entrepreneurs are moving in and making money.

Tim Loving has found his business paradise. As he surveys cubicles full of programmers tapping on computers, the campus-like park outside the window and the rolling, tree-clad hills beyond, the Australian head of accounting-software firm Acctrack says he expects to chalk up sales of $1.1 billion in the next five years. He plans to triple its staff in the next year to keep up with demand. Loving says there isn't anywhere in the world he'd rather he operating. 'Our costs are 70 percent lower than existing competitors.'

Where is this hi-tech Mecca? Boston or San Antonio? Hong Kong or Singapore?

Try the much-maligned Multimedia Super Corridor outside Kuala Lumpur. Brainchild of Malaysian Premier Mahathir Mohamad, the MSC was launched three years ago amid much government-orchestrated fanfare. The MSC would be an Asian Silicon Valley, Mahathir boasted, a 'global gift to the information age'.

Then came the Asian economic meltdown. Malaysia circled the wagons, imposing capital controls and freezing the exchange rate of the ringgit. That was followed by the arrest and imprisonment of Mahathir's former deputy, Anwar Ibrahim, which threw the country into political turmoil. Suddenly, the big promises dried up. Gloomy assessments of the MSC's future started appearing in the regional and international press, along with questions about the wisdom of continuing to pour money into the project during a severe recession. Microsoft's talk of locating its South-east Asian headquarters in the MSC came to nothing, and to this day the global technology giants have committed only nominal amounts of investment to the project.

But just when some pundits had written off the MSC as another white elephant spawned by Mahathir's grandiose visions, stories like Loving and Acctrack's have started causing many technology players to take a second look. Could it be that Malaysia has stumbled onto something despite its initial preoccupation with bagging big players, the continuing red tape and a looming lack of skilled workers? And, if it has, will the MSC become the driving force behind an information-technology industry that is crucial to the country's economic well-being?

'At first, we heard a lot of thunder about the MSC but we didn't see much fruit', reflects Alex Kong, chief executive of Web site Asia Travel Network, which has been operating in the MSC since October 1998. Kong says a core of viable companies that are actually generating revenue is now forming in the corridor. 'We're starting to see the first technopreneurs, companies starting to reap the fruit of the MSC.'

Peter Hitchen, who tracks developments in Asia's Internet business for Solomon Smith Barney, sees it in similar terms. 'South-east Asia is fertile ground' for the new breed of technology-driven companies, Hitchen says. The promise of long-term backing, such as some 3 billion ringgit ($790 million) spent on infrastructure, tax breaks of 5 to 10 years and other incentives by the Malaysian government will allow a lot of smaller start-ups to flourish in the MSC, he says.

'The real benefit to Malaysia', agrees Loving of Acctrack, 'is lots of start-ups. Some will fail and some will become mighty oak trees. That ferment of activity is required for the development of a world-class software industry.'

Malaysia needs that entrepreneurial energy. Once primarily a producer of commodities such as tin and rubber, the country now gains about a third of its gross domestic product from largely export-oriented manufacturing. But with fierce competition from the likes of Thailand and China for manufacturing investment, economists say relatively developed—and expensive—Malaysia must pull itself up the value-added ladder if it's to continue to grow at the booming pace of the last two decades. That's where the MSC was intended to come in. Powered by the money and technology of giants like Microsoft, it was to be the country's bridge to the Internet age, an engine of growth that would drag the rest of Malaysia into the 21st century.

That giddy prospect is still a long way off. The MSC today boasts 187 companies, employing some 9000 people, 800 of them foreigners. So far, firms have invested a total of 2.1 billion ringgit in setting up businesses in the corridor. A further 113 companies have applied for and been granted MSC status and there are 170 more applications in the pipeline.

Of the companies with MSC status, about a third are foreign-owned—34 of them multinationals like Lucent, Siemens and Motorola, all of which have small-scale operations in the corridor. The rest range from Web-based ventures such as on-line stock traders and content providers to telecoms' concerns and software developers, which make up a third of the total.

The majority of companies, however, share one characteristic: they are small start-ups like Loving's Acctrack and Kong's Asia Travel Network. Together, they could provide the seedbed for a new, more modest, roots-up MSC that may yet help to transform the country's economy.

'The MSC will never become Silicon Valley', says James Yao, executive director at AsiaTechVentures, a venture-capital firm with investments in both California and Asia. 'But the government does understand that they have to promote technological innovation in Malaysia. Something good will come out of the MSC. It won't be as good as Mahathir says, but it won't be as bad as some people are slamming it.'

For Akio Hotta, who heads operations in the MSC for Japanese telecoms giant NTT, it will take one or two breakouts by MSC-bred companies to really put the place on the map. 'I think you have to have some sort of success-story model' for other companies to follow, says Hotta, whose company has invested 60 million ringgit in a research and development centre—by a big margin the largest investment in the MSC by a multinational.

Unfortunately for the MSC, of course, it isn't operating in a vacuum. Both Hong Kong and Singapore have rival programs—albeit launched with less grandiose ambitions—that seek to attract the same investors and nurture the same start-ups. So what is Malaysia's competitive advantage?

Why set up in the MSC and not Cyberport in Hong Kong or Singapore One? Analysts say the MSC certainly has some things going for it: better English than Hong Kong, substantially cheaper costs than both, and an export-friendly exchange rate. It has drawbacks, too: a much smaller talent pool to draw from, for example. And then there is the vexed question of censorship. While the government hasn't meddled with the Internet, there continues to be concern that it might. Also, despite government promises, executives say working in the MSC is no bed of roses. They complain of excessive red tape, tech-ignorant bureaucrats who until recently were preoccupied with hooking the multinationals, slow visa approval and poor infrastructure—ranging from slow and expensive Internet access to a simple lack of shops. 'We moved all our guys from Singapore', complains one executive at a large technology multinational. 'The cost was much cheaper, but our guys were so preoccupied with everyday issues, with visas, that the opportunity costs were much higher than the money we saved.'

Of much graver concern in the long run for the MSC is a lack of technological skill among Malaysian workers. For the moment, most companies operating in the MSC say getting qualified staff isn't much of an issue. 'So far, we've looked for 50 software engineers', says Ramli Abbas, vice-president and country manager for Motorola. 'Six hundred people applied.'

But according to other executives, the glut of skilled workers was caused by the financial crisis and now it's dwindling fast. The government is well aware of the problem and even before the crisis hit had set up an incentive program to lure back Malaysians working in high-tech companies overseas. But the issue goes far beyond simple staffing problems. Critics worry it could be the most important factor in limiting the MSC's transformation into a crucible of ideas and innovations.

'Where's the skill base?' asks Annalee Saxenian, professor of city and regional planning at the University of California at Berkeley. The MSC has the resources to build the infrastructure, but that's not what drives the IT industry, she says. 'It's all about talent. If you have it, you have it. If you don't, you don't.'

Source: Elegant, S. & Hibert, M. (2000).

Activities for discussion, analysis and further research

1 Consider the elements required for change. Are those elements present in the MSC? What is lacking and how could this lack be overcome?
2 Do some research to discover what organisations have set up in the MSC and what their developmental plans might be.
3 Tim Loving is obviously benefiting by his move to the MSC. Find the Web address for Acctrack and investigate how the company is going.
4 What are some of the issues which Malaysia will need to face if the MSC region is to fulfil its potential?

PART 6

ACROSS ALL FUNCTIONS

Previous parts of this book introduce management and examine its four major functions: planning, organising, leading and controlling. Now, in Part 6, we see how these various functions apply in the significant management situation of conducting business in the international arena.

As managers must take an increasingly world-wide perspective, **Chapter 18** focuses on strategic issues and alternative structures to conduct business across national boundaries. Essential to the international manager is adapting to cultural differences and dealing with special social and ethical concerns which arise in international areas.

More recently concern has grown with regional communities which comprise countries with shared trade, economic and political interests. These include groupings such as the European Economic Community and the North American Free Trade Area. The region of most interest here is the Asia Pacific Region, otherwise known as the South-East Asia Region. **Chapter 19** considers the region, looking at the role and nature of each key member. It also discusses the role Australia has in the region and the continuing impact the region has on the global community.

International Management

Chapter 18

CHAPTER OUTLINE

The nature of international management
Organisations engaging in international
  management
Orientations toward international management

Assessing the international environment
Environmental elements
Promoting innovation: The competitive advantage
  of nations

Gauging international strategic issues
Methods of international entry
Multinational corporation strategies

Organising international business
World-wide functional divisions

World-wide product divisions
International division
Geographic regions
Global matrix
Networked structure

**Managing diversity: Adapting to cultural
  differences**
Managing international human resources
Adjusting leadership styles

**Handling social responsibility and ethical
  issues**
International social responsibility
Questionable-payments issue

LEARNING OBJECTIVES

After studying this chapter, you should be able to:

○ Explain the concept of a multinational corporation and describe four major orientations
  toward international management.
○ Delineate several elements important in assessing the international environment.
○ Explain the concept of competitive advantage of nations and its linkage to innovation.
○ Outline the major methods of entry into international business.
○ Contrast four major strategies for multinational corporations.
○ Enumerate the main structural alternatives for conducting international business.
○ Explain the principal issues related to assignment policies and recruitment, selection, training
  and repatriation of managerial personnel.
○ Describe adjustments in leadership style needed due to cultural differences.
○ Delineate the major social responsibility and ethics issues related to international management.

Striving for excellence

With a global organisation which spans some 30 countries, the parent company has a dual structure with corporate divisions such as marketing and sales, research, engineering, finance, and human resources. The focus internationally is very much concerned with finance, technology and manufacturing. Autoliv is undeniably a global organisation with a need to control and co-ordinate resources.

With that many skilled and talented people available to it, the organisation frequently utilises them to transfer knowledge and technology from one part of the organisation to another. This process, which is supported by a strong expatriate policy, is a key strategy for ensuring a healthy spread of the corporate culture and the key objectives of the parent organisation.

Because of the diversity of the organisation, Auloliv Corporate has a perfect opportunity to form joint research ventures among the various country operations with key personnel encouraged to share their learning and developments with other facilities around the world.

It is argued that organisations must adopt a global view of planning and other activities. By viewing the whole world as their operating area, managers can tap into world-wide markets and be active where conditions support organisational goals. Main (1989) argues that a world-wide outlook is a necessity to compete effectively in many industries, such as cars, banking, consumer electronics, entertainment, pharmaceuticals, publishing, travel services and washing machines.

Managers can engage in international business, face competition from international organisations or deal with them as suppliers or customers. This means managers must grasp international management issues firmly. Accordingly, in this chapter, we explore the basic nature of international management, building on the coverage of international management issues across this text. We also probe environmental factors affecting managerial international success, and we consider the idea of the competitive advantage of nations and its relationship to innovation. We then examine strategic issues associated with international management and consider structural alternatives for conducting international business. We next investigate how to adapt to cultural differences. Finally, we address ethical questions from organisations operating across the world.

THE NATURE OF INTERNATIONAL MANAGEMENT

international business

Profit-related activities conducted across national boundaries

international management

Process of planning, organising, leading and controlling in organisations engaged in international business

If you inventoried your belongings, you would find items demonstrating international activity. For example, shoes from Italy or Brazil, a Japanese television and VCR, and a shirt made in China. Even items with brand names of companies based in one country may have been made in another through international business. **International business** is profit-related activities across national boundaries. These include supplies from other countries, products or services sold to customers abroad, and fund transfers to subsidiaries in other countries. **International management** is planning, organising, leading and controlling in organisations engaged in international business (Auerback 1987).

Organisations engaging in international management

Organisations engaging in international management vary in size and in the extent that their business activities cross national boundaries. One type of organisation involved in international management is the multinational corporation. Although definitions differ, a **multinational corporation (MNC)** is an organisation engaged in production or service activities through affiliates in other countries, maintaining control over their policies, and managing from a global perspective (Root 1984; Rugman & Hodgetts 1995; Pacelle 1996). With this perspective, top managers allocate resources and co-ordinate activities to take best advantage of business conditions.

Multinational corporations may be hard to identify from the outside, in terms of how much control management has over affiliate policies or whether management uses a global perspective. As a result, an arbitrary percentage (25 percent of sales from foreign sources) distinguishes multinational corporations from other business types. However, no single universal foreign sales percentage separates multinational corporations from others (Rugman & Hodgetts 1995). The 25 largest multinational corporations are listed in Table 18.1.

Although multinational companies tend to be large and engage in many activities across borders, an increasing number of middle-sized and small companies conduct international business. According to one estimate about 10 percent of companies with 100 or less employees export (Aley 1995). Regardless of size, their managers hold a basic view of international management.

Orientations toward international management

Top-level managers in companies expanding internationally (particularly in multinational corporations) take one of four orientations regarding how much operating methods are influenced by headquarters or by company members in other parts of the world. These orientations are ethnocentric (home-country oriented), polycentric (host-country oriented), regiocentric (region oriented) and geocentric (world oriented) (Perlmutter 1969; Balagi, Chakravarthy & Perlmutter 1985; Morrison, Ricks & Roth 1991). A home country is the country where an organisation's headquarters is located, while a host country is a foreign country an organisation conducts business in.

An **ethnocentric** (or home-country) **orientation** is where executives assume that practices working in the headquarters or home country must work elsewhere (Trachtenberg 1986; *Financial Times* 1996; Fernandez & Barr 1994). Although an ethnocentric orientation is often a phase organisations go through when they enter the international arena, it can be hard to eradicate.

A **polycentric** (or host-country) **orientation** is an approach where executives believe organisation parts located in a given host country should be staffed by local individuals as much as possible. Locals—or nationals, as sometimes called—are seen to know their own culture, mores, work ethics and markets best. As a result, subsidiaries in various countries operate under direction of locals and are tied to the parent company by financial controls. The parent company may have a low public profile relative to the subsidiary.

multinational corporation (MNC)

Organisation engaging in production or service activities through its affiliates in several countries, maintaining control over policies of those affiliates, and managing from a global perspective

ethnocentric orientation

Approach to international management where executives assume practices which work in the headquarters or home country must necessarily work elsewhere

polycentric orientation

Approach to international management where executives believe the parts of the organisation located in a given host country should be staffed by local individuals to the fullest extent possible

Table 18.1 The world's largest 25 multinational corporations

Rank 1999	1995	Company	Headquarters	Industry
1	4	General Motors	USA	Motor vehicles
2	–	DaimlerChrysler	Germany	Motor vehicles
3	7	Ford Motor	USA	Motor vehicles
4	12	Wal-Mart Stores	USA	General merchandisers
5	2	Mitsui	Japan	Trading
6	3	Itochu	Japan	Trading
7	1	Mitsubishi	Japan	Trading
8	9	Exxon	USA	Petroleum refining
9	20	General Electric	USA	Electronics
10	8	Toyota Motor	Japan	Motor vehicles
11	10	Royal Dutch/Shell Group	Britain/Netherlands	Petroleum refining
12	6	Marubeni	Japan	Trading
13	5	Sumitomo	Japan	Trading
14	18	International Business Machines	USA	Computers
15	–	AXA	France	Insurance
16	–	Citigroup	USA	Finance
17	24	Volkswagen	Germany	Motor vehicles
18	15	Nippon Telegraph & Telephone	Japan	Telecommunications
19	–	BP Amoco	England	Petroleum refining
20	11	Nissho Iwai	Japan	Trading
21	14	Nippon Life Insurance	Japan	Insurance
22	25	Siemens	Germany	Electronics
23	–	Allianz	Germany	Insurance
24	13	Hitachi	Japan	Electronics
25	–	US Postal Service	USA	Mail/freight delivery

Source: Adapted from *Fortune* (17 April 2000).

regiocentric orientation

Approach to international management where executives believe geographic regions have commonalities which make a regional focus advantageous, and that company problems related to the region are generally best solved by individuals from the region

A **regiocentric** (or regional) **orientation** is an approach where executives believe geographic regions have commonalities making a regional focus advantageous and regional company problems best solved by people from there. Typically, regional headquarters co-ordinate efforts among local subsidiaries in the region, while world headquarters manage overall issues, such as global strategy, basic research and development, and long-term financing (Moran, Harris & Stripp 1993). For example, forming a more unified multination European Union by 'harmonising' national rules (e.g. adopting common standards for electric plugs) gives new opportunities for a regional focus. Previously, manufacturers in Europe often established plants in host countries serving the host country's, and perhaps small neighbours', specific needs. The plant produced the full product range sold in the particular host country.

With a more unified European Union, it is possible to achieve economies of scale with different products made in different factories located in the region. Products are then shipped over a broad geographical area to customers (Morrison et al. 1991).

The **geocentric** (or world) **orientation** is an approach where executives believe a global view is needed in both parent company headquarters and subsidiaries, and the best individuals, regardless of home- or host-country origin, should be used to solve company problems. Major issues are viewed globally by both headquarters and subsidiaries, which pose questions such as 'Where in the world shall we raise money, build our plant, conduct R&D, and develop and launch new ideas to serve our present and future customers?' (Perlmutter 1969, p. 13). The geocentric approach is hardest to achieve as managers must acquire both local and global knowledge.

A geocentric approach helped Boeing save its 737 aeroplane. When sales slowed in the early 1970s, a group of engineers saw they had not attended to a potential market, developing regions. Through visits, the engineers found runways in developing countries were too short for the 737 and mainly asphalt, softer than concrete. They then redesigned the wings allowing shorter landings on soft pavement and changed the engine for quicker takeoffs. They also developed new landing gear and installed low-pressure tyres. Boeing began with small 737 developing-country orders, and later larger Boeing planes because of the experiences with the 737. The 737 became the best-selling commercial jet in aviation history and still sells well (Kupfer 1988; Holmes 1995; Cole 1996). The Boeing approach shows how important understanding the international environment is.

geocentric orientation

Approach to international management where executives believe a global view is needed in both the headquarters of the parent company and its various subsidiaries and the best individuals, regardless of host- or home-country origin, should be utilised to solve company problems anywhere in the world

◖ The cost of being an expatriate   case in point

One effect of the increasing Asian focus for Australian business is that more and more Australians spend time working overseas. These international workers soon discover they face complex issues and there are costly pitfalls to be avoided with little to do with their direct job performance.

Since the early 1980s when a few companies posted a small number of senior executives overseas, matters have altered considerably. These days, large companies with well established international operations are sending large numbers of staff overseas. One example is BHP Petroleum which has an average of 70 to 80 Australians on posting overseas at any given time.

These individuals need to be cautious about arranging their affairs back home if they wish to avoid unnecessary complications regarding investments, superannuation, the value of their family home to name just a few.

These are issues which expatriates must consider in conjunction with other aspects of their overseas assignments.

Source: Adapted from Kavanagh, J. (1996).

Activities for discussion, analysis and further research

1 What might an organisation which posts an employee overseas do to support that individual in the effectiveness of their posting?
2 Should they assist that employee in sorting out their local affairs before departure? Why?

ASSESSING THE INTERNATIONAL ENVIRONMENT

While international management opens great opportunities, it poses the challenge of trying to understand a broader set of environmental factors than met in a strictly domestic business. In this section, we explore various elements of the effects of the international environment and also a broader concept, the competitive advantage of nations.

Environmental elements

The idea of a general environment, or mega-environment, helps us understand the nature of international management. The general environment is the external environment segment of broad societal conditions and trends where an organisation operates (see Chapter 3). Major general environment elements, such as economic, legal-political, sociocultural and technological factors, help us describe the international area more fully.

The economic element   Various economic systems of countries are discussed in Chapter 3. Other economic factors that influence organisations' ability to operate internationally are the level of economic development in particular countries, presence of adequate infrastructure, a country's balance of payments, and exchange rates.

Countries (other than Communist ones) fall into two groups based on economic or industrial development level. The first group, known as **developed countries**, with high economic or industrial development levels, includes Australia, New Zealand, Singapore, Canada, the United States, Western Europe and Japan. The second group is the **less developed countries (LDCs)** or developing countries (often called the 'third world'), and consists of relatively poor nations with low per capita income, little industry and high birth-rates. Within LDCs, countries emerging as major manufactured goods exporters are referred to as **newly industrialised countries (NICs)**, including such nations as Malaysia, Taiwan and South Korea.

We may think multinational corporations operate across the world. Actually, about 95 percent are based in developed countries with about 75 percent of foreign investment channelled to developed countries. However, the rising prosperity of many LDCs (particularly the NIC group) has great potential for market expansion (Mendenhall, Punnett & Ricks 1995).

Deciding to conduct business in a given area also depends on adequate infrastructure. **Infrastructure** refers to highways, railways, airports, sewage facilities, housing, educational institutions, communications networks, recreation facilities, and other economic and social amenities signalling an area's economic development level. Due to information technology's growing importance, communications and information infrastructure is most critical. According to an estimate from the Asian Development Bank, countries in the region must spend $150 billion over the next 10 years to upgrade telecommunications infrastructure. Another $300 billion will be needed for regional transportation, power and water systems. Hence, building infrastructure to support economic development is expensive (Marchand 1996).

---

developed countries

Group of countries that is characterised by a high level of economic or industrial development and includes Australia, the United States, Western Europe, Canada, Australia, New Zealand and Japan

less developed countries (LDCs)

Group of non-communist countries, often called the 'third world', consisting primarily of relatively poor nations characterised by low per capita income, little industry and high birth-rates

newly industrialised countries (NICs)

Countries within LDCs emerging as major exporters of manufactured goods, including such nations as Taiwan and South Korea

infrastructure

Highways, railways, airports, sewage facilities, housing, educational institutions, recreation facilities, and other economic and social amenities signalling the extent of an area's economic development

Another economic variable is a country's **balance of payments**, the account of goods and services, capital loans, gold and other items entering and leaving the country. **Balance of trade**, the difference between a country's exports and imports, is a critical determinant of a country's balance of payments. Constant trade deficits means a country's wealth is exported, and surpluses enhance a country's ability to expand and conduct more international trade (Knowlton 1988; Rugman & Hodgetts 1995).

Related to this is the **exchange rate**, the rate at which one country's currency can be exchanged for another's currency. Since exchange rates affect relative prices of goods from various countries, rate changes can influence a firm's ability to engage in international business (Melloan 1988; Magnusson 1992; Rose 1996).

The legal-political element

Both legal and political conditions affect a firm's ability to conduct business in other countries. Considerations include level of political risk of operating in a country, and trade barriers put up by governments.

Corporations must assess the political risk of setting up in a given country (Micallef 1981). **Political risk** is how likely political actions will result in loss of ownership or benefits (Hofheinz 1994). A host-country's government seizure of a foreign company's assets is **expropriation**. Countries including Cuba, Zambia and Iran have expropriated foreign-owned corporations' assets within their borders. Iran seized many companies' assets, valued at over $5 billion, when Ayatollah Khomeini took over the Iranian government in 1979. Since 1960, 76 nations have expropriated over 1535 companies (Jodice 1980). A related risk is presence of **indigenisation laws**, requiring host-country citizens to hold a majority interest in firms operating inside the country's borders. Other risks are less severe but make business harder or more expensive in a host country.

Another legal-political environment aspect is trade control, which involves barriers or limitations on goods entering or leaving a country (Rugman & Hodgetts 1995). These are often put up so domestic goods will be competitive with foreign competitors. The most common barrier type is a **tariff**, a customs duty, or tax, levied on imports. For example, Ford Motor Company's efforts to sell in Russia are restricted by high import tariffs. A combination of tariffs, excises and value-added taxes raises Ford cars' price by 100 percent (Serenyi 1996). Another barrier is an **import quota**, a limit on the amount of a product to be imported over a period of time. Import quotas can protect a domestic market by restricting foreign competitors' product availability (Daniels & Radebaugh 1989).

As tariffs and quotas provoke direct reprisals from countries with affected products, the more subtle approach of **administrative protections** may be used. These rules and regulations make it hard for foreign firms to operate in a country. In one case, Japanese video recorders had to pass through French customs at a small facility at Poitiers, to be inspected one by one. This caused great delays, and importation of recorders slowed to a dribble. As a result, Japanese manufacturers agreed to a 'voluntary export quota', limiting recorders shipped to France (*New York Times* 1983).

The sociocultural element

The sociocultural environmental element includes attitudes, values, norms, beliefs, behaviours and associated demographic trends characteristic of a geographic area. Comparing people in different nations, it is common to speak about cultural differences.

---

balance of payments

Account of goods and services, capital loans, gold, and other items entering and leaving a country

balance of trade

Difference between a country's exports and imports

exchange rate

Rate at which one country's currency can be exchanged for another's

political risk

Probability of occurrence of political actions resulting in either loss of enterprise ownership or significant benefits from conducting business

expropriation

Seizure of a foreign company's assets by a host-country's government

indigenisation laws

Laws which require that citizens of a host country hold a majority interest in all firms operating within the country's borders

tariff

Type of trade barrier in the form of a customs duty, or tax, levied mainly on imports

import quota

Type of trade barrier in the form of a limit on the amount of product which may be imported over a period of time

administrative protections

Type of trade barrier in the form of various rules and regulations making it more difficult for foreign firms to conduct business in a particular country

power distance

Cultural dimension involving the degree to which individuals in a society accept differences in power distribution as reasonable and normal

uncertainty avoidance

Cultural dimension involving the extent to which members of a society feel uncomfortable with and try to avoid situations they see as unstructured, unclear or unpredictable

individualism– collectivism

Cultural dimension involving the degree to which individuals concern themselves with their own interests and those of their immediate family, as opposed to the larger group's interests

achievement– nurturing orientation

Cultural dimension involving the extent to which a society emphasises values such as assertiveness, competitiveness and material success, rather than values such as passivity, co-operation and feelings

Geert Hofstede developed a framework to study societal culture's effects on individuals (Jackofsky, Slocum & McQuaid 1988; Hofstede 1980, 1984). In his work, he researched values and beliefs of over 100 000 IBM employees in 40 countries across the world. Hofstede's approach uses five cultural dimensions to analyse societies: power distance, uncertainty avoidance, individualism–collectivism, achievement–nurturing orientation, and long-term–short-term orientation. Each is a continuum from high to low.

Power distance is how much individuals in a society see power distribution differences as reasonable and normal. In low-power-distance societies (Sweden, Denmark and Israel) those from different backgrounds often interact, and members of lower-status groups easily move to higher-status positions. In contrast, in high-power-distance societies (Mexico, the Philippines and India) high-status people have limited interaction with lower-status individuals, and it is hard to raise one's status. These differences affect how much subordinates and their bosses collaborate. If power distance is high, managers are more likely to tell subordinates what to do, not consult them. On the other hand, managers and subordinates are more likely to collaborate in a low-power-distance society.

The second dimension in Hofstede's framework, **uncertainty avoidance**, is the extent to which a society's members are uncomfortable with and try to avoid situations seen as unstructured, unclear or unpredictable. For example, in low-uncertainty-avoidance countries (Australia, Sweden and Great Britain) organisations have fewer written rules and regulations. This develops generalists (knowing many different areas) rather than specialists (knowing a great deal on a narrow area) and encourages managerial risk taking. Organisations in high uncertainty-avoidance countries operate in reverse (Japan, Peru and France).

Individualism–collectivism, the third dimension, is how much individuals focus on their own and their immediate families' interests as opposed to the larger group's interests. In cultures valuing individualism (e.g. New Zealand, Great Britain and Canada) managers will change companies easily, feel less responsible for employee welfare, and rely on individual not group decision making. In contrast, in cultures valuing collectivism (e.g. Venezuela, Taiwan and Mexico) managers focus on team achievements not individual ones and emphasise employee welfare, viewing the organisation as if a family.

The fourth dimension, **achievement–nurturing orientation,** is how much a society emphasises values such as assertiveness, competitiveness and material success, rather than values such as passivity, co-operation and emotions. In competitive societies (e.g. Japan, Italy and Mexico) employees believe jobs should give recognition, growth and challenge. In more nurturing societies, (e.g. the Netherlands, Sweden and Finland) more emphasis is put on good working conditions, security, feelings and intuitive decision making. Competitive societies have different roles for men and women. As a result, women's opportunities in organisations are limited.

The final of Hofstede's dimensions is orientation to life and work. A society with a **long-term orientation** values thrift (saving) and goal persistence (e.g. Singapore, Hong Kong and Taiwan). In contrast a society with a **short-term orientation** is more concerned with living in the here-and-now and with maintaining personal stability or happiness (e.g. Australia, the United States and France); members spend more and save less.

The technological element   The technological element is significant in the international environment as technology levels in various countries affect market nature and companies'

ability to conduct business. In fact, much technology transfer occurs during international business. **Technological transfer** is transmission of technology from those possessing it to those who do not. Technology can be goods or processes such as component parts or machinery, or intangible know-how, such as advanced road-building techniques. For example, after buying Tungsram, a state-owned bulb maker in Budapest, Hungary, to boost its European position, General Electric overhauled the technology of Tungsram's factories and computer systems (Levine 1990; Syrett & Kingston 1995; Perlez 1994).

**long-term–
short-term**

Cultural dimension involving the degree to which members of a society value thrift and goal persistence rather than living in the here-and-now and maintaining personal stability or happiness

 # Crossing the boundaries for partnerships

gaining the edge

Companies world-wide are building myriad bridges to each other. The resulting alliances may not work. But they may well represent the new shape of global business.

For most people, unbeknown to them, the world is just a big whirl of alliances. The petrol pumped into my car may very well be the product of an alliance between Shell and Texaco. I pay for this with a credit card co-branded by a bank and a telecommunication company. A cup of coffee I grab at the airport is sold through a partnership between Starbucks Corporation and Host Marriott. The airline that transports me to my next destination is a member of a grouping of several international carriers. For most organisations, the basis of competition has shifted to groups of companies competing against groups of companies.

Through the 1990s, the corporate world was dominated by take-overs. The trend seems to have shifted to alliances, joint ventures and partnerships. These activities have been involving all areas of industry and business, media, entertainment, airlines, financial services, pharmaceuticals, biotech, and information technology.

Most alliances are created to share risks. As projects become larger and more complex, even the larger companies would rather have partners to share the costs of research and development. Others involve players with complementary operations; for example, a producer and a distributor. Alliances can span countries and continents, and many do for the purpose of access to different markets.

Source: Adapted from Sparks, D. (1999).

Activities for discussion, analysis and further research

1 In what ways might international alliances add to the competitive advantage of organisations?
2 What are the factors which might detract from the competitive advantage of an alliance or joint venture which involves nationals from countries with vastly different ethnic cultures and traditions?

Promoting innovation: The competitive advantage of nations

**technological
transfer**

Transmission of technology from those who possess it to those who do not

In considering the impact of environmental factors on organisations, Michael E. Porter (1990a, 1990b) developed the idea of the competitive advantage of nations. The **competitive**

**competitive
advantage of
nations**

Concept that environmental
elements within a nation can
foster innovation in certain
industries, thereby
increasing prospects for the
success of home-based
companies operating
internationally within those
industries

advantage of nations holds that a nation's environmental elements foster innovation in some industries, increasing success prospects of home-based companies operating internationally in those industries. These companies' competitive success has positive national prosperity consequences too.

Porter's idea is based on the view of companies gaining competitive advantage by innovation. These may be radical breakthroughs or small incremental improvements (see Chapter 11), so long as organisations continually innovate to stay ahead of the competition. Innovation's incidence among companies in particular industries is influenced by national characteristics where those companies are based.

The diamond of national advantage   To explain why some companies can innovate consistently, Porter identifies four national attributes which individually and in combination set the diamond of national advantage (see Fig. 18.1).

Factor conditions are production components, such as skilled labour or infrastructure, needed to compete in an industry. Factors influence competitive success most when they are highly specialised, need ongoing heavy investment, and relate directly to industry needs. For example, Holland's research institutes in flower cultivation and shipping build expertise, making the country the world's principal exporter of flowers.

Demand conditions are domestic demand characteristics for an industry's products and services. When domestic buyers are sophisticated and exacting, companies must innovate and meet high standards. For example, environmental concerns in Denmark have made companies there develop world-class water-pollution control equipment and windmills.

The attribute of *related and supporting industries* refers to availability of supplier and other related industries competing effectively internationally. Such industries give cost-effective inputs and latest developments rapidly to home-based companies. Companies can become test sites for potential supplier breakthroughs, speeding the rate of innovation.

Fig. 18.1   Determinants of national competitive advantage (Porter 1990)

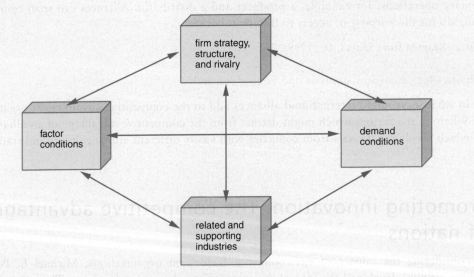

Firm strategy, structure and rivalry are national major conditions affecting how organisations are created, organised and managed, as well as the nature of domestic rivalries. For example, internationally successful firms in Italy tend to be small- or medium-sized companies privately owned and functioning as extended families. This suits industries Italian firms tend to do well in, such as lighting, furniture, footwear and woollen fabrics—requiring strategies with customised products, fast change and flexibility. German companies, in contrast, are likely to be hierarchical and have top managers with strong technical backgrounds. The German approach has been successful in industries needing strong technical and engineering expertise, such as optics, chemicals and complex machinery. Porter sees domestic rivalry as vital because it makes all local industry members innovate and upgrade their efforts. For example, rivalry between Swiss drug firms (Hoffman-La Roche and Novartis) enhances their global positions.

Implications for organisations and their managers   According to Porter, companies must act on factors in the diamond of national advantage and recognise the 'central role' innovation plays achieving competitive advantage. A company should expand international business dealings selectively, enabling it to tap other nations' advantages, such as sophisticated buyers or important research (Skrzycki 1987). Porter's issues further show how important long-range planning and strategic management is to international business.

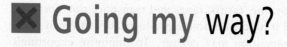

Going my way?

crossroads

Since the 1970s, engineers and IT specialists from Taiwan, India and China have been going to the United States to work in the Silicon Valley. However, the past two or three years have seen a changing trend. Engineers are still going but then, so are venture capitalists. These Asian investors have been a growing source of funds for start-ups and at the same time are brokering a special process of two-way trade. On one hand, they're building bridges to Asia for the valley's latest dot.com innovations, but on the other hand they are helping their region's own entrepreneurs take a foothold in this highly competitive market.

Source: Hiebert, M. (2000).

Reflection points

1   What are the issues these young investors must consider as they make their move?
2   They are obviously welcome and significant sources of funds for start ups. What factors should the recipients of those investments be considering as they accept this support?

Decision point

1   Locate the Web sites for Acer Technology and Asia Tech and see what you can find out about how they make their decisions on where to park their venture capital funds.

GAUGING INTERNATIONAL STRATEGIC ISSUES

Many companies in international business, particularly multinationals, engage in long-range planning. The planning period normally has a three-, five- or seven-year frame. Studies of multinationals show much planning occurs at headquarters, with some subsidiary involvement (Steiner & Cannon 1966; Negandhi & Welge 1984).

Although most companies in international business use long-range planning, their initial efforts at operating in other countries focus on narrower goals than becoming a fully-fledged multinational corporation. So, we consider major international entry methods before examining the strategic approaches of multinational corporations.

Methods of international entry

The four main methods organisations can use to expand into other countries are: exporting, licensing, establishing strategic alliances, and operating wholly owned subsidiaries (Schnitzer, Liebrenz & Kubin 1985; Rugman & Hodgetts 1995).

exporting

Process of making a product in the home country and sending it overseas

Exporting   For manufacturing organisations, **exporting**, making a product in the home country and sending it overseas, is a common way to enter international markets. Exporting requires little additional capital if the product does not need further modifications. It is low risk, particularly if the product is shipped after payment is guaranteed.

Exporting has potential disadvantages. For one, tariffs, taxes and transportation costs are involved. In addition, the exporter may find it hard to promote products adequately in other countries. If a product succeeds, local competition may emerge. To minimise exporting's disadvantages, companies may get foreign sales representatives, locals who understand product and market needs and whose activities may deter competition emerging.

licensing

Agreement in which one organisation gives limited rights to another to use certain of its assets, such as expertise, patents, copyrights or equipment, for an agreed-upon fee or royalty

Licensing   **Licensing** is an agreement where one organisation gives limited rights to another to use assets, such as expertise, patents, copyrights or equipment, for a fee or royalty. Typically, this allows them to use assets in a certain territory for a specified time. Licensing's main advantage is an organisation can make a profit and not lay out large sums to conduct business directly. Since the licensee is usually from the country involved, they are familiar with its culture and business methods.

Licensing has potential disadvantages, however. Most important is the licenser is usually not allowed to conduct business with the licensed product or service in a territory for 5, 10 or even 20 years. If the product or service succeeds, the licenser will miss much more profits from directly doing business. Another disadvantage is the licenser may establish a future competitor, since licensees may be able to produce equivalent product or service after the licence expires. Finally, the licensee may not perform as desired, impacting licensing revenues and long-term potential business.

strategic alliance

Where two or more independent organisations set up a co-operative partnership to gain mutual strategic advantage

Strategic alliances   A **strategic alliance** is where two or more independent organisations set up a co-operative partnership to gain mutual strategic advantage. In this arrangement no organisation is owned by another alliance member. Often strategic alliances involve a joint venture. A joint venture is where two or more organisations arrange to produce a product or service through a jointly owned enterprise (see Chapter 3) (Miller & Dess 1996; Yoshino & Rangan 1995; Inkpen 1995).

According to estimates, about 20 percent of direct investments are joint ventures (Christelow 1987; Ono 1993). Many companies seek to hold majority interest in joint ventures, to maintain operational control.

One advantage of strategic alliances is they give access to countries where full equity is not permitted. Other advantages include lower risk of new product introduction, keeping up with new technology, and combining home-country partner's technical expertise and capital with host-country partner's local knowledge. Possible disadvantages are losses if the venture is unsuccessful, expropriation, and disagreements among partners that are difficult and time-consuming to resolve.

Wholly-owned subsidiaries   A **wholly-owned subsidiary** is an operation on foreign soil totally owned and controlled by a company with headquarters outside the host country. Like joint ventures, wholly-owned subsidiaries are direct investments. However, one company owns the productive facilities. Wholly-owned subsidiaries can be established by acquisition (buying an existing company in the host country) or start-ups (building a company from scratch).

Wholly-owned subsidiaries have benefits. For one, the parent company has sole management authority over the subsidiary under the host-country laws where it is located. Similarly, the parent company keeps control over the technology and expertise. In addition, profits need not be shared. Moreover, the subsidiary may help a parent company's ability to service world-wide customers. The major disadvantage, apart from substantial costs involved, is facilities and expertise—a substantial investment and located within foreign borders—which may be expropriated if the political environment shifts.

Multinational corporation strategies

As companies expand internationally, they must develop appropriate strategies. Multinational corporations, and to a lesser extent other organisations operating internationally, must weigh two factors: the need to make optimum economic decisions globally and be responsive to host-country differences. Accordingly, multinationals have four strategy options: world-wide integration, national responsiveness, regional responsiveness and multifocal emphasis.

World-wide integration   A **world-wide integration strategy, or globalisation** (or globalism), aims to develop standardised products with global appeal, while rationalising global operations. Rationalising operations, or **rationalisation**, involves assigning activities to those organisation parts, regardless of location, that are best suited to producing the results desired and then selling finished products where they yield best profits. So a multinational might consider costs, expertise, raw materials and available capacity, in deciding where work is to be done. Rationalisation uses economies of scale, making best use of world-wide organisational resources.

wholly-owned subsidiary
Operation on foreign soil totally owned and controlled by a company with headquarters outside the host country

world-wide integration strategy, or globalisation
Strategy aimed at developing relatively standardised products with global appeal, as well as rationalising operations across the world

rationalisation
Strategy of assigning activities to parts of the organisation, regardless of their location, that are best suited to produce desired results, and then selling finished products where they will yield the best profits

Globalisation is based on the idea of products which can be used around the globe with little change to specification. Coca-Cola, sold in over 160 countries, is an example of a global product needing only small formula alterations. Few products and situations are suited to full globalisation.

National responsiveness   A **national responsiveness strategy** gives subsidiaries latitude adapting products and services to suit the specific needs and political realities of host countries. This strategy loses many world-wide integration advantages. Subsidiaries operate almost as national companies, though retaining many benefits of affiliation with a multi-national company, such as shared financial risks and access to global R&D resources. A national responsiveness strategy may be useful when globalisation is impossible due to national differences.

Parker Pen Ltd was using a national responsiveness strategy with about 500 pen styles from 18 plants. In about 150 countries local offices created packaging and advertising for local tastes. Then company officials read a *Harvard Business Review* article highlighting globalisation's advantages. The article argued that technology creates vast global markets for standardised consumer products and 'different cultural preferences, national tastes and standards, and business institutions are vestiges of the past'. (Levitt 1983, p. 96).

Taking the argument to heart, Parker officials consolidated pen styles to 100 choices made in eight plants. They designed one advertising campaign and translated it into several local languages. Profits dropped when local managers resisted the single advertising approach, which failed. After a $12 million loss in 1985, Parker was sold to a group of British managers. Profits came when a national responsiveness strategy was re-established (Lipman 1988; Koselka 1994). Thus, managers must evaluate the situation carefully, testing for a global market before making moves to develop an international strategy,

Regional responsiveness   A **regional responsiveness strategy** gives regional offices great latitude co-ordinating local subsidiaries and adapting products and services to suit their region's needs and political realities. This sacrifices some of the potential advantages of world-wide integration but keeps others because regions cover large areas, such as Europe, Africa or the Asia-Pacific region. Regional offices can get some economies of scale and adjust to regional tastes, but retain many benefits of affiliation with a multinational company, such as shared financial risks and access to global R&D resources. For example, France-based Thomson Consumer Electronics Inc., a major television-set manufacturer, switched from a national to a regional responsiveness strategy. To do so, Thomson set up four factories in Europe assembling specific set types for the European market. For instance, the German facility makes high-feature large television sets for the whole European region, while the Spanish factory produces low-cost, small-screen sets (Morrison et al. 1991).

Multifocal emphasis   A **multifocal strategy** aims to achieve the advantages of world-wide integration where possible, while trying to respond to national needs. Thus the strategy includes both world-wide integration and national responsiveness. Organisations with multi-focal strategies are more difficult to manage as they are concerned with two dimensions at once.

---

national responsiveness strategy

Strategy of allowing subsidiaries to have substantial latitude in adapting products and services to suit the particular needs and political realities of countries they operate in

regional responsiveness strategy

Strategy of allowing regional offices to have substantial latitude in co-ordinating the activities of local subsidiaries and adapting products and services to suit the particular needs and political realities of the regions in which they operate

multifocal strategy

Strategy aimed at achieving the advantages of world-wide integration where possible, while still attempting to be responsive to important national needs

@ B2B

The business-to-business segment is Asia's fastest growing area of e-commerce. Demand for software to automate supply chains and manage sales and inventories is rising fast. The pressure on businesses to go online is mounting daily. Taiwan wants 50 000 companies on line by 2001, Thailand recently passed a law requiring all export and import documents to go online before 2000.

Building this new model isn't going to be easy. The supply chains and networks of East Asian companies often stretch from Taiwan to mainland China to the Philippines—and to other countries with their own currencies, laws, languages and business practices. Asian business people also prefer dealing face-to-face and relying on relationships cultivated over years rather than through intermediaries they have never met.

Many entrepreneurs are taking the risk that these attitudes will change and setting up ventures to break down cultural and geographic barriers for thousands of small Asian manufacturers.

Western software and equipment makers are arriving in droves hoping to persuade Asian companies to outsource back-office functions such as billing, e-mail, customer databases, accounting and shipping, using the Web.

The sort of activities expected require a large change in mindset, especially for family-owned companies accustomed to secrecy. The reluctance to outsource such important functions as accounting and billing is a big obstacle. Supply-chain management requires users to open their inventory and procurement processes to suppliers and customers.

Source: Adapted from Moore, J. & Einhorn, B. (1999).

Activities for discussion, analysis and further research

1 New ways of doing business which have been accepted more or less easily by Western organisations are going to be more difficult for Asian firms to accept. Discuss the reasons.
2 What changes to attitudes and practices are required for e-business to work in Asia?

ORGANISING INTERNATIONAL BUSINESS

In addition to strategic issues, managers in international business must choose an appropriate organisation structure, given the company's global pursuits. Most research on organisation designs has looked at multinational corporations. The tendency is to adopt one of five types of structure: world-wide functional divisions, world-wide product divisions, international division, geographic regions and global matrix (Robock & Simmonds 1989).

World-wide functional divisions

With world-wide functional divisions, the parent company's top-level functional executives have world-wide responsibility for functions, such as manufacturing, marketing and finance (see Fig. 18.2). Thus a foreign subsidiary's functional units report directly to the respective parent company's functional units. This structure's strength is that it gives strong functional expertise to foreign subsidiaries in manufacturing and engineering. However, as actions need co-ordination across functional units, the structure hampers quick reactions to events in

Fig. 18.2   World-wide functional divisions structure

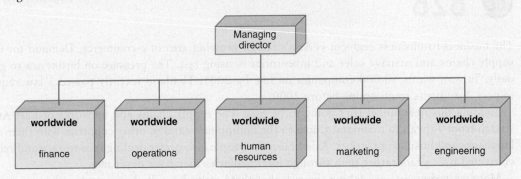

different countries and competition if products are diverse. The structure works best with a few related products sold in a fairly uniform world-wide market and with few foreign subsidiaries.

World-wide product divisions

With world-wide product divisions, top-level executives manage particular product areas world-wide (see Fig. 18.3). With this type of structure, the parent company emphasises co-ordination of product-related decisions but lets foreign subsidiaries run other business aspects. Because of the product focus, the structure is most effective with products technologically complex, highly diverse, or subject to rapid change. It is compatible with a world-wide integration strategy with several diverse products to consider.

International division

With an international division structure, a division is created and all foreign subsidiaries report to it. Figure 18.4 shows a multinational company with domestic product divisions and

Fig. 18.3   World-wide product divisions structure

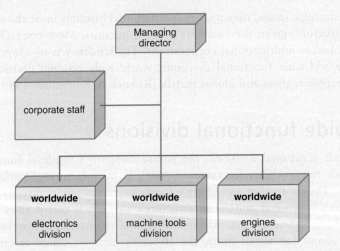

Fig. 18.4 International division structure

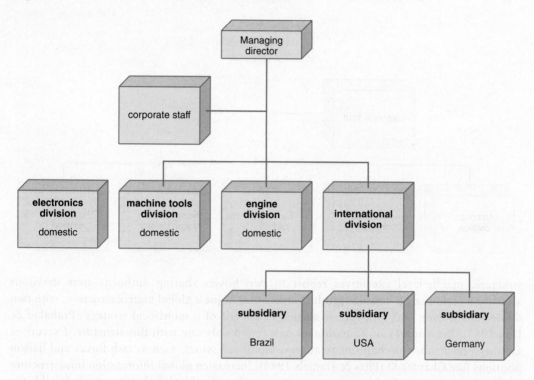

an international division. (An international division could be added to a functional structure, but is less prevalent.) (Daniels, Pitts & Tretter 1985). The international division structure allows geographic and product interests to be represented at the same level. However, the arrangement means that co-ordinating information between domestic product divisions and the international division is difficult. One study of 37 large multinationals showed the international division was the most common structure (Robock & Simmonds 1989).

Geographic regions

In this organisation design, the world is divided into regional divisions, with subsidiaries reporting to an appropriate one according to location (see Fig. 18.5). This structure aids information flow in regions but inhibits information exchange across them. As a result, it caters to regional and national differences and supports a regional or national responsiveness strategy. The geographic regions structure is often used by European multinationals (Robock & Simmonds 1989).

Global matrix

In a global matrix structure, equal authority and responsibility are assigned on at least two dimensions, with one dimension being region and the second either product or function. A global matrix, with region and product as the dimensions, is shown in Figure 18.6. In this

Fig. 18.5   Geographic regions structure

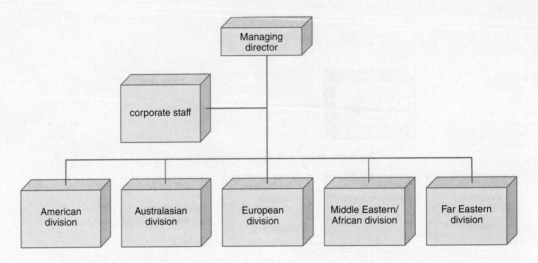

structure, middle-level executives report to two bosses sharing authority over decisions affecting a region and a business product area. Some argue a global matrix structure, with two dimensions (region and product), is needed in pursuit of a multifocal strategy (Prahalad & Dox 1987). Yet a survey of 93 multinationals found only one with this structure. Executives say they prefer other mechanisms to address multifocal issues, such as task forces and liaison positions (see Chapter 8) (Pitts & Daniels 1984). Increasing global information infrastructure of telecommunications and computer companies will make the global matrix more feasible for multinationals in future.

Networked structure

The networked structure is an organisation form where functions are contracted to independent firms and co-ordinated through information technology networks to operate as if in a single corporation. This structure is called the virtual corporation as it performs as if virtually one corporation (see Chapter 9). Given rapid growth of sophisticated telecommunications capacity, such a structure is feasible for those wanting to engage in international business who need great flexibility, need to be able to contract out functions and still maintain control over the core competencies of their competitive advantage.

MANAGING DIVERSITY: ADAPTING TO CULTURAL DIFFERENCES

Structural issues are important; however, another element of effective international management is adapting to cultural differences. Issues include managing international human resources and adjusting leadership styles.

Fig. 18.6   Global matrix structure

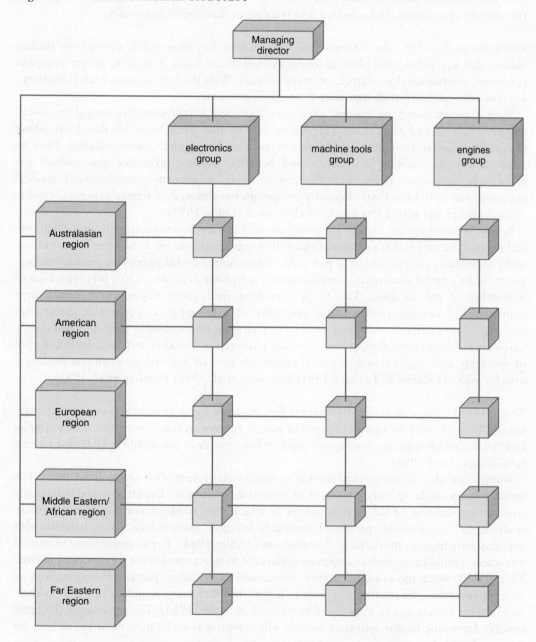

Managing international human resources

According to researchers on international management, companies operating internationally must emphasise strategic human resource management for a competitive edge internationally (Tung 1984; Dowling, Schuler & Welch 1995). Multinationals, particularly, need a developed pool of managerial talent to function effectively. Particular concerns are assignment policies, recruitment approaches, and selection and training of managerial personnel.

Assignment policies   An international organisation has four policy options on staffing sources for key managerial slots in overseas operations: local nationals, parent company personnel, international personnel, or mixed sources. With the local option, each subsidiary's key positions are filled with nationals from the host country.

With a parent company option, each subsidiary has a representative versed in overall company policies and procedures. This person may be more knowledgeable than locals about the parent's latest technological developments and have good communication lines to headquarters. In addition to salaries and benefits, position expenses may include car allowances, education costs, housing, cost-of-living adjustments, international medical coverage, and relocation costs. Recently companies have moved to reduce expenses, emphasising frugality and giving less generous allowances (Lohse 1995).

With a regional option, significant positions are filled by those qualified from a geographical region. The idea is that commonalities within regions and major differences between them make individuals experienced in a particular region suited to fill important regional assignments. In an international option, multinationals assign the best person to a job, regardless of nationality or job location. This helps a multinational foster a geocentric management approach and develop multinational managers able to apply a world-wide integration strategy. Most multinationals tend to follow a mixed option, mostly putting host-country nationals in foreign subsidiaries, home-country nationals in headquarters, and develop a pool of managers with regional and/or global experience to staff higher-level positions needing a broader view (Hodgetts & Luthans 1991; Morrison et al. 1991; Dowling et al. 1995).

Recruitment   Regardless of assignment policy, evidence suggests companies operating internationally must work to recruit competent people for key overseas positions. For example, locally-educated foreign students are an underutilised source of management talent for foreign subsidiaries (Tung 1984).

Women are also an under-used source of managerial talent. One study from the 1980s found women made up only 3 percent of expatriate managers. **Expatriates** are individuals who are not citizens of the host countries in which they work. According to a follow-up study, firms' international personnel managers felt that women face major barriers with overseas assignments compared to domestic ones (Adler 1984). For example, they identified foreigners' prejudice, as well as company reluctance to select women for foreign assignments. Nevertheless, when the same researcher interviewed 52 female expatriate managers, almost all were successful. Interestingly, almost half reported that being female was useful in their assignments, largely due to high visibility (Jelinick & Adler, 1984). The situation is changing rapidly. According to one estimate, women will comprise over 20 percent of expatriates by the year 2005.

Because many marriages now involve dual-career couples, posting employees abroad is increasingly complex. Foreign assignments may be declined over concern about negative impact on the spouse's career. To get suitable candidates for foreign assignments, organisations will need to aid 'trailing' spouses' job-seeking. Without assistance it is likely the trailing spouse will experience depression and other health problems, limited engagement with the new community, and need emotional support from the working expatriate spouse (Harvey 1995).

expatriates

Individuals who are not citizens of countries in which they are assigned to work

Selection and training   Expatriate failure rate is substantial, ranging from 25 to 40 percent. Such failures are costly in terms of direct costs of an early return and a replacement. There are other costs, such as loss of self-esteem and resulting problems in the subsidiary (Mendenhall & Oddou 1985). It is probable part of the high expatriate failure rate comes from serious lacks in their selection and training.

Multinational corporations use technical skills as the main criteria for selecting people for overseas assignments. While technical skills are important for expatriate success, organisations must consider *relational skills*, an expatriate's ability to relate and communicate effectively with host nationals. Needed communication skills involve being willing to use host nationals' language; confident communication; ability to engage in local small talk, such as anecdotes, jokes, and

Management in any level of industry requires sensitivity towards the family demands of its staff, especially when members are working in overseas countries.

comment on movies and sports; and desire to understand and relate to host nationals (Mendenhall & Oddou 1985). Showing needed flexibility, Australian Ben Lochtenberg, at one point chairman of Great Britain's Imperial Chemical Industries (ICI) American subsidiary and now heading ICI's Australian subsidiary, had to adjust communication style even in countries with a common language. For example, in England, his direct Australian manner caused problems, so he learned the indirect British approach. He would say 'Perhaps you ought to think about this a little more' to mean 'You must be mad—forget it'. In the United States, though, when Lochtenberg said the same the subordinate interpreted him literally and went on with the project (Main 1989; Kearns 1995).

Unfortunately, expatriate training before assignments is often poor. Inadequate training comes from feelings among human resource administrators that training is ineffective, expatriate trainee dissatisfaction with training, insufficient time to train before departure, or seeing assignments as too short to need expensive training (Mendenhall & Oddou 1985). Yet poor training leads to problems, as an American manager found. After arriving in France, he rented a luxury apartment and invited all staff to a large party. Unfortunately, he did not realise it is unusual for French employees to be invited to a superior's home. Furthermore, at the party were people from all organisation levels, as well as their spouses, who did not normally mix socially. This got things off to a bad start, and the manager never recovered (Copeland & Griggs 1986).

Repatriation   Another area for effective human resource management is **repatriation**, the return to one's home country after assignment in a host country (Rugman & Hodgetts 1995; Adler 1991). For expatriates, foreign assignments normally last two to three years. Major reasons for expatriates to return are (1) the end of the agreed-upon period of foreign assignment, (2) desire to have children's further education in home-country schools, (3) being unhappy in the foreign assignment, and (4) being ineffective in the foreign assignment.

Problems with adjustment during repatriation are common, as it may be difficult to adjust to returning home. For one, authority and status may be lower in the home office than in the foreign assignment. Moreover, the returned expatriate may see their foreign experience as insufficiently valued at the home office. They may find their previous job has changed and/or their technical expertise become obsolete.

repatriation

Process of returning to one's home country after an assignment in a host country

It can take months, possibly a year, for a returning manager to regain effectiveness. One way to ease repatriation and reduce anxiety is to develop an agreement promising a home country position equal at least in level to the position the individual left to accept the foreign assignment. Other steps include renting or maintaining the individual's home while they are on foreign assignment, giving a senior executive a mentor to help keep their career on track during foreign assignment and repatriation, and communicating with expatriates to avoid isolation from home-office activities (Finney 1996).

Adjusting leadership styles

Although some argue organisation behaviour is increasingly similar across nations, managers overseas may need to adjust leadership styles due to cultural factors (Adler, Dokter & Redding 1986; Kelley, Whatley & Wothley 1987). Studying leadership issues, researchers find it hard to isolate the effects of culture from differences in economic development and resources in various countries. As a result, much is to be learned about effective leadership in different nations and cultures.

From his study of an American multinational, Hofstede (1980) believes managers must consider the power-distance index in particular to determine leadership styles appropriate in different countries. In high-power-distance countries (e.g. Mexico, the Philippines and India), individuals accept large power-distribution differences in organisations. Subordinates expect superiors to act autocratically, be paternalistic, subject to different rules to subordinates, and enjoy privileges unavailable to them. In medium-power-distance countries (e.g. Australia, Japan and Italy), subordinates expect to be consulted but will accept some autocratic behaviour. They also expect laws and rules to apply to all, but accept some degree of privilege and status symbols for superiors unavailable to subordinates. In low-power-distance countries (e.g. Sweden, Denmark, and Israel), subordinates expect consultation on most issues, prefer participative democratic leadership, and rebel or strike if superiors seem to step beyond their authority. Typically, laws and rules are seen as applicable to all employees, and privileges and status symbols for superiors as unacceptable. Hofstede's research gives a frame for considering leadership issues in different cultures, such as needing to adjust leadership styles. Organisational social responsibility and managerial ethics are other areas needing special consideration when companies operate internationally.

HANDLING SOCIAL RESPONSIBILITY AND ETHICAL ISSUES

Organisational social responsibility and managerial ethics were addressed at length in Chapter 4. Here we examine several concerns particularly relevant to international management.

International social responsibility

Many social responsibility issues compound when an organisation has a great deal of international business. This is due to increased social stakeholders (customers and communities in various countries, etc.; see Chapter 4), particularly when business is done through subsidiaries in other countries. During the 1970s, multinational corporations were criticised for harmful activities in developing nations. Concerns focused on exhausting natural resources, diverting wealth to developed nations, and manipulating LDC governments. Currently, criticisms have lessened, for many reasons. These include stronger LDC governments, multinationals emerging based in several developed countries, emerging LDC multinationals, more smaller multinationals, increasing multinational adaptability to local conditions, and increased concern for environment (Rugman & Hodgetts 1995; Smith 1994; *Economist* 1994). Still, controversies continue, such as concern about 'sweatshops' which came with testimony about clothing being made by 13- and 14-year-olds working 18-hour days in Honduran factories (Strom 1996). There is still debate about the benefits versus harm wrought by large, powerful corporations, particularly in LDCs (Paul & Barbato 1985; Haour 1996).

Questionable-payments issue

A pervasive international ethical issue involves **questionable payments**, payments with ethical questions of right or wrong either in host or other countries (Frederick, Davis & Post 1992; Mahoney 1995). Difficulties come with differences in customs, ethics and laws of countries about different payment types. The most common questionable payments are:

○ political payments—usually funds to support a political party or candidate
○ bribes—money or valuables given to a powerful person to influence decisions in favour of the giver
○ extortion—payments made to protect a business against a threatened action, such as cancellation of a franchise
○ sales commissions—payments of a percentage of a sale, which become questionable if paid to a government official or political figure or if unusually large
○ expediting payments—normally, money given to lower-level government officials to ensure co-operation and prompt handling of routine transactions

Many payment types are considered to be legal and acceptable in many parts of the world, but in general are seen as unethical and/or illegal.

questionable payments

Business payments raising significant ethical questions of right or wrong either in the host country or in other nations

■ The MD's diary   the reflective practitioner

We both export and import people. The technology that we are introducing into the Australian market place here is typically technology that has been introduced three to five years earlier in other parts of the world. Our strategy here is to try and take technology that has been already developed and applied from our global organisation and introduce it as early as possible into the local industry. The way we do that is that we both import the human resources to kick-start technology within our own organisation, and we also have a strategic policy of exporting our own people into international environments so that they can get the experience early and bring back the knowledge and continue the implementation here.

Our previous experience was that we were only importing the technology. People would come in and use the opportunity to gain some expatriate experience in Australia for a couple of years. The constraints on the way we operate are such that there is a limited opportunity for them to transfer the knowledge into other people's heads while they're here, and at the end of the contract, they'd go home. And we were back to where we'd started. So we find the most effective way is to export the human resource from Australia into the other countries early and then bring them back. We transfer in reverse. It provides the experience overseas that some of our people are looking for and it brings people back here who are likely to stay for some period of time. They've made a personal investment in themselves—understanding this technology and developing the expertise. So we then have people who will remain with the organisation. Part of that is to make sure we recognise their capability when they do come back. We need to recognise it as part of their progression and career path. They generally come back at a higher classification than they left with. We also encourage a lot of cross fertilisation in terms of travel. Our people are travelling constantly. International travel these days is a given. In the past it may have been a reward, these days it is part of the job. For young engineers, it's exciting. They are soaking up so much information, so much experience in such a short period of time that it has an enormously positive effect on their motivation, their commitment and their self worth. They come back different people, much more competent, much more comfortable in themselves and contribute at a much higher level.

We have a role to support the Asia Pacific region out of here with technology and some marketing activities. The people we transfer into Asia are those who have come back from overseas with some four or five years experience that we can use in a start-up mode in some of our joint venture partners. It's a more mature person generally that we are exporting into those countries so they are more able to cope with the differences in culture. Hopefully, they have already had a fair bit of contact through technical exchanges. We are trying to promote such experiences in their career development. We want them to see any Asia Pacific experience as a contribution towards their own development.

We have a structure that rewards people for their contribution rather than their position so we can take people out of functional responsibilities and send them overseas for a couple of years and guarantee hat they will have a role back here consistent with the qualifications and experience that they will bring back with them. So there is a level of security for them.

■ The subordinate's log   the reflective practitioner

The global offices were managed by frequent reporting; frequent phone calls and frequent visits. Office heads had a fair degree of autonomy due to the logistics of managing globally. However, the constant communication with the CEO meant that international management was manageable.

Translating methodologies across languages presented little problem. We had bi-lingual consultants and much business is conducted in English even in non-English speaking countries. Some consultants are less able to work in foreign cultures so we occasionally organised training in multicultural communications.

My international management experience involved communicating with clients and consultants who are working in other countries. Frequent communication was the key here. Consultants need a high level of support when working in other countries for extended periods of time. These needs range from client-consulting needs to administrative support tasks.

Focus on practice—Strategies for improving

1 Consider how conditions are changing in relation to neighbouring countries and consider how those changes may impact on the way your organisation might conduct business there.
2 Develop a plan to successfully manage the changes across the region, which will enable your organisation to continue to expand internationally.

Source: Jones et al. (2000).

Chapter summary

International management is the planning, organising, leading and controlling in organisations operating internationally. Considerable international business is conducted by multinational corporations. These are organisations engaging in production or service activities through affiliates in several countries, that maintain control over those affiliates' policies, and manage from a global perspective. Multinationals and other organisations engaged in international business typically subscribe to one of four basic orientations, or philosophies, to international management: ethnocentric, polycentric, regiocentric and geocentric.

Various international environment elements affect organisations' ability to engage in business outside national borders. The economic element includes level of economic development in a country, presence of adequate infrastructure, a country's balance of payments, and monetary exchange rates. Major legal-political element issues are the degree of political risk associated with a particular country and degree to which governments erect trade barriers. Within the sociocultural element, Hofstede identified five major dimensions related to cultural values: power distance, uncertainty avoidance, individualism–collectivism, achievement–nurturing, and long-term-short-term. The technological element includes methods of technological transfer, an important aspect of international business. The concept of competitive advantage of nations holds that elements in a nation can foster innovation in certain industries, increasing prospects for success of home-based companies operating internationally within those industries. The elements comprising the diamond of national advantage include factor conditions, demand conditions, related and supporting industries, and firm strategy, structure and rivalry.

Organisations have four entry methods to expand into other countries: exporting, licensing, establishing strategic alliances, and wholly owned subsidiaries. Multinational corporations' strategies include world-wide integration, national responsiveness, regional responsiveness, and multifocal emphasis. Organisation structures for multinational corporations are world-wide functional divisions, world-wide product divisions, international division, geographic regions and global matrix.

Adapting to cultural differences requires careful management of international human resources, including assignment policies, recruitment approaches, personnel selection and training, and repatriation. Although scholars argue leadership issues are converging across nations, there are still differences in leadership styles that are likely to be effective in various cultures.

Conducting international business raises complex issues regarding social responsibility, international value conflicts, and questionable payments.

Questions for discussion and review

1 Explain the concept of a multinational corporation. Identify several major companies which are probably multinationals. Give reasons for your selections.

2 Describe four major orientations toward international management. Find a newspaper or magazine article about a company engaged in international business. Which orientation best depicts the company's approach to international management?

3 Outline several elements useful in assessing the international environment. How could you use these to help provide advice to a foreign company interested in doing business in your country?

4 Explain the concept of competitive advantage of nations. Use the concept to assess the ability of conditions in your country to foster innovation among home-based companies in an industry of your choice. What suggestions do you have to improve conditions?

5 Enumerate the principal methods of entry into international business. Explain the advantages and disadvantages of each. Which would you use if you were running a small company with few resources but had a product with potentially broad international appeal? Would you use a different approach if running a large company with considerable funds available? Give your reasons.

6 Explain the four major strategic alternatives for conducting international business. For each, recommend a type of business likely to be successful if it adopted that strategy.

7 Describe five main organisation structures used by international businesses. Identify a type of business you would like to manage internationally, and explain the organisation structure you believe would be most appropriate. Explain your reasoning.

8 Discuss principal issues related to assignment policies and recruitment, selection, training and repatriation of managerial personnel for international assignments. What recommendations would you make to companies just beginning their international expansions?

9 Assess types of adjustments in leadership style that managers may need to make because of cultural differences. What advice might you give to members of a local company going to set up a wholly-owned subsidiary in the Philippines? How would your advice differ if the subsidiary was to be in Denmark?

10 Explain the social responsibility and ethical issues international managers may confront. What steps would you, as a manager, take to prevent subordinates from making questionable payments while engaged in international business for your company?

Exercises for managing in the 21st century

Exercise 1
Skill building: Identifying international management orientations

Senior managers normally adopt an ethnocentric, polycentric, regiocentric or geocentric orientation or philosophy in dealing with the overseas parts of their organisations. Examples of these orientations follow. In each example indicate the orientation being exhibited.

Ethnocentric Polycentric
Regiocentric Geocentric

1 ____ The best people are selected from all parts of the organisation across the world.

2 ____ Basic market decisions are made by local employees.

3 ____ The system used at the multinational headquarters is always best.

4 ____ This firm attempts to develop managers who excel in a particular part of the world.

5 ____ The firm is run by host-country nationals.

6 ____ The corporate goal is to produce a product used in many countries globally.

7 ____ The organisation is focused on the western European approach to managing.

8 ____ Managers from the home country are given the best jobs and promoted ahead of their peers, regardless of their performance.

9 ____ The subsidiary is highly visible to the local population, whereas the multinational headquarters is relatively invisible.

10 ____ The multinational considers the world as the base for money, resources, suppliers and customers.

Exercise 2
Management exercise: Going international

You have spent many years working on a revolutionary combination automatic washer and dryer, which went into production for the first time last year. It has been an astounding success in Australia, and you are considering going international with your new product. You have had numerous inquiries and offers from businesses around the world but believe that you will concentrate on business in Canada, Great Britain, Western Europe, Australia and New Zealand for the near future. You are going to meet with your director of marketing tomorrow to discuss expanding your business into New Zealand. You recognise several options are available to you, including exporting, licensing, strategic alliances and wholly-owned subsidiaries. In addition, you must consider your philosophy of international management, select a strategy, decide on a structure, determine how to select and train your managers, and determine the appropriate leadership style to use.

Consider the issues above. Then, with two other classmates, discuss how you would proceed with the possibility of conducting business in New Zealand. You want to expand internationally and believe this is the place to start. Explain your rationale for the decisions you make, pointing out the advantages and disadvantages of each of your choices.

One country's food...

on the rim—
in China

Throughout the second half of 1999, China was very active in seeking admission to the World Trade Organisation (WTO). This was seen as a good thing in many quarters. However, in other quarters, it was not seen quite the same way.

More than 120 car factories could be facing going out of business because of the mainland's entry into the WTO. Entry is good news for globally competitive firms but not so good for those that are not competitive. Many of those latter ones are car plants which the government has been trying to close for years.

High tariffs and government protection have made car-production one of the mainland's least efficient industries. Its plants last year produced 1.6 million cars, less than any of the world's top 10 car-makers, of which 507 100 were passenger cars. Toyota, Japan's largest car-maker and the world's third biggest, made 5.3 million vehicles last year.

The mainland's 10 biggest plants make more than 90 percent of national output. Beijing wants to centralise production in these 10 but cannot because of the protection of local governments and special interests which see the automotive as a pillar industry. However, most of them produce less than 10 000 vehicles a year. And one on Beijing's outskirts made just 1000 last year.

High-costs, over-manning and small-scale production make mainland car prices two to three times higher than world averages. Import tariffs of 80 to 100 percent allow big domestic manufacturers to remain profitable.

With WTO entry, these would fall drastically. The world's most efficient car plants, operated by Toyota, Honda and Mazda in Japan, are just two days away by ship over the East China Sea.

As tariffs fall and the mainland is forced to give import quotas, the market would be open to new Japanese and other models. 'The result of a closed market is high prices and low quality and a big gap with global manufacturers', the *China Business Times* said. Zhu Yangfeng, general manager of First Automotive Works, one of the top two makers with 34.7 billion Yuan worth of truck and passenger-car sales, said that domestic manufacturers were ill-prepared to meet the challenge of WTO entry.

'The impact of WTO entry will be enormous,' said Mr Zhu. 'China's car industry has always been heavily protected. Unlike advanced countries, we do not have a modern company system or diverse source of funds,' he said. 'We are far behind international companies. Our passenger-car industry has a short history, is immature and is especially weak in its basic components. We are far behind advanced countries in developing new products.'

'Our wages are low but we have far too many workers so that our production costs are very high, making it difficult for us to compete.'

During the next five years, his company plans to switch its focus from trucks to passenger cars, which should account for 60 percent of outputs by 2004, and plans to train managers and technical staff to international standard.

Mr Zhu said he wanted the government to provide a good legal and regulatory environment to keep bureaucrats out of business, to improve social welfare so as to lighten the burden of his company and to encourage individuals to buy cars. 'In the last resort, a company can only rely on itself to survive in the market. Protection can only be temporary.' Beijing is hoping that the discipline of WTO rules will push local government to give up the subsidies and protection of their car factories and force them to close. It wants to exert external pressure to achieve what central government directives have been unable to do.

If anyone survives the shake-out, it will be the foreign-invested companies that are the most efficient producers, such as Volkswagen's two joint ventures which between them manufacture more than half of the mainland's passenger cars.

Those companies with the best chances of survival are the ones which have a strong business plan. In order to remain competitive, some of those organisations are carrying out the following strategies:

O focusing resources on areas of comparative strengths,
O honing English-language skills of top managers,
O searching for foreign partners,
O introducing performance-based pay and other incentive schemes,
O investing in research and development,
O building Internet abilities,
O hiring Western consulting firms.

In the field of retailing, WTO entry will mean that foreign companies will be allowed to set up distribution networks within three years, making it easier for foreign retailers to penetrate the Chinese market. That frightening prospect has lit a fire under Shanghai No1 Department Store, China's biggest retailer by sales. In November

1999, the store formed a joint venture with Japan's Marubeni Corp. to build a $10 million hypermarket in Shanghai that will compete with increasingly popular megastores like France's Carrefour. The Group deputy general manager Liu Fuqun admits that there is not much time and they are feeling the pressure. They have faced increasing pressure already from domestic and foreign competitors and that competition is now going to get tougher. The store intends to start selling over the Internet and it plans to improve its own distribution network with a view to partnering foreign firms. There is the expectation that the WTO will offer many opportunities because Western manufacturers will want to sell their goods in China and will need the help of Chinese distributors.

Sources: O'Neill, M. (1999); Saywell, T. & Yan Zhihua, (2000).

Activities for discussion, analysis and further research

1 How will the entry of China into the WTO affect expatriate managers operating in China?
2 Discuss the impact on foreign companies who wish to enter the Chinese market place.
3 Compare the Chinese way of doing business to the Western way.

The Regional Context

Chapter 19

CHAPTER OUTLINE

The regional context

Focus on Singapore
Issues confronting Singaporean managers
Directions for the future
Relationship with Australia

Focus on New Zealand
Economic reforms
Issues confronting New Zealand managers
Directions for the future
Relationship with Asia
Relationship with Australia

Focus on Indonesia
Issues confronting Indonesian managers
Directions for the future
Relationship with Australia

Focus on Malaysia
Issues confronting Malaysian managers
Directions for the future
Relationship with Australia

Focus on Thailand
Issues confronting Thai managers
Relationship with Australia

Japan's impact on the region
Relationship with Australia

Australia's position within South-East Asia

LEARNING OBJECTIVES

After studying this chapter, you should be able to:

O Identify geographic and economic regions your current country of residence fits into and reasons for the positioning.

O Demonstrate an awareness of similarities between philosophical approaches to management existing in the South-East Asia region.

O Demonstrate an understanding of differences in management practices between ASEAN countries.

O Understand the development of your own country's management practices and factors impacting upon it.

O Identify factors affecting future relationships between trading partners of the South-East Asia region.

Striving for excellence

Being part of the Asia Pacific Region is exciting and challenging. Aultoliv Australia is part of the regional team and must work in concert with the facilities and concerns in other countries. The challenge comes about because the infrastructure, processes and practices in other countries are sometimes very different from those in Australia. Furthermore, they vary dramatically from one Asian country to another.

Because Autoliv, as an organisation, believes that the leadership of a facility is best when it is native to that country, efforts must be made to maintain effective relationships between sister facilities. Care must be taken that communication is clear and non-ambiguous.

Working in the region does not only entail working with other Autoliv facilities but also with the regional sites of customers who are global in their activities. It also means interacting with regional suppliers. Therefore the inter-actions cover the whole spectrum of suppliers, related facilities and customers. This sometimes makes for complex interactions and sensitive communication situations.

In this chapter we will examine driving forces and changes happening in the East-Asian Pacific region. It is a region which, over the past two decades or so, has come to be a significant force. In this chapter, we will track some changes in specific countries and draw conclusions on issues that managers operating regionally must consider.

THE REGIONAL CONTEXT

This chapter is perhaps the most difficult to develop. Most aggregated trade statistics reach to the first part of 1998. The 'Asian crisis' became much more apparent in trade and other figures from late 1997. The problem for scholars and writers is that we are aware of the subsequent events, which were not all clear by the middle of 1998.

This means that what the statistics showed as a small drop in trade growth ultimately became a much more significant force in the region. This force has changed trading, borrowing and other financial patterns in the region, some possibly very long term. Some of the regional economies suffered much more as a result of the 'crisis' than others.

However, as the American President J.F. Kennedy said, 'When written in Chinese, the word "crisis" is composed of two characters—one represents danger and one represents opportunity.'

Thus the 'Asian crisis' has proven to be both a danger to regional economies and an opportunity for many structural changes. So please remember much of the following material relates to very fluid circumstances.

In the past few years, investment funds flowed into Asian countries. Some, such as Hong Kong, Korea, Singapore and Taiwan, known as Newly Industrialised Countries (NICs), have shown their ability to change to the world.

Over the last 10 years, many multinational companies invested heavily in Asian countries and transferred technologies

Engendering positive attitudes towards the cultures of other people can begin at an early age, something that managers of international relations should keep in mind.

there, only to discover it is harder to transfer management techniques. It is only after making the financial investment and commitment that organisations find management conformity less easily transferred.

As discussed in Chapter 18, understanding how management is viewed and practised in the country where investment is planned is vital to establish and manage enterprises there.

Brunei Darussalam, Indonesia, Laos, Malaysia, the Philippines, Singapore, Thailand and Vietnam form the group known as ASEAN (Association of South-East Asian Nations). There has been continuing debate as to whether Australia legitimately belongs to such a grouping. There are benefits for Australia to be a member of this group, and Australia's government is pursuing the issue.

Table 19.1   Australia's trade with ASEAN in 12 months ending March quarter 1998 ($A million)

	Exports	Imports
Brunei Darussalam	58	1
Indonesia	3390	2266
Laos	7	0
Malaysia	2361	2101
Myanmar	24	11
Philippines	1326	377
Singapore	3872	2489
Thailand	1651	1332
Vietnam	237	586
Total ASEAN	12926	9163

Source: ABS Catalogue No 5422.0.

Table 19.2   Australian trade with ASEAN by commodity group in 12 months ended March quarter 1998 ($A million)

Commodity grouping	Exports	Imports
Food and live animals	2202	681
Crude materials, inedible, except fuels	1022	470
Mineral fuels, lubricants and related materials	1075	2013
Manufactured goods classified chiefly by material	2136	983
Machinery and transport equipment	2021	3419
Miscellaneous manufactured articles	0	901
Commodities and transactions not classified elsewhere	3250	343
Other	1220	353
Total trade with ASEAN	12926	9163
Total Australian trade	84790	83418

Source: ABS Catalogue No 5422.0.

It is important that companies working to establish themselves in another country know the significant cultural elements of much of the local population's lives. Two points to recall are that the major religions such as Christianity, Buddhism, Islam and Hinduism are represented in most of those Asian countries; and that the majority are known politically as 'democratic'. Further, managers must realise more than half the world's population is in Asia and this region has cultural roots far stronger than the Western world's in their influence over various parts of life, including management practice.

FOCUS ON SINGAPORE

Singapore's turning point was its 1965 withdrawal from the Malaysian federation. This allowed a flood of American, Japanese, German, French and British multinational investors who introduced their own management systems, often with an expatriate as the operation's head. Singapore was perfectly located and its low labour costs meant management often viewed workers as an extension of the machinery foreign investors imported (Wong 1991). Singapore was used mostly as an assembly centre for home-based technologies and production, which then fed an international marketing network.

A tripartite body of employer groups, unions and government representatives was formed in 1972 as the The National Wages Council (NWC). Their goals were clear:

○ to recommend annual wage increases;
○ to ensure orderly wage determination so as to promote economic and social development; and
○ to assist in the development of incentive schemes to improve national productivity.

The NWC played a major part in maintaining harmonious industrial relations. However, the resulting poor personnel practices led to job hopping rather than training and staff development. As well, organisations poached staff from each other shamelessly by offering better pay.

In 1979, the Singaporean government set up the Skills Development Fund (SDF) to encourage organisations to upgrade workers' skills and so increase productivity (Wong 1991). This was followed by formation of the National Productivity Council (NPC) in 1981, emphasising higher worker productivity through upgrading skills.

Growth in productivity is often seen as the driver of economic growth. This is especially true in Singapore where gains in productivity have enabled continuing economic expansion. In fact, according to the NPC's figures, between 1981 and 1991, two-thirds of the 7.1 per cent average gross domestic product (GDP) growth was a direct result of higher productivity. Had productivity remained stagnant, the GDP would have been 36 per cent below the actual level attained (NPC 1991).

This is important because the only other source of increase in GDP would have been employing more workers. Singapore's tight labour market still prevents this being a major source of future economic growth for Singapore.

Then between 1997 and 1999, GDP growth dropped from 8.4% (1997) to 0.4% (1998) before beginning to recover to 5.4% (1999) as the Singaporean economy was buffeted by the regional turmoil (Statistics Singapore 2000).

Issues confronting Singaporean managers

Singapore faces several issues in the next decade. These are the same for multinational corporations and Singaporean enterprises.

Economic restructuring   Global competition is accelerating. Singapore was one of the first Asian countries to undergo significant economic and technological change, and now other Asian countries face these changes (Dodd 2000). It is therefore vital that Singapore continue economic restructuring and adopting high technology and value-adding industries. In part, this is demonstrated by the government's continuing drive to encourage multinational corporations to set up their regional headquarters in Singapore.

Tight labour market   The pace of industrialisation has resulted in an acute labour shortage, which means escalating wage costs and job hopping. To overcome this, many employers source workers from other parts of the region. The Singaporean government attempts to discourage this by imposing high permit fees. These workers also tend to job hop, playing employers off against each other, and lack company loyalty and a feeling of belonging.

Human resource development and management   Singapore still has considerable unskilled labour. Though the Singaporean educational level is rising, much of the manufacturing sector has workers possessing only the most basic of primary education (Wong 1991). Human resource management and development is crucial to Singapore. This means innovative personnel practices have to be developed and introduced to use employees most effectively.

Productivity and quality of work life   With increasing educational levels come higher standard of living expectations and increased work-life quality. This means Singaporean workers want to be more involved in workplace decision-making processes, and more interested in consultative management approaches.

The tight labour market results in wage escalation and lowers competitiveness, particularly for businesses with slim profits. Improving productivity is the key organisational objective. Increased efficiency can be achieved through job redesign and task flexibility.

Directions for the future

Singapore's past determination is still evident in its leader's plans. Singapore has a vision, that of being 'the intelligent island'. This vision sees every Singaporean home, office, school and factory linked by computer (Dodds 2000). Their commitment matches their vision, and much infrastructure is in place now. Furthermore, this vision is not simply an ideal means to bring about national competitive advantage and to enhance its citizens' lives.

There are four strategic thrusts (Birch 1993):

○ to develop a global hub to turn Singapore into a highly efficient traffic switching centre;
○ to boost the economic engine towards greater value-adding manufacturing;
○ to improve the quality of life and increase discretionary time; and
○ to enhance the potential of individuals as skills, creativity and knowledge are
   increasingly important.

Singapore's political environment contributes to this vision. This is because the political leadership has been the key in the island country's remarkable 25 years of growth and development. Singaporean society is one where conformity and compliance is expected and enforced. This has produced some attributes which the country's leaders are trying to eliminate.

One of these is *kiasu*, a Hokein word which means 'fear of losing out'. It is best summed up in a phrase popularised by a cartoon character, Mr Kiasu, in Singlish (the local idiom): 'Better grab first, later no more'.

This trait gives Singaporeans an unfortunate reputation abroad, and can show Singaporeans as risk aversive. With a government promoting expanding Singapore's overseas business activities, the *kiasu* syndrome, deterring risk-taking, is viewed as an obstacle to the development of home-grown entrepreneurs (Stewart 1993).

An enterprising spirit is seen as vital for the future. Despite its economic successes, Singapore has not yet nurtured a widespread entrepreneurship or enterprising spirit, and the country now needs to acquire these skills.

The island republic's prosperity can be traced to a relentlessly far-sighted government, not individual deal makers. Singaporeans, as noted, are risk aversive and conservative. State-controlled companies expand slowly internationally, and private enterprises are reluctant to back risky enterprises (Bromby 1993). This does not fit with the increasingly sophisticated, knowledgeable, well-travelled and cosmopolitan Singaporean.

Relationship with Australia

Singapore's government wants business to invest overseas to achieve growth beyond their domestic market. Following support offered to offshore investors, there is increasing interest in Australia as companies seek to diversify under the republic's plan for establishing external economic arms (Chong 1993).

Traditionally, Singapore invests heavily in Australian property. Singapore companies are the third largest investors in hotel and tourism after the United States and Japan.

In trade, Singapore has become Australia's eighth largest export partner (ABS Catalogue 5422.0). However, many exports to Singapore are re-exported to other South-East Asian countries. For example, Indonesia has imported capital equipment from Australia via Singapore because of how customs duties are calculated (Chong 1993).

Australian businesses investing in Singapore import Australian-made capital equipment to outfit their Singaporean plants. For example, Goodman Fielder imported bakery equipment for its bakery in Singapore. Cladding-material producer Permasteel-ISA brings 40 per cent of its product (glass and aluminium) from Australian factories for assembly in its two Singapore plants.

The relationship between Singapore and Australia is an enduring one, with projects dating from the early 1960s, such as construction of Changi Airport and land-reclamation. It does seem the relationship is to become a strategic alliance. Eventually, Singapore will become Australia's competitor rather than business partner. Either way, this relationship will expand. In the 12 months ending in the March quarter 1998, Australia's exports to Singapore were $A3871 million and imports from Singapore were $A2489 million.

FOCUS ON NEW ZEALAND

Since 1984 New Zealand has undertaken significant economic reform transforming from a heavily controlled country to a far more liberal one (Bollard & Mayes 1993). The process required managers (in private and public sectors) to consider all of their operations aspects. The major changes are summarised below using the task-environment model (Chapter 3).

Economic reforms

Customers and clients Reduction in trade restrictions and deregulation in foreign exchange markets have provided more options for New Zealand organisations to find international customers. In domestic markets, reduced regulatory limits (e.g. shop-trading hours and liquor sales) has meant firms must become more responsive to customers and their expectations.

Competitors Greater competition (particularly in finance, transport and energy) was seen as crucial to making New Zealand businesses more competitive internationally. Entry restrictions, price controls, monopolies and other advantages of existing firms (banks and airlines) were removed. Government monopolies such as Telecom and Air New Zealand competed with new entrants Clear and Ansett. For other businesses, the increased competition came from overseas. Trade barrier and protection removal freed up imports, and domestic producers had to meet international quality and price standards to survive.

Suppliers Deregulating finance, transport and energy sectors gave more choice (with increased complexity and risk) to New Zealand companies. Local and international companies now own, wholly or in part, government services (rail and air transport, and electricity supply). Phasing out import licensing and changed tariff structures gave greater flexibility for managers to seek sources of material from overseas (and increased competitive pressure on local import-substitute manufacturers).

Labour supply The strength of labour unions in New Zealand let them restrict labour supply (e.g. by compulsory membership and blanket coverage), and lift wages to uncompetitive levels. The *Employment Contracts Act 1991* (ECA) swung the balance of power back to employers. Unions lost the monopoly right to represent workers, and some union membership benefits (access to legal remedies for unfair dismissal) became universal—even chief executives could use the Employment Court for personal grievances and disputes. The implication for managers was that they had to communicate more with their workforce, and develop an employment strategy tailored to the organisation's needs; they no longer had a rigid pay award, set by unions and employer representatives in Wellington. Unions, unable to restrict labour supply, needed to increase demand for their membership to use their power for higher wages. As a result, they emphasised productivity bargaining, workplace reform, and performance agreements (*National Business Review* 1993).

Issues confronting New Zealand managers

Skill levels   During the last recession, few firms (including public sector apprentice employers) took on new trainees. When companies expanded, a shortage of technically skilled staff emerged and affected companies needed to look offshore for employees. Workforce planning with staff training and development will be needed to avoid such limits on growth.

Labour relations   The ECA required greater manager skills to reach agreements with workers. With high unemployment levels, employers have a strong bargaining position, and some exploit this. However, where demand is high or supply limited, employees have power (*National Business Review* 1993).

Workplace reform   Labour market deregulation let New Zealand companies create more flexible work practices. The Council of Trade Unions supported the general trend to increased employee involvement in decisions affecting them at work; for example, the job design and teamwork strategies set out in Chapters 9 and 15 (New Zealand Council of Trade Unions 1992). Managers must use these to maintain quality and productivity levels.

Social problems   These reforms have caused pain for many. While benefits are apparent (lower home-loan interest rates and taxes, improved business confidence), some community sectors suffer. Unemployment is still high, and educational user-pays policies limit tertiary education access. There are concerns over corporatisation's impact (creation of business structures) in government-funded health service delivery. Unless these issues (particularly unemployment) are resolved, the government will be pressured to become more interventionist.

Relationship with Asia

Asia is an increasingly important market for New Zealand companies, and business initiatives are actively supported by government. While East Asian and Japanese exports have increased since 1970, rapid growth has occurred since 1990. Now, six Asian countries are among New Zealand's top 10 export customers (see Table 19.3).

Agriculture and forestry products form the backbone of New Zealand exports; however, exports of clothing, software, domestic appliances and machinery are increasing.

Ministry of Foreign Affairs and Trade figures for the year ended June 1993 show Japan to be New Zealand's third largest source of imports (behind Australia and the USA). China and Taiwan are in sixth and seventh places, with Korea, Malaysia and Singapore appearing in the top 15.

Asian investment in New Zealand is significant, particularly forestry, property and tourism. Most of Auckland's main hotels belong to Asian investors (Smith 1993) and other investments include retail operations and golf courses. New Zealand and Asian joint ventures are planned or underway in projects such as Asian television broadcasting (Hudson 1993), brewing beer in China (Morrison 1993), and telecommunications in Vietnam (*National Business Review* 1993).

Table 19.3   New Zealand's main export markets in the year ended June
              1998 ($NZ million)

Country	Value
Australia	4 196.7
Japan	2 957.0
USA	2 480.6
UK	1 285.1
South Korea	706.6
Hong Kong	611.9
China	597.3
Taiwan	547.2
Belgium	457.5
Malaysia	453.9

Source: Trade New Zealand 2000.

Table 19.4   Australian trade with New Zealand ($A billion)

Year	Exports	Imports
1997–98	7.47	4.03
1996–97	5.68	3.65
1991–92	2.82	2.40
1990–91	2.54	2.15
1989–90	2.61	2.17
1988–89	2.22	1.97
1987–88	2.18	1.73
1986–87	1.77	1.43
1985–86	1.51	1.45
1984–85	1.54	1.10
1983–84	1.39	0.91
1982–83	1.16	0.69
1981–82	1.03	0.73
1980–81	0.92	0.64
1979–80	0.86	0.55
1978–79	0.74	0.42

Source: ABS 5410.0 and Trade New Zealand 2000.

Relationship with Australia

Australia is New Zealand's biggest export market, and source of imports, while New Zealand
is Australia's third largest export market. The two economies have close cultural, sporting and
economic ties, and these, coupled with the closer economic relationship agreement (CER)
between the two countries, facilitate trade in both goods and services.

Recent New Zealand reforms have led to reduced business costs, and some companies moving manufacturing operations from Australia to New Zealand. This includes manufacture of appliances by PDL, toiletry products by Gillette, powder detergent by Unilever PLC and toothbrushes by Johnson and Johnson (Doman 1993). These shifts highlight the importance to managers of giving close attention to the international environment; changing a company's mega-environmental political and economic fields can significantly alter its competitiveness, and mean a reassessment of strengths, weaknesses, opportunities and threats.

FOCUS ON INDONESIA

The Republic of Indonesia is a product of Asia's post–World War II decolonisation. The territory which was known as the Netherlands Indies became a state of its own. Ki Hadjar Dewantara, founder of the Indonesian educational system, set out three basic characteristics of the Indonesian style of leadership in the following quotation:

Ing ngarso sung tulodo,
Ing madya mangun karso,
Tut sari handayani.
　　Ki Hadjar Dewantara

Ing ngarso sung tulodo means leaders must build themselves up by changing their attitudes and practices to become exemplary models to subordinates. *Ing madya mangun karso* means leaders must be able to motivate and generate a spirit of self-help and creativity among subordinates. *Tut sari handayani* means leaders must be able to persuade their subordinates and be brave enough to become forerunners in bearing responsibilities (Widyahartono 1991).

The above certainly describes what many management students feel is the essence of management practice. It is congruent with the Indonesian state philosophy stated in its constitution's preamble. It comprises the Five Pillars (principles) known as *Panchasila*, *pancha* meaning five, and *sila* meaning principles.

1 Belief in God the Almighty, hence communism is totally rejected. There is no one state religion. All religions are fostered equally.
2 Humanism, that is treating people as human beings, being kind to them and respecting and helping each other.
3 Nationalism, that is putting the nation above all self-interest. The country's welfare and progress are the primary goals of individuals, institutions and organisations.
4 Sovereignty, that is the rights of the people are cared for and respected.
5 Justice, that is fairness in rendering justice to all, regardless of status differences.

The above principles are built into every Indonesian organisation and reflected in the principles and practices of management in every aspect of Indonesian society.

Issues confronting Indonesian managers

The relevance of management to Indonesian society　Indonesia is a country with a range of cultural settings. Could one managerial style apply to all or would a distinctive cultural flavour prevail? The tendency for managers is to adopt an American or European methodology. The challenge for Indonesia, currently a developing country, is to develop a style of its own which does not mimic Western, Chinese or Japanese styles. In many Indonesian organisations, the conflict therefore is of cultures, between modernity and tradition (Widyahartono 1991).

Indonesian society is still quite traditionally hierarchical and honour oriented. It prescribes the way relations between people should be structured and maintained. All is done to prevent conflict. Unlike most Western value systems, Indonesian society is in general not materialistic.

In seemingly Western organisations people work with the expectation of achieving organisational objectives but in a harmonious manner. Indonesian society is traditionally geared towards the practice of consultation, agreement and solidarity, with a strong hierarchical orientation (The Expatriate Web Site Association 2000).

In Indonesian organisations work is the means of achieving objectives but also the establishment and guarantee of harmony. Therefore the manager's main interest is to achieve and maintain this harmony while accumulating power and authority. It must be noted though that the concept of power and authority in this context is different to the Western view. It is not based on contract or appointment. It is a status embodied in the manager based on their age, class, expertise and so on. Given those circumstances, the Indonesian manager uses organisational assets to achieve the goal of harmony.

Indonesians of Chinese origins also apply the teachings of Confucius to their dealings. These are the five principles of filial piety, fidelity, obedience, kindness, and loyalty to one's superior.

While these two philosophies may appear different, their similarities give Indonesia a philosophical homogeneity not often seen in Western countries.

Directions for the future

Indonesia, the world's fourth most populous state with 212.9 million people, showed impressive growth until the last couple of years. Once the relative pauper of South-East Asia, Indonesia stood poised to become the region's newest industrialised power. As recently as 1976, half of Indonesia's population lived in what the World Bank designated as developing-world poverty. Until 1997 that number reduced dramatically, but since then the economic outlook has become considerably less favourable. Until 1997 year-on-year growth averaged 6 per cent, on much the same economic formula as its ASEAN neighbours (Ellis 1993).

The gross national product per person was just $US60 in 1967, growing to $US600 in 1993, and was targeted to $US1000 by the turn of the century. Instead it was $US45 in 1999.

Indonesia is responding to these and other challenges. One area to be addressed is telecommunications infrastructure to deliver business-integration and rebuilding solutions. Indonesia is a sprawling country and development requires linkages with Jakarta.

This would be a move away from its labour-intensive areas of electronics, clothing, textiles, footwear and furniture industries. In fact one World Bank Review expected the manufacturing sector to continue as the main engine of growth, but now it would be difficult to make the changes without assured funding.

Other areas needing development are railways, power generation and distribution. This is because the Indonesian economy is changing from an agriculture and resource base, to one with higher technology levels. This means training and industrial relations will again feature on the agenda of managers in the country over the next decade.

Relationship with Australia

The Australian view of Indonesia is changing. Previously there were misconceptions held about the Indonesian market. Economic reform in Indonesia saw changes in taxation, banking and customs procedures. However, there was a general lack of information about different business cultures in interpersonal relationships, corporate structures and business customs.

This point is evidenced by involvement of the 'big five' chartered accounting firms in Indonesia. For them, Indonesia was seen as a major expansion area with strong growth in joint ventures, mining, manufacturing and infrastructure projects. Note was made of increased interest in Indonesia by Australian companies due to proximity and market potential, particularly in food processing and distribution, construction and engineering services, mining and textiles (Jay 1993). Since the Australian involvement in East Timor, most business interactions have been slowed or halted

Ultimately, for Australia, a return to growth will mean an increase in trade opportunities. The issue Australian companies will have to remember as they look for these opportunities is that Indonesia must be judged by Indonesian standards and not those of the West.

Table 19.5   **Australian trade with Indonesia ($A million)**

Year	Exports	Imports
1997–98	3390	2266
1996–97	3233	1753
1991–92	1635	995
1990–91	1462	784
1989–90	1030	441
1988–89	734	419
1987–88	595	587
1986–87	528	310
1985–86	522	209
1984–85	431	363
1983–84	375	299
1982–83	384	561
1981–82	416	515
1980–81	358	416
1979–80	293	241
1978–79	217	99

Source: ABS 5410.0 and 5422.0.

FOCUS ON MALAYSIA

Malaysia is a multiracial nation with a population of over 20 million. The population of Malaysia consists of Malays (about 58 per cent of the population), Chinese (about 26 per cent), Indians (about 7 per cent) and other minor racial groups (about 9 per cent). By the time Malaysia gained its independence in 1957, a situation had evolved where general livelihood of the three main racial groups was segregated largely according to economic calling. The economic returns derived from small holdings in the agricultural sector and wages derived from working in the estates were small, which meant the Malays (Bumiputras—sons of the soil) were not as well off financially as were the Chinese population who tended to be in business.

The Second (1971–1975) and Third (1976–1980) Malaysia Plans concentrated on two objectives:

○ eradication of poverty among the population irrespective of race, and
○ restructuring society to eliminate identification of race with economic function.

These objectives were promulgated to influence national planning and development for the 20-year period from 1971 to 1990 (Thong 1991). Through a program of social engineering, it was planned that by 1990, as a general guideline, 30 per cent of the ownership of Malaysian companies would be in the hands of Bumiputras, 40 per cent in the hands of Chinese and Indians, and the remaining 30 per cent in the hands of foreign investors. The intention was to make employment of Bumiputras at various levels of private enterprise representative of the country's racial composition.

Issues confronting Malaysian managers

Multiculturalism   As a result of Malaysian encouragement of foreign investments since the early 1970s, management has increasingly professionalised. Thus many Malaysians have gone to foreign head offices for training, and there has been a high incidence of in-plant training by foreign consultants and trainers, integrating motivation programs used on sites in other countries.

Programs such as management by objectives (MBO), critical path methods (CPM), just in time (JIT), and quality control circles (QCC) have been implemented. These were often introduced by chief executives who brought them back from their training periods overseas. The issue crucial in all of these approaches has been that the method's success depends on the facilitator's ability to transfer concepts to local operations.

This is complicated by Malaysians' tendency to use an indirect approach. For example, first time contact is often made through an intermediary. This person assumes an informal role of guarantor of trustworthiness and goodwill of the party seeking the contact. This, of course, reflects on the intermediary's future credibility. While this takes time, the degree of success is much greater than a direct approach.

A great deal of importance is also placed on 'face'—the observance of courtesy and sensitivities to what is right and wrong. A win–win situation must be maintained at all times, if the transaction is to be successful.

Malaysia's multiracial composition means foreign managers must be constantly aware of issues specific to each racial group. For example, Malays, being Muslims, will not eat pork, and will not use crockery contaminated by pork. All meat must be slaughtered according to a specific religious ceremony. As well, Indians who are Hindus will not eat beef, and may be vegetarian. Managers should be aware of these issues, and organisations with canteen facilities must cater to these needs (Thong 1991). Finally, as religion plays such an important part in Malaysian life, staffing at particular times of the year will need to take religious calendars into consideration.

Decision-making practices   Some Malaysian managers may consistently seek second opinions when they have an important decision to make, by consulting experts in astrology and occult sciences. Meanwhile many Chinese also believe in *feng shui* or geomancy (Thong 1991). An example of this is that it is generally believed even placement of a building's front door will bring an organisation either good or bad luck.

While these practices may seem strange to students of Western management, they are a matter of belief; and in Malaysia many successful managers and businessmen take these very seriously. They may not openly advocate them, and may even have received Western education and training in management, but are still able to integrate the two styles effectively.

Directions for the future

Vision 2020 is aimed at giving Malaysians affluence now only widely available in leading Western economies. This vision has as its goal an industrialised Malaysia where citizens will have the purchasing power available to the average American citizen today. This would have required doubling of national income every 10 years, so by 2000, an eightfold increase would have been achieved (Doraisami 1993). The challenge in achieving this vision has become much greater recently. Firstly, it became more difficult to maintain the economy's momentum as it slowed during the regional crisis. Then other challenges stem from transformation of relatively fragile manufacturing sectors and manufactured exports' destinations within the region.

Malaysia's manufactured export performance has been influenced by its competitiveness relative to neighbouring South-East Asian countries. Malaysia was successful in attracting investments from Taiwan and South Korea as their currency appreciated, labour costs rose and their preferential treatment by the United States was lost, forcing them to seek off-shore bases.

However, as the cycle continues, labour markets will tighten up and wage rises will produce a new generation of lower-cost producers who will undercut Malaysia. This is important, for while manufactured exports account for about 70 per cent of total exports, the Malaysian manufacturing base is very narrow (Doraisami 1993).

Malaysia is working overtime to promote development of its medium- and small-scale industries. This requires upgrading of its generally low-level technology, particularly if Malaysia is to achieve newly developed country status in the near future.

Malaysia also faces shortages of both skilled and unskilled indigenous labour as production increases. Furthermore, it faces growing concern around environmental issues, and the temporary acceleration in economic growth will force exhaustion of its forestry and petroleum reserves. These difficulties are then coupled with little attention being given to occupational health and safety standards, waste disposal, and environmental hazards caused by irresponsible investors.

Malaysia is currently playing a leading role in fostering greater economic co-operation in the region through ASEAN. Increasingly, this co-operation is the critical path to prosperity. As a part of the process, growth triangles are being developed to take advantage of complementary conditions between neighbouring countries, in response to growing gaps between labour costs, capital flows and technology levels.

Relationship with Australia

The past few years have seen an encouraging broadening of the business base—from Australia's perspective—in Malaysia. Many small to medium-sized companies have won contracts in a wide range of areas, specifically in service sectors of the construction and development industry (Chong 1993). For example, the architectural firm Davenport Campbell is involved with a $200 million Tampoi Retail Centre in Johore, and John Holland won a contract to build a 12-storey apartment building in Kuala Lumpur. In addition, one of Australia's largest current investment plans is a petrochemical refinery worth more than $1 billion which BHP has proposed to build in Sarawak, although this is not proceeding at present due to financial limitations.

While Australia's investment base is coming from a low level, Australia's trade with Malaysia is modest compared with other Asian countries, due to Malaysia's reduced imports of raw materials. This is expected to change as Malaysia needs technology transfer. Traditionally, Australian companies have been better at this transfer than have Japanese companies, for example. Furthermore, Australian technology built to be robust and operate under a variety of climatic conditions is suited to Malaysian conditions. To illustrate, Nilson's Transformers, Melbourne based, won a $12 million contract with Tenaga Nasional Berhad, Malaysia's electricity-generating body.

While there is no doubt opportunities exist and will increase for Australian investments and developments in Malaysia, the challenge for Australian managers and their organisations will be adjustments to a very different culture.

FOCUS ON THAILAND

Thailand's population is 60 million, of whom 14 per cent are of Chinese origin and 95 per cent are Buddhists. The most pervasive characteristic of Thai society is a love of freedom, and this basic value has greatly affected development of the country, which is richly endowed with natural resources. Thai businessmen are mostly engaged in producing commodities and importing manufactured goods, and most financial institutions have been built on trading activities. While currently the more influential businessmen are traders, manufacturers are a new social group.

The systems of beliefs and values in Thai society are deeply rooted in Buddhism. The Buddhist approach to life and understanding of human behaviour is exemplified by Buddha's passive and contemplative way of dealing with the problems of life. The following are the tenets for consideration by Buddhists (Siengthai & Vadhanasindhu 1991):

1 Self-realisation—know who you are, and what your strengths and weaknesses are.
2 Knowing others—know whom you have to deal with and how to deal with them.
3 Causality—know about cause and effect of what you are doing.
4 Appropriate timing—know the appropriate time for dealing with problems or confronting them.
5 Appropriate place—know where to do things appropriately.
6 Knowing potentiality—know your ability and your limitations.

If you compare these tenets with those of Western society, which is conflict-resolution oriented, you will find Thai society geared to conflict avoidance. As Western society has developed values and institutions which require people to deal with others in a particular way, so has Thai society. The difference is in Thai society there is a strong desire to keep relationships peaceful and on an even keel. There is also a tendency to shrug off small frustrations and disagreements, preventing anger surfacing. To achieve this, relationships must be kept under control. This approach often leads to social relationships with Westerners being kept at a superficial level and results in involvement avoidance (Siengthai & Vadhanasindhu 1991).

Traditionally an agrarian community, Thailand has developed rapidly until it now combines a multi-faceted society with technology. In fact it hopes to exploit its geographic advantage as a central point in Asia to compete with Singapore and Hong Kong as established aviation hubs. Thailand has one natural advantage in this strategy, as it is a few flying hours closer to Europe than most established stopovers.

Issues confronting Thai managers

Incompatible business law   Unlike many other countries in the region, Thailand was never colonised by the British as were Singapore and Malaysia. As a result, Thai business law bears little similarity to the common law heritage of Australia's other Asian trading partners. Thai business law seems largely dependent upon a system of discretion, favours and patronage (Castellari 1993).

Demand for infrastructure   Thailand's middle class is demanding better infrastructure, creating opportunities in the country but also putting stress on the government to provide incentives to satisfy those demands through foreign investments and imports. Many projects are still on hold, however some resources are becoming available now.

An under-educated workforce   Although 90 per cent of the workforce is literate, their level of education is only primary school. Thus in 1993, Thailand needed to import thousands of engineers and technicians to satisfy its needs in those areas.

Cheap labour base   Thailand's competitive advantage rests heavily on a combination of cheap labour, foreign money and foreign technology. Many Thai industries such as textiles could easily migrate to lower-wage countries if a competitive economic environment is not maintained.

A critical issue currently facing Thailand is whether it has the infrastructure to make the transition from low-cost producer dependent on foreign investment to an economy supported by domestic and high-value-added production. This is an urgent issue as other countries with lower wage costs covet Thailand's markets and may soon prove to be attractive to offshore manufacturing (Edwards & Edwards 1993).

Fuelled by a labour shortage, the shopfloor wage in greater Bangkok has recently doubled to between $A10 and $A12 a day. This is as much as three times higher than in Vietnam and double that of China. The result is that the Japanese, Taiwanese and Hong Kong investments in light industry, which lead Thailand to think of itself as Asia's newest industrialised economy, are being lured elsewhere.

Relationship with Australia

Thailand in the 1990s was Australia's twelfth largest export market. In the 1997–98 year, Australia sold $A1.6 billion worth of goods, mostly gold, dairy products, wool and crude petroleum (ABS 5422.0). Australia's relationship with Thailand has traditionally been very friendly. Of all six ASEAN members, it is Thailand which seems most enthusiastic about Australia's thrust into Asia.

Table 19.6   Australian trade with Thailand ($A million)

Year	Exports	Imports	Difference
1997–98	1651	1332	319
1996–97	1660	1132	528
1992–93	1215	756	459
1991–92	816	647	168
1990–91	665	505	160

Source: ABS.

In 1993 a new Thai Australian Chamber of Commerce was established in Melbourne, to provide information to companies interested in exploring business opportunities in Thailand. With needs in infrastructure, support for its continuing manufacturing growth, and increased services in areas like quality control and training, Thailand offers many opportunities to Australian organisations as its economy continues to recover.

JAPAN'S IMPACT ON THE REGION

Traditionally, Japan's economy depends on importing raw materials and exporting high-value-added goods. Japan's export dependency on the United States is extremely high, matched only by the aggressively export-oriented economies of Malaysia, Thailand and China.

To maintain its export capacity, Japan has established facilities and assembly plants in South-East Asian countries. The pattern is to place expatriate Japanese managers in charge, with technology and managerial skills transfer not occurring readily. However, Japan has been the source of many of this decade's new management practices. Quality circles and just in time, for example, are Japanese management developments.

Since the end of World War II, the Japanese economy and industrial infrastructure's restructuring has given birth to the second largest economy in the world. It has brought with it a generally stable work environment for the Japanese worker. Lifetime employment, the seniority system and in-house labour unions were the three major system features. Loyalty to the company was assumed, while promotion involved years of rotation through many departments and locations. Talent was a negligible asset and generalists ruled the day. Women had equal opportunity so long as their work involved a supporting role to male managers.

In the 1990s this began to change. Presently, Japan is in the midst of a transformation. While the new Japan will still have a vast economic structure, deregulation will confront the nation with new dilemmas such as unemployment. Deregulation is urgently required. For example, to open a small business, some 250 forms must be filled in to satisfy local governmental regulations.

The themes of the new Japan are liberation of the economy from rigid regulation, liberation of consumer and worker from industry's interests, and dismantling of the iron triangle—the collusion between politicians, bureaucrats and industrialists (Hartcher 1993). This will result in a freer Japan but most probably a less passive one too. Japan is waking to a realisation of its impact on the world and there appears to be a growing determination to influence world politics and trade and the systems through which they are conducted. Traditionally, Japan has been content to do business in its own way, interacting remotely with its trading partners. The next decade may see changes to this practice.

Relationship with Australia

Japan's relationship with Australia has been one of the principal foundations for development of Australia's broader relationships with East Asia. In the last few years, dynamic growth has turned East Asia into a market which, in 1998, absorbed almost 60 per cent of Australia's trade, more than six times the value of Australia's exports to the United States (Australian Bureau of Statistics 2000).

Australia is a large commodities trader and as such has a huge direct stake in Asia-Pacific economic diplomacy, supporting an open, non-discriminatory global trading system. Furthermore, Australia has an indirect stake in the open trading system which has been critical to the region's development.

In the past, bilateral dialogue between Australia and Japan focused on the strategic-energy and raw-materials trade relationship between the two countries. Australia supplies about half the raw materials Japan uses for steel production as well as large volumes of coal and natural gas for its energy uses.

Japan is by far Australia's largest trading partner and has been its largest export market since the late 1960s, and its second largest source of imports since the early 1970s. Japan has also become Australia's most important source of tourism revenue, and in 1993 was the largest direct foreign investor in the Australian economy. Australia's manufactured exports to Japan are now larger than its total exports to the United Kingdom (Drysdale & Yamazawa 1993).

Table 19.7   **Trade between Australia and Japan in 12 months ending March quarter 1998**

Bilateral trade $25.6 billion
Australian exports to Japan $15.4 billion
Australian imports from Japan $10.17 billion

Main exports to Japan	$ million	Main imports from Japan	$ million
Coal	3600	Road vehicles	4100
Meat and meat preparation	1180	Office and automatic data processing machines	963
Cork and wood	532	Telecommunications and sound equipment	516
Petroleum	504	Specialised machinery	479
Fish	414	Photographic apparatus	240
Cereals	220		

Source: ABS March 1999.

Social, cultural and educational contacts and exchanges are increasing, bringing with them increased co-operation between both governments on a wide range of international affairs. Also many Australian students undertake Japanese language studies with a view to their future.

In short, Australia's Asia-Pacific partnership with Japan promises great practical economic benefits. Time will, however, demonstrate it to have enormous political significance as well.

AUSTRALIA'S POSITION WITHIN SOUTH-EAST ASIA

Traditionally, Australia's heritage and culture place it squarely in the Western nation category. Historically, its closest relationships have been with Great Britain and Europe and then the United States. The corollary to this overwhelmingly Western orientation has been the tyranny of distance. The importance of this orientation was emphasised by World War II and it was not until the Whitlam years with the end of the 'white Australia policy' that Australia ended its self-imposed cultural quarantine (Tye 1993).

Then when Britain joined the European Economic Community in the 1970s the resulting severance of trade ties with Australia gave real impetus to the exploration of our closest neighbours for trade purposes.

Though economics may seem to be the spur, the Hawke government in the 1980s was guided by a need to espouse a regional viewpoint which recognised where Australia's strategic interests lay. Under the Colombo Plan, Australia opened its doors to Asian scholars; through the Five Power Defence Arrangement, it helps maintain regional stability along with New Zealand, Great Britain, Singapore and Malaysia. History shows Australia pursued geo-political interests before it pursued an economic agenda in the region. Then over the past decade both political and economic involvement of Australia in South-East Asia has grown. It is therefore no surprise Australia's position and sense of belonging within the region is an important issue.

There is a strong difference of opinion, both on the part of Australians and non-Australians, as to Australia's legitimate membership of Asia. Consider the headline 'Wish as hard as we like, we cannot become part of Asia' (Davidson 1993, p. 15). Davidson quotes Mr Paul Cheng, president of the Hong Kong General Chamber of Commerce as saying, 'Asians may be very polite publicly, saying sure, sure we welcome you. But privately you're not part of Asia—ethnically, culturally, geographically . . . To keep on the [Keating] policy and keep saying "We are part of Asia" to me it jars. It's not being realistic'.

This debate is likely to continue. Economically and politically, Australia cannot afford not to be a part of Asia. Australia's economic importance to the region is diminishing as Asian countries' growing sources of supply and industrial sophistication mean Australia's commodity exports are of diminishing importance (Davidson 1993). The real question for Australia is not whether we are part of Asia or not. Our geographic location on the edge of the Asian continental shelf is not at issue in any form. The issue is whether Australia will develop the cultural maturity to be its own country and enter into equal partnership with our neighbours for the benefit of all.

■ The MD's diary

the reflective practitioner

I find working in the Asia Pacific fascinating because you do have a quite different level of infrastructure and sophis-tication in terms of management, in terms of organisations in so many different countries. You have some that are very developed in terms of their infrastructure such as Taiwan and Singapore and then you have the ones that are not so developed. That presents some incredible challenges to multinational Australian organisations which operate in those areas—particularly in our case where you have global customers. We deal with the automotive industry so our customers are the Fords, the General Motors, the Toyotas, etc. of the world, and as a global supplier to them

Ford Australia.

you'd like to think that you are able to offer a consistent level of service and technology and support irrespective of where the customer is in the world. This is the customer's demand. The customer demands of us that wherever they decide to set up, we will support them in exactly the same way—with the same product, with the same technological support and the same management support, and that creates enormous problems for us.

We, as an organisation, have taken a fundamental view that the chief executives in the Asian countries will be local people. We will support them technically, with financial systems and the necessary infrastructure internally but our whole approach is to make sure that it is local managers that are actually running those businesses. As an organisation we devote an enormous amount of time to ensure that the chief executive work together so they understand the difficulties, the problems, the peculiarities of those specific countries and develop trust levels. It only works on trust and understanding and closeness and almost an absence of the shallowness of professionalism. You have to be close and achieve relationships which are personal.

For instance, we had an incident where one of my people wrote a letter to our sister organisation in Korea where he attempted to explain why a particular outcome had not been reached. In this letter he mentioned someone's name. This, which under normal circumstances might have been acceptable, is not so in Korea. It caused a great deal of problems in terms of restoring that person's self esteem and had extreme career and personal consequences for that person. This process caused lack of co-operation between the two organisations at a very critical period. To resolve the issues required a very open and honest relationship between the chief executives.

■ The subordinate's log   *the reflective practitioner*

We worked in various countries on the Pacific Rim. Contrary to popular perception, these are quite different from each other and required different personal skills from consultants. Being sensitive to cultural differences and being able to complete a project within those cultures was a skill that only a handful of consultants were instinctively good at. Most required some sort of 'teaming'. It was found that it is more effective to resource projects in teams with a more experienced consultant being able to guide the junior consultant where appropriate.

 # The price of corruption   *going global*

Western business executives have often operated on the assumption it is culturally acceptable to gain a sale in a developing country through the use of a 15 to 20 percent bribe. In fact, many corporations, in preparing their budgets for new ventures in some parts of the world, have inflated them to include those 'invisible costs'.

The OECD has announced a new set of recommendations to fight bribery and corruption in international business transactions. The first treaty draft recommends member countries introduce extraterritorial laws to criminalise bribery of foreign officials. The proposed legislation was expected to be enacted by the end of 1998. This ambitious timeline emphasised the importance which the OECD attached to the issue. The problem of corruption has traditionally be dismissed as an endemic, incurable disease of some cultures. This legislation signalled very clearly that grand-scale bribery was no longer acceptable as a matter of course in the practice of western business in developing countries.

The chairman of the OECD working party on bribery claimed the group's aim is not to see many western executives in jail but instead to establish a level playing field to secure appropriate governance by operating an international convention binding on all business entities.

This was not the first attempt to change the way organisations operate internationally. The Unites States introduced the Foreign Corrupt Practices Act in 1977 under the Carter Administration. This was a response to the disclosure that leading US corporations had used bribes to ensure foreign orders. The companies mentioned in that particular action were Lockheed and United Brands. Consequently, US companies violating the Act are liable to fines of up to $US2 million per violation and individuals up to $US100 000 including imprisonment for up to five years. While it has not stopped all bribery by US companies, the Act has decreased it significantly.

The above is an example of the responsibility shift from the recipient (those being bribed) to the suppliers (individuals or companies doing the bribing). Given the Asia Pacific Region's expansion and the infrastructure levels being invested in, bribery levels and the sums of money involved are huge. With corruption seen as the rule rather than the exception, decision quality is questionable when decision makers are bought off.

It is sometimes hard to get to the truth as a result of the need, sometimes legitimate, for high secrecy levels. For example, Pakistan's top naval officer retired in April of 1997 amid bribery allegations in a $A1.26 billion purchase of submarines from DCN, the French submarine manufacturer.

The OECD move was a brave one. However, the distance from legislation to implementation is still large. Cleaning up and changing trade culture will be monumental. In spite of the OECD measure, 11 OECD member countries allow a legitimate business expenditure tax deduction of offshore bribes. However, the OECD is not fighting alone. The United Nations, the Council of Europe and the Organisation of African States are all altering their regulatory environments to criminalise foreign official bribery. All are working to remove tax deductibility from such payments and improve accounting demands. In addition, the World Bank is moving to strengthen these remedies by proposing to cancel contracts and to blacklist companies suspected of corruption.

All these initiatives take time to implement in all OECD member countries and even longer in non-member states such as some Asian and South American countries, though there will be an attempt to link those by means of the World Trade Organisation or the United Nations.

Source: Adapted from Pitman, J. (1997).

Activities for discussion, analysis and further research

1 Is it a good idea to criminalise offshore bribes? Why?
2 Examine a local paper and, if you can, a copy of a paper from another country. See if you can find articles describing instances of impropriety concerning offshore activities. Discuss the circumstances. Would an Act such as the OECD one described have helped prevent such an instance? Why?

Glossary

acceptance theory of authority Theory arguing authority does not depend as much on 'persons of authority' who give orders as on the willingness to comply of those who receive the orders

accommodation Conflict-handling mode focusing on solving conflicts by allowing the other party's desires to prevail

accountability Requirement to provide satisfactory reasons for significant deviations from duties or expected results

achievement–nurturing Cultural dimension involving the extent to which a society emphasises values such as assertiveness, competitiveness and material success, rather than values such as passivity, co-operation and feelings

achievement-oriented Leader behaviour involving setting challenging goals, expecting subordinates to perform at their highest level, and conveying a high degree of confidence in subordinates

acquired-needs theory Theory (developed by McClelland) stating that our needs are acquired or learned on the basis of our life experiences

acquisition Purchase of all or part of one organisation by another

active listening Process in which a listener actively participates in attempting to grasp facts and feelings being expressed by the speaker

activity Work component to be accomplished

ad hoc committee Another term for a task force

adjourning Stage in which group members prepare for disengagement as the group nears successful completion of its goals

administrative management Approach focusing on principles used by managers to co-ordinate the organisations' internal activities

administrative protections Type of trade barrier in the form of various rules and regulations making it more difficult for foreign firms to conduct business in a particular country

aggregate-production planning Process of planning how to match supply with product or service demand over a time horizon of about one year

alternative work schedules Schedules based on adjustments in the normal work schedule rather than in the job content or activities

amoral management An approach that is neither immoral nor moral, but ignores or is oblivious to ethical considerations

anchoring and adjustment Tendency to be influenced by an initial figure, even when the information is largely irrelevant

anti-freeloader argument An argument holding that since businesses benefit from a better society, they should bear part of the costs by actively working to bring about solutions to social problems

applications software packages Software programs available for sale or lease from commercial sources

artificial intelligence Field of information technology aimed at developing computers with human-like capabilities, such as seeing, hearing and thinking

asset ratios Financial ratios measuring how effectively an organisation manages its assets management

attribution theory Theory attempting to explain how individuals make judgments or attributions about the causes of another's or their own behaviour

authority Right to make decisions, carry out actions, and direct others in matters related to the duties and goals of a position

autocratic Behavioural style of leaders who tend to make unilateral decisions, dictate work methods, limit worker knowledge about goals to just the next step to be performed, and sometimes give feedback that is punitive

autonomy Amount of discretion allowed in determining schedules and work methods for achieving required output

availability Tendency to judge the likelihood of an occurrence on the basis of the extent to which other like instances or occurrences can easily be recalled

avoidance Conflict-handling mode involving ignoring or suppressing a conflict in the hope it will go away or become less disruptive

balance of payments Account of goods and services, capital loans, gold, and other items entering and leaving a country

balance of trade Difference between a country's exports and imports

balance sheet Financial statement showing an organisation's assets and claims against those assets at a point in time

BCG growth-share matrix Four-cell matrix (developed by the Boston Consulting Group) comparing various businesses in an organisation's portfolio on the basis of relative market share and market growth rate

behaviour modification Use of techniques associated with reinforcement theory

behavioural displacement Condition in which individuals engage in behaviours encouraged by controls and reward systems though they are inconsistent with organisational goals

behavioural science Approach emphasising scientific research as the basis for developing theories about human behaviour in organisations, that is used to establish practical guidelines for managers

behavioural viewpoint Perspective on management emphasising the importance of attempting to understand various factors affecting human behaviour in organisations

belongingness needs Needs involving the desire to affiliate with and be accepted by others

benchmarking Process of identifying best practices and approaches by comparing productivity in specific areas within one's own company with that of other organisations both within and outside the industry

bill of materials (BOM) Listing of all components, including partially assembled pieces and basic parts, making up an end product

boundary spanning Creating roles within the organisation interfacing with important elements in the

bounded rationality Concept suggesting the ability of managers to be perfectly rational in making decisions is limited by factors such as cognitive capacity and time constraints

brainstorming Technique encouraging group members to generate as many novel ideas as possible on a given topic without evaluating them

break-even analysis Graphic model helping decision makers understand relationships between sales volume, costs and revenues in an organisation

budgeting Process of stating in quantitative terms, usually dollars, planned organisational activities for a given period of time

buffering Stockpiling either inputs into or outputs from a production or service process to cope with environmental fluctuations

bureaucratic control Managerial approach relying on regulation through rules, policies, supervision, budgets, schedules, reward systems and other administrative mechanisms aimed at ensuring employees exhibit appropriate behaviours and meet performance standards

bureaucratic management Approach emphasising the need for organisations to operate in a rational manner rather than relying on owners' and managers' arbitrary whims

business-level strategy Type of strategy concentrating on the best means of competing within a particular business while also supporting corporate-level strategy

capacity argument An argument stating that the private sector, because of its considerable economic and human resources, must make up for government cutbacks in social programs

capacity planning Process of determining people, machines and major physical resources, such as buildings, necessary to meet production objectives of the organisation

capacity-requirements planning Technique for determining what personnel and equipment are needed to meet short-term production objectives

capital expenditures budget Plan for acquisition or divestiture of major

fixed assets, such as land, buildings or equipment

capitalist economy Economy in which economic activity is governed by market forces and the means of production are owned by individuals

carrying, or holding, cost Expenses associated with keeping an item on hand (storage, insurance, theft, breakage)

centralisation Extent to which power and authority are retained at the top organisational levels

ceremonial System of rites performed in conjunction with a single occasion or event

chain of command Unbroken line of authority ultimately linking each individual with the top organisational position through a managerial position at each successive layer in between

change Any alteration of the status quo

charisma Leadership factor comprising the leader's ability to inspire pride, faith and respect; to recognise what is really important; and to articulate effectively a sense of mission, or vision, to inspire followers

clan control Managerial approach relying on values, beliefs, traditions, corporate culture, shared norms and informal relationships to regulate employee behaviours and facilitate reaching of organisational goals

classical viewpoint Perspective on management emphasising finding ways to manage work and organisations more efficiently

closed system System doing little or no interacting with its environment and receiving little feedback

code of ethics A document prepared for the purpose of guiding organisation members when they encounter an ethical dilemma

coercive power Power depending on the ability to punish others when they do not engage in desired behaviours

cognitive theories Theories attempting to isolate thinking patterns we use in deciding whether or not to behave in a certain way

collaboration Conflict-handling mode striving to resolve conflicts by devising solutions allowing both parties to achieve desired outcomes

collectivism Condition where the demands and interests of group interests are given precedence over desires and needs of individuals.

command or **functional group** Formal group consisting of a manager and all the subordinates who report to them

communication channels Patterns of organisational communication flow representing potential established conduits through which managers and other organisation members can send and receive information

communication Exchange of messages between people to achieve common meanings

communication network Pattern of information flow among task-group members

competition Conflict-handling mode involving attempting to win a conflict at the other party's expense

competitive advantage of nations Concept that environmental elements within a nation can foster innovation in certain industries, thereby increasing prospects for the success of home-based companies operating internationally within those industries

competitive advantage Significant edge over competition in dealing with competitive forces

competitors Other organisations either offering or with a high potential of offering rival products or services

complacency Condition in which individuals either do not see signs of danger or opportunity or ignore them

compressed work-week Work schedule whereby employees work four ten-hour days or some similar combination, rather than the usual five eight-hour days.

compromise Conflict-handling mode aiming to solve issues by having each party give up some desired outcomes to get other desired outcomes

computer hardware Physical computer equipment, including the computer itself and related devices

computer software Set of programs, documents, procedures and routines associated with the operation of a computer system which makes hardware capable of various activities

computer virus Small program, usually hidden inside another program, which replicates itself and surfaces at a set time to cause disruption and possibly destruction

computer-aided design (CAD) System using computers to geometrically prepare, review and evaluate product designs

computer-aided manufacturing (CAM) System using computers to design and control production processes

computer-based information systems (CBISs) Information systems involving computer technology use

computer-integrated manufacturing (CIM) Computerised integration of all major functions associated with production of a product

concentration Approach focusing on effecting growth of a single product or service or a small number of closely related products or services

conceptual skills Skills related to the ability to visualise the organisation as a whole, discern interrelationships among organisational parts, and understand how the organisation fits into the wider context of the industry, community and world

concurrent control Regulation of ongoing activities which are part of the transformation process to ensure they conform to organisational standards

conflict Perceived difference between two or more parties resulting in mutual opposition

consideration Degree to which a leader builds mutual trust with subordinates, respects their ideas and shows concern for their feelings

contingency planning Development of alternative plans for use in the event that environmental conditions evolve differently than anticipated, rendering original plans unwise or unfeasible

contingency theory Viewpoint arguing that appropriate managerial action depends on the particular parameters of the situation

continuous-process production Type of technology where products are liquids, solids or gases made through a continuous process

control system Set of mechanisms designed to increase probability of meeting organisational standards and goals

controlling Process of regulating organisational activities so actual performance conforms to expected organisational standards and goals

controlling The process of regulating organisational activities so that actual performance conforms to expected organisational standards and goals

convergent thinking Effort to solve problems by beginning with a problem and attempting to move logically to a solution

co-opting Absorbing key members of important environmental elements into an organisation's leadership or policy-making structure

corporate culture Term sometimes used for organisational culture

corporate philanthropy Corporate contributions for charitable and social responsibility purposes

corporate social responsibility A term used in reference to the concept of organisational social responsibility as applied to business organisations

corporate social responsiveness A term used in reference to the concept of organisational social responsiveness as applied to business organisations

corporate-level strategy Type of strategy addressing what businesses the organisation will operate, how strategies of those businesses will be co-ordinated to strengthen the organisation's competitive position, and how resources will be allocated among businesses

cost leadership strategy Strategy outlined by Porter involving emphasising organisational efficiency so overall costs of providing products and services are lower than those of competitors

creativity Cognitive process of developing an idea, concept, commodity or discovery viewed as novel by its creator or a target audience

crisis problem A serious difficulty requiring immediate action

critical path Path in the network taking the longest to complete

customer divisions Divisions set up to service particular types of clients or customers

customers and clients Individuals and organisations purchasing an organisation's products and/or services

cybernetic control system Self-regulating control system which, once operating, can automatically monitor the situation and take corrective action when necessary

data Unanalysed facts and figures

data workers Individuals who mainly process and disseminate documents, messages and related information

database management system Software which allows an organisation to build, manage and provide access to its stored data

database Set of data organised efficiently in a central location to serve a number of information-system applications

debt ratios Financial ratios assessing the extent to which an organisation uses debt to finance investments, as well as indicating to management the degree to which it is able to meet its long-term obligations

decentralisation Extent to which power and authority are delegated to lower levels

deciding to decide Response in which decision makers accept the challenge

of deciding what to do about a problem and follow an effective decision-making process

decision making The process by which managers identify organisational problems and try to resolve them

decision-support system (DSS) Computer-based information system supporting the process of managerial decision making in poorly structured situations

decision tree Graphic model displaying structure of a sequence of alternative courses of action and usually showing payoffs associated with various paths and probabilities associated with potential future conditions

decode Process of translating symbols into the interpreted message

dedundancy A forced termination of the employment relationship resulting from the permanent deletion of specific positions within an organisation due to the positions no longer being required

defensive avoidance Condition in which individuals either deny the importance of a danger or an opportunity or deny any responsibility for taking action

defensive strategies Strategies focusing on the desire or need to reduce organisational operations, usually through cost and/or asset reductions

delegation Assignment of part of a manager's work to others, along with both responsibility and authority necessary to achieve expected results

Delphi method Structured approach to gaining judgments of a number of experts on a specific issue relating to the future

democratic Behavioural style of leaders who tend to involve the group in decision making, let the group determine work methods, make overall goals known, and use feedback as an opportunity for helpful coaching

departmentalisation Clustering of individuals into units and of units into

departments and larger units to facilitate achieving organisational goals

dependent demand inventory Type of inventory consisting of raw materials, components and subassemblies used in production of an end product or service

descriptive decision-making models Models of decision making attempting to document how managers actually make decisions

developed countries Group of countries that is characterised by a high level of economic or industrial development and includes Australia, the United States, Western Europe, Canada, Australia, New Zealand and Japan

development To broadly prepare the employee for future opportunities through the acquisition of new knowledge, skills and attitudes

devil's advocates Individuals assigned the role of making sure negative aspects of any attractive decision alternatives are considered

dialectical inquiry Procedure in which a decision situation is approached from two opposite points of view

differentiation Extent to which organisational units differ from one another in terms of behaviours and orientations of members and their formal structures

differentiation paradox Idea that although separating innovation efforts from the rest of the organisation increases the likelihood of developing radical ideas, such differentiation also decreases the likelihood radical ideas will be implemented

differentiation strategy Strategy outlined by Porter involving attempting to develop products and services viewed as unique in the industry

direct contact Communication between two or more persons at similar levels in different work units to co-ordinate work and solve problems

directive Leader behaviour involving

letting subordinates know what is expected of them, providing guidance about work methods, developing work schedules, identifying work evaluation standards, and indicating the basis for outcomes or rewards

discretionary expense centre Responsibility centre whose budgetary outcomes are based on achieving its goals by operating within predetermined expense constraints set through managerial judgment or discretion

dismissal The employer giving the required notice to terminate the employment relationship

distinctive competence Unique strength competitors cannot easily match or imitate

divergent thinking Effort to solve problems by generating new ways of viewing a problem and seeking novel alternatives

diversification Approach entailing effecting growth through development of new areas clearly distinct from current businesses

divestiture Strategy involving an organisation's selling or divesting of a business or part of a business

divisional structure Structure in which positions are grouped according to similarity of products, services, or markets

domain shifts Changes in product and service mix offered so an organisation will interface with more favourable environmental elements

downsizing Process of significantly reducing middle-management layers, increasing spans of control, and shrinking workforce size

downward communication Vertical communication flowing from a higher level to one or more lower levels in the organisation

driving forces Factors pressuring for a particular change

econometric models Systems of simultaneous multiple regression equations using several predictor variables used to identify and measure relationships or interrelationships that exist in the economy

economic element Systems of producing, distributing and consuming wealth

economic order quantity (EOQ) Inventory control method developed to minimise ordering plus holding costs, while avoiding stockout costs

effectiveness The ability to choose appropriate goals and achieve them

efficiency The ability to make the best use of available resources in the process of achieving goals

effort-performance (E→P) expectancy Our assessment of the probability our efforts will lead to the required performance level

electronic mail system Mail system which allows high-speed exchange of written messages by use of computerised text-processing and communication networks

electronic monitoring Practice of using computers to continually assess employee performance

encode Process of translating an intended message into words and gestures

end user Same as a user

end-user computing Development and/or management of information systems by users

enlightened self-interest argument An argument holding that businesses exist at society's pleasure and that, for their own legitimacy and survival, businesses should meet the public's expectations regarding social

entrepreneurial team Group of individuals with diverse expertise and backgrounds brought together to develop and implement innovative ideas aimed to create new products or services or significantly improve existing ones

environmental bounty Extent to which the environment can support sustained growth and stability

environmental complexity Number of elements in an organisation's environment and their degree of similarity

environmental dynamism Rate and predictability of change in the elements of an organisation's environment

environmental uncertainty Condition in which future environmental circumstances affecting an organisation cannot be accurately assessed and predicted

equity theory Theory arguing that we prefer situations of balance, or equity, which exists when we perceive the ratio of our inputs and outcomes to be equal to the ratio of inputs and outcomes for a comparison other

ERG theory Alternative (proposed by Alderfer) to Maslow's hierarchy-of-needs theory which argues there are three levels of individual needs

escalation situations Situations signalling a strong possibility of escalating commitment and accelerating losses

esteem needs Needs related to the two-pronged desire to have a positive self-image and to have our contributions valued and appreciated by others

ethics audits Systematic efforts to assess conforming to organisational ethical policies, aid understanding of those policies, and identify serious breaches requiring remedial action

ethics committee A group charged with helping to establish policies and resolve major questions involving ethical issues confronting organisation members in the course of their work

ethics hot line A special telephone line established to enable employees to bypass the normal chain of command in reporting grievances and serious ethical problems

ethnocentric orientation Approach to international management where executives assume practices which work in the headquarters or home country must necessarily work elsewhere

exchange rate Rate at which one country's currency can be exchanged for another's

executive-support system (ESS) Computer-based information system supporting decision making and effective functioning at the top levels of an organisation

existence needs Needs including various forms of material and physiological desires, such as food and water, as well as such work-related forms such as pay, fringe benefits and physical working conditions

expatriates Individuals who are not citizens of countries in which they are assigned to work

expectancy theory Theory (proposed by Vroom) arguing that we consider three main issues before we expend effort necessary to perform at a given level

expected value Sum of payoffs times respective probabilities for a given alternative

expert power Power based on possession of expertise valued by others

expert systems Computer-based systems that apply an expert's substantial knowledge to help solve specialised problems

explanatory, or causal models Models attempting to identify major variables related to or causing particular past conditions and then using current measures of those variables (predictors) to predict future conditions

exporting Process of making a product in the home country and sending it overseas

expropriation Seizure of a foreign company's assets by a host-country's government

external environment Major forces outside the organisation with potential to influence significantly a product or service's likely success

extinction Technique involving withholding previously available positive consequences associated with a behaviour to decrease that behaviour

Extranets Closed networks of information systems between a group of organisations

extrinsic rewards Rewards provided by others, such as bonuses, awards or promotions

facilities Land, buildings, equipment and other major physical inputs that substantially determine productivity capacity, require time to alter, and involve significant capital investments

feedback control Regulation exercised after a product or service has been completed to ensure the final output meets organisational standards and goals

feedback Degree to which the job provides for clear, timely information about performance results

feedback Information about results and organisational status relative to the environment

feedback Receiver's basic response to the interpreted message

feedforward control Regulation of inputs to ensure they meet standards necessary for the transformation process

Fiedler's contingency model Situational approach (developed by Fiedler and his associates) which suggests leaders differ in the degrees of their orientation toward the task versus toward the people

financial statement Summary of a major aspect of an organisation's financial status

finished-goods Stock of items produced and awaiting sale or transit to a customer inventory

first-line managers/ supervisors Managers at the lowest level of the hierarchy who are directly responsible for the work of operating (non-managerial) employees

five competitive forces model Porter's approach to analysing the nature and intensity of competition in a given industry in terms of five major forces

fixed-interval schedule of reinforcement Pattern in which a reinforcer is

administered on a fixed time schedule, assuming the desired behaviour has continued at an appropriate level

fixed-position layout Production configuration in which the product or client remains in one location and tools, equipment and expertise are brought to it, as necessary, to complete the productive process

fixed-ratio schedule of reinforcement Pattern in which a reinforcer is provided after a fixed number of occurrences of the desired behaviour

flat structure Structure with few hierarchical levels and wide spans of control

flexible manufacturing system (FMS) Manufacturing system using computers to control machines and the production process automatically so different types of parts or product configurations can be handled on the same production line

flexitime Work schedule specifying certain core hours when individuals are expected to be on the job and then allowing flexibility in starting and finishing times as long as individuals work the total number of required hours per day

focus strategy Strategy outlined by Porter entailing specialising by establishing a position of overall cost leadership, differentiation or both, but only within a particular portion, or segment, of an entire market

force-field analysis Method involving analysing the two types of forces, driving forces and restraining forces, that influence any proposed change then assessing how best to overcome resistance

forecasting Process of making predictions about changing conditions and future events that may significantly affect the business of an organisation

formal communication Vertical and horizontal communication which follows paths specified by the official hierarchical organisation structure and related task requirements

formal group Group officially created by an organisation for a specific purpose

formalisation Degree to which written policies, rules, procedures, job descriptions and other documents specify what actions are (or are not) to be taken under a given set of circumstances

forming Stage in which group members try to assess ground rules applying to a task and to group interaction

framing Tendency to make different decisions depending on how a problem is presented

frustration-regression principle Principle stating that if we are continually frustrated in our attempts to satisfy a higher-level need, we may cease to be concerned about that need

functional authority Authority of staff departments over others in the organisation in matters related directly to their respective functions

functional managers Managers with responsibility for a specific, specialised area of the organisation who

functional structure Structure in which positions are grouped according to their main functional (or specialised) area

functional-level strategy Type of strategy focusing on action plans for managing a particular functional area within a business in a way that supports business-level strategy

fundamental attribution error Tendency to underestimate importance of situational influences and overestimate the importance of dispositional influences in explaining behaviour

futurists Individuals who track significant trends in the environment and attempt to predict their impact on the organisation

Gantt chart Specialised bar chart developed by Henry L. Gantt showing current progress on each major project activity relative to necessary completion dates

general managers Managers with responsibility for a whole organisation or a substantial subunit including most of the common specialised areas

geocentric orientation Approach to international management where executives believe a global view is needed in both the headquarters of the parent company and its various subsidiaries and the best individuals, regardless of host- or home-country origin, should be utilised to solve company problems anywhere in the world

geographic divisions Divisions designed to serve different geographic areas

goal commitment One's attachment to, or determination to reach, a goal

goal Future target or end result an organisation wishes to achieve

goal incongruence Condition where there are major incompatibilities between goals of an organisation member and those of the organisation

government agencies Agencies providing services and monitoring compliance with laws and regulations at local, state or regional, and national levels

grand strategy Master strategy providing the basic strategic direction at corporate level

grapevine Another term for informal communication

group cohesiveness Degree to which members are attracted to a group, are motivated to remain in it, and are mutually influenced by one another

group decision-support system (GDSS) Computer-based information system supporting decision makers working together to solve structured problems

group-maintenance roles Roles not directly addressing a task itself but, instead, helping foster group unity, positive interpersonal relations among group members and development of their ability to work effectively together

group technology Classification of parts into families (groups of parts or products with similarities in how they are manufactured) so members of the same family can be manufactured on the same production line

group Two or more interdependent individuals interacting and influencing each other in collective pursuit of a common goal

group-task roles Roles helping a group develop and accomplish its goals

groupthink Tendency of cohesive groups to seek agreement about an issue at the expense of realistically appraising the situation

groupware Software designed to support collaborative efforts among group members, such as scheduling meetings, holding meetings, collaborating on projects and sharing documents

growth needs Needs impelling creativity and innovation, along with the desire to have a productive impact on our surroundings

growth strategies Grand strategies involving organisational expansion along some major dimension

growth-need strength Degree to which an individual needs personal growth and development on the job

hackers Individuals who are knowledgeable about computers and who gain unauthorised entry to, and sometimes tamper with, computer networks and files of organisations with which they have no affiliation

halo effect Tendency to use a general impression based on one or a few characteristics of an individual to judge other characteristics of that same individual

hand of government A view arguing that the interests of society are best served by having the regulatory hands of the law and the political process, rather than the invisible hand, guide the results of corporations' endeavours

hand of management A view stating that corporations and their managers are expected to act in ways that protect and improve society's welfare as a whole as well as advance corporate economic interests

harvest A strategy entailing minimising investments while attempting to maximise short-run profits and cash flow, with the long-run intention of exiting the market

Hawthorne effect Possibility that individuals singled out for a study may improve their performance simply because of the added attention received from researchers, rather than because of any specific factors being tested

Hawthorne studies Group of studies conducted at the Hawthorne plant of the Western Electric Company during the late 1920s and early 1930s, the results of which ultimately led to the human relations view of management

hierarchy-of-needs theory Theory (developed by Maslow) arguing that individual needs form a five-level hierarchy

high-context cultures Cultures where the emphasis in the communication process is on establishing and strengthening relationships in the course of exchanging information

Horizontal communication Lateral or diagonal message exchange either within work-unit boundaries, involving peers reporting to the same supervisor, or across work-unit boundaries, involving individuals who report to different supervisors

horizontal co-ordination Linking of activities across departments at similar levels

human resource management Those management functions concerned with attracting, maintaining and developing people in the employment relationship

human resource planning Determining future human resource needs in relation to an organisation's business objectives or strategic plan, then devising ways to meet the objectives

human skills Skills associated with a manager's ability to work well with others, both as a member of a group and as a leader who gets things done through others

hybrid structure Structure adopting both functional and divisional structures at the same management levels

hygiene factors Factors seeming to make individuals feel dissatisfied with their jobs

hypercompetition State of rapidly escalating competition in which competitors make frequent, daring, and aggressive moves cumulatively creating conditions of continual disequilibrium and change in the industry

idea champion An individual who generates a new idea or believes in the value of a new idea and supports it in the face of numerous potential obstacles

immoral management An approach not only lacking ethical principles but actively opposed to ethical behaviour

import quota Type of trade barrier in the form of a limit on the amount of product which may be imported over a period of time

income statement Financial statement summarising financial results of company operations over a specified time period, such as a quarter or a year

incremental model Model stating managers make the smallest response possible to reduce the problem to at least a tolerable level

incrementalist approach Approach to controlling an innovative project that relies on clan control but also involves a phased set of plans and accompanying bureaucratic controls beginning at a general level and growing more specific as the project progresses

independent demand inventory Type of inventory consisting of end products, parts used for repairs, and other items whose demand is tied more directly to market issues than

for dependent demand inventory items

indigenisation laws Laws which require that citizens of a host country hold a majority interest in all firms operating within the country's borders

individualised consideration Leadership factor involving delegating projects to help develop each follower's capabilities, paying personal attention to each follower's needs, and treating each follower as an individual worthy of respect

individualism Condition where personal interests are given more weight than the group's interests

individualism–collectivism Cultural dimension involving the degree to which individuals concern themselves with their own interests and those of their immediate family, as opposed to the larger group's interests

informal communication Communication which takes place without regard to hierarchical or task requirements

informal group Group established by employees, not the organisation, to serve group members' interests or social needs

informal leader Individual, other than the formal leader, emerging from a group as a major influence and perceived by members as a leader

information architecture Long-range plan for investing in and organising information technology to facilitate reaching organisational goals

information Data which have been analysed or processed into a meaningful form for decision makers

information power Power resulting from access to and control over the distribution of important information about organisational operations and future plans

information system Set of procedures designed to collect (or retrieve), process, store and disseminate information to support planning, decision making, co-ordination and control

infrastructure Highways, railways, airports, sewage facilities, housing, educational institutions, recreation facilities, and other economic and social amenities signalling the extent of an area's economic development

initiating structure Degree to which a leader defines their own role and the roles of subordinates in terms of achieving unit goals

innovation A new idea applied to initiating or improving a process, product or service

innovation New idea applied to initiating or improving a process, product or service

inputs Various human, material, financial, equipment and informational resources required to produce goods and services

institutional power Need for power in which individuals focus on working with others to solve problems and further organisational goals

integration Extent to which there is collaboration among departments needing to co-ordinate their efforts

intellectual stimulation Leadership factor involving offering new ideas to stimulate followers to rethink old ways of doing things, encouraging followers to look at problems from multiple vantage points, and fostering creative breakthroughs in obstacles which seemed insurmountable

internal environment General conditions existing within an organisation

international business Profit-related activities conducted across national boundaries

international element Developments in countries outside an organisation's home country with potential to influence the organisation

international management Process of planning, organising, leading and controlling in organisations engaged in international business

Internet A global connection of computer servers interconnected by telecommunication systems through which individuals can access stored information from their own computer and modem

Intranets Closed networks of information databases and systems within an individual organisation

intrapreneurs Individuals who engage in entrepreneurial roles inside organisations

intrapreneurship The process of innovating within an existing organisation

intrinsic rewards Rewards related to our own internal experiences with successful performance, such as feelings of achievement, challenge and growth

inventory Stock of materials used to facilitate production or to satisfy customer demand

investment centre Responsibility centre whose budgetary outcomes are based on return on investment

invisible hand A view holding that the entire social responsibility of a corporation can be summed up as 'make profits and obey the law'

iron law of responsibility A law stating that 'in the long run, those who do not use power in a manner that society considers responsible will tend to lose it'

issues management The process of identifying a relatively small number of emerging social issues of particular relevance to the organisation, analysing their potential impact and preparing an effective response

item cost Price of an inventory item

Japanese management An approach focusing on aspects of management in Japan that may be appropriate for adoption in other countries

job analysis The systematic collecting and recording of information about the purpose of a job, its major duties, the conditions under which it is performed, the required contacts with others and the knowledge, skills and abilities needed to effectively perform it

job characteristics model Model developed to guide job-enrichment efforts including consideration of core job characteristics, critical psychological states, and outcomes

job depth Degree to which individuals can plan and control work involved in their jobs

job design Specification of task activities associated with a particular job

job enlargement Allocation of a wider variety of similar tasks to a job to make it more challenging

job enrichment Process of upgrading the job-task mix in order to increase significantly potential for growth, achievement, responsibility and recognition

job rotation Practice of periodically shifting workers through a set of jobs in a planned sequence

job scope Number of different tasks an employee performs in a particular job

job sharing Work practice in which two or more people share a single full-time job

job simplification Process of configuring jobs so job-holders have only a small number of narrow activities to perform

joint venture Agreement involving two or more organisations arranging to produce jointly a product or service

judgmental forecasting Type of forecasting relying mainly on individual judgments or committee agreements regarding future conditions

jury of executive opinion Means of forecasting in which organisation executives hold a meeting and estimate, as a group, a forecast for a particular item

just-in-time (JIT) inventory control Approach to inventory control emphasising having materials arrive just as needed in the production process

Kanban Simple parts-movement system depending on cards and containers to pull parts from one work centre to another

kinesic behaviour Body movements, such as gestures, facial expressions, eye movements and posture

knowledge-work system (KWS) Computer-based information system which assists knowledge workers in creation of new knowledge for the organisation

knowledge workers Specialists, such as engineers, architects or scientists, who design products, services or processes and create new knowledge for organisations

labour supply Individuals potentially employable by an organisation

laissez-faire Behavioural style of leaders who generally give the group complete freedom, provide necessary materials, participate only to answer questions, and avoid giving feedback

large-batch and mass production Type of technology where products are manufactured in large quantities, frequently on an assembly line

lateral relations Co-ordination of efforts through communicating and problem solving with peers in other departments or units, rather than referring most issues up the hierarchy for resolution

law of effect Concept stating that behaviours having pleasant or positive consequences are more likely to be repeated and behaviours having unpleasant or negative consequences are less likely to be repeated

leadership Process of influencing others to achieve organisational goals

leading indicators Variables tending to be correlated with the phenomenon of major interest but also to occur in advance of that phenomenon

leading The process of influencing others to engage in the work behaviours necessary to reach organisational goals

legal-political element Legal and governmental systems within which an organisation must function

legitimate power Power stemming from a position's placement in the managerial hierarchy and the authority vested in the position

less developed countries (LDCs) Group of non-communist countries, often called the 'third world', consisting primarily of relatively poor nations characterised by low per capita income, little industry and high birth-rates

liaison role Role to which a specific individual is appointed to facilitate communication and resolution of issues between two or more departments

licensing Agreement in which one organisation gives limited rights to another to use certain of its assets, such as expertise, patents, copyrights or equipment, for an agreed-upon fee or royalty

life cycles Predictable stages of development organisations typically follow

line authority Authority following the chain of command established by the formal hierarchy

linear programming (LP) Quantitative tool for planning how to allocate limited or scarce resources so a single criterion or goal (often profits) is optimised

liquidation Strategy entailing selling or dissolving an entire organisation

liquidity ratios Financial ratios measuring the degree to which an organisation's current assets are adequate to pay current liabilities (current debt obligations)

local-area networks (LANs) Interconnections (usually cable) allowing communications between computers within a single building or in close proximity

logical office Concept that portable microcomputers allow an individual's office to be where the individual is, not restricted to a specific location

long-term–short-term Cultural dimension involving the degree to which members of a society value thrift and goal persistence rather than living in the here-and-now and maintaining personal stability or happiness

low-context cultures Cultures where the emphasis in the communication process is on exchanging information and is less focused on building relationships

LPC (least preferred value on coworker) orientation Personality trait indicating the extent to which an individual places a higher priority on task accomplishment than on personal relationships

management by exception Control principle suggesting managers should be informed of a situation only if control data show a significant deviation from standards

management by objectives (MBO) Process through which specific goals are set collaboratively for the organisation as a whole and every unit and individual within it; the goals are then used as a basis for planning, managing organisational activities, and assessing and rewarding contributions

management-information system (MIS) Computer-based information system that produces routine reports and often allows online access to current and historical information needed by managers mainly at the middle and first-line levels

management information systems Field of management focused on designing and implementing computer-based information systems for use by management

management science Approach aimed at increasing decision effectiveness through use of sophisticated mathematical models and statistical methods

management The process of achieving organisational goals by engaging in the four major functions of planning, organising, leading and controlling

managerial ethics Standards of conduct and moral judgment used by managers of organisations in carrying out their business

managing diversity The planning and implementing of organisational systems and practices that maximise the potential of employees to contribute to organisational goals and develop their capabilities unhindered by group identities such as race, gender, age or ethnic group

manufacturing-resource planning (MRP II) Computer-based information system integrating production planning and control activities of basic MRP systems with related financial, accounting, personnel, engineering and marketing information

market control Managerial approach relying on market mechanisms to regulate prices for certain clearly specified goods and services needed by an organisation

master production schedule (MPS) Schedule translating the aggregate plan into a formalised production plan encompassing specific products to be produced or services to be offered and specific capacity requirements over a designated time period

materials-requirements planning (MRP) Computer-based inventory system developing materials requirements for goods and services specified in the master schedule, and initiating actions needed to acquire materials when needed

matrix structure Structure superimposing a horizontal set of divisional reporting relationships onto a hierarchical functional structure

mechanistic characteristics Characteristics such as highly centralised decision making, many rules and regulations, and mainly hierarchical communication channels

medium Method used to convey the message to the intended receiver

mega-environment The broad conditions and trends in societies in which an organisation operates

merger Combining of two or more companies into one organisation

message Encoding-process outcome, which consists of verbal and non-verbal symbols developed to convey meaning to the receiver

middle managers Managers beneath the top levels of the hierarchy who are directly responsible for the work of managers at lower levels

mission statement Broad declaration of the basic, unique purpose and scope of operations distinguishing the organisation from others of its type

mission The organisation's purpose or fundamental reason for existence

modelling Actually observing and attempting to imitate behaviours of others

moral management An approach that strives to follow ethical principles and precepts

motivation Force energising behaviour, giving direction to behaviour, and underlying the tendency to persist

motivators Factors seeming to make individuals feel satisfied with their jobs

multifocal strategy Strategy aimed at achieving the advantages of worldwide integration where possible, while still attempting to be responsive to important national needs

multinational corporation (MNC) Organisation engaging in production or service activities through its affiliates in several countries, maintaining control over policies of those affiliates, and managing from a global perspective

multiple control systems Systems using two or more of the feedforward, concurrent and feedback control processes and involving several strategic control points

national responsiveness strategy Strategy of allowing subsidiaries to have substantial latitude in adapting products and services to suit the particular needs and political realities of countries they operate in

natural selection model Term sometimes used for the population ecology model

need for achievement (nAch) Desire to accomplish challenging tasks and achieve a standard of excellence in one's work

need for affiliation (nAff) Desire to maintain warm, friendly relationships with others

need for power (nPow) Desire to influence others and control one's environment

negative entropy Ability of open systems to bring in new energy, in the form of inputs and feedback from the environment, to delay or arrest entropy

negative reinforcement Technique, aimed at increasing a desired behaviour, that involves providing noxious stimuli so an individual will engage in the desired behaviour to stop the noxious stimuli

negative synergy Force resulting when group-process losses are greater than gains achieved from combining the forces of group members

network A set of co-operative relationships with individuals whose help is needed in order for a manager to function effectively

network diagram Graphic depiction of interrelationships among activities

networked structure Form of organising where many functions are contracted out to other independent firms and co-ordinated by use of information technology networks to operate as if they were within a single corporation

neutralisers Situational factors making it impossible for a given leader behaviour to have an impact on subordinate performance and/or satisfaction

new venture teams Temporary task forces or teams made up of individuals relieved of normal duties to develop a new process, product or program

new venture units Either separate divisions or specially incorporated companies created to develop new products or business ideas and initiatives

newly industrialised countries (NICs) Countries within LDCs emerging as major exporters of manufactured goods, including such nations as

Hong Kong, Taiwan and South Korea

node, or event Indication of beginning and/or ending of activities in the network

noise Any factor in the communication process interfering with exchanging messages and achieving common meaning

nominal group technique Technique integrating both individual work and group interaction within certain ground rules (NGT)

non-crisis problem An issue requiring resolution but without the simultaneous importance and immediacy characteristics of a crisis

non-cybernetic control system Control system relying on human discretion as a basic part of its process

non-programmed decisions Decisions for which predetermined decision rules are impractical due to novel and/or ill-structured situations

non-rational escalation Tendency to increase commitment to a previously selected course of action beyond the level expected if the manager followed an effective decision-making process; also called escalation phenomenon

non-rational models Models suggesting information-gathering and processing limitations make it difficult for managers to make optimal decisions

non-verbal communication Communication by means of elements and behaviours that are not coded into words

normative decision-making models Models of decision making attempting to prescribe how managers should make decisions

normative leadership model Model helping leaders assess critical situational factors affecting the extent to which they should involve subordinates in particular decisions

norming Stage in which group members begin to build group cohesion, as well as develop a consensus about

norms for performing a task and relating to each other

norms Expected behaviours sanctioned by a group that regulate and foster uniform member behaviour

not-for-profit organisation An organisation whose main purposes centre on issues other than making profits

object language Communicative use of material things, including clothing, cosmetics, furniture and architecture

office-automation system (OAS) Computer-based information system aimed at facilitating communication and increasing the productivity of managers and office workers through document and message processing

one-way communication Communication resulting when the communication process does not allow for feedback

open system System operating in continual interaction with its environment

operating budget Statement that presents the financial plan for each responsibility centre during the budget period and reflects operating activities involving revenues and expenses

operational control Control type involving overseeing implementation of operating plans, monitoring day-to-day results, and taking corrective action as required

operational goals Targets or future results set by lower management that address specific measurable outcomes required from the lower levels

operational plans Means devised to support implementation of tactical plans and achievement of operational goals

operations management Function or field of expertise primarily responsible for managing production and delivery of an organisation's products and services

operations management Management of productive processes converting inputs into goods and services

operations research Another name used for management science

opportunity problem A situation offering strong potential for significant organisational gain if appropriate actions are taken

orchestrator A high-level manager who explains the need for innovation, provides funding for innovating activities, creates incentives for middle managers to sponsor new ideas, and protects idea people

ordering cost Expenses of placing an order (paperwork, postage and time)

organic characteristics Characteristics such as decentralised decision making, few rules and regulations, and both hierarchical and lateral communication channels

organisation chart Line diagram depicting broad outlines of an organisation's structure

organisation design Process of developing an organisation structure

organisation structure Formal pattern of interactions and co-ordination designed by management to link the tasks of individuals and groups in achieving organisational goals

organisation Two or more persons engaged in a systematic effort to produce goods or services

organisational citizenship behaviours Discretionary actions that are not part of job requirements but contribute to attaining organisational goals

organisational culture System of shared values, assumptions, beliefs and norms uniting members of an organisation

organisational development (OD) Change effort planned, focused on an entire organisation or a large subsystem, managed from the top, aimed at enhancing organisational health and effectiveness, and based on planned interventions

organisational problems Discrepancies between a current state or condition and what is desired

organisational social responsibility The

obligation of an organisation to seek actions protecting and improving society's welfare along with its own interests

organisational social responsiveness A term referring to the development of organisational decision processes where managers anticipate, respond to, and manage areas of social responsibility

organisational termination Process of ceasing to exist as an identifiable organisation

organising The process of allocating and arranging human and non-human resources so that plans can be carried out successfully

outputs Products, services and other outcomes produced by the organisation

outsourcing Process of employing an outside vendor to perform a function normally carried on within the organisation

overconfident Tending to be more certain of judgments regarding the likelihood of a future event than one's actual predictive accuracy warrants

overcontrol Limiting individual job autonomy to the point where it seriously inhibits effective job performance

panic Reaction in which individuals become so upset they frantically seek a way to solve a problem

paralanguage Vocal aspects of communication that relate to how something is said rather than to what is said

partial-factor productivity Productivity approach considering the total output relative to a specific input, such as labour

participative Leader behaviour characterised by consulting with subordinates, encouraging their suggestions, and carefully considering their ideas when making decisions

path–goal theory Theory attempting to explain how leader behaviour can positively influence the motivation and job satisfaction of subordinates

payoff Amount of decision-maker value associated with a particular decision alternative and future condition

payoff table or decision matrix Two-dimensional matrix allowing a decision maker to compare how different future conditions are likely to affect respective outcomes of two or more decision alternatives

perception Process individuals use to acquire and make sense out of information from the environment

perceptual defence Tendency to block out or distort information one finds threatening or which challenges one's beliefs

performance appraisal A judgmental process of the job performance of employees

performance-outcome (P→O) expectancy Our assessment of the probability our successful performance will lead to certain outcomes

performing Stage in which energy is channelled toward a task and in which norms support teamwork

personal power Need for power in which individuals want to dominate others for the sake of demonstrating their ability to wield power

physiological needs Survival needs such as food, water and shelter

plan Means devised for attempting to reach a goal

planned change Change involving actions based on a carefully thought-out process anticipating future difficulties, threats and opportunities

planning staff Small group of individuals who assist top-level managers in developing various components of the planning process

planning The process of setting goals and deciding how best to achieve them

policy General guide specifying broad parameters within which organisation members are expected to operate in pursuit of organisational goals

political risk Probability of occurrence of political actions resulting in either loss of enterprise ownership or

significant benefits from conducting business

polycentric orientation Approach to international management where executives believe the parts of the organisation located in a given host country should be staffed by local individuals to the fullest extent possible

pooled interdependence Relationship in which units operate independently but individual efforts are important to the whole organisation's success

population ecology model Model focusing on populations or groups of organisations and arguing that environmental factors cause organisations with appropriate characteristics to survive and others to fail

portfolio strategy approach Method of analysing an organisation's mix of businesses in terms of both individual and collective contributions to strategic goals

positive reinforcement Technique, aimed at increasing a desired behaviour, which involves providing a pleasant, rewarding consequence to encourage that behaviour

positive synergy Force resulting when combined gains from group interaction are greater than group-process losses

power Capacity to affect the behaviour of others

power distance Cultural dimension involving the degree to which individuals in a society accept differences in power distribution as reasonable and normal

procedure Prescribed series of related steps to be taken under certain recurring circumstances

process layout Production configuration in which processing components are grouped according to type of function performed

process structure Type of departmentalisation where positions are grouped by a complete flow of work

product divisions Divisions created to concentrate on a single product or service or at least a relatively homogeneous set of products or services

product layout Production configuration in which processing components are arranged in a specialised line along which the product or client passes during the production process

product/market evolution Fifteen-cell matrix (developed by Hofer) in which businesses are plotted according to the business unit's business strength, or competitive position, and the industry's stage in the evolutionary product/market life-cycle matrix

productivity Efficiency concept gauging the ratio of outputs relative to inputs into a production process

profit centre Responsibility centre whose budgetary outcomes are measured by difference between revenues and costs—in other words, profits

profitability ratios Financial ratios helping measure management's ability to control expenses and earn profits by use of organisational resources

program Comprehensive plan co-ordinating a complex set of activities related to a major non-recurring goal

program evaluation and review technique (PERT) Network planning method for managing large projects

programmed decisions Decisions made in routine, repetitive, well-structured situations by use of predetermined decision rules

project managers Managers with responsibility for co-ordinating efforts involving individuals in several different organisational units all working on a particular project

project Plan co-ordinating a set of limited-scope activities which do not need to be divided into several major projects to reach a major non-recurring goal

projection Tendency of an individual to assume others share their thoughts, feelings and characteristics

prospect theory Theory positing that decision makers find the prospect of an actual loss more painful than giving up the possibility of a gain

prototyping Process of building a rough, working model of all or parts of a proposed information system for purposes of preliminary evaluation and further refinement

proxemics Influence of proximity and space on communication

public affairs department A permanent department that co-ordinates various ongoing social responsibilities and identifies and recommends policies for new social issues

punishment Technique involving providing negative consequences to decrease or discourage a behaviour

purchasing Process of acquiring necessary goods or services in exchange for funds or other remuneration

quality teams Small groups of employees who work on solving specific problems related to quality and improvement of productivity, often with stated targets for improvement

quality Totality of features and characteristics of a product or service bearing on its ability to satisfy needs stated or implied

quantitative forecasting Type of forecasting that relies on numerical data and mathematical models to predict future conditions

questionable payments Business payments raising significant ethical questions of right or wrong either in the host country or in other nations

queuing, or waiting-line, models Mathematical models describing operating characteristics of queuing situations, in which service is provided to persons or units waiting in line

ratio analysis Process of determining and evaluating financial ratios

rational model Model suggesting managers engage in completely rational decision processes, ultimately make optimal decisions, and

possess and understand all information relevant to their decisions at the time they make them

rationalisation Strategy of assigning activities to parts of the organisation, regardless of their location, that are best suited to produce desired results, and then selling finished products where they will yield the best profits

rationing Providing limited access to a product or service in high demand

raw materials inventory Stock of parts, ingredients and other basic inputs to a production or service process

reactive change Change occurring when one takes action in response to perceived problems, threats or opportunities

receiver Person with whom the message is exchanged

reciprocal interdependence Relationship in which one unit's outputs become inputs to another unit and vice versa

recruitment The process of finding and attracting job candidates capable of effectively filling job vacancies

re-engineering Thorough analysis and radical redesign of existing business processes to achieve breakthrough improvements by focusing on critical performance criteria, such as cost, quality, service and speed

referent power Power resulting from being admired, personally identified with, or liked by others

regiocentric orientation Approach to international management where executives believe geographic regions have commonalities which make a regional focus advantageous, and that company problems related to the region are generally best solved by individuals from the region

regional responsiveness strategy Strategy of allowing regional offices to have substantial latitude in co-ordinating the activities of local subsidiaries and adapting products and services to suit the particular needs and political realities of the regions in which they operate

regression models Equations expressing fluctuations in the variable being forecast in terms of fluctuations in one or more other variables (predictors)

reinforcement theory Theory arguing that our behaviour can be explained by consequences in the environment

relatedness needs Needs addressing our relationships with significant others, such as families, friendship groups, work groups and professional groups

reliability The degree to which the decision process will measure the same thing consistently

remuneration The financial payment to employees in return for their work

reorder point (ROP) Inventory level at which a new order should be placed

repatriation Process of returning to one's home country after an assignment in a host country

representativeness Tendency to be overly influenced by stereotypes in making judgments about the likelihood of occurrences

reservations Organisational units devoted to the generation of innovative ideas for future business

resource dependence Approach to controls which argues managers need to consider controls mainly in areas in which they depend on others for resources necessary to reach organisational goals

resource dependence model Model highlighting the organisation's dependence on the environment for resources and arguing that organisations attempt to manipulate the environment to reduce dependence

responsibility centre Subunit headed by a manager responsible for achieving one or more goals

responsibility Obligation to carry out duties and achieve goals related to a position

restraining forces Factors pressuring against a change

restructuring Process of making a major change in organisation structure often involving reducing management levels and possibly changing components of the organisation through divestiture and/or acquisition, as well as shrinking workforce size

retrenchment The forced termination of the employment relationship due to financial, technological or organisational circumstances, often reflecting an attempt by an employer to reduce labour costs in order to remain in business

revenue centre Responsibility centre whose budgetary outcomes are measured primarily by its ability to generate a specified revenue level

revitalisation Renewal of innovative vigour of organisations

reward power Power based on the capacity to control and provide valued rewards to others

risk The possibility a chosen action could lead to losses rather than intended results

rite Relatively elaborate, dramatic, planned set of activities intended to convey cultural values to participants and, usually, an audience

role An organised set of behaviours associated with a particular office or position

role Set of behaviours expected of an individual occupying a particular position in a group

routing, or distribution, models Quantitative models assisting managers in planning the most effective and economical approaches to distribution problems

rubbish-bin model Model stating managers behave in virtually a random way in making non-programmed decisions

rule Statement spelling out specific actions to be taken or not taken in a given situation

safety needs Needs pertaining to the desire to feel safe, secure and free from threats to our existence

sales-force composite Means of forecasting used mainly to predict future sales and typically by obtaining views of various salespeople, sales managers, and/or distributors regarding the sales outlook

satisfaction-progression principle Principle stating that satisfaction of one level of need encourages concern with the next level

satisficing model Model stating managers seek alternatives only until they find one which looks satisfactory, rather than seeking an optimal decision

scenario analysis Approach that addresses a variety of possible futures by evaluating major environmental variables, assessing likely strategies of other significant actors, devising possible counter-strategies, developing ranked hypotheses about the variables, and formulating alternative scenarios

schedules of reinforcement Patterns of rewarding that specify the basis for and timing of positive reinforcement

scientific management Approach emphasising the scientific study of work methods to improve worker efficiency

selection process The decision-making system used to identify which job applicants are best suited to the vacant position

self-actualisation needs Needs pertaining to the requirement of developing our capabilities and reaching our full potential

self-control Our ability to exercise control over our own behaviour by setting standards and providing consequences for our own actions

self-efficacy Belief in one's capabilities to perform a specific task

self-managing team Work group with responsibility for a task area without supervision, and given authority to influence and control group membership and behaviour

self-oriented roles Roles related to the personal needs of group members and often negatively influencing group effectiveness

self-serving bias Tendency to perceive oneself as responsible for successes and others as responsible for failures

semantic blocks Blockages or communication difficulties arising from word choices

semantic net Network of words and word meanings a given individual has available for recall

sender Initiator of the message

sequential interdependence Relationship in which one unit must complete its work before the next in the sequence can begin work

shaping Successive rewarding of behaviours closely approximating the desired response until the actual desired response is made

simulation Mathematical imitation of reality

single-use plans Plans aimed at achieving a specific goal which, once reached, will most likely not recur in the future

situational leadership theory Theory (developed by Hersey and Blanchard) based on the premise leaders need to alter their behaviours depending on one major situational factor—the readiness of followers

situational theories Theories of leadership taking into consideration important situational factors

skill variety Extent to which the job entails a number of activities requiring different skills

slack Latitude about when various activities on the non-critical paths can be started without endangering the entire project's completion date

slack resources Cushion of resources that facilitates adaptation to internal and external pressures, as well as initiation of changes

smoothing Taking actions aimed at reducing the impact of fluctuations, given the market

social audit A systematic study and evaluation of the social, rather than economic, performance of an organisation

social forecasting The systematic process of identifying social trends, evaluating the organisational importance of those trends, and integrating these assessments into the organisation's forecasting program

social learning theory Theory arguing learning occurs through continuous reciprocal interaction of our behaviours, various personal factors and environmental forces

social loafing or **free riding** Tendency of individuals to expend less effort when working in groups than when working alone and to benefit from the group's work without bearing a proportional share of costs involved

social scanning The general surveillance of various elements in the task environment to detect evidence of impending changes affecting the organisation's social responsibilities

socialist economy Economy in which means of production are owned by the state and economic activity is co-ordinated by plan

sociocultural element Attitudes, values, norms, beliefs, behaviours and associated demographic trends characteristic of a given geographic area

soldiering Deliberately working at less than full capacity

span of management or **span of control** Number of subordinates who report directly to a specific manager

sponsor A middle manager who recognises the organisational significance of an idea, helps obtain the necessary funding for development of the innovation, and facilitates its actual implementation

stability strategy Strategy involving maintaining the status quo or growing in a methodical, but slow, manner

standard cost centre Responsibility centre whose budgetary outcomes depend on achieving its goals by operating within standard cost constraints

standing committee Permanent task group of individuals charged with handling recurring matters in a narrowly defined subject area over an indefinite, but generally long, time period

standing plans Plans providing ongoing guidance for performing recurring activities

statistical process control Statistical technique using periodic random samples taken during actual production to determine whether acceptable quality levels are being met or production should be stopped for remedial action

stereotyping Tendency to attribute characteristics to an individual on the basis of an assessment of the group to which they belong

stockout cost Economic consequences of running out of stock (loss of customer goodwill and sales)

storming Stage in which group members frequently are in conflict with each another as they locate and resolve differences of opinion about key issues

story Narrative based on true events, which may be embellished to highlight intended value

strategic alliance Arrangement where two or more independent organisations form a co-operative partnership to gain mutual strategic advantage

strategic alliance Where two or more independent organisations set up a co-operative partnership to gain mutual strategic advantage

strategic business unit (SBU) Distinct business, with its own set of competitors, which can be managed relatively independently of other businesses within the organisation

strategic control Control type involving monitoring critical environmental factors which could affect viability of strategic plans, assessing effects of organisational strategic actions, and ensuring strategic plans are implemented as intended

strategic control points Performance areas chosen for control because they are particularly important in meeting organisational goals

strategic goals Broadly defined targets or future results set by top management

strategic management Process through which managers formulate and implement strategies geared to optimising strategic goal achievement, given available environmental and internal conditions

strategic plans Detailed action steps mapped out to reach strategic goals

strategies Large-scale action plans for interacting with the environment to achieve long-term goals

strategy formulation Process of identifying mission and strategic goals, conducting competitive analysis, and developing specific strategies

strategy implementation Process of carrying out strategic plans and maintaining control over how those plans are carried out

substitutes for leadership Approach attempting to specify some main situational factors likely to make leader behaviours unnecessary or to negate their effectiveness

substitutes Situational factors making leadership impact not only impossible but also unnecessary

sunk costs Costs which, once incurred, are not recoverable and should not enter into considerations of future courses of action

supervisors Mainly individuals with expertise and training in an area

suppliers Organisations and individuals supplying resources an organisation needs to conduct its operations

supportive Leader behaviour entailing showing concern for the status, wellbeing and needs of subordinates; doing small things to make work more pleasant; and being friendly and approachable

SWOT analysis Method of analysing an organisation's competitive situation involving assessing organisational strengths (S), weaknesses (W), environmental opportunities (O) and threats (T)

symbol Object, act, event or quality

serving as a vehicle for conveying meaning

symbolic processes Various ways we use verbal and imagined symbols to process and store experiences in representational forms to serve as guides to future behaviour

synergy Ability of the whole to equal more than the sum of its parts

system Set of interrelated parts operating as a whole in pursuit of common goals

systems-development life cycle Series of stages used in the development of most medium- and large-sized information systems

systems theory Approach based on the idea that organisations can be visualised as systems

tactical control Control type focusing on assessing implementation of tactical plans at department levels, monitoring associated periodic results, and taking corrective action as needed

tactical goals Targets or future results usually set by middle management for specific departments or units

tactical plans Means charted to support implementation of the strategic plan and achievement of tactical goals

tall structure Structure with many hierarchical levels and narrow spans of control

tariff Type of trade barrier in the form of a customs duty, or tax, levied mainly on imports

task environment Specific outside elements with which an organisation interfaces in the course of conducting its business

task force Temporary task group formed to recommend on a specific issue

task group Formal group created for a specific purpose, supplementing or replacing work normally done by command groups

task identity Degree to which the job allows completion of a major identifiable piece of work, rather than just a fragment

task significance Extent to which a

worker sees job output as having an important impact on others

team Temporary or ongoing task group with members charged to work together to identify problems, form a consensus about what should be done, and implement necessary actions in relation to a particular task or organisational area

technical skills Skills reflecting both an understanding of and a proficiency in a specialised field

technological element Current state of knowledge regarding production of products and services

technological interdependence Degree to which different organisation parts must exchange information and materials to perform required activities

technological transfer Transmission of technology from those who possess it to those who do not

technological, or qualitative forecasting Type of forecasting aimed primarily at predicting long-term trends in technology and other important, environmental aspects

technology Knowledge, tools, equipment and work techniques used by an organisation in delivering its product or service

telecommunications Electronic communication of information over a distance

telecommuting Form of working at home made possible by using computer technology to remain in touch with the office

teleconferencing Simultaneous communication among a group of individuals by telephone or via computer using specially designed software

Theory Z Concept combining positive aspects of American and Japanese management into a modified approach aimed at increasing managerial effectiveness while remaining compatible with the norms and values of American society and culture

time-series methods Methods using

historical data to develop future forecasts

top managers Managers at the very top levels of the hierarchy who are ultimately responsible for the entire organisation

total quality management (TQM) Management system integral to an organisation's strategy and aimed at continually improving product and service quality so as to achieve high levels of customer satisfaction and build strong customer loyalty

total quality management Approach highlighting collective responsibility for product and service quality, and encouraging individuals to work together to improve quality

total-factor productivity Productivity approach considering all inputs involved in producing outputs

trade associations Organisations composed of individuals or firms with common business concerns

training The process of equipping people with skills and competencies in a systematic manner

traits Distinctive internal qualities or characteristics of an individual, such as physical characteristics, personality characteristics, skills and abilities, and social factors

transactional leaders Leaders who motivate subordinates to perform at expected levels by helping them recognise task responsibilities, identify goals, acquire confidence about meeting desired performance levels, and understand how their needs and the rewards they desire are linked to goal achievement

transaction-processing system (TPS) Computer-based information system which executes and records routine day-to-day transactions needed to conduct an organisation's business

transformation processes Organisation's managerial and technological abilities used to convert inputs into outputs

transformational leaders Leaders who motivate individuals to perform

beyond normal expectations by inspiring subordinates to focus on broader missions transcending their own immediate self-interests, to concentrate on intrinsic higher-level goals rather than extrinsic lower-level goals, and to have confidence in their abilities to achieve the extraordinary missions articulated by the leader

turnaround Strategy designed to reverse a negative trend and restore the organisation to appropriate levels of profitability

two-factor theory Herzberg's theory that hygiene factors are necessary to keep workers from feeling dissatisfied, but only motivators can lead workers to feel satisfied and motivated

two-way communication Communication resulting when the communication process explicitly includes feedback

uncertainty A condition in which the decision maker must choose a course of action with incomplete knowledge of consequences following implementation

uncertainty avoidance Cultural dimension involving the extent to which members of a society feel uncomfortable with and try to avoid situations they see as unstructured, unclear or unpredictable

undercontrol Granting autonomy to an employee to the point where the organisation loses its ability to direct individual effort toward achieving organisational goals

unions Membership groups formed to represent employees and to negotiate collective agreements with management that determine the terms and conditions of employment

unit and small-batch production Type of technology where products are custom-produced to meet customer specifications or are made in small quantities primarily by craft specialists

upward communication Vertical flow of communication from a lower level to

one or more higher levels in the organisation

user Individual, other than an information system professional, engaged in the development and/or management of computer-based information systems

valence Our assessment of anticipated value of various outcomes or rewards

validity Whether the decision process actually measures what it sets out to measure

variable-interval schedule of reinforcement Pattern in which a reinforcer is administered on a varying, or random, time schedule which averages out to a predetermined time frequency

variable-ratio schedule of reinforcement Pattern in which a reinforcer is provided after a varying, or random, number of occurrences of the desired behaviour in such a way the reinforcement pattern averages out to a predetermined ratio of occurrences per reinforcement

verbal communication Written or oral use of words to communicate

vertical communication Communication involving a message exchange between two or more levels of the organisational hierarchy

vertical co-ordination Linking of activities at the top of the organisation with those at the middle and lower levels to achieve organisational goals

vertical integration Approach involving effecting growth through production of inputs previously provided by suppliers or through replacement of a customer role by disposing of one's own outputs

vicarious learning Our ability to learn new behaviours and/or assess their probable consequences by observing others

videoconferencing Holding meetings with individuals in two or more locations by means of closed-circuit television

virtual team Physically dispersed work group using information technology as a means to interact but rarely, if ever, meeting physically

voice mail Recording system providing senders with opportunity to leave messages for receivers by telephone

whistle-blower An employee who reports a real or perceived wrongdoing under the control of their employer to those able to take appropriate action

wholly owned subsidiary Operation on foreign soil totally owned and controlled by a company with headquarters outside the host country

wide-area networks (WANs) Networks providing communications between computers over long distances, usually through telecommunications companies

work agenda A loosely connected set of tentative goals and tasks that a manager is attempting to accomplish

work specialisation Degree to which work necessary to achieve organisational goals is broken down into various jobs

work-in-process inventory Stock of items currently being transformed into a final product or service

world-wide integration strategy, or globalisation Strategy aimed at developing relatively standardised products with global appeal, as well as rationalising operations across the world

References

Abrahamson, E. and Fombrun, C.J. 1994, Macrocultures: Determinants and consequences, *Academy of Management Review*, 19, pp. 728–55.

Ackerman, L.S. 1982, Transition management: An in-depth look at managing complex change, *Organizational Dynamics*, Summer, pp. 46–66.

Adair, J.G. 1984, The Hawthorne effect: A reconsideration of the methodological artifact, *Journal of Applied Psychology*, 69, pp. 334–45.

Adam, Jr, E.E. and Ebert, R.J. 1992, *Production and Operations Management*, Prentice-Hall, Englewood Cliffs.

Adams, J.R. and Kirchof, N.S. 1984, The practice of matrix management, in D.I. Cleland (ed.), *Matrix Management Systems Handbook*, Van Nostrand Reinhold, New York.

Adams, J.S. 1965, Inequity in social exchange, in L. Berkowitz (ed.), *Advances in Experimental Social Psychology*, 2, Academic, New York.

Adhikari, R. 1996, Do vendors feel your pain?, *Information Week*, 4 March, pp. 44–7.

Adler, N.J. 1984, Expecting international success: Female managers overseas, *Columbia Journal of World Business*, Fall, pp. 79–85.

Adler, N.J. 1991, *International Dimensions of Organizational Behavior*, P. W.S.-Kent, Boston.

Adler, N.J., Dokter, R. and Redding, S.G. 1986, From the Atlantic to the Pacific century: Cross-cultural management reviewed, *Journal of Management*, 12, pp. 295–318.

Alabanese, R. and Van Fleet, D.D. 1985, Rational behavior in groups: The free-riding tendency, *Academy of Management Review*, 10, pp. 244–55.

Albert, A. 1985, Citicorp shuffles units to emphasize management of institutional assets, *American Banker*, 5 July, p. 1.

Aldag, R.J. and Fuller, S.R. 1994, Beyond fiasco: A re-appraisal of the groupthink phenomenon and a new model of group decision processes, *Psychological Bulletin*, 113, pp. 533–52.

Alderfer, C.P. 1972, *Existence, Relatedness, and Growth: Human Needs in Organizational Settings*, Free Press, New York.

Alderfer, C.P. 1987, An intergroup perspective on group dynamics, in J.W. Lorsch (ed.), *Handbook of Organizational Behavior*, Prentice-Hall, Englewood Cliffs.

Aldrich Jr, N.W. 1986, Lines of communication, *INC.*, June, pp. 140–44.

Aldrich, H. and Herker, D. 1977, Boundary spanning roles and organization structure, *Academy of Management Review*, 2, pp. 217–30.

Aldrich, H.E. 1979, *Organizations and Environments*, Prentice-Hall, Englewood Cliffs.

Aley, J. 1995, New lift for the U.S. export boom, *Fortune*, 13 Nov., pp. 73–8.

Allcorn, S. 1985, What makes groups tick, *Personnel*, September, pp. 52–8.

Alster, N. 1989, Unlevel playing field, *Forbes*, 26 June, pp. 53–7.

Altier, W.J. 1986, SMR forum: Task forces—an effective management tool, *Sloan Management Review*, Spring, pp. 69–75.

Amabile, T.M. 1983, *The Social Psychology of Creativity*, Springer-Verlag, New York.

Amabile, T.M. 1988, A model of creativity and innovation in organizations, *Research in Organizational Behavior*, 10, pp. 123–67.

American Society for Quality Control 1992, Quality glossary, *Quality Progress*, Feb., p. 26.

Amit, R. and Livnat, J. 1988, A concept of conglomerate diversification, *Journal of Management*, 14, pp. 593–604.

Ancona, D.G. and Caldwell, D.F. 1992, Demography and design: Predictors of new product team performance, *Organization Science*, 3, pp. 321–41.

Anderson, E. 1990, Two firms, one frontier: On assessing joint venture performance, *Sloan Management Review*, Winter, pp. 19–26.

Andrews, J.D.W., The achievement motive and advancement in two types of organizations, *Journal of Personality and Social Psychology*, 6, pp. 163–68.

Andrews, K.R. 1968, Introduction to the thirtieth-anniversary edition of Chester I. Barnard, *The Function of the Executive*, Harvard, Cambridge.

Annual Report 1998, Harvey Norman Holdings Limited.

Ansberry, C. 1991, Utah's Geneva steel, once called hopeless, is racking up profits, *Wall Street Journal*, 20 Nov., p. A1.

Anthony, R.N., Dearden, J. and Bedford, N.M. 1984, *Management Control Systems*, Irwin, Homewood.

Applegate, L.M., Cash, Jr, J.I. and Mills, D.Q. 1988, Information technology and tomorrow's manager, *Harvard Business Review*, Nov.–Dec., pp. 128–36.

Arlow, P. and Gannon, M.J. 1982, Social responsiveness, corporate structure, and economic performance, *Academy of Management Review*, 7, pp. 235–41.

Armstrong, L. and Holyoke, L. 1995, NASA's tiny camera has a wide-angle future, *Business Week*, 6 March, pp. 54–5.

Arnold, H.J. 1981, A test of the validity of the multiplicative hypothesis of expectancy-valence theories of work motivation, *Academy of Management Journal*, 24, pp. 128–41.

Arnold, H.J. and Feldman, D.C. 1986, *Organizational Behavior*, McGraw-Hill, New York.

Arthur, L.J., Quick and dirty, *Computerworld*, 14 Dec., p. 4.

Arveny, R.D. and Campion, J.E. 1982, The employment interview: A summary and recent review of recent research, *Personnel Psychology*, Summer, pp. 281–322.

Arveny, R.D. and Ivancevich, J.M. 1980, Punishment in organizations: A review, propositions, and research suggestions, *Academy of Management Review*, 5, pp. 23–132.

Ashmos, D.P. and Huber, G.P. 1987, The systems paradigm in organization theory: Correcting the record and suggesting the future, *Academy of Management Review*, 12, pp. 607–21.

Astley, W.G. 1985, Organizational size and bureaucracy, *Organization Studies*, 6, pp. 201–28.

Atkinson, B. 1996, USF&G turning 100, a gleam in its eye, *Sun* (Baltimore), 24 March, p. 1E.

Attewell, P. and Rule, J. 1984, Computing and organizations: What we know and what we don't know, *Communications of the ACM*, Dec., pp. 1184–92.

Auerback, S. 1987, America, the 'diminished giant', *Washington Post*, 15 April, pp. A1, A18.

Aupperle, K.E., Carroll, A.B. and Hatfield, J.D. 1985, An empirical examination of the relationship between corporate social responsibility and profitability, *Academy of Management Journal*, 28, pp. 446–63.

Avishai, B. 1989, A CEO's common sense of CIM: An interview with J. Tracy O'Rourke, *Harvard Business Review*, Jan.–Feb. pp. 110–17.

Avishai, B. and Taylor, W. 1989, Customers drive a technology driven company, *Harvard Business Review*, Nov.–Dec., pp. 107–14.

Axley, S.R. 1984, Managerial and organizational communication in terms of the conduit metaphor, *Academy of Management Review*, 9, pp. 428–37.

Babbage, C. 1963, *On the Economy of Machinery and Manufactures*, Knight, London, 1832, reprinted by Kelly, New York.

Bahree, B. 1995, BP comes back even as oil prices sink, *Wall Street Journal*, 8 Sept., p. A6.

Baig, E. 1995, Taking care of business—without leaving the house, *Business Week*, 17 April, pp. 106–7.

Bailey, G. and Sherman, D. 1988, Downsizing: The alternatives may be cheaper, *Management Review*, April, pp. 54–5.

Bailey, G. and Szerdy, J. 1988, Is there life after downsizing?, *Journal of Business Strategy*, Jan.–Feb., pp. 8–11.

Bailey, J. 1987, The fine art of leading a meeting, *Working Woman*, Aug., pp. 68–70, 103.

Bailey, J. 1990, Ousted chairman of Abbott accuses company in filing, *Wall Street Journal*, 6 June, p. A6.

Baker, H.K. 1987, *Financial Management*, Harcourt Brace Jovanovich, San Diego.

Baliga, B.R. and Hunt, J.G. 1987, An organizational life cycle approach to leadership, in J.G. Hunt, B.R. Baliga, H.P. Dachler and C.A. Schriesheim (eds), *Emerging Leadership Vistas*, Heath, Boston.

Bamford, J. and McHenry, S. 1995, The Working Woman 50 top women business owners, *Working Woman*, May, p. 37.

Banagham, M. 1999, Fast food down to the wire, *Business Review Weekly*, 21 May, p. 103.

Bandura, A. 1977, *Social Learning Theory*, Prentice-Hall, Englewood Cliffs.

Bandura, A. 1986, *Social Foundations of Thought and Action: A Social Cognitive Theory*, Prentice-Hall, Englewood Cliffs.

Banerjee, N. 1995, For Mary Kay sales reps in Russia, hottest shade is the color of money, *Wall Street Journal*, 30 Aug., p. A8.

Banks, H. 1994, Superjumbo, *Forbes*, 24 Oct., pp. 180–6.

Barbash, F. 1995, Barings executives blamed for fall, *Washington Post*, 19 July, p. F3.

Barkdull, C.W. 1963, Span of control: A method of evaluation, *Michigan Business Review*, 15, pp. 25–32;

Barling, J. and Beattie, R. 1983, Self-efficacy beliefs and sales performance, *Journal of Organizational Behavior Management*, 5, pp. 41–51.

Barnard, C.I. 1968, *The Functions of the Executive*, Harvard, Cambridge.

Barnes, S. and Greller, L.M. 1994, Computer-mediated communication in organizations, *Communication Education*, 43, pp. 129–42.

Barnett, W.P. 1990, The organizational ecology of a techno-logical system, *Administrative Science Quarterly*, 35, pp. 31–60.

Barney, J.B. 1986, Organizational culture: Can it be a source of sustained competitive advantage? *Academy of Management Review*, 11, pp. 656–65.

Barney, J.B. 1995, Look inside for competitive advantage, *Academy of Management Executive*, 9, 4, pp. 49–61.

Barney, J.B. and Griffin, R.W. 1992, *The Management of Organizations*, Houghton Mifflin, Boston.

Barrett, P. M. 1995, How a young lawyer is making his mark at a Washington firm, *Wall Street Journal*, 15 Feb., pp. A1, A11.

Barrett, R.B. and Kistka, D.J. 1987, Forecasting system at Rubbermaid, *Journal of Business Forecasting*, Spring, pp. 7–9.

Barron, F.H. 1985, Payoff matrices pay off at Hallmark, *Interfaces*, July–Aug., pp. 20–5.

Bart, C.K. 1988, New venture units: Use them wisely to manage innovation, *Sloan Management Review*, Summer, pp. 35–43.

Bartholomew, D. 1996, Boost to response time, *Information Week*, 19 Feb., p. 73.

Bartino, J. 1992, At these shouting matches, no one says a word, *Business Week*, 11 June, p. 78.

Bartlett, C.A. and Ghoshal, S. 1992, *Transnational Management*, Irwin, Homewood.

Bartol, K.M. and Martin, D.C. 1986, Women and men in task groups, in R.D. Ashmore and F.K. Del Boca (eds), *The Social Psychology of Female-Male Relations*, Academic, Orlando.

Baskin, O.W. and Aronoff, C.E. 1980, *Interpersonal Communication in Organizations*, Scott, Foresman, Santa Monica.

Bass, B.M. 1981, *Stogdill's Handbook of Leadership*, Free Press, New York.

Bass, B.M. 1983, *Organizational Decision Making*, Irwin, Homewood.

Bass, B.M. 1985, *Leadership and Performance Beyond Expectations*, Free Press, New York.

Bass, B.M., Krusell, J. and Alexander, R.A. 1971, Male managers' attitudes toward working women, *American Behavioral Scientist*, 15, pp. 221–36.

Baucus, M.S. and Near, J.P. 1991, Can illegal corporate behavior be predicted? An event history analysis, *Academy of Management Journal*, 34, pp. 9–36.

Baum, L. 1987, Delegating your way to job survival, *Business Week*, 2 Nov., p. 206.

Baumeister, R.F. and Leary, M.R. 1995, The need to belong: Desire for interpersonal attachments as a fundamental human motivation, *Journal of Applied Psychology*, 117, pp. 497–529.

Bazerman, M.H. 1986, *Judgment in Managerial Decision Making*, Wiley, New York.

Beckhard, R. 1969, *Organizational Development: Strategies and Models*, Addison-Wesley, Reading.

Beer, M. 1980, *Organization Change and Development: A Systems View*, Goodyear, Santa Monica.

Beer, M. and Spector, B. 1985, Corporate wide transformations in human resource management, in R.E. Walton and P. R. Lawrence (eds), *Human Resource Management, Trends and Challenge*, Harvard Business School Press, Boston.

Begley, S. 1998, The boss feels your pain, *Newsweek*, 12 Oct., p. 74.

Behar, R. 1988, How the rich get richer, *Forbes*, 31 Oct., p. 70.

Behar, R. 1995, Stalked by Allstate, *Fortune*, 2 Oct., pp. 128–42.

Bell, D. 1987, The world and the United States in 2013, *Daedalus*, Summer, pp. 1–31.

Ben & Jerry's 1995, Annual Report.

Benjamin, R.I. 1982, Information technology in the 1990s: A long-range planning scenario, *MIS Quarterly*, June, pp. 11–31.

Benjamin, R.I., Rockart, J.F., Morton, M.S.S. and Wyman, J. 1984, Information technology: A strategic opportunity, *Sloan Management Review*, Spring, pp. 3–10.

Benne, K. and Sheats, P. H. 1948, Functional roles of group members, *Journal of Social Issues*, 4, pp. 41–9.

Bennet, J. 1993, A stronger yen is hurting sales of Japan's cars, *New York Times*, 5 Nov., pp. A1, C2.

Bennett, J.K. 1994, The 12 building blocks of the learning organization, *Training*, June, p. 41.

Bernstein, A. 1992, Teaching business how to train, *Business Week/Reinventing America*, 23 Oct., pp. 82–90.

Berry, M.M.J. and Taggart, J.H. 1994, Managing technology and innovation: A review, *R&D Management*, 24, pp. 341–53.

Berton, L. 1995, It's audit time! Send in the clowns, *Wall Street Journal*, 18 Jan., pp. B1, B6.

Bettenhausen, K. and Murnighan, J.K. 1985, The emergence of norms in competitive decision-making groups, *Administrative Science Quarterly*, 30, pp. 350–72.

Betton, J. and Dess, G.G. 1985, The application of population ecology models to the study of organizations, *Academy of Management Review*, 10, pp. 750–7.

Betts, M. 1992, Big things come in small buttons, *Computerworld*, 3 Aug., p. 30.

Beyer J.M. and Trice, H.M. 1984, A field study of the use and perceived effects of discipline in controlling work performance, *Academy of Management Journal*, 27, pp. 743–64.

Bhambri, A. and Sonnenfeld, J. 1987, The man who stands alone, *New Management*, Spring, pp. 29–33.

Bhambri, A. and Sonnenfeld, J. 1988, Organization structure and corporate social performance: A field study in two contrasting industries, *Academy of Management Journal*, 31, pp. 642–62.

Birchard, B. 1995, Power to the people, *CFO*, March, pp. 38–43.

Bird, L. 1994, Lazarus's IBM coup was all about relationships, *Wall Street Journal*, 26 May, pp. B1, B7.

Bird, L. and Jereski, L. 1996, Warnaco may buy authentic fitness corp., *Wall Street Journal*, 7 June, p. A2.

Birdwhistell, R. 1972, *Kenesics and Context*, University of Pennsylvania, Philadelphia.

Blackmon, D.A. 1998, A factory in Alabama is the merger in microcosm, *Wall Street Journal*, 5 May, pp. B1, B10.

Blake, R.R. and McCanse, J.S. 1991, *The Managerial Grid*, Gulf, Houston.

Blank, W., Weitzel, J.R. and Green, S.G. 1990, A test of the situational leadership theory, *Personnel Psychology*, 43, pp. 579–97.

Blomberg N. 1999, Bill-paying becomes focus of online war, *Taiwan News*, 13 Aug., p. 15.

Bluedorn, A.C. (ed.) 1986, Special book review section on the classics of management, *Academy of Management Review*, 11, pp. 442–64.

Blumenstein, R. 1996, Ohio strike that is crippling GM plants is tied to plan to outsource brake work, *Wall Street Journal*, 12 March, pp. A3, A4.

Bohn, R.E. 1994, Measuring and managing technological knowledge, *Sloan Management Review*, 22 Sept., p. 61.

Bongiorno, L. 1996, The Pepsi regeneration, *Business Week*, 11 March, pp. 70–3.

Boone, M.E. 1991, Computers reshape Phillips 66, *Industry Week*, 1 July, p. 12.

Booth, C. 1992, Against the time, *Time*, 17 Feb., pp. 54–6.

Bormann, E.G. 1983, Symbolic convergence: Organizational communication and culture, in L. Putnam and M.E. Pacanowsky (eds), *Communication and Organizations: An Interpretive Approach*, Sage, Beverly Hills.

Boslet, M. 1994, Metal buttons toted by crop pickers act as mini databases, *Wall Street Journal*, 1 June, p. B3.

Boulding, K.E. 1956, General systems theory—the skeleton of science, *Management Science*, 2, pp. 197–208.

Bounds, G., Yorks, L., Adams, M. and Ramney, G. 1994, *Beyond Total Quality Management: Toward the Emerging Paradigm*, McGraw-Hill, New York.

Bounds, W. 1995, Kodak reorganizes its sales force at imaging group, *Wall Street Journal*, 24 Jan., p. B3.

Bourgeois, L. J. 1981, On the measurement of organizational slack, *Academy of Management Review*, 6, pp. 29–39.

Bowen, E. 1987, Looking to its roots, *Time*, 25 May, pp. 26–9.

Bower, J.L. and Christensen, C.M. 1995, Disruptive technologies: Catching the wave, *Harvard Business Review*, Jan.–Feb., pp. 43–53.

Boyatzis, R.E. 1982, *The Competent Manager: A Model for Effective Performance*, Wiley, New York.

Boyd, B.K., Dess, G.G. and Rasheed, A.M.A. 1993, Divergence between archival and perceptual measures of the environment: Causes and consequences, *Academy of Management Review*, 18, pp. 204–26.

Brady, K. 1987, The power of positive stress, *Working Woman*, July, pp. 74–7.

Brahm, J. 1995, High-tech tools speed, *Machine Design*, 26 Jan., pp. 36–40.

Bramel, D. and Friend, R. 1981, Hawthorne, the myth of the docile worker, and class bias in psychology, *American Psychologist*, Aug., pp. 867–78.

Brand, D.C. and Scanlan, G. 1995, Strategic control through core competencies, *Long Range Planning*, 28, 2, pp. 102–14.

Bray, D.W., Campbell, R.J. and Grant, D.L. 1974, *Formative Years in Business: A Long Term AT&T Study of Managerial Lives*, Wiley, New York.

Brealey, R.A. and Myers, S.C. 1991, *Principles of Corporate Finance*, McGraw-Hill, New York.

Breeze, J. 1986, Paul Devinat's scientific management in Europe—A historical perspective, in D.A. Wren and J.A. Pearce II (eds), *Papers Dedicated to the Development of Modern Management*, Academy of Management.

Brief, A.P., Dukerich, J.M., Brown, P.R. and Brett, J.F. 1996, What's wrong with the Treadway commission report? *Journal of Business Ethics*, Feb., pp. 183–98.

Brockner, J. 1992, The escalation of commitment to a failing course of action: Toward theoretical progress, *Academy of Management Review*, 17, pp. 39–61.

Brown, B. 1988, James Bildner's spectacular rise and fall, *Wall Street Journal*, 24 Oct., p. B1.

Brown, C. 1995, The body-bending business, *Forbes*, 11 Sept., pp. 196–204.

Brown, M.G., Hitchcock, D.E. and Willard, M.L. 1994, *Why TQM Fails and What to Do about It*, Irwin, Burr Ridge.

Brown, P.B. 1988, The anti-marketers, *INC.*, March, pp. 62–72.

Brown, W. 1988, Electronic pulses replacing paper in workplace, *Washington Post*, 2 Sept., pp. F1, F2.

Brown, W. 1991, Perrier's market share fizzles in the aftermath of its recall, *Washington Post*, 4 Jan., p. F3.

Browning, E.S. 1990, Long-term thinking and paternalistic ways carry Michelin to top, *Wall Street Journal*, 5 Jan., pp. A1, A8.

Browning, E.S. 1992, Nestlé appears to win battle to acquire Source Perrier, *Wall Street Journal*, 24 March, p. A13.

Browning, E.S. 1993, Perrier tries to rejuvenate stodgy image, *Wall Street Journal*, 2 Sept., p. B1.

Browning, E.S. 1994, Computer chip project brings rivals together, but the cultures clash, *Wall Street Journal*, 3 April, pp. A1, A8.

Brull, S.V. and Gross, N. 1996, Sony's new world, *Business Week*, 27 May, pp. 100–8.

Bryan, M. 2000, Every step you take, every move you make, *Australian Financial Review*, 4–5 March, p. 27.

Bryant, G. 1999, Be part of the e-boom, *Business Review Weekly*, 21 May, p. 162.

Budescu, D.V. and Weiss, W. 1987, Reflection of transitive and intransitive preferences: A test of prospect theory, *Organizational Behavior and Human Decision Processes*, 39, pp. 184–202.

Bulkeley, W.M. 1990, When laptop computers go on the road, the hassles can cancel out the benefits, *Wall Street Journal*, 16 May, pp. B1, B4.

Bulkeley, W.M. 1995, Will ultimate voice mail make secretaries obsolete? *Wall Street Journal*, 20 Oct., pp. B1, B5.

Bulkeley, W.M. and Stecklow, S. 1994, Harvard's president, citing exhaustion, is going on leave during fund drive, *Wall Street Journal*, 29 Nov., p. B7.

Burck, C.G. 1982, Can Detroit catch up? *Fortune*, 8 Feb., pp. 34–9.

Burgelman, R.A. 1985, Managing the new venture division: Research findings and implications for strategic management, *Strategic Management Journal*, 6, pp. 39–54.

Burgess, J. 1987, Prankster's Christmas greeting generates few ho-ho-hos at IBM, *Washington Post*, 18 Dec., pp. F1, F10.

Burgess, J. 1988, Searching for a better computer shield, *Washington Post*, 13 Nov., p. H1.

Burgess, J. 1992, IBM finishes one race, starts another, *Washington Post*, 31 March, p. C1.

Burne, J.A. 1994, The pain of downsizing, *Business Week*, 9 May, p. 61.

Burns, J.M. 1978, *Leadership*, Harper and Row, New York.

Burns, T. and Stalker, G.M. 1961, *The Management of Innovation*, Tavistock, London.

Burrough, B. 1987, Broken barrier: More women join ranks of white-collar criminals, *Wall Street Journal*, May 29, p. 29.

Burt, D.N. and Soukup, W.R. 1985, Purchasing's role in new product development, *Harvard Business Review*, Sept.–Oct., pp. 90–7.

Burton, T.M. 1995, Visionary's reward: Combine 'simple ideas' and some failures; result: Sweet revenge, *Wall Street Journal*, 3 Feb., pp. A1, A5.

Business Review Weekly 1999, 100 fastest-growing private companies, 15 March, p. 54.

Business Review Weekly 2000, Race to be first and best makes instant managers, 31 March, p. 36.

Business Week 1983a, The antibribery act splits executives, 19 Sept., p. 16.

Business Week 1983b, The shrinking of middle management, 25 April, p. 56.

Business Week 1984a, After its recovery, new headaches for Tylenol, 14 May, p. 137.

Business Week 1984b, The new breed of strategic planner, 17 Sept., pp. 62–8.

Business Week 1988, Public service, 11 Jan., p. 156.

Business Week 1989, Why a big steelmaker is mimicking the minimills, 27 March, p. 92.

Business Week 1995a, Groupware requires a group effort, 26 June, p. 154.

Business Week 1995b, Prejudice: Still on the menu, 3 April, p. 42.

Bylinsky, G. 1987, Trying to transcend copycat science, *Fortune*, 30 March, pp. 42–6.

Bylinsky, G. 1996, To create products, go into a cave, *Fortune*, 5 Feb., pp. 80A–D.

Byrne, H.S. 1995, Lifting off, *Barron's*, 27 March, pp. 17–18.

Byrne, J.A. 1987, Culture shock at Xerox, *Business Week*, 22 June, pp. 106–10.

Byrne, J.A. 1992a, Here's what to do next, Dow Corning, *Business Week*, 24 Feb., p. 33.

Byrne, J.A. 1992b, The best laid ethics programs, *Business Week*, 9 March, pp. 67–9.

Byrne, J.A. 1995, Virtual B-schools, *Business Week*, 23 Oct., pp. 64–8.

Byrne, J.A. 1996a, Gross compensation? *Business Week*, 18 March, pp. 32–3.

Byrne, J.A. 1996b, How high can CEO pay go? *Business Week*, 22 April, pp. 100–6.

Cahill, P. 1999, Video Ezy holds course for Asia, *Business Review Weekly*, 11 June, p. 54–5.

Calori, R. and Dufour, B. 1995, Management European style, *Academy of Management Executive*, 9, 3, pp. 61–70.

Cameron, K.S., Whetten, D.A. and Kim, M.U. 1987, Organizational dysfunctions of decline, *Academy of Management Journal*, 30, pp. 126–38.

Caminiti, S. 1992, The payoff from a good reputation, *Fortune*, 10 Feb., pp. 74–7.

Campbell, J.P. and Prichard, R.D. 1976, Motivation theory in industrial and organizational psychology, in M.D. Dunnette (ed.), *Handbook of Industrial and Organizational Psychology*, Rand McNally, Chicago.

Campion, M.A. and McClelland, C.L. 1993, Follow-up and extension of the interdisciplinary costs and benefits of enlarged jobs, *Journal of Applied Psychology*, 78, pp. 339–51.

Campion, M.A., Cheraskin, L. and Stevens, M.J. 1994, Career-related antecedents and outcomes of job rotation, *Academy of Management Journal*, 37, pp. 1518–42.

Cane, A. 1994, From a caterpillar to butterfly, *Financial Times*, 27 May, p. 11.

Capowski, G.S. 1993, Designing a corporate identity, *Management Review*, June, p. 37–8.

Capowski, G.S. 1996, Managing diversity, *Management Review*, June, pp. 13–19.

Carey, A. 1967, The Hawthorne studies: A radical criticism, *American Sociological Review*, June, pp. 403–16;

Carley, W.M. 1995, Salesman's treatment raises bias questions at Schering-Plough, *Wall Street Journal*, 31 May, p. A1, A8.

Carlisle, H.M. 1974, A contingency approach to decentralization, *Advanced Management Journal*, July, pp. 9–18.

Carlyle, R.E. 1988, Managing IS at multinations, *Datamation*, 1 March, pp. 54–66.

Carnevale, A.P. and Stone, S.C. 1994, Diversity: Beyond the golden rule, *Training & Development*, Oct., pp. 22–39.

Carnevale, M.L. 1994, Marketing and media: FCC would allow higher charges as cable TV systems add channels, *Wall Street Journal*, 24 Oct., p. B12.

Carroll S.J. and Tosi, H.L. 1973, *Management by Objectives: Applications and Research*, Macmillan, New York.

Carroll, A. 1989, *Business and Society: Ethics and Stakeholder Management*, South-Western, Cincinnati.

Carroll, A.B. 1979, A three-dimensional conceptual model of corporate performance, *Academy of Management Review*, 4, pp. 499–500.

Carroll, A.B. 1987, In search of the moral manager, *Business Horizons*, March–April, pp. 7–15.

Carroll, S.J. and Gillen, D.J. 1987, Are the classical management functions useful in describing managerial work?, *Academy of Management Review*, 12, pp. 38–51.

Carson, P.P., Carson, K.D. and Roe, C.W. 1993, Social power bases: A meta-analytic examination of interrelationships and outcomes, *Journal of Applied Social Psychology*, 23, pp. 1150–69.

Carton, B. 1994, Muscled out? At Jenny Craig, men are ones who claim sex discrimination, *Wall Street Journal*, 29 Nov., pp. A1, A7.

Carton, B. 1995, Gillette faces wrath of children in testing on rats and rabbits, *Wall Street Journal*, 5 Sept., p. A1.

Carver, C.S., DeGregoria, E. and Gillis, R. 1980, Field-study evidence of an attribution among two categories of observers, *Personality and Social Psychology Bulletin*, 6, pp. 44–50.

Castrogiovanni, G.J. 1991, Environmental munificence: A theoretical assessment, *Academy of Management Review*, 16, pp. 542–65.

Caudron, S, 2000a, Learning revives training, *Workforce*, Jan., 79, 1, pp. 34–7.

Caudron, S, 2000b, Jobs disappear when work becomes more important, *Workforce*, Jan., 79, 1, pp. 30–2.

Chakravarthy, B.S. and Perlmutter, H.V. 1985, Strategic planning for a global business, *Columbia Journal of World Business*, Summer, pp. 5–6.

Chakravarty, S.N. 1994, Back in focus, *Forbes*, 6 June, pp. 72–6.

Chandler, A.D. 1962, *Strategy and Structure*, M.I.T., Cambridge.

Chase, M. 1986, Robot apprentices, *Wall Street Journal*, 16 Nov., p. D16.

Chase, M. 1998, HMOs send doctors to school to polish bedside manners, *Wall Street Journal*, 13 April, p. B1.

Chase, R.B. 1978, Where does the customer fit in a service operation?, *Harvard Business Review*, Nov.–Dec., pp. 137–42.

Chase, R.B. and Aquilano, N.J. 1992, *Production & Operations Management*, Irwin, Homewood.

Chatman, J.A. and Jehn, K.A. 1994, Assessing the relationship between industry characteristics and organizational culture: How different can you be? *Academy of Management Journal*, 37, pp. 522–53.

Cheng, A.T. 1999, Leaps of faith, *Asia Inc.*, Aug., pp. 54–5.

Chesanow, N. 1987, Quick, take this memo, *Washington Post*, 7 Sept., p. C5.

Chesbrough, H.W. and Teece, D.J. 1996, Organizing for innovation, *Harvard Business Review*, Jan.–Feb., pp. 65–73.

Child, C. 1995a, GMAC reorganizes field staff for better service, *Automotive News*, Dec. p. 8.

Child, C. 1995b, Olds hires new brand manager from cereal maker, *Automotive News*, Dec. 25, p. 5.

Child, J. 1984, *Organization: A Guide to Problems and Practice*, Harper and Row, London.

Chong, C.K. 2000, Seven hurt in rush for Hello Kitty, *Straits Times*, 14 Jan., p. 3.

Chopra, V. 1982a, Productivity improvement through closed loop MRP (Part one), *Production and Inventory Management Review and APCIS News*, March, pp. 18–21.

Chopra, V. 1982b, Productivity improvement through closed loop MRP (Part two), *Production and Inventory Management Review and APCIS News*, April, pp. 49–51.

Christelow, D.B. 1987, International joint ventures: How important are they? *Columbia Journal of World Business*, Summer, pp. 7–13.

Clark, R. 1992, *Human Resource Management*, McGraw Hill, Sydney.

Clemons, E.K. 1995, Using scenario analysis to manage the strategic risks of reengineering, *Sloan Management Review*, Summer, pp. 61–71.

Clifford, M.L. 1999, Daewoo boss is playing a dangerous game, *Business Week*, 16 Aug., p. 18.

Cockel, B. 1986, Textronix, *Distribution*, Aug., p. 54.

Cohen, M. 2000, Breaking the chains, *Far Eastern Economic Review*, 16 March, p. 28.

Cohen, M.D., March, J.G. and Olsen, J.P. 1972, A garbage can model of organizational choice, *Administrative Science Quarterly*, 17, pp. 1–25.

Cohn, D.V. 1995, Workers double up to get a job done, *Washington Post*, 23 Jan., p. D5.

Cole, J. 1995, Boeing teaches employees how to run small businesses, *Wall Street Journal*, 7 Nov., pp. B1, B2.

Cole, J. 1996, Boeing will offer a luxury 737 as entry to business-jet market, *Wall Street Journal*, 2 July, p. B4.

Collins, G. 1995, Ten years later, Coca-Cola laughs at 'New Coke', *New York Times*, 11 April, p. C4.

Collins, P. D. and Hull, F. 1986, Technology and span of control: Woodward revisited, *Journal of Management Studies*, March, pp. 143–64.

Collins, R. and Schmenner, R. 1996, Pan-regional manufacturing: The lessons from Europe, *Financial Times*, 2 Feb., p. 8.

Conference Board 1991, *Employee Buy-in to Total Quality*, New York, 1991.

Conference Board 1994a, *Linking Quality to Business Results*, New York.

Conference Board 1994b, *Quality Outlook*, New York.

Conference Board 1994c, *TQM and Supplier Relationships*, New York.

Conger, J.A. and Kanungo, R.N. 1987, Toward a behavioral theory of charismatic leadership in organizational settings, *Academy of Management Review*, 12, pp. 637–47.

Connors, M. 1996, Baxter's big makeover in logistics, *Fortune*, 8 July, pp. 106C–N.

Contractor 1995, Roto-Rooter continues growth as residential service giant, April, p. 8.

Cook, J. 1986, We are the market, *Forbes*, 7 April, pp. 54–5.

Cook, J. 1989, We're the low-cost producer, *Forbes*, 25 Dec., pp. 65–6.

Cook, P. 1999, I heard it through the grapevine: Making knowledge management work by learning to share knowledge, skills and experience, *Industrial and Commercial Training*, 31, 3, pp. 101–5.

Copeland, L. and Griggs, L. 1986, Getting the best from foreign employees, *Management Review*, June, pp. 19–26.

Coradetti, W.R. 1994, Teamwork takes time and a lot of energy, *HRMagazine*, June, pp. 74–7.

Cordery, J.L., Mueller, W.S. and Smith, L.M. 1991, Attitudinal and behavioral effects of autonomous group working: A longitudinal field study, *Academy of Management Journal*, 4, pp. 464–76.

Cornish, E. 1990, A short list of global concerns, *Futurist*, Jan.–Feb., pp. 29–36.

Cosier, R.A. and Dalton, D.R. 1983, Equity theory and time: A reformulation, *Academy of Management Review*, 8, pp. 311–19.

Cotts, C. 1998, Starr has left, but K&E is fine, *Wall Street Journal*, 31 Aug., p. A6.

Court, M. 1994, Removing macho management lessons from the field of education, *Gender Work and Organisation*, 6,1, pp. 33–249.

Cowan, A.L. 1986, Getting rich on other people's pay checks, *Business Week*, 17 Nov., pp. 148–9.

Cowan, D.A. 1986, Developing a process model of problem recognition, *Academy of Management Review*, 11, pp. 763–76.

Cowen, S.S. and Middaugh II, J.K. 1988, Designing an effective financial planning and control system, *Long Range Planning*, 21, pp. 83–92.

Cox Jr, T. 1994, *Cultural Diversity in Organizations: Theory, Research & Practice*, Berrett-Koehler, San Francisco.

Cox, T.H. and Blacke, S. 1991, Managing cultural diversity: Implications for organizational competitiveness, *Academy of Management Executive*, Aug., pp. 45–56.

Cranwell, J.R. 1969, How to have a well-informed boss, *Supervisory Management*, May, pp. 5–6;

Crawford, A.B. 1982, Corporate electronic mail—a communication-intensive application of information technology, *MIS Quarterly*, 6, pp. 1–14.

Cringeley, R.X. 1993, *Accidental Empires*, Harper Business, New York.

Croghan, L. 1996, Why it's time for local 7232 to make peace with Briggs & Stratton, *Financial World*, 30 Jan., p. 30.

Cronin, M.J. 1997, Intranets reach the factory floor, *Fortune*, 17 June, p. 122.

Cronin, M.J. 1998, Ford's intranet success, *Fortune*, 30 March, p. 158.

Cullen, J.B., Anderson, K.S. and Baker, D.D. 1986, Blau's theory of structural differentiation revisited: A theory of structural change or scale? *Academy of Management Journal*, 29, pp. 203–29.

Cummings, L.L., Huber, G.P. and Arendt, E. 1974, Effects of size and spatial arrangements on group decision making, *Academy of Management Journal*, 17, pp. 460–75.

D'Aveni, R.A. 1995, *Hypercompetitive Rivalries*, Free Press, New York.

Daft, R.L. 1998, *Organization Theory and Design*, West, St Paul.

Daft, R.L., Sormunen, J. and Parks, D. 1988, Chief executive scanning, environmental characteristics, and company performance: An empirical study, *Strategic Management Journal*, 9, pp. 123–39.

Dallas, S. 1995, Rock bottom restaurants: Brewing up solid profits, *Business Week*, 22 May, p. 74.

Dalton, D.R. and Mesch, D.J. 1990, The impact of flexible scheduling on employee attendance and turnover, *Administrative Science Quarterly*, 35, pp. 370–87.

Daniels, J.D. and Radebaugh, L.H. 1989, *International Business*, Addison-Wesley, Reading.

Daniels, J.D. Pitts, R.A. and Tretter, M.J. 1985, Organizing for dual strategies of product diversity and international expansion, *Strategic Management Journal*, 6, p. 301.

Datamation 1988, Ocean freighters turn to high tech on the high seas, 1 March, pp. 25–6.

David, F.R. 1987, *Concepts of Strategic Management*, Merrill, Ohio.

David, F.R. 1989, How companies define their mission, *Long Range Planning*, 22, pp. 90–7.

Davidson, J.P. 1986, A way to work in concert, *Management World*, March, pp. 9–12.

Davies, C. 1995, Growing elderly population prompts rise in businesses catering to seniors, *Warfield's*, 14 July, pp. 9, 13.

Davies, E. 1998a, Management style on trial, *Fortune*, 11 May, pp. 30–2.

Davies, E. 1998b, Dad! Billy keeps suing me! *Fortune*, 20 July, pp. 16–18.

Davis, G.B. and Olson, M.H. 1985, *Management Information Systems: Conceptual Foundations, Structure, and Development*, McGraw-Hill, New York.

Davis, K. 1972, *Human Behavior at Work*, McGraw-Hill, New York.

Davis, K. 1980, Management communication and the grapevine, in S. Ferguson and S.D. Ferguson (eds), *Intercom: Readings in Organizational Communication*, Hayden, Rochelle Park.

Davis, K.R. and McKeown, P. G. 1984, *Quantitative Models for Management*, Kent, Boston.

Davis, S.M. and Lawrence, P. R. 1977, *Matrix*, Addison-Wesley, Reading.

Davis, T.R.V. and Luthans, F. 1980, A social learning approach to organizational behavior, *Academy of Management Review*, 5, pp. 281–90.

Davison III, W.N. and Worrell, D.I. 1988, The impact of announcements of corporate illegalities on shareholder returns, *Academy of Management Journal*, 31, pp. 195–200.

Dawson, C. 2000, Pioneer's uncharted territory, *Far Eastern Economic Review*, 9 March, pp. 48–9.

Dawson, D. 1988, Place for a store, *Marketing*, 7 April, pp. 35–6.

de Bono, E. 1968, *New Think*, Basic Books, New York.

De Cordoba, J. 1995, Mellon heir's labor of love for Haitians survives his death, *Wall Street Journal*, 30 Jan., pp. A1, A8.

Deal, T.E. and Kennedy, A.A. 1982, *Corporate Cultures: The Rites and Rituals of Corporate Life*, Addison-Wesley, Reading.

Delbecq, A.L., Van de Ven, A.H. and Gustafson, D.H. 1975, *Group Techniques for Program Planning*, Scott, Foresman, Glenview.

Dembo, R.S., Chiarri, A., Martin, J.G. and Paradinas, L. 1990, Managing Hidroeléctrica Española's hydroelectric power system, *Interfaces*, Jan.–Feb., pp. 115–35.

Demetrakes, P. 1995, Food plants: Apt to adapt, *Food Processing*, March, p. 52.

Deming, W.E. 1986, *Out of the Crisis*, M.I.T., Center for Advanced Engineering Study, Cambridge.

Dennis, A.R. and Valacich, J.S. 1994, Group, sub-group, and nominal group idea generation: New rules for a new media? *Journal of Management*, 20, pp. 723–36.

Denton, D.K. 1995, Process mapping trims cycle times, *HRM Magazine*, Feb., p. 56–9.

Dess, G.G. and Beard, D.W. 1984, Dimensions of organizational task environments, *Administrative Science Quarterly*, 29, pp. 52–73.

Dess, G.G., Gupta, A., Hennart, J-F. and Hill, C.W.L. 1995, Conducting and integrating strategy research at the international, corporate, and business levels: Issues and directions, *Journal of Management*, 21, pp. 357–93.

Detroit News 1995, Ford-Mazda to cut white-collar jobs, 23 May, p. B1.

Deutsch, C. 1999, Working wide of the mark, *Business Review Weekly*, 30 July, p. 48.

Deveny, K. 1986a, Bag those fries, squirt that ketchup, fry that fish, *Business Week*, 13 Oct., p. 86.

Deveny, K. 1986b, McWorld? *Business Week*, 13 Oct., pp. 79–86.

Dewar, R.D. and Simet, D.P. 1981, A level specific prediction of spans of control examining the effects of size, technology, and specialization, *Academy of Management Journal*, 24, pp. 5–24;

Dilworth, J.B. 1993, *Production and Operations Management*, McGraw-Hill, New York.

Discount Store News 1996, Expansion abroad outpaces domestic growth. The power retailers: Toys 'R' Us, 5 Feb., p. 52.

Dixon, J.R., Arnold, P., Heineke, J., Kim, J.S. and Mulligan, P. 1994, Business process reengineering: Improving in new strategic directions, *California Management Review*, 36, Spring, pp. 9–31.

Dobbins, G.H. and Platz, S.J. 1986, Sex differences in leadership: How real are they? *Academy of Management Review*, 11, pp. 118–27.

Dobbins, G.H. and Zaccaro, S.J. 1986, The effects of group cohesion and leader behavior on subordinate satisfaction, *Group and Organizational Studies*, 11, pp. 203–219.

Dodds, T. 2000, Singapore paddles in the global ocean, *Australian Financial Review*, Thurs. 27 April, p. 16.

Donaldson, T. and Preston, L.E. 1995, The stakeholder theory of the corporation: Concepts, evidence, and implications, *Academy of Management Review*, 20, pp. 65–91.

Donovan, J.J. 1994, *Business Re-engineering with Information Technology*, Prentice-Hall, Englewood Cliffs.

Dorfman, J.R. and Gupta, U. 1995, Choice positions for four black mask problems, *Wall Street Journal*, 3 Feb., pp. B1, B2.

Dow Jones Newswires 2000, Service comes with the wash, *Australian Financial Review*, 22 Feb., p. 13.

Dowling, P. J., Schuler, R.S. and Welch, D.E. 1995, *Human Resource Management*, Wadsworth, Belmont.

Dozier, J.B. and Miceli, M.P. 1985, Potential predictors of whistle-blowing: A prosocial behavior perspective, *Academy of Management Review*, 10, pp. 823–36.

Dressler, C. 1995, We've got to stop meeting like this, *Washington Post*, 31 Dec., p. H2.

Drucker, P. F. 1954, *The Practice of Management*, Harper, New York.

Drucker, P. F. 1967, *The Effective Executive*, Harper and Row, New York.

Drucker, P. F. 1985, A prescription for entrepreneurial management, *Industry Week*, 29 April, pp. 33–4.

Dubashi, J. 1987, Through a glass lightly, *Financial World*, 19 May, pp. 20–9.

Dumaine, B. 1990, Who needs a boss? *Fortune*, 7 May, pp. 52–60.

Dumaine, B. 1992, Is big still good? *Fortune*, 20 April, pp. 50–60.

Dun's Business Month 1986, Citicorp loses top investment talent abroad, November, p. 21.

Duncan, R. 1979, What is the right organization structure? Decision tree analysis provides the answer, *Organizational Dynamics*, Winter, pp. 59–80.

Duncan, W.J. 1989, *Great Ideas in Management*, Jossey-Bass, San Francisco.

Dunegan, K.J. 1993, Framing, cognitive modes, and image theory: Toward an understanding of a glass half full, *Journal of Applied Psychology*, 78, pp. 491–503.

Dunkel, T. 1996, The front runners, *Working Woman*, April, pp. 30–5.

Dunkin, A. and O'Neal, M. 1987, Power retailers, *Business Week*, 21 Dec., pp. 86–92.

Dwyer, P. 1992, Air raid: British Air's bold global push, *Business Week*, 24 Aug., pp. 54–61.

Economist 1988, Japan makes a bid for the merger business, 17 Sept., pp. 85–6.

Economist 1992, Survey of the car industry, 17 Oct., pp. 13–15.

Economist 1993, The price is high, 14 Aug., p. 63.

Economist 1994, The war between the sexes, 5 March, pp. 80–1.

Economist 1995a, An ex-swordsman ploughs into the peace business, 23 Sept., p. 59.

Economist 1995b, The uncommon good, 19 Aug., p. 55.

Economist 1995c, The outing of outsourcing, 25 Nov., p. 27.

Economist 1996, In praise of the blue suit, 13 Jan., p. 59.

Eddy, W.B. 1985, *The Manager and the Working Group*, Praeger, New York.

Edgardio, P. 1994, A new high-tech dynasty? *Business Week*, 15 Aug., pp. 90–1.

Eichenwald, K. 1992, Two sued by S.E.C. in bidding scandal at Salomon Bros., *New York Times*, 3 Dec., p. A1.

Eisen, A. 1978, The meanings and confusions of Weberian 'rationality', *British Journal of Sociology*, March, pp. 57–70.

Eisenhardt, K.M. and Brown, S.L. 1998, *Competing on the Edge*, Harvard Business School Press, Boston.

Elbing, A. 1978, *Behavioral Decisions in Organizations*, Scott, Foresman, Glenview.

Eldridge, E. 1996, Ben & Jerry's gears up for CEO search, *USA Today*, 30 Sept., p. 58.

Elegant, S. and Hibert, M. 2000, Tech Mecca, *Far Eastern Economic Review*, 16 March, p. 48–50.

Elkin, G. 1999, based on course work by Kesh Gilmore, University of Otago.

Elkin, G. with acknowledgment to the *Otago Daily Times*, 28 July 1997.

Elkin, G.R. 2000, adapted from Tremaine, M. Different ways of making a difference, in J. Sayers, and M. Tremayne (eds) 1994, *The Visions and the Reality: EEO in the New Zealand Workplace*, Dunmore Press, Palmerston North.

Eller, D. 1995, Motorola trains VPs to become growth leaders, *HRMagazine*, June, pp. 82–7.

Eng, P. M. 1995, Big business on the net? Not yet, *Business Week*, 26 June, pp. 100–1.

Engardio, P. 1988, The Peace Corps' new frontier, *Business Week*, 22 Aug., pp. 62–3.

Engardio, P. 1994, A hothouse of high-tech talent, *Business Week/21st Century Capitalism*, p. 126.

Epstein, S. 1998, *Constructive Thinking*, Praeger, Westport.

Erlick, J.C. 1995, IKEA bites the big apple, *HFN The Weekly Newspaper for the Home Furnishing Network*, 18 Sept., p. 6.

Ettorre, B. 1995, GE brings a new washer to life, *Management Review*, Sept., pp. 33–8.

Ettorre, B.A 1996, A conversation with Charles Handy, On the future of work and an end to the 'century of the organization', *Organizational Dynamics*, 25, 1, Summer, pp. 15–26.

Evans, J.R. and Lindsay, W.M. 1996, *The Management and Control of Quality*, West, Minneapolis/St Paul.

Evans, M.G. 1986, Organizational behavior: The central role of motivation, *Journal of Management*, 12, pp. 203–22.

Executive File: Hot Employment Issues 1996a, Whose mail is it anyway?, Smith Publishers, Nashville.

Executive File: Hot Employment Issues 1996b, Defensive driving on the information superhighway, July, Smith, Nashville.

Expat Web Site Association 2000, *Business Across Cultures*, www.expat.or.id/business/e-mail.html

Fabris, P. 1996, Ground control, *CIO*, 1 April, pp. 40–5.

Fagley, N.S. and Miller, P. M. 1987, The effects of decision framing on choice of risky vs. certain options, *Organizational Behavior and Human Decision Processes*, 39, pp. 264–77.

Fallon, J. 1994, Joan & David debuts London flagship, signature line, *Footwear News*, 12 Sept., p. 5.

Farnham, A. 1994, America's most admired company, *Fortune*, 7 Feb., pp. 50–4.

Featherstone, T. (ed.), 1999, *Shares*, Business Review Weekly Media, Hannanprint Victoria, Victoria.

Feldman, D.C. 1984, The development and enforcement of group norms, *Academy of Management Review*, 9, pp. 47–53.

Fenn, D. 1995a, Service teams that work, *INC.*, Aug., p. 99.

Fenn, D. 1995b, When to go pro, *INC. 500*, p. 72.

Ferguson, A. 2000, The next Internet peak looks like serious business, *Business Review Weekly*, 21 Feb., p. 34.

Ferguson, A. and De Clercq, K. 1999, Boss cocky, *Business Review Weekly*, 5 Nov., p. 60–5.

Ferguson, D.H. and Selling, T.I. 1985, Probability analysis: A system for making better decisions, *Cornell H.R.A. Quarterly*, Aug., pp. 35–42.

Fiedler, F.E. 1967, *A Theory of Leadership Effectiveness*, McGraw-Hill, New York.

Fiedler, F.E. and Chemers, M.M. 1976, *Improving Leadership Effectiveness: The Leader Match Concepts*, Wiley, New York.

Fiedler, F.E. and Garcia, J.E. 1987, *New Approaches to Effective Leadership: Cognitive Resources and Organizational Performance*, Wiley, New York.

Fierman, J. 1987, The entrepreneurs: The best of their class, *Fortune*, 12 Oct., p. 144.

Fierman, J. 1990, Fidelity's secret: Faithful service, *Fortune*, 7 May, pp. 86–92

Fierman, J. 1995, Winning ideas from maverick managers, *Fortune*, 6 Feb., pp. 66–80.

Financial Times 1996, Lessons from doing business in Japan, 12 April, p. 10.

Finch, B.J. and Cox, J.F. 1988, Process-oriented production planning and control: Factors that influence system design, *Academy of Management Journal*, 31, pp. 123–53.

Finlay, P. 1994, *Introducing Decision Support Systems*, NCC Blackwell, Manchester.

Finn Jr, E.A. 1987, Megatort mania, *Forbes*, 1 June, pp. 114–20.

Finney, H.C. and Lesieur, H.R. 1982, A contingency theory of organizational crime, *Research in the Sociology of Organizations*, 1, pp. 255–99.

Finney, M.I. 1996, Global success rides on keeping top talent, *HR Magazine*, April, pp. 69–72.

Fisher, A.B. 1992, Welcome to the age of overwork, *Fortune*, 30 Nov., pp. 64–71.

Fisher, A.B. 1995, Making change stick, *Fortune*, 17 April, pp. 121–8.

Fisher, L.M. 1996, Chip index dips for 6th month in row, *New York Times*, 10 May, p. D3.

Fitzsimmons, J.A. and Fitzsimmons, M.J. 1994, *Service Management for Competitive Advantage*, McGraw-Hill, New York.

Flamholtz, E. 1979, Behavioral aspects of accounting/control systems, in S. Kerr (ed.), *Organizational Behavior*, Grid, Ohio.

Flamholtz, E.G. 1996, *Effective Management Control: Theory and Practice*, Kluwer, Boston.

Fleming, J.E. 1981, Public issues scanning, in L. Preston (ed.), *Research in Corporate Social Performance and Policy*, 3, JAI, Greenwich, pp. 154–74.

Flint, J. 1995, Can you tell applesauce from pickles, *Forbes*, 9 Oct., pp. 106–8.

Flint, J. with Heuslein, W. 1989, An urge to service, *Forbes*, 18 Sept., pp. 172–6.

Flynn, J. and Del Valle, C. 1992, Did Sears take its customers for a ride? *Business Week*, 3 Aug., pp. 24–5.

Flynn, J. and Nayeri, F. 1995, Continental divide over executive pay, *Business Week*, 3 July, pp. 40–1.

Foley, M.J. 1988, Post-MRPII: What comes next? *Datamation*, 1 Dec., pp. 24–36.

Fombrun, C. Tichy, N.M. and Devanna, M.A. 1984, *Strategic Human Resource Management*, Wiley, New York.

Footwear News 1995, The innovators: Designs aside, these are the preeminent minds and personalities that have spearheaded the footwear industry, 17 April, p. S36.

Forbes 1987a, It's tough up there, 13 July, pp. 145–60.

Forbes 1987b, The top 25, 15 June, p. 151.

Forbes 1995, Swatch out!, 5 June, pp. 150–2.

Ford, R.C. and Randolph, W.A. 1992, Cross-functional structures: A review and integration of matrix organization and project management, *Journal of Management*, 18, pp. 267–94.

Fortune 1995, A conversation with Roberto Goizueta and Jack Welch, 11 Dec., pp. 96–102.

Fowler, E.M. 1988, Management participation by workers, *New York Times*, 27 Dec., p. D6.

Frank, R. 1995, Coca-Cola is shedding its once-stodgy image with swift expansion, *Wall Street Journal*, 22 Aug., pp. A1, A5.

Frederick, W.C., Davis, K. and Post, J.E. 1992, *Business and Society: Corporate Strategy, Public Policy, Ethics*, McGraw-Hill, New York.

Frederickson, J.W. 1986, The strategic decision process and organizational structure, *Academy of Management Review*, 11, pp. 280–97.

Freeman, S.J. and Cameron, K.S. 1993, Organizational downsizing: A convergence and reorientation framework, *Organization Science*, Feb., pp. 10–29.

French, J.R.P. and Raven, B. 1959, The bases of social power, in D. Cartwright (ed.), *Studies in Social Power*, Institute for Social Research, Ann Arbor.

French, W.L. and Bell Jr, C.H. 1978, *Organization Development: Behavioral Interventions for Organizational Improvement*, Prentice-Hall, Englewood Cliffs.

Friedland, J. 1995, Did IBM unit bribe officials in Argentina to land a contract? *Wall Street Journal*, 11 Dec., pp. A1, A5.

Friedman, M. 1962, *Capitalism and Freedom*, University of Chicago, Chicago.

Friedman, S. 1981, Where employees go for information: Some surprises, *Administrative Management*, 42, pp. 72–3.

Fry, L.W. 1976, The maligned F. W. Taylor: A reply to many of his critics, *Academy of Management Review*, 1, pp. 124–9.

Fry, L.W. 1982, Technological-structure research: Three critical issues, *Academy of Management Journal*, 25, pp. 532–52.

Fuchsberg, G. 1992, Total quality is termed only partial success, *Wall Street Journal*, 1 Oct., pp. B1, B9.

Fuhrman, P. 1988, The workers' friend, *Forbes*, 21 March, pp. 124–8.

Fuhrman, P. 1992, Jewelry for the wrist, *Forbes*, 23 Nov., pp. 173–8.

Fuld, L.M. 1988, *Monitoring the Competition*, Wiley, New York.

Fuld, L.M. 1989, How to get the scoop on your competition, *Working Woman*, Jan., pp. 39–42.

Funk, D. 1996, Insurance industry on rebound after recent wave of consolidations, *Warfield's Business Record*, 3 June, pp. 9, 12.

Gabor, A. 1994, The making of a new-age manager, *Working Woman*, Dec., pp. 18–22.

Gaither, N. 1986, Historical development of operations research, in D.A. Wren and J.A. Pearce II (eds), *Papers Dedicated to the Development of Modern Management*, Academy of Management.

Galbraith, J.K. 1962, *The New Industrial State*, University of Chicago, Chigago.

Galbraith, J.K. 1975, *The Age of Uncertainty*, Houghton-Mifflin, Boston.

Galbraith, J.R. 1977, *Organization Design*, Addison-Wesley, Reading.

Galbraith, J.R. 1982, Designing the innovating organization, *Organizational Dynamics*, 10, Winter, pp. 5–25.

Galbraith, J.R. 1995, *Designing Organizations*, Jossey-Bass, San Francisco.

Galbraith, J.R. and Kazanjian, R.K. 1986, *Strategy Implementation: Structure, System, and Process*, West, St Paul.

Gallagher C.A. and Watson, H.J. *Quantitative Methods for Business Decisions*, McGraw-Hill, New York.

Galloway, P. 1990, Counterattack, *Chicago Tribune*, 19 Dec., p. C1.

Gallupe, R.B., Cooper, W.H., Grisé, M-L. and Bastianutti, L.M. 1994, Blocking electronic brainstorms, *Journal of Applied Psychology*, 79, pp. 77–86.

Gargan, E.A. 1994, For a furniture maker, a taste of a global future, *New York Times*, 17 March, pp. C1, C3.

Garland, S.B. 1998, Finally, a corporate tip sheet on sexual harassment, *Business Week*, 13 July, p. 39.

Garran, R. 2000, Hackers breach treasury site, *Australian*, 20 March, p. 3.

Garvin, D.A. 1987, Competing on the eight dimensions of quality, *Harvard Business Review*, Nov.–Dec., pp. 101–9.

Gatewood, R.D. and Carroll, A.B. 1991, Assessment of ethical performance of organization members: A conceptual framework, *Academy of Management Review*, 16, pp. 667–90.

Gavin, M.B., Green, S.G. and Fairhurst, G.T. 1995, Managerial control strategies for poor performance over time and the impact on subordinate reactions, *Organizational Behavior and Human Decision Processes*, 63, pp. 207–21.

Geber, B. 1986, Quality circles: The second generation, *Training*, Dec., pp. 54–61.

Gelbspan, R. 1987, Keeping a close watch on electronic work monitoring, *Washington Post*, 13 Dec., p. H4.

Gelfond, S.M. 1988, The computer age dawns in the corner office, *Business Week*, 27 June, pp. 84–6.

Genasci, L. 1995, That was the workweek that was, *Washington Post*, 15 Oct., p. H4.

Gentile, M.C. 1994, *Differences That Work: Organizational Excellence Through Diversity*, Harvard Business School Press, Boston.

George Jr, C.S. 1972, *The History of Management Thought*, Prentice-Hall, Englewood Cliffs.

George, J.M. 1997, AIDS/AIDS-related complex, in L. Peters, B. Greer, and S. Youngblood (eds), *The Blackwell Encyclopedic Dictionary of Human Resource Management*, Blackwell, Oxford.

Gerrity, T.P. and Rockart, J.F. 1986, End-user computing: Are you a leader or a laggard? *Sloan Management Review*, Summer, pp. 25–34.

Gersick, C.J.G. 1991, Revolutionary change theories: A multilevel exploration of the punctuated equilibrium paradigm, *Academy of Management Review*, 16, pp. 10–36.

Gibbons, P. 2000, Privacy: Senate searchlight on web, *Business Review Weekly*, 4 August.

Gibbs, B. 1994, The effect of environment and technology on managerial roles, *Journal of Management*, 20, pp. 581–604.

Gibson, R. 1994, General Mills tries to cook up fix for restaurant unit, *Wall Street Journal*, 16 Nov., p. B4.

Gilbreth, L.M. 1921, *The Psychology of Management*, Sturgis and Walton, 1914, reissued by Macmillan, New York.

Gittler, H. 1985, Decisions are only as good as those who can change them, *Wall Street Journal*, 7 Oct., p. 22.

Glain, S. 1995, Samsung is spending billions to diversify, *Wall Street Journal*, 10 Feb., p. B6.

Glenn, E.C. and Pood, E.A. 1989, Listening self-inventory, *Supervisory Management*, Jan., pp. 12–15.

Goggins, W.C. 1974, How the multidimensional structure works at Dow Corning, *Harvard Business Review*, Jan.–Feb.

Goldbaum, E. 1988, How quality programs win respect and get results, *Chemical Week*, 5 Oct., pp. 30–3.

Goldhaber, G.M. 1993, *Organizational Communication*, Brown, Iowa.

Goldsmith, C. 1995, British Airways' new CEO envisions a marriage of travel and amusement, *Wall Street Journal*, 6 Nov., p. B11.

Goleman, D. 1998, *Working with Emotional Intelligence*, Bantam Books, New York.

Golembiewski R.T. and Proehl, C.W. 1978, A survey of the empirical literature on flexible workhours: Character and consequences of a major innovation, *Academy of Management Review*, 3, pp. 837–53.

Gome, A. 1999, The brand that fell to earth, *Business Review Weekly*, 11 June, pp. 98–103.

Gome, A. 2000, A counsel of elders, *Business Review Weekly*, 24 March, pp. 70–3.

Gomez-Mejia, L.R., McCann, J.E. and Page, R.C. 1985, The structure of managerial behaviors and rewards, *Industrial Relations*, Winter, pp. 147–54.

Gomory, R.E. 1989, From the ladder of science to the product development cycle, *Harvard Business Review*, Nov.–Dec., pp. 99–105.

Goodling, R.Z. and Wagner III, J.A. 1985, A meta-analytic review of the relationship between size and performance: The productivity and efficiency of organizations and their subunits, *Administrative Science Quarterly*, 30, pp. 462–81.

Goodman, P. S., Ravlin, E. and Schminke, M. 1987, Understanding groups in organizations, *Research in Organizational Behavior*, 9, pp. 121–73.

Goodman, P.S., Ravlin, E.C. and Argote, L. 1986, Current thinking about groups: Setting the stage for new ideas, in P.S. Goodman and associates (eds), *Designing Effective Work Groups*, Jossey-Bass, San Francisco.

Goodpaster, K.E. and Matthews Jr, J.B. 1982, Can a corporation have a conscience? *Harvard Business Review*, Jan.–Feb., pp. 134–41.

Gordon, J. 1987, Learn how to listen, *Fortune*, 17 Aug., pp. 107–8.

Gordon, J. 1992, Work teams—how far have they come? *Training*, 29, pp. 59–65.

Gordon, J.R. 1987, *A Diagnostic Approach to Organizational Behavior*, Allyn and Bacon, Boston.

Gordon, J.R. 1996, *Organizational Behavior: A Diagnostic Approach*, Allyn and Bacon, Boston.

Gordon, S.R. and Gordon, J.R. 1996, *Information Systems: A Managerial Approach*, Dryden, Fort Worth.

Gourlay, R. 1994, Back to basics on the factory floor, *Financial Times*, 4 Jan., p. 12.

Graeff, C.L. 1983, The situational leadership theory: A critical view, *Academy of Management Review*, 8, pp. 285–91.

Grandori, A. 1984, A prescriptive contingency view of organizational decision making, *Administrative Science Quarterly*, 29, pp. 192–209.

Grant, R.A., Higgins, C.A. and Irving, R.H. 1988, Computerized performance monitors: Are they costing you customers? *Sloan Management Review*, Spring, pp. 39–45.

Gray, B. and Ariss, S.S. 1985, Politics and strategic change across organizational life cycles, *Academy of Management Review*, 10, pp. 707–23.

Gray, D.H. 1986, Uses and misuses of strategic planning, *Harvard Business Review*, Jan.–Feb., pp. 89–97.

Green, S.G. and Welsh, M.A. 1988, Cybernetics and dependence: Reframing the control concept, *Academy of Management Review*, 13, pp. 287–301.

Greenberger, D.B. and Strasser, S. 1986, Development and application of a model of personal control in organizations, *Academy of Management Review*, 11, pp. 164–77.

Greene, C.N. 1979, Questions of causation in the path-goal theory of leadership, *Academy of Management Journal*, 22, pp. 22–41.

Greenwald, A.G. and Banaji, M. 1995, Implicit social cognition: Attitudes, self-esteem, and stereotypes, *Psychological Review*, 102, pp. 4–27.

Greenwood, R.G. 1981, Management by objectives: As developed by Peter Drucker, assisted by Harold Smiddy, *Academy of Management Review*, 6, pp. 225–30.

Greenwood, R.G. and Wrege, C.D. 1986, The Hawthorne studies, in D.A. Wren and J.A. Pearce II (eds), *Papers Dedicated to the Development of Modern Management*, Academy of Management.

Greenwood, R.G., Bolton, A.A. and Greenwood, R.A. 1983, Hawthorne a half century later: Relay assembly participants remember, *Journal of Management*, 9, pp. 217–31.

Greising, D. 1994, Quality: How to make it pay, *Business Week*, 8 Aug., pp. 54–8.

Gremillion, L.L. and Pyburn, P.J. 1988, *Computers and Information Systems in Business: An Introduction*, McGraw-Hill, New York.

Griffin, R.W. 1991, Effects of work redesign on employee perceptions, attitudes, and behaviors: A long-term investigation, *Academy of Management Journal*, 34, pp. 425–35.

Griffiths, J. 1994, Europe's manufacturing quality and productivity still lag far behind Japan's, *Financial Times*, 4 Nov., p. 11.

Gross, N. 1989, A wave of ideas, drop by drop, *Business Week*, Innovation 1989 issue, 16 June, pp. 22–30.

Grossman, R.J. 1996, Damaged, downsized souls, *HR Magazine*, May, pp. 54–62.

Grove, A. 1993, How Intel makes spending pay off, *Fortune*, 22 Feb., pp. 56–61.

Guest, R.H. 1956, Of time and the foreman, *Personnel*, 32, pp. 478–86.

Gupta, A.K. and Govindarajan, V. 1984, Build, hold, harvest: Converting strategic intentions into reality, *Journal of Business Strategy*, March, pp. 34–47.

Gupta, U. 1995, Starting out; how much? Figuring the correct amount of capital for starting a business can be a tough balancing act, *Wall Street Journal*, 22 May, p. R7.

Gupte, P. 1988, Merge in haste, repent in leisure, *Forbes*, 22 Aug., p. 85.

Guyon, J. 1988a, GE to acquire Borg-Warner's chemical lines, *Wall Street Journal*, 17 June, 1, p. 3.

Guyon, J. 1988b, GE chairman Welch, though much praised, starts to draw critics, *Wall Street Journal*, 4 Aug., pp. 1, 8.

Guzzo, R.A. 1988, Productivity research: Reviewing psychological and economic perspectives, in J.P. Campbell, R.J. Campbell, and associates, *Productivity in Organizations*, Jossey-Bass, San Francisco.

Guzzo, R.A. and Dickson, M.W. 1996, Teams in organizations: Recent research on performance and effectiveness, *Annual Review of Psychology*, 47, pp. 307–38.

Hack, M. 1989, Harvard project manager serves pros, casual users, *InfoWorld*, 30 Jan., pp. 54–5.

Hackman, J.R. 1987, The design of work teams, in J.W. Lorsch (ed.), *Handbook of Organizational Behavior*, Prentice-Hall, Englewood Cliffs.

Hackman, J.R. and Oldham, G.R. 1980, *Work Redesign*, Addison-Wesley, Reading.

Hackman, J.R. and Wagemen, R. 1995, Total quality management: Empirical, conceptual, and practical issues, *Administrative Science Quarterly*, 40, pp. 309–42.

Haefele, J.W. 1962, *Creativity and Innovation*, Reinhold, New York.

Hafner, K.M. 1988, Is your computer secure, *Business Week*, 1 Aug., pp. 64–72.

Hall, E.T. 1959, *The Silent Language*, Doubleday, New York.

Hall, E.T. 1976, *Beyond Culture*, Anchor Press/Double Day, Garden City.

Hall, R.H. 1996, *Structures, Processes, and Outcomes*, Prentice-Hall, Englewood Cliffs.

Hambrick, D.C., MacMillan, I.C. and Day, D.L. 1982, Strategic attributes and performance in the BCG matrix: A PIMS-based analysis of industrial product businesses, *Academy of Management Journal*, 25, pp. 510–31.

Hamilton, J.O'C. 1987, Why rivals are quaking as Nordstroms heads east, *Business Week*, 15 June, pp. 99–100.

Hammer, M. and Champy, J. 1993, *Reengineering the Corporation*, Harper Business, New York.

Hamner, W.C. 1991, Reinforcement theory and contingency management in organizational settings, in R.M. Steers and L.W. Porter (eds), *Motivation and Work Behavior*, McGraw-Hill, New York.

Haney, W.V. (ed.), 1986, *Communication and Interpersonal Relations*, Irwin, Homewood.

Hannah, J. 1996, GM workers agree to end strike, *Bryan–College Station Eagle*, 23 March, p. A12.

Hannan, M.T. and Freeman, J. 1977, The population ecology of organizations, *American Journal of Sociology*, 82, pp. 929–64.

Hanvey, M. 1999, Web site steers trucker's business, *Business Review Weekly*, 21 May, p. 51.

Haour, G. 1996, Environmental concerns: Are they a threat or an opportunity? *Financial Times*, 15 March, p. 4.

Harcourt, J., Richerson, V. and Wattier, M. 1991, A national study of middle managers' assessment of organizational communication quality, *Journal of Business Communication*, 28, pp. 348–65.

Hardy, Q. 1999, Ask ehow to turn knowledge into power, *Business Review Weekly*, 8 Oct., p. 55.

Harmsen, P. 2000, Going solo pays off for foreign firms in China, *Business Times*, 11 Jan., p. 10.

Harrigan, K.R. 1985, Vertical integration and corporate strategy, *Academy of Management Journal*, 28, pp. 397–425.

Harris, C.L. and Foust, D. 1987, An electronic pipeline that's changing the way America does business, *Business Week*, 3 Aug., pp. 80–2.

Harrison, E.F. 1981, *The Managerial Decision-Making Process*, Houghton Mifflin, Boston.

Harvard Business Review 1985, Managing innovation: Controlled chaos, May–June, pp. 73–84.

Harvard Business School Press 1995, *Mary Parker Follett–Prophet of Management: A Celebration of Writings from the 1920s*, Boston.

Harvey, M.G. 1995, The impact of dual-career families on international relocations, *Human Resource Management Review*, 3, pp. 223–44.

Hater, J.J. and Bass, B.M. 1988, Superiors' evaluations and subordinates' perceptions of transformational and transactional leadership, *Journal of Applied Psychology*, 73, pp. 695–702.

Haveman, H.A. 1992, Between a rock and a hard place: Organizational change and performance under conditions of fundamental environmental transformation, *Administrative Science Quarterly*, 37, pp. 48–75.

Hayes, M.A. 1973, Nonverbal communication: Expression without word, in R.C. Huseman, C.M. Logue, and D.L. Freshley (eds), *Readings in Interpersonal and Organizational Communication*, Holbrook, Boston.

Hays, L. 1995a, IBM's helmsman indicates that bulk of layoffs is over, *Wall Street Journal*, 6 Jan., p. B3.

Hays, L. 1995b, The outsider's new in crowd: Five IBM lifers, *Wall Street Journal*, 12 Jan., p. B1, B8.

Hays, L. 1995c, IBM chief unveils top-level shake-up, consolidating sales arm, software line, *Wall Street Journal*, 10 Jan., p. B6.

Head, A. 1999, Wake in fright on January 1, *Business Review Weekly*, 22 Oct., p. 62.

Head, A. 2000, Small business should log on and write off, *Business Review Weekly*, 24 March, p. 56.

Heartly, J.R. 1992, *Concurrent Engineering*, Productivity Press, Cambridge.

Hellweg, S., Freiberg, K. and Smith, A. 1984, The pervasiveness and impact of electronic communication technologies in organizations: A survey of major American corporations, paper presented at a meeting of the Speech Communication Association, Chicago.

Helm, L. and Edid, M. 1994, Life on the line: Two auto workers who are worlds apart, *Business Week*, 30 Sept., pp. 76–8.

Hersey, P. and Blanchard, K.H. 1988, *Management of Organizational Behavior: Utilizing Human Resources*, Prentice-Hall, Englewood Cliffs.

Herzberg, F. 1966, *Work and the Nature of Man*, World Publishing, Ohio.

Heskett, J.L. 1986, *Managing in the Service Economy*, Harvard Business School, Boston.

Hiebert, M. 2000, Two way vision, *Far Eastern Economic Review*, 17 Feb., p. 51–2.

Hildebrant, H.W., Bon, F.A., Miller, E.L. and Swinyard, A.W. 1982, An executive appraisal of courses which best prepare one for general management, *Journal of Business Communication*, Winter, pp. 5–15.

Hill, C.W.L. 1994, *International Business: Competing in the Global Economy*, Irwin, Homewood.

Hill, C.W.L. 1995, The computer industry: The new industry of industries, in C.W.L. Hill and G.R. Jones (eds) *Strategic Management: An Integrated Approach*, Houghton Mifflin, Boston.

Hill, C.W.L. 1997, *International Business*, Irwin, Homewood.

Hill, C.W.L. and Jones, G.R. 1997, *Strategic Management: An Integrated Approach*, Houghton Mifflin, Boston.

Hinton, T. and Schaeffer, W. 1998, *Customer-Focused Quality: What to Do on Monday Morning*, Prentice-Hall, Englewood Cliffs.

Hirsch, J.S. 1996, A high-tech system for sending the mail unfolds at Fidelity, *Wall Street Journal*, 20 March, pp. A1, A5.

Hodgetts, R.M. and Luthans, F. 1991, *International Management*, McGraw-Hill, New York.

Hoerr, J. 1988, Work teams can rev up paper-pushers, too, *Business Week*, 28 Nov., pp. 64–72.

Hoerr, J. 1989, The payoff from teamwork, *Business Week*, 10 July, pp. 56–62

Hof, R.D. 1992, From dinosaur to gazelle, *Business Week/Reinventing America*, 23 Oct., p. 65.

Hof, R.D. 1995a, How to kick the mainframe habit, *Business Week*, 26 June, pp. 102–4.

Hof, R.D. 1995b, Intel: Far beyond the Pentium, *Business Week*, 20 Feb., pp. 88–90.

Hofer, C.W. and Schendel, D. 1978, *Strategy Formulation: Analytical Concepts*, West, St Paul.

Hofstede, G. 1980, Motivation, leadership, and organization: Do American theories apply abroad? *Organizational Dynamics*, Summer, pp. 42–63.

Hofstede, G. 1984, The cultural relativity of the quality of life concept, *Academy of Management Review*, 9, pp. 389–98.

Hollinger, R.D. and Clark, J.P. 1983, *Theft by Employees*, Lexington Books, Lexington.

Hollingshead, A.B. and McGrath, J.E. 1995, Computer-assisted groups: A critical review of the empirical research, in R.A. Guzzo and E. Salas, *Team Effectiveness in Organizations*, Jossey-Bass, San Francisco.

Holloman, C.R. 1968, Leadership and head: There is a difference, *Personnel Administration*, July–Aug., pp. 38–44.

Holloran, T.J. and Burn, J.E. 1986, United Airlines station manpower planning system, *Interfaces*, Jan.–Feb., pp. 39–50.

Holmes, S. 1995, Politics key to Boeing sales in China? *Seattle Times*, 10 April, p. A1.

Holmes, S.L. 1978, Adapting corporate structure for social responsiveness, *Business Horizons*, Fall, pp. 47–54.

Holmqvist, M. 1999, Learning in imaginary organisations: Creating interorganizational knowledge, *Journal of Organizational Change Management*, 12, 5, pp. 419–38.

Homans, G. 1950, *The Human Group*, Harcourt, Brace, New York.

Horton, N.R. 1988, Restructurings and dismemberments, *Management Review*, March, pp. 5–6.

Hostage, G.M. 1975, Quality control in a service business, *Harvard Business Review*, July–Aug., pp. 98–106.

Houghton, J. 1987, For better quality, listen to the workers, *New York Times*, Forum, 18 Oct., section 3, p. 3.

House, R.J. and Mitchell, T.R. 1974, Path-goal theory of leadership, *Journal of Contemporary Business*, 3, pp. 81–97.

House, R.J. and Singh, J.V. 1987, Organizational behavior: Some new directions for I/O psychology, *Annual Review of Psychology*, 38, pp. 669–718.

Howarth, B. 1999, Information is the key, *Business Review Weekly*, 8 Oct., p. 90.

Howarth, B. 2000, E-commerce dabblers create a new market, *Business Review Weekly*, 7 April, p. 12.

Howell, J.M. and Frost, P. J. 1989, A laboratory study of charismatic leadership, *Organizational Behavior and Human Decision Processes*, 43, pp. 243–69.

HRMagazine 1994, Maverick: The success story behind the world's most unusual workplace, April, pp. 88–9.

Huber, G.B. 1993, *Managerial Decision Making*, Scott, Foresman, Glenview.

Hull, F.M. and Collins, P.D. 1987, High-technology batch production systems: Woodward's missing type, *Academy of Management Journal*, 30, pp. 786–97.

Huse, E.F. and Cummings, T.G. 1985, *Organization Development and Change*, West, St Paul.

Huseman, R.C. and Miles, E.W. 1988, Organizational communication in the information age: Implications of computer-based systems, *Journal of Management*, 14, pp. 181–204.

Hwang, S. 1992, Getting personal, *Wall Street Journal*, 6 April, p. R19.

Hymowitz, C. 1988, A survival guide to the office meeting, *Wall Street Journal*, 21 June, p. 41.

Hymowitz, C. 1995, How a dedicated mentor gave momentum to a woman's career, *Wall Street Journal*, 24 April, p. B1, B3.

Ihrcke, J. 2000, The key to corporate success, *Economic Bulletin*, Jan., pp. 13–16.

Ilgen, D.R. and Klein, H.J. 1988, Individual motivation and performance: Cognitive influences on effort and choice, in J.P. Campbell, R.J. Campbell, and associates, *Productivity in Organizations*, Jossey-Bass, San Francisco.

INC. 1989, Thriving on order, Dec., pp. 47–62.

INC. 1992, Can you afford to be ethical?, Dec., p. 16.

INC. 1996, Apprentices make the grade, Feb., p. 98.

Ingersoll, B. 1989, Generic-drug scandal at the FDA is linked to deregulation drive, *Wall Street Journal*, 13 Sept., pp. A1, A14.

Ingrassia, P. and Stertz, B.A. 1988, Ford's strong sales raise agonizing issue of additional plants, *Wall Street Journal*, 26 Oct., pp. A1, A10.

Inkpen, A. 1995, *The Management of International Joint Ventures*, Routledge, London.

Irvine, V.B. 1970, Budgeting: Functional analysis and behavioral implications, *Cost and Management*, March–April, pp. 6–16.

Ivancevich, J.M. and Lyon, H.L. 1977, The shortened workweek: A field experiment, *Journal of Applied Psychology*, 62, pp. 34–7.

Jackofsky, E.F., Slocum Jr, J.W. and McQuaid, S.J. 1988, Cultural values and the CEO: Alluring companions? *Academy of Management Executive*, 11, pp. 39–49.

Jackson, J.M. and Harkins, S.G. 1985, Equity in effort: An explanation of the social loafing effect, *Journal of Personality and Social Psychology*, 49, pp. 1199–206.

Jackson, L. 1990, Steel zeal, *Detroit Free Press*, 12 March, pp. 1E, 5E.

Jackson, S.E. and Associates 1992, *Diversity in the Workplace: Human Resources Initiatives*, Guilford Press, New York.

Jackson, S.E., May, K.E. and Whitney, K. 1995, Understanding the dynamics of diversity in decision-making teams, in R.A. Guzzo and E. Salas (eds), *Team Effectiveness and Decision Making in Organizations*, Jossey-Bass, San Francisco.

Jacob, R. 1992, The search for the organization of tomorrow, *Fortune*, 18 May, pp. 93–4.

Jacob, R. 1995a, Corporate reputations, *Fortune*, 6 March, pp. 54–64.

Jacob, R. 1995b, How one red hot retailer wins customer loyalty, *Fortune*, 10 July, pp. 72–9.

Jaffe, A.M. 1994, At Texaco, the diversity skeleton still stalks the halls, *New York Times*, 11 Dec., sec. 3, p. 5.

Jago, A.G. 1982, Leadership: Perspectives in theory and research, *Management Science*, 28, pp. 315–36.

James, D. 1999, We are empowering you to deal with change–better get used to it, *Business Review Weekly*, 8 Feb., p. 55–6.

James, D. 2000, Build a funky business with attitude, *Business Review Weekly*, 31 March, p. 70–4.

Janis, I.L. 1982, *Groupthink*, Houghton Mifflin, Boston.

Jaworski, B.J., Stathakopoulos, V. and Krishnan, H.S. 1993, Control combinations in marketing: Conceptual framework and empirical evidence, *Journal of Marketing*, 57, pp. 57–69.

Jay, A. 1976, How to run a meeting, *Harvard Business Review*, March–April, pp. 120–34.

Jefferson, D.J. 1990, Dream to nightmare: When growth gets out of hand, *Wall Street Journal*, 23 Jan., p. B2.

Jegers, M. 1991, Prospect theory and the risk-return relation: Some Belgian evidence, *Academy of Management Journal*, 34, pp. 215–25.

Jelinek, M. and Adler, N.J. 1988, Women: World-class managers for global competition, *Academy of Management Executive*, 11, pp. 11–19.

Jereski, L. 1988, I'm a bad manager, *Forbes*, 8 Feb., pp. 134–5.

Jerkovsky, W. 1983, Functional management in matrix organizations, *IEEE Transactions on Engineering Management*, May, pp. 89–97.

Jiang Jingen 1999, First shots fired in cross-straits war of the Web, *China Daily*, 14 Aug., p. 2.

Jodice, D.A. 1980, Sources of change in third world regimes for direct investment, *International Organization*, Spring, pp. 177–206.

Johns, G. 1996, *Organizational Behavior*, HarperCollins, New York.

Johnston, W.B. 1991, Global work force 2000: The new world labor market, *Harvard Business Review*, March–April, pp. 115–27.

Jones, D. 1995, On-line surfing costs firms time and money, *USA Today*, 8 Dec., pp. A1, A2.

Jones, G.R. 1998, *Organizational Theory: Text and Cases*, Addison-Wesley, Reading.

Jones, G.R. and Hill, C.W.L. 1988, Transaction cost analysis of strategy–structure choice, *Strategic Management Journal*, 9, pp. 159–72.

Jones, G.R., George, J.M. and Hill, C.W.L. 2000, *Contemporary Management*, McGraw-Hill, New York.

Jones, J.E. and Pfeiffer, J.W. 1975, *The 1975 Annual Handbook for Group Facilitators*, University Associates, La Jolla.

Joyce, W.F. 1986, Matrix organization: A social experiment, *Academy of Management Journal*, 29, pp. 536–61.

Judge, P. C. 1996, Is it rainforest crunch time? *Business Week*, 15 July, pp. 70–1.

Juran, J.M. 1988, *Juran on Planning for Quality*, Free Press, New York.

Kadlec, D. 1996, Here's the scoop on Ben & Jerry's, *USA Today*, 31 Jan., p. 4B.

Kanter, R.M. 1982, The middle manager as innovator, *Harvard Business Review*, July–Aug., pp. 95–105.

Kanter, R.M. 1983, *The Change Masters*, Simon and Schuster, New York.

Kanter, R.M. 1988, When a thousand flowers bloom: Structural, collective, and social conditions for innovation in organizations, *Research in Organizational Behavior*, 10, pp. 169–211.

Kanter, R.M. 1989, The new managerial work, *Harvard Business Review*, Nov.–Dec., pp. 85–92.

Kaplan, R.E., Drath, W.H. and Kofodimos, J.R. 1984, *Power and Getting Criticism*, Center for Creative Leadership Issues and Observations.

Karau, S.J. and Williams, K.D. 1995, Social loafing: Research findings, implications, and future directions, *Current Directions in Psychological Science*, 4, October, pp. 134–40.

Karpin, D. 1995, *Enterprising Nation: Renewing Australia's Managers to Meet the Challenges of the Asia-Pacific Century*, AGPS, Canberra.

Kast, F.E. and Rosenzweig, J.E. 1972, General systems theory: Applications for organization and management, *Academy of Management Journal*, 15, pp. 447–65.

Kast, F.E. and Rosenzweig, J.E. 1974, *Organization and Management: A Systems Approach*, McGraw-Hill, New York.

Katz, D. and Kahn, R.L. 1978, *The Social Psychology of Organizations*, Wiley, New York.

Katz, R.L. 1974, Skills of an effective administrator, *Harvard Business Review*, Sep.–Oct., pp. 90–102.

Katz, S. 1982, An about-face in TI's culture, *Business Week*, 5 July, p. 77.

Kaufman, J. 1995, How Cambodians came to control California doughnuts, *Wall Street Journal*, 22 Feb., pp. A1, A8.

Kavanagh, J. 1996, Postings overseas can end up as costly affairs, *Weekend Australian*, 14–15 Sept., p. 63.

Kearns, L. 1995, Australia: Imperial chairman, *Age* (Melbourne), 28 Jan., p. C1.

Keinan, G. 1987, Decision making under stress: Scanning of alternatives under controllable and uncontrollable threats, *Journal of Personality and Social Psychology*, 52, pp. 639–44.

Keller, J.J. 1990, Software glitch at AT&T cuts off phone service for millions, *Wall Street Journal*, 16 Jan., pp. B1, B4.

Keller, J.J. 1995, High anxiety: AT&T breakup jolts managers, *Wall Street Journal*, 21 Nov., pp. B1, B10.

Kelley, B. 1994, A day in the life of a card shark, *Journal of Business Strategy*, Spring, pp. 36–9.

Kelley, H.H. Attribution theory in social psychology, *Nebraska Symposium on Motivation*, 15, pp. 192–238.

Kelley, L., Whatley, A. and Worthley, R. 1987, Assessing the effects of culture on managerial attitudes: A three-culture test, *Journal of International Business Studies*, Summer, pp. 17–31.

Kennedy, J.and Everest, A. 1991, Put diversity in context, *Personnel Journal*, Sept., pp. 50–4.

Keren, G. 1996, Perspectives of behavioral decision making: Some critical notes, *Organizational Behavior and Human Decision Processes*, 65, pp. 169–78.

Kerr, S. and Jermier, J.M. 1978, Substitutes for leadership: Their meaning and measurement, *Organizational Behavior and Human Performance*, 22, pp. 375–403.

Kerr, S., Schriesheim, C.A., Murphy, C.J. and Stogdill, R. 1975, Toward a contingency theory of leadership based on the consideration and initiating structure literature, *Organizational Behavior and Human Performance*, May, pp. 62–82.

Kesner, I.F. and Johnson, R.B. 1990, An investigation of the relationship between board composition and stock-holder suits, *Strategic Management Journal*, 11, pp. 327–36.

Keys, J.B., Denton, L.T. and Miller, T.R. 1994, The Japanese management theory jungle—revisited, *Journal of Management*, 20, pp. 373–402.

Kidwell Jr, R.E. and Bennett, N. 1993, Employee propensity to withhold effort: A conceptual model to intersect three avenues of research, *Academy of Management Review*, 18, pp. 429–56.

Kiechel III, W. 1982, The big presentation, *Fortune*, 26 July, pp. 98–100.

Kiechel III, W. 1991, The art of the corporate task force, *Fortune*, 29 Jan., pp. 104–5.

Kilbridge, M.D. 1960, Reduced costs through job enrichment: A case, *Journal of Business*, 33, pp. 357–62.

Kilmann, R.H. 1985, Five steps for closing culture-gaps, in R.H. Kilmann, M.J. Saxton, R. Serpa, and associates (eds) *Gaining Control of the Corporate Culture*, Jossey-Bass, San Francisco.

Kilmann, R.H., Saxton, M.J. and Serpa, R. 1986, Issues in understanding and changing culture, *California Management Review*, 28, pp. 87–94.

Kindel, S. 1988, The 10 worst managed companies in America, *Financial World*, 26 July, pp. 28–39;

Kindel, S. 1995, Eye-opening management: Luxottica Group S.p.a. A., *Hemisphere Magazine*, Aug., pp. 31–4.

King, N. 1970, Clarification and evaluation of the two-factor theory of job satisfaction, *Psychological Bulletin*, 74, pp. 18–31.

King, T. 1995, How a hot ad agency, undone by arrogance, lost its independence, *Wall Street Journal*, 11 April, pp. A1, A5.

Kirby, J. 2000, The heavies hit back, *Business Review Weekly*, 25 Feb., p. 60–7.

Kirkpatrick, D. 1986, What givebacks can get you, *Fortune*, 24 Nov., p. 61.

Kirkpatrick, D. 1992, Here comes the payoff from PCs, *Fortune*, 23 March, pp. 93–102.

Kleinfield, N.R. 1989, Wanted: CFO with 'Flair for funk,' *New York Times*, 26 March, p. D5.

Knowlton, C. 1988a, Making it right the first time, *Fortune*, 28 March, p. 48.

Knowlton, C. 1988b, The new export entrepreneurs, *Fortune*, 6 June, pp. 89–102.

Knox, A. 1992, The downside and dangers of downsizing, *Washington Post*, 15 March, p. H2.

Kodama, M. 1999, Community management support through community-based information networks, *Information Management & Computer Security*, 7, 3, pp. 140–50.

Kodama, M. 2000a, Business innovation through customer-value creation, *Journal of Management Development*, 19, 1, 49–70.

Kodama, M. 2000b, Strategic business applications and new virtual knowledge-based business through community-based information networks, *Information Management & Computer Security*, 7, 4, pp. 186–99.

Koepp, S. 1987, Having it all, then throwing it all away, *Time*, 25 May, pp. 22–3.

Koh, L. 2000, Fruits on the net, *Straits Times*, 11 Jan., p. 35.

Kohn, A. 1987a, *No Contest: The Case against Competition*, Houghton Mifflin, Boston.

Kohn, A. 1987b, Art for art's sake, *Psychology Today*, Sept., p. 54.

Kohn, A. 1987c, It's hard to get left out of a pair, *Psychology Today*, Oct., pp. 53–7.

Kolodny, H.F. 1979, Evolution to a matrix organization, *Academy of Management Review*, 4, pp. 543–53.

Kolodny, H.F. 1981, Managing in a matrix, *Business Horizons*, March–April, pp. 17–24.

Koriat, A., Lichtenstein, S. and Fischoff, B. 1980, Reasons for confidence, *Journal of Experimental Psychology: Human Learning and Memory*, 6, pp. 107–18.

Koselka, R. 1994, It's my favorite statistic, *Forbes*, 12 Sept., pp. 162–76.

Kotlowitz, A. 1987, Working at home while caring for a child sounds fine—in theory, *Wall Street Journal*, 30 March, p. 21.

Kotter, J.P. 1979, Managing external dependence, *Academy of Management Review*, 4, pp. 87–92.

Kotter, J.P. 1982a, *The General Managers*, Free Press, New York.

Kotter, J.P. 1982b, What effective general managers really do, *Harvard Business Review*, Nov.–Dec., pp. 156–67.

Kotter, J.P. 1995, Leading change: Why transformation efforts fail, *Harvard Business Review*, March–April, pp. 59–67.

Kotter, J.P. and Heskett, J.L. 1992, *Corporate Culture and Performance*, Free Press, New York.

Kotter, J.P. and Schlesinger, L.A. 1979, Choosing strategies for change, *Harvard Business Review*, March–April, pp. 106–14.

Kotter, J.P., Schlesinger, L.A. and Sathe, V. 1979, *Organization: Text, Cases, and Readings on the Management of Organizational Design and Change*, Irwin, Homewood.

Kraar, L. 1994, The overseas Chinese: Lessons from the world's most dynamic capitalists, *Fortune*, 31 Oct., pp. 91–114.

Krietner, R. and Luthans, F. 1991, A social learning approach to behavioral management: Radical behaviorists 'Mellowing out', in R.M. Steers and L.W. Porter (eds), *Motivation and Work Behavior*, McGraw-Hill, New York.

Krone, K.J., Jablin, F.M. and Putnam, L.L. 1987, Communication theory and organizational communication: Multiple perspectives, in F.M. Jablin, L.L. Putnam, K.H. Roberts, and L.W. Porter (eds), *Handbook of Organizational Communication: An Interdisciplinary Perspective*, Sage, Newbury Park.

Kruglanski, A.W. 1986, Freeze-think and the challenger, *Psychology Today*, Aug., pp. 48–9.

Kumpecb, T. and Bolwijn, P. T. 1988, Manufacturing: The new case for vertical integration, *Harvard Business Review*, March–April, pp. 75–81.

Kuntz, M. 1995, Reinventing the store, *Business Week*, 27 Nov., pp. 84–96.

Kupfer, A. 1988, How to be a global manager, *Fortune*, 14March, pp. 52–8.

Kurke, L.B. and Alrich, H.E. 1983, Mintzberg was right! A replication and extension of the nature of managerial work, *Management Science*, 29, pp. 975–84.

Kurylko, D.T. 1995, Opel says empowerment was factor in wrongdoing, *Automotive News*, 17 July, pp. 1, 36.

Kusumoto, S. 1991, We're not in Honshu anymore, *Across the Board*, June, pp. 49–50.

LaBarre, P. 1994, Management tools must be managed, *Industry Week*, 5 Sept., pp. 78–82.

LaBarre, P. 1995, Patagonia comes of age, *Industry Week*, 3 April, p. 42.

Labate, J. 1993, Deal those workers in, *Fortune*, 19 April, p. 26.

Labich, K. 1995, Winners in the air wars, *Fortune*, 11 May, pp. 68–79.

Lachman, R. 1985, Public and private sector differences: CEOs' perceptions of their role environments, *Academy of Management Journal*, Sept., pp. 671–80.

Laderman, J.M. 1988, The family that hauls together brawls together, *Business Week*, 29 Aug., pp. 64–8.

Lai, F. 2000, McDonald's acts on throwaway burgers, *Straits Times*, 11 Jan., p. 42.

Landro, L. and Sease, D.R. 1987, General Electric to sell consumer electronics lines to Thomson S.A. for its medical gear business, cash, *Wall Street Journal*, 23 July, p. 3.

Landy, F.J. 1992, Hugo Münsterberg: Victim or visionary, *Journal of Applied Psychology*, 77, pp. 787–802.

Langlois, C.C. and Schlegelmilch, B.B. 1990, Do corporate codes of ethics reflect national character? Evidence from Europe and the United States, *Journal of International Business Studies*, 21, pp. 519–39.

Larson, E. 1988, Forever young, *INC.*, July, pp. 50–62.

Larson, L.L., Hunt, J.G. and Osborn, R.N. 1976, The great hi-hi leader behavior myth: A lesson from Occam's razor, *Academy of Management Journal*, 19, pp. 628–41.

Latham, G.P. and Wexley, K.N. 1981, *Increasing Productivity through Performance Appraisal*, Addison-Wesley, Reading.

Laudon, K.C. and Laudon, J.P. 1994, *Management Information Systems*, Macmillan, New York.

Lawler III, E.E. 1981, *Pay and Organization Development*, Addison-Wesley, Reading.

Lawler III, E.E. 1994, Total quality management and employee involvement: Are they compatible?, *Academy of Management Executive*, 8, 1, pp. 68–76.

Lawrence, P. R. and Lorsch, J.W. 1969, *Organization and Environment*, Irwin, Homewood.

Leana, C.R. 1985, A partial test of Janis' groupthink model: Effects of group cohesiveness and leader behavior on defective decision making, *Journal of Management*, 11, pp. 5–17.

Leana, C.R. 1986, Predictors and consequences of delegation, *Academy of Management Journal*, 29, pp. 754–74.

Leavitt, H.J. 1964, Applied organization change in industry: Structural, technical, and human approaches, in W.W. Cooper, H.J. Leavitt, and M.W. Shelly II (eds), *New Perspectives in Organization Research*, Wiley, New York.

Leavitt, H.J. and Whisler, T.L. 1958, Management in the 1980s, *Harvard Business Review*, Nov.–Dec., pp. 41–8.

Lee, C. 1994, The feminization of management, *Training*, Nov., pp. 25–31.

Lee, M.K. 1999, A hoarder ready to spring, *Asia Inc.*, Aug., pp. 10–11.

Lee, S.M., Luthans, F. and Olson, D.L. 1982, A management science approach to contingency models of organizational structure, *Academy of Management Journal*, 25, pp. 553–66.

Lee, T.W., Locke, E.A. and Latham, G.P., 1989, Goal setting theory and job performance, in L.A. Pervin (ed.), *Goal Concepts in Personality and Social Psychology*, Erlbaum, New Jersey.

Leibman, M.S. 1992, Getting results from TQM, *HR Magazine*, Sept., pp. 34–8.

Leibowitz, M.R. 1988, Clash of the high speed titans, *High Technology Business*, July, pp. 50–1.

Lengnick-Hall, C.A. 1992, Innovation and competitive advantage: What we know and what we need to learn, *Journal of Management*, 18, pp. 399–429.

Lenzner, R. 1995, The reluctant entrepreneur, *Forbes*, 11 Sept., pp. 162–7.

Leonard, J.W. 1986, Why MBO fails so often, *Training and Development Journal*, June, pp. 38–9;

Leonard-Barton, D. and Sviokla, J.J. 1988, Putting expert systems to work, *Harvard Business Review*, March–April, pp. 91–8.

Lesly, E. 1995, Are these 10 stretched too thin? *Business Week*, 13 Nov., p. 78.

Levine, J. 1992, Beer barrel blues, *Forbes*, 22 June, pp. 98–100.

Levine, J.B. 1990, GE carves out a road east, *Business Week*, 30 July, pp. 32–3.

Levine, J.B. and Byrne, J.A. 1986, Corporate odd couples, *Business Week*, 21 July, pp. 100–5.

Levitt, T. 1983, The globalization of markets, *Harvard Business Review*, May–June, p. 96.

Lewin, K. 1947, Frontiers in group dynamics: Concept, method, and reality in social science, *Human Relations*, 1, pp. 5–41.

Lewin, K. 1951, *Field Theory in Social Science: Selected Theoretical Papers*, Harper, New York.

Lewin, K. and Lippitt, R. 1938, An experimental approach to the study of autocracy and democracy: A preliminary note, *Sociometry*, 1, pp. 292–300.

Lewis, M.H. and Reinsch Jr, N.L. 1988, Listening in organizational environments, *Journal of Business Communication*, Summer, pp. 49–67.

Lewis, P.V. 1980, *Organizational Communication: The Essence of Effective Management*, Prentice-Hall, Englewood Cliffs.

Lichtenstein, S., Slovic, P., Fischhoff, B., Layman, M. and Combs, B. 1978, Judged frequency of lethal events, *Journal of Experimental Psychology: Human Learning and Memory*, 4, pp. 551–78.

Licker, P.S. 1985, *The Art of Managing Software Development People*, Wiley, New York.

Lieber, R.B. 1996, The fight to legislate incompetence out of the cockpit, *Fortune*, 5 Feb., p. 30.

Liebowitz, S.J. and Holden, K.T. 1995, Are self-managing teams worthwhile? A tale of two companies, *SAM Advanced Management Journal*, 22 March, p. 11.

Likert, R. 1961, *New Patterns of Management*, McGraw-Hill, New York.

Likert, R. 1979, From production- and employee-centeredness to systems 1–4, *Journal of Management*, 5, pp. 147–56.

Linden, D.W. 1995, The mother of them all, *Forbes*, 16 Jan., pp. 75–6.

Lipman, J. 1988, Marketers turn sour on global sales pitch Harvard guru makes, *Wall Street Journal*, 12 May, pp. 1, 13.

Lipner, M. 1991, Ben & Jerry's: Sweet ethics evince social awareness, *COMPASS Readings*, July, pp. 22–30.

Lippert, J. and Lupo, N. 1988, A not-so-happy birthday, *Detroit Free Press*, 28 Aug., pp. F1, F2;

Lloyd, S. 1999a, Amway says hello to profit growth, *Business Review Weekly*, 8 Oct., pp. 76–9.

Lloyd, S. 1999b, No pride without lions, *Business Review Weekly*, 25 Aug., pp. 44–5.

Lloyd, S. 2000, The culling game, *Business Review Weekly*, Ap. 7, pp. 96–9.

Locke, A., Shaw, K.N., Saari, L.M. and Latham, G.P. 1981, Goal setting and task performance, *Psychological Bulletin*, 90, pp. 125–52.

Locke, E.A. 1976, The nature and causes of job satisfaction, in M. Dunnette (ed.), *Hand book of Industrial and Organizational Psychology*, Rand McNally, Chicago.

Locke, E.A. 1982, The ideas of Frederick W. Taylor: An evaluation, *Academy of Management Review*, 7, pp. 14–24.

Locke, E.A. 1994, The nature and causes of job satisfaction, H.C. Triandis, M.D. Dunnette, and L.M. Hough (eds), *Handbook of Industrial and Organizational Psychology*, Consulting Psychologists Press, California.

Locke, E.A. and Latham, G.P. 1984, *Goal Setting: A Motivational Technique That Works*, Prentice-Hall, Englewood Cliffs.

Locke, E.A. and Latham, G.P. 1990, *A Theory of Goal Setting and Task Performance*, Prentice-Hall, Englewood Cliffs.

Locke, E.A., Latham, G.P. and Erez, M. 1988, The determinants of goal commitment, *Academy of Management Review*, 31, pp. 23–39.

Locke, E.A., Shaw, K.N., Saari, L.M. and Latham, G.P. 1982, Goal setting and task performance: 1969–1980, *Psychological Bulletin*, 90, pp. 125–52.

Lockheed Martin 1992, *Gray Matters: The Ethics Game Manual*, pp. 9, 25, and 29.

Loeb, M. 1994, How to grow a new product every day, *Fortune*, 14 Nov., pp. 269–70.

Loeb, M. 1999, Ten commandments for managing creative people, *Fortune*, 16 Jan., pp. 135–6.

Lohner, B.T., Noe, R.A., Moeller, N.L. and Fitzgerald, M.P. 1985, A meta-analysis of the relation of job characteristics to job satisfaction, *Journal of Applied Psychology*, 70, pp. 280–9.

Lohr, S. 1987, Manufacturing cars the Volvo way, *New York Times*, 23 June, pp. D1, D5.

Lohse, D. 1995, For foreign postings, the accent is on frugality, *Wall Street Journal*, 23 June, p. 1C.

Lopez, J.A. 1994, A better way? Setting your own pay—and other unusual compensation plans, *Wall Street Journal*, 13 April, p. R6.

Lorange, P., Morton, M.F.S. and Ghoshal, S. 1986, *Strategic Control Systems*, West, St Paul.

Lord, R.G., De Vader, C.L. and Alliger, G.M. 1986, A meta-analysis of the relation between personality traits and leadership perceptions: An application of validity generalization procedures, *Journal of Applied Psychology*, 71, pp. 402–10.

Lorsch, J.W. 1976, Contingency theory and organization design: A personal odyssey, in R.H. Kilmann, L.R. Pondy, and D.P. Slevin (eds), *The Management of Organization Design: Strategies and Implementation*, 1, North-Holland, New York.

Lorsch, J.W. 1979, Making behavioral science more useful, *Harvard Business Review*, March–April, pp. 171–80.

Lorsch, J.W. 1986, Managing culture: The invisible barrier to strategic change, *California Management Review*, Winter, pp. 95–109.

Lovdal, M.L., Bauer, R.A. and Treverton, N.H. 1977, Public responsibility committees on the board, *Harvard Business Review*, May–June, pp. 41–64.

Lublin, J.S. 1994a, It's shape-up time for performance reviews, *Wall Street Journal*, 3 Oct., pp. B1, B2.

Lublin, J.S. 1994b, Turning the tables: Underlings evaluate bosses, *Wall Street Journal*, 4 Oct., pp. B1, B14.

Lublin, J.S. 1995, My colleague, my boss, *Wall Street Journal*, 12 April, pp. R4, R12.

Lublin, J.S. 1996, AT&T outplacement manager's phone rings nonstop, *Wall Street Journal*, 25 Jan., pp. B1, B5.

Lubman, S. 1995, Hubris and ambition in Orange County: Robert Citron's story, *Wall Street Journal*, 18 Jan., pp. A1, A8.

Lubove, S. 1995a, New-tech, old-tech, *Forbes*, 17 July, pp. 58–60.

Lubove, S. 1995b, Salad in a bag, *Forbes*, 23 Oct., pp. 201–3.

Luthans, F. 1973, The contingency theory of management, *Business Horizons*, June, pp. 67–72.

Luthans, F. 1988, Successful vs. effective real managers, *Academy of Management Executive*, 2, no. 2, pp. 127–32.

Luthans, F. 1995, *Organizational Behavior*, McGraw-Hill, New York.

Luthans, F. and Kreitner, R. 1975, *Organizational Behavior Modification*, Scott, Foresman, Glenview.

Machan, D. 1991, Eager pupils, *Forbes*, 16 Sept., p. 118.

Maciariello, J.A. 1984, *Management Control Systems*, Prentice-Hall, Englewood Cliffs.

Macintosh, N.B. 1995, *The Social Software of Accounting Information Systems*, Wiley, New York.

Magnet, M. 1988, The resurrection of the rust belt, *Fortune*, 15 Aug., pp. 40–8.

Magnet, M. 1992, Who's winning the information revolution, *Fortune*, 30 Nov., pp. 110–17.

Magnusson, P. 1992, Grabbing new world orders, *Business Week, Reinventing America*, 23 Oct., pp. 110–18.

Mahoney, J. 1995, Gifts, grease and graft—business ethics, *Financial Times*, 8 Dec.

Mahoney, T.A. 1988, Productivity defined: The relativity of efficiency, effectiveness, and change, in J.P. Campbell, R.J. Campbell, and associates, *Productivity in Organizations*, Jossey-Bass, San Francisco.

Mahoney, T.A., Jerdee, T.H. and Carroll, S.J. 1965, The job(s) of management, *Industrial Relations*, February, pp. 97–110.

Maidique, M.A. 1980, Enterpreneurs, champions, and technological innovation, *Sloan Management Review*, Winter, pp. 59–76.

Maier, N.R.F. 1963, *Problem-Solving Discussions and Conferences: Leadership Methods and Skills*, McGraw-Hill, New York.

Maier, N.R.F. 1989, Assets and liabilities in group problem solving: The need for an integrative function, in M.T. Matteson and J.M. Ivancevich (eds), *Management and Organizational Behavior Classics*, BPI/Irwin, Homewood.

Main, J. 1989, How to go global—and why, *Fortune*, 28 Aug., pp. 70–6.

Main, J. 1992, How to steal the best ideas around, *Fortune*, 19 Oct., pp. 102–6.

Malone, M. and Davidow, W. 1992, Virtual corporation, *Forbes ASAP*, 7 Dec., pp. 103–7.

Management Review 1995, Flower power: A talk with Jim McCann, March, pp. 9–12.

Mangelsdorf, M.E. 1989, Beyond just-in-time, *INC.*, Feb., p. 21.

Mann, R.D. 1959, A review of the relationships between personality and performance in small groups, *Psychological Bulletin*, 56, pp. 241–70.

March, J.G. and Sevon, G. 1984, Gossip, information, and decision making, in L.S. Sproull and P. D. Larkey (eds), *Advances in Information Processing in Organizations*, 1, JAI, Greenwich.

Marchand, D. 1996, The information infrastructure—Promises and realities, *Financial Times*, 5 Jan., p. 8.

Marcia, J. Just doing it, *Distribution*, Jan., pp. 36–40.

Marcom Jr, J. 1991, Blue blazers and guacamole, *Forbes*, 25 Nov., pp. 64–8.

Marcus, A.A. 1988, Responses to externally induced innovation: Their effects on organizational rerformance, *Strategic Management Journal*, 9, pp. 387–402.

Markels, A. 1995, A power producer is intent on giving power to its people, *Wall Street Journal*, 3 July, pp. A1, A12.

Marketing 1995, P&G divides to rule, 23 March, p. 15.

Marketing News TM 1995, Lynn Shostack receives AMA services award, 2 Jan., p. 22.

Marsh, B. 1989, Going for the golden arches, *Wall Street Journal*, 1 May, p. B1.

Martin, J. 1992, *Cultures in Organizations: Three Perspectives*, Oxford University Press, New York.

Maruca, R.F. 1994, The right way to go global: An interview with Whirlpool CEO David Whitwam, *Harvard Business Review*, March–April, pp. 135–45.

Maslow, A.H. 1943, A theory of human motivation, *Psychological Review*, 50, pp. 370–96.

Maslow, A.H. 1954, *Motivation and Personality*, Harper and Row, New York.

Mathews, J. 1994, Increasingly, coffee isn't our cup of tea, *Washington Post*, 4 Nov., p. C3.

Mathews, J. 1995, Utensile strength: Rubbermaid's relentless innovation gains success, respect, *Washington Post*, 2 April, p. 1H.

Mathewson, W. 1988, Shop talk, *Wall Street Journal*, 30 Sept., p. 29.

Mathis, R.L. and Jackson, J.H. 1994, *Human Resource Management*, West, St Paul.

Max, R.R. 1985, Wording it correctly, *Training and Development Journal*, March, pp. 50–1.

McCall Jr, M.W. and Lombardo, M.M. 1983, What makes a top executive? *Psychology Today*, February, pp. 26–31.

McCartney, S. 1994, Compaq borrows Wal-Mart's idea to boost production, *Wall Street Journal*, 17 June, p. B4.

McClelland, D.C. 1965, Achievement motivation can be developed, *Harvard Business Review*, Nov.–Dec., pp. 6–25.

McClelland, D.C. 1976, Power is the great motivator, *Harvard Business Review*, March–April, pp. 100–10.

McClelland, D.C. 1985, *Human Motivation*, Scott, Foresman, Glenview.

McClelland, D.C. 1995, Retrospective commentary, *Harvard Business Review*, Jan.–Feb., pp. 138–9.

McClelland, D.C. and Boyatzis, R.E. 1982, Leadership motive pattern and long-term success in management, *Journal of Applied Psychology*, 67, pp. 737–43.

McClelland, D.C. *Human Motivation*, Scott, Foresman, Glenview.

McComas, M. 1986, Cutting costs without killing the business, *Fortune*, 13 Oct., pp. 70–8.

Mcgee, S. 1995, Garish jackets add to clamor of Chicago pits, *Wall Street Journal*, 31 July, p. C1.

McGregor, D. 1960, *The Human Side of Enterprise*, McGraw-Hill, New York.

McGuire, J.B., Sundgren, A. and Schneeweis, T. 1988, Corporate social responsibility and firm financial performance, *Academy of Management Journal*, 31, pp. 854–72.

McKean, K. 1985, Decisions, *Discover*, June, pp. 22–31.

McLeavey, D.W. and Narasimhan, S.L. 1985, *Production Planning and Inventory Control*, Allyn and Bacon, Boston.

McLeod Jr, R. 1986, *Management Information Systems*, Science Research Associates, Chicago.

McLeod, P. L. 1996, An assessment of the experimental literature on electronic support of group work: Results of a meta-analysis, *Human-Computer Interaction*, 7, 3, pp. 257–80.

McMenamin, B. 1995, Diversity hucksters, *Forbes*, 22 May, pp. 174–6.

McMorris, F.A. 1995, Is office voice mail private? Don't bet on it, *Wall Street Journal*, 28 Feb., p. B1.

Mecham, M. 1995, Instant success fuels Korean air expansion, *Air Transport*, 143, p. 28.

Meeks, F. 1988, Live from Dallas, *Forbes*, 26 Dec., pp. 112–13.

Meeks, F. 1989a, The man is the message, *Forbes*, 17 April, pp. 148–52.

Meeks, F. 1989b, Tom Golisano and the red tape factory, *Forbes*, 15 May, pp. 80–2.

Meeks, F. 1992, We all scream for rice and beans, *Forbes*, 30 March, p. 20.

Mehrabian, A. 1972, *Silent Messages*, Wadsworth, Belmont.

Meigs W.B. and Meigs, R.F. 1993, *Accounting: The Basis for Business Decisions*, McGraw-Hill, New York.

Meising, P. 1998, Using electronic networks in management and executive learning, *Journal of Workplace Learning*, 10, 6/7, pp. 324–7.

Melloan, G. 1988, Caterpillar rides the economic policy bumps, *Wall Street Journal*, 5 April, p. 37.

Mendenhall, M. and Oddou, G. 1985, The dimensions of expatriate acculturation: A review, *Academy of Management Review*, 10, pp. 39–47.

Mendenhall, M., Punnett, B.J. and Ricks, D. 1995, *Global Management*, Blackwell, Cambridge.

Mentzer, J.T. and Cox, J.E. 1984, Familiarity, application and performance of sales forecasting techniques, *Journal of Forecasting*, 3, pp. 27–36.

Merchant, K.A. 1982, The control function of management, *Sloan Management Review*, Summer, pp. 43–55.

Merchant, K.A. 1985, *Control in Business Organizations*, Pitman, Boston.

Metcalf, H.C. and Urwick L. (eds), 1940, *Dynamic Administration: The Collected Papers of Mary Parker Follett*, Harper and Row, New York.

Micallef, J.V. 1981, Political risk assessment, *Columbia Journal of World Business*, Summer, pp. 47–52.

Michaelsen, L.K., Watson, W.E. and Black, R.H. 1989, A realistic test of individual versus group consensus decision making, *Journal of Applied Psychology*, 74, pp. 834–9.

Milbank, D. 1995, Long viewed as kaput, many European firms seem to be reviving, *Wall Street Journal*, 14 Feb., pp. A1, A8.

Milkovich, G.T. and Glueck, W.F. 1985, *Personnel/Human Resource Management: A Diagnostic Approach*, Business Publications, Texas.

Miller, A. and Dess, G.G. 1996, *Strategic Management*, McGraw-Hill, New York.

Miller, A. and Dess, G.G. 1996, *Strategic Management*, McGraw-Hill, New York.

Miller, D. 1986, Configurations of strategy and structure: Toward a synthesis, *Strategic Management Journal*, 7, pp. 233–49.

Miller, D. 1988, Relating Porter's business strategies to environment and structure: Analysis and performance implications, *Academy of Management Journal*, 31, pp. 280–308.

Miller, D. and Friesen, P.H. 1982, Structural change and performance: Quantum versus piecemeal-incremental approaches, *Academy of Management Journal*, 25, pp. 867–92.

Miller, D. and Shamsie, J. 1996, The resource-based view of the firm in two environments: The Hollywood film studios from 1936 to 1965, *Academy of Management Journal*, 39, pp. 519–43.

Miller, J. 1978, *Living Systems*, McGraw-Hill, New York.

Miller, J.R. and Feldman, H. 1983, Management science—theory, relevance, and practice in the 1980s, *Interfaces*, Oct., pp. 56–60.

Miller, M.W. 1987, At many firms, employees speak a language that's all their own, *Wall Street Journal*, 29 Dec., p. 17.

Mintzberg, H. 1980, *The Nature of Managerial Work*, Prentice-Hall, Englewood Cliffs.

Mintzberg, H. 1983, *Power in and around Organizations*, Prentice-Hall, Englewood Cliffs.

Mintzberg, H., Raisignhani, D. and Theoret, A. 1976, The structure of 'unstructured' decision processes, *Administrative Science Quarterly*, 21, pp. 246–75.

Mishkoff, H.C. 1986, The network nation emerges, *Management Review*, Aug., pp. 29–31.

Mishra, J. 1990, Managing the grapevine, *Public Personnel Management*, Summer, pp. 213–28.

Mitchell, T.R., Daniels, D., Hopper, H., George-Falvy, J. and Ferris, G.R. 1996, Perceived correlates of illegal behavior in organizations, *Journal of Business Ethics*, April, pp. 439–55.

Mitchell, V.F. and Moudgill, P. 1976, Measurement of Maslow's need hierarchy, *Organizational Behavior and Human Performance*, 16, pp. 334–49.

Mizruchi, M.S. 1983, Who controls whom? An examination of the relation between management and boards of directors in large American corporations, *Academy of Management Review*, 8, pp. 426–35.

Mohrman Jr, A.M., Mohrman, S.A., Ledford Jr, G.E., Cummings, T.G., Lawler III, E.E. and associates 1989, *Large-Scale Organizational Change*, Jossey-Bass, San Francisco.

Monks, J.G. 1987, *Operations Management*, McGraw-Hill, New York.

Montgomery, C.A., Thomas, A.R. and Kamath, R. 1984, Divestiture, market valuation, and strategy, *Academy of Management Journal*, 27, pp. 830–40.

Moore, J. and Einhorn, B., 1999, A Biz-to-biz e-boom, *Business Week*, 25 Oct., pp. 26-7.

Moore, T. 1987, Goodbye, corporate staff, *Fortune*, 21 Dec., pp. 65–76.

Morais, R.C. 1995, If you stand still, you die, *Forbes*, 30 Jan., pp. 44–5.

Moran, R.T., Harris, P. R. and Stripp, W.G. 1993, *Developing the Global Organization*, Gulf, Houston.

Morgenthaler, E. 1989, A 19th-century firm shifts, reinvents itself and survives 100 years, *Wall Street Journal*, 9 May, pp. A1, A16.

Morris, B. 1987, Shaking things up at Coca-Cola Foods, *Wall Street Journal*, 3 April, p. 36.

Morrisey, G.L. 1988, Who needs a mission statement? You do, *Training and Development Journal*, March, pp. 50–2.

Morrisey, G.L. 1996, *A Guide to Long-Range Planning*, Jossey-Bass, San Francisco.

Morrison, A.J., Ricks, D.A. and Roth, K. 1991, Globalization versus regionalization: Which way for the multinational? *Organizational Dynamics*, Winter, pp. 17–29.

Moser, P. 1988, The McDonald's mystique, *Fortune*, 4 July, pp. 112–16.

Moskowitz, M.R. 1989, Company performance roundup, *Business and Society Review*, Winter, pp. 72–8.

Moss, L. 1998, Disney ups Sweeney to Laybourne's old post, *Multichannel News*, 24 Aug., p. 10.

Moutkheiber, Z. 1995, I'm just a peddler, *Fortune*, 17 July, pp. 42–3.

Mowday, R.T. 1991, Equity theory predictions of behavior in organizations, in R.M. Steers and L.W. Porter (eds), *Motivation and Work Behavior*, McGraw-Hill, New York.

Muczyk, J.P. 1979, Dynamics and hazards of MBO application, *Personnel Administrator*, May, pp. 51–61.

Mueller, R. 1979, Criteria for the appraisal of directors, *Harvard Business Review*, 57, pp. 48–56.

Mullen, B. and Copper, C. 1994, The relation between group cohesiveness and performance: An integration, *Psychological Bulletin*, 115, pp. 210–27.

Mullen, B., Anthony, T., Salas, E. and Driskell, J.E. 1994, Group cohesiveness and quality of decision making: An integration of tests of the groupthink hypothesis, *Small Group Research*, 25, pp. 189–204.

Munter, M. 1987, *Business Communication: Strategy and Skill*, Prentice-Hall, Englewood Cliffs.

Muris, T., Scheffman, D. and Spiller, P. 1992, Strategy and transaction costs: The organization of distribution in the carbonated soft drink industry, *Journal of Economics and Management Strategy*, 1, pp. 77–97.

Murray, K. 1994, A cool commander for Murdoch's assault on cable, *New York Times*, 7 Aug., p. 14.

Myers, D.G. 1983, *Social Psychology*, McGraw-Hill, New York.

Myers, R.N. 1992, At Martin Marietta, this board game is lesson in ethics, *Wall Street Journal*, 25 Sept., p. B7A.

Nabers, W. 1995, The new corporate uniforms, *Fortune*, Nov., 13, pp. 132–56.

Nadler, D. and Tushman, M. 1988, *Strategic Organization Design*, Scott, Foresman, Glenview.

Nadler, D.A. and Lawler III, E.E. 1983, Motivation: A diagnostic approach, in J.R. Hackman, E.E. Lawler III, and L.W. Porter (eds), *Perspectives on Behavior in Organizations*, McGraw-Hill, New York.

Nakarmi, L. 1995, A flying leap toward the 21st Century? Pressure from competitors and Seoul may transform the chaebol, *Business Week*, 20 March, pp. 78–80.

Narisetti, R. 1995, Manufacturers decry a shortage of workers while rejecting many, *Wall Street Journal*, 8 Sept., pp. A1, A4.

Nash, L. 1988, Mission statements—mirrors and windows, *Harvard Business Review*, March–April, pp. 155–6.

Nash, L.L. 1981, Ethics without the sermon, *Harvard Business Review*, Nov.–Dec., p. 81.

National Business Employment Weekly 1987, A question of ethics, Special Edition, *Managing Your Career*, Spring 1987, p. 4.

National Law Journal, 1995, Verdicts, 6 Feb., Supplement, C2.

Naughton, K. and Kerwin, K. 1995, At GM, two heads may be worse than one, *Business Week*, 14 Aug., p. 46.

Nayak, P. R. and Ketteringham, J.M. 1986, *Break-Throughs*, Rawson Associates, New York.

Neale, M.A., Huber, V.L. and Northcraft, G.B. 1987, The framing of negotiations: Contextual versus task frames, *Organizational Behavior and Human Decision Processes*, 39, pp. 228–41.

Near, J.P. and Miceli, M.P. 1995, Effective whistle-blowing, *Academy of Management Review*, 20, pp. 679–708.

Neff, R. 1995, They fly through the air with the greatest of ... Ki? *Business Week*, 23 Jan., p. 60.

Negandhi, A.R. and Welge, M.K. 1984, *Beyond Theory Z*, JAI, Greenwich.

Nemetz, P. and Fry, L.W. 1988, Flexible manufacturing organizations: Implications for strategy formulation and organizational design, *Academy of Management Review*, 13, pp. 627–38.

Neumann, S. 1994, *Strategic Information Systems*, Macmillan, New York.

New Steel 1994, Birmingham steel will build new bar and rod mill in Ohio, November, p. 12.

New York Times 1983, Japan to curb VCR exports, 21 Nov., p. D5.

New York Times 1992, Buns run out at McDonald's, 10 Oct., p. 39.

New York Times 1995, Little IKEA in Manhattan, 7 Sept., p. 5C.

Newman, B. 1995, Global chatter, *Wall Street Journal*, 22 March, pp. A1, A15.

Newman, W.H. 1975, *Constructive Control*, Prentice-Hall, Englewood Cliffs.

Newman, W.H. and Logan, J.P. Strategy, *Policy, and Central Management*, South-Western, Cincinnati.

Newsweek 1995, The risky new bonuses, 16 Jan., p. 42.

Nienstedt, P. and Wintermantel, R. 1987, Motorola restructures to improve productivity, *Management Review*, Jan., p. 47.

Nienstedt, P.R. 1989, Effectively downsizing management structures, *Human Resource Planning*, 12, pp. 155–6.

Noble, D.F. 1977, *America by Design: Science, Technology and the Rise of Corporate Capitalism*, Knopf, New York.

Norman, J.R. 1988, A hardheaded takeover by McLouth's hardhats, *Business Week*, 6 June, pp. 90–1.

Norman, J.R. 1994, Choose your partners, *Forbes*, 21 Nov., pp. 88–9.

Nossiter, V. 1979, A new approach toward resolving the line and staff dilemma, *Academy of Management Review*, 4, pp. 103–6.

Novack, J. 1995a, Lender's best friend, *Forbes*, 18 Dec., pp. 198–9.

Novack, J. 1995b, What if the guy shoots somebody? *Forbes*, 4 Dec., p. 37.

Nutt, P. C. 1984, Types of organizational decision processes, *Administrative Science Quarterly*, 29, pp. 414–50.

Nutt, P. C. 1986, Tactics of implementation, *Academy of Management Journal*, 29, pp. 230–61.

Nyce, E.H. and Groppa, R. 1983, Electronic mail at MHT, *Management Technology*, May, pp. 65–72.

O'Neal, M. 1988, Gould is so thin you can hardly see it, *Business Week*, 29 Aug., p. 74.

O'Neill, M. 1999, Industry faces day of reckoning over entry, *South China Morning Post*, 9 Nov., p. 4.

O'Reilly III, C.A. and Roberts, K.H. 1974, Information filtration in organizations: Three experiments, *Organizational Behavior and Human Performance*, 11, pp. 253–65.

O'Reilly, B. 1997, The curse of the Koch brothers, *Fortune*, 17 Feb., pp. 112–16.

O'Toole, J. 1985, *Vanguard Management: Redesigning the Corporate Future*, Doubleday, New York.

Oldenburg, D. 1989, What do you say? *Washington Post*, 23 Aug., p. C5.

Olian, J.D. and Rynes, S.L. 1991, Making total quality work: Aligning organizational processes, performance measures, and stakeholders, *Human Resource Management*, Fall, pp. 303–33.

Olins, R. and Waples, J. 1996, Cunard sails into unknown waters, *Times* (London), 10 March, Business, p. 1.

Onsman, Harry 1999, Workplace: the secret of a happy office, *Business Review Weekly*, 11 June.

Ono, Y. 1993, 'King of Beers' wants to rule more in Japan, *Wall Street Journal*, 28 Oct., p. B1.

Ono, Y. and Brauchli, M.W. 1989, Japan cuts the middle-management fat, *Wall Street Journal*, 8 Aug., p. B1.

Organ, D.W. and Ryan, K. 1995, A meta-analytic review of attitudinal and dispositional predictors of organizational citizenship behavior, *Personnel Psychology*, 48, pp. 775–802.

Ortega, B. 1994, Nearing 80, founder of Dillard stores seeks to keep on growing, *Wall Street Journal*, 11 May, pp. A1, A5.

Ortega, B. 1995, Broken rules, conduct codes garner goodwill for retailers but violations go on, *Wall Street Journal*, 3 July, pp. A1, A4.

Osborn, A.F. 1963, *Applied Imagination*, Scribner, New York.

Otten, A.L. 1986, Ethics on the job: Companies alert employees to potential dilemmas, *Wall Street Journal*, 14 July, p. 21.

Ouchi, W.G. and Maguire, M.A. 1975, Organizational control: Two functions, *Administrative Science Quarterly*, 20, pp. 559–69.

Pace, R.W. 1983, *Organizational Communication: Foundations for Human Resource Development*, Prentice-Hall, Englewood Cliffs.

Papalia, D.E. and Olds, S.W. 1988, *Psychology*, McGraw-Hill, New York.

Pape, W.R. 1997, Group insurance, *INC.* (Inc. Technology Supplement), 17 June, pp. 29–31.

Parets, R.T. 1995, Payout, *Investor's Business Daily*, 23 Aug., p. A6.

Parker, D.F. and Dyer, L. 1976, Expectancy theory as a within person behavioral choice model: An empirical test of some conceptual and methodological refinements, *Organizational Behavior and Human Performance*, 17, pp. 97–117.

Parker, L.D. 1984, Control in organizational life: The contribution of Mary Parker Follett, *Academy of Management Review*, 9, pp. 736–45.

Pastore, R. 1996, Great expectations, *CIO*, 15 Jan., pp. 46–50.

Patrick, F., 1994, IBM one day, Lexmark the next, *Management Review*, Jan., pp. 38–44.

Patterson, A. 1995, Target 'Micromarkets' its way to success; no 2 stores are alike, *Wall Street Journal*, 31 May, pp. A1, A9.

Paul, K. and Barbato, R. 1985, The multinational corporation in the less developed country: The economic development model versus the north–south model, *Academy of Management Review*, 10, pp. 8–14.

Pavett, C.M. and Lau, A.W. 1983, Managerial work: The influence of hierarchical level and functional specialty, *Academy of Management Journal*, 26, pp. 170–7.

Pearce II, J.A. and David, F. 1987, Corporate mission statements: The bottom line, *Academy of Management Executive*, 1, pp. 109–16.

Pearce II, J.A. and Harvey, J.W. 1990, Concentrated growth strategies, *Academy of Management Executive*, 4, 1, pp. 61–8.

Pearce II, J.A. and Robinson Jr, R.B. 1988, *Strategic Management: Strategy Formulation and Implementation*, Irwin, Homewood.

Pearson, A.E. 1988, Tough-minded ways to get innovative, *Harvard Business Review*, May–June, pp. 99–106.

Pereira, J. and Lublin, J.S. 1995, A new CEO for Cherry Garcia's creators, *Wall Street Journal*, 2 Feb., p. 1B.

Pereira, J. and Rebello, J. 1995, Production problems at generic-drug firm lead to serious claims, *Wall Street Journal*, 2 Feb., p. A1.

Perlmutter, H.V. 1969, The tortuous evolution of the multinational corporation, *Columbia Journal of World Business*, Jan.–Feb., pp. 9–18.

Perrow, C. 1961, The analysis of goals in complex organizations, *American Sociological Review*, 26, pp. 854–66.

Peters, L.H., Hartke, D.D. and Pohlmann, J.T. 1985, Fiedler's contingency theory of leadership: An application of the meta-analysis procedures of Schmidt and Hunter, *Psychological Bulletin*, 97, pp. 274–85.

Peters, T.J. and Waterman, R.H. 1982, *In Search of Excellence*, Harper and Row, New York.

Petrozzello, D. 1998, Sweeney heads Disney/ABC cable, *Broadcasting & Cable*, 24 Aug., p. 47.

Petzinger Jr, T. 1995, All happy businesses are alike, but heirs bring unique conflicts, *Wall Street Journal*, 17 Nov., p. B1.

Petzinger, T. 1997, Dave Hurley gets a lesson in business, *Wall Street Journal*, 14 March, p. B1.

Pfeffer, J. 1981, *Power in Organizations*, Pitman, Boston.

Pfeffer, J. and Salancik, G. 1978, *The External Control of Organizations*, Harper and Row, New York.

Pfeiffer, J.W. 1994, *The 1994 Annual: Developing Human Resources*, University Associates, California.

Phalon, R. 1989, Roto-Rooter's new drill, *Forbes*, 11 Dec., pp. 176–8.

Pinchot III, G. 1985, *Intrapreneuring*, Harper and Row, New York.

Pinney, W.E. and McWilliams, D.B. 1982, *Management Science: An Introduction to Quantitative Analysis for Management*, Harper and Row, New York.

Pitman, J. 1997, Kicking the kickbacks, *Australian*, 13 June, p. 27.

Pitts, R.A. and Daniels, J.D. 1984, Aftermath of the matrix mania, *Columbia Journal of World Business*, Summer, pp. 48–54.

Planty, E. and Machaver, W. 1952, Upward communications: A project in executive development, *Personnel*, 28, pp. 304–18.

Podsakoff, P.M., Niehoff, B.P., MacKenzie, S.B. and Williams, M.L. 1993, Do substitutes for leadership really substitute for leadership? An empirical examination of Kerr and Jermier's situational leadership model, *Organizational Behavior and Human Decision Processes*, 54, pp. 1–44.

Pollock, E.J. 1995, Workers want more money, but they also want to control their own time, *Wall Street Journal*, 28 Nov., pp. B1, B12.

Pongvutitham, A. 2000, Small firm thrives on honesty, *Nation*, 14 Feb., p. B1.

Port, O. 1987, The push for quality, *Business Week*, 8 June, pp. 130–6.

Port, O. 1988, The software trap: Automate—or else, *Business Week*, 9 May, pp. 142–54.

Porter, L.W. and Roberts, K. 1976, Communication in organizations, in M.D. Dunnette (ed.), *Handbook of Industrial and Organization Psychology*, Rand McNally, Chicago.

Porter, L.W. and Roberts, K. 1990, Communication in organizations, in M.D. Dunnette and L.M. Hough (eds), *Handbook of Industrial and Organization Psychology*, Consulting Psychologists Press, California.

Porter, M.E. 1980, *Competitive Strategy: Techniques for Analyzing Industries and Competitors*, Free Press, New York.

Porter, M.E. 1985, *Competitive Advantage: Creating and Sustaining Superior Performance*, Free Press, New York.

Porter, M.E. 1990a, The competitive advantage of nations, *Harvard Business Review*, March–April, pp. 73–93.

Porter, M.E. 1990b, *The Competitive Advantage of Nations*, Free Press, New York.

Porter, M.E. and Millar, V.E. 1985, How information gives you competitive advantage, *Harvard Business Review*, July–Aug., pp. 149–60.

Posner, B.G. 1989, If at first you don't succeed, *INC.*, May, pp. 132–4.

Posner, B.Z. and Schmidt, W.H. 1984, Values and the American manager: An update, *California Management Review*, 26, pp. 202–16.

Post, J.E. and the Foundation for Public Affairs 1993, The state of corporate public affairs in the United States, *Research in Corporate Social Performance and Policy*, 14, pp. 81–91.

Post, J.E., Frederick, W.C., Lawrence, A.T. and Weber, J. 1996, *Business and Society: Corporate Strategy, Public Policy, Ethics*, McGraw-Hill, New York.

Post, J.E., Murray Jr, E.A., Dickie, R.B. and Mahon, J.F. 1983, Managing public affairs: The public affairs function, *California Management Review*, Fall, pp. 135–6.

Pottinger, J. 1994, Brazilian maverick reveals his radical recipe for success, *Personnel Management*, Sept., p. 71.

Potts, M. 1987, Bic stock dives after report about lighters, *Washington Post*, 11 April, p. D10.

Potts, M. 1989, Toys 'R' US and McDonald's take on Japanese toy market, *Washington Post*, 27 Sept., p. B1.

Powell, G.N. 1993, *Women and Men in Management*, Sage, Newbury Park.

Powers, T.L. 1987, Breakeven analysis with semi-fixed costs, *Industrial Marketing Management*, 16, pp. 35–41.

PR Newswire 1995a, Rockwell marks 10-year anniversary of Allen-Bradley purchase, 20 Feb., pp. 1–3.

PR Newswire 1995b, Tennant reveals fourth quarter results, 8 Feb.

Prahalad, C. K. and Dox, Y.L. 1987, *The Multinational Mission: Balancing Local Demands and Global Vision*, Free Press, New York.

Preble, J.F. 1984, The selection of delphi panels for strategic planning purposes, *Strategic Management Journal*, 5, pp. 157–70.

Prinzinsky, D. 1996, New bar mill guaranteed fast start, *Crain's Cleveland Business*, 5 Feb., p. 3.

Pritchard, R.D., Jones, S.D., Roth, P. L., Stuebing, K.K. and Ekeberg, S.E. 1988, Effects of group feedback, goal setting, and incentives on organizational productivity, *Journal of Applied Psychology*, 73, pp. 337–58.

Pritchard, R.D., Roth, P. L., Jones, S.D., Galgay, P. J. and Watson, M.D. 1988, Designing a goal-setting system to enhance performance: A practical guide, *Organizational Dynamics*, Summer, pp. 69–78.

Puchalsky, A. 1996, GM recouping ground lost in strike, *Wall Street Journal*, 24 June, p. B2.

Pyatt Jr, R.A. 1986, AAA's lesson for Fairfax, *Washington Post*, 3 Oct., pp. F1–F2.

Queenan, J. 1988, Juice men, *Barrons*, 20 June, pp. 37–8.

Queenan, J. 1989, Purveying yuppie porn, *Forbes*, 13 Nov., pp. 60–4.

Quinn, J.B. 1979, Technological innovation, entrepreneurship, and strategy, *Sloan Management Review*, Spring, pp. 19–30.

Quinn, J.B., Anderson, P. and Finkelstein, S. 1996, Managing professional intellect: Making the most of the best, *Harvard Business Review*, March–April, pp. 71–80.

Quintanilla, C. and Gibson, R. 1994, 'Do call us': More companies install 1-800 phone lines, *Wall Street Journal*, 20 April, p. B1.

Rachlin, H. 1989, *Judgment, Decisions, and Choice*, Freeman, New York.

Rahim, M.A. and Magner, N.R. 1995, Confirmatory factor analysis of the styles of handling interpersonal conflict: First-order factor model and its invariance across groups, *Journal of Applied Psychology*, 80, pp. 122–32.

Raia, A.P. 1974, *Managing by Objectives*, Scott, Foresman, Glenview.

Ramanujam, V. and Varadarajan, P. 1989, Research on corporate diversification: A synthesis, *Strategic Management Journal*, 10, pp. 523–51.

Ramaprasad, A. 1983, On the definition of feedback, *Behavioral Science*, Jan., pp. 4–13.

Rapaport, R. 1993, To build a winning team: An interview with head coach Bill Walsh, *Harvard Business Review*, Jan.–Feb., pp. 111–20.

Raven, B.H. 1993, The bases of power: Origins and recent developments, *Journal of Social Issues*, 49, pp. 227–51.

Raven, B.H. and Kruglanski, A.W. 1970, Conflict and power, in P. Swingle (ed.), *The Structure of Conflict*, Academic, New York.

Rebello, J. 1995, Radical ways of its CEO are a boon to bank, *Wall Street Journal*, 20 March, pp. B1, B3.

Rebello, K. and Burrows, P. 1996, The fall of an American icon, *Business Week*, 5 Feb., pp. 34–42.

Redwood, R. 1996, Giving credit where credit is due: The work of the federal glass ceiling commission, *Credit World*, May–June, pp. 34–6.

Reeves, C.A. and Bednar, D.A. 1994, Defining quality: Alternatives and implications, *Academy of Management Review*, 19, pp. 419–45.

Regan, M.B. 1995, Shattering the AFL-CIO's glass ceiling, *Business Week*, 13 Nov., p. 46.

Reibstein, L. 1986, A finger on the pulse: Companies expand use of employee surveys, *Wall Street Journal*, 27 Oct., p. A31.

Reich, R.B. 1987, Entrepreneurship reconsidered: The team as hero, *Harvard Business Review*, May–June, pp. 77–83.

Reichheld, F.F. 1996, Learning from customer defections, *Harvard Business Review*, March–April, pp. 56–69.

Reiste, K.K. and Hubrich, A. 1996, Work-team implementation, *Hospital Management Quarterly*, Feb. pp. 47–53.

Reitman, V. 1995, Toyota names a chief likely to shake up global auto business, *Wall Street Journal*, 11 Aug., pp. A1, A4.

Reitz, H.J. 1987, *Behavior in Organizations*, Irwin, Homewood.

Rensberger, B. 1987, Lessons of the VCR revolution: How U.S. industry failed to make American ingenuity pay off, *Washington Post*, 13 April, pp. 1, 10.

Reuter Textline El Pais 1993, *Spain: Fewer Operators in Spain's Restructured Electricity Sector*, June 8, p. 1.

Reuters 2000, E-jobs boom in China, *Straits Times*, 12 Jan. p. Life 6.

Reynolds, E.V. and Johnson, J.D. 1982, Liaison emergence: Relating theoretical perspectives, *Academy of Management Review*, 7, pp. 551–9.

Rice, B. 1982, The Hawthorne defect: Persistence of a flawed theory, *Psychology Today*, Feb., pp. 70–4.

Rice, F. 1994, How to make diversity pay, *Fortune*, 8 Aug., pp. 78–86.

Rice, R.E. and Case, D. 1983, Electronic message systems in the university: A description of use and utility, *Journal of Communication*, 33, pp. 131–52.

Richards, M.D. 1986, *Setting Strategic Goals and Objectives*, West, St Paul.

Richman, R. 1993, Christmas: Science of the sell, *Chicago Sun Times*, 5 Dec., p. 14.

Richman, T. 1988, In the black, *INC.*, May, pp. 116–20.

Riechheld, F.F. 1996, Learning from customer defections, *Harvard Business Review*, March–April, pp. 56–69.

Rifkin, G. 1994, Don't ever judge this consultant by her cover, *New York Times*, 1 May, p. 5.

Rifkin, G. 1995, A skeptic's guide to groupware, *Forbes ASAP*, pp. 76–91.

Rigdon, J.E. 1991, PepsiCo's KFC scouts for blacks and women for its top echelons, *Wall Street Journal*, 13 Nov., p. A1.

Robbins, S.P. 1990, *Organization Theory: The Structure and Design of Organizations*, Prentice-Hall, Englewood Cliffs.

Robinson, G. and Dechant, K. 1997, Building a case for business diversity, *Academy of Management Executive*, 3, pp. 32–47.

Robock, S.H. and Simmonds, K. 1989, *International Business and Multinational Enterprises*, Irwin, Homewood.

Rockett, L., Valor, J., Miller, P. and Naude, P. 1998, Technology and virtual teams: Using globally distribute groups in MBA learning, *Campus-Wide Information Systems*, 15, 5, pp. 174–82.

Rodes, L. 1988, At the crossroads, *INC.*, Feb., pp. 66–76.

Rodgers, R. and Hunter, J.E. 1991, Impact of management by objectives on organizational productivity, *Journal of Applied Psychology*, 76, 2, pp. 322–36.

Romanelli, E. and Tushman, M.L. 1994, Organizational transformation as punctuated equilibrium: An empirical test, *Academy of Management Journal*, 37, pp. 1141–66.

Ronen, S. 1994, An underlying structure of motivational need taxonomies: A cross-cultural confirmation, in H.C. Triandis, M.D. Dunnette, and L.M. Hough (eds), *Handbook of Industrial and Organizational Psychology*, Consulting Psychologists Press, California.

Ronen, S. and Primps, S.B. 1981, The compressed work week as organizational change: Behavioral and attitudinal outcomes, *Academy of Management Review*, 6, pp. 61–74.

Root, F.R. 1984, *International Trade & Investment*, South-Western, Cincinnati.

Rose, R.L. 1993, After turning around Giddings and Lewis, Fife is turned out himself, *Wall Street Journal*, 22 June, p. A1.

Rose, R.L. 1996, Caterpillar's profit is surprisingly strong, *Wall Street Journal*, 19 Jan.

Rosen, B. and Jerdee, T.H. 1978, Perceived sex differences in managerially relevant characteristics, *Sex Roles*, 4, pp. 837–43.

Ross, J. and Staw, B.M. 1993, Organizational escalation and exit: Lessons from the Shoreham nuclear power plant, *Academy of Management Journal*, 36, pp. 701–32.

Rowland, M. 1988, Creating a plan to reshape a business, *Working Woman*, Aug., pp. 70–4.

Rubel, C. 1996, Treating coworkers right is the key to Kinko's success, *Advertising Age*, 29 Jan., p. 5.

Rubin, J.Z. 1980, Experimental research on third party intervention in conflict: Toward some generalizations, *Psychological Bulletin*, 87, pp. 379–91.

Rudnitsky, H. 1982, How Sam Walton does it, *Forbes*, 16 Aug., pp. 42–4.

Rudnitsky, H. 1987, Play it again, Sam, *Forbes*, 10 Aug., p. 48.

Rue, L.W. and Holland, P.G. 1989, *Strategic Management: Concepts and Experiences*, McGraw-Hill, New York.

Rugman, A.M. and Hodgetts, R.M. 1995, *International Business: A Strategic Management Approach*, McGraw-Hill, New York.

Russell, G. 1987, Rebuilding to survive, *Time*, 16 Feb., p. 44.

Sadker, M., Sadker, D, and Klein, S. 1986, Abolishing misconceptions about sex equality in education theory and practice, 25, p. 4.

Sager, I. and Cortese, A. 1995, IBM: Why the good news isn't good enough, *Business Week*, 23 Jan., pp. 72–3.

Salpukas, A. 1994, Hurt in expansion, airlines cut back and may sell hubs, *New York Times*, 1 April, pp. A1, C8.

Sampson, H. 1988, The army's Clausewitz of the meeting room, *Army*, Jan., pp. 49–50.

Sandberg, J. 1995, Internet's popularity in North America appears to be soaring, *Wall Street Journal*, 30 Oct., p. B2.

Sanders, D.H. 1987, *Computer Concepts and Applications*, McGraw-Hill, New York.

Santamaria, S. 2000, Long queues for cutie Kitty collectibles, *Straits Times*, 7 Jan., p. 3.

Santosus, M. 1996, Tactical maneuvers, *CIO*, 1 April, pp. 54–6.

Saporito, B. 1985, Heinz pushes to be the low cost producer, *Fortune*, 24 June, pp. 44–54.

Saporito, B. 1986, The revolt against 'Working smarter,' *Fortune*, 21 July, pp. 58–65.

Saporito, B. 1988, The tough cookie at RJR Nabisco, *Fortune*, 18 July, pp. 32–46.

Saporito, B. 1992, A week aboard the Wal-Mart express, *Fortune*, 24 Aug., pp. 77–84.

Saporito, B. 1993, This Bud's for them, *Fortune*, 9 Aug., pp. 12–14.

Sathe, V. 1983, Implications of corporate culture: A manager's guide to acting, *Organizational Dynamics*, Autumn, pp. 5–23.

Sawaya Jr, W.J. and Giauque, W.C. 1986, *Production and Operations Management*, Harcourt Brace Jovanovich, San Diego.

Saywell, T. and Yan, Z. 2000, Ready for the deluge, *Far Eastern Economic Review*, 23 March, pp. 44–5.

Schein, E.H. 1992, *Organizational Culture and Leadership*, Jossey-Bass, San Francisco.

Schilit, W.K. 1987, An examination of the influence of middle-level managers in formulating and implementing strategic decisions, *Journal of Management Studies*, May, pp. 271–93.

Schiller, Z. 1988, The marketing revolution at Procter & Gamble, *Business Week*, 25 July, pp. 72–6.

Schine, E. 1995, The fall of a timber baron, *Business Week*, 2 Oct., pp. 85–92.

Schlesinger, J.M. 1987, Plant-level talks rise quickly in importance; Big issue: Work rules, *Wall Street Journal*, 16 March, p. A16.

Schmidt, L. 1999a, Harvey Norman, a structured success, *Business Review Weekly*, pp. 72–5.

Schmidt, L. 1999b, She who dares, wins, *Asia Inc.*, Aug., pp. 52–3.

Schmitt, R.B. 1997, Judges try curbing lawyers' body-language antics, *Wall Street Journal*, 11 Sept., pp. B1, B7.

Schneider, B. and Bowen, D.E. 1995, *Winning the Service Game*, Harvard Business School Press, Boston.

Schnitzer, M.C., Liebrenz, M.L. and Kubin, K.W. 1985, *International Business*, South-Western, Cincinnati.

Schoemaker, P.J.H. 1993, Multiple scenario development: Its conceptual and behavioral foundation, *Strategic Management Journal*, 14, pp. 193–213.

Schoemaker, P.J.H. 1995, Scenario planning: A tool for strategic thinking, *Sloan Management Review*, Winter, pp. 25–40.

Schofield, M. and Arnold, D. 1988, Strategies for mature businesses, *Long Range Planning*, 21, pp. 69–76.

Schonberger, R.J. 1984, An assessment of just-in-time implementation, in *Readings in Zero Inventory*, APICS 27th Annual International Conference proceedings, Las Vegas, Oct. 9–12, p. 57.

Schrage, M. 1987, Bell labs is long on genius but short in the marketplace, *Washington Post*, 1 March, pp. H1, H4.

Schreyoff, G. and Steinmann, H. 1987, Strategic control: A new perspective, *Academy of Management Review*, 12, pp. 91–103.

Schriesheim, C.A. and Bird, B.J. 1979, Contributions of the Ohio state studies to the field of leadership, *Journal of Management*, 5, pp. 135–45.

Schroeder, M. 1991, Charity doesn't begin at home anymore, *Business Week*, 25 Feb., p. 91.

Schroeder, R.G. 1989, *Operations Management*, McGraw-Hill, New York.

Schuler, R.S. and Huber, V.L 1990, *Personnel and Human Resource Management*, West, Minnesota.

Schwartzman, H.B. 1986, The meeting as a neglected social form in organizational studies, *Research in Organizational Behavior*, 8, pp. 233–58.

Schwenk, C. and Valacich, J.S. 1992, Effects of devil's advocacy and dialectical inquiry on individuals versus groups, *Organizational Behavior and Human Decision Processes*, 59, pp. 210–22.

Schwenk, C.R. 1990, Effects of devil's advocacy and dialectical inquiry on decision making: A meta-analysis, *Organizational Behavior and Human Decision Processes*, 47, pp. 161–76.

Scott, R.S. 1996, The mandate is still being honored: In defense of Weber's disciples, *Administrative Science Quarterly*, 41, pp. 163–71.

Seashore, S. 1954, *Group Cohesiveness in the Industrial Work Group*, Institute for Social Research, Ann Arbor.

Sedwick, D. 1996, Competitive brake market at strike's root, *Automotive News*, 18 March, pp. 1, 50.

Seeger, J.A. 1983, No innate phases in group problem solving, *Academy of Management Review*, 8, pp. 683–9.

Segal, T. 1992, Saving our schools, *Business Week*, 14 Sept., pp. 70–8.

Sellers, P. 1988, How to handle customers' gripes, *Fortune*, 24 Oct., pp. 88–100.

Sellers, P. 1998, The 50 most powerful women in American business, *Fortune*, 12 Oct., pp. 76–98.

Senge, P. 1990, *The Fifth Disciple: The Art and Practice of the Learning Organization*, Doubleday, New York.

Serenyi, P. 1996, Ford opens office to boost sales, *Moscow Times*, 29 March, p. 1.

Serwer, A.E. 1994, McDonald's conquers the world, *Fortune*, 17 Oct., pp. 103–16.

Serwer, A.E. 1995, An odd couple aims to put Lionel on the fast track, *Fortune*, 30 Oct., p. 21.

Sharpe, R. 1994, Women make strides, but men stay firmly in top company jobs, *Wall Street Journal*, 29 March, pp. A1, A8.

Shaw, M.E. 1981, *Group Dynamics: The Psychology of Small Group Behavior*, McGraw-Hill, New York.

Shaw, W.H. and Barry, V. 1995, *Moral Issues in Business*, Wadsworth, Belmont.

Shellenbarger, S. 1994, Reviews from peers instruct–and sting, *Wall Street Journal*, 4 Oct., pp. B1, B4.

Shepard, J.M. 1971, On Alex Carey's radical criticisms of the Hawthorne studies, *Academy of Management Journal*, March, pp. 23–32.

Shepperd, J.A. 1993, Productivity loss in performance groups: A motivational analysis, *Psychological Bulletin*, 113, pp. 67–81.

Sherden, W.A. 1988, Gaining the service quality advantage, *Journal of Business Strategy*, March–April, pp. 45–8.

Sherman, S.P. 1989, Inside the mind of Jack Welch, *Fortune*, 27 March, pp. 39–50.

Shirouzu, N. 1995, Daiwa bank's oversight is called lax in letter by trader who hid losses, *Wall Street Journal*, 12 Dec., p. A16.

Shleifer, A. and Vishny, R.W. 1994, Takeovers in the 1960s and 1980s: Evidence and implications, in R.P. Rumelt, D.E. Schendel and D.J.Teece (eds) *Fundamental Issues in Strategy*, Harvard Business School Press, Boston.

Shull Jr, F.A., Delbecq, A.L. and Cummings, L.L. 1970, *Organizational Decision Making*, McGraw-Hill, New York.

Siler, C. 1989, The goal is 0%, *Forbes*, 30 Oct., pp. 95–8.

Siler, J.F. 1989a, A warning shot from the king of beers, *Business Week*, 18 Dec., p. 124.

Siler, J.F. 1989b, The slippery ladder at Abbott Labs, *Business Week*, 30 Oct., pp. 136–7.

Siler, J.F. and Atchison, S. 1991, The Rx at work in Utah, *Business Week/Quality*, 25 Oct., p. 113.

Simon, H.A. 1955, A behavioral model of rational choice, *Quarterly Journal of Economics*, 69, pp. 99–118.

Simon, H.A. 1956, Rational choice and the structure of the environment, *Psychological Review*, 63, pp. 129–38.

Simon, R. 1987, The morning after, *Forbes*, 19 Oct., pp. 164–8.

Simons, R. 1995, *Levers of Control: How Managers Use Innovative Control Systems to Drive Strategic Renewal*, Harvard Business School Press, Boston.

Sims Jr, H.P. 1995, Challenges to implementing self-managing teams—part 2, *Journal for Quality & Participation*, March, pp. 24–31.

Siwolop, S. and Eklund, C. 1986, The capsule controversy: How far should the FDA go? *Business Week*, 3 March, p. 37.

Skinner, W. 1986, The productivity paradox, *Harvard Business Review*, July–Aug., pp. 55–9.

Skrzycki, C. 1987, How some firms become foreign success stories, *Washington Post*, 15 Nov., p. H1.

Skrzycki, C. 1989, Just who's in charge here, anyway? *Washington Post*, 29 Jan., pp. H1, H8.

Sloan Jr, A.P. 1964, *My Years with General Motors*, Doubleday, New York.

Slovic, P. 1995, The construction of preference, *American Psychologist*, 50, pp. 364–71.

Smallwood, W.N. and Jacobsen, E. 1987, Is there life after downsizing? *Personnel*, Dec., pp. 42–6.

Smart, T. 1995, A lot of the weaknesses Carbide had are behind it, *Business Week*, 23 Jan., pp. 83–4.

Smeltzer, L.L. and Fann, G.L. 1989, Comparison of managerial communication patterns in small, entrepreneurial organizations and large, mature organizations, *Group and Organization Studies*, 14, pp. 198–215.

Smircich, L. 1983, Concepts of culture and organizational analysis, *Administrative Science Quarterly*, 28, pp. 339–58.

Smith, A. 1910, *The Wealth of Nations*, Dent, London.

Society for Human Resource Management 1995, *Mosaics*, March, p. 1.

Soloman, R.C. 1992, *Ethics and Excellence*, Oxford University Press, New York.

Sonnenfeld, J.A. 1985, Shedding light on the Hawthorne studies, *Journal of Occupational Behavior*, 6, pp. 111–30.

Sounder, W.E. 1988, Managing relations between R&D and marketing in new product development projects, *Journal of Product Innovation Management*, 5, pp. 6–19.

Southerland, D. 1994, They want the card-carrying customer, *Washington Post*, 19 Oct., p. G1.

Spangler, W.D. 1992, Validity of questionnaire and TAT measures of need for achievement: Two meta-analyses, *Psychological Bulletin*, 112, pp. 140–54.

Sparks, D. 1999a, Partners, *Business Week*, 25 Oct., pp. 72–5.

Sproull, L. and Kiesler, S. 1986, Reducing social context cues: Electronic mail in organizational communication, *Management Science*, 32, pp. 1492–512.

Sprout, A.L. 1995, The internet inside your company, *Fortune*, 27 Nov., pp. 161–8.

Stahl, S. and Violino, B. 1996, Viruses still pose a threat, *Information Week*, 4 March, p. 30.

Stalk, G. and Hout, T.M. 1990, *Competing Against Time*, Free Press, New York.

Standard & Poor's Industry Surveys 1993, Autos—auto parts, 24 June.

Stauffer, D. 1999, Workers just like to have fun productively, *Business Review Weekly*, 29 Oct., pp. 56–7.

Staw, B.M. 1984, Organizational behavior: A review and reformulation of the field's outcome variables, *Annual Review of Psychology*, 35, pp. 627–66.

Stech, E. and Ratliffe, S.A. 1985, *Effective Group Communication: How to Get Action by Working in Groups*, National Textbook, Lincolnwood.

Stecklow, S. 1994a, Chief prerequisite for college president's job: Stamina, *Wall Street Journal*, 1 Dec., pp. B1, B10.

Stecklow, S. 1994b, Harvard's president, too slow to delegate, got swamped in detail, *Wall Street Journal*, 9 Dec., pp. A1, A10.

Steers, R.M. 1987, Murray's manifest needs theory, in R.M. Steers and L.W. Porter (eds), *Motivation and Work Behavior*, McGraw-Hill, New York.

Steers, R.M. and Porter, L.W. 1991, *Work and Motivation*, McGraw-Hill, New York.

Steers, R.M., Porter, L.W. and Bigley, G.A. 1996, *Motivation and Leadership at Work*, McGraw-Hill, New York.

Steiner, G. and Cannon, W.M. 1966, *Multinational Corporate Planning*, Macmillan, New York.

Stepanek, M. 1999, How fast is Netfast?, *Business Review Weekly*, 1 Nov., pp. 30–2.

Stepp, L.S. 1991a, In search of ethics: Alcoa pursues a corporate conscience through emphasis on 'core values', *Washington Post*, 31 March, pp. H1, H4.

Stepp, L.S. 1991b, New test of values, *Washington Post*, 4 Aug., pp. H1, H4.

Stern, R.N. and Barley, S.R. 1996, Organizations and social systems: Organization theory's neglected mandate, *Administrative Science Quarterly*, 41, pp. 146–62.

Stevens, A. 1995a, Boss's brain teaser: Accommodating depressed worker, *Wall Street Journal*, 11 Sept., p. B1.

Stevens, A. 1995b, Lawyers and clients, *Wall Street Journal*, 19 June, p. B7.

Stevens, T. 1995, Where the rubber meets the road, *Industry Week*, 20 March, pp. 14–18.

Stevenson, H.H. and Gumpert, D.E. 1985, The heart of entrepreneurship, *Harvard Business Review*, March–April, pp. 85–94.

Stewart, R. 1982, A model for understanding managerial jobs and behavior, *Academy of Management Review*, 7, pp. 7–13.

Stogdill, R.M. 1948, Personal factors associated with leadership: A survey of the literature, *Journal of Psychology*, 25, pp. 35–71.

Stogdill, R.M. 1972, Group productivity, drive, and cohesiveness, *Organizational Behavior and Human Performance*, 8, pp. 26–43.

Stogdill, R.M. 1974, *Handbook of Leadership*, Free Press, New York.

Stoner, J.A.F. and Wankel, C. 1986, *Management*, Prentice-Hall, Englewood Cliffs.

Straits Times 2000a, Pride and hope to profit, 7 January, p. 21.

Straits Times 2000b, X-mas trees recycled in Ikea's green scheme, 11 Jan, p. 37.

Strand, R. 1987, A systems paradigm of organizational adaptations to the social environment, *Academy of Management Review*, 8, pp. 93–4.

Strauss, G. 1964, Work flow frictions, interfunctional rivalry, and professionalism: A case study of purchasing agents, *Human Organization*, 23, pp. 137–49.

Strebel, P. 1994, Choosing the right change path, *California Management Review*, 36, pp. 29–51.

Strom, S. 1996, A sweetheart becomes suspect; Looking behind those Kathie Lee labels, *New York Times*, 27 June, p. D1.

Strube, M. and Garcia, J. 1981, A meta-analysis investigation of Fiedler's contingency model of leadership effectiveness, *Psychological Bulletin*, 90, pp. 307–21.

Studer, M. 1992, SMH leads a revival of Swiss watchmaker industry, *Wall Street Journal*, 20 Jan., p. B4.

Sugawara, S. 1996, Japan Inc. finds a way to keep the lid on layoffs, *Washington Post*, 12 March, p. D11.

Sullivan, R.L. 1995, Lawyers à la carte, *Forbes*, 11 Sept., p. 44.

Sullivan-Trainorm, AM.L. and Maglitta, J. 1990, Competitive advantage fleeting, *Computerworld*, 8 Oct., p. 28.

Supervisory Management 1995, After reengineering what's next? May, p. 1.

Switzer, P. 2000, There's bread in them thar loaves, *Australian*, 24 Jan., p. 37.

Syrett, M. and Kingston, K. 1995, GE's Hungarian light lwitch, *Management Today*, April, p. 52.

Tabakoff, N. 1999a, The go-between, *Business Review Weekly*, 8 Oct., pp. 82–4.

Tabakoff, N. 1999b, Workers second-class labor, says union, *Business Review Weekly*, 8 Oct., p. 84.

Tait, P. and Vessey, I. 1988, The effect of user involvement on system success: A contingency approach, *MIS Quarterly*, March, pp. 91–108.

Talbott, S.P. 1994, Peer review drives compensation at Johnsonville, *Personnel Journal*, Oct., pp. 126–32.

Tang T.L-P. and Crofford, A.B. 1995-96, Self-managing work teams, *Employment Relations Today*, Winter, pp. 29–39.

Tannen, D. 1995a, The power of talk, *Harvard Business Review*, Sept.–Oct., pp. 138–48.

Tannen, D. 1995b, *Talking from 9 to 5*, Avon Books, New York.

Tannenbaum, R. and Schmidt, W.H. 1973, How to choose a leadership pattern, *Harvard Business Review*, May–June, pp. 162–80.

Tanzer, A. 1987, Create or die, *Forbes*, 6 April, p. 57.

Taylor III, A. 1989, The U.S. gets back in fighting shape, *Fortune*, 24 April, pp. 42–8.

Taylor III, A. 1992, U.S. cars come back, *Fortune*, 16 Nov., pp. 52–85.

Taylor III, A. 1993, Why GM leads the pack in Europe, *Fortune*, 17 May, pp. 83–6.

Taylor III, A. 1994, The auto industry meets the new economy, *Fortune*, 5 Sept., pp. 52–60.

Taylor, A. 1995, Boeing—sleepy in Seattle, *Fortune*, Aug., pp. 92–8.

Taylor, F.W. 1985, *The Principles of Scientific Management*, Hive, Easton.

Taylor, M.S., Locke, E.A., Lee, C. and Gist, M. 1984, Type A behavior and faculty research productivity: What are the mechanisms?, *Organizational Behavior and Human Performance*, 34, pp. 402–18.

Taylor, R.N. 1984, *Behavioral Decision Making*, Scott, Foresman, Glenview.

Teng, J.T.C., Grover, V. and Fiedler, K.D. 1994, Business process reengineering: Charting a strategic path for the information age, *California Management Review*, 36, Summer, pp. 93–108.

Thackray, J. 1985, Planning an Avon turnaround, *Planning Review*, Jan., pp. 6–11.

Wall Street Journal 1989a, How you play the game says whether you win, 18 April, p. B1.

Wall Street Journal 1989b, Out of sight, not out of mind, 20 June, p. B1.

Washington Post 1995, Leesson sentenced to 6½ years for causing Barings collapse, 2 Dec., p. 1F.

Therrien, L. 1989, The rival Japan respects, *Business Week*, 13 Nov., pp. 108–18.

Thite, M. 1999, Identifying key characteristics of technical project leadership, *Leadership and Organization Development*, 20, 5, pp. 253–61.

Thomas, E.G. 1987, Flextime doubles in a decade, *Management World*, April–May, pp. 18–19.

Thomas, J. and Sireno, P. 1980, Assessing management competency needs, *Training and Development Journal*, 34, pp. 47–51.

Thomas, K.W. 1977, Toward multi-dimensional values in teaching: The example of conflict behaviors, *Academy of Management Review*, 2, pp. 484–90.

Thomas, T. 1999a, Loan arranger prefers the solo practice life, *Business Review Weekly*, 29 Oct., pp. 130–1.

Thomas, T. 1999b, Nursery firm looks after the littlies until they grow big, *Business Review Weekly*, 21 May, pp. 98–9.

Thompson Jr, A.A. and Strickland III, A.J. 1987, *Strategic Management: Concepts and Cases*, Business Publications, Texas.

Thompson Jr, A.A. and Strickland III, A.J. 1999, *Strategic Management: Concepts and Cases*, McGraw-Hill: New York.

Thompson, J.D. 1967, *Organizations in Action*, McGraw-Hill, New York.

Thyfault, M.E. 1996, The intranet rolls in, *Information Week*, 29 Jan., pp. 15, 76–8.

Tichy, N. and DeRose, C. 1995, Roger Enrico's master class, *Fortune*, 27 Nov., pp. 105–6.

Tichy, N.M. and Ulrich, D.O. 1984, The leadership challenge—a call for the transformational leader, *Sloan Management Review*, Fall, pp. 59–68.

Tjosvold, D. 1984, Making conflict productive, *Personnel Administrator*, June, pp. 121–30.

Tjosvold, D. 1993, *Teamwork for Customers*, Jossey-Bass, San Francisco.

Tomsho, R. 1990, U-Haul patriarch now battles offspring in bitterest of feuds, *Wall Street Journal*, 16 July, pp. A1–A6.

Torrington, D. and Weightman, J. 1987, Middle management work, *Journal of General Management*, 13, pp. 74–89.

Tosi Jr, H.L. 1974, The human effects of budgeting systems on management, *MSU Business Topics*, Autumn, pp. 53–63.

Tosi Jr, H.L. and Slocum Jr, J.W. 1984, Contingency theory: Some suggested directions, *Journal of Management*, 10, pp. 9–26.

Tosi, H.L., Rizzo, J.R. and Carroll, S.J. 1986, *Managing Organizational Behavior*, Pitman, Marshfield.

Towne, H.R. 1886, The engineer as an economist, *Transactions of the American Society of Mechanical Engineers*, 7, pp. 428–32;

Townsend, A.M., DeMarie, S.M. and Hendrickson, A.R. 1996, Are you ready for virtual teams? *HRMagazine*, Sept., pp. 122–6.

Townsend, A.M., DeMarie, S.M. and Hendrickson, A.R. 1998, Virtual teams: Technology and the workplace of the future, *Academy of Management Executive*, 12, 3, pp. 17–29.

Toy, S. 1989, Waiter, a magnum of your best Portland champagne, *Business Week*, 11 Dec., pp. 92–4.

Trachtenberg, J.A. 1986, They didn't listen to anybody, *Forbes*, 15 Dec., pp. 168–9.

Trade New Zealand 2000, *New Zealand Country Profile*, www.tradenz.govt.nz/nz/nz.html

Treadgold, T. 1999, From the bottom drawer, a top dollar money manager, *Business Review Weekly*, 29 Oct., p. 59.

Trevino, L.K. 1986, Ethical decision making in organizations: A person–situation interactionist model, *Academy of Management Review*, 11, pp. 601–17.

Trice, H.M. and Beyer, J.M. 1993, *The Cultures of Work Organizations*, Prentice-Hall, Englewood Cliffs.

Trost, C. 1985, Bhopal disaster spurs debate over usefulness of criminal sanctions in industrial accidents, *Wall Street Journal*, 7 Jan., p. 18.

Trost, C. 1992, To cut costs and keep the best people, more concerns offer flexible work plans, *Wall Street Journal*, 2 Feb., p. B1.

Tuckman, B.W. 1965, Developmental sequence in small groups, *Psychological Bulletin*, 63, pp. 384–99.

Tuckman, B.W. and Jensen, M.A.C. 1977, Stages of small-group development revisited, *Group and Organization Studies*, 2, pp. 419–27.

Tuckey, Bill 1999, Debt struck Daewoo buys into the small car war, *Business Review Weekly*, 29 Oct., p. 46.

Tuleja, T.F. 1985, Beyond the bottom line: How business leaders are turning principles into profits, *Facts on File*, New York.

Tully, S. 1994, Why to go for stretch targets, *Fortune*, 14 Nov., pp. 145–58.

Tully, S. 1995, Purchasing's new muscle, *Fortune*, 20 Feb., pp. 75–83.

Tung, R.L. 1984, Strategic management of human resources in the multinational enterprise, *Human Resource Management*, 23, pp. 129–43.

Turban, E. and Watkins, P.R. 1986, Integrating expert systems and decision support systems, *MIS Quarterly*, June, pp. 121–38.

Turner, G. 1986, Inside Europe's giant companies: Daimler-Benz goes top of the league, *Long Range Planning*, 19, pp. 12–17.

Tushman, M. and Nadler, D. 1986, Organizing for innovation, *California Management Review*, 28, pp. 74–92.

Tushman, M.L. and Anderson, P. 1986, Technological discontinuities and organization environments, *Administrative Science Quarterly*, 31, pp. 439–65.

Tushman, M.L. and Scanlan, T.J. 1981, Boundary spanning individuals: Their role in information transfer and their antecedents, *Academy of Management Journal*, 24, pp. 289–305.

Ulrich, D. and Barney, J.B. 1984, Perspectives in organizations: Resource dependence, efficiency, and population, *Academy of Management Review*, 9, pp. 471–81.

Ulvila, J.W. 1987, Postal automation (ZIP 14) technology: A decision analysis, *Interfaces*, March–April, pp. 1–12.

Updike, E.H., Woodruff, D. and Armstrong, L. 1995, Honda's civic lesson, *Business Week*, 18 Sept., pp. 71–6.

USA Today 1992, *Low Grade Government*, 3 Sept., 1992, p. A1.

Uttal, B. 1985, Behind the fall of Steve Jobs, *Fortune*, 5 Aug., pp. 20–4.

Uttal, B. 1987, Companies that serve you best, *Fortune*, 7 Dec., pp. 98–116.

Van de Ven, A.H. 1986, Central problems in the management of innovation, *Management Science*, 32, pp. 590–607.

Van de Ven, A.H. and Delbecq, A.L. 1974, The effectiveness of nominal, delphi, and interacting group processes, *Academy of Management Journal*, 17, pp. 605–21.

Van Fleet, D.D. 1983, Span of management research and issues, *Academy of Management Journal*, 26, pp. 546–52.

Van Velsor, E. and Leslie, J.B. 1995, Why executives derail: Perspectives across time and cultures, *Academy of Management Executive*, 9, pp. 62–72.

Vecchio, R.P. 1987, Situational leadership theory: An examination of a prescriptive theory, *Journal of Applied Psychology*, 72, pp. 444–51.

Verity, J.W. and Hof, R. 1995, Bullet-proofing the net, *Business Week*, 13 Nov., pp. 98–9.

Violino, B. 1996, Internet insecurity: Your worst nightmare, *Information Week*, 19 Feb., pp. 34–6.

Vlasic, B. 1996, Can the UAW put a brake on outsourcing? *Business Week*, 17 June, pp. 66, 70.

Vlasic, B. and Kerwin, K. 1996, GM's man in merging traffic, *Business Week*, 4 March, p. 38.

Vokola, M., Rezgul, Y. and Wood-Harper, T. 2000, The Condor business process re-engineering model, *Managerial Auditing Journal*, 15, 1, pp. 42–6.

von Bertalanffy, L. 1951, General systems theory: A new approach to the unity of science, *Human Biology*, Dec., pp. 302–61.

von Bertalanffy, L. 1962, General systems theory—a critical review, *General Systems*, 7, pp. 1–20.

Vroom, V.H. and Jago, A.G. 1988, *The New Leadership: Managing Participation in Organizations*, Prentice-Hall, Englewood Cliffs.

Wagner III, J.A. 1995, Studies of individualism—collectivism effects on co-operation in groups, *Academy of Management Journal*, 28, pp. 152–72.

Wahba, M.A. and Bridwell, L.G. 1976, Maslow reconsidered: A review of research on the need hierarchy theory, *Organizational Behavior and Human Performance*, 16, pp. 212–40.

Wakizaka, A. 1995, Faxes, e-mail, help the deaf get office jobs, *Wall Street Journal*, 3 Oct., pp. B1, B5.

Waldman, P. 1989, New RJR chief faces a daunting challenge at debt-heavy firm, *Wall Street Journal*, 14 March, pp. A1, A19.

Waldon, H. 1985, Putting a new face on Avon, *Planning Review*, July, pp. 18–25.

Wall Street Journal 1994a, Staples taps Hanaka from Lechmere inc. to become its CEO, 29 July, p. B2.

Wall Street Journal 1994b, Team selling catches on, but is sales really a team sport?, 29 March, p. A1.

Wall Street Journal 1995a, E-mail etiquette starts to take shape for business messaging, 12 Oct., p. A1.

Wall Street Journal 1995a, Motorola inc.: Company is chosen to build cellular system in Calcutta, 5 Jan., p. B4.

Wall Street Journal 1995b, Formosa plastics corp.: Company says pretax profit doubled in the first quarter, 28 April, p. A1.

Wall Street Journal 1995b, Motorola inc. plans to increase business with Chinese ventures, 13 Feb., p. B11.

Wall Street Journal 1995c, Glass ceiling is a heavy barrier for minorities, blocking them from top jobs, 14 March, p. A1.

Wall Street Journal 1995d, Life is good for telecommuters, but some problems persist, 3 Aug., p. A1.

Wall Street Journal 1995e, Miscommunications plague pilots and air-traffic controllers, 22 Aug., p. A1.

Wall Street Journal 1995f, Wanted: Middle managers, audition required, 28 Dec., p. A1.

Wall Street Journal 1995g, Diversity is up, 'Goal-setting' is down in workplace-training programs, 21 March, p. A1.

Wall Street Journal 1995h, Chevron settles claims of 4 women at unit as part of sex bias suit, 22 Jan., p. B12.

Wall Jr, J.A. and Callister, R.R. 1995, Conflict and its management, *Journal of Management*, 21, pp. 515–58.

Walters, K. 1999a, Rag traders get some help from an experienced hand, *Business Review Weekly*, 12 November, p. 77.

Walters, K. 1999b, When a deal goes out of its tree, *Business Review Weekly*, 21 May, pp. 45–6.

Walters, K. 1999c, Freight innovator no longer running on empty, *Business Review Weekly*, 29 Oct., p. 61.

Walton, R.E. 1985, From control to commitment in the workplace, *Harvard Business Review*, March–April, pp. 77–84.

Walton, R.E. and Dutton, J.M. 1969, The management of interdepartmental conflict: A model and review, *Administrative Science Quarterly*, March, pp. 73–84.

Wanous, J.P., Keon, T.L. and Latack, J.C. 1983, Expectancy theory and occupational/organizational choices: A review and test, *Organizational Behavior and Human Performance*, 32, pp. 66–86.

Want, J.H. 1986, Corporate mission: The intangible contributor to performance, *Management Review*, August, pp. 46–50.

Wartick, S.L. and Cochran, P.L. 1985, The evolution of the corporate social performance model, *Academy of Management Review*, 10, pp. 758–69.

Waterman Jr, H. 1988, The power of teamwork, *Best of Business Quarterly*, Spring, pp. 17–25.

Watson, H.J., Rainer Jr, R.K. and Koh, C.E. 1991, Executive information systems: A framework for development and a survey of current practices, *MIS Quarterly*, March, pp. 13–30.

Watson, W.E., Kumar, K. and Michaelsen, L.K. 1993, Cultural diversity's impact on interaction process and performance: Comparing homogeneous and diverse task groups, *Academy of Management Journal*, 36, pp. 590–602.

Way, N. 1999, Juggling and struggling, *Business Review Weekly*, 22 Oct., pp. 69–75.

Way, N. 2000, The kings of culture, *Business Review Weekly*, 7 April, pp. 100–4.

Weatherly, J.D. 1992, Dare to compare for better productivity, *HR Magazine*, Sept., pp. 42–6.

Weber, J. 1991, Meet Du Pont's 'In-house conscience', *Business Week*, 24 June, pp. 62–5.

Webster's New World Dictionary 1984, College Edition, Simon & Schuster, New York.

Weick, K.E. 1995, *Sensemaking in Organizations*, Sage, Thousand Oaks.

Weick, K.E. and Browning, L.D. 1986, Argument and narration in organizational communication, *Journal of Management*, 12, pp. 243–59.

Weiner, S. 1987, Taking the pledge, *Forbes*, 29 June, pp. 41–2;

Weisman, K. 1989, Safe harbor, *Forbes*, 4 Sept., pp. 58–62.

Weiss, E. 1996, Employees: Stop goofing off on net, *Warfield's Business Record*, 11 March, p. 18.

Weiss, R.M. 1983, Weber on bureaucracy: Management consultant or political theorist? *Academy of Management Review*, 8, pp. 242–8.

Welch, J.F. 1992, Service quality measurement at American Express traveler's cheque group, *National Productivity Review*, 22 Sept., p. 463.

Welles, C. 1988, What led Beech-Nut down the road to disgrace, *Business Week*, 22 Feb., pp. 124–8.

Werther Jr, W.B. and Davis, K. 1989, *Personnel Management and Human Resources*, McGraw Hill, New York.

Wessel, D. 1987, Computer finds a role in buying and selling, reshaping business, *Wall Street Journal*, 8 March, pp. 1, 10.

Wheeler, D.D. and Janis, I.L. 1980, *A Practical Guide for Making Decisions*, Free Press, New York.

Wheelwright, S.C. and Hayes, R.H. 1985, Competing through manufacturing, *Harvard Business Review*, Jan.–Feb., pp. 99–109.

Wheelwright, S.C. and Makridakis, S. 1989, *Forecasting Methods for Management*, Wiley, New York.

Whetten, D.A. and Cameron, K.S. 1998, *Developing Management Skills*, Scott, Foresman, Glenview.

White, J.B. 1988, U.S. car-parts firms form Japanese ties, *Wall Street Journal*, 12 April, p. 6.

White, J.B. 1989, Toyota wants more managers out on the line, *Wall Street Journal*, 2 Aug., p. A10.

White, J.B. 1997, Chrysler's intranet: Promise vs. reality, *Wall Street Journal*, 13 May, pp. B1, B6.

Whyte, G. 1989, Groupthink reconsidered, *Academy of Management Review*, 14, pp. 40–56.

Wildstrom, S.H. 1987, A risky tack for Democrats, *Business Week*, 20 July, p. 71.

Wildstrom, S.H. 1995, This 'secretary' really listens, *Business Week*, 24 April, p. 19.

Wilkes, M.V. 1992, Charles Babbage—The great uncle of computing?, *Communications of the ACM*, March.

Willoughby, J. 1987, The last iceman, *Forbes*, 13 July, pp. 183–204.

Winberg, N. 1996, Shaking up an old giant, *Forbes*, 20 May, pp. 68–80.

Winslow, R. 1995, Hospitals' weak systems hurt patients, study says, *Wall Street Journal*, 5 July, pp. B1, B6.

Wiseman, C. and MacMillan, I.C. 1984, Creating competitive weapons from information systems, *Journal of Business Strategy*, Fall, pp. 42–9.

Wokutch, R.E. and Spencer, B.A. 1987, Corporate saints and sinners: The effects of philanthropic and illegal activity on organizational performance, *California Management Review*, 29, pp. 62–77.

Wolff, W.F. 1996, Japan study team probes management of R&D, *Research-Technology Management*, March–April, pp. 4–5.

Wood, R.E., Mento, A.J. and Locke, E.A. 1987, Task complexity as a moderator of goal effects: A meta analysis, *Journal of Applied Psychology*, 72, pp. 416–25.

Woodman, R.W., Sawyer, J.E. and Griffin, R.W. 1993, Towards a theory of organizational creativity, *Academy of Management Review*, 18, pp. 293–321.

Woodruff, D. and Miller, K.L. 1995, Mercedes' maverick in Alabama, *Business Week*, 11 Sept., pp. 64–5.

Woodward, J. 1958, *Management and Technology*, Her Majesty's Stationery Office, London.

Woodward, J. 1965, *Industrial Organisations: Theory and Practice*, Oxford University, London.

World Airlines News 1995, Product news, 9 Jan., p. 1.

Worthy, F.S. 1989, When somebody wants a payoff, *Fortune*, Pacific Rim issue, Fall, pp. 117–22.

Wrege, C.D. and Perroni, A.G. 1974, Taylor's pig tale: A historical analysis of Frederick W. Taylor's pig iron experiment, *Academy of Management Journal*, 17, pp. 6–27.

Wrege, C.D. and Stotka, A.M. 1978, Cooke creates a classic: The story behind F. W. Taylor's principles of scientific management, *Academy of Management Review*, 3, pp. 736–49.

Wren, D.A. 1979, *The Evolution of Management Thought*, Wiley, New York.

Wren, D.A. 1986, Years of good beginnings: 1886 and 1936, in D.A. Wren and J.A. Pearce II (eds), *Papers Dedicated to the Development of Modern Management*, Academy of Management.

Wright, P. M. and Kacmar, K.M. 1994, Goal specificity as a determinant of goal commitment and goal change, *Organizational Behavior and Human Decision Processes*, 29, pp. 242–60.

www.brw.com.au (accessed 14/9/99)

www.brw.com.au (accessed 14/9/99),

www.businesssunday.ninemsn.com.au/ (accessed 16/9/99)

www.cck.com.au

www.comsec.com.au (accessed 07/10/99)

www.immi.gov.au/facts/11fifty.htm

www.immi.gov.au/facts/13pop. htm

www.kirkland.com

www.Pacifica.com.au

www.statistics.gov.au/websitedbs/c311

Wyman, L. 1996, Rugs roll at IKEA; Latest theme at Manhattan store, *HFN The Weekly Newspaper for the Home Furnishing Network*, 8 April, p. 11.

Wysocki Jr, B. 1995, Some companies cut costs too far, suffer 'Corporate Anorexia,' *Wall Street Journal*, 5 July, p. A1.

Yerak, B. 1994, Castite owner lets dream have its way, *Plain Dealer*, 1 June, p. 1C.

Yoshino, M.Y. and Ranga, U.S. 1995, *Strategic Alliance: An Entrepreneurial Approach to Globalization*, Harvard Business School, Boston.

Young, J. 1996, Digital octopus, *Forbes*, June 17, pp. 102–106.

Yukl, G. 1989, Managerial leadership: A review of theory and research, *Journal of Management*, 15, pp. 251–89.

Yukl, G. 1994, *Leadership in Organizations*, Prentice-Hall, Englewood Cliffs.

Zaccaro, S.J. 1984, Social loafing: The role of task attractiveness, *Personality and Social Psychology Bulletin*, 10, pp. 99–106.

Zachary, G.P. 1989, Software makers get a chill from Microsoft's Windows, *Wall Street Journal*, 10 Oct., pp. B1, B8.

Zachary, G.P. 1994, It's a mail thing: Electronic messaging gets a rating—ex, *Wall Street Journal*, 22 June, p. A1.

Zachary, G.P. 1995a, Can unions organize low-paid workers? Watch this woman, *Wall Street Journal*, 23 Oct., pp. A1, A10.

Zachary, G.P. 1995b, Some unions step up organizing campaigns and get new members, *Wall Street Journal*, 1 Sept., pp. A1, A2.

Zaheer, S. 1995, Overcoming the liability of foreignness, *Academy of Management Journal*, 38, pp. 341–63.

Zaleznik, A. 1977, Managers and leaders: Are they different? *Harvard Business Review*, May–June, pp. 47–60.

Zaleznik, A. 1990, The leadership gap, *Academy of Management Executive*, 4, pp. 7–22.

Zaltman, G., Duncan, R. and Holbek, J. 1973, *Innovations and Organizations*, Wiley, New York.

Zaremba, A. 1988, Working with the organizational grapevine, *Personnel Journal*, July, pp. 38–42.

Zemke, R. 1988, Putting the SQUEEZE on middle managers, *Training*, Dec., pp. 41–6.

Ziegler, B. 1995a, IBM fires three Argentine executives amid investigation of bank contract, *Wall Street Journal*, 15 Sept., p. A6.

Ziegler, B. 1995b, Virtual power lunches will make passing the salt an impossibility, *Wall Street Journal*, 28 June, p. B1.

Zinger, B.J. and Madique, M.M. 1990, A model of new product development: An empirical test, *Management Science*, 36, pp. 867–83.

Credits

Adapted by permission of Prentice Hall, Englewood Cliffs, New Jersey; 13.8 reprinted with the permission of The Free Press, Macmillan Publishing, from *Leadership and Performance Beyond Expectations* by Bernard M. Bass. Copyright © 1985 by The Free Press; 14.2 Phillip V. Lewis, *Organizational Communication: The Essence of Effective Management*, 2e, © 1980. Reprinted by permission of Prentice Hall, Englewood Cliffs, New Jersey; 14.5 R. Wayne Pace, *Organizational Communication: Foundations for Human Resource Development*, © 1983, p. 40. Adapted by permission of Prentice Hall, Englewood Cliffs, New Jersey; 14.6 Phillip V. Lewis, *Organizational Communication: The Essence of Effective Management*, 2e, © 1980. Reprinted by permission of Prentice Hall, Englewood Cliffs, New Jersey, and Edward E. Scannell, *Communication for Leadership*, McGraw-Hill, New York, © 1970. Reprinted by permission; 16.2 modified by permission from page 12 of *Strategic Control* by Peter Lorange, Michael F. Scott Morton & Sumantra Ghoshal. Copyright © 1986 by West Publishing Company. All rights reserved; 16S2.3 reprinted by permission of *Harvard Business Review*. From 'How to choose a leadership pattern' by R. Tannenbaum & W. Schmidt, May–June 1973. Copyright © 2000 by the President and Fellows of Harvard College, all rights reserved; 16S2.7, 16S2.8 E. S. Buffa, *Modern Production/Operations Management*, Wiley, New York, 1983; 18.1 reprinted by permission of *Harvard Business Review*. From 'How to choose a leadership pattern' by R. Tannenbaum & W. Schmidt, May–June 1973. Copyright © 2000 by the President and Fellows of Harvard College, all rights reserved.

Tables
The following tables are from K. Bartol & D. Martin, *Management*, 3rd edition, McGraw-Hill Inc., New York, 1997: 2.1, 2.2, 2.3, 2.5, 2.6, 3.2, 4.2, 4.4, 5.1, 5.2, 5.4, 6.4, 8.3, 10.1, 10.2, 10.3, 10.4, 11.1, 13.1, 13.3, 16S2.1, 16S2.2, 17.2.

Table 2.4 reprinted with permission from General and Industrial Management © 1987. Published by The Centre for Effective Performance, 4250 Perimeter Park South, Suite 131, Atlanta GA30341; 3.1 Australian Bureau of Statistics; 3.3 reprinted by permission of *Harvard Business Review*. Adapted from 'The heart of entrepreneurship' by H. H. Stevenson & D. E. Gumpert, March–April 1985. Copyright © 1985 by the President and Fellows of Harvard College. All rights reserved; 5.3 adapted and reprinted with the permission of The Free Press, a Division of Simon & Schuster, from *A Practical Guide for Making Decisions* by Daniel D. Wheeler & Irving L. Janis. Copyright © 1980 by The Free Press; 5S.1 S. Makridakis & S. C. Wheelwright. 'Forecasting an organi-

zation's futures', in P. C. Nystrom & W H. Starbuck (eds), *Handbook of Design*, Oxford University Press, 1981. By permission of Oxford University Press; 6.1 reprinted from *Long Range Planning*, vol. 22, F. R. David 'How companies define their mission', pp. 92–3. Copyright 1989, with kind permission from Elsevier Science Ltd, The Boulevard, Langford Lane, Kidlington OX5 lGB; 6.2 P. F. Drucker, *Management: Tasks, Responsibilities and Practices*, Harper & Row, New York; 7.1, 7.3 adapted and reprinted with the permission of The Free Press, a Division of Simon & Schuster, from *Competitive Strategy: Techniques for Analyzing Industries and Competitors* by Michael E. Porter. Copyright © 1980 by The Free Press; 8.1 reprinted by permission of *Harvard Business Review*. Based on an exhibit from 'Evolution and revolution as organizations grow', L. Greiner, July–August, 1972. Copyright © 1972 by the President and Fellows of Harvard College. All rights reserved; 8.2 K. S. Cameron, D. A. Whetten & Myung U. Kim, 'Organizational dysfunctions of decline', *Academy of Management Review*, vol. 30, 1987; 10.5 J. Woodward, *Industrial Organization: Theory and Practice*, Oxford University Press, 1965. By permission of Oxford University Press; 13.2 reprinted from *Leadership and Decision-Making* by Victor H. Vroom & Philip W. Yetton, by permission of the University of Pittsburgh Press. © 1973 by University of Pittsburgh Press; 14.1 R. M. Hodgetts & S. A. Altman, *Organizational Behavior*, Saunders, Philadelphia, 1979, p. 305; 16S1.4 reprinted from *Long Range Planning*, vol. 21, S. S. Cowen & J. K. Middaugh II, 'Designing an effective financial planning and control system', pp. 83–92, copyright 1988, with kind permission from Elsevier Science Ltd, The Boulevard, Langford Lane, Kidlington OX5 1GB, UK; 17.1 reprinted by permission of *Harvard Business Review*. An exhibit from 'Choosing strategies for change', J. P. Kotter & L. A. Schlesinger, March–April, 1979. Copyright © 1979 by the President and Fellows of Harvard College. All rights reserved.

Photographs
Photographs are reproduced by courtesy of the following: pp. 4, 94, 398, 456 Autoliv Australia Pty Ltd; p. 29 CCK Financial Solutions Ltd; p. 54 Fusion Design Consultants Pty Ltd; p. 69 Electrolux Pty Ltd; p. 85 Turbosoft; p. 147 Freshdirect Pty Ltd; p. 191 Australiawide Loading; p. 216 Cuisine Courier Pty Ltd; p. 300 Allied Express Transport; p. 320 Boyd Partners Ltd; p. 326 Singapore Computer Systems Limited;, p. 342 Tripac International Pty Ltd; p. 346 HiTech Personnel; p. 384 Fusion Design Consultants Pty Ltd; p. 452 China Rich Holdings Ltd; p. 483 Tania Kearney, Fisher and Paykel, New Zealand; p. 511 Ausdoc Group Limited; p. 519 The Body Shop International; p. 658 Ford Australia.

Index

A

ability
  situational leadership theory, 413
acceptability
  control process and cost
    acceptability, 500–1
  solutions, of, 134
accommodation, reducing and
  resolving conflict and, 592, 594
accountability, 281
achievement, need for, 371
achievement–nurturing orientation, 616
achievement-oriented leaders, 416
acquired-needs theory, 371
acquisition, 215
  organisational termination, 240
active listening, 437
  guidelines, 438
activity, in network diagram, 165
ad hoc committees, 475
adaptation, as approach to managing
  environment, 78–9
adjourning stage of group
  development, 471
administrative culture, 85
administrative management, 40–1
administrative protections, 615, 616
advertising, 79–80
  awards for, 488–90
  recruitment, 338
aesthetics, quality and, 524
aggregate production planning, 545
aggressor role, 465
agreement, overcoming resistance to
  change and, 581
alternative solutions, 133
alternative work schedules, 274
alternatives to control, 501
America Online, 144
amoral management, 108
anchoring and adjustment, 140

Ansett Australia, 135, 501
anti-freeloader argument, 96
artificial intelligence, 564
Asian crisis, 640–1
asset management ratios, 530, 531
assignment policies, international
  business and, 628
Association of South-East Asian
  Nations (ASEAN), 641
  Australian trade with, 641
Atlantic Gulf & West Indies Steam
  Ship Lines, 74
attention stage of modelling, 386
attitudes, negative, control systems
  and, 512, 542
attribution theory, 434
  fundamental attribution error, 434
  processes, 434
audits
  ethics, 115
  social, 104
Ausdoc, 510–11
Australian workforce, 72–3
Australia's position in South-East Asia,
  657–8
Australiawide Loading, 190–1
authority, 281
  decentralising, 280
  delegation of (see delegation)
  functional, 283
  line, 282, 283
autocratic leaders, 401
Autoliv Integrated Management System
  (AIMS), 4, 32, 64, 94–5, 126, 172,
  204, 234, 266, 298, 330, 366,
  398, 426, 456, 492, 576, 610, 640
  code of ethics, 95
  communication, 426
  departmental organisation, 266
  human resources, 330
  leadership, 398

  motivation, 366
  strategies, 204
autonomy, as core job characteristic,
  274
availability bias, 139–40
avoidance
  reducing and resolving conflict and,
  592, 593

B

Babbage, Charles, 33, 34–5, 57
baby boomers, 72–3
backward integration, 215
balance of payments, 615
balance of trade, 615
balance sheet, 528–30
Baldwin Locomotive, 74, 84
bankruptcy
  organisational termination, 240
bargaining power
  customers, of 209
  suppliers, of 209
Barings Bank, 136
Barnard, Chester, 40, 41, 58
BCG growth-share matrix, 217–18
behaviour modification, 380
behavioural displacement, control and,
  512
behavioural science approach, 48
behavioural theories of management,
  42–8, 55
behaviourism (see reinforcement theory)
behaviours
  identifying leader, 401
belief systems, 507
belongingness needs, 368
benchmarking, as control mechanism,
  504–5, 527
biases
  communication, in, 138
  decision making, recognising, 138

bill of materials (BOM), 547
blocker role, 463
boundary spanning, 80
boundary systems, 509
bounded rationality, 130
brainstorming, 133, 150
break-even analysis, 169–70
bribes, 113
budget(s), 534–5
    capital expenditures, 535
    operating, 534–5
budgetary control, 522, 533–4
    impacts of budgeting process and,
        535
    responsibility centres, 533–4
    types of budgets, 534–5
budgeting, 533–4
    (*see also* budget(s); budgetary
        control)
buffering, 78–9
bureaucratic control, 506–7, 594
bureaucratic management, 38–9, 594
business-level strategies, 207, 221
    cost leadership, 221–2, 318, 566
    differentiation, 223
    focus, 223
    formulating, 221

C
capacity argument, 96
capacity planning, 543–5
capacity-requirements planning, 545
capital expenditures budget, 535
capitalist economy, 66
careers in management
    ethical issues and, 111
Carnival Cruise Lines, 78
carryover behaviours, norms and, 468
cash cows, 218
categorisation stage of problem
        identification, 132
causal models, 158–60
CCK Financial Solutions, 29–30
centralisation, 280
ceremonials, organisational culture
        and, 83
chain network, 439
chain of command, 269
change, 21, 22–3, 234–5
    conflict, relationship to, 596
    cultural components of, 254
    defined, 21, 235

diagnosing the need for, 576–7
external factors, 577
forces for, 235–6
human resource components of, 253
innovation and, 21–2, 234–5
internal factors, 577
interrelationship among components
    of, 254
managing change and innovation,
    21–2, 576–8
organisational, components of, 252
planned, 241
processes of, 241, 591–3
reactive, 241
resistance to, 578–80
structural components of, 252
technological, 21, 253
change cycle, 578, 579
charisma, 416
chief executive officer (CEO) (*see* top
        managers)
circle network, 439
Citicorp, 106
clan control, 506, 507
classical management theories, 36–41
clients, 70
closed system, 51
co-optation, overcoming resistance to
        change and, 581
Coca-Cola, 22, 128, 134
code of ethics, 114–15
    Autoliv, 95
coercion, overcoming resistance to
        change, 581
coercive power, 399
cognitive theories of motivation, 374
    assessing, 378
collaboration, reducing and resolving
        conflict and, 593
collectivism
    work groups, in, 465
collectivity stage of organisational life
        cycle, 237, 238
combination approach, social response
        mechanism, 106
command groups, 457
committees
    ad hoc, 475
    permanent, 107
    temporary, 105
communication
    basic components of process, 429

conflict and, 587
decoding and, 430
definition of, 427
downward, 441–2
electronic, 445
encoding and, 430
face-to-face, 445
feedback and, 430, 437
formal, 444
formal report, by
horizontal, 443
informal, 444
limited, 595
managerial, 425–53
managers' preferences for form of,
    428
message and, 430
noise and, 430
non-verbal, 428
one-way, 430
oral, 427, 428
overcoming resistance to change
    and, 581
patterns, 572
perceptual processes and, 431
receiver and, 430
semantics and, 434–6
sender and, 430
skills in, 437
styles, conflict and, 589
two-way, 431
upward, 442
verbal, 427
vertical, 441
voice mail, 446
written, 427, 428
communication channels, 440–1
    horizontal, 443
    informal, 444
    multiple, 441–3
    vertical, 441
communication networks, 438–9
    centralised, 439
    chain, 439
    circle, 439
    decentralised, 439
    star, 439
    wheel, 439
    Y, 439
community, social responsibility and,
    100
competence, distinctive, 212

competition
    five competitive forces model and,
        208–9
    operations management strategy
        and, 542
    reducing and resolving conflict and,
        592, 593
    (see also business-level strategies)
competitive advantage, 77, 205
    arguments in favour of managing
        diversity for, 99
    disruption of, 210
    innovation and, 246
    nations, of, 617–18
    new work patterns, 283–4
    Singapore, 643
    sustaining, 567
competitive strategies (see business-
        level strategies)
    requirements for, 222
competitors
    definition, 70
    keeping tabs on, 71–3
    task environment and, 70
    threat of new, 210
complacency, as reaction to problems,
        136
complex environments, 75
complex situations, handling, 494
compressed work-week, 275
compromise, reducing and resolving
        conflict and, 591, 593
computer-based information systems
        (CBISs), 558–60
    developing, 567–9
    hardware, 558–9
    software, 559–60
computer virus, 573
concentration strategies, 214
concentric diversification, 215
conceptual skills, 13, 16, 27
concurrent control, 502–3, 522
concurrent engineering, 247
conflict, 583–98
    benefits and losses, 590–1
    causes of, 589–91
    change, relationship to, 596
    changing views on, 598
    goal differences and, 589
    individuals and organisations,
        between, 584–6
    reducing and resolving, 592–4

    stimulating, 597–8
    structural factors, 587
conformance, quality and, 523
confrontation and negotiation in
        conflict resolution, 595
conglomerate diversification, 215
consideration
    individualised, 402, 416–17
contemporary management theories,
        50–5
content theories of motivation, 368
context characteristics, path–goal
        theory and, 414
Continental Airlines, 505
contingency factors, organisation
        design and, 299
contingency planning, 190
contingency theory, 51
    of leadership (see situational
        theories of leadership)
continuous improvement, quest for,
        23
continuous-process production,
        organisation design and, 314
contraction decisions, 551
control(s)
    accuracy of, 513
    alternatives to, 501
    behavioural displacement and, 512
    benchmarking, 503–5, 527
    bureaucratic, 506–7, 594
    clan, 506, 507
    concurrent, 502–3, 522
    conditions for, 500–1
    cost acceptability of, 500–1
    cost-effective system, 513
    cybernetic, 504
    deciding what to control, 499–501
    determining areas to, 496
    establishing standards, 496–8
    feedback, 503, 522
    feedforward, 502, 522
    financial, 522, 528–33
    flexibility of, 514, 599–601
    formalisation and control stage of
        organisational life cycle and,
        237, 239
    future-oriented system, 513
    game playing and, 512
    incrementalist approach to, 509–10
    information processing and, 557–8
    levels of, 495–6

    levers for strategic control, 508–10,
        516
    managerial implementation, 506–11
    market, 507–8
    MD's diary, 226, 514–15
    measuring performance, 336, 498
    monitorable system, 514
    multi-dimensional system, 513
    multiple control systems, 503–4
    negative attitudes and, 512, 542
    non-cybernetic, 504
    operating delays and, 512
    operational, 496
    outsourcing, 507–8
    overcontrol, 513
    performance v. standards, 498–9
    process feasibility, 501
    process of, 496–502
    promoting innovation and, 508–11
    quality, 522
    role of, 494–5
    significance of process, 493
    span of, 278, 279
    steps in control process, 496–9
    strategic, 494–5, 508–9, 514–15
    subordinate's log, 226, 514–15
    tactical, 496
    timeliness and, 502–4
    types of, 502–5
    undercontrol, 513
    (see also budgetary control,
        financial control, inventory
        control)
control systems, 493, 521–2
    acceptability to members, 515
    assessing, 512–16
    effective, characteristics of, 513–14,
        515
    flexibility of, 514
    overcontrol v. undercontrol, 513
    potential dysfunctional aspects of,
        512
    timely data, importance of, 513
controlling, 492
    definition of, 6, 492, 516
    management function, as a, 492–3
    role of, 494–5
    significance of, 493
    steps in process, 496–9
    (see also control(s); control systems)
convergent thinking, 145
co-opting, 80

co-ordination (*see* horizontal
    co-ordination; vertical
    co-ordination)
co-ordinator role, 463
core job characteristics, 273, 275
Corning Inc, 82
corporate culture
    definition, 82
    (*see also* organisational culture)
corporate-level strategy, 213
    formulating, 213
    grand, 213–14
    portfolio, 217
corporate philanthropy, 101
    philanthropic contributions, 98
corporate social responsibility, 95–102
corporate social responsiveness), 104
    (*see also* social responsiveness)
corrective action, 499, 508
    manager's levers for strategic
        control, 509, 516
corruption and bribery, 659–61
cost(s)
    carrying, 536
    discretionary, 533–4
    fixed and variable, 170
    holding, 536
    inventory, 536
    item, 536
    ordering, 536
    solutions, of, 134
    stockout, 536
    sunk, 141
cost effective control systems, 513
cost leadership, 221, 318, 566
cost leadership strategies, 221–2, 318,
    566
countries
    developed, 614
    less developed (LDCs), 614
    newly industrialised (NICs), 614
creativity
    advertising and, 486–8
    decision making, in, 144–50
    definition, 144
    stages of, 149
    techniques for enhancing group
        creativity, 149–50
creativity-relevant skills, 145
crisis problem, 128
critical events, norms and, 468
critical path method (CPM), 163–5

cross-marketing, 188
cultural differences, 22–3
    leadership styles and, 406, 630
    managing, in work force, 22–3,
        72–3
    managing human resources and,
        627–8
    managing international
        management, 626–30
culture, organisational (*see*
    organisational culture)
currency cross rates, 102
customer(s), 70
    contact, managing, 548–50
    social responsibility and, 99–100
    strategic linkages, 567
    task environment and, 70
customer divisions, 305
customer loyalty programs, 501–3
customer service, 77
cybernetic control systems, 504

D
Daewoo Motors, 91–2
Daiwa Bank, New York office, 494
data, information compared with, 557
data workers, 560
database, 559
database management system, 559–60
debt management ratios, 530, 531–3
decentralisation, 280
    of authority, 281, 495
deciding to decide, as reaction to
    problems, 136
decision(s)
    escalation situations and, 141
    expansion and contraction, 551
decision making, 126, 594
    aids to, 157–70
    alternative solutions in, 133
    avoiding decision-escalation
        phenomenon, 140–1
    break-even analysis, 169–70
    creativity in, 144–50
    decision trees, 168–9
    definition, 126
    directive, 151
    evaluating and choosing alternative,
        133–4
    group, 594
    implementing and monitoring
        chosen solution, 134

managers as decision makers, 130–1
managing conflict, 594
nature of, 127–9
non-rational models of, 130
overcoming barriers to, 135–41
payoff tables and, 167–8
rational model of, 130
recognising biases in, 138
sufficient alternatives in, 137
types of problems faced, 127–8
decision matrix, 167
decision processes
    strategic plan implementation and,
        225
decision-support system (DSS), 564
decision trees, 168–9
decoding, 430
defamation by e-mail, 474
defensive avoidance, as reaction to
    problems, 136
defensive strategies, 215
delegation, 281
    in situational leadership theory, 413
Delphi method, 160–1
Deming, W. Edwards, 53–4, 524–5
democratic leaders, 401
department(s)
    social response mechanism, as, 106
departmentalisation, 319
dependent demand inventory, 546
descriptive decision-making models,
    131
developed countries, 614
devil's advocates, 143
diagnosis stage of problem
    identification, 132, 576–7
dialectical inquiry, 143
differentiation
    innovative, 318, 321
    market, 318
    niche, 318
    organisation design and, 317, 318
    strategic thrust, as, 223, 566
differentiation paradox, 321
differentiation strategies, 223, 566
Digital Equipment Corporation (DEC),
    109
direct contact, lateral relations and,
    290
directive leaders, 414
discretional responsibilities of
    management, 97–8

discretionary expense centre, 533–4
dismissal, 353
distribution models, 166
divergent thinking, 145
diversification, concentric and
    conglomerate, 215
diversification strategies, 215
diversity
    cultural context, 436
    managing, in work force, 22–3,
        72–3, 98–9, 114
    managing, in work groups, 461–2
divestiture strategies, 216, 217
divisional structure, 277, 303–7
    advantages of, 306
    disadvantages of, 306
    forms of, 303, 305
    uses of, 307
dogs, 218
domain-relevant skills, 145
domain shifts, as approach to
    managing environment, 81
dominator role, 463
downsizing, 279
downward communication, 441–2
driving forces, 583
Du Pont, 98–9
Dun & Bradstreet, 66
durability, quality and, 523
dyad, 464
dysfunctional conflict, 596–7
    changes within groups, 597

E
e-commerce
    benefits, 510–11
    growth of, 18
    risks, 210–11
    strategy, 300
e-mail
    misuse in workplace, 474–5
    virtual teams and, 476–7
E-Records, 415
economic element
    definition, 66
    external environment, 66
    international environment, 614
economic order quantity (EOQ),
    536–7
education
    overcoming resistance to change
        and, 581

(*see also* training and development)
effect, law of, 380
effectiveness, of performance, 13
efficiency, of performance, 13–14
elaboration of structure stage of
    organisational life cycle, 237, 239
Electrolux, 68–9
electronic communications policy, 474
electronic mail systems, 445
electronic monitoring, 571
electronic procurement, 510–11
employees, social responsibility and,
    98–9
employment relationship
    dismissal, 353
    flexibility, 351–2
    redundancy, 353
    retrenchment, 353
    termination of, 352
encoding, 430
encourager role, 463
end user, 569
    computing, 569–71
energiser role, 463
enlightened self-interest argument, 96,
    97
enterprise resource planning (ERP)
    companies, 54
entrepreneurial culture, 85
entrepreneurial role, 18
entrepreneurial stage of organisational
    life cycle, 237
entrepreneurial teams, 476
environment(s)
    assessment of, 208–10
    characteristics of, 75–6
    external, defined, 64
    internal, defined, 64
    international (*see* international
        environment)
    mega-environment, 65–8
    (*see also* external environments;
        organisational culture)
environmental bounty, 76
    ethics, and, 113
environmental characteristics, path-
    goal theory and, 413–14
environmental competitiveness, ethics
    and, 112
environmental complexity, 75
environmental conditions, analysis of,
    73–7

environmental dynamism, 75
environmental uncertainty, 75
    assessing degree of, 75–6
equity theory, 377
    implications for managers, 377
    reducing or eliminating inequity
        and, 377
ERG theory, 370
escalation situations, 141
esteem needs, 368
ethical dilemmas, 111
ethical responsibilities of management,
    97–8
ethical standards of managers, 108–10
    career issues, 111
ethics, 103
    code of ethics, 95, 114–15
ethics audits, 115
ethics committees, 115
ethics hotlines, 115
ethics in management, 103, 106–16
    mechanisms for, 114–16
    quandaries, 103
    questionable-payments issue and, 629
    situational factors affecting, 112–14
    solutions, of, 134
    unethical behaviour, 112–14
ethics training, 115
ethnocentric orientation toward
    international management, 611
event, in network diagram, 165
exchange rates, 102–3, 613
executive career derailment, causes
    of, 17
executive-support (information) system
    (ESS), 564–5
executives, individual social response
    mechanism, 105
existence needs, 370
expansion decisions, 551
expatriates, 628
expectancy theory, 374
    combining elements, 375
    components, 374
    effort-performance expectancy
        and, 374
    managerial implications, 376
    performance-outcome expectancy
        and, 375
    valence and, 375
expectations
    goal commitment, 183

expected value, 168, 169
expert power, 399
expert systems, 564
explanatory models, 158–60
explicit statements, norms and, 468
exporting, 620
expropriation, 615
external environments, 64
    adaptation approach to managing,
      78–9
    analysing conditions, 73–7
    characteristics of, 75–6
    definition, 64
    domain shifts in managing, 81
    managing environmental elements,
      78–81
    types of, 64–73
external forces, change and innovation
    and, 235
extinction, 382
extranets, 349
extrinsic rewards, 375

F
facilitation overcoming resistance to
    change and, 581
facilities, 541
    designing and utilising, 551–2
    layout, 552
    location, 551–2
family life
    employees balancing work and,
      98–9, 116
    managers balancing work and,
      20–1, 116
favourability influence, as approach to
    managing environment, 79–81
Fayol, Henri, 40–1, 58
feasibility
    control process, of, 500
    solutions, of, 133
features, quality control and, 523
feedback, 522
    communication, in, 430, 437
    conflict and, 590
    core job characteristic, as, 274
    systems theory, in, 50
feedback control, 503, 522
feedforward control, 502, 522
Fiedler's contingency theory, 407
    LPC (least preferred co-worker)
      and, 407

matching leadership style and
    situation and, 408
    situational factors and, 407
financial control, 522, 528–33
    comparative financial analysis,
      532–3
    financial statements, 528–30
    ratio analysis, 530–32
financial goals, 532
financial statements, 528
finished-goods inventory, 535
first-line managers, 14–15, 25
five competitive forces model, 208–9
fixed costs, 170
fixed-interval schedule of
    reinforcement, 382–3
fixed-position layout, 552
fixed-ratio schedule of reinforcement,
    383
flat structure, 278
flexible employees, 352
flexible work, 350–1
flexitime, 274
focus strategies, 223
Follett, Mary Parker, 43, 58
follower role, 463
Forbes magazine study, 74
force-field analysis, overcoming
    resistance to change, 583–4
Ford Motor Company, 22, 52, 60–1,
    92
    downsizing, 279–80
forecasting, 157
    choosing method for, 161–2
    judgmental, 161
    qualitative, 160–1
    quantitative, 157–60
    technological, 160–1
formal communication, 444
formal groups, 457–8
    diagrams, 458, 459
formalisation, 277
formalisation and control stage of
    organisational life cycle, 237, 239
forming stage of group development,
    470
forward integration, 215
framing, 139
free riding, 464
Fresh-Direct, 147
frustration-regression principle, 370
functional authority, 283

functional conflict, 596
functional divisions, worldwide, 623–4
functional-level strategy, 223
functional managers, 19
functional structure, 277, 301–3
    advantages of, 302
    disadvantages of, 302–3
    divisional structures, versus, 304
    functions and, 301
    uses of, 303
fundamental attribution error, 434
future-oriented control systems, 513

G
Gantt, Henry L., 38, 58
Gantt charts, 163–3
gatekeeper role, 463
General Electric, 190, 191
general managers, 19
General Motors, 15, 52, 92, 107, 108–9
geocentric orientation toward
    international management, 613
geographic divisions, 303, 625
Gilbreth, Frank and Lillian, 37–8, 58
global matrix structure, 625, 627
global perspective, development of, 21
global problems and social
    responsibilities, 101
globalisation, 621–2
    automotive industry, 60–1
    virtual teams and, 476–7
    (*see also* international management)
globalisation strategy, 621–2
goal, 173
    (*see also* organisational goals)
goal attainment, conflict and, 590
goal commitment, 183–4
goal content, 181
goal incongruence, controlling and,
    497–8
goal-setting theory, 378
government agencies, task environment
    and, 73
grapevine, 444–5, 447
group(s)
    command, 457
    communication networks, and (*see*
      communication networks)
    conflict within, 586
    decision making (*see* group decision
      making)
    definition of, 457

development of (*see* group
   development)
formal, 457–60
heterogeneous, 461
informal, 458–61
management of, 493
managing diversity in, 461–2
size of, 464–5
stages of, 470–6
(*see also* work groups)
group cohesiveness, 468–70
   benefits from conflict, 590
   consequences of, 468–9
   determinants of, 470
group decision making, 141–4
   advantages and disadvantages of,
      141–2
   computer assisted, 143–4, 564
   enhancing process of, 142–3
group decision-support system (GDSS),
      564
group development, 470–2
   adjourning stage in, 471
   forming stage in, 470
   norming stage in, 470
   performing stage in, 471
   storming stage in, 470
group maintenance roles, 463
group management, 456–88
   (*see also* work group)
group norms, 467–8
group observer role, 463
group pressure, goal commitment, 183
group size, 464
   conflict and, 587
   interactions and, 464
   performance and, 464–5
group task roles, 463
groupthink, 142
groupware, 143, 446, 563
growth needs, 274, 370

H
hackers, 573
halo effect, and communication, 432
hand of government
   definition, 96
   economic and legal responsibilities
      of management, 97
   ethical and discretionary
      responsibilities of management,
      97–8

perspective on social responsibility,
      96
hand of management
   definition, 96
   economic and legal responsibilities
      of management, 97, 281
   ethical and discretionary
      responsibilities of management,
      97–8, 281
   perspective on social responsibility, 96
hardware, computer, 558–9
Harley-Davidson, 99–100
harmoniser role, 463
harvest and/or divest strategies, 216
Hawthorne studies, 44–6
   impact of, 45–6, 58
Henley Clothing Company, 24
heterogeneous work group, 461
hierarchy
   span of management and, 278
hierarchy of needs theory, 368
high-context cultures, 436
holding cost, 536
home-country orientation toward
      international management, 611
Honeywell, 102
horizontal communication, 443
horizontal co-ordination, 287
   informational systems and, 288
   lateral relations and, 289
   methods, 288
   slack resources and, 287
horizontal dimension of manager's
      responsibility, 19
horizontal integration, concentration
      strategies and, 214
host-country orientation toward
      international management, 611
   indigenisation laws, 615
human relations movement, 46–7
human resource management (HRM),
      330–61
   cultural diversity and, 627–8
   definition of, 330
   extranets, 349
   Internet and, 349
   intranets, 349
   MD's diary, 354
   unions and, 331
human resource planning, 335
human resources
   acquisition of, 335

change, and, 253
   functional structure, and, 302
   in strategy implementation, 225
human skills, 13, 16–17
   definition, 13
humour in the workplace, 473–4
hybrid structure, 277, 307–9
   advantages of, 307
   disadvantages of, 307
   uses of, 309
hygiene factors, 369
hypercompetition, 210

I
IBM, 74, 80
idea champion, 18, 249, 321
Ikea, 111–2
illumination stage of creativity, 149
immoral management, 107
implementing and monitoring chosen
      solution, 134
import quotas, 615
incentives, goal commitment, 183–4
income statement, 530
incremental model of managerial
      decision making, 131
incrementalist approach to control,
      509–10
incubation stage of creativity, 149
independent demand inventory, 542
indigenisation laws, 615
individualised consideration, 402,
      416–17
individualism
   work groups, in, 465
individualism–collectivism dimension,
      in international environment, 616
Indonesia, 648–50
   directions for the future, 649–50
   management issues, 648–9
   overseas labour force, 373
   relationships with Australia, 650
   relevance of management to society,
      648–9
industrial relations, recent history of
   Australia, 331–3
   New Zealand, 333–4
industrial relations legislation
   Australia, 334
   New Zealand, 334
inequity, reducing or eliminating, 377
influence (*see* power)

informal communication, 444
informal groups, 458–9
    development of, 460
    diagrams, 458, 459, 460
informal leader, 464
information architecture, 560
information-giver role, 463
information power, 399
information-seeker role, 463
information systems, 558
    computer-based (CBIS), 557, 558–9
    data v. information, 557
    horizontal co-ordination, 288
    information processing and, 557–8
    management information systems,
        49, 557–74
    nature of, 557–8
    organisation structure, 571
    organisational risk and, 572
    promoting innovation, 565
    resistance, 574
    types, 562
information technology, 21
infrastructure, 614
initiating structure, 402
initiator-contributor role, 463
innovation, 18, 234–5
    competitive advantage, for, 246
    control and, 508–10
    cultural barriers to, 236
    definition, 18, 235
    differentiation paradox and, 321
    entrepreneurship and, 18
    ethics and, 102
    forces for, 235–6
    horizontal co-ordination, 287
    intrapreneurship and, 249–50
    MD's diary, 254
    organisational, 235
    processes of, 241
    promoting (see promoting
        innovation)
    reservations and, 321
innovative differentiation, 318
inputs
    information processing and, 558
    systems theory, in, 50
institutional power, 372
integration
    backward, 215
    forward, 215
    horizontal, 214

organisation design and, 317, 318
vertical, 214–15
intellectual stimulation, 419
interactive monitoring systems, 509
intergroup
    conflict, types of, 596
    training for conflict resolution, 595
internal environment, 81–7
    definition, 64
    (see also organisational culture)
internal forces, change and innovation
    and, 235
international business, 610, 623–6
    changing character of, 610
    organising, 623–6
international community, social
    responsibility and, 101
international divisions, 624–5
international element, in external
    environment, 68
international (mega) environment
    assessing, 614–17
    diagram, 67
    economic element of, 66
    international element, 68
    legal-political element of, 67, 613
    sociocultural element of, 68, 615–16
    technological element of, 65,
        616–17
international management, 609–37
    changing character of international
        business and, 610
    competitive advantage of nations
        and, 617–18
    cultural differences and, 626–7
    environment of (see international
        environment)
    geographic regions and, 625
    global matrix and, 625, 627
    international division structure and,
        624–5
    leadership styles and, 630
    orientations toward, 611–12
    questionable-payments issue, 631
    strategic issues in (see international
        strategy)
    worldwide functional divisions and,
        623–4
    worldwide product divisions and,
        624
international strategy
    methods of entry and, 620–1

multinational corporations and,
    621–2
Internet, 349
    bill paying, 144
    buying and selling goods, 18,
        510–11
    classified advertising, 188
    corporate portal, 54
    electronic communication, 445
    horizontal co-ordination, 288
    LEXIS/NEXIS, 66
    Peakhour, 83
    personal use in workplace, 474–5
    reinvention of manufacturers as
        service providers, 68–9
    TTWIN, 85–6
    virtual teams and, 476–7
interpreting, in perception, 431
    conflict and, 589
interview
    conducting an effective, 340
    performance appraisal, 336
    selection, 339
intranets, 349
intrapreneur(s), 18, 249
intrapreneurial ideas checklist, 250
intrapreneurial roles, 249
intrapreneurship, 18
    innovation and, 249–50
intrinsic rewards, 375
inventory, 535
    dependent demand, 544
    finished-goods, 535
    independent demand, 546
    raw materials, 535
    significance of, 535–6
    work-in-process, 535
inventory control, 522, 535–8
    costs of inventory and, 536
    just-in-time (JIT), 537–8
    significance of inventory and, 5
        35–6
investment centre(s), 534
invisible hand
    definition, 96
    economic and legal responsibilities
        of management, 97
    ethical and discretionary
        responsibilities of management,
        97–8
    perspective on social responsibility,
        96

involvement, overcoming resistance to change and, 581
iron law of responsibility, 96, 97
irregularities, detecting, 494
issues management, 104–5
item cost, 536

J
Japan, 655–7
  impact on the region, 655–6
  relationship with Australia, 656–7
Japanese management, 52–3, 58, 60
jargon, professional, 435
job(s)
  core job characteristics and, 273–5
  information technology and, 571–2
  managerial (*see* managerial job types)
  nature of, 571
job analysis, 335–6
  methods, 336
  process, 335
job characteristics model, 273, 275
  motivational value, 274
job depth, 273
job design, 271, 336
  alternative work schedules and, 274
  approaches to, 271–2
  job enlargement and, 273
  job enrichment and, 273
  job rotation and, 273
  job simplification and, 271, 273
job enlargement, 273
job enrichment, 273
job rotation, 273
job scope, 273
job sharing, 275
job simplification, 271, 273
John Deere, 102
joint ventures, 80–1
judgmental forecasting, 161
jury of executive opinion, 161
just-in-time (JIT) inventory control, 537–8

K
Kanban, 535
key management skills, 7, 12, 13, 16, 27
kinesic behaviour, 428
knowledge base, management, 7, 12–13
knowledge-work systems (KWS), 563

knowledge workers, 560
Korean automobile manufacturer, 91–2

L
La Prospective, 161
labour force by birthplace, 72
labour-management relations in Australia, 331–4
labour-management relations in New Zealand, 333–4
labour supply, 72–3
laissez-faire leaders, 401
large-batch production, organisation design and, 314
lateral relations, 289
  direct contact and, 290
  liaison roles and, 290
  managerial integrators and, 291
  task forces and teams and, 290
law of effect, 380
leader(s)
  achievement-oriented, 414
  autocratic, 401
  cultural change and, 406
  democratic, 401
  directive, 414
  informal, 464
  laissez-faire, 401
  participative, 414
  power, effective use of, 399
  role of, 462–3
  sources of power for, 399
  supportive, 414
  traits of, 400
  transactional, 416
  transformational, 416
leader behaviour
  behaviours in, 401
  choosing, 414
  female v. male, 404
  Iowa and Michigan studies of, 401
  Ohio State studies of, 402–4
  path-goal theory and, 413–414
  situational theories and, 407
leader, role of, 463–4
leadership, 398–424
  boss-centred, 402
  cultural differences and, 406
  Fiedler's contingency model of, 407
  grid, 404, 405
  international business and, 630
  MD's diary, 419–20

meetings, of, 472–3
normative model of, 131, 409
organisational life cycle and, 418
path-goal theory of, 413
styles across cultures, 406
subordinate-centred, 402
transformational, 416
  (*see also* leader(s); power)
leading
  definition, 5
  meeting, 472–3
leading indicators, 160
legal-political element, 67
  external environment, in, 67–8
  international environment, 615
legal responsibilities of management, 97, 281
legitimate power, 398
less developed countries (LDCs), 614
Levi Strauss, 102, 106
liaison roles, 290
  lateral relations and, 290
licensing, 620
life cycle(s), organisational, 236
  stages of, 237
life-cycle portfolio matrix, 218
line authority, 283
  managerial integrators and, 291
line position, 282, 284
  conflict, 588
linear programming (LP), 166
liquidation
  organisational termination, 240
  strategies, 216, 217
liquidity ratios, 530, 531
listening skills, 437
local-area networks (LAN), 561
local community, social responsibility and, 100
Lockheed Martin Corp, 106, 163
  ethics game, 118
logical office, 572
long-range capacity planning, 544
long-term orientation, 616
low-context cultures, 436
LPC orientation, 407
Luxottica Group S.p.A., 494

M
McCulloch Corporation, 108
McDonald's
  breakfast service, 13

McDonald's, continued
  control systems, 493, 498, 490–1
  corporate creed, 82
  joint venture, 81
  toys promotion, 119–20
McGregor, Douglas, 46–8, 58
  Theory X and Theory Y, 46–7, 58
Malaysia, 651–3
  decision-making practices, 652
  directions for the future, 652–3
  issues for managers, 651–2
  multiculturalism, 652
  relationship with Australia, 653
management
  administrative, 40–1, 85
  amoral, 108
  behavioural viewpoint, 42–8, 55
  bureaucratic, 38–9, 594
  challenge of, 112
  change, and innovation process, 241
  classical theories, 36–41, 55
  contemporary viewpoints, 49–55, 404
  contingency theory of, 51
  definition of, 5
  discretional responsibilities of, 97–8
  ethical responsibilities of, 97–8
  functions of, 6, 7, 16
  hand-of-management perspective on social responsibility and, 96
  Hawthorne studies of, 44–6, 58
  hierarchical levels of, 14–16
  human relations movement, 46–7
  human resources (*see* human resource management)
  immoral, 107
  Indonesia, 648–9
  international (*see* international management)
  issues, 104–5
  Japanese, 52–3, 58, 60
  Malaysia, 651–2
  moral, 108
  New Zealand, 646
  operations (*see* operating systems; operations management)
  performance and, 336
  personal contact, 77
  preclassical theories of, 33–5
  process of, 6–7
  production-operations (*see* operations management)

quantitative viewpoint of, 48–9, 55
  responsibilities of, 281
  scientific, 36–8, 49
  Singapore, 643
  skills, development of, 345
  span of, 278
  strategic (*see* strategic management)
  styles, 56, 57
  systems theory of, 50–1
  Thailand, 654–5
  theories of (*see* management theories)
management by exception, 498–9
management by objectives (MBO), 191
  assessing, 194
  steps in, 192–4
  strengths and weaknesses of, 194
management-information system (MIS), 49, 557–74
  definition, 49, 563
management science, 49
  (*see also* operations research)
management skills, 7, 12, 13, 16, 27
management theories, 33–55
  acceptance theory of authority, 40
  behavioural, 42–8, 55
  classical, 36–41, 55
  contemporary, 49–55
  evolution of, 33
  major contributions of, 55
  preclassical, 33–5
  quantitative, 48–9, 55
  Theory Z, 52–3, 58
manager(s)
  activities and responsibilities of, 281
  balancing work and family, 20–1
  causes of executive career derailment, 17
  communication and (*see* communication)
  competitive advantage's implications for, 619
  decisional roles, 10
  effective, 400
  equity theory's implications for, 377
  ethical (*see* managerial ethics)
  ethical guidelines for, 108–10
  first-line, 14–15, 25
  functional, 19
  future trends and, 21–2
  general, 19
  informational roles, 10
  interpersonal roles, 10

job types of (*see* managerial job types)
  key management skills, 7, 12, 13, 16, 27
  knowledge base, 7, 12–13
  middle, 14, 15, 19
  need-profile of successful, 372
  network building, 8–12
  product, 19
  roles of, 9–10
  social response mechanism, 106
  social responsibilities of, 97
  sponsor of innovation, 19
  top, 14, 15, 19
  work methods of, 7–8
managerial communication (*see* communication)
managerial ethics, 95, 106–16
  guidelines for, 108–10
  mechanisms for, 114–5
  quandaries, 103
  situational factors affecting, 112–14
  types of, 107–8
managerial integrators, lateral relations and, 291
  line authority, 291
managerial job types, 14–17
  hierarchical levels, 14–17
managerial roles, 9–10
managerial work agendas, 7, 11–12
  definition, 11
managing in the 21st century
  continuous improvement, quest for, 23
  diversity in work force, 22–3, 72–3, 99, 114
  global perspective, development of, 21, 99
  total quality, quest for, 23
manipulation, overcoming resistance to change, 581
manufacturing
  virtualisation of, 508
manufacturing organisations
  service organisations compared with, 540–1
  technology and (*see* technology)
manufacturing resource planning (MRP II), 548
market control, 507
market development, 214
market differentiation, 318

Maslow, Abraham, 46, 48, 58, 368
master production schedule (MPS), 546
    advantages, 546
materials requirements planning
        (MRP), 546–8
    benefits, 548
    inputs, 547
matrix of service characteristics, 549
matrix structure, 277, 309–12
    advantages of, 311
    disadvantages of, 311
    stages of, 310
    when to consider, 311–12
mechanistic characteristics,
        organisation design and, 317
medium of communication, 430
medium-range capacity planning, 542
    agenda, 472
    leading, 472–3
    objectives, 472
mega-environment, 65–8
    diagram, 67
    economic element of, 66
    international element, 68
    legal-political element of, 67, 615
    sociocultural element of, 68, 615–16
    technological element of, 65, 616–17
merger, 215
    organisational termination, 240
message, 430
Metarlong, 462
Microsoft, 74, 144
Minolta, 105
mission, organisational, 173–4
mission statement, 173–4
misunderstanding, resistance to change
        and, 579
modelling, 386
Monsanto, 105
moral management, 108
motivation, 366–95
    cognitive theories and, 374, 378
    goals and, 378
    MD's diary, 387–8
    need (content) theories of, 368
    process, 367
    reinforcement theory of, 380
    social learning theory of, 385, 386
motivation stage of modelling, 386
motivators, 369
multi-dimensional control systems, 513
multifocal strategy, 622

multiple control systems, 501–2
Munsterberg, Hugo, 42–3, 58

N
NAFTA (North American Free Trade
        Agreement), 68
national advantage, diamond of,
        618–19
national responsiveness strategy, 622
natural selection model, 74
need for achievement (nAch), 371
need for affiliation (nAffl), 372
need for power (nPow), 372
    institutional power, 372
    personal power, 372
need theories of motivation, 368
    assessing, 373
needs analysis, for training and
        development, 344
negative attitudes, control systems and,
        512, 542
negative entropy, 51
negative reinforcement, 381
negative synergy, 467
negotiating
    contracts, 80
    overcoming resistance to change
        and, 581
Nestle, 108
NetComm, 474
network(s)
    building, 8–12
    communication (see communication
        networks)
    definition, 8
    local area (LAN), 561
    verbal contacts and, 8
    wide area (WAN), 561
network diagram, 164
networked structure, 312, 626
neutralisers, 418
new entrants, threat of, 210
new venture teams, 321
new venture units, 321
New Zealand, 645–8
    competitors, 645
    customers and clients, 645
    economic reforms, 645
    Fisher and Paykel and EDWT,
        483–6
    issues confronting New Zealand
        managers, 646

labour relations, 646
labour supply, 645
relationship with Asia, 645–7
relationship with Australia, 647–8
skill levels, 646
social problems, 646
supplier, 645
workplace reform, 646
newly industrialised countries (NICs),
        614
NGOs (non-government organisations),
        56
niche differentiation, 318
node, in network diagram, 165
noise, in communication, 430
nominal group technique (NGT), 150
non-crisis problem, 128
non-cybernetic control systems, 504
non-government organisations (NGOs),
        56
non-profit organisation, 6
non-programmed decisions, 129
non-rational escalation, 141
non-rational models of managerial
        decision making, 130
non-verbal communication, 428
norm(s)
    surfacing actual norms, 86
normative decision-making models,
        409–10
normative leadership model, 131, 409
norming stage of group development,
        470
North American Free Trade Agreement
        (NAFTA), 68
not-for-profit organisation, 6
    ethics and environmental
        competitiveness, 112

O
object language, 428
office-automation systems (OAS), 563
Ohio State studies on leadership,
        402–4
one-way communication, 430
open system, 51
operant conditioning (see
        reinforcement theory)
operating budgets, 534–5
operating systems, 541
    aggregate production planning and,
        545

operating systems, continued
  capacity planning, 543–5
  forecasting and, 543
  purchasing and, 548–9
  scheduling and, 546
operational control, 496
operational goals, 176–8
operational plans, 186
operations management, 49
  definition of, 49, 539
  facilities (*see* facilities)
  manufacturing v. service
    organisations, 540–1
  operations strategy, 541–2
  process, 541
  process technology and, 541, 552–5
  productivity and, 539–40
  productivity improvement and,
    555–6
  service delivery system, 549–50
  (*see also* operating systems)
operations strategy, formulating, 541–2
opinion surveys, 104
opportunities
  identifying, 494
  in SWOT analysis, 208
opportunity problem, 128
oral communication, 427, 428
orchestrator, 19
ordering costs, 536
organic characteristics, organisation
  design and, 317
organisation(s), 5
  assessment of, 211
  capabilities of, 211
  change and 21st century, 22–3, 252
  competitive advantage's implications
    for, 212, 617
  culture of (*see* organisational
    culture)
  definition, 5
  design of (*see* organisation design)
  development of (*see* organisational
    development)
  goals of (*see* organisational goals)
  interface with environment, 73–5
  life cycle of (*see* organisational life
    cycles)
  not for profit, 6, 112
  resources of (*see* resources)
  structure of (*see* organisation
    structure)

systems view of, 50
  total quality, quest for, 23
organisation chart, 267–9
organisation design, 267, 299
  contingency factors and, 299
  factors influencing, 578
  structure and (*see* organisation
    structure)
organisation structure, 265
  change and, 252
  contingency factors in, 314
  definition of, 252, 267
  departmentalisation and, 276, 319
  designing, 298
  divisional, 277, 303–7
  elaboration-of-structure stage of
    organisational life cycle and,
    237, 239
  emerging, 312
  environment and, 317
  factors influencing, 576
  flat, 278
  flexible, 351
  franchising, 269–70
  functional, 277, 301–3
  horizontal co-ordination methods
    and, 287
  human resource components, 253
  hybrid, 277
  information technology and, 21, 569
  job design and, 271
  matrix, 83–4, 277, 309–12
  mechanistic, 317
  nature of, 267
  networked, 312, 624
  organic, 317
  process, 312
  promoting innovation using, 320,
    508–10
  size and, 316
  strategic plan implementation and,
    225
  systems development approach and,
    571
  tall, 278
  technological components, 253, 314
  vertical co-ordination and, 277
organisational citizenship behaviours,
  468
organisational culture, 64, 254
  changing, 77, 86–7
  definition, 64, 254

diagram, 66
  entrepreneurial characteristics, 85
  leaders' influence on, 87–8
  manifestations of, 82–6
  nature of, 81–2
organisational culture change, 77,
  86–7, 254
organisational development (OD), 244,
  255
  diagnosis and, 245
  evaluation and, 245
  intervention and, 245
organisational goals, 173
  attainable, 181
  benefits of, 174–6
  challenging, 181
  commitment to, 183–4
  content of, 181
  effectiveness, 13
  efficiency, 13–14
  linking with plans, 185–8
  measurable, 181
  nature of, 174–85
  operational, 176–8
  organisational citizenship
    behaviours and, 468
  problems with, 185
  process components affecting,
    184–5
  relevant, 181
  setting, 181–3
  specific, 181, 192
  strategic, 176–8
  tactical, 176–8
  time horizons of, 187–8, 546
  time-limited, 181
  work behaviour, 184
organisational life cycles, 236
  leadership and, 418
  organisational termination and,
    236, 240
  stabilisation and decline, 240
  stages of, 237
organisational mission, 173–4
organisational problems, 132
  identifying, 132–3
organisational requirements, demand
  for human resources and, 253
organisational risk, information
  technology and, 572
organisational social responsibility,
  95–103

organisational social responsiveness, 104–6
organisational termination, 236, 240
organising, 5
  definition, 5
  international business, 610, 623–6
orienter role, 463
output(s)
  information processing and, 558
  systems theory, in, 50
outsourcing, 507–8, 570
overconfident bias, 140
overcontrol, 513
Owen, Robert, 33, 34, 57

P
panic, as reaction to problems, 136
paralanguage, 428
partial-factor productivity, 540
participation
  conflict and, 587
  goal commitment, 184
  overcoming resistance to change and, 581
  situational leadership theory and, 413
participative leaders, 414
path–goal theory, 413–415
  leader behaviours and, 414
  situational factors and, 414
payoff, 113, 167
payoff tables, 167–8
  expected value, 168
peer pressure and goal commitment, 183
PeopleSoft, 54
perception(s)
  communication in, 431
perceptual defence, 432
performance
  comparing against standards, 336, 496–7
  how goals facilitate, 180–5
  management and, 7, 13–14
  measuring, control and, 336, 498
  positive, recognition of, 380, 499
  pressure for, ethics and, 112–13
  quality, 523
  relationship to ability, motivation and working conditions, 367
performance appraisal, 336, 347
  feedback, 348
  methods for, 347

performance–outcome expectancy, 375
performance management systems, 509
performing stage of group development, 471
personal behaviour and conflict, 589
personal power, 372
PERT (program evaluation and review technique), 163–5
philanthropy, 98
  corporate philanthropy, defined, 101
physiological needs, 368
plan(s), 173
  categorised by extent of recurring use, 186–7
  levels of, 185–6
  linking with goals, 185–8
  operational, 186
  single-use, 186
  standing, 187
  strategic, 185–6
  tactical, 186
  time horizons of, 187–8, 542–3, 546
planned change, 241
planning, 5
  aids to, 157–70
  capacity, 543–4
  capacity-requirements, 545
  components of, 173
  definition, 5
  goals, 173
  human resource (*see* human resource planning)
  linear programming, 166
  organisational mission, 173–4
  overall process of, 173–4
  potential obstacles to, 190
  production, aggregate, 545
  projects, 162–5
  promoting innovation, 188–9
  queuing models, 166
  routing models, 166
  simulation models, 166
  techniques, 165–6
  (*see also* organisational goals)
planning staff, 190
policy, 187
political activity, 81
political element
  external environment, in, 67–8
  international environment, in, 613
political payments, questionable, 631

political risk, in international environment, 615
polycentric orientation toward international management, 611
pooled interdependence, 315
population ecology model, 73–4
portal, 54
portfolio matrix, 217–20
  assessment of, 220
portfolio strategy approaches, 217
position power, Fiedler's contingency theory, 408
positive reinforcement, 380
positive synergy, 467
power
  coercive, 399
  conflict and, 588
  effective use of, by leaders, 400
  empowerment, 399–400
  expert, 399
  information, 399
  institutional, 372
  leadership, 398
  legitimate, 398
  need for (nPow), 372
  personal, 372
  position, Fiedler's contingency theory and, 407
  referent, 399
  reward, 398
power distance, in international environment, 616
preclassical management theories, 33–6
preparation stage of creativity, 149
price, competitive, 77
primacy, 468
privacy issues, 573
problem(s)
  crisis, 128
  non-crisis, 128
  opportunity, 128
  solving (*see* decision making)
problem child, 218
procedure, 187
process consultation, 245
process layout, 552, 553
process structure, 312
process technology (*see* technology)
process theories of motivation, 367
processing batch, 314
  information processing and, 558
product(s), substitute, threat of, 210

product development
    concentration strategies, 214
    principles, 246–9
    sequential and parallel development
        processes, 249
product divisions, 303
    worldwide, 624
product layout, 552, 554
product liability, social responsibility
        and, 99–100
product/market evolution matrix,
        218–19
production-operations management
        (see operations management)
productivity, 539–40
    improving, 555–6
    lost productivity and use of Internet,
        474
    operations management and, 539
    partial-factor, 540
    total-factor, 540
professional jargon, 435
profit centres, 534
profitability ratios, 530, 532
program, 186
program evaluation and review
        technique (PERT), 163–5
programmed decisions, 128
project(s), 187
    planning and control models for,
        162–3
project managers, 19
projection, 432
promoting innovation, 18, 55
    adaptive, entrepreneurial culture,
        by, 83–5
    change and innovation process and,
        21–2
    competitive advantage and, 246
    control and, 508–11
    creativity factor in decision making,
        144–50
    entrepreneurial role, 18
    idea champion, 18, 249, 321
    planning process role, 188–9
    process technology and, 541, 552–5
    qualitative forecasting, 160–1
    social responsibility and, 102
    task forces and teams and, 290,
        475–7
    technological forecasting and,
        160–1

transformational leadership and,
        416–417
prospect theory, 139
prototyping, 569
proxemics, 428
public affairs department, 106
public display, goal commitment, 183
public relations, 79–80
punishment, 382

Q
Qantas, 135, 501–2
qualitative forecasting, 160–1
quality, 523
    competing on, 524
    controlling (see quality control)
    criterion in decision making, 134
    dimensions of, 523–4
    perceived, 524
    strategic implications, 421–2
quality control, 522
    Deming's 14 points to improve, 53,
        524–5
    statistical aids to, 527
    total quality management (TQM),
        23, 32, 53, 58, 520, 514–8
quality improvement teams, 526
quantitative aids for decision making,
        167–70
quantitative forecasting, 157–60
    explanatory methods for, 158–60
    time-series methods for, 157–8
quantitative theories of management,
        48–9, 55
quapple, 82
question marks, 218
questionable-payments issue, 631
queuing (waiting-line) models, 166
quotas, import, 615

R
ratio analysis, 530
rational model of managerial decision
        making, 130
rationalisation, 621
rationing, 79
raw materials inventory, 535
reactive change, 241
receiver, 430
reciprocal interdependence, 316
reciprocity
    definition, 8

recognition-seeker role, 463
recruitment, 336–8
    contractors, 338
    executive, 338
    external, 80, 337
    internal, 337
    international business, 628
    interviews (see interview)
    processes, 337
    selection methods, 336, 338, 339
Red Earth, 138
redundancy, 353
re-engineering, 553–4
referent power, 399
regiocentric orientation towards
        international management, 612
regional context, 639–60
    Australia's position in South-East
        Asia, 657–8
    Indonesia, 648–50
    Japan, 655–7
    Malaysia, 651–3
    New Zealand, 645–8
    Singapore, 642–4
    Thailand, 643–5
regional responsiveness strategy, 622
regression models, 159–60
reinforcement theory, 380–4
    behaviourism, 380
    extinction and, 382
    negative reinforcement and, 381
    positive reinforcement and, 380
    punishment and, 382
    schedules of reinforcement and, 382
    situations, 381
    using, 384
relatedness needs, 370
relational skills, international business
        and, 629
relationship behaviour, situational
        leadership theory and, 412
reliability
    quality control and, 523
    selection, in, 339
remuneration, 336, 343
reorder point (ROP), 536
repatriation, 629–30
representativeness, 139
reproduction stage of modelling, 386
reservations, innovation and, 321
resource(s)
    competitive implications of, 211

expansion of, 594
expected resource flow, 500
high dependence on, 500
imitability of, 212
interdependence, conflict and, 588
organisation of, 212
rarity of, 211
slack, 287
value of, 211
resource dependence, 499–500
resource dependence model, 74–5, 500
definition, 74
responsibility, 281, 479–80
responsibility centres, 533–4
uses of, 534
restraining forces, 583
restructuring, 279
retention stage of modelling, 386
retrenchment strategies, 353
revenue centres, 534
reversibility, of solutions, 134
revitalisation, 239
reward
extrinsic and intrinsic, 375
goal commitment, 183–4
power, 398
reward structures, conflict and, 589
reward systems
conflict, 588
strategic plan implementation, 225
risk, 129
outsourcing of physical
manufacturing, 508
rites, organisational culture and, 83
rivalry, 209
competitive advantage and, 209
roles
definition, 9
entrepreneurial, 18
flexibility in, 479–80
group leaders, 463–4
group maintenance, 463
group members, of, 462–3
group task, 463–4
informal leader, 464
intrapreneurs, 18, 249
intrapreneurship, 18, 249
liaison, lateral relations and, 290
managers, of, 7, 9–10, 25
self-oriented, 463
vital for promoting innovation, 320
work group, 462–3

routing (distribution) models, 166
rubbish-bin model of decision making,
131
rule, 187

S
sabotage and security breaches, 573
safety needs, 368
sales commissions, questionable, 631
sales-force composite, 161
satisfaction-progression principle, 370
satisficing model of managerial
decision making, 131
scanning stage of problem
identification, 132
scenario analysis, 161
schedules of reinforcement, 382
fixed interval, 382–3
fixed ratio, 383
variable interval, 383
variable ratio, 383–4
scheduling, 546
science research, 48
scientific management, 36–8
selection, 336, 339
devices, 339
international business and, 629
process, 339
validity of selection methods and,
339
selection interview, 339
self-actualisation needs, 368
self-control, 386
self-efficacy, 385
self-interest, resistance to change and,
579
self-managing teams, 476
self-oriented roles, 463
self-serving bias, 434
selling, situational leadership theory
and, 413
semantic blocks, 434–5
semantic net, 434
semantics, 434–6
sender, 430
sequential interdependence, 316
service delivery system, 549–50
customer contact, 549–50
matrix of service characteristics, 549
service organisations
manufacturing operations compared
with, 540–1

serviceability, quality and, 524
services, substitute, threat of, 210
shaping, 380
shareholders, social responsibility
and, 98
short-range capacity planning, 544–5
short-term orientation, 616
simulation models, 166
Singapore
call-back operations, 213
directions for the future, 643–4
economic restructure, 643
human resource development and
management, 359, 643
information technology, 326–7
management issues, 643
National Productivity Council
(NPC), 642
National Wages Council (NWC),
642
productivity and quality of work
life, 643
relationship with Australia, 644
retraining and retrenchment, 358
Skills Development Fund (SDF), 642
Skills Redevelopment Program
(SRP), 358
tight labour market, 643
single-use plans, 186
situational factors
ethical behaviour, influencing,
112–14
Fiedler's contingency theory and,
407
path–goal theory and, 414
reducing and resolving conflict and,
592
situational theories of leadership, 407,
412–13
Fiedler's contingency model, 407
normative leadership model, 131,
409
path–goal theory, 413
situational leadership theory,
412–13
size
conflict and, 587
group interaction and, 464
optimum management group, 464–5
organisation design and, 316
skill variety, as core job characteristic,
273

skills
   communication, 437
   conceptual, 13, 16–17, 27
   creativity-relevant, 145
   domain-relevant, 145
   human, 13, 16–17, 27
   key management, 7, 12, 13, 16, 27
   listening, 437
   technical, 13, 16–17, 27
   variety in, 273
slack, 165
slack resources, 287
small-batch production, organisation
   design and, 314
SMEs (small and medium enterprises),
   83
smoothing, 79, 594
social audits, 104
social forecasting, 104
social learning theory, 385
   self-control and, 386
   symbolic processes and, 385
   using, 386
   vicarious learning and, 385–6
social loafing, 464–5
social responsibility
   customers and, 99–100
   employees and, 98–9
   financial performance and, 101
   global community and, 101
   impact on financial success, 101
   international community, 101, 630–1
   local community and, 101
   management, of, 97
   organisational, 95–101
   perspectives on, 95–7
   promoting innovation and, 102
   shareholders and, 98
   social stakeholders, 98–101, 102
   society and, 100
social responsiveness, 104
   corporate, 104
   internal mechanisms for, 105–6
   monitoring social demands and
      expectations and, 104–5
   organisational, 104–6
social scanning, 105
socialist economy, 66
society, social responsibility and, 100
sociocultural element
   international environment, in, 68,
      615–6

software, computer, 559–60
   applications software packages, 569
span of management (span of control),
   278
   factors influencing, 278
sponsor, 19
stability strategies, 215
staff positions, 282, 284
   conflict, 588
staffing
   recruitment and, 336–8
   selection and, 336, 339
stage-gate development funnel, 246–7
Standard & Poor, 67
standard(s)
   adjusting, 499
   comparing performance against,
      498–9
   employee behaviour and, 497–8
   establishing, for control process,
      496–8
standard cost centres, 533
standard operating procedures (SOPs),
   187
standard setter role, 463
standing committee, 458
star(s), 218
star network, 439
statistical process control, 527
stereotyping, 432
stockout cost, 536
stories, organisational culture and,
   82–3
storming stage of group development,
   470
strategic alliance, 80–1, 620–1, 567
strategic business unit (SBU), 207
strategic control, 495–6, 515–16
   maintaining, 225
   manager's levers for, 508–10
strategic control points, 499
strategic goals, 176–8
   major areas for, 177
strategic linkages, 567
   alliance, 567
   customer, 567
   supplier, 567
strategic management, 203
   concept of, 205
   definition, 205
   importance of, 205–206
   levels of strategies and, 208

   organisational assessment and, 211
   process of, 205, 206, 224
strategic plans, 185–6
   carrying out, 224
strategies, 205
   business-level, 207, 221
   competitive, 221–2, 566–7
   concentration, 214
   co-ordinating levels of, 208
   corporate-level, 207, 213
   cost leadership, 221, 318, 566
   defensive, 215
   departmentalisation, 319
   differentiation, 223, 566
   diversification, 215
   divestiture, 216, 217
   e-commerce, 244, 300
   focus, 223
   functional-level, 207–8, 223
   globalisation, 619–20
   grand, 213–14
   growth, 214
   harvest, 216
   harvest and/or divest, 216
   human resource management 225
   implementation of, 224
   innovative differentiation, 318
   international (see international
      strategy)
   levels of, 207
   liquidation, 216, 217
   market differentiation, 318
   multifocal, 622
   national responsiveness, 622
   niche differentiation, 318
   operations, formulating, 541–2
   operations management-based, 542
   portfolio, 217
   regional responsiveness, 622
   retrenchment, 353
   stability, 215
   turnaround, 216
   vertical integration, 214–15
   worldwide integration, 621
strategy formulation, 205, 206
   competitive analysis, role of, 208
strategy implementation, 205, 206, 224
strengths
   growth-need, 274
   in SWOT analysis, 208
stress and health consequences, 571
structure (see organisation structure)

subordinate characteristics, path–goal theory and, 414
substitutes, 418
substitutes for leadership, 417
sunk costs, 141
superordinate goals, reducing and resolving conflict and, 592
supervisory authority, goal commitment and, 183
suppliers, 72
  strategic linkages, 567
  task environment and, 72
support, overcoming resistance to change and, 581
supportive leaders, 414
SWOT analysis, 208, 210, 227
symbols, organisational culture and, 82
synergy, 51, 467
  definition, 51
  negative, 467
  positive, 467
systems, 50
  definition, 50
  operating (see operating systems)
  service delivery, 549–50
systems development approaches
  alternative, 569
  selecting, 570
systems-development life cycle, 568–9
  assessing, 568
  stages, 568
systems theory, 50–1

T
tactical control, 494
tactical goals, 176–8
tactical plans, 186
takeover
  organisational termination, 240
tall structure, 278
tariffs, 615
task behaviour, situational leadership theory and, 412
task environment, 70
  competitors and, 70–1
  customers and clients and, 70
  diagram, 70
  government agencies and, 73
  labour supply and, 72–3
  suppliers and, 72
task focus, 590

task forces (groups), 290–1, 458, 475–7
  social response mechanism, as, 106
task identity, as core job characteristic, 273
task interdependence, conflict and, 588
task response times, 77
task significance, as core job characteristic, 274
task structure, Fiedler's contingency theory and, 408
Taylor, Frederick Winslow, 36–7, 58
team building, 245
team development, 483–6
teams, 290, 476
  employee involvement, 456–7
  entrepreneurial, 476
  everyday workplace teams (EDWT), 483–5
  horizontal co-ordination and, 287
  new venture, 321
  quality improvement, 526
  self-managing, 476
  virtual, 476–7
  (see also work groups)
technical skill(s), 13, 16
  definition, 13
  international business selection and, 629
technological change, 21, 253
technological element
  definition, 65
  external environment, 64–7
  international environment, 616–17
technological forecasting, 160–1
technological interdependence, 315
  organisation design and, 315
technological transfer, 617, 618
technology, 314
  change and, 21, 29–30, 253
  computer-aided design, 555
  computer-aided manufacturing, 555
  computer-based information systems (CBIS), 557, 558–60
  computer-integrated manufacturing, 554–5
  contingency factor, as, 314
  flexible manufacturing systems, 555
  group, 555
  information (see information systems)
  process, 541, 551–5
  service industries, in, 555

strategic plan implementation and, 224
  (see also technological element)
telecommunications, 560
technostructural activities, 245
telecommunications technology, 560
telecommuting, 572
teleconferencing, 446, 563
telephone calls
  employer's expense, at, 465–7
telephone discussions, 39
teleworking, 350
telling, situational leadership theory and, 413
temporary task forces, 106, 290
Thailand, 643–5
  cheap labour base, 654
  demand for infrastructure, 654
  exchange rates, 102–3
  incompatible business law, 654
  issues for managers, 654–5
  relationship with Australia, 655
  undereducated workforce, 654
theft, 572
Theory X and Theory Y, 46–7
Theory Z, 52–3, 58
therblig, 37
third-party intervention, 245
threats
  new entrants, 210
  substitute products or services, 210
  SWOT analysis, in, 208
time horizons
  capacity planning and, 544–5
  goals and plans, of, 544–5, 546
time-series methods, 157–8
timing, control types and, 522
top managers, 15
  commitment to ethical management, 114
  orchestrator of innovation, 19
total-factor productivity, 540
total quality control (TQC), 53
total quality management (TQM), 23, 32, 53, 58, 522, 514–8
  change principles, 525–6
  definition, 53, 523
  does it work, 527–8
  intervention techniques, 526–7
  philosophy, 525
Towne, Henry R., 33, 35, 57
Toys 'R' Us, 81

trade, balance of, 615
trade associations, 81
training and development, 336, 344
    definitions, 344
    intergroup, 595
    international business and, 629
    quality improvement, 526
    remuneration, 343
    strategic rationales, 344
    (see also education)
traits, of leaders, 400
transaction-processing systems (TPS), 562
transactional leaders, 416
transfer process, innovation and, 322
transformation processes
    definition, 50
    systems theory, in, 50
transformational leadership, 416–17
trust, lack of, resistance to change and, 579–80
Turbosoft, 85–6
turnaround strategies, 216
two-factor theory, 369
two-way communication, 431

U
uncertainty, 129
    control and, 494
    non-programmed decisions and, 129
uncertainty avoidance, 616
undercontrol, 513
unions, 331
    membership, 332
unit production, organisation design and, 314
United Nations Conference of Trade and Development (UNCTAD), 56
upward communication, 442
user, 569
user-developed systems, 569

V
valence, 375
validity
    selection processes, 339
vanguard corporations, 102
variable interval schedule of reinforcement, 383
variable ratio schedule of reinforcement, 383–4
verbal communication, 428
verification stage of creativity, 149

vertical communication, 441
vertical co-ordination, 277
    centralisation versus decentralisation and, 280
    delegation and, 281
    formalisation and, 277
    line and staff positions and, 282, 284
    span of management and, 278
vertical integration strategies, 214–15
Vertigo Tree Services, 179–80
vicarious learning, 385–6
Video Ezy, 120–2
videoconferencing, 446
    virtual teams and, 476–7
virtual team, 476–7
virtualisation of manufacturing, 508
virus computer, 573
voice mail, 446, 563

W
waiting-line models, 166
watchmakers, 132–4
weaknesses, in SWOT analysis, 208
web sites
    attacks on, 101
    Australian government information, 73
    Australiawide Loading, 191
    Career Post, 188
    CCK Financial Solutions, 30
    Fresh-Direct, 147
    Red Earth, 138
Weber, Max, 38, 58
    characteristics of ideal bureaucracy, 39
WebSpy, 474
wheel network, 439
whistle-blower, 115
wholly owned subsidiary, 621
wide-area networks (WAN), 561
willingness, situational leadership theory and, 413
Wood Veneer Products, 198–200
work agendas, 7
    definition, 11
    factors influencing, 12
    managerial, 11–12
    nature of, 11–12
work behaviour, organisational goals, 184
work groups
    attraction to, 462

behaviour, model of, 461
    cohesiveness of, 468–70
    command (functional), 457
    composition of, 461–2
    definition, 457
    development stages of, 470–2
    formal, 457–60
    foundations of, 457–62
    group processes and, 467–75
    heterogeneous work group, 461
    informal, 458–61
    inputs, 461–7
    managing conflict in, 461–2
    managing diversity in, 461–2
    member characteristics, 461
    member roles, 462–3
    model of, 461
    norms, 467–8
    operation of, 460–1
    processes, 467–75
    promoting innovation and, 475–9
    size, 464–5
    task, 458
    types of, 457
    (see also groups)
work in process inventory, 535
work methods, of managers, 7
work specialisation, 271
    conflict and, 590
WorkCover
    Victorian WorkCover awards, 61
workforce diversity, conflict and, 589
workweek, compressed, 275
world orientation toward international management, 611, 621
World Trade Organisation (WTO), 56
worldwide integration strategy, 621
worldwide product divisions structure, 624

X
Xerox Corporation
    benchmarking of competitors, 71
    diagram of elements of the mega-environment, 67
    diagram of elements of the task environment, 70
    force-field analysis of, 584
    suppliers, 72

Y
Y network, 439